ADVANCED
BREAD AND PASTRY
A PROFESSIONAL APPROACH

ADVANCED
BREAD AND PASTRY

A PROFESSIONAL APPROACH

Michel Suas

Photography by
Frank Wing
Photography

DELMAR
CENGAGE Learning™

Detroit • New York • San Francisco • New Haven, Conn • Waterville, Maine • London

Advanced Bread and Pastry: A Professional Approach, First Edition
Michel Suas

Vice President, Career and Professional Editorial: Dave Garza

Director of Learning Solutions: Sandy Clark

Acquisitions Editor: James Gish

Managing Editor: Larry Main

Product Manager: Patricia Osborn

Editorial Assistant: Sarah Timm

Vice President, Career and Professional Marketing: Jennifer McAvey

Marketing Director: Wendy Mapstone

Marketing Manager: Kristin McNary

Marketing Coordinator: Scott Chrysler

Production Director: Wendy Troeger

Production Manager: Stacy Masucci

Senior Content Project Manager: Glenn Castle

Art Director: Joy Kocsis

Technology Project Manager: Sandy Charette

Production Technology Analyst: Thomas Stover

For product information and technology assistance, contact us at
Professional & Career Group Customer Support, 1-800-648-7450

For permission to use material from this text or product, submit all requests online at **www.cengage.com/permissions**
Further permissions questions can be emailed to
permissionrequest@cengage.com

Cover and Interior Design by Kerry Gavin

Library of Congress Control Number: 2008920842

ISBN-13: 978-1-4180-1169-7

ISBN-10: 1-4180-1169-X

Delmar Cengage Learning
5 Maxwell Drive
Clifton Park, NY 12065-2919
USA

Cengage Learning products are represented in Canada by Nelson Education, Ltd.

For your lifelong learning solutions, visit **delmar.cengage.com**

Visit our corporate website at **www.cengage.com**

Notice to the Reader

Publisher does not warrant or guarantee any of the products described herein or perform any independent analysis in connection with any of the product information contained herein. Publisher does not assume, and expressly disclaims, any obligation to obtain and include information other than that provided to it by the manufacturer. The reader is expressly warned to consider and adopt all safety precautions that might be indicated by the activities described herein and to avoid all potential hazards. By following the instructions contained herein, the reader willingly assumes all risks in connection with such instructions. The publisher makes no representations or warranties of any kind, including but not limited to, the warranties of fitness for particular purpose or merchantability, nor are any such representations implied with respect to the material set forth herein, and the publisher takes no responsibility with respect to such material. The publisher shall not be liable for any special, consequential, or exemplary damages resulting, in whole or part, from the readers' use of, or reliance upon, this material.

Printed in the United States of America
1 2 3 4 5 XX 10 09 08

DEDICATION

I would like to dedicate this book to all the people who supported me during my journey in the industry. It was a bumpy road at times but always enjoyable for a 14-year-old dropout student.

I would like to start in France, from my first pastry chef, Mr. Hingouet, who gave me the opportunity to be his apprentice, to chef Mr. Blaise who gave me the value of the food and craft in the kitchen. To Mr. Barrier who offered me the position of executive pastry chef at the age of 22, at his three star restaurant. To all my mentors and coworkers.

In the United States, to all my customers at TMB Baking Inc., to all the students at the San Francisco Baking Institute who help me achieve my goals. To the people who trusted me and sought out my advice and consulting for their ventures, or kept attending classes at SFBI.

This book is to say *thank you* for all your support, encouragement, and trust. I hope this book will fulfill your expectations, and that it will help you teach the new generation or discover the value of the craft.

Likewise, thank you to all the persons who participated in the creation of this book, everyone at SFBI and TMB Baking Inc., and my family, especially my daughter Julie Marie who gave the strength and spirit to move forward whenever I thought the book was more than I could handle. She always managed to make me laugh.

Thank you all!

contents

Advanced Bread and Pastry: A Professional Approach

PREFACE

Advanced Bread and Pastry: A Professional Approach is a comprehensive guide to bread and pastry, designed as a resource for colleges and universities, private culinary schools, and professionals. Balancing a respect for tradition with modern approaches to method and technique, *Advanced Bread and Pastry* unites appealing presentation and indispensable instruction. It is written to help today's instructor, baker, and pastry chef respond to the recent evolution of ingredients, products, and presentation in the industry. The recipes (called formulas) are based on a variety of classic and contemporary methods and processes. With this strong foundation of knowledge, bakers and pastry chefs are ready to develop advanced skills, experiment with new ideas, and understand any formula.

THE FORMULAS

A formula can be seen as the composition of different ingredients that have been properly and thoughtfully selected. It is a procedure followed with an observation and a final product with an evaluation.

Product evaluation should be made during the whole process of the formula, not just when it is finished. By doing this you know what to change in the formula or the process and how to correct the problem. Through the process of creation, we learn the properties of each ingredient by noticing their reactions within the process and examining the end results.

Each formula is presented here with the best knowledge of the name applied to it. Some of these formulas or compositions are very classic; they are presented here because we realize the importance of knowing where we have come from. These classics are bases for you; they allow you to evolve the product with your own style and flavor. Even with this license though, do not call bread shaped like a boule a baguette. All the terminology in this book, presented as key words by chapter, is accurate. You can use these terms with confidence. For example, it is important to know that a biga is a biga and that it is not a sponge or a poolish or anything else because it's a biga. In the glossary you will find all of the key words that are and are not part of our common language, which you need to remember, use properly, and teach to each other.

HOW TO USE THIS BOOK

In using this book, you should review the explanations in each chapter for information on ingredients and processes (including mixing, baking, and finishing) in order to understand how to succeed with the formulas presented. The most important part of any formula is the process; you need to take full control of all the steps in order to be able to observe what is happening and to be able to correct it if necessary.

First, read the chapter to understand the context. Use the glossary to go further on key words and use the ingredient section in the online companion at http://www.delmarlearning.com/companions/, as well as the ingredients lists in the chapters, to understand the properties and uses of ingredients for different purposes.

The goal of this book is to educate and improve skills through the information provided as well as hands-on learning. For this, we have provided a spectrum of formulas that represent a range of techniques and processes to yield different end results. By creating different formulas with different ingredients and processes you are able to achieve a knowledge of different products and their characteristics. For example, the section on cake mixing presents sponge cake, liquid shortening cake, and creaming method cakes in order for you to understand the relationship between ingredients, process, and the final product. In the sections that deal with fermentation, we have presented a range of options for formulas, including baguette, croissant, Danish, and brioche. This is because the use of different preferments and mixing techniques will give you an understanding of the specific formulas' effects on mixing and fermentation and the effect they can have on work schedules, as well as the rheological properties of the dough, flavor, and shelf life.

TROUBLESHOOTING

This book is written with troubleshooting tips throughout the chapters. If the product does not turn out properly, go back to the chapter and read. Look for answers to help you understand what could have gone wrong and why. The best part of the baking and pastry industry is that you can discover something new every time you make a product.

Again, this book provides the best of the classical preparations and processes. Sometimes you will be faced with a formula with a different ingredient selection, a different approach to the formula, or a different appearance of the finished product from this book. Embrace the differences to understand and learn from them. This is the beauty of our industry. You can create your own product like an artist, musician, or painter.

ABOUT THE AUTHOR

Michel Suas, founder of the San Francisco Baking Institute (SFBI) and TMB Baking, was trained in France, his native country, where he earned diplomas in cooking, pastry, and baking. After nearly four decades in the industry, Michel has demonstrated his expertise in all areas of baking and pastry, including form, formula, production, bakery layout, bakery equipment, and training. In 1996, Michel founded SFBI, which has since educated thousands of professional and aspiring bakers from all over the world. The school has acted as a training site for several award-winning Baking USA teams and has hosted a variety of international groups from countries including Russia, China, and Japan. Michel's commitment to establishing the education needed for students entering the baking trade, and professionals motivated to strengthen their skills, continues to grow. His devotion to education is Michel's primary focus as he expands SFBI's curriculum and travels around the world sharing his extensive knowledge and passion for the trade.

ORGANIZATION OF THE TEXT

This book is organized in relation to the step-by-step progression of the method and procedure for each product. The organization is in parallel with each formula, making it easy for the reader and instructor to develop a clear understanding of the correlation between procedures and the relative importance and differences of each.

The book is divided into four parts: Introduction, Bread, Viennoiserie, and Pastry, and then followed by three appendices: Conversions, Baker's Percentages, and Temperature Conversions.

FEATURES

Advanced Bread and Pastry: A Professional Approach is an attractive bridge between a comprehensive textbook and the kind of elegant collection book on the art of baking and pastry you might find written and illustrated by a celebrity chef.

Some features include:

- Beautifully designed full color photographs of the finished products, along with more practical photographs showing step-by-step processes, engage readers and provide important visual reference.
- Chapter objectives are listed to help students understand the purpose of each chapter.
- A key terms list reinforces relevant terminology for each chapter.
- A glossary of key terms and their definitions is provided at the back of the book for quick reference.
- Detailed colorful illustrations and are provided throughout the text to assist in the understanding more difficult concepts.
- Tables and charts provide a visual representation of essential information for student comprehension.

INSTRUCTOR AND STUDENT RESOURCES

An Instructor's Manual to accompany *Advanced Bread and Pastry: A Professional Approach* is available providing chapter outlines, answers to end-of-chapter review questions, and test questions and answers.

An Online Companion, available at http://www.delmarlearning.com/companions/, provides additional resources for both the instructor and student. It provides PowerPoint slides, a test bank, lesson plans, and additional resources. Comprehensive information on equipment and ingredients is also provided.

ACKNOWLEDGEMENTS AND SPECIAL THANKS

This book became a reality thanks to many people. The name of the author reflects only the person responsible for thinking of it in the first place and then directing the creation of his views with a clear objective in mind. "The Book" is the result of multitalented people with a wide array of experience and expertise. All share credit for the final outcome. For a book of this scale, with so much information compiled into one volume, the only way to write it is to seek proven expertise in each area.

The following people deserve special recognition for their contributions.

Didier Rosada This project could not have existed without the participation of Didier Rosada in the bread section. His knowledge, passion, and devotion are evident in the text. Those who know Didier personally will attest that his skills as an instructor, and integrity as a human being, surpass all expectations. He has an open mind, sharing his knowledge fully and teaching the mysteries of bread dough with simplicity, humor, and a firm hand, and always in-depth. It does not matter if you are a beginner or an advanced student—you will always find something to learn from Didier Rosada.

Brian Wood The organization of this book would not have been possible without Brian Wood. At his young age and an already excellent pastry chef, he demonstrated remarkable drive and persistence. Brian's participation in writing the introduction, Viennoiserie, and pastry sections, as well as contributing to many other areas of the book, showed his dedication to perfection. His personal stamp of quality contributed greatly to the positive outcome of this project.

Miyuki Togi Miyuki's writing and editing support was invaluable as we created this book. Taking care to develop a deep understanding of the message we wanted to share, Miyuki was able to expertly deliver information, just as it was needed, in several chapters. In addition, her detailed work on the baking tests strengthened our confidence in the quality of the formulas. Miyuki's involvement in the décors and plated desserts sections is a preview of the skills this talented young person will bring to the industry.

Steve Hartz For his contributions to the sanitation chapter, Steve Hartz was irreplaceable. His thorough understanding of sanitation problems and his experience in the baking industry allowed him to share the perspective of practical day-to-day knowledge, along with theory.

Juliette Lelchuk With her creative mind and exceptional understanding of flavor and presentation, Juliette had a strong influence on the plated desserts development. Her smile and considerate nature were also of help to us in many ways.

Stéphane Tréand We could not have hoped for a better person to handle the décors with pastillage and sugar than Stéphane Tréand. His skill and professionalism are apparent in everything he does. Stéphane was not afraid to work for 14 hours straight to make sure that every photo was right. Even under a lot of pressure his positive and friendly attitude never wavered. He made each task more enjoyable for everyone involved in the process as we watched him create elements of decoration with precision and style.

Lisa Curran Researching, reviewing, and adding components in the flour chapter, Lisa proved to be a wealth of information, always presented with modesty and a friendly approach. It is always a pleasure to work with Lisa.

Kelly O'Connell Kelly was consistently available whenever we needed her for research and review. Her involvement in the ice cream chapter was most valuable, and her calm, positive attitude made the work seem easy.

Julie Marie Suas Julie Marie deserves special thanks for her involvement in the photo shoots and selection of pictures, along with her suggestions for some chapters to make the book more fun.

Evelyne Suas For keeping track of all of our photo shoots, but mostly for her constant positive support, thank you Evelyne.

Frank Wing Frank's enthusiasm and eccentric devotion to the photographs he set up made the pictures seem even better than the real thing. We learned so much from Frank. All the products we photographed for the book are authentic products. No food stylist came into play. Without Frank's patience and understanding of food we would never have come close to the outstanding photos featured in this book.

Jamie Williams Jamie worked on the first draft copyedit. She helped to maintain consistency in the chapters and to present a single voice from all the contributing writers. Her enthusiasm and attention to detail were very helpful and greatly appreciated.

Nikki Lee We would like to thank Nikki and her team from Lachina Publishing Services for their patience and attention to detail for the layout and production of the book. Always under a deadline, she maintained a consistently high level of attention to detail. Thank you Nikki.

Cengage Learning We would like to thank all of the people at Cengage Learning who worked on this project. From its acquisition by Matt Hart, to the overseeing of the writing and production process by Patricia Osborn, to the production and art design with Glenn Castle, the team was very helpful in assisting us to achieve the book we wanted to have published. Thank you.

TMB Baking Staff During the tests and writing of this book the patience and support of the TMB Baking staff was tremendously encouraging. Special thanks go to Richard Abitbol for his overall support, and for developing the graphics and other media for the cakes. His assistance in putting the final information into detailed works, as well as documenting equipment, was very helpful.

Baking Industry Professionals, Students, and Enthusiasts We would not be here without all of the dedicated students who have attended the San Francisco Baking Institute (SFBI). We appreciate your continued support as well as your great excitement and eager anticipation for this book.

Tim Kitzman For his patience and determination as he tried each bread formula over and over again, and then carefully compiled all the data, thank you to Tim Kitzman.

REVIEWERS

Cengage Learning would like to thank the following reviewers for their invaluable feedback and contributions to this book.

Elena Clement, CEPC
Associate Instructor
Johnson & Wales–Denver Campus
Denver, CO

Joseph A. DiPaolo Jr., AOS CEPC
Pastry Chef Instructor
Le Cordon Bleu College of Culinary Arts Atlanta
Duluth, GA

Elizabeth K. Fackler, CCE, CEPC
Pastry Arts Instructor
Alaska Culinary Academy, Alaska Vocational Technical Center
Seward, AK

Christopher Harris
Pastry Chef Instructor
South Seattle Community College
Seattle, WA

Lisa Inlow, AOS
Chef Instructor
Saddleback Junior College
Mission Viejo, CA

Paul V. Krebs
Professor
Schenectady County Community College
Schenectady, NY

Ken Morlino, MAB, CEC
Associate Professor, Coordinator of Culinary Arts
Nashville State Community College
Nashville, TN

Dominic O'Neill, CEC
Executive Chef and Instructor
Scottsdale Community College
Scottsdale, AZ

William Darrel Smith, MAED
Chef Instructor
The Art Institute International Minnesota (AiM)
Minneapolis, MN

Chris Thielman, MA, CEC, CCE
Chef Instructor
College of DuPage
Glen Ellyn, IL

Michelle R. Walsh, CEPC
Adjunct Instructor
Oakland Community College
Farmington Hills, MI

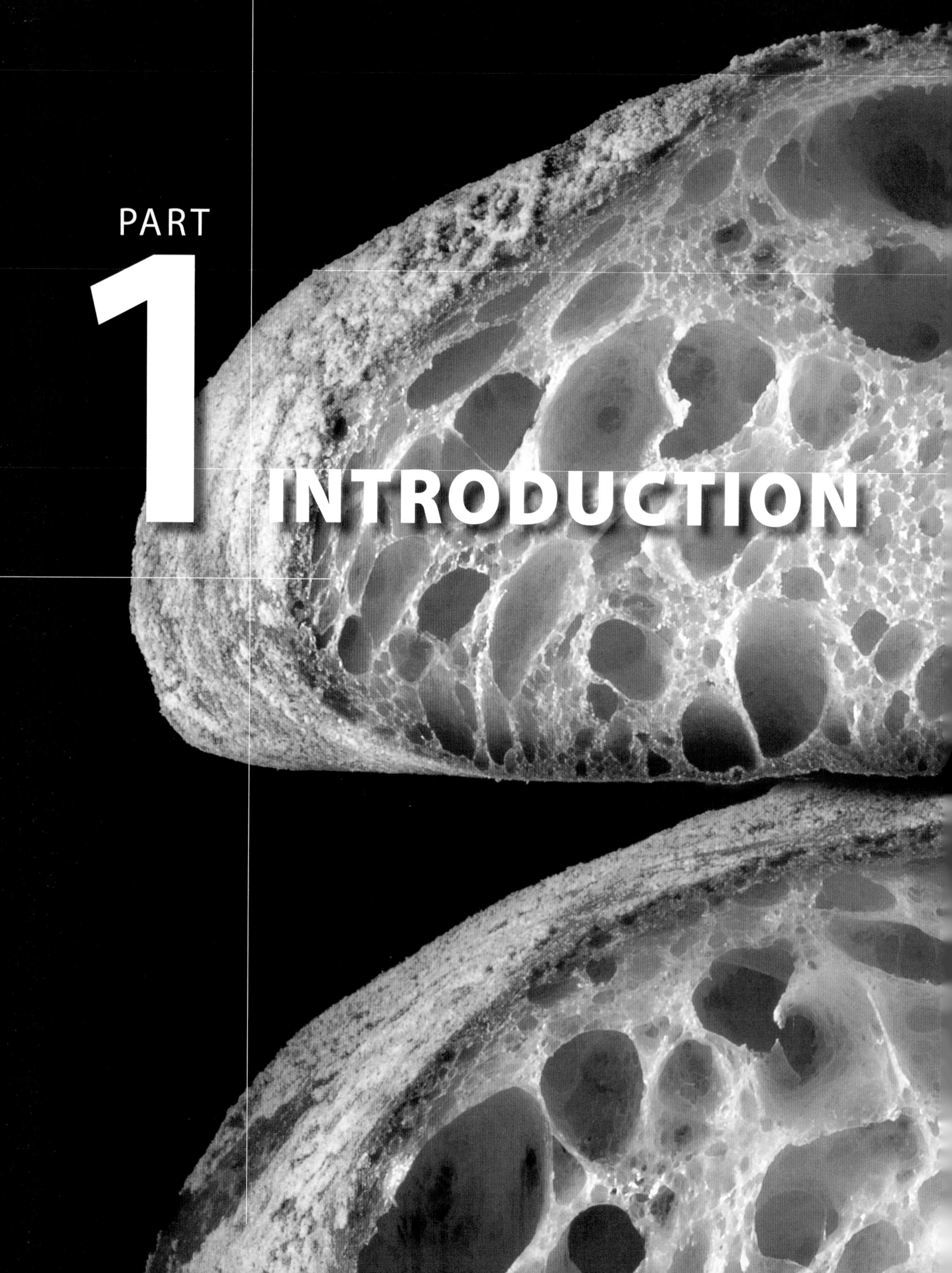

PART 1 INTRODUCTION

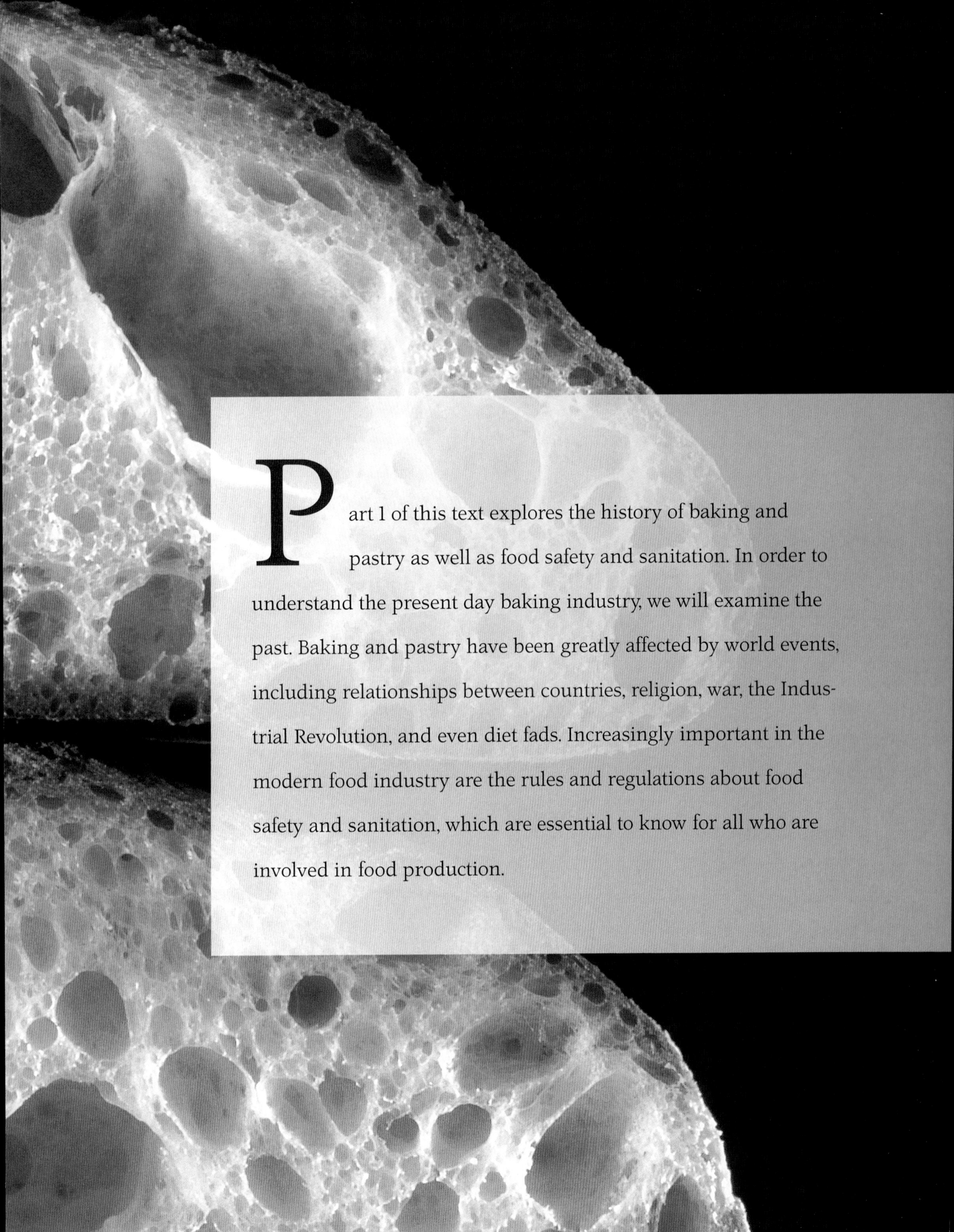

Part 1 of this text explores the history of baking and pastry as well as food safety and sanitation. In order to understand the present day baking industry, we will examine the past. Baking and pastry have been greatly affected by world events, including relationships between countries, religion, war, the Industrial Revolution, and even diet fads. Increasingly important in the modern food industry are the rules and regulations about food safety and sanitation, which are essential to know for all who are involved in food production.

chapter
1

BREAD AND PASTRY: A HISTORICAL PERSPECTIVE AND CURRENT OPPORTUNITIES

OBJECTIVES

After reading this chapter, you should be able to

- present the history and developments of baking and pastry making, including their effects on various civilizations.
- explain the culture of baking in the United States and elsewhere.
- explain the loss and return of artisan baking, the reasons for its loss and return, and the people who helped to reintroduce the methods of artisan baking.
- explain requirements and challenges bakers and pastry chefs face today.
- understand the industry and the opportunities it presents.

AN INTRODUCTION TO BREAD AND PASTRY

Throughout history, humans have sought out foods that are beneficial to health, and that will ensure survival as a species. Although our lives have become considerably more complex since the days of the hunter-gatherer, this requirement for nourishment has remained the same. The difference is that advances in science and technology have provided us with ways to better meet the need.

To achieve a comprehensive understanding of baking, it's necessary to thoroughly explore both the breadth and depth of its history. A number of developments—including new agricultural technology, the threat of famine, the rise and fall of nation-states, the marriages of kings and queens, the Industrial Revolution, improved information access, religion, and wars—have all left their mark on the bread and pastry we make and consume today.

NEOLITHIC PERIOD (10,000 BCE–4000 BCE)

The Neolithic period is marked by the shift from mobile hunting and gathering societies to fixed, agrarian-based communities. Approximately half of the Neolithic diet consisted of hunted foods, including deer, fish, or pheasant. The remaining half was made up of gathered nuts, berries, and grains, including **rye**, **spelt**, **millet**, and **wheat**. During this time, predecessors to primitive breads emerged, such as a simple **porridge** made first by soaking, and later by boiling, foraged and grown grains in water. Not only was the softened grain texture more digestible than raw, but the subsequent boiling process also provided access to more of the grain's nutrients.

The transition from mobile to fixed communities also marked a slow turning away from the wild (Flandrin & Montanari, 1999, pp. 71–72). Europeans who lived in more temperate areas enjoyed a diverse landscape that provided a nourishing, balanced diet consisting of numerous cereals, primarily wheat and rye, and meat from livestock such as sheep, goats, cows, and pigs (Flandrin & Montanari, p. 28). As this predominantly agrarian culture eventually spread west through Europe, their diet became the foundation of what Westerners eat today (Flandrin & Montanari, p. 28).

As ancient technology developed, the process of preparing grain for consumption changed, as well. The original porridge was eventually heated on hot stone slabs or even baked under embers to create a crude flatbread that was less prone to spoilage and was easily transported. These grain products provided vital nutrients not readily accessible from meat and were an essential staple of the Neolithic diet. Because they may have meant the difference between life and death, grains were cared for and eaten by entire communities, which increased both collaboration and sharing.

Another major development during the Neolithic period was the creation and use of stoneware ceramic vessels, elementary grain mills, and raised ovens. Archaeological excavations have uncovered mills and ovens as centerpieces of the home, revealing their roles as integral parts of life. These advances in basic technology also laid the groundwork for the Greeks and Egyptians to move forward the art of making bread (Flandrin & Montanari, 1999, p. 28).

CLASSIC ANTIQUITY (EGYPT AND GREECE 5500 BCE–300 CE)

As civilization in Europe and the Near and Middle East advanced, a growing number of people lived in densely populated areas and relied on grains as their primary food source. During this period, the Egyptians and Greeks became the first cultures to truly advance the science of bread through experimentation with ingredients and techniques.

Sediment examined from the Nile River delta in Egypt has shown signs that as early as 4000 BCE, farmers grew spelt, wheat, and **barley** for domestic bread, pastry, and beer production and for export to Greece. These exports supplied Greece with extra grain necessary for domestic bread and pastry production (Flandrin & Montanari, 1999, p. 39).

Most of what is known regarding bread and pastry in ancient Egypt comes from archaeological finds, as there is little written record. Excavations of Egyptian tombs have revealed "funeral meals," an assortment of breads and pastries, sometimes numbering in the thousands, and intended as food for the afterlife (Flandrin & Montanari, 1999, p. 38).

What we do know is that the breads and porridge of antiquity were made from both local and imported grains, and that the type of bread or porridge eaten was generally related to one's status in society. The wealthiest of people ate the whitest breads, the middle class ate breads with some whole grain present, and the poorest of people ate whole grain and spelt breads.

Those people who ate their grains in the form of bread often milled the flour at their own houses. Grains were lightly toasted or dried in the sun to help separate the chaff from the grain, and the chaff was subsequently removed. The grain was then crushed using a mortar and pestle, milled between two stones, and sifted to the desired degree. Examined Egyptian remains show excessively worn teeth, which archeologists have attributed to the incidental mixing of fine sand with flour during the milling process (Flandrin & Montanari, 1999, p. 39).

Initial Egyptian flatbreads were made from wheat, barley, or spelt flour, water, and salt. Hieroglyphics show us that people kneaded dough with their hands, and that larger quantities were processed using the feet. Although flatbreads were typically baked on hot stone slabs or on a stone hearth of an oven, there is also speculation that they may have been baked on the oven wall, much like authentic Naan is baked today (Flandrin & Montanari, 1999, p. 39).

As cited by the Greek historian Athenaeus, the Greeks from antiquity were known to have 72 distinct types of bread (Revel, 1982, p. 65). The scope of their products is indicative of the significant sociological and technological developments during that period, including the redesign and use of wood-fired ovens and an advanced milling process capable of producing multiple grades of flour. The diversity of available ingredients provided many different flavor combinations, with a large selection of grains, herbs, oils, fruits, and nuts used to create a wide array of breads. In time, the art of bread advanced to the degree that specialty shapes and flavor profiles were created for different occasions, including conical loaves that were coated with cumin seeds and used for religious ceremonies. Other shapes included flat, round, oval, and triangular loaves. With these important developments, the use of grain as simply a means of nutrition shifted, and bread came to be associated with civility and gastronomic innovation (Revel, pp. 64–65).

Leavened breads were produced from about 1500 BCE onward (Flandrin & Montanari, 1999, p. 39). There are two dominant theories concerning the development of yeasted bread. The first is that the Egyptians, who had mastered the process of brewing beer, used beer instead of water in bread making and thus introduced yeast into the dough. The second theory is that a piece of dough was forgotten about, inoculated by ambient wild yeast and later baked (Tannahill, 1988, p. 52).

Although this second dough would not have produced a very light bread, it may have been lighter than what was previously experienced by the Egyptians. On the other hand, if yeasted dough was first made by ale, the Egyptians would easily make the connection between fermentation of grain to produce beer and the fermentation of grain to leaven bread. The ale theory is more common and possibly more realistic, as it continued to be the most popular method for producing leavened breads in Egypt (Tannahill, 1988, p. 52).

Areas outside Egypt developed methods to leaven dough in accordance with regional resources and customs. The Greeks and Italians used methods related to the wine-making process to generate fermentation; the three most popular methods were millet flour and grape juice, bran and white wine, and old porridge (Tannahill, 1988, p. 52). The Gauls (an ancient culture that inhabited what is now roughly France and Belgium) and the Iberians (who inhabited what is now an area by Georgia, Armenia, and Azerbaijan) used the foam from ale to leaven their breads (Tannahill, p. 52). The most common method of fermentation was to hold back a portion of the dough to be added to the next batch, a technique used in many bakeries today.

EARLY PASTRIES

In addition to producing breads, the Egyptians and the Greeks made rudimentary pastries. Egyptians are known to have been making cakes as early as 3000 BCE (Tannahill, 1988, p. 53). Popular ingredients for pastry and cake making included milk, eggs, butter, honey, sesame seeds, pine nuts, walnuts, almonds, poppy seeds, and dates (Revel, 1982, p. 69). A typical cake may have been sweetened bread that was rolled in honey and coated with seeds.

In his book *Culture and Cuisine*, Jean-Francois Revel presents a pastry formula from the Greek historian Athenaeus, dated approximately 200 CE:

> *Take walnuts from Thasos in the Pont, almonds and poppy seeds and toast them carefully. Then crush them well in a clean mortar, mix these three fruits together, grind them by adding strained honey to them, and pepper, and blend the whole together well; the mixture will become black because of the pepper. Make a flat square of this paste, then grind some white sesame, mix it with flour and strained honey, and make two flat cakes of it, between which you will place the proceeding black paste, fastening it securely in the middle. (Revel, 1982, p. 69)*

Apicius, an epicurean and writer from Greco-Roman times, recorded many cake preparations popular during the transition to the Common Era. His are some of the only written descriptions of pastry making and cake preparation during antiquity and the Middle Ages. A previous author, Chrysippus of Tyanus, wrote *Treatise on Baking*, which detailed more than 30 cakes from the time; unfortunately, this book did not survive. Fortunately, there are other existing examples of ancient cakes, such as this second recipe recorded by Jean-Francois Revel:

> *Domestic cakes: Grind dates, walnuts or pine nuts with spelt cooked in water. Work fine-ground pepper and honey into this gruel; make little balls of it, salting the outside of them lightly. Fry them in oil and then moisten them with strained honey (Revel, 1982, p. 69).*

Like many formulas that survived the Classical Greek and Ancient Egyptian eras, only the basic preparations are described, and it is believed that quantities and specific instructions were commonly known. Another interesting note is that both preparations include pepper, a very common spice for the time.

BREAD AND CULTURE IN ANTIQUITY

The congregation of people into densely populated areas and the emergence of bread and grain as the main food source had a large impact on the culture of Ancient Greece and Egypt, and for most emerging European communities to come. The people of these regions transitioned into a sedentary, urban life and abandoned what was considered the "barbaric lifestyle" by nurturing their immediate needs (Flandrin & Montanari, 1999, p. 69).

The hallmark of civilization in Greece and Egypt was marked by the food the people ate. The models needed to sustain this civilized culture have been recognized as "conviviality, type of food eaten and the art of cooking and dietary regiments" (Flandrin & Montanari, 1999, p. 69). Conviviality, or the interaction of social groups, promoted networking and group identity, while the type of food eaten by a specific group created an identity that separated it from others. For the Greeks and the Egyptians, the fabrication of bread came to symbolize what it meant to live in a civilized society. In Egypt, it was believed that "He whose belly is empty is the one who complains" (Flandrin & Montanari, p. 38). A stomach full of bread ensured order.

Bread and cakes also played a major role in the religious life. During funerals and sacrificial offerings in Egypt, for example, tombs were filled with sweet items for the dead to enjoy in the afterlife, and cakes and breads were often sacrificed to the gods. According to some accounts, Rameses III annually sacrificed 9,000 cakes and 200,000 loaves of bread to the gods (Bachmann, 1955, p. 2).

Just as importantly, control over the basic needs of nutrition meant that more time was available for intellectual and social growth. The Greeks and Egyptians were the earliest masters of philosophy, the arts, construction, and agriculture. From Greece, the art and science of baking made its way to Rome and became a dominant part of the culture during the Roman Empire, supplying the army and people with food. In 100 CE, Emperor Trajan created a guild of bakers who were to supply bread to the public at the state's expense. By keeping the needs of the poorest people fulfilled, Trajan was able to control social order, in much the same way the Egyptians did earlier (Montagné, 2001, p. 66.)

THE MIDDLE AGES

The Middle Ages spanned the 5th to the 15th century, beginning with the fall of the Roman Empire and ending with the rise of industry and the arts that brought on the Renaissance. The Middle Ages were marked by drastic grain shortages, growing urbanization, starvation, disease, and a polar change in baking. At their onset, bread consumption was on the decline, but toward the end of the era, the organization of the profession and rules surrounding bread making had become more developed. The most notable advances in baking and pastry were the technological improvements made to ovens, the introduction of new ingredients in pastry items, the organization of pastry cooks and bakers, and the formation of guilds.

The decline in bread production and consumption can be attributed to a dominant, nomadic Germanic culture that relied heavily on meats and left the land largely uncultivated. This way of life was in stark contrast with the earlier Egyptian, Greek, and Roman models of domesticity, sustainability, and separation from the wild. While this Germanic culture prevailed, the use of the staple Mediterranean ingredients (grain, oil, wine) fell off. People returned to hunting in the wild, or converted their farms to pasture land for domesticated animals.

Agriculture was reintroduced around 1000 CE, and baking finally began to progress from the status quo it had achieved in antiquity. This sweeping change was initiated by the Catholic Church as a way to settle nomadic people and create grains for bread, which held an important role in the sacrificial rituals of the church. Catholic priests learned to farm from agricultural texts written hundreds of years earlier by their Greco-Roman ancestors, who described the intricacies of tending the land (Jacob, 1944, pp. 115–116).

The 1100s saw the development of the baking profession, along with guidelines of what it meant to be a baker. Toward the latter part of the 12th century, an important distinction arose between those who solely baked bread (**fornarii**) and those who made dough and baked it (**pistores**). Specifically, the role of the fornarii was to bake dough that was brought to them from the townspeople. Oven tending was considered a dangerous job, and this skilled trade was based on knowledge passed down from previous generations. But use of the communal ovens of the fornarii came with a price. Bribes were offered and accepted, preference was given to those who could afford to pay more, and power struggles inevitably erupted (Flandrin & Montanari, 1999, p. 277).

As the consumption of bread increased in Mediterranean areas, the local fornarii realized it would benefit them to sell it as well, and they gained that right with support from the church. By comparison, the pistores of Paris in 1200 CE sought and gained the right to be the city's sole bread makers and bakers. For this right, they were required to make payments (in bread) to royalty, and to submit to regular inspection to ensure that proper sanitation and weight regulations were being followed (Flandrin & Montanari, 1999, p. 277).

The first baker's guild, called the Tameliers, was formed in France at this time. The name *Tameliers* refers to the sifting of flour that was required upon its receipt. In order to become a Tamelier, one had to go through a four-year apprenticeship, pass various tests, and be awarded the right to bake from the king. Through the guild, bakers provided various industries with bread and received privileges in return. For example, bakers who supplied bread to hospitals could be assured of free and expeditious medical care (Montagné, 2001, p. 66).

During the 13th century, breads were made primarily from wheat and were an integral part of the growing urbanization of Western Europe. The quality of the wheat varied widely, and the type of flour used continued to depict one's rank in society—the wealthier the family, the softer and whiter the bread. The loaves of the upper classes were known as pain de bouche or pain mollet in France, Semmelbrot in Germany, and pandemain or white bread in England (Flandrin & Montanari, 1999, p. 281). The bread for the working class contained more bran and wheat germ and was referred to as brown bread, while whole wheat bread was made for the poorest of people (Flandrin and Montanari, p. 281).

With the production of bread well established, bakers soon started to make "sweet" items to be sold for church offerings, holidays, and when grain prices were low. The first items created were primitive wafers and waffles that were made by pressing batter between two hot pieces of metal. Depending on the availability of supplies, the batter was enriched with ingredients such as honey, milk, eggs, and sometimes sugar. These sweets became popular in no time, with people of royalty and privilege placing orders for them on a daily basis. In addition to being eaten as a light dessert, they also may have been morning fare (Flandrin & Montanari, 1999, p. 281).

The Crusades played an integral role in the development of pastry. Westerners brought back sugar, thought to be a new and exciting "spice," from Persia, as well as a primitive form of puff pastry and assorted fruits, nuts, and spices. The introduction of sugar and puff pastry eventually caused some problems among the three main guilds of Paris (bakers, pastry cooks, and restaurateurs), because each wanted exclusive rights over their use and sale (Montagné, 2001, pp. 855–856).

From the late Middle Ages into the Renaissance, the specialization of and distinction between bread and pastry grew considerably throughout Western Europe. Along with these distinctions came strict management by royalty, who issued rights to specific guilds for the production of certain baked items, determined the rules of trade, created standards, controlled prices, and tested quality.

Examples of this include French King John the Good, who in 1351 defined the scope of pastry making and the products it encompassed, including wafers and various cookies, numerous sweet and savory fritters, marzipan, and tarts (Montagné, 2001, p. 856). In 1366, Charles V of France set rules regarding when and where bread could be sold and set the prices for breads with various flours (Montagné, p. 66). In 1397 and again in 1406, his successor, Charles VI, revised the original rights of cookie makers by creating guidelines that dictated what they could sell, set standards for quality, and created a job description for **oubloyers**, or journeyman cookie makers. In Charles VI's time, an oubloyer was expected to manufacture, in one day, 500 large **oublies** (wafers), 300 supplications (for religious holidays and church offerings), and 200 esterels (Flandrin & Montanari, 1999, p. 281).

THE RENAISSANCE INTO INDUSTRIAL REVOLUTION

Royalty maintained tight controls over bread and pastry making throughout the Renaissance. In 1440, Charles VIII of France issued a directive conferring the rights of baked savory items to the **pâtissiers**, a new guild that was given exclusive rights to make and sell tarts and pies filled with various meats, fish, and cheeses. Along with these rights came responsibilities to ensure proper food safety. For example, it was unlawful to sell old pastries or to use rotten meats and dairy ingredients that had spoiled or were of poor quality. Charles VIII also created production rules for pâtissiers and pâtissiers assistants that mirrored those of the oubloyers. In time, the pâtissiers and oubloyers would merge into one guild to gain control over weddings and banquets, a monopoly that lasted from 1556 until the elimination of the French guilds by Turgot in 1776 (Montagné, 2001, p. 856).

Laws surrounding the production and sale of flour, breads, and pastries reached new heights in France during the 1600s, primarily due to a reduction in the availability of grain. In 1635, Richelieu ordered that "bakers of bread rolls and pastry cooks will not buy grain before eleven o'clock in winter and noon in summer; bakers of large loaves will not buy grain before two o'clock. This will enable the people of the town to obtain their supply first. Bakers shall put a distinctive trademark on their loaves, and keep weights and scales in their shops, under penalty of having their licenses removed" (Montagné, 2001, p. 856).

Most notable was the setting of prices and standards for identity and weight, as well as the requirement of scoring bread with distinctive trademarks so that it could be tracked to a specific baker. Later, when urban markets were formed in cities like Paris, laws governing the sale of breads often specified that a baker could sell his bread only with the assistance of his wife and children (Montagné, 2001, p. 856).

During the 16th and 17th centuries, the danger of famine in Western Europe was a constant reality. Not only were grain yields variable, but the growing proportion of poor urban populations strained the supply. As the poor flocked to "food-stable" cities and the price of bread rose along with demand, kings and queens were ultimately responsible for ensuring "nutritional equilibrium" among their subjects. Failure to do so could lead to civil unrest, the looting of bakeries, and even rebellion against the monarchy itself (Flandrin & Montanari, 1999, p. 108).

As wheat-growing technology improved during the 1700s, yields increased and the threat of famine slowly declined. In order to maintain a subdued peasantry, the government of France ordered merchants to build up reserve stocks of grain for times of need. These increased reserves did not calm the public, however, because large wheat purchases by merchants created higher consumer prices, and the people still went hungry (Flandrin & Montanari, 1999, p. 281). Their response was to accuse the government of price fixing in conjunction with the merchants, an outcry that resulted in a restoration of grain prices in 1773.

Unfortunately, renewed confidence in the agrarian model resulted in sweeping changes in distribution and laws regarding the sale of wheat in France. Within one year of Turgot's nullification of all laws restricting the sale of wheat, the price for a loaf of bread was almost as high as a day laborer's wages (Tannahill, 1988, p. 283). The "war of famine" ensued (Montagné, 2001, p. 67), which culminated in the famous 1789 march from a Paris marketplace to Versailles, with the people shouting "Let's get the Baker and the Baker's wife."

The crisis in France had little, if anything, to do with the absence of raw goods. Throughout Europe, trade between nations was becoming more common, and large quantities of wheat imported from the Baltic States to Western Europe often provided relief during poor harvests (Flandrin & Montanari, 1999, p. 281). Ironically, the problems that led to the downfall of the French monarchy lay not so much in wheat and bread production, but rather in the lack of a means to distribute it to the masses (Tannahill, 1988, p. 283).

THE EVOLUTION OF PASTRY

The baking and pastry arts went through their most drastic evolution from the 16th century onward, ultimately establishing the bases that exist today. Enjoyed by a limited, wealthy audience, the advancement of pastry had its roots in savory preparations: pâtissiers were primarily makers of meat, fish, and cheese pies. Although the pastries of the 16th century may not be recognizable to a modern pastry chef, some resemblances can be seen. One of the most common bases found in today's pastry kitchen originated in the town of Pithivier, France, in 1506, when a local pastry chef invented the "almond cream" widely used as cake bases and pastry fillings such as that of the Pithivier Cake (Chaboissier & Lebigre, 1993, p. 12). Another major pastry base that has its roots in France is the predecessor to pâte à choux, also known as choux paste. Pâte à choux was created when Popelini, the pastry chef of Catherine de Medici, accompanied her from Italy to France upon her marriage to Henry II in 1540. Although the original version is not the one used today, it was nonetheless an innovative preparation of the time (Chaboissier & Lebigre, p. 12).

Additional innovation in the 1500s was made possible by the increasing availability of sugar, which brought advances in egg whites and whipped cream. From these base preparations came madeleines and macarons, although they were probably not as refined as those enjoyed today. According to legend, another of Catherine de Medici's pastry chefs from Italy, Della Pigna, introduced **pastillage**, a decorative medium he used to create **pièces montées**, or centerpieces of artistic design (Chaboissier & Lebigre, 1993, p. 12).

The 17th and 18th centuries saw further advancement of the pastry arts through refinement of processes and incorporation of new ingredients such as coffee from Africa, tea from China, and chocolate from the Americas (Revel, 1982, p. 166). The end of the 17th century saw a large increase in the consumption of ices and sherbets originating from Spain and Sicily. In addition, sugar beets brought a new source of sucrose to Europe for the first time.

Important developments of the 17th century include the sweet almond tartlets of Rageuneau in 1638, which represented a major departure from the basic cookies of the time, especially in light of years of unpredictable wheat availability and rationing. In 1686, bakers in Budapest created the croissant as a reward for detecting an invading Turkish army and alerting the city. After its successful defense, they were allowed to develop a specialty pastry honoring the crescent of the Ottoman flag (Montagné, 2001, p. 372). In 1770, Marie Antoinette is credited with bringing the croissant and other Viennese pastry to France (Chaboissier & Lebigre, 1993, p. 13) after her marriage to Louis XVI.

The 18th century brought some important technological innovations for processing raw materials. In the late 1700s, a German chemist worked on extracting beet sugar and crystallizing it in order to create an economical alternative to the more costly imported cane sugar. The process proved to be very expensive, though, and the resulting product was of poor quality. The process was not refined enough to produce a sweetener comparable to cane sugar until 1812 (Chaboissier & Lebigre, 1993, p. 16). The 18th century also saw further refinement of pastry processes, such as the 1740 introduction of Baba au Rhum to France by the Polish King Stanislas Leszczynski, and the 1760 creation of toasted choux by famous pastry chef Avice. The year 1783 was notable for the birth of Marie-Antonin Carême, whose accomplishments in the development of pastry were unmatched in his time.

Carême contributed volumes to the world of pastry, but he was also a chef and avid developer of kitchens and equipment, both large and small. He was abandoned at the age of 12 by his father, who informed him that society had more to offer "an enterprising soul" than did he (Revel, 1982, p. 246). Carême was initially taken in by a low-end restaurant owner and put to work in the kitchen. By the age of 16, he was apprenticed to one of the best pastry chefs in Paris, Bailly on the rue Vivienne (Revel, p. 250), and was credited with being one of the most influential chefs of modern times by the time he was 20. He carefully studied the work of the food masters of his time to develop styles and presentation never before used in the culinary world. In *Culture and Cuisine*, Revel describes Carême's attention to other people's detail in the following passage:

> *Like all creators, he was a stealer of ideas—a stealer I emphasize, not a plagiarist. He was passionately attached to all the masters who had something to say to him, Avice for pastry, Laquipiere for sauces—it is only the weak who are afraid of being influenced, Goethe said—*

but none of their conceptions was ever followed by him down to the last detail, and, he always rendered them affectionate and generous homage. (Revel, 1982, p. 246)

While working for Bailly, Carême was exposed to new forms of pastry and was given the responsibility for making tourtes and showpieces. His inspiration came from the National Print Museum, where he would spend his free time studying and copying various works of art. The famous diplomat Talleyrand was responsible for Carême's next career move. A frequent diner at Bailly's during Carême's tenure, Talleyrand soon had him in his own employ, working directly under Boucher (Revel, 1982, pp. 250–251).

Carême is also credited with inventing or greatly improving many of the bases of pastry used today. He is most famous for his development of the modern version of puff pastry, which is used for both sweet and savory applications. To improve earlier versions of this dough (previously "perfected" by Guillaume Tirel, a.k.a. Taillevent, in the late 15th century (Chaboissier & Lebigre, 1993, p. 11)), Carême pioneered the technique of puff pastry, the lamination that carefully layers butter and dough to create upward of several hundred layers. Other people get credit for puff pastry too, from Feuillet to Claude Gelé. We can leave it to the historians and to your own preference to take sides for such a versatile and wonderful dough as the potential "creator" has with so many variations and applications. Furthermore, Carême was the creator of nougat, meringue, croquant, poupelins (a pâte-à-choux-based cake filled with fresh cream) and solilemmes, a brioche-like dough with warm salted butter drizzled over it once baked (Revel, 1982, p. 251).

Carême's attention to detail and personal drive were almost as unique and unprecedented as his work with pastry. His interdisciplinary approach to food and presentation styles not only impacted French cuisine for generations, it still creates inspiration for aspiring chefs. Gauging the impact of his work, Carême once reflected, "When in order to forget envious men I cause my eye to wander in Paris, I note with joy the increase in the number of pastry shops and the improvement in them. Nothing of all that existed before my labor and books. As I have predicted, pastry makers have become very skillful and very meticulous" (Revel, 1982, p. 251).

Carême also reached new heights in the presentation of food, with abundance and surprise as key elements. This new form of dining, called service à la française, relied heavily on assistance from chefs, cooks, butlers, and stewards. Although enjoyed almost exclusively by royalty and nobility, service à la française fundamentally changed food preparation, as well as how people ate socially. It soon trickled down to the middle class, where it was enjoyed in the form influenced by the next great chef: Auguste Escoffier.

BAKING IN AMERICA

As Europeans migrated to North America, they brought with them the culture of baking as a primary source of nutrition. During the first voyages into the New World, the unprepared explorers were forced to rely on the sea and foraging for survival. One of their first culinary discoveries was **maize**. Native Americans had relied on more than 200 varieties of maize, also known as corn, for possibly as long as the Europeans had relied on wheat. The grain was brought back to Europe, where its use rapidly spread, but ultimately it did not replace wheat as the preferred choice for baking (Tannahill, 1988, pp. 204–205).

GASTRONOMIC GROWTH

The Pilgrim Fathers who landed at Plymouth Rock in 1620 brought with them wheat and rye to use as their staple food (Tannahill, 1988, p. 222). To their surprise and dismay, these grains did not take well to the rocky soil of New England, and they were forced to look elsewhere for their food supply. With the help of Native Americans, the settlers learned how to make simple gruels and griddle cakes from maize, including hominy, johnnycakes, and cornpone, which are still consumed today.

As a growing number of immigrants began to settle in America, they brought with them a variety of baked items that formed a large portion of their diets. Much of the influence initially came from England, but as European settlers arrived, so did their baking traditions (Meyer, 1998, p. 4). It is no surprise, then, that from the mid-1700s through the early 1800s, American baking reflected the foodstuffs grown and the cultures settled in various areas. This time period saw the introduction and growing prevalence of pies, johnnycakes, pandowdies, steamed pudding, Indian puddings, and biscuits (Meyer, p. 5).

The advent of additional baking ingredients in America propelled the craft closer to what we know today. In 1750, the first chemical leavening agent was used. Known as pearl ash (potassium carbonate), it was created from natural ash of wood and other natural resources. Before potash was available, cake textures were dense. Ammonia was used also as a leavening agent. A solution of water and ammonia was made and a drop of that solution was inserted on top of the cake batter. The center of the cake would rise as in the madeleine's. Yeast was also commercially produced from the late 1800s, and was relied upon more and more over perpetuated natural starters. Additional chemical leavening agents (potassium bicarbonate and sodium bicarbonate) were created by the turn of the 19th century, but it wasn't until the 1850s that these inventions were accepted and used regularly (Meyer, 1998, p. 10). One of the barriers to widespread use was that a specific list of ingredients was needed to activate the leavening agents. The first baking powder was not introduced until the 1940s, eliminating the need to balance acidic and base ingredients.

By the mid- to late 19th century, the stage was set for the rebirth of the baking industry. Commercial baking was about to make a comeback, for better or worse, thanks to significant technological developments in several areas.

The first was the modern mill, which was created in 1830. This invention mechanized the work of men and enabled massive amounts of grain to be processed for various end products. In 1875, the mill was adapted to hydraulic power, with many mills located close to Niagara Falls (Jacob, 1944, p. 350). The second development was the dough mixer, which was developed in France by the 1850s and became standardized and used in many bakeries a half century later. The next was the increasing prevalence of ovens by the late 1800s, with the first commercial and automated ovens making their initial appearance in the United States around the time of World War I, and later in Europe (Jacob, p. 354). Other innovations in automatic dough dividers, proofing systems, and packaging systems provided faster production times and better sanitation (Jacob, p. 356).

As the 20th century began, regional commercial bakeries across the United States supplied vast quantities of bread to the public. Small town–oriented, "artisan" bakeries began to be less and less common as the efficiency and cost-cutting measures of these large conglomerates were established.

These commercial bakeries of the early 20th century were large enterprises that could afford overproduction, as well as buy back their unsold bread. A 1923 study through Stanford University found that, on average, 6 to 10 percent of bread production went unsold, with the US Food and Drug Administration (FDA) estimating that as many as 600,000 barrels of flour, worth millions of dollars, were being wasted annually. As a result, the FDA set into place measures that extended the shelf life of bread, conserving resources and ensuring public health. Some penny-wise bakers took creative measures to recycle their unsold bread into new bread, until federal laws passed during the Second World War prohibited its reworking. Bread was to be eaten fresh, or it was to be eaten stale (Jacobs, 1944, p. 354).

A Transition Back to Artisan Foods

Through World War II, much of the bread produced in the United States and Europe was made using highly mechanized processes. High-speed mixers, paired with strong wheat flours, mixed dough efficiently and produced a final product with a tight, white crumb and full volume. Dough could now be mixed, baked, and packaged without ever being touched by a human hand. Bakers favored the new mixers because they meant less manual labor, and the public enjoyed the full-volume, soft white bread. Everyone was happy for a short period of time. However, excessive dough oxidation, a lack of preferments for flavor, and the excessive use of dough emulsifiers and stabilizers gave a long shelf life to bread and took out all the flavor and special characteristics of each bakery, from the crust to the crumb. Good quality bread was difficult to find.

In the 1970s, the so-called French bread or baguette became a new trend for the baking industry in the United States. Large companies from France came to the United States to supply the demand. Entrepreneurs started small, establishing first specialty shops and later multiple stores. This brought a new type of bread, not baked in a pan, to the market. The crust was crispy, and the crumb was more open. In general, the quality of this bread was mediocre, the flavor was bland, and the shelf life was only one day. Problems similar to those of pan bread production caused this mediocre quality: overmixing, the addition of dough conditioners (to give it a white open crumb), and a lack of preferments. The low quality of bread brought ambitious newcomers to the baking industry who desired to produce a higher quality of bread. Not many technical publications were available at that time, and those that existed were only in French.

In France, the quality of bread was no better, and the old-fashioned way of making bread was disappearing. Traditions were no longer passed on, and the skilled labor force was shrinking.

One man, Raymond Calvel, was on a mission to bring back the quality of bread to the highest level. Calvel was very opinionated in his views of bread; he was not afraid to say what was on his mind whether talking to the small baker or to larger institutions. His impact in the industry was slow, but he began by building solid foundations.

As Calvel's knowledge and techniques slowly disseminated through sectors of the baking industry, the reaction was wholeheartedly positive, and for good reason. A fresh-baked hearth loaf with a creamy-colored open crumb, a complex flavor, and a thin, crisp, golden crust converted the most stubborn of pan bread eaters. Students of Calvel learned his theories on dough mixing, fermentation, and baking; took them on as their own; and educated fellow bakers and the public in this more refined approach. Most notably, Calvel introduced the world to the autolyse, a technique that can have many positive results on the bread.

The development of the artisan bread movement in the United States was the result of many trials and errors. What may have pushed the movement so far is that there were no limits to the creativity with flavors. This brought us variations on familiar breads such as the seeded baguette and olive, semolina, multigrain, ciabatta, and sourdough bread. To provide the best flavor, texture, and shelf life, most of these breads were produced with preferments from sourdough, liquid starter, poolish, or fermented dough.

Through the evolution of artisan baking, the use of preferments became more popular, dough was allowed to ferment at a longer, slower pace, and the final proof was extended. The time it took to produce baguettes in the 1970s was 3 hours timed from the mixing of the dough to the bake. Today, the average time is from 6 to 16 hours with some processes approaching 24 hours. The result of this increase in fermentation has improved flavor and shelf life. Additionally, by employing new techniques, the breads came to have a more open crumb and for the first time, a darker crust color. The artisan bread movement evolved as a result of crossbreeding specialty bread techniques from different countries.

The most interesting part of the artisan bread evolution in the United States was the creation of techniques unique to individual bakeries. These techniques were sometimes kept secret.

With these new developments in the making of bread, consumers were ready to support the product, and for a change it was not just a fad. Quality bread came to be a part of many people's daily diet. Even when low-carb diets became popular, the market that made quality bread was not affected.

Along with the bread evolution came a revolution in the wheat and flour industry. Bakers were looking for low-protein flour with more ash content. Organic flours are now easily available and affordable. The names of a few bakeries that were pioneers in the artisan movement are Acme Bread Co., Semifreddi's, La Brea Bakery, Della Factoria, Grace Baking, Essential Baking Company, Ecce Panis, Balthazar, Marvelous Market, Artisan Bakers, and Amy's Breads. Because these smaller businesses were successful with artisan breads, the supermarkets also wanted to be involved as there was clearly a growing demand for quality hearth-style breads in the market. Because of the long production procedures, the lack of skilled labor, and regional demand, the supermarkets needed to resolve the problem of distributing bread that did not contain shelf-extension chemicals. The ultimate solution was to par-bake and freeze bread. Larger bakeries that had contracts with supermarkets set up new production systems to accommodate the procedure. The first bread factory of this kind was built in the United States. This factory was such a success that Europeans came to the United States to learn about these production and distribution systems and to get some new ideas about artisan bread in order to improve their product and quality.

We can conclude that the artisan bread has enough flavors to complement a dish or a sandwich due to such large selection of flavors coming from the fermentation and ingredients added to the dough.

The artisan bread movement is still happening and moving to Asia and Australia.

This technology is also expanding and has turned toward Viennoiserie: Laminated dough such as croissant and Danish underwent a transition in processing that established new levels of quality, flavor, and shelf life. Pastry is going through a revival with new ingredients, superior raw materials, and enhanced flavors, textures, and decorations.

BAKING: A WELL-ROUNDED, COMPLEX HISTORY

From the humble beginning of the Neolithic time to the current era, people have been drawn toward grain, and specifically wheat, for its nutritious and cultural significance. The rise and fall of nation-states, disease, plague, war, and hope have all been attributed to an abundance or lack of wheat. Although the information and technology that have been applied to milling, mixing, and baking have changed little through the ages, we are undoubtedly at one of the high points today: the blend of mechanization with artisan processes to create European-style bread for the masses.

The craft is constantly evolving, and though many say that there is nothing new in baking and pastry, innovation and the revitalization of ideas continue to propel the industry forward. A current survey of the best breads and pastries is sure to depict unique presentation and flavor achieved through strict attention to detail and craftsmanship. We need to recognize that many phases and fads come and go within the baking and pastry industry, but we also need to understand them. These are the transformations that mark the evolution of the trade, even while they show where it has been. To understand the history of baking and pastry is also to have a glimpse into its future.

COMMERCIAL BAKING AND PASTRY MAKING TODAY

People who aspire to become a baker or a pastry chef today must be prepared to delve into a career that can be both challenging and rewarding, in an environment that is often invigorating, and sometimes exhausting. They must be curious, creative and precise, ready to contribute to a dynamic field that offers numerous specialty niches and regional variations.

OPPORTUNITIES FOR BAKERS AND PASTRY CHEFS

Traditionally, bakers and pastry chefs spent their entire career exploring one specialty bread or pastry. Today, broader access to ingredients and learning materials makes it more common to master multiple parts of the trade, including specialties like chocolate work, sugar work, bread, Viennoiserie, pie, and wedding cakes.

The baking and pastry arts are under constant refinement through new techniques and presentations. Far from being exhausted, the prestige and surprise elements of pastry established by Carême some 200 years ago are still being explored and built upon.

TRAINING TO BE A BAKER OR PASTRY CHEF

The traditional road to a baking career was through familial connections, with family bakeries typically passed from father to son. When the baking industry took off on an industrial level in the late 1800s, training began to evolve into the model that exists today: school or on-the-job learning. In both situations, aspiring bakers learn from more experienced bakers and/or pastry chefs. Each course of training has pros and cons, and each person must decide which option is best on an individual level.

Going to School

Baking schools typically offer theory-based learning materials about ingredients, equipment, management, and composition; a broad range of ingredients and formulas; different methods of production; and hands-on practice. Many schools offer basic training courses for aspiring bakers and pastry chefs, as well as continuing education for professionals. Classes can range from a couple of days to several years.

The major benefit of attending a school is that students are able to learn a great deal of information in a relatively short amount of time, which they can then put into practice through practical, on-the-job experience. For beginners, this approach establishes a strong foundation that can be very helpful throughout their careers.

Learning on the Job

On-the-job training is great for learning efficient, production-oriented work habits. One drawback to this approach, however, is that the rate of learning new formulas and processes may be significantly slower than at school. When learning on the job, bakers must take their education into their own hands and take full advantage of every opportunity to train. Depending on their individual goals, they may seek out a situation where they can learn a number of skills and take on additional responsibilities. The benefits of on-the-job training are compounded when the trainees can work under several bakers and/or pastry chefs, learning the best from each one to come up with their own unique styles.

Continuing Education

Many experienced bakers and pastry chefs supplement their education and experience with continuing education classes or seminars that further their professional development. These intensively focused courses are meant to teach a highly specialized topic in a short amount of time. Specialized classes can motivate and inspire students to improve the quality of their work, strengthen industry connections, and elevate the craft of baking and pastry. They add real value, both to the individual and to the establishment that sends them.

Another common approach to ongoing professional development is for the baker or pastry chef to complete a **stage** (a short work period to learn techniques and processes) at a workplace other than his or her own. Although the amount of time at a stage may vary, the goal is to gain new skills and inspiration.

Whatever path of training an aspiring baker or pastry chef takes, it is important to remain educated on current trends, new techniques, and new ingredients. Attending specialty seminars and classes and completing stages are great ways to stay ahead of the pack.

OPPORTUNITIES IN BAKING AND PASTRY

Bakers and pastry chefs who have proven their competency often reach for new opportunities in management, research and development, teaching or consulting, competition baking, and more. These new directions often require additional training to expand marketable skills, including food science classes, management classes, and teacher certification programs.

Succeeding beyond the bench takes a lot of individual motivation, drive, and enthusiasm. Those who are up to the challenge are often responsible for training and motivating the next generation of bakers and pastry chefs, and for elevating the craft of the bread and pastry arts to new levels.

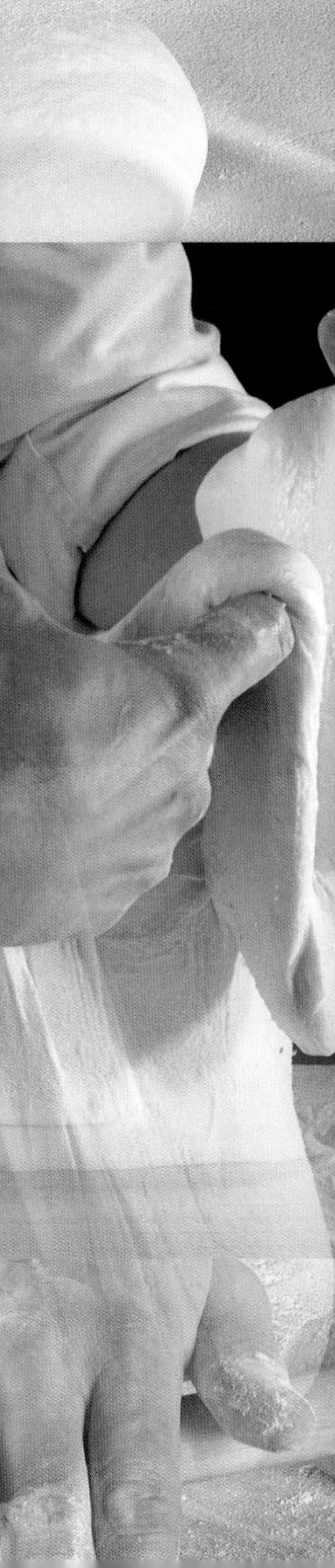

CHAPTER SUMMARY

To fully understand baking and its influence upon humanity, one must look to the many historical moments that baking or pastry have had upon human culture. From famine, the rise and fall of nation-states, the Industrial Revolution, religion, and wars, the influence of baking and pastry has been immense and lasting. The many cultures of the world have developed their own styles of baked goods that represent their land, their struggles, and their successes, and these baked goods are forever enmeshed within their lives. Though the milling, mixing, and baking of breads and pastries have been influenced by technology, we as a people still consume the baked goods that people have eaten throughout history. For a time, highly mechanized processes had altered the basic principles, and we lost quality baked goods. After several years of lesser-quality products being produced, a renaissance of artisan baking took root and has since flourished. With this revival, more and more opportunities exist for bakers and pastry chefs. The interest of the consumer to obtain a high-quality baked good is increasing, and the new bakers and pastry chefs must meet that desire.

KEY TERMS

- ❖ Barley
- ❖ Fornarii
- ❖ Maize
- ❖ Millet
- ❖ Oat
- ❖ Oublies
- ❖ Oubloyers
- ❖ Pastillage
- ❖ Pâtissiers
- ❖ Pièces montées
- ❖ Pistores
- ❖ Porridge
- ❖ Rye
- ❖ Spelt
- ❖ Stage
- ❖ Wheat

REVIEW QUESTIONS

1. **What function did grain play in the lives of people during the Neolithic period?**
2. **What were the results of advancements in baking and pastry during antiquity?**
3. **What was the function of the guilds of the Middle Ages?**
4. **What effect did Carême have on pastry?**
5. **How were measures taken to refresh the quality of bread into what may be considered artisan bread today?**

chapter
2

FOOD SAFETY AND SANITATION IN THE BAKERY

OBJECTIVES

After reading this chapter, you should be able to

- discuss the importance of the food hygiene and sanitation practices that define food safety in a baking or pastry-making environment and gain a basic understanding of the laws and regulations that govern them.
- describe the basic laws and regulations of food hygiene and sanitation.
- explain the Hazard Analysis Critical Control Point system.
- explain the Standard Sanitation Operating Procedures.

FOOD SERVICE INDUSTRY SAFETY AND SANITATION

The food service industry has a duty to those they serve to deliver a product that is free of any potential harm. This is a simple statement to make, but it is not a simple act to perform and perpetuate. The rules and regulations for bakery sanitation and food hygiene must be followed and practiced so that the products being manufactured are safe and clear of any and all hazards. Bakery owners and their employees must follow the food safety and sanitation laws that have been set. They must learn and adhere to these laws. The **Hazard Analysis Critical Control Point (HACCP)** system and the **Sanitation Standard Operating Procedures (SSOPs)** are systems that have been established to provide the basic understanding and the practical execution of these laws necessary for a safe food product and a safe food-producing environment. Much of this chapter is dedicated to the rules and regulations that govern the industry and the methods used to counter potentially hazardous problems.

HOW FOOD LAWS AND REGULATIONS AFFECT BAKING AND PASTRY MAKING

In the nearly 70 years since it was enacted, the **Federal Food, Drug, and Cosmetic Act (FDCA)** of 1938 has not only retained its relevance to the baking industry but also serves as the basis of a safe food supply. As significant as the FDCA is, however, it did not mark the beginning of food laws and regulations. It was the culmination of thousands of years of history and experience in attempting to prevent unsafe and misleading practices in the production and marketing of foods, coupled with the application of knowledge gained through advances in science and technology.

Two of the foremost objectives of food law are to prevent **adulteration** and to punish those who perpetrate it, when and where necessary. The two general types of adulteration are economic and foreign material. Economic adulteration refers to the act of reducing the value of a food by mixing it with a less valuable ingredient (such as diluting orange juice with water) or by removing a more valuable material from a food (such as marketing cookies as being made with butter when they actually contain shortening).

Foreign material adulteration describes aesthetically displeasing (rodent hairs, insect fragments, and so on) or potentially harmful (pathogenic microorganisms, glass, unsafe chemicals, and so on) materials that are contained in the bread or pastry product.

Historical references to food adulteration are plentiful. In early Rome, merchants frequently claimed that artificial oil was pure olive oil, and early Roman law prohibited the practice of adding good grain to spoiled grain to mask deterioration. In approximately 200 BCE, Cato described a method for determining whether wine had been watered down. Later on in 15th-century Europe, a proclamation was made prohibiting the sale of wine that misrepresented the region of its origin.

Early food laws also related to baking. For example, in 1202, King John of England prohibited the adulteration of bread with ingredients of lower economic value than flour, such as ground peas or beans.

Other examples of concern over food safety include a 1723 English law prohibiting the use of lead pipes in the liquor distillation process, as well as an 1898 Virginia law that considered candy to be adulterated if it contained any of a number of mineral substances, poisonous colors or flavors, or other ingredients that could prove injurious to health.

Today, it is a credit to the baking industry that the industrialized countries of the world have an extremely safe baked goods supply. Even so, foreign material and/or unapproved chemicals occasionally do make their way into breads and pastries. If these materials are not detected prior to release for sales and distribution, they can become the subjects of product recalls or actions taken to remove those products from the market.

Recalls can be conducted on a bakery owner's initiative or at the request of the **US Food and Drug Administration (FDA)**. All bread- and pastry-producing companies, regardless of size, are subject to the possibility of recalls and must have systems in place to allow the tracking of products from production through distribution for the duration of their shelf lives. Recalls are classified as Class I, II, or III, with Class I representing the highest probability that use of or exposure to the product will cause serious health consequences or death.

Whether intentional or unintentional, food adulteration continues to be a potential problem that is specifically addressed and prohibited by modern food laws and regulations. Additionally, much of the effort of federal, state, and local regulatory agencies is devoted to uncovering and taking action against companies and individuals who engage in these practices.

The **Nutrition Labeling and Education Act of 1990 (NLEA)** amended the FDCA and contained provisions that mandated nutritional labeling on all commercially produced bakery products. This critical piece of legislation marked the beginning of a new era in the regulation of the US food supply. By requiring proactive labeling to prevent false and misleading statements about food products, it enabled consumers to make informed decisions when choosing foods. The NLEA also acknowledged the vital relationship between diet and health, giving consumers tools that would allow them to choose baked goods based on complete, accurate, and truthful information.

Today, a combination of federal, state, and local government regulations work together to ensure that any bread item or pastry that reaches the public is safe. For this reason, new bakeries should contact their local health department prior to start-up to ensure compliance with necessary legal requirements. Some states, local jurisdictions, and academic institutions offer sanitation certification programs for bakeries. The location and availability of these certification programs varies from state to state and is easily researched online.

GOOD MANUFACTURING PRACTICES IN THE BAKERY

Good Manufacturing Practices (GMPs) are guidelines that provide a system of processes, procedures, and documentation to ensure that the bread or pastry produced has the identity, strength, composition, quality, and purity that it is represented to possess.

The legal basis for GMPs was established with the passage of the FDCA in 1938, but it was not until the late 1960s that regulations regarding food adulteration were finalized to help the food industry deal with the provisions of the Act. The regulations are written as requirements and make consistent use of the term *shall* rather than *should*. This terminology is used for a specific reason: *shall* means "required," while *should* means "suggested or recommended." GMPs are enforcement tools that are primarily used in conjunction with the inspection of a food plant or warehouse. They are a valuable tool for producers of baked goods, and when properly implemented, they may help avoid a charge of adulteration under the FDCA.

Detailed GMP regulations can be found in the *Code of Federal Regulations*, Title 21. Subpart A, Section 110.10 covers personnel issues:

(a) *Disease control.* Any person who, by medical examination or supervisory observation, is shown to have, or appears to have, an illness, open lesion, including boils, sores, or infected wounds, or any other abnormal source of microbial contamination by which there is a reasonable possibility of food, food-contact surfaces, or food-packaging materials becoming contaminated, shall be excluded from any operations which may be expected to result in such contamination until the condition is corrected. Personnel shall be instructed to report such health conditions to their supervisors.

(b) *Cleanliness.* All persons working in direct contact with food, food-contact surfaces, and food-packaging materials shall conform to hygienic practices while on duty to the extent necessary to protect against contamination of food. The methods for maintaining cleanliness include, but are not limited to: (1) Wearing outer garments suitable to the operation in a manner that protects against the contamination of food, food-contact surfaces, or food-packaging materials. (2) Maintaining adequate personal cleanliness. (3) Washing hands thoroughly (and sanitizing if necessary to protect against contamination with undesirable microorganisms) in an adequate hand-washing facility before starting work, after each absence from the work station, and at any other time when the hands may have become soiled or contaminated. (4) Removing all unsecured jewelry and other objects that might fall into food, equipment, or containers, and removing hand jewelry that cannot be adequately sanitized during periods in which food is manipulated by hand. If such hand jewelry cannot be removed, it may be covered by material which can be maintained in an intact, clean, and sanitary condition and which effectively protects against contamination by these objects of the food, food-contact surfaces, or food-packaging materials. (5) Maintaining gloves, if they are used in food handling, in an intact, clean, and sanitary condition. The gloves should be of an impermeable material. (6) Wearing, where appropriate, in an effective manner, hair nets, headbands, caps, beard covers, or other effective hair restraints. (7) Storing clothing or other personal belongings in areas other than where food is exposed or where equipment or utensils are washed. (8) Confining the following to areas other than where food may be exposed or where equipment or utensils are washed: eating food, chewing gum, drinking beverages, or using tobacco. (9) Taking any other necessary precautions to protect against contamination of food, food-contact surfaces, or food-packaging materials with microorganisms or foreign substances including, but not limited to, perspiration, hair, cosmetics, tobacco, chemicals, and medicines applied to the skin.

(c) *Education and training*. Personnel responsible for identifying sanitation failures or food contamination should have a background of education or experience, or a combination thereof, to provide a level of competency necessary for production of clean and safe food. Food handlers and supervisors should receive appropriate training in proper food handling techniques and food-protection principles and should be informed of the danger of poor personal hygiene and unsanitary practices.

(d) *Supervision*. Responsibility for assuring compliance by all personnel with all requirements shall be clearly assigned to competent supervisory personnel. (Current good manufacturing . . . , 2007)

FOOD SAFETY IN THE BAKERY

Consumers expect to buy breads and pastries that are safe to eat. Whether it is purchased for preparation in the home, or prepared by others and purchased for consumption at a restaurant or other food service establishment, baked goods are expected to be free of hazards that might cause discomfort, illness, or death.

The use of Hazard Analysis Critical Control Points (HACCP) was initiated in the early 1960s as a cooperative effort between the Pillsbury Company, the National Air and Space Administration (NASA), the Natick Laboratories of the US Army, and the US Air Force Space Laboratory Project Group. The original purpose of HACCP was to produce defect- and hazard-free food for astronauts to consume during space flights.

Today, that mission has expanded. The FDA has taken the position that it cannot guarantee the safety of the general food supply because it simply does not have the necessary resources in existing oversight, policing, and inspection programs. All segments of the food industry, including bakeries, need to share in the responsibility by taking steps to avoid failures in the food production, processing, and supply system. This has led to the development and potential regulatory requirement of HACCP programs as essential elements of food safety in bakery operations throughout the United States.

THE SEVEN ELEMENTS OF AN HACCP PROGRAM

A properly developed and implemented HACCP program should be designed to prevent hazards in the baking process, rather than to detect them once they have occurred. This is accomplished through an end-product testing program.

Analyzing Hazards

In developing an HACCP program, it is first necessary to determine what hazards might exist in the bread or pastry being produced. These can only be identified after the word *hazard* has been accurately defined.

In technical terms, a hazard is the presence in a food of a poisonous or deleterious substance in violation of Section 402(a)(1) of the FDCA. A hazard is more specific than an adulterant. A food containing a hazard is considered to be adulterated, but the presence of an adulterant does not necessarily constitute a hazard. For example, a food can be adulterated with substances such as insect parts, which, while aesthetically displeasing, are not a hazard to a consumer of that food.

Instead, a hazard is commonly defined as either a microorganism, chemical, or physical substance. If the hazard is a microorganism, it must be pathogenic; if it is a chemical, it must be considered harmful at the levels consumed; and if it is a physical substance, it must be capable of causing injury when ingested. Examples of physical hazards include pieces of glass or fragments of metal that might find their way into a baked good.

Once a good understanding of what constitutes a hazard has been attained, the next step is to review bakery production processes to discover where a hazard might enter the baked good. A thorough review of the ingredients, formula, process, and storage conditions, conducted by a knowledgeable person, will determine what hazards might occur in the finished bread item. One obvious source is the ingredients and other raw materials used. Another source might be a breakdown in some aspect of the processing system, such as failure in a sterilization process.

Figures 2-1 and 2-2 are examples of a process flowchart and a process hazard assessment matrix that might be used in the production of a sourdough baguette. Note that, on the flowchart, every step in the production process is listed and the critical control point(s) are clearly identified. The process hazard assessment matrix is a detailed report that helps the bakery staff determine which hazards could possibly be introduced into the baked good, and at which step in the process this would likely occur.

Identifying Critical Control Points in the Baking Process

A critical control point (CCP) is defined as a point at which a hazard might develop or enter the baked good if the operation is out of control. If the loss of control might lead to a potential hazard, the point is considered

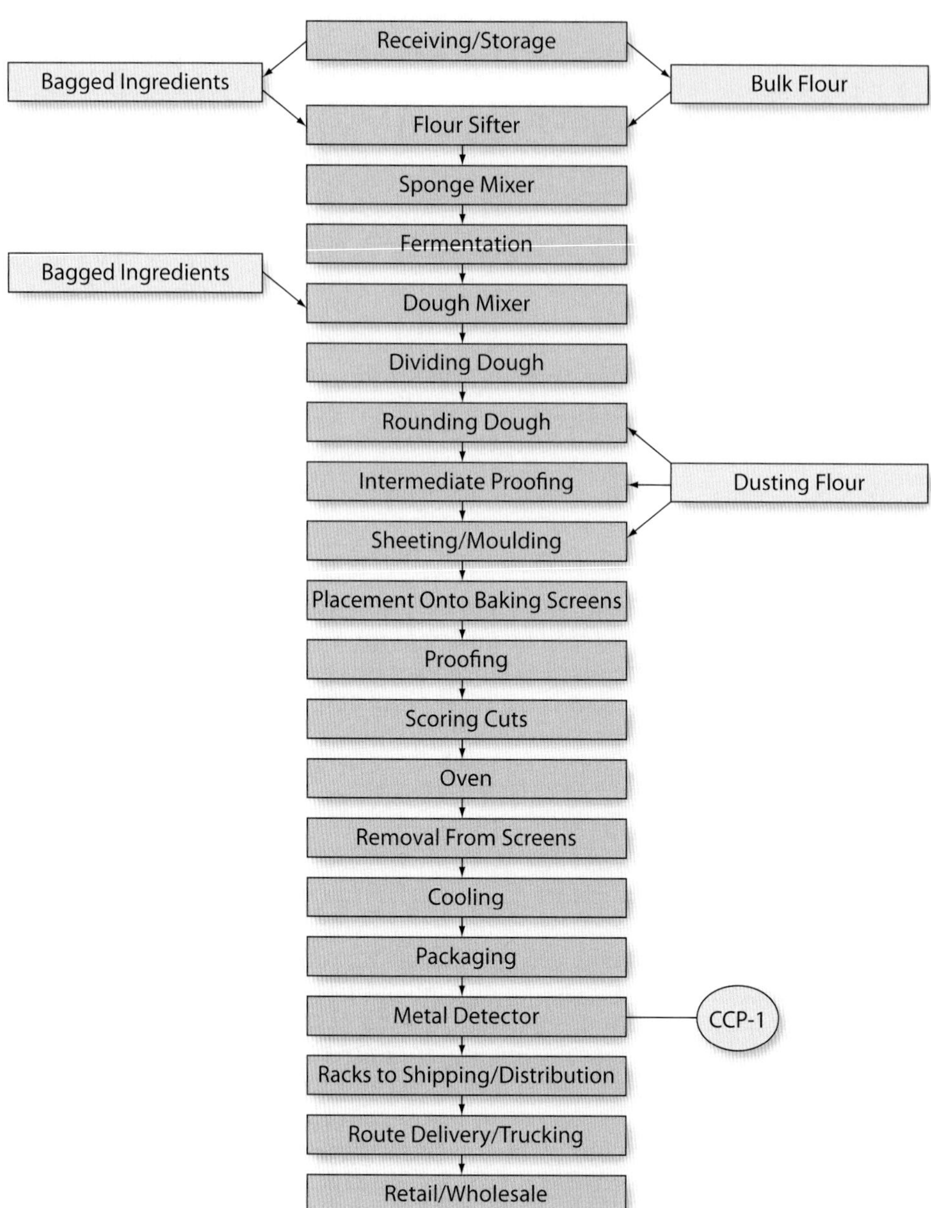

Figure 2-1
Sourdough Baguette Production Flowchart

a *critical* control point. However, if the loss of control might result in a deviation from quality standards, the point is considered a *quality* control point. Although HACCP programs are only concerned with critical control points, a reputable bakery is concerned with both critical and quality control points.

When determining where critical control points exist in a baking operation, the use of a decision tree is often helpful. An example of this approach, as developed by the National Advisory Committee on Microbiological Criteria for Foods (NACMCF), is presented in Figure 2-3.

Establishing Limits for Critical Control Points

In general, a critical control point must be operating out of control for a hazard to develop or enter the bread or pastry item. To effectively prevent this from occurring, it is necessary to determine the point at which the potential for a hazard arises. This ability to establish limits is only possible if a thorough knowledge of both hazards and process exists.

Figure 2-2 Process Hazard Assessment of Sourdough Baguette Production

1	2	3	4	5	6
Processing Step	**Hazard INTRODUCED by Ingredient or This Process Step (B) biological, (C) chemical, (P) physical**	**Is Hazard CONTROLLED by Pre-Req. Program (Yes or No)? If Yes, List.**	**Is Hazard ELIMINATED by Later Step (Yes or No)?**	**Identify the Later Step Which Controls/Eliminates Potential Hazard**	**Critical Control Point (CCP)**
Bulk Ingredient Receiving	(B) *Salmonella*, aflatoxin, vomitoxin (C) Allergen cross contamination (P) Paper, plastic, wood, metal	(B) Yes, product specs (C) Yes, receiving procedures (P) Yes, GMPs	(B) Yes (C) (P) Yes	(B) Baking, product reaches internal temp of 200°F (C) (P) Metal Detector CCP#1	
Incidental Ingredient Receiving	(B) *Salmonella*, aflatoxin, vomitoxin (C) Allergen cross contamination (P) Paper, plastic, wood, metal	(B) Yes, product specs (C) Yes, receiving procedures (P) Yes, GMPs	(B) Yes (C) (P) Yes	(B) Baking, product reaches internal temp of 200°F (C) (P) Metal Detector CCP#1	
Storage of Ingredients	(B) Mold related to bulk silos (C) Allergen cross contamination (P) Paper, plastic, metal	(B) MCS (C) Yes, production GMPs, allergen control protocols (P) Paper/plastic: Yes: GMPs. Metal: No	(B) (C) (P) Yes	(B) (C) (P) Metal Detector CCP#1	
Bulk Flour Sifter	(B) None (C) None (P) Paper, plastic, metal	(B) (C) (P) Paper/plastic: Yes: GMPs. Metal: No sifter screen size #30 mesh	(B) (C) (P) Yes	(B) (C) (P) Metal Detector CCP#1	
Scaling of Ingredients	(B) Mold (C) Allergen cross contamination, from previous products (P) Metal	(B) MCS (C) Yes, production GMPs, allergen control protocols (P) Paper/plastic: Yes: GMPs. Metal: No	(B) NA (C) (P) Yes	(B) Baking, product reaches internal temp of 200°F (C) (P) Metal Detector CCP#1	
Sponge/Dough Mixing	(B) None (C) Allergen cross contamination, from previous products (P) Metal	(B) NA (C) Yes, production GMPs, allergen control protocols (P) Paper/plastic: Yes: GMPs. Metal: No	(B) NA (C) (P) Yes	(B) (C) (P) Metal Detector CCP#1	
Fermentation	(B) Mold (C) Allergen cross contamination, from previous products (P) Metal	(B) MCS (C) Yes, production GMPs, allergen control protocols (P) Paper/plastic: Yes: GMPs. Metal: No	(B) (C) (P) Yes	(B) (C) (P) Metal Detector CCP#1	
Machining (divider & moulder)	(B) None (C) Allergen cross contamination, from previous products (P) Metal	(B) NA (C) Yes, production GMPs, allergen control protocols (P) Metal	(B) NA (C) (P) Yes	(B) (C) (P) Metal Detector CCP#1	

(continues)

Figure 2-2 Process Hazard Assessment of Sourdough Baguette Production *(continued)*

1	2	3	4	5	6
Processing Step	**Hazard INTRODUCED by Ingredient or This Process Step (B) biological, (C) chemical, (P) physical**	**Is Hazard CONTROLLED by Pre-Req. Program (Yes or No)? If Yes, List.**	**Is Hazard ELIMINATED by Later Step (Yes or No)?**	**Identify the Later Step Which Controls/Eliminates Potential Hazard**	**Critical Control Point (CCP)**
Screening and/or Peelboards	(B) Mold (C) Allergen cross contamination, from previous products (P) Metal, wood	(B) Rotation of peelboards (C) Yes, production GMPs, allergen control protocols (P) No	(B) Yes (C) (P) Yes	(B) Baking, product reaches internal temp of 200°F (C) (P) Metal Detector CCP#1	
Proofer	(B) None (C) Allergen cross contamination, from previous products (P) Metal	(B) NA (C) Yes, production GMPs, allergen control protocols (P) No	(B) NA (C) (P) Yes	(B) NA (C) (P) Metal Detector CCP#1	
Scoring	(B) None (C) Allergen cross contamination, from previous products (P) Metal	(B) NA (C) Yes, production GMPs, allergen control protocols (P) No	(B) NA (C) (P) Yes	(B) NA (C) (P) Metal Detector CCP#1	
Depanning	(B) None (C) Allergen cross contamination, from previous products (P) Metal	(B) NA (C) Yes, production GMPs, allergen control protocols (P) Metal: No	(B) NA (C) (P) Yes	(B) NA (C) (P) Metal Detector CCP#1	
Cooling	(B) None (C) Allergen cross contamination, from previous products (P) Metal	(B) NA (C) Yes, production GMPs, allergen control protocols (P) Plastic: Yes: GMPs. Metal: No	(B) NA (C) (P) Yes	(B) NA (C) (P) Metal Detector CCP#1	
Packaging	(B) None (C) Printed film allergen legend errors/wrong packaging, contamination from previous products (P) None	(B) NA (C) Yes, receiving and production allergen control protocols (P)	(B) NA (C) (P)	(B) NA (C) (P)	
Metal Detector	(B) None (C) Allergen cross contamination, from previous products (P) Metal	(B) (C) Yes, production GMPs, allergen control protocols (P) No	(B) (C) (P) Yes	(B) (C) (P) Metal Detector CCP#1	CCP#1
Distribution & Storage	(B) None (C) Printed film allergen legend errors/wrong packaging, contamination from previous products (P) Foreign material	(B) (C) Yes, receiving and production allergen control protocols (P) Pest control	(B) (C) (P)	(B) (C) (P)	

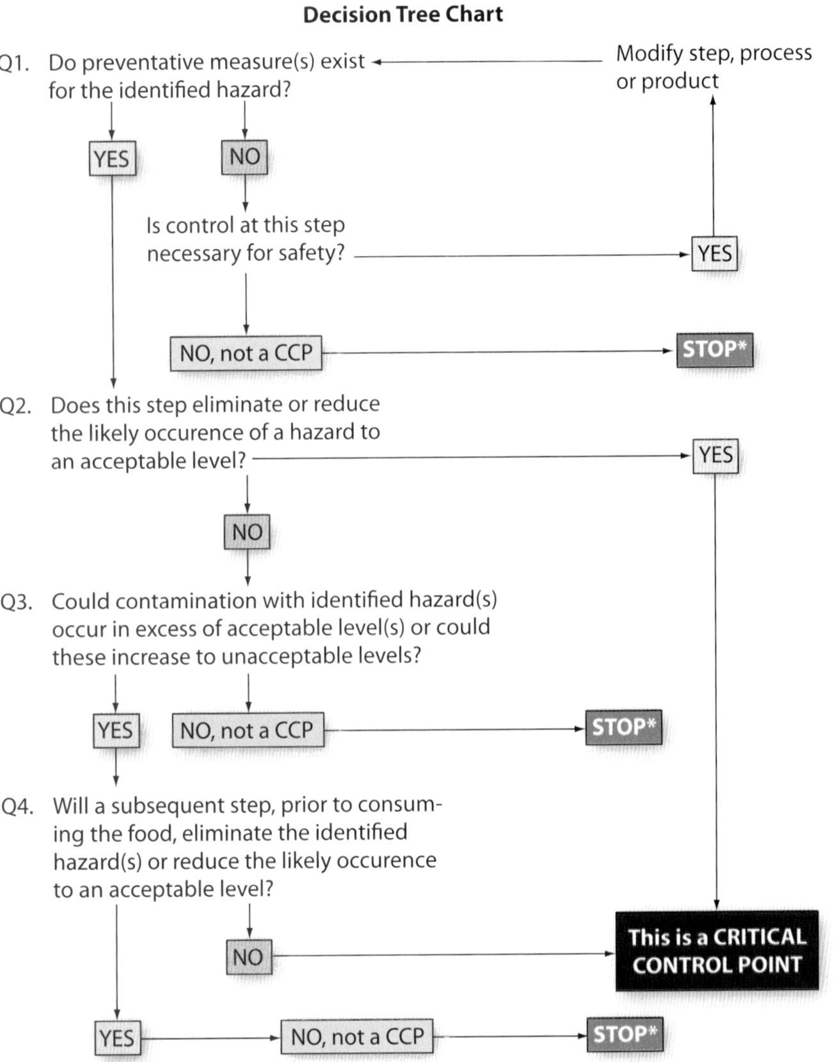

Figure 2-3
Decision Tree Chart

Setting limits for each CCP is not an easy task, but it is an essential step in developing an effective HACCP program.

Monitoring Critical Control Points

After a CCP's acceptable limits have been established, a monitoring system must be implemented. This will ensure that if a process exceeds limits and a hazard potential exists, corrective action may be taken promptly. To keep potential product losses to a minimum, a continuous monitoring system is preferred. If continuous or frequent monitoring is used, it is also often possible to identify trends that might result in an out-of-control situation.

Detailing Proper and Effective Corrective Action

Identification and monitoring of critical control points are only the beginning of the process. A complete HACCP plan for the bakery also specifies the corrective action that must be taken when the monitoring system reveals that a critical control point is outside established limits. This can even include shutting down a bread-processing line until corrective actions are completed. Sample corrective actions include rejecting a shipment of an ingredient, such as flour, that contains a pathogenic microorganism at a level above the acceptable maximum, or adjusting the calibration of a measuring device, such as a divider or moulder, that has allowed an operation to drift out of control. Flour, for example, could have unacceptable levels of aflatoxins (mold), which is commonly found in this ingredient. If a load of flour came into a facility with a COA (Certificate of Analysis) from the vendor showing a higher-than-normal percentage of moisture, then the ingredient would be suspected to have levels of aflatoxins that exceed the boundaries set forth in the HACCP plan. Based on this information, the customer would reject this load of flour.

Developing a Record-Keeping System for the Bakery

A comprehensive record-keeping system for the bakery is essential to demonstrate the establishment of a system, to document its utilization, and to verify its effectiveness in the production of safe consumable baked goods. Although HACCP programs represent a cooperative effort and shared responsibility for ensuring the safety of the food supply, a regulatory agency such as the FDA needs more than verbal assurances that an effective plan has been developed and is being used. An organized and up-to-date written plan provides required evidence and provides the agency with tools to assess the plan and its validity for the bakery operation.

Both bakery management and regulatory officials typically examine monitoring data and records of corrective action to ascertain that the HACCP system is being used properly. These records can also include documentation of training received by the bakery employees responsible for implementing the program. These training records add further verification that an effective system is being practiced.

Verifying Procedures

The final step in developing and implementing an HACCP program is to verify that all of the previously described actions and procedures are effective. Critical control points should be reviewed periodically, and changes should be made when needed. Bakery management should regularly verify that control point limits are still appropriate, and that records are complete and easily available. There should be evidence that effective corrective action has been taken when a control point is found to be outside of limits and the results of those verification procedures should be recorded so that the efficacy of the HACCP program can be demonstrated to regulatory officials and others.

HACCP Summary

Although HACCP programs are not a new concept in food safety, they are receiving favorable attention as a means toward achieving total and comprehensive prevention of food safety problems. An effective HACCP program contains these seven components:

- Determination of potential hazards for each process
- Identification of potential hazard control points
- Establishment of limits for critical control points
- Establishment of procedures to monitor control points
- Establishment of corrective actions when control points exceed limits
- Establishment of an appropriate record-keeping system
- Establishment of a program to verify efficacy of the HACCP program

FOOD HYGIENE IN THE BAKERY

Proper food hygiene is essential to ensure that bread and pastry products meant for the marketplace are safe for customers to consume. When recommended practices are followed, the reputation of a business and the health of its customers are protected. Of course, observance of good hygiene practices is also a requirement of the law.

Because harmful bacteria that cause food poisoning are easily spread, everything possible must be done to prevent this from happening. Food poisoning can, at the very least, cause severe discomfort; in extreme cases, it can lead to serious illness or even death.

There are four main defenses against the growth and spread of bacteria:

- Ensure that food areas are clean and good standards of **personal hygiene** are maintained.
- Store, prepare, and cook foods properly.
- Keep foods at the right temperature.
- Prevent cross contamination.

To achieve good hygiene, these actions must be implemented at every step of the process, from the moment a food or raw ingredient is received to the sale of the final product. If hygiene standards fail at any stage along the way, the result can be food poisoning.

PERSONAL HYGIENE

Food can be contaminated very easily when it is handled. For this reason, all bakery staff who handle doughs or other ingredients must maintain good standards of personal hygiene at all times, and systems must be in place to ensure that the product does not get contaminated with harmful germs, dirt, or foreign material.

In particular, hands must be washed and dried regularly during the preparation process:

- Before starting work
- Before handling ready-to-eat foods
- After touching raw food, especially raw meat or poultry
- After using the toilet
- After a break

Employees must be instructed in proper hand-washing methods and practice these techniques. To wash hands thoroughly, use warm water and liquid soap. Work up a good lather and make sure to wash wrists, hands, fingers, thumbs, fingernails, and in between the fingers. Rinse the soap off and dry hands thoroughly using disposable towels or a hot-air dryer; do not dry hands on an apron or other piece of clothing.

Staff working in food preparation areas should also

- Wear clean clothes and an apron or other clean protective garment.
- Refrain from touching their hair or faces.
- Cover cuts or sores with clean, waterproof dressings with a disposable outer glove.
- Wash hands after blowing their noses.
- Refrain from coughing or sneezing over food.

- Refrain from smoking.
- Avoid wearing jewelry or false nails that might fall into food.

Training and Supervision

Bakery owners or those who supervise the preparation of breads and pastries must ensure that food handlers receive instruction in food hygiene, as well as supervision that is appropriate for their work. Local environmental health agencies should be able to provide information, including details about available training programs, along with advice.

Staff Illness

Staff members who arrive at work exhibiting food poisoning symptoms like diarrhea, vomiting, or stomach pain must not be allowed to work in food preparation areas or handle food as they can easily contaminate it and make others ill.

INGREDIENTS

To ensure food safety, reputable food suppliers should be chosen, and measures should be taken to ensure the products purchased have been stored, processed, and treated safely. When ingredients are delivered, they should be checked to verify that

- The order is correct.
- Chilled and frozen food is at the right temperature.
- The packaging is undamaged and intact.

Storing Food

Food must be stored correctly to keep it safe. In particular, make sure that

- Temperature control is observed.
- Raw food, especially meat and dairy products, is kept away from ready-to-eat food, ideally in separate refrigerators.
- Meat and eggs are stored in sealable containers at the bottom of the refrigerator, so that they cannot touch or drip onto ready-to-eat food.
- Refrigerators are not overloaded and circulation of cool air is not restricted, which can result in food not being kept at cool enough temperatures.
- Dry goods such as flour, grains, and nuts are stored off the floor, ideally in sealable containers, to protect them from pests.
- Food is never used after the use-by date has elapsed, since it may not be safe to eat.
- Food with a short shelf life is checked every day to make sure the use-by date has not passed.
- Storage instructions on the product label or packaging are followed.

As a practical tip, the **first-in, first-out (FIFO)** rule should be followed when storing foods. This involves rotating stock to move foods with a closer use by or best before date to the front of the shelf, so they get used first.

Preparing Food

Food can become contaminated very easily during preparation. To avoid contamination, food handlers should

- Observe good personal hygiene.
- Use different chopping boards/work surfaces for raw food and ready-to-eat food.

- Use different equipment and utensils for raw and ready-to-eat food, wherever possible.
- Clean equipment and surfaces thoroughly before and after use.
- Avoid using hands to transfer food, using clean tongs, plates, or trays instead.
- Return chilled food to the refrigerator as soon as possible during preparation.

Cooking/Baking

Proper cooking or baking kills poisonous bacteria such as *Salmonella, Campylobacter, Escherichia coli* 0157:H7, and *Listeria*. For this reason, it is important to cook and reheat food thoroughly, especially dairy products and meat, if used. Food should not be reheated more than one time, and foods should be allowed to cool somewhat before placing in the refrigerator. This will prevent heat from these items from warming up other foods stored nearby. Furthermore, the FDA guidelines state that food must cool from 135°F (57°C) to 70°F (21°C) within 2 hours and that foods must cool from 70°F (21°C) to 41°F (5°C) in an additional 4 hours.

TEMPERATURE CONTROL

Strict temperature control must be maintained in order to keep certain foods safe. Prepared ready-to-eat foods, cooked foods, smoked meat or fish, and certain dairy products must, by law, be kept hot or chilled until they are served to a customer. If they are not, harmful bacteria can grow or toxins (poisons) can form in the food, causing consumers to become ill.

Certain **pathogens** or disease-causing microorganisms can survive at all temperature ranges. For many of those capable of causing foodborne illness, however, the most hospitable environment is one with temperatures 41°F (5°C) to 135°F (57°C)—a range known as the **danger zone**. Above 135°F (57°C), most pathogens are either destroyed or will not reproduce. Below 41°F (5°C), the cycle of reproduction will be slowed or interrupted.

For these reasons, foods that are being kept hot before serving should remain above 145°F (63°C) and their temperatures should be continuously monitored. Foods that are being held to be served chilled should be kept at 40°F (4°C) or below.

CROSS CONTAMINATION

The term **cross contamination** describes the transfer of bacteria from one food, typically raw, to other foods. The bacteria can be transferred directly, when the contaminated food touches another food, or indirectly, via hands, equipment, work surfaces, knives, and/or other utensils. Such cross contamination can easily occur in the bakery where eggs and dairy products are a common ingredient. Cross contamination occurs frequently and is one of the major causes of food poisoning. Some of the most common causes include storing raw and ready-to-eat food together, not washing hands after touching raw foods, and using the same chopping board or knife for raw and ready-to-eat food.

FOODBORNE ILLNESS

In all, 76 million cases of foodborne illness occur each year in the United States. Five thousand of these result in death.

CAUSES

Although bacteria or their toxins cause most foodborne illness, it can also be related to parasites (trichinosis), viruses (hepatitis), and chemicals (mushrooms). Contamination of foods can occur during cultivation, harvesting, handling, storage, transportation, or preparation.

RISK FACTORS

Pregnant women, the elderly, small children, and persons with chronic health problems such as diabetes, liver cirrhosis, chronic kidney failure, AIDS, and cancer are at an increased risk for contracting foodborne illnesses.

A total of 79 percent of foodborne outbreaks in the United States are attributable to bacteria, with *Salmonella* constituting over half of confirmed cases. *Salmonella* can be contracted by consuming eggs, meat, and poultry. In all, one in 20,000 eggs carries *Salmonella* inside the eggshell. *Campylobacter*, which is spread through milk, chicken, beef, and companion animals, causes 4 million cases of foodborne illness each year in the United States. It is typically more sporadic and not associated with an outbreak.

DIAGNOSIS

The symptoms of foodborne illness resemble stomach flu. Sufferers complain of stomach cramps, nausea, vomiting, and diarrhea. In some cases, fever, headache, body aches, and dehydration can occur. A proper diagnosis is based on the history of ingestion of particular foods and laboratory testing. Examination of the suspected food, if it is available, is helpful.

TREATMENT

Most foodborne illnesses are relatively mild and require no treatment other than increased intake of fluids to replace those lost. Patients exhibiting serious symptoms such as bleeding, fever, neurological symptoms, shallow breathing, and dizziness should consult a physician immediately. In some cases, hospitalization is necessary for hydration or other medical treatment.

FOODBORNE PATHOGENS

Those involved in the food preparation business are responsible for becoming knowledgeable about pathogens, including where they come from and how to avoid them. The most commonly encountered and problematic of these include

- *Campylobacter*, the most common bacterial cause of diarrhea in the United States—Its sources are raw milk, untreated water, and raw or undercooked meat and poultry.
- *Clostridium botulinum*, an organism that produces a toxin that causes botulism—This life-threatening illness, which can prevent the breathing muscles from moving air in and out of the lungs, can be caused by home-prepared foods and herbal oils. Also, due to the possible presence of *Clostridium botulinum*, honey should not be fed to children younger than 12 months old.
- *Escherichia coli* 0157:H7, a bacterium that can produce a deadly toxin—*E. coli* 0157:H7 causes approximately 73,000 cases of foodborne illness

each year in the United States. Its sources are raw milk, produce, and meat, especially undercooked or raw hamburger.

- *Listeria monocytogenes*, the cause of listeriosis, a serious disease for pregnant women, newborns, and adults with a weakened immune system—Its main sources are soil and water, and it has been found in dairy products, including soft cheese, as well as in raw and undercooked meat, poultry, seafood, and produce.
- *Norovirus*, the leading cause of diarrhea in the United States—Any food can be contaminated with norovirus if handled by someone who is infected with it.
- *Salmonella*, responsible for millions of cases of foodborne illness every year—As the most common cause of foodborne death, its sources include raw and undercooked eggs, undercooked poultry and meat, dairy products, seafood, fruits, and vegetables.
- *Staphylococcus aureus*, a bacterium with toxins that cause vomiting shortly after ingesting—It is found in cooked foods that are high in protein such as cooked ham, salads, bakery products, and dairy products.
- *Shigella*, the cause of an estimated 3 million cases of diarrhea illnesses annually—Poor hygiene causes *Shigella* to be easily passed from person to person. Its sources are salads, milk and dairy products, and unclean water.
- *Toxoplasma gondii*, a parasite that causes toxoplasmosis—This serious disease can produce central nervous system disorders, particularly mental retardation and visual impairment in children. Pregnant women and people with weakened immune systems are at higher risk. The primary sources of *Toxoplasma gondii* are pork and other meats.
- *Vibrio vulnificus*, a bacterium that causes gastroenteritis or a syndrome known as primary septicemia—People with liver diseases are at especially high risk of contracting *Vibrio vulnificus*. It is found in raw or undercooked seafood.

ALLERGENS

A **food allergen** is a product or ingredient that contains certain proteins that can potentially cause severe, occasionally fatal, reactions in a person who is allergic to that food. Allergen proteins occur naturally and cannot be eliminated by cooking or baking. Note that many of the most common and dangerous allergens, listed in the next section, are used in the baking industry.

Food allergies cause a response in the immune system that can range from discomfort to a life-threatening reaction. Currently no medications that cure food allergies are available, although epinephrine, or adrenaline, is commonly used to control the allergic reaction to a food protein. The only way to prevent a reaction from occurring is for the allergic person to avoid the food.

THE BIG EIGHT

According to the *FDA Guidance Document for Food Investigators*, eight foods contain the proteins that cause 90 percent of all food-allergic reactions. In compiling this list, the FDA focused on the primary foods that cause anaphylaxis, including

- Milk
- Eggs

- Peanuts
- Tree nuts
- Fish
- Shellfish
- Soy
- Wheat

In Canada, the list of major allergens has been expanded to include sesame seeds and sulfites. Note that the category of tree nuts includes walnuts, almonds, pecans, hazelnuts/filberts, pistachios, cashews, pine nuts, macadamia nuts, and Brazil nuts. Shellfish includes crab, crawfish, lobster, shrimp, mussels, and oysters. Wheat includes barley, rye, oats, and spelt, either as the grain, flour, or in another other form. In all categories, the exact amount of allergenic protein required to bring on an allergenic response is not yet known.

All food allergens are proteins, but not all proteins are allergens. Approximately 170 different food materials have been identified as capable of causing an allergic response and should be of particular concern to producers of baked goods. These foods include cottonseed, poppy seed, sunflower seed, sesame seed, legumes, and sulfites, and the list continues to grow. Chemical sensitivities to sulfites and FD&C yellow #5 are also generally included as part of the allergen review; however, sulfites added at a level of less than 10 parts per million (ppm) do not have to be listed on the ingredient label.

Allergens should be included as part of the ingredient hazard analysis in a baking facility's HACCP program. If the facility does not have an HACCP plan, then ingredients should be reviewed independently for allergen content. A methodology for differentiating allergenic ingredients from nonallergenic ingredients should be developed, and allergens should be identified as a single ingredient or component ingredients within a mix on the ingredient specification. Bakeries can use many different methods to identify ingredients as long as the program is followed. The ingredient hazard analysis should also include processing aids or incidental additives that may contain an allergen, sulfites, or FD&C yellow #5.

The key to managing allergens in processing is to avoid cross contamination. For informational purposes, the area in the process flow where each allergen is added should be listed. If the same allergenic ingredient is used in all product formulations, there is no risk of cross contamination. Unfortunately, this is generally not the case. The possibility of cross contamination in the bakery environment might occur, for example, when going from production of a seeded or nut bread to one that will not be labeled as containing nuts or seeds. Proper sanitation or changeover cleanup of equipment and surfaces, coupled with segregation of pans and screens, will help to avoid allergen cross contamination.

LABELING

Ingredient legends must include all the ingredients used in the manufacture of specific baked goods, and all allergens must be clearly listed. In addition, the ingredients used to produce a selected product must be compared to the actual ingredient legend to ensure that they are identical.

On January 1, 2006, FDA rules that require all food products labeled for sale in the United States meet new standards for declaring the presence of trans fats and food allergens went into effect. Specific information regarding labeling requirements for trans fat content can be obtained at the FDA Web site: <http://www.fda.gov/oc/initiatives/transfats>. For information on food allergen labeling, please refer to the FDA's Center for Food Safety and Applied Nutrition site: <http://www.cfsan.fda.gov/~dms/alrguid.html>.

PROPER BAKERY CLEANING AND SANITIZING PRACTICES

In any food production process, the premises and all equipment and surfaces that come into contact with food must be kept clean and, when necessary, disinfected. A cleaning schedule and the right cleaning compounds are good ways to ensure that appropriate levels of cleanliness are achieved.

A comprehensive sanitation plan for the bakery should consist of a written schedule for sanitation activities that take place daily, weekly, and monthly or periodically. It should also include Sanitation Standard Operating Procedures (SSOPs), or written, step-by-step cleaning and sanitizing procedures for each sanitation application. Finally, there should be checklists for documenting sanitation activities as they are completed. These should be faithfully maintained.

CLEANING VERSUS SANITIZING

Cleaning removes visible dirt and debris, including dust and food waste, whereas **sanitizing** decreases the number of illness-causing microorganisms to safe levels. A food contact surface cannot be properly sanitized without first having been thoroughly cleaned because dirt and food waste residue can shield bacteria from the effects of a sanitizer.

Basic Cleaning/Sanitizing Process

The following is the process for basic cleaning and sanitizing of food contact surfaces:

- Wipe up dirt, debris, and food waste.
- Rinse with clean water.
- Wash/scrub with detergent to loosen remaining particles.
- Second rinse with hot water.
- Sanitize with a chemical approved for use on food contact surfaces.
- Air dry (using paper or cloth toweling can result in cross contamination).

This procedure may also be used on non food surface areas such as floors, walls, and ceilings.

CLEANING AGENTS

Proper cleaning procedures provide the foundation for an effective bakery sanitation program. As stated, cleaning with the appropriate detergent must be accomplished before sanitizing can occur. Selection of the right cleaner depends on the type of soil being removed, the amount of cleaning required, the type of surface to be cleaned, and the type of equipment used for cleaning.

Factors Affecting Cleaning

Two factors affect cleaning: the concentration of the cleaner and the types of detergent or cleaner used. Concentration includes the specificity of cleaner because different cleaners work best on different types of soil. Other factors in this category include the amount of time the cleaner is in contact with the area to be cleaned, the degree of foaming, the temperature of the cleaning solution, the mechanical action of scrubbing, the type and amount of soil, and the water used, including its degree of hardness.

Four types of detergents or cleaners are appropriate for use in a bakery environment:

- General-purpose cleaners are mild, in the neutral pH range. They are safe for use on painted or corrodible surfaces.
- Alkaline cleaners contain moderate-to-high alkaline (caustic) levels that are more effective against food soils.
- Chlorinated or chlorinated alkaline cleaners are effective in loosening protein-based soils.
- Acid cleaners are best for removing inorganic mineral deposits like scale and lime.

SANITIZERS

Chlorine, iodine-containing compounds, and quaternary ammonia are the three most commonly used chemical sanitizers. When heat is used as a sanitation step, the temperature of the water must be kept at not less than 170°F (76.7°C) and not more than 190°F (90.6°C) for 30 seconds.

Factors Affecting Sanitizing

Adding too much sanitizer can create a toxic and ineffective solution, whereas adding too little will make the solution weak and ineffective. When the solution is prepared, it should be tested at the beginning and regularly during the process to ensure that a proper concentration is maintained. The following components should be considered when developing a sanitizing program:

- A plan for sanitizer rotation to prevent buildup of **biofilm**, or a community of microorganisms that attaches to solid surfaces exposed to water and excretes a slimy, glue-like substance—Biofilms readily colonize upon many surfaces, including sinks, countertops, and other food contact surfaces. Poor disinfection practices and ineffective cleaning products can increase the incidence of illnesses associated with them.
- The type of surface to be sanitized—Different sanitizers work best on different surfaces.
- The amount of time a sanitizer is in contact with the area to be sanitized
- The temperature of the sanitizing solution
- The likelihood that the sanitizer will come into contact with organic material, reducing its effectiveness

Most Commonly Used Sanitizer Concentrations

Figure 2-4 shows the four most commonly used sanitizers, along with their recommended concentrations for food and nonfood contact surfaces. The high end of the listed range indicates the maximum concentration permitted without a required rinse. To arrive at the correct concentrations, follow the product label directions for dilution ratios. Paper test strip kits are commercially available and can be used as a follow-up to ensure that proper concentrations have been achieved.

Figure 2-4
Sanitizer Concentrations

Sanitizer	Food Contact Surface (ppm)	Nonfood Contact Surface (ppm)
Chlorine	100–200	400
Iodine	25	25
Quats (Quaternary ammonium compounds)	200	400–800
Peroxyacetic acid	200–315	200–315

PEST CONTROL IN THE BAKERY

One of the many precautions that will ensure a clean, safe, and wholesome product during baked goods production and storage is an **Integrated Pest Management (IPM)** approach to pest control. This has become the preferred method for food processors and bakery operations today. Whether the pest control program is contracted out or managed in-house, a basic understanding of pest management is required.

INSECT INFESTATION IN STORED FOOD PRODUCTS

Literally thousands of insects are associated with the baking industry. At the highest risk for attracting insects are cereals, nuts, fruit, and candy, all common ingredients in breads and pastries.

The most common **food-stored insects** in the bakery environment are

- Confused flour beetles
- Red flour beetles
- Sawtooth grain beetles
- Cigarette beetles
- Indian meal moths
- Mediterranean flour moths
- Merchant grain beetles

The life cycle or **complete metamorphosis** of food-stored insects consists of four stages: (1) egg, (2) larva, (3) pupa, and (4) adult. The cycle begins when insect eggs are laid within or near food supplies. During the larva stage, the insect does the most damage to the food product and surrounding environment. The small larva hatches and begins to feed at once. As the larva grows, it molts and enters the pupa stage. The pupa then sheds its skin and the adult emerges.

Secondary Insects

A second group of insects can infest storage facilities and stored food products. Known as secondary insects, they are related to exclusion and sanitation.

American and German cockroaches are the most common secondary insects found in the bakery environment. They can be controlled through an organized program that includes inspection of all incoming raw materials and packaging materials to make sure they are not infested. Additionally, all cracks and crevices throughout a facility must be sealed or filled to eliminate any areas that can potentially provide insect harborage. Finally, a consistent practice of good sanitation techniques, and application of pesticides or baited traps when necessary, can control these insect populations.

Flies, which carry disease and are associated with filth, are another serious problem in bakeries. Flies can be controlled using many of the same methods described for controlling cockroaches. Additionally, the use of mechanical barriers such as screens, air curtains, and electric flytraps can be very effective in controlling fly infestation.

RODENT SPECIES, HABITS, AND CHARACTERISTICS

The Norway rat, roof rat, and common house mouse can cause trouble for the baker. Rats and mice travel along walls and baseboards. Mice need less water and are easier to trap than rats, which in major US cities can have a population equal to or greater than the human population. In addition to sheer numbers, rats can transmit diseases such as typhus and plague.

Rodent control is first accomplished by creating barriers. In other words, it is essential to properly seal all doors. Older buildings with structural deficiencies such as cracks and crevices that can allow rodents to enter should be sealed or repaired.

Bait stations can be used along the exterior perimeters of a baking facility. They should be tamper-resistant, secured in place, and clearly identified. Rodent bait should never be placed inside the production or storage areas of a processing facility. For interior perimeters, nonbaited trapping devices can be used, but they should be clearly identified and inspected on a weekly basis.

BIRD SPECIES, HABITS, AND CHARACTERISTICS

English sparrows, starlings, and pigeons are considered to be pests in and around food production facilities.

Birds in a bakery can be controlled by taking three precautionary measures: eliminating all food and water sources, preventing entrance and harbor by excluding them or constructing barriers, and trapping or baiting with avicides.

PESTICIDES

Two types of **pesticides** are commonly used in the baking industry. They are general-use pesticides, which offer little hazard to people or the environment when used according to label directions, and restricted-use pesticides, which can pose potential hazards even when used as directed.

GENERAL OPERATIONAL PROCEDURES FOR CONTROLLING PESTS

The following are recommended procedures for receiving and storing ingredients and packaging materials to prevent the introduction of pests into the bakery:

- Inspect all material deliveries coming into the bakery before accepting them, to ensure the absence of pests or to discover pest contamination that might have occurred in transit.
- Establish an effective FIFO stock rotation for all materials, not just for food items.
- Store all products and materials 18 inches (45 centimeters) away from walls and not directly on the floor.
- Keep toxic materials (cleaning compounds, pesticides) secure and a safe distance from all food to avoid the possibility of contamination.
- Clean up any wet or dry spillage immediately. Damaged or punctured bags where product is exposed must be checked daily for infestation.
- Strongly consider mechanical pest control devices such as multiple-catch rodent traps, glue boards, and insect light traps. Rodent baits

and/or other toxic poisons should be used as a last resort and only under the supervision of a certified individual.

- Maintain a record or log of all pest activity and control measures taken. A pest management program manual consisting of contracts, insurance, and service reports should be kept in the bakery.
- Perform internal and/or external inspections to evaluate the overall effectiveness of the pest control program. These inspections should be performed on a regular basis and should take into account the needs and exposure of the bakery.
- Provide employee awareness sessions on pest exclusion practices and good sanitation on an ongoing basis.

BIOSECURITY

One outcome of the terrorist attacks of September 11, 2001, has been an increased awareness of the need to enhance the security of the United States. Congress responded by passing the Public Health Security and Bioterrorism Preparedness and Response Act of 2002 (**Bioterrorism Act**), which President Bush signed into law on June 12, 2002.

The Bioterrorism Act is divided into five titles. The FDA is responsible for carrying out certain provisions of the Bioterrorism Act, particularly Title III, Subtitle A—Protecting Safety and Security of Food and Drug Supply.

HIGHLIGHTS OF BIOTERRORISM ACT TITLE III, SUBTITLE A

Section 305 (Registration of Food Facilities) required the owner, operator, or agent in charge of a domestic or foreign facility to register with the FDA no later than December 12, 2003. Facilities are defined as a factory, warehouse, or establishment, including importers. The Bioterrorism Act exempts farms, restaurants, other retail food establishments, and nonprofit food establishments in which food is prepared for or served directly to the consumer. Foreign facilities subject to the registration requirement are limited to those that manufacture, process, pack, or hold food only if food from such a facility is exported to the United States without further processing or packaging outside the United States.

FOOD SECURITY

To prevent intentional tampering, larger companies are now looking at developing food security programs for their operations. These programs cover, but are not limited to, the following components:

- Vulnerability assessments and risk management
- Development of written policies and programs
- Establishment of a food security team
- Facility review
- Security measures for buildings and grounds
- Access control
- Security for warehouses
- Preparation for a recall
- Crisis management programs
- Security inspections
- Customer-supplier relationships

GETTING STARTED IN THE BAKING BUSINESS

Whether it's a small entrepreneur just starting out or an established business wishing to expand, operating a baked goods or pastry business in an ever-changing regulatory environment can be a daunting task.

The following information provides a basic framework for getting started and can be used to create a solid foundation for a new or expanding bakery business. The local health department is a good resource to learn what will be required for the type of operation being contemplated, as well as for the particular segment of the market being catered to—whether retail, food service, wholesale, or some of each. Once this information has been gathered, it will be possible to move forward.

Whether the operation is conducted out of a 300-square-foot home kitchen or a 30,000-square-foot commercial facility, the owner's exposures and responsibilities are the same. The only difference is that, in the larger operation, the components of the food safety program will be more involved and complex.

PROCEDURE FOR SIZING UP THE BAKERY OPERATION

Depending on what item is being produced, there may be many variables to consider. The following are some general practices to follow:

- Calculate the size of the facility or area (number of square feet/square meters).
- Determine the types of breads and/or pastries to be produced.
- Take inventory of equipment to be used in the process(es).
- Create a roster of ingredients to be used in the process(es).
- If employees will be used, decide how many and whether training will be needed.
- If ingredients and packaging materials will be stored on site, determine size and type of warehousing/storage space needed.
- Designate how products will be distributed, whether by owner vehicles, common carrier, or other means.

PROCESS FOR DETERMINING FACILITY SIZE AND PROCESSING EQUIPMENT LAYOUT

The components of a successful food safety program are dictated by the size of the facility and types of equipment being used in production. When planning a work space, take time to implement an efficient process flow and provide ample space to help to establish an organized, clean workplace. Some guidelines follow:

- Create a schematic of the bakery, including the layout of processing equipment and any separation of areas related to processing.
- Locate on the schematic all main doors and roll-up doors leading into or out of the bakery or processing areas.
- Identify areas that will be used for storing raw materials or other materials used in processing or in support of the operation.
- Identify housekeeping/mop sink area for performing general cleaning/sanitizing activities.
- If applicable, identify employee facilities (restroom/locker room).

CONSIDERATIONS FOR PEST CONTROL

After the plan for the bakery operation has been laid out, consult or contract with an outside pest control company. Smaller bakeries can benefit from the pest control contractor's expertise on the specific area in which the operation is located. A contractor will also be able to provide both internal and external protection from pests such as rats, mice, birds, and insects that may enter the facility.

When hiring an outside pest control service, the bakery owner should ensure that the service has experience in the food industry. Even when an outside pest control contractor is hired, it is still the bakery owner's ultimate responsibility if a process or finished product is exposed to a pesticide. Bakery owners must keep their liability in mind when controlling for pests.

When hired, pest control contractors can and should provide service logs of their activities. Only licensed contractors who agree to provide all necessary documentation when performing a service should be retained. The contractor should be required to check in and out with a designated person within the operation, so that any questions or concerns can be dealt with in a timely fashion.

If a pesticide application is necessary, documentation known as **Material Safety Data Sheets (MSDS)** must be provided to ensure that both workers and emergency personnel know the proper procedures for handling or working with a particular substance.

PROCESS FOR CREATING PRODUCT PROFILES

Once the baker or pastry chef completes the finished baked good, the job is not done. The handling and storage of finished baked goods are as important as their fabrication. Items, especially pastry items, that contain fresh fruit, fresh or cooked creams, and nuts should be stored and labeled properly to limit chances of foodborne illness. Basic guidelines follow:

- Develop a product profile for each baked good or pastry item to be produced so that parameters on controls such as temperature sensitivity or allergen concerns can be implemented.
- Establish the shelf life of the product in relation to safety and freshness.
- Determine what labeling and packaging requirements, if any, apply to each item.
- Specify the staging or storage requirements for finished products.
- Establish the distribution requirements and/or processes.

PROCESS FOR RAW MATERIALS AND PACKAGING MATERIALS

The storage of raw materials and packaging materials is considered a control point. The safety of the final baked item is dependent upon the safety of the raw materials that went into it, and the materials used to package it. What follows are some basic considerations:

- Perform an inventory of raw materials needed for processing.
- Determine any special requirements that may apply to the handling and storage of raw materials, including temperature control, special handling/storage of allergen ingredients, and so on.

- Designate proper storage space that allows for the separation of ingredients and packaging materials.
- Ensure that any and all labels used on packaging meet all regulatory requirements.

PROCESS FOR ESTABLISHING CLEANING AND SANITIZING PROCEDURES

Establishing standard procedures for cleaning and sanitizing is the best way to ensure a facility is clean and sanitary. Working with a chemical supply company and with employees to establish guidelines, ensure all employees are aware of the importance of cleaning and sanitizing and are following established SSOPs. Tracking cleaning and sanitizing activities daily or even by shift ensures accountability and is helpful toward maintaining a clean production environment.

- Consult with a local chemical supply company that is accustomed to working with food processors to determine the cleaning and sanitizing product needs of the bakery.
- Request assistance from the chemical supplier in drawing up cleaning procedures on various applications in the facility.
- Obtain MSDS for any and all cleaners and sanitizers used at the facility.
- Ask the chemical supplier to assist with training employees in safe chemical handling practices for the chemicals to be used, including application, especially as the business grows.

CONSIDERATIONS FOR OUTSIDE CONSULTANTS AND LOCAL EDUCATIONAL INSTITUTIONS

The operator of a baking establishment must have a basic knowledge of the laws and procedures which are required for operating their business. Often there are courses in sanitation and food handling through community colleges or the local health department. For a more in-depth and situation-specific solution, consultants may be helpful.

- When starting out, use consultants or attend courses at a local college, both of which are valuable resources.
- If using the services of a consultant, always check references and credentials.
- Money spent on consulting services in the beginning can help avoid costly problems down the road.

CHAPTER SUMMARY

The basic principles of food hygiene and sanitation are set by law. Managers of a bakery or pastry shop who understand these basic principles and can maintain hazard-free production can offer consumers a safe product. Potentially hazardous products can be avoided if the shop follows HACCP and SSOP procedures. Once the procedures are incorporated into daily production, the chances of food contamination are greatly reduced. If those procedures are followed daily, any and all problems will likely be prevented.

KEY TERMS

- Adulteration
- Biofilm
- Bioterrorism Act
- Complete metamorphosis
- Cross contamination
- Danger zone
- Federal Food, Drug, and Cosmetic Act (FDCA)
- First-in, first-out (FIFO)
- Food allergen
- Food-stored insects
- Good Manufacturing Practices (GMPs)
- Hazard Analysis Critical Control Point (HACCP)
- Integrated Pest Management (IPM)
- Material Safety Data Sheets (MSDS)
- Nutrition Labeling and Education Act of 1990 (NLEA)
- Pathogens
- Personal hygiene
- Pesticides
- Sanitation Standard Operating Procedures (SSOPs)
- Sanitizing
- US Food and Drug Administration (FDA)

REVIEW QUESTIONS

1. **What is the difference between the words *shall* and *should* as they pertain to Good Manufacturing Practices (GMPs)?**
2. **What are the four main defenses against the growth and spread of bacteria?**
3. **Foodborne illness is caused by bacteria or its toxins, parasites, viruses, and what other exposure?**
4. **Can allergen proteins be eliminated by the cooking or heating process?**
5. **What must be done before a food contact surface can be fully sanitized?**

PART 2 BREAD

Part 2 explores the ingredients and processes involved in making bread, beginning with the traditional baguette and extending to the more contemporary Carmelized Hazelnut Squares. In order to give students the knowledge to be able to make a selection of breads with great crust, crumb and flavor, we will begin this section with an overview of the baking process as well as a detailed look at mixing, fermentation, the baking of the bread, advanced flour technology, and alternative baking processes.

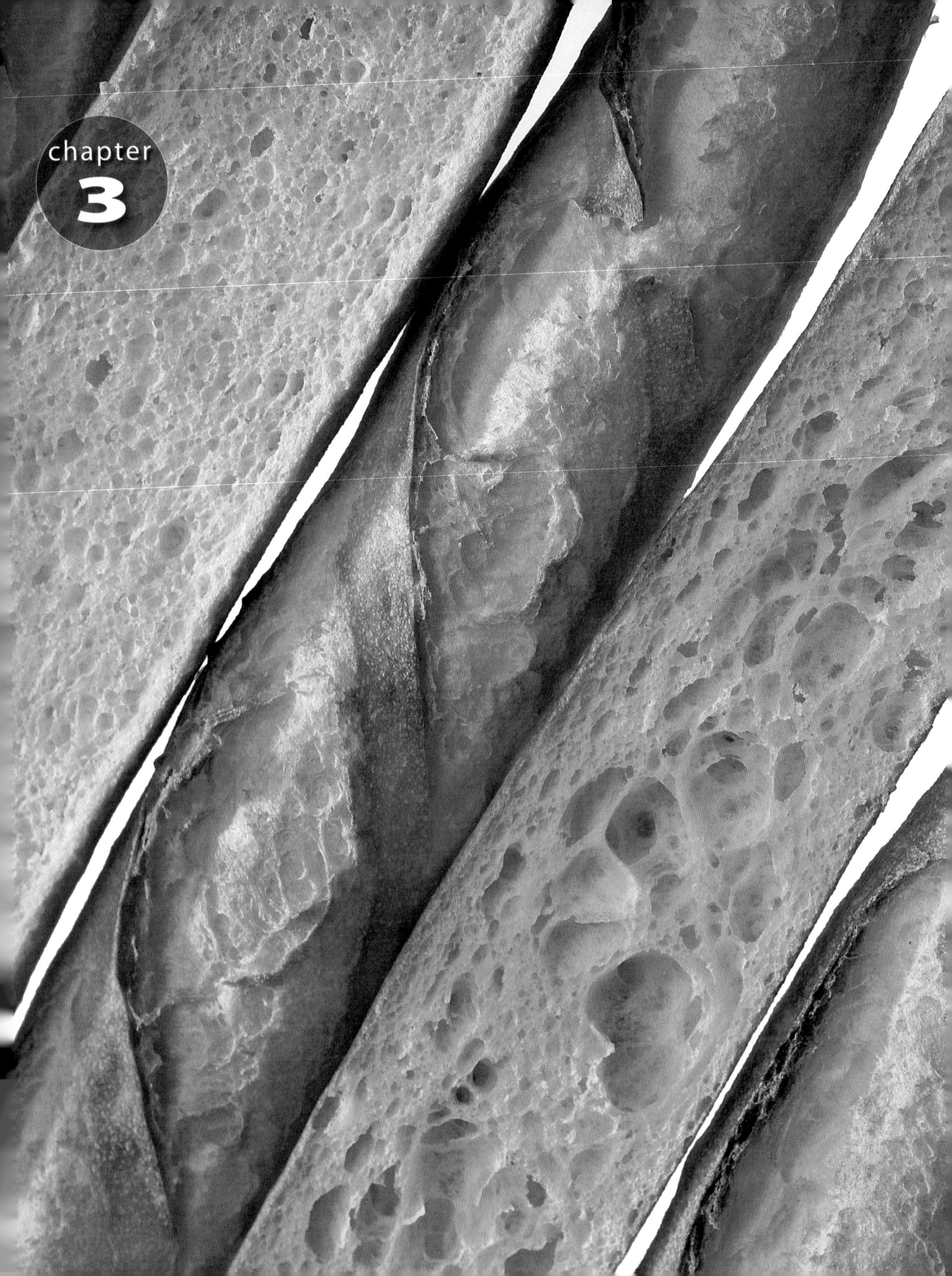
chapter
3

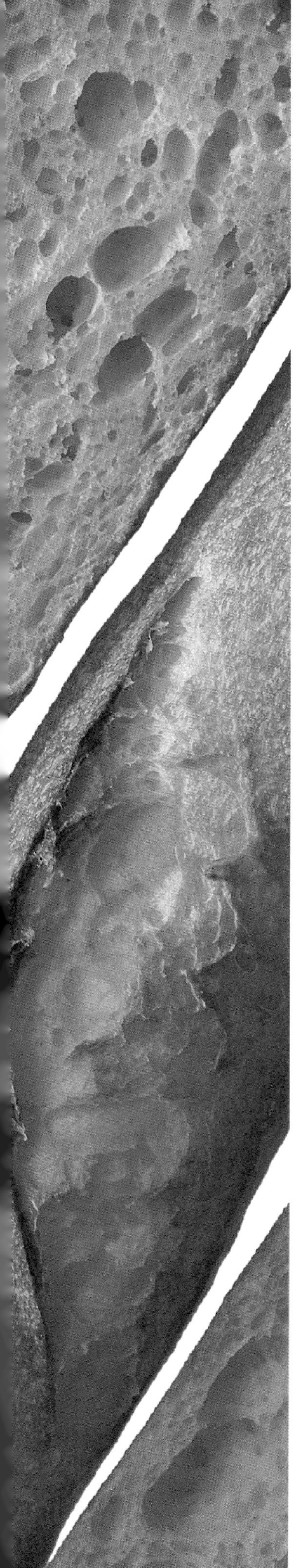

THE BAKING PROCESS AND DOUGH MIXING

OBJECTIVES

After reading this chapter, you should be able to

- present the 10 steps of the baking process.
- present an historical point of view of dough mixing and how it has evolved over time.
- explain the basic theory of dough mixing and the proper steps involved.
- explain the three main mixing techniques and understand their respective results on the dough and on the final products.
- explain the concept of strength and how it relates to the various mixing techniques.
- properly mix dough using the methods presented in this chapter.

INTRODUCTION

This chapter begins with a brief overview of the baking process and continues with a detailed look at mixing.

THE BAKING PROCESS

The baking process can be defined as a natural and logical succession of steps that will ensure the proper transformation of basic ingredients into a loaf of bread. As detailed in Chapter 6, the baking process has a direct effect on the characteristics of the finished product.

When the baker accomplishes all of the steps properly, the integrity of the ingredients is retained and the loaf of bread has the right appearance and a very nice, complex flavor. If any of the steps are incomplete or ignored (especially mixing and fermentation time), or if the dough is handled the wrong way, the quality of the finished product will be diminished. (See Figure 3-1.)

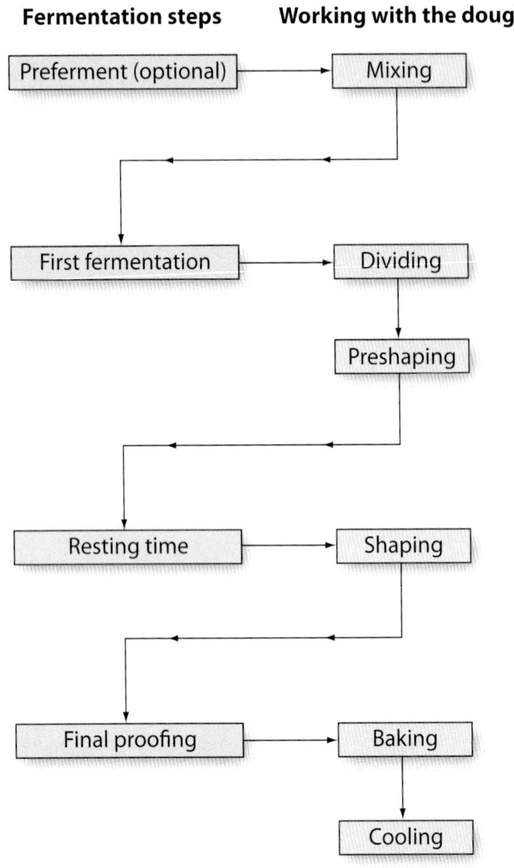

Figure 3-1
The 10 Steps of the Baking Process

TRADITIONAL METHOD

Despite the evolution of baking technology, modern baking processes still follow the same basic steps as the traditional baking processes used for thousands of years. The **traditional method** starts with the elaboration of the **preferment** (a portion of the dough that is fermented and then added to the final dough) using natural yeast, like sourdough, or commercial yeast. Once elaborated, the preferment is allowed to ferment to develop the benefits that will be transmitted to the final dough and bread. When it is properly matured, the preferment is returned to the mixer and final dough mixing begins.

The dough is developed to its proper stage according to the final product characteristics described later in this chapter in Figure 3-23. Then, the dough is allowed to ferment in bulk for a period of time that is directly related to the mixing time and proportion of ingredients in the formula. Crucial to developing optimal flavor, bulk fermentation is considered to be the most important step of fermentation in terms of bread quality. During this process, the dough benefits from its own mass effect, and conditions are perfect to achieve the complete benefits of fermentation.

After the dough has properly matured, it is divided and preshaped according to its final weight and shape, and allowed to rest until final shaping. The shaped pieces of dough then go through the next fermentation step, where gas is produced by the yeast and trapped into the dough. This gas generates the typical volume and texture of the bread.

Once enough gas has been produced, the dough is scored and loaded into the oven. As the baking process begins, an important jump-start can be noticed. Sometimes referred to as "oven kick," this is when the loaf reaches its final volume. After baking, the bread is unloaded and allowed to cool before it is packed or enjoyed by customers.

Even if complex pieces of equipment have replaced the baker's hands for certain operations, the same steps should be followed to create, ferment and make the dough evolve into its final presentation as a loaf of bread.

The remainder of this chapter provides the correct terminology for each step, and briefly explains what is happening during each.

Preferment

This optional step in the baking process, which takes place before mixing, can be a very valuable tool for the baker to improve product quality. During preferment, a portion of the dough is allowed to ferment for a certain time in specific conditions. Then, it is added back into the final dough to improve its physical characteristics, as well as the appearance, flavor, and shelf life of the finished product. As described in Chapter 7, different kinds of preferment can be used according to the type of product and its required final characteristics.

Mixing

Mixing is the first important step of the baking process. During this step, the baker combines all of the ingredients together to make the dough.

Several important principles must be respected to achieve optimum quality for the dough and bread.

First Fermentation

Also called **bulk fermentation** or **floor time**, **first fermentation** takes place when the dough is allowed to ferment as a large mass. This mass effect creates conditions that are optimum for the development of all of the benefits fermentation brings to the dough (see Chapter 4), including increased dough strength and development of flavor.

Dividing

During the **dividing** step, the bulk of the dough is divided into small pieces according to the final weight of the bread and the weight loss that will occur during baking. For manual dividing, the baker must handle the dough very carefully to avoid damaging or disorganizing the gluten structure. Also, when cutting portions of the dough, an effort should be made to have one piece of dough, as opposed to many little pieces that have been put together to obtain the desired weight.

For mechanical dividing, the equipment choice is critical to preserve the precise weight, gluten structure, and gas retention that ensure the integrity of the dough. Hydraulic and stress-free dough dividers are preferred, because they minimize damage to the dough and maintain proper volume and crumb structure in the product.

Preshaping

In this step, cut pieces of dough are preshaped by hand or by machine using an automatic rounder. **Preshaping** is done with the desired final shape in mind; for example, loose balls are appropriate for short shapes like batards or boules, while rectangles are used for longer shapes like baguettes.

During preshaping, the strength of the dough can be adjusted if necessary. Weaker dough will benefit from a tighter preshaping that will reinforce the gluten structure, while stronger dough should be very gently preshaped. It is very important for the baker to carefully assess the dough characteristics and adjust preshaping accordingly. Over- or underworking the dough at this stage can be detrimental to final product quality.

Finally, the simple manipulation of preshaping will form a smooth "skin" on the outside of the dough that will promote proper and better shaping, as well as better crust characteristics.

Resting Time (or Intermediate Proof)

Between preshaping and shaping, the dough is allowed to **rest** (Figure 3-2) which allows the gluten to relax and makes it easier to work with during **shaping**. The **intermediate proof** continues to produce gas that will contribute to the cell structure of the crumb in the final products.

During resting, the dough should always be protected to avoid the surface drying that makes shaping very difficult. While it is easy to prevent drying, it is very difficult to rehydrate dough once it happens. Enclosed cabinets or plastic sheets are two options to protect dough from air drafts.

Figure 3-2
Preshaped Dough Resting

Shaping

After a period of rest, the dough is formed to its final shape. This operation can be achieved by hand or by machine. At this stage, the baker should carefully judge the characteristics of the dough and adapt the

FIGURE 3-3 SHAPING BAGUETTE

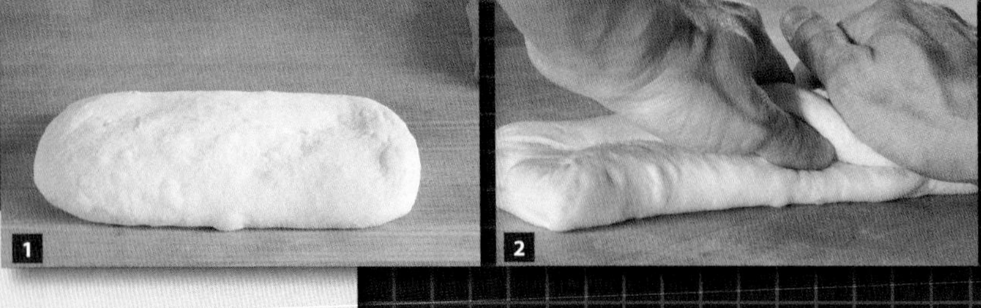

1 The preshaped rectangle is ready for final shape.

2 By folding over the dough piece, the loaf is seamed.

3 The dough piece is ready to roll out.

hand shaping or adjust the machine settings accordingly. Weak dough should be shaped tighter, while strong dough will benefit from a gentler shaping. In fact, this is the last chance for the baker to modify the dough, if necessary, in order to get optimum product quality. For mechanical shaping, equipment that provides minimum pressure and stress on the dough should be selected. This will ensure maintenance of the gluten structure that provides great crumb cell structure after baking. (See Shaping Baguette Figure 3-3, Shaping Batard Figure 3-4, and Shaping Boule Figure 3-5.)

Final Proof

This fermentation period takes place between shaping and the beginning of the bake. During **final proof**, the gas produced by the yeast will accumulate and create internal pressure on the gluten structure. Because of its physical properties, the gluten can stretch while maintaining its shape to create a loaf with great volume and a nice texture. The dough should also be protected during this stage to avoid surface dryness that can cause a thick, hard crust with poor, dull color. Enclosed cabinets or rack covers can be used to prevent dryness when bread is proofed at room temperature (or at a proper setting of the humidity level in a proof box). Linen is also used to maintain the right level of moisture on the loaves while proofing (see Figure 3-6), or a proofer-retarder with humidity control may be used.

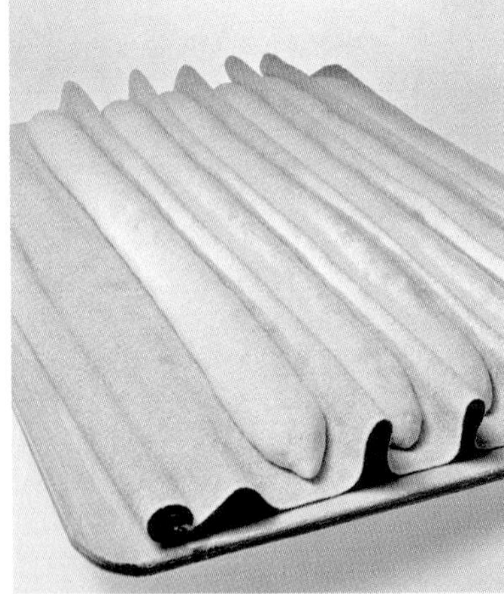

Figure 3-6
Baguettes Proofing on Linen

Oven Loading

After proper fermentation, the loaves are placed in the oven for baking. **Oven loading** can be done by hand, using an oven peel or loader, or with an automatic loading system for larger production. Several precautions should be taken to handle the dough as gently as possible to avoid deflation, and it is sometimes wiser to use a transfer peel to minimize damage during transfer from the proofing board to the loader. When loading, even spacing of the loaves is crucial to ensure the heat distribution necessary for an even bake and a uniform crust color on the finished products.

Scoring

Scoring creates an incision on the skin of the dough. Scoring has a direct impact on the volume and final appearance of the bread, as desribed in Chapter 5.

Unloading the Oven

Unloading can be accomplished with an oven peel or with a loader. In either case, it should be done very carefully to avoid damaging

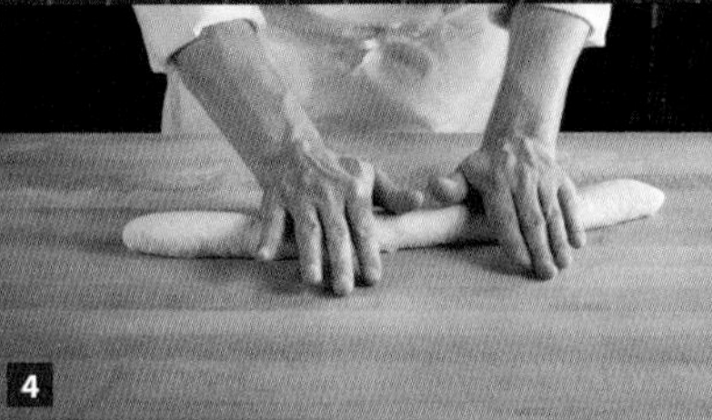

4 The baguette is rolled out with both hands.

5 The final shaped baguette is complete.

FIGURE 3-4 SHAPING BATARD

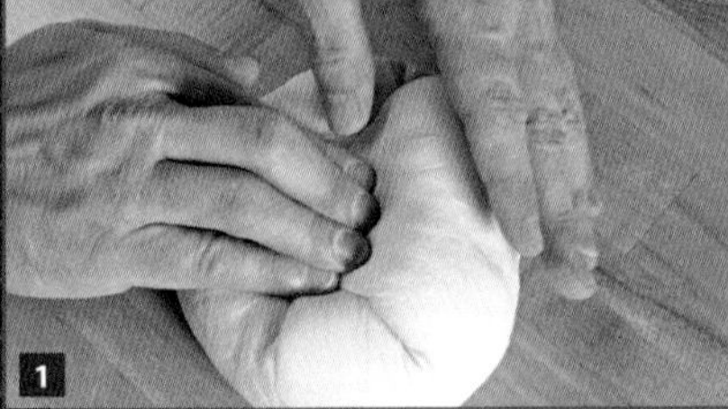

Perform the first fold for the batard.

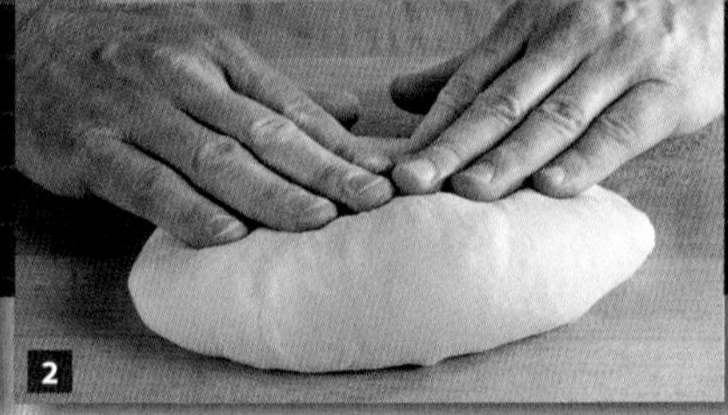

Perform the second fold for the batard.

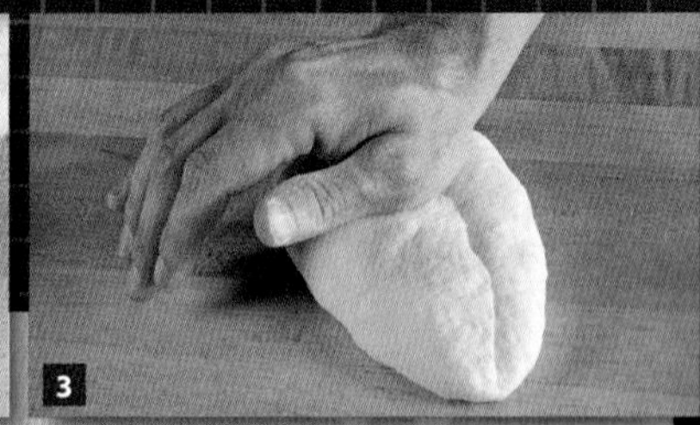

A seam is created with the palm, and is now ready for final fold. After seaming with the palm, fold over the dough piece for final seam.

The final shaped batard is complete.

FIGURE 3-5 SHAPING BOULE

The preshaped ball is ready for final shape.

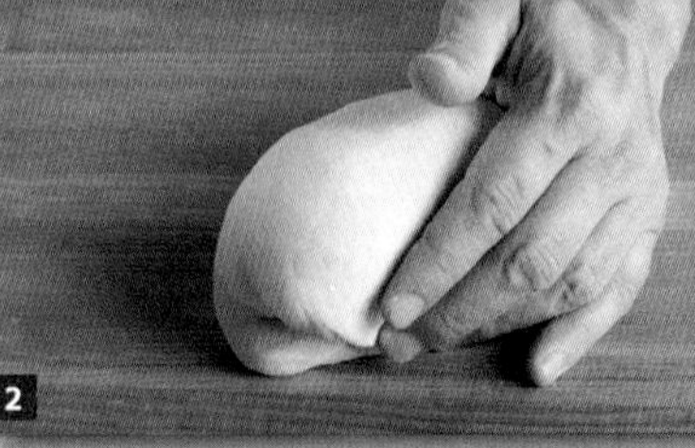

Perform the second fold and tightening of the boule.

Perform the tightening of the boule.

The final tightening of the boule is shown.

Figure 3-7
Bread Cooling on Racks

the crust, which is very delicate and fragile at this stage of the baking process.

COOLING

Bakers typically underestimate the importance of **cooling** (see Figure 3-7) and believe that the baking process ends when the bread comes out of the oven. However, the bread goes through a series of transformations during the cooling process. If the precautions described in Chapter 5 are not respected, quality can be compromised.

These 10 steps of the traditional method are required in order to bake bread. The quality of the final loaf depends on the attention to detail given to all of the steps.

THE DOUGH MIXING PROCESS

Many bakers consider mixing to be the most important step in the baking process. Although all the steps in the baking process are connected, and each is important, mixing is the first mandatory step in producing bread. For this reason, a great deal of attention must be given to this stage of the baking process.

Numerous functional and crucial dough characteristics, such as **consistency**, or level of hardness or softness of the dough system, and **gluten development**, also described as the formation of the structure of the dough and dough temperature, are determined during mixing. While analyzing what is happening when dough is mixed, this section of the chapter considers the following topics:

- Steps to follow for successful dough mixing
- What happens during mixing
- Precautions to take when mixing in extra ingredients
- Different mixing techniques and their applications
- How to determine mixing time
- Factors that affect mixing time
- What technique to choose in a production environment

FOUR CRITICAL STEPS OF DOUGH MIXING

Mixing is a procedure that can be divided into four important steps: scaling the ingredients, checking the temperature, incorporating the ingredients, and developing the dough. If all those steps are carefully achieved, the result will be properly mixed dough and a very consistent final product.

SCALING THE INGREDIENTS

Before mixing, it is important to scale all ingredients precisely. This first step might sound very simple, but it is definitely important because proper scaling will ensure a well-balanced formula and consistent end product.

MONITORING THE WATER TEMPERATURE

The temperature of the final dough is a critical factor in mixing, as it is directly related to the rate of fermentation. The ideal temperature to create an environment favorable for fermentation of most dough is 74°F (23°C) to 77°F (25°C). This is known as **desired dough temperature**, or **DDT**. If the dough is too warm, the yeast will move too quickly, and fermentation tolerance will be reached before the proper balance of strength and flavor has been reached. If it is too cold, the yeast will be very sluggish, and fermentation will take a very long time.

Several factors contribute to the final temperature of dough. These include the temperature of the room, flour, and water; the amount of heat created by the action of the mixer (also known as friction factor); and the temperature of the preferment, if one is being used.

The only temperature factor under the control of the baker is the temperature of the water, as the temperature of the room and flour are typically already set. As for the friction factor, it will vary depending on the type of dough and type of mixer used. To calculate the friction factor, first find the number of degrees the dough will rise when mixed in second speed for one minute. Then, multiply this number by the number of minutes the dough will be mixed in second speed. This test should be done on the first dough of the day and logged. It can then be applied to the remaining dough mixed during that day. The average friction factor for a spiral mixer is 2°F (3.6°C) per minute of mixing. When working with a planetary mixer, some experiments might be done to find the right mixing friction factor. No precise factor can be provided, as the size of the bowl and shape of the dough hook will affect the mixing friction factor.

The following example illustrates the process used to determine the correct water temperature required to arrive at the DDT. In this example, the room and flour temperature is 65°F, the friction factor is 8°F, and the DDT is 75°F. In this example, no preferment is used.

To find the base temperature, multiply the DDT by the number of factors contributing to that temperature: 75°F × 3 = 225°F. The friction factor is not included in the average because it is not a temperature but a value that designates a change in temperature. The known temperatures can then be subtracted from the base temperature to determine what the water temperature should be.

CALCULATION

Base Temperature	225° F
Less Room Temperature	−65° F
Less Flour Temperature	−65° F
Less Friction Factor	− 8° F
Water Temperature	87° F

225°F − (65°F + 65°F + 8°F) = 87°F

If all the temperatures are accurate, and the friction factor has been determined properly, using 87°F (22°C) water will yield dough with a final temperature of 75°F (24°C).

If a preferment like sourdough is used, it must be considered as a fourth factor in the calculation. The DDT is multiplied by four instead of three (75°F × 4 = 300°F), and the preferment temperature is subtracted from the base temperature.

CALCULATION

Base Temperature	300° F
Less Room Temperature	−65° F
Less Flour Temperature	−65° F
Less Preferment Temperature	−68° F
Less Friction Factor	− 8° F
Water Temperature	94° F

300°F − (65°F + 65°F + 68°F + 8°F) = 94°F

If all the temperatures are accurate and the friction factor has been determined properly, using 94°F water will yield dough with a final temperature of 75°F.

It is important to remember that this formula should only be used as a guideline. A log should be kept in the bakery to record temperatures, so that there is a guide to follow and any changes are noticed immediately. This will allow adjustments to be made before the consistency of the final product is jeopardized.

INCORPORATING THE INGREDIENTS

Ensuring Clean Equipment

Next, it is necessary to make sure that the mixer bowl and hook are clean. It takes just a few seconds to clean scraps of dried dough that are still stuck to the bowl, which, if left, may not dissolve properly into the next dough and leave a hard lump in the final product.

Adding Ingredients to the Mixing Bowl

Finally, in order to prevent changing the weight of the flour, add it to the bowl first, followed by water and the other ingredients. Following this order is important because formulas are designed in baker's percentages, where all the ingredients are based on the total weight of the flour. For example, if the water is added before the flour, and the dough is too soft, more flour will have to be added. Because all the other ingredients were calculated on the original weight of the flour, if the quantity of added flour is fairly large, the formula will be out of balance.

For dough mixed in a planetary mixer or a mixer without a bowl-reverse option, if flour is placed in the bowl first, some of it might get stuck in the bottom without being incorporated into the dough. One way to prevent this problem is to add half of the water first, then all of the flour and the rest of the water, until the proper dough consistency is achieved.

When the ingredients are scaled and the water temperature is determined, flour and water are placed in the bowl and the mixer is turned on at first speed for incorporation. If preferments are used, they should be incorporated into the dough at this stage. Depending on the type of preferment (high or low hydration), the consistency of the dough might be changed, and some water adjustments may be necessary. During the next 3 to 4 minutes, flour, water, and preferment will be combined by the mechanical action of the mixer's dough hook. During this time, the baker must carefully watch the consistency of the dough to determine if more water is needed, as this is the best time to add it.

When mixing a formula for the first time, it is better to hold back some of the water just in case the flour used has a lower absorption. If needed, the withheld water can be added to obtain the desired consistency.

When the proper consistency is achieved, two options are possible. The baker can continue mixing and incorporate the other ingredients of the dough, such as fresh yeast and then salt. The other option is to "autolyse" the dough.

Autolyse

The **autolyse** is a process developed by **Professor Raymond Calvel**, a French Master Baker known for his in-depth studies of the dough system wherein the flour and water are mixed and rest for a minimum of 15 to 20 minutes. During this time, two important reactions happen in the dough. First, the proteins of the flour become better hydrated, leading to better gluten structure properties of strength and gas retention. The second is a natural action of a specific **enzyme** called **protease**, which is naturally present in the flour. In general, an enzyme is an organic component with a specific and natural action of degradation. Proteases are responsible for protein degradation. When allowed enough time to work, they will react on the protein and degrade some of the gluten bonds. As a result, the dough will become more extensible, and its machinability will be improved.

A minimum of 15 to 20 minutes is necessary to provide sufficient time for the activation of the enzymes. Autolyse can last up to 1 hour for the bulk of the dough. Another option is to autolyse only a portion of the dough made with a portion of the total flour for the formula but for a longer period of time (in general, 8 to 12 hours or overnight). The autolysed portion of dough is returned to the mixer the next day, and mixing resumes in a normal way. This technique allows the baker to get the benefit of the autolyse without having to stop the mixing process to wait for the enzymatic activity to happen.

Yeast, salt, and stiff preferments are added to the dough after an autolyse because both ingredients work to counter its effects. Salt slows the action of the proteases of the flour, while the fermentation process initiated from the yeast creates acidity that increases dough strength and decreases **extensibility**. Extensibility could be described as the property of the dough to elongate easily or not under a stretching action.

Special Considerations for Autolyse One important exception to the no-yeast-before-an-autolyse rule is when using dried instant yeast. In this case, it is better to incorporate the yeast with the flour for 1 minute at the beginning of the mixing time because the cells in dried instant yeast have a low water content and require more time for rehydration. If incorporated late in the process, they will not completely dissolve into the dough and fermentation will be negatively affected.

The same principle can be applied for an autolyse. Because mixing time is reduced, it is better to incorporate the dry instant yeast just before the autolyse. By the time the cells are dissolved into the dough, the autolyse time will be almost over and the fermentation of the dough will still be minimal.

Liquid preferments like poolish or liquid levain must be incorporated at the beginning of the mixing process even if an autolyse is done because their low yeast content won't really affect dough strength. However, stiffer preferments with more yeast, such as prefermented dough, should be incorporated after the autolyse.

Technically speaking, when no autolyse is made, flour, water, yeast, and salt can be incorporated at the beginning of mixing. Despite the common belief that salt will kill the yeast, no change will happen in the dough or bread characteristics. The salt and yeast are in contact in the dough for 4 to 6 hours after mixing, so if something negative were to happen, there would be plenty of time.

However, in order to have a better control of ingredient incorporation and to make sure that nothing has been forgotten, it is better to follow a standard procedure when adding ingredients into the dough. For example, if the baker always adds yeast and then salt before going into second speed, there is less chance of error.

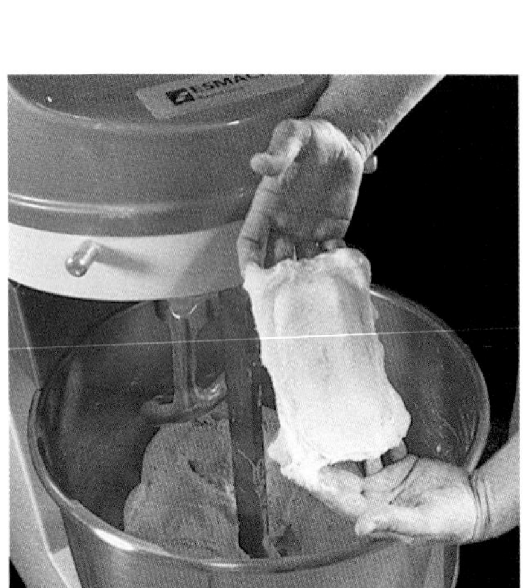

Figure 3-8
Checking the Development of the Dough

DEVELOPING THE DOUGH

When all ingredients are well incorporated and proper dough consistency has been achieved, the baker proceeds to the next step: **dough development** (see Figure 3-8). Depending on desired gluten development, this step can be done in first or second speed. A long mixing time in second speed is used for well-developed dough, and a short mixing time in first speed is used for underdeveloped dough. The method used will be determined by the desired characteristics of the final product. More precise guidelines will be presented later in the chapter.

Dough Temperature

Because fermentation activity is dependent on the temperature of the dough, the baker should confirm that the desired temperature has been reached. If the temperature is good, the baker can follow the regular baking process. If it is too cold, the first fermentation time will need to be lengthened; if it is too warm, it should be shortened. These differences should be taken into consideration for the next batch of dough by increasing or decreasing the water temperature.

A common mistake made by many bakeries is to continue mixing when the temperature of the dough is too cold. While the extra friction created by this process will warm up the dough, the extra mixing time will also continue to develop the gluten of the dough. The end result may be the desired dough temperature, but the dough will likely be overdeveloped, creating gluten with an excess of extensibility (due to the breaking of some gluten strength) and a lack of **elasticity.** Elasticity is the property of dough to retract to its initial position after being stretched. The dough will also be sticky and very difficult to work with, and the final product will have the tendency to be flat, with a dense inside and little cut opening. Adjusting the first fermentation time is a much safer procedure, and is strongly advised.

Physical Changes During the Formation of Dough

As soon as flour and water come into contact, the water hydrates the flour components, which are primarily starch and protein. The two main types of starch are native starch and damaged starch. The structure of the native starch remains the same, but the structure of the damaged starch has been broken during the milling process. The native starch absorbs water on the outside of the particle only, while damaged starch absorbs close to its own weight in water. Both play the role of filling agent in a dough system.

The two primary proteins in wheat—**glutenin** (protein that will have some effect on the elasticity of the dough) and **gliadin** (protein that will affect the extensibility of the dough)—are responsible for the formation of the dough. Depending on their quality, these proteins can absorb 200 to 250 percent of their weight in water. As they inflate, they become attracted to each other and form chains of proteins called **gluten**. (See Figure 3-9.)

After the gluten has formed, the mechanical operation of the dough hook will work it into an organized structure through two distinct movements. The first stretches the chains of gluten, while the second folds the chains over onto themselves. After a period of mixing, these chains become longer and longer, finer and finer, and more and more overlapped. This creates the three-dimensional gluten structure of the dough.

A longer mix will generate a well-developed gluten structure, while a shorter mix will generate an underdeveloped one. Care must be taken to prevent mixing for too long, as it will stretch the gluten chains to the point where they will break. This is called overmixing the dough.

Due to the overlapping and better organization of the gluten chains, the structure of the gluten will get stronger, and a noticeable change in the **dough rheology** (properties of the dough to deform and flow during the baking process) can be observed. (See Figures 3-10 and 3-11.) Viscoelastic properties will develop, or, more simply, the dough will become less extensible, more elastic, and able to trap and retain gas.

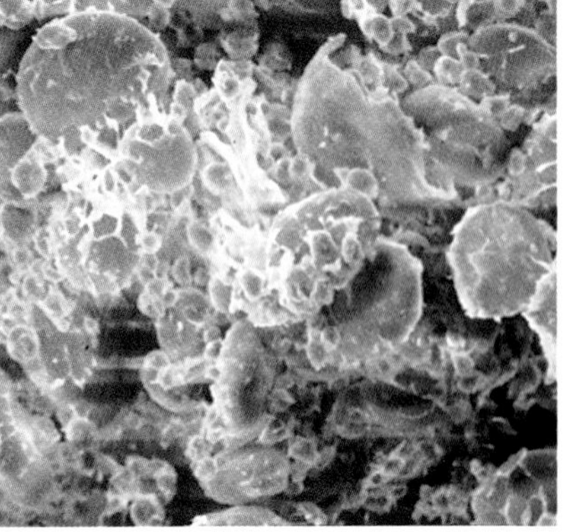

Figure 3-9
Microscopic View of Gluten Formation

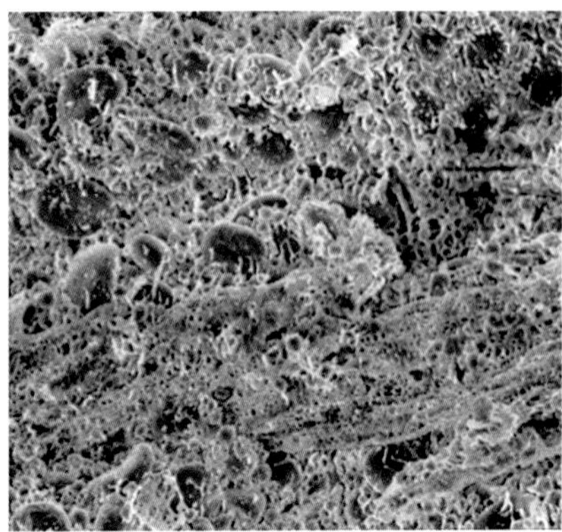

Figure 3-10
Microscopic View of Improved Mix

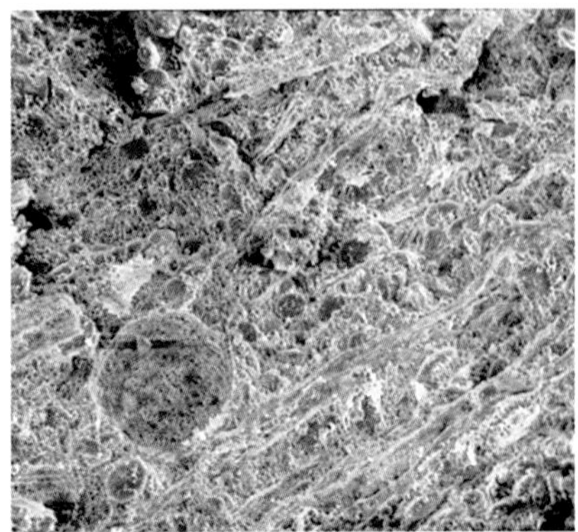

Figure 3-11
Microscopic View of Intensive Mix

Protein Hydration and Mixing Time in First Speed Protein hydrates at a slower pace than starch, which makes it necessary to mix in first speed for at least 5 or even 6 minutes for a larger batch of dough to ensure a good gluten quality. If the mixer is switched to second speed too early, it may start to organize gluten that is barely created, and the overall gluten development of the dough will be negatively affected.

Chemical Changes During the Formation of Dough

When water is introduced into the mix, the two main natural chemical reactions are fermentation activity and enzyme activity. The rate of these reactions depends on the quantity of water used. For example, wet dough will generate faster fermentation activity. Consequently, the level of yeast needed in the formula in order to maintain control may need to be reduced over the process.

Oxidation of the Dough Another important chemical change that happens during mixing is dough **oxidation**. Oxidation occurs when naturally occurring oxygen is incorporated into the dough during mixing. Most of the effects from this reaction are positive. As the oxygen chemically reacts with the molecules of protein, better gluten bonds are formed; they reinforce the gluten structure and the tolerance of the dough.

If the dough is overmixed, too much oxygen will be incorporated, and the **carotenoid pigments** (natural components of the kernel of wheat that are responsible for the creamy color of the flour and some aroma production) will be negatively affected. Too much oxygen will deteriorate these pigments and automatically lead to a final product with a whiter crumb color and a blander flavor.

Although too much oxygen is bad, some is necessary. The micro cells of air that are introduced into the dough system during mixing play an important role later in the baking process by forming the core of the crumb structure. During fermentation, the gas produced by the yeast accumulates in these micro cells and forms the cell structure of the crumb or **alveoles**.

FIGURE 3-12 INCORPORATION OF FAT

1 A large percentage of butter is added at the end of dough development.

2 The butter should be pliable to be incorporated properly.

To minimize the negative effect of oxidation, the baker can utilize salt's natural property of slowing down chemical reactions (which is why it is used to increase the shelf life of foods like cured meats or salted fish). By incorporating salt into the dough at the beginning of the mixing time (while the mixer is still in first speed), the oxidation process will be retarded. Conversely, should the baker want to achieve a very white crumb structure, the incorporation of the salt must be delayed, but flavor will also be penalized.

Incorporation of Secondary Ingredients Into a Dough System

Even though we cannot discuss every ingredient added to dough in every bakery, some observations about primary ingredients will be helpful.

Incorporation of Fat A small percentage (2 to 4 percent) of solid fat, such as butter or margarine, can be incorporated with the flour and water at the beginning of mixing. A larger percentage (5 to 15 percent) of solid fat should be incorporated when the dough is halfway through development (in general, at the middle of the second speed time). An earlier incorporation (at the beginning of the mixing time) will "lubricate" the chains of proteins, delaying the bonding and development of the gluten.

More than 15 percent solid fat should be incorporated when the gluten is almost fully developed. This will ensure a strong dough structure that is able to support this massive incorporation of fat. (See Incorporation of Fat Figure 3-12.)

Liquid fats, like oil, are in general part of the hydration of the flour and should be incorporated into the dough at the beginning of the mixing time. If a large quantity of oil is required, it can also be incorporated after the full gluten development (very slowly in first speed).

Incorporation of Sugar A small amount of sugar (up to 12 percent) can be incorporated into the dough at the beginning of the mixing time. Higher levels should be incorporated in several steps. Because it is a hydroscopic ingredient, sugar will absorb a lot of water. If too much sugar is introduced to the dough at once, it may take some water away from the protein and disorganize the whole gluten structure.

When levels of sugar are very high (20 to 30 percent), some bakers use the same technique as for a high level of butter, leaving it out of the dough until the gluten is well developed.

Incorporation of Eggs Eggs should be incorporated at the beginning of the mixing because they play a major role in the hydration of the flour. Even

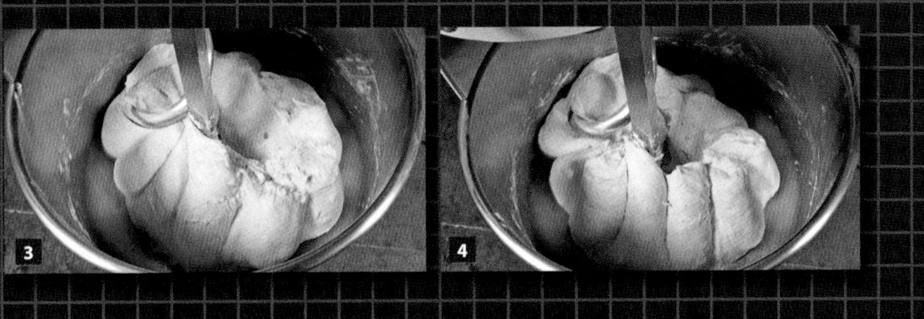

3 At 80 percent incorporation, small butter chunks still remain on the surface of the dough.

4 At 100 percent incorporation, no butter is visible.

though some formulas only call for eggs to hydrate the flour, they don't have the same flour hydration characteristics as water. To ensure a good gluten quality, at least 10 percent of water should be added in addition to the eggs. The final product will have a lighter, moister crumb texture.

Incorporation of Dry Ingredients Ingredients like malt or milk powder can be incorporated with flour and water at the beginning of the mixing time.

Incorporation of Solid Ingredients Like Nuts, Dry Fruits, and Chocolate Chips Any chunky ingredients that won't dissolve into the dough must be incorporated at the end of the mixing time. After the gluten has been properly developed, turn the mixer to first speed and gradually add the ingredients until they are well distributed into the dough.

This gentle incorporation will have two positive effects for the dough and the bread. First, the added ingredients will stay intact within the dough. Second, incorporating the ingredients in a gentle way will reduce damage to the gluten structure. If second speed is used, the ingredients will act like razor blades into the dough and cut all the gluten bonds that were formed during mixing. (See Incorporating Solid Ingredients Figure 3-13.)

MIXING PROCESS CONCLUSION

Mixing dough involves four distinct stages: scaling the ingredients, checking the temperature, incorporating the ingredients, and developing the dough. Following these steps with precision and attention to detail typically results in properly mixed dough and a predictable, consistent final product.

MIXING TECHNIQUES

A thorough knowledge of the various mixing techniques used for bread production is essential to consistently achieve desired results for different products. The goal of the second half of this chapter is to describe the different mixing techniques used in bakeries and to discuss how bread quality can be changed depending on gluten development. The three main mixing techniques covered in this chapter are short mixing, intensive mixing, and improved mixing. In addition, there is a brief discussion of the double hydration technique used for super-hydrated breads.

FIGURE 3-13 INCORPORATING SOLID INGREDIENTS

1 Mix on first speed when adding nuts into dough.

2 At 80 percent incorporation, the nuts are still showing on the surface.

SHORT MIX

To understand the three main mixing techniques, it is necessary to examine the recent history of baking. Before mechanical mixers became widely available 50 to 60 years ago, bakers mixed their dough by hand. The energy provided to the dough during hand mixing is not sufficient to accomplish a lot of gluten development; in fact, the resulting gluten structure is very underdeveloped. To complete gluten development and make the dough strong enough for shaping and proofing, a long fermentation time is necessary. This entire process is referred to as a **short mix.**

INTENSIVE MIX

After World War II, mechanical mixers increased in availability. The first mixers were very basic, running only with one speed. Mixing was still very gentle and gluten was underdeveloped. When faster, two-speed mixers became available, bakers realized that the more intensive development of the gluten enabled them to reduce the first fermentation time. This brought up an interesting point: Producing more bread during one shift meant more sleep. Also, consumers of the time enjoyed bread with a large volume and a white crumb. This convergence led to the creation of the **intensive mix** technique, which is characterized by a long mixing time with short first fermentation.

As time passed, consumers began to notice that the flavor of bread was lacking, and staling was happening much faster than before. At first, they pointed the finger at mechanical mixers, blaming the baker and the machinery for the changes. However, with the evolution of the science and a better understanding of the baking process, it has become clear that the mixers themselves were not responsible for the lower bread quality. Instead, it was the way the mixers were used.

By mixing the dough until full development, two major factors were created that compromised bread quality. The first was overoxidation of the dough, which led to the whiter crumb and a blander flavor. The second was related to the fermentation activity of the dough. By reducing the first fermentation time to almost zero, acidity was given no time to develop, aromas were not created, and shelf life was considerably reduced.

IMPROVED MIX

In order to sell a larger quantity of higher-quality bread, bakers started to think about ways to improve the baking process. Of course, giving up on mechanical mixers and returning to hand mixing was out of the question. With the help of baking's scientific community, the **improved mix** method was created. This technique improves the quality of the bread by reducing the mixing time in second speed. As a result, gluten isn't fully developed and dough still requires some first fermentation time to gain strength.

This technique completes two positive actions: The shorter mixing time limits oxidation and preserves the integrity of the wheat kernel, and the longer first fermentation develops acidity that increases the product aroma and shelf life.

Today's bakers still have a choice of techniques when mixing dough. The following sections describe each technique more precisely and explore their effects on final product characteristics.

SHORT MIX DESCRIPTION

Short mix, the gentle mixing method that utilizes first speed only, most closely approximates the characteristics of hand mixing. Short mixing incorporates the ingredients and does very little gluten development, resulting in an underdeveloped gluten structure and a long fermentation time (see Figure 3-14). Typically, two to four folds are necessary during the first fermentation to develop strength (see Folding the Dough Figure 3-15). Because good extensibility is needed for easy dough folding, a soft dough consistency is preferable. Also, due to the long first fermentation, a low percentage of yeast must be used. At the shaping stage, dough is fairly gassy and soft, but it is still easy to work with.

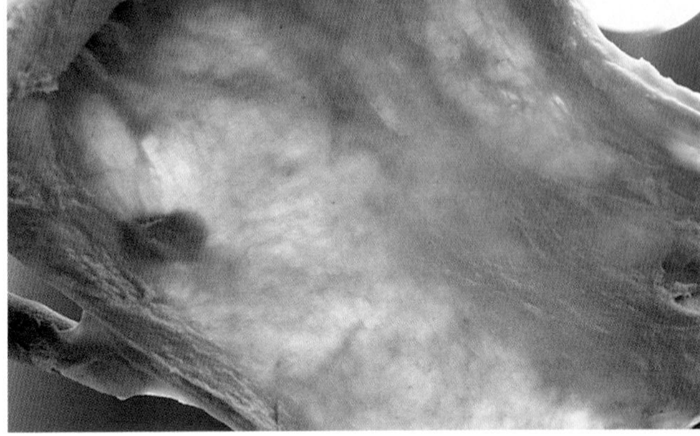

Figure 3-14
Gluten Window for Short Mix

SHORT MIX EFFECTS ON BREAD CHARACTERISTICS

Short mixing creates almost no oxidation, resulting in a very creamy crumb color. Due to the low development of the gluten, the crumb cell structure will be open and irregular as gas accumulates in uneven air pockets in the dough. In addition, the long first fermentation will produce a great deal of acid, greatly enhancing the flavor and shelf life of the final product. Finally, because the gluten is not well organized, it won't retain much gas, and the volume of the bread will be slightly reduced.

INTENSIVE MIX DESCRIPTION

During intensive mixing, ingredients are incorporated in first speed, and the dough is developed to the maximum in second speed. It is a fast, efficient mixing method that produces dough that runs easily through heavily mechanized processes.

Intensive mixing produces a stiff, fully developed dough that is strong enough to shape almost immediately. The typical length of bulk fermentation is limited to 15 to 20 minutes and is, in fact, more of a resting time than fermentation time. For some dough, a too-long first

FIGURE 3-15 FOLDING THE DOUGH

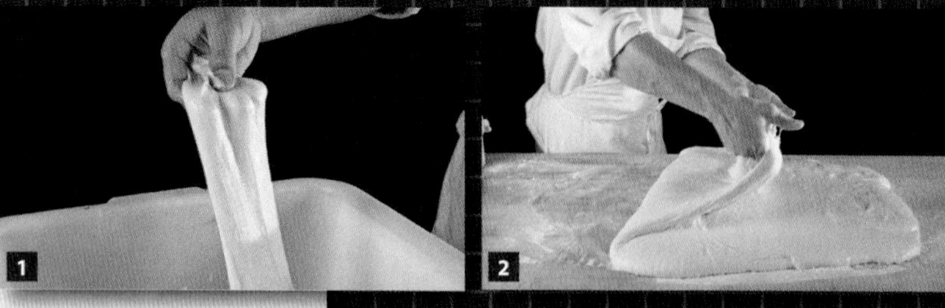

1 Partway through the first fermentation, the dough is very extensible.

2 Turn the dough out onto a floured table and fold over one-third of the dough from the right.

3 Fold the dough from the left side.

fermentation after mixing automatically results in an excess of strength and a dough that is difficult to work with. (See Figure 3-16.)

INTENSIVE MIX EFFECTS ON BREAD CHARACTERISTICS

A long mixing time automatically incorporates more air into the dough, increasing oxidation and its negative effects, including a very white crumb color. Due to the full gluten development, the cell structure of the bread is very tight and regular, creating a crumb structure with a very even grain. In addition, the perfect organization of the gluten structure retains a lot of gas into the dough system, resulting in a fairly large volume of the final product. Unfortunately, flavor profiles and shelf life are much diminished due to the very short first fermentation time involved.

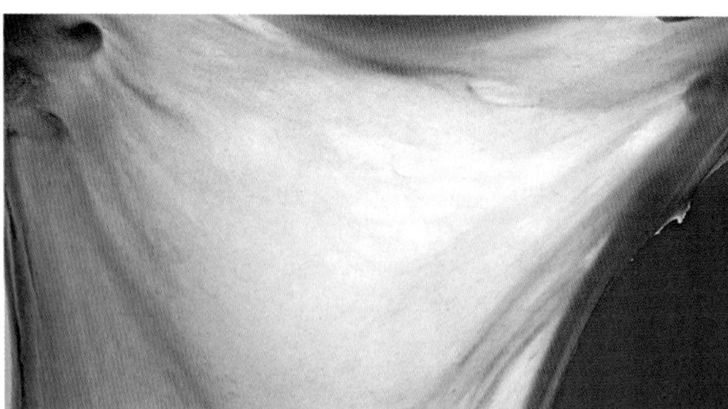

Figure 3-16
Gluten Window for Intensive Mix

IMPROVED MIX DESCRIPTION

The improved mix is a compromise between the short mix and the intensive mix. It allows the baker to achieve more of the efficiencies of intensive mixing, while retaining most of the product quality obtained with a short mix method.

With this technique, ingredients are incorporated in first speed, and dough is mixed to half development in second speed. Dough consistency should be medium soft (extensible enough), since the strength of the dough will increase even more during the fairly long first fermentation. The dough obtained will be perfectly adapted for hand shaping or a semi-mechanized process. (See Figure 3-17.)

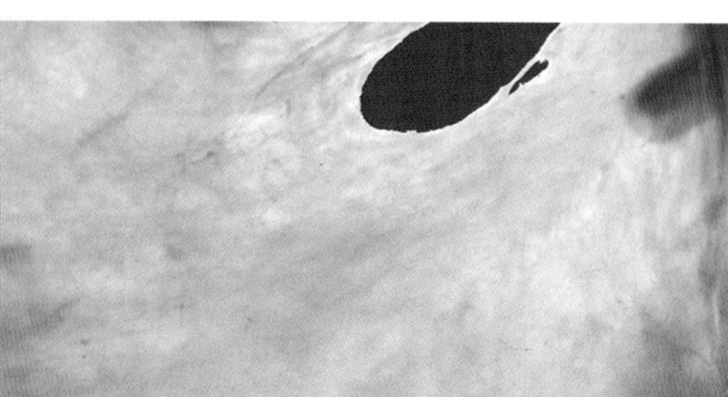

Figure 3-17
Gluten Window for Improved Mix

IMPROVED MIX EFFECTS ON BREAD CHARACTERISTICS

The gentler mixing process in this technique helps to retain a creamy color and open crumb, while longer fermentation results in a more flavorful product with a good shelf life. Volume is a compromise between the smaller loaves characteristic of a short mix and the larger ones achieved by an intensive mix. (See Figure 3-18.)

4 Fold the dough from the front to the back.

5 Fold the dough from the back to the front.

6 The short mix dough now has one complete fold.

Figure 3-18
Intensive, Improved, and Short Crumb Comparison (top to bottom)

DOUBLE HYDRATION

The end of the 1990s saw the growing popularity of super-hydrated dough like ciabatta, pugliese, and francese. To mix these types of dough in a large production environment, another method called the double hydration technique can be used.

The double hydration technique involves incorporating water in two phases. First, enough water is incorporated at the beginning of the mixing time to make a medium-soft dough consistency. Then, the dough is mixed, and the gluten is developed. Once the gluten reaches approximately two-thirds of its full development, the rest of the water is added little by little, until it is well incorporated into the dough. (See Double Hydration Technique Figure 3-19.)

FIGURE 3-19 DOUBLE HYDRATION TECHNIQUE

1 For the double hydration technique, water is added once the gluten is developed.

2 Water is added in stages to achieve full incorporation.

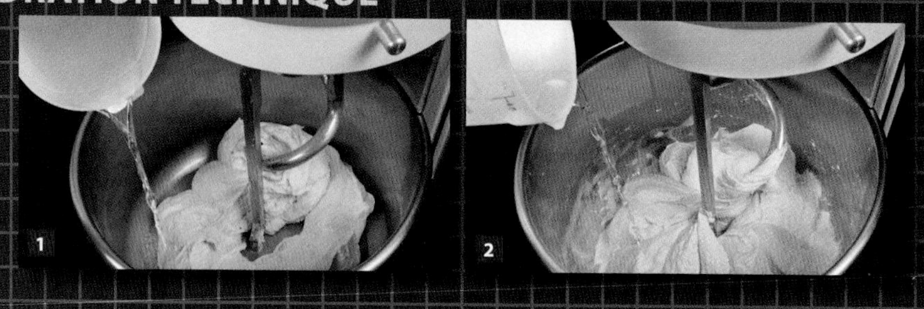

Double hydration can create a very soft dough with sufficient strength for machinability. This technique works well when using equipment that uses stress-free technology, which requires good machinability properties like good flow and strength.

HOW TO CALCULATE MIXING TIME

For each mixing technique, the baking scientific community has developed guidelines to determine the amount of mixing time required to obtain the desired gluten structure. These guidelines are based on the movement of the dough hook during mixing and its effect on gluten organization. Because each movement or revolution stretches and folds the gluten, it is necessary to know the number of revolutions needed for appropriate gluten structure.

For gluten structure for a short mix, the hook needs to make 600 revolutions in the dough in first speed. For an improved mix, 1,000 revolutions of the hook in second speed are needed. Intensive mix requires 1,600 revolutions of the hook in second speed. Each of these calculations takes into account the fact that all ingredients have already been incorporated and the gluten formed before the number of revolutions begins. These calculations specifically apply to the mixing time, where the gluten is being developed. (See Figures 3-20 and 3-21.)

The formula for calculating mixing time serves as a starting point to define proper mix times on specific equipment. The mixing times listed in Figure 3-21 are only guidelines, based on standard mixer speeds and full batch sizes. A variety of factors can affect mix time; this is why the texture of the dough and gluten development (window test) should always be the final guide. (See Figure 3-19, Step 3.)

Figure 3-20
Calculation of Mixing Time

The following calculation can be used to determine the mixing time for the dough:

$$\frac{\text{Total revolutions required (as specified by mix method)}}{\text{Revolutions per minute (RPM) of the mixer}} = \text{Total mixing time}$$

Revolutions per minute can vary with the brand of mixer, so before calculating mixing time, it is important to check the mixer's technical manual for its specific RPM. This information is also available from your equipment supplier.

3 After incorporating all the water, the dough is very wet but has a well developed gluten structure.

4 Shown here are the crumb and crust of ciabatta made using the double hydration technique.

FACTORS AFFECTING MIXING TIME

Mixing time can be adjusted to compensate for variables that can affect the development of the dough, including type and design of mixer, batch size, flour characteristics, dough hydration, and incorporation of additional ingredients.

Type and Design of Mixer

Motor speed, the shape of the hook, and mixer design can all affect the stretch-and-fold motion of the hook against the dough. A good example is to compare spiral mixers and oblique mixers. For an improved mix, a spiral mixer requires only 5 minutes of mixing in second speed, while an oblique mixer will require 12 1/2 minutes. If different styles of mixers are used in a bakery, the same dough may require different mixing times, depending on the type of mixer used.

Batch Size

Batch size may be one of the most important factors to consider in mix time. Because mixers are generally designed to perform optimally at full capacity, smaller batches will generally mix faster than full batches because the dough comes in contact with the hook more often.

Figure 3-21
Example of Mixing Time Calculation

The RPM of the mixer used in these examples will be as follows:

Spiral mixer:	100 RPM in first speed	200 RPM in second speed
Oblique mixer:	40 RPM in first speed	80 RPM in second speed
Planetary mixer (20-qt Hobart):	107 RPM in first speed	198 RPM in second speed
Planetary mixer (60-qt Hobart):	70 RPM in first speed	124 RPM in second speed

Note: With respect to other planetary mixers, please refer to the technical manual to find out the exact RPM for various speeds.

These values represent the average RPM for most of these styles of mixers.

Short Mix

Spiral mixer:	600/100 = 6 minutes in first speed
Mixing time will be:	4 to 5 minutes in first speed for ingredients incorporation 6 minutes in first speed for gluten development
Oblique mixer:	600/40 = 15 minutes in first speed
Mixing time will be:	4 to 5 minutes in first speed for ingredients incorporation 15 minutes in first speed for gluten development

(continues)

Figure 3-21
Example of Mixing Time Calculation *(continued)*

Improved Mix

Spiral mixer:	1000/200 = 5 minutes in second speed
Mixing time will be:	4 to 5 minutes in first speed for ingredients incorporation 5 minutes in second speed for gluten development
Oblique mixer:	1000/80 = 12.5 minutes in second speed
Mixing time will be:	4 to 5 minutes in first speed for ingredients incorporation 12.5 minutes in second speed for gluten development

Intensive Mix

Spiral mixer:	1600/200 = 8 minutes in second speed
Mixing time will be:	4 to 5 minutes in first speed for ingredients incorporation 8 minutes in second speed for gluten development
Oblique mixer:	1600/80 = 20 minutes in second speed
Mixing time will be:	4 to 5 minutes in first speed for ingredients incorporation 20 minutes in second speed for gluten development

You should reduce mix time for partial batches, but there is no direct correlation between bowl size and mix time (a half batch won't mix in half the time, for example). Some experimentation will be necessary to determine the mixing time more precisely.

Flour Characteristics

Strong flour may require longer mixing time because the gluten is less extensible and requires a longer time to reach the desired structure. Rye flour, for example, contains a lower quality and amount of protein, which makes it preferable to mix more in first speed and less in second speed. The gentler action of the hook in first speed will protect the fragile gluten structure of rye dough.

Dough Hydration

Lower hydration creates stiffer dough with less-extensible gluten that requires longer mixing time in comparison with medium-soft dough consistency.

Incorporation of Extra Ingredients

As mentioned earlier, if seeds, fruits, nuts, or other ingredients are added to the dough, they must be added after development has been completed. This incorporation should be done in first speed. Otherwise, these "chunky" ingredients can cut the gluten strands and slow down development.

COMPARISON OF THE MAIN MIXING TECHNIQUES

Figure 3-22 summarizes information about calculating mixing times and provides guidelines for each mixing technique's formulas and baking processes. Some explanations regarding different technical points are also included.

Figure 3-22
Comparison of Main Mixing Techniques

Typical Formulation

	Short Mix	Improved Mix	Intensive Mix
Flour	100%	100%	100%
Water[1]	70%	67%	65%
Fresh yeast[2]	0.5%	1.5%	2%
Salt[3]	2%	2%	2%

Baking Process

	Short Mix	Improved Mix	Intensive Mix
Water temperature[4]	63°F (17°C)	55°F (13°C)	38°F (3°C)
Dough temperature	76°F (24°C) to 77°F (25°C)	76°F (24°C) to 77°F (25°C)	76°F (24°C) to 77°F (25°C)
First speed (100 RPM)[5]	3–4 minutes + 6 minutes	3–4 minutes	3–4 minutes
Second speed (200 RPM)[6]	0 minutes	5 minutes	8 minutes
First fermentation	3.5 hours	1.5 hours	20 minutes
Punch and fold	3	0 or 1	0
Resting time	20–25 minutes	20–25 minutes	20–25 minutes
Final proof[7]	45 minutes to 1 hour	1 to 1.5 hours	1.5 to 2 hours

[1]The water ratio in short mix and improved mix formulas is higher because extra water is necessary to give the dough the extensibility needed for the folds during first fermentation.

[2]Lower yeast quantities keep fermentation activity from happening too fast, allowing for longer first fermentation with short and improved mixes.

[3]A higher salt ratio adds flavor to intensive mix, but less salt is needed with the other methods because fermentation allows dough to develop more flavor of its own. Some short mix formulas reduce salt as low as 1.8 percent; some intensive mix formulas increase salt as high as 2.5 percent.

[4]Mixing friction creates heat. Adjusting water temperature compensates for heat generated during mixing, allowing the baker to achieve a final dough temperature of 75° (24°C) to 77°F (25°C). The temperatures listed here are only guidelines and may need to be adjusted depending of the conditions of the bakery.

[5]In the short mix method, use first speed to both incorporate ingredients and develop gluten. This enables the baker to duplicate more closely the effects of hand mixing.

[6]Mix time is based on a full batch size and standard revolutions. Mix time may need to be adjusted depending on the type of mixer used, batch size, type of flour, and so on.

[7]Final proof time increases with improved and intensive mixes because these doughs are stronger and can retain more CO_2 gas.

COMPARISON OF MIXING PROCESSES AND EFFECTS ON THE FINAL PRODUCTS

Figure 3-23 summarizes the effects of each mixing method on the dough and the final product characteristics. Explanations regarding different characteristics are also provided.

Figure 3-23
Chart: Mixing Processes and Effects on Final Products

Effect on Dough	Short Mix	Improved Mix	Intensive Mix
Consistency	Fairly soft [1]	Medium soft	Stiff
Strength	Lacks strength	Slightly lacking in strength	OK to strong
First fermentation	Long	Medium	Short
Machining	Difficult [2]	Possible	Ideal
Final proof	Short [3]	Medium	Long

Effect on Bread	Short Mix	Improved Mix	Intensive Mix
Volume	Small	Medium	Big
Color	Creamy	Less creamy [4]	White
Crumb	Open, irregular	Open, irregular	Tight, regular
Flavor	Very complex	Complex	More bland
Shelf life	Longer	Medium	Shorter

[1]A soft dough is needed in order to get enough gluten extensibility to be able to fold the dough efficiently. Punching and folding is necessary to develop the underdeveloped gluten structure.

[2]The dough will be difficult to machine using a fully automated process, but semimechanized processes are still possible using equipment such as hydraulic dough dividers and regular baguette molders.

[3]Less CO_2 can be retained in the dough due to the more underdeveloped gluten structure.

[4]Though less creamy than breads produced with the short mix, the crumb color is still definitely acceptable.

DEVELOPING YOUR OWN PROCESS

Mixing and fermentation can be "balanced" to achieve desired bread characteristics and production parameters. The right way to mix depends mainly on the attributes the baker wishes to achieve in the dough, and each technique has its own benefits and tradeoffs.

Although only three main mixing techniques are described in this chapter, once the baker can control and understand each of them, it can be said that there are as many ways to mix as there are ways to make bread. The baker must, however, keep in mind that mixing and fermentation work together, and if mixing is changed, fermentation time may have to be changed as well.

WHICH METHOD TO USE?

Some principles also apply to any type of bread produced in a bakery, including whole wheat and sourdough, which is why it is important to know how different mix methods will affect the final product before a technique is chosen.

Once the baker understands the differences between each method and their effects on the outcome of the final product, the method that works best in the individual baking environment can be devised. Begin this process by answering the following questions:

- What characteristics do I want my bread to have?
- What schedule/time issues do I have to work within?
- What equipment issues are involved (batch size, type of mixer, and the like)?

The answers will determine which mixing technique will provide the qualities most important to the particular product being made.

Sometimes, some adjustments to the method might be necessary. For example, when making pan bread, the required characteristics of the final product are the tight and even crumb provided by intensive mixing. Unfortunately, as has been discussed, an intensive mix will dull flavor. In order to counteract this, the baker can involve a preferment in the formula rather than resorting to short or improved mixing, which will produce a more irregular crumb.

It is important to keep in mind that when mixing methods are altered to achieve one characteristic, all the other characteristics that go with that method will be there as well. For example, dough cannot be developed to achieve a tight crumb and allowed to ferment for a long time, or it will be overdeveloped and lose its extensibility. The end result will be very difficult to work with.

In the same way, choosing a method to extend fermentation will result in all of its effects, including gassier dough that's harder to work with.

Understanding these important interconnections gives bakers more flexibility to balance the product attributes they want with the methods that best fit their production schedules.

MIXING AND TRAINING

In a large production environment, the baker in charge of mixing should see all the final products that were the result of his or her mixing shift. This can be a great learning experience, for, as we said earlier, a number of bread characteristics such as volume, crumb, and cut openings can be positively or negatively affected by the mixing time.

Standardizing the mixing procedure in large bakeries is also very important to guarantee a good consistency in production, regardless of which baker or which shifts mixed the dough.

There are several critical points during the mixing process where it is possible for mistakes to happen. However, through regimented and careful execution of each task, results should be fairly consistent and good.

SCALING

If a dough is not scaled properly, the ratio of ingredients will be off, and the intended result of the formula will be difficult, if not impossible, to achieve. The results may be noticeable within the first few minutes, as in the case of water that is improperly scaled. Problems with salt or yeast, on the other hand, may not be noticeable until the first fermentation or after the baking process is complete. You can ensure that all ingredients are properly scaled by double-checking measurements against the printed formula.

INCORPORATING INGREDIENTS

Even though all ingredients may have been properly scaled, they may not all make it into the dough. The implications of this depend on the missing ingredient, the most common of which include yeast, salt, sugar, and butter. On the other hand, it is hard to imagine someone forgetting the olives for olive bread.

How to remedy the situation will depend on what was forgotten and how much time has passed. If salt or yeast has been forgotten and the dough has just finished mixing, the salt or yeast should be dissolved in a small quantity of water and added to the dough in first speed. The same technique can be used for yeast that has been forgotten for up to 1 hour after mixing, if no preferment is being used. A missed addition of salt is trickier because the dough has been through a process of fermentation. Mixing the dough after this will have a negative effect on its rheology.

DEVELOPING DOUGH

Under- or overmixing the dough will change the physical characteristics of both the dough and the bread. This may affect the first fermentation time, which in turn can affect the rest of the baking process. Please refer to the charts in this chapter for specific results linked to under- or overdeveloping dough.

Sourdough Bread

CHAPTER SUMMARY

Mixing is not a very complicated step, but it does require a great deal of care and accuracy. It is fairly simple to understand that if mixing is done carefully, all of the steps after it will be easy. But if the dough is not right after mixing, the baker will have to know how to adjust and troubleshoot the baking process in order to produce a good-quality product. This can quickly turn a smooth production day into a difficult one. The incorporation of ingredients must be done in the proper order, dough should be developed using the correct mixing techniques, and the ideal dough temperature should be achieved in order to get the desired final product characteristics.

KEY TERMS

- ❖ Alveoles
- ❖ Autolyse
- ❖ Bulk fermentation
- ❖ Carotenoid pigments
- ❖ Consistency
- ❖ Cooling
- ❖ Desired dough temperature (DDT)
- ❖ Dividing
- ❖ Dough development
- ❖ Dough rheology
- ❖ Elasticity
- ❖ Enzyme
- ❖ Extensibility
- ❖ Final proof
- ❖ First fermentation
- ❖ Floor time
- ❖ Gliadin
- ❖ Gluten
- ❖ Gluten development
- ❖ Glutenin
- ❖ Improved mix
- ❖ Intensive mix
- ❖ Intermediate proof
- ❖ Mixing
- ❖ Oven loading
- ❖ Oxidation
- ❖ Preferment
- ❖ Preshaping
- ❖ Professor Raymond Calvel
- ❖ Protease
- ❖ Rest
- ❖ Scoring
- ❖ Shaping
- ❖ Short mix
- ❖ Traditional method

REVIEW QUESTIONS

1. **What are the three primary mixing methods and what effect does each one have on a final loaf of bread?**
2. **Why is it important to know and control the water temperature when mixing dough?**
3. **True or False: If mixing a baguette to an improved mix and the final temperature is 72°F (22°C), it is recommended to continue mixing until the desired dough temperature is reached.**
4. **What is oxidation of the dough? How can it be controlled?**
5. **What is double hydration and when and how is it used?**

chapter
4

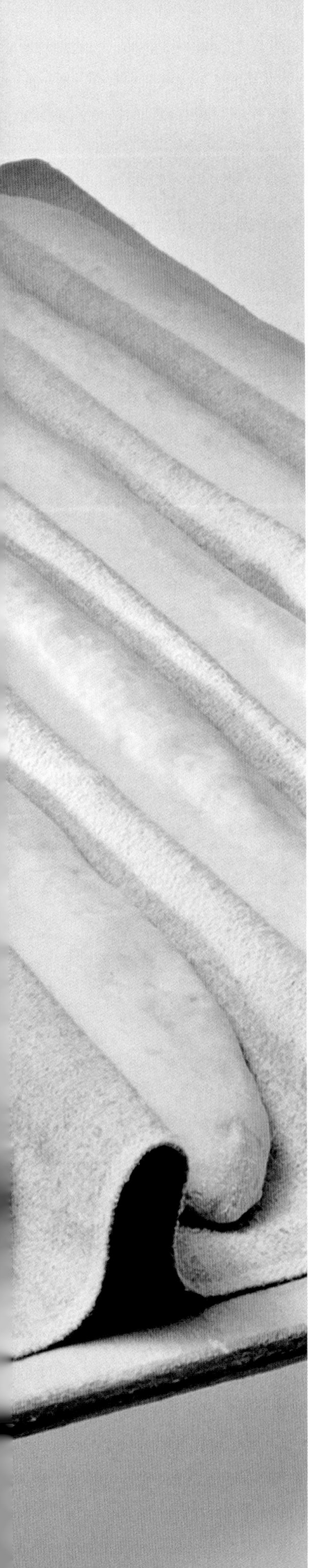

FERMENTATION

OBJECTIVES

After reading this chapter, you should be able to

- explain what fermentation is and why it is a very important step in baking.
- explain the different ways to use fermentation and how to control it to ensure consistent quality product.
- put into practice several retarding techniques.
- explain the connection between fermentation and flavor.

FERMENTATION

The baking process is a harmonious balance between the skill of the baker and the natural transformation that happens during fermentation. Fermentation begins when the baker joins together the two main components of bread: flour and water. With the addition of salt, yeast, time, and temperature, the baker balances all aspects of fermentation. It can be divided into two different phases: the handling period, when the baker physically works with the dough to mix, divide, and shape it, and the fermentation period, when dough characteristics are transformed. Both phases are critical to the final quality of the product. The style or path of fermentation dictates the bread's final flavor and aroma. To understand fermentation is to understand the baker's preference and expectations of the product.

Fermentation refers to the breakdown of compound molecules in organic substances under the effect of yeast or bacteria (ferments). Different types of fermentation are responsible for a number of products consumed in everyday life. For example, lactic fermentation is used to make cheese, butter, and some yogurts; acetic fermentation is used to produce vinegar from wine; and alcoholic fermentation is used to produce alcohol, cider, beer, and a number of other products.

In bread baking, fermentation occurs when some of the sugars or **glucides** (the group of carbohydrates that includes sugars, starches, cellulose, and many other compounds found in living organisms) naturally present in the flour are converted into alcohol and carbon dioxide under the effect of commercial or naturally occurring yeast and bacteria. This type of fermentation is categorized as an alcoholic fermentation. (See Figure 4-1.)

SUGAR TRANSFORMATION

Wheat flour contains different types of glucides that are used at different times during fermentation. These glucides can be classified according to the complexity of their structures. Some are used as is. Other glucides with more complex composition must be degraded by enzymes, or organic substances with different degradation proprieties that either are naturally present in flour and yeast or are added during the milling process. (See Figure 4-2.)

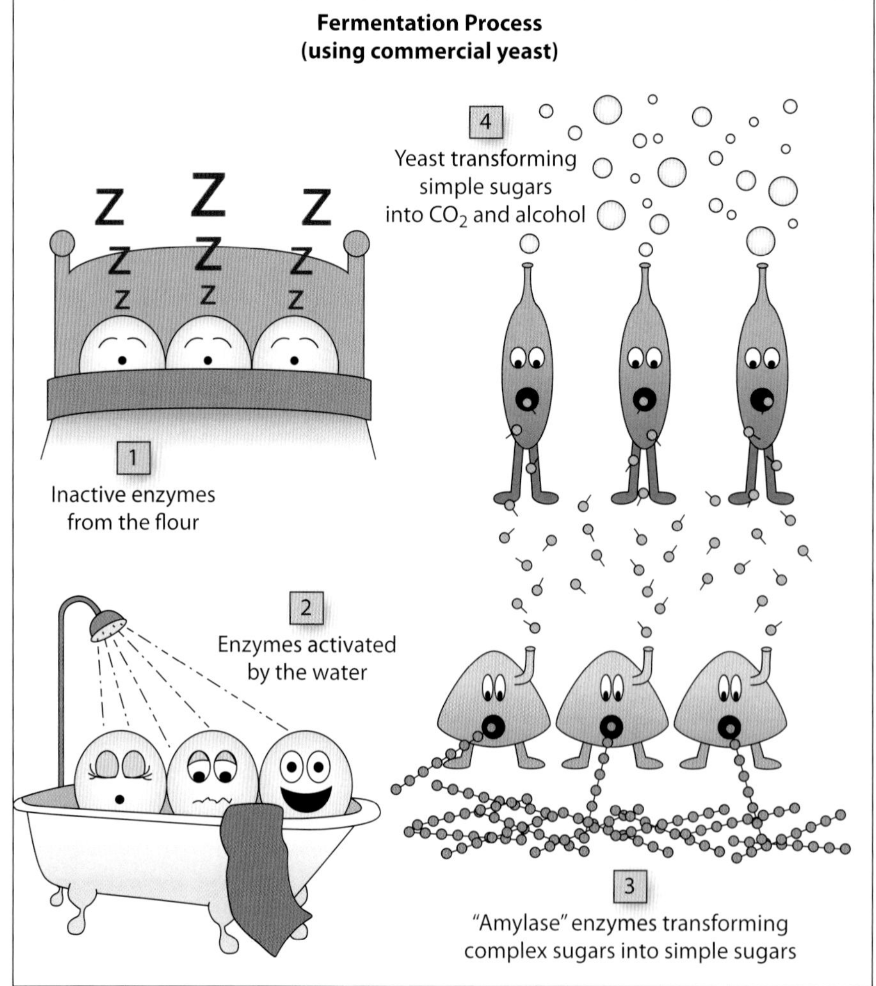

Figure 4-1
Fermentation Process

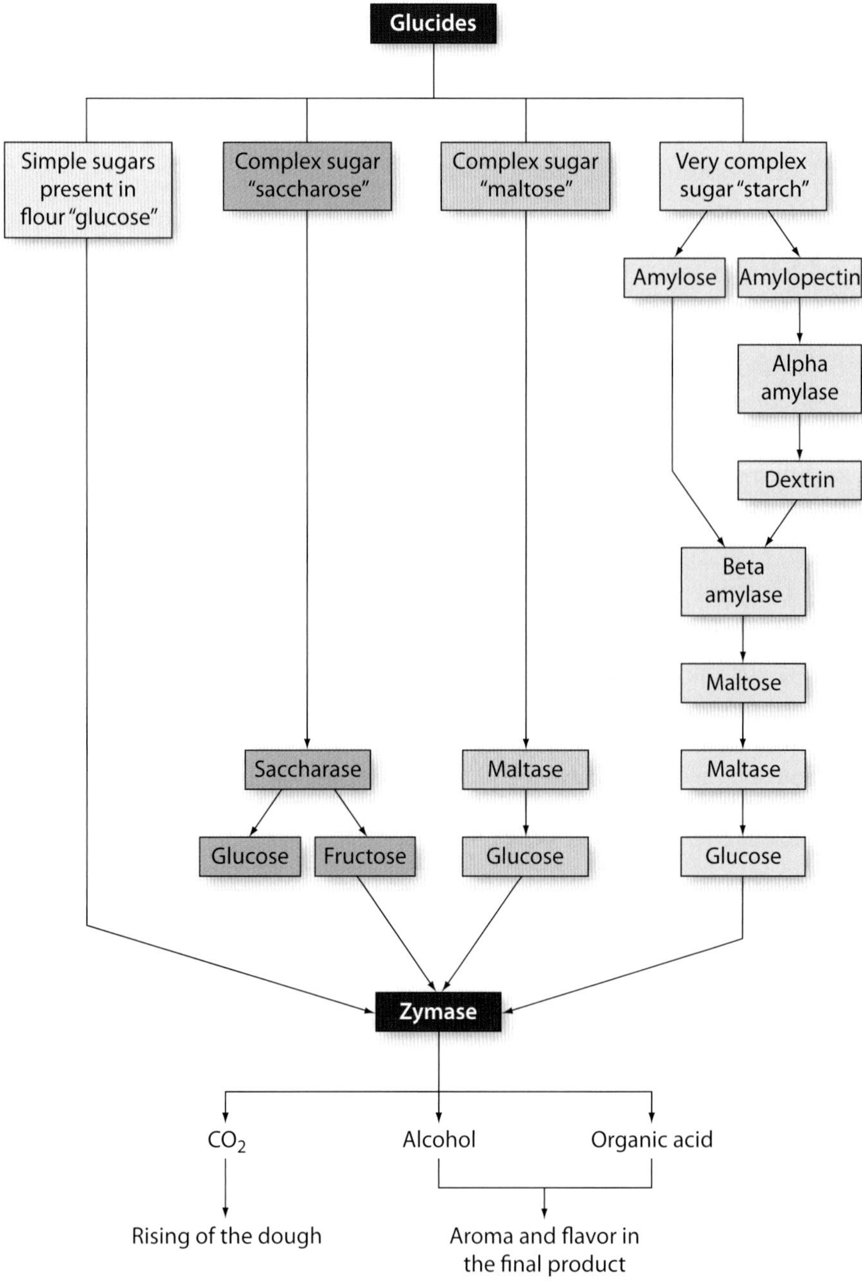

Figure 4-2
Sugar Degradation

Simple Glucides (Carbohydrates)

The basic simple glucides (**simple sugars**) are glucose and fructose, which together represent about 0.5 percent of flour. They are directly assimilated when the yeast penetrates the membrane of the cell. Simple sugars are transformed into alcohol and carbon dioxide by zymase, the naturally present enzyme contained in the yeast cells. Easy absorption causes these sugars to be used first, during the first 30 minutes of the fermen-tation process.

Complex Glucides (Carbohydrates)

Saccharose and maltose, the two main complex glucides, represent approximately 1 percent of the flour. Because of their complex composition, they spend the first 30 minutes of fermentation undergoing enzymatic transformation into simple sugars that are used later in the fermentation process. Saccharose is transformed into glucose and fructose by the saccharase enzyme, and maltose is transformed into glucose by the maltase enzyme. Both of these enzymes are naturally present in the flour and yeast cells. The glucose and fructose produced is then transformed in carbon dioxide and alcohol by the zymase enzyme that occurs in the yeast cell.

Very Complex Glucides (Carbohydrates)

The main complex glucide is starch, which represents about 70 percent of the flour. Two types are found: amylose and amylopectin. Amylose is degraded into maltose by the beta amylase enzyme, and the maltose is then degraded into glucose by the maltase enzyme. The amylopectin is degraded into dextrin by the alpha amylase enzyme, and the dextrin is degraded into maltose by beta amylase. The resulting maltose is then degraded into glucose by the maltase. Finally, the yeast uses the glucose to generate carbon dioxide and alcohol.

Most of the starch used during fermentation was damaged during the milling process. These damaged particles easily absorb water during dough elaboration, which in turn triggers the enzymatic activity. A non-damaged particle of starch will only retain water at its periphery, and not inside the particle itself.

IMPORTANCE OF ENZYMATIC BALANCE IN THE FLOUR

Even though alpha and beta amylase enzymes are naturally present in the flour, the amount of alpha amylase can vary, depending on the **germination** or sprouting stage of the wheat. When the wheat is preparing to start a new cycle of life (sprouting), the germ sends enzymes to the **endosperm**, the nutritive tissue of the seed. These enzymes transform the complex components of the endosperm in smaller nutrients that the germ can use.

Typically, flour lacks the alpha amylase enzymes, due to storage quality issues that require harvesting before wheat sprouts. To simplify work for the baker and to keep fermentation as regular and consistent as possible, millers compensate for this lack of enzymes by adding malted flour or fungal enzymes.

Only a minimum amount of starch is used during the fermentation process. Technically, fermentation can last a very long time, but dough does have limits for gas retention. For this reason, it is important for the baker to understand and control fermentation activity.

EFFECTS OF FERMENTATION ACTIVITY ON DOUGH

The most visible effect of fermentation activity is rising due to carbon dioxide production. In the beginning, the gas is dispersed in free water (not fixed by the flour). As the water becomes saturated with gas, an increasing accumulation creates internal pressure that stretches the gluten structure of the dough. Because of its physical properties of extensibility and elasticity, the gluten is able to hold the structure of the dough and retain the carbon dioxide needed to accomplish a good rise.

The second effect of fermentation is the **acidification** of dough, the production of organic acids that lower its pH. Dough acidification provides an indication of good fermentation activity, and measuring it is a good way to ensure consistent fermentation on a daily basis (pH meters remain the best tool to measure dough acidification). Another very important aspect of acidity is that it delays the staling process and increases product shelf life.

The final important effect of fermentation is the production of aroma. Some aromas are created by alcohol production, others are obtained from organic acids, and still others are created by the secondary reactions that take place during fermentation. Aroma formation takes time, a fact that is especially true during the secondary stage of fermentation. For example, bacteria and different types of "wild" yeast naturally present in the flour generate the aromas related to secondary reactions. This explains why a long fermentation time at the beginning of the baking process is necessary to obtain bread with a good complexity of flavor.

Independent of the physical changes that take place during handling, fermentation changes dough characteristics. During the long first (or bulk) fermentation, the dough develops and strengthens, producing reduced extensibility and increased elasticity.

Because the concepts of extensibility, elasticity, and strength are extensively discussed in this chapter, we need to have a clear understanding at the outset of how these terms are used. Extensibility refers to the stretching property of dough, with easy-to-stretch dough commonly described as having good extensibility. Elasticity refers to the dough's ability to return to its initial position after stretching. Strength refers to the balance between extensibility, elasticity, and a third property called tenacity.

FACTORS AFFECTING FERMENTATION

Different factors will affect fermentation during the baking process, including the amount of yeast, salt, and sugar used; the temperature; and the pH. The baker must control each of these to achieve predictable, consistent results.

Amount of Yeast

The rate of fermentation is directly related to the amount of yeast used in the dough. Specifically, the quantity of yeast must be limited to control fermentation and allow the dough enough time to benefit. Depending on the product and baking process, it should be in the range of 0.5 to 2 percent (fresh compressed yeast) based on the flour for lean dough. A higher amount is necessary for sweet dough.

Temperature

Yeast activity is faster at higher temperatures and slower at lower ones. To obtain the optimum production of gas and acidity, dough must be kept at approximately 76°F (24°C). If it is too warm, gas production will increase, but aroma production will suffer.

Amount of Salt and Sugar

Salt slows down fermentation activity. In general, the amount of salt for a regular and consistent fermentation is 2 percent, based on the total flour in the formula. A small amount of sugar (5 percent) will increase fermentation activity due to higher amounts of nutrients for the yeast. A larger amount (12 percent) will have the opposite effect, slowing fermentation due to a change in yeast cell function.

Dough pH

Commercial yeast works best when the pH of the dough is in between 4 and 6. One of the effects of lower pH is a reduction in fermentation activity that changes the characteristics of the dough. "Wild" yeast and bacteria are better adapted to lower pH, which is why they work so well in these conditions present in the sourdough process.

RELATIONSHIP BETWEEN FERMENTATION AND DOUGH HANDLING

The baking process will determine most of the final characteristics of bread, including flavor, crumb texture, volume, and shelf life. The baking process is best described as a succession of steps that include the handling of the dough (such as mixing, dividing, shaping, scoring, and baking) and its fermentation.

The baking process is so interesting because all these steps are interconnected; technically, it's not possible to isolate any of them. Any change in dough characteristics during one step will, for better or worse, affect all subsequent steps of the baking process.

Relationship Between First Fermentation and Mixing

A long first fermentation considerably increases dough strength and brings several benefits to bread, the two most significant being increased flavor and shelf life.

The process begins during mixing. At this stage, water creates cohesion in all the flour components, creating gluten. The hook of the mixer gives structure to the gluten by stretching its strands and folding them over onto themselves. The more the dough is mixed, the more the gluten structure will be organized, and the stronger the dough will be. This effect continues until the structure of the gluten reaches the overmixed stage, at which point the strands begin to tear.

If the baker opts to increase strength through a long fermentation, it is necessary to decrease mixing time. The longer the first fermentation lasts, the more the structure of the dough is reinforced by the production of acidity. Limiting the mixing time in this case will avoid a double increase in strength that will negatively impact the dough during the subsequent steps of the baking process.

A shorter mixing time also reduces the negative effects of oxidation that occur when oxygen is incorporated into the dough during the mixing process. A small amount of oxygen is necessary to reinforce the binding of the gluten strains, but too much has a negative effect on the components of the flour that are responsible for flavor and crumb color.

It is possible to obtain the advantages and characteristics of bread made by hand with a mechanical mixer by adapting the mixing time. To compensate for the underdeveloped gluten structure created by the mechanical mixing of a short mix, the baker should combine a long first fermentation with a folding technique. The two benefits of folding the dough are

- Reorganization of the gluten structure, duplicating the physical action of the hook during the mixing process
- Expulsion of the carbon dioxide accumulated in the dough during the first fermentation, which optimizes yeast activity (The physical and chemical transformations of the yeast cell are affected when the environment is saturated in carbon dioxide and alcohol.)

Bakers who couple a long mixing time with a long first fermentation can end up with an excess of dough strength that will hurt extensibility during shaping. It will also result in bread with a cross section that is too round, unopened cuts, and a tight crumb structure, as opposed to a natural opening and irregular hole structure. Conversely, underdeveloped dough requires a longer first fermentation with the help of folding to prevent a flat, unappealing appearance.

Relationship Between First Fermentation and Dividing

The dough is divided after first fermentation is complete. At this point, the strands of gluten have been stretched and are more fragile, and the dough is gassier and more difficult to work with. For these reasons, it is important to avoid damaging the dough during this step.

If dividing is done by hand, the baker should find the desired weight within two or three attempts. Too many small pieces of dough will disorganize the gluten structure and will increase dough strength as a secondary effect. In this case, some extra work is needed to reorganize the gluten during the next step of the process, which is preshaping.

If dividing is done by machine, the baker should opt for one that won't damage or tear the gluten during the process. Dividers that work by sucking action, for example, are typically not suitable for gassy dough due to the gluten tearing and damage that occurs. This damage makes preshaping harder and produces dough with excessive strength. Gassy dough also provides some irregularity in the weight of the loaves because the varying levels of carbon dioxide create different ratios of volume and weight in each piece of dough. Instead, hydraulic dividers or stress-free dividers are more suitable for dough with a long first fermentation time.

Relationship Between Dough Characteristics and Preshaping

If the relationship between mixing and first fermentation is respected, the dough should be well balanced in strength at this point of the baking process. However, some factors can prevent this from happening, including using flour that is too strong or that has poor protein quality or dough that is an inappropriate temperature.

Should the dough have insufficient or excessive strength, corrections can be made during preshaping. If the dough is too extensible, the baker can increase strength by making a tighter preshaping that folds the strands of gluten over onto themselves one more time. If the dough is too strong, it must be handled gently to avoid excessively folding the gluten strands.

Relationship Between Dough Characteristics and Shaping

If dough characteristics are not well balanced at this point in the baking process, shaping is the last opportunity to correct them. Dough lacking strength requires tighter shaping. This can be achieved by tightening or folding the dough a little more if hand shaping or by decreasing the space between the two first rollers of the shaping machine. If the dough is too strong, a light shaping is more suitable. Dough should be handled just enough to provide the final shape and to maintain it during the final proof.

Relationship Between Final Proof and Shaping

Compared to dough that has been hand-shaped, dough that has been shaped by machine will last longer through the final proof. The molder makes dough stronger and expels more gas during flattening. Since the dough is stronger and less-gassy, final proofing takes more time to reach the point where the dough is ready to bake. Hand-shaped dough, with its higher gas content and less tightly organized gluten structure, is ready to bake after a shorter period of time.

Relationship Between Dough Characteristics and Scoring

Scoring must be adapted to fit the dough characteristics at the end of the final proof. If the dough is slightly overproofed, scoring should be shallow to avoid deflation. If it is underproofed, it will benefit from deeper scoring, which creates better expansion during oven spring and provides some compensation for lack of volume.

The method in which scoring is done on the surface of the loaf also changes its appearance. A sausage (transversal) cut or a chevron cut gives the bread a rounded cross section, whereas cuts done parallel to the length of the bread create a flatter cross section. For this reason, weak dough looks better when it is scored with a sausage or chevron cut.

PREFERMENTS

Another form of fermentation widely used in baking is preferment. Preferments provide a simple and inexpensive way to improve bread quality, as well as dough and bread characteristics like strength and aroma.

Preferment is a dough or batter that is created from a portion of the total formula's flour, water, yeast (natural or commercial), and sometimes salt. It is prepared prior to mixing the final dough, allowed to ferment for a controlled period of time, and added to the final dough.

Types of Preferments

Depending on the type of product to be baked, production scheduling, and available equipment, bakers can select from a number of different preferments. These include prefermented dough, poolish, sponge, and biga. It is also possible to develop unique preferment formulas and processes that rely on the same basic concepts.

Prefermented Dough **Prefermented dough** (sometimes referred to as old dough) is a fairly new, uncomplicated method that was originally developed to compensate for the mediocre quality of bread produced by using a short first fermentation. Prefermented dough allows the baker to produce a better-quality product even when the first fermentation must be shortened due to production scheduling or mechanization.

The process is fairly simple: A piece of regular dough (made with white flour, water, yeast, and salt) is allowed to ferment for a period of time before being incorporated back in the final mix. In order for the baker to achieve the greatest benefit from the process, prefermentation should last at least 3 hours and should not exceed 6 hours at room temperature.

For longer periods of time before use, it is preferable to let the dough ferment for 1 to 2 hours at room temperature and then to hold it in the refrigerator until incorporation into the final dough. At 35°F (2°C) to 45°F (7°C), prefermented dough can be stored up to 48 hours. If using this procedure, the baker should remove the prefermented dough from storage 1 or 2 hours before incorporating it into the final dough. If this is not practical, the water temperature in the final dough should be adjusted to compensate for the colder prefermented dough.

Prefermented dough can also be a piece of dough that is saved from a previous mix. For example, a piece of whole wheat dough can be used as preferment for the next day's whole wheat production. In general, however, bakers prefer to save baguette dough because it contains only the four basic ingredients of any dough (flour, water, yeast, and salt), which provides the versatility needed to be used in any kind of final mix.

The amount of prefermented dough needed for various formulas ranges from 10 to 180 percent, based on the flour of the final mix. In general, 40 to 50 percent is the most commonly used proportion. The most convenient way for the baker to procure the quantity required for the next production is to remove the dough to be used as a preferment just after the first fermentation, and to store it in the refrigerator.

One other alternative for prefermenting dough is to mix it as separate dough the day before, or at least 3 hours prior to incorporation in the final dough. In this case, usually about 20 to 30 percent of the flour from the total formula is used in the preferment. The absorption should be adjusted to obtain a medium consistency (generally 64 to 66 percent). Salt is 2 percent, and yeast is 1 to 1.5 percent (fresh). All percentages are calculated based on the amount of flour in the preferment.

No matter how it is made, prefermented dough can be used in many different products, from Viennoiserie like croissants, brioche, and Danish to many different breads, including baguettes, pan breads, and whole wheat and rye breads. The biggest drawback to this method is the large amount of refrigerated space required for overnight storage.

Poolish **Poolish** is one of the first preferments ever elaborated with commercial yeast. The name is derived from the Polish bakers who are credited with inventing this preferment in Poland at the end of the 19th century. The process was then adapted in Austria and later brought to France by some Viennese bakers. Bread made with a poolish was lighter in texture and less acidic than the sourdough bread common at the time. This feature, coupled with the availability of commercial yeast, led to a quick rise in its popularity.

Technically, we can consider poolish to be a transition between baking with sourdough and baking with commercial yeast using a straight process. Even today, in the windows of some older Paris bakeries, you will find two signs. One will say, "Pain Viennois," or bread from Vienna made with commercial yeast, and the other will say, "Pain Francais," or bread from France made with sourdough. Poolish can be used in many different bread or sweet products, and it is generally the preferment of choice for baguette dough.

Traditionally, the size of a poolish has been calculated based on the water involved in the total formula. Bakers use from 20 to 80 percent of the water to prepare a poolish, which is elaborated using the same amount of flour as water. This creates a hydration of 100 percent and provides a liquid consistency. Poolish does not usually contain salt. It is important to note that poolish is allowed to ferment at room temperature; therefore, the quantity of yeast is calculated depending on the fermentation time. Despite the fact that it is difficult to give precise numbers, Figure 4-3 provides some guidelines to calculate the quantity of yeast required.

Fermentation time	3 hours	7 to 8 hours	12 to 15 hours
Quantity of yeast (fresh)*	1.5%	0.7%	0.1%

* Based on the amount of flour used in the poolish.

Figure 4-3
Yeast Quantity Calculation for Poolish

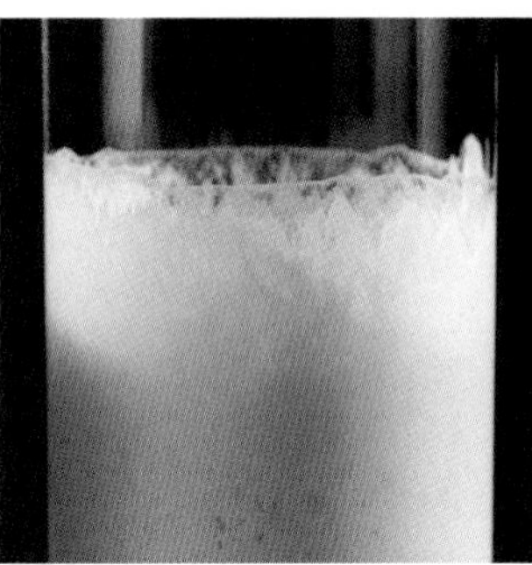

Figure 4-4
Mature, Undermature, and Overmature Poolish (top to bottom)

These guidelines are applicable for a bakery temperature of 80°F (27°C) to 85°F (29°C) and a water temperature of 60°F (16°C). If the temperature of the bakery is warmer, the yeast quantity or the water temperature should be decreased. The goal is for the baker to obtain a poolish that is perfectly matured at the time of mixing the final dough. Full maturation is indicated when the poolish has domed slightly on top and has just begun to recede, which creates some areas on the surface that are a bit more concave. A poolish that has not matured adequately does not provide the full benefit of the acidity. One that has overmatured can create other types of acidity that can negatively affect the flavor of the final product. (See Figure 4-4.)

If production and storage are adequate, it is better for the baker to opt for an overnight poolish. This produces more favorable aromas and requires less yeast, increasing the amount of time for use to up to $2^{1}/_{2}$ hours without overmaturing.

Tip: If large amounts of poolish are required for various doughs, it is much easier to divide it into separate containers for each final dough right after it is mixed, instead of measuring after it matures.

Sponge Originally, **sponge** was used as preferment in pan bread production in England. Today, the sponge process for pan bread production has largely been replaced by the straight dough method, with dough conditioners replacing the sponge. Sponges were also, and still are, used in the production of sweet dough in other European countries as well as the United States.

The sponge process is similar to the poolish process; it differs primarily in dough hydration. While poolish has a liquid consistency, the absorption of sponge is around 60 to 63 percent, creating a stiffer consistency that makes the dough easier to handle. Like poolish, the sponge usually does not contain salt, and the quantity of yeast is calculated depending on the length of the fermentation. In fact, the yeast guidelines for a poolish can be applied to the sponge process. When it comes to taste, sponges and poolish generate very similar aromas; however, it tastes slightly sweeter than the poolish.

A sponge should be used after it has reached full maturation. Its surface contains vital clues to help the baker determine its readiness, including numerous bubbles and the formation of cracks that create some collapse. At this point, the sponge is ready for incorporation into the final dough. An undermature sponge will not be as beneficial because of inadequate acid development, whereas an overmature sponge will have too much, negatively affecting the strength of the dough and the flavor of the bread. (See Figure 4-5.)

A sponge that uses minimal yeast and ferments overnight offers the baker a longer period of time between undermaturation and overmaturation. This longer fermentation time generates enough acidity to ensure good flavor and a longer shelf life.

A sponge can be used in many products. Sweet dough will get the most benefit from the sponge method because the stiffer consistency of the sponge improves the strength of the dough. This increase in strength is usually enough to compensate for the potential weakening of the gluten that is created by the sugar and fat frequently found in sweet bread formulas.

Biga Many Italian bread formulas are made with **biga**. A close study of these formulas shows that even if the basic ingredients of a biga are the same, the finished preferment can have very different characteristics. Some biga are liquid, some are stiff, some are sour, some are fermented at room temperature, and still others are fermented in a cold environment.

After research (including conversations with Italian bakers), the conclusion can be made that biga is more a generic term for preferment than a reference to a specific process. In the United States, the term is occasionally used instead of "prefermented dough," "poolish," or "sponge" to add a touch of "Italian authenticity" to the bread. Like the preceding preferments, its advantages are good flavor and extended shelf life.

Originally, biga was a very stiff preferment used to reinforce the weaker strength of dough that was, by then, elaborated with weaker wheat. A traditional biga is prepared using flour, water, and yeast, with a hydration of approximately 50 to 55 percent. Unlike the poolish and sponge processes, the quantity of yeast, fermentation temperature, and fermentation time are constant, with 0.8 to 1 percent of fresh commercial yeast typically used. Biga is held at approximately 60°F (16°C) for about 18 hours.

True biga can be used for products that require stronger dough characteristics, such as brioche or stollen. It is also a good choice for dough with high hydration. Because of its higher level of yeast, very stiff consistency, and cooler, longer fermentation time, biga naturally develops a superior amount of acidity. Therefore, bakers should use biga properly when also using stronger flour to avoid penalizing extensibility. If extensibility is compromised, higher hydration or autolyse will help regain a better balance.

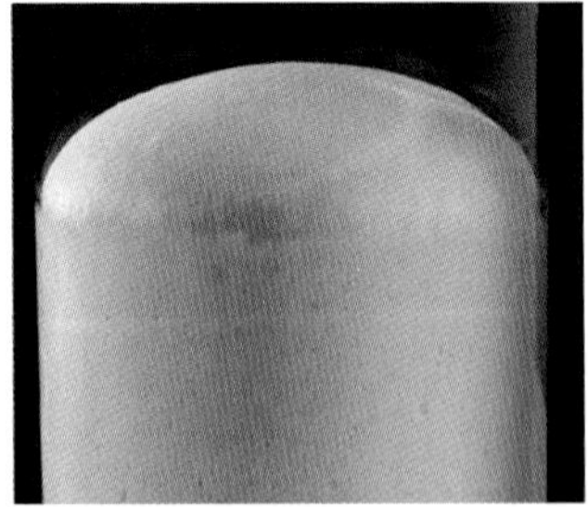

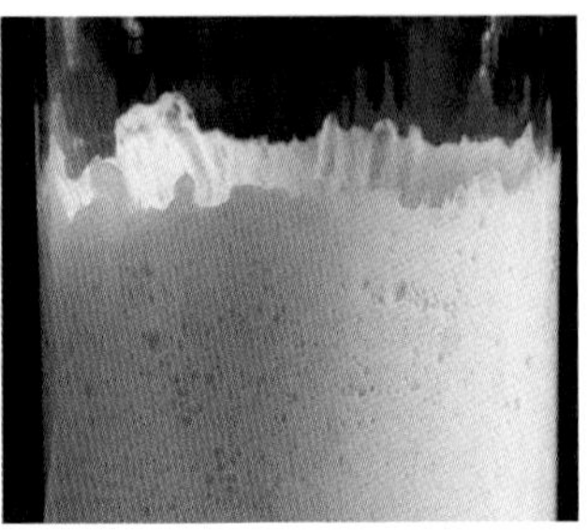

Figure 4-5
Mature, Undermature, and Overmature Sponge (top to bottom)

Advantages and Drawbacks of Preferments

By reviewing the advantages and drawbacks of preferments, bakers should learn how to take full advantage of each method and decide which preferment will work best with a specific flour or dough. Even with the downsides, preferments are worthwhile for bakers, especially when the increased quality of the final product is taken into consideration.

Advantages The main advantage of preferment is to bring all of the benefits of fermentation to the final dough, including gas, alcohol, and acidity.

- *Gas production:* At this stage of the baking process, gas does not have the same importance as it does after the final dough is mixed because preferments are used to make the final dough, not the final product.
- *Alcohol production:* During preferment, alcohol reacts with other substances to generate **esters**, the aromatic components of bread that are very important in producing the flavor of the final product.
- *Acid production:* At this stage, acidity plays a more important role than gas or alcohol. Its three main effects on the dough and final product are tightening protein to strengthen the dough, lowering the pH triggering an increase in shelf life of the bread by delaying the staling process, and inhibiting mold growth. Finally, as a result of secondary fermentation, organic acids are formed, producing aromas in the dough. Those aromas are very important for the flavor of the final product.

There are two other advantages worth mentioning. First, when the quality of the flour is not optimal, preferment can be a great help in strengthening the dough and compensating for flour deficiencies.

Second, preferments facilitate better organization of work. By experimenting with the quantity of preferment involved in the formula, bakers can increase or decrease the length of the first fermentation without jeopardizing the quality of the final product. For example, a longer first fermentation requires less preferment, while the shorter first fermentation, which is more common in bakeries, requires more.

Drawbacks The main drawback to using preferment is the additional work required before final dough mixing. In order to prepare the preferment, additional mixing and scaling are required, either the day before or at least 3 hours prior to mixing the final dough.

Another drawback is the amount of extra space at ideal conditions (room temperature or sometimes refrigerated) necessary to allow prefermentation to happen. For heavy production, this shortcoming can present a significant problem, especially if the production area is small or refrigeration space is limited. In designing a new bakery, it is a good idea to plan a room reserved specifically for preferment. To keep the fermentation activity as consistent as possible, an additional temperature control system can be beneficial.

A final drawback is the potential inability to plan the exact amount of preferment needed relative to the quantity of production. One way to bypass this obstacle is to require customers to place orders at least a day in advance.

Technical Considerations

The main factors to consider when opting for a specific type of preferment are production and space requirements, flour characteristics, and flavor. Within these parameters, the baker should be able to decide what kind of preferment is best for production. Once the choice is made, it is best to limit the type of preferment to two or three kinds.

In order to obtain the full benefits from using preferments, the baker must understand and respect certain precise technical points in the process. These include mixing the preferment and incorporating it into the final dough.

Mixing Preferments A very basic but extremely important step in mixing is the precise scaling of all the ingredients. This is critical for regulating fermentation activity and ensuring consistency in the final product.

Water temperature should be at approximately 60°F (16°C), but it can be adjusted if the baker wants to increase or decrease prefermentation time. Water that is too cold can have a negative effect on the work of the yeast, making it necessary to decrease the quantity of yeast when a longer prefermentation is necessary.

Because gas retention is not important, the gluten structure does not need to be developed. Mixing time should be long enough to fully incorporate the ingredients but short enough to avoid overoxidizing the dough. Depending on the size of the batch, a spiral mixer can complete mixing at first speed in 5 to 8 minutes. For slower mixers, like an oblique or vertical mixer, 2 to 3 minutes at second speed can be added to the mixing time after incorporation to ensure complete incorporation of ingredients.

For liquid preferments, a paddle attachment is preferable to achieve a perfect blend in a shorter period of time. When making a poolish overnight (using a very small amount of yeast), dilute the yeast in water first to diffuse it completely.

Incorporating Preferments Into the Final Dough Timing and quantity must be considered when adding preferment to the final dough.

Preferments are generally added to the final dough at the beginning or during the incorporation period of the mixing process. However, it is sometimes preferable to delay incorporating preferments, as is the case with prefermented dough from a prior, fully mixed batch. This must be incorporated toward the end of the mixing time to avoid double-mixing.

When making dough using autolyse, the preferment should be added to the final dough, along with yeast and salt, only after the autolyse resting period. This is done to avoid any incorporation of yeast into the autolyse. (As discussed in Chapter 3, liquid preferments are added to the dough before the autolyse because their high water content are part of the total dough hydration.) Because of slower fermentation activity, sourdough is a possible exception to this rule. Levain can be incorporated before the autolyse starts; however, if the water temperature is very cold, it is better to incorporate the **levain** (sourdough culture matured enough to be used to ferment the final dough) after autolyse to avoid delaying the culture's fermentation process.

The quantity of preferment the baker can include in formulas depends on the baking process. A number of factors, such as the strength of the flour, hydration, and the type of preferment help determine the final amount. As a general rule, any time the first fermentation is shorter, the quantity of preferment should be increased to avoid penalizing the quality of the final product. There are, of course, certain limits. For example, if an excessive amount of preferment is added, the acidity level in the dough may be too high. It is possible to determine the optimal percentage of preferment through a series of baking tests. Also, practical considerations like floor space and/or production requirements must sometimes play a part in the decision.

Note: Preferment can also be used to alter water temperature. For example, prefermented dough coming from the cooler is a good substitute for ice or cold water for regulating dough temperature. On the other hand, when using a high-quantity of poolish that has been allowed to ferment at room temperature, the water temperature in the final dough should be decreased. (In certain circumstances, at least half the water used for the poolish is already at room temperature.)

Secondary Effects of Preferment

When flour and water are incorporated, enzyme activity begins. Some enzymes generate sugar degradation (amylase), while others provoke protein degradation (protease).

During prefermentation, the yeast uses up most of the flour's simple sugars, especially during a long fermentation time at room temperature. When this portion of flour is added back into the final dough, the overall quantity of fermentable sugar is lower than what is usually available for the yeast in a straight dough method. As a result, satisfactory crust coloration is difficult to obtain. This defect is sometimes noticeable when a high percentage of overnight poolish or sponge is used in the final dough, or when the enzyme activity of the flour is on the low side. To troubleshoot this problem, 0.5 to 1 percent of diastatic malt (based on the total flour) can be added to the final dough.

Preferments like poolish or sponge sometimes generate low levels of fermentable sugars, which are available at the end of the prefermentation time. In certain cases, these sugars can be used to the baker's advantage. A higher quantity of preferment should be added to the final dough when working with a high level of enzyme in the flour (low falling number). By increasing the percentage of preferment, the portion of the flour with less sugar available to the yeast also increases. This reduces both the fermentation activity and the reddish crust color that is usually obtained when too many enzymes are present in the flour.

Because of their consistency, liquid preferments like poolish favor amylase and protease activity. As a result, the final dough is more extensible. The same protease effect also happens in preferments like sponge that do not have salt and ferment for a long time at room temperature, as opposed to cooler temperatures, which inhibit enzyme activity. The absence of salt in the preparation also encourages a higher rate of protease activity because protease is very salt-sensitive. Cold doughs with salt do not generate the same level of enzyme activity, it is more useful to apply an autolyse process when using prefermented dough than when using a poolish or levain. In addition, flour with a tendency to generate strong dough will give better baking performance when used with a poolish.

An excess of enzyme activity can cause the inside of the preferment to liquefy, especially at the end of the maturation stage, which can compromise the characteristics of the final dough. To correct this problem, add 0.1 to 0.2 percent salt during the preparation of the preferment. The addition of salt can also slow down preferment activity and reduce the risk of overmaturation in hot climates or during summer months.

When it comes to flavor, each preferment generates different aromas depending on its characteristics. Consistency, temperature, salt content, and type of yeast all have some effect on the types of aromas produced and the final flavor of the product. Although it is difficult to describe all the flavors of each preferment, poolish is generally described as having a nutty flavor, sponge is sweeter with more acidity, and prefermented dough is a little bit more acetic without being sour.

SOURDOUGH

Some historians claim that sourdough bread originated in Egypt somewhere between 4000 and 3000 BCE. Legend says that while preparing the unleavened bread of the time, a woman forgot a piece of dough and left it out in the warm, humid Nile River countryside. When she later discovered her mistake, the dough had greatly expanded. She incorporated it into a new batch of dough and baked it. As a result of the mistake, the sourdough process was discovered. For a very long period of time, this method of baking mystified most bakers. However, with the recent evolution of baking science, and microbiology in particular, this natural fermentation process is becoming better understood.

General Sourdough Process

The general sourdough process involves starting a culture of **microorganisms** (mainly yeast and bacteria), cultivating them to increase their quantity, and using them to ferment the final dough. After this last step, the baker perpetuates some of the reserved **culture** (the growing of microorganisms in controlled conditions) by adding more flour and water to maintain its activity. (See Figure 4-6.)

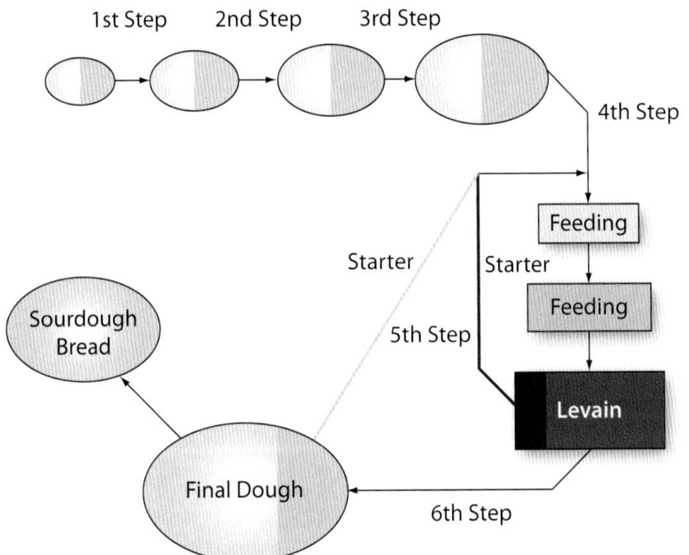

Steps

1. Creating a culture.
2. Elaborating the culture.
3. Preparing the culture for use when it is sufficiently strong and active. At this stage, the culture is called a starter.
4. Feeding the starter. After one or more feedings, the culture is called a feeding. After the final feeding before incorporation into the final dough, the culture is called a levain.
5. Perpetuating the culture. A piece of dough is saved from either 1) the levain, or 2) the final dough. At this stage, the culture is again called the starter.
6. Incorporating the levain into a final dough and making bread.

Figure 4-6
Sourdough Process

Microorganisms Involved in the Sourdough Process

Yeast and bacteria are the two main types of microorganisms that make up the flora present in the sourdough process. Because every microorganism needs a specific environment with favorable conditions for reproduction, the type and quantity of each will be affected by the characteristics of the sourdough, including hydration, ingredients, temperature, acidity, and more.

Both of these microorganisms can be found everywhere: in air, water, on the equipment—even on the baker! The largest source is the flour itself, where one gram contains a total of about 13,000 cells of wild yeast and approximately 320 cells of lactic bacteria.

Yeast Yeast transforms simple sugars like glucose and fructose into alcohol (ethanol) and gas (carbon dioxide) during the fermentation process. Yeast is classified as "wild" because it is present in any natural environment. Most wild yeast cells are members of the *Saccharomyces cerevisiae* family, the same as commercial yeast, but their genetic characteristics are slightly different. Other species of wild yeast, such as *Saccharomyces exiguus*, *Candida tropicalis*, and *Hansenula anomala* have also been identified. Generally speaking, wild yeast is more resistant to acidity compared to commercial yeast, making it better adapted to the sourdough process.

Bacteria Lactic bacteria are part of the "bacillus" family (Lactobacillus) or "coque" family (Lactocoque) and are divided in two types: **homofermentative** and **heterofermentative**. Each has different morphology and a different reaction in the dough. Lactic bacteria also work on certain sugars, converting them into organic acids that are transformed into aromas. Two main types of acid are lactic and acetic. Lactic acid plays a direct role in bread flavor, whereas acetic acid seems to reinforce the flavor provided by the other aromas and accentuates the acid flavor of the final product with a much sharper flavor.

Figure 4-7
Transformation Made by Microorganisms in the Sourdough Process

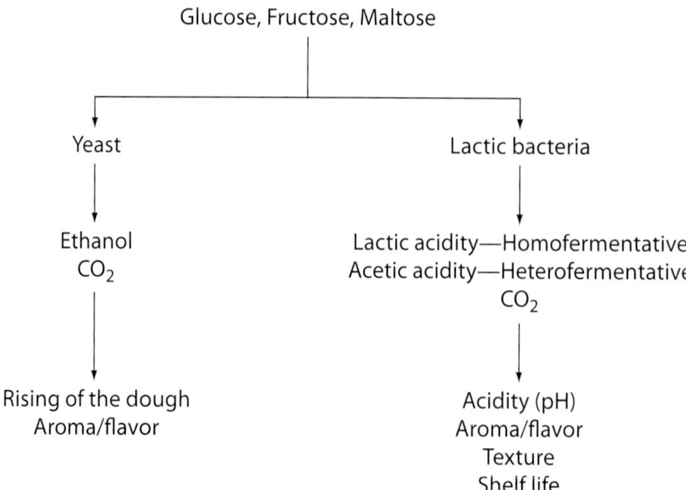

Homofermentative bacteria produce only lactic acid; heterofermentative bacteria produce lactic acid, acetic acid, and carbon dioxide. (See Figure 4-7.)

Starting the Culture

There are many ways to start a sourdough culture, but the principle is always the same. The initial microorganisms come from the flora naturally contained in the flour. To start a successful sourdough process, the baker develops this flora and activates it enough to ferment the final dough. All necessary environmental conditions have to be respected for this to happen.

Microorganisms need three things to reproduce and generate the proper transformations: food, which is provided by the simple sugars naturally contained in flour or from enzymatic activity; water, which is added to the flour; and oxygen, which is supplied by air that is naturally incorporated during mixing.

Organic flour can increase the chance of starting a successful culture. Because it lacks chemical herbicides and pesticides, it is richer in microorganisms. Rye flour is another alternative. By nature, rye flour contains more wild yeast and bacteria than wheat flour and is richer in minerals, another source of nutrients that jump-starts culture activity. Diastatic malt, which is very rich in simple sugars, can also be added to the culture to increase the nutrients available to feed the microorganisms. (See Figure 4-8.)

Culture Elaboration

During the first step of culture elaboration, flour and water are mixed, and oxygen is incorporated to start the microorganisms' activity. At this stage, many different types of microorganisms are present in the culture.

At the beginning, sufficient oxygen in the dough and limited flora create conditions for aerobic activity favorable to the reproduction of microorganisms. After several hours, an increase in the flora starts to reduce the amount of available oxygen, and the microorganisms switch to an anaerobic way of life. Fermentation activity begins, enhanced by a constant, relatively warm temperature. After about 22 hours, the culture has risen to twice its original volume.

During elaboration, a natural balance (quantity and quality) of yeast and bacteria occurs. The selection is made based on the fact that some microorganisms are more or less resistant to the lack of food, lack

Figure 4-8 Starting the Starter

Schedule	Flour	Water	Starter	Time Before Next Feeding
Day One a.m.[1]	1 lb 1.5 oz (0.500 kg) whole wheat flour 1 lb 1.5 oz (0.500 kg) bread flour	2.2 lb (1.000 kg)	—	24 hours
Day Two a.m.	1 lb 1.5 oz (0.500 kg) bread flour	1 lb 1.5 oz (0.500 kg)	1 lb 1.5 oz (0.500 kg)	6–8 hours
Day Two p.m.	1 lb 1.5 oz (0.500 kg) bread flour	1 lb 1.5 oz (0.500 kg)	1 lb 1.5 oz (0.500 kg)	16 hours
Day Three a.m.	1 lb 1.5 oz (0.500 kg) bread flour	1 lb 1.5 oz (0.500 kg)	1 lb 1.5 oz (0.500 kg)	6–8 hours
Day Three p.m.	1 lb 1.5 oz (0.500 kg) bread flour	1 lb 1.5 oz (0.500 kg)	1 lb 1.5 oz (0.500 kg)	16 hours
Day Four a.m.	1 lb 1.5 oz (0.500 kg) bread flour	1 lb 1.5 oz (0.500 kg)	1 lb 1.5 oz (0.500 kg)	6–8 hours
Day Four p.m.	1 lb 1.5 oz (0.500 kg) bread flour	1 lb 1.5 oz (0.500 kg)	1 lb 1.5 oz (0.500 kg)	16 hours
Day Five a.m.	1 lb 1.5 oz (0.500 kg) bread flour	1 lb 1.5 oz (0.500 kg)	1 lb 1.5 oz (0.500 kg)	6–8 hours
Day Five p.m.	1 lb 1.5 oz (0.500 kg) bread flour	1 lb 1.5 oz (0.500 kg)	1 lb 1.5 oz (0.500 kg)	16 hours

[1]Add ½ oz (0.015 kg) of malt to the first feeding to help initiate fermentation.

This schedule is a guide for starting a starter from scratch. During this process, the starter should be held at 80°F (27°C) to encourage fermentation. A mature culture will be able to multiply three times in volume in 8 to 10 hours.

of oxygen, or acidification of the culture. Cohabitation of the yeast and bacteria is also possible because they are not competing for the same type of nutrients.

Studies have shown that due to this natural selection, the flora of some levains constituted with the same types of yeast and bacteria differ in element quantity, depending on the conditions of the culture preparation. Other minor populations of wild yeast and bacteria specific to a particular place or a particular process can also be found. This is why, even if the main types of bacteria are the same, each levain is different and will produce breads with different appearance and flavor.

To keep the flora alive and active, it is necessary to ensure that its vital conditions (food/sugar from the flour/water/air) are renewed. This process, completed several times during elaboration, is called **feeding** the culture. A helpful indication of when the culture needs to be fed is when the surface starts to become concave, or collapsed, in the center.

The time between two feedings depends on the characteristics of the culture, including temperature, activity, hydration, and ingredients. A well-established culture in terms of fermentation activity and acid production should rise to four times its initial volume in 6 to 8 hours of fermentation at room temperature. When this level of activity is reached, the culture becomes a **starter**. The name comes from the fact that starter is the culture that will start the sourdough process.

The elaboration of the culture can also be sped up by using ingredients other than flour and water, such as malt, honey, water in which dry fruits have been soaked, milk powder, yogurt, fresh fruits, and grapes. The goal is to add extra nutrients in the form of simple sugars to assist the beginning of the fermentation process, as well as to sometimes host a different flora.

From Starter to Levain

Once the starter has been elaborated, the baker needs to keep its activity lively enough to ensure the fermentation of the final dough. A feeding process where flour and water are added to the starter at certain intervals achieves this goal. (See Figure 4-9.) The proportion of flour and water depends on the activity of the culture, the feeding schedule (once, twice, or three times a day), and the production schedule.

The process in Figure 4-9 involves two feedings per day. The last feeding (second feeding, in this example) is called the levain. Levain is the natural preferment used to ferment the final dough.

Depending on the fermentation time between the two feedings, the ratio of starter or first feeding must be adapted. A longer fermentation at room temperature requires a lower amount of starter or first feeding during the feeding preparation. A shorter fermentation time requires more of the starter.

Perpetuating the Culture

There are two possible methods for obtaining the starter used to perpetuate the culture. In the first method, a piece of final dough removed just before salt is incorporated becomes the first feeding (flour and water have been added during the final dough incorporation). This method has the advantage of eliminating one feeding, but there is a risk of changing the culture characteristics because final dough ingredients and tempera-

Figure 4-9
Sourdough Feeding Example

Flour	100%
Water	50%
Starter	50%
Total first feeding	200%

Fermentation for 12 hours at room temperature [75°F (24°C) to 80°F (27°C)]

Flour	100%
Water	50%
First feeding	50%
Total first feeding	200%

Fermentation for 12 hours at room temperature [75°F (24°C) to 80°F (27°C)] and final dough preparation.

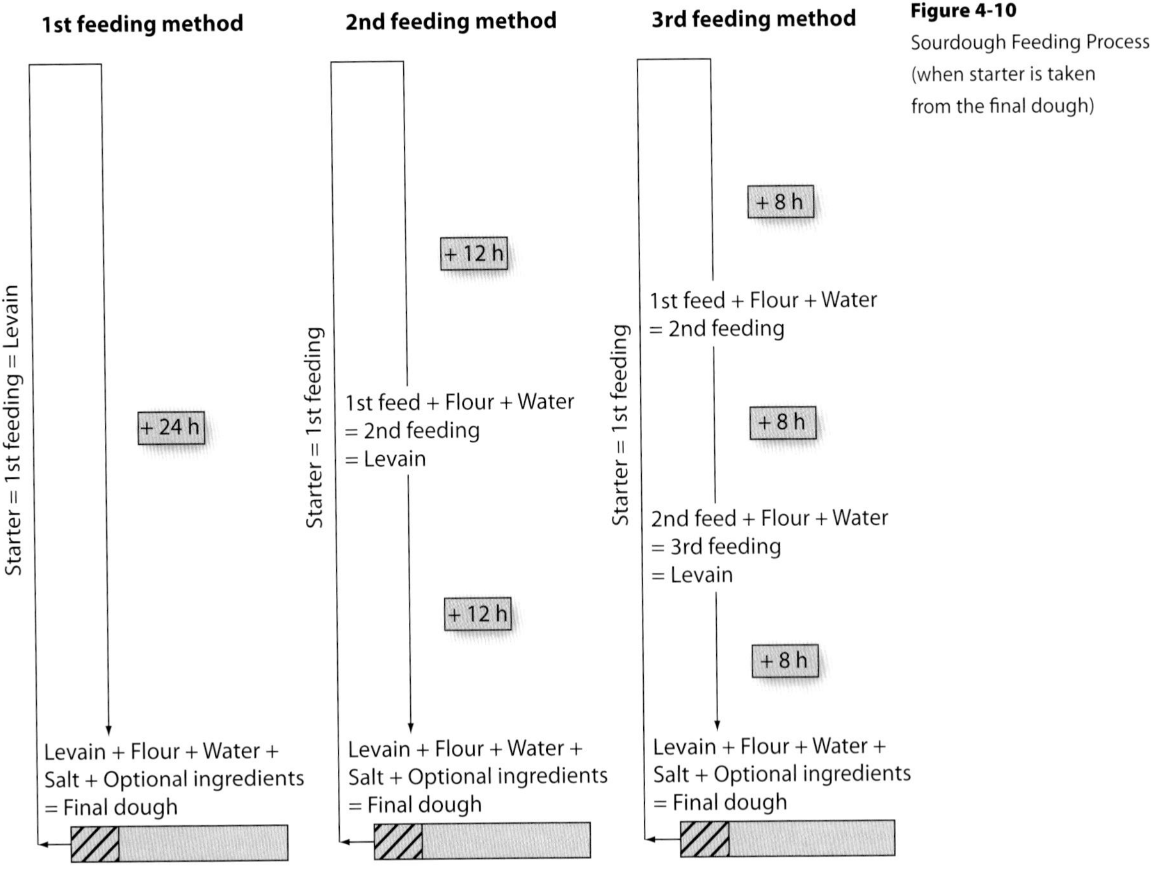

Figure 4-10
Sourdough Feeding Process (when starter is taken from the final dough)

ture are generally different from the ones used to feed the culture. (See Figure 4-10.)

In the second method, the starter is removed from the levain just before the levain is incorporated into the final dough. This process has the advantage of keeping the starter purer because it will never be in contact with the final dough. However, it does require an extra feeding. (See Figure 4-11.)

Factors Affecting Culture Characteristics

Several factors can change the microbiological activity of the culture during the feeding process and affect the final characteristics of the bread. Figure 4-12 summarizes the main factors that can affect the sourdough culture and will help the baker to better visualize all these important considerations.

Hydration A stiff culture will have the tendency to develop more acetic acidity, whereas liquid levain will increase the production of lactic acidity.

Temperature High temperatures [85°F (29°C) to 90°F (32°C)] favor bacterial activity and the production of lactic acidity, but fermentation is more difficult to control due to a higher yeast activity. Low temperatures favor the production of acetic acid and suppress fermentation activity.

Figure 4-11
Sourdough Feeding Process (when starter is taken from levain)

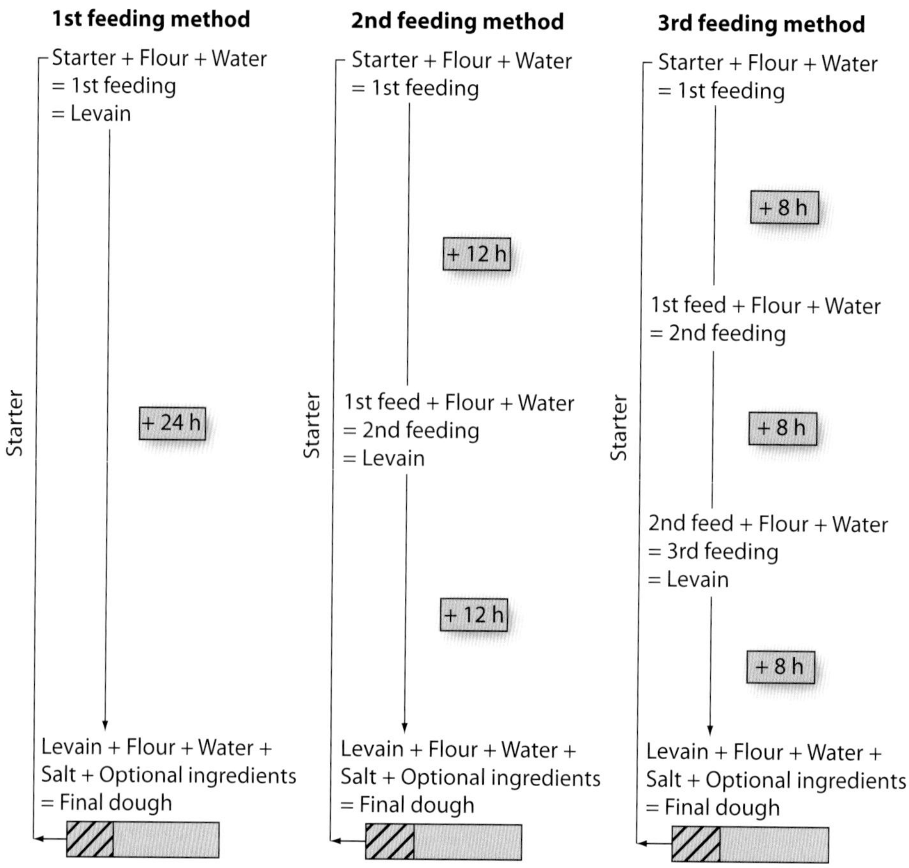

Temperatures around 77°F (25°C) seem to optimize fermentation activity, the development of the dough, and the production of aromas. Yeast activity also favors lactic acid production.

Flour Enzyme activity and bran content determine the amount of simple sugar and minerals available for the microorganism. In general, flour with a higher extraction provides better activity and higher acid production. San Francisco sourdough culture is also generally elaborated with high gluten flour to offset the high level of acidity that will negatively degrade the gluten structure of the dough after long fermentation time.

Salt A small amount of salt (0.1 percent) can be beneficial for a culture with high protease activity, whereas amounts higher than 0.1 percent can inhibit the activity of some microorganisms.

Maintaining the Culture

Maintaining the correct proportion of ingredients, feeding schedule, water temperature, fermentation temperature, and fermentation time are critical for a consistent and healthy culture. To keep the levain in its purest condition, the baker must also pay strict attention to sanitation. Tables and mixers must be cleaned during the feeding process and the

Figure 4-12 Important Sourdough Considerations

Ingredients	Cultural Elaboration	Final Dough Elaboration
Flour High extraction has a positive effect on gas production, but a negative effect on the volume of the bread.	**Hydration** Liquid levain increases the production of lactic acid (positive effect on the volume of the bread, and makes bread less acidic). Stiff levain increases the production of acetic acid.	**Hydration** Higher hydration increases the volume of the bread and the microbiological activity.
The Enzyme Activity Determines the nutrients available for the microorganism. **Rye Flour** Assists the microbiological activity. Negative effect on the volume of the bread.	**Temperature** Low temperature helps the production of acetic acid. Higher temperature helps the production of lactic acid and bacterial activity. Also available for the storage of the levain during fermentation time.	**Temperature** At the end of the mixing, the temperature which provides the best development is 77°F (25°C) to 78°F (26°C).
Salt Delays the ferment's multiplication. Limits protease activity of the lactic bacteria.	**Levain Activity** Growth of the yeast increases lactic activity.	**Fermentation** Long fermentation time (at least 1 hour 30 minutes) is necessary to allow the activity to take place in the dough (slower process in comparison with commercial yeast).
Water High chlorine content will delay the sourdough activity.		**Oxygenation of the Dough** Factor which helps aroma production. Punch and fold increases aroma production.

mixing of the final dough, taking care to remove scraps of dry dough made with commercial yeast to avoid "contaminating" the culture.

Troubleshooting Sourdough Culture

Sourdough culture activity can be affected by several factors, including fermentation activity and acid production. It is important for the baker to immediately correct problems before characteristics have changed too much and bread quality is negatively affected. Figure 4-13 summarizes some of the deficiencies that sourdough culture can take on and how to efficiently correct them.

Use in Final Dough

The quantity of levain used in the final dough depends on its characteristics, as well as the characteristics desired in the final product. A large amount of levain, for example, increases the acidity level (or lowers the pH) of the dough. It is important to keep in mind that there are some limits to the amount of sourdough that can be incorporated into a formula.

Figure 4-13 Main Defects of Sourdough Culture

Defects	Origin	Solutions
Lack of acidity Lack of strength Bread not very tasty	• Levain too young • Lack of fermentation (length of activity) • Fermentation time too short between two feedings • Quantity of sourdough too small in the final dough	• Increase the maturation process • Allow to ferment at higher temperature and at a higher humidity • Use flour with a higher amount of bran • Make sure the water is not too chlorinated • Longer fermentation time (8 to 10 hours, for example) • Increase the amount of levain (50%, for example)
Excess of acidity Bread with a sharp flavor	• Dough liquification • Old sourdough • Not enough consistency in the feeding schedule • Fermentation time too long between two feedings or at too high of a temperature. • Bacteria activity too intense • Quantity of levain too big in the final dough	• Start a new culture • Shorten the fermentation time between the two feedings and lower the temperature • Add a litle bit of salt to decrease the activity • Reduce the amount of levain (30%, for example)
Lack of development of the bread	• Not enough fermentation activity (low gas production) • Not enough yeast to make yeast production • Excess of acidity which inhibits the yeast activity (even with a large enough population) • Long storage at cold temperature • Long storage in the freezer	• Add a small amount of commercial yeast (max 2%) • Make final dough a little bit warmer and a little bit softer • Make dough a little bit warmer and let the levain ferment at a higher temperature • Keep the sourdough at a temperature higher than 50°F (10°C) • Avoid putting the sourdough in the freezer for a long time
Lack of strength in the levain	• Lack of acidity • Lack of gas production • Dough too cold at the end of the mixing • Not enough levain in the final dough	• Longer first fermentation • More punch and fold • Use warmer temperature • Increase the amount of levain

Formula

The formula in Figure 4-14 will yield 44 loaves scaled at 1 lb 1.5 oz (500 g) each.

Figure 4-14
Example Formula for First Feeding, Levain, and Final Dough

First Feeding

	Baker's %	Kilogram	Lb & Oz
Flour	100	0.85 kg	1 lb 14 oz
Water	50	0.65 kg	15 oz
Starter	80	0.65 kg	1 lb 7 oz
Total first feeding	230	1.95 kg	4 lb 4.6 oz

Fermentation for 8 hours at room temperature [75°F (24°C) to 80°F (27°C)][1]

Levain

	Baker's %	Kilogram	Lb & Oz
Flour	95	2.32 kg	5 lb 1.8 oz
Rye flour[2]	5	0.12 kg	4.2 oz

(continues)

Water	50	1.22 kg	2 lb 11 oz
First feeding	80	1.95 kg	4 lb 4.6 oz
Total levain[3]	230	5.65 kg	12 lb 7.2 oz

Figure 4-14
Example Formula for First Feeding, Levain, and Final Dough *(continued)*

Fermentation for 8 hours at room temperature [75°F (24°C) to 80°F (27°C)][1]

Final Dough

	Baker's %	Kilogram	Lb & Oz
Flour	100	10 kg	22 lb 6.4 oz
Water	70	7 kg	15 lb 6.9 oz
Salt[5]	2.66	266 g	9.4 oz
Levain	50	5 kg	11 lb 3.2 oz
Total dough	222.5	22.25 kg	49 lb 0.8 oz

Mix[6]	Improved mix
First Fermentation	3 hours
Dividing	500 g (l lb 1.5 oz)
Resting time	30 to 40 minutes
Shaping	Batards
Final proof	5 hours
Baking[7]	460°F (238°C) for 45 minutes; open the oven door for the last 10 to 15 minutes to allow the crust to dry

Notes

[1] Fermentation time can change, depending on culture fermentation activity

[2] Using a small amount of rye flour in the levain preparation has several small but significant effects on the final product. Because rye flour is higher in minerals, it helps to maintain the activity of the levain. Rye flour contains less protein, with lower protein quality than wheat flour, which helps to keep the structure of the levain from becoming too strong

[3] Amount of levain includes the levain needed for the final dough plus the starter used to perpetuate the culture

[4] Amount of water can change depending on the flour absorption.

[5] Salt is 2 percent based on the total flour weight (flour involved in the levain plus flour from the final dough).

[6] Incorporate all of the ingredients on first speed for 3 to 4 minutes. Then, switch the mixer to second speed and mix just until the dough starts to get smooth. The goal is to achieve a lightly developed gluten structure.

[7] Baking time and temperature will vary depending on the type of oven.

FERMENTATION CONCLUSION

Fermentation is a crucial step in the baking process; it is necessary for a good-tasting and long-lasting product. Equally important, fermentation contributes to certain physical changes in the dough related to mechanical reactions, like carbon dioxide pressure, and chemical reactions, like acid production.

Successful bread baking depends on the ability of the baker to understand and control each step of the sequence. The capacity to feel the dough and anticipate eventual changes or defects is also very important in order to make needed corrections and maintain desired results.

Unfortunately, a feeling for the dough cannot be learned in books; it must be assimilated through the everyday experience of working with the dough. This learning experience can be a little frustrating at the beginning, but the pleasure of a good loaf of bread is ample reward for time spent mastering its complexities.

RETARDING PROCESS

Retarding delays fermentation of the dough at any time during the baking process. This fairly new method of baking has been developed not only to meet customer expectations of fresh bread throughout the day, but also to offer the baker a better quality of life by reducing night work.

Despite its advantages, this technique also includes some drawbacks. Specific equipment, the energy needed to produce the required temperatures, and additional floor space all increase the fabrication cost of the final product. In addition, very precise baking methods including temperature, hydration, and fermentation time require that bakers develop good technical knowledge in order to produce consistently high-quality bread.

TECHNICAL CONSIDERATIONS

Four different factors need to be taken into consideration when delaying the fermentation of dough: temperature, gas production, gas retention, and dough's natural degradation process.

Temperature

All the methods used in retarding are based on the fact that the ferments used in baking are very sensitive to changes in temperature. Commercial yeast, wild yeast, and bacteria generate optimum fermentation activity when the temperature of the dough is between 74°F (23°C) and 80°F (27°C). At higher temperatures, these microorganisms increase their activity, and commercial and wild yeasts produce more gas. At lower temperatures, yeast and bacteria slow down their metabolism, and carbon dioxide and acidity production decrease. When the temperature drops to 40°F (4°C), yeast and bacteria become dormant and most activity is stopped.

Gas Production

The rate of carbon dioxide production depends on both temperature and quantity of yeast. Depending on the retarding method chosen by the baker, the amount of yeast will have to be adjusted. When dough remains at a low temperature for a long period of time, the metabolism of the yeast cell can be altered, affecting fermentation activity later on in the process.

The freshness and quality of the yeast are very important when long delays at a low temperature are planned. It is interesting to note that some yeast companies offer different types of yeast, depending on the baking process for which it will be used (for example, yeast specifically designed for frozen dough is now available to the baker).

In a sourdough process, gas production will depend on the culture fermentation activity. A culture maintained in a liquid stage at room temperature usually produces more gas, compared to a culture maintained in a stiff stage at lower temperatures. The percentage of levain used in the final dough will also affect carbon dioxide production.

Gas Retention

Because gluten is elastic and extensible, it can be stretched when the pressure of the gas produced by the yeast increases, and it will hold its structure until its coagulation during baking. The goal of the retarding process is to delay as long as possible the point where the gluten reaches maximum extensibility and breaks under the pressure of the gas. To be more precise, the length of time needed to delay the dough depends completely on how much gas is produced in the dough before it is placed in the retarder.

This is why, in most cases, a short first fermentation time is necessary to delay the point where the dough reaches its gas retention limit. However, this reduced time slows acid production. For this reason, a larger amount of preferment should be used in the final dough to compensate for the lack of acidity.

Another factor that slows fermentation activity is flour with low starch damage. Enzymes use and transform right away damaged particles of starch, providing simple sugars and therefore increasing the availability of nutrients for the yeast.

To delay gas production at the beginning of the process, before dough is placed at cold temperatures, the temperature after mixing should be kept at approximately 73°F (23°C).

Natural Dough Degradation

To understand degradation fully, remember that dough evolves significantly during the baking process. This evolution is mainly due to two types of transformation: physical reactions related to changes in gluten and biochemical reactions related to enzyme activity and fermentation.

Like any living thing, dough deteriorates. This deterioration naturally occurs when flour and water are put in contact at the mixing stage, and it continues as the fermentation progresses. Its intensity is proportional to the length of the fermentation time.

Most dough degradation happens because of the action of protease, the enzyme that breaks down the proteins that are the major components of gluten. As these proteins deteriorate, the dough structure itself degrades. Because protease is naturally present in wheat, flour with slightly-lower-than-normal enzyme activity is preferable for retarding. This delays fermentation at the beginning of the baking process and diminishes the risk of red crust color that can happen when there is a longer period of contact between flour and water. When this enzyme activity is triggered, sugar degradation increases, along with the risk of residual sugars that emphasize caramelization at the end of the baking process.

Note: Low enzyme activity doesn't mean that flour with a noncorrected falling number should be used. Whenever possible, flours with a slightly higher falling number (around 350 to 380 seconds) indicating a slightly lower enzyme level are preferable. (Please refer to Chapter 6 to learn more about falling number.)

Another way to delay degradation is to start with dough that is strong enough to withstand retarding. Flour with good protein quality must be used to obtain a gluten structure with good tolerance to fermentation. When the quality is not sufficient, dough oxidizers like ascorbic acid or a higher percentage of preferment may be necessary to reinforce the gluten. It is important to note that quality and quantity of protein are two different things. For a good retarding process, a higher protein quality is more important than a higher quantity. High levels of protein can produce an excess of elasticity that makes the dough difficult to work with after a long stay at low temperatures.

Some adaptations must also be made during mixing. First, hydration should be slightly lower to decrease the amount of water available to the enzymes, which in turn decreases their activity (particularly protease). Second, stiffer dough will provide a stronger gluten structure. Finally, mixing time must be calculated to sufficiently develop the dough and to obtain a strong and fairly well organized gluten structure. Gluten development between improved mix and intensive mix is required for a long retarding time, and the dough temperature should be cooler than usual [around 73°F (23°C)].

As a final consideration, smaller batches of dough that are faster to process ensure that the fermentation doesn't start too soon before the retarding process. Tighter shaping also will increase dough strength.

BASIC RETARDING TECHNIQUES

Three basic techniques can be used to delay dough fermentation: delayed first fermentation, slow final proof, and retarding-proofing process. Depending on the method used, retarding can be done at different stages of the baking process. (See Figures 4-15 and 4-16.)

Delayed First Fermentation

For the delayed first fermentation technique, the dough is mixed using an improved mix process; the amount of fresh yeast is around 1.2 percent. Hydration must be sufficient to obtain a medium-soft consistency in the final dough. To reinforce the structure of the gluten, use of preferment is advised. Dough temperature should be 73°F (23°C) at the end of the mixing.

Method

- After mixing, place the dough in containers in the retarder set at 45°F (7°C) to 48°F (9°C). The retarding time can last from 12 to 18 hours.
- After retarding, take the dough out of the retarder and divide it right away, or wait about 1 hour before scaling.

Figure 4-15
Overview of Retarding Processes

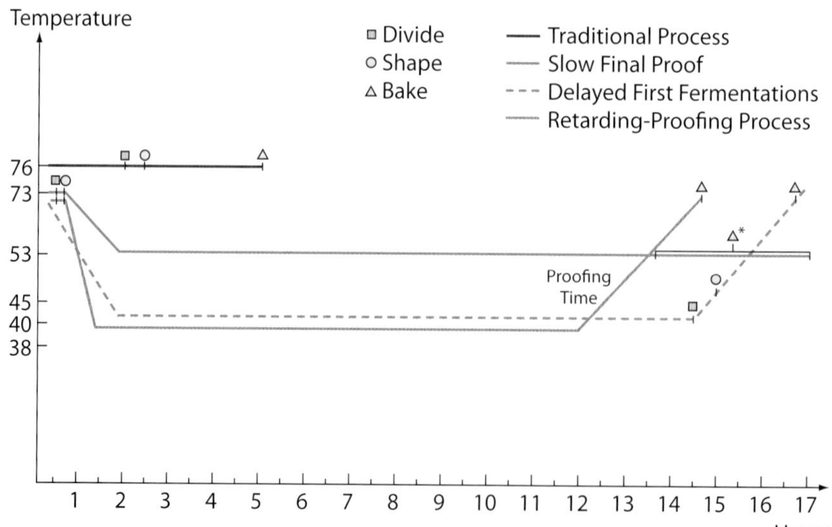

* When using the slow final proof, it is possible to bake the bread during a window of several hours.

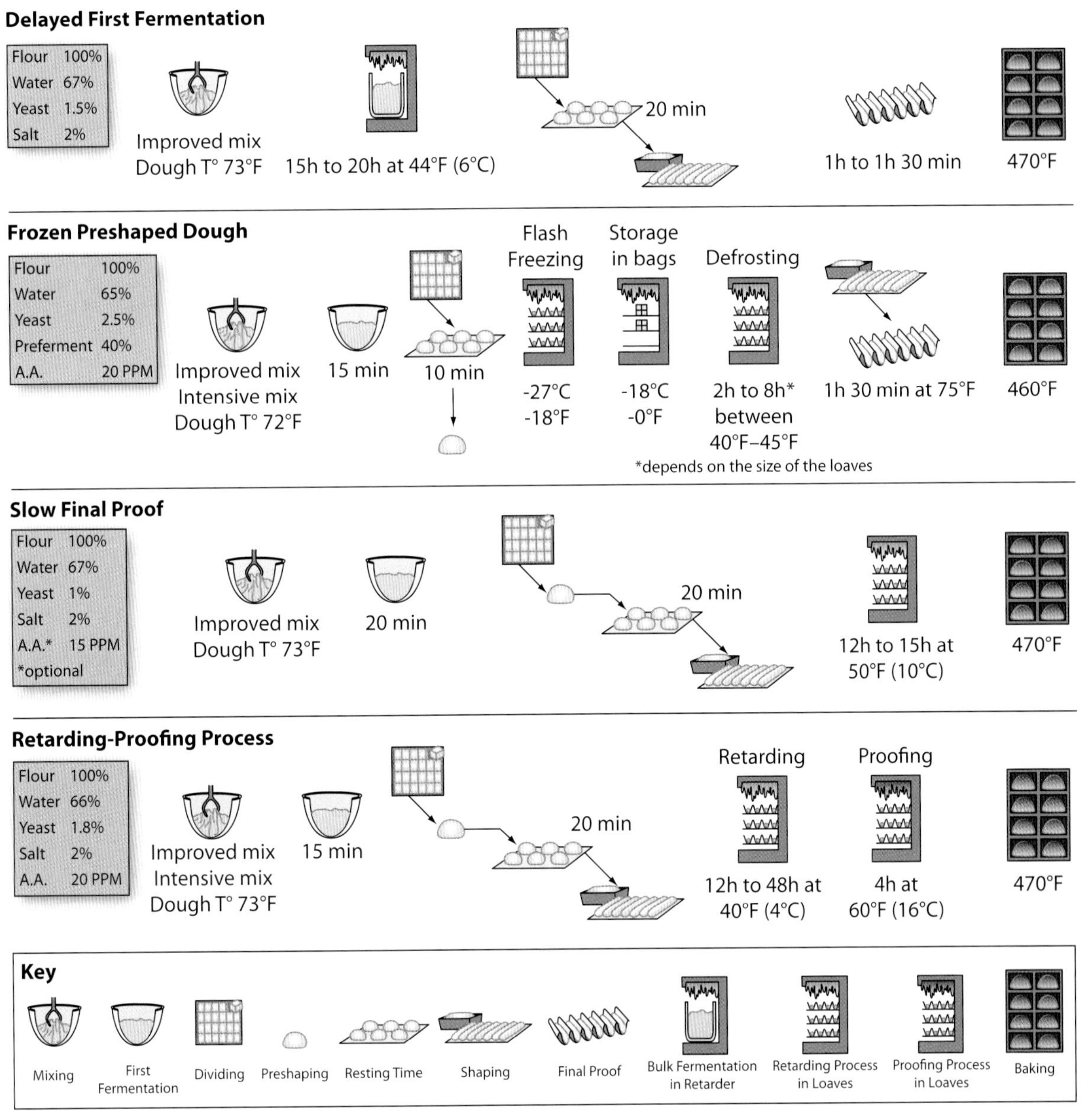

Figure 4-16
Chart of Retarding Processes

- Divide and preshape as normal. A longer resting time will be necessary to allow the dough to warm up and restart fermentation.
- Follow these steps with normal shaping and a regular final proof.
- Complete baking at the usual temperature and time.

Advantages

- At 45°F (7°C) to 48°F (9°C), the fermentation of the dough is not completely stopped. The gas and acidity production is still happening at a lower rate but for a longer period of time. Quality of the final product is not affected by the retarding time.
- When good quality flour is used, there is no need for dough conditioners such as ascorbic acid, keeping the product labeling cleaner.

- Dough with a high water content like ciabatta can be delayed without problems using this technique.
- Because the dough is retarded in bulk before shaping, no blisters are formed during baking.
- The baker can organize production in such a way to offer customers fresh bread all day long without mixing too many batches of dough.

Drawbacks

- The main drawback is the need of retarder with enough capacity to store a large amount of dough.
- The bread cannot be baked immediately after its retarding time. Three to four hours are necessary to divide, shape, proof, and bake the bread. The final product is not immediately available.

Slow Final Proof

With the slow final proof method, mixing time should be adjusted to obtain a gluten structure between an improved mix and an intensive mix, and dough consistency should be a bit stiffer. The amount of fresh yeast generally used is between 0.8 and 1 percent, but it can be adapted depending on the length of the retarding period (a longer fermentation time calls for a lower percentage of yeast). Preferment is advised in the final dough, and dough temperature should be 73°F (23°C).

Method

- After mixing, allow the dough to ferment 20 to 30 minutes and then divide and preshape. Rest for 20 to 30 minutes, and shape as normal.
- Place the shaped pieces of dough in the retarder set at 50°F (10°C).
- Retard for 12 to 15 hours. When ready, loaves can be baked right away, directly from the retarder.

Advantages

- At 50°F (10°C), fermentation is not completely stopped, but the yeast produces only a small amount of carbon dioxide. This small production for a long period of time allows the baker to obtain the right quantity of carbon dioxide necessary to bake the dough just after removing it from the retarder.
- Dough can be ready to bake after 12 hours. However, the biggest advantage is that due to the slow carbon dioxide production, dough from the same batch can also be baked after 15 hours.
- The baker can plan production to have fresh bread for breakfast and lunch without mixing too many batches of dough.

Drawbacks

- Typically, 15 to 20 ppm of ascorbic acid is necessary to reinforce the gluten structure of the dough.
- The surface of the loaves can become dehydrated. For this reason, it is important to have a good humidifier system.

Retarding-Proofing Process

For this method, mixing time is adjusted to obtain a gluten structure between an improved mix and an intensive mix, and dough consistency should be stiffer. The amount of yeast generally used is between 1.8 and 2 percent. Preferment is definitely advised in the final dough to provide strength and flavor, and dough temperature should be 73°F (23°C).

Method

- After mixing, divide and preshape the dough; then allow it to ferment for 20 to 30 minutes. Let it rest for 20 minutes and shape, when possible, more tightly than usual.
- Place the shaped pieces of dough in the retarder set at 38°F (3°C) to 40°F (4°C). Retard from 12 to 48 hours.
- There are two options for the next step. The first is to remove the dough from the retarder and leave it at room temperature for the final proof.
- If the retarder is also a proofer-retarder, the second option is to set the clock for an automatic increase in temperature [72°F (22°C) to 75°F (24°C)] after the retarding time to achieve final proof.

Advantages

When the second method is used, the baker can bake right away the next day and can obtain fresh bread 1 hour after arriving at the bakery.

Drawbacks

- Dough conditioners are necessary to reinforce the strength of the dough, and sometimes to avoid the formation of blisters during baking.
- Large proofer-retarders are necessary if all production is retarded, which increases the fabrication cost of the final product.
- Because air is drier at low temperatures, equipment must be able to provide enough humidity to avoid dehydration of the surface of the loaves, which generally happens at a higher rate.

SOURDOUGH IN THE RETARDING PROCESS

When sourdough is used as a preferment, retarding becomes a bit simpler. The high level of acidity naturally reinforces the dough characteristics, and the gluten can handle a longer fermentation time without too much degradation. Dough conditioners are not typically necessary. Because of the strength attained via the acidity of the sourdough culture, rye and whole wheat flours (which are generally too weak to delay fermentation) can also be used in the retarding process.

EQUIPMENT

Many types of equipment can be used in a retarding process. And, even though a number of equipment suppliers offer different types of retarders or proofer-retarders, the key points of focus should be on temperature, humidity production, and air diffusion.

To ensure humidity in a retarder, water is automatically atomized to keep the atmosphere moist enough to avoid dry skin formation on loaves. When a retarding-proofing process is used, enough humidity must be produced during proofing to rehydrate the surface of the loaves that are typically baked right out of the proofer. Sometimes, the condensation effect from the transition from cold to warmer temperatures is enough to create a necessary thin film of water on the dough.

RETARDING CONCLUSION

Retarding bread provides the baker with a good way to organize production more efficiently and can increase quality of life. But these improvements come with a cost. The right choices of ingredients (especially flour), method, and equipment are crucial in order to avoid compromising quality.

For the retarding process to be successful, bakers must possess good knowledge and technical skill. Lack of attention to technical considerations will inevitably lead to lower quality in the final product. But when the process is done correctly, night hours can be substantially cut down, to the great enjoyment of the baker.

DOUGH STRENGTH

Dough strength is a direct result of ingredient selection, mixing, and fermentation. Even though having a clear idea of dough strength is very important, it is one of the properties that is the most difficult to assess. It is virtually impossible to learn how to judge strength by reading a technical book. Only a great deal of practical work with a lot of dough at the bakery will educate the hands to feel (or evaluate) strength and make corrections when necessary.

Many parameters can affect the strength during the entire baking process. The remainder of this chapter covers the main issues in order to help the baker understand what can go wrong and how to fix it.

DEFINITION OF STRENGTH

Strength is a balance among three physical dough characteristics: extensibility, elasticity, and tenacity.

Extensibility

Extensibility is the property of the dough to be stretched. Dough with good extensibility is easy to stretch. This characteristic is fairly important for manual shaping of long products like baguettes, as well as for producing laminated dough.

Elasticity

Elasticity refers to the dough's ability to return to its initial position after being stretched. Dough that will noticeably spring back after being stretched is judged too elastic.

Tenacity

Tenacity is the property that resists a stretching action. This property can influence the elongation part of the shaping process. If the dough puts up a lot of resistance to the baker's efforts to make it longer, it is described as tenacious.

A solid relationship or connection exists between tenacity and elasticity. Elastic dough will naturally resist the stretching action, and dough with a lot of tenacity has the tendency to retract to its initial position very quickly. For this reason, at a bakery level, strength is often described as a balance between extensibility and elasticity. However, in a laboratory environment, the three characteristics are taken into consideration when evaluating flour characteristics, and especially gluten properties.

STRONG DOUGH VERSUS WEAK DOUGH

Elastic dough, extensible dough, strong dough, and weak dough are common terms in the bakery. Quite often, these important descriptions are confused.

Strong dough is precisely defined as dough with a lack of extensibility and an excess of elasticity. For the baker, this translates as dough that is difficult to stretch during hand or machine shaping, along with a tendency to retract once the desired length is achieved. Strong dough results in shorter finished breads with a rounder cross section and inferior cuts openings. These defaults can easily be explained by the lack of gluten extensibility, which penalizes the development of the bread during proofing and/or oven spring.

In contrast, weak dough has so much extensibility that it is easy to stretch, and so little elasticity that it will not spring back during shaping. Despite good machinability, the gluten lacks the strength to retain much gas during the proofing and baking. As a direct result, finished products have a very low volume, a flat cross section, dense crumb structure, and poorly developed cut openings.

FACTORS AFFECTING DOUGH STRENGTH

Dough strength is affected by ingredients, mixing, and fermentation.

Ingredients

Flour Because flour is the main ingredient in dough, it has a huge impact on strength. Flour with a high level of protein will provide more gluten, resulting in dough with high elasticity and low extensibility. Low protein has the opposite effect, and very low protein flour will generate dough with a definite lack of strength.

Protein Quality Flour made with soft wheat, such as pastry flour, doesn't have the same gluten-forming ability compared to flour made with hard wheat, such as bread flour. As a result, bread made with a soft wheat flour leads to dough with poor strength and gas retention. At the same time, different kinds of hard wheat contain varying levels of protein and can create very different dough and bread characteristics. For this reason, it is difficult to provide the exact amount of protein needed, but on average, flour between 10.5 and 12 percent should provide a good balance between extensibility and elasticity.

Ash Content A lot of bran left in the flour after the milling process will interfere with gluten formation and generally lead to dough with less strength. For example, whole wheat flours create dough that is always more extensible, with lower gas retention than doughs made from regular bread flours. Flour with a low ash content like patent flour generates dough with a tendency to develop a little extra strength. Again, it is difficult to give precise ash content, but in general ash content of around 0.5 percent is desirable.

Flour Treatments Some flour treatments, such as oxidizers like ascorbic acid or potassium bromate, automatically generate an increase in strength. The bleaching agent benzoyl peroxide doesn't really affect strength as much as it does the color of the crumb in the finished product. ADA or azodicarbonamide, a maturing agent, also increases dough strength. Malt or fungal amylase has only a secondary effect on strength by promoting enzyme and fermentation activity.

Natural Maturation Natural maturation, which is directly related to the natural oxidation of the flour, has an impact on the strength of the dough. Fresh flour has the tendency to lack strength, while properly matured flour is more balanced. This is why it is always recommended to allow the flour to mature for 2 to 3 weeks before using it in baking.

Water Water quality and quantity can have an effect on dough characteristics. The minerals found in hard and soft water are used as yeast nutrients in a dough system and play an important role during fermentation activity. Hard water, because of its higher mineral content, generates dough with higher fermentation activity and leads to dough with higher strength, compared to dough made with soft water and lower mineral content.

Dough hydration, which is directly related to the amount of water used in the formula, will also affect strength. Underhydrated proteins create gluten that lacks extensibility and has an excess of elasticity. Overhydrated proteins create very extensible dough with a lack of elasticity that requires some changes in the baking process. These can include using a longer mixing time, more folds, or a longer fermentation time.

Other Ingredients Some ingredients, like butter or a high level of sugar (15+ percent), increase dough extensibility. Others, such as seeds or other chunky ingredients like nuts, chocolate chips, or fruit, weaken gluten. In the latter case, certain precautions must be taken to bring the dough back to a good balance, including a longer mixing or more folds. To avoid any damage to the gluten and to preserve structure and strength as much as possible, chunky ingredients should be added at the end of the mixing time after the gluten structure has been properly formed.

Mixing

Autolyse By using an autolyse process, the baker automatically changes the characteristics of the gluten. By allowing the incorporated flour and water to rest for an average of 20 minutes to 1 hour, the proteins will have more time to absorb water and create better boundaries. This improves the structure of the gluten network. At the same time, the protease will degrade some of the chains of proteins, slightly weakening the gluten structure and creating a positive effect on extensibility. Mixing time can be reduced, since the more extensible gluten will organize faster under the mechanical action of the mixer's hook.

In addition, the working characteristics and machinability of the dough will be improved. Breads will have a better crumb cell structure (more open and creamier due to lower mixing time), a slightly larger volume, and better cut openings due to better expansion during the first stage of baking.

Deactivated Yeast Deactivated yeast can be used to improve dough extensibility without using the autolyse process. Because deactivated yeast is a natural product with a "clean" label, it is increasingly used in laminated dough and formulas of long, shaped bread like baguettes. This type of yeast does not generate any fermentation activity.

Mixing Time Mechanically mixing for longer periods of time stretches and folds gluten strands so that they are longer and more tightly bound, creating a more organized, stronger gluten structure. Shorter mixing times create less binding and generate weaker gluten structure. The baker can compensate for the latter by increasing first fermentation time and using one or several stretches and folds.

Temperature Dough temperature has an indirect impact on strength. Warmer dough generates more fermentation activity and stronger dough, while cooler dough lowers fermentation activity and produces weaker dough.

Fermentation

In its advanced stages, fermentation creates acidity, which is responsible for three important reactions. The first is the creation of aromas through acids like organoleptic acids. The second is the lowering of dough pH that increases the shelf life of the bread. The last reaction, which is more related to strength, is the physical and chemical reinforcement of gluten bonds.

All three reactions occur at the same time. This means that bakers who want to achieve good flavor characteristics through long fermentation will also get stronger dough (sometimes excessively strong). To avoid this, adjustments should be made in the baking process, including shorter mixing time and higher hydration in the formula. For dough made without first fermentation, longer mixing time and sometimes dough oxidizers are needed. This step is necessary to build up enough strength to the dough to compensate for the fact that no acidity will be produced after mixing.

Mass Effect The quantity or "mass" of dough allowed to ferment also plays a role in strength, with a larger piece of dough increasing in strength faster than a smaller one. The chemical reactions happen faster in larger masses of dough, creating a better environment for microorganism activity. This is what we refer to in the baking industry as the "mass effect." Mass effect is particularly important to consider when adapting formulas developed for home baking to a production environment, and vice versa. For smaller batches of dough, up to 6 lb (2.724 kg), longer fermentation time may be necessary, while larger batches of 50 lb (22.7 kg) and more require slightly shorter fermentation time.

Preferments As a general rule, any time a preferment is added, strength increases. However, other factors concerning preferments must also be taken into consideration, including type, quantity, and the degree of maturation when incorporated.

Types of Preferments Because of the large amount of water involved in their formulas, liquid preferments like poolish develop more enzymatic activity. In this case, protease activity is particularly interesting, as it brings all of the advantages of autolyse. Preferment allowed to ferment at room temperature and without salt (like sponge) also brings some protease activity. If sponges are stiff, less enzyme activity is generated, but the amount is typically sufficient to generate positive effects. When a sourdough process is used, the dough automatically develops more strength due to the higher level of acidity. This increase in strength can retard some of the dough. Due to its consistency, liquid sourdough promotes better dough extensibility and is recommended for the production of long shapes, like sourdough baguettes.

Quantity Used in the Final Dough When using preferments, the increase in strength is proportional to the quantity used. Bakers consider this factor when developing formulas.

The amount of preferment directly relates to the length of first fermentation. When a short first fermentation time exists, a larger amount of preferment can and should be used. If a long first fermentation time is possible, the amount should be lowered. This is a common mistake in some bakeries, where bakers think about preferment solely in terms of flavor.

Preferment can also be used for troubleshooting. For example, flour with a lack of fermentation tolerance or a lack of maturation will benefit from a higher percentage of fermented flour in formulas.

Degree of Maturation Preferments must be properly matured for maximum benefit. Overmatured preferment can lead to excessive strength and, eventually, to acid levels that are so high they cause gluten deterioration. Dough takes longer to mix and starts to break down during the first fermentation, resulting in very low final product quality. When this happens, it is necessary for the baker to decrease the amount of preferment in the final dough and to recalculate percentages to take this into consideration. Undermatured preferment requires a longer first fermentation time to compensate for the lack of acidity.

Dough Handling The way the dough will be handled, whether by hand or with machinery, will also have a direct effect on strength. Tight preshaping and shaping increase elasticity and decrease extensibility, whereas light preshaping and shaping preserve extensibility but hurt elasticity. Bakers must learn how to evaluate the strength of the dough in order to handle it properly. This strength judgment, or evaluation of the feeling of the dough, is probably the most difficult lesson in the baking profession and is best mastered simply by working with dough.

In many bakeries, it is commonly believed that the harder or stronger the dough is worked, the better it is. In fact, if all the appropriate steps have been carefully followed, a gentle preshaping and shaping are all that is needed.

Scoring is also important for the strength of the dough. Cuts perpendicular to the side of the loaves favor an upright expansion of the bread during oven kick and are more suitable for weaker dough like rye or whole wheat. The upright expansion naturally favors the cross section of the bread and, therefore, its volume and final appearance. Cuts parallel to the side of the loaves favor a sideways expansion of the bread. These cuts create great openings that are more suitable for stronger dough like baguettes or sourdough.

CHAPTER SUMMARY

It is easy to understand why fermentation is the most important step in baking. The quality of bread is greatly dependent on a number of factors, including duration of fermentation, temperature, hydration, and quantity of yeast among others. The development of aromas and the flavor profile are accomplished with fermentation and its handling.

From straight dough with short or long first fermentation, from yeasted preferments to sourdough, or from baked the same day to delayed overnight, the baker has numerous choices. Regardless of the fermentation process selected, it is important for the baker to have a comprehensive understanding of the biochemical reactions and physical changes that happen in dough during this crucial step. Not only will they be able to produce consistently high-quality bread day after day, but they will also be able to develop many different flavor profiles to accommodate their customers' needs.

KEY TERMS

- ❖ Acidification
- ❖ Biga
- ❖ Culture
- ❖ Endosperm
- ❖ Esters
- ❖ Feeding
- ❖ Fermentation
- ❖ Germination
- ❖ Glucides
- ❖ Heterofermentative
- ❖ Homofermentative
- ❖ Levain
- ❖ Microorganisms
- ❖ Poolish
- ❖ Prefermented dough
- ❖ Simple sugars
- ❖ Sponge
- ❖ Starter

REVIEW QUESTIONS

1. **What is fermentation?**
2. **What are the results of the fermentation activity on the dough and on the bread?**
3. **What is the relationship between mixing and fermentation?**
4. **What are the technical factors to take into consideration when using preferments?**
5. **What are the two main microorganisms involved into a sourdough process? What are their effects on the dough and on the finished product?**

chapter
5

BAKING BREAD

OBJECTIVES

After reading this chapter, you should be able to

- exhibit competency in the baking process of yeasted dough.
- evaluate the fermentation of dough and determine the final proof of the dough.
- explain and demonstrate the goal and techniques of scoring.
- explain the evolution of products and precautions to take after baking.

THE BAKING PROCESS

After mixing and fermentation have been properly achieved, the next step is baking the dough in an oven. In their quest to create the perfect loaf, bakers benefit from an extensive selection of ovens that take into account production capacity, the types of bread to be baked, and the cost of energy. But equally important to producing consistent loaves of bread is a solid understanding of the chemical and physical changes that occur in dough during the baking process. The challenge for the baker is to maintain enough control over these changes to produce flavorful and appealing results on a consistent basis. The goal of this chapter is to explain the baking process, step by step, in order to help the baker ensure consistent results.

BEFORE BAKING

EVALUATION OF THE FINAL PROOF

Successful baking starts before the dough is placed in an oven. The first important parameter is to properly judge the end of the final proof. Bakers rely on practices like elapsed time after shaping, visual judgment, and feel. All of these techniques are good and necessary for breads that must be baked at certain times for production purposes, but the most precise is dough feel. (See Figures 5-1 and 5-2.)

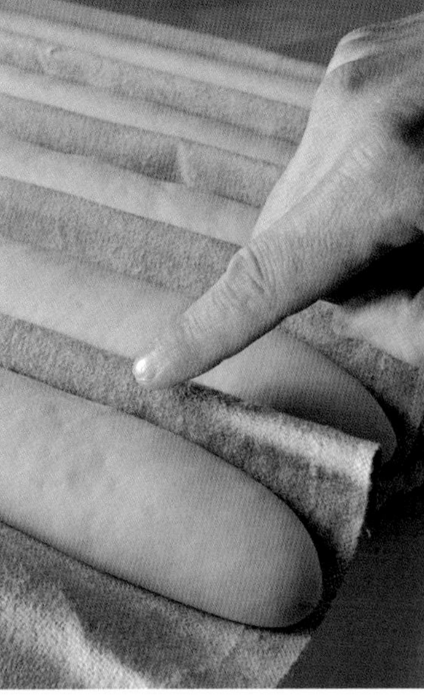

Figure 5-1

When pressed with a finger, a properly proofed baguette should spring back and leave a slight indentation.

The baker should be able to determine if dough has proofed enough by applying gentle pressure with the fingers. A loaf that is ready to bake should spring back a little after being pressed and retain a light indentation. Underproofed dough will spring back very quickly and feel firm to the touch, while overproofed dough will keep the indentation and remain flat (or start to deflate) where the baker presses down.

An experienced baker can also feel the gas produced by the yeast during fermentation in properly proofed dough. The sensation is a little bit like pressing on an inflated balloon. This evaluation requires experience, but a baker can learn by observing the bread after baking and taking the results into consideration for future judgment.

Bakers should keep in mind that fermentation is not over when the bread is loaded in the oven. In fact, the most intense step of fermentation takes place during the first few minutes of the baking process. The gluten will only develop properly and reach the expected volume if its physical characteristics (mainly extensibility) allow it to trap the large quantity of gas produced during this stage. Otherwise, the volume of the bread will remain small and the final product will be unattractive.

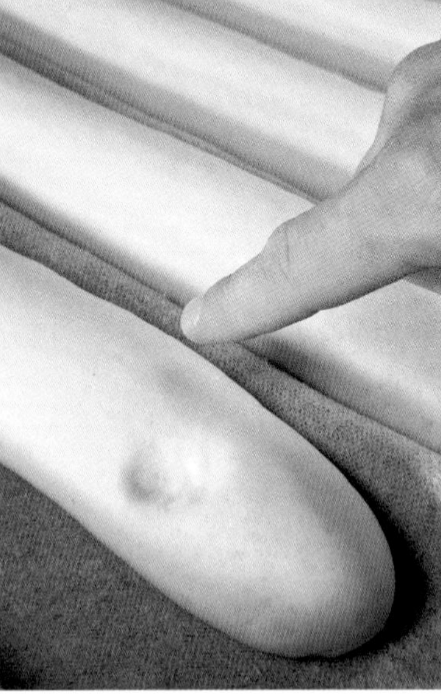

Figure 5-2

When pressed with a finger, an overproofed baguette leaves an indentation and does not spring back.

If dough is coming out of a retarder, the cold temperature will tighten the gluten and possibly make the dough feel underproofed. In this case, the baker should evaluate the volume and size of the bread to determine if the dough is ready.

Common thinking holds that retarded dough must be at room temperature before it goes into the oven; however, the most important factor is the amount of gas trapped in the gluten. The dough can be baked if enough gas has been produced, regardless of temperature. To avoid the problem of cracking on the sides of larger loaves during baking, it is best to bake them when the internal temperature of the dough is approximately 50°F (10°C).

SCORING

Once bread is properly proofed, the baker can move on to the next step: **scoring** the loaves, or making incisions on the surface of the dough before baking.

Origin

The origin of scoring dates to 1834, when Vaudry mentions "breads with cuts on their surface" (Guinet & Godon, 1994, p. 23). A French scientist who wrote several books on the craft of bread baking, Vaudry describes these cuts as an improvement in the appearance of bread. Initially, scored breads were baked only for wealthy families and the famous restaurants of Paris, and so made up only a small part of overall bread production.

Scoring is one of the characteristics of bread made in France, but it does not apply only to breads of French origin. When done properly, most types of bread will benefit from "cuts on their surface."

There are three primary reasons to score dough. The first involves the overall aesthetics of the loaf. The baker can score bread in different ways to improve appearance, bearing in mind that each scoring technique will produce a different result once baked.

The second reason is technical. Surface incisions create weak points in the skin of the dough that reduce the dough's "tenacity," or resistance to expansion. Consequently, scored dough will expand more during the oven spring (where carbon dioxide pressure is very important), and the loaf will increase in volume.

Finally, by scoring the loaves, the baker creates precise paths for carbon dioxide to escape when the pressure becomes too great inside the dough during oven spring. Each scoring technique will allow the baker to control in a precise manner the expansion of the bread during the baking and therefore its final appearance.

If loaves aren't cut before baking, the finished product will have less volume and, frequently, ruptures on the surface. These ruptures are created when expanding carbon dioxide creates pressure inside the dough and looks for an escape route during oven spring. When the pressure becomes too great, the skin of the dough splits at its weakest points and creates abscesses that are not visually appealing. (See Figure 5-3.)

Figure 5-3
Effect of No Scoring, Improper Scoring, Proper Scoring, and No Steam (from left to right, top to bottom)

Tools

Scoring cuts can be made with several different utensils. Originally, bakers used metallic blades (or *lames* in French) with a variety of curves that created different cut effects. They sharpened the blades with a small sharpening stone between oven loadings. Today, razor blades are commonly used. Even though they are typically fixed on metal handles (or *porte lames*), the baker should ensure safety by verifying that each blade is securely attached to its support.

Other tools for scoring bread include knives, cutters, and scissors. To obtain as precise and neat a cut as possible, the sharpest tools will yield the best results. This is especially true for delicate dough like baguette or whole wheat. To ensure the neatness of cuts, blades should also be very clean at all times. This can be achieved by storing them in a cup of water next to the oven. There are two advantages to this method of storage: improved sanitation, provided the water is replaced frequently, and a better slide across the surface of the dough.

Technique

Even if it seems like a simple movement, scoring bread requires precision, dexterity, flexibility, regularity, lightness, and experience.

Before scoring, the baker must pay attention to the strength and degree of fermentation of the dough. Underfermented dough with an excess of strength will require deeper scoring in order to form a good opening during the more intense oven spring. Overproofed doughs, or those that are not very strong, must be scored very lightly to avoid deflating the loaf.

Cuts for Elongated Shapes

For breads with an elongated shape, four main types of cuts can be used: classic, "sausage," "polka" or criss-cross, and chevron.

Classic Cut The **classic cut** is used for baguettes and batards or any time a nice, neat opening is desired. It is one of the most difficult cuts to perform properly. To make a classic cut, the baker holds the blade as flat as possible, or at least with a 45-degree angle to the surface, and creates a horizontal incision. Only a thin film of dough is cut to form the "ear" that will detach from the surface during the oven spring.

It is important to note that the angle used also has a technical effect. If the angle is not achieved and the cut is done with the blade vertical to the loaf, the two sides of the dough will spread very quickly during oven spring and expose an enormous surface area to the heat. The crust will begin to form too soon—sometimes before the end of oven spring—penalizing the development of the bread. If the cut is properly horizontal, the sides of the loaf will spread slower. The layer of dough created by the incision will partially and temporarily protect the surface from the heat and encourage a better oven spring and development.

If only one classic cut is done, it must be made parallel to the side of the dough, following a straight line at half inch to the right of the middle of the loaf (for a right-handed baker). In order to obtain a regular development during the bake, the incision should start at one extremity and finish at the other end of the loaf. It is not necessary to curve the cut. If the loaf has been shaped properly, the curving will happen naturally during bread development.

If several incisions are placed, they must be made as parallel as possible to the side of the loaf and concentrated on the middle. They should never be made as diagonal cuts on the side of the loaf in order to get a nicer appearance. The second cut should overlap one-third of the length of the first one, and so on. If this overlapping is not observed, the dough will develop irregularly, and the finished bread will have an irregular shape. In addition, each cut should be of the same length. The number of cuts is up to the baker, but, in general, fewer cuts will open better. As an example, a baguette can be scored with five to eight cuts, depending on its length. (See Figures 5-4 and 5-5.)

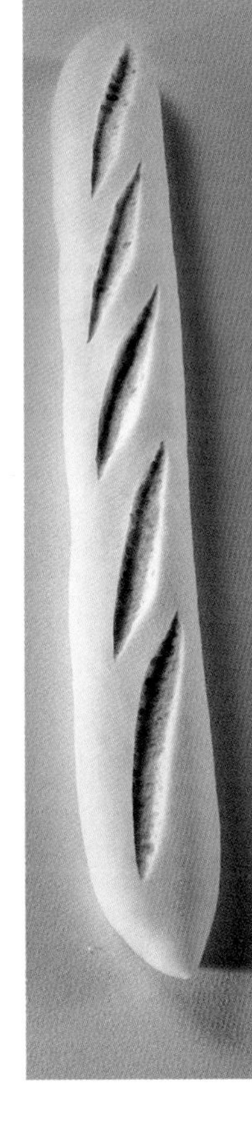

Figure 5-4
Improperly Scored Baguette (left) and Properly Scored Baguette (right)

"Sausage" Cut The **sausage cut** is used for batards, specialty breads (rye, whole wheat), and Viennese baguettes. It is typically used when the baker is looking for a round cross section in the final product. For this technique, the baker holds the blade perpendicular to the dough and makes cuts diagonally, almost perpendicular to the side of the loaf. The number of cuts is the baker's choice, but for a better appearance, the space between each cut should not be more than 1/2 inch (1.5 cm). The first cut should start at one extremity of the loaf and the last cut should cover the opposite extremity. (See Figure 5-5 "Sausage" Cut.)

"Polka" or Criss-Cross Cut The **polka cut**, or criss-cross cut, is used when the baker wants to achieve a flat top surface on batards and specialty breads and rolls. As with the sausage cut, the blade is held perpendicular to the dough. Cuts are made diagonally, starting from one side of the loaf and finishing on the opposite side. Then, using the same movement,

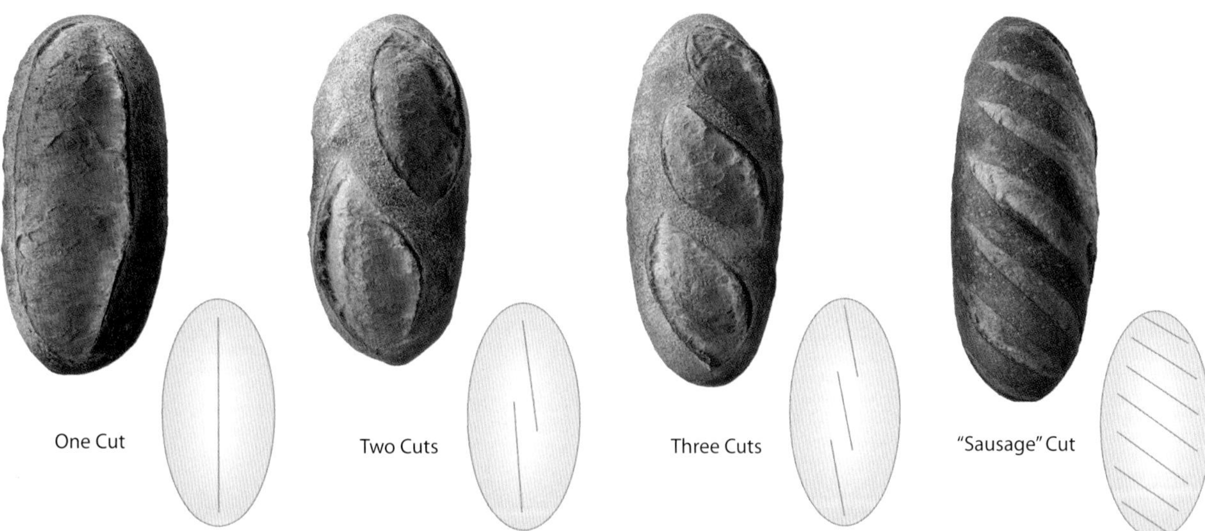

Figure 5-5
Scoring Techniques for Batards

the baker makes another cut with an opposite angle to create a cross. The number of crosses depends on the length of the loaf, but they should cover its entire surface.

Chevron Cut The **chevron cut** is typically used for short, elongated shapes like batards. Like the sausage cut, the chevron cut gives the bread a round cross section. To make the cut, the blade is held perpendicular to the dough. Incisions are made on two sides, leaving about 1/4 inch (0.5 cm) in the middle of the top of the surface, as if the baker were making a sausage cut on the two sides of the loaf. As with the other cuts, the whole surface should be covered for a better regularity.

Cuts for Other Loaf Shapes

Scoring techniques or patterns for other loaf shapes include leaf cuts, wave cuts, and diamond cuts. Although bakers are limited only by their imaginations, they must keep in mind that each technique will have a different effect on the final shape of the loaf.

If, for example, a baker decides to cut a ball of dough with only one-way parallel cuts, the ball will turn into an oval shape during oven spring. In this case, the weakness created on the dough allows the carbon dioxide pressure to expand the volume of the bread in only one direction. To maintain the round shape, the cuts should be done in a square shape (though the four cuts do not need to meet) to allow the bread to expand in all directions. (See Figure 5-6.)

It is also possible to cut the loaf with scissors to create different designs like épi, which is a bread with a cut shaped like a stalk of wheat, or with a dough cutter to make breads like fougasse.

Which Technique to Use The choice of the technique will depend on the type of dough, the type of bread, and the desired final appearance.

For dough that tends to develop little strength, such as rye or whole wheat, it is better to opt for a sausage or chevron cut. Because they are done perpendicularly to the side of the dough, these cuts encourage vertical expansion and a rounder cross section that is more appealing to the customer. Classic cuts used for these types of dough will have a flatter

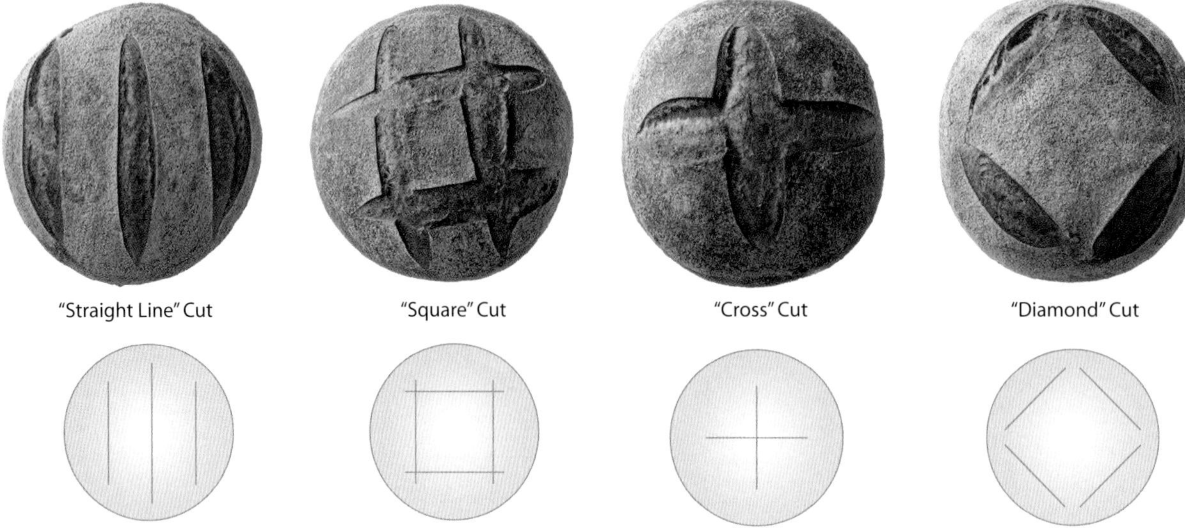

Figure 5-6
Scoring Techniques for Boules

appearance, because parallel cuts encourage horizontal expansion. On the other hand, any kind of cut can be used for dough made with regular white flour. Tradition often dictates the technique; for example, a traditional baguette typically has five to eight classic cuts.

When bakers consider all of the technical and aesthetic factors that determine the type of cut to use for a particular kind of bread, they should keep using it. Not only will this ensure consistent production, but customers who typically identify bread by its distinctive scoring will not be confused.

In addition to the technical considerations related to scoring, the baker's artistic side should also be considered. Some breads, like sourdough, are tolerant enough to support many different scoring designs. For those types of bread, the baker can use their creativity to find original patterns and differentiate bread from the competition.

When to Score

Most loaves are scored just before oven loading, but some doughs require particular attention. Doughs made from flour with poor gluten quality, like rye flour, should be cut just after the shaping to avoid deflating dough that is more fragile after the final proof. Dense doughs, like multigrain, can also be cut after the shaping to better hold the design on the loaf surface after the baking.

Scoring as an Art Form

For the professional baker, achieving perfect cuts is a sign that all the steps of the baking process have been respected, from flour selection through baking. From a customer's point of view, displays of bread with regular, finished appearances create a positive feeling about the bakery. If, on the other hand, breads look messy and unattractive, customers will have a bad first impression.

The scoring of bread is often considered the baker's signature. Looking at the cuts enables the customer to judge the quality and fineness of the bread, and the precision of the baker. In short, scoring bread is an art form that requires much attention and care.

OVEN LOADING

When loaves have been scored, the baker begins to load the oven. This operation can be done manually, or it can be automated. In either case, a considerable amount of care should be given to the dough, which is quite fragile and cannot tolerate much abuse. If it is treated roughly, the gas trapped by the gluten structure will start to escape, and the final product characteristics will be negatively affected. For example, cuts may not open, the crumb may be dense, and sections of the bread may be flat.

When loaves are placed in the oven, there should be enough space between them to obtain optimal heat circulation for proper crust crispness and color. Additionally, as common sense might suggest, the deck of the oven should be clean before loading to prevent the final products from having an unappealing, "dirty" bottom.

Steaming

During baking, steam plays a major role in bread development, crust crispness, and color. After the loaves have been loaded in the oven, hot steam comes into contact with the cooler surface of the bread, and the resulting condensation causes a thin film of water to lightly coat the bread. This makes the surface of the dough more extensible and better able to develop under the gas pressure at the beginning of the bake, leading to a larger volume.

By slowing down evaporation on the surface of the dough, the coating of moisture delays crust formation, making the crust thinner and crisper. It also generates a slight dilution of the starch present on the surface of the dough, resulting in a glossy effect after baking.

To achieve the greatest benefits from condensation, steam should be injected into the bake chamber before and after the loaves have been loaded. If injection is late, and the surface of the loaves is allowed to increase in temperature, a skin will form on the loaves before the steam reaches them, automatically lowering the condensation effect and minimizing the positive effects of the steam.

When rack ovens or convection ovens are used, the baker does not have the option of steaming before loading. However, these ovens are generally well equipped with powerful and efficient steam generators that quickly fill up the bake chamber right after the racks have been introduced.

The quantity of steam should be sufficient to form a light coating of water on the dough's surface. Because different ovens are equipped with steam generators of varying efficiency, it is very difficult, if not impossible, to give an exact steaming time in seconds. The baker should look at the surface of the loaves, which should be lightly covered with moisture and slightly shiny. Another visual clue is the appearance of steam on the oven door, indicating that the bake chamber has sufficient moisture.

If drops of water are running on the surface of the loaves, too much steam has been injected. This can potentially penalize the final product quality, including a crust that is not crispy enough, cuts that do not open sufficiently, and a very shiny surface that looks almost artificial.

Steam is only necessary at the beginning of the bake. Once bread starts to bake, it will release some moisture that will have the same effect as the steam.

DURING BAKING

As soon as the heat reaches the dough and increases its temperature, a succession of chemical and physical reactions transforms it into bread. During the first 4 to 6 minutes of the baking time, yeast and enzyme activity are stimulated by the quick temperature increase. This causes a large amount of **carbon dioxide** (gas) to be produced and retained by the gluten structure, which in turn develops the volume of the bread. This is what we generally refer to as the **oven kick** or **oven spring**. Bakers should always keep this intense gas production in mind when evaluating the end of the final proof, to ensure that the gluten is able to retain a sufficient extra amount of gas when the dough goes in the oven.

When the temperature inside the dough reaches 122°F (50°C), the starch granules start to swell, and the yeast begins to reach a dying stage. At 140°F (60°C), the starch begins to gelatinize as the starch granules burst, liberating numerous chains of starch that form a very complex, gelatin-like matrix. This process is known as the **starch gelatinization.** After cooling, this matrix creates the crumb of the bread.

At 145°F (63°C), all yeast cells have been killed, and yeast activity ends. However, the gas produced by the yeast starts to expand under the effect of the heat, and the bread continues to increase in volume. At 153°F (67°C), starch gelatinization is complete. At 165°F (74°C), the gluten starts to coagulate, and the chains of protein begin to solidify. This process is called **gluten coagulation.** At that point, the structure of the bread is completely set. At 180°F (82°C), all enzymatic activity is over, and no more chemical transformations take place.

When the surface of the bread reaches the temperature of 212°F (100°C), some moisture evaporates, creating the beginning of the crust. Increasing the temperature for a longer period of time will create the final crust with thin, crisp characteristics.

Coloration of the crust happens at a higher temperature, when the sugars naturally present in the dough will start to caramelize. These sugars, which are the result of the enzymatic activity of the flour, are also called **residual sugars**. This is because the yeast has not used them during the fermentation activity.

Breads made from flour that lacks enzymes frequently do not attain good coloration during baking. Less enzyme activity produces less simple sugar and thus less residual sugar. As a result, the bread will remain pale and will not be as attractive. Adding some diastatic malt (0.5 to 1 percent, based on the total flour weight) to the dough will solve this issue.

When coloration is proper, the crust initially takes on a golden-orange hue. At higher temperatures, coloration intensifies, somewhat like cooking caramel on a stove. It is interesting to note that the aroma produced during the caramelizing process plays a significant role in the flavor of the final product and helps to explain why bread connoisseurs always enjoy a good crust color.

During the baking process, another very important chemical reaction takes place: the **Maillard reaction**. This refers to the dark color and

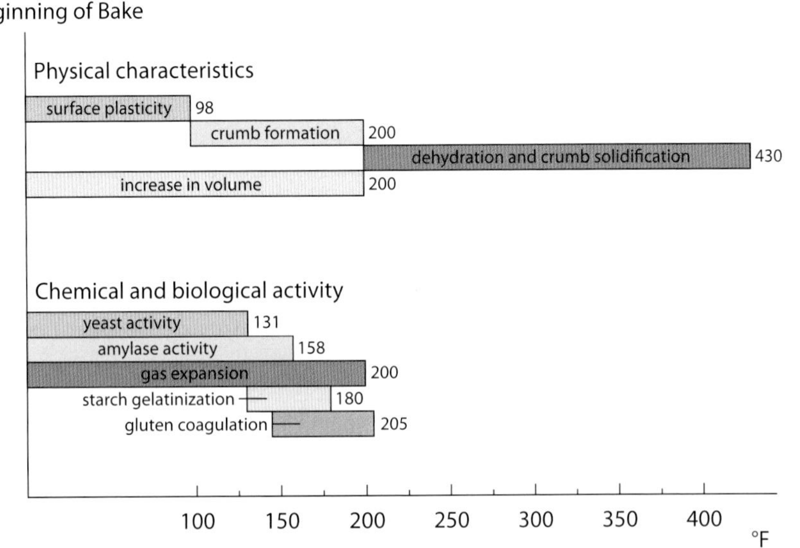

Figure 5-7
Dough Transformation During Baking

aromas that occur when the **simple sugars** that are not used by yeast during the fermentation process mix with **amino acids** (the basic components of the proteins) and are heated. As the bread bakes, the crust color and aroma become more intense; in fact, the fragrance caused by the Maillard reaction has a major effect on bread flavor.

It is important to note that if one of the components of the reaction increases, the entire reaction will be more intense. For example, if the dough contains an excess of sugar, the Maillard reaction happens at a greater intensity and produces a crust with a very dark color and potentially a bitter aroma. To counterbalance the excess of sugar, the baker should bake at a lower temperature. This is the case with breads made from sweet dough.

If the protein level of the flour increases due to the use of high gluten flour, the amount of amino acids will automatically be higher, and the rate of the Maillard reaction will increase. This also generates a crust with an overly brown color, and sometimes creates a slightly bitter aftertaste.

Figure 5-7 summarizes the important transformations that happen to the dough during the baking process.

HOW TO KNOW WHEN BREAD IS BAKED

It is sometimes difficult to assess if bread is properly baked. Bakers usually rely on time, color, sound, or pressure on the crust.

Color is not always the best way to determine when baking has ended because a hot oven can color the bread very quickly without properly baking the inside the loaf. If it is associated with a time factor, however, color is one of the main parameters when evaluating doneness. It is interesting to note that in the United States, different regions have definite preferences in crust color, from light golden to dark brown.

Many bakers test for doneness by listening for a hollow sound when they gently knock the bottom of the bread with a finger. While there is nothing scientific in this technique, a baker with a little bit of experience can really trust it to determine if the bread is ready to take out of the oven.

Pressing the side of bread after it is removed from the oven can also provide some guidance about baking. Excessive softness is a sure sign that the bread has spent insufficient time in the oven for crusty bread. It is important to note that sometimes the crust seems hard and sufficiently baked, but becomes soggy as the bread cools. This is often the case with bread made from whole wheat flour with a high ash content.

Sogginess occurs when the bran of the wheat absorbs water that is not allowed to evaporate during baking and is instead released into the crust during cooling. The baker can avoid this by allowing the crust to dry out before taking the bread out of the oven, simply by opening the oven door for a few minutes at the end of the bake. The bread will then bake in a dry atmosphere and will lose moisture without further coloring. If the oven is equipped with dampers, it is also possible to open them at the end of the bake to allow steam to escape. Of course, the dampers will have to be closed again before steam is injected into the oven for a new bake.

OVEN TEMPERATURE

There is not really a standard oven temperature for baking bread simply because there are too many oven parameters that can affect the temperature. These include the type of oven, its size and energy use, as well as any one of numerous dough characteristics like type, size of loaf, hydration, and shape.

It is commonly said that lean dough like that used for baguettes must be baked at 480°F (248°C). Even though this is true for deck ovens, rack ovens should be set lower at 440°F (227°C) to 460°F (238°C) because of the hot air blown on the surface of the dough.

There are more precise guidelines to ensure good control when baking bread. In general, a 350 g (12 oz) baguette (in dough) should bake in about 20 to 23 minutes. If it bakes faster, the oven temperature is too hot and should be adjusted. Longer baking time indicates a too-low oven temperature and will result in a drier final product.

Another important guideline for setting proper oven temperature is that larger pieces of dough require a longer baking time at a lower temperature to avoid an excessively dark color before the inside of the bread is properly baked. Smaller loaves like dinner rolls benefit from a shorter bake at a higher temperature to avoid drying out.

COOLING BREAD

All the reactions are not yet over when bread is taken out of the oven. The first, very noticeable reaction is the equalization of heat: As the bread cools down, the bakery warms up. This seems pretty simple and logical, but it is quite important. For example, in the case of a bakery working with rack ovens, every time a rack goes out of the oven, the bakery heats up quite a bit. This can affect the fermentation activity of dough proofing in the bakery, which is why some bakeries have a room designed specifically to cool the bread after baking.

During the cooling process, enough moisture is released to generate a loss of weight in the final product. If this moisture is not allowed to dissipate in the air, it will condense on the surface of the loaf, reabsorb, and make the crust soggy. For this reason, cooling the bread on a wire rack in a well-ventilated area is advised. It is also important to allow the bread to cool down completely before packaging it. This will minimize negative changes in the crumb and crust characteristics.

Pressure inside the bread will also equalize during the cooling process. When the gas that expands during baking leaves the bread, the cold air that replaces it occupies less volume. As a result, the bread contracts and shrinks. The crumb can retract with no problem because of its elastic property. The crust, however, can't retract and will crack at some points. These crackling sounds, which are always a good sign, make the little "song" that the baker hears when the bread cools down. A crust that won't crack and "sing" is retracting too easily and won't be crusty after cooling.

The final important reaction that happens during cooling is the distribution of aroma. To fully appreciate the real flavor of the bread, the bread must cool down completely before eating. The aroma from the crumb will be diffused into the crust and the aroma from the crust will be diffused into the crumb, creating the complexity of flavor characteristic of a good loaf of bread.

Aromas are very volatile substances; subsequently, many of them escape from the bread. It is said that the baker gets the best of the flavor of the bread because when the bread cools down, the bakery smells wonderful. Some bakers take advantage of this smell to attract customers. For example, when baking chocolate croissants in the morning or pizzas at lunch or dinner time, the smell never fails to attract customers who want to buy these products.

STALING BREAD

As soon as the bread cools down, degradation (**staling**) begins to take place in different parts of the loaf.

The degradation of the crumb is mostly due to migration of water. Water that surrounds the starch particles in the dough moves to the inside during gelatinization and baking, bursting the starch particle and extending some chains of starch molecules. As the bread cools, these chains retract to their original position, making the crumb denser and causing it to lose softness. This process is more active when the bread is kept at approximately 40°F (4°C), which is why keeping bread in the refrigerator should be avoided.

This change in the structure of bread is thermoreversible. When stale bread is heated up, the crumb regains some softness and becomes more pleasant to eat. Unfortunately, this improvement doesn't last very long and can only be obtained once.

When some breads are frozen, they go through the staling phase twice (once during cooling, once during warming). It is important to freeze and warm bread as quickly as possible to avoid the critical temperature zone between 40°F (4°C) and 50°F (10°C). For best freezing results, a flash freezer is recommended.

During staling, the crust loses some shine, and crispiness changes, depending on the weather. The crust will become harder in dry weather, soggier in humid weather, and in either case, more unpleasant to eat.

A great deal of aroma is evaporated into the air during cooling, and even more disappears during staling. In addition, changes in the structure of the bread modify the aromas of both the crust and the crumb, making them less pleasant and not as attractive to customers.

DELAYING STALING

The baking process can make a large difference in the rate of staling. Dough with higher hydration generates bread that stales more slowly, as does longer fermentation time, which naturally produces more acidity. Keeping the volume of the bread to a reasonable size also helps to avoid too much drying. After baking, the surface of the bread should not be exposed to drafts, which can cause a significant loss of moisture.

Another way to slow down staling is the freezing process. Technically, at very low temperatures −8°F (−22°C) to 25°F (−4°C), the staling process is almost stopped. But after 4 or 5 days at these temperatures, the crust may start to fall apart, especially on bread with longer shapes, like baguettes. Shorter shapes or breads with fat in the formula will last longer in the freezer without significant degradation.

When freezing bread, some precautions are necessary. The baker should freeze only freshly baked bread, which should be placed on a screen to facilitate cold air circulation and speed up the freezing process. Once frozen, bread should be stored in plastic bags to avoid potentially bad smells and drying (**freezer burn**).

There are two ways to defrost breads efficiently. The first is to place frozen loaves in a 400°F (204°C) oven for 4 or 5 minutes with steam, remove them, and complete the defrosting at room temperature while avoiding drafts. The second is to hold the bread at room temperature until completely defrosted, still avoiding draft. Then it should be placed in a 480°F (248°C) oven for 2 to 3 minutes with steam. When freezing and defrosting are done properly, both methods result in good-quality product.

Other than this, staling cannot be avoided or stopped. It is natural for the bread to change its characteristics as it ages. What is not natural is bread that remains fresh for 3 to 4 weeks on the shelf. For this to happen, the formula must contain a significant amount of chemicals.

Specialty Sourdough Bread

CHAPTER SUMMARY

From judging when the dough is ready to bake, to choosing the type of score and the amount of steam necessary, to unloading the loaves from the oven, baking is a very important succession of steps that when well achieved will lead to great quality bread.

Oven choice is also crucial in a bakery. In times past, bakers said that the oven was the soul of the bakery, a sentiment that is still true. When baking bread, it is very important to keep important parameters like temperature and baking time under control to obtain the right crust and crumb in the final product.

For breads to be properly produced, it is also important for the baker to understand the succession of transformations that take place as the dough changes into bread during the baking process. Even though bakers like to "blame it on the oven," it is not always to blame when bread doesn't turn out as it should.

KEY TERMS

- ❖ Amino acids
- ❖ Carbon dioxide
- ❖ Chevron cut
- ❖ Classic cut
- ❖ Freezer burn
- ❖ Gluten coagulation
- ❖ Maillard reaction
- ❖ Oven kick or oven spring
- ❖ Polka cut
- ❖ Residual sugars
- ❖ Sausage cut
- ❖ Scoring
- ❖ Simple sugars
- ❖ Staling
- ❖ Starch gelatinization

REVIEW QUESTIONS

1. **How should the final proof be evaluated?**
2. **What are the main goals of scoring the dough?**
3. **What is the effect of steaming on the bread?**
4. **What is the Maillard Reaction? What are its effects on the finished products?**
5. **What is happening during the staling of the bread? How can it be delayed?**

chapter
6

ADVANCED FLOUR TECHNOLOGY AND DOUGH CONDITIONERS

OBJECTIVES

After reading this chapter, you should be able to

- explain the scientific tests used to assess bread flour baking performance.
- explain how to perform a baking test to assess bread flour baking performance.
- know how to compensate for flour deficiency.
- explain the different types of dough conditioners and their effects on dough and finished products.
- present the various types of specialty flours and their uses.

INTRODUCTION

Once the baker attains a good level of control over the baking process, it is also important to attain a deeper understanding of flour characteristics and how to select the proper flour. Flour specification sheets are a great tool to learn more about flour baking performance, but in general they cannot provide a complete picture of finished product quality. This information can only be achieved with a baking test. The first part of this chapter explains how to properly read a flour specification sheet, how to interpret the provided data, and how to conduct a baking test to evaluate baking performance.

HOW TO READ A FLOUR SPECIFICATION SHEET

Each stage of flour production can affect its baking performance, including wheat variety, cultivation, watering, fertilization, harvest, storage, variety blending, conditioning, milling, and distribution. The baker is challenged on a daily basis to consistently produce bread from flour that can exhibit different characteristics due to its complex transformation process.

To help bakers predict performance, the miller supplies with the flour a type of "identity form" that is commonly referred to as the **product specification sheet (spec sheet)**. The objective of this chapter is to explain, from a baker's perspective, the information present on a flour spec sheet. More importantly, it explains how this information relates to the physical and chemical characteristics of the dough and the quality of the final product.

Spec sheets vary from mill to mill, but they generally include the same type of information. (See Figures 6-1 and 6-2.)

GENERAL INFORMATION

This section of the spec sheet includes the name and address of the mill and the brand identity of the flour. The name of the lab and the person who performed the testing can also be included.

Figure 6-1
Specification Sheet #1

PRODUCT SPECIFICATION INFORMATION

PRODUCT NAME AND DESCRIPTION

ARTISAN BAKERS CRAFT PLUS ORGANIC UNBLEACHED MALTED FLOUR
-Unbleached Wheat Flour
-Item No:0501800

INGREDIENT STATEMENT

Blend of Hard Red Winter and Hard Red Spring Wheat

FLOUR TREATMENT

Organic Malted Barley Flour

PHYSICAL CHARACTERISTICS

Product is creamy/off-white in color. Odor shall be fresh, clean, sweet, and free of the slightest musty, smutty, or garlicky smell, or any other objectionable odors.

PACKAGING SPECIFICATIONS

Product shall be shipped in properly sealed and labeled multi-walled bags or in approved pneumatic bulk trailers.

STORAGE RECOMMENDATIONS

When due care has been taken by owner of this product to maintain a clean, dry, ambient condition, the shelf-life is in excess of six months. Central Milling Company has recommended that the product be rotated every thirty days with storage conditions that are 65 degrees Fahrenheit and below 60% humidity.

ANALYTICAL SPECIFICATIONS

Moisture: 13.00% Minimum | **Ash:** maximum 0.65%
Protein: 11.0 Minimum | **Falling Number:** 240-260

**Protein Disclaimer: The protein may change from year to year depending on growing conditions of the wheat.
**All products made at Central Milling are GMO free.

TYPICAL PROCESSING SPECIFICATIONS

All products are produced under the following guidelines: [FC: 1999, FDA: Part 123.6, REF FDA: 123.7 (C)(5) 123.8 (A) 123.8 (C),: USDA [*used as a guideline {416.1, incl. Sections 2, 3, 4, 6, 12, 13, 14, 16}*] Products labeled "*ORGANIC*" are produced under the above referenced guidelines in addition to the following: [OTA; Sections 2-4, 7-9, 12; U.S. Department of Agriculture 7 CFR part 205 {Docket # TMD-00-02-FR} RIN 051-AA40/Action: Final Rule}]

ORGANIC CERTIFYING AGENCY CERTIFIER	KOSHER
Utah Department of Agriculture and Food	

Figure 6-2 Specification Sheet #2

Product Specification/ Technical Data Sheet

HARVEST KING, WHEAT FLOUR, Enriched, Malted	Code 53722	Size 50#	Mills AV BF KC GF VN	Revision Date 01/01/05 HARVEST KING ENR MT ING Code 249896

DEFINITION

- This product shall be of food grade and in all respects, including labeling, in compliance with the Federal Food, Drug and Cosmetic Act of 1938 as amended and all applicable regulations there under. It shall meet FDA Food Standards for Enriched Wheat Flour as found in 21 CFR 137.165.
- A high quality patent bread flour milled from a selected blend of hard wheat. Wheat selection is to be consistent with optimum baking characteristics and performance. Wide variations in the type of wheat utilized for this flour are not permitted. The flour shall be produced under sanitary conditions in accordance with GMPs.

PACKAGING/SHELF LIFE/STORAGE CONDITIONS/PALLET CONFIGURATION

1. The package consists of 50 lb. multi-wall paper bags.
2. Stored according to GMPs at <80°F and 70% R.H., the shelf life is 1 year from the date of manufacture.
3. To preserve quality, dry storage at room temperature with regular inspection and rotation is recommended.

Size	Bags/Pallet	Bags/Layer	Gross Wt./Bag	Cube	Pallet Dimension
50# (West)	55	5	50.5	1.3	53"H/41.5"W/52"D
50# (East)	50	5	50.5	1.3	48"H/41.5"W/52"D

PHYSICAL CHARACTERISTICS

1. Color – Clean, creamy white, free of bran specks.
2. The product shall be free of rancid, bitter, musty or other undesirable flavors or odors.
3. The product shall be as free of all types of foreign material as can be achieved through GMPs.
4. Falling Number – 240 – 280 sec.

KOSHER APPROVAL: Orthodox Union

ALLERGEN INFORMATION: Allergen - Wheat

INGREDIENT LEGEND:

Wheat flour, malted barley flour, niacin, iron, thiamin mononitrate, riboflavin, folic acid.

CHEMICAL COMPOSITION (14.0% Moisture basis)		
1. Moisture	14.0%	Maximum
2. Protein	12.0%	+/- 0.3%
3. Ash	0.52%	+/- 0.03%

TREATMENT:	
1. Enriched	2. Barley Malt

NUTRITION (Approx. per 100G)					
Calories	357		Thiamin (B1)	0.64	mg
Protein	11.9	g	Riboflavin (B2)	0.40	mg
Fat	1.0	g	Niacin	5.30	mg
Saturated	0.14	g	Folic Acid	0.15	mg
Trans Fat	0.0	g	Iron	4.40	mg
MonoUnsaturated	0.08	g	Sodium	1.0	mg
PolyUnsaturated	0.45	g	Potassium	105	mg
Carbohydrate	73.1	g	Phosphorus	95	mg
Complex	71.7	g			
Sugars	1.4	g			
Dietary Fiber	2.9	g			
Soluble	1.8	g			
Insoluble	1.2	g			

MICROBIAL GUIDELINES: Listed as guidelines as opposed to controllable specifications	
Standard Plate Count	<50,000/g
Coliforms	<500/g
Yeast	<500/g
Mold	<500/g
C.P Staph	<10/g
E. Coli	<3/g
Salmonella	Negative

PRODUCT DESCRIPTION

The product description section of the spec sheet describes the origin and type of wheat used to produce the flour (see Figure 6-3) and guarantees that the wheat was selected and cleaned in compliance with the US Federal Food, Drug and Cosmetic Act.

INGREDIENT DECLARATION

This specification lists the ingredients present in the flour. Besides wheat flour, other ingredients may be added to improve dietetic quality or to increase baking performance. The following is a list of the most common ingredients and their significance in the baking process.

Enrichment

In order to increase its nutritional value, vitamins like thiamin, niacin, and riboflavin and minerals like iron have been added to flour since the 1930s. Since January 1998, folic acid has also been included. Referred to as **enrichment**, this process has no noticeable effects on the baking process.

Potassium Bromate

Potassium bromate is an oxidizer; its effects are evident near the end of the baking process (at the end of final proof and beginning of the bake). It strengthens gluten and increases the fermentation tolerance of dough. Because bromate manifests later in the baking process, it has little effect on steps in which the dough is physically worked and requires good extensibility, such as dividing and shaping. When potassium bromate is used, the final product exhibits increased volume with larger cut openings. California, Oregon, and several countries around the world have banned the use of potassium bromate because it possesses carcinogenic properties.

Ascorbic Acid

Ascorbic acid is a synthesized vitamin C product and is classified in the same oxidizer category as potassium bromate. The effects of ascorbic acid are noticeable early in the baking process. Unlike potassium bromate, it can decrease the extensibility of the dough during shaping.

Note: A long first fermentation will naturally increase dough oxidation, and when protein quality is sufficient, it can be substituted for bromate or ascorbic acid.

Benzoyl Peroxide

A bleaching agent added to whiten flour, benzoyl peroxide reacts with the carotenoid pigments naturally contained in wheat. This reaction negatively affects the natural creaminess of the crumb color and the flavor of the bread because carotenoid pigments are responsible for some dough aromas.

Azodicarbonamide

Though classified as a bleaching agent, azodicarbonamide (ADA) behaves more like an oxidizer with maturing proprieties. It chemically induces flour **maturation**, or aging, in order to improve baking performance. Freshly milled or "green" flour does not usually perform well due to a lack of oxidation and maturation.

Note: Maturing agents can be avoided when flour is allowed to rest for 2 to 3 weeks after milling. The natural oxidation process improves protein quality and the baking performance of the flour.

Figure 6-3 Chart of Wheat Categories

Wheat Categories: Abbreviations are used to designate different classes of wheat.
The order of abbreviation is always the same on the spec sheet: hardness, season, and color.

Category	Description	Performance
Hard, Soft, or Durum (H/S/D)	Refers to the "hardness" of the wheat kernel, determined by its molecular structure (the shape and density of the kernel).	This characteristic affects the baking performance of the flour, specifically its ability to form gluten. Bread flour is made from hard wheat, while soft wheat flour is generally used in making pastry. Durum kernels are very hard and are used for pasta or specialty flours like semolina.
Winter or Spring (W/S)	The season of year when the wheat was planted. Spring wheat is cultivated in northern states (MN, ND, etc.) where it is sown in April and harvested by late August or early September. Winter wheat is grown in milder climates. Seeds are sown in the fall, reach a grass stage before temperatures lower, and then stay dormant through the winter. When temperatures climb again, the growing cycle of the plant resumes until its harvest in June or July.	Winter wheat tends to perform better when long fermentation times are required.
Red or White (R/W)	The color refers to the "envelope" around the wheat kernel, which naturally contains a chemical that produces a reddish coloration. Studies have shown this chemical can cause bitterness in the final product. To eliminate bitterness, scientists have developed a new variety of wheat called "white" because of the lighter coloration in the envelope.	The coloration of the bran does not seem to affect the baking performance of the flour. Flavor, especially in whole wheat breads, is the main beneficiary of the relatively new white wheat class.

Malt

Malt is a form of malted barley flour added to correct enzyme activity (see the "Falling Number" section of this chapter for more information).

Fungal Amylase

Fungal amylase refers to enzymes produced in the laboratory from a base of fungus cultures. Like malt, amylases are added to flour to supplement enzyme activity.

Note: Although malt naturally contains enzymes besides amylase that can produce other, less-controllable effects on the dough, fungal amylases allow the miller to add only amylase (the most important enzyme for sugar degradation) to the flour.

ANALYTICAL SPECIFICATION

The spec sheet details the results (**analytical data**) of several analytical tests performed on the flour that precisely determine its characteristics. Data such as moisture content, ash content, protein content, and enzyme activity can then be provided to the baker.

Moisture Content

According to regulations, flour must not possess moisture content above 14 percent at the end of the milling process. Later on, moisture content may vary depending on climatic and storage conditions.

Ash Content

Ash content represents the amount of bran present in flour after milling. The term "ash" refers to the lab test used to determine bran content, in which a flour sample is incinerated at 1,652°F (900°C). The organic components burn completely, and only the ash of the mineral components remains. An ash content of 0.5 represents 0.5 g of minerals contained in 100 g of flour (14 percent moisture content).

Ash content also correlates to the extraction rate during the milling process. In whole wheat flour, 100 percent extraction renders an ash content of approximately 1.5. A lower extraction rate (75 to 77 percent) produces an ash content of approximately 0.48 to 0.50.

The flour's ash content affects the dough characteristics and fermentation activity. High bran content produces dough with more extensibility because envelope particles interfere with protein strand bonding and impact gluten formation, increasing dough porosity. Conversely, low bran quantity can form dough that is less extensible.

Because minerals contained in the bran envelope supply nutrients to commercial or wild yeast, flour with high bran content generates additional fermentation activity. The baker can compensate for this by decreasing the amount of yeast called for, in order to maintain the balance of gas and acidity production during fermentation. For long fermentation and proper extensibility, ash content between 0.47 and 0.52 is preferred.

Protein Content

Protein content is especially useful data for bakers because the protein levels in flour directly affect dough characteristics. To measure protein, a sample of flour is subjected to a lengthy combustion process that assesses its nitrogen content (the main component of protein). The results are expressed in percentage form. For example, a protein content of 13 percent simply means that 13 percent of the flour (14 percent moisture content) is protein. A faster, but less accurate test uses an infrared signal to provide almost immediate results.

High protein (at least 12.5 to 13 percent) creates a strong gluten structure and can result in longer mixing times, depending on protein quality. Protein also affects dough extensibility and bread volume. Bread made from high-gluten flour tends to have a tough or rubbery crust and a too-tight crumb structure. It can also have a browner color and possess a slightly bitter aftertaste due to a more pronounced Maillard reaction. For most artisan or traditional products, flour with protein content between 10.5 and 12 percent is ideal. However, high-gluten flours have excellent benefits for the more mechanized production processes of certain types of bread like pan breads, bagels, or sourdough when chewy crust and crumb are desired (typical San Francisco sourdough, for example).

Enzyme Activity (Falling Number)

Wheat naturally contains enzymes that originate in the germ and progress to the endosperm during the plant's maturation. These enzymes break down complex nutrients like starch and protein into simple nutrients for use in the next life cycle. The enzyme activity of flour depends upon how advanced the wheat's germination was at harvest time.

The **falling number** test measures the enzyme activity of the flour. Because a certain activity level is necessary to sustain long fermentation times, the result is an important performance indicator. The test is performed using a homogenous solution of flour and water. A test tube of the sample is placed in boiling water and agitated with a ski-pole-shaped apparatus. The solution is heated until it begins to coagulate. When the apparatus is able to "stand" on the surface of the solution, agitation ceases.

The heat and consistency of the solution stimulate enzyme activity, the mixture starts to liquefy due to enzyme degradation, and the "ski-pole" descends into the test tube as the solution breaks down. The number of seconds it takes for the pole to "fall" through the sample is timed. This is referred to as the falling number.

A falling number between 250 and 350 seconds represents the preferred level of enzyme activity for artisan baking. A number less than 200 seconds indicates that the flour is too rich in enzymes and will result in a fast fermentation and bread with a reddish crust coloration and sticky crumb. A falling number greater than 350 seconds suggests an enzyme deficiency. In this case, fermentation will be slow, and the bread may have less volume and a pale crust color.

Millers sometimes use additives like fungal amylase or malt to supplement low enzyme content. When fungal amylase is used, a modified version of the falling number test must be performed to ensure the enzyme activity of the flour has been reestablished.

FARINOGRAPH

The **farinograph** characterizes the quality of the flour by measuring the mixing properties of the dough to determine absorption capacity, development time, and structure stability. (See Figure 6-4.)

This scientific instrument is composed of three main parts:

- Bowl with mixing blades to mix the dough
- Dynamometer to measure the force or friction of the dough against the mixing blades during mixing
- Computer to calculate and illustrate a curve that identifies the different values

Figure 6-4
Farinograph

With a farinograph the following values can be recorded:

- The flour's capacity to absorb water is expressed with a percentage. This value does not refer to the amount of water to use when making dough in the bakery, but it can be helpful to gauge hydration or compare flour. For example, bakers can use this value to determine if a new batch of flour may require more or less water than the previous one.

- Peak time, or **dough development time**, measures the amount of time between the first addition of water and the development of the dough to maximum consistency.
- The **stability** establishes how long the dough can be mixed before its gluten structure breaks down.
- The **mixing tolerance index (MTI)** indicates how fast the gluten structure breaks down after reaching its full development.

How to Read the Farinograph Curve

The two curves in Figure 6-5 show farinograph curves for high-gluten flour and bread flour. Their different characteristics (especially protein content) will affect the curves during the farinograph test. The following section will focus on how to interpret these two graphs.

It is first important to understand the graph: The numbers on the bottom of the chart (horizontal reading) are minutes, while the numbers for the vertical reading are farinogram units (FU). *Note:* FU used to be referred to as Brabender unites (BU). The most important line is the 500 FU line. It is used as a reference for dough development during the mixing process.

Arrival Time **Arrival time** is the time required for the top of the curve to reach the 500 FU line after the mixer has been started and the water introduced. This value is a measurement of the rate at which flour absorbs water during the formation of the dough. On a given variety of wheat, arrival time generally increases as protein increases.

The arrival time of the high-gluten flour is higher compared to the arrival time of the bread flour. This indicates to the baker that the incorporation phase of the mixing time will be longer when working with the high-gluten flour.

Dough Development Time The dough development time is measured in minutes between the first addition of water and the development of dough's maximum consistency. This value does not directly relate to mixing dough in a bakery as the type of mixing differs, but, as a general rule, the higher the peak time is, the longer the mixing time will be to achieve full development. This value is also helpful in assisting in making flour comparisons.

Stability Stability is expressed on the graph by calculating the difference in time between the point at which the top of the curve intercepts the 500 FU line (arrival time) and the point at which the top of the curve leaves the 500 FU line (departure time). The stability gives some indication of the flour's tolerance during mixing.

The stability of the high-gluten flour is much longer compared to that of the bread flour. This indicates to the baker that the bread flour will reach its optimum development faster but won't stay very long at this stage. In other words, the dough will have the tendency to be in an overmixed stage much sooner in the mixing process compared to the high-gluten flour. Therefore, extra care must be taken during mixing time to avoid overdeveloping the gluten structure when working with lower protein flour.

Departure Time The **departure time** value represents (in minutes) the time from the first addition of water until the top of the curve leaves the

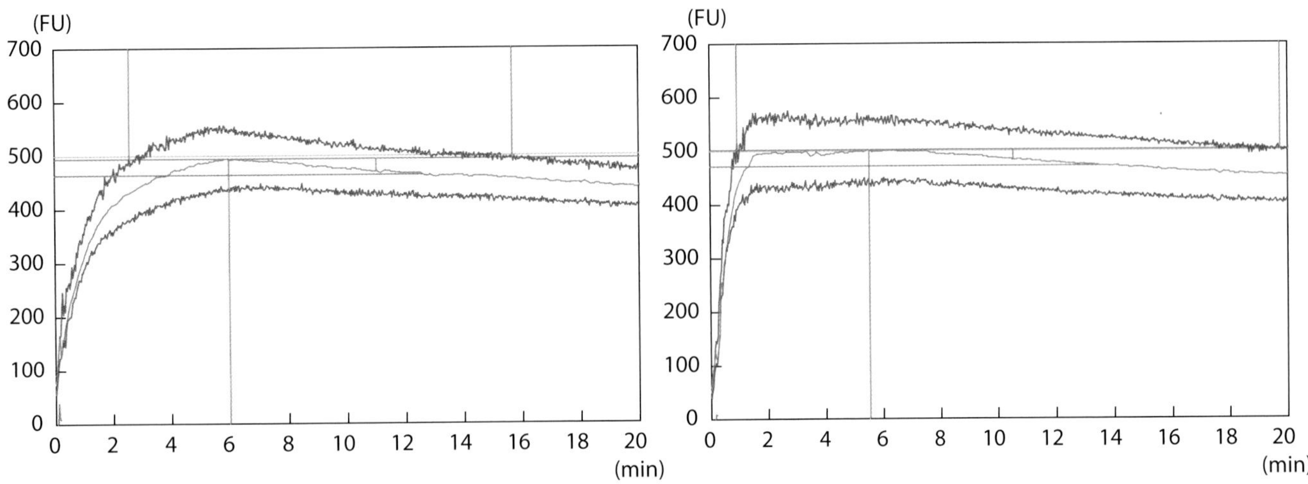

Sample: High-Gluten Bread Flour

Consistency: 494 FU with water absorption 65%	
Protein	13.95
Moisture	13.9
FN	400+
Ash	0.56%
Water absorption (corrected for 500 FU)	64.90%
Water absorption (corrected to 14%)	64.80%
Development time	6.0 min
Stability	13.1 min
Tolerance index (MTI)	23 FU
Time to break down	12.6 min
Farinograph quality number	126

Sample: Low-Protein Bread Flour

Consistency: 502 FU with water absorption 59.5%	
Protein	11.93
Moisture	13.23
FN	400+
Ash	0.58%
Water absorption (corrected for 500 FU)	59.60%
Water absorption (corrected to 14%)	58.70%
Development time	5.5 min
Stability	18.8 min
Tolerance index (MTI)	19 FU
Time to break down	13.8 min
Farinograph quality number	138

Figure 6-5
Farinograph Curves: High-Gluten Bread Flour (left) and Low-Protein Bread Flour (right)

500 FU line. Longer time indicates stronger flour as the mixing time can be longer without degradation of the gluten structure.

The departure time of the high-gluten flour is much longer compared to the bread flour. Again, this tells the baker that the lower protein flour doesn't have the ability to be mixed for a longer period of time without any degradation.

Mixing Tolerance Index The MTI is the difference in FU between the top of the curve at the peak and the top of the curve measured 5 minutes after the peak is reached. The higher the MTI is, the weaker the flour will be, as the curve goes down quicker, indicating an early degradation of the gluten during mixing.

The MTI of the high-gluten flour is lower compared to that of the bread flour. This indicates to the baker that the high-gluten flour can be mixed longer after its full development without a lot of degradation.

Some Values Figure 6-6 gives some general farinograph values that can be used to compare three different types of flour: high-gluten flour, bread flour (lower protein content), and pastry flour (made with soft wheat).

Figure 6-6
General Farinograph Values

	Bread Flour	High-Gluten Flour	Pastry Flour
Absorption	60–62	63–68	52–55
Peak	5.5–6.5	7–9	1–4
Stability	9.5–12.5	12–18	2–4
MTI	25–30	15–20	40–60

Farinograph Conclusion

Farinograph values relate primarily to the mixing characteristics of the dough. In traditional baking, where dough is not mixed to full development to avoid excessive oxidation, farinograph values become less important.

ALVEOGRAPH

The **alveograph** is a scientific instrument that discerns specific physical characteristics of dough, including elasticity, extensibility, the balance between elasticity and extensibility, and strength. These values appear on the spec sheet as *P*, *L*, *P/L*, and *W*, respectively. (See Figure 6-7.)

The alveograph is composed of four main parts:

- Mixer to mix dough under specific conditions: same consistency (determined according to moisture content of the flour), same temperature (jacketed mixer), and same amount of salt. The mixer is also equipped with an extruding system to take the dough out once mixing is completed.
- Dough sheeting assembly to create an even band of dough that will be cut into disks.
- Dough bubble-blowing apparatus that will pressure each disk of dough between two plates and allow an airflow under the bottom of the disk of dough. The edge of the disk of dough is compressed, but the center remains open. The air will increase the pressure under the disk of dough, which will start to inflate once the pressure gets too high.
- Recording dough manometer that measures the amount of air pressure needed to inflate the dough, the amount of air trapped into the bubble of dough, and the point at which the dough breaks under the air pressure. These measurements are recorded in the form of a curve on graph paper.

How to Read an Alveograph Curve

- P *Value—Elasticity:* A high *P* value (≅ 90) indicates ample dough elasticity and strong flour. A low *P* value (≅ 50) signifies a lack of elasticity and weaker flour. The curve of the strong flour is much higher compared to the weak flour. A baker can expect that a flour with a lot of elasticity will be difficult to work with if no changes are made in the baking process. Autolyse, working with liquid preferment (favoring protease activity), or the addition of deactivated yeast would be some ways to decrease dough elasticity and get better working characteristics.
- L *Value—Extensibility:* Dough extensibility is represented by an *L* value. The lower the value is, the less extensible the dough will be and the stronger the flour is. The curve of the weak flour is much longer compared to that of the strong flour, indicating an excess of extensi-

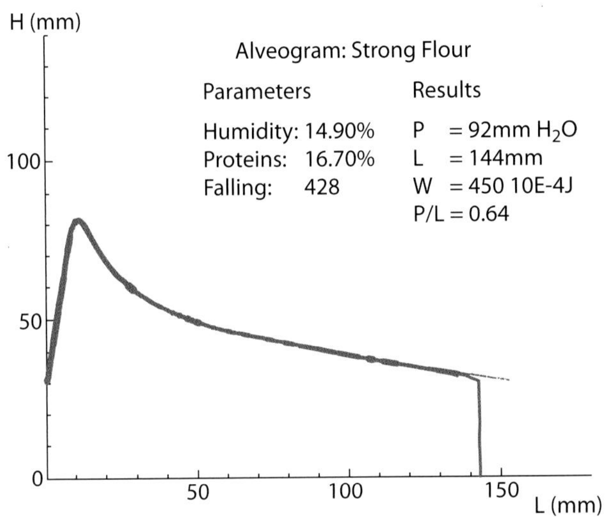

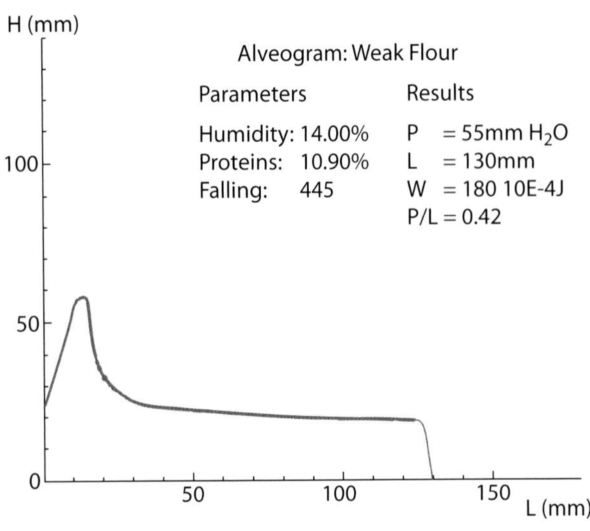

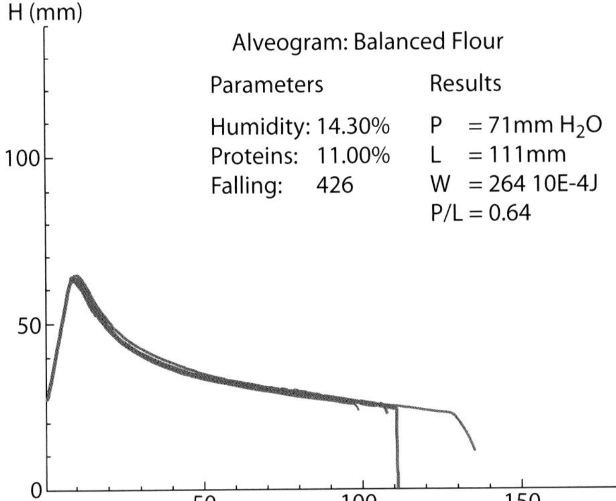

Figure 6-7
Alveograph Curve for Strong, Weak, and Balanced Flour

bility. The baker will have to modify the baking process to decrease dough extensibility to avoid getting a dough that is too weak. Working with preferment, lengthening first fermentation with folds, or adding 20 to 30 ppm of ascorbic acid would decrease dough extensibility and increase its strength. **Parts per million (ppm)** refers to the controlled measurement of very strong agents such as ascorbic acid by diluting a known quantity of the stronger agent in a known quantity of flour to lower the dose. See page 153 for a detailed explanation of the process for using ppm.

- P/L *Value—Ratio of Elasticity/Extensibility:* A $P/L \geq 1$ signifies strong dough, and because elasticity is more prominent than extensibility, the baker can anticipate problems during the elongating part of the shaping process. A very low *P/L* indicates dough with ample extensibility and a lack of elasticity that may not be strong enough to endure a normal baking process. It is difficult to specify the ideal *P/L* because there are other factors to consider. In general, a $P/L \cong 0.6$ indicates an appropriate balance between extensibility and elasticity. The curve of the strong flour is much higher than it is long, indicating that *P/L* is greater than 1, while the curve of the weak flour is much longer than it is high, indicating that *P/L* is less than 1. When *P/L* is greater than 1, the baker must use all the necessary ways to decrease the strength of the dough and improve its extensibility. On the other hand, when *P/L* is very low, the baking process must be adjusted to improve the strength of the dough.

- W *Value—Strength:* A high *W* value (> 300) indicates a strong dough, and *W* < 200 indicates a relatively weak dough. The surface under the curve of the strong flour is much larger compared to the weak flour, indicating to the baker that the flour will be very strong.

Alveograph Conclusion

Alveograph values provide bakers with an early indication of dough strength. Because strength is a crucial factor in the baking process for dough and bread characteristics, these values are very helpful in flour selection.

ADDITIONAL INFORMATION

This specification includes kosher status, organic certification, and storage recommendations. Even though having complete knowledge about the flour is important, these qualities do not really affect the baking process.

FLOUR SPECIFICATION SHEET CONCLUSION

The information detailed on the product specification sheet can help bakers better understand and utilize their flour. It is an important resource not only in flour selection but also as a basis to promote communication between millers and bakers.

Although it provides extensive information about the flour, a spec sheet cannot completely predict its performance. Alveographs and farinographs are predictive tests, but some fundamental characteristics, such as protein quality, appearance, and flavor of the final product simply cannot be evaluated with current methodology. A comprehensive baking test, based on real-world artisan baking and adhering to specific protocols, is the ultimate way to assess flour characteristics at each stage of the baking process. Such testing may well allow the baker to ascertain even the most elusive final product qualities, such as flavor and aroma, from a sample of flour.

It is important to differentiate between the spec sheet and the **Certificate of Analysis (COA)**. The spec sheet just provides a general range of information about the flour, whereas the COA refers to a specific batch of flour (usually being delivered to the bakery). (See Figure 6-8.)

EVALUATION OF FLOUR BAKING PERFORMANCE: HOW TO PERFORM A BAKING TEST

INTRODUCTION

Because of the high availability of baking flours, bakers sometimes select the ones that best fit production. The type of wheat, protein content, and ash content are important guidelines that assist in the selection process, but none of these are a precise representation of what the final product characteristics will be. The only way to gain a complete understanding of baking performance is to perform a baking test.

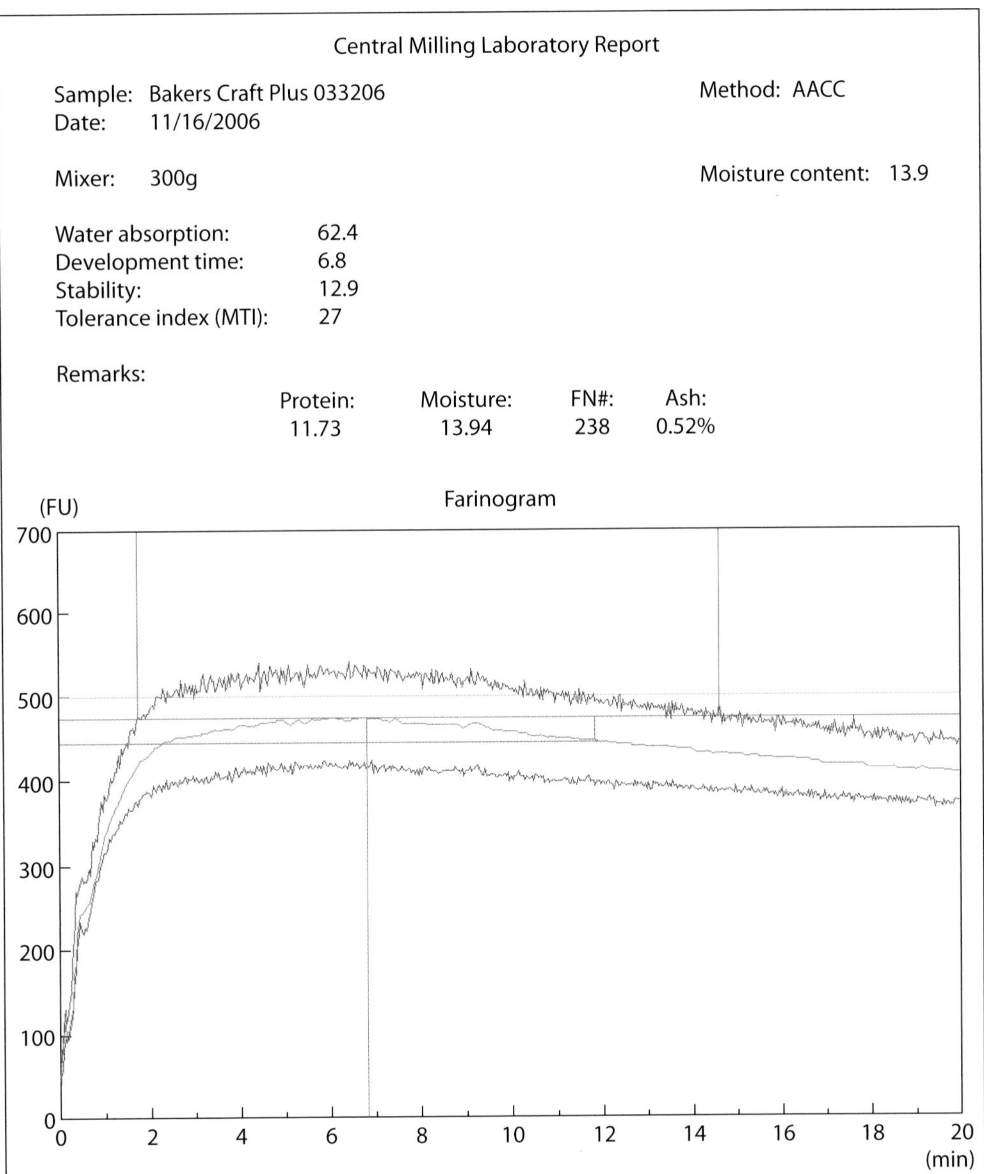

Central Milling Laboratory Report

Sample: Bakers Craft Plus 033206
Date: 11/16/2006

Method: AACC

Mixer: 300g

Moisture content: 13.9

Water absorption:	62.4
Development time:	6.8
Stability:	12.9
Tolerance index (MTI):	27

Remarks:

Protein:	Moisture:	FN#:	Ash:
11.73	13.94	238	0.52%

Figure 6-8

Certificate of Analysis

In France, where artisan baking is still the predominant baking style and additives are minimally used, baking tests are commonly made at the mill level to properly blend wheat and bring to the market flours that are well balanced with optimum baking performance.

In the United States, baking tests are primarily designed to demonstrate whether baking performance is right for pan bread products, including large volume, tight and even crumb, and whiter crumb color. It is up to the baker to establish individual testing procedures that will properly evaluate flour quality.

GOAL

When a very precise baking process is followed, baking tests demonstrate the properties of flour that are not noticeable with common scientific tests, such as fermentation tolerance, crispiness of the crust, crumb color, and flavor.

All tests should be performed by an experienced baker capable of carefully determining dough consistency and neutrally assessing dough characteristics throughout the baking process and bread characteristics at the end of it. These tests are always conducted in comparison to a control flour with known baking performances for point of reference and to demonstrate that the test can be reproduced.

BASIC METHOD

The method and ingredients used should not improve flour characteristics.

- No preferment should be involved, as flavor should primarily come from the flour and not from the aromas developed during prefermentation.
- Only basic ingredients (no fat or sugar) should be part of the formula to avoid altering the flavor and to minimize changes in the fermentation activity (from sugar) or dough extensibility (from fat).
- Improved mix, the most common in traditional baking, is the best mixing technique for flour testing.
- To easily compare the general appearance of bread and assess bread interior characteristics, a batard or baguette shape is recommended.
- In order to evaluate fermentation tolerance, two lengths of final proof are made.
- Normal production baking times and temperatures are set according to the type of oven.
- A cooling time of 90 minutes in proper conditions is necessary to preserve the integrity of the bread.

FORMULA

The following formula is a good starting point for any kind of baking test: 100 percent flour, 62 percent water, 1.5 percent fresh yeast, and 2 percent salt. Hydration starts at 62 percent but must be adapted to achieve dough with a medium-soft consistency. This consistency should remain constant with all the tested flour samples to avoid penalizing flour characteristics (by working with too stiff or soft dough). The extra amount of water (when necessary) must be carefully recorded as it will become an important value for the baker in charge of mixing in a production environment. The yeast used should be compressed yeast. However, if dry instant yeast is used, the percentage will have to be adjusted.

BAKING PROCESS

Mixing

Mixing time should be adjusted for an improved mix method and the type of mixer used. Water temperature should be calculated to achieve a final dough temperature of 75°F to 76°F (24°C), which is crucial for a successful baking test. If a mistake is made and the dough temperature is not correct, mixing must begin again with the necessary water temperature correction.

First Fermentation

For the quantity of yeast mentioned in the formula, first fermentation must be 90 minutes. For better control of the fermentation activity, the dough should be placed in a well-controlled environment with a temperature of 75°F (24°C) to 77°F (25°C) and relative humidity of 80 percent.

Dividing

Dough is typically scaled at 12 1/2 oz (350 g) for both baguettes and batards. This arbitrary weight can be changed as long as all of the dough pieces are scaled the same to ensure a correct comparison of loaves at the end of the process.

Preshaping

Round preshaping for batards and rectangle shaping for baguettes should be achieved using a standard operative procedure to preserve dough characteristics. If the dough is too weak, no effort should be made to correct it. The weakness of the tested flour will have to be factored in during evaluation.

Shaping

Shaping is usually done by hand by an experienced baker who can duplicate the same shaping process, in terms of tightness and length, with all of the dough pieces. As with preshaping, shaping must be neutral to preserve dough characteristics without positively or negatively affecting its strength.

Final Proof

Two lengths of final proof must be done to evaluate fermentation tolerance. Half of the loaves are baked after one hour, and the other half are baked after 90 minutes. This staggered baking time will indicate whether the dough can tolerate a longer-than-usual fermentation (a common occurrence in production) without any degradation of the gluten structure or negative impact on appearance.

Baking

For baking, a deck oven with steam is advised. Depending on the type of oven, a baking time of 20 to 25 minutes for baguettes and 25 to 30 minutes for batards is required. Once the baking time and temperature have been established with a control flour, it is important to bake all of the dough being tested at this temperature and for the same amount of time. This will make it possible to identify any potential defects in crust coloration of the bread, such as a lack of lack of residual simple sugar.

Cooling

Before the final evaluation of finished products, cooling should take place on a wire cooling rack for 90 minutes at room temperature. This allows the flavor and moisture level of the bread to stabilize.

Alternative Method

It is also possible to assess the baking performance of flour under specific conditions. For example, a specific formula already in use at the bakery or a specific baking process (short or intensive mix) with specific dough shapes can also be used. However, the same precision in the method and working of the dough is necessary to ensure realistic flour evaluation.

EVALUATION OF FLOUR PERFORMANCE

The flour is evaluated during the entire process, and the results are reported on an evaluation form. (See Figure 6-9.)

The evaluation of flour performance is made with a numerical grading system that is based on 10 for optimum quality and on 1, 4, or 7, according to the degree of lack or excess for specific dough properties. For example, dough with an important lack of extensibility during shaping will be noted as a 1, whereas dough lacking just a bit of extensibility will be noted as a 7. Intermediate totals are then calculated to make it easier to compare specific dough characteristics at some point of the baking process, such as mixing, first fermentation, or shaping.

Finally, the overall total is calculated to classify the flour. A higher total means that the baking performance of the flour is outstanding; lower totals indicate that a number of defects will need to be corrected.

EVALUATIONS AT EACH STEP OF THE PROCESS

The following evaluations take place at each stage of the baking process:

- Dough evaluation is made at mixing, at first fermentation, at shaping, and at the end of the final proof.
- Fermentation tolerance is evaluated by the general appearance of the loaf after baking and by bread volume. (See Figure 6-10.)
- The bread exterior is evaluated by the cross section, appearance, volume, and crust.
- The bread interior is evaluated by color, hole, and crumb structure.
- Flavor, which is based on 20, demonstrates the importance of this characteristic in the evaluation. It is given greater importance because off flavors cannot always be corrected.

Figure 6-10
The baguettes on the left were proofed for 1.5 hours; the baguettes on the right were proofed for 1 hour.

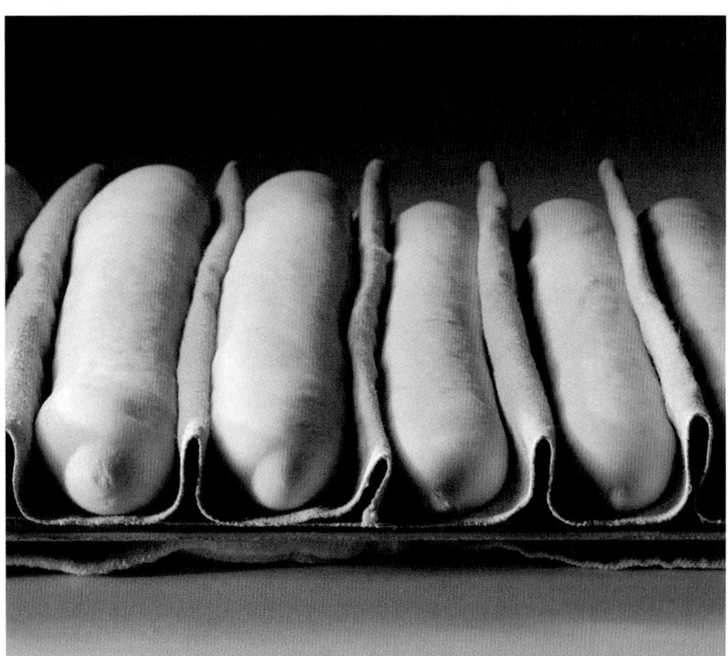

AFTER THE EVALUATION

Once the baking test is done, the baker must decide whether or not the flour can be used in production. Flour with too many defects should not be used because producing consistent products might be very challenging. If not too pronounced, some defects can easily be corrected. For example, a lack of extensibility can be fixed with the use of an autolyse, while a lack of crust color can be adjusted by adding malt to the formula.

COMPENSATING FOR FLOUR DEFICIENCIES

Although millers do their best to supply customers with consistent flour quality, several factors can affect wheat properties during the growing cycle and can naturally trigger negative or positive variations in the

Figure 6-9 Example of Baking Text Evaluation Form

Baking Test Evaluation Form

Sample number : ____________
Date : ____________

Flour
Moisture content : ____________
Ash content : ____________
Protein content : ____________
Falling # : ____________

Treatments : ____________

Others analytical specifications
Alveograph
P value : ____________
L value : ____________
P/L value : ____________
W value : ____________

Wheat
Variety : ____________
Category : ____________

Milling
Location : ____________
Date : ____________

Temperature
Bakery : ____________
Flour : ____________
Water : ____________
Dough : ____________

Hydration : ____________

		Insufficient				Excessive			
		1	4	7	10	7	4	1	
Mixing	Mixing Time								
	Extensibility								
	Elasticity								
								Total Mixing / 30	
First Fermentation	Slackness								
								Total First Fermentation / 10	
Shaping	Extensibility								
	Elasticity								
	Stickiness								
								Total Shaping / 30	
Proof	Fermentation Activity								
	Tearing								
								Total Proof / 20	
Fermentation	Tolerance								
								Total Tolerance / 10	
								TOTAL DOUGH / 100	

		Insufficient				Excessive			
		1	4	7	10	7	4	1	
Bread - Exterior	Cross-section								
	Crust Color								
	Crust Crispness								
	Development of Cuts								
	Volume								
								Total Bread - Exterior / 50	
Bread - Interior	Color								
	Hole Structure								
								Total Bread - Interior / 30	
								TOTAL BREAD / 80	

		1	5	10	15	20	4	1	
Flavor	Flavor								
								Total Flavor / 20	
								Total Score / 200	

baking performance of flour. Weather-related factors like the quantity of rain or sun at certain times during the growing cycle, fertilizing, and harvesting can change wheat and flour characteristics. In addition, millers must consider economic factors related to their industry, like wheat market prices and availability, as well as transportation costs from grain elevators to the mill.

Not much can be done to control these natural and economic variations in flour quality at the bakery level. Instead, the baker must use technical knowledge to adjust the formula and baking process in order to produce consistent loaves of bread. The main inconsistencies that artisan bakers can find in flour include maturation, water absorption, mixing tolerance, maturation, lack or excess of strength, fermentation tolerance, enzyme activity, coloration, and flavor.

MATURATION

Flour baking performance improves as flour ages. The natural oxidation of the proteins in flour during resting time creates better gluten structure and better fermentation tolerance during the baking process. In general, 2 weeks of maturation are recommended in summer, whereas 3 weeks are required in winter due to the slower chemical reactions in lower temperatures.

Maturation can naturally occur during transportation from the mill and storage at the distribution center warehouse. However, customers who are located close to the milling location and who deal directly with the mill have a high probability of receiving "green" flour that is very fresh. The milling date that is typically printed on the side of the flour bag or listed in the spec sheet that accompanies bulk delivery provides the exact flour maturation.

Bakers who work with green flour notice a tendency for the flour to absorb more water at the beginning of the mixing process. As mixing progresses, the dough appears to release water that creates a shiny, sticky surface. Toward the end of the first fermentation, the dough will have the tendency to slacken and lose its strength. Fermentation tolerance and oven kick will also be poor.

Unfortunately, there are not many ways to naturally compensate for lack of maturation. Using more preferment when possible and folding the dough to improve strength during the first fermentation are among the few possibilities. Chemically, ADA replaces maturation as soon as it comes into contact with water during mixing. Because of the small quantity necessary, the miller typically adds ADA; when used, it is usually mentioned on the ingredients list on the bag of flour or on the spec sheet. Ascorbic acid is also used to improve the baking performance of green flour. Its oxidation action reinforces gluten properties and fermentation tolerance. In general, at a bakery level, 15 to 20 ppm can be added to dough. This amount can vary depending on the length of first fermentation. A process with very short fermentation time (15 to 30 minutes) will require a larger quantity of ascorbic acid.

WATER ABSORPTION

Bakers realize that they need to add or subtract water to achieve desired dough consistency. Flour can absorb more or less water depending on several factors. The humidity level (or moisture content) can vary depending on the origin of the flour or storage conditions, including the length of storage and humidity level in the warehouse. For example, flour stored in a dry environment for 2 to 3 weeks will have the tendency to lose some moisture and will probably require more water during mixing.

The protein quantity and quality of the flour also have a direct impact on dough hydration. Proteins have a natural property to absorb 150 to 200 percent of their own weight in water, depending on their quality. The higher the protein level in the flour, the more water will be necessary to reach the desired dough consistency.

The level of starch damage also affects dough hydration, with a damaged particle of starch able to absorb four to six times more water compared to a native particle of starch, which typically absorbs 40 percent of its weight in water. Flour with a higher level of starch damage requires a larger amount of water during mixing. Flours with higher ash content also require more water. Bran is very rich in cellulose, and this component alone will retain a large amount of water.

The best way to deal with changes in water absorption is to make a test batch every time a new lot of flour is used in production. An experienced baker who knows how to assess dough consistency must conduct the test, in which the amount of water necessary to reach the specific consistency is carefully measured. If changes need to be made, the production manager should simply adjust the percentage of water in the formula. This new number will work until a new lot of flour is delivered to the bakery.

Even though flour absorption rates change during the year, bakers should remember that proper dough consistency is more important than the quantity of water used to reach it. In addition, flour with higher absorption is economically more interesting because it will increase the dough yield using the same amount of flour.

MIXING TOLERANCE

Bakers sometimes notice that dough develops faster or slower with a new batch of flour. This is generally due to the quality of the wheat protein, and it is not necessarily a flour deficiency as long as the final product quality remains the same. This change in mixing time can be noticed from the end of August to end of September when the miller uses wheat from a new crop year. Just as with flour, wheat needs to age in order to reach full baking performance. Millers typically transition from an old crop to a new one by blending the two crops for a period of time to let the new wheat age and allow the baker to transition to baking properties of the new wheat. As the wheat ages, mixing times generally go back to normal.

If lower-quality products are obtained with flour that requires a shorter mixing time, it can signify lower protein quality that will probably generate dough with lack of strength.

Artisan bakers should be careful during mixing and check gluten development often until the perfect mixing time is determined. As with water absorption, an experienced baker can run a test batch to determine exact mixing time and the best mixing procedure to use in production. In the case of a heavily automated production line, knowing the correct mixing time is crucial. These times are typically preset in the mixer computer, so the results of the test batch are very important.

LACK OF STRENGTH

With bread flour, lack of strength is very rare in the United States. The good-quality hard wheat that is commonly utilized in bread flours typically carries a sufficient amount of protein to generate dough with enough strength for the baking process. However, for bakers using all-purpose flours, a lack of strength can sometimes be noticed. In general, this depends on the blend of wheat used in the all-purpose flour. If it contains a significant amount of soft wheat, the protein will not have the same gluten-forming ability as hard wheat. Strength can also be a problem if the miller includes too great a percentage of lower-quality hard wheat in the wheat blend.

To compensate for this flour deficiency, the baker should lower dough hydration and increase, when possible, the amount of preferment. The first fermentation can also be lengthened with an extra fold to improve dough strength. Preshaping and shaping should be done a little bit tighter by hand or by machine, and the length of the final proof should be shortened. Extra care should be taken when loading the loaves in the oven. When possible, baking can be done at a slightly higher temperature at the beginning of the bake to encourage oven kick and dough development.

Depending on the baker's philosophy, a quick fix to this problem would be to add 20 to 40 ppm of ascorbic acid to the dough. Because of its oxidizing properties, ascorbic acid will reinforce the gluten as the fermentation advances, recreating the right balance in dough strength.

EXCESS OF STRENGTH

Wheat in the United States is mostly developed for the large commercial bakery industry, which requires stronger gluten properties for the dough to handle the abuse of machinery. As a result, much of the flour that reaches artisan bakeries generates dough with strong characteristics. Fortunately, a growing number of milling companies are carefully selecting their wheat to offer flour that is more suitable for artisan baking.

When working with strong flours, the dough requires higher absorption and sometimes a longer mixing time. During shaping, the dough will be difficult to stretch and will have the tendency to retract a little after being elongated. The bread might have a very round cross section, and sometimes, if strength is really excessive, cuts won't open and the volume of the bread will be penalized. Crumb can also be more dense than usual.

Bakers have several methods for decreasing strength and improving dough extensibility. During mixing, they can use more water to make the dough a bit softer than usual. An autolyse should also be used to allow the proteins to better absorb water and enough time for the protease to degrade some gluten bonds.

Decreasing the percentage of preferment is another way to cut down the strength of the dough. However, doing so also penalizes flavor and shelf life. A better option is to use more liquid preferment, as the softer consistency encourages enzyme activity during prefermentation. Reducing the number of folds or eliminating them altogether also reduces dough strength.

Preshaping and shaping will have to be done more gently by hand or by machine to avoid tightening up the gluten and to preserve some dough extensibility. Bread should be baked well proofed, and scoring can be done a little deeper.

Using additives in the dough is another option. Reducing agents such as deactivated yeast can be added to improve dough extensibility. This is particularly interesting for the production of long shaped breads like baguettes or the production of laminated dough. Deactivated yeast that is produced using only natural ingredients can keep the finished product free from chemicals. Other additives like L-cysteine can also be used to improve dough extensibility.

FERMENTATION TOLERANCE

Fermentation tolerance is generally related to wheat quality. Among the factors that can naturally affect wheat characteristics are climatic conditions, class of wheat (spring or winter, hard or soft), and varieties of wheat. Green flours will also often generate dough with poor fermentation tolerance.

For the artisan baker, two main characteristics should be taken into consideration when judging the quality of the protein. The first is the ability of the wheat to form the gluten of the dough, which will have a direct effect on the working properties or machinability of the dough. The second is the ability of the gluten structure to maintain its shape in a dough system during long fermentation times.

For a baker, a great tolerance to fermentation is a major advantage. A poor protein quality will generate dough that will start to degrade at the end of the final proof, providing a short window of opportunity to bake loaves before the dough starts to collapse. Good protein quality will create dough that can last a little longer, even if the loaves are ready to bake, without penalizing the quality of the final product.

It is difficult to know the fermentation tolerance of flour in advance because no scientific apparatus can assess this characteristic. The only way to know is to perform a baking test with different fermentation times and to compare the products obtained at the end of the tests. However, even if it is difficult to scientifically prove, a number of baking tests have demonstrated that in an artisan baking process winter wheats have better fermentation tolerance than spring wheats.

When fermentation tolerance is lacking, bakers have several ways to naturally improve it, including increasing the amount of preferment in the final dough, lengthening the first fermentation time, and giving an extra fold to the dough. Adding a small percentage of sourdough (10 to 15 percent based on the flour weight in the final dough) will increase fermentation tolerance in most cases without changing the flavor of the bread. The use of 15 to 30 ppm of ascorbic acid in the final dough will also have a positive effect.

ENZYME ACTIVITY

Enzyme activity, which is easily controlled by the miller, is very important for the fermentation process. Enzymes are responsible for breaking down complex sugars into a more digestible form that the yeast can use to generate fermentation. A lack or excess of enzymes in the flour can create problems during the baking process. Not enough will generate dough that lacks fermentation; too many will generate dough with fermentation that is too fast and bread with an excess of crust color. Flour rarely contains too many enzymes because farmers and millers carefully monitor the enzyme content of the wheat to ensure good keeping quality in grain elevators.

However, a lack of enzymes is fairly common. An easy way to know if enzyme activity is well balanced is to check the falling number. If it is between 250 and 300 seconds, the enzyme activity is correct. A higher falling number indicates a lack of enzyme. If no information is available on the flour, the baker needs to bake with the flour to monitor fermentation activity and crust color.

Adding some enzymes to the flour is possible at the bakery level. The addition of diastatic malt in the form of malted barley flour or syrup is the best and easiest way to accomplish this. Diastatic signifies that the enzymes are still active in the malt (as opposed to nondiastatic malt, which is generally used for flavor). In general, 0.5 to 1 percent of malt based on the total flour weight in the final dough is sufficient to achieve a normal fermentation activity and a normal crust color. A simple way to find out if the flour contains the correct amount of enzymes is to look at the ingredient list on the flour bag. If malted barley flour or enzymes are listed, then the miller has already corrected the flour in terms of enzyme activity.

Crust coloration can also be affected by the amount of preferment used in the dough. A large amount will use up a lot of the flour's simple sugar during prefermentation, generating lower caramelization during baking, even if the amount of enzyme is correct at the beginning of the process. In this case, adding some malt to the final dough can also reestablish normal crust color.

COLORATION

The color of the flour will have a direct effect on the color of the crumb of the bread. In general, a creamy color indicates good wheat pigmentation and is desirable for final product quality. A scientific test can provide some indication of flour coloration. The result is expressed as the B-value of the flour. Few mills report this characteristic on their spec sheets because it doesn't have an impact on flour baking performance and can vary depending on the age of the flour. The only way that the miller can control the flour coloration is by selecting wheat with certain pigmentation. However, because pigmentation is natural, only bleaching can change flour coloration.

Ash content in relation to the extraction used at the mill can also have an effect on the color of the flour. Flour with higher ash content will have a darker color, compared to flour with lower ash content.

FLAVOR

Just as different types of grapes can change the flavor of wine, so too can flour impact the flavor of the final product. This is another area where only a baking test can determine if the flavor of the bread will be acceptable. Even so, flour processed with the same baking process can lead to a wide range of flavor in the final product, from a sweet and complex flavor to one that is slightly bitter.

COMPENSATING FOR FLOUR DEFICIENCIES CONCLUSION

Because each mill uses its own wheat blend and milling process, bakers can multiply their chances for variation when they buy flour from different milling companies during the course of the year. With some technical knowledge and the potential use of an additive, maintaining flour consistency can be relatively easy. However, the challenge remains to maintain quality while respecting the nature and integrity of the ingredient and process. The more educated the baker is, the easier it will be to deal with changes in flour characteristics and to provide a consistent final product to the customer.

WORKING WITH SPECIALTY FLOURS

INTRODUCTION

In addition to regular bread flour, a variety of other types of flour milled from wheat or different grains can be used in baking. These flours allow bakers to diversify the production line and offer customers bread with different flavors and added nutritional value.

Because of the different nature of grains, some of these flours have a baking performance different from that of wheat flour. Higher bran content, particle size, and different protein quality and/or quantity are just a few of the factors that affect final dough characteristics. Many types of flours or meals come from a variety of seeds that can be used in baking. The goal of this section is to describe the main options available to the baker and how to adjust the baking process to achieve the best results in the final product.

MAIN TYPES OF SPECIALTY FLOUR

Whole Wheat Flour

Whole wheat flour is made from 100 percent of the wheat kernel, whereas white flour uses about 75 percent of the kernel. The granulation (extra fine, fine, medium, coarse, or extra coarse) will have a direct effect on the texture of the finished product. Products made with a coarse granulation will have a tendency to be denser with earthier, unrefined crumb texture. Finer granulation will provide more refined crumb texture with a smoother mouth feel. Sometimes, a small percentage of extra-fine whole wheat flour is used in formulas to give a slightly darker crumb color to the finished product that imitates traditional crumb characteristics.

Cracked whole wheat is not technically considered whole wheat flour, but it is sometimes used to add a touch of crunchiness in the finished product. If cracked whole wheat is used, it should be soaked in water until it becomes tender (in general, 3 to 4 hours before mixing). Longer soaking time must be avoided because the soaking water can trigger some enzymatic activity that can negatively affect the final dough. If a longer soaking time must be done, place the soaker in the cooler (colder temperatures slow down chemical reactions) or add salt to control the enzymatic activity. In general, 0.5 to 1 percent of salt is enough. The amount of salt used in the soaker needs to be considered when calculating the salt for the final dough.

Changes in the Baking Process The first noticeable change is the hydration of the dough. When whole wheat flour is used, a higher amount of water is necessary to maintain dough consistency. Whole wheat flour is very rich in bran that contains a lot of fiber and cellulose. By nature, it absorbs a large amount of water. In general, the higher the percentage of whole wheat flour is, the higher the required percentage of water will be. For large amounts of whole wheat flour (60 percent and more), the mixer should be stopped for about 10 minutes after the incorporation of all ingredients to allow the flour components to absorb water and become fully hydrated. This resting or swelling time allows the proteins to become better hydrated and form a better and stronger gluten structure.

In general, shorter mixing times are necessary to avoid overworking and tearing gluten made more fragile by the presence of large particles of bran in the dough. When working with 100 percent whole wheat flour, the double hydration technique can be used to maximize water absorption and gluten development. Add approximately 80 percent of the total quantity of water at the beginning of the mixing time; when the gluten is half developed, add the remaining water until optimum dough consistency and gluten development are achieved.

Fermentation activity happens much faster when whole wheat flour is used in a formula because bran is rich in minerals that are a natural nutrient for yeast. To compensate for the faster fermentation activity, a lower percentage of yeast should be used.

The high level of bran also creates more fragile dough with a tendency to become porous faster. For this reason, gas production and proofing should be kept under good control to avoid tears in the structure of the dough and overproofing. The use of preferment is advised to reinforce gluten development.

When working with a large amount of whole wheat flour in a dough, shorter shapes are better because gas production will be more concentrated in one point and will provide better loaf expansion during oven kick. Scoring can be done after shaping or before baking according to the percentage of whole wheat flour involved in the formula. Bread with a high level of whole wheat (70 percent and more) should be scored after shaping. The cut will retain better definition during baking, and also there is less chance of the loaf collapsing if it is slightly overproofed. Cuts perpendicular to the side of the loaf are preferable because they favor a rounder cross section and better bread development.

Whole wheat breads should be baked at a lower temperature [10°F (6°C) to 20°F (11°C) less] for a longer period of time. When possible, the damper or the oven door should be opened once the bread has reached its final coloration to maximize evaporation at the end of the bake. Because bran naturally absorbs and retains a lot of moisture, moisture that is not allowed to leave the bread will naturally migrate from the inside to the outside during cooling. Whole wheat bread must be cooled a bit longer before eating for the aroma to completely diffuse into the loaf.

Rye Flour

More information about rye flour is available in the online companion. To download information on ingredients, go to http://www.delmarlearning.com/companions/.

Changes in the Baking Process When using rye flour, higher hydration is necessary during mixing to maintain normal dough consistency. This is necessary due to the high level of fibers naturally present in the kernel of rye, as well as the presence of a larger amount of pentosans, which attract and retain a lot of water. Pentosans play a positive role in dough viscosity and help with the gas retention during proofing, but they create dough that is on the "sticky" side in that it is more difficult to work with and harder to clean from the hands.

When working with a high level of rye flour (50 percent and more), it is necessary to adjust the mixing time. More mixing should be done in first speed and less in second speed. The protein structure is very fragile so it should be protected as much as possible. In first speed, the mixer's hook should develop the gluten in a more gentle way. The reduction of mixing time in second speed protects the gluten from the more "aggressive" action of the hook and decreases the chances of damaging the dough structure or overmixing.

Rye is, by nature, a grain rich in minerals that speed up fermentation activity and require a lower amount of yeast to keep fermentation activity under control. In addition, it is necessary to work with a shorter fermentation time because rye dough doesn't have very good fermentation tolerance and becomes porous very quickly. The loaves can easily become overproofed if they are fermented too long.

The use of a preferment is advised in order to maximize the reinforcement of the gluten network. Because of its higher acidity level, sourdough physically optimizes the strength of rye dough and makes it more tolerant to fermentation. Even with the use of sourdough, some commercial yeast should be used in rye dough to speed up gas production and shorten fermentation time.

Like whole wheat dough, rye bread should be shaped as short loaves to favor optimum expansion during oven kick. Shaping must be done very gently to avoid damaging and tearing the gluten. Loaves should be scored right after shaping. If scored after proofing, the incision can excessively weaken the dough and cause the bread to collapse.

Rye bread should be baked at a lower temperature for a longer period of time to dry out the moisture retained into the dough as much as possible. Opening the door at the end of the bake will also ensure crispier crust characteristics. Just as with whole wheat dough, it is important to allow rye breads to cool down long enough before eating. If consumed too early, the crumb of rye bread will be very sticky and unpleasant to eat. A longer cooling time will also ensure better aroma diffusion and greater and more complex flavor.

Semolina Flour

More information about semolina flour is available in the online companion. To download information on ingredients, go to http://www.delmarlearning.com/companions/.

Changes in the Baking Process Basically all the changes that apply to the use of strong flour will apply to semolina or durum flour. The higher level of protein requires more hydration, and the higher number of gluten chains require longer mixing time to properly develop gluten structure. Autolyse is also necessary when a high percentage of semolina or durum flour is used. The resting time allows better hydration, creating dough with better viscosity and gluten structure. The autolyse also breaks down the strength of the flour and improves dough extensibility. Any percentage of semolina or durum flour can be used in the formula (up to 100 percent), but increasing amounts make adjustments even more important. No other major modifications need to be made to the rest of the baking process.

Spelt Flour

More information about spelt flour is available in the online companion. To download information on ingredients, go to http://www.delmarlearning.com/companions/.

Changes in the Baking Process Due to lower and more fragile proteins, spelt dough should be mixed for a shorter period of time, and a great deal of care must be taken to avoid overmixing. A good starting point is to reduce mixing by 50 percent, then to check the gluten structure and continue mixing if needed. Usually, when mixing with spelt flour, the mixing time can be reduced by 30 percent compared to a mixing time for dough using wheat flour. No autolyse is necessary as it can excessively weaken the already fragile gluten network.

Fermentation of spelt dough must also be carefully monitored. Carbon dioxide accumulation will stretch weaker and more extensible gluten strains quickly and easily. The lack of gluten elasticity also makes the dough intolerant to fermentation and very delicate to handle. Use of preferment is recommended to reinforce gluten bonding and to improve the strength of the dough.

By nature, spelt flours make bread that has the tendency to dry faster than regular bread. Despite the natural property of the protein to absorb less water, higher hydration is advised to improve the moistness of the crumb and overall shelf life. If the higher level of water weakens the dough too much, some punch and folds may be necessary during the first fermentation to reestablish the balance between extensibility and elasticity.

Other Grains

Quinoa flour, soy flour, amaranth flour, millet flour, buckwheat flour, oat meal, flax meal, and sunflower meal are just a few examples of other options available to the baker. When working with these specialty flours and meals, bakers should carefully monitor the amount incorporated into the final dough. Even if these ingredients are rich in proteins, these proteins are usually soluble in water and won't form any gluten structure. When used in large quantities in the final dough, they can excessively weaken the gluten structure of the regular flour and will produce very dense loaves with a flat cross section. A good starting point is to use about 20 percent of the total flour in specialty flour, but only a good deal of experimentation, taking into consideration all the factors mentioned previously regarding dough hydration, strength, shaping, and baking, will determine the exact amount to use to get the best balance between optimum dough characteristics, desired appearance, and flavor for the finished product. Note that when regular wheat flour is added to specialty flours, the products can't be identified as "wheat free."

Specialty Flours and Preferments

When the baker decides to work with specialty flour in a formula, all of it (or a percentage of it, depending on the amount) should be used in the preferment. There are two main reasons for this.

The first is that, during fermentation, a number of different aromas specific to the specialty flour are transformed by the yeast to develop finished products with very unique flavor. For example, sourdough culture elaborated with rye gives the bread a very complex and interesting spicy flavor, and a whole wheat–yeasted sponge creates sweet and nutty aromas with a hint of honey. The list of flavors that can be obtained is long and limited only by the imagination; nevertheless, the baker should consider all the precautions applicable to each specialty flour. For example, due to the faster fermentation activity of rye or whole wheat flour, it is necessary to work with a much smaller percentage of starter or commercial yeast when these flours are involved in a sourdough culture or yeasted preferment.

The second advantage is related to the rheological properties of the dough. When prefermented flour is added back to the final dough, it will automatically lower baking performance. By nature, specialty flours have lower protein quality or quantity. When combined with white flour, it is better to have the weaker flour weaken during prefermentation and keep the stronger white flour intact for the final dough. This will create dough with a higher-quality gluten structure and breads with nicer appearance and superior volume.

SPECIALTY FLOURS CONCLUSION

Regardless of the type of specialty flour used, the baker should still have a good understanding of the flour's functionality and adjust the baking process accordingly. Many steps, from mixing to baking, may have to be modified to achieve optimum bread quality. Bakers can develop an array of formulas that, when done correctly, will lead to a complete variety of day-to-day or special occasion breads.

DOUGH CONDITIONERS

INTRODUCTION

Dough conditioners are sometimes used in baking to improve the processing characteristics of the dough and the final product characteristics. Some of these optional ingredients are natural, others are chemical, and some are processed from microbial sources. Bread can be produced without any of these products, but when used properly, they can sometimes be helpful to compensate for flour deficiency or to achieve more consistent performance. The use of dough conditioners requires a solid understanding of their functionality and effect on the dough and finished products. While a large selection of dough conditioners is available to the baker, the active ingredients can be classified in the categories listed below.

Scaling very small amounts of dough conditioners can be a real challenge in a bakery environment. Instead of scaling the concentrated additives, an easy method is to disperse the ingredient in flour using the concept of ppm. For example, if we need to add ascorbic acid to a dough, we can make our own ppm blend by thoroughly combining 0.4 oz (10 g) of AA with 34.7 oz (990 g) of flour. Of this blend, 0.1 percent based on the total flour involved in the formula will bring 10 ppm of AA into the batch of dough, and 0.2 percent will bring 20 ppm. For a batch of dough made with 220 lb (100 kg) of flour, 3.5 oz (100 g) of the in-house dough conditioner will bring 10 ppm of AA.

OXIDIZERS OR OXIDIZING AGENTS

Description

Oxidizers work by fixing the oxygen incorporated into the dough during mixing. This triggers a chemical process that reinforces the bonding of gluten chains by creating disulfide bonds leading to a stronger gluten structure. Oxidizers must be used when the baker opts for a no-time dough process, where first fermentation time, which promotes natural oxidation and increases strength and tolerance, is absent. Oxidizers are also necessary when the gluten needs to be reinforced for a long fermentation time such as a retarding process.

If the rheological properties of the dough will be negatively affected by processes like freezing, the baker must use an oxidizer to build as much strength as possible at the beginning of the process. By improving the quality of the gluten structure and the ability of the protein to better retain water, the dough will be improved, and the surface will be a bit drier and easier to work with.

Some oxidizers react at the beginning of the process, when oxygen becomes available in the dough, and others react later on. Ascorbic acid, a synthesized product of vitamin C, is a fast-acting oxidizer. Too much will increase elasticity too much and penalize extensibility, making the dough difficult to work with by hand or with a machine. However, when properly dosed, ascorbic acid can be a great help when flour protein quality or quantity is deficient. By reinforcing the gluten structure, ascorbic acid will improve flour's baking performance by reestablishing the balance between elasticity and extensibility. In addition, fermentation tolerance of the dough will be improved. This can provide a great advantage for large production environments because they give the baker a larger window of opportunity to organize the baking schedule after final proofing.

Slow-acting oxidizers like potassium bromate start to work toward the end of the baking process. Their most beneficial action happens at the end of the final proof and during the oven kick. Due to this late action, the strength of dough isn't affected, and its workability properties are preserved. As mentioned previously in this chapter, potassium bromate can leave some residues in the finished baked product that could represent a potential health threat. Despite still being allowed in most of the United States and in many countries, potassium bromate is being eliminated by a growing number of bakeries.

Fast oxidizers like azodicarbonamide are also sometimes added to the flour or are part of the composition of certain dough conditioners. These fast-acting oxidizing agents react right away in the process. In addition to its oxidizing properties, ADA is also described as a maturing agent that is sometimes used in freshly milled flour without any natural aging or maturation time. Ascorbic acid will also improve the baking performance of fresh flour, but not as much and as fast as ADA. Other oxidizers like calcium peroxide, potassium iodate, or calcium iodate are used in some countries for their fast oxidizing properties.

Usage Level

The US Food and Drug Administration regulates maximum oxidizer levels in its standards of identity; however, it is very difficult to recommend a precise quantity to use at a bakery level. The amount must be adjusted according to the process and the flour characteristics. However, some guidelines have been established.

If any first fermentation time (or prefermentation) is used in the process, a lower level or no dough oxidizer will be necessary. Fermentation will naturally provide sufficient maturation. The acidity produced during this step will also naturally reinforce the protein chains and create stronger bonds and gluten structure. In this case, a low level of ascorbic acid (preferable to potassium bromate) should be added to the dough, with 10 to 15 ppm typically a good starting point. A higher level of 20 to 30 ppm may be necessary if the flour proteins are not at optimum quality, or if the baker is looking to improve the fermentation tolerance of the dough. For no-time dough processes, a higher level (up to 100 ppm) must be used to compensate for the lack of dough maturation.

Ascorbic acid, a very powerful oxidizer, will start to react in the dough at levels as low as 5 ppm. To avoid any potentially negative effect on dough characteristics like extensibility, it is very important to precisely control the amount added. Tablets of AA can be commercially found and can provide an easy (but not as precise) way to add AA to the dough. The baker must know the concentration of AA per tablet because this will determine the number of tablets (or the size) to add to the final dough.

Effect on the Finished Product

Because the gluten bonds are stronger, and if dough extensibility is not penalized by an excessive amount of oxidizers, more carbon dioxide can be trapped during final proof and oven kick. This will lead to baked products with larger volume. In addition, because of greater expansion during oven kick, cuts will better and more consistently open. Since the bread will expand a bit more during baking, the crust will have the tendency to be thin, and crispiness will be improved after baking.

REDUCING AGENTS

Description

Reducing agents are used to reduce dough elasticity and improve extensibility. They act on the gluten in essentially the reverse of oxidizing agents. By removing oxygen, they inhibit the formation of disulfide bonds, creating a gluten network that is easier to stretch. These reducing agents are used to decrease mixing time and to improve dough flow and machinability. Although they have many applications in baking, their use is more justified when the baker wants to stretch dough while minimizing the stress and potential tearing of gluten that can affect gas retention and volume. For example, they are useful for laminated dough, pizza dough, and cracker dough, which need to be easily stretched without any shrinkage after cutting.

The baking industry's most common reducing agents are L-cysteine and deactivated yeast. L-cysteine has a chemical origin, whereas deactivated yeast (sometimes called nonleavening yeast) is manufactured with a base of regular baker's yeast that undergoes a specific process that deactivates the yeast cells. As a direct result of this deactivation, the yeast cells release a component called glutathione that contains gluten-reducing properties. A large advantage of this product is to keep the label of packaged breads cleaner, with fewer chemical additives.

Usage Level

The desired level of extensibility and finished product characteristics determine the amount of dough reducer, with stronger dough requiring more reducing agent.

The level of L-cysteine can range between 10 and 90 ppm based on the total flour. The level of deactivated yeast (0.1 to 1 percent) depends on the manufacturer, and the amount should be calculated based on the manufacturer's recommended level. Overdosage must be avoided because too much automatically generates a lack of strength and excess of extensibility.

Effect on the Finished Product

In addition to noticeably improving dough characteristics, reducing agents also have a positive effect on finished products. In the case of laminated dough, shrinkage and dough deformation are reduced or eliminated, ensuring a more consistent shape. The gluten's ability to trap more gas generates products of superior volume, better cell structure, and, when applicable, cuts with better openings. To a certain degree, autolyse during mixing time can achieve all of these benefits as well.

COMBINED ACTION OF REDUCING AGENTS AND OXIDIZERS

For optimum gluten development and dough processing performance, it is possible to combine reducing agents and oxidizers for certain applications. Oxidizers will create a better-quality and stronger-quality gluten structure. At the same time, the reducing agent will maintain its extensibility and workability and will create optimum final products. The goal of the baker is to find the appropriate dosage to maximize flour properties, baking processes, and desired final product characteristics.

EMULSIFIERS

Description

Emulsifiers are chemical or natural substances that are soluble at low concentrations in both water and fat. Their main function in a dough system is to better link water and the lipids naturally contained in the flour. As a result of this better molecular interaction, the dough has a stronger texture and is better able to withstand mechanical mixing. Some emulsifiers also have the beneficial effect of slowing down starch retrogradation, which reduces the crumb's firming process during the natural staling of bread. Emulsifiers can be used individually to improve strength or in combination to achieve both strengthening and softening effects.

Lecithin is a natural emulsifier that is mostly used for its crumb-softening effects. Diacetyl tartaric acid ester and mono- and diglycerides (DATEM) improve the strength of the dough with limited impact on the crumb of the bread. Sodium stearoyl lactylate (SSL) improves dough structure and softens the crumb. Other emulsifiers used in dough conditioners include calcium stearoyl lactylate (CSL), polysorbate 60, and mono- and diglycerides.

Usage Level

Emulsifier usage levels are determined by the quality of the flour and the desired final product characteristics. Lecithin and SSL are typically used at a level of 0.25 to 1 percent, and DATEM at approximately 0.1 to 0.5 percent.

Effect on the Finished Product

Due to their dough-reinforcing properties, emulsifiers generate bread with larger volume. Some emulsifiers also generate bread with a softer crumb and longer shelf life. An excess of emulsifier can negatively affect the crust by making it less crispy with a "cardboard" texture.

VITAL WHEAT GLUTEN

Description

For some applications, such as frozen dough, when using a combination of weak flours or flour of poor protein quality, vital wheat gluten can be added to the formula to reinforce the gluten structure and provide the necessary strength to the final dough. It is made with the insoluble portion of the protein of the flour that has been separated by washing out the rest of the other flour components and then dried. Vital wheat gluten contains about 75 to 80 percent of protein. It is used to increase the level of protein in the flour and to create a very strong gluten structure.

Usage Level

The percentage of vital wheat gluten (based on the total flour) should be calculated according to the required dough strength. Due to its high price, bakers try to limit the quantity of gluten to the required minimum level. Although the amount can range from 1 to 5 percent, 3 percent is a good average. When gluten percentage increases, dough hydration increases as well, due to the high water absorption of the protein. A level of gluten that is too high penalizes dough extensibility and can create some problems during shaping.

Effect on the Finished Product

Reinforced gluten structure is able to resist the natural dough degradation that happens with long fermentation. At the same time, it traps more fermentation gas and creates bread with superior volume. However, high levels of vital wheat gluten penalize crust crispiness and make it more leathery. Also, due the higher level of protein, the Maillard reaction that occurs during the final bake will be more intense, creating a crust with a redder color and a bitter aftertaste. For these reasons, it is best to limit or even avoid these ingredients if a golden, crispy crust is desired in the finished product.

YEAST NUTRIENTS

When water mineral content is lacking, yeast nutrients can be used in the final dough. These inorganic salts supply minerals in a readily usable form for the yeast and allow more consistent fermentation activity. This is an important aspect for a no-time dough process where fermentation activity must happen fairly quickly. For artisan and traditional baking, which generally involves long fermentation time, yeast nutrients are not necessarily needed.

ENZYMES

Description

Enzymes are large proteins that act as catalysts to speed reactions in a dough system. Although they are produced by plants, animals, or microorganisms, enzymes are not living organisms. Each enzyme is genetically coded to perform a specific transformation of a defined product, called a substrate, into a useful derived substance that will improve dough and finished product characteristics. Because they are highly active, only very small quantities of enzymes are needed. They are increasingly used to replace chemical ingredients and to perform other functions that cannot be accomplished with traditional dough conditioners. They enable the baker to preserve a label-friendly list of ingredients on final packaging.

Enzymes are named by attaching the suffix "ase" to the name of the substrate with which the enzymes react; for example, protease reacts with protein. Each enzyme has its own range of pH and temperature and performs best when placed within optimum conditions with sufficient time for reaction. Understanding the functions and characteristics of enzymes can help bakers to decide whether any enzymes are needed for a specific baking process and to use them more effectively when they are.

Main Classes of Enzymes Used in Baking

Amylase The function of amylase is to break down a portion of the starch naturally contained in the flour into dextrin, so it can be broken down into more simple sugars, including mactose and glucose. This enzyme is necessary to maintain good, lengthy, and constant fermentation activity by transforming complex molecules of starch into smaller fermentable sugars that yeast can use. Alpha-amylase and beta-amylase are already present at a natural state in the kernel of wheat. However, to avoid sprouting damage, their quantity is limited at the harvest stage. Millers and sometimes bakers typically supplement some amylase to compensate for this natural deficiency in the flour.

The two forms of amylase used to correct the indigenous concentration of the wheat are malt and fungal amylase. Malt is obtained by processing a cereal (usually barley or wheat) that has been allowed to sprout under specific conditions to increase its enzymatic activity. Malt naturally brings alpha-amylase to the flour when it is added at the mill or to the dough when it is added at a bakery level. Malt is used in two forms: diastatic malted flour in a powder form or diastatic malted syrup. Even though both perform equally well, malted flour is neater and easier to scale compared to malted syrup. In general, a good starting point is to use 0.5 percent. This can increase to 1 percent based on total flour weight. Too little malt will trigger slow fermentation activity and pale crust color, whereas excessive malt will make fermentation happen too quickly and will create a reddish crust color and a sticky crumb. Nondiastatic malt is also available to the baker, but its enzymatic power has been deactivated. It is only used to add a touch of sweetness and malted flavor in some formulas, but it does not have any effect on the enzymatic activity of the flour.

Some milling companies prefer to correct enzymatic activity with fungal amylases instead of malted flour because they provide a more controlled way to correct natural amylase's deficiency. Malt can contain other enzymes that are undesirable in certain cases. Malted flour also usually has enough light sweetness to attract insects. To minimize the risk of infestation, millers sometimes prefer the more neutral fungal amylase. There is no noticeable difference in baking between the use of malt and fungal amylase when used properly. Additional fungal amylases are sometimes added to dough conditioners to emphasize gas production and oven spring and to achieve bread of superior volume.

To improve shelf life, other forms of amylases that are resistant to higher temperature and work at later stages of the baking process are sometimes used. Their actions last longer compared to the heat-sensitive amylase contained in malt. They positively affect the structure of the starch and make it able to resist becoming firm during staling.

Glucoamylase **Glucoamylases** break down the dextrin chains generated by amylases into glucose sugar, which is easier for the yeast to process and improves yeast activity during fermentation. These enzymes are sometimes used to partially replace other sugars in the formula and to create a final product that is a bit leaner but retains a sweet flavor.

Protease Protease, which breaks down gluten-forming proteins in dough, provides the same function as a reducing agent. The improved dough extensibility allows gluten to stretch more and accumulate more gas, but enzymatic gluten degradation reduces dough tolerance. For this reason, these enzymes are not commonly used for bread baking.

Protease is more commonly used for lamination or thin sheeting applications like puff pastry, crackers, and pizza, as well as when shrinkage issues need to be corrected. It improves dough machinability and consistency in finished products.

Hemicellulase **Pentosans** or **hemicelluloses** are long-chained carbohydrate molecules that are naturally present in flour. These complex molecules can be described as gums and fiber supplements with very high water absorption power. Their function in a dough system is to attract and distribute water. The two types of pentosans found in cereals are soluble and insoluble. Soluble pentosans help bind water to the flour components, improving its rheological properties and viscosity. Insoluble pentosans attract and retain a lot of water that remains fixed. Insoluble pentosans strongly disturb the formation of the gluten network.

When hemicellulases (also called pentosanases) are added to dough, they break down the insoluble pentosans and transform them into soluble pentosans. This action naturally releases some water into the dough, improving gluten structure and workability. More gas will be trapped during fermentation, and bread will have a higher volume. In some countries, hemicellulase is added directly in the flour at the mill. They are also active ingredients in certain dough conditioners.

Glucose Oxidase **Glucose oxidase** converts glucose into gluconic acid, forming some hydrogen peroxide in the process. This component acts as an oxidizer and increases gluten strength. In some cases, glucose oxidase can replace chemical oxidizers like potassium bromate or ascorbic acid. Glucose oxidase oxidizes the AA to dehydroascorbic acid that modifies the gluten-forming protein, forming more links to increase dough strength and viscosity. All the benefits of oxidizers can be obtained with this enzyme.

Lipase Flour naturally contains some lipids, or molecules of fat, which impede the formation of the gluten during mixing by interfering with the protein. Adding lipases enzyme to a dough system will modify the structure of these naturally present lipids. As a result, gluten becomes more tolerant and dough has better baking performance. Some lipases also transform fat into emulsifiers. Although not as efficient, the same results can be obtained when SSL or DATEM are used. In general, the use of lipase is limited to lean dough. These enzymes are not used in formulas with dairy products or other types of fat because their reaction can create bad aromas that generate breads with off flavors.

Usage Level

It is very rare to use only one enzyme in a dough system. Typically, enzymes are blended into complex mixtures that provide more than one activity. Even if mixtures are sold under a standardized form of a single activity, "other side effects or secondary effects" may be obtained and create quality issues. Enzymes are also sometimes associated with other additives like ascorbic acid or emulsifiers to obtain the best synergy between component functions and optimum results.

Enzyme activity is measured in laboratories using analysis procedures that differ from bakery conditions. Activity measurement can also vary among enzyme suppliers. For these reasons, providing specific usage levels or recommended starting points is difficult. Baking tests should be conducted using the enzyme suppliers' recommended levels and in controlled conditions to finalize ideal enzymatic levels for ingredients, formulas, and baking processes.

FILLERS

Using one or a combination of pure active ingredients can be difficult at a bakery level, mainly because scaling such small quantities and blending them homogenously with the flour can be challenging. Most dough conditioners contain a cocktail of active ingredients that are typically diluted in fillers to ease the scale and avoid the formation of lumps. The fillers have no functionality in the dough system and do not affect dough or bread characteristics. The most frequently used fillers are flour, starch, and sometimes calcium sulfate.

DOUGH CONDITIONERS CONCLUSION

When choosing a dough conditioner, bakers with a good understanding of the function of each active ingredient can make the best choice for production and avoid adverse effects. It is also important to keep in mind that some of these additives are added at the mill, and it is not always necessary to add them again at a bakery level.

Additives and enzymes are very active and powerful substances that can affect dough characteristics, even at very low levels. For this reason, precision is essential when working with dough conditioners. A judicious combination of high-quality ingredients with an appropriate baking process remains the best way to produce high-quality products, and dough conditioners are completely optional. However, production constraints, ingredient quality, and lack of baker experience are a few reasons why the baker may opt for properly selected dough conditioners.

CHAPTER SUMMARY

Flour is a very simple ingredient, but, as seen in this chapter, its characteristics can largely affect the baking process. The properties of flours are influenced by the complex intricacy of the wheat growing cycle, milling process, and flour treatment. Millers and bakers must know how to control all these parameters in order to produce consistent bread on a day-to-day basis.

The advanced technical information in this chapter may not be used on an everyday basis at a bakery level, but it will be very helpful for bakers who want to better understand flour and experiment with more advanced baking processes.

KEY TERMS

- ❖ Alveograph
- ❖ Analytical data
- ❖ Arrival time
- ❖ Ash content
- ❖ Certificate of Analysis (COA)
- ❖ Departure time
- ❖ Dough conditioners
- ❖ Dough development time
- ❖ Emulsifiers
- ❖ Enrichment
- ❖ Falling number
- ❖ Farinograph
- ❖ Glucoamylases
- ❖ Glucose oxidase
- ❖ Maturation
- ❖ Mixing tolerance index (MTI)
- ❖ Oxidizers
- ❖ Parts per million (ppm)
- ❖ Pentosans (hemicelluloses)
- ❖ Product specification sheet (spec sheet)
- ❖ Reducing agents
- ❖ Stability

REVIEW QUESTIONS

1. **What is the purpose of a flour spec sheet? What are the main analytical data that it provides?**
2. **What information is provided by the alveograph and the farinograph?**
3. **What is the falling number?**
4. **What can be done to improve the fermentation tolerance of dough?**
5. **What are the main additives used in baking? What are their functions in a dough system and their effects on the finished products?**

chapter
7

ALTERNATIVE BAKING PROCESSES

OBJECTIVES

After reading this chapter, you should be able to

- control the alternative baking processes available to bakers.
- explain the par-baked bread process.
- explain the frozen dough process.
- explain the preproof frozen dough process.

ALTERNATIVE METHODS OF BAKING

Bakers have many choices in how to develop and bake their product. This chapter will introduce and explain several alternative baking processes that can produce a high-quality product using methods that influence the timing of fermentation, baking, cooling, storage, and distribution of the product. Alternative bread-baking processes provide convenience and variety to bakers and their customers. Par-baked bread, for example, allows end users to have "fresh" bread that is ready to serve or to sell in about 10 to 15 minutes, while frozen dough products allow bakers to limit the amount of production at the bakery. For example, some bakers may choose to bake their bread fresh every day and buy frozen Viennoiserie. Par-baked, frozen dough, and preproof frozen dough have vastly influenced the baking industry and have become common in many bakeries throughout the world. Regardless of the alternative process used, a good understanding of technique and proper equipment is required to ensure good results on finished products.

PAR-BAKED

Par-baked bread first appeared in the United States in the 1950s, under the name "brown and serve." Its primary market was the food service industry. In Europe, especially France, the par-baked process gained popularity in the 1990s and is typically used for French products like baguettes, demi-baguettes, and dinner rolls. (See Figure 7-1.)

Figure 7-1
Comparison of Par-Baked and Fully Baked Bread

At the same time, it became popular again in the United States for the distribution of artisan breads. The par-baked process is the only way to do a large distribution without using chemicals to preserve the freshness of the finished products.

PAR-BAKED PROCESS

Formulation

In the **par-baked process**, the dough is baked until the starch is gelatinized and the protein coagulates. At this point, the structure of the product is solid, and its volume is almost final. Par-baked breads are taken out of the oven when the crust is still a light beige color. Although any traditional formulation can be used for par-baked bread, the following special considerations should be taken:

- Preferment and/or a long first fermentation time should be used to obtain maximum flavor development.
- Dough hydration should be reduced to help the loaf maintain its structure after the first bake and to avoid sagging.
- If applicable, sugar levels should be lowered to minimize crust color in the first part of the bake and to prevent early removal from the oven, which will increase the risk of collapse.
- Fat content should be reduced to avoid excessive weakening of dough structure.

Any kind of specialty flour can be used in a par-baked formula, including whole wheat, rye, and spelt. The typical protein weakness in these flours is not a problem because the bread is baked until its final structure is set.

Mixing and Fermentation

No major changes should be made to the process during mixing and fermentation. The major advantage of the par-baked process is that dough produced with a short mix (which has a very fragile gluten structure) and long fermentation time can be par-baked easily. Like a regular baking process, preferments are recommended for optimum flavor development.

Dividing and Preshaping

The ability of par-baked products to maintain structure after the first bake is based on the weight, shape, and diameter of the dough pieces. For example, large round breads that weigh more than 1 lb (450 g), like boules or miches, won't usually par-bake well and will have the tendency to collapse. In addition to their large diameter, the large mass of dough will naturally trigger a slow setup of the internal structure of the bread, while the crust in the meantime will start to take. Too short of a first bake will result in a collapsed loaf, but baking until the internal structure is properly set will result in a crust that is too thick and dry and that can flake off during the second bake. The only way to successfully par-bake this type of product, without its collapsing, would be to increase the first baking time until the inside structure is just set enough and the crust is formed with a light coloration.

Preshaping should be done the usual way. Dough with a tendency to be on the weak side will benefit from a tighter preshaping to reinforce strength and create a finished product with a stronger and rounder cross section.

Resting and Shaping

Resting time and precautions for par-baked bread are the same as those for a regular baking process. Shaping, whether by hand or machine, is done the same way as for a regular baking process. Longer, narrower shapes are better than shorter and wider ones.

Proofing and Scoring

When par-baking, it is better to bake the dough when it is slightly underproofed. It is very important to avoid overproofing because this will create bread with a larger volume and a very fragile structure that will certainly collapse after the first bake. If the dough is a bit underproofed, scoring can be done a little bit deeper than usual to emphasize dough development and cuts opening.

First Bake

The first bake step is the only one that is unique to the par-baking process. The goal is to bake the product until its structure is set, the "skin" or the beginning of the crust is formed, and the crust is starting to color without browning. If crust formation is too advanced, two major problems can occur. First, the excessive loss of moisture during the first bake will dry the crust very quickly and cause it to flake off during the second bake. Second, so much moisture will be lost during the first bake that staling will take place much more quickly than normal.

Two baking curves are possible. For smaller loaves, a high temperature for a short period of time at the beginning of the bake will emphasize oven kick and bread development while preventing excessive browning. On the other hand, low temperature for a longer period of time will prevent browning but will negatively affect oven kick, final volume, and moisture.

The best approach, when the type of oven allows it, is to start at a high temperature to promote oven kick, and then to decrease the temperature for the rest of the baking time quickly. To achieve this temperature profile, tunnel ovens with separate temperature controls for the length of the oven are best. Deck ovens also work well because the direct contact between the dough and the deck naturally promotes the required oven kick. Unfortunately this contact also gives the bread a darker bottom and slightly higher moisture loss, which can compromise shelf life. When using a rack oven, the staging feature would allow the setting of different temperatures during the baking cycle.

Cooling

Normal cooling conditions that emphasize lateral support will work for par-baked breads, but because of their more fragile structure, they should not be stacked or they will sag and easily collapse.

Par-baked products do not have a thick enough crust to interfere with water evaporation from the crumb. Because of this, they are more likely to lose moisture during cooling. A temperature- and humidity-controlled room can help.

After Cooling

After cooling, par-baked bread can be processed fresh or frozen.

Fresh Par-Baked Bread The shelf life of fresh par-baked products is fairly limited. Depending on the formulation and the preferment used, they begin to dry and stale in an average of 2 days. Mold growth can also be an issue in humid climates. If par-baked bread is packaged and treated with a mixture of carbon dioxide and nitrogen, shelf life can be extended up to 10 weeks. New "under vacuum" air technology also allows long shelf life without freezing. In this relatively new process, the bread is cooled under specific conditions before being packaged and stored.

After being par-baked and cooled, bread is stored in shelved racks fitted with a protective cover. This prevents excessive drying due to ambient air movement and maintains the humidity in the racks. Because the structure of par-baked bread is so fragile, it should be transported in baking trays to avoid excessive stacking.

Frozen Par-Baked Bread Under specific conditions, par-baked products can be frozen. This process naturally stops the development of microorganisms and mold, as well as staling. Using the normal process, par-baked breads cool until the inside temperature reaches about 82°F (28°C). Then, they are placed in a blast freezer set at approximately −40°F (−40°C) using automatic conveyor belt or wired racks for better temperature distribution. The **blast freezer** is used to freeze products quickly, minimizing the dryness and ice crystal formation inside products. Because the maximum rate of bread staling occurs at temperatures from 40°F (4°C) to 50°F (10°C), it is very important to go through this critical zone as quickly as possible.

To retain moisture and preserve freshness after the second bake, par-baked bread that is warmer than 82°F (30°C) can be placed in a blast freezer. However, there are two significant drawbacks to this technique. The first is the higher cost of energy necessary to bring down the inside temperature of the bread. The second is the risk of creating excessive condensation and frost in the freezer, which will decrease long-term performance and increase maintenance.

Once the inside of the bread has reached 10°F (−12°C) to 0°F (−18°C), it is removed and packaged in plastic bags and cardboard boxes. It is important to limit the length of time the bread is in the blast freezer or excessive drying will occur. Packaging is a very important step for product quality. It protects the bread from drying and potential breakage, eases handling, and provides a way to display product information.

After they are properly packaged, par-baked breads are placed in a holding freezer at regular freezer temperature [0°F (−18°C)]. If the entire process from baking to freezing is respected, the shelf life of the bread in the holding freezer can be up to 7 to 10 weeks without any major loss of moisture.

Distribution Par-baked products defrost quite rapidly, which makes it important to transport them in trucks equipped to maintain freezer temperature. Even partial defrosting will result in condensation that can cause the fragile crust to flake off and can begin the staling process. Customers must store par-baked breads in a holding freezer until the second bake.

Second or Final Bake

During this final step, the crust temperature rises, the crust continues to form, and colorization begins due to caramelizing sugars and the

Maillard reaction. The crumb, which has already formed, will regain its freshness and take on characteristics very similar to freshly baked bread.

The biggest advantage of the par-baked process is that the end user can perform the final bake in any type of oven. For optimum results, ovens that inject steam in the bake chamber are preferable because they generate a shinier crust and prevent excessive moisture loss. When possible, par-baked bread should be placed on perforated sheet pans. Placing the breads directly on the oven hearth can create a dry, hard bottom crust that is not very pleasant to eat. Like bread baked with a traditional process, oven temperature depends on the type of oven and the size of the loaves. However, par-baked bread should be baked at a slightly higher temperature than normal [about 50°F (10°C) to 60°F (16°C) higher] and for a shorter period of time to avoid excessive drying of the crust and overall moisture loss.

Cooling

Even more than traditional freshly baked bread, par-baked bread must cool in perfect conditions to limit moisture loss and avoid dry and flaky crust.

PAR-BAKED CONCLUSION

The par-bake process is a compromise between frozen dough technology and traditional fresh baking. Until the first bake, the first part of the process is the same as the traditional one, and the second part is comparable to a freezing process. The par-bake process has several advantages:

- The use of preferment and/or long fermentation time creates good product quality.
- The ability to use specialty flours like rye, spelt, or buckwheat allows bakers to offer a diverse product line to customers without having to mix specialty dough on a daily basis.
- Longer runs of the same product make the production process more efficient and lower labor costs.
- Par-baked breads can be ready to sell (at a bakery) or to serve (at a restaurant) within 15 to 30 minutes after being taken out of the freezer. This fast reaction time makes it possible to sell or serve fresh bread until the end of the day without a lot of leftovers.

It is important to mention that the par-baked process also has some major drawbacks. The primary ones are floor space and the major investment in equipment required to efficiently accomplish the process. In addition, if products are not frozen in a blast freezer or are not stored properly, quality will be highly compromised. Finally, the baker has to ensure that end users have enough training in proper baking times and temperatures to achieve optimum product quality.

FROZEN DOUGH

In the **frozen dough process**, dough can be frozen right after shaping. Once required for baking, it is defrosted and then proofed as usual. Even though this alternative baking process is not widely used in artisan or traditional baking, it can be a valuable tool in some circumstances. Low-volume, occasional, or weekend-only products can be made using this technique in order to avoid mixing small batches of dough daily or adding to the workload on the weekend, which is generally the busiest production time.

From the characteristics of the ingredients to the process itself, a few important points should be respected for best product quality. The two main issues for the freezing process are gas production by the yeast and gas retention in the dough. The baker must be able to keep yeast active enough to maintain its gas production. At the same time, the physical properties of the gluten must be retained to avoid degradation and to ensure that the dough will be able to retain carbon dioxide once the dough is defrosted and the fermentation process begins again.

FROZEN INGREDIENT SELECTION

Flour

Flour should be carefully selected for optimum protein quality. The gluten structure needs to be strong enough to cope with freeze-related damage such as the formation of ice crystals that interfere with gluten bonding, yet it must still be extensible enough to maintain good machinability properties. Protein content can be a little higher than flour used for the traditional baking process.

Water

Water content is usually lowered for frozen dough. The goal is to minimize the "free" water activity in the dough system and to reduce the formation of ice crystals. Also, stiffer dough will ensure that the dough holds its shape better during the freezing process.

Yeast

There are basically only two yeast options for the frozen dough process: fresh compressed yeast and yeast specially designed for frozen dough. Fresh yeast, the less expensive option, performs well only if freshly manufactured. If it is too old, it already contains a number of damaged cells, which are even more negatively affected by the freezing process. Also, due to the high moisture level of fresh yeast, its fermentation activity is quite unstable, especially after 5 to 7 days in the freezer.

Yeast specially designed for frozen baking is sold in a dry form. Its cells are specifically engineered to resist freezer temperatures for longer periods of time without excessive loss of gassing power. Due to its lower moisture content, it is more stable and will perform better in frozen dough systems. Frozen baking yeast, which should always be stored at freezer temperature, can be found in two versions: one for lean dough and one for high sugar dough. As with traditional baking, the choice of yeast depends on the percentage of sugar involved in the formula.

Active or dry instant yeast is not appropriate for a long freezing process because it contains more damaged cells than fresh yeast. These damaged cells release a component called glutathione, which weakens gluten structure and penalizes gas retention and dough strengthening, all of which create bread with a tendency to be flat after baking.

Salt

To strengthen the gluten and add a bit more flavor to compensate for the lack of first fermentation, the percentage of salt used can stay the same or increase to 2.2 to 2.5 percent. Any type of salt can be used. Higher levels of salt will also naturally slow down fermentation activity and gas production after mixing, which has a positive effect on bread quality.

Sugar

If any sugar is included in the formula, the amount should be slightly reduced to compensate for the very limited first fermentation. An excessive amount of residual sugar can lead to bread with a reddish crust color. At the same time, sugar can have a positive effect in the frozen dough process. Because of its hygroscopic properties, sugar reduces the level of "free" water in the dough system, reducing the formation of ice crystal and limiting the damage they can inflict on yeast cells.

Dough Conditioners

In most cases, dough conditioners must be used to reinforce the gluten structure. Chemical oxidizers, such as ascorbic acid, play a major role in compensating for the lack of natural oxidation due to minimal first fermentation. Where still allowed, potassium bromate can also be used.

In combination with the oxidizing agents, reducing agents are sometimes necessary to improve dough extensibility and machinability. L-cysteine, ascorbic acid, and deactivated yeast are the most commonly used reducing agents.

Vital wheat gluten is used to reinforce the natural protein levels in flour, when necessary. However, using over 5 percent of vital wheat gluten can trigger higher water absorption and increase the formation of ice crystals in the dough.

Other dough conditioners like emulsifiers, enzymes, or gums can be used to improve dough and bread characteristics. Emulsifiers generate stronger gluten that can retain more gas and create a softer and moister crumb. Gums greatly aid in gas retention but penalize crust crispness.

FROZEN DOUGH PROCESS

Mixing

When using the frozen method, the goal for the baker is to adjust the mixing process to obtain optimal gluten development. This intensive mix process automatically leads to stronger dough that has good gas retention and won't sag during thawing.

Dough consistency should be firm enough to limit water movement and strengthen the gluten enough to resist the damage that can occur during the freezing process. Longer mixing times that favor dough oxidation are preferred, but they have a negative effect due to the loss of carotenoid pigments, which in turn creates a whiter crumb color and inferior flavor. Salt can also be delayed to emphasize oxidation and create stronger gluten.

To compensate for the friction generated by longer mixing time and to limit gas production before freezing, water temperatures should be cold, and sometimes ice will need to be added. This is necessary to keep the dough temperature under control. The goal is to obtain a final dough temperature after mixing between 64°F (18°C) and 68°F (20°C). It is also possible, although not really convenient for large production, to keep flour temperature as cold as possible by storing some in the freezer.

Fermentation

To avoid the beginning of gas production, first fermentation should be very short or simply avoided. Because limited or no fermentation activity will happen due to the cold temperature of the dough, this step is more a resting time to relax the gluten before dividing.

First fermentation should be restricted as much as possible to avoid gas accumulation that will increase internal pressure and stress on the gluten. Also, fermentation byproducts like alcohol can create some damage in yeast cells, which can be detrimental to their survival during the freezing process and will create some problems during the final proofing stage after thawing.

Dividing

Dividing must be done as quickly as possible to preserve the dough from too high an increase in temperature, which can trigger fermentation activity. In general, high-speed volumetric dividers are used in large production settings. Smaller production environments should mix smaller batches of dough in order to process them as quickly as possible.

Resting Time

Resting time is another process that should be as short as possible to avoid or minimize fermentation activity. It should be long enough to relax the gluten and enable shaping without tearing. Sometimes, especially for lean dough without fat and sugar, a reducing agent should be added to the formula to improve extensibility without extended resting.

Cold dough has the tendency to dry out faster, so an extra effort should be made to protect it by covering it or working in an atmosphere humid enough to avoid the formation of dry skin on its surface.

Shaping

Shaping should be done as quickly as possible to limit fermentation activity and gas production.

Blast Freezing

Blast freezing, the crucial step in this process, should be done immediately after shaping to avoid excessive gas production. It is important to cool the dough as quickly as possible to minimize the size of ice crystals. A slower cooling rate will create larger ice crystals that can interfere with gluten strands and damage yeast cells, leading to several problems, including glutathione production. When the dough system starts its chemical activity after the freezing process, an excess of glutathione can cause excessive degradation to dough structure.

The temperature of the blast freezer should be set around −22°F (−30°C) to −31°F (−35°C). Lower temperatures can cause irreversible damage to the yeast and gluten structure. The amount of time required in the blast freezer depends on the following factors:

- The type of freezer. Mechanical blast freezers take about twice as long as cryogenic blast freezers. However, blast freezing that occurs too rapidly can break some protein chains, especially on the surface of the dough. This can result in some visible cracks on the surface of the crust on the final product.

- The initial temperature of the dough before it is introduced in the blast freezer.
- The weight and shape of the piece of dough. For example, an elongated dinner roll will freeze faster than a 1 lb (0.454 kg) boule.
- The temperature of the blast freezer when the dough is placed into it. If the blast freezer is prechilled, then the freezing process will be faster; if not, it might take longer.

Basically, the goal is to bring the inside or core temperature of the dough within the range of 10°F (−12°C) to 0°F (−18°C), which is, in general, the storage temperature of the dough after the blast freezing and packaging process.

Packaging

After the blast-freezing process, the frozen pieces of dough are immediately packaged. The packaging is very important to protect the dough from dehydration during storage at freezer temperatures, where the air has a lower level of relative humidity. To prevent loss of moisture, packaging material must be airtight but also flexible and temperature-resistant.

Storage

The temperature of a common **storage freezer** is in general 0°F (−18°C) to −4°F (−20°C), plus or minus a couple of degrees. At this temperature, and if blast freezing is done properly, the packaged pieces of frozen dough can be kept from 2 weeks to 6 months, depending on inventory, stock rotation, market (local or export), and size of the storage freezer. The level of yeast in the final dough must be adjusted to compensate for storage length because its fermentation power decreases over time. A very long storage time will require more than double the amount of yeast used in the traditional baking process.

Transportation

During distribution, it is very important to maintain cold temperatures to ensure that dough remains frozen. Products must be kept at 0°F (−18°C) to −4°F (−20°C) to avoid thawing or partial thawing, which can be detrimental for final product quality. The bags or boxes of products must be handled very carefully because shapes like long, thin baguettes can be very fragile.

Thawing

During the thawing process, a very high level of moisture will condense on the surface of the dough, greatly increasing its stickiness and making it impossible to proof on linen. For this reason, the only way to thaw and ferment frozen dough is on sheet pans, or on fluted trays for longer and thinner pieces.

Three thawing methods can be used to reactivate dough fermentation. The first one consists of removing the dough from the freezer and placing it on trays with sufficient space for proofing and heat distribution during baking. These trays are placed directly in the proof box set up to a maximum temperature of 85°F (29°C). This is a fast process that can be fairly inconsistent. The temperature on the surface of the dough will increase faster than the core. As a result, the yeast will tend to be more active on the surface than in the core, creating bread with low volume and dense crumb at the center.

The second thawing process consists of thawing the dough at room temperature and then placing it in the proofer. Like the first technique, this will create a fair amount of condensation and a greater rate of fermentation activity at the dough surface.

The third technique provides end users with much better results. After placement on trays, frozen pieces of dough are allowed to thaw in a proofer-retarder. The initial thawing stage happens at a low temperature [around 40°F (4°C)], which slowly brings the core of the dough from 0°F (−18°C) to 32°F (0°C). This method greatly reduces the condensation process at the surface of the dough and ensures an even temperature throughout.

The second part of the process is to switch the proofer-retarder at a warm temperature to raise the core temperature of the dough from 32°F (0°C) to 77°F (25°C) or higher until the dough has proofed enough and is ready to bake. During this step, humidity should be used to ensure proper proofing conditions. This technique creates optimum quality for frozen breads. If no proofer-retarder is available at the bakery, a combination of walk-in cooler and regular proofer will achieve the same results. The racks of dough should be manually transferred from the walk-in cooler to the proofer at the appropriate time.

Baking

Baking can be done in rack ovens or convection ovens equipped with steam generators. Deck ovens can be used, but because the dough is proofed in sheet pans or fluted trays, the benefit of direct contact with the hearth is lost. Oven temperature should be lowered a little to compensate for the higher level of residual sugar still present in the dough.

Frozen dough should be baked by qualified bakers who can properly thaw it, judge when it is correctly proofed, and obtain good scoring. Compared to par-baked breads that simply need rebaking, frozen dough requires more experienced staff at the end location. The location must also be better equipped, with a storage freezer, baking accessories like sheet pans or fluted trays, and a walk-in cooler and proofer (or proofer-retarder).

Other Options

The challenge is to protect frozen dough from too much degradation. The breakdown that can happen to protein chains is reversible by reshaping the dough to reform the gluten and restore its initial property of extensibility or elasticity. Another alternative is to blast freeze after preshaping using the same process and taking the same precautions. The blocks of dough are then thawed in the walk-in cooler and shaped. The reshaping will bring the gluten chains back together so that they reform a strong gluten structure. Another advantage of this technique is that the bread can be proofed on linen or cornmeal and baked directly on the stone of a hearth oven, providing better crumb and crust characteristics.

The frozen dough process can also be used with enriched dough like egg bread and brioche. The fat and eggs generally included in the formulas for these products protect gluten and add stability during the freezing and thawing processes. Egg bread or brioche-type dough can be frozen in its final shape or in blocks to be reshaped after the thawing process. When freezing enriched dough in blocks, then thawing and shaping, full strength is restored to the gluten and better-quality products are produced.

The frozen dough process can also be applied to laminated dough such as croissant and Danish because it allows the baker to obtain better efficiencies in production and labor costs. The dough can be frozen in blocks or after shaping. When freezing in blocks, it is preferable to fold the dough one time after the thawing process. This last fold will automatically rebind the gluten strands and create dough with better strength properties than it had before shaping. In both cases, final proofing and baking are done in the same way as in a traditional baking process.

FROZEN DOUGH CONCLUSION

Like most alternative baking processes, the frozen dough process improves quality of life and production efficiency for the baker, as well as provides a measure of convenience for the customer or end user. However, the ingredient, equipment, and transportation costs associated with this technique must be taken into consideration. The lower quality of products is another important drawback to consider. For very short freezing times of 1 to 3 days, a normal baking process with a slight increase in yeast and shorter fermentation time can lead to good results in small bakery settings.

A final drawback is that the number of products that can be frozen as dough is fairly limited. For example, natural sourdough bread dough won't freeze well because wild yeast and bacteria are very cold-sensitive and will be greatly damaged by a long stay in the freezer.

However, this technique can be very interesting for Viennoiserie (see Chapter 9). Croissants, Danish, and other breakfast items can easily be frozen at different points in the process with very little compromise in quality.

PREPROOF FROZEN

In addition to the par-baked and frozen dough process, this newer alternative baking process is now gaining popularity in both Europe and the United States where the demand for freshly baked products is growing. The **preproof frozen process** allows the final consumer to have freshly baked products available to sell or serve in about 20 minutes without thawing and proofing, and the necessity of having qualified bakers or a lot of equipment available. The degree of proofing can vary; however, 75 percent proofed is the most common. Since all of the work required to prepare preproof frozen products is completed at the bakery, the end user just needs to take the preproof frozen product out of the box, place it in the oven, and in 20 minutes have a sellable product.

PROCESS

The biggest challenge for the baker is to make sure that the gluten structure will be strong enough to retain the gas produced during the preproofing period, to retain it during the freezing process, and be able to develop furthermore during the final baking of the dough. The type of flour, dough conditioner, and baking process are crucial for a successful preproofing process.

- Flour should have enough quality gluten. It does not necessarily need a lot of protein, but it does need good quality protein. Sometimes the addition of vital wheat gluten is necessary to obtain a gluten structure strong enough.
- The dough conditioner is in general a special blend of enzymes, oxidizers, and emulsifiers. Special gums are also used to improve dough viscosity and gas retention.
- The dough should be mixed to obtain optimum gluten development that will ensure a strong gluten structure. Undermixing or overmixing would be detrimental to the quality of the finished products because the gluten might collapse during the final bake of the product. The dough temperature at the end of mixing is crucial. A dough that is too cold could have difficult machinability properties, whereas a dough that is too warm could be too active in terms of fermentation activity and create an excessive amount of gas before the freezing process.
- After shaping, two possible processes can be applied depending on the technique and formula (percentage of yeast and dough conditioners) used.
- The products are placed in the freezer without any or very limited final proofing time. These products are designed to go directly to the oven, and the rising of the dough will happen at the beginning of the baking time.
- The products are egg washed (for breakfast pastries), proofed under specific conditions, and frozen. Then the products are packaged, stored, and delivered to the final customers. The end users just need to take the product out of the freezer, place it on a sheet pan, and bake it.

PREPROOF FROZEN CONCLUSION

The big advantage of this technique is that it is very convenient, requiring very limited equipment at the level of the end user (the oven is the only necessary piece of equipment).

But due to the lack of first fermentation time or the difficulty in involving some preferment in the formula (an excess of gas production might penalize the process), the quality of the bread produced with this technique is definitively lower compared to the regular baking process or the par-baked process. Monitoring the amount of chemicals used is also very important when applying this technique. However, the quality could be acceptable for breakfast pastries, but only when fabricated with good quality butter and eaten as fresh as possible. Hotels and restaurants, as well as coffee shops that bake frequently, are in general great customers of breakfast pastries made with the preproof frozen technique. Transportation and frozen storage are also critical points that must be respected in order to maintain the properties of the product during that delicate phase of the process.

CHAPTER SUMMARY

Par-baked, frozen dough, and preproof frozen processes are great alternatives for the baker. Each technique has its own advantages and drawbacks in term of production and product quality. Also, each process requires a great deal of precision and attention to the baking step to ensure that the quality of the final product does not suffer. The cost of these alternate baking processes is also higher because special equipment such as a blast freezer and a storage freezer should be used. Due to the lack of qualified bakers, more and more baked products are being made using these techniques.

KEY TERMS

- ❖ Blast freezer
- ❖ Frozen dough process
- ❖ Par-baked process
- ❖ Preproof frozen process
- ❖ Storage freezer

REVIEW QUESTIONS

1. **What are the advantages of the par-baked technique?**
2. **Why is blast freezing necessary when working with a par-baked process and a frozen dough process?**
3. **Why can't long first fermentation time be used in a frozen dough process?**
4. **What are the advantages of freezing dough in blocks?**
5. **What are the advantages and limitations of the preproof frozen dough technique?**

chapter
8

BREAD FORMULAS

AN INTRODUCTION TO BREAD FORMULAS

The formulas in this book express the procedures by which to create the product. While reading the formula sheets from top to bottom, the necessary steps are stated in the order that the process requires. These formulas are written for production purposes, but they can very easily be understood if you wish to make only a few loaves. Most formula are written to show the original or total formula by which the preferment and final dough are derived. These are considered simple formulas. Formulas that require a sourdough culture or a feeding process are considered complex; therefore, the original or total formula is not shown. In the following discussion, we break down a simple formula to show how preferments are derived. We also break down a complex formula to show how a sourdough culture relates to the original formula and the final dough. The sourdough formulas are written with the assumption that the baker has a sourdough culture (refer to Figure 4-6 on page 91 for how to create a sourdough culture). Considering that the formulas are written for production purposes, the final formula for the sourdough product is stated in a sequence that follows the steps necessary to create the product. The following discussion should provide you with the tools you need to read and comprehend the format of these formulas. This objective list will refer to those portions of the text that are necessary to understand before you begin to make the product. You should read the text and review baker's percentages (Appendix B) before trying to make any of the products in this book.

HOW TO READ A BREAD FORMULA SHEET

- Understand that the formulas are written to be followed from beginning to end and that the steps provide the sequence of events that will allow you to prepare and make your product.
- Formulas with prefermented items (sponge, poolish, prefermented dough) show the preferment formula first, then the Final Dough Ingredients, with the Total Formula Ingredients showing where the preferment and final values are derived.
- Any formula that has a preferment shows the percentage of the preferment. The percentage is based upon the amount of flour taken from the Total Formula to make the preferment.
- The term *starter* refers to a portion of a sourdough culture that is mixed in a feeding process as stated in the formula.
- The term *levain* refers to a fully mature sourdough culture that is to be used in the Final Dough.
- A "stiff" or "liquid" starter refers to the sourdough culture's hydration.
- If the sourdough culture is anything other than a white bread flour-based culture, then the formula will state as such.
- DDT is desired dough temperature. (Refer to Chapter 3, page 57 on how to calculate water temperature to arrive at the proper DDT.)
- Rh represents the percentage of relative humidity, which allows for the proper humidity level to proof any bread product. If a humid environment is not available, consider and avoid factors that may begin to dry the surface of the product, such as a dry heat source or a draft.
- Hydration may vary with the quality and moisture content of the flour.
- Mixing times are not stated (refer to Chapter 3, pages 68–70); rather the mixing procedure is stated knowing that mixing times will vary according to the type of mixer (planetary mixers generally take longer for dough development than do spiral mixers), the hydration of the product, the type of flour being used, and the amount of dough being mixed.
- While mixing, the dough's consistency—being soft, medium soft, medium, or stiff—has been stated; this allows the baker to understand the flour's hydration not the absolute water calculation (meaning the baker adds or subtracts the scaled water according to the proper dough consistency the baker wishes to achieve).
- All formulas are presented with dry instant yeast (DIY). If you need to convert to fresh yeast, use this conversion: DIY × 2.5 = Fresh Yeast.
- First fermentation may also be referred to as bulk time or floor time.
- Second fermentation may also be referred to as bench time or rest time.
- If mixing a small batch of dough, add approximately 20 percent extra time for first fermentation to compensate for a lower mass effect (refer to Chapter 4, page 109 to understand the mass effect).
- The bread flour listed in the formulas refers to low-protein bread flour, having approximately 11 to 12 percent protein.
- Time and temperature will vary from oven to oven and with the weight of the loaves.

HOW TO DEVELOP A SIMPLE FORMULA

We start with a straight dough formula when we need to develop a formula that has a preferment. We call these formulas simple formulas rather than complex formulas that have levain feedings as well as the possibility of prefermented items. (In more complex formulas that have levain feedings, the salt must be calculated based upon the total flour content, and the calculations become a bit more complex because the starters used to feed the levain have flour as an ingredient.) After an original formula is developed, the baker may then begin to calculate a preferment from that original formula.

Note: This example is written in one unit of measure to simplify the page. The kilogram (kg) is the chosen measurement for its ease of division. We could also use pounds measured as a decimal fraction just as easily. Always convert one unit of measure to another unit of measure with a decimal point value.

Baguettes With Poolish

	Total Formula		Poolish		Final Dough	
	Baker's %	Quantity	Baker's %	Quantity	Baker's %	Quantity
Bread flour	100	5.900 kg				
Water	67	3.950 kg				
Yeast	0.6	0.035 kg				
Salt	2	0.118 kg				
Poolish	—	—				
Total	169.6	10.000 kg				

When beginning to calculate a preferment from an original formula, the baker must choose what type of preferment is to be used (such as sponge, poolish, prefermented dough).

Once the type of preferment is chosen, the percentage of flour to be used in its making must be chosen.

In this case, 33% of the original formula's flour value is calculated: 5.900 × 33% = 1.980.

	Total Formula		Poolish		Final Dough	
	Baker's %	Quantity	Baker's %	Quantity	Baker's %	Quantity
Bread flour	100	5.900 kg	100	1.980 kg		
Water	67	3.950 kg	100	1.980 kg		
Yeast	0.6	0.035 kg	0.1	0.002 kg		
Salt	2	0.118 kg	—			
Poolish	—	—	—	—		
Total	169.6	10.000 kg		3.962 kg		

With this new value calculated, the preferment can be calculated. For this example, a poolish that is 100% water is calculated in relationship to the flour value taken for the preferment: 1.980 × 100% = 1.980.

Based on the flour value of the preferment, 0.1% yeast is then calculated: 1.980 × 0.1 = 0.002.

	Total Formula		Poolish		Final Dough	
	Baker's %	Quantity	Baker's %	Quantity	Baker's %	Quantity
Bread flour	100	5.900 kg	100	1.980 kg	100	3.920 kg
Water	67	3.950 kg	100	1.980 kg	50	1.980 kg
Yeast	0.6	0.035 kg	0.1	0.002 kg	0.9	0.033 kg
Salt	2	0.118 kg	—		3	0.118 kg
Poolish	—	—	—	—	101	3.962 kg
Total	169.6	10.000 kg		3.962 kg	254.9	10.000 kg

After the preferment calculations have been made the values of the components taken for the preferment are then subtracted from the Total Formula values to create the Final Dough values:

5.900 − 1.980 = 3.920 = Final Flour Value

3.950 − 1.980 = 1.980 = Final Water Value

0.035 − 0.002 = 0.033 = Final Yeast Value

0.118 − 0 = 0.118 = Final Salt Value

1.980 + 1.980 = 0.002 = 3.962 = Final Poolish Value

Since all percentages are based on the flour value of a formula, the percentages in the Final Dough column represent each component's percentage value in relationship to the Final Flour Value.

After the preferment has matured, it is then incorporated with the Final Dough ingredients, and the dough is mixed.

HOW TO READ AND DEVELOP A COMPLEX FORMULA

This book provides many formulas that have multiple preferments and sourdough feedings. These formulas are stated in a manner that allows the baker to follow a sequence that will create the final product. The formulas with sourdough feedings are not given the original or total formula from which they are derived for it would be a confusing page layout to provide that information. This section provides an example of a complex formula and an explanation on how to originate the values of a Total Formula and its relationship to the Final Dough.

Note: This example is written in one unit of measure to simplify the page. The kilogram (kg) is the chosen measurement for its ease of division. We could also use pounds measured as a decimal fraction just as easily. Always convert one unit of measure to another unit of measure with a decimal point value.

Caramelized Hazelnut Squares was chosen as the formula to examine due to its complexity of ingredients and multiple preparations. The formula has examples of prefermented items, two different levain feedings using two different starters for the feedings, as well as the addition of caramelized hazelnuts. With so many components to this formula, we have used multiple columns and rows in Figure 8-1 (see pages 182–183) to show the source of the preferments and levains. A color system is provided to show the sequence of ingredients from the Total Formula to the Final Dough Formula.

To understand the composition of the total ingredients and the relationship of these ingredients to their percentage composition, we must first understand the composition of the sourdough starters. Knowing that the sourdough starters involved have both flour and water, the baker must calculate these values into the total ingredients percentage to understand the total flour value, the total water value, and the total salt value. This is important to understand because all values of all formulas are based on total flour values. (See Figure 8-2.)

Figure 8-2

Example A: Calculating Values of Flour and Water

White Starter	%	Quantity
Bread flour	100	0.640 kg
Water	50	0.320 kg
Total	150	0.960 kg

The white starter is considered a "stiff" starter and its composition is 100 parts flour and 50 parts water for a total of 150 parts.

To calculate flour: [0.960 stiff starter (cell C14) / 150 parts] × 100 = 0.640 flour (cell C12).

To calculate water: [0.960 stiff starter (cell C14) / 150 parts] × 50 = 0.320 water (cell C13).

Note: The starter used to trigger fermentation is not listed as an ingredient; it is made with the same parts of flour and water, respectively (100% flour and 50% water).

Rye Starter	%	Quantity
Medium rye flour	100	0.290 kg
Water	120	0.350 kg
Total	220	0.640 kg

The rye starter composition is 100 parts flour and 120 parts water for a total of 290 parts.

To calculate flour: [0.640 rye starter (cell C17) / 220 parts] × 100 = 0.290 (cell C15).

To calculate water: [0.640 rye starter (cell C17) / 220 parts] × 120 = 0.350 (cell C15).

Note: The starter used to trigger fermentation is not listed as an ingredient; it is made with the same parts of flour and water respectively (100% flour and 120% water).

- The values of both the flour and water are then recalculated with the total formula values so that the water hydration and salt calculation at the chosen percentage is consistent throughout the formula.
- In this example, the addition of

White flour	80.000 kg + 0.640 kg	= 80.670 kg
Whole wheat flour	12.000 kg + 0	= 12.000 kg
Medium rye flour	8.000 kg + 0.290 kg	= 8.270 kg
Total flour		= 100.930 kg

- The desired percentage of salt in the final dough (based on total flour) is 2%.
- Salt now is calculated given the total flour values by including the flour values of each sourdough starter.

Total flour = 100.930 kg × 2% = 2.020 kg of salt.

- Salt needs to be calculated as a baker's percentage (based on flour used in formula without the flour involved in the 2 levain.

(2.020 × 100%) = 2.02 Now the percentage of salt is 2.02%.

Figure 8-1 Example of How to Break Down a Complex Formula

CARAMELIZED HAZELNUT SQUARES

Loaves	Weight	Total Dough
190	1.000 kg	190.000 kg

+ 9.270 kg of extra dough = 199.927 kg of dough total (cell C line 21)

USE FOR FORMULA DEVELOPMENT AND TROUBLESHOOTING							
	A	B	C	D	E	F	G
1					40%		80%
2	Total ingredients	Total values		White Sponge		Whole Wheat Sponge	
3		%	Quantity	%	Quantity	%	Quantity
4	Bread flour	80	80.000 kg	100	32.000 kg		
5	Whole wheat flour	12	12.000 kg			100	9.600 kg
6	Medium rye flour	8	8.000 kg				
7	*Flour pretotal*	*100*	*100.000 kg*				
8	Water	75	75.000 kg	60	19.200 kg	70	6.720 kg
9	Instant Yeast	0.25	0.250 kg	0.1	0.032 kg	0.1	0.010 kg
10	Salt	2.02	2.020 kg				
11	Malt	0.4	0.400 kg				
12	*Flour used in white starter*	*100*	*0.640 kg*				
13	*Water*	*50*	*0.320 kg*				
14	White starter	0.96	0.960 kg				
15	*Rye flour used in rye starter*	*100*	*0.290 kg*				
16	*Water*	*120*	*0.350 kg*				
17	Rye starter	0.64	0.640 kg				
18	White sponge	—	—				
19	Whole wheat sponge	—	—				
20	Caramelized hazelnuts	20	20.000 kg				
21	Total	199.27	199.270 kg	160.1	51.232 kg	170.1	16.330 kg

- Ingredients in italic (lines 7, 12, 13, 15, 16) are not scaled in the formula (they represent the ingredients used to make the starter). Note that some sourdough culture is necessary to initiate fermentation of the starter.
- The water and flour used in the two starters was taken into consideration when first determining total flour absorption and dough consistency. (See Example A in Figure 8-2). Generally, those amounts are so low that they are not part of calculation when determining flour absorption.
- To create sponge, see Example B in Figure 8-3.

	H	I	J	K
1		12%		100%
2	Stiff Levain		Rye Levain	
3	%	Quantity	%	Quantity
4	100	9.600 kg		
5				
6			100	8.000 kg
7				
8	50	4.800 kg	120	9.600 kg
9				
10				
11				
12				
13				
14	10	0.960 kg		
15				
16				
17			8	0.640 kg
18				
19				
20				
21	160	15.360 kg	228	18.240 kg

USE FOR PRODUCTION		
L	M	N
Final Dough Ingredients	Final dough values	
	%	Quantity
Bread flour	94.0	38.400 kg
Whole wheat flour	6.0	2.400 kg
Medium rye flour	0.0	0.000 kg
Total	*100.0*	*40.800 kg*
Water	85.0	34.680 kg
Instant yeast	0.5	0.208 kg
Salt	5.0	2.020 kg
Malt	1.0	0.400 kg
Stiff levain	37.6	15.360 kg
Rye levain	44.7	18.240 kg
White sponge	125.6	51.232 kg
Whole wheat sponge	40.0	16.330 kg
Caramelized hazelnuts	49.0	20.000 kg
Total	488.4	199.270 kg

- Cells E, G, I, and K on line 1 represents the chosen percentage of flour used in the preferment (prefermented flour).
- The percentage of ingredients involved in the total formula is based on the total of the three flours used in the formula (flour pre-total).
- The percentage of ingredients in the final dough is based on the flour to scale for mixing the final dough (they represent the total flour minus the quantity of flour used in the preferment).
- These percentages (column M) are important to easily increase or decrease dough yield in production.
- Note that total dough values are similar in cells C and N on line 21.

When creating a formula with a portion of the total formula becoming a prefermented item, the baker must choose a percentage of flour from the original flour components in which to ferment. Once a percentage of flour is chosen for the preferment, the flour value now becomes 100 percent, as if in its own separate formula. The ingredients to create each preferment, as shown in Figure 8-3, are now based upon that flour value and calculated according to the desired final preferment characteristics: consistency, fermentation time, and the like.

Figure 8-3

Example B: Choosing Percentage of Flour for Prefermentation

White Sponge	%	Quantity
Bread flour	100	32.000 kg
Water	60	19.200 kg
Yeast	0.1	0.032 kg
Total	160.1	

The chosen percentage of bread flour to be fermented is 40% [represented by the % row above the white sponge (cell E1)].

This value now becomes 100%, upon which all subsequent values are now based.

80.000 × 40% = 32.000 (cells C4 × E1 = E4)

32.000 × 60% = 19.200 (cells E4 × D8 = E8)

32.000 × 0.1% = 0.032 (cells E4 × D9 = E9)

Total Value = 51.232 (cells E4 + E8 + E9 = E21)

Whole Wheat Sponge	%	Quantity
Whole wheat flour	100	9.600 kg
Water	70	6.720 kg
Yeast	0.1	0.010 kg
Total	170.1	16.330 kg

The chosen % of whole wheat flour to be fermented is 80% [represented by the % row above the whole wheat sponge (cell G1)].

This value now becomes 100%, upon which all subsequent values are now based.

12.000 × 80% = 9.600 (cells C5 × G1 = G5)

9.600 × 70% = 6.720 (cells G5 × F8 = G8)

9.600 × 0.1% = 0.010 (cells G5 × F9 = G9)

Total Value = 16.330 (cells G5 + G8 + G9 = G21)

- After all preferment and levain feedings are devised, the values of each of their components are then subtracted from the Total Formula column and now comprise the ingredient values in the Final Dough Ingredients column.

Bread flour	80.000 − 32.000 − 9.600 = 38.400	(cells C4 − E4 − I4 = N4)
Whole wheat flour	12.000 − 9.600 = 2.400	(cells C5 − G5 = N5)
Medium rye flour	8.000 − 8.000 = 0.000	(cells C6 − K6 = N6)
Water	75.000 − 19.200 − 6.720 − 4.800 − 9.600 = 34.680	(cells C8 − E8 − G8 − I8 − K8 = N8)
Instant yeast	0.250 − 0.032 − 0.010 = 0.208	(cells C9 − E9 − G9 = N9)

- To make the product, all preferments and levain feedings must be processed according to instructions, and the Final Dough ingredients need to be scaled.
- After all this is done, the mature preferments and levains are incorporated with the Final Dough ingredients, and the dough is mixed.

HOW TO DEVELOP A FORMULA

- To develop a formula, the baker must first choose the ingredients for the bread: flour composition, hydration, salt, yeast (type of yeast, wild or commercial), sugars, fats, eggs, and added ingredients (such as fruits, nuts, seeds, etc.), among others.
- After choosing the ingredients, the baker must calculate the relationship of each ingredient in terms of the total flour content. With the flour total always being 100 percent, hydration, salt content, yeast content plus other ingredients will show a relationship to the flour as a percentage.
- After calculating total ingredients, the baker will then choose the style of fermentation (straight fermentation, prefermentation, or sourdough fermentation) and length of fermentation.
- After calculating the dough with ingredients and fermentation considerations, the baker then tests the formula by producing the newly developed bread.
- After the product is baked, the baker will consider the performance of the dough, the flavor profile, and the bread's aesthetics. At this point, the baker can manipulate the formula to achieve the desired product.

When a product is developed, the baker now must consider how to implement the procedures involved in creating the baked product. For production purposes, the formula sheet will have a Final Dough Ingredients column and the percentages that compose the final measurements. Those percentages are necessary so that a baker can increase or decrease the amount of dough desired for that day's production. Often a bakery will create a spread sheet that will do the calculations for each day's production.

Assorted Shapes of Baguettes

FORMULA

BAGUETTES

Now almost universally associated with France, the baguette is actually a derivation of an Old World Viennese recipe. Before the early 1900s, *boules* (round loaves) reigned supreme with the French, thus their word for baker: *boulanger.* Technology introduced early in the 20th century accelerated the baguette's rise to prominence in France, particularly in Paris. By the 1920s, most French bakeries were finally equipped with the steam ovens needed to create a proper baguette crust. The long, thin, more rapidly prepared baguette made an attractive alternative to the traditional boule. Over the years, the baguette became a symbol of France, but the quality of the original slowly waned with the introduction of whiter and whiter flours and less and less proofing time. In the 1990s, a revival took hold, and the baguette was reborn as bakers in France and all over the world returned to the values of traditional baking methods for this most rewarding of daily breads.

BAGUETTE, SHORT MIX, STRAIGHT

Final Dough Formula

Ingredients	Baker's %	Kilogram	US decimal	Lb & Oz		Test
Bread flour	100.00	2.625	5.787	5	12⅝	1 lb 2½ oz
Water	70.00	1.837	4.051	4	⅞	13 oz
Yeast (instant)	0.30	0.008	0.017		¼	½ tsp
Salt	2.00	0.052	0.116		1⅞	⅜ oz
Malt	0.50	0.013	0.029		½	⅛ oz
Total	172.80	4.536	10.000	10	0	2 lb

Yield: 13 [12 oz (0.350 kg)] loaves
Test: 2½ [12 oz (0.350 kg)] loaves

Process, Final Dough	
Mix	Short mix (soft consistency)
DDT	73°F (23°C) to 76°F (24°C)
First fermentation	3 hours with 2 to 3 folds
Divide	12 oz (0.350 kg)
Preshape	Light rectangle

Resting time	20 to 30 minutes
Shape	Baguette
Final proof	45 minutes to 1 hour at 80°F (27°C) at 65% rh
Scoring	5 to 6 scores
Steam	2 seconds
Bake	Deck oven, 22 to 25 minutes at 460°F (238°C)

BAGUETTE WITH POOLISH

% of Flour Prefermented 33%

Poolish Formula

Ingredients	Baker's %	Kilogram	US decimal	Lb & Oz	Test
Bread flour	100.00	0.875	1.930	1 14⅞	6⅛ oz
Water	100.00	0.875	1.930	1 14⅞	6⅛ oz
Yeast (instant)	0.10	0.001	0.002	<⅛	⅛ tsp
Total	200.10	1.752	3.862	3 13¾	12⅜ oz

Process, Poolish

1. Mix all the ingredients until well incorporated with a DDT of 70°F (21°C).
2. Allow to ferment 12 to 16 hours at room temperature [65°F (18°C) to 70°F (21°C)].

Final Dough Formula

Ingredients	Baker's %	Kilogram	US decimal	Lb & Oz	Test
Bread flour	100.00	1.777	3.918	3 14¾	12½ oz
Water	52.24	0.928	2.047	2 ¾	6½ oz
Yeast (instant)	0.70	0.012	0.027	⅜	⅛ oz
Salt	2.99	0.053	0.117	1⅞	⅜ oz
Malt	0.75	0.013	0.029	½	⅛ oz
Poolish	98.56	1.752	3.862	3 13¾	12⅜ oz
Total	255.24	4.536	10.000	10 0	2 lb

Yield: 13 [12 oz (0.350 kg)] loaves
Test: 2½ [12 oz (0.350 kg)] loaves

Process, Final Dough

Mix	Improved mix (medium soft consistency)
DDT	73°F (23°C) to 76°F (24°C)
First fermentation	1 hour
Divide	12 oz (0.350 kg)
Preshape	Light rectangle

Resting time	20 to 30 minutes
Shape	Baguette
Final proof	1 hour to 1 hour 15 minutes at 80°F (27°C) at 65% rh
Scoring	5 to 6 scores
Steam	2 seconds
Bake	Deck oven, 22 to 25 minutes at 460°F (238°C)

Total Formula

Ingredients	Baker's %	Kilogram	US decimal	Lb & Oz		Test
Bread flour	100.00	2.653	5.848	5	13⅝	1 lb 2¾ oz
Water	68.00	1.804	3.977	3	15⅝	12¾ oz
Yeast (instant)	0.50	0.013	0.029		½	⅛ tsp
Salt	2.00	0.053	0.117		1⅞	⅜ oz
Malt	0.50	0.013	0.029		½	⅛ oz
Total	171.00	4.536	10.000	10	0	2 lb

BAGUETTE WITH PREFERMENTED DOUGH

% of Flour Prefermented 30%

Prefermented Dough Formula

Ingredients	Baker's %	Kilogram	US decimal	Lb & Oz		Test
Bread flour	100.00	0.796	1.754	1	12⅛	5⅝ oz
Water	65.00	0.517	1.140	1	2¼	3⅝ oz
Yeast (instant)	0.60	0.005	0.011		⅛	⅛ tsp
Salt	2.00	0.016	0.035		½	⅛ oz
Total	167.60	1.334	2.940	2	15	9⅜ oz

Process, Prefermented Dough

1. Mix all the ingredients until well incorporated with a DDT of 70°F (21°C).
2. Allow to ferment 1 to 1½ hours at room temperature [65°F (18°C) to 70°F (21°C)].
3. Then refrigerate overnight.

Final Dough Formula

Ingredients	Baker's %	Kilogram	US decimal	Lb & Oz	Test
Bread flour	100.00	1.857	4.094	4 1½	13⅛ oz
Water	69.29	1.287	2.836	2 13⅜	9⅛ oz
Yeast (instant)	0.46	0.008	0.019	¼	¼ tsp
Salt	2.00	0.037	0.082	1¼	¼ oz
Malt	0.71	0.013	0.029	½	⅛ oz
Prefermented dough	71.83	1.334	2.940	2 15	9⅜ oz
Total	244.29	4.536	10.000	10 0	2 lb

Yield: 13 [12 oz (0.350 kg)] loaves
Test: 2½ [12 oz (0.350 kg)] loaves

Process, Final Dough

Mix	Improved mix (medium consistency)
DDT	73°F (23°C) to 76°F (24°C)
First fermentation	1 hour
Divide	12 oz (0.350 kg)
Preshape	Light rectangle
Resting time	20 to 30 minutes
Shape	Baguette
Final proof	1 hour to 1 hour 15 minutes at 80°F (27°C) at 65% rh
Scoring	5 to 6 scores
Steam	2 seconds
Bake	Deck oven, 22 to 25 minutes at 460°F (238°C)

Total Formula

Ingredients	Baker's %	Kilogram	US decimal	Lb & Oz	Test
Bread flour	100.00	2.653	5.848	5 13⅝	1 lb 2¾ oz
Water	68.00	1.804	3.977	3 15⅝	12¾ oz
Yeast (dry instant)	0.50	0.013	0.029	½	⅛ tsp
Salt	2.00	0.053	0.117	1⅞	⅜ oz
Malt	0.50	0.013	0.029	½	⅛ oz
Total	171.00	4.536	10.000	10 0	2 lb

BAGUETTE WITH SPONGE

% of Flour Prefermented 30%

Sponge Formula

Ingredients	Baker's %	Kilogram	US decimal	Lb & Oz	Test
Bread flour	100.00	0.796	1.754	1 12⅛	5⅝ oz
Water	65.00	0.517	1.140	1 2½	3⅝ oz
Yeast (instant)	0.10	0.001	0.002	< ⅛	⅛ tsp
Total	165.10	1.314	2.896	2 14⅜	9¼ oz

Process, Sponge

1. Mix all the ingredients until well incorporated with a DDT of 70°F (21°C).
2. Allow to ferment 12 to 16 hours at room temperature [65°F (18°C) to 70°F (21°C)].

Final Dough Formula

Ingredients	Baker's %	Kilogram	US decimal	Lb & Oz	Test
Bread flour	100.00	1.857	4.094	4 1½	13⅛ oz
Water	69.29	1.287	2.836	2 13⅜	9⅛ oz
Yeast (instant)	0.67	0.012	0.027	½	⅛ tsp
Salt	2.86	0.053	0.117	1⅞	⅜ oz
Malt	0.71	0.013	0.029	½	⅛ oz
Sponge	70.76	1.314	2.896	2 14⅜	9¼ oz
Total	244.29	4.536	10.000	10 0	2 lb

Yield: 13 [12 oz (0.350 kg)] loaves
Test: 2½ [12 oz (0.350 kg)] loaves

Process, Final Dough

Mix	Improved mix (medium soft consistency)
DDT	73°F (23°C) to 76°F (24°C)
First fermentation	1 hour
Divide	12 oz (0.350 kg)
Preshape	Light rectangle
Resting time	20 to 30 minutes
Shape	Baguette
Final proof	1 hour to 1 hour 15 minutes at 80°F (27°C) at 65% rh
Scoring	5 to 6 scores
Steam	2 seconds
Bake	Deck oven, 22 to 25 minutes at 480°F (249°C)

Total Formula

Ingredients	Baker's %	Kilogram	US decimal	Lb & Oz		Test
Bread flour	100.00	2.653	5.848	5	13⅝	1 lb 2¾ oz
Water	68.00	1.804	3.977	3	15⅝	12¾ oz
Yeast (instant)	0.50	0.013	0.029		½	⅛ tsp
Salt	2.00	0.053	0.117		1⅞	⅜ oz
Malt	0.50	0.013	0.029		½	⅛ oz
Total	171.00	4.536	10.000	10	0	2 lb

FORMULA

CIABATTA WITH POOLISH

Named after its distinctive shape, ciabatta or "slipper" is one of the newest breads to come out of Italy, and one of the most popular in the United States. At least two Italian bakers claim to have invented ciabatta, and its origins have been traced to both the Lake Como region and Trentino. One theory holds that the rustic bread may have been the result of a baker adding too much water to a dough and then continuing the baking process anyway, which would have created a final result like the ciabatta: flat and long, with a large and open crumb cell structure. Ciabatta is often used in America to create rustic panini sandwiches.

% of Flour Prefermented 38%

Poolish Formula

Ingredients	Baker's %	Kilogram	US decimal	Lb & Oz		Test
Bread flour	100.00	0.951	2.097	2	1½	6¾ oz
Water	100.00	0.951	2.097	2	1½	6¾ oz
Yeast (instant)	0.10	0.001	0.002		<⅛	⅛ tsp
Total	200.10	1.903	4.196	4	3⅛	13½ oz

Process, Poolish

1. Mix all the ingredients until well incorporated with a DDT of 70°F (21°C).
2. Allow to ferment 12 to 16 hours at room temperature [65°F (18°C) to 70°F (21°C)].

Final Dough Formula

Ingredients	Baker's %	Kilogram	US decimal	Lb & Oz		Test
Bread flour	100.00	1.552	3.422	3	6¾	10⅞ oz
Water	61.29	0.951	2.097	2	1½	6¾ oz
Yeast (instant)	0.26	0.004	0.009		⅛	⅛ tsp
Salt	3.23	0.050	0.110		1½	⅜ oz
Oil	4.84	0.075	0.166		2⅝	½ oz
Poolish	122.64	1.903	4.196	4	3⅛	13½ oz
Total	292.26	4.536	10.000	10	0	2 lb

Yield: 13 [12 oz (0.350 kg)] loaves
Test: 2½ [12 oz (0.350 kg)] loaves

Process, Final Dough

Mix	Short mix
DDT	73°F (23°C) to 76°F (24°C)
First fermentation	3 hours with 2 to 3 folds
Divide	1 lb (0.454 kg)
Preshape	None
Resting time	None
Shape	Rectangular pieces, placed upon well-dusted linen
Final proof	30 to 45 minutes at 80°F (27°C) at 65% rh
Scoring	None
Steam	2 seconds
Bake	Deck oven, 35 minutes at 450°F (232°C)

Total Formula

Ingredients	Baker's %	Kilogram	US decimal	Lb & Oz		Test
Bread flour	100.00	2.503	5.519	5	8¼	1 lb 1⅝ oz
Water	76.00	1.903	4.194	4	3⅛	13⅜ oz
Yeast (instant)	0.20	0.005	0.011		⅛	⅛ tsp
Salt	2.00	0.050	0.110		1¾	⅜ oz
Oil	3.00	0.075	0.166		2⅝	½ oz
Total	181.20	4.536	10.000	10	0	2 lb

Note

Ciabatta is allowed to ferment in a large container; then, it is divided at one time all at the same height and size.

FORMULA

COUNTRY BREAD
(VARIETY OF DECORATIVE SHAPES)

Most of the shapes shown on page 195 were created by the *Compagnons du Devoir* (a guild of bakers in France that exists to this day). At the end of apprenticeship, *Compagnon* bakers took a graduation exam, which included a requirement to create breads with new shapes. The bakers' ideas were sometimes inspired by cultural observations, such as the Auvergnat, or, "bread covered with a hat shape," which reflected the fact that men in Auvergne at that time always wore hats. Other new shapes were purely from the artistic imagination of the bakers. Some of these shapes remain particular to a region of France and are still sold today. For example, the Tordu (crocked or twisted bread) and the Fendu (split) bread remain typical of the southwest of France, while the Fleur (daisy flower) continues to be popular in Lyon. The Charleston was named after the bread's many criss-cross indentations, which evoke dancing the Charleston. The Pain d'Aix, shaped like a bow tie, celebrated the students of the famous university of Aix en Provence (near Marseille), who wore a signature suit and a bow tie to school every day. The Tabatiere ("tobacco pouch") is still popular in Paris where people (used to) smoke cigarettes fervently.

% of Flour Prefermented 50%

Prefermented Dough Formula

Ingredients	Baker's %	Kilogram	US decimal	Lb & Oz	Test
Bread flour	100.00	1.321	2.912	2 14⅝	9⅜ oz
Water	65.00	0.859	1.893	1 14¼	6 oz
Yeast (instant)	1.20	0.016	0.035	½	⅛ tsp
Salt	2.00	0.026	0.058	⅞	⅛ oz
Total	168.20	2.222	4.898	4 14⅜	15⅝ oz

Process, Prefermented Dough

1. Mix all the ingredients until well incorporated with a DDT of 70°F (21°C).
2. Allow to ferment 1 hour at room temperature [65°F (18°C) to 70°F (21°C)].
3. Refrigerate overnight.

Final Dough Formula

Ingredients	Baker's %	Kilogram	US decimal	Lb & Oz		Test
Bread flour	90.00	1.189	2.621	2	9⅞	8⅜ oz
Medium rye flour	10.00	0.132	0.291		4⅝	⅞ oz
Water	71.00	0.938	2.068	2	1⅛	6⅝ oz
Yeast (instant)	1.20	0.016	0.035		½	⅛ oz
Salt	2.00	0.026	0.058		⅞	⅛ oz
Malt	1.00	0.013	0.029		½	⅛ oz
Prefermented dough	168.20	2.222	4.898	4	14⅜	15⅝ oz
Total	343.40	4.536	10.000	10	0	2 lb

Yield: 10 [1 lb (0.454 kg)] loaves
Test: 2 [1 lb (0.454 kg)] loaves

Process, Final Dough

Mix	Improved mix (medium consistency)
DDT	73°F (23°C) to 76°F (24°F)
First fermentation	1 hour
Divide	As needed
Preshape	Light ball
Resting time	20 to 30 minutes
Shape	Boule or batard
Final proof	1 hour 15 minutes at 80°F (27°C) at 65% rh
Scoring	Refer to the scoring charts in Chapter 5
Steam	2 seconds
Bake	Deck oven, 25 to 30 minutes at 460°F (238°C)

Total Formula

Ingredients	Baker's %	Kilogram	US decimal	Lb & Oz		Test
Flour	95.00	2.510	5.533	5	8½	1 lb 1¾ oz
Medium rye flour	5.00	0.132	0.291		4⅝	⅞ oz
Water	68.00	1.796	3.960	3	15⅜	12⅝ oz
Yeast (instant)	1.20	0.032	0.070		1⅛	¼ oz
Salt	2.00	0.053	0.116		1⅞	⅜ oz
Malt	0.50	0.013	0.029		½	⅛ oz
Total	171.70	4.536	10.000	10	0	2 lb

Note

This dough is often used to make the French regional shapes shown on the next page.

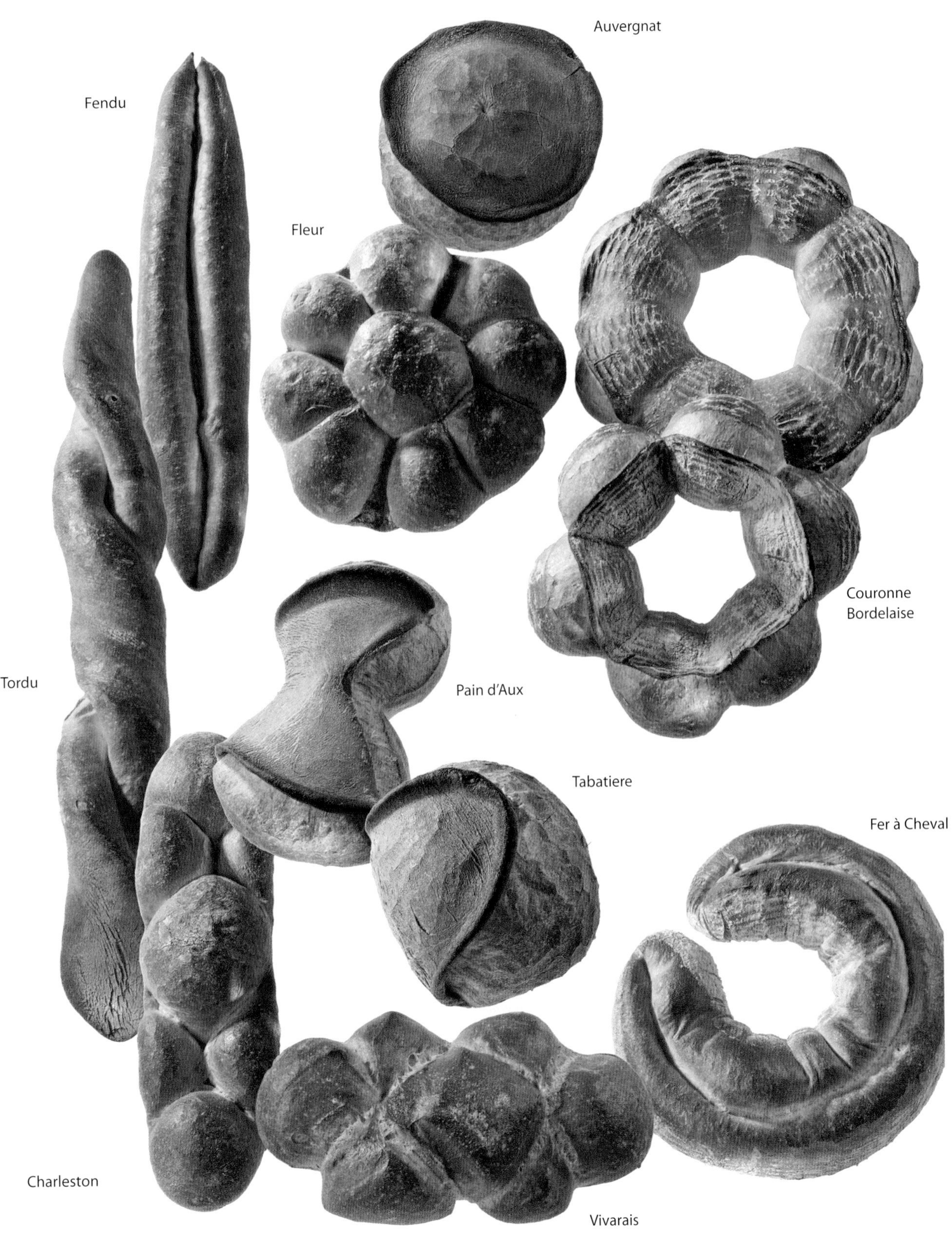

Country Bread

AUVERGNAT

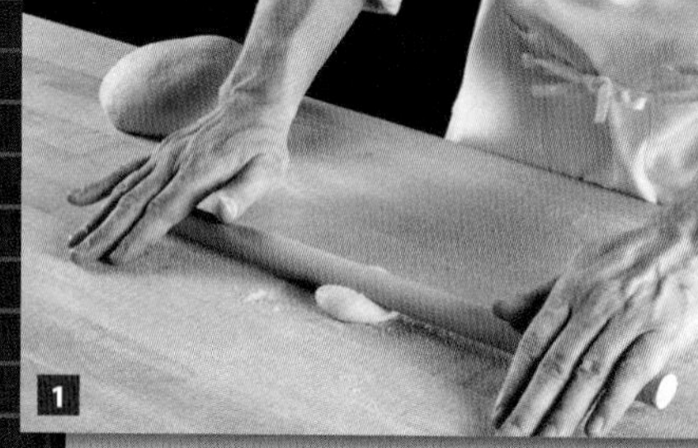

Roll out the smaller portion of dough.

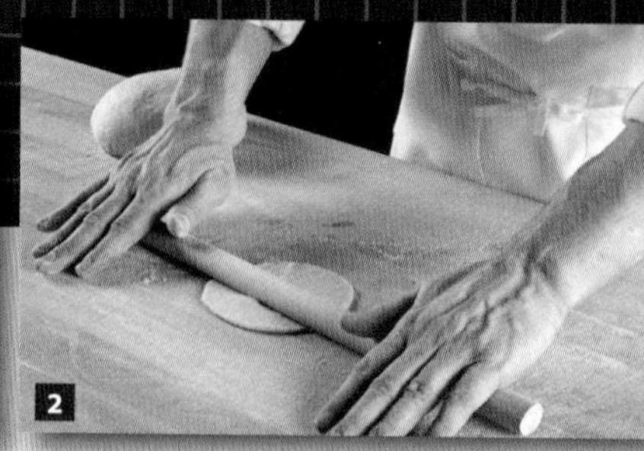

Roll to a round shape with an even thickness.

Brush the edge of the dough with oil.

Place the dough oiled side-down onto a larger portion of dough, and make a deep indentation on the center with one finger.

FLEUR

After preshaping into boule, create a deep indentation in the center with a skinny rolling pin.

Rotate the dough 90 degrees, and make another indentation.

Make two more indentations to create eight equal portions.

Place a small boule on the center.

TORDU

After preshaping into a long batard, sprinkle some flour on the center so that the dough does not stick to the rolling pin.

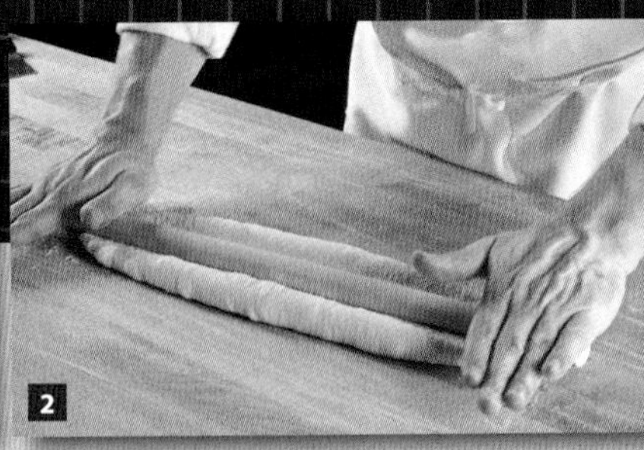

Roll out the center of the dough using a skinny rolling pin.

Roll the dough from your side away from you.

Twist the dough to create a Tordu shape.

FENDU WITH FER À CHEVAL VARIATION

After preshaping into a long batard, sprinkle some flour on the center so that the dough does not stick to the rolling pin.

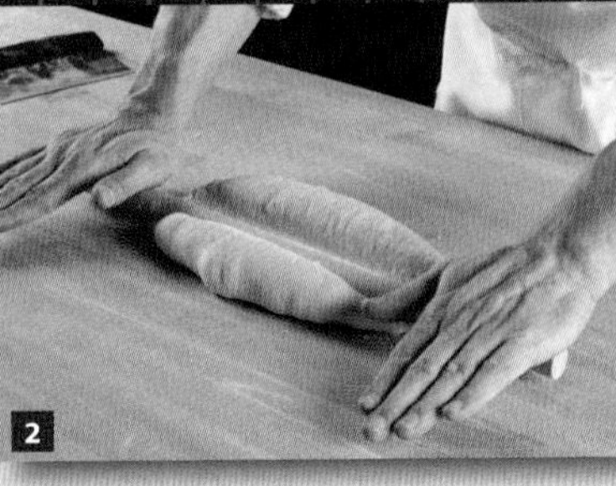

Roll out the center of the dough using a skinny rolling pin.

Roll the dough from your side away from you.

Hang the finished Fendu upside-down.

For Fer à Cheval, make the Fendu into a curved shape. Proof upside-down in a couronne basket.

VIVERAIS

After preshaping into a batard, cut an "X" shape on one side with a bench scraper.

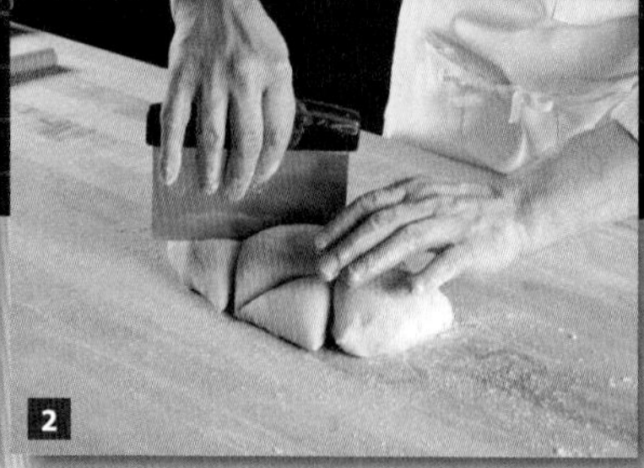

Next, cut one more "X" shape next to it.

Gather the whole piece with two hands, transfer onto a dusted couche, and place upside-down.

TABATIERE WITH PAIN D'AIX VARIATION

Preshape into a tight boule.

Once the dough is rested, roll out one side of the dough to about the length of the diameter of the boule.

Brush the edge of the rolled out part with oil.

The Tabatiere is finished.

For Pain d' Aix, split the Tabatiere from the center with a bench knife.

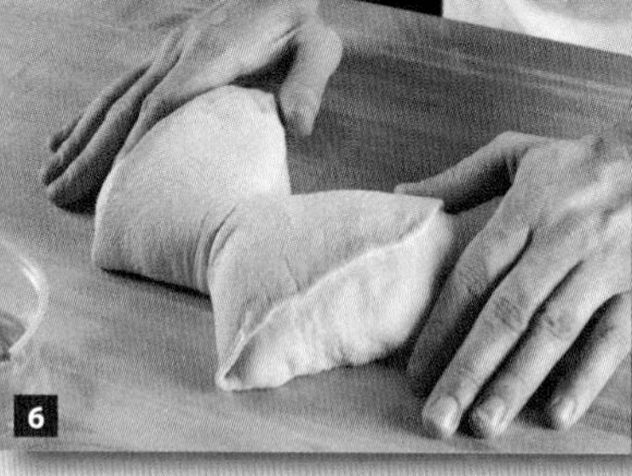

Adjust to create a bow-tie shape. Proof upside-down on a dusted couche.

CHARLESTON

After preshaping into a batard, sprinkle some flour on the center so that the dough does not stick to the rolling pin.

Make an "X" shaped indentation on one side of the dough with a skinny rolling pin

Make another "X" indentation on the other side of the dough.

The Charleston is finished. Proof on a dusted couche, upside-down.

COURONNE BORDELAISE

Roll out the center portion of the dough into a flat, even round. Place it on the center of a couronne basket.

Place six boules in the basket, seam-up.

Cut the center portion into six wedges.

Place the wedges onto the boules so that they stick to each other.

FORMULA

SOURDOUGH BREAD

One of the first forms of baking bread, sourdough breads have been baked for over 3,000 years (some research indicates that it might even be 5,000 years). The bread originated in the Nile River valley where wheat was first cultivated. Legend tells us that sourdough was probably invented accidentally, when some dough was forgotten and not baked. To avoid waste, the lady of the house (in charge of the bread production at that time) may have decided to keep the unbaked dough. The flour-based dough, the heat, and the humidity of the area would have created the perfect combination to trigger fermentation and the involuntary start of a sourdough culture, creating a final bread that was lighter, more digestible, and possessed better flavor. Thousands of years later, sourdough bread retains its essential goodness and simplicity, even as variations continue to be invented.

Sourdough Bread

SAN FRANCISCO SOURDOUGH BREAD

Levain Formula

Ingredients	Baker's %	Kilogram	US decimal	Lb & Oz	Test
Bread flour	95.00	0.348	0.767	12¼	2½ oz
Medium rye flour	5.00	0.018	0.040	⅝	⅛ oz
Water	50.00	0.183	0.404	6½	1¼ oz
Starter (stiff)	80.00	0.293	0.646	10⅜	2⅛ oz
Total	230.00	0.843	1.858	1 13¾	6 oz

Process, Levain

1. Mix all the ingredients until well incorporated with a DDT of 70°F (21°C).
2. Allow to ferment 12 hours at room temperature [65°F (18°C) to 70°F (21°C)].

Final Dough Formula

Ingredients	Baker's %	Kilogram	US decimal	Lb & Oz	Test
Flour	100.00	2.106	4.644	4 10¼	14⅞ oz
Water	72.80	1.534	3.381	3 6⅛	10⅞ oz
Salt	2.53	0.053	0.118	1⅞	⅜ oz
Levain	40.00	0.843	1.858	1 13¾	6 oz
Total	215.33	4.536	10.000	10 0	2 lb

Yield: 10 [1 lb (0.454 kg)] loaves
Test: 2 [1 lb (0.454 kg)] loaves

Process, Final Dough

Mix	Improved mix (medium consistency)
DDT	75°F (24°C) to 78°F (25°C)
First fermentation	3 hours with 1 fold
Divide	1 lb (0.454 kg)
Preshape	Light ball
Resting time	20 to 30 minutes
Shape	Boule or batard
Final proof	12 to 16 hours at 48°F (9°C) at 65% rh
Scoring	Refer to the scoring charts in Chapter 5
Steam	2 seconds
Bake	Deck oven, 35 minutes at 450°F (232°C)

SOURDOUGH WITH LIQUID LEVAIN

Levain Formula

Ingredients	Baker's %	Kilogram	US decimal	Lb & Oz		Test
Bread flour	95.00	0.390	0.859		13¾	2¾ oz
Medium rye flour	5.00	0.021	0.045		¾	⅛ oz
Water	100.00	0.410	0.905		14½	2⅞ oz
Starter (liquid)	60.00	0.246	0.543		8⅝	1¾ oz
Total	260.00	1.067	2.352	2	5⅝	7½ oz

Process, Levain

1. Mix all the ingredients until well incorporated with a DDT of 70°F (21°C).
2. Allow to ferment 24 hours at room temperature [65°F (18°C) to 70°F (21°C)].

Final Dough Formula

Ingredients	Baker's %	Kilogram	US decimal	Lb & Oz		Test
Bread flour	100.00	2.134	4.704	4	11¼	15 oz
Water	60.00	1.280	2.822	2	13⅛	9 oz
Yeast (instant)	0.10	0.002	0.005		⅛	⅛ tsp
Salt	2.50	0.053	0.118		1⅞	⅜ oz
Levain	50.00	1.067	2.352	2	5⅝	7½ oz
Total	212.60	4.536	10.000	10	0	2 lb

Yield: 10 [1 lb (0.454 kg)] loaves
Test: 2 [1 lb (0.454 kg)] loaves

Process, Final Dough

Mix	Improved mix (medium consistency)
DDT	75°F (24°C) to 78°F (25°C)
First fermentation	2 hours
Divide	1 lb (0.454 kg)
Preshape	Light ball
Resting time	20 to 30 minutes
Shape	Boule or batard
Final proof	1 hour 30 minutes to 2 hours at 80°F (27°C) at 65% rh
Scoring	Refer to the scoring charts in Chapter 5
Steam	2 seconds
Bake	Deck oven, 35 minutes at 440°F (227°C)

SOURDOUGH BREAD ONE FEEDING

Levain Formula

Ingredients	Baker's %	Kilogram	US decimal	Lb & Oz		Test
Bread flour	95.00	0.457	1.008	1	⅛	3 ¼ oz
Medium rye flour	5.00	0.024	0.053		⅞	⅛ oz
Water	50.00	0.241	0.530		8 ½	1 ¾ oz
Starter (stiff)	25.00	0.120	0.265		4 ¼	⅞ oz
Total	175.00	0.842	1.857	1	13 ¾	6 oz

Process, Levain

1. Mix all the ingredients until well incorporated with a DDT of 70°F (21°C).
2. Allow to ferment 24 hours at room temperature [65°F (18°C) to 70°F (21°C)].

Final Dough Formula

Ingredients	Baker's %	Kilogram	US decimal	Lb & Oz		Test
Bread flour	100.00	2.106	4.642	4	10 ¼	14 ⅞ oz
Water	72.80	1.533	3.379	3	6 ⅛	10 ⅞ oz
Yeast (instant)	0.10	0.002	0.005		⅛	⅛ tsp
Salt	2.53	0.053	0.118		1 ⅞	⅜ oz
Levain	40.00	0.842	1.857	1	13 ¾	6 oz
Total	215.43	4.536	10.000	10	0	2 lb

Yield: 10 [1 lb (0.454 kg)] loaves
Test: 2 [1 lb (0.454 kg)] loaves

Process, Final Dough

Mix	Improved mix (medium consistency)
DDT	75°F (24°C) to 78°F (25°C)
First fermentation	2 hours
Divide	1 lb (0.454 kg)
Preshape	Light ball
Resting time	20 to 30 minutes
Shape	Boule or batard
Final proof	1 hour 30 minutes to 2 hours at 80°F (27°C) at 65% rh
Scoring	Refer to the scoring charts in Chapter 5
Steam	2 seconds
Bake	Deck oven, 35 minutes at 440°F (227°C)

FORMULA

WHITE PAN BREAD (OPEN TOP AND PAIN DE MIE)

Pan breads—breads that are shaped, proofed, and baked in a pan—are the result of the baking industrialization that happened after World War II. Engineers of the time were looking for efficient ways to produce breads that could be baked uniformly and then quickly packaged, stored, and shipped throughout the United States. The pan breads of that time were usually baked with white flour and an accelerated baking process; the modern versions included here use healthier ingredients and higher quality methods.

% of Flour Prefermented 23%

Prefermented Dough Formula

Ingredients	Baker's %	Kilogram	US decimal	Lb & Oz		Test
Bread flour	100.00	0.574	1.266	1	4¼	4 oz
Water	68.00	0.373	0.823		13⅛	2⅝ oz
Yeast (instant)	0.50	0.003	0.006		⅛	⅛ tsp
Salt	2.00	0.011	0.025		⅜	⅛ oz
Total	170.50	0.962	2.120	2	1⅞	6¾ oz

White Pan Bread

Process, Prefermented Dough

1. Mix all the ingredients until well incorporated with a DDT of 70°F (21°C).
2. Allow to ferment 1 hour at room temperature [65°F (18°C) to 70°F (21°C)].
3. Then refrigerate overnight.

Final Dough Formula

Ingredients	Baker's %	Kilogram	US decimal	Lb & Oz		Test
Bread flour	100.00	1.922	4.237	4	3¾	13½ oz
Water	62.99	1.211	2.669	2	10¾	8½ oz
Salt	2.00	0.038	0.085		1⅜	¼ oz
Yeast (instant)	0.99	0.019	0.042		⅝	⅛ oz
Sugar	5.00	0.096	0.212		3⅜	⅝ oz
Butter	9.99	0.192	0.423		6¾	1⅜ oz
Milk powder	5.00	0.096	0.212		3⅜	⅝ oz
Prefermented dough	50.03	0.962	2.120	2	1⅞	6¾ oz
Total	236.00	4.536	10.000	10	0	2 lb

Process, Final Dough

Mix	Intensive mix (medium consistency)
DDT	73°F (23°C) to 76°F (24°C)
First fermentation	45 minutes to 1 hour
Divide	1 lb (0.454 kg)
Preshape	Light ball
Resting time	25 to 30 minutes
Shape	Batard in pan
Final proof	1 hour 30 minutes to 2 hours at 80°F (27°C) at 65% rh
Scoring	One down the center or no score
Steam	5 seconds
Bake	Convection oven, 35 minutes at 385°F (196°C)

Total Formula

Ingredients	Baker's %	Kilogram	US decimal	Lb & Oz		Test
Bread flour	100.00	2.496	5.503	5	8	1 lb 1⅝ oz
Water	63.45	1.584	3.492	3	7⅞	11⅛ oz
Salt	2.00	0.050	0.110		1¾	⅜ oz
Yeast (instant)	0.88	0.022	0.048		¾	⅛ oz
Sugar	3.85	0.096	0.212		3⅜	⅝ oz
Butter	7.69	0.192	0.423		6¾	1⅜ oz
Milk powder	3.85	0.096	0.212		3⅜	⅝ oz
Total	181.72	4.536	10.000	10	0	2 lb

Note

When shaping, allow the loaf to relax; then fold in both sides of the ball to the middle of the loaf, flatten, and roll up tightly. The objective is to create a tight crumb, so do not allow the dough to become too gassy and shape tightly. Place the loaf in the pan seam side down.

FORMULA

EGG BREAD

Somewhere between bread and brioche, egg bread was once baked for special occasion such as weddings or baptisms. Although it has earned is reputation as a celebration bread, this enriched dough can also be enjoyed every day.

% of Flour Prefermented 37%

Prefermented Dough Formula

Ingredients	Baker's %	Kilogram	US decimal	Lb & Oz		Test
Bread flour	100.00	0.880	1.940	1	15	6 ¼ oz
Water	68.00	0.598	1.319	1	5 ⅛	4 ¼ oz
Yeast (instant)	0.60	0.005	0.012		⅛	⅛ tsp
Salt	2.00	0.018	0.039		⅝	⅛ oz
Total	170.60	1.501	3.309	3	5	10 ⅝ oz

Process, Prefermented Dough

1. Mix all the ingredients until well incorporated with a DDT of 70°F (21°C).
2. Allow to ferment 1 hour at room temperature [65°F (18°C) to 70°F (21°C)].
3. Then refrigerate overnight.

Final Dough Formula

Ingredients	Baker's %	Kilogram	US decimal	Lb & Oz		Test
Bread flour	100.00	1.498	3.303	3	4 ⅞	10 ⅝ oz
Water	39.43	0.591	1.302	1	4 ⅞	4 ⅛ oz
Eggs	20.00	0.300	0.661		10 ⅝	2 ⅛ oz
Yeast (instant)	1.00	0.015	0.033		½	⅛ oz
Salt	2.00	0.030	0.066		1	¼ oz
Sugar	20.00	0.300	0.661		10 ⅝	2 ⅛ oz
Butter	15.08	0.226	0.498		8	1 ⅝ oz
Milk powder	5.08	0.076	0.168		2 ⅝	½ oz
Prefermented dough	100.19	1.501	3.309	3	5	10 ⅝ oz
Total	302.78	4.536	10.000	10	0	2 lb

Yield: 10 [15 oz (0.450 kg)] braided loaves
Test: 2 [15 oz (0.450 kg)] braided loaves

Process, Final Dough

Mix	Intensive mix (medium consistency)
DDT	73°F (23°C) to 76°F (24°C)
First fermentation	45 minutes to 1 hour
Divide	3 [5 oz (0.150 kg)]
Preshape	Light rectangle
Resting time	20 to 30 minutes
Shape	Braided
Final proof	1 hour 30 minutes to 2 hours at 80°F (27°C) at 65% rh
Scoring	Refer to the braiding chart at http://www.delmarlearning.com/companions/
Steam	2 seconds
Bake	Convection oven, 40 minutes at 335°F (168°C)

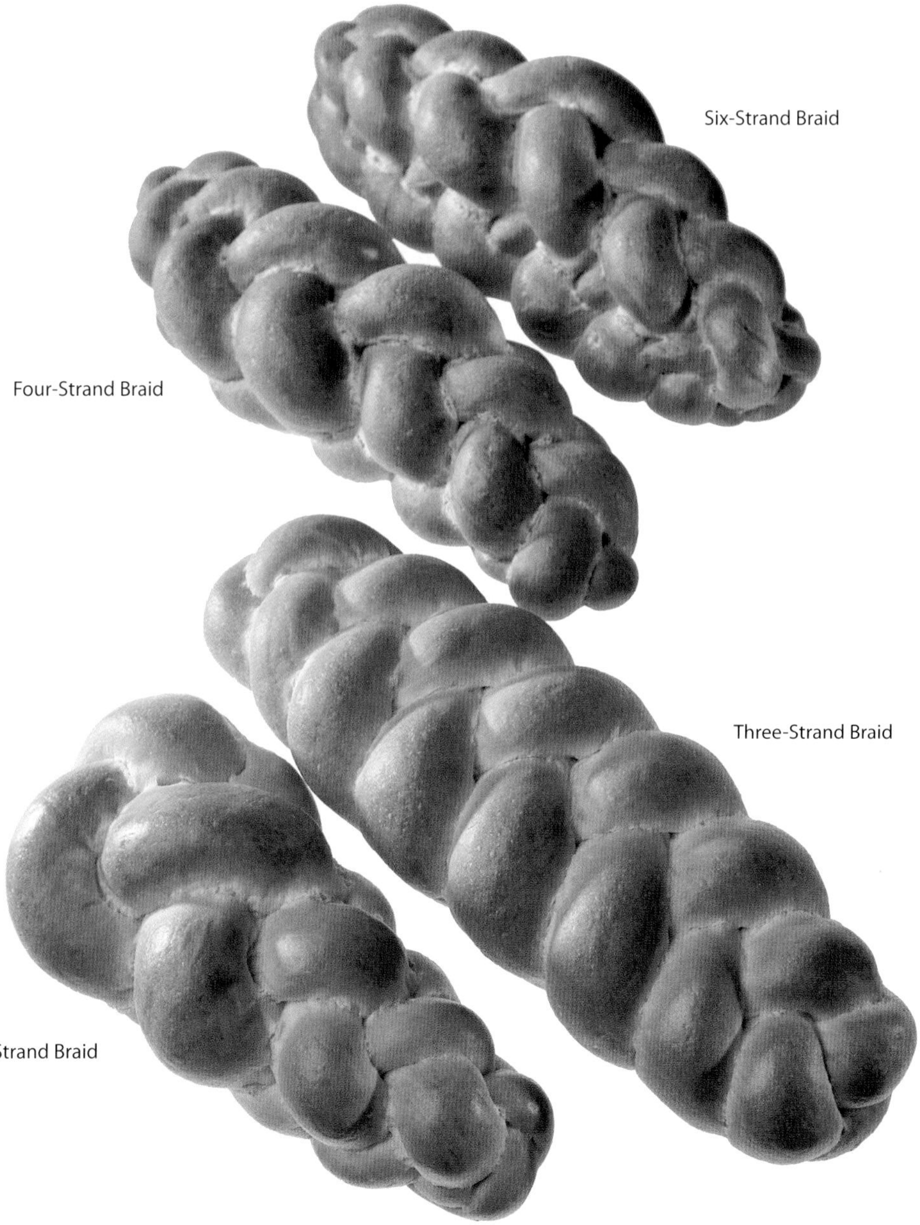

Egg Bread

Six-Strand Braid

Four-Strand Braid

Three-Strand Braid

Two-Strand Braid

Total Formula

Ingredients	Baker's %	Kilogram	US decimal	Lb & Oz	Test
Bread flour	100.00	2.378	5.242	5 3⅞	1 lb ¾ oz
Water	50.00	1.189	2.621	2 10	8⅜ oz
Eggs	12.60	0.300	0.661	10⅝	2⅛ oz
Yeast (instant)	0.85	0.020	0.045	¾	⅛ oz
Salt	2.00	0.048	0.105	1⅝	⅜ oz
Sugar	12.60	0.300	0.661	10⅝	2⅛ oz
Butter	9.50	0.226	0.498	8	1⅝ oz
Milk powder	3.20	0.076	0.168	2⅝	½ oz
Total	190.75	4.536	10.000	10 0	2 lb

FORMULA

100 PERCENT WHOLE GRAIN BREAD

By now, everyone knows the importance of whole wheat to the diet, and Americans have learned to seek out breads that offer unadulterated whole grains. This simple, yet undeniably delicious recipe for 100 percent whole wheat bread is the one of the more satisfying ways to enjoy a healthful portion of whole grains.

Levain Formula

Ingredients	Baker's %	Kilogram	US decimal	Lb & Oz	Test
Whole wheat flour	100.00	0.166	0.806	12⅞	2⅝ oz
Water	80.00	0.133	0.645	10⅜	2⅛ oz
Starter (stiff)	25.00	0.041	0.202	3¼	⅝ oz
Total	205.00	0.750	1.653	1 10½	5¼ oz

Process, Levain

1. Mix all the ingredients until well incorporated with a DDT of 70°F (21°C).
2. Allow to ferment 12 hours at room temperature [65°F (18°C) to 70°F (21°C)].

Soaker Formula

Ingredients	Baker's %	Kilogram	US decimal	Lb & Oz		Test
Flax seeds	15.25	0.086	0.189		3	⅝ oz
Sunflower seeds	15.25	0.086	0.189		3	⅝ oz
Sesame seeds	15.25	0.086	0.189		3	⅝ oz
Rolled oats	15.25	0.086	0.189		3	⅝ oz
Water	39.00	0.219	0.483		7¾	1½ oz
Total	100.00	0.562	1.240	1	3⅞	4 oz

Process, Soaker

Allow seeds to soak at least 2 hours.

Final Dough Formula

Ingredients	Baker's %	Kilogram	US decimal	Lb & Oz		Test
Whole wheat flour	65.00	1.218	2.686	2	11	8⅝ oz
Rye meal	25.00	0.469	1.033	1	½	3¼ oz
Medium rye flour	10.00	0.187	0.413		6⅝	1⅜ oz
Water	69.00	1.293	2.851	2	13⅝	9⅛ oz
Salt	2.70	0.051	0.112		1¾	⅜ oz
Yeast (instant)	0.30	0.006	0.012		¼	⅛ tsp
Soaker	30.00	0.562	1.240	1	3⅞	4 oz
Levain	40.00	0.750	1.653	1	10½	5¼ oz
Total	242.00	4.536	10.000	10	0	2 lb

Yield: 10 [1 lb (0.454 kg)] loaves
Test: 2 [1lb (0.454 kg)] loaves

Process, Final Dough

Mix	Improved mix (medium consistency) Add soaker after dough has been developed on first speed only until incorporated
DDT	73°F (23°C) to 76°F (27°C)
First fermentation	1 hour 30 minutes at 80°F (27°C) at 65% rh
Divide	1 lb (0.454 kg)
Preshape	Light ball
Resting time	25 to 30 minutes
Shape	Batard
Final proof	1 hour at 80°F (27°C) at 65% rh
Scoring	Refer to the scoring charts in Chapter 5
Steam	2 seconds
Bake	Deck oven, 30 to 35 minutes at 450°F (232°C)

FORMULA

SOURDOUGH WHOLE WHEAT BREAD

This sourdough whole wheat bread is the perfect blend of white and whole wheat flours, providing excellent nutritional value, with a lighter texture than 100 percent whole wheat bread.

Levain Formula

Ingredients	Baker's %	Kilogram	US decimal	Lb & Oz		Test
Bread flour	95.00	0.342	0.753		12	2⅜ oz
Medium rye flour	5.00	0.018	0.040		⅝	⅛ oz
Water	50.00	0.180	0.397		6⅜	1¼ oz
Starter (stiff)	80.00	0.288	0.634		10⅛	2 oz
Total	230.00	0.827	1.824	1	13⅛	5⅞ oz

Process, Levain

1. Mix all the ingredients until well incorporated with a DDT of 70°F (27°C).
2. Allow to ferment 12 hours at room temperature [65°F (18°C) to 70°F (21°C)].

Final Dough Formula

Ingredients	Baker's %	Kilogram	US decimal	Lb & Oz		Test
Bread flour	40.00	0.827	1.824	1	13⅛	5⅞ oz
Whole wheat flour	60.00	1.241	2.736	2	11¾	8¾ oz
Water	76.60	1.584	3.493	3	7⅞	11⅛ oz
Yeast (instant)	0.16	0.003	0.007		⅛	⅛ tsp
Salt	2.53	0.052	0.116		1⅞	⅜ oz
Levain	40.00	0.827	1.824	1	13⅛	5⅞ oz
Total	219.29	4.536	10.000	10	0	2 lb

Yield: 10 [1 lb (0.454 kg)] loaves
Test: 2 [1 lb (0.454 kg)] loaves

Process, Final Dough

Mix	Improved mix (medium consistency)
DDT	75°F (24°C) to 78°F (25°C)
First fermentation	2 hours
Divide	1 lb (0.454 kg)
Preshape	Light ball
Resting time	20 to 30 minutes
Shape	Boule or batard

Final proof	1 hour to 1 hour 30 minutes at 80°F (27°C) at 65% rh
Scoring	Refer to the scoring charts in Chapter 5
Steam	2 seconds
Bake	Deck oven, 35 minutes at 450°F (232°C)

FORMULA

SOURDOUGH RYE BREAD

Strongly flavored rye flour combined with equally recognizable sourdough flavor brings exceptional depth and character to sourdough rye bread, which is best enjoyed with seafood, fish, or soft cheese.

Levain Formula

Ingredients	Baker's %	Kilogram	US decimal	Lb & Oz	Test
Bread flour	95.00	0.348	0.767	12 ¼	2 ½ oz
Medium rye flour	5.00	0.018	0.040	⅝	⅛ oz
Water	50.00	0.183	0.404	6 ½	1 ¼ oz
Starter (stiff)	80.00	0.293	0.646	10 ⅜	2 ⅛ oz
Total	230.00	0.842	1.857	1 13 ¾	6 oz

Process, Levain

1. Mix all the ingredients until well incorporated with a DDT of 70°F (21°C).
2. Allow to ferment 12 hours at room temperature [65°F (18°C) to 70°F (21°C)].

Final Dough Formula

Ingredients	Baker's %	Kilogram	US decimal	Lb & Oz	Test
Bread flour	40.00	0.842	1.857	1 13 ¾	6 oz
Medium rye flour	60.00	1.263	2.785	2 12 ½	8 ⅞ oz
Water	72.80	1.533	3.379	3 6 ⅛	10 ⅞ oz
Yeast (instant)	0.12	0.003	0.006	⅛	⅛ tsp
Salt	2.53	0.053	0.118	1 ⅞	⅜ oz
Levain	40.00	0.842	1.857	1 13 ¾	6 oz
Total	215.45	4.536	10.000	10 0	2 lb

Yield: 10 [1 lb (0.454 kg)] loaves
Test: 2 [1 lb (0.454 kg)] loaves

Process, Final Dough

Mix	Improved mix (medium consistency)
DDT	75°F (24°C) to 78°F (25°C)
First fermentation	2 hours
Divide	1 lb (0.454 kg)
Preshape	Light ball
Resting time	20 to 30 minutes

Shape	Batard
Final proof	1 hour to 1 hour 30 minutes at 80°F (27°C) at 65% rh
Scoring	Refer to the scoring charts in Chapter 5
Steam	2 seconds
Bake	Deck oven, 35 minutes at 450°F (232°C)

FORMULA

SOURDOUGH MULTIGRAIN BREAD

The multiple flour and seed combinations found in the sourdough multigrain bread offer a healthy blend of minerals, vitamins, and other important nutrients for a well-balanced diet.

Levain Formula

Ingredients	Baker's %	Kilogram	US decimal	Lb & Oz		Test
Bread flour	95.00	0.365	0.804		12⅞	2⅝ oz
Medium rye flour	5.00	0.019	0.042		⅝	⅛ oz
Water	50.00	0.192	0.423		6¾	1⅜ oz
Starter (stiff)	80.00	0.307	0.677		10⅞	2⅛ oz
Total	230.00	0.883	1.947	1	15⅛	6¼ oz

Process, Levain

1. Mix all the ingredients until well incorporated with a DDT of 70°F (21°C).
2. Allow to ferment 12 hours at room temperature [65°F (18°C) to 70°F (21°C)].

Soaker Formula

Ingredients	Baker's %	Kilogram	US decimal	Lb & Oz		Test
Flax seeds	39.13	0.199	0.472		7½	1½ oz
Sunflower seeds	39.13	0.199	0.472		7½	1½ oz
Sesame seeds	39.13	0.199	0.472		7½	1½ oz
Rolled oats	39.13	0.199	0.472		7½	1½ oz
Water	100.00	0.508	1.207	1	3¼	3⅞ oz
Total	256.52	1.302	3.095	3	1½	9⅞ oz

Final Dough Formula

Ingredients	Baker's %	Kilogram	US decimal	Lb & Oz		Test
Bread flour	65.00	1.435	3.163	3	2⅝	10⅛ oz
Whole wheat flour	25.00	0.552	1.217	1	3½	3⅞ oz
Medium rye flour	10.00	0.221	0.487		7¾	1½ oz
Water	72.80	1.607	3.543	3	8⅝	11⅜ oz
Yeast (instant)	0.16	0.004	0.008		⅛	⅛ tsp
Salt	2.53	0.056	0.123		2	⅜ oz
Soaker	59.00	1.302	3.095	3	1½	9⅞ oz
Levain	40.00	0.883	1.947	1	15⅛	6¼ oz
Total	274.49	4.536	10.000	10	0	2 lb

Process, Final Dough

Mix	Improved mix (medium consistency) Add soaker on first speed after dough has been developed, only until incorporated
DDT	75°F (24°C) to 78°F (25°C)
First fermentation	2 hours
Divide	1 lb (0.454 kg)
Preshape	Light ball
Resting time	20 to 30 minutes
Shape	Batard
Final proof	1 hour to 1 hour 30 minutes at 80°F (27°C) at 65% rh
Scoring	Refer to the scoring charts in Chapter 5
Steam	2 seconds
Bake	Deck oven, 35 minutes at 450°F (232°C)

FORMULA

SOURDOUGH OLIVE BREAD

While still somewhat exotic in the United States, olive bread is typical of the Mediterranean regions where olives and thyme are familiar elements of the local cuisines.

Levain Formula

Ingredients	Baker's %	Kilogram	US decimal	Lb & Oz		Test
Bread flour	95.00	0.236	0.521		8⅜	1⅝ oz
Medium rye flour	5.00	0.012	0.027		½	⅛ oz
Water	100.00	0.249	0.548		8¾	1¾ oz
Starter (stiff)	80.00	0.199	0.439		7	1⅜ oz
Total	280.00	0.696	1.535	1	8⅝	4⅞ oz

Process, Levain

1. Mix all the ingredients until well incorporated with a DDT of 70°F (21°C).
2. Allow to ferment 12 hours at room temperature [65°F (18°C) to 70°F (21°C)].

First Dough Formula

Ingredients	Baker's %	Kilogram	US decimal	Lb & Oz		Test
Bread flour	100.00	2.321	5.118	5	1⅞	1 lb ⅜ oz
Water	63.00	1.462	3.224	3	3⅝	10⅜ oz
Yeast (instant)	0.10	0.002	0.005		⅛	⅛ tsp
Salt	2.30	0.053	0.118		1⅞	⅜ oz
Levain	30.00	0.696	1.535	1	8⅝	4⅞ oz
Total	195.40	4.536	10.000	10	0	2 lb

Final Dough Formula

Ingredients	Baker's %	Kilogram	US decimal	Lb & Oz		Test
Thyme	0.15	0.007	0.015		¼	¼ tsp
Olives	14.00	0.635	1.400	1	6⅜	4½ oz
Whole wheat flour	5.00	0.227	0.500		8	1⅝ oz
Dough	100.00	4.536	10.000	10	0	2 lb
Total	119.15	5.405	11.915	11	14⅝	2 lb 6⅛ oz

Toss olives with whole wheat and thyme.
Yield: 10 [1 lb (0.454 kg)] loaves
Test: 2 [1 lb (0.454 kg)] loaves

Process, Final Dough

Mix	Improved mix (medium consistency) At the end of mixing, add olives on first speed
DDT	75°F (24°C) to 78°F (25°C)
First fermentation	2 hours
Divide	1 lb (0.454 kg)
Preshape	Light ball
Resting time	20 to 30 minutes
Shape	Boule or batard
Final proof	2 hours at 80°F (27°C) at 65% rh
Scoring	Refer to the scoring charts in Chapter 5
Steam	2 seconds
Bake	Deck oven, 35 minutes at 450°F (232°C)

FORMULA

SOURDOUGH CHEESE BREAD

This modern take on the classic sourdough puts the cheese that people sometimes enjoy as an accompaniment to bread right inside the dough! Filling and fragrant, sourdough cheese bread can be a meal in itself.

Levain Formula

Ingredients	Baker's %	Kilogram	US decimal	Lb & Oz		Test
Bread flour	95.00	0.216	0.476		7⅝	1½ oz
Medium rye flour	5.00	0.011	0.025		⅜	⅛ oz
Water	100.00	0.227	0.501		8	1⅝ oz
Starter (liquid)	60.00	0.136	0.300		4¾	1 oz
Total	260.00	0.591	1.302	1	4⅞	4⅛ oz

Process, Levain

1. Mix all the ingredients until well incorporated with a DDT of 70°F (21°C).
2. Allow to ferment 12 hours at room temperature [65°F (18°C) to 70°F (21°C)].

Final Dough Formula

Ingredients	Baker's %	Kilogram	US decimal	Lb & Oz		Test
Bread flour	100.00	1.969	4.340	4	5½	13⅞ oz
Water	63.00	1.240	2.734	2	11¾	8¾ oz
Yeast (instant)	0.10	0.002	0.004		⅛	⅛ tsp
Salt	2.30	0.045	0.100		1⅝	⅜ oz
Levain	30.00	0.591	1.302	1	4⅞	4⅛ oz
Asiago, shredded	35.00	0.689	1.519	1	8¼	4⅞ oz
Total	230.40	4.536	10.000	10	0	2 lb

Yield: 10 [1 lb (0.454 kg)] loaves
Test: 2 [1 lb (0.454 kg)] loaves

Process, Levain

Mix	Improved mix (medium consistency) At the end of mixing, add cheese on first speed until incorporated
DDT	75°F (24°C) to 78°F (25°C)
First fermentation	2 hours
Divide	1 lb (0.454 kg)
Preshape	Light ball

Resting time	20 to 30 minutes
Shape	Boule or batard
Final proof	2 hours at 80°F (27°C) at 65% rh
Scoring	Refer to the scoring charts in Chapter 5
Steam	2 seconds
Bake	Deck oven, 30 minutes at 450°F (232°C)

FORMULA

MICHE

Miche is one of the oldest known breads and was once baked in communal ovens. The higher extraction flour currently used in the formula aims to duplicate the flour used by bakers in the old days when the milling process was not as refined. Sourdough, of course, is the fermentation process of this bread, providing characteristic flavor and a long shelf life.

First Feeding Levain Formula

Ingredients	Baker's %	Kilogram	US decimal	Lb & Oz	Test
High-extraction flour	100.00	0.202	0.446	7⅛	1⅜ oz
Water	120.00	0.243	0.535	8½	1¾ oz
Salt	0.60	0.001	0.003	<⅛	⅛ tsp
Starter (stiff)	10.00	0.020	0.045	¾	⅛ oz
Total	230.60	0.466	1.028	1 ½	3¼ oz

Process, First Feeding Levain

1. Mix all the ingredients until well incorporated with a DDT of 70°F (21°C).
2. Allow to ferment 16 hours at room temperature [65°F (18°C) to 70°F (21°C)].

Levain Formula

Ingredients	Baker's %	Kilogram	US decimal	Lb & Oz	Test
High-extraction flour	100.00	1.165	2.569	2 9⅛	8¼ oz
Water	120.00	1.399	3.083	3 1⅜	9⅞ oz
Salt	0.60	0.007	0.015	¼	¼ tsp
First feeding	40.00	0.466	1.028	1 ½	3¼ oz
Total	260.60	3.037	6.696	6 11⅛	5⅜ oz

Process, Levain

1. Mix all the ingredients until well incorporated with a DDT 70°F (21°C).
2. Allow to ferment 8 hours at room temperature [65°F (18°C) to 70°F (21°C)].

Final Dough Formula

Ingredients	Baker's %	Kilogram	US decimal	Lb & Oz		Test
Bread flour	60.00	0.790	1.742	1	11⅞	5⅝ oz
High-extraction flour	20.00	0.263	0.581		9¼	1⅞ oz
Medium rye flour	20.00	0.263	0.581		9¼	1⅞ oz
Water	10.00	0.132	0.290		4⅝	⅞ oz
Salt	3.80	0.050	0.110		1¾	⅜ oz
Levain	230.60	3.037	6.696	6	11⅛	5⅜ oz
Total	344.40	4.536	10.000	10	0	2 lb

Yield: 5 [2 lb (0.908 kg)] loaves

Test: 1 [2 lb (0.908 kg)] loaf

Process, Final Dough

Mix	Improved mix (medium consistency)
DDT	75°F (24°C) to 78°F (25°C)
First fermentation	15 minutes
Divide	2 lb (0.900 kg)
Preshape	Light ball
Resting time	20 to 30 minutes
Shape	Boule: 2 lb (0.900 kg)
Final proof	Retard overnight in a basket at 48°F (9°C)
Scoring	Diamonds
Steam	2 seconds
Bake	Deck oven, 45 to 50 minutes at 440°F (227°C)

FORMULA

PAIN DE BEAUCAIRE

Named after Beaucaire, a region in Southeastern France, the Pain de Beaucaire is one of the first breads to be made "free form," or not formally shaped. The bread is produced by placing two layers of dough on top of each other and then cutting with Râcle à Beaucaire, strips of dough that are baked side by side, giving this bread its unique appearance. Pain de Beaucaire was very popular until people started to prefer the lighter and crunchier baguette. However, this authentic regional bread is currently enjoying a resurgence as a new generation discovers its many appealing characteristics.

Levain Formula

Ingredients	Baker's %	Kilogram	US decimal	Lb & Oz	Test
Bread flour	95.00	0.334	0.736	11¾	2⅜ oz
Medium rye flour	5.00	0.018	0.039	⅝	⅛ oz
Water	100.00	0.352	0.775	12⅜	2½ oz
Starter (stiff)	60.00	0.211	0.465	7½	1½ oz
Total	260.00	0.914	2.015	2 ¼	6½ oz

Process, Levain

1. Mix all the ingredients until well incorporated with a DDT of 70°F (21°C).
2. Allow to ferment 8 hours at room temperature [65°F (18°C) to 70°F (21°C)].

Final Dough Formula

Ingredients	Baker's %	Kilogram	US decimal	Lb & Oz	Test
Bread flour	100.00	2.285	5.038	5 ⅝	1 lb ⅛ oz
Water	56.00	1.280	2.821	2 13⅛	9 oz
Yeast (instant)	0.10	0.002	0.005	⅛	⅛ tsp
Salt	2.40	0.055	0.121	1⅞	⅜ oz
Levain	40.00	0.914	2.015	2 ¼	6½ oz
Total	198.50	4.536	10.000	10 0	2 lb

Yield: 10 [1 lb (0.454 kg)] loaves
Test: 2 [1 lb (0.454 kg)] loaves

Process, Final Dough

Mix	Improved mix (medium consistency)
DDT	75°F (24°C) to 78°F (25°C)
First fermentation	1 hour 30 minutes
Divide	1 lb (0.454 kg)
Preshape	Light ball
Resting time	20 to 30 minutes
Shape	Batard
Final proof	2 hours at 80°F (27°C) at 65% rh
Scoring	None
Steam	2 seconds
Bake	Deck oven, 35 minutes at 450°F (232°C)

For Shaping

1. Make a paste with 1 lb (0.454 kg) of water and 3 oz (0.085 kg) of flour. Reserve.
2. After preshaping and the dough has relaxed, flatten out the dough to 1 ½ inch (5 cm) rectangular pieces and cut in half.
3. Brush the dough pieces with the paste mixture and cover with course bran.
4. Divide the pieces into long strips.
5. Proof with the seams on the side of the loaf.
6. Bake with the seam side up.

FORMULA

TWO CASTLE RYE

Legend has it that, in medieval Germany, two proud lords were always fighting to conquer each other's territory. When they finally made peace, the bakers of the lords' territories decided to create a bread to celebrate the end of the war. The two loaves of sourdough rye used to make Two Castle Rye are proofed and baked together; they represent the unity of the two castles.

Levain Formula

Ingredients	Baker's %	Kilogram	US decimal	Lb & Oz	Test
Medium rye flour	100.00	0.419	0.923	14¾	3 oz
Water	80.00	0.335	0.739	11⅞	2⅜ oz
Starter (rye)	12.00	0.050	0.111	1¾	⅜ oz
Total	192.00	0.804	1.773	1 12⅜	5⅝ oz

Process, Levain

1. Mix all the ingredients until well incorporated with a DDT of 70°F (21°C).
2. Allow to ferment 12 hours at room temperature [65°F (18°C) to 70°F (21°C)].

Soaker Formula

Ingredients	Baker's %	Kilogram	US decimal	Lb & Oz		Test
Coarse whole wheat flour	10	0.266	0.266		4 ¼	⅞ oz
Oat flakes	10	0.266	0.266		4 ¼	⅞ oz
Sunflower seeds	10	0.266	0.266		4 ¼	⅞ oz
Pumpkin seeds	20.00	0.532	0.532		8 ½	1 ¾ oz
Water	50.00	1.330	1.330	1	5 ¼	4 ¼ oz
Total	100.00	1.206	2.660	2	10 ½	8 ½ oz

Process, Soaker

Combine all ingredients and soak at least 2 hours.

Final Dough Formula

Ingredients	Baker's %	Kilogram	US decimal	Lb & Oz		Test
Bread flour	40.00	0.643	1.418	1	6 ¾	4 ½ oz
High-extraction flour	40.00	0.643	1.418	1	6 ¾	4 ½ oz
Medium rye flour	20.00	0.322	0.709		11 ⅜	2 ¼ oz
Water	50.00	0.804	1.773	1	12 ⅜	5 ⅝ oz
Salt	2.80	0.045	0.099		1 ⅝	⅜ oz
Yeast (instant)	1.20	0.019	0.043		⅝	⅛ oz
Honey	2.00	0.032	0.071		1 ⅛	¼ oz
Roasted malt	1.00	0.016	0.035		⅝	⅛ oz
Rye levain	50.00	0.804	1.773	1	12 ⅜	5 ⅝ oz
Soaker	75.00	1.206	2.660	2	10 ½	8 ½ oz
Total	282.00	4.536	10.000	10	0	2 lb

Yield: 5 [2 lb (0.900 kg)] loaves
Test: 1 [2 lb (0.900 kg)] loaf

Process, Final Dough

Mix	Improved mix (medium consistency) Add soaker after the dough has been developed back in first speed only until incorporated
DDT	75°F (24°C) to 78°F (25°C)
First fermentation	1 hour 30 minutes at 80°F (27°C) at 65% rh
Divide	2 [1 lb (0.454 kg)]
Preshape	Light ball
Resting time	25 to 30 minutes

Shape	Boule or batard; allow two pieces to proof into one another
Final proof	1 hour at 80°F (27°C) at 65% rh
Scoring	None
Steam	2 seconds
Bake	Deck oven, 30 to 35 minutes at 450°F (232°C)

FORMULA

MOUNTAIN BREAD

Combining rye levain and white flour, this bread began as a staple in the mountainous regions of Switzerland. The long shelf life created by the sourdough process was an advantage in a time and place when bread was baked only once a week. The hole in the middle of the crown was used to hang the mountain bread to a pole fixed high on the wall to store the bread safely.

Levain Formula

Ingredients	Baker's %	Kilogram	US decimal	Lb & Oz		Test
Medium rye flour	100.00	0.385	0.848		13⅝	2¾ oz
Water	120.00	0.462	1.018	1	¼	3¼ oz
Rye starter	8.00	0.031	0.068		1⅛	¼ oz
Total	228.00	0.877	1.934	1	15	6¼ oz

Process, Levain

1. Mix all the ingredients until well incorporated with a DDT of 70°F (21°C).
2. Allow to ferment 8 hours at room temperature [65°F (18°C) to 70°F (21°C)].

Final Dough Formula

Ingredients	Baker's %	Kilogram	US decimal	Lb & Oz		Test
Bread flour	85.00	1.864	4.110	4	1¾	13⅛ oz
Whole wheat flour	15.00	0.329	0.725		11⅝	2⅜ oz
Water	64.00	1.404	3.095	3	1½	9⅞ oz
Yeast (instant)	0.10	0.002	0.005		⅛	⅛ tsp
Salt	2.70	0.059	0.131		2⅛	⅜ oz
Levain	40.00	0.877	1.934	1	15	6¼ oz
Total	206.80	4.536	10.000	10	0	2 lb

Yield: 10 [1 lb (0.454 kg)] loaves
Test: 2 [1 lb (0.454 kg)] loaves

Process, Final Dough

Mix	Improved mix (medium consistency)
DDT	75°F (24°C) to 78°F (25°C)
First fermentation	2 hours with 1 fold
Divide	1 lb (0.454 kg)
Preshape	Light ball
Resting time	20 to 30 minutes
Shape	Ring or crown
Final proof	2 hours at 80°F (27°C) at 65% rh
Scoring	Refer to the scoring charts in Chapter 5
Steam	2 seconds
Bake	Deck oven, 40 minutes at 450°F (232°C)

FORMULA

NEW YORK RYE

Rye flour and caraway seeds are a typical flavor combination found in breads from Eastern Europe. When people from this area of the world immigrated to New York City, they brought their bread-making traditions along. Rye bread came to be thought of as being native to New York City, where it was particularly associated with Jewish delicatessens.

% of Flour Prefermented 20%

Prefermented Dough Formula

Ingredients	Baker's %	Kilogram	US decimal	Lb & Oz		Test
Bread flour	100.00	0.523	1.153	1	2½	3¾ oz
Water	65.00	0.340	0.749		12	2⅜ oz
Yeast (instant)	0.50	0.003	0.006		⅛	⅛ tsp
Salt	2.00	0.010	0.023		⅜	⅛ oz
Total	167.50	0.876	1.931	1	14⅞	6⅛ oz

Process, Prefermented Dough

1. Mix all the ingredients until well incorporated with a DDT of 70°F (21°C).
2. Allow to ferment 1 hour at room temperature [65°F (18°C) to 70°F (21°C)].
3. Then refrigerate overnight.

Final Dough Formula

Ingredients	Baker's %	Kilogram	US decimal	Lb & Oz		Test
Bread flour	50.00	1.046	2.305	2	4⅞	7⅜ oz
Medium rye flour	50.00	1.046	2.305	2	4⅞	7⅜ oz
Water	71.25	1.490	3.285	3	4⅝	10½ oz
Yeast (instant)	0.50	0.010	0.023		⅜	⅛ oz
Salt	2.00	0.042	0.092		1½	¼ oz
Caraway seeds	1.25	0.026	0.058		⅞	⅛ oz
Prefermented dough	41.88	0.876	1.931	1	14⅞	6⅛ oz
Total	216.88	4.536	10.000	10	0	2 lb

Yield: 10 [1 lb (0.454 kg)] loaves
Test: 2 [1 lb (0.454 kg)] loaves

Process, Final Dough

Mix	Improved mix (medium consistency)
DDT	73°F (23°C) to 76°F (24°C)
First fermentation	1 hour to 1 hour 30 minutes
Divide	1 lb (0.454 kg)
Preshape	Light ball
Resting time	20 to 30 minutes
Shape	Batard
Final proof	20 to 30 minutes at 80°F (27°C) at 65% rh
Scoring	Refer to the scoring charts in Chapter 5
Steam	2 seconds
Bake	Deck oven, 35 minutes at 450°F (232°C)

Total Formula

Ingredients	Baker's %	Kilogram	US decimal	Lb & Oz		Test
Flour	60.00	1.569	3.458	3	7⅜	11⅛ oz
Medium rye	40.00	1.046	2.305	2	4⅞	7⅜ oz
Water	70.00	1.830	4.035	4	½	12⅞ oz
Yeast (instant)	0.50	0.013	0.029		½	⅛ oz
Salt	2.00	0.052	0.115		1⅞	⅜ oz
Caraway seeds	1.00	0.026	0.058		⅞	⅛ oz
Total	173.50	4.536	10.000	10	0	2 lb

FORMULA

NAAN

Naan, which originated in Afghanistan, is a flatbread that gets its flavor from yogurt (typically made with goat's milk) and the black onion seeds sprinkled on top of the bread before baking.

% of Flour Prefermented 25%

Sponge Formula

Ingredients	Baker's %	Kilogram	US decimal	Lb & Oz		Test
Bread flour	100.00	0.633	1.395	1	6⅜	4½ oz
Water	62.00	0.392	0.865		13⅞	2¾ oz
Yeast (instant)	0.10	0.001	0.001		<⅛	⅛ tsp
Total	162.10	1.026	2.261	2	4⅛	7¼ oz

Process, Sponge

1. Mix all the ingredients until well incorporated with a DDT of 70°F (21°C).
2. Allow to ferment 12 to 16 hours at room temperature [65°F (18°C) to 70°F (21°C)].

Final Dough Formula

Ingredients	Baker's %	Kilogram	US decimal	Lb & Oz		Test
Bread flour	93.00	1.792	3.951	3	15¼	12⅝ oz
Whole wheat flour	7.00	0.106	0.234		3¾	¾ oz
Water	48.67	0.924	2.037	2	⅝	6½ oz
Goat milk yogurt	67.61	1.283	1.283	1	4½	4⅛ oz
Yeast (instant)	0.37	0.007	0.015		¼	¼ tsp
Salt	2.13	0.040	0.089		1⅜	¼ oz
Olive oil	3.07	0.058	0.128		2	⅜ oz
Sponge	54.03	1.026	2.261	2	4⅛	7¼ oz
Total	275.88	5.237	10.000	10	0	2 lb

Yield: 10 [1 lb (0.454 kg)] loaves
Test: 2 [1 lb (0.454 kg)] loaves

Process, Final Dough

Mix	Improved mix (medium soft consistency)
DDT	73°F (23°C) to 76°F (24°C)
First fermentation	3 hours with 1 fold
Divide	1 lb (0.454 kg)
Preshape	Light ball

Resting time	20 to 30 minutes
Shape	Boule
Final proof	1 hour to 1 hour 15 minutes at 80°F (27°C) at 65% rh
Scoring	Flatten out, dock, and season to taste
Steam	2 seconds
Bake	Deck oven, 12 minutes at 500°F (260°C)

Total Formula

Ingredients	Baker's %	Kilogram	US decimal	Lb & Oz		Test
Bread flour	95.80	2.425	5.346	5	5½	1 lb 1⅛ oz
Whole wheat flour	4.20	0.106	0.234		3¾	¾ oz
Water	52.00	1.316	2.902	2	14⅜	9¼ oz
Goat milk yogurt	23.00	0.582	1.283	1	4⅝	4⅛ oz
Yeast (instant)	0.30	0.008	0.017		¼	¼ tsp
Salt	1.60	0.040	0.089		1⅜	¼ oz
Olive oil	2.30	0.058	0.128		2	⅜ oz
Total	179.20	4.536	10.000	10	0	2 lb

FORMULA

TORTILLA

The French have their baguette, and the Mexicans their tortilla. The traditional tortilla has been made of corn or maize since pre-Columbian times. This flat bread is a mainstay of Mexican life, used as an important staple during the three meals of the day. Now made from corn flour, wheat flour, or a combination of the two, the tortilla has become popular with the mainstream in the United States and is no longer considered an ethnic food. An authentic tortilla is baked on a hot metal plate, but it can also be baked in a deck oven.

Final Dough Formula

Ingredients	Baker's %	Kilogram	US decimal	Lb & Oz		Test
Corn flour	60.00	1.690	3.727	3	11⅝	11⅞ oz
Bread flour	40.00	1.127	2.484	2	7¾	8 oz
Water	60.00	1.690	3.727	3	11⅝	11⅞ oz
Salt	1.00	0.028	0.062		1	¼ oz
Total	161.00	4.536	10.000	10	0	2 lb

Yield: 53 [3 oz (0.085 kg)] tortilla
Test: 10 [3 oz (0.085 kg)] tortilla

Process, Final Dough

Mix	Improved mix (stiff consistency)
DDT	73°F (24°C) to 76°F (24°C)
Resting time	15 to 20 minutes
Divide	3 oz (0.085 kg)
Shape	Flatten ⅛ inch (2 to 3 mm) thick
Bake	Hot skillet on both sides

FORMULA

LAVASH

Lavash, originally from Armenia, has been in existence since mankind started harvesting wheat thousands of years ago. A soft, thin flatbread made with flour, water, and salt, it is the most common type of bread in Armenia and Iran today. Traditionally it was rolled out flat and slapped against the hot walls of a tandoori oven, also called *tonir* in Armenian, *tanur* in Persian, and *tandır* in Turkish. This is still the method used throughout Armenia, Iran, Turkey, and sometimes the United States. Sprinkled with a blend of seeds and coarse salt, lavash can be enjoyed on its own or as an accompaniment to hummus, yogurt-based dips, or other Middle Eastern dips.

Final Dough Formula

Ingredients	Baker's %	Kilogram	US decimal	Lb & Oz		Test
Bread flour	100.00	2.939	6.479	6	7⅝	1 lb 4¾ oz
Water	50.00	1.469	3.239	3	3⅞	10⅜ oz
Yeast (instant)	0.60	0.018	0.039		⅝	⅛ tsp
Salt	0.75	0.022	0.049		¾	⅛ tsp
Honey	3.00	0.088	0.194		3⅛	⅝ oz
Total	154.35	4.536	10.000	10	0	2 lb

Yield: 22 [7 oz (0.200 kg)] ½ sheet pans
Test: 4½ [7 oz (0.200 kg)] ½ sheet pans

Process, Final Dough

Mix	Improved mix
DDT	73°F (23°C) to 76°F (24°C)
First fermentation	3 hours
Divide	7 oz (0.200 kg) light ball for ½ sheet pan

Resting time	25 to 30 minutes
Shape	Sheet out to ⅛ inch (2 mm) thick
Final proof	10 minutes at 80°F (27°C) at 65% rh
Steam	2 seconds
Bake	Deck oven, 10 minutes at 460°F (238°C)

For Shaping

1. Roll out the dough piece with a rolling pin or sheeter to ⅛ inch (2 mm) thickness.
2. Lay across the back of the sheet pan, trying to maintain the thickness and not allow shrinkage. (*Optional:* Brush with olive oil and season to taste.)

FORMULA

PITA

Pita, Greek for "flat," has been in use for thousands of years in Middle Eastern and Mediterranean cuisines. In many areas of the world, this flat bread is used to scoop sauces or dip, or to wrap into simple sandwiches, such as kebabs, gyros, or falafel. In the Western world, pita gained popularity with the invention of "pita pockets" which allowed for ingredients to be placed inside the bread like a more familiar Western sandwich.

% of Flour Prefermented 15%

Sponge Formula

Ingredients	Baker's %	Kilogram	US decimal	Lb & Oz	Test
Bread flour	100.00	0.397	0.874	14	2¾ oz
Water	78.00	0.309	0.682	10⅞	2⅛ oz
Yeast (instant)	12.00	0.048	0.105	1⅝	⅜ oz
Sugar	6.50	0.026	0.057	⅞	⅛ oz
Total	196.50	0.779	1.718	1 11½	5½ oz

Process, Sponge

1. Mix all the ingredients until well incorporated with a DDT of 70°F (21°C).
2. Allow to ferment 30 minutes at room temperature [65°F (18°C) to 70°F (21°C)].

Final Dough Formula

Ingredients	Baker's %	Kilogram	US decimal	Lb & Oz	Test
Bread flour	100.00	2.247	4.953	4 15¼	15⅞ oz
Water	62.00	1.393	3.071	3 1⅛	9⅞ oz
Yeast (instant)	0.00	0.000	0.000	0	0
Salt	1.18	0.026	0.058	⅞	⅛ oz
Sugar	0.03	0.001	0.001	<⅛	⅛ tsp
Butter	4.00	0.090	0.198	3⅛	⅝ oz
Sponge	34.68	0.779	1.718	1 11½	5½ oz
Total	201.89	4.536	10.000	10 0	2 lb

Yield: 53 [3 oz (0.085 kg)] pita
Test: 10 [3 oz (0.085 kg)] pita

Process, Final Dough

Mix	Improved mix (medium consistency)
DDT	73°F (23°C) to 76°F (24°C)
First fermentation	1 hour 30 minutes
Divide	3 oz (0.085 kg)
Preshape	Loose ball
Resting time	20 to 30 minutes
Shape	Flat, rolled with a pin or sheeter
Final proof	30 minutes at 80°F (27°C) at 65% rh
Scoring	None
Steam	2 seconds
Bake	Deck oven, 5 minutes at 500°F (260°C)

Total Formula

Ingredients	Baker's %	Kilogram	US decimal	Lb & Oz	Test
Bread flour	100.00	2.643	5.828	5 13¼	1 lb 2⅝ oz
Water	64.40	1.702	3.753	3 12	12 oz
Yeast (instant)	1.80	0.048	0.105	1⅝	⅜ oz
Salt	1.00	0.026	0.058	⅞	⅛ oz
Sugar	1.00	0.026	0.058	⅞	⅛ oz
Olive oil	3.40	0.090	0.198	3⅛	⅝ oz
Total	171.60	4.536	10.000	10 0	2 lb

Assorted Flat Breads

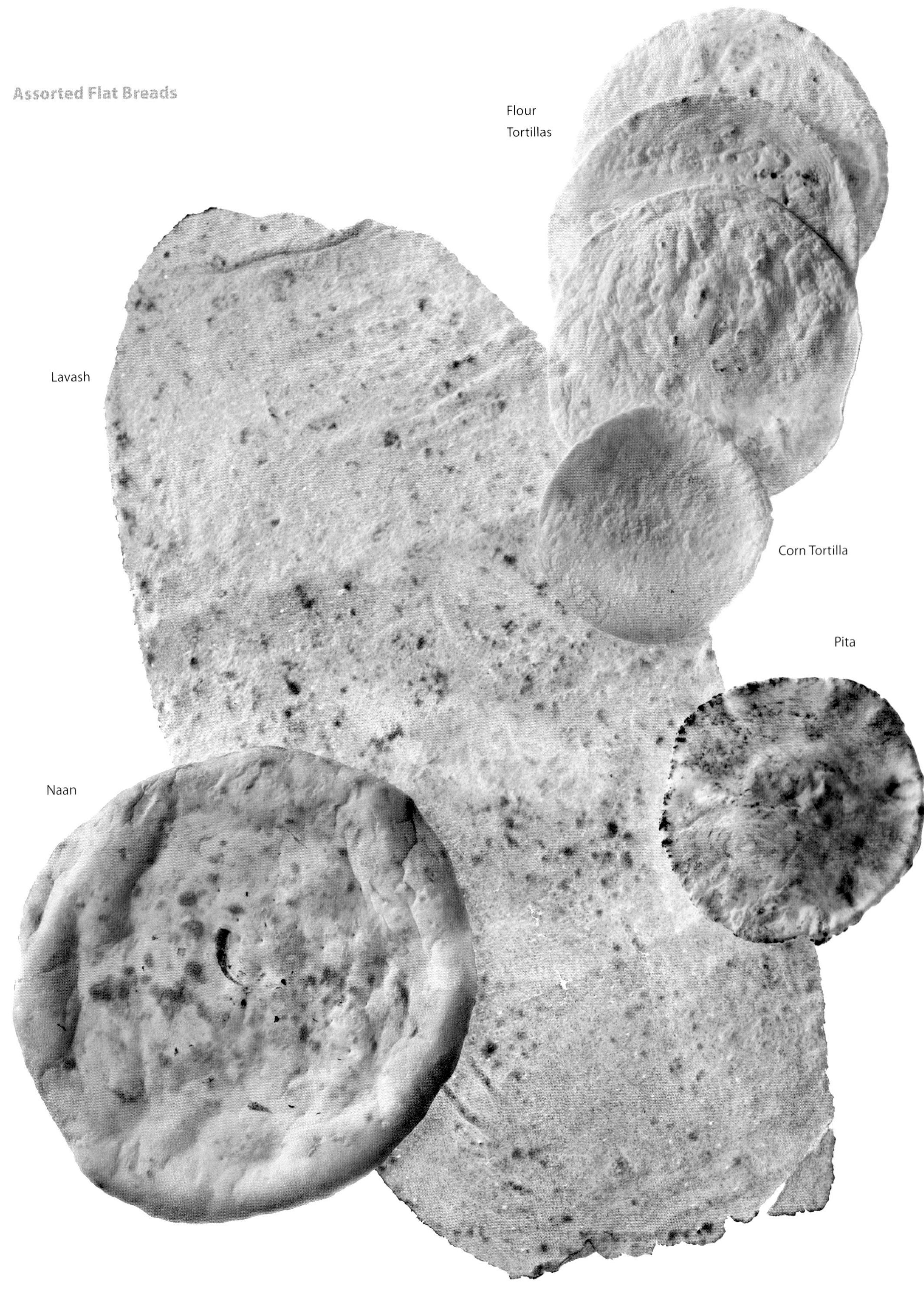

FORMULA

FOCACCIA

Focaccia is a classic Italian flatbread rich in olive oil and often flavored with fragrant herbs such as rosemary. It can be served as is or used for making sandwiches. Our version has prefermented dough and parmesan cheese in the dough to add an extra flavor dimension.

% of Flour Prefermented 25%

Prefermented Dough Formula

Ingredients	Baker's %	Kilogram	US decimal	Lb & Oz		Test
Bread flour	100.00	0.639	1.408	1	6½	4½ oz
Water	65.00	0.415	0.915		14⅝	2⅞
Yeast (instant)	0.60	0.004	0.008		⅛	¼ tsp
Salt	2.00	0.013	0.028		½	⅛ oz
Total	165.60	1.071	2.361	2	5¾	7½ oz

Process, Prefermented Dough

1. Mix all the ingredients until well incorporated with a DDT of 70°F (21°C).
2. Allow to ferment 1 to 1½ hours at room temperature [65°F (18°C) to 70°F (21°C)].
3. Then refrigerate overnight.

Final Dough Formula

Ingredients	Baker's %	Kilogram	US decimal	Lb & Oz		Test
Bread flour	100.00	1.917	4.225	4	3⅝	13½ oz
Water	66.33	1.271	2.803	2	12⅞	9 oz
Yeast (instant)	0.47	0.009	0.020		⅜	⅛ oz
Salt	2.00	0.038	0.085		1⅜	¼ oz
Oil	8.00	0.153	0.338		5⅜	1⅛ oz
Cheese, grated	4.00	0.077	0.169		2¾	½ oz
Prefermented dough	55.87	1.071	2.361	2	5¾	7½ oz
Total	236.67	4.536	10.000	10	0	2 lb

Yield: 3 [3 lb 5 oz (1.5 kg)] pieces
Test: 1 [2 lb (0.900 kg)] piece

Process, Final Dough

Mix	Short mix (soft consistency)
DDT	73°F (23°C) to 76°F (26°C)
First fermentation	2 hours with 1 fold
Divide	Rectangle—3.2 to 3.5 kg per full sheet pan
Shape	On oiled pan, stretch out to edges
Final proof	1 hour at 80°F (26°C) at 65% rh
Steam	2 seconds
Bake	Deck oven

Total Formula

Ingredients	Baker's %	Kilogram	US decimal	Lb & Oz		Test
Bread flour	100.00	2.555	5.634	5	10⅛	1 lb 2 oz
Water	66.00	1.687	3.718	3	11½	11⅞ oz
Yeast (instant)	0.50	0.013	0.028		½	⅛ oz
Salt	2.00	0.051	0.113		1¾	⅜ oz
Oil	6.00	0.153	0.338		5⅜	1⅛ oz
Cheese, grated	3.00	0.077	0.169		2¾	½ oz
Total	177.50	4.536	10.000	10	0	2 lb

Assorted Focaccia

Fougasse

FORMULA

FOUGASSE

Very popular in the Provence region of southern France, fougasse is a bread similar to Italy's focaccia. It is traditionally rolled out thin and cut into decorative, open shapes, sometimes representing a sheath of wheat or a ladder. Additional ingredients are frequently added to the dough such as cheese (hard or soft), olives, chorizo, lardon, nuts, and herbs.

Levain Formula

Ingredients	Baker's %	Kilogram	US decimal	Lb & Oz		Test
Bread flour	95.00	0.387	0.853		13⅝	2⅝ oz
Water	100.00	0.387	0.853		13⅝	2⅞ oz
Starter	60.00	0.232	0.512		8¼	1¾ oz
Total	255.00	1.006	2.219	2	3½	7⅜ oz

Process, Levain

1. Mix all the ingredients until well incorporated with a DDT of 70°F (21°C).
2. Allow to ferment 12 hours at room temperature [65°F (18°C) to 70°F (21°C)].

Final Dough Formula

Ingredients	Baker's %	Kilogram	US decimal	Lb & Oz		Test
Bread flour	100.00	2.078	4.581	4	9¼	14⅝ oz
Water	60.00	1.247	2.749	2	12	8¾ oz
Yeast (instant)	0.40	0.008	0.018		¼	⅛ tsp
Salt	2.50	0.052	0.115		1⅞	⅜ oz
Olive oil	5.00	0.104	0.229		3⅝	¾ oz
Rosemary	0.40	0.008	0.018		¼	⅛ tsp
Levain	50.00	1.039	2.290	2	4⅝	7⅜ oz
Total	218.30	4.536	10.000	10	0	2 lb

Yield: 5 [2 lb (0.900 kg]) pieces
Test: 1 [2 lb (0.900 kg)] piece

Process, Final Dough

Mix	Improved mix (medium consistency)
DDT	75°F (24°C) to 78°F (26°C)
First fermentation	1 hour
Divide	Rectangle
Shape	Roll out to a rectangle; cut in traditional, decorative shapes
Final proof	1 hour to 1 hour 30 minutes at 80°F (27°C) at 65% rh
Steam	2 seconds
Bake	Deck oven , 35 minutes at 450°F (232°C)

Note

After dividing dough, let it relax. Roll out to desired thickness [½ to ¾ inch (1.5 cm)], cut into desired shape, and then allow to proof.

FORMULA

HAWAIIAN PINEAPPLE SWEET BREAD

Pineapple juice is the subtle sweetener in this Hawaiian sweet bread, which actually comes from the Portuguese, who were brought to Hawaii from the Portuguese islands of Madeira and the Azores as laborers in the late 1800s. Many of the immigrants brought along an inherited talent for making bread, particularly *pao doce*, or sweet bread. Sweet bread became an enduring part of the Hawaiian culture, usually served at breakfast or as dessert.

Levain Formula

Ingredients	Baker's %	Kilogram	US decimal	Lb & Oz	Test
Bread flour	100.00	0.108	0.239	3 ⅞	¾ oz
Water	50.00	0.054	0.119	1 ⅞	⅜ oz
Starter (stiff)	60.00	0.065	0.143	2 ¼	½ oz
Total	210.00	0.227	0.501	8	1 ⅝ oz

Process, Levain

1. Mix all the ingredients until well incorporated with a DDT of 70°F (21°C).
2. Allow to ferment 8 hours at room temperature [65°F (18°C) to 70°F (21°C)].

Final Dough Formula

Ingredients	Baker's %	Kilogram	US decimal	Lb & Oz		Test
Bread flour	100.00	2.274	5.014	5	¼	1 lb
Water	30.00	0.682	1.504	1	8 ⅛	4 ⅞ oz
Eggs	10.00	0.227	0.501		8	1 ⅝ oz
Pineapple juice	15.00	0.341	0.752		12	2 ⅜ oz
Sugar	20.00	0.455	1.003	1	0	3 ¼ oz
Osmotolerant instant yeast	1.80	0.041	0.090		1 ½	¼ oz
Salt	2.00	0.045	0.100		1 ⅝	⅜ oz
Vegetable oil	10.00	0.227	0.501		8	1 ⅝ oz
Ginger	0.15	0.003	0.008		⅛	⅛ tsp
Vanilla extract	0.50	0.011	0.025		⅜	⅛ oz
Levain	10.00	0.227	0.501		8	1 ⅝ oz
Total	199.45	4.536	10.000	10	0	2 lb

Yield: 10 [1 lb (0.454 kg)] loaves
Test: 2 [1 lb 0.454 kg)] loaves

Process, Final Dough

Mix	Intense mix (medium consistency)
DDT	75°F (24°C) to 78°F (25°C)
First fermentation	2 hours
Divide	1 lb (0.454 kg)
Preshape	Light ball
Resting time	20 to 30 minutes
Shape	Ring or crown
Final proof	2 hours 30 minutes at 80°F (27°C) at 65% rh
Scoring	None
Steam	2 seconds
Bake	Convection oven, 35 to 40 minutes at 400°F (204°C)

FORMULA

PORTUGUESE SWEET BREAD

During the late 19th century, there was a large influx of Portuguese to America, primarily to New England and Hawaii. When the new immigrants arrived, they brought their *pao doce*, or sweet bread, along. The Portugese immigrants, who were overwhelmingly Catholic, traditionally served sweet bread on Easter, but it was also used as everyday bread, as it still is, to be enjoyed at any meal, but most often with breakfast.

% of Flour Prefermented 7%

Sponge Formula

Ingredients	Baker's %	Kilogram	US decimal	Lb & Oz		Test
Bread flour	100.00	0.147	0.324		5 ¼	1 oz
Water	192.00	0.282	0.623		10	2 oz
Osmotolerant instant yeast	32.00	0.047	0.104		1 ⅝	⅜ oz
Milk powder	90.00	0.132	0.292		4 ⅝	⅞ oz
Sugar	45.00	0.066	0.146		2 ⅜	½ oz
Total	459.00	0.675	1.489	1	7 ⅞	4 ¾ oz

Process, Sponge

1. Mix all the ingredients until well incorporated with a DDT of 70°F (21°C).
2. Allow to ferment 1 hour at room temperature [65°F (18°C) to 70°F (21°C)].

Final Dough Formula

Ingredients	Baker's %	Kilogram	US decimal	Lb & Oz		Test
Bread flour	100.00	1.925	4.243	4	3 ⅞	13 ⅝ oz
Water	39.90	0.768	1.693	1	11 ⅛	5 ⅜ oz
Eggs	15.07	0.290	0.639		10 ¼	2 oz
Osmotolerant instant yeast	0.39	0.007	0.016		¼	¼ tsp
Salt	1.29	0.025	0.055		⅞	⅛ oz
Sugar	29.93	0.576	1.270	1	4 ⅜	4 ⅛ oz
Butter	13.99	0.269	0.594		9 ½	1 ⅞ oz
Sponge	35.08	0.675	1.489	1	7 ⅞	4 ¾ oz
Total	235.65	4.536	10.000	10	0	2 lb

Yield: 10 [1 lb (0.454 kg)] loaves
Test: 2 [1 lb (0.454 kg)] loaves

Process, Final Dough

Mix	Intensive mix (medium consistency)
DDT	73°F (23°C) to 76°F (24°C)
First fermentation	45 minutes to 1 hour
Divide	1 lb (0.454 kg)
Preshape	Light ball
Resting time	20 to 30 minutes
Shape	Boule in a pie plate
Final proof	1 hour 30 minutes to 2 hours at 80°F (27°C) at 65% rh
Scoring	None
Steam	2 seconds
Bake	Convection oven, 30 minutes at 380°F (193°C)

Total Formula

Ingredients	Baker's %	Kilogram	US decimal	Lb & Oz		Test
Bread flour	100.00	2.072	4.568	4	9 ⅛	14 ⅝ oz
Water	50.70	1.050	2.316	2	5	7 ⅜ oz
Eggs	14.00	0.290	0.639		10 ¼	2 oz
Osmotolerant instant yeast	2.63	0.054	0.120		1 ⅞	⅜ oz
Salt	1.20	0.025	0.055		⅞	⅛ oz
Sugar	31.00	0.642	1.416	1	6 ⅝	4 ½ oz
Butter	13.00	0.269	0.594		9 ½	1 ⅞ oz
Milk powder	6.40	0.133	0.292		4 ⅝	⅞ oz
Total	218.93	4.536	10.000	10	0	2 lb

FORMULA

CORONA DULCE

This sweet enriched bread, flavored with anise, has been shaped like a crown since the days of old, when the bakers of Spain invented a creative way to honor their royalty.

Final Dough Formula

Ingredients	Baker's %	Kilogram	US decimal	Lb & Oz		Test
Bread flour	100.00	2.067	4.556	4	8⅞	14⅝ oz
Milk	35.00	0.723	1.595	1	9½	5⅛ oz
Water	10.00	0.207	0.456		7¼	1½ oz
Eggs	20.00	0.413	0.911		14⅝	2⅞ oz
Osmotolerant instant yeast	5.00	0.103	0.228		3⅝	¾ oz
Salt	1.50	0.031	0.068		1⅛	¼ oz
Sugar	25.00	0.517	1.139	1	2¼	3⅝ oz
Butter	20.00	0.413	0.911		14⅝	2⅞ oz
Vanilla extract	2.00	0.041	0.091		1½	¼ oz
Anise seed	1.00	0.021	0.046		¾	⅛ oz
Total	219.50	4.536	10.000	10	0	2 lb

Yield: 10 [1 lb (0.454 kg)] loaves
Test: 2 [1 lb (0.454 kg)] loaves

Process, Final Dough

Mix	Intensive mix (medium soft consistency)
DDT	73°F (23°C) to 76°F (24°C)
First fermentation	45 minutes to 1 hour at 80°F (27°C) at 65% rh
Divide	6 [2½ oz (0.075 kg)]
Preshape	Light ball
Resting time	25 to 30 minutes
Shape	Refer to the photograph on the next page
Final proof	1 hour 30 minutes to 2 hours at 80°F (27°C) at 65% rh
Scoring	None
Steam	2 seconds
Bake	Convection oven, 30 minutes at 380°F (193°C)

Portuguese Sweet Breads (boule, braid, and batard with sugar)

Hawaiin Pineapple Sweet Bread

Corona Dulce

Sweet Breads

FORMULA

PUGLIESE

Originating in Puglia, a region of southern Italy, pugliese was originally "the bread of the poor people." It was (and sometimes still is) produced with moderately refined flour, and mashed potatoes were added when flour was not available in sufficient quantity. This created a filling bread with a chewy and moist crumb texture, while the dense, round shape ensured a naturally longer shelf life.

% of Flour Prefermented 50%

Sponge Formula

Ingredients	Baker's %	Kilogram	US decimal	Lb & Oz		Test
Bread flour	80.00	0.901	1.986	1	15¾	6⅜ oz
Whole wheat flour	20.00	0.225	0.497		8	1⅝ oz
Water	55.00	0.619	1.365	1	5⅞	4⅜ oz
Yeast (instant)	0.40	0.004	0.008		⅛	⅛ tsp
Total	155.40	1.749	3.856	3	13¾	12⅜ oz

Process, Sponge

1. Mix all the ingredients until well incorporated with a DDT of 70°F (21°C).
2. Allow to ferment 6 to 8 hours at room temperature [65°F (19°C) to 70°F (21°C)].

Final Dough Formula

Ingredients	Baker's %	Kilogram	US decimal	Lb & Oz		Test
Bread flour	93.00	0.721	1.589	1	9⅜	5⅛ oz
Whole wheat flour	7.00	0.405	0.894		14¼	2⅞ oz
Water	60.00	0.676	1.490	1	7⅞	4¾ oz
Mashed potatoes	82.00	0.923	2.036	2	⅝	6½ oz
Yeast (instant)	0.48	0.005	0.012		¼	⅛ tsp
Salt	5.00	0.056	0.124		2	⅜ oz
Sponge	155.32	1.749	3.856	3	13¾	12⅜ oz
Total	402.80	4.536	10.000	10	0	2 lb

Yield: 10 [1 lb (0.454 kg)] loaves
Test: 2 [1 lb (0.454 kg)] loaves

Process, Final Dough

Mix	Improved mix (soft consistency)
DDT	73°F (22°C) to 76°F (24°C)
First fermentation	2 hours with 1 fold
Resting time	25 to 30 minutes
Divide	1 lb (0.454 Kg)
Preshape	Light ball
Shape	Light rectangle
Final proof	1 hour 30 minutes to 2 hours at 80°F (27°C) at 65% rh
Scoring	None: bake seam side up
Steam	2 seconds
Bake	Deck oven, 30 minutes at 450°F (232°C)

Total Formula

Ingredients	Baker's %	Kilogram	US decimal	Lb & Oz		Test
Bread flour	72.00	1.622	3.575	3	9¼	11½ oz
Whole wheat flour	28.00	0.631	1.390	1	6¼	4½ oz
Water	57.50	1.295	2.855	2	13⅝	9⅛ oz
Mashed potatoes	41.00	0.923	2.036	2	⅝	6½ oz
Yeast (instant)	0.40	0.009	0.020		⅜	⅛ oz
Salt	2.50	0.056	0.124		2	⅜ oz
Total	201.40	4.536	10.000	10	0	2 lb

FORMULA

ROASTED POTATO BREAD

The selection of just the right type of potatoes is a must for roasted potato bread. If they are too starchy, they will dissolve into the dough; too cakey, they will give a poor texture to the finished product. Yukon Gold potatoes are a good choice. The addition of fresh rosemary adds savory fragrance and flavor, while cracked wheat provides excellent texture contrast with the softness of the crumb.

% of Flour Prefermented 17%

Sponge Formula

Ingredients	Baker's %	Kilogram	US decimal	Lb & Oz		Test
Bread flour	50.00	0.184	0.406		6 ½	1 ¼ oz
Whole wheat flour	50.00	0.184	0.406		6 ½	1 ¼ oz
Water	68.00	0.251	0.553		8 ⅞	1 ¾ oz
Yeast (instant)	0.10	0.000	0.001		< ⅛	⅛ tsp
Total	168.10	0.620	1.366	1	5 ⅞	4 ⅜ oz

Process, Sponge

1. Mix all the ingredients until well incorporated with a DDT of 70°F (21°C).
2. Allow to ferment 12 to 16 hours at room temperature [65°F (18°C) to 70°F (21°C)].

Soaker Formula

Ingredients	Baker's %	Kilogram	US decimal	Lb & Oz		Test
Cracked wheat	100.00	0.090	0.198		3 ⅛	⅝ oz
Water	100.00	0.090	0.198		3 ⅛	⅝ oz
Total	200.00	0.179	0.395		6 ⅜	1 ¼ oz

Process, Soaker

Combine the cracked wheat and water and allow to soak overnight.

Final Dough Formula

Ingredients	Baker's %	Kilogram	US decimal	Lb & Oz		Test
Bread flour	89.76	1.615	3.562	3	9	11⅜ oz
Whole wheat flour	5.42	0.098	0.215		3½	¾ oz
Medium rye flour	4.82	0.087	0.191		3	⅝ oz
Water	64.99	1.170	2.579	2	9¼	8¼ oz
Salt	2.59	0.047	0.103		1⅝	⅜ oz
Yeast (instant)	0.29	0.005	0.012		⅛	⅛ tsp
Soaker	9.96	0.179	0.395		6⅜	1¼ oz
Potatoes (large diced and roasted)	39.76	0.716	1.578	1	9¼	5 oz
Sponge	34.43	0.620	1.366	1	5⅞	4⅜ oz
Total	252.02	4.536	10.000	10	0	2 lb

Yield: 10 [1 lb (0.454 kg)] loaves
Test: 2 [1 lb (0.454 kg)] loaves

Process, Final Dough

Mix	Improved mix (medium consistency) Add the potatoes and soaker after the dough has been developed on first speed
DDT	73°F (23°C) to 76°F (24°C)
First fermentation	1 hour 30 minutes to 2 hours at 80°F (27°C) at 65% rh
Divide	1 lb (0.454 kg)
Preshape	Light ball
Resting time	20 to 30 minutes
Shape	Boule
Final proof	1 hour 30 minutes to 2 hours at 80°F (27°C) at 65% rh
Scoring	Refer to the scoring charts in Chapter 5
Steam	2 seconds
Bake	Deck oven, 35 to 40 minutes at 440°F (227°C)

Total Formula

Ingredients	Baker's %	Kilogram	US decimal	Lb & Oz		Test
Bread flour	83.00	1.800	3.968	3	15½	12¾ oz
Whole wheat flour	13.00	0.282	0.621		10	2 oz
Medium rye flour	4.00	0.087	0.191		3	⅝ oz
Water	65.50	1.420	3.131	3	2⅛	10 oz
Salt	2.15	0.047	0.103		1⅝	⅜ oz
Yeast (instant)	0.26	0.006	0.012		¼	⅛ tsp
Soaker	8.27	0.179	0.395		6⅜	1¼ oz
Potatoes (roasted)	33.00	0.716	1.578	1	9¼	5 oz
Total	209.18	4.536	10.000	10	0	2 lb

FORMULA

PEAR BUCKWHEAT BREAD

Traditionally used for pancakes, buckwheat flour is a flavorful and healthy addition to bread formula. The heady combination of buckwheat flour, dry pears soaked in white wine, and lightly toasted walnuts makes pear buckwheat bread the perfect match for blue cheese or salads.

% of Flour Prefermented 41%

Poolish Formula

Ingredients	Baker's %	Kilogram	US decimal	Lb & Oz		Test
Buckwheat flour	20.00	0.186	0.411		6⅝	1⅜ oz
Bread flour	80.00	0.685	1.509	1	8⅛	4⅞ oz
Water	100.00	0.871	1.920	1	14¾	6⅛ oz
Yeast (instant)	0.10	0.001	0.002		<⅛	⅛ tsp
Salt	0.10	0.001	0.002		<⅛	⅛ tsp
Total	200.20	1.743	3.844	3	13½	12¼ oz

Process, Poolish

1. Mix all the ingredients until well incorporated with a DDT of 70°F (21°C).
2. Allow to ferment 12 to 16 hours at room temperature [65°F (18°C) to 70°F (21°C)].

Final Dough Formula

Ingredients	Baker's %	Kilogram	US decimal	Lb & Oz		Test
Bread flour	100.00	1.403	3.092	3	1½	9⅞ oz
Water	47.48	0.666	1.468	1	7½	4¾ oz
Salt	3.19	0.045	0.099		1⅝	⅜ oz
Yeast (instant)	0.76	0.011	0.024		⅜	⅛ oz
Walnuts (toasted)	14.26	0.200	0.441		7	1⅜ oz
Dry pears, soaked in white wine	33.39	0.468	1.033	1	½	3¼ oz
Poolish	124.30	1.743	3.844	3	13½	12¼ oz
Total	323.38	4.536	10.000	10	0	2 lb

Soak pears for 1 hour, then strain.

Yield: 10 [1 lb (0.454 kg)] loaves

Test: 2 [1 lb (0.454 kg)] loaves

Process, Final Dough

Mix	Improved mix (medium consistency) Add pears and walnuts after dough has developed in first speed
DDT	73°F (23°C) to 76°F (24°C)
First fermentation	1 hour 30 minutes at 80°F (27°C) at 65% rh
Divide	1 lb (0.454 kg)
Preshape	Light ball
Resting time	20 to 30 minutes
Shape	Pear (refer to the photo on page 251)
Final proof	1 hour at 80°F (27°C) at 65% rh
Scoring	Refer to the photo on page 251
Steam	2 seconds
Bake	Deck oven, 30 to 35 minutes at 450°F (232°C)

Total Formula

Ingredients	Baker's %	Kilogram	US decimal	Lb & Oz		Test
Bread flour	91.80	2.087	4.602	4	9⅝	14¾ oz
Buckwheat flour	8.20	0.186	0.411		6⅝	1⅜ oz
Water	67.60	1.537	3.388	3	6¼	10⅞ oz
Salt	2.00	0.045	0.100		1⅝	⅜ oz
Yeast (instant)	0.50	0.011	0.025		⅜	⅛ oz
Walnuts (toasted)	8.80	0.200	0.441		7	1⅜ oz
Pears, soaked in white wine	20.60	0.468	1.033	1	½	3¼ oz
Total	199.50	4.536	10.000	10	0	2 lb

FORMULA

SESAME SEMOLINA BREAD

Milled from the harder of the amber-colored wheat variety, semolina flour is usually used in pasta production. Its use in bread formula takes advantage of semolina's natural yellow color, which gives the final product a nice crumb color. Sesame seeds are usually added to the dough or sprinkled on top of the loaf to enhance the somewhat neutral flavor of this flour.

Levain Formula

Ingredients	Baker's %	Kilogram	US decimal	Lb & Oz		Test
Bread flour	95.00	0.344	0.757		12⅛	2⅜ oz
Medium rye flour	5.00	0.018	0.040		⅝	⅛ oz
Water	100.00	0.362	0.797		12¾	2½ oz
Starter (liquid)	60.00	0.217	0.478		7⅝	1½ oz
Total	260.00	0.940	2.073	2	1⅛	6⅝ oz

Process, Levain

1. Mix all the ingredients until well incorporated with a DDT of 70°F (21°C).
2. Allow to ferment 12 hours at room temperature [65°F (18°C) to 70°F (21°C)]

Final Dough Formula

Ingredients	Baker's %	Kilogram	US decimal	Lb & Oz		Test
Bread flour	31.00	0.648	1.428	1	6⅞	4⅝ oz
Semolina flour	34.00	0.710	1.566	1	9	5 oz
Durum flour	35.00	0.731	1.612	1	9¾	5⅛ oz
Water	65.00	1.358	2.994	2	15⅞	9⅝ oz
Yeast (instant)	0.10	0.002	0.005		⅛	⅛ tsp
Salt	3.00	0.063	0.138		2¼	½ oz
Levain	45.00	0.940	2.073	2	1⅛	6⅝ oz
Sesame seeds	4.00	0.084	0.184		3	⅝ oz
Total	217.10	4.536	10.000	10	0	2 lb

Yield: 10 [1 lb (0.454 kg)] loaves
Test: 2 [1 lb (0.454 kg)] loaves

Process, Final Dough

Mix	Improved mix (medium consistency) At the end of mixing, incorporate the seeds in first speed
DDT	75°F (24°C) to 78°F (25°C)
First fermentation	2 hours
Divide	1 lb (0.454 kg)
Preshape	Light ball
Resting time	20 to 30 minutes
Shape	Batard
Final proof	2 hours at 80°F (27°C) at 65% rh
Scoring	"S" shape
Steam	2 seconds
Bake	Deck oven, 35 minutes at 450°F (232°C)

FORMULA

CARAMELIZED HAZELNUT SQUARES

A touch of honey, the spiciness of rye levain, and the texture of slightly caramelized hazelnuts combine to make this unusually delicious bread. It is perfect alone, or paired with salad or soft cheese at the end of a meal.

Levain Formula

Ingredients	Baker's %	Kilogram	US decimal	Lb & Oz	Test
Bread flour	100.00	0.215	0.475	7⅝	1½ oz
Water	50.00	0.108	0.237	3¾	¾ oz
Starter (stiff)	10.50	0.023	0.050	¾	⅛ oz
Total	160.50	0.346	0.762	12¼	2½ oz

Process, Levain

1. Mix all the ingredients until well incorporated with a DDT of 70°F (21°C).
2. Allow to ferment 12 hours at room temperature [65°F (18°C) to 70°F (21°C)].

Rye Levain Formula

Ingredients	Baker's %	Kilogram	US decimal	Lb & Oz	Test
Medium rye flour	100.00	0.162	0.357	5¾	1⅛ oz
Water	120.00	0.194	0.428	6⅞	1⅜ oz
Rye starter	8.00	0.013	0.029	½	⅛ oz
Total	228.00	0.369	0.813	13	2⅝ oz

Process, Rye Levain

1. Mix all the ingredients until well incorporated with a DDT of 70°F (21°C).
2. Allow to ferment 12 hours at room temperature [65°F (18°C) to 70°F (21°C)].

White Sponge Formula

Ingredients	Baker's %	Kilogram	US decimal	Lb & Oz	Test
Bread flour	100.00	0.717	1.580	1 9¼	5 oz
Water	62.00	0.444	0.980	15⅝	3⅛ oz
Yeast (instant)	0.10	0.001	0.002	<⅛	⅛ tsp
Total	162.10	1.162	2.561	2 9	8¼ oz

Process, White Sponge

1. Mix all the ingredients until well incorporated with a DDT of 70°F (21°C).
2. Allow to ferment 12 hours at room temperature [65°F (18°C) to 70°F (21°C)].

Wheat Sponge Formula

Ingredients	Baker's %	Kilogram	US decimal	Lb & Oz	Test
Whole wheat flour	100.00	0.233	0.514	8¼	1⅝ oz
Water	70.00	0.163	0.360	5¾	1⅛ oz
Yeast (instant)	0.10	0.000	0.001	<⅛	⅛ tsp
Total	170.10	0.397	0.874	14	2¾ oz

Process, Wheat Sponge

1. Mix all the ingredients until well incorporated with a DDT of 70°F (21°C).
2. Allow to ferment 12 hours at room temperature [65°F (18°C) to 70°F (21°C)].

Caramelized Hazelnuts Formula

Ingredients	Baker's %	Kilogram	US decimal	Lb & Oz	Test
Hazelnuts	100.00	0.306	0.674	10¾	2⅛ oz
Sugar	36.67	0.112	0.247	4	¾ oz
Water	11.11	0.034	0.075	1¼	¼ oz
Butter	10.00	0.031	0.067	1⅛	¼ oz
Total	157.78	0.452	0.996	16	3¼ oz

Process, Caramelized Hazelnuts

1. Roast the nuts in a low oven until the core of the nuts are golden brown.
2. Combine the sugar and water and cook until 240°F (116°C).
3. Add the nuts and stir constantly until the sugar starts to caramelize.
4. Add the butter to retard sticking, and cook further until it reaches the desired color of caramelization.

5. Pour the caramelized nuts onto a silicone baking mat or a lightly oiled granite surface, and separate the nuts.
6. Allow to cool and then reserve until needed.

Final Dough Formula

Ingredients	Baker's %	Kilogram	US decimal	Lb & Oz		Test
Bread flour	94.00	0.867	1.911	1	14⅝	6⅛ oz
Whole wheat flour	6.00	0.055	0.122		2	⅜ oz
Water	90.00	0.830	1.830	1	13¼	5⅞ oz
Yeast (instant)	0.40	0.004	0.008		⅛	⅛ tsp
Salt	5.00	0.046	0.102		1⅝	⅜ oz
Malt	1.00	0.009	0.020		⅜	⅛ oz
Levain	37.50	0.346	0.762		12¼	2½ oz
Sponge	126.00	1.162	2.561	2	9	8¼ oz
Whole wheat sponge	43.00	0.397	0.874		14	2¾ oz
Rye levain	40.00	0.369	0.813		13	2⅝ oz
Caramelized hazelnuts	49.00	0.452	0.996	1	0	3¼ oz
Total	491.90	4.536	10.000	10	0	2 lb

Yield: 10 [1 lb (0.454 kg)] loaves
Test: 2 [1 lb (0.454 kg)] loaves

Process, Final Dough

Mix	Improved mix (soft consistency)
	At the end of mixing, add the hazelnuts in first speed
DDT	75°F (24°C) 78°F (25°C)
First fermentation	2 hours with 1 fold
Divide	1 lb (0.454 kg)
Preshape	None
Resting time	None
Shape	Rectangular pieces, placed upon well-dusted linen
Final proof	30 to 45 minutes at 80°F (27°C) at 65% rh
Scoring	None
Steam	2 seconds
Bake	Deck oven, 35 to 40 minutes at 440°F (227°C)

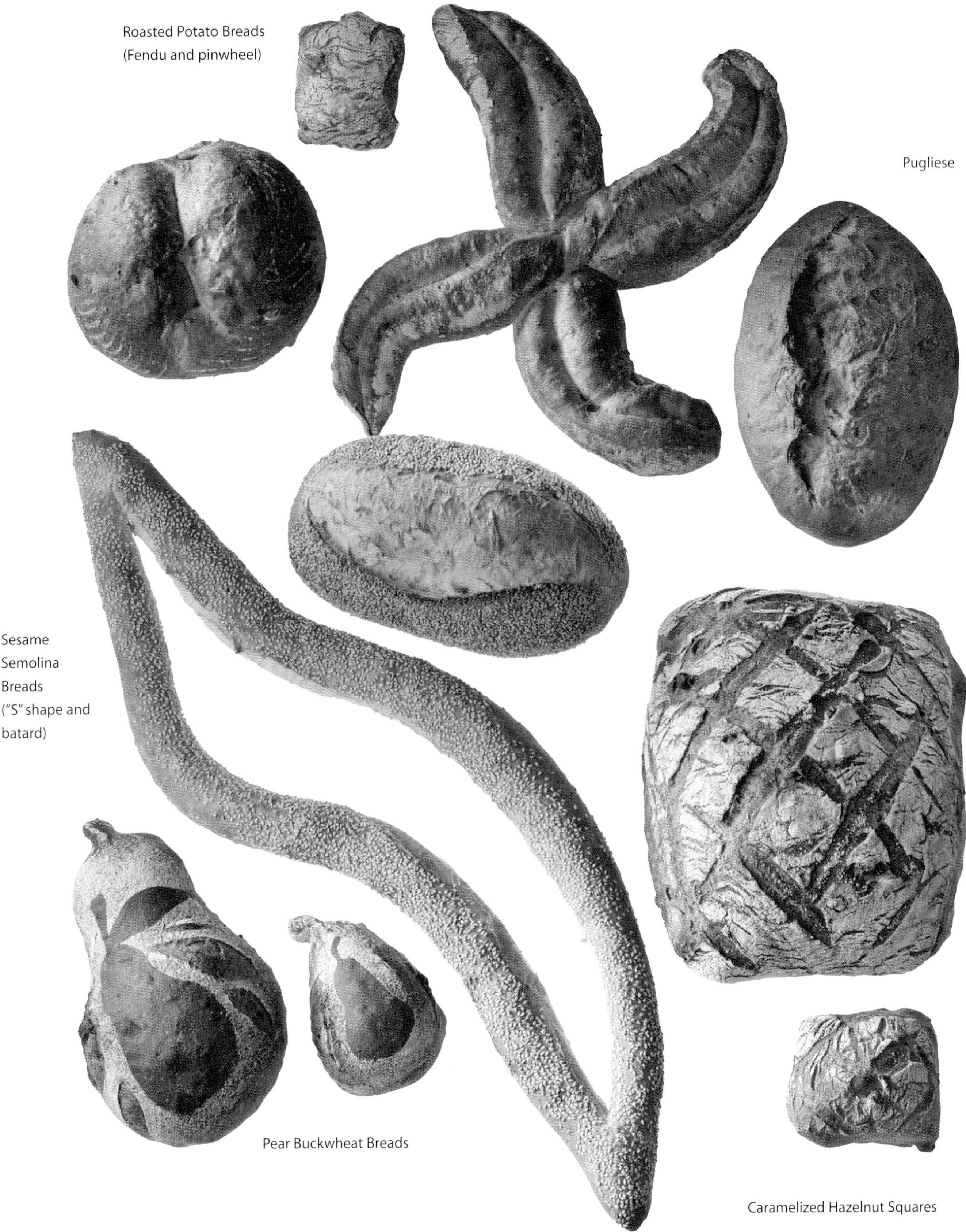

Roasted Potato Breads (Fendu and pinwheel)

Pugliese

Sesame Semolina Breads ("S" shape and batard)

Pear Buckwheat Breads

Caramelized Hazelnut Squares

FORMULA

SPELT BREAD

Distant cousin to modern wheat, the origin of spelt can be traced back to approximately 5000 BC in the area now known as Iran. Once commonly grown in North America, spelt was replaced at the beginning of this century by modern wheat varieties more suited to the high-volume production techniques used on most American farms. Modern wheat varieties have been bred to be easier to grow and harvest, to increase yield, or to have higher protein content. On the other hand, spelt has retained much of its original character because fewer chemicals are used during the growing cycle. Gluten-sensitive individuals have been able to include spelt-based food in their diets. This bread is also a good source of fiber and B complex vitamins. Spelt has become more sought after as Americans pay greater attention to their health and search for foods that are easier on the environment.

% of Flour Prefermented 33%

Poolish Formula

Ingredients	Baker's %	Kilogram	US decimal	Lb & Oz	Test
White spelt flour	90.00	0.791	1.743	1 11⅞	5⅝ oz
Whole spelt flour	10.00	0.088	0.194	3⅛	⅝ oz
Water	100.00	0.879	1.937	1 15	6¼ oz
Yeast (instant)	0.10	0.001	0.002	<⅛	⅛ tsp
Total	200.10	1.758	3.876	3 14	12⅜ oz

Process, Poolish

1. Mix all the ingredients until well incorporated with a DDT of 70°F (21°C).
2. Allow to ferment 12 to 16 hours at room temperature [65°F (18°C) to 70°F (21°C)].

Final Dough Formula

Ingredients	Baker's %	Kilogram	US decimal	Lb & Oz		Test
White spelt flour	90.00	1.606	3.540	3	8⅝	11⅜ oz
Wheat spelt flour	10.00	0.178	0.393		6¼	1¼ oz
Water	52.24	0.932	2.054	2	⅞	6⅝ oz
Yeast (instant)	0.43	0.008	0.017		¼	¼ tsp
Salt	2.69	0.048	0.106		1¾	⅜ oz
Poolish	98.56	1.758	3.876	3	14	12⅜ oz
Total	253.92	4.530	9.986	9	15¾	2 lb

Yield: 10 [1 lb (0.454 kg)] loaves
Test: 2 [1 lb (0.454 kg)] loaves

Process, Final Dough

Mix	Short mix
DDT	73°F (23°C) to 76°F (24°C)
First fermentation	3 hours with 3 folds
Divide	1 lb (0.454 kg)
Preshape	None
Resting time	None
Shape	Rectangular pieces, placed upon well-dusted linen
Final proof	30 to 45 minutes at 80°F (27°C) at 65% rh
Scoring	None
Steam	2 seconds
Bake	Deck oven, 40 minutes at 440°F (238°C)

Total Formula

Ingredients	Baker's %	Kilogram	US decimal	Lb & Oz		Test
White spelt flour	90.00	2.396	5.283	5	4½	1 lb ⅞ oz
Whole spelt flour	10.00	0.266	0.587		9⅜	1⅞ oz
Water	68.00	1.811	3.992	3	15⅞	12¾ oz
Salt	2.00	0.048	0.106		1¾	⅜ oz
Yeast (instant)	0.36	0.009	0.019		¼	½ tsp
Total	170.36	4.536	10.000	10	0	2 lb

FORMULA

PAIN MEUNIER

To honor and thank their millers for delivering consistent flour, bakers of old created pain meunier, or Miller's bread. The formula was creatively designed to involve all the components of the kernel of wheat in the dough. As a result, in addition to possessing great flavor, this bread also has exceptional nutritional value.

% of Flour Prefermented 52%

Prefermented Dough Formula

Ingredients	Baker's %	Kilogram	US decimal	Lb & Oz		Test
Bread flour	100.00	1.204	2.655	2	10½	8½ oz
Water	65.00	0.783	1.726	1	11⅝	5½ oz
Yeast (instant)	0.60	0.007	0.016		¼	¼ tsp
Salt	2.00	0.024	0.053		⅞	⅛ oz
Total	167.60	2.019	4.450	4	7¼	14¼ oz

Process, Prefermented Dough

1. Mix all the ingredients until well incorporated with a DDT of 70°F (21°C).
2. Allow to ferment 1 hour at room temperature [65°F (18°C) to 70°F (21°C)].
3. Then refrigerate overnight.

Soaker Formula

Ingredients	Baker's %	Kilogram	US decimal	Lb & Oz		Test
Cracked wheat	100	0.280	0.616		9⅞	2 oz
Water	100	0.280	0.616		9⅞	2 oz
Total	200	0.559	1.233	1	3¾	4 oz

Process, Soaker

Allow to soak for at least 2 hours.

Final Dough Formula

Ingredients	Baker's %	Kilogram	US decimal	Lb & Oz		Test
Bread flour	85.80	1.013	2.234	2	3¾	7⅛ oz
Whole wheat flour	9.47	0.112	0.247		4	¾ oz
Wheat germ	4.73	0.056	0.123		2	⅜ oz
Water	63.90	0.755	1.664	1	10⅝	5⅜ oz
Salt	1.91	0.023	0.050		¾	⅛ oz
Yeast (instant)	0.00	0.000	0.000		<⅛	0
Soaker	47.34	0.559	1.233	1	3¾	4 oz
Prefermented dough	170.91	2.019	4.450	4	7¼	14¼ oz
Total	384.06	4.536	10.000	10	0	2 lb

Yield: 10 [1 lb (0.454 kg)] loaves
Test: 2 [1 lb (0.454 kg)] loaves

Process, Final Dough

Mix	Improved mix (medium consistency) Add soaker after the dough has developed on first speed only until incorporated
DDT	73°F (22°C) to 76°F (24°C)
First fermentation	1 hour 30 minutes at 80°F (27°C) at 65% rh
Divide	1 lb (0.454 kg)
Preshape	Light ball
Resting time	20 to 30 minutes
Shape	Batard, Fendu
Final proof	1 hour at 80°F (27°C) at 65% rh
Scoring	None
Steam	2 seconds
Bake	Deck oven, 30 to 35 minutes at 450°F (232°C)

Total Formula

Ingredients	Baker's %	Kilogram	US decimal	Lb & Oz		Test
Bread flour	95.20	2.218	4.889	4	14¼	15⅝ oz
Whole wheat flour	4.80	0.112	0.247		4	¾ oz
Wheat germ	2.40	0.056	0.123		2	⅜ oz
Water	66.00	1.538	3.390	3	6¼	10⅞ oz
Salt	2.00	0.047	0.103		1⅝	⅜ oz
Yeast (instant)	0.31	0.007	0.016		¼	⅛ tsp
Malt	0.48	0.011	0.025		⅜	⅛ oz
Soaker	24.00	0.559	1.233	1	3¾	4 oz
Total	195.19	4.536	10.000	10	0	2 lb

FORMULA

RUSTIC FILONE

Filone, or "stick," is named for its long, thin shape. This recipe is elaborated with rye poolish, combining its "spicy" aromas with the more sour aromas of the levain for a truly unique taste.

Poolish Formula

Ingredients	Baker's %	Kilogram	US decimal	Lb & Oz		Test
Bread flour	70.00	0.491	1.083	1	1⅜	3½ oz
Medium rye flour	30.00	0.211	0.464		7⅜	1½ oz
Water	100.00	0.702	1.547	1	8¾	5 oz
Yeast (instant)	0.10	0.001	0.002		<⅛	⅛ tsp
Total	200.10	1.404	3.096	3	1½	9⅞ oz

Process, Poolish

1. Mix all the ingredients until well incorporated with a DDT of 70°F (21°C).
2. Allow to ferment 12 to 16 hours at room temperature [65°F (18°C) to 70°F (21°C)].

Levain Formula

Ingredients	Baker's %	Kilogram	US decimal	Lb & Oz	Test
Bread flour	100	0.387	0.387	6¼	1¼ oz
Water	50	0.193	0.193	3⅛	⅝ oz
Starter (stiff)	50	0.193	0.193	3⅛	⅝ oz
Total	200.00	0.774	0.774	12⅜	2½ oz

Process, Levain

1. Mix all the ingredients until well incorporated with a DDT of 70°F (21°C).
2. Allow to ferment 12 hours at room temperature [65°F (18°C) to 70°F (21°C)].

Final Dough Formula

Ingredients	Baker's %	Kilogram	US decimal	Lb & Oz		Test
Bread flour	90.00	1.580	3.483	3	7¾	11⅛ oz
Whole wheat flour	10.00	0.176	0.387		6¼	1¼ oz
Water	55.00	0.965	2.128	2	2	6¾ oz
Salt	3.00	0.053	0.116		1⅞	⅜ oz
Yeast (instant)	0.40	0.007	0.015		¼	¼ tsp
Poolish	80.00	1.404	3.096	3	1½	9⅞ oz
Levain	20.00	0.351	0.774		12⅜	2½ oz
Total	258.40	4.536	10.000	10	0	2 lb

Yield: 10 [1 lb (0.454 kg)] loaves
Test: 2 [1 lb (0.454 kg)] loaves

Process, Final Dough

Mix	Improved mix (medium consistency)
DDT	73°F (23°C) to 76°F (24°C)
First fermentation	1 hour 30 minutes at 80°F (27°C) at 65% rh
Divide	1 lb (0.454 kg)
Preshape	Light ball
Resting time	20 to 30 minutes
Shape	Long batard
Final proof	1 hour at 80°F (27°C) at 65% rh
Scoring	Score as for baguette or batard
Steam	2 seconds
Bake	Deck oven, 30 to 35 minutes at 450°F (232°C)

FORMULA

CORNBREAD

The following yeasted cornbread was inspired by the more classic chemically leavened cornbread. This version highlights the flavor of corn by using a high ratio of corn flour in the dough and a small amount of cornmeal for texture. Because this dough has a high percentage of corn flour, a prefermented dough is used to help add strength (and flavor) to the dough and a poolish is used for additional complexity. This versatile bread can be enjoyed just as would traditional cornbread, or it can be used for items like sandwiches, toast, croutons, and even stuffing.

% of Flour Prefermented 16%

Poolish Formula

Ingredients	Baker's %	Kilogram	US decimal	Lb & Oz	Test
Bread flour	100.00	0.441	0.973	15 ⅝	3 ⅛ oz
Water	100.00	0.441	0.973	15 ⅝	3 ⅛ oz
Salt	0.20	0.001	0.002	< ⅛	⅛ tsp
Yeast (instant)	0.10	0.000	0.001	< ⅛	⅛ tsp
Total	200.30	0.884	1.948	1 15 ⅛	6 ¼ oz

Process, Poolish

1. Mix all the ingredients until well incorporated with a DDT of 70°F (21°C).
2. Allow to ferment 12 to 16 hours at room temperature [65°F (18°C) to 70°F (21°C)].

% of Flour Prefermented 35%

Prefermented Dough Formula

Ingredients	Baker's %	Kilogram	US decimal	Lb & Oz	Test
Bread flour	100.00	0.971	2.141	2 2 ¼	6 ⅞ oz
Water	65.00	0.631	1.392	1 6 ¼	4 ½ oz
Yeast (instant)	0.60	0.006	0.013	¼	⅛ tsp
Salt	2.00	0.019	0.043	⅝	⅛ oz
Total	167.60	1.628	3.589	3 9 ⅜	11 ½ oz

Process, Prefermented Dough

1. Mix all the ingredients until well incorporated with a DDT of 70°F (21°C).
2. Allow to ferment for 1 hour at room temperature [65°F (18°C) to 70°F (21°C)].
3. Refrigerate overnight.

Final Dough Formula

Ingredients	Baker's %	Kilogram	US decimal	Lb & Oz	Test
Bread flour	25.05	0.341	0.752	12	2⅜ oz
Corn flour	64.77	0.882	1.945	1 15⅛	6¼ oz
Coarse cornmeal	10.18	0.139	0.306	4⅞	1 oz
Water	44.91	0.612	1.349	1 5⅝	4⅜ oz
Salt	2.38	0.032	0.071	1⅛	¼ oz
Yeast (instant)	0.50	0.007	0.015	¼	⅛ oz
Butter	0.79	0.011	0.024	⅜	⅛ oz
Prefermented dough	119.47	1.628	3.589	3 9⅜	11½ oz
Poolish	64.86	0.884	1.948	1 15⅛	6¼ oz
Total	332.91	4.536	10.000	10 0	2 lb

Yield: 10 [1 lb (0.454 kg)] loaves
Test: 2 [1 lb (0.454 kg)] loaves

Process, Final Dough

Mix	Improved mix (medium consistency)
DDT	73°F (23°C) to 76°F (24°C)
First fermentation	1 hour 30 minutes at 80°F (27°C) at 65% rh
Divide	1 lb (0.454 kg)
Preshape	Light ball
Resting time	20 to 30 minutes
Shape	Refer to the photo on page 262
Final proof	1 hour at 80°F (27°C) at 65% rh
Scoring	Refer to the photo on page 262
Steam	2 seconds
Bake	Deck oven, 30 to 35 minutes at 450°F (232°C)

Total Formula

Ingredients	Baker's %	Kilogram	US decimal	Lb & Oz	Test
Bread flour	63.20	1.754	3.866	3 13⅞	12⅜ oz
Corn flour	31.80	0.882	1.945	1 15⅛	6¼ oz
Coarse corn	5.00	0.139	0.306	4⅞	1 oz
Water	60.70	1.684	3.713	3 11⅜	11⅞ oz
Salt	1.90	0.053	0.116	1⅞	⅜ oz
Yeast (instant)	0.47	0.013	0.029	½	⅛ oz
Butter	0.39	0.011	0.024	⅜	⅛ oz
Total	163.46	4.536	10.000	10 0	2 lb

FORMULA

FRANCESE

Sometimes referred to as the Italian version of a baguette, francese is generally not shaped, but cut, creating a long and thin strip of dough to achieve the same eating characteristics as a baguette. *Pane Francese* means "French bread" in Italian.

% of Flour Prefermented 20%

Poolish Formula

Ingredients	Baker's %	Kilogram	US decimal	Lb & Oz		Test
Bread flour	100.00	0.508	1.119	1	1⅞	3⅝ oz
Water	100.00	0.508	1.119	1	1⅞	3⅝ oz
Yeast (instant)	0.10	0.001	0.001		<⅛	⅛ tsp
Total	200.10	1.016	2.240	2	3⅞	7⅛ oz

Process, Poolish

1. Mix all the ingredients until well incorporated with a DDT of 70°F (21°C).
2. Allow to ferment 12 to 16 hours at room temperature [65°F (18°C) to 70°F (21°C)].

Final Dough Formula

Ingredients	Baker's %	Kilogram	US decimal	Lb & Oz		Test
Bread flour	79.52	1.686	3.716	3	11½	11⅞ oz
Whole wheat flour	20.48	0.345	0.761		12⅛	2⅜ oz
Water	70.00	1.422	3.134	3	2⅛	10 oz
Yeast (instant)	0.35	0.007	0.016		¼	¼ tsp
Salt	2.00	0.041	0.090		1⅜	¼ oz
Malt	0.98	0.020	0.044		¾	⅛ oz
Poolish	50.03	1.016	2.240	2	3⅞	7⅛ oz
Total	223.36	4.536	10.000	10	0	2 lb

Yield: 13 [12 oz (0.350 kg)] loaves
Test: 2½ [12 oz (0.350 kg)] loaves

Process, Final Dough

Mix	Short mix (soft consistency)
DDT	73°F (23°C) to 76°F (24°C)
First fermentation	3 hours with 2 to 3 folds
Divide	12 oz (0.350 kg)
Preshape	None
Resting time	None
Shape	Long strips, placed upon well-dusted linen
Final proof	30 to 45 minutes at 80°F (27°C)
Scoring	None
Steam	2 seconds
Bake	Deck oven, 22 to 25 minutes at 460°F (238°C)

Total Formula

Ingredients	Baker's %	Kilogram	US decimal	Lb & Oz		Test
Bread flour	86.40	2.193	4.835	4	13⅜	15½ oz
Whole wheat flour	13.60	0.345	0.761		12⅛	2⅜ oz
Water	76.00	1.929	4.253	4	4	13⅝ oz
Yeast (instant)	0.30	0.008	0.017		¼	½ tsp
Salt	1.60	0.041	0.090		1⅜	¼ oz
Malt	0.78	0.020	0.044		¾	⅛ oz
Total	178.68	4.536	10.000	10	0	2 lb

Francese

Spelt Bread

Cornbread

Pain Meunier

FORMULA

PIZZA DOUGH

Serving as the base for one of America's favorite foods, this pizza dough is a simple, basic recipe that is waiting to welcome tomato sauce, cheese, and imaginative toppings of choice.

% of Flour Prefermented 25%

Poolish Formula

Ingredients	Baker's %	Kilogram	US decimal	Lb & Oz		Test
Bread flour	100.00	0.614	1.354	1	5⅝	4⅜ oz
Water	100.00	0.614	1.354	1	5⅝	4⅜ oz
Yeast (instant)	0.10	0.001	0.001		<⅛	⅛ tsp
Total	200.10	1.229	2.708	2	11⅜	8⅝ oz

Process, Poolish

1. Mix all the ingredients until well incorporated with a DDT of 70°F (21°C).
2. Allow to ferment 12 to 16 hours at room temperature [65°F (18°C) to 70°F (21°C)].

Final Dough Formula

Ingredients	Baker's %	Kilogram	US decimal	Lb & Oz		Test
Bread flour	100.00	1.842	4.061	4	1	13 oz
Water	69.33	1.277	2.815	2	13	9 oz
Yeast (instant)	0.23	0.004	0.009		⅛	⅛ tsp
Salt	2.67	0.049	0.108		1¾	⅜ oz
Malt	0.67	0.012	0.027		⅜	⅛ oz
Oil	6.67	0.123	0.271		4⅜	⅞ oz
Poolish	66.70	1.229	2.708	2	11⅜	8⅝ oz
Total	246.27	4.536	10.000	10	0	2 lb

Yield: 10 [16 inch (42 cm)] pizzas
Test: 2 [16 inch (42 cm)] pizzas

Process, Final Dough

Mix	Short mix
DDT	73°F (23°C) to 76°F (24°C)
First fermentation	2 hours with 2 folds

Divide	1 lb (0.454 kg)
Preshape	Light ball
Resting time	20 to 30 minutes
Shape	Flatten out to the desired thickness
Toppings	As desired
Bake	Deck oven, 6 minutes at 550°F (288°C)

Total Formula

Ingredients	Baker's %	Kilogram	US decimal	Lb & Oz		Test
Bread flour	100.00	2.456	5.414	5	6⅝	1 lb 1⅜ oz
Water	77.00	1.891	4.169	4	2¾	13⅜ oz
Yeast (instant)	0.20	0.005	0.011		⅛	⅛ tsp
Salt	2.00	0.049	0.108		1¾	⅜ oz
Malt	0.50	0.012	0.027		⅜	⅛ oz
Oil	5.00	0.123	0.271		4⅜	⅞ oz
Total	184.70	4.536	10.000	10	0	2 lb

FORMULA

MULTIGRAIN PAN BREAD AND HONEY WHEAT PAN BREAD

Pan breads—breads that are shaped, proofed, and baked in a pan—are the result of the baking industrialization that happened after World War II. Engineers of the time were looking for efficient ways to produce breads that could be baked uniformly, then quickly packaged, stored, and shipped throughout the United States. Pan breads of that time were usually baked with white flour and an accelerated baking process; however, the modern versions included here use healthier ingredients and higher-quality methods.

MULTIGRAIN PAN BREAD

Prefermented Dough Formula

Ingredients	Baker's %	Kilogram	US decimal	Lb & Oz	Test
Bread flour	100.00	0.612	1.350	1 5⅝	4⅜ oz
Water	65.00	0.398	0.878	14	2¾ oz
Salt	2.00	0.012	0.027	⅜	⅛ oz
Yeast (instant)	0.60	0.004	0.008	⅛	⅛ tsp
Total	167.60	1.027	2.263	2 4¼	7¼ oz

Process, Prefermented Dough

1. Mix all the ingredients until well incorporated with a DDT of 70°F (21°C).
2. Allow to ferment 1 hour at room temperature [65°F (18°C) to 70°F (21°C)].
3. Then refrigerate overnight.

Levain Formula

Ingredients	Baker's %	Kilogram	US decimal	Lb & Oz	Test
Bread flour	50.00	0.096	0.212	3⅜	⅝ oz
Whole wheat flour	50.00	0.096	0.212	3⅜	⅝ oz
Water	60.00	0.115	0.255	4⅛	⅞ oz
Starter (stiff)	40.00	0.077	0.170	2¾	½ oz
Total	200.00	0.385	0.849	13⅝	2¾ oz

Process, Levain

1. Mix all the ingredients until well incorporated with a DDT 70°F (21°C).
2. Allow to ferment 12 hours at room temperature [65°F (18°C) to 70°F (21°C)].

Soaker Formula

Ingredients	Baker's %	Kilogram	US decimal	Lb & Oz		Test
Flax seeds	20.00	0.110	0.242		3 ⅞	¾ oz
Sunflower seeds	20.00	0.110	0.242		3 ⅞	¾ oz
Sesame seeds	20.00	0.110	0.242		3 ⅞	¾ oz
Rolled oats	30.00	0.165	0.364		5 ⅞	1 ⅛ oz
Water	50.00	0.275	0.606		9 ¾	2 oz
Total	140.00	0.770	1.697	1	11 ⅛	5 ⅜ oz

Process, Soaker

Allow seeds to soak at least 2 hours.

Final Dough Formula

Ingredients	Baker's %	Kilogram	US decimal	Lb & Oz		Test
Bread flour	60.00	0.770	1.697	1	11 ⅛	5 ⅜ oz
Whole wheat flour	20.00	0.257	0.566		9	1 ¾ oz
Medium rye flour	10.00	0.128	0.283		4 ½	⅞ oz
Semolina flour	5.00	0.064	0.141		2 ¼	½ oz
Rice flour	5.00	0.064	0.141		2 ¼	½ oz
Water	68.00	0.873	1.924	1	14 ¾	6 ⅛ oz
Salt	2.50	0.032	0.071		1 ⅛	¼ oz
Yeast (instant)	1.00	0.013	0.028		½	⅛ oz
Honey	6.00	0.077	0.170		2 ¾	½ oz
Oil	6.00	0.077	0.170		2 ¾	½ oz
Levain	30.00	0.385	0.849		13 ⅝	2 ¾ oz
Prefermented dough	80.00	1.027	2.263	2	4 ¼	7 ¼ oz
Soaker	60.00	0.770	1.697	1	11 ⅛	5 ⅜ oz
Total	353.50	4.536	10.000	10	0	2 lb

Yield: 5 [2 lb (0.900 kg)] loaves
Test: 1 [2 lb (0.900 kg)] loaf

Process, Final Dough

Mix	Improved mix (medium consistency) Add soaker after the dough has been developed on first speed until incorporated
DDT	73°F (23°C) to 76°F (24°C)
First fermentation	1 hour 30 minutes at 80°F (27°C) at 65% rh
Divide	1 lb (0.454 kg)
Preshape	Light ball
Resting time	20 to 30 minutes
Shape	Batard in pan
Final proof	1 hour at 80°F (27°C) at 65% rh

Scoring	Refer to the scoring charts in Chapter 5, Figures 5-5 and 5-6
Steam	2 seconds
Bake	Convection oven, 40 minutes at 385°F (197°C)

Note

When shaping, allow the loaf to relax; then, fold in both sides of the ball to the middle of the loaf, flatten, and roll up tightly. The objective is to create a tight crumb, so do not shape the dough too loose. Place the dough in the pan seam side down.

HONEY WHEAT PAN BREAD

Levain Formula

Ingredients	Baker's %	Kilogram	US decimal	Lb & Oz		Test
Bread flour	100.00	0.302	0.667		10⅝	2⅛ oz
Water	90.00	0.272	0.600		9⅝	1⅞ oz
Starter (stiff)	8.00	0.024	0.053		⅞	⅛ oz
Total	198.00	0.599	1.320	1	5⅛	4¼ oz

Process, Levain

1. Mix all the ingredients until well incorporated with a DDT of 70°F (21°C).
2. Allow to ferment 8 hours at room temperature [65°F (18°C) to 70°F (18°C)].

Final Dough Formula

Ingredients	Baker's %	Kilogram	US decimal	Lb & Oz		Test
Whole wheat flour	100.00	1.996	4.401	4	6⅜	14⅛ oz
Water #1	72.00	1.437	3.169	3	2¾	10⅛ oz
Water #2	8.00	0.160	0.352		5⅝	1⅛ oz
Salt	2.20	0.044	0.097		1½	¼ oz
Yeast (instant)	1.00	0.020	0.044		¾	⅛ oz
Honey	8.00	0.160	0.352		5⅝	1⅛ oz
Sunflower oil	6.00	0.120	0.264		4¼	⅞ oz
Levain	30.00	0.599	1.320	1	5⅛	4¼ oz
Total	227.20	4.536	10.000	10	0	2 lb

Yield: 5 [2 lb (0.900 kg)] loaves

Test: 1 [2 lb (0.900 kg)] loaf

Process, Final Dough

Mix	Improved mix (medium consistency) Double hydration technique (refer to Chapter 3, page 68)
DDT	75°F (24°C) to 78°F (25°C)

First fermentation	2 hours
Divide	1 lb (0.454 kg)
Preshape	Light ball
Resting time	20 to 30 minutes
Shape	Batard in pan
Final proof	1 hour at 80°F (27°C) at 65% rh
Scoring	None
Steam	2 seconds
Bake	Convection oven, 35 to 40 minutes at 400°F (204°C)

Note

When shaping, allow the loaf to relax; then, fold in both sides of the ball to the middle of the loaf, flatten, and roll up tightly. The objective is to create a tight crumb, so do not roll the dough to become too gassy but shape tightly. Place the dough in the pan seam side down.

Honey Wheat Pan Bread

FORMULA

HAMBURGER BUNS

This traditional bun envelops the iconic all-American burger, from the rare to the well-done.

% of Flour Prefermented 25%

Sponge Formula

Ingredients	Baker's %	Kilogram	US decimal	Lb & Oz		Test
Bread flour	100.00	0.627	1.381	1	6 ⅛	4 ⅜ oz
Water	62.00	0.388	0.856		13 ¾	2 ¾ oz
Yeast (instant)	0.10	0.001	0.001		< ⅛	⅛ tsp
Total	162.10	1.016	2.239	2	3 ⅞	7 oz

Process, Sponge

1. Mix all the ingredients until well incorporated with a DDT of 70°F (21°C).
2. Allow to ferment 12 to 16 hours at room temperature [65°F (18°C) to 70°F (21°C)].

Final Dough Formula

Ingredients	Baker's %	Kilogram	US decimal	Lb & Oz		Test
Flour	100.00	1.880	4.144	4	2 ¼	13 ¼ oz
Water	63.33	1.191	2.625	2	10	8 ⅜ oz
Yeast (instant)	1.01	0.019	0.042		⅝	⅛ oz
Salt	2.67	0.050	0.111		1 ¾	⅜ oz
Sugar	5.07	0.095	0.210		3 ⅜	⅝ oz
Butter	10.13	0.190	0.420		6 ¾	1 ⅜ oz
Milk powder	5.07	0.095	0.210		3 ⅜	⅝ oz
Sponge	54.03	1.016	2.239	2	3 ⅞	7 ⅛ oz
Total	241.31	4.536	10.000	10	0	2 lb

Yield: 53 [3 oz (0.085 kg)] buns
Test: 10 [3 oz (0.085 kg)] buns

Process, Final Dough

Mix	Improved mix (medium soft consistency)
DDT	73°F (23°C) to 76°F (24°C)
First fermentation	45 minutes to 1 hour
Divide	3 oz (0.085 kg)
Preshape	None

Resting time	20 to 30 minutes
Shape	Bun
Final proof	1 hour 30 minutes to 2 hours at 80°F (27°C) at 65% rh
Scoring	None
Steam	2 seconds
Bake	Convection oven, 20 minutes at 380°F (193°C)

Total Formula

Ingredients	Baker's %	Kilogram	US decimal	Lb & Oz		Test
Bread flour	100.00	2.506	5.525	5	8⅜	1 lb 1⅝ oz
Water	63.00	1.579	3.481	3	7¾	11⅛ oz
Yeast (instant)	0.78	0.020	0.043		¾	⅛ oz
Salt	2.00	0.050	0.111		1¾	⅜ oz
Sugar	3.80	0.095	0.210		3⅜	⅝ oz
Butter	7.60	0.190	0.420		6¾	1⅜ oz
Milk powder	3.80	0.095	0.210		3⅜	⅝ oz
Total	180.98	4.536	10.000	10	0	2 lb

FORMULA

SOFT DINNER ROLLS

An American classic, warm dinner rolls with a generous pat of butter were once a given at any family supper. This recipe for soft dinner rolls, equally delicious for sandwiches, mealtime, or hot out of the oven on their own, inspires bakers to bring rolls back to their proper place on the table.

% of Flour Prefermented 25%

Sponge Formula

Ingredients	Baker's %	Kilogram	US decimal	Lb & Oz		Test
Bread flour	100.00	0.578	1.275	1	4⅜	4⅛ oz
Water	62.00	0.359	0.791		12⅝	2½ oz
Yeast (instant)	0.10	0.001	0.001		< ⅛	⅛ tsp
Total	162.10	0.938	2.067	2	1⅛	6⅝ oz

Process, Sponge

1. Mix all the ingredients until well incorporated with a DDT of 70°F (21°C).
2. Allow to ferment 12 to 16 hours at room temperature [65°F (18°C) to 70°F (21°C)].

Final Dough Formula

Ingredients	Baker's %	Kilogram	US decimal	Lb & Oz		Test
Bread flour	100.00	1.735	3.826	3	13¼	12¼ oz
Water	52.67	0.914	2.015	2	¼	6½ oz
Eggs	16.00	0.278	0.612		9¾	2 oz
Yeast (instant)	1.03	0.018	0.040		⅝	⅛ oz
Salt	2.67	0.046	0.102		1⅝	⅜ oz
Sugar	8.00	0.139	0.306		4⅞	1 oz
Butter	20.00	0.347	0.765		12¼	2½ oz
Milk powder	7.00	0.121	0.268		4¼	⅞ oz
Sponge	54.03	0.938	2.067	2	1⅛	6⅝ oz
Total	261.40	4.536	10.000	10	0	2 lb

Yield: 53 [3 oz (0.085 kg)] rolls

Test: 10 [3 oz (0.085 kg)] rolls

Process, Final Dough

Mix	Improved mix (medium soft consistency)
DDT	73°F (23°C) to 76°F (24°C)
First fermentation	45 minutes to 1 hour
Divide	3 oz (0.085 kg)
Preshape	Light ball
Resting time	20 to 30 minutes
Shape	Rolls
Final proof	1 hour 30 minutes to 2 hours at 80°F (27°C) at 65% rh
Scoring	None
Steam	2 seconds
Bake	Convection oven, 380°F (193°C)

Total Formula

Ingredients	Baker's %	Kilogram	US decimal	Lb & Oz	Test
Bread flour	100.00	2.314	5.101	5 1⅝	1 lb ⅜ oz
Water	55.00	1.273	2.805	2 12⅞	9 oz
Eggs	12.00	0.278	0.612	9¾	2 oz
Yeast (instant)	0.80	0.019	0.041	⅝	⅛ oz
Salt	2.00	0.046	0.102	1⅝	⅜ oz
Sugar	6.00	0.139	0.306	4⅞	1 oz
Butter	15.00	0.347	0.765	12¼	2½ oz
Milk powder	5.25	0.121	0.268	4¼	⅞ oz
Total	196.05	4.536	10.000	10 0	2 lb

FORMULA

BAGELS

The first printed mention of bagels may have been found in 1610, Krakow, Poland, where community regulations stating that "bagels would be given as a gift to any woman in childbirth" indicate that the ring shape could have been seen as a symbol of life. In the 1880s, the arrival of hundreds of thousands of Jewish immigrants brought the bagel to New York City, where vendors threaded the hole-shaped bread onto dowels and hawked them on street corners. Bagels slowly gained popularity but continued to be rare in United States communities without large Eastern European Jewish populations until the last quarter of the 20th century. Now enjoyed all over the United States and the world, bagels were first a popular breakfast food, then evolved to become snack food and sandwich bases.

% of Flour Prefermented 30%

Sponge Formula

Ingredients	Baker's %	Kilogram	US decimal	Lb & Oz	Test
High-gluten flour	100.00	0.888	1.958	1 15⅜	6¼ oz
Water	65.00	0.577	1.273	1 4⅜	4⅛ oz
Yeast (instant)	0.30	0.003	0.006	⅛	⅛ tsp
Total	165.30	1.468	3.237	3 3¾	10⅜ oz

Process, Sponge

1. Mix all the ingredients until well incorporated with a DDT of 70°F (21°C).
2. Allow to ferment 6 to 8 hours at room temperature [65°F (18°C) to 70°F (21°C)].

Final Dough Formula

Ingredients	Baker's %	Kilogram	US decimal	Lb & Oz		Test
High-gluten flour	100.00	2.073	4.569	4	9⅛	14⅝ oz
Water	43.57	0.903	1.991	1	15⅞	6⅜ oz
Yeast (instant)	0.30	0.006	0.014		¼	⅛ tsp
Salt	1.86	0.038	0.085		1⅜	½ oz
Malt	2.29	0.047	0.104		1⅝	⅜ oz
Sponge	70.84	1.468	3.237	3	3¾	10⅜ oz
Total	218.86	4.536	10.000	10	0	2 lb

Yield: 53 [3 oz (0.085 kg)] bagels
Test: 10 [3 oz (0.085 kg)] bagels

Process, Final Dough

Mix	Improved to intensive mix (stiff consistency)
DDT	73°F (23°C) to 76°F (24°C)
First fermentation	30 minutes
Divide	3 oz (0.085 kg)
Preshape	None
Resting time	20 to 30 minutes
Shape	Bagel
Final proof	12 to 18 hours in a retarder
Blanch	Blanch in simmering water for 45 seconds
Steam	2 seconds
Bake	Deck oven, 15 minutes at 460°F (238°C)

Total Formula

Ingredients	Baker's %	Kilogram	US decimal	Lb & Oz		Test
High-gluten flour	100.00	2.961	6.527	6	8½	1 lb 4⅞ oz
Water	50.00	1.480	3.264	3	4¼	10½ oz
Yeast (instant)	0.30	0.009	0.020		⅜	⅛ oz
Salt	1.30	0.038	0.085		1⅜	¼ oz
Malt	1.60	0.047	0.104		1⅝	⅜ oz
Total	153.20	4.536	10.000	10	0	2 lb

FORMULA

PRETZELS

Although the task of determining the history of the pretzel is as twisty as its shape, folklore assures us that pretzels were invented in 610 BCE, in southern France or northern Italy, by a monk preparing unleavened bread for Lent. Christians of the day prayed with their arms folded across their chests, each hand on the opposite shoulder. The monk decided to twist the leftover dough from his bread into this shape and use it as a treat for the children of his village who memorized their prayers. He named his creation *pretiola*, Latin for "little reward." The pretzel continued to be a popular treat throughout Europe, where it came to symbolize good fortune. Some historians believe that the pretzel came to America on the *Mayflower* in 1620.

% of Flour Prefermented 9%

Poolish Formula

Ingredients	Baker's %	Kilogram	US decimal	Lb & Oz	Test
Bread flour	100.00	0.243	0.535	8 ½	1 ¾ oz
Water	100.00	0.243	0.535	8 ½	1 ¾ oz
Yeast (instant)	0.10	0.000	0.001	< ⅛	⅛ tsp
Total	200.10	0.486	1.070	1 1 ⅛	3 ⅜ oz

Process, Poolish

1. Mix all the ingredients until well incorporated with a DDT of 70°F (21°C).
2. Allow to ferment 12 to 16 hours at room temperature [65°F (18°C) to 70°F (21°C)].

Final Dough Formula

Ingredients	Baker's %	Kilogram	US decimal	Lb & Oz	Test
Bread flour	100.00	2.454	5.409	5 6 ½	1 lb 1 ½ oz
Water	29.67	0.728	1.605	1 9 ⅝	5 ⅛ oz
Milk	29.67	0.728	1.605	1 9 ⅝	5 ⅛ oz
Yeast (instant)	0.79	0.019	0.043	⅝	⅛ oz
Salt	1.98	0.049	0.107	1 ⅝	⅜ oz
Butter	2.97	0.073	0.160	2 ⅝	½ oz
Poolish	19.79	0.486	1.070	1 1 ⅛	3 ⅜ oz
Total	184.87	4.536	10.000	10 0	2 lb

Yield: 53 [3 oz (0.085 kg)] pretzels
Test: 10 [3 oz (0.085 kg)] pretzels

Process, Final Dough

Mix	Improved mix
DDT	73°F (23°C) to 76°F (24°C)
First fermentation	30 minutes
Divide	3 oz (0.085 kg)
Preshape	Light ball
Resting time	20 to 30 minutes
Shape	Pretzel or batard
Final proof	1 hour 30 minutes at 80°F (27°C) at 65% rh
Dipping in caustic solution*	Caustic soda 1 lb 6 oz (630 g) + 4¾ gal (18 liters) water
Steam	2 seconds
Bake	Convection oven, 15 minutes at 420°F (215°C)

Notes

* Lye Solution: up to 4% caustic soda to water.
Use caution when handling lye. Wear protective gear including heavy rubber gloves and protective eyeware. Follow manufacturers' directions for use.

Total Formula

Ingredients	Baker's %	Kilogram	US decimal	Lb & Oz		Test
Bread flour	100.00	2.696	5.944	5	15⅛	1 lb 3 oz
Water	36.00	0.971	2.140	2	2¼	6⅞ oz
Milk	27.00	0.728	1.605	1	9⅝	5⅛ oz
Yeast (instant)	0.73	0.020	0.043		¾	⅛ oz
Salt	1.80	0.049	0.107		1¾	⅜ oz
Butter	2.70	0.073	0.160		2⅝	½ oz
Total	168.23	4.536	10.000	10	0	2 lb

Traditional Pretzel
Mini Batard
Pretzels
Soft Dinner
Rolls
Bagel

FORMULA

CONCHAS

A staple in Mexico, concha is a sweet roll named after its topping, which is reminiscent of a shell (similar to the shell topping a boule of dough). This bread is eaten all day long in Mexico—with coffee in the morning, and soda during the day. Its popularity is just beginning to increase in the United States.

% of Flour Prefermented 20%

Sponge Formula

Ingredients	Baker's %	Kilogram	US decimal	Lb & Oz		Test
Bread flour	100.00	0.433	0.955		15 ¼	3 oz
Water	60.00	0.260	0.573		9 ⅛	1 ⅞ oz
Yeast (instant)	0.10	0.000	0.001		< ⅛	⅛ tsp
Total	160.10	0.693	1.529	1	8 ½	4 ⅞

Process, Sponge

1. Mix all the ingredients until well incorporated with a DDT of 70°F (21°C).
2. Allow to ferment 12 to 16 hours at room temperature [65°F (18°C) to 70°F (21°C)].

Final Dough Formula

Ingredients	Baker's %	Kilogram	US decimal	Lb & Oz		Test
Bread flour	100.00	1.733	3.820	3	13 ⅛	12 ¼ oz
Water	40.00	0.693	1.528	1	8 ½	4 ⅞ oz
Eggs	25.00	0.433	0.955		15 ¼	3 oz
Yeast (instant)	1.98	0.034	0.075		1 ¼	¼ oz
Salt	1.80	0.031	0.069		1 ⅛	¼ oz
Sugar	30.00	0.520	1.146	1	2 ⅜	3 ⅝ oz
Butter	11.00	0.191	0.420		6 ¾	1 ⅜ oz
Milk powder	11.00	0.191	0.420		6 ¾	1 ⅜ oz
Vanilla	1.00	0.017	0.038		⅝	⅛ oz
Sponge	40.03	0.693	1.529	1	8 ½	4 ⅞ oz
Total	261.81	4.536	10.000	10	0	2 lb

Yield: 53 [3 oz (0.085 kg)] conchas
Test: 10 [3 oz (0.085 kg)] conchas

Process, Final Dough

Mix	Intensive mix (medium consistency)
DDT	73°F (24°C) to 76°F (24°C)
First fermentation	45 minutes to 1 hour
Divide	3 oz (0.085 kg)
Preshape	Light ball
Resting time	20 to 30 minutes
Shape	As a ball, then cover with paste
Final proof	1 hour 30 minutes to 2 hours at 80°F (27°C) at 65% rh
Scoring	Mark the paste with a cross
Steam	2 seconds
Bake	Convection oven, 18 minutes at 360°F (182°C)

Paste Formula

Ingredients	Baker's %	Kilogram	US decimal	Lb & Oz		Test
Bread flour	100.00	0.972	2.143	2	2¼	6⅞ oz
Shortening	66.66	0.648	1.429	1	6⅞	4⅝ oz
Powdered sugar	66.66	0.648	1.429	1	6⅞	4⅝ oz
Colorant	SQ					
Total	233.32	2.268	5.000	5	0	1 lb

Process, Paste

1. Mix the shortening and powdered sugar until light and fluffy.
2. Mix in the pastry flour until smooth.
3. Add a sufficient quantity (SQ) of colorant as desired.
4. Topping: Form a small ball and flatten it. Place it on top of the dough.
5. Cut a line in the topping before baking.

Total Formula

Ingredients	Baker's %	Kilogram	US decimal	Lb & Oz		Test
Bread flour	100.00	2.166	4.775	4	12⅜	15¼ oz
Water	44.00	0.953	2.101	2	1⅝	6¾ oz
Eggs	20.00	0.433	0.955		15¼	3 oz
Yeast (instant)	1.60	0.035	0.076		1¼	¼ oz
Salt	1.44	0.031	0.069		1⅛	¼ oz
Sugar	24.00	0.520	1.146	1	2⅜	3⅝ oz
Butter	8.80	0.191	0.420		6¾	1⅜ oz
Margarine	8.80	0.191	0.420		6¾	1⅜ oz
Vanilla	0.80	0.017	0.038		⅝	⅛ oz
Total	209.44	4.536	10.000	10	0	2 lb

Conchas

FORMULA

ONION POPPY SEED ROLLS

Some think this bread must originally have been developed for a steak house restaurant because it is a perfect match with a great piece of red meat. Frequently used for sandwiches in pubs and other simple establishments, onion poppy seed rolls are satisfyingly hearty and flavorful.

% of Flour Prefermented 25%

Sponge Formula

Ingredients	Baker's %	Kilogram	US decimal	Lb & Oz		Test
Bread flour	100.00	0.528	1.164	1	2⅝	3¾ oz
Water	62.00	0.327	0.722		11½	2¼ oz
Yeast (instant)	0.10	0.001	0.001		<⅛	⅛ tsp
Total	162.10	0.856	1.887	1	14⅛	6 oz

Process, Sponge

1. Mix all the ingredients until well incorporated with a DDT of 70°F (21°C).
2. Allow to ferment 12 to 16 hours at room temperature [65°F (18°C) to 70°F (21°C)].

Final Dough Formula

Ingredients	Baker's %	Kilogram	US decimal	Lb & Oz		Test
Bread flour	100.00	1.584	3.492	3	7⅞	11⅛ oz
Water	48.67	0.771	1.699	1	11¼	5½ oz
Eggs	16.00	0.253	0.559		9	1¾ oz
Yeast (instant)	1.03	0.016	0.036		⅝	⅛ oz
Salt	2.67	0.042	0.093		1½	¼ oz
Sugar	8.00	0.127	0.279		4½	⅞ oz
Butter	20.00	0.317	0.698		11⅛	2¼ oz
Milk powder	6.67	0.106	0.233		3¾	¾ oz
Onions (small diced and sauteed until translucent)	24.00	0.380	0.838		13⅜	2⅝ oz
Poppy seeds	5.33	0.084	0.186		3	⅝ oz
Sponge	54.03	0.856	1.887	1	14⅛	6 oz
Total	286.40	4.536	10.000	10	0	2 lb

Yield: 53 [3 oz (0.085 kg)] rolls
Test: 10 [3 oz (0.085 kg)] rolls

Process, Final Dough

Mix	Improved mix Add sautéed onions and poppy seeds after the dough is developed on first speed
DDT	73°F (23°C) to 76°F (24°C)
First fermentation	45 minutes to 1 hour
Divide	3 oz (0.085 kg)
Preshape	None
Resting time	20 to 30 minutes
Shape	Bun
Final proof	1 hour 30 minutes to 2 hours at 80°F (27°C) at 65% rh
Scoring	None
Steam	2 seconds
Bake	Convection oven, 15 minutes at 380°F (193°C)

Total Formula

Ingredients	Baker's %	Kilogram	US decimal	Lb & Oz		Test
Bread flour	100.00	2.112	4.655	4	10½	14⅞ oz
Water	52.00	1.098	2.421	2	6¾	7¾ oz
Eggs	12.00	0.253	0.559		9	1¾ oz
Yeast (instant)	0.80	0.017	0.037		⅝	⅛ oz
Salt	2.00	0.042	0.093		1½	¼ oz
Sugar	6.00	0.127	0.279		4½	⅞ oz
Butter	15.00	0.317	0.698		11⅛	2¼ oz
Milk Powder	5.00	0.106	0.233		3¾	¾ oz
Onions	18.00	0.380	0.838		13⅜	2⅝ oz
Poppy seeds	4.00	0.084	0.186		3	⅝ oz
Total	214.80	4.536	10.000	10	0	2 lb

FORMULA

POTATO DILL ROLLS

The flavors of dill and potato are meant for each other, nowhere more so than in this tasty little potato dill roll. The texture is also pleasantly soft.

Prefermented Dough Formula

Ingredients	Baker's %	Kilogram	US decimal	Lb & Oz	Test
Bread flour	100.00	0.372	0.820	13 ⅛	2 ⅝ oz
Water	67.00	0.249	0.549	8 ¾	1 ¾ oz
Yeast (instant)	0.60	0.002	0.005	⅛	⅛ tsp
Salt	2.00	0.007	0.016	¼	¼ tsp
Total	169.60	0.631	1.391	1 6 ¼	4 ½ oz

Process, Prefermented Dough

1. Mix all the ingredients until well incorporated with a DDT of 70°F (21°C).
2. Allow to ferment 1 hour at room temperature [65°F (18°C) to 70°F (21°C)].
3. Then refrigerate overnight.

Liquid Levain Formula

Ingredients	Baker's %	Kilogram	US decimal	Lb & Oz	Test
Bread flour	100.00	0.121	0.267	4 ¼	⅞ oz
Water	100.00	0.121	0.267	4 ¼	⅞ oz
Starter	60.00	0.073	0.160	2 ⅝	½ oz
Total	260.00	0.315	0.695	11 ⅛	2 ¼ oz

Process, Liquid Levain

1. Mix all the ingredients until well incorporated with a DDT of 70°F (21°C).
2. Allow to ferment 12 hours at room temperature [65°F (18°C) to 70°F (21°C)].

Final Dough Formula

Ingredients	Baker's %	Kilogram	US decimal	Lb & Oz		Test
Bread flour	80.00	1.682	4.636	4	10⅛	14⅞ oz
Whole wheat flour	12.00	0.252	0.556		8⅞	1¾ oz
Potato flour	8.00	0.168	0.371		5⅞	1⅛ oz
Water	68.00	1.430	3.153	3	2½	10⅛ oz
Salt	2.30	0.048	0.107		1¾	⅜ oz
Yeast (instant)	0.20	0.004	0.009		⅛	¼ tsp
Levain (liquid)	15.00	0.315	0.695		11⅛	2¼ oz
Prefermented dough	30.00	0.631	1.391	1	6¼	4½ oz
Dill	0.20	0.004	0.009		⅛	2 tsp
Total	215.70	4.536	10.000	10	0	2 lb

Yield: 53 [3 oz (0.085 kg)] rolls
Test: 10 [3 oz (0.085 kg)] rolls

Process, Final Dough

Mix	Improved mix (medium soft consistency)
DDT	73°F (23°C) to 76°F (24°C)
First fermentation	45 minutes to 1 hour
Divide	3 oz (0.085 kg)
Preshape	None
Resting time	20 to 30 minutes
Shape	Rolls
Final proof	1 hour 30 minutes to 2 hours at 80°F (27°C) at 65% rh
Scoring	None
Steam	2 seconds
Bake	Convection oven, 15 minutes at 380°F (193°C)

FORMULA

CARROT ROLLS

The shredded carrot used in this tasty German bread adds visual appeal, as well as a nice, chewy crumb texture.

% of Flour Prefermented 25%

Prefermented Dough Formula

Ingredients	Baker's %	Kilogram	US decimal	Lb & Oz	Test
Bread flour	100.00	0.422	0.930	14⅞	3 oz
Water	100.00	0.422	0.930	14⅞	3 oz
Yeast (instant)	0.20	0.001	0.002	< ⅛	⅛ tsp
Salt	0.10	0.000	0.001	< ⅛	⅛ tsp
Total	200.30	0.845	1.862	1 13¾	6 oz

Process, Prefermented Dough

1. Mix all the ingredients until well incorporated with a DDT of 70°F (21°C).
2. Allow to ferment 1 hour at room temperature [65°F (18°C) to 70°F (21°C)].
3. Then refrigerate overnight.

Soaker Formula

Ingredients	Baker's %	Kilogram	US decimal	Lb & Oz	Test
Seven grain mix	100	0.422	0.930	14⅞	3 oz
Water	100	0.422	0.930	14⅞	3 oz
Total	200	0.844	1.860	1 13¾	6 oz

Process, Soaker

Allow to soak at least 2 hours.

Final Dough Formula

Ingredients	Baker's %	Kilogram	US decimal	Lb & Oz		Test
Bread flour	100.00	1.300	2.865	2	13⅞	9⅛ oz
Water	65.96	0.857	1.890	1	14¼	6 oz
Salt	3.52	0.046	0.101		1⅝	⅜ oz
Yeast (instant)	1.15	0.015	0.033		½	⅛ oz
Malt	3.44	0.045	0.099		1⅝	⅜ oz
Carrots (shredded)	45.03	0.585	1.290	1	4⅝	4⅛ oz
Soaker	64.90	0.844	1.860	1	13¾	6 oz
Poolish	65.00	0.845	1.862	1	13¾	6 oz
Total	349.00	4.536	10.000	10	0	2 lb

Yield: 53 [3 oz (0.085 kg)] rolls
Test: 10 [3 oz (0.085 kg)] rolls

Process, Final Dough

Mix	Improved mix (medium consistency) Add soaker and carrots after development in first speed
DDT	73°F (23°C) to 76°F (24°C)
First fermentation	1 hour 30 minutes at 80°F (27°C) at 65% rh
Divide	3 oz (0.085 kg)
Preshape	None
Resting time	20 to 30 minutes
Shape	Square
Final proof	1 hour at 80°F (27°C) at 65% rh
Scoring	None
Steam	2 seconds
Bake	Deck oven, 30 to 35 minutes at 440°F (232°C)

Total Formula

Ingredients	Baker's %	Kilogram	US decimal	Lb & Oz		Test
Bread flour	100.00	1.721	3.795	3	12¾	12⅛ oz
Water	74.30	1.279	2.820	2	13⅛	9 oz
Salt	2.68	0.046	0.102		1⅝	⅜ oz
Yeast (instant)	0.92	0.016	0.035		½	⅛ oz
Malt	2.60	0.045	0.099		1⅝	⅜ oz
Carrots	34.00	0.585	1.290	1	4⅝	4⅛ oz
Soaker	49.00	0.844	1.860	1	13¾	6 oz
Total	263.50	4.536	10.000	10	0	2 lb

FORMULA

FILONCINI BURRO Y NOCCI

Literally translating to "small stick with butter and walnuts," Filoncini Burro y Nocci is made all over Italy but is most popular in the Piedmont region where walnuts are produced in abundance.

% of Flour Prefermented 11%

Biga Formula

Ingredients	Baker's %	Kilogram	US decimal	Lb & Oz	Test
Bread flour	100.00	0.239	0.526	8⅜	1⅝ oz
Water	55.00	0.131	0.289	4⅝	⅞ oz
Yeast (instant)	1.00	0.002	0.005	⅛	⅛ tsp
Total	156.00	0.372	0.820	13⅛	2⅝ oz

Process, Biga

1. Mix all the ingredients until well incorporated with a DDT of 70°F (21°C).
2. Allow to ferment 16 to 18 hours at 60°F (18°C).

Final Dough Formula

Ingredients	Baker's %	Kilogram	US decimal	Lb & Oz	Test
Bread flour	100.00	1.872	4.128	4 2	13¼ oz
Water	5.12	0.096	0.211	3⅜	⅝ oz
Milk	50.01	0.936	2.064	2 1	6⅝ oz
Eggs	8.00	0.150	0.330	5¼	1 oz
Sugar	6.47	0.121	0.267	4¼	⅞ oz
Yeast (instant)	0.64	0.012	0.026	⅜	⅛ oz
Salt	2.19	0.041	0.090	1½	¼ oz
Butter	19.99	0.374	0.825	13¼	2⅝ oz
Walnuts, ground	29.98	0.561	1.237	1 3¾	4 oz
Biga	19.87	0.372	0.820	13⅛	2⅝ oz
Total	242.27	4.536	10.000	10 0	2 lb

Yield: 53 [3 oz (0.085 kg)] rolls
Test: 10 [3 oz (0.085 kg)] rolls

Process, Final Dough

Mix	Intensive mix (medium soft consistency) Add soft butter at intensive mix stage and once fully incorporated add the walnuts in first speed
DDT	73°F (23°C) to 76°F (24°C)
First fermentation	1 hour 30 minutes to 2 hours at 80°F (27°C) at 65% rh
Divide	3 oz (0.085 kg)
Preshape	Light ball
Resting time	20 to 30 minutes
Shape	Batard
Final proof	1 hour 30 minutes to 2 hours at 80°F (27°C) at 65% rh
Scoring	None
Steam	2 seconds
Bake	Convection oven, 30 minutes at 400° F (204°C)

Total Formula

Ingredients	Baker's %	Kilogram	US decimal	Lb & Oz		Test
Bread flour	100.00	2.111	4.653	4	10½	14⅞ oz
Water	10.76	0.227	0.501		8	1⅝ oz
Milk	44.36	0.936	2.064	2	1	6⅝ oz
Eggs	7.10	0.150	0.330		5¼	1 oz
Sugar	5.74	0.121	0.267		4¼	⅞ oz
Yeast (instant)	0.68	0.014	0.032		½	⅛ oz
Salt	1.94	0.041	0.090		1½	¼ oz
Butter	17.73	0.374	0.825		13¼	2⅝ oz
Walnuts, ground	26.59	0.561	1.237	1	3¾	4 oz
Total	214.90	4.536	10.000	10	0	2 lb

Carrot Rolls
Onion Poppy Seed Rolls
Potato Dill Rolls
Filoncini Buro e Noci

FORMULA

PAN DE LOS MUERTOS

This traditional celebratory bread, made in the shape of a skull and cross bones, is baked in very large quantities as part of the feasts during El Dia de los Muertos or Day of the Dead, observed on November 2 all over the world, but most prominently in Mexico. It may seem morbid to the uninitiated, but the purpose of the holiday is to remember the dead and celebrate ancestors in a joyful, reflective way that honors the continuation of life. Pan de los Muertos has been an important part of this ritual for many years.

% of Flour Prefermented 24%

Sponge Formula

Ingredients	Baker's %	Kilogram	US decimal	Lb & Oz	Test
Bread flour	100.00	0.524	1.155	1 2½	3¾ oz
Water	66.00	0.346	0.762	12¼	2½ oz
Yeast (instant)	0.10	0.001	0.001	<⅛	⅛ tsp
Total	166.10	0.870	1.919	1 14¾	6⅛ oz

Process, Sponge

1. Mix all the ingredients until well incorporated with a DDT of 70°F (21°C).
2. Allow to ferment 12 hours at room temperature [65°F (18°C) to 70°F (21°C)].

Anise Water Formula

Ingredients	Baker's %	Kilogram	US decimal	Lb & Oz	Test
Water	100.00	0.080	0.176	2¾	½ oz
Anise seeds	6.00	0.005	0.011	⅛	1 tsp
Total	106.00	0.085	0.186	3	⅝ oz

Process, Anise Water

Boil seeds and water together; then allow to cool. Strain water.

Final Dough Formula

Ingredients	Baker's %	Kilogram	US decimal	Lb & Oz	Test
Bread flour	100.00	1.643	3.622	3 10	11⅝ oz
Water	0.00	0.000	0.000	0	0
Orange water	3.30	0.054	0.119	1⅞	⅜ oz
Anise water	5.14	0.085	0.186	3	⅝ oz
Eggs	19.99	0.328	0.724	11⅝	2⅜ oz
Egg yolks	26.00	0.427	0.942	15⅛	3 oz
Sugar	26.00	0.427	0.942	15⅛	3 oz
Osmotolerant instant yeast	1.19	0.020	0.043	¾	⅛ oz
Salt	1.50	0.025	0.054	⅞	⅛ oz
Lard	18.00	0.296	0.652	10⅜	2⅛ oz
Butter	21.00	0.345	0.760	12⅛	2⅜ oz
Vanilla extract	1.00	0.016	0.036	⅝	⅛ oz
Sponge	52.97	0.870	1.919	1 14¾	6⅛ oz
Total	276.09	4.536	10.000	10 0	2 lb

Yield: 8 [1 lb 4 oz (0.545 kg)] loaves
Test: 1½ [1 lb 4 oz (0.454 kg)] loaves

Process, Final Dough

Mix	Intensive mix
DDT	73°F (23°C) to 76°F (24°C)
First fermentation	45 minutes
Divide	Body: 1 lb (0.450 kg); skull (ball): ¾ oz (0.020 kg); bones (2): 2½ oz (0.075 kg)
Preshape	Light ball
Resting time	30 minutes
Shape	Refer to the photo on page 295
Final proof	2 hours at 85°F (29°C) at 65% rh
Scoring	None
Steam	2 seconds
Bake	Convection oven, 25 minutes at 350°F (177°C)

Total Formula

Ingredients	Baker's %	Kilogram	US decimal	Lb & Oz	Test
Bread flour	100.00	2.167	4.777	4 12⅜	15¼ oz
Water	15.96	0.346	0.762	12¼	2½ oz
Orange water	2.50	0.054	0.119	1⅞	⅜ oz
Anise water	3.90	0.085	0.186	3	⅝ oz
Eggs	15.16	0.328	0.724	11⅝	2⅜ oz
Egg yolks	19.71	0.427	0.942	15⅛	3 oz
Sugar	19.71	0.427	0.942	15⅛	3 oz
Osmotolerant instant yeast	0.93	0.020	0.044	¾	⅛ oz
Salt	1.14	0.025	0.054	⅞	⅛ oz
Lard	13.65	0.296	0.652	10⅜	2⅛ oz
Butter	15.92	0.345	0.760	12⅛	2⅜ oz
Vanilla extract	0.76	0.016	0.036	⅝	⅛ oz
Total	209.34	4.536	10.000	10 0	2 lb

FORMULA

PAN DE CIOCCOLATE

This sumptuous Italian delicacy combines the flavors of honey and chocolate, creating a perfect breakfast bread or dessert with fresh fruits.

Levain Formula

Ingredients	Baker's %	Kilogram	US decimal	Lb & Oz	Test
Bread flour	95.00	0.162	0.358	5¾	1⅛ oz
Medium rye flour	5.00	0.009	0.019	¼	1 tsp
Water	50.00	0.086	0.189	3	⅝ oz
Starter (stiff)	80.00	0.137	0.302	4⅞	1 oz
Total	230.00	0.393	0.867	13⅞	2¾ oz

Process, Levain

1. Mix all the ingredients until well incorporated with a DDT of 70°F (21°C).
2. Allow to ferment 8 hours at room temperature [65°F (18°C) to 70°F (21°C)].

Final Dough Formula

Ingredients	Baker's %	Kilogram	US decimal	Lb & Oz		Test
Bread flour	100.00	1.967	4.337	4	5⅜	13⅞ oz
Water	63.00	1.239	2.732	2	11¾	8¾ oz
Honey	18.00	0.354	0.781		12½	2½ oz
Vanilla extract	1.00	0.020	0.043		¾	⅛ oz
Cocoa powder	6.00	0.118	0.260		4⅛	⅞ oz
Osmotolerant instant yeast	0.30	0.006	0.013		¼	¼ tsp
Salt	2.30	0.045	0.100		1⅝	⅜ oz
Levain	20.00	0.393	0.867		13⅞	2¾ oz
Chocolate chips	20.00	0.393	0.867		13⅞	2¾ oz
Total	230.60	4.536	10.000	10	0	2 lb

Yield: 10 [1 lb (0.454 kg)] loaves
Test: 2 [1 lb (0.454 kg)] loaves

Process, Final Dough

Mix	Improved mix (medium consistency)
DDT	75°F (24°C) to 78°F (25°C)
	At the end of mixing, add the chips on first speed
First fermentation	2 hours
Divide	1 lb (0.454 kg)
Preshape	Light ball
Resting time	20 to 30 minutes
Shape	Boule or batard
Final proof	2½ to 3 hours at 80°F (27°C) at 65% rh
Scoring	Refer to Chapter 5, Figure 5-5
Steam	2 seconds
Bake	Rack oven, 35 to 40 minutes at 400°F (204°C)

FORMULA

ROTOLO DI NATALE

This ring of dough is usually baked in Italy for Christmas celebrations. The combination of soft enriched dough and crunchy filling creates an unusual texture, while the appealing presentation makes Rotolo di Natale a festive centerpiece.

% of Flour Prefermented 20%

Sponge Formula

Ingredients	Baker's %	Kilogram	US decimal	Lb & Oz		Test
Bread flour	100.00	0.451	0.994		15⅞	3⅛ oz
Milk	60.00	0.271	0.597		9½	1⅞ oz
Yeast (instant)	0.10	0.000	0.001		<⅛	⅛ tsp
Total	160.10	0.722	1.592	1	9½	5⅛ oz

Process, Sponge

1. Mix all the ingredients until well incorporated with a DDT of 70°F (21°C).
2. Allow to ferment 12 hours at room temperature [65°F (18°C) to 70°F (21°C)].

Final Dough Formula

Ingredients	Baker's %	Kilogram	US decimal	Lb & Oz		Test
Bread flour	100.00	1.804	3.977	3	15⅝	12¾ oz
Water	33.75	0.609	1.342	1	5½	4¼ oz
Eggs	15.00	0.271	0.597		9½	1⅞ oz
Rum	5.00	0.090	0.199		3⅛	⅝ oz
Salt	2.20	0.040	0.087		1⅜	¼ oz
Osmotolerant instant yeast	2.48	0.045	0.098		1⅝	⅜ oz
Sugar	28.00	0.505	1.114	1	1⅞	3⅝ oz
Butter	25.00	0.451	0.994		15⅞	3⅛ oz
Sponge	40.03	0.722	1.592	1	9½	5⅛ oz
Orange zest	To taste	0.005	0.011		0	1 tsp
Lemon zest	To taste	0.005	0.011		0	1 tsp
Total	251.46	4.546	10.022	10	0	2 lb

Filling Formula (for 10 lb dough)

Ingredients	Baker's %	Kilogram	US decimal	Lb & Oz		Test
Walnuts	200.00	0.469	1.034	1	½	2 ⅛ oz
Pine nuts	100.00	0.235	0.517		8 ¼	1 oz
Sugar	100.00	0.235	0.517		8 ¼	1 oz
Cacao powder	66.67	0.156	0.345		5 ½	⅝ oz
Raisins	200.00	0.469	1.034	1	½	2 ⅛ oz
Rum	100.00	0.235	0.517		8 ¼	1 oz
Beaten egg whites	200.00	0.469	1.034	1	½	2 ⅛ oz
Total	966.67	2.268	5.000	5	0	10 oz

Yield: 4 [2.21 lb (1 kg)] loaves
Test: 1 [2 lb (0.9 kg)] loaf

Process, Filling

Mix all the ingredients until fully incorporated.

Process, Final Dough

Mix	Intensive mix At intensive mix, add the rum, orange, and lemon zest in first speed
DDT	73°F (23°C) to 76°F (24°C)
First fermentation	Overnight in the refrigerator
Divide	2.21 lb (1 kg)
Preshape	Roll the dough to a rectangular shape
Resting time	None
Shape	Apply filling over the dough and roll up like a cinnamon roll; form into a crown shape
Final proof	3 hours at 85°F (29°C) at 65% rh
Scoring	None
Steam	2 seconds
Bake	Convection oven, 45 minutes at 315°F (157°C) Egg wash and sprinkle coarse sugar on the loaves prior to baking

Total Formula

Ingredients	Baker's %	Kilogram	US decimal	Lb & Oz		Test
Bread flour	100.00	2.255	4.971	4	15½	15⅞ oz
Water	27.00	0.609	1.342	1	5½	4¼ oz
Milk	12.00	0.271	0.597		9½	1⅞ oz
Egg yolks	12.00	0.271	0.597		9½	1⅞ oz
Rum	4.00	0.090	0.199		3⅛	⅝ oz
Salt	1.76	0.040	0.087		1⅜	¼ oz
Osmotolerant instant yeast	2.00	0.045	0.099		1⅝	⅜ oz
Sugar	22.40	0.505	1.114	1	1⅞	3⅝ oz
Butter	20.00	0.451	0.994		15⅞	3⅛ oz
Orange zest	To taste	0.005	0.011		0	1 tsp
Lemon zest	To taste	0.005	0.011		0	1 tsp
Total	201.16	4.546	10.022	10	0	2 lb

Corona Dulce

Rotolo di Natale

Pan de Cioccolate

Pan de los Muertos

FORMULA

CHALLAH

Challah is a Jewish Sabbath and holiday bread that has been in existence for thousands of years. The word *challah* refers to the portion of dough to be set aside for the high priests in the Temple of Jerusalem during ancient times. Biblical law dictated that following the rising of the dough, women were to separate a piece and burn it to remind them of the offerings to the Temple. Challah is served during many Jewish holidays, with shapes and preparations laden with traditional symbolism. For instance, poppy seeds and sesame seeds sprinkled on the bread symbolize manna from heaven, while braided loaves, with their intertwined portions, symbolize love.

% of Flour Prefermented 30%

Prefermented Dough Formula

Ingredients	Baker's %	Kilogram	US decimal	Lb & Oz		Test
Bread flour	100.00	0.687	1.514	1	8 ¼	4 ⅞ oz
Water	65.00	0.446	0.984		15 ¾	3 ⅛ oz
Yeast (instant)	0.60	0.004	0.009		⅛	⅛ tsp
Salt	2.00	0.014	0.030		½	⅛ oz
Total	167.60	1.151	2.537	2	8 ⅝	8 ⅛ oz

Process, Prefermented Dough

1. Mix all the ingredients until well incorporated with a DDT of 70°F (21°C).
2. Allow to ferment 1 hour at room temperature [65°F (18°C) to 70°F (21°C)].
3. Then refrigerate overnight.

Final Dough Formula

Ingredients	Baker's %	Kilogram	US decimal	Lb & Oz		Test
Bread flour	100.00	1.602	3.533	3	8 ½	11 ¼ oz
Water	42.14	0.675	1.489	1	7 ⅞	4 ¾ oz
Eggs	22.29	0.357	0.787		12 ⅝	2 ½ oz
Osmotolerant instant yeast	0.96	0.015	0.034		½	⅛ oz
Salt	2.00	0.032	0.071		1 ⅛	¼ oz
Sugar	17.86	0.286	0.631		10 ⅛	2 oz
Butter	22.43	0.359	0.792		12 ⅝	2 ½ oz
Milk powder	3.57	0.057	0.126		2	⅜ oz
Prefermented dough	71.83	1.151	2.537	2	8 ⅝	8 ⅛ oz
Total	283.08	4.536	10.000	10	0	2 lb

Yield: Varies with amount of strands chosen to braid

Process, Final Dough

Mix	Intensive mix
DDT	73°F (23°C) to 76°F (24°C)
First fermentation	45 minutes to 1 hour
Divide	5 oz (0.150 kg) strand
Preshape	Light rectangle
Resting time	25 to 30 minutes
Shape	Six-strand braid
Final proof	1 hour 15 minutes at 80°F (27°C) at 65% rh Egg wash prior to baking
Scoring	None
Steam	2 seconds
Bake	Convection oven, 25 minutes at 380°F (193°C)

Total Formula

Ingredients	Baker's %	Kilogram	US decimal	Lb & Oz		Test
Bread flour	100.00	2.289	5.047	5	¾	1 lb ⅛ oz
Water	49.00	1.122	2.473	2	7⅝	7⅞ oz
Eggs	15.60	0.357	0.787		12⅝	2½ oz
Osmotolerant instant yeast	0.85	0.019	0.043		⅝	⅛ oz
Salt	2.00	0.046	0.101		1⅝	⅜ oz
Sugar	12.50	0.286	0.631		10⅛	2 oz
Butter	15.70	0.359	0.792		12⅝	2½ oz
Milk powder	2.50	0.057	0.126		2	⅜ oz
Total	198.15	4.536	10.000	10	0	2 lb

Note

This challah formula is not kosher due to the dairy in the formula. To make kosher replace the butter with oil and delete the milk powder.

FORMULA

STOLLEN

First made in Dresden, Germany, around the 1400s, Stollen was meant to represent the baby Jesus wrapped in swaddling clothes. It was a popular Christmas pastry, but because Advent was a time of fasting, there was a ban on the use of butter in baked goods, so oil was used as a replacement, which made for a somewhat tasteless pastry. When the Pope finally lifted the ban for the general public in 1691, stollen (now baked with butter) became more popular and slowly evolved from the original to a sweeter version containing candied and liqueur-soaked fruits and nuts, which is similar to the kind eaten around the world today.

% of Flour Prefermented 26%

Sponge Formula

Ingredients	Baker's %	Kilogram	US decimal	Lb & Oz		Test
Bread flour	100.00	0.363	0.800		12¾	2½ oz
Water	66.70	0.242	0.534		8½	1¾ oz
Yeast (instant)	0.10	0.000	0.001		< ⅛	⅛ tsp
Total	166.80	0.605	1.335	1	5⅜	4¼ oz

Process, Sponge

1. Mix all the ingredients until well incorporated with a DDT of 70°F (21°C).
2. Allow to ferment 12 to 16 hours at room temperature [65°F (18°C) to 70°F (21°C)].

Final Dough Formula

Ingredients	Baker's %	Kilogram	US decimal	Lb & Oz		Test
Bread flour	100.00	1.053	2.321	2	5⅛	7⅜ oz
Milk	15.33	0.161	0.356		5¾	1⅛ oz
Osmotolerant instant yeast	5.34	0.056	0.124		2	⅜ oz
Salt	2.29	0.024	0.053		⅞	⅛ oz
Malt	2.29	0.024	0.053		⅞	⅛ oz
Sugar	14.52	0.153	0.337		5⅜	1⅛ oz
Eggs	15.33	0.161	0.356		5¾	1⅛ oz
Lemon zest	1.48	0.016	0.034		½	⅛ oz
Orange zest	1.48	0.016	0.034		½	⅛ oz
Spice mixture	1.21	0.013	0.028		½	⅛ oz
Butter	78.27	0.824	1.816	1	13⅛	5⅞ oz
Sponge	57.51	0.605	1.335	1	5⅜	4¼ oz
Rum-soaked fruits	135.83	1.430	3.152	3	2⅜	10⅛ oz
Total	430.88	4.536	10.000	10	0	2 lb

Yield: 10 [1 lb (0.454 kg)] loaves
Test: 2 [1 lb (0.454 kg)] loaves

Process, Final Dough

Mix	Intensive mix Add the butter and sugar from the beginning but withhold the rum-soaked fruits until after the dough has developed; mix in fruits on first speed
DDT	73°F (23°C) to 76°F (24°C)
First fermentation	½ hour
Divide	1 lb (0.454 kg)
Preshape	Light ball
Resting time	20 to 30 minutes
Shape	Batard, offset Fendu
Final proof	1 hour at 80°F (27°C) at 65% rh
Steam	3 seconds
Bake	Convection oven, 30 minutes at 375°F (190°C)
Finishing	Brush with clarified butter Dredge in granulated sugar Dust with powdered sugar

Total Formula

Ingredients	Baker's %	Kilogram	US decimal	Lb & Oz		Test
Bread flour	100.00	1.416	3.121	3	2	10 oz
Water	17.10	0.242	0.534		8 ½	1 ¾ oz
Milk	11.40	0.161	0.356		5 ¾	1 ⅛ oz
Osmotolerant instant yeast	4.00	0.057	0.125		2	⅜ oz
Salt	1.70	0.024	0.053		⅞	⅛ oz
Malt	1.70	0.024	0.053		⅞	⅛ oz
Sugar	10.80	0.153	0.337		5 ⅜	1 ⅛ oz
Eggs	11.40	0.161	0.356		5 ¾	1 ⅛ oz
Lemon zest	1.10	0.016	0.034		½	⅛ oz
Orange zest	1.10	0.016	0.034		½	⅛ oz
Spice mixture	0.90	0.013	0.028		½	⅛ oz
Butter	58.20	0.824	1.816	1	13 ⅛	5 ⅞ oz
Rum-soaked fruits	101.00	1.430	3.152	3	2 ⅜	10 ⅛ oz
Total	320.40	4.536	10.000	10	0	2 lb

Rum-Soaked Fruits Formula

Ingredients	Baker's %	Kilogram	US decimal	Lb & Oz		Test
Raisins	100.00	0.617	1.361	1	5 ¾	4 ⅜ oz
Candied orange peel	30.00	0.185	0.408		6 ½	1 ¼ oz
Candied lemon peel	45.00	0.278	0.612		9 ¾	2 oz
Slivered almond	40.00	0.247	0.544		8 ¾	1 ¾ oz
Rum	16.60	0.102	0.226		3 ⅝	¾ oz
Total	231.60	1.430	3.152	3	2 ⅜	10 ⅛ oz

Notes

Spice mixture: equal parts of cinnamon, cardamom, nutmeg, clove, and allspice.
During shaping a piped line of almond filling may be applied prior to folding over the dough in the traditional Fendu shape.

Stollen

PART

3 VIENNOISERIE

Part 3 explores Viennoiserie. This type of bread originated in Vienna, where it was first made exclusively for the monarchy. The butter, sugar, and eggs that transformed lean doughs into sweet pastries could only be afforded by the powerful. From the 18th century to today, Viennese style breads and pastries have evolved into sophisticated and refined items that are enjoyed globally in a variety of shapes and types. At the same time, all of them uniquely relate back to the regions from which they evolved.

chapter
9

VIENNOISERIE

OBJECTIVES

After reading this chapter, you should be able to

- describe the Viennoiserie ingredients used and their central functions.
- explain the mixing, fermentation, makeup, proofing, and baking of laminated and nonlaminated dough.
- produce a selection of various pastries from laminated doughs, exhibiting proper mixing, lamination, and makeup techniques.
- produce a selection of nonlaminated Viennoiserie.
- demonstrate and implement alternative baking processes for Viennoiserie.

AN INTRODUCTION TO VIENNOISERIE

Viennoiserie is the meeting point between pastry and bread. Professional bakers and pastry chefs use this term to refer to yeast-raised products that are sweetened with sugar and enriched with butter and eggs. The two major classes of Viennoiserie are **laminated dough** and **nonlaminated dough**.

Lamination is the process of creating layers of dough and butter to create light and flaky pastries. Examples of laminated Viennoiserie include croissant and Danish, while versions of nonlaminated Viennoiserie include brioche, Pan d'Oro, and Gibassier. Viennoiserie requires knowledge of bread-making principles such as dough mixing, fermentation, proofing time assessment, and baking, yet it can also require skills more commonly associated with the pastry chef, such as visual composition, uniqueness of flavor, and presentation.

THE BAKING PROCESS FOR VIENNOISERIE

Like bread, Viennoiserie is yeast raised, and many of the same basic principles apply. However, depending on the category of Viennoiserie and the characteristics of the dough, some special considerations should to be taken. The basic processes for Viennoiserie are listed in Figure 9-1.

The working stages of Viennoiserie are similar to bread and can be divided into two categories: physically working with the dough (mixing, laminating, dividing, preshaping, and shaping) and resting or undergoing fermentation (preferment, first fermentation, final fermentation, and oven spring). A review of mixing and fermentation from Chapters 3 and 4 will be helpful. The important difference is the process of lamination.

INGREDIENT SELECTION AND FUNCTIONALITY

The selection of ingredients for Viennoiserie will have an effect on the properties of the dough. As with bread, basic ingredients include flour, water, yeast, and salt. Additional ingredients commonly used in sweet, yeasted dough include sugar, fat, eggs, and milk.

FLOUR

The choice of flour is important because the dough needs go through the processes of mixing, fermentation, and makeup. Proper dough characteristics can be achieved through a good balance between extensibility and elasticity. Most bakers use low-protein bread flour milled from HRW (hard red winter) wheat, which provides enough strength to support the additional ingredients commonly found in doughs like croissant or brioche.

Other bakers use high-gluten flour milled from HRS wheat. This option may be desirable for dough with ingredients that weaken gluten structure, like hard fat and sugar. However, the use of high-gluten flour might create a product with a thicker crust with a leathery mouth feel and a crumb with a more chewy texture. Occasionally, the baker may come across a formula that uses a weaker flour like cake or pastry flour

Figure 9-1
Comparative Steps in Laminated and Nonlaminated Viennoiserie

Laminated	Nonlaminated
Preferment (optional)	Preferment (optional)
Mixing	Mixing
First fermentation	First fermentation
Lamination	Dividing
Dividing	Preshaping
Relaxing of dough	Resting time
Shaping	Shaping
Final proof	Final proof
Baking	Baking
Cooling	Cooling

in addition to stronger flour. This will slightly weaken the dough in order to make it more tender.

The ash content of flour is another important consideration, because a high level of minerals combined with the higher levels of sugar in Viennoiserie can prematurely increase dough's fermentation activity rate. When ash content is high, a lower quantity of yeast may be required to decrease the rate of fermentation. In addition, high ash content can interfere in the development of the dough, decreasing the chances of obtaining sufficient elasticity in the dough. Higher levels of ash content can also create a darker crumb color which is not as visually attractive for Viennoiserie. See Chapter 6 for more information on ash content and its effect on dough and fermentation.

HYDRATING COMPONENTS OF VIENNOISERIE: WATER, MILK, AND EGGS

Flour needs to be hydrated in order to link its components and start chemical reactions in the dough. For Viennoiserie, one has the option of using water, milk, eggs, or a combination of these ingredients. The choice will have an effect on the dough's physical properties and flavor. In addition, as in bread mixing, the temperature of the liquids controls the temperature of the dough.

Water

Water is commonly used in Viennoiserie, often in conjunction with milk or milk powder, especially for croissant dough. Water does not lend any unique flavors, as eggs or milk do, but it is very effective at hydrating flour. When 100 percent water is used, 100 percent of the water contributes to hydrating the dough, which helps produce a cohesive dough with good working properties.

Milk

Milk adds richness, flavor, nutritional benefits, and color to Viennoiserie. Although any type of milk can be used, whole milk is typically chosen for its more concentrated flavor and richness. Milk contains natural sugars and proteins that help facilitate browning effects, as well as natural fat that helps make dough smoother, resulting in a finer, softer crumb.

Milk is commonly used as a portion of the liquid for croissant, and as the majority of the liquid for Danish. Milk hydrates flour at about 87 percent, which must be taken into account when determining dough hydration.

When milk is indicated by a formula, some bakers choose to use milk powder in conjunction with water. This is often determined by the size of the bakery and the availability of dairy products. When milk powder is used in Viennoiserie formulas, it is measured at 10 percent milk powder by weight of the milk being replaced. The difference is added to the formula in the form of water.

Any dry milk can be used successfully, but the nonfat variety is preferred because it is stable and because it can be mixed directly with dry ingredients. High heat-processed dry milk is preferable to low heat-processed varieties because the enzymes that can break down dough have been killed in high heat. Some older formulas for croissant or Danish call for milk that has been scalded to destroy these enzymes. This step is no longer necessary because the pasteurization process used on all milk today has the same enzyme-killing effect.

Eggs

When eggs are used as a hydrating agent, their addition is more noticeable than either water or milk. Added flavor, color, and nutrition make eggs a common addition to richer forms of Viennoiserie such as Danish, brioche, and the extremely egg-rich Pan d'Oro and Panettone.

Eggs contain water, protein, and fats and hydrate flour at 73 percent of water. Dough hydration can be improved by adding 10 to 20 percent of milk or water when a large quantity of eggs is used in a formula. Higher quantities of egg increase dough plasticity. The protein coagulates during baking, providing structure and strength, and the fat in the yolks acts as a tenderizing agent and helps retain moisture.

The egg yolk, rich in carotenoid pigments, also adds richness in color and flavor. The fats, cholesterol, and lecithin help create a smooth, fine texture in baked goods, while higher levels of egg yolk help emulsify higher quantities of butter within the dough. The protein in the yolk also aids in the Maillard reaction and promotes browning during baking.

The type of egg used typically depends on the size and location of the bakery. Smaller bakeries often use fresh eggs. When a larger volume of egg is required and fresh eggs are no longer practical, frozen bucket eggs are likely to be used. If this is the case, the quantity of sugar added to the eggs for preservation must be taken into account in the final dough. If fresh or frozen eggs are not available, or are not economical, rehydrated dry eggs can be used. Pasteurized liquid egg products are another choice and are increasingly more common because they are easy to use (no defrosting is necessary) and very safe microbiologically.

SUGAR

Sugar is used in varying amounts in Viennoiserie. For example, puff pastry has no added sugars, croissant has a modest 12 to 13 percent, based on flour weight, and some brioche have upward of 20 percent. The amount of sugar in a sweet, yeasted dough will not only affect the flavor of the finished item but also affect the mixing, fermentation, and baking guidelines that need to be followed.

The point at which sugar has a significant impact on dough mixing and fermentation is 10 to 12 percent. These two steps are related to dough development and yeast activity, respectively.

Mixing

Because sugar is hygroscopic, it competes with protein from the flour for hydration in a dough system. If sugar is added too early in the mixing process, the gluten formation will be delayed and the dough will be more difficult to develop, resulting in increased mixing times. To give the gluten sufficient opportunity to form and develop, higher quantities of sugar (10 percent and greater) should be held back and slowly added as the dough develops.

Flavor

The amount of flavor that sugar contributes to Viennoiserie is dictated by the type and amount used. For example, even though croissants are described as sweet, yeasted pastries, they are not very sweet. The type of sugar used also has an influence on secondary flavor characteristics.

Brown sugar in Danish or croissant create a more complex sweetness and aroma, while honey adds a characteristic flavor inherent to its particular source and blend.

Color

Sugar may not color dough, but it does have an impact on crust color. As a result of the sugar caramelization and Maillard reaction, which is created as residual sugars and amino acids react under heat, higher quantities of sugar result in faster browning during baking. In this case, a lower oven temperature ensures that items bake before they become too dark. Sugars such as brown sugar or molasses can change the color of the crumb and are sometimes used in sweet dough for their unique flavor contributions.

Texture and Shelf Life

Sugar's hygroscopic properties improve the texture of baked goods. Its ability to attract and retain moisture creates a softer crust and crumb, both of which are characteristic of Danish and croissant. Sugar also creates denser dough with smaller alveoles that are typically regular in distribution and size. Shelf life is also related to the quantity of sugar used, with higher amounts ensuring longer freshness in finished products. Additionally, natural and commercially produced inverted sugars may be used to increase shelf life and help retain moisture.

Types of Sugar Used in Viennoiserie

Granulated white sugar is the most common type of sugar found in sweet, yeasted dough, with honey and brown sugar used significantly less often. Once the baker understands how to use sugar in dough and how to alter mixing, fermentation, and baking accordingly, other types of sugar can be substituted or quantities altered to achieve desired results.

SALT

Salt has the same functions in Viennoiserie as it does in bread. For a thorough review of salt and its effect on dough, please refer to Chapters 3 and 4. In Viennoiserie, salt helps to regulate fermentation, improves fermentation tolerance, and balances the sweet and acidic flavors within a baked item. The quantity of salt can be adjusted to accommodate longer or shorter fermentation time and/or higher quantities of sugar. For example, if a formula contains a high level of sugar, it may have a smaller percentage of salt (1 to 1.5 percent based on flour weight) to avoid slowing down the fermentation activity too much.

YEAST

Yeast guidelines are similar for Viennoiserie and bread. Yeast is incorporated into the dough in the same way as it is for bread dough, and the same precautions exist. However, a different type of yeast, **osmotolerant yeast**, is preferred for Viennoiserie. This is a particular strain or strains of yeast conditioned with specific culture processes that allow them to function well under the high osmotic pressure created from increased levels of sugar. In these situations, osmotolerant yeast ensures consistent results for fermentation activity and a fuller volume of the finished products.

FAT

The fat used in laminated dough affects the working properties of the dough, as well as the flavor and cost of the final product. Although unsalted butter is traditionally used, cost and working properties sometimes result in the substitution of alternative solid fats. The most common of these include margarine or other hydrogenated oils like **roll-in shortening** (a fat specifically designed for use with laminated doughs). Some bakers use a blend of butter and another hard fat to balance flavor, cost, and working properties of the dough.

Selection of Fat

To better understand the selection of fats used in Viennoiserie, please review the butter, margarine, and shortening sections of the online companion, including melting temperatures, working properties, and flavor and texture characteristics. To download the information on ingredients, go to http://www.delmarlearning.com/companions/.

Application of Fat in Viennoiserie

The selection of fat is always a determining quality of Viennoiserie. Whether it is used in brioche, croissant, or Panettone, it lends unique qualities. The two basic methods of incorporating fat into Viennoiserie are often used in conjunction for laminated dough. The baker can put fat in the dough and can laminate it to create thin layers of fat and dough.

Fat in the Dough

Practically all Viennoiserie dough contains fat. For laminated dough, this creates extensibility. For nonlaminated Viennoiserie, such as brioche, fat softens and enriches the crumb. The range of fat added to a dough can be anywhere from 4 to 70 percent of the flour weight. The higher the percentage of fat, the more precautions the baker needs to take during mixing, shaping, proofing, and baking. Quality Viennoiserie will always contain butter. Specific guidelines for working with high-fat dough appear later in this chapter.

Effects Color, flavor, crumb, and shelf life are all affected by the type and quantity of butter mixed into the dough. For example, margarine has a more golden color than butter, while butter has a more golden color than shortening. Butter can add a unique cultured flavor. In addition, as the quantity of fat increases, the texture of the crumb becomes softer and tighter, and staling is increasingly delayed.

Mixing Considerations The quantity of fat mixed into the final dough will affect its development and strength. When the percentage of butter increases beyond 10 to 12 percent based on flour weight, it is necessary to mix longer to ensure proper development and strength. For dough with a high content of fat, such as brioche or Panettone, an intensive mix is required. The fat should be added, in a softened, malleable state, just before full development has been achieved. If it is added too early, the dough will take much longer to develop and gain the strength required to support larger quantities of fat.

For leaner enriched dough, which contains only 4 to 10 percent fat based on flour weight, the fat can be added during ingredient incorporation. Development for these leaner sweet doughs (croissant and Danish) is typically limited to improved mix, and the butter should be malleable to ensure easy incorporation. For products with large quantities of fat, the temperature of the fat must be considered for proper control of dough temperature.

Fat for Lamination

Fat is also used to create the thin layer of butter and dough that creates the desired flaky texture. Special considerations, such as temperature and quantity in relation to the total amount of dough, must be followed when considering fat for lamination. Although the most popular choices are butter, margarine, shortening, or a blend of butter and shortening, the most prized is cultured butter with a fat content between 82 and 84 percent. This butter is also referred to as dry butter because it has lower water content than standard butter. Dry butter produces flakier pastries and typically has a more pronounced flavor due to the addition of unique cultures.

Quantity of Fat The quantity of roll-in fat in relation to dough in the formula will affect the lamination process and, in turn, the texture of the final product. The standard quantity of fat for croissant is 25 percent of total dough weight; for puff pastry, it is 50 percent of dough weight. As a general rule, higher ratios of fat to dough require more folds. For example, three single folds are standard for croissant, whereas five to six single folds are required for puff pastry.

Temperature and Texture of Fat Due to the various melting points of fats used in laminated dough, obtaining the proper working properties can be a challenge. For proper lamination to occur, the fat must have **plasticity**. Properties of plasticity include having the butter firm, yet pliable. The temperature of the fat should always be cold enough to resist absorption into the dough or oozing out of the **détrempe**, the dough portion of laminated Viennoiserie. This is why some bakers opt to use margarine or roll-in shortening. The melting point for each is higher than that of butter, water content is lower, and both are easily workable at moderate room temperatures. Some bakers mix 5 to 10 percent flour (based on the weight of the roll-in butter) into the butter to absorb water content, increase plasticity, and prevent the butter from becoming too firm. The dry butter must be softened slightly before the lamination process begins to ensure that the butter has good plasticity so that it will expand in thin even sheets along with the dough during the lamination process.

AN OVERVIEW OF THE LAMINATED DOUGH PROCESS

Six critical steps make up the laminated dough process. This process serves as a starting point for introducing different preferments and alternative fermentation techniques to create unique flavor profiles and adaptable production schedules.

MIXING

Proper mixing is the first step in making successful laminated dough. Throughout time, this step has evolved from a simple incorporation of ingredients to an improved mix. Although a short mix is sometimes still used today, an improved mix results in better volume and a more consistent production schedule. If mixing time is shorter, a longer first fermentation is required to build optimal strength before lamination.

Croissant made using a shorter mixing time will have a smaller volume, a crumb with a more golden color, and possibly a more complex flavor due to the limited amount of dough oxidation. The one typical adjustment required when mixing croissant over lean dough is that the sugar is held back until development occurs if sugar percentage is more than 10 percent based on the flour weight. Optimal dough temperature for laminated dough is 76°F (24°C).

Just as in lean dough mixing, the baker can choose to use an autolyse for laminated dough. This will reduce the mixing time and will increase the extensibility of the dough. Having a dough with good extensibility is beneficial especially if laminating the dough manually; however, it is indispensable for mechanical processing as well, especially during the final sheeting of the dough to help prevent shrinkage.

FIRST FERMENTATION

The typical duration of the first fermentation of yeasted laminated dough is 2 hours using two temperature zones. The purpose of the two temperature zones is to allow the dough to ferment and then to cool in preparation for the laminating process. After mixing is completed, the dough enters first fermentation and the temperature should be taken. Depending on the temperature of the dough, the baker may need to adjust the ambient temperature surrounding the dough to either warm it or cool it. The appropriate guidelines follow:

- Dough cooler than 72°F (22°C) should be placed in a warm area of the bakery for 1 hour.
- Dough between 73°F (23°C) and 78°F (26°C) should remain at room temperature for 1 hour.
- Dough 79°F (26°C) or warmer should go into the refrigerator for 1 hour.

After the dough has undergone the initial hour of first fermentation in its designated temperature zone, it may be divided into the appropriate weight per détrempe and put under refrigeration. During this time, the yeast activity is slowed, and the dough temperature becomes equal to the temperature of the butter used for lamination.

LAMINATION

Lamination is the process by which layers of dough and butter are created to make flaky pastries such as croissant and Danish. Among the important things to consider when laminating are the temperature and preparation of the butter (also known as the **beurrage** or **roll-in fat**), the temperature and consistency of the dough, the process of rolling out the dough, and the types and quantity of folds given to the dough. During the process of lamination, it is crucial that the temperature of the dough and butter remains cold and that the butter remains extensible.

Preparing the Beurrage

The first step in lamination is the preparation of the butter. This important step has been ill-achieved in several "creative" but misguided ways. In one such method, butter was grated over the dough like cheese, which actually produces a final product more like bread than pastry. In another innovative process, warmed, spreadable butter was used. Because this technique requires that the dough be refrigerated before sheeting, the butter is absorbed and the layers of fat and dough are less distinct.

The most commonly used techniques to prepare butter for lamination all lead to the creation of a cold block of fat that is smooth, pliable, and extensible. Some of the following techniques may be more applicable than others, depending on production requirements and equipment availability. The two most important aspects for the pastry chef or baker are knowing what characteristics to look for and how to control them.

- Larger bakeries that produce thousands of pieces of pastry per day benefit from using a **butter press**, a hydraulic press that efficiently and consistently forms uniform blocks of butter at the push of a button.
- The dough sheeter technique is useful for bakeries that cannot afford a butter press yet want to quickly and efficiently produce butter blocks. Room temperature butter is sheeted out to the desired size and shape between two silicone baking mats (see Dough Sheet Technique Figure 9-2, Steps 1–2). Once prepared, it can be transferred to parchment paper and reserved under refrigeration until needed. (See Dough Sheet Technique Figure 9-2, Steps 3–4.)
- For the small bakery or the serious home baker, the rolling pin technique is simple in theory but loud in practice. The cold butter is placed between heavy plastic sheets and is hit with a heavy French rolling pin until it is the desired shape and size (see Rolling Pin Technique Figure 9-3, Step 1). The action of the pin softens the butter, making it extensible and pliable, but the quick process maintains the cool temperature. (See Rolling Pin Technique Figure 9-3, Step 2.)

Bakers from any production environment should be able to successfully prepare the butter for lamination using any one of these three options. The process can be simplified by using commercially available sheets of butter when available, but the choice of butter in prepared blocks is more limited than with bulk butter, and the cost is higher.

Dough and Butter Characteristics

A successful lamination process creates great laminated dough. To achieve both, the dough and butter used must exhibit particular characteristics. If the dough is too wet, it will cause indistinct layers within the pastry; if it is too stiff, it will cause an excessive amount of strength and problems during lamination and makeup. Depending on the type of flour used and the quantity of butter in the dough, a hydration of 60 to 65 percent of flour weight is standard. If less water is used in the dough, the fat can be increased up to 10 percent of flour weight to increase extensibility. In addition, the butter enclosed in the dough must be at a similar temperature and texture.

Enclosing the Fat into the Dough

There are several ways to enclose fat into the dough, and some work better than others. The method used will determine the number of layers. The most common and easiest way to accomplish this is to enclose the beurrage over 50 percent of the dough, creating an initial single layer of fat. (See Enclosing Fat Into Dough Figure 9-4, Steps 1–2.) The fat should extend to the edges so that the dough is not stretched to enclose the fat. Altering the thickness of the dough can create uneven layers of dough and fat that can throw off the lamination. When done correctly, the end result of this method is two layers of dough and one layer of butter. (See Enclosing Fat Into Dough Figure 9-4, Step 3.)

FIGURE 9-2 DOUGH SHEET TECHNIQUE

1

Place the butter in an even layer between two silicon baking mats.

2

Sheet the butter using the dough sheeter.

3

Once the butter is the desired size, remove the silicon mats and place butter on parchment paper.

4

The butter is now ready for storage.

FIGURE 9-3 ROLLING PIN TECHNIQUE

1

Place the butter in an even layer, enclosed in a heavy-duty plastic sheet, and hit the butter to soften it and form the shape.

2

The finished butter block is ready for use.

FIGURE 9-4 ENCLOSING FAT INTO DOUGH

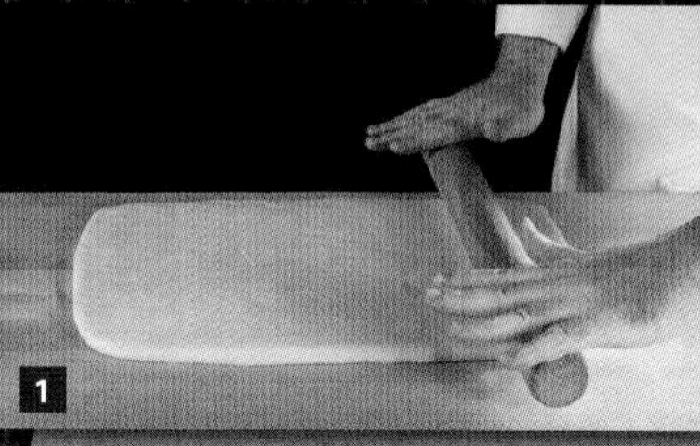
1

Roll the dough to double the size of the fat.

2

Place the fat in the center of the dough and fold the sides toward the center.

3

The seam should run down the center of the dough, and the butter should come to the edge.

An alternate method is to lay the fat over two-thirds of the dough, justified to the left or right (see Alternative Method: Enclosing Fat Into Dough Figure 9-5, Step 1). Next, the third that is not covered is folded over the butter (see Alternative Method: Enclosing Fat Into Dough Figure 9-5, Step 2). After this, the third that is topped with butter is folded toward the center (see Alternative Method: Enclosing Fat Into Dough Figure 9-5, Step 3). The end result is three layers of dough and two layers of butter (see Alternative Method: Enclosing Fat Into Dough Figure 9-5, Step 4).

Sheeting the Dough and the Folding Process

The next step in the process is to sheet or roll out the dough. After this, the dough is given a series of folds. There are two options for folds: a **single** or **letter fold** (see Single Fold Figure 9-6) and a **double** or **book fold** (see Double Fold Figure 9-7). Single fold refers to folding one third of the dough from the left and then the right, as if folding a business letter. A double fold can be done by folding the sheeted dough in four, with the center spine offset to ensure consistent layering.

A proper resting time is required between folds. For example, croissant typically get three single folds, the first two of which may be done back to back. After resting for at least a half hour, the third fold can be completed. When making croissant dough by hand, it is beneficial to rest the dough for up to 45 minutes after each fold.

Sheeting guidelines are the same whether the pastry chef or baker is making laminated dough by hand or with a reversible dough sheeter. It is essential to sheet the dough out as evenly as possible in order to create even layers of dough and fat. In addition, the dough must be sheeted in the direction of the open ends to help prevent it from distorting and creating excessive scrap dough. Caution must be taken to not sheet the dough out too much in one pass of the sheeter or one roll of the pin because even, gradual sheeting will help ensure even layering. The degree to which the dough is sheeted out largely depends on the size of the détrempe. In general, the dough should be sheeted to three times its width for a single fold and to four times its width for a double fold.

After the dough has been sheeted out to the appropriate length, the fold can be given. When a dough sheeter is used, it is possible to give a second fold right away; however, if the dough is processed by hand, it is beneficial to let it rest for at least 30 minutes in the refrigerator. Before making the second fold, rotate the dough 90° to ensure the sheeting is congruent with the open ends of the dough. After the second fold, the dough should rest for at least 30 minutes in the refrigerator.

The final fold may be given to the détrempe after the minimum resting time is completed. After the third fold is complete, the dough must then rest again before being sheeted out for product makeup. Allowing the dough to rest is important to ensure that the dough does not shrink during makeup, which can produce narrow, thick strips of dough.

The Effect of Sheeting and Folding the Dough Beside the obvious effect of creating layers of dough and fat, other things happen as dough is sheeted and folded. As the folds are completed, dough strength increases, much as it does with punches and folds for bread dough. This increase in dough strength due to sheeting is one of the reasons it is possible to undermix a dough, yet still end up with an acceptable laminated pastry.

FIGURE 9-5 ALTERNATIVE METHOD: ENCLOSING FAT INTO DOUGH

Place the prepared fat over two-thirds of the dough.

Fold the uncovered dough toward the center of the fat.

Fold the dough with the butter on it toward the opposite side.

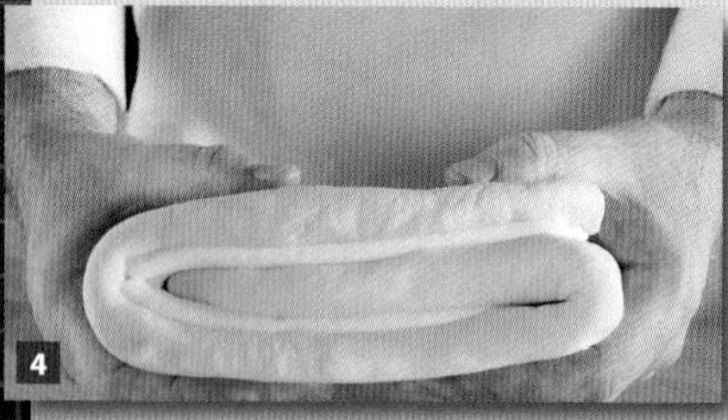

The finished détrempe will have three layers of dough and two layers of fat.

FIGURE 9-6 SINGLE FOLD

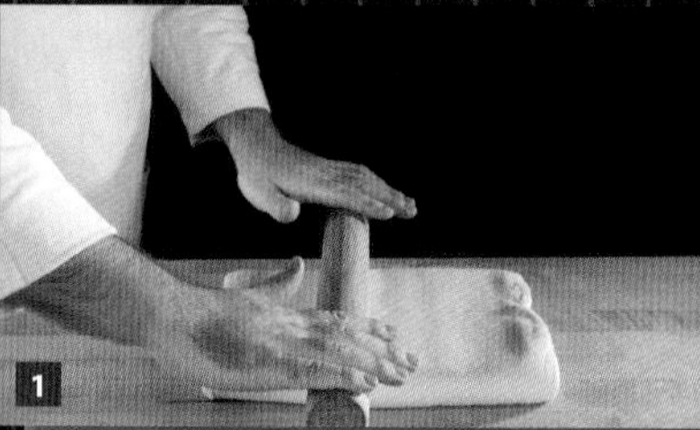

Roll out the dough on a lightly floured surface to about three times its width.

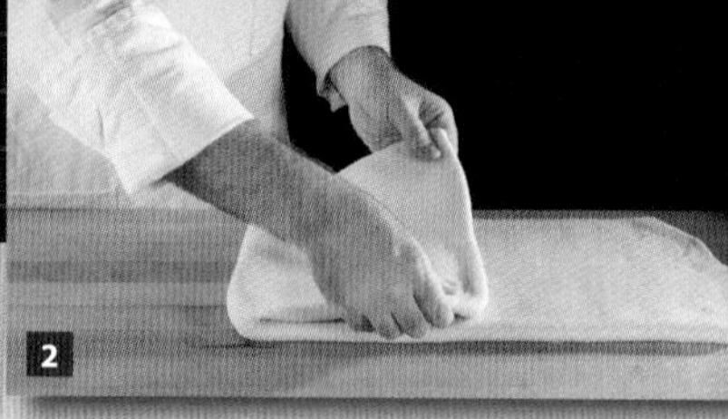

Fold one-third of the dough toward the center.

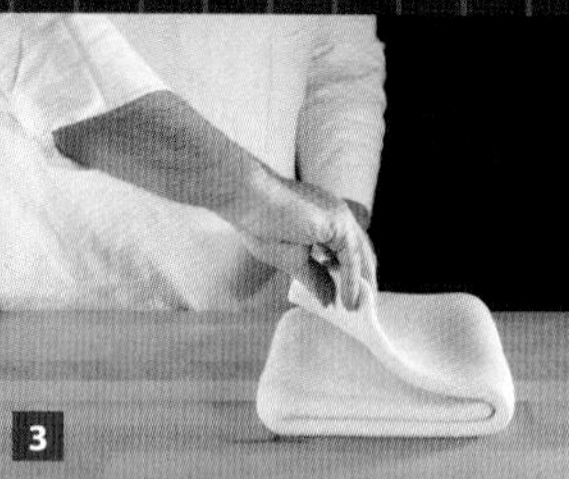

From the other side, fold the remaining third toward the center.

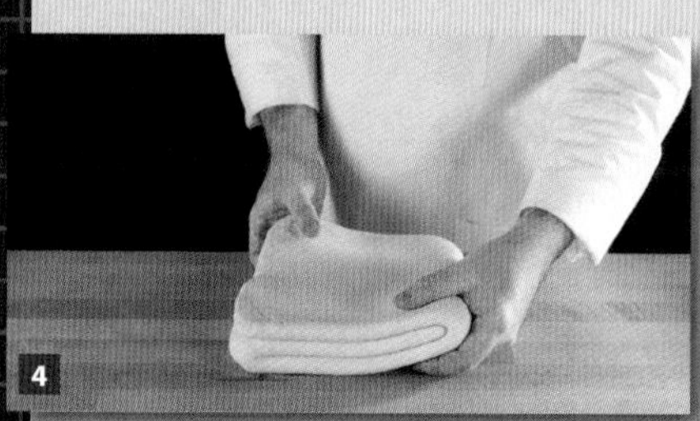

The single fold is complete.

The type and number of folds have a large impact on the final product. For example, when making croissant, the first two folds can be done back to back, but at least 30 minutes should pass before the third fold can be completed. To speed up production time and reduce dough handling, some pastry chefs and bakers use a single and a double fold back to back, or two double folds back to back. This method is useful to keep production moving because dough is ready for sheeting, cutting, and makeup within 30 minutes. When combining single and double folds, the single fold should always be completed first.

The degree of flakiness in the final product is largely dependent on the quality of the lamination, but it is also the result of the number and types of folds that are put into the dough. The larger layers of fat and dough that are created by a combination of double and single folds create a flakier pastry than one made using the same formula, but with three single folds. Doing less than a single and a double fold is not advisable because the layers of dough will be too thick, easily flaking off the finished products.

MAKEUP

Makeup can happen after the dough has had its final fold and has rested in the refrigerator for at least 30 minutes. During the final sheeting, establish the proper width first and then rotate the dough 90° to sheet it down to the proper thickness. On most reversible sheeters, dough thickness should be about 1/8 inch (3 to 3.5 mm) for the average size croissant.

Before dividing and shaping begins, the dough must be relaxed. During this process, the dough shrinks, which helps to prevent shrinking after cutting. When cutting laminated dough, it is essential to use rulers for proper measurement and to work quickly with sharp tools. The dough will warm at an accelerated rate because it has been sheeted so thinly.

The type of Viennoiserie being made will determine the shape of the cuts and the ease of effort. Although the varieties may seem endless, shaping must remain consistent. The makeup techniques for the laminated Viennoiserie vary. (See Shaping Traditional Croissant Figure 9-8; Shaping Chocolate Croissant Figure 9-9; Shaping Half Pocket Danish Figure 9-10; Shaping Pocket Danish Figure 9-11; Shaping Pinwheel Danish Figure 9-12; Shaping Snail Danish Figure 9-13; Filling Danish with Cream and Jam Figure 9-14; Filling Danish with Cream and Fruit Figure 9-15.)

Egg Washing Pastries

After the pastries have been made up, they are panned and egg washed. When panning, allow sufficient space for each pastry and bake on parchment paper. The goal of egg washing is to coat each pastry with a thin coat of egg wash. It should not pool on the pastry or around the base of the pastry. Egg washing prevents a skin from forming on the pastry, and the yolk enhances the crust color. All Viennoiserie is typically egg washed twice: once after makeup and again before baking. This practice ensures even coloration over the pastry, taking into consideration the part of the dough that was not exposed before proofing.

Care must be taken when egg washing to prevent deflating or damaging the delicate pastries. When egg washing croissant, use a brush with soft bristles and brush in strokes parallel to the shoulders of the croissant to avoid gluing together the layers of dough and smearing together the layers on the finished product.

FIGURE 9-7 DOUBLE FOLD

Roll out the dough on a lightly floured surface to about four times its width.

Fold approximately one-eighth of the dough toward the center.

From the other side, fold the dough to meet the first fold.

Fold the dough in half to complete the double fold.

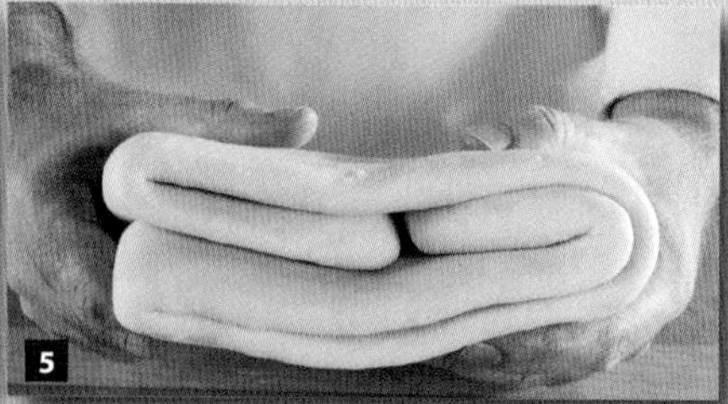

The "offset" double fold is complete.

FIGURE 9-8 SHAPING TRADITIONAL CROISSANT

Roll out the dough to 16 inches (41 cm) wide. Cut it into two 8 inch (20 ½ cm) wide strips from which the triangles are cut having a 4 inch (10 ¼ cm) wide base.

Gently stretch the dough.

Gently stretch out the base.

Roll the croissant toward the tip.

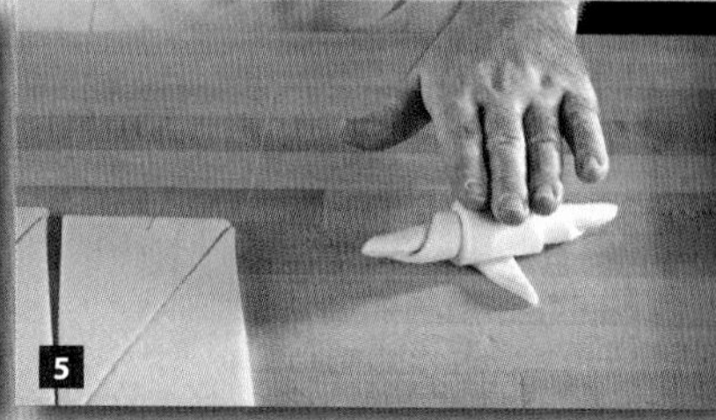

Use caution to not damage the shoulders of the croissant.

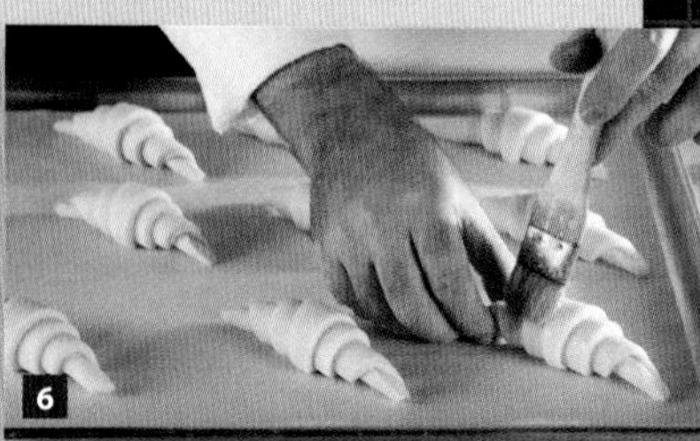

After panning, apply a light coat of egg wash.

FIGURE 9-9 SHAPING CHOCOLATE CROISSANT

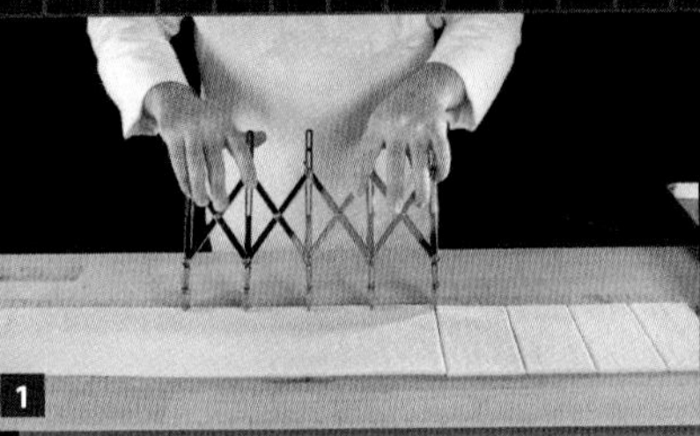

1 Cut strips of dough measuring 5 ¼ inches (13 ½ cm) in width (lengthwise) and then cut them into sections approximately 3 inches (8 cm) wide (or as wide as the chocolate baton).

2 Step-by-step view of shaping for chocolate croissant.

3 The seam should always be centered on the bottom of the pastry.

4 Using the same shaping principle as in Figure 9-10, Step 2, the same technique can be applied to an uncut strip of croissant dough.

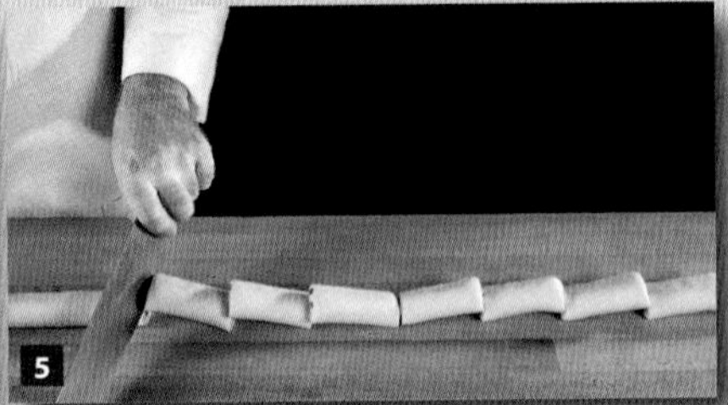

5 After the strip is complete, it can be cut to the desired size.

FIGURE 9-10 SHAPING HALF POCKET DANISH

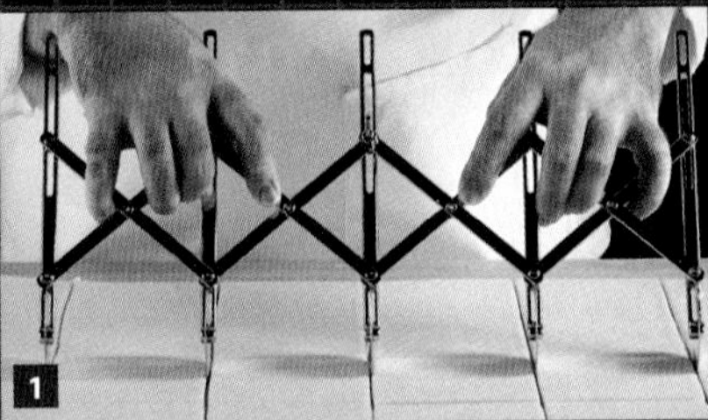

1 Cut squares to the desired size.

2 From two opposing corners, gently pull them outward.

3 Fold the extended corners toward the center of the dough piece and press to secure.

4 The half pocket Danish is ready for proofing.

FIGURE 9-11 SHAPING POCKET DANISH

Start with the shape for the half pocket Danish.

Rotate the dough, stretch the two unfolded sides outward, and bring them toward the center.

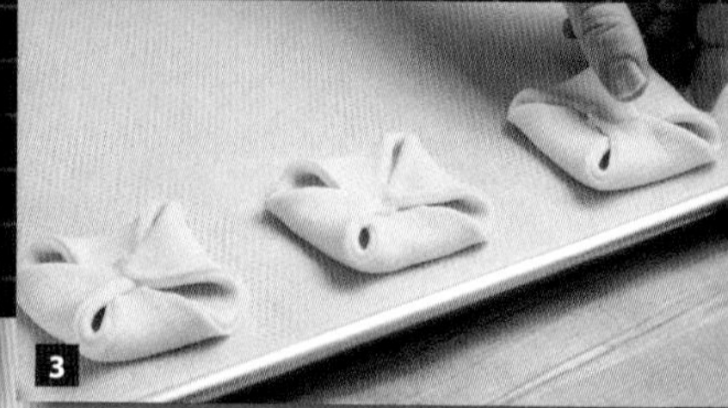

The completed pocket Danish ready for proofing.

FIGURE 9-12 SHAPING PINWHEEL DANISH

Cut out squares of dough and cut them from the corners in toward the center, taking caution to not cut through the center.

Fold the tips of the dough in to the center.

In the center, press them down to secure the shape.

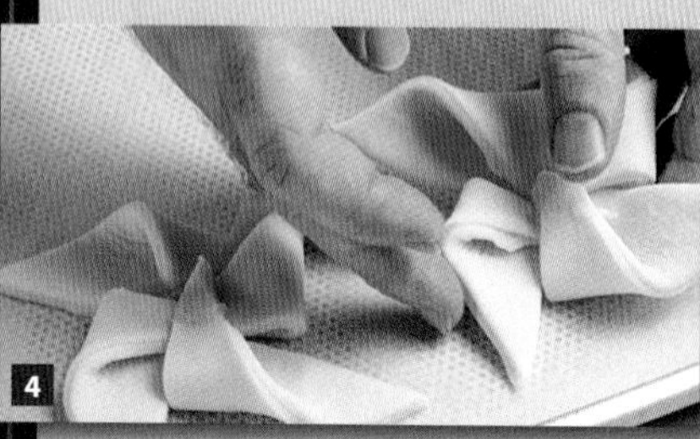

The pinwheel Danish is ready for proofing.

FIGURE 9-13 SHAPING SNAIL DANISH

Brush a 16 inch (41 cm) wide strip of Danish dough lightly with egg wash and then sprinkle it with cinnamon sugar.

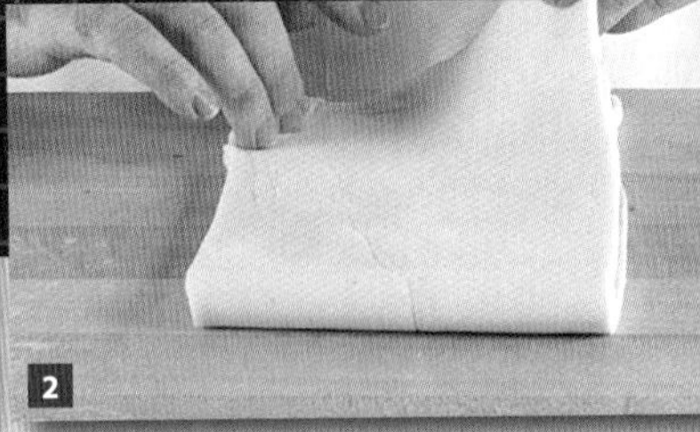

Fold the dough in half to form a layer of cinnamon sugar sandwiched between the Danish dough.

Cut the dough into strips ¾ inch (2 cm) wide and gently stretch them.

Twist the strip of dough on the table.

Secure the closed end of the strip on the table and wrap the twisted strip around the center.

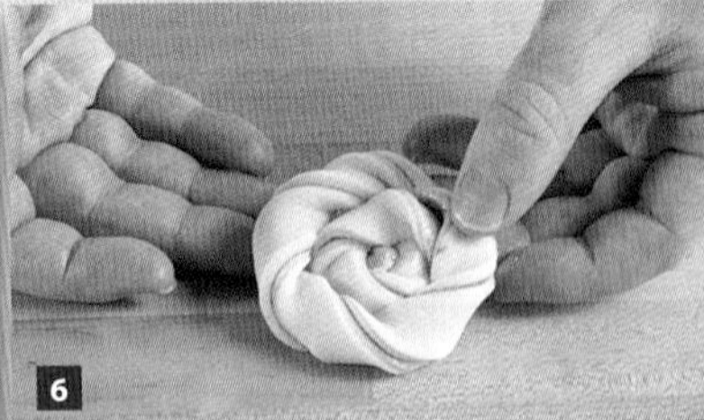

Secure the tail under the pastry.

FIGURE 9-14 FILLING DANISH WITH CREAM AND JAM

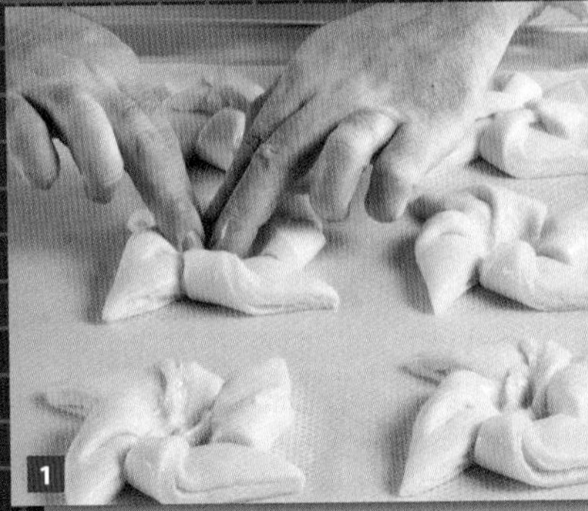

Once proofed, egg wash the pastry a second time and degas the center of the pastry.

Pipe in the pastry cream.

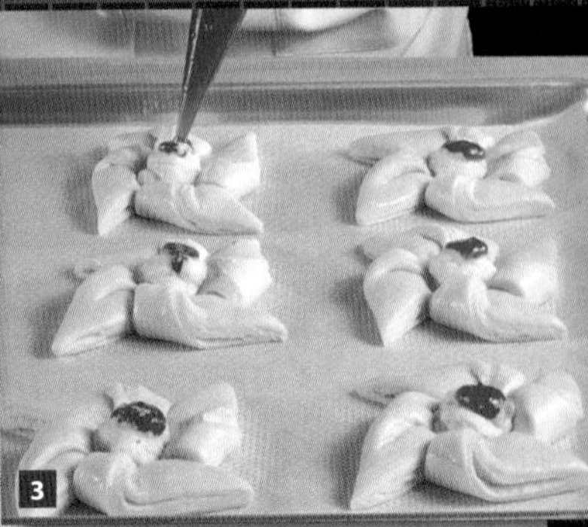

Pipe jam into the pastry cream and bake.

FIGURE 9-15 FILLING DANISH WITH CREAM AND FRUIT

Once proofed, egg wash the pastry a second time and degas the center of the pastry.

Pipe the desired filling into the center of the pastry (cream cheese filling shown).

Top the filling with frozen or fresh fruit and bake.

THE FINAL PROOF

Yeasted laminated dough undergoes a final proof before baking. Due to the elevated level of sugar, this process can take up to 90 minutes. This can be done at room temperature [68°F (20°C) to 70°F (21°C)] or in a proof box. Proof boxes are more consistent, but the temperature and humidity settings should be closely controlled. The ideal temperature for proofing laminated dough is at 78°F (26°C) with approximately 80 percent humidity. Excessive heat can potentially melt the butter within the layers of the dough, whereas too much humidity can cause excessive blistering or wrinkling of the pastry.

BAKING

Once the final proof has been assessed, the Viennoiserie is ready to bake. Before baking, an additional coat of egg wash is required and additional preparation may be needed for items like Danish and specialty croissant. Creams, fillings, or jams should be added just before baking. The area where the filling will go should be slightly degassed so that the filling does not migrate off the pastry due to oven spring. Only the portion of the pastry where the filling will be deposited should be degassed.

Steam is just as important in baking Viennoiserie as it is in baking bread because it allows full oven spring to occur and leads to a product with higher volume and lighter texture. However, because of the egg wash coating the product, a lower amount of steam is needed in comparison to bread.

Proper oven temperature is critical for yeasted, laminated dough. Ideally, it is baked at a high temperature to ensure steam production and ample oven spring. If the temperature is too cold, the water content of the butter will not turn to steam fast enough and the texture and volume will suffer. Additionally, if the oven is too cool, the pastry will dry out excessively before proper coloration is reached. A too-hot oven temperature will promote premature browning, and the inside of the pastry may very well be underbaked if removed from the oven too soon. If browning happens at an accelerated rate, the temperature can be lowered or the tray can be double-panned.

Once pastries are baked, handling should be minimal to prevent damage. They will set and become more stable during the cooling process, making them less prone to damage when moved for finishing or packaging.

The finishing of croissant and Danish varies with type and desired presentation. Powdered sugar, apricot glaze, pastry cream, assorted creams, fresh fruit, and whipped cream can all be used to garnish specialty pastries.

NONLAMINATED VIENNOISERIE

Nonlaminated Viennoiserie is also known as sweet, yeasted dough. It is characterized by higher levels of sugar and eggs and by fats of variable quantities. One of the most popular of these is brioche, described by Professor Raymond Calvel as a typically French product that is "one of the oldest examples of yeast-raised sweet goods. Its origins are lost so far back in the depths of times that it would be foolish to try and determine exactly the period during which it was developed" (Calvel, 2001, p. 149).

The evolution of brioche is an interesting example of how enriching ingredients have changed throughout time. Before sugar was readily available, honey was commonly used as a sweetener. To supplement the flavor of the honey, orange flour water was often used and can still be seen today in regional brioche and other sweet, yeasted specialty breads. In addition, vegetable oils and animal fats were historically used as enriching ingredients instead of butter.

As the popularity of brioche spread, enterprising bakers added local ingredients to the dough, adopting characteristic formulas with varying levels of sweetness and richness, along with a variety of specialty shapes that mirrored local tastes and preferences.

The basic process for sweet, yeasted dough is very similar to that of traditional bread. Because of the inherent differences in formulation, however, mixing, fermentation, makeup, proofing, and baking procedures have changed. As a general rule, all specific instructions that accompany formulas should be followed. Due to the large variation of regional specialties, we cannot present them all.

MIXING

Because sweet, yeasted dough always contains sugar and butter in higher ratios, the dough must be further developed than most laminated dough. The goal of the intensive mix is to limit the weakening action of the butter and sugar by creating a strong gluten network.

When mixing sweet, yeasted dough, several basic principles should be closely followed. When adding quantities of sugar and butter greater than 10 percent based on flour weight, the dough must first be developed toward an improved mix, and sugar must be added slowly as the dough develops. Adding sugar too quickly will require a longer mixing time, which will result in a greater dough oxidation and warmer dough.

Longer mixing times and higher levels of oxidation will also occur if fat is added too early in the mixing process. Quantities of fat higher than 10 percent based on flour weight should be added once the dough is near full development. For easy incorporation, the butter should be pliable and slightly softened. Once the fat is completely incorporated and the dough shows signs of proper development, mixing should stop.

FIRST FERMENTATION

The first fermentation for sweet, yeasted dough is much the same as for traditional baking and Viennoiserie, except for certain regional preparations that are noted in the formula section of this text.

Depending on strength, the dough may require one to two punches and folds during the first fermentation. Because most of the bread in this category is so high in fat, it is difficult to work with at room temperature or the temperature at which the dough comes off the mixer. After 1 hour at room temperature, it is standard to cool most sweet, yeasted dough for 1 hour in the retarder or refrigerator to ensure ease of handling. In addition, retarding the dough slows the rate of fermentation and encourages the production of acidity, which is beneficial to flavor, aroma production, and shelf life.

DIVIDING, PRESHAPING, AND RESTING

The basic theory behind dividing, preshaping, and resting sweet dough is the same as for lean dough, but the process for dough handling and the tightness of the preshape differ.

As quantities of sugar and butter increase in the dough, changes should be made in the preshaping process. If the dough lacks strength, it may need to be shaped tightly. Conversely, if the dough already has a sufficient amount of strength, a loose preshape is recommended.

Even though the dough may be sticky, it is essential to not add too much flour, which can dry out the product and leave a dull matte finish after baking. For some regional specialties such as traditional Panettone and Pan d'Oro, the bread is preshaped and shaped on a buttered table to ensure silky smoothness throughout the makeup process.

The resting time for sweet yeast dough should be at least 20 minutes. Depending on the temperature of the bakery and product composition, this may best be done under refrigeration in warmer working environments. Keep in mind that a dough that is too cold won't shape well because the stiff butter impedes gluten extensibility and dough viscosity. Guidelines for preshaping and resting time should be followed for individual formulas.

SHAPING

After the dough has been appropriately preshaped and rested, it can be shaped and deposited into the baking mold or onto the baking tray. As with lean yeasted dough, the strength of the dough must be considered when determining how tightly to shape the product, and all products should be egg washed after shaping unless otherwise noted. Shaping guidelines and instructions should be followed for individual formulas.

FINAL PROOF

Depending on the composition of the product, the proofing time for sweet, yeasted dough can last from 30 minutes to 15 hours. Because the quantities of sugar, fat, and yeast are highly variable, it is necessary to refer to specific formulas for final proof guidelines.

Temperatures for the final proof can vary from room temperature [70°F (21°C)] to between 78°F (26°C) and 80°F (27°C) in a proof box. Because most sweet, yeasted dough contains high levels of butter, the proofing temperature must not be too high. Although guidelines for assessing the final proof of sweet, yeasted dough are similar to that for lean dough, the process is a bit trickier because the surface of the dough is typically tacky.

BAKING

All nonlaminated Viennoiserie should be egg washed before baking. The temperature for baking will vary by oven type, product selection, and product size. Steam is typically used for sweet, yeasted dough items but may not be required in some instances, such as Panettone. Baking guidelines for individual formulas should be followed.

After items are baked, they typically need to cool slightly before being removed from the pan. Preparations like traditional Panettone and Columba di Pasqua may require upside-down cooling to prevent collapse (due to their large volume and high levels of butter and sugar). If these are regularly produced in a bakery, pinzes are used to hang them upside-down. Smaller quantities can be hung between tables using thick wooden skewers. In general, finishing sweet, yeasted dough is less involved than finishing laminated dough. Powdered sugar, pearl sugar, apricot glaze, and flat icing or fondant are all common garnishes.

ALTERNATIVE PROCESSES FOR VIENNOISERIE

The basic processes described for laminated dough and nonlaminated sweet, yeasted dough can be altered to include variations in the mixing process, including the addition of preferments, autolyse, and various retarding techniques. The purpose of these alternative measures is to improve dough characteristics, accommodate production and scheduling, improve or alter flavor characteristics, and improve shelf life and physical qualities like crumb structure and appearance of the crust.

PREFERMENTS

The use of preferments is highly beneficial in Viennoiserie because fermentation creates the major flavor profiles of yeasted products. Even though it can contain high levels of sugar, butter, eggs, and other ingredients, Viennoiserie would probably taste bland without extended fermentation. Preferments are an ideal way to add the benefits of a long fermentation, and the final characteristics will depend on the type of preferment used and its quantity in the final dough. To determine which one best suits products and the production schedule, the baker should run tests and use the one where the best flavors are obtained.

This section will review commercially yeasted preferments like prefermented dough, sponge, poolish, and biga, as well as naturally leavened preferments like liquid levain and Italian levain. For an in-depth discussion of preferments, please refer to Chapter 4.

Prefermented Dough

The best type of prefermented dough for Viennoiserie is lean dough that has a formulation similar to basic baguette dough. If a prefermented dough is used in Viennoiserie, it should be its own mix to control overdevelopment and fermentation. Traditionally, prefermented dough is not used as often as a sponge for Viennoiserie, but it is valued for the strength it brings to the final dough. This may be important if weaker flour is used and strength has been a problem with dough such as brioche. Pulling a piece of yeasted dough off to ferment and introduce to the next batch on a continual basis is not advised, as it can cause off flavors and inconsistent characteristics.

Sponge

A sponge preferment is the classic choice for Viennoiserie because the characteristic, sweet notes of this preferment are complementary to the flavor of sweet, yeasted dough. Sponges also add strength to the dough.

Poolish

The slightly acidic qualities of poolish that has fermented longer create complex flavors and aromas in Viennoiserie that are sometimes described as nutty. Because of the more important secondary effect of the protease activity in a wet environment, poolish is beneficial for dough that requires a larger degree of extensibility for lamination, such as croissant made by hand using a rolling pin, or for makeup purposes, such as forming Danish snails.

Biga

In Italy, biga is traditionally used in conjunction with weaker flours. The stiff consistency and long fermentation time at a lower temperature of this preferment add mellow acidity to Viennoiserie and also help to improve dough strength if only weaker flour is available.

Liquid Levain

Although sourdough has limited uses in Viennoiserie, it brings beneficial qualities to the dough when used properly. When sourdough is used, it is usually in the form of a liquid levain in small quantities of about 10 to 15 percent of the flour weight. Used in these quantities, liquid levain brings subtle acidity to the dough that adds strength, flavor, and keeping qualities. Its use in small quantities is especially easy if a fermentation tank, which limits the need to mix another preferment specifically for the dough, is on hand. The milder lactic acidity of liquid levain complements very nicely the butter flavor of breakfast pastries.

Italian Levain

An Italian levain is a stiff levain that differs from the "stiff levain" discussed in the sourdough section of this text in Chapter 4. Its characteristics are different because of the alteration in the feeding and storage process and the percentage of starter in the levain. A basic formula for Italian levain contains 100 percent flour, 50 percent water, and 100 percent starter.

Feedings should take place with warm water to ensure a final dough temperature of 85°F (29°C). Once fed, the levain is left to ferment at 85°F (29°C) and is fed again every 4 hours, ensuring a very active culture. Because the dough is so active, it produces very mild acidity and although it is a "stiff starter," there are no real sour characteristics to it.

Italian levain is ideal for producing naturally leavened Viennoiserie in both laminated and sweet, yeasted dough preparations. Examples include sourdough croissant, Pan d'Oro, and traditional Panettone. Italian levain brings all the benefits of sourdough without the signature intense flavors, including enhanced shelf life, crust color, dough strength, fermentation tolerance, aroma production, and flavor.

Summary of Preferments

Good lamination technique alone is not enough to produce high-quality Viennoiserie. The starting point is sufficient and proper fermentation, which is simplified by preferments. Through a series of tests that mimic production needs, the pastry chef or baker can achieve desired flavor-building characteristics, as well as total control over the fermentation process.

RETARDING VIENNOISERIE

The process of retarding dough or made-up Viennoiserie provides the pastry chef or baker with flexibility and convenience in managing production, building flavor, managing inventory, and providing fresh pastries throughout the day. Each of the options for retarding Viennoiserie—including retarding in bulk, retarding shaped, freezing in bulk, freezing shaped, and freezing preproofed frozen—has its own benefits and considerations.

Retarding in Bulk

Retarding in bulk can be used for both laminated and nonlaminated Viennoiserie. The basic procedure is to refrigerate or retard the dough for up to 16 hours after it has undergone its first fermentation. This technique is helpful for the production of laminated dough because the long, slow fermentation produces desirable acidity and aids in the baking process, flavor production, and shelf life. After retarding is complete, the dough can be laminated or processed as required for sweet, yeasted dough.

Laminated dough can also be retarded for up to 18 hours in the middle of the lamination process. When using this technique, it is important that the last fold in the dough is not performed before retarding begins. During extended retarding, the dough will accumulate some gas, and the butter will lose some of its plasticity. When the dough is ready to be used, the final fold is given, which helps to degas the dough and soften the butter. The dough can then be processed as usual after the appropriate resting period under refrigeration.

Retarding Shaped

Retarding shaped provides the pastry chef with flexibility as to when products are baked. Once made up and egg washed, pastries can be held under refrigeration for up to 24 hours. The pastries can be transferred to a proof box on an as-needed basis to undergo final fermentation before being baked. When using this technique, it is essential that pastries be put into a retarder as soon as possible to control fermentation.

Freezing in Bulk

The goal of freezing in bulk is to have frozen and ready for use détrempes of dough that have all but the last fold completed. The process is to mix the dough (a lower dough temperature of 68°F (20°C) to 72°F (22°C) is advised), give it a very limited first fermentation, portion and cool the dough, give all but one fold, wrap it well, and then freeze it. The night before it is needed, transfer the dough to the refrigerator. After the dough is fully defrosted and the final fold has been put into it, the process resumes as normal.

This method is convenient as it condenses mixing and most of the lamination to one day. For each day's production, the required amount of dough can be removed from the freezer to be used for the following day's sales.

Some precautions must be taken when using this method. If freezing the dough for a week or longer, dough conditioners should be used to maintain the integrity of dough strength. When freezing dough, it is also recommended that the quantity of yeast be increased by as much as double to ensure that not all of it dies during the freezing process. In addition, the faster dough freezes, the better. Slow freezing encourages more ice crystals, which increase the breakdown of dough strength. Proper air circulation is required, and a blast freezer is ideal.

Freezing Shaped

Freezing Viennoiserie shaped is a good technique to use if a limited bake off is needed every day. The process is unchanged for both laminated and nonlaminated dough to the point of the final proof, at which time the pastries are put into the freezer. The pastries must be covered, and if they are to be frozen for longer than a week, the quantity of yeast must be increased to up to double the normal dosage, and dough conditioners must be used to reinforce the strength of the gluten.

Before baking off frozen, shaped Viennoiserie, the pastry must first be totally thawed under refrigeration or at room temperature and then proofed and baked as normal. Pastry chefs and bakers should avoid placing frozen pastry into a warm proof box because it will cause the outside to defrost and begin proofing before the center of the pastry has had a chance to thaw.

Preproofed Frozen

Preproofed frozen products are made from dough that has gone through an adapted process that quickly freezes the pastry just before the optimal proof is reached. For this technique to be successful, specialty equipment is required. Changes in the formulation include the addition of preferment for added flavor and strength, the addition of dough conditioners for strength (required), a limited first fermentation, and cold dough for processing.

Preproofed frozen pastry can be baked directly out of the freezer, but it should be baked at a lower temperature to ensure a balance between thawing and oven spring. Bake time can increase by as much as 40 percent. These pastries are valued for their versatility for pastry shops, restaurants, and hotels that want freshly baked products on demand. They are not valued for their flavor or shelf life and are best served while still warm because they stale and lose flavor quickly.

Putting Alternative Processes Into Production

Although preferments and retarding processes can be used in conjunction with each other, there are situations in which combining techniques can be detrimental to the final dough. Autolyse is not part of this discussion because its effects are primarily on the dough and have a limited impact on planning production.

To adapt to scheduling and to build flavor and strength in products, many of the preferment and retarding techniques can be used together. Precautions should be taken when combining techniques regarding fermentation activity, specifically for gas retention. To ensure a longer, slower fermentation, the dough should contain less yeast.

Another important consideration is that products can be frozen only once. Several problems will be created otherwise, including decreased yeast activity, extensive loss of dough strength, the production of off flavors and aromas, and an inefficient work schedule. For example, freezing dough in bulk, defrosting it, making up croissants, freezing them, and finally defrosting, proofing, and baking them at a later date will make for an inferior product.

Examples of Production Scenarios for Viennoiserie Using Preferments and/or Retarding

Note: All scenarios will result in fresh-baked pastries by 6:00 a.m. Friday.

- Croissant with Poolish (retarded shaped)

8:00 p.m.	Wednesday:	Mix poolish.
11:00 a.m.	Thursday:	Mix dough for 76°F (24°C) final temperature. Give 1 hour at room temperature.
12:00 p.m.	Thursday:	Retard dough for second hour of first fermentation.
1:00 p.m.	Thursday:	Prepare dough and give two single folds.
1:30 p.m.	Thursday:	Give last single fold.
2:00 p.m.	Thursday:	Final sheeting of the dough. Shape and retard.
3:30 a.m.	Friday:	Remove from retarder, transfer to proofer.
5:30 a.m.	Friday:	Bake.

- Danish (retarded in bulk with two single folds)

12:00 p.m.	Thursday:	Mix dough.
1:00 p.m.	Thursday:	Retard dough 1 hour.
2:00 p.m.	Thursday:	Prep dough and give two single folds.
1:30 a.m.	Friday:	Give last single fold.
2:00 a.m.	Friday:	Sheet dough and form pastries.
2:30 a.m.	Friday:	Proof pastries.
5:30 a.m.	Friday:	Bake.

- Brioche with Prefermented Dough (frozen shaped)

6:00 p.m.	Sunday:	Mix prefermented dough.
8:00 p.m.	Sunday:	Retard prefermented dough.
9:00 a.m.	Monday:	Mix brioche, give 1 hour at room temperature.
10:00 a.m.	Monday:	Transfer brioche to refrigerator.
11:00 a.m.	Monday:	Divide and preshape brioche.
11:20 a.m.	Monday:	Shape brioche, egg wash, and freeze.
5:00 p.m.	Thursday:	Pull brioche and place in proofer/retarder.
2:30 a.m.	Friday:	Retarder turns on to proofer.
5:00 a.m.	Friday:	Bake.

- Croissant with Sponge (bulk frozen and shaped retarded)

6:00 p.m.	Sunday:	Mix sponge.
9:00 a.m.	Monday:	Mix croissant dough and give 1 hour at room temperature.
10:00 a.m.	Monday:	Put dough in refrigerator.
11:00 a.m.	Monday:	Prepare dough, give two single folds, and freeze.
5:00 a.m.	Thursday:	Pull détrempe from freezer and put in refrigerator to thaw.
3:00 p.m.	Thursday:	Give last single fold.
3:30 p.m.	Thursday:	Sheet out dough and shape croissants.
4:00 p.m.	Thursday:	Retard shaped croissant in proofer/retarder.
2:30 a.m.	Friday:	Retarder turns on to proofer.
5:30 a.m.	Friday:	Bake.

Retarding Technique Conclusion

Retarding techniques can be of great benefit in the production of breakfast pastry. The goal is to spread out the process of dough handling and to encourage changes in the dough that can benefit and improve flavor and shelf life. At the same time, retarding reduces continuous workload and increases productivity. For example, it is easier for a small bakery to process a larger amount of dough once a week rather than smaller batches every day. Once the drawbacks of retarding in the refrigerator or freezer are understood, the pastry chef can implement quality control and appropriately adjust formulas and processing as needed.

CROISSANTS

According to legend, the croissant was invented in Vienna to celebrate the end of the second invasion of Vienna by Ottoman troops in 1683. The enemy decided to attack at night to avoid being seen, but the Viennese bakers, who were at work at the time, realized the city was under siege and gave the alert. To immortalize this victory, the bakers created the *Hörnchen* ("small horn" in German), with a crescent shape to symbolize the Ottoman flag. Marie-Antoinette d'Autriche, originally from Vienna, officially introduced and promoted the popularity of the croissant in France, starting in the late 1700s. However, the croissant may have existed in France well before Marie Antoinette's introduction. In the culinary inventory of the *Patrimoine Français*, mention is made of a cake in the shape of a croissant served during a banquet given in Paris by the Queen of France in 1549 to commemorate the alliance of François Ier with le Grand Turc. Today, the croissant is a traditional element of the French breakfast, and one of the most familiar French pastries to those living outside France, ubiquitous in bakeries throughout the world. It has transcended breakfast in some instances, serving delicious duty as a quick and simple sandwich. While deviations abound, the perfect croissant is memorable for its sultry layers of buttery, flaky dough.

Classic Croissants
(back to front)
Traditional, Almond, and Chocolate

FORMULA

CROISSANT DOUGH

Made with no preferments, this croissant dough can withstand retarding for up to 18 hours in bulk. Longer retarding builds acidity, which adds a fine complexity to the flavor of croissants made from this dough. For an interesting comparison to note the effect of fermentation on flavor and rheological properties, process the dough after it has cooled for an hour, following an hour of fermentation.

Final Dough Formula

Ingredients	Baker's %	Kilogram	US decimal	Lb & Oz		Test
Bread flour	100.00	2.496	5.504	5	8	1 lb 1⅝ oz
Water	38.00	0.949	2.091	2	1½	6¾ oz
Milk	23.00	0.574	1.266	1	4¼	4 oz
Sugar	13.00	0.325	0.715		11½	2¼ oz
Salt	2.00	0.050	0.110		1¾	⅜ oz
Osmotolerant instant yeast	1.20	0.030	0.066		1	¼ oz
Malt	0.50	0.012	0.028		½	⅛ oz
Butter	4.00	0.100	0.220		3½	¾ oz
Total	181.70	4.536	10.000	10	0	2 lb
Butter for roll-in	25.00	1.134	2.500	2	8	8 oz

Process, Final Dough

Mix	Improved mix
DDT	72°F (22°C) to 77°F (25°C)
First fermentation	45 minutes to 1 hour, retard for 8 to 15 hours at 40°F (4°C)
Divide	None
Lamination	Three single folds
Resting time in refrigerator	30 minutes between each fold or series of folds
Shaping	Assorted shapes
Final proof	1.5 to 2 hours at 78°F (26°C) at 65% rh
Steam	2 seconds
Bake	Convection oven, 13 to 15 minutes at 385°F (96°C)

Note

Butter for roll-in is a percentage of the total dough weight.

FORMULA

CROISSANT DOUGH WITH POOLISH

This croissant uses a lot of poolish as a preferment. The result is a dough with good machinability because of the higher levels of protease activity. The poolish lends a complex, slightly nutty flavor, and the higher levels of acidity add a blistered appearance to the crust.

Poolish Formula

Ingredients	Baker's %	Kilogram	US decimal	Lb & Oz		Test
Bread flour	100.00	0.791	1.744	1	11⅞	5⅝ oz
Water	100.00	0.791	1.744	1	11⅞	5⅝ oz
Yeast (instant)	0.10	0.001	0.002		< ⅛	⅛ tsp
Total	200.10	1.583	3.490	3	7⅞	11⅛ oz

Process, Poolish

1. Mix all the ingredients until well incorporated with a DDT of 70°F (21°C).
2. Allow to ferment 12 to 16 hours at room temperature [65°F (18°C) to 70°F (21°C)].

Final Dough Formula

Ingredients	Baker's %	Kilogram	US decimal	Lb & Oz		Test
Bread flour	100.00	1.809	3.989	3	15⅞	12¾ oz
Milk	34.00	0.615	1.356	1	5¾	4⅜ oz
Sugar	18.50	0.335	0.738		11¾	2⅜ oz
Salt	2.90	0.052	0.116		1⅞	⅜ oz
Osmotolerant instant yeast	1.40	0.025	0.056		⅞	⅛ oz
Malt	0.70	0.013	0.028		½	⅛ oz
Butter	5.70	0.103	0.227		3⅝	¾ oz
Poolish	87.50	1.583	3.490	3	7⅞	11⅛ oz
Total	250.70	4.536	10.000	10	0	2 lb
Butter for roll-in	25.00	1.134	2.500	2	8	8 oz

Process, Final Dough

Mix	Improved mix
DDT	72°F (22°C) to 77°F (25°C)
First fermentation	45 minutes to 1 hour, then 1 hour at 40°F (4°C)
Divide	None
Lamination	Three single folds

Resting time in refrigerator	30 minutes between each fold or series of folds
Shaping	Assorted shapes
Final proof	1.5 to 2 hours at 78°F (26°C) at 65% rh
Steam	2 seconds
Bake	Convection oven, 13 to 15 minutes at 385°F (196°C)

Total Formula of Détrempe

Ingredients	Baker's %	Kilogram	US decimal	Lb & Oz		Test
Bread flour	100.00	2.601	5.733	5	11¾	1 lb 2⅜ oz
Water	30.42	0.791	1.744	1	11⅞	5⅝ oz
Milk	23.66	0.615	1.356	1	5¾	4⅜ oz
Sugar	12.87	0.335	0.738		11¾	2⅜ oz
Salt	2.02	0.052	0.116		1⅞	⅜ oz
Osmotolerant instant yeast	1.00	0.026	0.058		⅞	⅛ oz
Malt	0.49	0.013	0.028		½	⅛ oz
Butter	3.97	0.103	0.227		3⅝	¾ oz
Total	174.43	4.536	10.000	10	0	2 lb

Note

Butter for roll-in is a percentage of the total dough weight.

SHAPING OPTIONS

Lunette Shape With Fig Filling

Sheet out the dough to 16 inches (41 cm) wide and down to ⅛ inch (3 to 3½ mm) thick. Spread the fig filling in a thin layer evenly over the dough. (Do not use too much filling, or the makeup and baking process will be difficult.) Roll the dough inward from both edges to meet in the middle. Cut into 1 inch (2½ cm) wide portions. Line 12 to 15 on a parchment lined sheet pan and egg wash. Proof and bake as normal.

Twisted "S" Shape With Praline and Chocolate

Sheet out the dough to 16 inches (41 cm) wide and down to ⅛ inch (3 to 3½ mm) thick. Spread the praline filling over the dough, leaving a 1½ inch (4 cm) wide gap without filling running down the center of the dough. (Do not use too much filling, or the makeup and baking process will be difficult.) Sprinkle semi-sweet chocolate chips over the surface of the dough. As for the lunette, roll the dough from both edges toward the center, leaving a 1 inch (2½ cm) gap between the two rolls. Cut into 1 inch (2½ cm) wide portions. When placing on a parchment-lined sheet pan, flip one side of the pastry to create the "S" shape. Egg wash the top and the sides of the pastry. Proof and bake as normal.

Pain au Raisin

Sheet out the dough to 16 inches (41 cm) wide and down to ⅛ inch (3 to 3 ½ mm) thick. Brush the far edge of the dough with water, about 1 inch (2 ½ cm) wide. Spread pastry cream thinly over the dough, leaving the part that has been brushed with water. Sprinkle raisins evenly over the pastry cream, and dust lightly with granulated sugar. Roll the dough toward the far side, without tightening too much. Cut into 1 inch (2 ½ cm) wide portions, place 15 per parchment-lined sheet pan and egg wash. Proof and bake as normal.

Croissant Specialty Shapes

FORMULA

CROISSANT DOUGH WITH PREFERMENTED DOUGH

Utilizing prefermented dough adds a fair amount of strength to this croissant dough. Extensibility is slightly reduced, and the flavor is complex and deep, while the crust appears blistered from acidity. This is a good formula to use with less consistent, weaker bread flours.

Prefermented Dough Formula

Ingredients	Baker's %	Kilogram	US decimal	Lb & Oz		Test
Bread flour	100.00	0.490	1.080	1	1¼	3½ oz
Water	65.00	0.318	0.702		11¼	2¼ oz
Yeast (instant)	0.60	0.003	0.006		⅛	⅛ tsp
Salt	2.00	0.010	0.022		⅜	⅛ oz
Total	167.60	0.821	1.810	1	13	6 oz

Process, Prefermented Dough

1. Mix all the ingredients until well incorporated with a DDT of 70°F (21°C).
2. Allow to ferment 1 hour at room temperature [65°F (18°C) to 70°F 21°C)].
3. Refrigerate until needed.

Final Dough Formula

Ingredients	Baker's %	Kilogram	US decimal	Lb & Oz		Test
Bread flour	100.00	2.003	4.415	4	6⅝	14⅛ oz
Water	33.00	0.661	1.457	1	7¼	4⅝ oz
Milk	29.00	0.581	1.280	1	4½	4⅛ oz
Sugar	15.00	0.300	0.662		10⅝	2⅛ oz
Salt	2.00	0.040	0.088		1⅜	¼ oz
Osmotolerant instant yeast	1.20	0.024	0.053		⅞	⅛ oz
Malt	0.30	0.006	0.013		¼	¼ tsp
Butter	5.00	0.100	0.221		3½	¾ oz
Prefermented dough	41.00	0.821	1.810	1	13	5¾ oz
Total	226.50	4.536	10.000	10	0	2 lb
Butter for roll-in	25.00	1.134	2.500	2	8	8 oz

Process, Final Dough

Mix	Improved mix
DDT	72°F (22°C) to 77°F (25°C)
First fermentation	45 minutes to 1 hour, then 1 hour at 40°F (4°C)
Divide	None
Lamination	Three single folds
Resting time in refrigerator	30 minutes between each fold or series of folds
Shaping	Assorted shapes
Final proof	1.5 to 2 hours at 78°F (26°C) at 65% rh
Steam	2 seconds
Bake	Convection oven, 13 to 15 minutes at 385°F (196°C)

Total Formula of Détrempe

Ingredients	Baker's %	Kilogram	US decimal	Lb & Oz		Test
Bread flour	100.00	2.493	5.495	5	7⅞	1 lb 1⅝ oz
Water	39.29	0.979	2.159	2	2½	6⅞ oz
Milk	23.30	0.581	1.280	1	4½	4⅛ oz
Sugar	12.05	0.300	0.662		10⅝	2⅛ oz
Salt	2.00	0.050	0.110		1¾	⅜ oz
Osmotolerant instant yeast	1.08	0.027	0.059		1	¼ oz
Malt	0.24	0.006	0.013		¼	¼ tsp
Butter	4.02	0.100	0.221		3½	¾ oz
Total	181.98	4.536	10.000	10	0	2 lb

Note

Butter for roll-in is a percentage of the total dough weight.

FORMULA

CROISSANT DOUGH WITH SPONGE

Using sponge as the preferment in sweet dough is a common choice, and in croissant, the use of a sponge enhances the natural flavors of the rich, buttery croissant with slightly acidic sweet tones.

Sponge Formula

Ingredients	Baker's %	Kilogram	US decimal	Lb & Oz		Test
Bread flour	100.00	0.520	1.146	1	2⅜	3⅝ oz
Water	62.00	0.322	0.710		11⅜	2¼ oz
Yeast (instant)	0.10	0.001	0.001		< ⅛	⅛ tsp
Total	162.10	0.842	1.857	1	13¾	6 oz

Process, Sponge

1. Mix all the ingredients until well incorporated with a DDT of 70°F (21°C).
2. Allow to ferment 12 to 16 hours at room temperature [65°F (18°C) to 70°F (21°C)].

Final Dough Formula

Ingredients	Baker's %	Kilogram	US decimal	Lb & Oz		Test
Bread flour	100.00	2.106	4.643	4	10¼	14⅞ oz
Water	20.00	0.421	0.929		14⅞	3 oz
Milk	30.00	0.632	1.393	1	6¼	4½ oz
Sugar	16.00	0.337	0.743		11⅞	2⅜ oz
Salt	2.50	0.053	0.116		1⅞	⅜ oz
Osmotolerant instant yeast	1.60	0.034	0.074		1¼	¼ oz
Malt	0.30	0.006	0.014		¼	¼ tsp
Butter	5.00	0.105	0.232		3¾	¾ oz
Sponge	40.00	0.842	1.857	1	13¾	6 oz
Total	215.40	4.536	10.000	10	0	2 lb
Butter for roll-in	25.00	1.134	2.500	2	8	8 oz

Process, Final Dough

Mix	Improved mix
DDT	72°F (27°C) to 77°F (25°C)
First fermentation	45 minutes to 1 hour, then 1 hour at 40°F (4°C)
Divide	None
Lamination	Three single folds

Resting time in refrigerator	30 minutes between each fold or series of folds
Shaping	Assorted shapes
Final proof	1.5 to 2 hours at 78°F (26°C) at 65% rh
Steam	2 seconds
Bake	Convection oven, 13 to 15 minutes at 385°F (196°C)

Total Formula of Détrempe

Ingredients	Baker's %	Kilogram	US decimal	Lb & Oz		Test
Bread flour	100.00	2.625	5.788	5	12⅝	1 lb 2½ oz
Water	28.31	0.743	1.639	1	10¼	5¼ oz
Milk	24.06	0.632	1.393	1	6¼	4½ oz
Sugar	12.83	0.337	0.743		11⅞	2⅜ oz
Salt	2.01	0.053	0.116		1⅞	⅜ oz
Osmotolerant instant yeast	1.30	0.034	0.075		1¼	¼ oz
Malt	0.24	0.006	0.014		¼	¼ tsp
Butter	4.01	0.105	0.232		3¾	¾ oz
Total	172.76	4.536	10.000	10	0	2 lb

Note

Butter for roll-in is a percentage of the total dough weight.

FORMULA

CROISSANT DOUGH WITH NATURAL STARTER

The combination of sourdough and croissant is natural. The key to success is controlling the degree of acidity that accumulates in the dough. The levain required for this is an Italian levain, prized for its mild acidity. This croissant is comprised of two doughs, in the Italian tradition (think Pan d'Oro and Panettone). The first dough is allowed to ferment for 12 to 15 hours and is then mixed into the final dough. The flavor of this croissant is quite pleasant, and mildly acidic.

Italian Levain Formula

Ingredients	Baker's %	Kilogram	US decimal	Lb & Oz
Bread flour	100.00	0.018	0.040	⅝
Water	50.00	0.009	0.020	⅜
Starter	100.00	0.018	0.040	⅝
Total	250.00	0.045	0.100	1 ⅝

Process, Italian Levain

1. Mix all the ingredients until well incorporated with a DDT of 85°F (29°C).
2. Feed every 4 hours.
3. When the levain is mature, mix all the ingredients until well incorporated with a DDT of 70°F (21°C).
4. Allow to ferment 12 to 16 hours at room temperature [73°F (23°C) to 76°F (25°C)].

First Dough Formula

Ingredients	Baker's %	Kilogram	US decimal	Lb & Oz	Test
Bread flour	100.00	0.223	0.492	7 ⅞	1 ⅝ oz
Water	50.00	0.112	0.246	4	¾ oz
Milk	13.00	0.029	0.064	1	¼ oz
Eggs	4.00	0.009	0.020	⅜	⅛ oz
Sugar	14.00	0.031	0.069	1 ⅛	¼ oz
Butter	4.00	0.009	0.020	⅜	⅛ oz
Levain	15.00	0.034	0.074	1 ⅛	¼ oz
Total	200.00	0.447	0.985	15 ¾	3 ⅛ oz

Process, First Dough

1. Incorporate all the ingredients for 4 minutes in first speed.
2. Mix just until the gluten starts to develop in second speed.
3. Allow to ferment 12 hours at 70°F (21°C).

Final Dough Formula

Ingredients	Baker's %	Kilogram	US decimal	Lb & Oz		Test
Bread flour	100.00	2.233	4.924	4	14¾	15¾ oz
Water	30.00	0.670	1.477	1	7⅝	4¾ oz
Milk	25.00	0.558	1.231	1	3¾	4 oz
Eggs	5.00	0.112	0.246		4	¾ oz
Sugar	14.00	0.313	0.689		11	2¼ oz
Salt	2.20	0.049	0.108		1¾	⅜ oz
Osmotolerant instant yeast	1.50	0.034	0.074		1⅛	¼ oz
Malt	1.40	0.031	0.069		1⅛	¼ oz
Butter	4.00	0.089	0.197		3⅛	⅝ oz
First dough	20.00	0.447	0.985		15¾	3⅛ oz
Total	203.10	4.536	10.000	10	0	2 lb

Process, Final Dough

Mix	Improved mix
DDT	72°F (22°C) to 77°F (25°C)
First fermentation	45 minutes to 1 hour, then 1 hour at 40°F (4°C)
Divide	None
Lamination	Three single folds
Resting time in refrigerator	30 minutes between each fold or series of folds
Shaping	Assorted shapes
Final proof	1.5 to 2 hours at 78°F (26°C) at 65% rh
Steam	2 seconds
Bake	Convection oven, 13 to 15 minutes at 385°F (196°C)

Total Formula of Détrempe

Ingredients	Baker's %	Kilogram	US decimal	Lb & Oz		Test
Bread flour	100.00	2.479	5.465	5	7½	1 lb 1½ oz
Water	31.98	0.793	1.748	1	12	5⅝ oz
Milk	23.69	0.587	1.295	1	4¾	4⅛ oz
Eggs	4.86	0.121	0.266		4¼	⅞ oz
Sugar	13.87	0.344	0.758		12⅛	2⅜ oz
Salt	1.98	0.049	0.108		1¾	⅜ oz
Osmotolerant instant yeast	1.35	0.034	0.074		1⅛	¼ oz
Malt	1.26	0.031	0.069		1⅛	¼ oz
Butter	3.96	0.098	0.217		3½	¾ oz
Total	182.95	4.536	10.000	10	0	2 lb

FORMULA

CROISSANT DOUGH—HAND MIX

The luxury of possessing both a dough mixer and a reversible dough sheeter is not always reality. This croissant dough is formulated to be mixed and processed by hand. The use of poolish in this formula lends to extensibility of the dough, which is beneficial for the lamination process. After the dough is mixed, it should be refrigerated right away to limit any fermentation, as that would increase the strength of the dough. For easier lamination, allow the dough to rest 1 hour in the refrigerator between each fold, rather than the standard 30 minutes.

Poolish Formula

Ingredients	Baker's %	Kilogram	US decimal	Lb & Oz		Test
Bread flour	100.00	0.734	1.617	1	9⅞	5⅛ oz
Water	100.00	0.734	1.617	1	9⅞	5⅛ oz
Yeast (instant)	0.10	0.001	0.002		< ⅛	⅛ tsp
Total	200.10	1.468	3.236	3	3¾	10⅜ oz

Process, Poolish

1. Mix all the ingredients until well incorporated with a DDT of 70°F (21°C).
2. Allow to ferment 12 to 16 hours at room temperature [65°F (18°C) to 70°F (21°C)].

Final Dough Formula

Ingredients	Baker's %	Kilogram	US decimal	Lb & Oz		Test
Bread flour	100.00	1.678	3.698	3	11 ⅛	11 ⅞ oz
Water	34.00	0.570	1.257	1	4 ⅛	4 oz
Milk	20.00	0.336	0.740		11 ⅞	2 ⅜ oz
Sugar	18.50	0.310	0.684		11	2 ¼ oz
Salt	2.90	0.049	0.107		1 ¾	⅜ oz
Osmotolerant instant yeast	1.40	0.023	0.052		⅞	⅛ oz
Malt	0.40	0.007	0.015		¼	½ tsp
Butter	5.70	0.096	0.211		3 ⅜	⅝ oz
Poolish	87.50	1.468	3.236	3	3 ¾	10 ⅜ oz
Total	270.40	4.536	10.000	10	0	2 lb
Butter for roll-in	25.00	1.134	2.500	2	8	8 oz

Process, Final Dough

Mix	Hand mix
DDT	72°F (22°C) to 77°F (25°C)
First fermentation	2 hours in the refrigerator
Divide	None
Lamination	Three single folds
Resting time in refrigerator	1 hour between each fold
Shaping	Assorted shapes
Final proof	1.5 to 2 hours at 78°F (26°C) at 65% rh
Steam	2 seconds
Bake	Convection oven, 13 to 15 minutes at 385°F (196°C)

Total Formula of Détrempe

Ingredients	Baker's %	Kilogram	US decimal	Lb & Oz		Test
Bread flour	100.00	2.411	5.315	5	5	1 lb 1 oz
Water	54.08	1.304	2.875	2	14	9 ¼ oz
Milk	13.92	0.329	0.740		11 ⅞	2 ⅜ oz
Sugar	12.87	0.310	0.684		11	2 ¼ oz
Salt	2.02	0.049	0.107		1 ¾	⅜ oz
Osmotolerant instant yeast	1.00	0.024	0.053		⅞	⅛ oz
Malt	0.28	0.007	0.015		¼	½ tsp
Butter	3.97	0.096	0.211		3 ⅜	⅝ oz
Total	188.14	4.536	10.000	10	0	2 lb

Note

Butter for roll-in is a percentage of the total dough weight.

FORMULA

WHOLE WHEAT CROISSANT DOUGH

Using whole wheat flour in this dough is a fairly new variation on the classic and adds a pleasing flavor and aroma. Egg yolk helps make the dough smoother (balancing the texture of the whole wheat) because of its natural lecithin. This dough is excellent for making a savory croissant.

Final Dough Formula

Ingredients	Baker's %	Kilogram	US decimal	Lb & Oz		Test
Bread flour	75.00	1.924	4.242	4	3⅞	13⅝ oz
Whole wheat flour	25.00	0.641	1.414	1	6⅝	4½ oz
Water	50.00	1.283	2.828	2	13¼	9 oz
Egg yolks	8.00	0.205	0.452		7¼	1½ oz
Sugar	11.00	0.282	0.622		10	2 oz
Salt	2.00	0.051	0.085		1⅜	¼ oz
Osmotolerant instant yeast	1.60	0.041	0.090		1½	¼ oz
Malt	0.20	0.005	0.011		⅛	⅛ tsp
Butter	4.00	0.103	0.226		3⅝	¾ oz
Total	176.80	4.536	10.000	10	0	2 lb
Butter for roll-in	25.00	1.134	2.500	2	8	8 oz

Process, Final Dough

Mix	Improved mix
DDT	72°F (22°C) to 77°F (25°C)
First fermentation	45 minutes to 1 hour, retard for 8 to 15 hours at 40°F (5°C)
Divide	None
Lamination	Three single folds
Resting time in refrigerator	30 minutes between each fold or series of folds
Shaping	Assorted shapes
Final proof	1.5 to 2 hours at 78°F (26°C) at 65% rh
Steam	2 seconds
Bake	Convection oven, 13 to 15 minutes at 385°F (196°C)

Note

Butter for roll-in is a percentage of the total dough weight.

SHAPING OPTIONS: SAVORY CROISSANT

Ham and Cheese Croissants

Sheet out the dough to 16 inches (41 cm) wide and down to ⅛ inch (3 to 3 ½ mm) thick.

For the square ham and cheese croissant, cut the dough into 3 ¼ inch (8 ⅜ cm) × 5 ⅓ inch (13 ½ cm) portions. Place a slice of black forest ham and a slice of Swiss cheese on one side, and fold the dough twice so that the end edge without filling ends up on the bottom of the pastry. Place 15 per parchment-lined sheet pan. Egg wash and score if desired. Proof and bake as normal.

For the traditional shape ham and cheese croissant, sheet out the dough to 16 inches wide and down to 3 to 3 ½ mm thick. Cut the dough into 4 inch × 8 inch triangles. Place the ham and cheese on the wide end of the triangle, and shape as for traditional croissant. Place 15 per parchment-lined sheet pan and egg wash. Proof and bake as normal.

Spinach and Feta Croissants

Sheet out the dough to 16 inches (41 cm) wide and down to ⅛ inch (3 to 3 ½ mm) thick. Cut into three 5 ⅓ inch (13 ½ cm) wide strips. For each strip, place the spinach and feta filling down the center in one line. (Spinach and feta filling is on page 394.) Roll the dough over the filling and place the seam on the bottom to seal. Cut into 3 inch (7 ½ cm) wide pieces, or as desired. Place 15 per parchment-lined sheet pan. Proof and bake as normal.

Savory Croissant With Whole Wheat Croissant Dough

Spinach and Feta

Ham and Cheese

FORMULA

WHOLE WHEAT CROISSANT DOUGH WITH PREFERMENTED DOUGH

Based on the same formula as the whole wheat croissant dough, this version uses prefermented dough, which gives it additional flavor and strength.

Prefermented Dough Formula

Ingredients	Baker's %	Kilogram	US decimal	Lb & Oz		Test
Bread flour	100.00	0.500	1.103	1	1⅝	3½ oz
Water	65.00	0.325	0.717		11½	2¼ oz
Yeast (instant)	0.60	0.003	0.007		⅛	⅛ tsp
Salt	2.00	0.010	0.022		⅜	⅛ oz
Total	167.60	0.838	1.849	1	13⅝	5⅞ oz

Process, Prefermented Dough

1. Mix all the ingredients until well incorporated with a DDT of 70°F (21°C).
2. Allow to ferment 1 hour at room temperature [65°F (18°C) to 70°F (21°C)].
3. Refrigerate until needed.

Final Dough Formula

Ingredients	Baker's %	Kilogram	US decimal	Lb & Oz		Test
Bread flour	75.00	1.534	3.381	3	6⅛	10⅞ oz
Whole wheat flour	25.00	0.502	1.127	1	2	3⅝ oz
Water	48.00	0.982	2.164	2	2⅝	6⅞ oz
Egg yolks	10.00	0.205	0.451		7¼	1½ oz
Sugar	13.00	0.266	0.586		9⅜	1⅞ oz
Salt	2.00	0.041	0.090		1½	¼ oz
Osmotolerant instant yeast	1.60	0.032	0.072		1⅛	¼ oz
Malt	0.20	0.004	0.009		⅛	¼ tsp
Butter	6.00	0.123	0.271		4⅜	⅞ oz
Prefermented dough	41.00	0.838	1.849	1	13⅝	5⅞ oz
Total	221.80	4.536	10.000	10	0	2 lb
Butter for roll-in	25.00	1.134	2.500	2	8	8 oz

Process, Final Dough

Mix	Improved mix
DDT	72°F (22°C) to 77°F (25°C)
First fermentation	45 minutes to 1 hour, then 1 hour at 40°F (5°C)
Divide	None
Lamination	Three single folds
Resting time in refrigerator	30 minutes between each fold or series of folds
Shaping	Assorted shapes
Final proof	1.5 to 2 hours at 78°F (26°C) at 65% rh
Steam	2 seconds
Bake	Convection oven, 13 to 15 minutes at 385°F (196°C)

Total Formula

Ingredients	Baker's %	Kilogram	US decimal	Lb & Oz		Test
Bread flour	80.00	2.036	4.484	4	7¾	14⅜ oz
Whole wheat flour	20.00	0.509	1.127	1	2	3⅝ oz
Water	51.34	1.307	2.881	2	14⅛	9¼ oz
Egg yolks	8.03	0.204	0.451		7¼	1½ oz
Sugar	10.45	0.266	0.586		9⅜	1⅞ oz
Salt	2.00	0.051	0.112		1¾	⅜ oz
Osmotolerant instant yeast	1.40	0.036	0.079		1¼	¼ oz
Malt	0.16	0.004	0.009		⅛	¼ tsp
Butter	4.82	0.123	0.271		4⅜	⅞ oz
Total	178.20	4.536	10.000	10	0	2 lb
Butter for roll-in	25.00	1.134	2.500	2	8	8 oz

Note

Butter for roll-in is a percentage of the total dough weight.

DANISH

In Denmark, Danish is known as *wienerbrød*, or "bread of Vienna." A popular explanation goes back to an 18th or 19th century strike by Danish journeyman bakers, which created a shortage of bakers in Denmark. Austrian bakers who traveled to Denmark to replace the striking workers introduced their traditional recipe for sweet pastry. The Viennese dough relied on a high amount of butter and resulted in a light, flaky product that became a sensation in Denmark and soon spread to surrounding lands. In other countries, the name "Danish" was applied to the newly discovered pastries, but in Denmark, it retained its reference to Viennese origins. Danish pastries are now popular throughout the world in a wide variety of flavors and shapes. In the United States, the current pervasiveness of Danish can be attributed to New York City and its Jewish delicatessens, which helped to popularize the pastries beginning in the early 1900s.

Assorted Danish
(left to right) Half Pockets, Cinnamon Snails, Half Pockets, and Pinwheels

FORMULA

DANISH DOUGH

This Danish dough has no preferments but can withstand a longer retarding for up to 18 hours in bulk. The retarding builds acidity, which leads to a pleasant complexity in the flavor of the Danish made from this dough. For an interesting experiment to note the effect of fermentation on flavor and rheological properties, process the dough after it has cooled for an hour, following an hour of fermentation.

Final Dough Formula

Ingredients	Baker's %	Kilogram	US decimal	Lb & Oz	Test
Bread flour	100.00	2.588	5.705	5 11¼	1 lb 2¼ oz
Milk	46.00	1.190	2.624	2 10	8⅜ oz
Sugar	12.00	0.311	0.685	11	2¼ oz
Eggs	11.00	0.285	0.627	10	2 oz
Salt	2.00	0.052	0.114	1⅞	⅜ oz
Osmotolerant instant yeast	1.30	0.034	0.074	1⅛	¼ oz
Butter	3.00	0.078	0.171	2¾	½ oz
Total	175.30	4.536	10.000	10 0	2 lb
Butter for roll-in	27.00	1.225	2.700	2 11¼	8⅝ oz

Process, Final Dough

Mix	Improved mix
DDT	72°F (22°C) to 77°F (25°C)
First fermentation	45 minutes to 1 hour, retard for 8 to 15 hours at 40°F (5°C)
Divide	None
Lamination	Three single folds
Resting time in refrigerator	30 minutes between each fold or series of folds
Shaping	Assorted shapes
Final proof	1.5 to 2 hours at 78°F (26°C) at 65% rh
Steam	2 seconds
Bake	Convection oven, 13 to 15 minutes at 385°F (196°C)

Note

Butter for roll-in is a percentage of the total dough weight.

FORMULA

DANISH DOUGH WITH BIGA

The long, slow fermentation that is characteristic of the biga gives the Danish made with this dough multifaceted flavor and aroma. Slightly sweet and acidic, the resulting pastries retain moisture and resist staling longer. This formula is well suited to those times when only weaker or inconsistent bread flours are available.

Biga Formula

Ingredients	Baker's %	Kilogram	US decimal	Lb & Oz	Test
Bread flour	100.00	0.771	1.699	1 11⅛	5⅜ oz
Milk	55.00	0.424	0.934	15	3 oz
Yeast (instant)	0.40	0.003	0.007	⅛	⅛ tsp
Total	155.40	1.197	2.640	2 10¼	8½ oz

Process, Biga

1. Mix all the ingredients until well incorporated with a DDT of 70°F (21°C).
2. Allow to ferment for 16 hours at 60°F (16°C).

Final Dough Formula

Ingredients	Baker's %	Kilogram	US decimal	Lb & Oz	Test
Bread flour	100.00	1.787	3.940	3 15	12⅝ oz
Milk	45.00	0.804	1.773	1 12⅜	5⅝ oz
Eggs	16.00	0.286	0.630	10⅛	2 oz
Sugar	17.00	0.304	0.670	10¾	2⅛ oz
Salt	3.00	0.054	0.118	1⅞	⅜ oz
Osmotolerant instant yeast	1.80	0.032	0.071	1⅛	¼ oz
Butter	4.00	0.071	0.158	2½	½ oz
Biga	67.00	1.197	2.640	2 10¼	8½ oz
Total	253.80	4.536	10.000	10 0	2 lb
Butter for roll-in	27.00	1.225	2.700	2 11¼	8⅝ oz

Process, Final Dough

Mix	Improved mix
DDT	72°F (22°C) to 77°F (25°C)
First fermentation	45 minutes to 1 hour, then 1 hour at 40°F (5°C)
Divide	None

Lamination	Three single folds
Resting time in refrigerator	30 minutes between each fold or series of folds
Shaping	Assorted shapes
Final proof	1.5 to 2 hours at 78°F (26°C) at 65% rh
Steam	2 seconds
Bake	Convection oven, 3 to 15 minutes at 385°F (196°C)

Total Formula of Détrempe

Ingredients	Baker's %	Kilogram	US decimal	Lb & Oz		Test
Bread flour	100.00	2.558	5.639	5	10¼	1 lb 2 oz
Milk	48.01	1.228	2.707	2	11⅜	8⅝ oz
Eggs	11.18	0.286	0.630		10⅛	2 oz
Sugar	11.88	0.304	0.670		10¾	2⅛ oz
Salt	2.10	0.054	0.118		1⅞	⅜ oz
Yeast (instant)	1.38	0.035	0.078		1¼	¼ oz
Butter	2.79	0.071	0.158		2½	½ oz
Total	177.34	4.536	10.000	10	0	2 lb

Note

Butter for roll-in is a percentage of the total dough weight.

FORMULA

DANISH DOUGH WITH SPONGE

Danish dough and sponge preferment complement each other nicely. Sponge, a common choice of preferments for sweet, yeasted doughs, adds an excellent flavor and aroma to the Danish.

Sponge Formula

Ingredients	Baker's %	Kilogram	US decimal	Lb & Oz		Test
Bread flour	100.00	0.771	1.701	1	11¼	5½ oz
Water	62.00	0.478	1.054	1	⅞	3⅜ oz
Yeast (instant)	0.10	0.001	0.002		< ⅛	⅛ tsp
Total	162.10	1.251	2.757	2	12⅛	8⅞ oz

Process, Sponge

1. Mix all the ingredients until well incorporated with a DDT of 70°F (21°C).
2. Allow to ferment 12 to 16 hours at room temperature [65°F (18°C) to 70°F (21°C)].

Final Dough Formula

Ingredients	Baker's %	Kilogram	US decimal	Lb & Oz		Test
Bread flour	100.00	1.807	3.984	3	15¾	12¾ oz
Milk	40.00	0.723	1.594	1	9½	5⅛ oz
Eggs	16.00	0.289	0.637		10¼	2 oz
Sugar	17.00	0.307	0.677		10⅞	2⅛ oz
Salt	3.00	0.054	0.120		1⅞	⅜ oz
Osmotolerant instant yeast	1.80	0.033	0.072		1⅛	¼ oz
Butter	4.00	0.072	0.159		2½	½ oz
Sponge	69.20	1.251	2.757	2	12⅛	8⅞ oz
Total	251.00	4.536	10.000	10	0	2 lb
Butter for roll-in	27.00	1.225	2.700	2	11¼	8⅝ oz

Process, Final Dough

Mix	Improved mix
DDT	72°F (22°C) to 77°F (25°C)
First fermentation	45 minutes to 1 hour, then 1 hour at 40°F (5°C).
Divide	None
Lamination	Three single folds
Resting time in refrigerator	30 minutes between each fold or series of folds
Shaping	Assorted shapes
Final proof	1.5 to 2 hours at 78°F (26°C) at 65% rh
Steam	2 seconds
Bake	Convection oven, 13 to 15 minutes at 385°F (196°C)

Total Formula

Ingredients	Baker's %	Kilogram	US decimal	Lb & Oz		Test
Bread flour	100.00	2.579	5.685	5	11	1 lb 2¼ oz
Water	18.55	0.478	1.054	1	⅞	3⅜ oz
Milk	28.03	0.723	1.594	1	9½	5⅛ oz
Eggs	11.21	0.289	0.637		10¼	2 oz
Sugar	11.91	0.307	0.677		10⅞	2⅛ oz
Salt	2.10	0.054	0.120		1⅞	⅜ oz
Osmotolerant instant yeast	1.29	0.033	0.073		1⅛	¼ oz
Butter	2.80	0.072	0.159		2½	½ oz
Total	175.89	4.536	10.000	10	0	2 lb

Note

Butter for roll-in is a percentage of the total dough weight.

FORMULA

DANISH DOUGH WITH PREFERMENTED DOUGH

The use of prefermented dough in this formula creates a well-developed yeasty flavor, while the acidity benefits shelf life.

Prefermented Dough Formula

Ingredients	Baker's %	Kilogram	US decimal	Lb & Oz		Test
Bread flour	100.00	1.049	2.312	2	5	7 ⅜ oz
Water	65.00	0.682	1.503	1	8	4 ¾ oz
Yeast (instant)	0.60	0.006	0.014		¼	¼ tsp
Salt	2.00	0.021	0.046		¾	⅛ oz
Total	167.60	1.758	3.875	3	14	12 ⅜ oz

Process, Prefermented Dough

1. Mix all the ingredients until well incorporated with a DDT of 70°F (21°C).
2. Allow to ferment 1 hour at room temperature [65°F (18°C) to 70°F (21°C)].
3. Refrigerate until needed.

Final Dough Formula

Ingredients	Baker's %	Kilogram	US decimal	Lb & Oz		Test
Bread flour	100.00	1.556	3.429	3	6 ⅞	11 oz
Water	21.00	0.327	0.720		11 ½	2 ¼ oz
Milk powder	11.00	0.171	0.377		6	1 ¼ oz
Eggs	18.00	0.280	0.617		9 ⅞	2 oz
Sugar	20.00	0.311	0.686		11	2 ¼ oz
Salt	2.00	0.031	0.069		1 ⅛	¼ oz
Osmotolerant instant yeast	1.60	0.025	0.055		1 ⅞	⅛ oz
Butter	5.00	0.078	0.171		2 ¾	½ oz
Prefermented dough	113.00	1.758	3.875	3	14	12 ⅜ oz
Total	291.60	4.536	10.000	10	0	2 lb
Butter for roll-in	27.00	1.225	2.700	2	11 ¼	8 ⅝ oz

Process, Final Dough

Mix	Improved mix
DDT	72°F (22°C) to 77°F (25°C)
First fermentation	45 minutes to 1 hour, then 1 hour at 40°F (5°C)
Divide	None
Lamination	Three single folds
Resting time in refrigerator	30 minutes between each fold, or series of folds
Shaping	Assorted shapes
Final proof	1.5 to 2 hours at 78°F (26°C) at 65% rh
Steam	2 seconds
Bake	Convection oven, 13 to 15 minutes at 385°F (196°C)

Total Formula

Ingredients	Baker's %	Kilogram	US decimal	Lb & Oz		Test
Bread flour	100.00	2.604	5.742	5	11⅞	1 lb 2⅜ oz
Water	38.72	1.008	2.223	2	3⅝	7⅛ oz
Milk powder	6.57	0.171	0.377		6	1¼ oz
Eggs	10.75	0.280	0.617		9⅞	2 oz
Sugar	11.95	0.311	0.686		11	2¼ oz
Salt	2.00	0.052	0.115		1⅞	⅜ oz
Osmotolerant instant yeast	1.20	0.031	0.069		1⅛	¼ oz
Butter	2.99	0.078	0.171		2¾	½ oz
Total	174.18	4.536	10.000	10	0	2 lb

Note

Butter for roll-in is a percentage of the total dough weight.

Assorted Miniature Viennoiserie
Plain and Chocolate Croissants, Assorted Danish

FORMULA

LAMINATED BRIOCHE

This formula for laminated brioche is based on a leaner, dryer brioche formula. Cutting back on the fat in the dough, and the hydration, is necessary to achieve the lamination. Because there is a fair amount of butter in the dough, it must be well chilled before beginning lamination and the butter should not be too firm. Laminated brioche is great for rolled-up pastries, such as the cinnamon roll. Common additions include pastry cream or frangipane, along with currants, citrus zests, chocolate chips, or almond meal, alone or in combination. Care must be taken not to overload the filling; otherwise, the pastry will not be able to support the filling once baked.

Sponge Formula

Ingredients	Baker's %	Kilogram	US decimal	Lbs & Oz	Test
Bread flour	100.00	0.445	0.982	15¾	3⅛ oz
Water	62.00	0.276	0.609	9¾	2 oz
Yeast (instant)	0.10	0.000	0.001	< ⅛	⅛ tsp
Total	162.10	0.722	1.592	1 9½	5⅛ oz

Process, Sponge

1. Mix all the ingredients until well incorporated with a DDT of 70°F (21°C).
2. Allow to ferment 12 to 16 hours at room temperature [65°F (18°C) to 70°F (21°C)].

Final Dough

Ingredients	Baker's %	Kilogram	US decimal	Lb & Oz	Test
Bread flour	100.00	1.805	3.979	3 15⅝	12¾ oz
Water	4.60	0.083	0.183	2⅞	⅝ oz
Eggs	67.00	1.209	2.666	2 10⅝	8½ oz
Sugar	15.60	0.282	0.621	9⅞	2 oz
Salt	2.50	0.045	0.099	1⅝	⅜ oz
Osmotolerant instant yeast	1.60	0.029	0.064	1	¼ oz
Butter	20.00	0.361	0.796	12¾	2½ oz
Sponge	40.00	0.722	1.592	1 9½	5⅛ oz
Total	251.30	4.536	10.000	10 0	2 lb
Butter for roll-in	25.00	1.134	2.500	2 8	8 oz

Process, Final Dough	
Mix	Intensive mix
DDT	72°F (22°C) to 77°F (25°C)
First fermentation	45 minutes to 1 hour, retard for 8 to 15 hours at 40°F (5°C)
Divide	None
Lamination	Three single folds
Resting time in refrigerator	30 minutes between each fold
Shaping	Assorted shapes
Final proof	1.5 to 2 hours at 78°F (26°C) at 65% rh
Steam	2 seconds
Bake	Convection oven, 12 to 13 minutes at 385°F (196°C)

Total Formula of Détrempe

Ingredients	Baker's %	Kilogram	US decimal	Lb & Oz		Test
Bread flour	100.00	2.250	4.961	4	15⅜	15⅞ oz
Water	15.96	0.359	0.792		12⅝	2½ oz
Eggs	53.74	1.209	2.666	2	10⅝	8½ oz
Sugar	12.51	0.282	0.621		9⅞	2 oz
Salt	2.01	0.045	0.099		1⅝	⅜ oz
Osmotolerant instant yeast	1.30	0.029	0.065		1	¼ oz
Butter	16.04	0.361	0.796		12¾	2½ oz
Total	201.56	4.536	10.000	10	0	2 lb

Note

Butter for roll-in is a percentage of the total dough weight.

SHAPING OPTIONS

Raisin Swirl

Sheet out the dough to 16 inches (41 cm) wide and down to ⅛ inch (3 to 3½ mm) thick. Brush one edge with water, about 1 inch (2½ cm) wide. Spread the pastry cream thinly over the dough, leaving the part that has been brushed with water. Sprinkle the raisins evenly over the cream, and dust lightly with granulated sugar. (Do not use too much filling, or the makeup and baking process will be difficult.) Roll from the nonwatered side, without tightening too much. Cut into 1 inch (2½ cm) wide strips. Place 15 per sheet pan. When placing on a parchment-lined sheet pan, place the outer end of the strip underneath the center of the swirl. Egg wash the top and the sides of the pastry. Proof and bake as normal.

Almond Swirl

Sheet out the dough to 16 inches (41 cm) wide and down to ⅛ inch (3 to 3 ½ mm) thick. Brush water on one edge, about 1 inch (2 ½ cm) wide. Spread the pastry cream thinly over the dough, leaving the part that has been brushed with water. Dust with almond meal evenly over the cream. (Do not use too much filling, or the makeup and baking process will be difficult.) Roll from the nonwatered side, without tightening too much. Cut into 1 inch (2 ½ cm) wide strips. Place 15 per sheet pan. When placing on a parchment-lined sheet pan, place the outer end of the strip underneath the center of the swirl. Egg wash the top and the sides of the pastry. Proof and bake as normal.

Laminated Brioche

Apple Chausson (sides) and Jalousie (center)

FORMULA

PAIN AU LAIT

Pain au lait, or bread made with milk, is slightly sweet with a soft crust and a delicate, rich crumb. It is commonly used for breakfast pastries but can be shaped and baked in loaf pans, or made into boules.

Final Dough Formula

Ingredients	Baker's %	Kilogram	US decimal	Lb & Oz		Test
Bread flour	100.00	2.010	4.431	4	6⅞	14⅛ oz
Milk	45.00	0.904	1.994	1	15⅞	6⅜ oz
Eggs	22.00	0.442	0.975		15⅝	3⅛ oz
Sugar	11.00	0.221	0.487		7¾	1½ oz
Salt	2.00	0.040	0.089		1⅜	¼ oz
Osmotolerant instant yeast	0.70	0.014	0.031		½	⅛ oz
Butter	45.00	0.904	1.994	1	15⅞	6⅜ oz
Total	225.70	4.536	10.000	10	0	2 lb

Process, Final Dough

Mix	Intensive mix
DDT	72°F (22°C) to 77°F (25°C)
First fermentation	45 minutes to 1 hour, refrigerate overnight
Divide	8 oz (225 g) × 2 for braids, 2.8 oz (80 g) for buns
Preshape	Light batard
Resting time	20 to 30 minutes
Shape	2-strand braid
Final proof	1 hour to 1 hour 30 minutes at 78°F (25°C) at 65% rh
Scoring	None
Steam	2 seconds
Bake	Convection oven, 30 minutes at 335°F (169°C)

Pain au Lait Loaf
and Buns

FORMULA

SWEET ROLL DOUGH

Sweet roll dough is a versatile choice for morning roll-style pastries. Its tender crumb can be attributed to the ample use of butter and eggs, as well as the use of cake flour for a portion of the dough. The dough is best worked with cold, and should be sheeted to about 1/8 inch (3 mm). It can then be filled with cinnamon sugar and raisins, white sugar, orange zest and raisins, or any imaginative combination of ingredients.

Final Dough Formula

Ingredients	Baker's %	Kilogram	US decimal	Lb & Oz		Test
Bread flour	80.00	1.696	3.738	3	11 ⅞	12 oz
Cake flour	20.00	0.424	0.748		12	2 ⅜ oz
Water	40.00	0.848	1.869	1	13 ⅞	6 oz
Milk powder	5.00	0.106	0.234		3 ¾	¾ oz
Eggs	15.00	0.318	0.701		11 ¼	2 ¼ oz
Sugar	20.00	0.424	0.935		15	3 oz
Salt	2.00	0.042	0.093		1 ½	¼ oz
Osmotolerant instant yeast	2.00	0.042	0.093		1 ½	¼ oz
Butter (cubed)	30.00	0.636	1.402	1	6 ⅜	4 ½ oz
Total	214.00	4.536	10.000	10	0	2 lb

Process, Final Dough

Mix	Intensive
DDT	72° (22°C) to 77°F (25°C)
First fermentation	45 minutes to 1 hour, refrigerate overnight
Divide	None
Preshape	None
Resting time	20 to 30 minutes
Shape	See "Shaping Process"
Final Proof	1 hour to 1 hour 30 minutes at 78°F (26°C) at 65% rh
Scoring	None
Steam	2 seconds
Bake	Convection oven, 15 minutes at 385°F (196°C)

Cinnamon Sugar Formula

Ingredients	Baker's %	Kilogram	US decimal	Lb & Oz	Test
Sugar	100.00	0.440	0.971	15 ½	3 ⅛ oz
Brown sugar	100.00	0.440	0.971	15 ½	3 ⅛ oz
Cinnamon	6.00	0.026	0.058	⅞	⅛ oz
Total	206.00	0.907	2.000	2 0	6 ⅜ oz

SHAPING PROCESS

Sheet out the dough into ⅛ inch (3 mm) thick and 16 inches (41 cm) wide. Brush the entire surface of the dough with water. Dust the cinnamon sugar over the dough, leaving 1 inch (2 ½ cm) wide area on one edge without the sugar so that it sticks. Roll the dough, cut into 1 inch (2 ½ cm) to 1 ½ inch (3 ⅞ cm) wide strips.

For Cinnamon Rolls

Smear the sticky bun glaze (formula on page 394) on a parchment-lined sheet pan. Place 24 rolls on one sheet pan. After baking, invert immediately and peel off the parchment paper.

For Sticky Buns

Smear the sticky bun glaze (formula on page 394) on the bottom of hamburger bun molds or large muffin tins that have been well sprayed. Place one roll per mold.

BRIOCHE

Every school child learns Marie Antoinette's infamous response to her subjects when they were rioting because they had no bread—"*Qu'ils mangent de la brioche,*" commonly translated in English to "Let them eat cake." A more correct English translation, "Let them eat brioche," casts the notorious queen in a more generous light, as 18th century brioche was only lightly enriched by small quantities of butter and eggs, and not very different from a typical loaf of bread at the time. Brioche may have originated in Normandy, famous for the quality of its butter since the Middle Ages. The word "brioche" comes from the old Norman verb "broyer," meaning to pound, and refers to the prolonged kneading of the dough. In the 17th century, brioche arrived in Paris, where it became customary to bake this delicacy, still nesting deliciously somewhere between the worlds of bread and cake, in a deep, round, fluted tin, narrow at the base and flaring widely at the top.

FORMULA

BRIOCHE

This brioche is rich with butter, at 60 percent of the flour weight. It is best prepared in advance to be retarded in bulk for 12 to 15 hours. This allows the dough to be cold for shaping and to build acidity for flavor development. Use this brioche dough for brioche à tête, sugar-topped brioche, loaves, tarts, and more.

Final Dough Formula

Ingredients	Baker's %	Kilogram	US decimal	Lb & Oz		Test
Bread flour	100.00	1.791	3.949	3	15 ¼	12 ⅝ oz
Milk	10.00	0.179	0.395		6 ⅜	1 ¼ oz
Eggs	60.00	1.075	2.370	2	5 ⅞	7 ⅝ oz
Osmotolerant instant yeast	1.20	0.021	0.047		¾	⅛ oz
Salt	2.00	0.036	0.079		1 ¼	¼ oz
Sugar	20.00	0.358	0.790		12 ⅝	2 ½ oz
Butter	60.00	1.075	2.370	2	5 ⅞	7 ⅝ oz
Total	253.20	4.536	10.000	10	0	2 lb

Process, Final Dough

Mix	Intensive
DDT	72°F (22°C) to 77°F (25°C)
First fermentation	1 hour, refrigerate 12 to 15 hours
Divide	1.75 oz (50 g) (rolls)
Preshape	Light boule
Resting time	20 to 30 minutes
Shape	Boule/brioche à tête
Final proof	1 hour to 1 hour 30 minutes at 78°F (26°C) at 65% rh
Scoring	None
Steam	2 seconds
Bake	Convection oven, 12 to 15 minutes at 385°F (196°C)

Note

For brioche sucrée, brush lightly with apricot glaze and garnish with pearl sugar.

FORMULA

BRIOCHE WITH PREFERMENTED DOUGH

Using prefermented dough builds flavor and strength, while the lower quantity of butter in relation to the straight dough brioche means this brioche is easier to handle. As there is no bulk-retarding time, this brioche dough must be thoroughly chilled before handling.

Prefermented Dough Formula

Ingredients	Baker's %	Kilogram	US decimal	Lb & Oz	Test
Bread flour	100.00	0.427	0.942	15 ⅛	3 oz
Water	65.00	0.278	0.612	9¾	2 oz
Yeast (instant)	0.60	0.003	0.006	⅛	⅛ tsp
Salt	2.00	0.009	0.019	¼	¼ tsp
Total	167.60	0.716	1.579	1 9¼	5 oz

Process, Prefermented Dough

1. Mix all the ingredients until well incorporated with a DDT of 70°F (21°C).
2. Allow to ferment 1 hour at room temperature [65°F (18°C) to 70°F (21°C)].
3. Refrigerate overnight.

Final Dough Formula

Ingredients	Baker's %	Kilogram	US decimal	Lb & Oz		Test
Bread flour	100.00	1.705	3.759	3	12⅛	12 oz
Water	0.00	0.000	0.000		0	0
Eggs	50.00	0.853	1.880	1	14⅛	6 oz
Milk	18.00	0.307	0.677		10⅞	2⅛ oz
Sugar	25.00	0.426	0.940		15	3 oz
Salt	2.00	0.034	0.075		1¼	¼ oz
Osmotolerant instant yeast	1.00	0.017	0.038		⅝	⅛ oz
Butter	28.00	0.477	1.053	1	⅞	3⅜ oz
Prefermented dough	42.00	0.716	1.579	1	9¼	5 oz
Total	266.00	4.536	10.000	10	0	2 lb

Process, Final Dough	
Mix	Intensive
DDT	72°F (22°C) to 77°F (25°C)
First fermentation	Refrigerate 1 hour
Divide	1.75 oz (50 g)
Preshape	Light boule, refrigerate
Resting time	20 to 30 minutes
Shape	Boule/brioche à tête
Final proof	1 hour to 1 hour 30 minutes at at 65% rh
Scoring	None
Steam	2 seconds
Bake	Convection oven, 12 to 15 minutes at 385°F (196°C)

Note

For brioche sucrée, brush lightly with apricot glaze and garnish with pearl sugar.

Total Formula

Ingredients	Baker's %	Kilogram	US decimal	Lb & Oz	Test
Bread flour	100.00	2.133	4.701	4 11¼	15 oz
Eggs	39.98	0.853	1.880	1 14⅛	6 oz
Water	13.02	0.278	0.612	9¾	2 oz
Milk	14.39	0.307	0.677	10⅞	2⅛ oz
Sugar	19.99	0.426	0.940	15	3 oz
Salt	2.00	0.043	0.094	1½	¼ oz
Osmotolerant instant yeast	0.92	0.020	0.043	¾	⅛ oz
Butter	22.39	0.477	1.053	1 ⅞	3⅜ oz
Total	212.69	4.536	10.000	10 0	2 lb

FORMULA

BRIOCHE WITH SPONGE

The sweetness of the sponge pairs nicely with this brioche dough to balance flavor with a tender and light crumb. Use this lighter version of brioche dough as an interesting alternative to the straight variation.

Sponge Formula

Ingredients	Baker's %	Kilogram	US decimal	Lb & Oz		Test
Bread flour	100.00	0.458	1.009	1	⅛	3 ¼ oz
Water	65.00	0.297	0.656		10 ½	2 ⅛ oz
Yeast (instant)	0.10	0.000	0.001		< ⅛	< ⅛ tsp
Total	165.10	0.756	1.666	1	10 ⅝	5 ⅜ oz

Process, Sponge

1. Mix all the ingredients until well incorporated with a DDT of 70°F (21°C).
2. Allow to ferment 12 to 16 hours at room temperature [65°F (18°C) to 70°F (21°C)].

Final Dough Formula

Ingredients	Baker's %	Kilogram	US decimal	Lb & Oz		Test
Bread flour	100.00	1.399	3.085	3	1 ⅜	9 ⅞ oz
Milk	7.00	0.098	0.216		3 ½	¾ oz
Eggs	72.00	1.007	2.221	2	3 ½	7 ⅛ oz
Osmotolerant instant yeast	1.60	0.022	0.049		¾	⅛ oz
Salt	2.60	0.036	0.080		1 ¼	¼ oz
Sugar	22.00	0.308	0.679		10 ⅞	2 ⅛ oz
Butter	65.00	0.909	2.005	2	⅛	6 ⅜ oz
Sponge	54.00	0.756	1.666	1	10 ⅝	5 ⅜ oz
Total	324.20	4.536	10.000	10	0	2 lb

Process, Final Dough

Mix	Intensive
DDT	72°F (22°C) to 77°F (25°C)
First fermentation	1 hour
Divide	1.75 oz (50 g)
Preshape	Light boule, refrigerate

Resting time	20 to 30 minutes
Shape	Boule
Final proof	1 hour to 1 hour 30 min. at 78°F (26°C) at 65% rh
Scoring	None
Steam	2 seconds
Bake	Convection oven, 12 to 15 minutes at 385°F (196°C)

Note

For brioche sucrée, brush lightly with apricot glaze and garnish with pearl sugar.

Total Formula

Ingredients	Baker's %	Kilogram	US decimal	Lb & Oz		Test
Bread flour	100.00	1.857	4.093	4	1½	13⅛ oz
Milk	5.27	0.098	0.216		3½	¾ oz
Water	16.02	0.297	0.656		10½	2⅛ oz
Eggs	54.24	1.007	2.221	2	3½	7⅛ oz
Osmotolerant instant yeast	1.23	0.023	0.050		¾	⅛ oz
Salt	1.96	0.036	0.080		1¼	¼ oz
Sugar	16.57	0.308	0.679		10⅞	2⅛ oz
Butter	48.97	0.909	2.005	2	⅛	6⅜ oz
Total	244.26	4.536	10.000	10	0	2 lb

SHAPING OPTION

Brioche Tropézienne

Preshape the dough into a light boule. Once the dough is relaxed, roll out into 4 inch (10¼ cm) disks and place in 4 inch (10¼ cm) tart pans. Brush with the egg wash. Before baking, place the streusel topping (see Coffee Cake formula in Chapter 11) on top. Once baked, and cooled, slice the brioche in half. Using a large round tip, pipe the Crème Chiboust onto the bottom half, making shells from the outside to the center to form a flower-like pattern. Place in freezer to set the cream. Once the cream is hardened, top with the remaining brioche half.

Brioche Tropézienne

Pear Bourdaloue

FORMULA

COLUMBA DI PASQUA

Traditionally served as an Easter delicacy in Italy, the Columba di Pasqua is a sweet bread made from a dough very similar to that used for Panettone, another famous Italian holiday bread. The Pasquale's unique charm is achieved in its shape—that of a dove, the universal symbol of peace. Our Pasquale is flavored with candied orange peel, almond paste, orange zest, and vanilla bean and covered with a chocolate hazelnut glaze and finally sprinkled with pearl sugar, resulting in a magnificent-looking centerpiece bread.

Italian Levain Formula

Ingredients	Baker's %	Kilogram	US decimal	Lb & Oz	Test
Bread flour	100.00	0.123	0.272	4⅜	⅞ oz
Water	50.00	0.062	0.136	2⅛	⅜ oz
Starter	100.00	0.123	0.272	4⅜	⅞ oz
Total	250.00	0.308	0.680	10⅞	2⅛ oz

Process, Italian Levain

1. Mix all the ingredients for 4 minutes on first speed or until well incorporated with a DDT of 85°F (29°C).
2. Feed three times allowing to ferment 4 hours at room temperature [85°F (29°C)].

First Dough Formula

Ingredients	Baker's %	Kilogram	US decimal	Lb & Oz	Test
Bread flour	100.00	0.985	2.172	2 2¾	7 oz
Water	40.00	0.394	0.869	13⅞	2¾ oz
Egg yolks	25.00	0.246	0.543	8⅝	1¾ oz
Sugar	37.50	0.369	0.814	13	2⅝ oz
Butter	37.50	0.369	0.814	13	2⅝ oz
Italian levain	31.30	0.308	0.680	10⅞	2⅛ oz
Yeast (instant)	0.20	0.002	0.004	⅛	⅛ tsp
Total	271.50	2.674	5.896	5 14⅜	1 lb 2⅞ oz

Process, First Dough

1. Mix to incorporation, for about 4 minutes on first speed.
2. Ferment 3 hours at 85°F (29°C).

Final Dough Formula

Ingredients	Baker's %	Kilogram	US decimal	Lb & Oz	Test
Bread flour	100.00	0.246	0.542	8 ⅝	1 ¾ oz
Water	18.00	0.044	0.098	1 ½	¼ oz
Egg yolks	100.00	0.246	0.542	8 ⅝	1 ¾ oz
Sugar	75.00	0.184	0.407	6 ½	1 ¼ oz
Honey	50.00	0.123	0.271	4 ⅜	⅞ oz
Salt	4.00	0.010	0.022	⅜	⅛ oz
Butter	150.00	0.369	0.813	13	2 ⅝ oz
Cocoa butter	10.00	0.025	0.054	⅞	⅛ oz
First dough	1087.40	2.674	5.896	5 14 ⅜	1 lb 2 ⅞ oz
Vanilla bean	Each	1 ¼	1 ¼	1 ¼	¼ each
Oranges zested	Each	1 ¼	1 ¼	1 ¼	¼ each
Candied orange peel	200.00	0.492	1.084	1 1 ⅜	3 ½ oz
Almond paste*	50.00	0.123	0.271	4 ⅜	⅞ oz
Total	1844.40	4.536	10.000	10 0	2 lb

*Roll out the almond paste to ¼ inch (6 mm), cut into cubes, and reserve in the freezer.

Process, Final Dough

1. Incorporate the flour, water, salt, first dough, orange zest, and vanilla bean in first speed.
2. Mix in second speed to start to develop the gluten.
3. Gradually add the sugar and half of the egg yolk as the dough increases in strength.
4. Mix in second speed to continue to develop the gluten; add the honey.
5. Continue to mix in second speed until the gluten has fully developed.
6. Add the butter and mix in second speed until fully incorporated.
7. Add the cocoa butter and mix in first speed until fully incorporated.
8. Add the remaining egg yolk and mix in first speed until fully incorporated.
9. Add the candied orange peel and frozen cubes of almond paste in first speed until incorporated.

Mix	Intensive
DDT	78°F (25°C) to 85°F (29°C)
First fermentation	45 minutes with 2 punch and folds after 15 minutes
Divide	11 oz (300 g) and 7 oz (200 g)
Preshape	Light boule
Resting time	10 to 15 minutes
Shape	Two batards crossed in Columba mold—the 11 oz (300 g) piece lengthwise and the 7 oz (200 g) piece widthwise
Final proof	7 hours at 85°F (29°C)

Scoring	See note on glazing
Steam	1 second
Bake	Convection oven, 35 minutes at 360°F (182°C)

Note

Glaze is optional before baking. Apply glaze using a piping bag, dust with powdered sugar, and garnish with pearl sugar.

Glaze Formula

Ingredients	Baker's %	Kilogram	US decimal	Lb & Oz		Test
Granulated sugar	100.00	0.101	0.222		3½	¾ oz
Hazelnut powder	50.00	0.050	0.111		1¾	⅜ oz
Vegetable oil	5.00	0.005	0.011		⅛	¼ tsp
Corn flour	10.00	0.010	0.022		⅜	⅛ oz
Flour	5.00	0.005	0.011		⅛	¼ tsp
Vanilla bean	Each	1	1	1		¼ each
Egg whites	55.00	0.055	0.122	2		⅜ oz
Total	225.00	0.227	0.500	8		1⅝ oz

Process, Glaze

Blend together all the ingredients using a whisk.

FORMULA

GIBASSIER

This celebration bread from Provence, France, is named after the summit Le Gibas in the mountains of Luberon. The Gibassier is reminiscent of this area of France as it is made with the region's specialty flavors and ingredients: olive oil, anise seed, and orange peel. After it is baked, it is brushed with clarified butter and dredged in sugar. This magically complex delicacy was traditionally served as the 13th dessert of the midnight meal during the supper of Christmas in Provence.

Sponge Formula

Ingredients	Baker's %	Kilogram	US decimal	Lb & Oz		Test
Bread flour	100.00	0.427	0.941		15	3 oz
Milk	45.00	0.192	0.423		6¾	1⅜ oz
Eggs	12.50	0.053	0.118		1⅞	⅜ oz
Yeast (instant)	0.10	0.000	0.001		< ⅛	⅛ tsp
Total	157.60	0.673	1.483	1	7¾	4¾ oz

Process, Sponge

1. Mix all the ingredients until well incorporated with a DDT of 70°F (21°C).
2. Allow to ferment 12 to 16 hours at room temperature [65°F (18°C) to 70°F (21°C)].

Final Dough Formula

Ingredients	Baker's %	Kilogram	US decimal	Lb & Oz		Test
Bread flour	100.00	1.603	3.600	3	9⅝	11½ oz
Water	8.00	0.131	0.288		4⅝	⅞ oz
Eggs	28.00	0.457	1.008	1	⅛	3¼ oz
Olive oil	18.80	0.307	0.677		10⅞	2⅛ oz
Orange flower water	6.30	0.101	0.227		3⅝	¾ oz
Osmotolerant instant yeast	2.80	0.046	0.101		1⅝	⅜ oz
Salt	1.90	0.031	0.068		1⅛	¼ oz
Sugar	25.00	0.408	0.900		14⅜	2⅞ oz
Butter	18.80	0.307	0.677		10⅞	2⅛ oz
Candied orange peel	25.00	0.408	0.900		14⅜	2⅞ oz
Anise seed	2.00	0.033	0.072		1⅛	¼ oz
Sponge	41.20	0.673	1.483	1	7¾	4¾ oz
Total	277.80	4.536	10.000	10	0	2 lb

Process, Final Dough

Mix	Intensive
DDT	72°F (22°C) to 77°F (25°C)
First fermentation	1 hour
Divide	1 lb (454 g)
Preshape	Light boule
Resting time	15 to 20 minutes
Shape	Refer to note
Final Proof	1 hour 30 minutes at 78°F (26°C) at 65% rh
Scoring	None
Steam	2 seconds
Bake	Convection oven, 12 to 15 minutes at 375°F (191°C)

Note

After preshaping, roll out to ¾ inch (2 cm) thickness, cut an "X" in the center and four smaller "X"s on the sides. Proof on sheet pans lined with parchment paper. After baking, brush with clarified butter and dredge in granulated sugar.

Total Formula

Ingredients	Baker's %	Kilogram	US decimal	Lb & Oz		Test
Bread flour	100.00	2.060	4.541	4	8⅝	14½ oz
Water	6.34	0.131	0.288		4⅝	⅞ oz
Milk	9.33	0.192	0.423		6⅝	1⅜ oz
Eggs	24.79	0.511	1.126	1	2	3⅝ oz
Olive oil	14.90	0.307	0.677		10⅞	2⅛ oz
Orange flower water	4.99	0.103	0.227		3⅝	¾ oz
Osmotolerant instant yeast	2.24	0.046	0.102		1⅝	⅜ oz
Salt	1.51	0.031	0.068		1⅛	¼ oz
Sugar	19.82	0.408	0.900		14⅜	2⅞ oz
Butter	14.90	0.307	0.677		10⅞	2⅛ oz
Candied orange peel	19.82	0.408	0.900		14⅜	2⅞ oz
Anise seed	1.59	0.033	0.072		1⅛	¼ oz
Total	220.23	4.536	10.000	10	0	2 lb

FORMULA

KUGELHOPF

Austrians, Germans, Poles, and the French of Alsace all claim credit for the invention of this wonderful special occasion bread. Kugelhopf is customarily baked in a fluted mold and dusted simply with powdered sugar. Alsatian legend recounts that in ancient days, a piece of Kugelhopf with wine for men and coffee for women was served before the lengthy marriage ceremonies held in churches and synagogues. The bride's mother also baked a Kugelhopf for the priest, pastor or rabbi, the mayor and schoolteacher, the midwife, and neighbors, as tokens of goodwill in case their help was ever needed during the couple's marriage. Similar to a brioche but with less egg and more milk, this bread acquires its distinctively rich flavor from the addition of rum-soaked raisins at the end of mixing. For a variation, try soaking the raisins in Kirsch.

Sponge Formula

Ingredients	Baker's %	Kilogram	US decimal	Lb & Oz	Test
Bread flour	100.00	0.482	1.063	1 1	3⅜ oz
Water	60.14	0.290	0.639	10¼	2 oz
Yeast (instant)	0.10	0.000	0.001	< ⅛	⅛ tsp
Total	160.24	0.773	1.703	1 11¼	5½ oz

Process, Sponge

1. Mix all the ingredients until well incorporated with a DDT of 70°F (21°C).
2. Allow to ferment 12 to 16 hours at room temperature [65°F (18°C) to 70°F (21°C)].

Final Dough Formula

Ingredients	Baker's %	Kilogram	US decimal	Lb & Oz	Test
Bread flour	100.00	1.331	2.935	2 15	9⅜ oz
Milk	48.02	0.639	1.409	1 6½	4½ oz
Eggs	20.98	0.279	0.616	9⅞	2 oz
Osmotolerant instant yeast	1.99	0.027	0.059	⅞	⅛ oz
Salt	2.70	0.036	0.079	1¼	¼ oz
Sugar	21.80	0.290	0.640	10¼	2 oz
Butter	38.14	0.508	1.119	1 1⅞	3⅝ oz
Raisins, dark and golden	40.87	0.544	1.199	1 3¼	3⅞ oz
Rum	8.17	0.109	0.240	3⅞	¾ oz
Sponge	58.04	0.773	1.703	1 11¼	5½ oz
Total	340.71	4.536	10.000	9 16	2 lb

Process, Final Dough

Mix	Intensive mix
DDT	72°F (22°C) to 77°F (25°C)
First fermentation	1 hour 30 minutes at 80°F (27°C) at 65% rh
Dividing	As desired
Resting time	25 to 30 minutes
Shaping	Assorted shapes (boule, loaf, braid, bun, etc.)
Final proof	1 hour 15 minutes to 1 hour 40 minutes at 80°F (27°C) at 65% rh
Bake	Convection oven, 25 minutes at 360°F (196°C)

Total Formula

Ingredients	Baker's %	Kilogram	US decimal	Lb & Oz		Test
Bread flour	100.00	1.814	3.998	3	16	12¾ oz
Milk	35.25	0.639	1.409	1	6½	4½ oz
Water	16.00	0.290	0.640		10¼	2 oz
Eggs	15.40	0.279	0.616		9⅞	2 oz
Osmotolerant instant yeast	1.49	0.027	0.060		1	¼ oz
Salt	1.98	0.036	0.079		1	¼ oz
Sugar	16.00	0.290	0.640		10¼	2 oz
Butter	28.00	0.508	1.119	1	1⅞	3⅝ oz
Raisins, dark and golden	30.00	0.544	1.199	1	3¼	3⅞ oz
Rum	6.00	0.109	0.240		3⅞	¾ oz
Total	250.12	4.536	10.000	10	0	2 lb

FORMULA

SAVORY KUGELHOPF

Walnuts, lardons, parsley, onion, and Swiss cheese all come together to make this savory Kugelhopf exceptional in flavor.

Sponge Formula

Ingredients	Baker's %	Kilogram	US decimal	Lb & Oz		Test
Bread flour	100.00	0.551	1.214	1	3⅜	3⅞ oz
Water	60.00	0.330	0.729		11⅝	2⅜ oz
Yeast (instant)	0.10	0.001	0.001		< ⅛	Pinch
Total	160.10	0.882	1.944	1	15⅛	6¼ oz

Process, Sponge

1. Mix all the ingredients until well incorporated with a DDT of 70°F (21°C).
2. Allow to ferment 12 to 16 hours at room temperature [65°F (18°C) to 70°F (21°C)].

Final Dough Formula

Ingredients	Baker's %	Kilogram	US decimal	Lb & Oz		Test
Bread flour	100.00	1.102	2.430	2	6⅞	7¾ oz
Milk, cold	21.00	0.231	0.510		8⅛	1⅝ oz
Eggs, cold	35.00	0.386	0.851		13⅝	2¾ oz
Sugar	7.50	0.083	0.182		2⅞	⅝ oz
Salt	4.00	0.044	0.097		1½	¼ oz
Yeast (instant)	1.00	0.011	0.024		⅜	⅛ oz
Sponge	80.00	0.882	1.944	1	15⅛	6¼ oz
Butter	40.00	0.441	0.972		15½	3⅛ oz
Pancetta, diced	50.00	0.551	1.215	1	3½	3⅞ oz
Onions, small, diced and sauteed	50.00	0.551	1.215	1	3½	3⅞ oz
Walnuts, chopped and roasted	15.00	0.165	0.365		5⅞	1⅛ oz
Parsley, minced	3.00	0.033	0.073		1⅛	¼ oz
Swiss cheese, shredded	5.00	0.055	0.122		2	⅜ oz
Total	411.50	4.536	10.000	10	0	2 lb

Process, Final Dough

Mix	Intensive
DDT	72°F (22°C) to 77°F (25°C)
First fermentation	1 hour 30 minutes
Divide	1 lb (454 g)
Preshape	Light boule
Resting time	20 to 30 minutes
Shape	Boule
Final proof	1 hour to 1 hour 30 minutes at 78°F (25°C) at 65% rh
Scoring	None
Steam	2 seconds
Bake	Convection oven, 30 to 35 minutes at 335°F (168°C)

Total Dough Formula

Ingredients	Baker's %	Kilogram	US decimal	Lb & Oz		Test
Bread flour	100.00	1.653	3.644	3	10 ¼	11 ⅝ oz
Water	19.99	0.330	0.729		11 ⅝	2 ⅜ oz
Milk, cold	14.00	0.231	0.510		8 ⅛	1 ⅝ oz
Eggs, cold	23.34	0.386	0.851		13 ⅝	2 ¾ oz
Sugar	5.00	0.083	0.182		2 ⅞	⅝ oz
Salt	2.67	0.044	0.097		1 ½	¼ oz
Yeast (instant)	0.70	0.012	0.026		⅜	⅛ oz
Butter	26.67	0.441	0.972		15 ½	3 ⅛ oz
Pancetta, diced	33.34	0.551	1.215	1	3 ½	3 ⅞ oz
Onions	33.34	0.551	1.215	1	3 ½	3 ⅞ oz
Walnuts	10.00	0.165	0.365		5 ⅞	1 ⅛ oz
Parsley, minced	2.00	0.033	0.073		1 ⅛	¼ oz
Swiss cheese	3.33	0.055	0.122		2	⅜ oz
Total	274.38	4.536	10.000	10	0	2 lb

PANETTONE

Some historians claim to have found references to *pan del ton* or "luxury bread," in Milanese dialect, as far back as the 1300s. Of the many stories about the origins of Panettone, the most commonly cited and romantic concerns a young noble in 15th-century Milan who fell in love with the daughter of a poor baker named Toni. He wanted to marry the girl, but he had to earn her father's esteem first, so he became an apprentice to her father, sharing some of his wealth to buy the best flour, eggs, and butter, as well as raisins and citron, which they added to their bread. The bread, known as "*Pan di Tonio*," brought the bakery great fame, which helped the young baker's apprentice win the hand of the baker's daughter. Today, Panettone is one of the most famous Italian celebration breads, made all over the world, and exported by some of Italy's largest bakeries. Most of the Panettone from Italy are made with natural yeast, which gives them a shelf life of several weeks.

FORMULA

PANETTONE WITH SPONGE

This "quick" Panettone is essentially a brioche dough with ingredients characteristic to Panettone added in. It is based on a sponge and has a slightly complex flavor. The keeping qualities are not as good as they are with the Panettone made with natural starter.

Sponge Formula

Ingredients	Baker's %	Kilogram	US decimal	Lb & Oz		Test
Bread flour	100.00	0.951	2.097	2	1½	6¾ oz
Water	60.00	0.571	1.258	1	4⅛	4 oz
Sugar	16.70	0.159	0.350		5⅝	1⅛ oz
Yeast (instant)	2.00	0.019	0.042		⅝	⅛ oz
Total	178.70	1.700	3.747	3	12	12 oz

Process, Sponge

1. Mix all the ingredients until well incorporated with a DDT of 70°F (21°C).
2. Allow to ferment 2 hours at room temperature [65°F (18°C) to 70°F (21°C)].

(opposite, back to front) Gibassier, Savory Kugelhopf, Kugelhopf

Final Dough Formula

Ingredients	Baker's %	Kilogram	US decimal	Lb & Oz		Test
Bread flour	100.00	0.659	1.452	1	7 ¼	4 ⅝ oz
Water	27.00	0.178	0.392		6 ¼	1 ¼ oz
Egg yolks	40.00	0.264	0.581		9 ¼	1 ⅞ oz
Orange flower water	5.00	0.032	0.073		1 ⅛	¼ oz
Osmotolerant instant yeast	1.00	0.007	0.015		¼	⅛ tsp
Salt	2.50	0.016	0.036		⅝	⅛ oz
Sugar	50.00	0.329	0.726		11 ⅝	2 ⅜ oz
Milk powder	5.00	0.033	0.073		1 ⅛	¼ oz
Butter	50.00	0.329	0.726		11 ⅝	2 ⅜ oz
Sponge	258.00	1.700	3.747	3	12	12 oz
Candied orange peel	75.00	0.494	1.089	1	1 ⅜	3 ½ oz
Raisins	75.00	0.494	1.089	1	1 ⅜	3 ½ oz
Total	688.50	4.536	10.000	10	0	2 lb

Process, Final Dough

Mix	Intensive
DDT	72°F (22°C) to 77°F (25°C)
First fermentation	10 minutes
Divide	1 lb (454 g)
Preshape	Light boule
Resting time	20 to 30 minutes
Shape	Boule
Final proof	3 hours and 30 minutes at 78°F (25°C) at 65% rh
Scoring	Score with an "X"
Steam	2 seconds
Bake	Convection oven, 335°F (168°C) for 35 minutes

Total Formula

Ingredients	Baker's %	Kilogram	US decimal	Lb & Oz		Test
Bread flour	100.00	1.610	3.549	3	8¾	11⅜ oz
Water	46.49	0.749	1.651	1	10⅜	5¼ oz
Egg yolks	16.36	0.263	0.581		9¼	1⅞ oz
Orange flower water	2.04	0.033	0.072		1⅛	¼ oz
Osmotolerant instant yeast	1.58	0.025	0.056		⅞	⅛ oz
Salt	1.02	0.016	0.036		⅝	⅛ oz
Sugar	30.32	0.488	1.076	1	1¼	3½ oz
Milk powder	2.04	0.033	0.072		1⅛	¼ oz
Butter	20.45	0.329	0.726		11⅝	2⅜ oz
Candied orange peel	30.68	0.494	1.089	1	1⅜	3½ oz
Raisins	30.68	0.494	1.089	1	1⅜	3½ oz
Total	281.66	4.536	10.000	10	0	2 lb

FORMULA

PANETTONE WITH NATURAL STARTER

The long slow, staged fermentation of this dough creates a delicate, enticing flavor, and an ultralight interior with a soft, tender crumb. Because of the acidity built from the first dough, and the quantity of liquid and sugar in the final dough, it is essential to follow the proper mixing techniques to not develop the dough too quickly or too slowly. Because the dough is so delicate, the Panettone must be hung upside-down after baking to prevent it from caving in on itself. In Italy this is done with a pinze, a long beam with metal rods to which the bread is stuck. For smaller productions it is fine to use heavy duty wooden skewers to hang the bread between two tables. Allow the bread to cool completely before taking out the skewer.

Levain Formula

Ingredients	Baker's %	Kilogram	US decimal	Lb & Oz	Test
Bread flour	100.00	0.098	0.216	3½	¾ oz
Water	50.00	0.049	0.108	1¾	⅜ oz
Starter	100.00	0.098	0.216	3½	¾ oz
Total	250.00	0.245	0.540	8⅝	1¾ oz

Process, Levain

1. Mix all the ingredients until well incorporated with a DDT of 85°F (29°C).
2. Feed three times a day and allow to ferment 4 hours at 85°F (29°C).

First Dough Formula

Ingredients	Baker's %	Kilogram	US decimal	Lb & Oz		Test
Bread flour	100.00	0.980	2.160	2	2½	6⅞ oz
Water	55.00	0.539	1.188	1	3	3¾ oz
Egg yolks	16.00	0.157	0.346		5½	1⅛ oz
Sugar	24.00	0.235	0.518		8¼	1⅝ oz
Malt	2.00	0.020	0.043		¾	⅛ oz
Butter	24.00	0.235	0.518		8¼	1⅝ oz
Levain (instant)	25.00	0.245	0.540		8⅝	1¾ oz
Osmotolerant instant yeast	0.30	0.003	0.006		⅛	⅛ tsp
Total	246.30	2.413	5.319	5	5⅛	1 lb 1 oz

Process, First Dough

1. Mix to ingredient incorporation.
2. Ferment for 12 hours at 72°F (22°C).

Final Dough Formula

Ingredients	Baker's %	Kilogram	US decimal	Lb & Oz		Test
Bread flour	100.00	0.234	0.515		8¼	1⅝ oz
Water	138.00	0.322	0.711		11⅜	2¼ oz
Egg yolks	30.00	0.070	0.154		2½	½ oz
Salt	6.00	0.014	0.031		½	⅛ oz
Oranges zested	Each	1.5	1.5		1.5	⅓ each
Vanilla bean	Each	2.5	2.5		2.5	½ each
First dough	1033.00	2.413	5.319	5	5⅛	1 lb 1 oz
Sugar	100.00	0.234	0.515		8¼	1⅝ oz
Butter	153.00	0.357	0.788		12⅝	2½ oz
Honey	23.00	0.054	0.118		1⅞	⅜ oz
Candied orange peel	153.00	0.357	0.788		12⅝	2½ oz
Candied lemon peel	53.00	0.124	0.273		4⅜	⅞ oz
Raisins	153.00	0.357	0.788		12⅝	2½ oz
Total	1942.00	4.536	10.000	10	0	2 lb

Process, Final Dough

1. Incorporate the flour, salt, first dough, egg yolks, orange zest, vanilla, and half of the water in first speed for 3 minutes.
2. Next, mix in second speed to start to develop the gluten.
3. Add half the sugar slowly as the dough continues to develop in second speed.
4. Slowly add the remaining sugar and mix until reaches consistency of intensive mix.
5. Add the softened butter and mix in second speed until the butter is fully incorporated and the gluten is developed.
6. Add the honey and the rest of the water as needed in first speed.
7. Add the candied orange, lemon peel, and the raisins in first speed and mix until well incorporated.

Process, Final Dough

Mix	Intensive
DDT	78°F (25°C) to 85°F (29°C)
First fermentation	1 hour with 1 punch and fold
Divide	1 lb 2 oz (500 g) for a mold with dimensions of [5 ¼ inch (13 ½ cm) diameter × 3 ¼ inch (11 ½ cm) height]
Preshape	Light boule on a buttered table
Resting time	15 to 20 minutes
Shape	Boule in Panettone mold
Final proof	4 to 6 hours at 80°F (27°C)
Scoring	Cross cut or glazing
Steam	2 seconds
Bake	Convection oven, 325°F (163°C) for 35 minutes
Cooling	Once baked, stick metal skewers through the base of the mold, invert the bread and cool hanging upside-down between two tables.

Chocolate Glaze Formula

Ingredients	Baker's %	Kilogram	US decimal	Lb & Oz		Test
Almond meal	5.00	0.025	0.055		⅞	⅛ oz
Granulated sugar	100.00	0.497	1.096	1	1½	3½ oz
Vegetable oil	7.50	0.037	0.082		1⅜	¼ oz
Corn flour	7.50	0.037	0.082		1⅜	¼ oz
Cocoa powder	7.50	0.037	0.082		1⅜	¼ oz
Egg whites	55.00	0.273	0.603		9⅝	1⅞ oz
Total	182.5	0.907	2.000	1	16	6⅜ oz

Process, Chocolate Glaze

1. Blend together all the ingredients using a whisk.
2. Glaze the Panettone and top with powdered sugar, whole blanched almonds, and pearl sugar.

FORMULA

PAN D'ORO

Within Italy, the Pan d'Oro, or bread of gold, is a celebration bread second only to Panettone in popularity. "Pandoro" was first mentioned as a dessert of the Venetian aristocracy during the 1700s. The formula for making Pan d'Oro was developed and perfected in Verona for over a century. Baked in a tall and conical star shape reminiscent of a Christmas tree, Pan d'Oro is sprinkled with powdered sugar just before serving, creating the illusion of fresh fallen snow.

Levain Formula

Ingredients	Baker's %	Kilogram	US decimal	Lb & Oz		Test
Bread flour	100.00	0.137	0.302		4 ⅞	1 oz
Water	50.00	0.068	0.151		2 ⅜	½ oz
Starter	140.00	0.192	0.423		6 ¾	1 ⅜ oz
Total	290.00	0.397	0.875		14	2 ¾ oz

Process, Levain

1. Mix all the ingredients until well incorporated with a DDT of 85°F (29°C).
2. Feed every 4 hours, or once mature.

First Dough Formula

Ingredients	Baker's %	Kilogram	US decimal	Lb & Oz		Test
Bread flour	100.00	0.274	0.604		9 ⅝	1 ⅞ oz
Water	50.00	0.137	0.302		4 ⅞	1 oz
Eggs	40.00	0.110	0.241		3 ⅞	¾ oz
Sugar	25.00	0.068	0.151		2 ⅜	½ oz
Levain	145.00	0.397	0.875		14	2 ¾ oz
Total	360.00	0.986	2.173	2	2 ¾	7 oz

Process, First Dough

1. Mix only until incorporated in first speed only.
2. Ferment 2 hours at 85°F (29°C).

Second Dough Formula

Ingredients	Baker's %	Kilogram	US decimal	Lb & Oz	Test
Bread flour	100.00	0.169	0.372	6	1¼ oz
Eggs	65.00	0.110	0.242	3⅞	¾ oz
Sugar	20.00	0.034	0.074	1¼	¼ oz
Osmotolerant instant yeast	2.00	0.003	0.007	⅛	⅛ tsp
Total	187.00	0.315	0.695	11⅛	2¼ oz

Process, Second Dough

1. Mix only until incorporated in first speed only.
2. Ferment 1½ hours at 85°F (29°C).

Third Dough Formula

Ingredients	Baker's %	Kilogram	US decimal	Lb & Oz	Test
Bread flour	100.00	0.246	0.543	8¾	1¾ oz
Eggs	44.00	0.108	0.239	3⅞	¾ oz
Sugar	20.00	0.049	0.109	1¾	⅜ oz
Butter	5.55	0.014	0.030	½	⅛ oz
First dough	400.00	0.986	2.173	2 2¾	7 oz
Second dough	128.00	0.315	0.695	11⅛	2¼ oz
Total	697.55	1.719	3.790	3 12⅝	12⅛ oz

Process, Third Dough

1. Mix only until incorporated in first speed only.
2. Ferment 3 hours at 85°F (29°C).

Final Dough Formula

Ingredients	Baker's %	Kilogram	US decimal	Lb & Oz	Test
Bread flour	100.00	0.905	1.994	1 15⅞	6⅜ oz
Eggs	75.75	0.685	1.511	1 8⅛	4⅞ oz
Salt	2.40	0.022	0.048	¾	⅛ oz
Third dough	190.00	1.719	3.790	3 12⅝	12⅛ oz
Honey	4.50	0.041	0.090	1⅜	¼ oz
Sugar	48.48	0.439	0.967	15½	3⅛ oz
Butter	75.75	0.685	1.511	1 8⅛	4⅞ oz
Cocoa butter, chopped	4.50	0.041	0.090	1⅜	¼ oz
Vanilla bean	Each	2	2	2	½ each
Total	501.38	4.536	10.000	10 0	2 lb

Process, Final Dough

Premixing Process

1. Using a paddle attachment in a vertical mixer, cream the butter with the vanilla bean seeds until very light.
2. Next, add the cocoa butter and allow it to blend in during two or three turns of the paddle.

Mixing Process

1. Mix the flour, half the egg, salt, third dough, and honey on first speed for 5 minutes.
2. Add one-third of the sugar and continue to mix in first speed until well incorporated.
3. Turn the mixer up to second speed and begin to develop the gluten.
4. When the gluten starts to develop, add a small amount of the egg. Keep mixing in second speed.
5. Add some of the sugar and mix until it is incorporated in the dough.
6. Repeat this step until all the sugar and the eggs are well incorporated into the dough and the gluten starts to be fully developed.
7. When the gluten structure is fully developed, add the butter preparation from the pre-mixing process, using first speed.
8. Mix in first speed to achieve butter incorporation and to reach the cleanup stage.

Process, Final Dough

Mix	Intensive
DDT	78°F (25°C) to 85°F (29°C)
First fermentation	2 hours with 1 punch and fold
Divide	1 lb 2 oz (500 g) for a mold with dimensions of 5 ¼ inch (13 ½ cm) diameter × 3 ¼ inch (11 ½ cm) height
Preshape	No preshape
Resting time	No resting time
Shape	Boule, place in Pan d'Oro mold or paper Panettone mold
Final proof	72°F (22°C) for 14 hours
Scoring	None
Steam	2 seconds
Bake	Convection oven, 35 minutes at 325°F (203°C)
Finishing	Once baked, turn out of the Pan d'Oro mold and dust with powdered sugar

(back to front) Pan d'Oro, Traditional Panettone, Panettone With Sponge, Columba di Pasqua

FORMULA

STRAWBERRY BRIOCHE

This moist and super light brioche is highlighted with the flavors of strawberries, almonds, and dark rum with a thin, crisp chocolate crust. If dried strawberries are not available, try using dried apricot or prunes for an interesting variation.

Poolish Formula

Ingredients	Baker's %	Kilogram	US decimal	Lb & Oz		Test
Bread flour	100.00	0.484	1.066	1	1	3⅜ oz
Water	100.00	0.484	1.066	1	1	3⅜ oz
Yeast (instant)	0.10	0.000	0.001		< ⅛	⅛ tsp
Total	200.10	0.967	2.133	2	2⅛	6⅞ oz

Process, Poolish

1. Mix all the ingredients until well incorporated with a DDT of 70°F (21°C).
2. Allow to ferment 12 to 16 hours at room temperature [65°F (18°C) to 70°F (21°C)].

Soaker Formula

Ingredients	Baker's %	Kilogram	US decimal	Lb & Oz		Test
Dried strawberry, diced	100.00	0.225	0.497		8	1 ⅝ oz
Dark rum	40.00	0.090	0.199		3 ⅛	⅝ oz
Total	140.00	0.316	0.696		11 ⅛	2 ¼ oz

Process, Soaker

Mix all the ingredients, and let sit for 24 hours.

Final Dough Formula

Ingredients	Baker's %	Kilogram	US decimal	Lb & Oz		Test
Bread flour	100.00	1.127	2.486	2	7 ¾	8 oz
Eggs	23.00	0.259	0.572		9 ⅛	1 ⅞ oz
Egg yolks	17.00	0.192	0.423		6 ¾	1 ⅜ oz
Salt	2.90	0.033	0.072		1 ⅛	¼ oz
Osmotolerant instant yeast	2.50	0.028	0.062		1	¼ oz
Vanilla extract	4.30	0.048	0.107		1 ¾	⅜ oz
Sugar	26.00	0.293	0.646		10 ⅜	2 ⅛ oz
Butter	71.30	0.804	1.772	1	12 ⅜	5 ⅝ oz
Almond paste, diced	21.50	0.242	0.534		8 ½	1 ¾ oz
Dried strawberry, diced	20.00	0.225	0.497		8	1 ⅝ oz
Strawberry soaker	28.00	0.316	0.696		11 ⅛	2 ¼ oz
Poolish	85.81	0.967	2.133	2	2 ⅛	6 ⅞ oz
Total	402.31	4.536	10.000	10	0	2 lb

Process, Final Dough

Mix	Intensive
DDT	73°F (23°C) to 78°F (25°C)
First fermentation	1 hour 30 minutes
Divide	1 lb 3 oz (550 g)
Preshape	Light boule, refrigerate
Resting time	20 to 30 minutes
Shape	Batard for loaf pan
Final proof	1 hour to 1 hour 30 min. at 78°F (26°C) at 65% rh
Glazing	Pipe chocolate glaze (formula follows) over dough, top with powdered sugar, whole blanched almonds, and pearl sugar

Scoring None
Steam 2 seconds, if glazed no steam
Bake Convection oven, 30 to 35 minutes at 325°F (163°C)

Total Formula

Ingredients	Baker's %	Kilogram	US decimal	Lb & Oz		Test
Bread flour	100.00	1.611	3.552	3	8⅞	11⅜ oz
Water	30.01	0.484	1.066	1	1	3⅜ oz
Eggs	16.10	0.259	0.572		9⅛	1⅞ oz
Egg yolks	11.90	0.192	0.423		6¾	1⅜ oz
Salt	2.03	0.033	0.072		1⅛	¼ oz
Osmotolerant instant yeast	1.78	0.029	0.063		1	¼ oz
Vanilla extract	3.01	0.048	0.107		1¾	⅜ oz
Sugar	18.20	0.293	0.646		10⅜	2⅛ oz
Butter	49.90	0.804	1.772	1	12⅜	5⅝ oz
Almond paste	15.05	0.242	0.534		8½	1¾ oz
Dried strawberry, diced	27.99	0.451	0.994		15⅞	3⅛ oz
Strawberry soaker	5.60	0.090	0.199		3⅛	⅝ oz
Total	281.56	4.536	10.000	10	0	2 lb

Chocolate Glaze Formula

Ingredients	Baker's %	Kilogram	US decimal	Lb & Oz		Test
Almond meal	5.00	0.121	0.05		16	⅛ oz
Granulated sugar	100.00	2.416	1.10	1	15	3½ oz
Vegetable oil	7.50	0.181	0.08		2	¼ oz
Corn flour	7.50	0.181	0.08		2	¼ oz
Cocoa powder	7.50	0.181	0.08		2	¼ oz
Vanilla bean	Each	1	1		1	½ each
Egg whites	55.00	1.329	0.60	1	1	1⅞ oz
Total	182.5	0.907	2.00	4	7	6⅜ oz

Process, Chocolate Glaze

1. Blend together all the ingredients using a whisk.
2. Glaze the brioche and top with the whole blanched almonds, powdered sugar, and pearl sugar.

FORMULA

HAZELNUT CREAM

Similar in formulation to almond cream, the use of hazelnuts gives hazelnut cream a dark, earthy color and a full robust flavor. Hazelnut cream can be used in place of almond cream, even in frangipane. It can also be used as a filling in Danish, croissants, and tarts.

Ingredients	Baker's %	Kilogram	US decimal	Lb & Oz		Test
Butter	100.00	0.754	1.662	1	10 ⅝	7 ⅞ oz
Sugar	100.00	0.754	1.662	1	10 ⅝	7 ⅞ oz
Eggs	83.33	0.628	1.385	1	6 ⅛	6 ⅝ oz
Vanilla extract	2.00	0.015	0.033		½	⅞ oz
Hazelnut meal	100.00	0.754	1.662	1	10 ⅝	7 ⅞ oz
Flan powder	12.50	0.094	0.208		3 ⅜	1 oz
Total	397.83	3.000	6.613	6	9 ¾	2 lb

Process

1. In a mixer with a paddle attachment, mix the butter and sugar until light.
2. Gradually add the eggs and vanilla.
3. Add the hazelnut meal and flan powder and mix until smooth.

FORMULA

LIGHT PISTACHIO CREAM

This pistachio-flavored cream is similar in composition to almond cream. After the base cream is made, cool pastry cream is blended in to lighten the texture further. Light pistachio cream can be used as a filling in Danish and other pastries, including croissants and tarts.

Ingredients	Baker's %	Kilogram	US decimal	Lb & Oz		Test
Pistachios, raw	320.10	0.587	1.293	1	4 ¾	6 ¼ oz
Sugar	320.51	0.587	1.295	1	4 ¾	6 ¼ oz
Butter	320.51	0.587	1.295	1	4 ¾	6 ¼ oz
Bread flour	100.00	0.183	0.404		6 ¾	2 oz
Pistachio paste	128.21	0.235	0.518		8 ¼	2 ½ oz
Pastry cream	301.28	0.552	1.217	1	3 ½	5 ⅞ oz
Eggs	146.15	0.268	0.590		9 ½	2 ⅞ oz
Total	1636.76	3.000	6.613	6	9 ¾	2 lb

Process

1. Grind the pistachios and sugar until fine.
2. Cream the butter and pistachio sugar mixture until light.
3. Gradually add the eggs.
4. Incorporate the flour.
5. Add the pistachio paste and mix until smooth.
6. Add the pastry cream and mix until well blended and creamy.

FORMULA

CREAM CHEESE FILLING

Rich and just slightly sweet, this cream cheese filling adds the ideal texture balance to Danish pastry. Try topping with frozen blueberries, raspberries, or blackberries.

Ingredients	Baker's %	Kilogram	US decimal	Lbs & Oz		Test
Cream cheese	100.00	1.630	3.594	3	9½	1 lb 1⅜ oz
Sugar	50.00	0.815	1.797	1	12¾	8¾ oz
Butter, softened	10.00	0.163	0.359		5¾	1¾ oz
Eggs	9.00	0.147	0.323		5⅛	1⅝ oz
Vanilla extract	2.00	0.033	0.072		1⅛	⅜ oz
Bread flour	13.00	0.212	0.467		7½	2¼ oz
Total	184.00	3.000	6.613	6	9¾	2 lb

Process

1. In a mixer with a paddle attachment, mix the cream cheese and sugar together until smooth.
2. Add the butter and mix until blended.
3. Mix in the eggs and vanilla.
4. Add the flour and mix until combined.

FORMULA

FIG FILLING

This filling is based on fig paste, which is generally available commercially. If it is not available, whole dried figs can be pureed until a paste consistency is achieved. Fig filling works well in roll-up style pastries such as lunettes or the twisted "S" shape.

Ingredients	Baker's %	Kilogram	US decimal	Lb & Oz		Test
Almond paste	100.00	1.408	3.105	3	1⅝	15 oz
Fig paste	70.00	0.986	2.173	2	2¾	10½ oz
Egg whites	38.00	0.535	1.180	1	2⅞	5¾ oz
Orange zest	5.00	0.070	0.155		2½	¾ oz
Total	213.00	3.000	6.613	6	9¾	2 lb

Process

1. Warm the almond paste and blend with the fig paste.
2. Add the egg whites to the paste.
3. Add the orange zest.

FORMULA

APPLE FILLING

Perfect for an apple Danish or an apple croissant, this filling benefits from the flavors of fresh apples, butter, sugar, and vanilla and is a wonderful accompaniment to any pastry. Be sure to not cook the apples too long, as they continue to soften in the oven and it is ideal to have some "fresh," slightly crisp texture in the finished filling.

Ingredients	Baker's %	Kilogram	US decimal	Lb & Oz		Test
Apples, diced ¼ inch (1 cm)	100.00	2.272	5.010	5	⅛	1 lb 8¼ oz
Water	10.00	0.227	0.501		8	2⅜ oz
Sugar	10.00	0.227	0.501		8	2⅜ oz
Cornstarch	2.00	0.045	0.100		1⅝	½ oz
Vanilla bean	Each	2	2		2	⅕ each
Butter	10.00	0.227	0.501		8	2⅜ oz
Total	132.00	3.000	6.613	6	9¾	2 lb

Process

1. Cook the apples with the water and the butter over medium high heat until the water boils.
2. Mix together the sugar, cornstarch, and scraped vanilla bean and add to the apples.
3. Continue to cook on medium heat until thickened.
4. Pour onto a sheet pan with parchment, cover to the surface with plastic, and refrigerate until needed.

FORMULA

LEMON FILLING

This filling, processed in much the same way as pastry cream, captures the intense flavor of lemon and is best prepared with fresh lemon juice. Sweet and tart harmonize nicely for a refreshing flavor, perfect for use in Danish or croissants.

Ingredients	Baker's %	Kilogram	US decimal	Lb & Oz		Test
Water	180.00	0.863	1.902	1	14⅜	9¼ oz
Lemon juice	100.00	0.479	1.056	1	⅞	5⅛ oz
Lemon zest	10.00	0.048	0.106		1¾	½ oz
Sugar	195.00	0.934	2.060	2	1	10 oz
Cornstarch	28.00	0.134	0.296		4¾	1⅜ oz
Egg yolks	63.00	0.302	0.666		10⅝	3¼ oz
Butter	50.00	0.240	0.528		8½	2½ oz
Total	626.00	3.000	6.613	6	9¾	2 lb

Process

1. Heat the water, lemon juice, and lemon zest.
2. When warm to the touch stir in half of the sugar.
3. Combine the remaining sugar with the cornstarch.
4. Add the egg yolks to this mixture and whisk until smooth.
5. When the lemon juice comes to a boil, temper in the egg yolk mixture.
6. Return the mixture to the heat and boil for 2 minutes, stirring constantly.
7. Remove from the heat and stir in the butter.
8. Pour onto a sheet pan with parchment, cover to the surface with plastic, and refrigerate until needed.

FORMULA

STICKY BUN GLAZE

This glaze provides the gooeyness of cinnamon rolls and sticky buns. Deposited under the pastry before baking, it melts in the oven, slightly bakes into the pastry and turns into a sticky glaze out of the oven. The flavor combination of butter, brown sugar, and honey makes every treat this sticky bun glaze touches irresistible.

Ingredients	Baker's %	Kilogram	US decimal	Lb & Oz		Test
Brown sugar	100.00	1.506	3.320	3	5⅛	1 lb ⅛ oz
Butter	56.67	0.854	1.882	1	14⅛	9⅛ oz
Salt	0.83	0.013	0.028		½	⅛ oz
Honey	38.33	0.577	1.273	1	4⅜	6⅛ oz
Vanilla extract	2.50	0.038	0.083		1⅜	⅜ oz
Cinnamon	0.83	0.013	0.028		½	⅛ oz
Total	199.16	3.000	6.613	6	9¾	2 lb

Process

1. Cream the sugar and butter until smooth.
2. Add the remaining ingredients and continue mixing until light and creamy.
3. Alternate process: Heat all the ingredients in a saucepan until the sugar is dissolved.

FORMULA

SPINACH AND FETA FILLING

Two simple, yet classically compatible, ingredients come together for this savory croissant filling. The spinach does not need to be blanched or sautéed, but it should be well coated with the feta to help weigh it down.

Ingredients	Baker's %	US decimal	Kilogram	Lb & Oz		Test
Spinach	70.00	1.235	2.723	2	11⅝	13⅛ oz
Feta	100.00	1.764	3.890	3	14¼	1 lb 2⅞ oz
Total	170.00	3.000	6.613	6	9¾	2 lb

Yield: 65 to 75 croissants

Process

1. Clean the spinach and drain well.
2. Add the crumbled feta and blend well.

FORMULA

CRÈME CHIBOUST FOR BRIOCHE TROPÉZIENNE

Popular in the seaside resort town of St. Tropez, France, this pastry is filled with Crème Chiboust: a pastry cream lightened with Italian meringue and stabilized with gelatin. This version is flavored with vanilla bean and rum. Follow the temperature guidelines in the formula closely. After piping the cream onto the bottom half of the brioche, allow it to cool in the freezer for about 15 to 20 minutes to firm up, then place the other half of the brioche atop the cream.

Ingredients	Baker's %	Kilogram	US decimal	Lb & Oz		Test
Gelatin	1.75	0.021	0.047		< ⅛	3 sheets
Water	10.00	0.123	0.270		4⅜	1¼ oz
Milk	100.00	1.226	2.703	2	11¼	13⅛ oz
Vanilla bean	Each	1	1		1	⅕ each
Sugar	5.00	0.061	0.135		2⅛	⅝ oz
Cornstarch	10.00	0.123	0.270		4⅜	1¼ oz
Egg yolks	24.00	0.294	0.649		10⅜	3⅛ oz
Butter	10.00	0.123	0.270		4⅜	1¼ oz
Water	10.91	0.134	0.295		4¾	1⅜ oz
Sugar	33.00	0.405	0.892		14¼	4⅜ oz
Glucose	6.00	0.074	0.162		2⅝	¾ oz
Egg whites	24.00	0.294	0.649		10⅜	3⅛ oz
Rum	10.00	0.123	0.270		4⅜	1¼ oz
Total	244.66	3.000	6.613	6	9¾	2 lb

Process

Make Pastry Cream

1. Bloom the gelatin in cold water; reserve.
2. Scale the whole milk, vanilla beans, and half of the sugar into a stainless steel pot and bring to a boil.
3. Meanwhile, scale the other half of the sugar and cornstarch into a bowl and mix to combine.
4. Scale the yolks into the sugar-cornstarch mixture and whisk until just combined; do not incorporate air.
5. Once the milk comes to a boil, temper one-third of it into the yolk mixture; stir to incorporate evenly.
6. Return this mixture back to the pot, stirring constantly.
7. Continue to cook the custard while stirring until it has boiled for 2 minutes.
8. Off heat, add the butter and bloomed gelatin; stir until mixed in completely.
9. Pour the pastry cream into a bowl and cover with plastic wrap to prevent a skin from developing. Reserve and make the Italian Meringue.

Make Italian Meringue

1. Heat the water, second sugar, and glucose until it reaches the boiling point.
2. Wash down the sides of the pan with water.
3. When the sugar reaches 241°F (116°C) start whipping the egg whites on medium speed.
4. When the sugar reaches soft ball stage 246°F (119°C) to 250°F (121°C), slowly pour it into the whipping egg whites.
5. Whip until 104°F (40°C).

Finishing Crème Chiboust

Once both mixtures are at 104°F (40°C), fold the warm meringue and the rum into the pastry cream and use immediately.

CHAPTER SUMMARY

Growing numbers of American consumers appreciate the high quality of Viennoiserie produced with good ingredients, a respectful fermentation, and the skill of the pastry chef or baker. Attention to detail in mixing, fermentation, lamination, makeup, proofing, and preparation for the oven must be mastered and well understood in order to create croissant, brioche, or Panettone that is as light as air. Formulas, ingredients, and processes should focus on ensuring a proper balance of fermentation and structure to create even layers of dough and fat for laminated doughs and for properly mixed nonlaminated Viennoiserie. Once the basic steps are understood, the pastry chef or baker can implement preferments and retarding processes that better build flavors, improve production schedules, and provide freshly baked Viennoiserie as needed.

KEY TERMS

- ❖ Beurrage
- ❖ Book fold
- ❖ Butter press
- ❖ Détrempe
- ❖ Double fold
- ❖ Laminated dough
- ❖ Lamination
- ❖ Letter fold
- ❖ Nonlaminated dough
- ❖ Osmotolerant yeast
- ❖ Plasticity
- ❖ Roll-in fat
- ❖ Roll-in shortening
- ❖ Single fold
- ❖ Viennoiserie

REVIEW QUESTIONS

1. **What is osmotolerant yeast? Why is it well suited for use in Viennoiserie?**
2. **What is the function of fat in croissant dough?**
3. **What are the three preferments commonly used in Viennoiserie? What are the benefits of each?**
4. **What are five retarding techniques commonly used for Viennoiserie? How are they put into practice?**
5. **What precautions must be taken if freezing unbaked Viennoiserie for more than one week?**

PART 4

PASTRY

Part 4 explores pastry, which is both a classic tradition and a quickly evolving sector of the food business. From its relatively simple beginnings, the category has evolved into highly refined techniques and presentations, thanks to higher-quality ingredients, better equipment, and high consumer expectations. Even so, many of the basic ingredients, knowledge, and formula processes have existed for more than a century. Whether simply blending wet and dry ingredients to create a quick bread, whipping egg whites for Parisian macarons, or tempering chocolate for delicate molded candies, the level of knowledge required goes far beyond just following a specific formula.

chapter
10

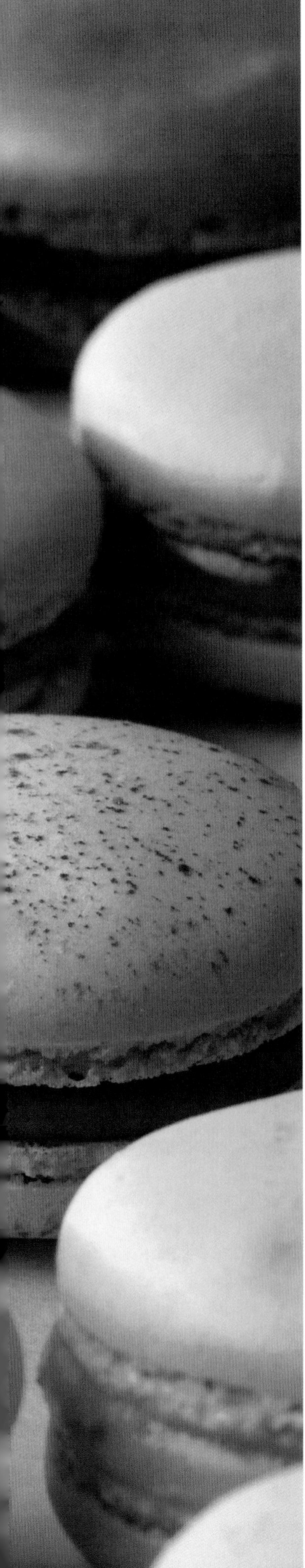

COOKIES

OBJECTIVES

After reading this chapter, you should be able to

- describe the functions of each ingredient in cookies as a tenderizer, a toughener, or an inclusion.
- identify the effects of different mixing methods.
- explain the causes of cookie spread and be able to control the factors that contribute to it.
- describe what affects the main characteristics of a cookie: crispness, softness, chewiness, sandiness.
- make a selection of cookies using the methods outlined in this chapter.

DEFINITION AND SCOPE OF COOKIES

Whether they're a treat for special celebrations, a midnight snack with milk, or a goodie for any occasion in between, cookies are enjoyed around the world. The history of the cookie is thousands of years old; however, cookies as we know them today are adapted from recipes and techniques created during the Middle Ages.

Cookies are made from a batter or dough that may be similar to some types of cake batter. A cookie is, essentially, a smaller, dryer version of a cake—the main difference between the two is the liquid content. The texture of cookies may be soft, chewy, hard, brittle, light, or dense. There are endless flavor combinations, due to a vast selection of base ingredients that include butter, sugar, eggs, flour, nut meals, and **inclusions**. Inclusions are ingredients that add different flavor and texture components to cookies. They do not have a structural function and are usually added into the dough near the end of the mixing process. Examples of inclusions are chocolate chips, rolled oats, nuts, and dried fruits.

INGREDIENT FUNCTIONS FOR COOKIES

The ingredients used in a cookie formula can be classified into two major groups: **tenderizing ingredients** and **toughening ingredients**. Both ingredient groups play a major role in the formation of cookie characteristics such as softness, chewiness, crispness, and spread. Tenderizing ingredients soften the cookie, enable spread, and prevent the cookie from becoming crisp and chewy. Toughening ingredients create a viable structure for the dough that reduces spread, retains a firmer shape, and creates an end product that is easily recognized as a cookie (Matz, 1987, p. 151).

TOUGHENERS

The major toughening ingredients include flour, water, cocoa powder, salt, egg whites, whole eggs, milk, and nonfat milk solids. Primarily consisting of starches and proteins, these ingredients help to hold the cookie together before and after the baking process.

Protein in flour becomes a toughening component because when it is hydrated with water the gluten is formed. The type of flour used for cookies depends on the type of cookie being produced. In the baking industry, typical flours used for cookies include pastry flour (7 to 9 percent protein) and low-protein bread flour (10.5 to 12 percent protein). Higher-protein flours are not suitable because they create an excessive amount of toughening action that results in a coarse crumb and the possibility of surface cracks.

Water acts as a toughening agent by hydrating and potentially toughening the gluten. Salt toughens the dough by reinforcing the strength of the gluten, but usually there is not a significant amount of salt in cookie formulas to create a noticeable difference. Salt is generally added in smaller quantities only to enhance flavor. The protein in whole eggs and egg whites provides essential structure and creates volume: As the cookie bakes, the proteins coagulate and help it to set. Milk and milk powders provide a degree of toughening because the protein binds water. A mix of approximately 5 percent dried milk powder, based on flour weight, will provide a slight toughening effect and will also improve crust color and shine.

TENDERIZERS

The tenderizing ingredients that balance toughening ingredients and create a softer cookie texture are primarily sugars and fats. The main tenderizers include granulated sugars, liquid or inverted sugars, natural and manufactured fats, egg yolks, starches derived from corn or wheat, and leavening agents.

Sugar

Sugar is **hygroscopic**, which means that it attracts and retains moisture. The size of the sugar granule will affect the spread of the cookie and, consequently, its tenderness. Evidently, the smaller the sugar granule, the more the cookie will spread with less mixing. Conversely, the larger the sugar grain, the longer mixing will have to occur to produce more spread. Lower concentrations of sugar granules in cookie dough encourage more water to be bound to the flour, allowing the gluten to develop which in turn retards the spread of the dough (Matz, 1992, p. 110). If the sugar granules are smaller in size, but of the same weight, they disperse in the dough at a higher concentration: They are located closer to each other, preventing gluten from forming strong bonds, and spread is encouraged.

Inverted or liquid sugars, such as Trimoline or corn syrup and glucose, may also be added to cookie formulas in small quantities to help maintain softness. The effect of too much inverted sugar is an early formation of the crust, and lighter color of the crust. Ten to fifteen percent inverted or liquid sugar, based on the weight of the flour, may be substituted in place of sucrose. An excessive amount of inverted or liquid sugar can cause an unpleasant hardness on the crust and too much sweetness in the finished product.

Fat

Fat tenderizes cookies by interfering with starch and gluten-forming proteins in the wheat. Butter and vegetable shortenings are the major fats used in cookie formulas; lard and liquid oils are used less often. Since butter is expensive compared to other fats, margarine or vegetable shortening can be substituted in cases when its flavor does not contribute greatly to the final product. Additionally, the large ratio of fat in egg yolks adds both richness in color and softness in texture. Lecithin, one of the fatty acids present in egg yolk, is a natural emulsifier and helps to generate a better distribution of liquids and fats, creating a more tender product.

Starch

Starches derived from wheat and corn act as tenderizing agents because they absorb moisture and create filler but no structural strength. Products derived from corn include cornmeal, corn flour, and cornstarch. Cornmeal is usually coarse ground corn kernels and comes in several textures, which give flavor and crunchy texture to cookies. Cornstarch does not have a corn flavor, and it is added to formulas to create a light, crumble-textured cookie. Cornstarch does not have a significant effect on spread. Potato flour, which is made from cooked, dried, and ground high-starch-content potatoes, is sometimes used in formulas to create soft and spongy, almost mealy texture. Both corn and potato starch have a high starch content, and they are very low in protein, when compared to wheat flour, which has about 8 to 15 percent protein.

Chemical Leavening Agents

Chemical leavening agents act as tenderizing ingredients because carbon dioxide is created during the baking process and gives rise to the cookies and provides a tender texture. Major leavening agents used in cookie formulas are baking soda (sodium bicarbonate) and double acting baking powder, which is a mixture of baking soda, acid salts, and cornstarch.

When the acid salts in a chemical leavening system are exposed to heat, they react with the sodium bicarbonate and begin the release of the carbon dioxide. Different acid salts can begin their reaction at different temperatures. Examples of the acid salts that react at low temperatures are cream of tartar (potassium hydrogen tartrate) and monocalcium phosphate. A high-temperature reacting acid salt, such as sodium aluminum sulfate, creates a larger amount of gas during baking, enabling the cookie to leaven in the oven.

When double acting baking powder is used, carbon dioxide is produced in two stages: when it is exposed to moisture and when it is exposed to heat. During mixing, a small amount of gas is created by the acid salts reacting with the dissolved sodium bicarbonate. The second reaction happens in the oven, guaranteeing a sufficient amount of leavening. Single acting baking powder contains only low-temperature reacting acid salt, but it is not largely manufactured in today's industry.

Baking soda can be used only when a formula contains an acidic ingredient, such as cocoa powder or buttermilk. This is because the baking soda needs an acidic component to trigger the reaction to create the carbon dioxide. When too much baking soda is used, an alkaline flavor may reside in the finished product because not all of the baking soda was able to react with the available acidic ingredients. Additionally, too much baking soda or powder can result in a slightly coarse texture and dark crust color.

Baking ammonia (ammonium bicarbonate) is a chemical leavening agent that is not often used in bakeshops today. When baking ammonia comes in contact with moisture and is exposed to high heat, it quickly breaks down into ammonia, carbon dioxide, and water, which all assist in leavening baked goods. Baking ammonia is appropriate to use in spiced products, such as gingerbread, or in cookies and crackers that will be baked until very dry, eliminating the chance for off flavors. Baking ammonia helps to maintain uniformity and spread in cookies by reacting very quickly. When it is used properly, in formulation, as well as in the baking process, there will be no residue of ammonia odor.

TYPES OF COOKIES

The eight classifications of cookies are primarily based on their method of formulation and production. (See Figure 10-1.) Because makeup and baking guidelines vary considerably from cookie to cookie, be sure to follow any instructions in the formula for specialized makeup techniques and baking times. Regardless of the type of cookie, it is important to portion them evenly so that they bake evenly.

- **Dropped cookie**: The name of this cookie classification comes from the portioning and releasing action of the dough. Dropped cookies, also known as wire-cut cookies, are made from thicker dough. Cookies are mixed, portioned using a scoop or cookie depositor, and baked, or they can be frozen after being portioned. Portion control can be maintained by the size of the scoop or the dye plate on the portioning unit. Chocolate chip and oatmeal raisin cookies are typical examples of dropped cookies.
- **Piped cookie**: Although piped cookies are made from softer dough than dropped cookies, they are still able to hold their shape. This type of cookie formula may sometimes contain almond meal or almond paste. Piped cookies are portioned using a piping bag, cookie press, or depositor and are often created in decorative shapes. Spritz cookies and sables à la poche are examples of piped cookies.
- **Cut-out cookie**: Cut-out cookies are formulated to limit spread during baking, so that their original shape may be retained. They are cut from rolled-out dough that has similar rheological properties to the dough used for dropped cookies. This dough must be able to handle the stress of rolling out without losing strength and breaking, yet it must also maintain a soft and crumbly texture. It is important that this dough is not overworked because excessively developed gluten causes shrinkage and a tough texture. Any scrap should be carefully kneaded together

with fresh dough and rolled out to minimize waste. Sugar cookies or gingerbread cookies are examples of cut-out cookies.

Figure 10-1
Assorted Cookies (top to bottom, left to right): Oatmeal Raisin Cookies, Tuiles, Assorted Diamonds, Sables à la Poche, Lemon Bars, Sugar Cookies, Double Chocolate Biscotti

- **Sheet cookie**: This classification represents a diverse range of products that are usually baked on a sheet pan and then portioned into individual-sized servings. The process of making sheet cookies is closely tied to the formula. Examples of sheet cookies include brownies, lemon bars, toscani, and granola bars.
- **Sliced cookie**: A sliced cookie is made from a long piece of dough that is baked, and then cut into individual pieces. Dough consistency is typically close to that of dropped cookies. Two common examples of sliced cookies include fig bars and biscotti. Biscotti literally translates as "twice baked" and is dried out in the oven after being sliced.
- **Icebox cookie**: Because of the mixing process and formulation of the dough, icebox cookies have very little spread and retain their definition of shape and color throughout the baking process. Icebox cookies may be constructed using traditional methods to create intricate geometric or marbled designs, as well as multiple flavors. They are then formed into cylinders or blocks of dough that are refrigerated, sliced and baked, or frozen until needed.
- **Stencil cookie**: Typically thin and crisp in texture, stencil cookies are made primarily to be a component of, or garnish for, plated desserts. Often called tuile, they are made from a thin, basic batter that is mixed, rested, and spread free form or into a template and then baked. The name "tuile" is derived from the classic, thin, rounded cookies that are topped with sliced almonds. Once out of the oven and while still hot, the cookies are formed into curve shapes to resemble a "tuile" (roof shingle). Contemporary tuile garnishes include cocoa nibs, coconut, nuts, spices, and seeds. A formula for tuile is found in Chapter 20.
- **Molded cookie**: Molded cookies vary considerably in composition. It is important that the dough be properly mixed using the one-stage or sanding method, so that if intricate designs are used, they do not bake out or deform. Once mixed, the dough is deposited into dye plates, and then extracted for baking. Historically, the most common type of molded cookie was shortbread, produced from molds that were made of wood or metal. Today, molded cookies typically come from large-scale commercial bakeries with highly specialized equipment.

COOKIE MIXING METHODS

Cookie mixing methods are closely associated with cake mixing methods, the main difference being the quantity of liquid used. As with cake mixing, very little gluten development should occur because gluten will toughen the cookie.

Before making any cookie formula, it is important to have all ingredients properly scaled and, in general, all ingredients to room temperature. An exception is the sanding method because the butter must be cold. The temperature of ingredients is essential for proper ingredient incorporation and proper emulsification of the fats and liquids. What follows is a description of the four major methods for mixing cookies.

CREAMING METHOD

The most common technique for mixing cookie dough, the **creaming method**, is defined by the mixing of fats and sugars to incorporate air. Just how much air is incorporated depends on the desired characteristics of the cookie. The more the fats and sugars are creamed, the more the cookies will spread during the baking process. Furthermore, if the cookie is high in fat and low in flour, only a short mixing time of the fat and sugar is required. Overmixing in this situation will create excessive spread and will overheat the cookie dough, which results in melting some of the fat and causes undesirable texture and volume of the final product.

Once the fat and sugar have been sufficiently creamed, eggs are gradually added. The rate of adding the eggs, along with the proper temperature of ingredients, must be maintained to help prevent curdling. If the eggs are added too quickly, the mixture may lose its emulsion because the structure of fat and sugar matrix is unable to absorb all the liquid at once. The temperature of the eggs must be similar to that of the butter [60°F (16°C) to 65°F (18°C)]. If the eggs are too cold, they will solidify the butter particles that are dispersed with sugar and the mixture will curdle.

It is rare that a cookie will contain additional liquids. However, if any liquids are to be added, they are added after the eggs and all at once. Next, the dry ingredients are mixed in just until incorporated. It is very important to achieve even distribution of dry ingredients in order to prevent lumps and minimize gluten development.

Mixing is a crucial step of cookie production. All ingredients must be incorporated evenly and to the proper degree specified in individual formulas. Even so, a common mistake is uneven mixing of the butter–sugar mixture into the remaining dough. For example, when using the creaming method, the paddle attachment never touches the bowl, which leaves a thin layer of the butter/sugar mixture. To ensure even distribution of the butter/sugar phase, the bowl must be scraped down throughout the mixing process. Failure to do so will result in this portion of the mix getting into the dough which results in **run out**. This is when the butter–sugar phase melts and flows out of the cookie. (See Figure 10-2.)

Figure 10-2
Cookie With Run Out

If any inclusions are added, it is done just before the dough is fully mixed, to avoid overmixing and crushing the inclusion. Once complete, the dough may be portioned, made up, and baked, or it can be reserved under refrigeration or in the freezer until needed.

Creaming Method Process

- Scale all the ingredients and have them at room temperature.
- In the bowl of an electric mixer fitted with the paddle attachment, cream the butter and sugar. (See Creaming Method Figure 10-3, Step 1.)
- Slowly add the eggs and then the vanilla. (See Creaming Method Figure 10-3, Steps 2–3.)

- Scrape down the bowl and mix to reincorporate ingredients evenly. (See Creaming Method Figure 10-3, Step 4.)
- Add the flour and mix just until combined. (See Creaming Method Figure 10-3, Step 5.)
- If adding additional ingredients, only mix in the flour 50 percent, then add the additional ingredients and continue mixing to incorporation. (See Creaming Method Figure 10-3, Step 6.)
- Reserve in the refrigerator or freezer and portion; then bake as needed.

SPONGE METHOD

This method is used for softer textured cookies, such as some types of brownies and some types of macarons. Ladyfingers, generally considered as cookies in Europe, are made using the sponge method; however, in the United States, they are more commonly used as a base for cakes. A cookie made using the **sponge method** may use whole eggs, egg whites, and sometimes egg yolks to create foam that is stabilized by a portion of the sugar from the formula. As the egg foam incorporates air, it gains volume. The degree to which the egg product is whipped greatly depends on the product being made and the type of egg product being used.

The stiffness of meringue is classified into three stages: **soft peak**, **medium peak**, and **stiff peak**. When the meringue has a smooth look and falls from the whisk without creating any peaks, it is called soft peak. If a peak forms when the whisk is lifted, but the top of the peak bends, this is medium peak. When meringue has been whipped to stiff peak, it has a glossy look and forms spikes when the whisk is lifted. Soft peak meringue is used for mousses and meringue pie fillings. Medium peak meringue is mainly used for cakes and cookies, and stiff peak meringue is usually used for baked meringue. For a full review of meringue and egg foams, refer to Chapter 15.

Once the egg product and sugar have been whipped to the desired stage, the sifted dry ingredients are folded in. If melted chocolate is being used, as in the case of brownies, it may be added before the flour. The batter may then be portioned and baked.

The sponge method is made up of two steps. First, egg products and sugar are whipped to a desired stage. Next, the sifted dry ingredients are folded in. From this basic procedure, there are three distinguishable variations wherein the egg foam may be based on whole eggs, egg whites and egg yolks, or just whites. For example, during the mixing of

FIGURE 10-3 CREAMING METHOD

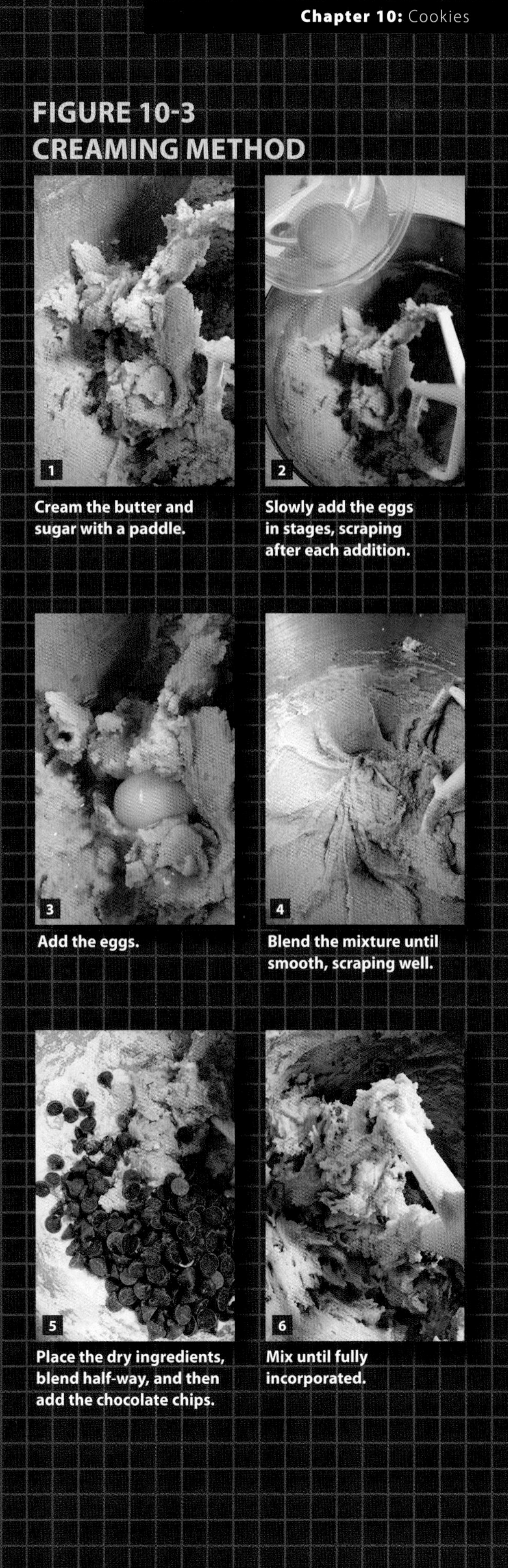

1 Cream the butter and sugar with a paddle.

2 Slowly add the eggs in stages, scraping after each addition.

3 Add the eggs.

4 Blend the mixture until smooth, scraping well.

5 Place the dry ingredients, blend half-way, and then add the chocolate chips.

6 Mix until fully incorporated.

FIGURE 10-4 MERINGUE METHOD FOR PARISIAN MACARONS

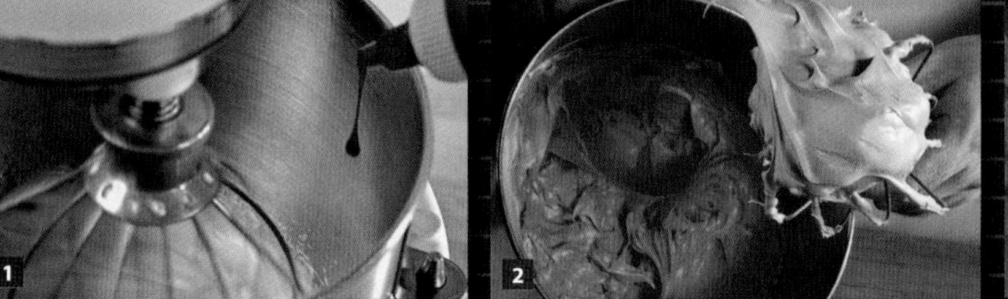

1 Add the desired colorant in the whipping egg whites.

2 Whip to a stiff peak.

3 Incorporate the sifted dry ingredients.

classic brownies, whole eggs are whipped with the sugar to **ribbon stage**, or until the mixture forms ribbon-like texture when the whisk is lifted. In the classic preparation of ladyfingers, egg yolks and whites are whipped separately and then combined to gain the maximum volume. For macarons, additional ingredients are folded into egg whites. An explanation of the three different methods follows.

Sponge Process—Whole Egg Method (Brownies)

- Scale all the ingredients and have them at room temperature.
- In the bowl of an electric mixer fitted with the whip attachment, whip the eggs and sugar until the ribbon stage.
- Add any additional ingredients such as vanilla, melted butter, or chocolate, and mix to incorporate.
- Add the sifted dry ingredients and fold just until combined, using the paddle attachment or a rubber spatula.
- Portion as needed and bake immediately.

Sponge Process—Separated Egg Method (Ladyfingers)

- Scale all the ingredients and have them at room temperature.
- In the bowl of an electric mixer fitted with the whip attachment, whip the egg yolk and sugar until ribbon stage.
- In the bowl of an electric mixer fitted with the whip attachment, whip the egg whites and sugar until medium peak.
- Gently fold meringue into the yolk mixture, using a rubber spatula.
- Add the sifted dry ingredients and fold just until combined, using the rubber spatula.
- Portion as needed and bake immediately.

Sponge Process—Meringue Method (Parisian Macarons)

- Scale all the ingredients and have them at room temperature.
- In the bowl of an electric mixer fitted with the whip attachment, whip the egg whites and sugar until stiff peaks are formed. Add colorant as needed. (See Meringue Method for Parisian Macarons Figure 10-4, Steps 1–2.)
- Add the dry ingredients, and mix to deflate the batter to the desired stage. (See Meringue Method for Parisian Macarons Figure 10-4, Steps 3–4.)

4 **Blend the mixture until smooth, scraping well.**

5 **Portion as desired, let skin form, and bake immediately.**

- Portion as desired, let a skin form, and then bake immediately. (See Meringue Method for Parisian Macarons Figure 10-4, Step 5.)

SANDING METHOD

The **sanding method**, or sablér method (*sablé* is the French term for "sandy"), produces products that can range from a crumbly and sandy texture to a crisper texture. Base ingredients used for these cookies include flour, butter, sugar, and eggs, with the option of adding additional flavoring or inclusions.

The process for this method starts off very differently from cookies that utilize the creaming method. The first step is to combine the flour, sugar, and any other dry ingredients such as salt or spices and then blend in cold butter using the paddle attachment on a stand mixer. To create the sandy texture of this cookie, it is necessary to coat most of the starch and protein content of the flour with fat. After the mixture looks like coarse cornmeal, eggs (or yolks) are added, and the dough is mixed until it comes together. The uncoated starch and fat will be hydrated by the egg and will ensure that cohesive dough is formed. Then, the dough can be portioned and made up as desired, baked right away, or reserved in the refrigerator or freezer for later baking. The sanding method is typically used for icebox cookies or cut-out cookies.

When utilizing the sanding method, a couple of precautions must be taken to ensure success. First, when incorporating the dry ingredients and the butter, it is essential to use cold butter. If the butter is warm, it will be absorbed by the flour and melt the sugar. Second, it is important not to overprocess the initial flour–sugar–butter mixture. If this happens, the three ingredients will form a dough prematurely, the cookie will not be able to absorb the egg, and the cookie texture will be too tender, because the starch is not hydrated to create the structure for the cookie.

Sanding Process

- Scale all the ingredients, keeping the butter and eggs (or yolks) cold.
- In the bowl of an electric mixer, fitted with the paddle attachment, mix the dry ingredients with the butter until mealy. (See Sanding Method Figure 10-5, Step 1.)
- Add the eggs (or yolks) and mix until the dough comes together. See Sanding Method Figure 10-5, Steps 2–4.)
- Cover the dough with plastic wrap, and refrigerate until cool.

FIGURE 10-5 SANDING METHOD

1 Blend the cold fat and dry ingredients in a mixing bowl fitted with a paddle attachment and mix until mealy.

2 Add the liquid ingredients at once.

3 At 50 percent incorporation, add almond meal (if applicable).

4 At 100 percent incorporation, do not overmix.

ONE-STAGE METHOD

The **one-stage method** is the most straightforward mixing method of all: The ingredients are all mixed together at once and are then portioned according to the consistency of the dough. Because all the ingredients are mixed in one stage, there is less control over the development of gluten, compared to other mixing method. Hence, the one-stage method is used less frequently.

Once all ingredients are scaled and brought to room temperature (if needed), they are placed in the bowl of a mixer with the paddle attachment and mixed until incorporation. Risks include overmixing the dough, which may toughen the cookie by overdeveloping the gluten. This method is used only when overdevelopment of gluten is not a considerable problem and when the dough is somewhat stiff, as with some types of chewy macaroons.

One-Stage Process

- Scale all the ingredients.
- Combine all the ingredients in the bowl of an electric mixer fitted with the paddle attachment.
- Mix until the dough comes together.
- Refrigerate the dough until cool; then portion according to its consistency and bake as desired.

COOKIES PROPERTIES AND CAUSES

To produce a wide selection of cookies, one must be able to manipulate their characteristics and textures. This requires an understanding of how the ingredients function, along with the formula processes and baking properties—any and all of which control whether a cookie is crisp, soft, chewy, or sandy.

CRISPNESS

Crispness is primarily controlled by limiting moisture in the cookie formula. The greater the amount of moisture, the softer the cookie will be. The following factors also contribute to crispness:

- A low or excessive amount of sugar content. When a very small amount of sugar is in the formula, the cookie becomes crispy. Sugar is hygroscopic and attracts moisture and promotes tenderness. If a cookie is low in sugar, it will not be moist or tender. However, when larger quantities of sugar are added or an alternative baking process is used, sugar will recrystallize during the longer baking processes as with biscotti. A shiny look from recrystallized sugar appears on the surface of biscotti, which is typically baked for a long time at a low temperature to dry out the cookie.
- The size of the cookie in relation to the baking temperature. A smaller, thinner cookie will bake to a dry texture faster than a larger cookie baked at the same temperature.
- A longer baking time at a lower temperature. This technique bakes the cookie beyond the point of setup and reduces the moisture content.
- Twice-baking to encourage excessive crispness, as with biscotti.

To retain their crisp qualities, cookies should be stored in an airtight container or packaging to avoid absorbing moisture from the air.

SOFTNESS

Softness is encouraged by factors in direct opposition to those that promote crispness.

- Higher moisture content, which creates a softer cookie and retards drying.
- A high fat content, since fat tenderizes and keeps moisture in cookies.
- Use of **humectants**, such as honey, molasses, corn syrup, inverted sugar, and glucose. These ingredients have hygroscopic properties, which attract moisture.
- Baking larger-sized cookies for shorter periods of time.
- Baking for briefer periods at higher temperatures.
- Covering soft-textured cookies will prevent staling and drying.

CHEWINESS

Moisture is necessary to create chewiness, and a fine balance of toughening and tenderizing ingredients are required for proper product development.

- A higher sugar content is required to create a softer texture.
- A higher degree of toughening ingredients such as higher protein flour or whole eggs or egg whites will provide needed body.
- A longer final mixing time increases the development of the gluten.

SANDINESS

The key to producing a sandy texture is a dry dough that is formulated using a high percentage of tenderizing ingredients. Typically, more butter, less sugar, and less liquid are utilized, with egg yolk used as the primary liquid to ensure minimal gluten development and a crisp cookie texture. An example of sandy textured cookie is shortbread.

Not much liquid is used in shortbread because the flour has been coated with fat and cannot absorb much liquid. Just as with pie dough, it is critical that the fat–flour phase not be overmixed; this would completely mix the flour into the butter, creating a cookie that is too tender.

COOKIE SPREAD

Cookie spread refers to a cookie's expansion outward from its unbaked state during the baking process. By understanding the factors that affect spread, including ingredient selection, formula processes, and baking conditions, formulas can be easily manipulated as desired.

Spread can be evaluated by using the spread factor, when flour is a variable in the formula. Spread factor can be determined by dividing the average cookie width (W) by the average cookie thickness (T), for both the baked and unbaked dough. When the two spread factors are compared, the spread factor of the variable product is divided by the original spread factor.

Spread Factor = W/T

% Spread Factor = (Spread Factor of Variable Product × 100)/Spread Factor (Matz, 1992, p. 348)

Example 1

Control product (what you originally have)—Cookies with average width of 3 inches, average height of 0.7 inches

Variable product (what is compared)—Cookies with average width of 2.5 inches, average height of 1 inch

Spread Factor (Control) = 3 / 0.7 = 4.286

Spread Factor (Variable) = 2.5 / 1 = 2.5

% Spread Factor = (2.5 × 100) / 4.28 = 58.32

The spread of variable product is 58.32 percent of the original product.

Example 2

Control Product (what you originally have)—Cookies with average width of 3 inches, average height of 0.7 inches

Variable product (what is compared)—Cookies with average width of 3.5 inches, average height of 0.5 inches

Spread Factor (Control) = 3 / 0.7 = 4.286

Spread Factor (Variable) = 3.5 / 0.5 = 7.00

% Spread Factor = (7.00 × 100) / 4.286 = 163.32

The spread of the variable product is 163.32 percent of the original product.

By knowing your spread factor you can control the size of the cookie by adjusting the height during depositing.

INCREASED SPREAD

Cookie spread is heavily influenced by the type and amount of sugar used, along with the length of time spent creaming the fats and sugar. Based on the same quantity of mixing, smaller granules of sugar create more spread than larger sugar granules. Smaller granules are further dispersed in dough and prevent gluten from developing. The same weight of coarse sugar granules are more scattered throughout the dough, allowing the gluten to have more strength. A high level of creaming promotes spreading because it incorporates air into the dough, which expands outward when heated. Chemical leavening agents have a similar effect, releasing gases during the baking process to create a lighter cookie that spreads outward.

Other factors that encourage spread include a lower baking temperature, which delays the gelatinization of starch and coagulation of protein, and the temperature of the dough, with a warmer cookie dough spreading more than a colder one. In addition, a softer flour with a lower protein content will allow more spread, as will greasing the pan to decrease spread resistance.

DECREASED SPREAD

The properties that deter spread are generally the opposite of the properties that promote it. Using larger granules of sugar is an effective approach, and less creaming of fats and sugars limits the incorporation of air into the dough. A similar effect is created by using less chemical leavening. Spread can also be limited by increasing toughening ingredients such as flour or by using stronger flour. A final technique, which is not recommended, is to use higher temperatures during the baking process, allowing the cookie to set up before it has a chance to spread too much. If employed, caution must be exerted to ensure the cookie does not burn on the outside before baking in the inside.

THE BAKING PROCESS

How and when to bake cookie dough largely depends on the formula as well as production needs. The baking guidelines for cookies vary incredibly, depending on the type and formulation. For example, some cookie doughs may be refrigerated or frozen for later use, depending on the chemical leavening agents present and the mixing process used. Cookie dough that contains baking powder has a high tolerance for storage in the refrigerator and freezer because the majority of the gas is created during exposure to heat. When only baking soda is used as the leavening agent and the acidic ingredient is within the dough, the storage tolerance is poor because the acidity triggers a reaction upon contact with moisture during mixing. The storage of cookie dough in the freezer is common in commercial bakeries, with large batches of dough mixed, portioned, and baked as needed throughout the week. Frozen cookie dough may be baked directly from the freezer without defrosting; however, the baking temperature should be lower and the baking time longer than if baking a cookie that is not frozen.

Although there are some general rules for the baking process, specific guidelines for each formulation should be followed. The first step of the baking process involves portioning and panning the cookies, with the size, shape, and quantity affecting baking time and temperature. Cookies are typically baked on parchment-lined flat sheet pans; however, they may be baked on silicone mats or even in tart molds. It is also important that cookies are portioned to accommodate spread during the baking process. The degree of spread will vary from product to product.

The second step of the baking process involves oven heat. Most cookies are baked as quickly as possible at a medium to high temperature in order to preserve desired qualities without drying out. Typical temperatures are 350°F (177°C) for convection ovens and 375°F (191°C) for deck or home ovens. Baking at too low of a temperature will dry the cookie and may encourage excessive spread and pale color. Baking at too high of a temperature may reduce spread and promote burning before baking the inside of the dough.

Several guidelines dictate when a cookie should come out of the oven, including the degree of doneness, crispness, or softness, as well as color, which may be light to golden brown. For a cookie to be edible, it needs to have some structure. Cookies often feel very soft coming out of the oven and then set up as they cool. To test doneness, lift the edge of the cookie while it is still in the oven. If it releases from the parchment paper, it is a good sign that it is done.

Once baked, cookies are very soft and susceptible to damage and should remain on the pan in which they baked until cool. If baked on a greased sheet pan, they should be transferred to a cool surface after being out of the oven for approximately 10 minutes. If stacked while warm, cookies may stick together, or warp if they do not remain level.

FORMULA

CHOCOLATE CHIP COOKIE

Chocolate chip cookies are not hard to like, even though some like them chewy while others prefer them crunchy, some like them with nuts but others can do without the nuts. Over half the cookies baked in American homes are chocolate chip, with an estimated seven billion consumed annually. The "Toll House Cookie" was invented by Ruth Graves Wakefield in the 1930s, when she and her husband Kenneth owned the Toll House Inn in Massachusetts. While cooking for her guests one day, Ruth had to substitute semi-sweet chocolate for baker's chocolate in a cookie recipe. She chopped the chocolate in bits, but when she took the cookies from the oven, the semi-sweet chocolate had not melted into the dough as the baker's chocolate usually did. These cookies with chocolate "chips" became an immediate hit with her guests. Eventually, Mrs. Wakefield sold the recipe to Nestlé in exchange for a lifetime supply of chocolate chips, and the rest is history.

Ingredients	Baker's %	Kilogram	US decimal	Lb & Oz		Test
Butter	70.79	0.775	1.709	1	11⅜	5½ oz
Sugar	44.21	0.484	1.068	1	1⅛	3⅜ oz
Brown sugar	52.63	0.576	1.271	1	4⅜	4⅛ oz
Eggs	31.58	0.346	0.763		12¼	2½ oz
Vanilla extract	1.58	0.017	0.038		⅝	1 tsp
Bread flour	100.00	1.095	2.415	2	6⅝	8¾ oz
Baking soda	1.11	0.012	0.027		⅜	½ tsp
Salt	1.68	0.018	0.041		⅝	1 tsp
Chocolate chips	110.53	1.211	2.669	2	10¾	8½ oz
Total	414.11	4.536	10.000	10	0	2 lb

Process

1. Cream the butter and the sugar.
2. Gradually add the eggs and then the vanilla.
3. Combine the bread flour, baking soda, and salt; mix to 50 percent incorporation.
4. Add the chocolate chips and mix just until incorporated.
5. Scale into 2 lb 3 oz (1,000 g) pieces and roll into 17 inch (43 cm) logs (sheet pan width).

6. Wrap each log in parchment, and refrigerate until ready to bake.
7. Cut to the desired size [2 oz (50 g) to 4 oz (100 g)], place on parchment-lined sheet pans, and bake at 350°F (177°C) in a convection oven for 10 to 12 minutes.

FORMULA

OATMEAL RAISIN COOKIE

When perfectly executed, the oatmeal raisin cookie is a delightful treat with an irresistible aroma. The key to achieving desired results is to avoid overbaking, as the texture of this cookie is essential. Earthy and humble, this classic American cookie demands a glass of milk as accompaniment.

Ingredients	Baker's %	Kilogram	US decimal	Lb & Oz		Test
Butter	68.75	0.607	1.339	1	5⅜	4¼ oz
Brown sugar	145.00	1.281	2.824	2	13⅛	9 oz
Eggs	32.50	0.287	0.633		10⅛	2 oz
Vanilla extract	3.50	0.031	0.068		1⅛	1½ tsp
Bread flour	100.00	0.883	1.947	1	15⅛	6¼ oz
Baking powder	3.50	0.031	0.068		1⅛	1½ tsp
Baking soda	1.75	0.015	0.034		½	½ tsp
Salt	1.00	0.009	0.019		¼	½ tsp
Rolled oats	85.00	0.751	1.655	1	10½	5¼ oz
Raisins	72.50	0.640	1.412	1	6⅝	4½ oz
Total	513.50	4.536	10.000	10	0	2 lb

Process

1. Cream the butter and the sugar on medium speed until mixed thoroughly, but not fluffy.
2. Gradually add the eggs and vanilla.
3. Combine the dry ingredients and add these to the bowl; mix to 50 percent incorporation.
4. Add the raisins and the oats and mix until incorporated.
5. Scale into 2 lb 3 oz (1,000 g) pieces and roll into 17 inch (43 cm) logs (sheet pan width).
6. Wrap each log in parchment, and refrigerate until ready to bake.
7. Cut to the desired size [2 oz (50 g) to 4 oz (100 g)], place on parchment-lined sheet pans, and bake at 350°F (177°C) in a convection oven for 12 to 15 minutes.

FORMULA

PEANUT BUTTER COOKIE

Today, over half the American peanut crop goes to making peanut butter, which was invented in the late 19th century by a St. Louis doctor who first introduced it as a health food at the 1904 St. Louis World's Fair. Crushed or chopped peanuts in baking were actively promoted by George Washington Carver, an African American educator, botanist, and scientist from Alabama's Tuskegee Institute, but peanut butter was not commonly used as an ingredient in cookies until the early 1930s. Now a staple in American bakeries and home baking, the peanut butter cookie, with its trademark crisscross pattern, is appreciated for its dense texture and rich taste.

Ingredients	Baker's %	Kilogram	US decimal	Lb & Oz		Test
Butter	60.71	0.748	1.650	1	10⅜	5¼ oz
Sugar	53.57	0.660	1.456	1	7¼	4⅝ oz
Brown sugar	52.68	0.649	1.431	1	6⅞	4⅝ oz
Eggs	26.79	0.330	0.728		11⅝	2⅜ oz
Vanilla extract	0.89	0.011	0.024		⅜	½ tsp
Peanut butter	68.75	0.847	1.868	1	13⅞	6 oz
Bread flour	100.00	1.233	2.717	2	11½	8¾ oz
Baking powder	3.93	0.048	0.107		1¾	2 tsp
Salt	0.71	0.009	0.019		¼	½ tsp
Total	368.03	4.536	10.000	10	0	2 lb

Process

1. Combine the dry ingredients and reserve.
2. Cream the butter and sugars.
3. Add the eggs and vanilla and then the peanut butter.
4. Add the dry ingredients and mix until well incorporated.
5. Scale into 2 lb 3 oz (1,000 g) pieces and roll into 17 inch (43 cm) logs (sheet pan width).
6. Wrap each log in parchment, and refrigerate until ready to bake.
7. Cut to the desired size [2 oz (50 g) to 4 oz (100 g)], place on parchment-lined sheet pans, and bake at 350°F (177°C) in a convection oven for 12 to 15 minutes.

FORMULA

SNICKERDOODLE

This whimsically named cookie could be from colonial New England times, when cooks were known for giving odd names to their creations. However, some food historians believe snickerdoodles were invented by the Pennsylvania Dutch, with their name derived from "St. Nick," or from the Germans and their *schneckennudeln*, a cinnamon-dusted sweet roll. Regardless of origin, these appealing cookies are notable for their soft texture and cinnamon sugar-dusted surface.

Ingredients	Baker's %	Kilogram	US decimal	Lb & Oz		Test
Butter	80.88	1.189	2.620	2	9⅞	8⅜ oz
Sugar	99.26	1.459	3.216	3	3½	10¼ oz
Eggs	23.53	0.346	0.762		12¼	2½ oz
Vanilla extract	2.94	0.043	0.095		1½	¼ oz
Bread flour	100.00	1.470	3.240	3	3⅞	10⅜ oz
Baking powder	1.18	0.017	0.038		⅝	1 tsp
Salt	0.88	0.013	0.029		½	½ tsp
Total	308.67	4.536	10.000	10	0	2 lb

Process

1. Cream the butter and the sugar.
2. Gradually add the eggs and vanilla.
3. Combine the dry ingredients and add them, being careful not to overmix the dough.
4. Scale into 2 lb 3 oz (1,000 g) pieces and roll into 17 inch (43 cm) logs (sheet pan width).
5. Wrap each log in parchment, and refrigerate until ready to bake.
6. Cut to the desired size [2 oz (50 g) to 4 oz (100 g)], roll pieces in cinnamon sugar (see ratio below), place on parchment-lined sheet pans, and bake at 350°F (177°C) in a convection oven for 10 to 12 minutes.

Cinnamon Sugar Formula

Ingredients	Baker's %	Kilogram	US decimal	Lb & Oz	
Sugar	100	0.454	1.000	1	0
Cinnamon	4–6	0.018–0.027	3–5 tbsp	3–5 tbsp	

FORMULA

GINGER MOLASSES COOKIE

Ginger and molasses demonstrate how much they belong together in these irresistibly chewy, aromatic cookies. With coffee or a fresh glass of milk, nothing could be better on an autumn afternoon.

Ingredients	Baker's %	Kilogram	US decimal	Lb & Oz		Test
Butter	44.67	0.787	1.736	1	11¾	5½ oz
Brown sugar	71.32	1.257	2.771	2	12⅜	8⅞ oz
Eggs	7.84	0.138	0.305		4⅞	1 oz
Molasses	26.65	0.470	1.035	1	⅝	3⅜ oz
Bread flour	100.00	1.762	3.885	3	14⅛	12⅜ oz
Baking soda	2.51	0.044	0.098		1½	2 tsp
Salt	1.10	0.019	0.043		⅝	1 tsp
Cloves, ground	0.63	0.011	0.024		⅜	½ tsp
Cinnamon	0.94	0.017	0.037		⅝	½ tsp
Ginger, ground	0.94	0.017	0.037		⅝	½ tsp
Nutmeg, ground	0.47	0.008	0.018		¼	¼ tsp
Allspice, ground	0.31	0.005	0.012		¼	⅛ tsp
Total	257.38	4.536	10.000	10	0	2 lb

Process

1. Cream the butter and sugar until well combined.
2. Add the eggs and then the molasses.
3. Add the dry ingredients and mix until well incorporated.
4. Scale into 2 lb 3 oz (1,000 g) pieces and roll into 17 inch (43 cm) logs (sheet pan width).
5. Wrap each log in parchment, and refrigerate until ready to bake.
6. Cut to the desired size [2 oz (50 g) to 4 oz (100 g)], place on parchment-lined sheet pans, and bake at 350°F (177°C) in a convection oven for 12 to 15 minutes.

FORMULA

GINGERSNAP

Characteristically crunchy and redolent, the diminutive gingersnap has been a favorite treat since medieval times. Some claim the combination of exotic spices and stimulating texture makes these cookies uniquely addictive. Gingersnaps are a traditional cookie for St. Lucy (Lucia) day in Sweden.

Ingredients	Baker's %	Kilogram	US decimal	Lb & Oz		Test
Butter	67.06	1.037	2.286	2	4⅝	7⅜ oz
Sugar	68.63	1.061	2.340	2	5⅜	7½ oz
Eggs	19.61	0.303	0.669		10¾	2⅛ oz
Molasses	30.59	0.473	1.043	1	⅝	3⅜ oz
Bread flour	100.00	1.546	3.409	3	6½	10⅞ oz
Baking soda	3.92	0.061	0.134		2⅛	2 tsp
Salt	0.78	0.012	0.027		⅜	½ tsp
Cloves, ground	0.39	0.006	0.013		¼	¼ tsp
Cinnamon	0.78	0.012	0.027		⅜	½ tsp
Ginger, ground	1.57	0.024	0.054		⅞	1 tsp
Total	293.33	4.536	10.000	10	0	2 lb

Process

1. Sift the dry ingredients together and reserve.
2. Cream the butter and sugar.
3. Add the eggs slowly.
4. Add the molasses and mix to incorporate.
5. Add the dry ingredients, and mix to incorporate.
6. Scale into 2 lb 3 oz (1,000 g) pieces, and roll into 17 inch (43 cm) logs (sheet pan width).
7. Wrap each log in parchment, and refrigerate until ready to bake.
8. Portion at 1.5 oz (45 g), roll into balls, and dredge in sanding sugar.
9. Place on parchment-lined sheet pans, 9 cookies per pan, and bake at 300° F (149°C) for 20 to 22 minutes.

Assorted American-Style Cookies
(top to bottom, left to right) Peanut Butter Cookie, Gingersnap, Ginger Molasses Cookie, Chocolate Chip Cookie, Snickerdoodle, Oatmeal Raisin Cookie

FORMULA

CHEWY COCONUT MACAROON

The word "macaroon" is derived from the Italian word for paste: *maccarone.* The pure almond version is usually credited to a group of Italian Carmelite nuns from the late 18th century. Legend has it that the most famous macaroons of the time, *Macaroons de Nancy* from the town of Nancy in France, went stale quickly, which is why coconut was originally added to the recipe as a natural preservative. With their crisp, toasted coconut outer layer and moist, chewy centers, macaroons are delectable treats that become even more delicious when half of the cookie is dipped in chocolate. Because they are flourless and free of egg yolks, macaroons meet the standards of Jewish dietary requirements and are a tradition during Passover.

Ingredients	Baker's %	Kilogram	US decimal	Lb & Oz		Test
Macaroon coconut	92.71	1.686	3.718	3	11 ½	11 ⅞ oz
Sugar	100.00	1.819	4.010	4	⅛	12 ⅞ oz
Egg whites	56.67	1.031	2.272	2	4 ⅜	7 ¼ oz
Total	249.38	4.536	10.000	10	0	2 lb

Process

1. Combine all the ingredients in a saucepan, place over medium heat, and stir constantly until mixture reaches 130°F (55°C).
2. Scoop the macaroons onto parchment-lined sheet pans.
3. Cookies should be approximately 2 inches (5 cm) in diameter and 1¾ inches (4.5 cm) tall.
4. Bake at 325°F (163°C) in a convection oven until golden brown, approximately 15 minutes.
5. When completely cool, dip the bottoms in tempered chocolate and allow to set up on clean parchment.

Chewy Coconut Macaroon

FORMULA

BISCOTTI

Many countries have their own variations of this centuries-old cookie, but the biscotti we are most familiar with today probably originated during the 15th century with an Italian baker who originally served them with Tuscan wines. They became so popular that each province developed its own version. Biscotti are said to have been a favorite of Christopher Columbus and other sailors of the time because of their long shelf life. In Italian, the word *biscotto* means "biscuit" or "cookie." More specifically, biscotti are named according to their original method of baking. The root words *bis* and *cotto* literally mean "twice" and "baked." Their long and thin shape and crunchy texture make biscotti the ideal dipping cookie for beverages hot and cold.

Double Chocolate Biscotti Formula

Ingredients	Baker's %	Kilogram	US decimal	Lb & Oz		Test
Butter	25.00	0.352	0.775		12⅜	2½ oz
Sugar	72.00	1.013	2.233	2	3¾	7⅛ oz
Eggs	48.00	0.675	1.488	1	7⅞	4¾ oz
Vanilla extract	4.00	0.056	0.124		2	⅜ oz
Bread flour	100.00	1.407	3.101	3	1⅝	9⅞ oz
Almond meal	20.00	0.281	0.620		9⅞	2 oz
Cocoa powder	14.50	0.204	0.450		7¼	1½ oz
Baking powder	2.50	0.035	0.078		1¼	1½ tsp
Salt	1.50	0.021	0.047		¾	½ tsp
Chocolate chunks	35.00	0.492	1.085	1	1⅜	3½ oz
Total	322.50	4.536	10.000	10	0	2 lb

Process, Double Chocolate Biscotti

1. Cream the butter and sugar until well combined.
2. Add the eggs and vanilla.
3. Combine the dry ingredients.
4. Add the dry ingredients, and mix until 50 percent incorporation. Then add the chocolate chunks and mix until combined.

5. Form the dough into 2 lb 3 oz (1,000 g) logs. Place on parchment-lined sheet pans and flatten to 1 inch (2.5 cm) height.
6. Bake at 325°F (163°C) convection for 35 to 40 minutes, until firm to touch.
7. When completely cooled, cut on a bias and return slices to the sheet pan.
8. Rebake the biscotti at 250°F (121°C) until well dried.

Orange Pecan Biscotti Formula

Ingredients	Baker's %	Kilogram	US decimal	Lb & Oz		Test
Butter	21.18	0.274	0.603		9⅝	1⅞ oz
Sugar	80.59	1.041	2.295	2	4¾	7⅜ oz
Eggs	42.94	0.555	1.223	1	3⅝	3⅞ oz
Vanilla extract	3.53	0.046	0.101		1⅝	2 tsp
Bread flour	100.00	1.292	2.848	2	13½	9⅛ oz
Cinnamon	1.76	0.023	0.050		¾	1 tsp
Baking ammonia	1.18	0.015	0.034		½	½ tsp
Salt	1.76	0.023	0.050		¾	1 tsp
Pecans, toasted and chopped	92.35	1.193	2.630	2	10⅛	8⅜ oz
Orange zest	5.88	0.076	0.167		2⅝	⅕ oz
Total	351.17	4.536	10.000	10	0	2 lb

Process, Orange Pecan Biscotti

1. In a bowl with a paddle attachment, cream together the butter and sugar.
2. Gradually add the eggs and vanilla.
3. Sift the flour with the cinnamon, baking ammonia, and salt.
4. Add the dry ingredients to the butter and mix until 50 percent incorporation.
5. Add the pecans and orange zest, and mix until distributed.
6. Form the dough into 2 lb 3 oz (1,000 g) logs. Place on parchment-lined sheet pans and flatten to 1 inch (2.5 cm) height.
7. Bake at 325°F (163°C) in a convection oven for 35 to 40 minutes, until firm to touch.
8. When completely cooled, cut on a bias, and return slices to the sheet pan.
9. Rebake the biscotti at 250°F (121°C) until well dried.

FORMULA

SABLES À LA POCHE

These tender and crumbly cookies get their name from a French phrase, which translates in English to "sand in your pocket." Rich in butter and flavored with cinnamon, sables à la poche are more likely to end up in mouths than in pockets, but their name is charming nonetheless!

Ingredients	Baker's %	Kilogram	US decimal	Lb & Oz		Test
Butter, softened	88.89	1.691	3.728	3	11⅝	11⅞ oz
Powdered sugar	33.33	0.634	1.398	1	6⅜	4½ oz
Egg whites	13.33	0.254	0.559		9	1¾ oz
Cinnamon	1.11	0.021	0.047		¾	1 tsp
Bread flour	100.00	1.902	4.194	4	3⅛	13⅜ oz
Baking powder	0.89	0.017	0.037		⅝	⅔ tsp
Salt	0.89	0.017	0.037		⅝	1 tsp
Total	238.44	4.536	10.000	10	0	2 lb

Process

1. Cream the butter with the paddle and then add the powdered sugar. Add the egg whites slowly and mix until incorporated.
2. Add the dry sifted ingredients; do not overmix.
3. Pipe into shell shapes using a large star tip and bake at 325°F (163°C) in a convection oven for 15 minutes.

FORMULA

DIAMONDS

Sparkling with a crisp sugar coating, diamond cookies live up to their name in both appearance and spirit, offering a luxurious treat to those who appreciate cookies as little treasures. Diamond cookies are very tender and also versatile, amenable to infinite flavor variations. Because the dough freezes well, bakers treasure diamonds for their ease of production.

Chocolate Diamonds Formula

Ingredients	Baker's %	Kilogram	US decimal	Lb & Oz		Test
Butter	100.00	1.700	3.749	3	12	12 oz
Powdered sugar	40.00	0.680	1.500	1	8	4¾ oz
Eggs	12.50	0.213	0.469		7½	1½ oz
Bread flour	100.00	1.700	3.749	3	12	12 oz
Cocoa powder	12.50	0.213	0.469		7½	1½ oz
Salt	1.75	0.030	0.066		1	1 tsp
Total	266.75	4.536	10.000	10	0	2 lb

Vanilla Diamonds Formula

Ingredients	Baker's %	Kilogram	US decimal	Lb & Oz		Test
Butter	88.80	1.728	3.810	3	13	12¼ oz
Powdered sugar	35.50	0.691	1.523	1	8⅜	4⅞ oz
Vanilla bean	Each	4	4		4	1 each
Egg yolks	8.80	0.171	0.378		6	1¼ oz
Bread flour	100.00	1.946	4.290	4	5	13¾ oz
Total	233.10	4.536	10.000	10	0	2 lb

Process, Diamonds (general)

1. Mix the soft butter, powdered sugar, scraped vanilla pod (vanilla only) and then add the egg yolks (whole eggs for chocolate) and mix until combined.
2. Add the sifted flour (and the cocoa powder and salt for chocolate) and mix to incorporation.
3. Portion into 7 oz (200 g) logs, 17 inch (43 cm) long (sheet pan width).
4. Refrigerate for a minimum of 4 hours.
5. Brush each log lightly with egg wash and roll in granulated sugar. Cut into slices, 0.4 inch (1 cm) thick, and place on a parchment-lined sheet pan.
6. Bake at 335°F (168°C) in a convection oven for 10 to 12 minutes.

FORMULA

CORNMEAL CURRANT COOKIE

This deceptively simple cookie is a balance of sweet and savory elements. Cornmeal lends a sturdy texture, just between dry and tender, while rosemary and currants tantalize the palate and create a wonderful aroma during baking.

Ingredients	Baker's %	Kilogram	US decimal	Lb & Oz		Test
Bread flour	100.00	1.055	2.326	2	5 ¼	7 ½ oz
Yellow cornmeal	76.00	0.802	1.767	1	12 ¼	5 ⅝ oz
Sugar	66.67	0.703	1.550	1	8 ¾	5 oz
Currants	66.67	0.703	1.550	1	8 ¾	5 oz
Rosemary, fresh	2.00	0.021	0.047		¾	1 tsp
Butter	95.33	1.006	2.217	2	3 ½	7 ⅛ oz
Vanilla extract	1.33	0.014	0.031		½	½ tsp
Egg yolks	22.00	0.232	0.512		8 ⅛	1 ⅝ oz
Total	430.00	4.536	10.000	10	0	2 lb

Process

1. Chop the rosemary very fine.
2. Combine the flour, cornmeal, sugar, currants, rosemary, and butter in the bowl of a mixer fitted with the paddle.
3. Blend until sandy, and then add the egg yolks and vanilla extract. Mix just until the dough comes together.
4. Scale into 2 lb 3 oz (1,000 g) pieces and roll into 17 inch (43 cm) logs (sheet pan width).
5. Wrap each log in parchment, and refrigerate until ready to bake.
6. Portion into 1.5 oz (45 g) slices, place on parchment-lined sheet pans, and bake at 325°F (163°C) in a convection oven for about 14 minutes.

FORMULA

CHOCOLATE INDULGENCE COOKIE

In the wonderful land where brownie meets cookie, the chocolate indulgence cookie was born. Made with couverture-grade chocolate, this intensely rich cookie is soft and chewy, leaving the chocolate lover completely satisfied.

Ingredients	Baker's %	Kilogram	US decimal	Lb & Oz		Test
Semi-sweet chocolate	735.29	1.704	3.758	3	12⅛	12 oz
Butter	100.00	0.232	0.511		8⅛	1⅝ oz
Eggs	529.41	1.227	2.706	2	11¼	8⅝ oz
Sugar	467.65	1.084	2.390	2	6¼	7⅝ oz
Vanilla extract	7.35	0.017	0.038		⅝	1 tsp
Cake flour, sifted	100.00	0.232	0.511		8⅛	1⅝ oz
Baking powder	12.65	0.029	0.065		1	1 tsp
Salt	4.41	0.010	0.023		⅜	½ tsp
Total	1956.76	4.536	10.000	10	0	2 lb

Process

1. Sift together the cake flour, baking powder, and salt; reserve.
2. Melt together the chocolate and butter.
3. Whip the sugar, eggs, and vanilla to the ribbon stage. When the chocolate reaches 90°F (33°C) add it to the whipped eggs.
4. Add the dry ingredients using the paddle attachment of the mixer or by hand with a spatula.
5. Using an ice cream scoop, portion onto parchment-lined sheet pans, and leave at room temperature for 30 minutes.
6. Bake at 325°F (163°C) in a convection oven for 12 to 15 minutes. (Insert a cake tester into a cookie. Remove from the oven when the tester shows some crumb structure and a slightly underbaked center.)

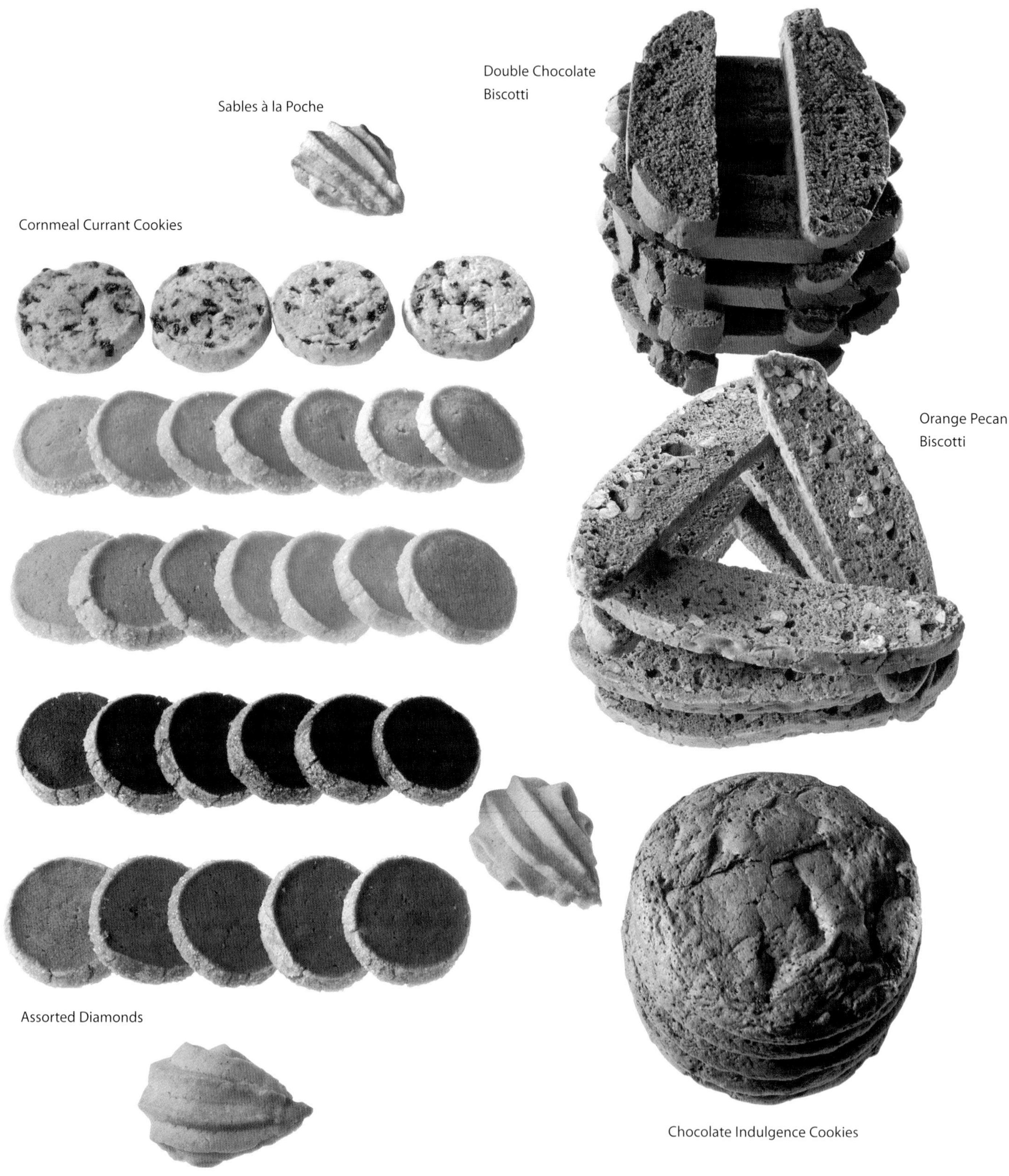

Assorted European-Style Cookies

FORMULA

PARISIAN MACARONS

Macaron confections can be traced back to the 17th century, but we had to wait until the early 20th century for Parisian pastry makers to begin creating the chic versions we delight in today. French-style macarons typically involve two meringue-like cookies, with a delicate exterior and a soft, spongy interior, sandwiched together with ganache or other cream. Modern-day macarons excite the imagination with vivid colors and unexpected flavor combinations, while their sublime texture triggers culinary euphoria.

Plain Parisian Macarons Formula

Ingredients	Baker's %	Kilogram	US decimal	Lb & Oz		Test
Egg whites	100.00	0.981	2.162	2	2⅝	6⅞ oz
Granulated sugar	36.50	0.358	0.789		12⅝	2½ oz
Egg white powder	9.40	0.092	0.203		3¼	1½ tbsp
Almond flour	117.60	1.153	2.543	2	8⅝	8⅛ oz
Powdered sugar	199.00	1.952	4.303	4	4⅞	13¾ oz
Color, as desired	~	~	~	~		~
Total	462.50	4.536	10.000	10	0	2 lb

Process, Plain Parisian Macarons

1. Sift the almond flour and powered sugar together.
2. Whip the egg whites, sugar, and egg white powder to stiff peaks.
3. Fold the almond sugar mixture into the meringue, color as desired, and pipe 1½ inch (4 cm) circles onto silpat-lined perforated sheet pans.
4. Let a skin form (time will vary according to climate) and bake at 310°F (154°C) in a convection oven with the vent open for 9 to 11 minutes.

Chocolate Parisian Macarons Formula

Ingredients	Baker's %	Kilogram	US decimal	Lb & Oz		Test
Egg whites	100.00	0.909	2.005	2	⅛	6⅜ oz
Granulated sugar	32.90	0.299	0.660		10½	2⅛ oz
Egg white powder	5.00	0.045	0.100		1⅝	2 tsp
Almond meal	126.60	1.151	2.538	2	8⅝	8⅛ oz
Powdered sugar	216.60	1.970	4.342	4	5½	13⅞ oz
Dark cocoa powder	17.70	0.161	0.355		5⅝	1⅛ oz
Total	498.80	4.536	10.000	10	0	2 lb

Process, Chocolate Parisian Macarons

1. Sift the almond meal, powdered sugar, and cocoa power together.
2. Whip the egg whites, egg white powder, and sugar to stiff peaks.
3. Fold the almond sugar mixture into the meringue and pipe 1.5 inch (4 cm) circles onto silpat-lined perforated sheet pans.
4. Let a skin form (time will vary according to climate), and bake at 310°F (154°C) in a convection oven with the vent open for 9 to 11 minutes.

Assorted Parisian Macarons

(opposite, top to bottom) Lemon, Chocolate, Raspberry, Passion Fruit, Pistachio, Vanilla Bean

FORMULA

ROCHER MERINGUE

These superb little cookies get their name from their resemblance to a rock, or *rocher* in French, even though they are undeniably soft and chewy. Rochers are wonderfully diverse, allowing for an array of variations, including coffee, chocolate, and raspberry. Typically, a large batch of the meringue is prepared, and then varying flavors are folded into separate portions. Before baking, the meringue can be portioned onto a baking tray, or dropped from a spoon for a more rustic appearance.

Ingredients	Baker's %	Kilogram	US decimal	Lb & Oz		Test
Sugar #1	100.00	1.184	2.611	2	10	8 oz
Water	33.00	0.391	0.862		14	3 oz
Egg whites	100.00	1.184	2.611	2	10	8 oz
Sugar #2	10.00	0.118	0.261		4	1 oz
Powdered sugar	60.00	0.711	1.567	1	9	5 oz
Sliced almonds, toasted	80.00	0.947	2.089	2	1	7 oz
Total	383.00	4.536	10.000	10	0	2 lb

Process

1. Mix together the powdered sugar and almonds.
2. Combine sugar #1 and the water in a saucepan to prepare an Italian meringue.
3. Once the sugar syrup is at 240°F (116°C), begin to whip the egg whites and sugar #2 to stiff peaks.
4. When the sugar syrup reaches 248°F (120°C), pour the syrup over the whipping whites to make an Italian meringue. Continue to whip until cooled to slightly warm temperature.
5. Fold the powdered sugar covered almonds into the meringue gently and divide the meringue to be flavored, as desired. Some flavoring suggestions include cocoa nibs, raspberry (jam), coffee (Trablit), cocoa powder, and chocolate chips.
6. Pipe or drop, using a large spoon, onto a parchment-lined sheet pan. Bake at 350°F (177°C) in a convection oven with the vent open for 25 minutes, or until dry to the touch.

Assorted Rocher Meringue

Almond, Raspberry, and Cocoa Nib

FORMULA

BROWNIES

In 1897, the Sears, Roebuck catalog published the first known recipe for brownies, and it quickly became a popular American dessert. The origin of the chocolate brownie is unknown; however, it was probably created by accident, the result of a forgetful cook neglecting to add baking powder to chocolate cake batter. Brownies have evolved over the years to include recipes for the both cake-like and chewy variations, sometimes using nuts or chocolate chips. For those who love chocolate, there are few scents in the world as seductive as brownies baking in the oven.

Ingredients	Baker's %	Kilogram	US decimal	Lb & Oz		Test
Bittersweet chocolate	100.00	1.000	2.205	2	3¼	9⅛ oz
Butter	74.00	0.740	1.631	1	10⅛	6¾ oz
Eggs	74.00	0.740	1.631	1	10⅛	6¾ oz
Sugar	172.80	1.728	3.809	3	13	15¾ oz
Salt	0.80	0.008	0.018		¼	½ tsp
Vanilla extract	3.40	0.034	0.075		1¼	2 tsp
Pastry flour	100.00	1.000	2.205	2	3¼	9⅛ oz
Total	525.00	5.250	11.574	11	9⅛	3 lb

Yield: 1 sheet pan
Test: ¼ sheet pan

Process

1. Sift the flour and reserve.
2. Place the chopped chocolate and butter in a bowl and melt over a double boiler or in the microwave.
3. Let the mixture cool to between 80°F (27°C) and 90°F (32°C).
4. Warm the eggs and sugar to 90°F (32°C) and whip with the salt and vanilla until the ribbon stage.
5. Fold in the melted chocolate and butter until smooth.
6. Fold the flour into the whipped mixture.
7. Spread the batter onto a parchment-lined sheet pan.
8. Bake at 325°F (163°C) in a convection oven for 30 to 35 minutes.
9. When cool, remove from the pan, and cut into bars of desired size.

FORMULA

LEMON BARS

With its crisp crust and supple filling, the lemon bar is an essential addition to any baker's repertoire. The combination of textures, along with a colorful presentation and tangy citrus bite, make this classic dessert a perennial favorite, particularly in the southern United States.

Ingredients	Baker's %	Kilogram	US decimal	Lb & Oz		Test
Sugar	722.58	2.448	5.398	5	6⅜	1 lb 3⅜ oz
Eggs	451.61	1.530	3.374	3	6	12⅛ oz
Lemon juice	216.13	0.732	1.615	1	9⅞	5¾ oz
Bread flour	100.00	0.339	0.747		12	2⅝ oz
Total	1490.32	5.050	11.133	11	2⅛	2 lb 8 oz

Yield: 1 sheet pan
Test: ¼ sheet pan

Mise en Place

Pâte sucrée, 3.3 lb (1.500 kg) per sheet pan

Process

1. Line a sheet pan with pâte sucrée and par bake. Cool and reserve. With pâte sucrée, patch any cracks or low points on the sides where the liquid filling could leak out.
2. Combine the sugar and eggs by hand; blend well.
3. Add the lemon juice and mix.
4. Let sit for about 20 minutes; skim off the white foamy layer.
5. Blend in the flour while mixing to avoid lumps.
6. Pour the batter into the prebaked short dough crust.
7. Bake at 300°F (149°C) in a convection oven for 30 minutes or until set.
8. When cool, dust with powdered sugar and cut into bars of desired size.

FORMULA

PUMPKIN PAVÉ

As the weather cools and the holidays approach, the baker's selection of fresh ingredients changes. Most notably fall brings a new crop of crisp apples and other specialty vegetables such as pumpkin and squash. These classic fruits and vegetables are the foundation of many traditional American holiday treats. *Pavé*, meaning "brick" or "slab," refers to the shape of this pastry. Fresh or canned pumpkin may be used, and an interesting variation may be made with fresh butternut squash. The nut meal in the streusel may be substituted; however, if nut pieces are used, the quantity of butter may need to be reduced by 15 to 20 percent.

Hazelnut Streusel Formula

Ingredients	Baker's %	Kilogram	US decimal	Lb & Oz	Test
Pastry flour	100.00	0.739	1.630	1 10⅛	7 oz
Brown sugar	62.00	0.458	1.011	1 ⅛	4¼ oz
Hazelnut meal	50.00	0.370	0.815	13	3½ oz
Butter	76.00	0.562	1.239	1 3⅞	5¼ oz
Total	288.00	2.130	4.695	4 11⅛	1 lb 4 oz

Yield: 1 sheet pan
Test: ¼ sheet pan

Process, Hazelnut Streusel

1. Place all the ingredients in the bowl of a mixer fitted with the paddle attachment, and mix until a streusel is formed.
2. Per formula, place half of the streusel onto a sprayed sheet pan with a pan collar.
3. Press the streusel down to form the bottom crust.
4. Bake at 350°F (177°C) in a convection oven for about 12 minutes, or until the crust starts to brown.
5. Reserve until cool.

Pumpkin Filling Formula

Ingredients	Baker's %	Kilogram	US decimal	Lb & Oz		Test
Cream cheese	100.00	1.463	3.225	3	3 5/8	10 7/8 oz
Vanilla bean	Each	2	2		2	½ each
Allspice	0.96	0.014	0.031		½	½ tsp
Cinnamon	1.92	0.028	0.062		1	1 ½ tsp
Sugar	74.65	1.092	2.407	2	6 ½	8 1/8 oz
Maple syrup	6.85	0.100	0.221		3 ½	¾ oz
Pumpkin puree	54.79	0.801	1.767	1	12 ¼	6 oz
Eggs	54.79	0.801	1.767	1	12 ¼	6 oz
Total	293.96	4.300	9.479	9	7 5/8	2 lb

Process, Pumpkin Filling

1. Scale all the ingredients and have all the ingredients at room temperature.
2. Cream the cream cheese, vanilla bean, allspice, and cinnamon together in a mixer fitted with the paddle attachment. Scrape down the bowl.
3. Once smooth, add the sugar slowly and mix until well incorporated. Scrape down the bowl.
4. Next, add the maple syrup and mix until incorporated.
5. Add the pumpkin puree and mix until smooth. Scrape down the bowl.
6. Add the eggs slowly and mix just to incorporation. Scrape down the bowl again and mix briefly.

Assembly

1. Pour the pumpkin filling over the prebaked hazelnut crust.
2. Sprinkle the remaining hazelnut streusel over the filling.
3. Bake at 300°F (149°C) in a convection oven for about 35 minutes or until the filling is set.
4. Cool overnight and portion the following day.

Assorted Bar-Style Cookies

FORMULA

PALMIERS

These buttery delicacies are made from puff pastry. Sugar is laminated into the dough for the last two folds and then coated on the outside, which caramelizes during baking, adding an enticingly crispy texture.

Mise en Place

Puff pastry with the last two single folds completed with sugar, additional sugar.

Process

1. Sheet the dough to 1/12 inch (2 mm) and unroll onto a table dusted with granulated sugar.
2. Sprinkle the surface of the puff pastry with granulated sugar.
3. Make a long and narrow band and double fold the two extremities of the band toward the center until the two bands meet in the center.
4. Fold each of the two pieces on top of each other.
5. Using a chef knife, cut ⅓ inch (1 cm) thick slices of the sugared and folded puff pastry.
6. Put the cut palmiers open faced on a sheet pan and bake at 350°F (177°C) for 20 minutes or until golden brown.

FORMULA

SACRISTANS

These corkscrew shaped cookies are formed from twisted puff pastry coated in granulated sugar, with the optional addition of sliced almonds. Said to be named after the official in charge of the sacred vessels in the Roman Catholic Church, sacristans are certainly delicious enough to inspire a religious following.

Mise en Place

Puff pastry with six single folds sheeted to 1/12 inch (2.5 mm), granulated sugar.

Process

1. Coat both sides of the puff pastry with sugar. Unroll the dough onto a table dusted with granulated sugar. Then, sprinkle the surface with granulated sugar.
2. Cut into bands 6 inches (15 cm) wide, and cut those into ½ inch (1 cm) strips.

3. Twist each strip twice before placing it on a parchment-lined sheet pan that has been lightly sprayed with water. The water helps to prevent the dough from shrinking. Push down on the ends to ensure proper shaping during the bake.
4. Refrigerate for a minimum of 30 minutes before baking.
5. Bake at 350°F (177°C) for 20 minutes until golden brown.

CHAPTER SUMMARY

Cookies are one of the simplest forms of pastry and are a basic repertoire of many kitchens and bakeshops. Cookies can be prepared as individual pastries or as an element for intricate plated desserts. Techniques required for assembling cookies includes many basic skills that are essential for every baker and pastry chef. By knowing the basic foundations of cookie making, the aspiring baker and pastry chef can produce consistent results, troubleshoot formulas and processes, and create new formulas.

KEY TERMS

- ❖ Cookie spread
- ❖ Creaming method
- ❖ Cut-out cookie
- ❖ Dropped cookie
- ❖ Humectants
- ❖ Hygroscopic
- ❖ Icebox cookie
- ❖ Inclusions
- ❖ Medium peak
- ❖ Molded cookie
- ❖ One-stage method
- ❖ Piped cookie
- ❖ Ribbon stage
- ❖ Run out
- ❖ Sanding method
- ❖ Sheet cookie
- ❖ Sliced cookie
- ❖ Soft peak
- ❖ Sponge method
- ❖ Stencil cookie
- ❖ Stiff peak
- ❖ Tenderizing ingredients
- ❖ Toughening ingredients

REVIEW QUESTIONS

1. **What are tenderizing and toughening ingredients and what role do they play in the composition of a cookie?**
2. **What effect will under- or over-creaming have on the final product? Why?**
3. **What factors contribute to crispness of cookies?**
4. **List all factors that have an influence on spread of cookies.**
5. **What are the signs that cookies are done baking?**

chapter
11

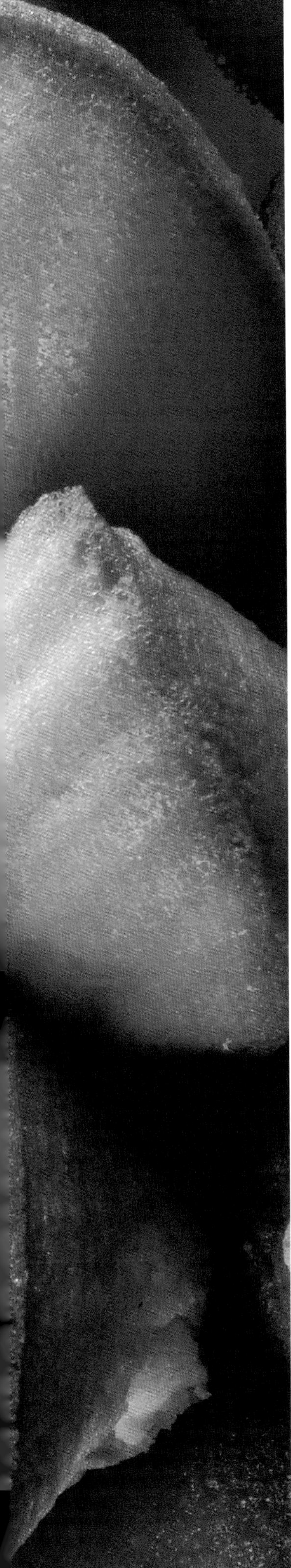

QUICK BREADS

OBJECTIVES

After reading this chapter, you should be able to

- describe the three mixing methods of quick breads.
- describe the role gluten plays in the physical structure of the final baked good.
- explain the makeup and baking processes of different quick breads.
- discuss characteristics of different chemical leavening agents and their functional properties.
- make a selection of quick breads using the techniques presented in this chapter.

DESCRIPTION AND SCOPE OF QUICK BREADS

The category of **quick breads** covers a wide range of nonyeasted products such as muffins, scones, biscuits, and coffee cakes. Leavened by chemical agents and steam, quick breads are staple bakery products that are quick and inexpensive to produce on a large scale. The technical skills involved in making quick breads are limited to several key concepts that include ingredient functions, mixing methods, and baking processes. Once these are understood, it is possible to make a wide array of products with relatively few ingredients and little expertise. Many commercial quick bread mixes are available in the market; the use of the mixes will yield more consistent products in shorter production time. It is very convenient to use the mixes in a larger production environment, although in a smaller production setting, the quality is better and the cost is lower when they are made from scratch.

CONTROLLING THE DEVELOPMENT OF GLUTEN

The most desirable physical characteristic of quick breads is tenderness. Even though the scope of the category encompasses diverse products such as scones, muffins, and fruit breads, each product should be of a tender texture in order to ensure a pleasurable eating experience. This is controlled through the mixing process.

The development of gluten plays an important role in controlling the texture of quick breads. The sugar and fat content of quick breads helps prevent excessive gluten development; however, formulas that contain higher levels of liquid may be prone to developing at a faster rate. In addition, overmixing muffin or coffee cake batter will cause a toughening of the crumb and may create holes in the pastry that run diagonally, a phenomenon referred to as **tunneling**. Products like biscuits and scones will have a dense and tough texture if overmixed. Proper mixing methods and precautions for each of the major mixing categories are covered in this chapter. (See Figure 11-1.)

THE ROLE OF CHEMICAL LEAVENING AGENTS

Chemical leavening agents play a crucial role in the development of quick breads. There are several kinds of chemical leavening agents, but all have the same functional purposes in the making of quick breads. First, every chemical leavening agent creates gas by reacting with water, heat, or leavening acid. The gas aerates and leavens the batter before and/or during baking. The aeration of batter results in the tenderizing of the product, providing a pleasurable mouthfeel. Second, baking soda has a high pH when it is dissolved, and it is used to balance out the total pH of the quick bread batter. Exact measurement of leavening agents is essential because a slight change can result in imperfect final products.

BAKING SODA AND BAKING POWDER

The most common leavening agents used for quick breads are **baking soda** and **baking powder**. Baking soda is the chemical sodium bicarbonate, and baking powder is a mixture of baking soda, **leavening acids**, and cornstarch. Leavening acids are added to react with sodium bicarbonate and produce carbon dioxides during mixing and/or baking. The starch prevents baking powder from caking, absorbs ambient moisture, and most importantly prevents the chemicals from prematurely reacting.

During mixing, a small amount of carbon dioxide is created by fast-acting leavening acids reacting with dissolved sodium bicarbonate.

Figure 11-1
Properly Mixed (left) and Undermixed (right) Muffins Showing Effect on Volume, Peak, and Crumb

Examples of the leavening acids that react at this point at low temperatures are cream of tartar (potassium hydrogen tartrate) and monocalcium phosphate.

High-temperature reacting leavening acids are usually aluminum salts, such as sodium aluminum sulfate (SAS) and sodium aluminum phosphate, and they create larger amounts of gas during baking, enabling the quick bread to rise in the oven. The alums do not react with bicarbonate of soda at a low temperature, but they rapidly react under the heat in the oven. The residue of this reaction is aluminum hydroxide, which is insoluble and undesirable in food, and it tends to leave an unpleasant flavor in final products. In the United States, the use of SAS in baking powder is permitted because the actual intake is only a trace amount. Sodium acid pyrophosphate, which also is a high-temperature reacting acid but does not contain alum, is commonly used in specialty baking powder for people who have concerns about aluminum intake.

Baking powder that contains both low- and high-temperature reacting leavening acids is called **double-acting baking powder**, and one with only low-temperature reacting acid salt is called **single-acting baking powder**. Single-acting baking powder is usually used in larger food processing operations. Both baking soda and baking powder need to be kept in a container with a tight lid and stored in a cool and dry place. The shelf life for both of these products is about one year after the date of manufacture.

HISTORY OF CHEMICAL LEAVENING AGENTS

Carbonates of soda and **potash** are known as the earliest leavening agents used in baking. Carbonates of soda were obtained from the ashes of sea plants, as well as from plants growing near the seashore. Potash comes from the ashes of land plants and was originally referred to as potashes. From potashes a purer form of leavening known as pearl ashes was made (Bennion & Bamford, 1973, p. 76). Both carbonate of soda and potash are alkalis, and when used with an acid ingredient, such as sour milk or buttermilk, they create a reaction resulting in the creation of carbon dioxide. Although lactic acid exists in those dairy products, the amount of acid is not sufficient to make the leavening agents fully react. However, it is truly believable that the acid reduced the alkaline taste and discoloration. At this time, domestic baking was widely practiced, but as commercial baking became more popular, it was necessary to discover more convenient and stable substances to aid in chemical aeration.

Until the 1830s, potash and **alum** were used in bakeries as leavening agents. Alum is not an acid, but it reacts with carbonate of soda producing carbon dioxide when exposed to heat in the oven. **Baking ammonia** appeared on the market at this point, and it was used by home bakers as well as in commercial bakeries. Ready-mixed baking powder made with tartaric acid and cream of tartar, mixed with bicarbonate of soda was introduced to the market at the end of 1840s. Many leavening acids were examined to be used in baking powder from 1860s to 1890s. Calcium acid phosphate and SAS, which are commercially used in production of baking powder today, were found during this period, and the first double-acting baking powder was manufactured.

Sodium acid pyrophosphate was the next leavening acid introduced to the United States in 1911. This material is completely nonhygroscopic in cold water, but it dissolves and reacts readily in a hot environment; this is an adequate "slow-acting" baking acid. In the current baking industry, the main leavening acid used in baking powder is cream of tartar, mono-calcium phosphate, SAS, sodium aluminum phosphate, and sodium acid pyrophosphate.

CHEMICAL LEAVENING AGENTS AND PH BALANCE

A proper balance of baking soda, as well as other leavening systems like baking powder, is essential for the final quality of the texture and flavor of baked goods. Baking soda balances the pH in quick breads when other chemical leavening systems are used. Furthermore, controlling pH is crucial in the process of quick bread making because lower pH relaxes gluten and a higher pH tightens gluten. Baking soda, which has pH around 8.0, is always used with cream of tartar or other acidic ingredients, such as honey, molasses, or cocoa powder. Baking soda also helps to balance out the flavor of the final product by making the acidity less pronounced. A small amount of cream of tartar in biscuits lowers the pH and weakens the gluten, yielding a more tender product. Cream of tartar also helps to yield a whiter crumb. When too much baking powder or baking soda is used, it results in a slightly coarse texture, metallic flavor, and yellow or greenish off-coloration.

CHOOSING CHEMICAL LEAVENING AGENTS IN QUICK BREAD FORMULAS

The proper leavening system for use in a specific formula depends on the ingredients and processes involved in the preparation. While chemical leavening agents are generally added as a ratio of the flour, the acidity of the batter must be taken into account. The more fat and sugar in a formula, the less baking powder and milk will be required; conversely, the less fat and sugar in a formula, the more baking powder and milk will be required. The fat has a tenderizing effect on gluten and reduces resistance to gas pressure. Batter is leavened slightly during the mixing process as air is incorporated; however, additional leavening agents are often used as well. (See Figures 11-2a and 11-2b.)

In large commercial bakeries, specially blended baking powders containing different leavening acids may be used to more closely control the release of carbon dioxide into the dough system. A combination of mono-calcium phosphate and sodium acid pyrophosphate, both leavening acids (the prior is fast acting and latter is slow acting), are commonly used for commercial baking powder.

MIXING METHODS FOR QUICK BREAD

Because of the range of products in the quick bread category, there are three mixing methods to consider: biscuit, creaming, and blending. The particular mixing method used will depend on the desired outcome for the final product.

BISCUIT METHOD FOR BISCUITS AND SCONES

What is known as biscuit in the United States was developed many years ago and gained its popularity mostly in the southern states. The neutral flavor of biscuits is often used as a flavor carrier for the food that is served with them. They may be prepared as either sweet or savory and

Figure 11-2a
Side-by-Side Comparison of Effects of Chemical Leavening on Quick Breads (none, 100 percent, 200 percent)

Figure 11-2b
Cross-Sectional Side-by-Side Comparison of Effects of Chemical Leavening on Quick Breads (none, 100 percent, 200 percent)

are commonly served for breakfast, lunch, or dinner. Scones are a much richer version of biscuits, often containing fruit, nuts, or dried fruits and sweeteners such as honey, molasses, or granulated sugar. Savory versions of scones can also be prepared by using various cheeses, spices, and herbs.

Ingredient Functions

The **biscuit method** is achieved by the cutting fat into the flour and other dry ingredients and then adding the liquid ingredients and blending to incorporation. The typical end result is to have small to medium-sized pieces of fat throughout the dough in order to create a flaky structure. The formulation for flaky biscuits and scones is similar, with common ingredients that include flour, solid fat, chemical leavening agents, milk, buttermilk or cream, sugar, and other ingredients.

A range of flour may be found in formulas for biscuits as scones. Bread flour, pastry flour, and sometimes cake flour are used for this method to give enough strength and to create flaky layers. The stronger the flour is, the more the height of the biscuit will increase and the more the width will decrease. If the flour is too weak, the shape will not remain uniform because the protein will be too minimal to hold the shape. Weaker flour also creates a lighter color on crust, but this phenomenon can be compensated by adding dry milk solids, approximately 5 percent of flour weight.

The most common sugars used in quick bread are granulated sugar and inverted sugar such as honey. Only a small amount of sugar is used in biscuit formulas; savory biscuits usually contain 2 to 5 percent sugar, and in sweet biscuits, which are often used for strawberry shortcake in the United States, up to 15 percent sugar can be added. In scone formulations, sugar is almost always present. When inverted sugar is used, it increases crust color and also keeps the product moist for a longer time. Honey is often used in scone formulas to yield a longer shelf life and add unique flavor.

Mixing Method

The key to producing excellent flaky biscuits and scones is the mixing process. Fats must be blended into the flour to the proper size, liquids must be added in the proper amount, and mixing should be minimal. To ensure flakiness in the final product, the fat in biscuits and scones must be cold and remain in visible, pea-sized pieces.

Biscuit dough is mixed lightly after the incorporation of liquid into the flour and fat phase. Next, the dough is sheeted to the desired thickness and cut out. It is essential to rest the portioned dough at least 20 minutes before baking to allow the gluten to relax, in order to obtain an even oven spring during baking. Egg wash should be applied to the top surface of the product and not to the sides in order to yield an even rise. Biscuits and scones freeze well after being portioned and covered in plastic. Before baking, they should be thawed completely to achieve full leavening and to prevent an underbaked center of the dough.

If scone and biscuit dough is overmixed, the fat will eventually coat all the starch granules. This creates a product that is too tender and that will not have enough structure. Another result of overmixing is shrinkage; as gluten is strengthened, the final product has less volume. However, undermixing can cause problems as well. Lumps of flour or large pieces of fat will lead to inconsistent final products. All dry ingredients of the dough should be moistened sufficiently. If they are overhydrated, the result will be a soft and weak dough that can barely hold together when lifted, which will result in poor volume and texture. Some degree of gluten development occurs during the sheeting or rolling out of the dough for cutting, but it will not cause significant damage unless it is overly done. Minimizing the waste of scrap dough is important because if it is reworked, it gains strength and toughens.

If scones with frozen fruit are being made, it is easiest to mix plain scone dough and add the frozen fruit to the dough during makeup. To do this, the dough is first divided and then the dough is sandwiched with the frozen fruit between two layers and additional fruit is pressed into the top of the scones. This is done to avoid crushing the fruits and to prevent the bleeding of color during mixing.

Biscuit Method Process

- Scale all the ingredients.
- Sift the chemical leavening agents and combine with the dry ingredients.
- Combine the liquid ingredients.
- Cut the fat into the flour by hand or with the paddle attachment on a mixer until the fat is the size of peas. (See Biscuit Method Figure 11-3, Step 1.)
- Add the liquid to the dry ingredients and mix just until combined. (See Biscuit Method Figure 11-3, Steps 2–3.)

FIGURE 11-3 BISCUIT METHOD

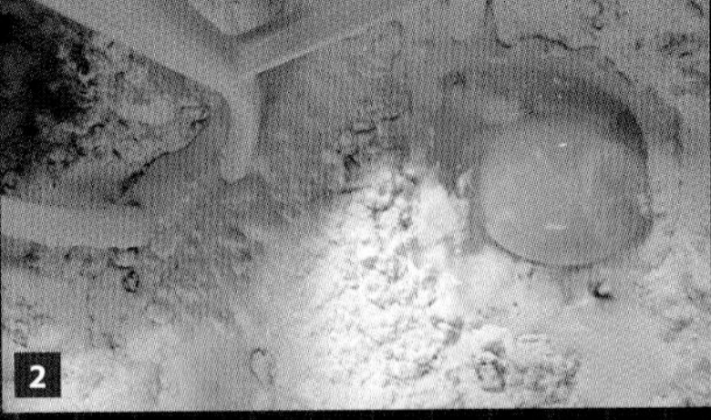

1 The cold fat is blended into the dry ingredients until the proper size.

2 The liquid ingredients are added to the dry ingredients.

3 The dough is mixed just to incorporation.

CREAMING METHOD FOR BISCUITS AND SCONES

Some biscuits and scones are mixed by the **creaming method** in which the fat and sugar are incorporated until they form a smooth paste. This makes a product with finer crumb and less flaky, cake-like texture when compared to ones produced by the biscuit method.

Ingredient Functions

The ingredients and ingredient functions in biscuits and scones made using the creaming method are very similar to the ones made using the biscuit method. The main difference is that formulas that use the creaming method tend to contain less solid fat. When a very tender texture is desired, heavy cream is added with eggs after the sugar and fat are incorporated instead of using a liquid with less fat, such as milk or water.

Mixing Method

In the creaming method for biscuits and scones, the fat and sugar are incorporated, and the fat spreads evenly throughout the dough in a continuous phase, limiting the chance for pockets of fat to provide a flaky product. Next, the liquid ingredients are added slowly and are mixed into the sugar and fat phase. The sifted flour and chemical leavening are added next, and mixing occurs until the ingredients are well incorporated. When compared to the biscuit method, it is easier to yield an even mix of ingredients when using this method. Compared to the biscuit method, the final effect on the dough is very different; the crumb is finer and more tender than flaky. If dried fruits and/or nuts are added, they should be added when the dry ingredients are 50 percent incorporated to prevent overmixing.

When using the creaming method for biscuits and scones, the fat and sugar should be creamed only to the point of incorporation because overmixing can add additional air into the batter and create a more cake-like texture, which is not desirable in biscuits and scones.

Makeup and baking are similar for the creaming and biscuit methods. For small retail production, biscuit and scone dough made by the creaming method is often deposited using an ice cream scoop, whereas larger operations may use an automated depositor. Additionally, the dough can be rolled out and cut into desired shapes with a knife or cutter. It is recommended to rest portioned dough for at least 15 minutes before baking for an even oven spring.

Creaming Method Process for Biscuits and Scones

- Scale all the ingredients. Prepare a mixing bowl with the paddle attachment. Sift the chemical leavening agents and combine with the flour and salt.

- Combine the fat and sugar and cream only until smooth, not light and fluffy.
- Add the eggs slowly, scraping down the bowl after they are all added.
- Add any liquid and mix in thoroughly.
- Add the dry ingredients and mix just until combined.

BLENDING METHOD FOR MUFFINS, LOAF CAKES, AND SCONES

Probably the most simple and familiar technique to the new home baker is the **blending method**, also known as the muffin method. In this method, the dry ingredients are simply combined with the liquid ingredients. It is a fast and easy mixing method that can be used for many products, including muffins, banana bread, and cream scones. The same mixing method is also used for pancakes, crepes, and waffles; however, the consistency of those batters is more fluid. These formulas are sometimes adapted by adding in egg foam to further lighten the texture, such as in the case of certain waffle batter. Larger-sized loaves tend to have a more dense and moist interior compared to small-portioned ones because larger mass keeps moisture longer during baking.

Ingredient Functions

The flour used for the blending method can range from pastry flour to low-protein bread flour. If a formula calls for all-purpose flour, low-protein bread flour can often be substituted without issue. The fat used in the blending method is in a liquid phase, which results in a dense and moist crumb. Butter is often used because it provides a rich, creamy flavor; however, margarine could be substituted as long as it is unsalted. Liquid oils such as canola or safflower are also common ingredients. It is important to use oil with a neutral flavor. Typically white or brown sugar is used. Not only does sugar help to prevent the development of the gluten, but it also helps to retain moisture and delay the staling process. Chemical leavening agents often are comprised of baking powder or a combination of baking powder and soda. The amount will vary depending on the ratio of the other ingredients in the formula. Inclusions can range from fruit (fresh, dried, canned, or frozen) to nuts and spices.

Mixing Method

Because the liquid-to-flour ratio is high in these types of formulas, it is important to keep the mixing to a minimum to prevent excessive development of the gluten: the wet and dry ingredients are mixed to incorporation. Sugar is treated as a wet ingredient in blending method formulas and should be combined with the wet ingredients. If there are any additional ingredients, such as fruit and/or nuts, they should be added when the batter is mixed halfway to prevent overmixing. To prevent the breakdown of frozen fruit in the mixing and makeup process, they must be completely frozen when being mixed in.

Batter made with the blending method is often deposited into greased molds or paper molds. The products can be baked into muffin-size portions or into loaves. Cornbread is usually baked on a sheet pan and then sliced into individual portions. Only products such as scones should be egg washed. The surfaces of loaves or muffins can be decorated with coarse sugar, seeds, or nuts. When baked in greased molds, the products should be unmolded 10 minutes after baking, to cool completely and prevent sweating.

Blending Method Process

- Scale all the ingredients. Sift the dry ingredients together.
- Combine the wet ingredients.
- Add all of the wet ingredients to the dry ingredients and mix just until the batter comes together. The batter may look lumpy. Do not overmix.
- Store for later use or deposit to be baked. (*Note:* Depending on the formula, prolonged holding may affect oven spring.)

CREAMING METHOD FOR MUFFINS, COFFEE CAKES, AND LOAVES

The creaming method for muffins, coffee cakes, and cake loaves is used less often than the blending method. It is a more time-consuming procedure, with more attention to the detail of the mixing process; nevertheless, it creates a moist textured product and is likely to be more tender than a product made using the blending method.

Ingredient Functions

In general, creaming method formulas tend to have a higher content of fat and sugar than blending method formulas, resulting in rich flavors and tender textures. Muffins and coffee cakes made with the creaming method are based on the creaming of a solid fat (butter, margarine, shortening, or a combination) and sugar. Sometimes cream cheese is included in the preparation and should be a part of the creaming process. The presence of cream cheese adds stability to the fat–sugar phase and assists in maintaining the emulsion after the eggs are added because cream cheese contains gums and stabilizers. Pastry flour is commonly used, but a blend of pastry flour and cake flour is sometimes used to create a less chewy and more tender crumb. Just like products made with the blending method, both sweet and savory applications are possible.

Mixing Method

For this application, air is incorporated into the fat–sugar mixture to aid in leavening and to lighten the crumb. In general, the sugar is creamed with the fat and any additional ingredients, such as cream cheese. For effective creaming, the fat must be at least 65°F (18°C) to ensure an appropriate consistency. Once the fat and sugar mixture is light and fluffy, the eggs can be added slowly. After they're added, the bowl should be scraped down to ensure even mixing. Next, any additional liquids can be added. Last, the dry ingredients should be added and mixed just to incorporation.

Creaming Method Process for Muffins, Coffee Cakes, and Loaves

- Scale all the ingredients. Prepare a mixing bowl with the paddle attachment. Sift together the flour, baking powder, and salt.
- Combine the fat and sugar and cream until light and fluffy.
- Add the eggs in three stages, mixing after each addition and scraping down the bowl after all the eggs are added.
- Add any liquid and mix in thoroughly.
- Add the sifted dry ingredients and mix just until smooth. If adding additional ingredients, add these once the mixing is three-fourths complete.

FIGURE 11-4 SCONE MAKEUP

1 Once the dough is mixed and divided, flatten a portion of dough into an 8 inch (20 cm) cake ring.

2 Divide into 8 pieces by using a chef's knife.

3 Brush the top lightly with egg wash.

4 Finish with a sprinkle of coarse sugar.

MAKEUP PROCESSES FOR QUICK BREADS

The makeup processes for quick breads are largely determined by the mixing method, or on a product-by-product basis. As with anything in baking, the baker needs to adapt to the situation and apply his or her skills to determine the best process. Some general guidelines for individual products follow.

SCONES

- Sheet or roll the dough out on a lightly floured surface to about 3/4 inch (2 cm) thick.
- Cut with a round or fluted pastry cutter or a chefs knife to the desired size and shape, minimizing waste.
- Creamed scones may be scooped.
- Alternatively, portion the dough into 2.2 lb (1 kg) pieces and press into an 8 inch (20 cm) cake ring. (See Scone Makeup Figure 11-4, Step 1.)
- Cut into eight equal wedges and transfer to a sheet pan. (See Scone Makeup Figure 11-4, Step 2.)
- Place the scones on a parchment-lined sheet pan and brush with egg or cream wash and garnish with sugar (optional). (See Scone Makeup Figure 11-4, Steps 3–4.)

Scones Made With Frozen Fruit (Blueberries)

- Process a plain scone dough.
- Scale the dough into 1 lb (0.450 kg) pieces.
- Spread 1 3/4 oz (0.050 kg) of frozen blueberries within an 8 inch × 2 inch (20 cm × 10 cm) ring mold.
- Round off a piece of scone dough and press it into the blueberries.
- Spread 1 3/4 oz (0.050 kg) of frozen blueberries over the scone dough and gently press in.
- Round off a second piece of scone dough and press it into the ring mold.
- Remove the ring mold and cut the round into eight wedges.

Note: Work with only the amount of blueberries that will remain frozen. Toss the blueberries in a small quantity of flour to prevent them from bleeding.

BISCUITS

- On the bench, knead the dough lightly by pressing it out and folding the dough in half. Repeat this approximately 10 times.
- Roll the dough out to about 3/4 inch (2 cm) thick and cut the biscuits to the desired size with a floured cutter.
- Place the biscuits on a sheet pan lined with parchment paper and brush with egg or cream wash and garnish with sugar (optional).

MUFFINS

- The quantity of muffin batter per portion varies according to the mixing technique and muffin tin size.
- All muffins pans need to be lined with paper cups or sprayed with nonstick spray.

FIGURE 11-5 COFFEE CAKE MAKEUP

1 After a portion of batter is spread on the bottom of the pan, fillings are applied on top.

2 Place second layer of batter on top; flatten evenly.

3 Spread streusel over the top layer.

- Creamed muffin batter should fill approximately half of each tin.
- Blending method batter can fill three-fourths of each tin.
- The quantity of batter in the tin will have an effect on the size of the muffin top. More batter will produce more top.
- In a production setting, muffins are generally portioned by volume, using various scoop sizes to maintain portion control.
- Once the tray is portioned, the muffins may be garnished and baked.

LOAF CAKES

- The guidelines for filling loaf pans are similar to the guidelines for filling muffin tins.
- Loaf pans should always be sprayed with nonstick spray and placed on a flat sheet pan.
- Loaf cakes are typically portioned by weight, rather than by volume, to ensure even baking and proper portion control.
- Some loafs breads may be "scored" using a bench knife that has been partially dipped in oil. When gently pressed 1/4 inch (0.6 cm) into the batter, it creates a means for the bread to split during baking.

COFFEE CAKES

- The makeup process for coffee cakes generally consists of several steps.
- First, the pans are prepared with nonstick pan spray. Next, a portion of the dough is placed into the pan and is spread out evenly.
- A filling of choice is then evenly distributed over the base layer. (If using jam or fruits, it is important that they do not touch the side of the pan.) (See Coffee Cake Makeup Figure 11-5, Step 1.)
- Next, the second layer of batter is placed over the filling and is pressed down flat. (See Coffee Cake Makeup Figure 11-5, Step 2.)
- If streusel is called for, it can be spread over the top layer. (See Coffee Cake Makeup Figure 11-5, Step 3.)

SHEET PAN APPLICATIONS

- Items such as coffee cake or cornbread may be baked in a sheet and then portioned.
- The pans are prepared with parchment paper.
- A pan-collar may be used to obtain fuller volume of the baked item.

- Deposit the batter depending on the pan size and product makeup.
- Bake at a lower temperature for a longer period of time to ensure an even bake.

BAKING QUICK BREADS

The common trait shared by quick breads is that they should bake as quickly as possible to ensure a palatable, enjoyable final product. Even so, baking temperatures and times vary. Items such as scones and biscuits will bake at a higher temperature and for a shorter amount of time than a coffee cake, while a loaf cake will bake at a lower temperature for a longer time than muffins to ensure that the center of the product is fully baked.

When it comes to determining whether a product is done, professional bakers who produce the same items on a daily basis can tell from a quick glance. For the novice, however, or in the case of a new formula, there are several key things to look for. For example, baked loaf cakes will have a definite cell structure that allows them to spring back to the touch once they are baked. The common method for testing doneness is to insert a cake tester in the center of the loaf. If it comes out clean, the product has baked enough. If it is not ready yet, the cake tester will be coated with batter. The same technique may be used for muffins. Other characteristics of muffins and loaf cakes that are done baking include a golden brown color, a surface center that springs back to the touch, and partial separation of the sides from the pan.

Loaf cakes and muffins should be removed from the pan 10 to 15 minutes after baking. If they are not removed, they may be harder to remove later, and condensation that can damage the integrity of the product will occur.

PRODUCTION OF BISCUITS AND SCONES

The production of scones and biscuits for retail bakeries ranges from completely by hand to completely by machine. A difference in quality may be evident depending on the product; however, there is a point where the demands of high-volume production will most likely result in the need to sacrifice some quality. This is due to problems that arise during the mixing stage. For bulk production, scones may be made up and then frozen or reserved in the refrigerator for later use. Flaky scones and biscuits should always go into the oven cold in order to maintain their structure.

STORAGE OF QUICK BREADS

Quick breads are best served fresh, but if they must be served at a later date, they keep well in the freezer. For example, items such as loaf cakes and coffee cakes can be produced in large quantities once a week and stored in the freezer until needed without much of a sacrifice in flavor or texture. Items to be stored in this way must be well wrapped after they have completely cooled. If they are wrapped with plastic when warm, moisture will be trapped that will cause faster molding and possible contamination with microorganisms at a faster rate. The good news is that quick breads are fast and simple to make, which makes them easy to serve fresh.

FORMULA

BANANA BREAD

Banana bread first became standard fare in American kitchens when baking soda and baking powder hit the mainstream in the 1930s, ushering in the popularity of quick breads of all kinds. Its reputation as a standby was renewed in the 1960s when hearty breads became fashionable, and the simplicity of the basic recipes for banana bread have contributed to its enduring popularity ever since.

Ingredients	Baker's %	Kilogram	US decimal	Lb & Oz		Test
Bananas	105.00	0.725	1.599	1	9⅝	5⅛ oz
Buttermilk	11.25	0.078	0.171		2¾	½ oz
Vanilla extract	0.50	0.003	0.008		⅛	⅛ tsp
Sugar	66.00	0.456	1.005	1	⅛	3¼ oz
Brown sugar	33.00	0.228	0.503		8	1⅝ oz
Eggs	40.70	0.281	0.620		9⅞	2 oz
Canola oil	42.00	0.290	0.640		10¼	2 oz
Bread flour	100.00	0.691	1.523	1	8⅜	4⅞ oz
Salt	1.00	0.007	0.015		¼	¼ tsp
Baking soda	2.00	0.014	0.030		½	½ tsp
Baking powder	2.00	0.014	0.030		½	½ tsp
Cinnamon	0.70	0.005	0.011		⅛	⅛ tsp
Walnuts	30.00	0.207	0.457		7¼	1½ oz
Total	434.15	3.000	6.613	6	9¾	1 lb 5 oz

Yield: 5 [8 inch (20 cm) × 4 inch (10 cm)] loaves
Test: 1 [8 inch (20 cm) × 4 inch (10 cm)] loaf

Process

1. In the bowl of a mixer fitted with the paddle attachment, premix the bananas, buttermilk, and vanilla extract until broken up. Reserve.
2. Combine the sugar, brown sugar, eggs, and canola oil in the bowl of a mixer fitted with the paddle attachment and mix until well incorporated.
3. Combine the dry ingredients and add to the wet ingredients and mix until 50 percent incorporation.

4. Add the banana buttermilk mixture and then add the walnuts and mix to incorporation.
5. Deposit into sprayed pans three-fourths up the pan.
6. "Score" along length of the loaf, ¼ inch (2 cm) deep with a scraper dipped in vegetable oil.
7. Bake until golden brown and the surface bounces back to the touch.
8. For an 8 inch (20 cm) × 4 inch (10 cm) [1 lb 5 oz (600 g)] loaf, bake at 335°F (168°C) in a convection oven for 40 to 45 minutes.

Variation: Caramel Pear Bread Formula

Adjustments	Baker's %	Kilogram	US decimal	Lb & Oz	Test
Add nutmeg	0.1	0.001	0.002	< ⅛	< ⅛
Add ginger	0.5	0.003	0.008	⅛	< ⅛
Replace bananas with diced pears, cut in ½ inch (1 cm) squares	112	0.774	1.706	1 11¼	5½ oz

Caramel Formula

Ingredients	Baker's %	Kilogram	US decimal	Lb & Oz	Test
Sugar	100	0.227	0.496	7⅞	1½ oz
Ginger	0.1	0.000	0.002	< ⅛	< ⅛
Nutmeg	0.1	0.000	0.002	< ⅛	< ⅛
Total	100.20	0.227	0.500	8	1½ oz

Process

1. Make a caramel with the sugar and spices and then add the diced pears. Cook until tender; reserve.
2. After the caramel pear mixture is cool, fold into the batter.
3. Deposit 1 lb 5 oz (600 g) batter per 8 inch (20 cm) × 4 inch (10 cm) loaf and continue as with the banana bread.

FORMULA

PUMPKIN BREAD

A hearty, dense bread served most often during the autumn and winter holidays, pumpkin bread really deserves to be appreciated all year round. Filled with spices, pumpkin, and walnuts, each bite is packed with flavor. It is a lovely bread to enjoy at breakfast or with an afternoon cup of coffee or tea.

Ingredients	Baker's %	Kilogram	US decimal	Lb & Oz		Test
Sugar	109.00	0.639	1.409	1	6½	4⅝ oz
Butter	91.00	0.533	1.176	1	2⅞	3⅞ oz
Eggs	31.00	0.182	0.401		6⅜	1¼ oz
Pumpkin puree	92.00	0.539	1.189	1	3	3⅞ oz
Low-protein bread flour	100.00	0.586	1.292	1	4⅝	4¼ oz
Baking soda	0.80	0.005	0.010		⅛	<⅛
Baking powder	0.40	0.002	0.005		⅛	<⅛
Salt	0.80	0.005	0.010		⅛	<⅛
Cinnamon	0.40	0.002	0.005		⅛	<⅛
Nutmeg	0.40	0.002	0.005		⅛	<⅛
Allspice	0.40	0.002	0.005		⅛	<⅛
Ginger	0.40	0.002	0.005		⅛	<⅛
Total	426.60	2.501	5.513	5	8¼	1 lb 2 oz

Yield: 5 [8 inch (20 cm) × 4 inch (10 cm)] loaves
Test: 1 [8 inch (20 cm) × 4 inch (10 cm)] loaf

Process

1. In the bowl of a mixer, cream the butter and sugar using the paddle attachment.
2. Mix the eggs and pumpkin together and slowly add to the creamed butter and sugar.
3. Sift all the dry ingredients together; add to the bowl and mix until the batter is smooth.
4. Deposit 1 lb 2 oz (500 g) batter per 8 inch (20 cm) × 4 inch (10 cm) loaf pan.
5. Bake at 350°F (177°C) in a convection oven for 45 minutes or until done.

FORMULA

CORNBREAD

The earliest makers of cornbread were the Native American tribes of the southern United States and Central America, who relied heavily upon corn as a food source. Early American settlers soon acquired the practice of using local ingredients, such as cornmeal, when the wheat they were accustomed to using was in short supply. Cornbread was popular during the Civil War because it was economical and easy to make. Today, cornbread is made in an endless array of varieties, most commonly in the southern United States, where authenticity of the recipes is prized. Notable for its crumbly simplicity, and incomplete without a generous slathering of butter, cornbread is often eaten hot, or at least warm.

Ingredients	Baker's %	Kilogram	US decimal	Lb & Oz		Test
Cornmeal	34.00	0.619	1.366	1	5⅞	4⅜ oz
Semolina flour	33.00	0.601	1.326	1	5¼	4¼ oz
Pastry flour	33.00	0.601	1.326	1	5¼	4¼ oz
Baking powder	5.00	0.091	0.201		3¼	⅝ oz
Salt	1.70	0.031	0.068		1⅛	¼ oz
Sugar	32.00	0.583	1.285	1	4⅝	4⅛ oz
Eggs	20.00	0.364	0.803		12⅞	2⅝ oz
Buttermilk	76.00	1.385	3.053	3	⅞	9¾ oz
Butter	26.00	0.474	1.044	1	¾	3⅜ oz
Total	260.70	4.750	10.472	10	7½	2 lb 1½ oz

Yield: 5 [8 inch (20 cm)] cake pans
Test: 1 [8 inch (20 cm)] cake pan

Process

1. Melt the butter and reserve until needed.
2. Sift the cornmeal, semolina flour, pastry flour, baking powder, salt, and sugar together and reserve.
3. Combine the eggs and buttermilk. Add the dry ingredients to the wet ingredients and mix until incorporated.
4. Next, add the melted butter and mix until smooth.
5. Pour the batter into prepared pans at 2 lb 1½ oz (0.950 kg) per pan. Bake at 350°F (177°C) for 16 to 18 minutes or until done.

FORMULA

SAVORY MUFFIN

Take some of the best elements of a hot breakfast, fold them into an egg-rich muffin batter, flavored with mustard and parsley, and put them in the oven, and what do you have? The mouth-watering ham and cheese muffin demands to be eaten with a cup of coffee on the side.

Ingredients	Baker's %	Kilogram	US decimal	Lb & Oz		Test
Parsley	6.00	0.044	0.097		1½	1 tbsp
Gruyere, grated	50.00	0.365	0.805		12⅞	2⅝ oz
Ham, small dice	75.00	0.548	1.208	1	3⅜	3⅞ oz
Eggs	150.00	1.096	2.416	2	6⅝	7⅞ oz
Mustard	25.00	0.183	0.403		6½	1¼ oz
Butter, soft	60.00	0.438	0.967		15½	3⅛ oz
Salt	2.00	0.015	0.032		½	1 tsp
Pepper	1.00	0.007	0.016		¼	¼ tsp
Bread flour	100.00	0.731	1.611	1	9¾	5¼ oz
Baking powder	10.00	0.073	0.161		2⅝	½ oz
Total	479.00	3.500	7.716	7	11½	1 lb 9 oz

Yield: 45 medium-sized muffins
Test: 9 medium-sized muffins

Process

1. Bring all the ingredients to room temperature and warm the butter to soften it.
2. Mince the parsley; prepare the cheese and ham.
3. Combine all of the wet ingredients (eggs, mustard, parsley, butter).
4. Combine all of the dry ingredients (salt, pepper, bread flour, baking powder).
5. Add the dry ingredients to the wet ingredients, and fold them in three-fourths of the way. Then add the cheese and ham and mix to incorporate.
6. Deposit into greased or papered muffin pans.
7. Bake the muffins at 375°F (191°C) in a convection oven for 15 minutes, or until done.

Note

Salt content of mustard, cheese, and ham will vary by source. Adjust salt amount in formula as necessary.

Assorted Quick Breads

FORMULA

BLUEBERRY MUFFIN

Every traditional American bakery has its version of a blueberry muffin. The color, texture, and tartness of blueberries, melded with a slightly sweet muffin batter, create a classic morning delicacy with unshakable appeal.

Ingredients	Baker's %	Kilogram	US decimal	Lb & Oz		Test
Canola oil	20.00	0.237	0.522		8⅜	1⅝ oz
Melted butter	20.00	0.237	0.522		8⅜	1⅝ oz
Sugar	76.50	0.906	1.997	2	0	6⅜ oz
Eggs	35.00	0.415	0.914		14⅝	2⅞ oz
Milk	59.50	0.705	1.554	1	8⅞	5 oz
Vanilla extract	1.50	0.018	0.039		⅝	1 tsp
Bread flour	100.00	1.184	2.611	2	9¾	8⅜ oz
Baking powder	3.75	0.044	0.098		1⅝	2 tsp
Salt	1.75	0.021	0.046		¾	1 tsp
Blueberries	65.00	0.770	1.697	1	11⅛	5⅜ oz
Total	383.00	4.536	10.000	10	0	2 lb

Yield: 45 medium-sized muffins
Test: 9 medium-sized muffins

Process

1. Sift the flour and baking powder. Add the salt and reserve.
2. Blend the oil, butter, and sugar.
3. Add the eggs, milk, and vanilla to the butter mixture.
4. Add the dry ingredients to the wet ingredients and mix in first speed to incorporation. Continue to mix on low speed 30 seconds to 1 minute. The extra mixing will promote a peaked muffin top.
5. Fold in the berries.
6. Scoop into greased or papered muffin pans of desired size.
7. Garnish with choice of pearl sugar, sliced almonds, streusel, or granulated sugar just before baking.
8. Bake at 375°F (190°C) in a convection oven for 18 minutes or until done.

Note

Batter may be kept under refrigeration for 2 days with good results.

FORMULA

BRAN MUFFIN

This is the kind of bran muffin that makes healthy eating seem not only endurable, but pleasurable. With its earthy, moist texture and generous portions of currants, wheat germ, and bran, this muffin offers a delicious dose of responsible fun.

Ingredients	Baker's %	Kilogram	US decimal	Lb & Oz		Test
Canola oil	35.00	0.334	0.737		11 ¾	2 ⅜ oz
Honey	9.50	0.091	0.200		3 ¼	⅝ oz
Molasses	21.00	0.201	0.442		7 ⅛	1 ⅜ oz
Brown sugar	59.50	0.568	1.253	1	4	4 oz
Vanilla extract	1.20	0.011	0.025		⅜	½ tsp
Eggs	41.60	0.397	0.876		14	2 ¾ oz
Buttermilk	123.00	1.175	2.591	2	9 ½	8 ¼ oz
Bread flour	100.00	0.955	2.106	2	1 ¾	6 ¾ oz
Baking soda	4.70	0.045	0.099		1 ⅝	2 tsp
Baking powder	2.30	0.022	0.048		¾	1 tsp
Cinnamon	1.20	0.011	0.025		⅜	½ tsp
Salt	0.50	0.005	0.011		⅛	⅛ tsp
Wheat germ	23.00	0.220	0.484		7 ¾	1 ½ oz
Bran	14.25	0.136	0.300		4 ¾	1 oz
Currants	38.00	0.363	0.800		12 ¾	2 ½ oz
Total	474.75	4.536	10.000	10	0	2 lb

Yield: 45 medium-sized muffins
Test: 9 medium-sized muffins

Process

1. Combine the dry ingredients and reserve.
2. Combine the wet ingredients, and add the dry ingredients to them.
3. Mix to 75 percent incorporation; fold in the wheat germ, bran, and currants and mix to incorporation.
4. Deposit 3 ½ oz (100 g) of batter into greased or papered muffin pans and garnish with a dusting of bran.
5. Bake at 375°F (190°C) in a convection oven for 15 to 17 minutes or until done.

Note

Batter may be kept under refrigeration for 2 days with good results.

COFFEE CAKE

Coffee cake is aptly named after the beverage with which it is most often enjoyed. Even though its traditional role is to make the morning routine noticeably more pleasurable, coffee cake has also served as a customary dessert to offer visiting guests, no matter the time of day.

FORMULA

COFFEE CAKE

The addition of cream cheese to this coffee cake creates a softer, moister crumb. Two layers of batter, divided by a layer of jam and fruit, add a pleasing sweetness with a touch of acidic flavors to help cleanse the palate. The batter of this cake can be stored under refrigeration for up to 24 hours, or the assembled cakes may be stored unbaked, frozen for up to one week with good results. The cake should be thawed before baking.

Streusel Topping Formula

Ingredients	Baker's %	Kilogram	US decimal	Lb & Oz		Test
Butter, cold	140.00	0.317	0.699		11 ¼	2 ¼ oz
Sugar	100.00	0.227	0.500		8	1 ⅝ oz
Almond meal	100.00	0.227	0.500		8	1 ⅝ oz
Pastry flour	100.00	0.227	0.500		8	1 ⅝ oz
Salt	0.80	0.002	0.004		⅛	⅛ tsp
Cinnamon	0.40	0.001	0.002		0	⅛ tsp
Total	441.20	1.000	2.204	2	3 ¼	7 oz

Yield: 5 [9 inch (23 cm)] cakes
Test: 1 [9 inch (23 cm)] cake

Process, Streusel Topping

1. Combine all the ingredients in the bowl of a mixer fitted with the paddle attachment.
2. Mix on medium speed until the mixture is crumbly. Do not overmix.
3. Refrigerate in an airtight container until needed (also stores well in the freezer for longer periods of time).

Batter Formula

Ingredients	Baker's %	Kilogram	US decimal	Lbs & Oz	Test
Butter	44.92	0.570	1.256	1 4⅛	4 oz
Cream cheese	56.25	0.713	1.573	1 9⅛	5 oz
Sugar	56.25	0.713	1.573	1 9⅛	5 oz
Eggs	39.06	0.495	1.092	1 1½	3½ oz
Vanilla extract	1.95	0.025	0.055	⅞	1 tsp
Bread flour	100.00	1.268	2.796	2 12¾	9 oz
Baking powder	1.56	0.020	0.044	¾	1 tsp
Baking soda	2.34	0.030	0.065	1	1 tsp
Salt	1.56	0.020	0.044	¾	⅔ tsp
Whole milk	31.25	0.396	0.874	14	2¾ oz
Total	335.14	4.250	9.370	9 5⅞	1 lb 14 oz

Yield: 5 [9 inch (23 cm)] cakes
Test: 1 [9 inch (23 cm)] cake

Process, Batter

1. Cream the butter, cream cheese, and sugar until light.
2. Gradually add the eggs and vanilla.
3. Sift the dry ingredients together and add these slowly, not overmixing the dough.
4. Add the whole milk and mix until smooth.

Coffee Cake Assembly Formula

Ingredients	Baker's %	Kilogram	US decimal	Lbs & Oz	Test
Batter	100.00	4.250	9.370	9 5⅞	1 lb 14 oz
Raspberries	13.99	0.595	1.311	1 5	4 oz
Raspberry jam	4.66	0.198	0.437	7	1 oz
Total	118.65	5.043	11.118	11 1⅞	2 lb 3 oz

Process, Coffee Cake Assembly

1. Spray 9 inch (23 cm) cake pans with pan release and deposit 14 oz (400 g) of batter into each pan and flatten it.
2. Pipe about 1 oz (40 g) of jam onto the batter and place about 4 oz (120 g) of berries over the jam.
3. Top this with an additional 1 lb (450 g) of batter. Top with about 7 oz (200 g) of streusel.
4. Bake at 335°F (168°C) in a convection oven for 50 to 55 minutes.
5. Allow to cool in the pan for 15 minutes; then remove from the pan.

FORMULA

SOUR CREAM COFFEE CAKE

This rich and tender coffee cake emphasizes the flavorful combination of apples and hazelnuts. The preparation is somewhat detailed for a coffee cake, but with advance planning, the process can be simplified. This coffee cake is best when baked in a large sheet and cut into squares for serving.

Hazelnut Streusel Topping Formula

Ingredients	Baker's %	Kilogram	US decimal	Lb & Oz	Test
Brown sugar	140.00	0.271	0.597	9 ½	2 ⅜ oz
Pastry flour	100.00	0.193	0.426	6 ⅞	1 ¾ oz
Butter, cold	100.00	0.193	0.426	6 ⅞	1 ¾ oz
Hazelnuts	100.00	0.193	0.426	6 ⅞	1 ¾ oz
Total	440.00	0.850	1.875	1 14 ⅛	7 ½ oz

Process, Hazelnut Streusel Topping

1. Chop the hazelnuts coarsely.
2. Combine all the ingredients and mix on medium speed using the paddle attachment.
3. Mix until crumbly; do not overmix.

Roasted Apple Filling Formula

Ingredients	Baker's %	Kilogram	US decimal	Lb & Oz	Test
Apples, diced	100.00	1.301	2.868	2 13 ⅞	11 ½ oz
Cinnamon sugar	10.80	0.141	0.310	5	1 ¼ oz
Butter, melted	4.61	0.060	0.132	2 ⅛	½ oz
Total	115.41	1.501	3.310	3 5	13 ¼ oz

Process, Roasted Apple Filling

1. Dice the apples to ¾ inch (2 cm); combine with the melted butter and cinnamon sugar.
2. Roast at 325°F (163°C) for 20 to 25 minutes. Cool and reserve.

Streusel Filling Formula

Ingredients	Baker's %	Kilogram	US decimal	Lb & Oz		Test
Brown sugar	1027.48	1.024	2.257	2	4⅛	9 oz
Pastry flour	100.00	0.100	0.220		3½	⅞ oz
Butter, cold	170.23	0.170	0.374		6	1½ oz
Hazelnuts	910.31	0.907	2.000	2	0	8 oz
Total	2208.02	2.200	4.850	4	13⅝	3⅜ oz

Process, Streusel Filling

1. Roast the hazelnuts at 325°F (163°C) for 15 minutes or until golden brown.
2. When cool, chop coarsely.
3. Mix the brown sugar, pastry flour, cold butter, and hazelnuts with the paddle attachment until the mixture is crumbly.
4. Reserve.

Cake Batter Formula

Ingredients	Baker's %	Kilogram	US decimal	Lb & Oz		Test
Butter	76.30	0.909	2.003	2	0	8 oz
Sugar	38.15	0.454	1.002	1	0	4 oz
Brown sugar	38.15	0.454	1.002	1	0	4 oz
Eggs	48.74	0.580	1.280	1	4½	5⅛ oz
Vanilla extract	1.68	0.020	0.044		¾	1 tsp
Pastry flour	100.00	1.191	2.625	2	10	10½ oz
Baking soda	1.85	0.022	0.049		¾	1 tsp
Baking powder	1.51	0.018	0.040		⅝	1 tsp
Sour cream	84.03	1.001	2.206	2	3¼	8⅞ oz
Total	390.41	4.649	10.250	10	4	2 lb 9 oz

Yield: 1 full sheet pan
Test: ¼ sheet pan

Process, Cake Batter

1. Sift together the pastry flour, baking soda, and baking powder and reserve.
2. Cream the butter and sugar until light with the paddle attachment.
3. Gradually add the tempered eggs and vanilla.
4. Scrape down the bowl.
5. Add half of the dry ingredients and mix to incorporation.
6. Add the sour cream and mix to incorporation.
7. Add the remaining dry ingredients and blend to incorporation.

Assembly

1. Deposit half of the batter onto a parchment-lined sheet pan with a collar.
2. Deposit the roasted apple filling over the batter. Then sprinkle with the streusel filling.
3. Cover with the remaining batter and spread out evenly.
4. Top with the hazelnut streusel topping.
5. Bake at 325°F (163°C) in a convection oven for 45 to 55 minutes.

Assorted Quick Breads
(clockwise from top) Coffee Cake, Blueberry Muffin, Bran Muffins, and Sour Cream Coffee Cake

SCONES

Some believe the first scones originated in Scotland, taking their name from the *Stone of Destiny* (or *Scone*), the place where Scottish kings were once crowned. Others believe the name is derived from the Dutch word *schoonbrot* meaning "fine white bread" or from the German word *sconbrot* meaning "fine or beautiful bread." Still others say it comes from the Gaelic *sgonn*, basically a "shapeless mass" or "large mouthful." Whatever their country of origin, scones were first made with oats, shaped into a large round, scored into four to six triangles, and then cooked on a griddle either over an open fire or on top of the stove. Today's versions are more often flour-based and are baked in the oven. Their shapes, including triangles, rounds, squares, and diamonds, are as diverse as their flavor combinations, from the sweet to the savory.

FORMULA

CREAM SCONE

The cream scone is a classic favorite that calls for a cream with a fat content of at least 35 percent. The simple mixing method allows for easy production, but one must be careful not to overmix the dough. These scones store well in the refrigerator for up to 18 hours or in the freezer well-wrapped for up to one week.

Ingredients	Baker's %	Kilogram	US decimal	Lb & Oz		Test
Bread flour	100.00	1.765	3.777	3	12⅜	12 oz
Sugar	20.00	0.343	0.755		12⅛	2 ⅜ oz
Baking powder	4.50	0.077	0.170		2¾	½ oz
Salt	0.63	0.011	0.024		⅜	½ tsp
Nuts, dried fruits, etc.	43.75	0.749	1.652	1	10⅜	5 ¼ oz
Heavy cream	105.00	1.799	3.965	3	15½	12 ⅝ oz
Honey	18.00	0.308	0.680		10⅞	2 ⅛ oz
Total	291.88	5.052	11.023	11	¾	2 lb 3 oz

Yield: 40 scones; cut from five 8 inch (20 cm) circles
Test: 8 scones; cut from one 8 inch (20 cm) circle

Process

1. Combine the flour, sugar, baking powder, and salt.
2. Add the dried fruit or nuts to incorporate.
3. Whisk together the cream and the honey.
4. Add the cream mixture to the dry ingredients and mix just until the dough comes together.
5. Divide the dough into 2 lb 3 oz (1 kg) pieces.
6. Flatten each portion into an 8 inch (20 cm) cake ring to mold.
7. Remove the ring and cut the circle into eight wedges.
8. Brush with the egg wash and garnish with sugar or nut meal.
9. Bake at 375°F (190°C) in a convection oven for 15 to 17 minutes or until golden brown and baked through.

FORMULA

BUTTER SCONE

The butter scone is defined by its flaky and tender texture. For the best texture, mixing should be done by hand. If machine mixing is required, the batch size should be limited to prevent overmixing the dough, which can easily happen when mixing upwards of 100 pounds (45 kg). These scones store well in the refrigerator for up to 18 hours or in the freezer well-wrapped for up to a week.

Ingredients	Baker's %	Kilogram	US decimal	Lb & Oz		Test
Bread flour	100.00	1.998	4.405	4	6½	14⅛ oz
Sugar	12.50	0.250	0.551		8¾	1¾ oz
Baking powder	5.60	0.112	0.247		4	¾ oz
Salt	0.80	0.016	0.035		⅝	½ tsp
Orange zest	1.00	0.020	0.044		¾	1 tsp
Butter, cold	25.00	0.500	1.101	1	1⅝	3½ oz
Currants	30.60	0.611	1.348	1	5⅝	4¼ oz
Cream	56.00	1.119	2.467	2	7½	7⅞ oz
Honey	7.50	0.150	0.330		5¼	1 oz
Eggs	11.25	0.225	0.496		7⅞	1⅝ oz
Total	250.25	5.000	11.024	11	⅞	2 lb 3 oz

Yield: 40 scones; cut from five 8 inch (20 cm) circles
Test: 8 scones; cut from one 8 inch (20 cm) circle

Process

1. Combine the cream, honey, and eggs; reserve.
2. Combine the flour, sugar, baking powder, salt, and zest in a mixing bowl.
3. With the paddle attachment, cut the butter into the dry ingredients until it is the size of peas. Add the currants, and mix to distribute evenly.
4. Add the liquid ingredients; mix to incorporation.
5. Divide the dough into 2 lb 3 oz (1 kg) pieces.
6. Flatten each portion into an 8 inch (20 cm) cake ring to mold.
7. Remove the ring and cut the circle into eight wedges.
8. Alternately, roll out on a lightly floured surface and cut out shapes as desired.
9. Store under refrigeration or in the freezer or brush lightly with egg wash and bake at 375°F (190°C) in a convection oven for about 15 to 17 minutes or until golden brown.

FORMULA

SAVORY SCONE

The best of the pastry and savory worlds meet in this tender savory scone, studded with goat cheese, pine nuts, and green onion. This scone is a satisfying alternative to sweeter versions in the morning or afternoon.

Ingredients	Baker's %	Kilogram	US decimal	Lb & Oz		Test
Bread flour	60.00	1.267	2.794	2	12¾	8⅞ oz
Semolina flour	17.00	0.359	0.792		12⅝	2½ oz
Durum flour	23.00	0.486	1.071	1	1⅛	3⅜ oz
Baking powder	4.50	0.095	0.210		3⅜	⅝ oz
Salt	1.00	0.021	0.047		¾	½ tsp
Butter, cold	23.50	0.496	1.094	1	1½	3½ oz
Cream	35.00	0.739	1.630	1	10⅛	5⅛ oz
Honey	18.00	0.380	0.838		13⅜	2⅝ oz
Eggs	11.70	0.247	0.545		8¾	1¾ oz
Scallion	11.00	0.232	0.512		8¼	1⅝ oz
Pine nuts	17.00	0.359	0.792		12⅝	2½ oz
Goat cheese	15.00	0.317	0.699		11⅛	2¼ oz
Total	236.70	5.000	11.023	11	⅜	2 lb 3 oz

Yield: 40 scones; cut from five 8 inch (20 cm) circles
Test: 8 scones; cut from one 8 inch (20 cm) circle

Process

1. Combine the cream, honey, and eggs, and reserve.
2. Combine the flours, baking powder, salt, and butter in a mixing bowl with the paddle attachment.
3. Mix until the butter is the size of peas.
4. With the machine on, add the wet ingredients and mix to 50 percent incorporation.
5. Add the scallions, pine nuts, and crumbled goat cheese.
6. Continue to mix until the dough just barely comes together.
7. Divide the dough into 2 lb 3 oz (1 kg) pieces.
8. Flatten each portion into an 8 inch (20 cm) cake ring to mold.
9. Remove the ring and cut the circle into eight wedges.
10. Brush with the egg wash.
11. Bake at 375° F (190°C) in a convection oven for about 15 to 17 minutes or until golden brown.

FORMULA

MADELEINES

Madeleines were first made famous by Marcel Proust in *Remembrance of Things Past*, in which he wrote: "She sent out for one of those short, plump little cakes called 'petites madeleines', which looked as though they had been moulded in the fluted scallop of a pilgrim's shell. . . . An exquisite pleasure had invaded my senses." Popular legend relates the story of madeleines originating in 18th century Commercy, in the region of Lorraine, when a girl named Madeleine made them for Stanislaw Lezczynski, Duke of Lorraine, who shared his love of the newly discovered delicacy with his daughter, Marie, the wife of Louis XV, thus ensuring their popularity. These enchanting little cakes are baked in oval molds with ribbed indentations in a distinctive shell shape.

Ingredients	Baker's %	Kilogram	US decimal	Lb & Oz		Test
Sugar	81.63	1.060	2.336	2	5⅜	7½ oz
Brown sugar	12.24	0.159	0.350		5⅝	1⅛ oz
Salt	0.41	0.005	0.012		¼	⅛ tsp
Honey	16.33	0.212	0.467		7½	1½ oz
Eggs	110.20	1.431	3.154	3	2½	10⅛ oz
Pastry flour	100.00	1.298	2.862	2	13¾	9⅛ oz
Baking powder	2.86	0.037	0.082		1¼	1½ tsp
Butter, 82% fat, melted	100.00	1.298	2.862	2	13¾	9⅛ oz
Total	423.67	5.500	12.125	12	4	2 lb 6½ oz

Yield: 5 sheets (Flexipan mold)
Test: 1 sheet (Flexipan mold)

Process

1. Sift the pastry flour and baking powder; reserve.
2. Melt the butter and reserve.
3. In a bowl, combine the sugars, salt, honey, and eggs just to incorporation with a whisk.
4. Add the sifted flour and baking powder; fold in using a rubber spatula.
5. Add the melted butter, and fold to incorporate.
6. Pipe into molds three-fourths full and refrigerate for a minimum of 1½ hours.
7. Bake in a staged convection oven: Start at 400°F (245°C) for 2 minutes and drop to 350°F (176°C) for 9 to10 minutes.
8. Remove from the molds 5 minutes after baking.

Madeleines

FORMULA

FINANCIER

The financier, sometimes called a *friand* (meaning "dainty" or "tasty"), is a light tea cake. The basis of the cake itself is *beurre noisette* (brown butter), almond meal, egg whites, flour, and powdered sugar. Like the madeleine, financiers are often baked in shaped molds and may have been named after their traditional rectangular mold, which resembles a bar of gold. Financiers are often topped with whipped cream, berries, or fresh fruit and can be served with ice cream or other frozen confections.

Ingredients	Baker's %	Kilogram	US decimal	Lb & Oz		Test
Powdered sugar	264.00	1.763	3.887	3	14¼	12½ oz
Almond meal	96.00	0.641	1.413	1	6⅝	4½ oz
Bread flour	100.00	0.668	1.472	1	7½	4¾ oz
Baking powder	2.40	0.016	0.035		⅝	⅔ tsp
Vanilla bean	Each	2.5	2.5		2.5	½ each
Trimoline	24.00	0.160	0.353		5⅝	1⅛ oz
Butter, browned	144.00	0.962	2.120	2	1⅞	6¾ oz
Egg whites	268.00	1.790	3.946	3	15⅛	12⅝ oz
Total	898.40	6.000	13.227	13	3⅝	2 lb 10 oz

Yield: 5 sheets (Flexipan mold)
Test: 1 sheet (Flexipan mold)

Process

1. Sift together the dry ingredients and add the vanilla and Trimoline to this mixture.
2. Blend until combined in the bowl of a mixer fitted with the paddle attachment.
3. Cook the butter to the browned butter stage using caution to not stir the mixture.
4. Strain the browned butter (*beurre noisette*) and add to the dry ingredients; mix well.
5. Add half of the egg whites and mix to incorporate.
6. Add the remaining egg whites and mix until the batter is smooth.
7. Pipe into greased molds or Flexipans three-fourths of the way up the mold.
8. Bake at 370°F (187°C) for about 10 to 12 minutes or until done.
9. Batter can be stored in bulk in the refrigerator for up to 4 days or frozen portioned for up to 10 days.

CHAPTER SUMMARY

Quick bread products are the cornerstone of many bakeries. The absence of yeast and uncomplicated mixing methods make these ideal products to make and serve at bakeries. The three main mixing methods for quick breads—the biscuit method, the creaming method, and the blending or muffin method—are simple; however, one needs to be concerned about the degree to which the gluten is developed. In some instances, mixing beyond incorporation, such as for some types of muffin, can improve the texture as well as appearance of the muffin by improving volume. Typically however, mixing is kept to a minimum to keep the products tender and light. It is critical to understand the properties of chemical leavening agents presented in this chapter in order to understand their role within the baking process of quick breads. Production of quick breads can happen daily, or some work can be done out of the freezer for easier scheduling and work organization. Working out of the freezer with products like scones and coffee cake allows one to present a larger selection of product, with less active work by the staff of the bakery.

KEY TERMS

- ❖ Alum
- ❖ Baking ammonia
- ❖ Baking powder
- ❖ Baking soda
- ❖ Biscuit method
- ❖ Blending method
- ❖ Carbonates of soda
- ❖ Chemical leavening agents
- ❖ Creaming method
- ❖ Double-acting baking powder
- ❖ Leavening acids
- ❖ Potash
- ❖ Quick breads
- ❖ Single-acting baking powder
- ❖ Tunneling

REVIEW QUESTIONS

1. **Describe the biscuit method and how the flaky structure of biscuits is created.**
2. **Explain the function of baking powder and of baking soda and how the chemical reactions occur.**
3. **Describe the process for making scones with frozen fruit. How is the process different than using dried fruit or nuts as an add-in ingredient?**
4. **What are the signs that the following are fully baked?**
   a. **Muffins**
   b. **Scones**
   c. **Loaf cake**
5. **What is tunneling? What are the causes of tunneling?**

chapter
12

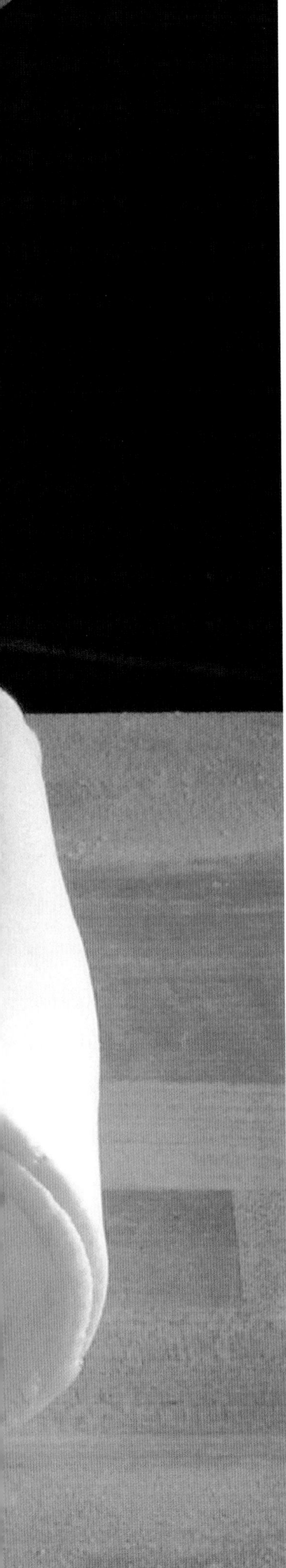

PASTRY DOUGH

OBJECTIVES

After reading this chapter, you should be able to

- explain the characteristics of various doughs, as well as their working properties and common uses.
- present the ingredient functions of various pastry doughs presented in this chapter.
- describe the mixing process for the different doughs presented.
- make a variety of doughs including pâte brisée, pâte sablée, sablé breton, puff pastry, pâte à foncer, and pie dough.

INTRODUCTION TO PASTRY DOUGH

The word "**pâte**" (French for "dough," "paste," or "batter") is classically used as a descriptor for a category of products, which are the building blocks of many traditional and contemporary creations. Dough bases are so important they are traditionally the responsibility of a department within the pastry shop or bakery. One who works in this department is referred to as a **tourrier**. This is an important job because the care in mixing and proper handling of various dough preparations ultimately determines the quality of the pastry shop's finished products.

There are several different styles of pastry dough. Although each of them has a different texture, many of them are all made with flour, fat, sugar, a liquid such as water, milk, and/or eggs in varying ratios. The texture of each dough is the result of which ingredients are used, how the fat is incorporated into the dough, and how much the gluten is developed.

Of the main pastry doughs presented in this chapter, they are divided into two categories based on their level of sweetness. The quantity of sugar in the dough, and its resulting flavors, determine not only the texture of the dough but also what it is typically used for. This chapter will present sweet and nonsweet versions of dough that are used for the bases of pastries. Nonsweet varieties include pie dough, pâte brisée, and pâte à foncer. Sweet varieties include pâte sucrée, pâte sablée, and sablé breton. Two additional products will be presented which include puff pastry and pâte à choux.

Between the terms that are commonly used in the United States and the terms used in Europe, specifically France, there are some differences between terminologies. Please refer to Figure 12-1 for a quick summary of how each type of dough is commonly used.

INGREDIENT FUNCTIONS FOR PASTRY DOUGH

Although dough may be composed of the same basic ingredients, depending on the formula and the process, there may be different results in the physical and textural characteristics. Many of these characteristics are established by the method in which they are prepared and the ratio of ingredients in the formula.

Five main ingredients form the foundation for the various types of pastry dough: flour, fat, liquid (milk or water), eggs, and sugar. Secondary ingredients such as salt and baking powder can also play a role. The choice of ingredients and the ratio in which they are present in comparison to the flour will determine many of the characteristics of the final product. Balancing the different protein, fat, free water, and sugars within doughs is critical in obtaining successful pastry with the desired results.

Figure 12-1

Pastry Dough and Common Uses

	Sweet	Not Sweet	Pie	Tart	Cookie	Texture	Comments/Uses
Pie dough		X	X	X		Tender/flaky	Pie, sweet and savory
Pâte brisée		X	X	X		Tender	Tarts, sweet and savory
Pâte à foncer	(X)	X	X	X		Tender/crisp	Tarts, sweet or savory; varieties based on usage; sugar can be up to 25% of FW
Pâte sucrée	X			X	X	Crisp	Sweet tart dough
Pâte sablée	X			X	X	Tender/crisp	Base for tarts
Sablé breton	X				X	Tender/crumbly	The traditional cookie from Bretagne
Pâte à sablé breton	X			X	X	Tender/crumbly	Used as a base for entremets or tart
Puff pastry		X		X	X	Flaky/light	For napoleons, apple turnover, savory tarts, vol-au-vent
Pâte à choux		X				Soft/crisp	For cream puffs, éclair, religiuse, etc.

FLOUR

The type of flour used in a pastry dough formula is typically from wheat and the variety of flour used largely depends on the item being made. Most types of dough use pastry flour or a low-protein bread flour to ensure tenderness in the final product. When little gluten development and a tender, crumbly, or flaky texture is desired, pastry flour is generally used to obtain these desired textures. For doughs that require more strength, such as when the dough contains sugar at 10 percent based on the flour weight or more, a low-protein or all-purpose flour is advised. With exception of pâte à choux, all of the dough presented in this chapter has a hydration of 50 percent or less based on the flour weight. When there is a larger ratio of flour to water, gluten can develop at a faster rate; therefore, it is important to use the proper flour. The starch coming from the flour will absorb the liquids from the dough and, upon being heated in the oven, will gelatinize in the oven giving way to a product with structure.

FATS

Although fats and oils are commonly classified as shortening agents, they can also be known as tenderizing ingredients. The term "shortening" is classically used to describe the ability to shorten or divide the gluten strands that can toughen flour-based dough. This term is misleading because something must first be long in order to be shortened. When mixing pie dough, the protein in the flour is not developed and then shortened. Instead, the high presence of fat, as well as the mixing process, inhibits the flour from forming gluten. The tenderizing effect occurs when the fat in the formula coats a portion of the flour and destroys its ability to easily form long, continuous strands of gluten. In formulas that use larger pieces of fat, the fat remains dispersed throughout the dough after mixing and creates flakier crust. Finer incorporation of fat, on the other hand, creates "shorter" dough that is less flaky.

Fat is used to add flavor, create texture, aid in leavening, and create mouth feel. Commonly used fats include butter, lard, vegetable oils, hydrogenated shortening, and emulsified shortenings. Fats used for pastry dough are typically unsalted.

The function of hard fat in dough is to create flakiness, tenderness, and moisture protection. Depending on the cost involved, as well as desired appearance, working properties, and flavor, it is possible to choose from a selection of fats that will deliver a variety of outcomes.

Butter, which is prized for its flavor and mouth feel, is the fat most commonly used in dough. Some dough, however, benefits from shortening, as is the case with pie dough. In this case, one should be aware of the water content in the fat to allow for appropriate changes that might be needed in the formula.

The type of fat has many effects on both the dough and the final product. The higher melting point of manufactured fats creates dough that is easier to work with and flakier. Specialty shapes and decorative borders on pie crust also benefit from manufactured fat because they do not bake out as much as all-butter crusts.

For artisan baking, the tendency is to use 100 percent butter because of its superior taste and the commitment to quality foods. The lower melting point means that dough made completely with butter is slightly harder to work with than dough made with shortening. However, as long as the environment is not too hot and one works efficiently, butter should pose no real workability challenge.

LIQUIDS

Water and/or milk are found in most formulas; however, some formulas call for other liquids, including cream, eggs, buttermilk, or even juice. Water, coming from the selected liquid ingredients, allows water-soluble ingredients such as salt, sugar, and chemical leavening agents to be dissolved evenly, and it allows the formation of dough by hydrating the starch and protein in the flour. The other components of the liquids, such as fats, protein, and carbohydrates, also have an effect on the texture and baking performance of the dough. Additionally, when water converts to steam at 212°F (100°C) in the oven, it transforms into steam and helps to leaven the product.

Milk and milk derivatives add additional functions to those of water. Lactose and proteins aid in the development of crust color, firmness, and crispness. Lactic acid tightens gluten and increases its stability, resulting in a fine grain and texture. Butterfat from milk aids in making dough softer.

The rate of hydration, or absorption of water into the flour, depends on the flour's moisture content, as well as on how thoroughly the butter is cut into it. This rate of hydration is critical because it determines the final texture and strength of the dough. If the butter is mixed into the dough too much, not enough flour will be able to hydrate the protein and starch, and the dough will be brittle and will not produce a good crust. If the fat is not worked into the dough enough, too much protein and starch will be hydrated, and the dough will become tough and hard to roll out.

The water used for dough should always be cold to help prevent the fat from softening and being absorbed by the flour, and the taste should be neutral. If the water is heavily chlorinated, it may be a good idea to use filtered water or to allow the water to sit for several hours. This allows the chlorine to naturally dissipate.

Alternative liquids that are sometimes used for dough, especially pie dough, include milk, cream, sour cream, and buttermilk. These liquids add additional sugar (lactose) and fat, along with acidity that makes the dough more flavorful and easier to roll out.

EGGS

Egg products, including for the most part whole eggs and egg yolks, are commonly used in pastry dough. Whether they are used whole, or separated into yolks and whites, egg products perform a number of functions that affect hydration, structure, texture, leavening, flavor, and color. These ingredients all contain a significant portion of water, which is able to hydrate protein and starch.

Egg whites are approximately 90 percent water, and yolks are roughly 50 percent water meaning whole eggs are approximately 72 percent water. The proteins found in whole eggs coagulate during the baking process and create structure. Dough made using whole egg should provide a crust that does not fall down the sides, or shrink into the mold after the baking process. Conversely, the high percentage of fats in egg yolk tends to promote tenderness and enrich the color of the dough. When egg yolks are the sole egg product/hydration in a formula, it is sometimes best suited for use as a flat base because the tenderizing properties can cause the dough to fall down the sides of the mold. Lecithin, a natural emulsifier in egg yolks, helps to generate a better distribution of liquids and fats, thus making the dough smoother. This is not always desirable though. Some varieties of pâte sablée include a process to precook the yolk to render the lecithin useless, enabling a more tender, crumblier texture. If only egg whites are used in a pastry dough, they have a high percentage of water as well as protein; therefore, the dough achieves strength during mixing, as well as during baking from the coagulation of the egg white protein.

SUGAR

Sugar is used to some degree in almost all pastry dough, except for most puff pastry. It is used in varying degrees to alter both the level of sweetness and the texture of the dough. The most common varieties used include powdered sugar, superfine sugar, and granulated sugar. Exotic sugars such as muscovado can be used to create unique flavor as well as variation in the color of the dough.

The size of the sugar grain has an effect on flavor, mouth feel, and dough properties as well as mixing processes (Figure 12-2).

The fine texture of powdered sugar enables the ingredient to spread easily throughout the dough and makes very smooth dough, which is highly regarded for its workability. The sheeting properties of dough made with powdered sugar are better than those of dough made with superfine sugar or granulated sugar. The one negative point of powdered sugar use is that the flavor of the crust from the use of this sugar is not ideal in comparison to the superfine sugar or granulated sugar.

The use of superfine sugar yields good results overall; however, the dough is noticeably more difficult to work with. The flavor from the dough is better; however, sheetability is reduced as the larger grains of sugar interfere with the sheeting of the dough.

Granulated sugar has the best flavor of the three sugars, but due to its larger crystal sizes, it creates a rougher texture for the sheeting of the dough, which is understandable.

Even though the creaming method may be used to make pastry dough, it should not be used to incorporate air. Air incorporation is detrimental to the structure of dough used for tarts because it alters its shape during the baking process. Sugar's hygroscopic properties help to retain moisture. It prolongs freshness by absorbing moisture from the other ingredients, as well as from the environment. Sugar has a denaturing effect on gluten, which creates a softer crumb, a finer grain, and a moister, more tender texture. Sugar also contributes to the Maillard reaction during the baking process, which imparts color and firmness to the crust.

LEAVENING AGENTS

Both chemical and physical leavening are used to produce pastry dough. Physical leavening occurs in all pastry dough on a range of levels depending on the application. For example, consider the slight leavening of a piecrust in contrast to the dramatic rise of puff pastry as the result of the water content in the dough and the butter turning to steam. Dough, in which the butter is incorporated to a higher degree,

Property	Powdered Sugar	Superfine Sugar	Granulated Sugar
Sheeting properties	XXX	XX	X
Shelf life	XXX	XX	X
Flavor/mouth feel	X	XX	XXX

Figure 12-2
Sugar and Dough Properties

will have a denser texture. A small amount of chemical leavening is commonly used in these doughs. Baking powder is commonly used in pastry dough for lining molds or specialty tarts. For pâte breton, baking powder contributes to the unique texture of the dough.

SALT

Salt is added to most pastry dough to add flavor, improve shelf life, and round out the flavors of the flour. It also has a slight tenderizing effect on the gluten and helps to make the dough less sticky. Salt should be measured by weight to ensure that the proper quantity is used: approximately 1.5 to 2 percent based on the flour weight is standard. Some specialty pastry dough, such as sablé breton, has a distinct salty flavor which is characteristic of that dough. In Bretagne, the region where sablé breton is common, salted butter is also used in the preparation of the cookie.

OTHER INGREDIENTS

Some formulas may call for a small quantity of lemon juice or vinegar to be added to the pastry dough. The addition of an acidic liquid will help relax the gluten so the dough is more extensible for rolling out. Acidity in the dough will also help prevent oxidation, or the slight gray discoloration that occurs when dough is left in the refrigerator for several days.

Variations in flavor as well as texture can be made by using various nut flours, spices, and flavoring extracts. A small percentage of almond meal is commonly used in pâte sucrée as well as pâte sablée, and vanilla bean rather than extract is also used to flavor the dough.

UNSWEETENED PASTRY DOUGH

Unsweetened pastry dough has a variety of functions and can be used for both savory and sweet applications. Depending on the filling, it may be better to have a crust that is not too sweet, even for a filling that has a noticeable level of sweetness. For example, to pair a pâte sucrée tart crust with a lemon curd filling would make a very different flavor than if the curd were in a pâte à foncer crust. Both can be good, but they will be noticeably different. The balancing of sweetness, tenderness, flakiness, and crispness is an important consideration in the creation of desserts and pastries.

The selection of unsweetened pastry dough covered in this chapter includes pie dough, pâte brisée, and pâte à foncer. The two doughs with the greatest difference between them are pie dough and pâte à foncer. Pâte brisée is slightly more enriched than pâte à foncer, and pie dough and is commonly used for savory applications.

Pie dough is mixed using the pie dough method, which is similar to the sanding method used in mixing cookies and butter scones. The method of mixing for pâte brisée and pâte à foncer can be either the creaming method or the sablér method. Both create dough that is generally stronger and easier to roll out into large pieces and that has a crisp texture. The makeup and baking techniques for pie and **tart dough** are covered in detail in Chapter 13. Tart dough encompasses all dough which may be used to make tarts; however, it is usually sweetened pastry dough. All dough should rest for a minimum of 4 hours before working. This will help to minimize shrinkage and ensure that the fats are cold and will not melt as easily into the dough.

PIE DOUGH

There are two types of **pie dough** commonly made: **mealy** and **flaky**. Both are tender, though mealy dough has a more compact texture. The type of pie dough is determined by the degree to which the fat has been incorporated into the flour. In order to create pie dough that is both tender and flaky, the proper types of ingredients, which include flour, fat, and water, should be used. Additional basic ingredients can include salt, sugar, and an acidic liquid such as lemon juice.

The protein content in pastry flour creates a fine balance of strength and tenderness that makes it the standard choice for piecrust. Bread flour, with its higher protein content, produces a tough crust that is hard to roll out thinly. Conversely, cake flour will not provide enough strength to hold its shape throughout the baking process and may be too fragile when rolled out. If a whole wheat crust is desired, whole wheat pastry flour creates a nice, wholesome crust. If no whole wheat pastry flour is available, it is possible to substitute 25 percent of the flour weight with whole wheat bread flour.

Manufactured fats and natural hard fats are most commonly used in pie dough; however, some formulations do call for liquid vegetable oil. Manufactured fats include all varieties of shortening and margarine, while natural fats include butter and lard.

Water is an essential ingredient for pie dough because it binds together the starches and proteins to form dough that has strength. The average ratio of water to flour is 20 to 30 percent.

Sugar, an optional ingredient in pie dough, is generally used in sweet pies at a low percentage of about 5 to 8 percent, based on the flour weight. A small addition of sugar to the dough will make the crust a little more tender and will also help to promote browning.

Mealy Pie Dough

Mealy pie dough is created when the fat is mixed in until the flour–fat mixture resembles coarse cornmeal. Because the hard fat coats a large portion of the flour, it repels moisture and ensures a crisper crust for longer periods of time. This property is essential for pies with wet fillings such as fruits, creams, and chiffons. Mealy pie dough is very versatile and may be used for both tops and bottoms of pies.

Flaky Pie Dough

Flaky pie dough is used for drier fillings and top crusts. The flour and fat are mixed until the fat is the size of walnuts, leaving large fat particles that create a flaky texture once rolled out. In flaky pie dough, more water is needed to hydrate the starch and protein. Flaky pie dough can be used for unbaked pies with wet fillings if the blind-baked crust is coated with a thin layer of chocolate or cocoa butter to help resist moisture damage.

Mixing Pie Dough

When the proper mixing technique is used, successful pie dough is usually the result. Knowing the working properties of the ingredients is important because the temperature and mixing of the dough will determine its workability and the quality of the final product. Pie dough can be mixed by hand or machine with good results, but care must be taken to prevent overmixing the dough when a machine is used.

The important stages of mixing are cutting in the fat and adding water to the fat–flour mixture. It is essential that the fat be cold for cutting in.

If it is too warm, it will be absorbed into the flour. The amount of water required depends on the degree to which the fat is mixed into the flour. To produce a flakier crust, larger pieces of fat are required, and more water is needed to hydrate the available protein and starch. For mealy dough, less water is used because more of the protein and starch have been coated with fat. If the dough is too wet or too dry, it will be difficult to work with, and quality will be compromised.

Mixing by Hand

- Combine the flour, salt, and sugar, and dice the cold butter into 1 inch (2.5 cm) cubes. (See Mixing by Hand Figure 12-3, Step 1.).
- Add the cold butter to the flour mixture. (See Mixing by Hand Figure 12-3, Step 2.)
- With a bowl scraper or bench knife, cut the butter into the flour mixture until the desired consistency is reached (coarse meal for mealy, walnut-sized for flaky). This may be done on a table or counter.
- Add the water and lemon juice (if using), reserving some, and mix until dough forms. (See Mixing by Hand Figure 12-3, Steps 3–5.)
- Add more liquid if needed.
- Transfer the dough to a parchment-lined sheet pan and cover with plastic.
- Place in the refrigerator for at least 4 hours before using.

Mixing by Machine

- In the bowl of a mixer fitted with the paddle attachment, combine the flour, salt, and sugar.
- Dice the cold butter into 1 inch (2.5 cm) cubes and toss them in the flour mixture. (See Mixing by Machine Figure 12-4, Step 1.)
- Mix on a medium speed until the desired consistency is reached (coarse meal for mealy, hazelnut-sized for flaky). (See Mixing by Machine Figure 12-4, Step 2.)
- Add the water and lemon juice (if using), reserving some, and mix until dough forms. (See Mixing by Machine Figure 12-4, Step 3.)
- Add more liquid if needed.
- Transfer the dough to a parchment-lined sheet pan and cover with plastic.
- Place in the refrigerator for at least 4 hours before using.

Precautions for Mixing One of the first steps to ensure success with pie dough is to make sure the temperature of the ingredients is correct. Both the fat and liquid should be cold. The next precaution is to mix the fat into the flour mixture to the proper degree. Insufficient mixing will require that you add more water to the dough, resulting in a crust that may absorb too much liquid. On the other hand, if the flour–fat phase is overmixed and the dough cannot be properly hydrated, the dough will not be strong enough and may shrink excessively during baking.

Finally, the proper amount of water in pie dough is critical. If there is enough water in the dough, overmixing can overwork and strengthen the gluten, resulting in a tough crust. If there is not enough water, the dough may be dry, crumbly, and difficult to work with.

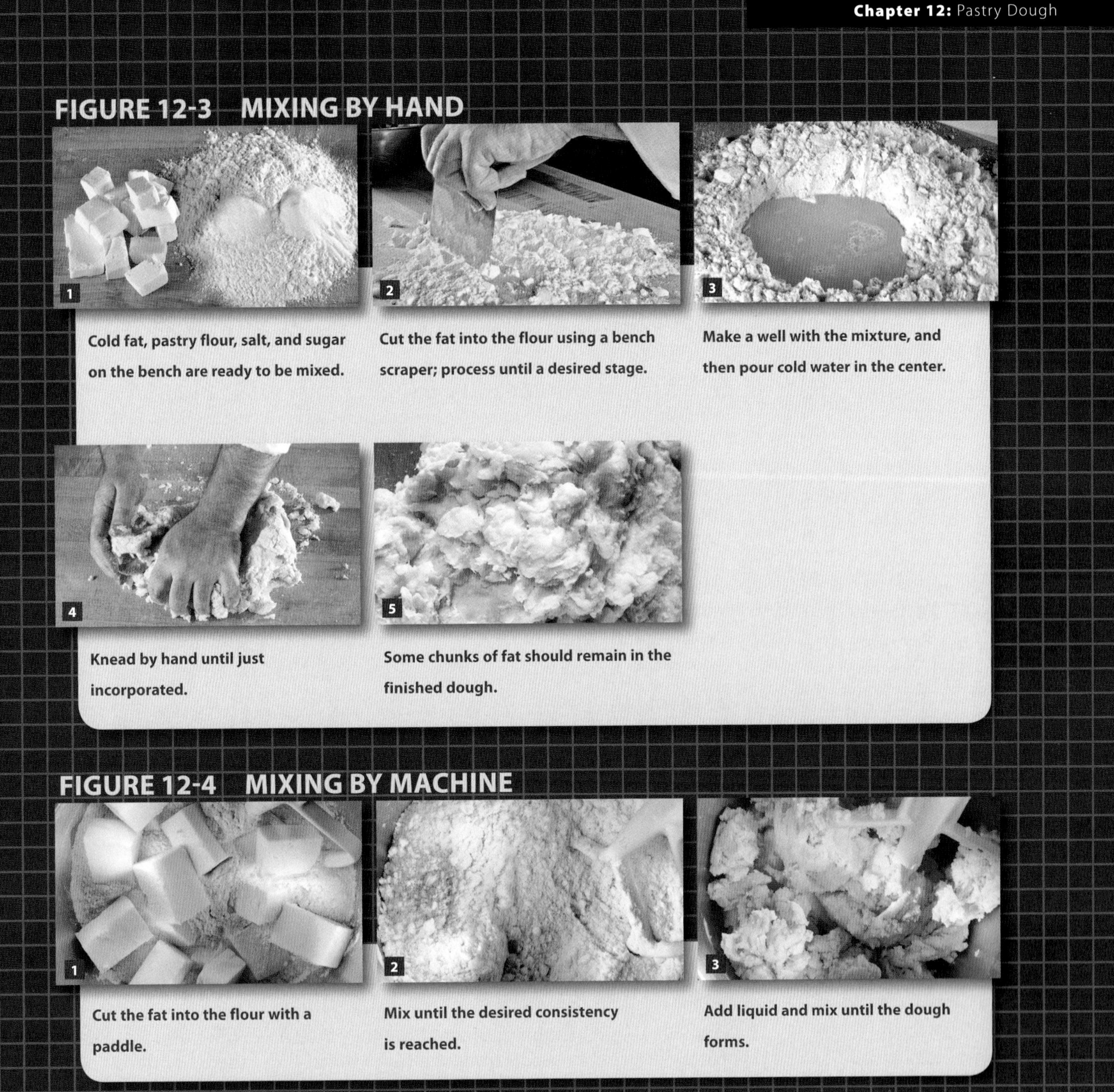

FIGURE 12-3 MIXING BY HAND

1. Cold fat, pastry flour, salt, and sugar on the bench are ready to be mixed.
2. Cut the fat into the flour using a bench scraper; process until a desired stage.
3. Make a well with the mixture, and then pour cold water in the center.
4. Knead by hand until just incorporated.
5. Some chunks of fat should remain in the finished dough.

FIGURE 12-4 MIXING BY MACHINE

1. Cut the fat into the flour with a paddle.
2. Mix until the desired consistency is reached.
3. Add liquid and mix until the dough forms.

PÂTE A FONCER

Pâte à foncer, which translates as "lining pastry," is used primarily for lining molds for pies and tarts. According to *Traite de Patisserie Moderne* (Darenne & Duval, 1974, pp. 54–55), there are five classic variations, which include pâte à foncer fine, pâte à foncer ordinare, pâte à foncer commune, pâte à foncer pour entremets, and foncer levee ordinare pour tarts, flans. It can have little to no sugar in it and can be used for sweet and savory applications. The basic formulation mirrors that of pie dough, but it is processed using butter that is at room temperature instead of cold butter. This produces a finer crumb as the butter disperses more easily throughout the dough.

Figure 12-5
Sample Formulas of Pâte à Foncer

Ingredient	Formula 1 (%)	Formula 2 (%)
Flour	100 (pastry)	100 (bread)
Butter	50	50–75
Salt	2	2
Water	12	—
Sugar	—	0–25
Eggs	—	15–20

A typical formulation (Formula 1) as well as an alternate, richer formulation (Formula 2) for pâte à foncer is shown in Figure 12-5. Depending on the quantity of sugar in the dough, as well as the quality of the flour being used, it may be beneficial to use bread or pastry flour in pâte à foncer. With higher quantities of sugar, the higher protein content of bread flour will add strength to the dough, making it easier to work with. This dough can be enriched with sugar [up to 25 percent of flour weight (FW)], butter can be increased (up to 25 percent more based on FW), and egg may replace water (15 to 20 percent based on FW). Like all rolled, cut dough, pâte à foncer should rest for a minimum of 4 hours before use to ensure the butter is well chilled and the gluten has relaxed.

PÂTE BRISÉE

Pâte brisée is a dough similar to pie dough and pâte à foncer, but it typically always has egg in it. Because pastry is such a dynamic field, and many like to make their own variations, formulas tend to vary significantly from source to source, and pâte brisée is a good example of this tendency. Some varieties may use bread flour, others pastry flour. Some may contain sugar, others not. However, according to *Traite de Patisserie Moderne*, a bible for pastry terminology, pâte brisée should not contain sugar (Darenne & Duval, 1974, p. 60). Some may contain water, others egg, some just yolk. Knowing the properties of the ingredients and how the ingredients work together to affect the dough as a whole is important in understanding the mixing, baking, shelf life, and eating qualities. The two examples of pâte brisée in Figure 12-6 show how they can vary considerably. Formula 1 features a higher percent of butter and utilizes pastry flour, whereas Formula 2 utilizes bread flour and less butter but adds tenderizing agents including egg yolk and powdered sugar.

REVIEW OF UNSWEETENED PASTRY DOUGH

Unsweetened pastry dough is a versatile group of dough, some types of which are very similar, and it can be used for both savory and sweet applications. The choices of ingredients, as for any item, as well as the mixing processes are very important to follow. For all pastry dough, it is necessary to allow it to rest at least 4 hours to ensure that the dough is well chilled and the gluten is well relaxed. After the dough is rolled out (this topic will be covered in more detail in Chapter 13), it should be cut efficiently to minimize waste. Any scrap dough should be added to the next sheeting, and when possible, it is best to preportion dough to prevent waste. Scrap pieces should not exceed 15 percent of the new dough weight.

Ingredients	Formula 1 (%)	Formula 2 (%)
Flour	100 (pastry)	100 (bread)
Butter	60	45
Water	20	18
Egg yolk	—	7
Powdered sugar	—	9
Salt	2	1.8

Figure 12-6
Sample Formulas of Pâte Brisée

SWEET PASTRY DOUGH

Sweet pastry dough has a larger quantity of sugar and egg than a typical pie dough formula, making it sweeter and richer. Several important and prevalent sweet pastry doughs are used, including pâte sucrée, pâte sablée, and pâte à sablé breton. Not only are these doughs used for making tarts, but they may also be used to make cookies or bases for cakes. **Pâte sucrée**, which literally means "sweet pastry," is a traditional French dough that is often used for lining tart molds. **Pâte sablée** is a more tender dough that can be used for lining tart molds, but it can also be used as a base for cake or other pastry. **Pâte à sablé breton** is a dough, originally used for traditional cookies from Brittany, France, that is now often used as a base for tarts and other pastries. Like other pastry dough, all sweet pastry doughs can be rolled thin to create a delicate crust, golden color, and crisp texture; however, when being used for alternate bases, such as for tarts or entremets, the dough is usually thicker. All sweet pastry dough may also be flavored with ingredients like vanilla bean, chocolate, almond, or pistachio to add uniqueness. As with any pastry, the ingredients and mixing processes used for pastry dough will affect its final taste and texture.

INGREDIENT FUNCTIONS FOR SWEET PASTRY DOUGH

If the flour used for sweet pastry dough is too weak, the dough will not have sufficient strength to be rolled out, transferred to the tart pan, and lined. If it is too strong, it will produce dough that is tough to roll out, requires more hydration, and shrinks excessively during baking. The best choice is low-protein bread flour or all-purpose flour, both of which provide sufficient strength yet allow tart dough to remain tender and crisp. The protein content of the flour is essential for adding strength because the sugar content makes the dough weaker, possibly making the dough tear during sheeting.

Unsalted butter is the standard choice for sweetened pastry dough because it lends a sweet, rich flavor. Salted butter, or half-salted butter, may be used for specialty versions of pâte à sablé breton as well as some pâte sablée. If this is the case, the salt in the formula should be balanced and adjusted to taste for the ideal outcome.

Three types of sugar are common in sweet pastry dough: granulated, superfine, and powdered. The choice will affect the dough's texture, workability, and flavor. Refer to Figure 12-2 for a review of these properties. The finer powdered sugar, depending on the method of production, will not incorporate any air into the dough, which will reduce spread and create a dough that is easier to work with for mass production. If white granulated sugar is used, flavor is improved; however, care must be taken to not incorporate too much air into the butter because tart dough should not spread much in the oven.

Eggs are used as the primary source of hydration in sweet pastry dough in larger quantity than in unsweetened pastry dough. The egg yolk adds richness in color as well as flavor, while natural emulsifiers in the yolk help make the dough easier to roll out and work with. In certain instances, the egg yolk is precooked and pressed through a sieve before being incorporated into the dough to create a less dense, more crumbly texture. If this is done, it is essential that the yolk not remain uncovered for too long after it is prepared because it will dry out and negatively affect the hydration of the dough. Though seldom used in sweet pastry dough preparations, the egg white adds crispness and stability to baked dough.

Salt is used to round off the flavors of the other ingredients in the dough, especially the flour. Some specialty preparations may use salted butter to intensify the flavor of a dough. Additionally, specialty salts, such as fleur de sel de Guérande, may be used to add a unique, surprising saltiness.

Baking powder is an optional ingredient but is often added to sweet pastry dough to lighten it up. It is generally added in small quantities of about 0.5 percent of the weight of the flour. Baking powder is usually used in the classic sablé breton and is largely responsible for its final texture as well as its golden brown color.

MIXING METHODS

There are two main mixing methods for sweet pastry dough: the sanding and creaming methods. The creaming method for sweet pastry dough is adapted from the standard creaming method and produces results similar to the sanding method. Please review Chapter 10 for a complete overview of the sanding method, as well as the traditional creaming method.

Sanding Method

For the sanding method, a large portion of the flour and sugar is coated with fat, and then eggs are added to hydrate the remaining flour and add strength. The result is a crisp and tender crust. If properly rolled out and blind baked, the crust should not shrink, and pie weights are typically not needed.

Creaming Method

For the creaming method for sweet pastry dough, the butter and sugar are creamed minimally, to limit the quantity of air introduced to the dough. It is important that the butter be very soft to help limit the incorporation of air and to ensure that the butter is thoroughly distributed throughout the dough. If mixed properly using the soft butter technique, the results should be similar to the sanding method. After the fat and sugar are blended, the eggs and then the flour are added and mixed to incorporation. More people have adapted formulas calling for the sanding method technique to the soft butter creaming method because the results are more consistent as the butter texture can be controlled. It is more difficult to control the exact incorporation of the butter into the dry ingredients, especially during warmer seasons.

PÂTE SUCRÉE

Pâte sucrée is a rich sweet dough that is usually made using the creaming method, but it can also be made using the sanding method. Pâte sucrée is used for lining pastry shells or as a base for cut-out cookies. The classic formulation for this dough is 100 percent flour, 50 percent butter, 50 percent sugar, and 20 percent egg. Some bakers add a small amount of baking powder to further lighten the texture. Pâte sucrée bakes into a crisp texture and is ideal for tarts because it is easy to handle for larger productions and generally has a good shelf life.

PÂTE SABLÉE

Sablé, a French term that means "sandy," is often used to refer to cookies. Pâte sablée, or shortbread pastry, is delicate, rich, and crumbly due to the high ratio of butter and sugar to flour. A classic formulation contains 100 percent flour, 60 percent butter, and 40 percent sugar. Pâte sablée can also contain baking powder, which gives it a lighter texture and, consequently, a shorter shelf life. Some versions add almond meal for added flavor and texture, and vanilla bean is also a common addition.

Though not traditional, some versions of pâte sablée contain egg yolk, which may be precooked. The addition of fresh egg yolk makes a slightly richer dough and gives the dough some extra strength due to the water content coming from the yolk. If cooked yolk is added, the dough becomes more tender (due to the nullification of the lecithin) and thus more difficult to process. Pâte sablée made using cooked yolk is generally used for cookies and bases for petit four or entremets. Pâte sablée can be mixed either by the creaming method or the sanding method, depending on the formula being used.

PÂTE BRETON AND PÂTE À SABLÉ BRETON

Pâte breton, a specialty dough that originated in Brittany, France, is baked traditionally as a cookie. The traditional mixing method for pâte breton begins by whipping egg yolks and sugar, adding soft butter and mixing just to incorporation, and then adding the flour sifted with baking powder and mixing just until incorporation. This technique results in a cookie with an open crumb and a very sandy texture.

Pâte à sablé breton is a variation on pâte breton and is commonly used for tarts and petit four bases. Pâte à sablé breton is not suitable for lining tart molds as it is such a tender dough and lacks the strength to line a vertical wall of a mold.

REVIEW OF SWEET PASTRY DOUGH

With just several sweet pastry dough bases, one can make a wide range of products that have different textures and flavors. Some preparations are better than others for larger production. For example, pâte sucrée can tolerate more handling than can pâte sablée with cooked egg yolks. The flavors and textures of the dough should complement the components of which they are paired. Understanding the range of sweet dough, one has the ability to create several styles of pastry bases.

PUFF PASTRY DOUGH

Puff pastry is a classic French pastry dough with a long history. In its rudimentary forms, it has been around since the 15th century. It is a laminated dough, but it is not technically considered Viennoiserie. Puff pastry is not yeasted, and typically no sugar is added to the dough. Its richness is due to the high quantity of butter used to create paper-thin layers of dough that bake into crisp, light pastry.

Puff pastry is often used as a component to make a dessert referred to as **mille feuille**, which literally translated means "thousand layers," a reference to the many layers created in the dough during the lamination process. Because it is not sweet, puff pastry dough applications extend to the savory kitchen. It can often be used for dishes such as beef Wellington, salmon en croute, rustic savory galette, or savory appetizers. In the pastry shop, a wide range of puff pastry is used for breakfast pastry, tarts, sweet galettes, cakes, and classic pastries such as napoleons, palmiers, apple turnovers, vol-au-vents, Jalousie, and cream horns.

Although puff pastry is made from a minimum of four basic ingredients (flour, water, butter, salt), the process of making the dough transforms it into one like none other. Additional ingredients such as lemon juice, white wine, sugar (in very small quantities), malt, and eggs can be added to the basic dough.

The choice of flour is typically low-protein bread flour. However, if the puff pastry is made by hand, up to 25 percent of the flour weight can be substituted with pastry flour for easier workability. The water used for puff pastry should always be cold, while salt will help even the flavors of the flour and butter. Ideally, the butter should be European-style cultured butter with a higher fat content. The butter is, on average, equal to half of the dough weight. Acidic ingredients such as lemon juice or white wine can help add some extensibility but also help prevent dough oxidization. The Italian variety has a small quantity of egg and sometimes sugar that slightly enriches the dough.

BASIC PROCESS

Like Viennoiserie, the basic process of puff pastry involves mixing dough that is classically referred to as the détrempe and enclosing the beurrage (butter block) in it. This package is then sheeted out and given a series of folds. Because too few folds will cause the butter to melt out of the dough, puff pastry requires at least four single folds, and five or a maximum of six is normal. The folds for puff pastry can be completed in the same way as for other laminated doughs by using single and double folds independently or combined. Refer to Chapter 9 for a review of lamination.

TYPES OF PUFF PASTRY

The four main types of puff pastry are blitz, traditional, Italian, and inverted. Each has its own virtues and followers, and it is beneficial to understand them all to know what is most appropriate for particular needs. In addition to these four basic formulas, there are a handful of possible variations based on inclusions such as cocoa powder or pistachio paste into the dough, or butter for roll-in.

Blitz Puff Pastry

Blitz puff pastry is the most basic of the puff dough selections. **Blitz puff pastry**, also known as quick puff pastry, is named for its fast preparation. It is essentially very flaky pie dough that has had turns completed on it. The average percentage of butter in the dough is 75 percent of the flour weight.

Blitz puff dough is mixed only until rough dough is formed, and it is essential to not overmix it. The butter chunks in the dough should be about golf-ball sized in order to provide proper layering for lamination. It may appear shaggy out of the mixer, but it will become more cohesive once lamination begins. After the dough is mixed, it should rest in the refrigerator for a minimum of 20 minutes. Four single folds are standard

FIGURE 12-7 TRADITIONAL PUFF PASTRY

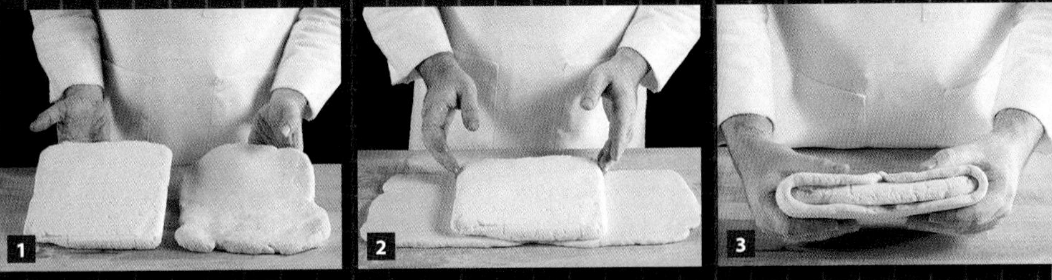

1 Prepared dough and butter are shown.

2 Roll out the dough to double the size of the butter.

3 Enclose the butter into the dough.

4 Rotate the dough 90 degrees, and then roll out the dough for the first fold.

for blitz puff because there is not a large, concentrated mass of butter in the dough. The dough should rest for a minimum of 20 minutes after the first two folds, as well as after the third and fourth folds. Too many folds can sacrifice the volume and flakiness of the final product.

Traditional Puff Pastry

Traditional puff pastry is made from a beurrage and détrempe and requires a more involved process than the blitz puff. The butter for traditional puff pastry is typically 50 percent of the dough weight. With an average of 50 percent of the flour hydrated, the dough is fairly stiff, which is required to create distinct layers of dough and butter.

The mixing of the détrempe is limited to ingredient incorporation only. After it is mixed, it should rest in the refrigerator for at least 1 hour before lamination begins. As with yeasted laminated doughs, it is possible to do two folds back to back. Between folds, the dough should rest in the refrigerator, or even possibly the freezer, to maintain a cold temperature. (See Traditional Puff Pastry Figure 12-7.)

Italian Puff Pastry

Italian puff pastry, also known as **pasta sfogliata**, varies in composition from blitz and traditional in that white wine and eggs are included in the dough. The mixing process is another difference. In the case of Italian puff, an intensive mix is required. The process for laminating Italian puff pastry is the same as traditional puff pastry, and the same guidelines should be followed.

Inverted Puff Pastry

Inverted puff pastry is best made using a reversible dough sheeter. As the name implies, the beurrage is on the outside of the dough. This creates a crisper, flakier puff pastry because the outside surfaces become one during the folding process, increasing the layers of fat.

The formulation of inverted puff dough varies significantly from other puff dough because the technique is so different. In order to make a sheetable butter that does not readily melt and is more extensible, the butter is first mixed with flour. In all, approximately 40 percent by weight of flour is added to the butter. The détrempe for this dough is richer as well, with an average of about 30 percent butter in the dough. It is essential that this butter be thoroughly mixed in and then chilled, as opposed to the beurrage for traditional and Italian puff, which can be used right away. The equivalent of five single folds is required for inverted puff pastry. (See Inverted Puff Pastry Figure 12-8.)

FIGURE 12-8 INVERTED PUFF PASTRY

1. Mix the butter and flour for the beurrage of inverted puff pastry.
2. Spread the butter mixture on a heavy plastic sheet into a flat block shape.
3. Mix the dough in a mixing bowl fitted with a hook attachment; process to incorporation only.
4. Prepare the beurrage and cold dough.
5. Roll out the beurrage to twice the size of the dough and place the dough on the center. 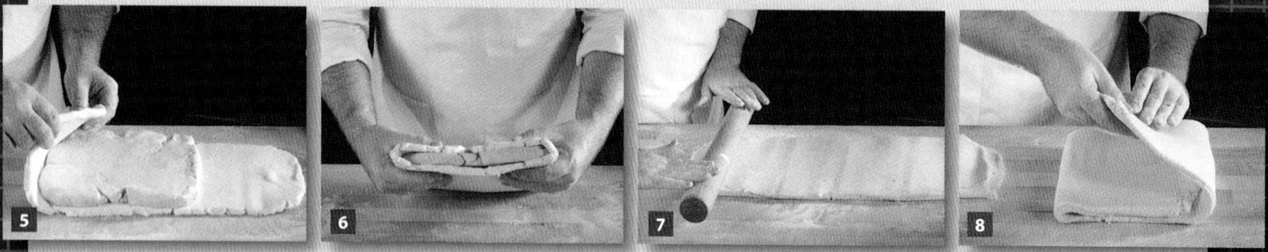
6. Enclose the dough in the beurrage.
7. Roll the dough out to three times its width.
8. Complete a single fold.

WORKING WITH PUFF DOUGH

When working with puff dough, it is imperative to work quickly and efficiently to avoid warming. Because the dough is typically sheeted very thin, this happens quickly. Once sheeted out, the dough must be relaxed, or it can shrink after it is cut. In addition, it is important to allow the puff dough to rest for at least 30 minutes in the refrigerator after the product is made up to prevent the pastry shape from shrinking during baking. (See Working with Puff Dough—Jalousie Figure 12-9.)

PÂTE À CHOUX

Pâte à choux is a classic French pastry preparation that uses two stages of preparation: cooking the paste and baking the paste. Pâte à choux has roots to the 16th century and was originally made by adding eggs to a paste made from potatoes. This dish is still made today and is known as pommes dauphine. The word derivation of *choux* (French for "cabbage") refers to the irregular shape it takes on as it bakes (historically). It is a versatile and important component of every chefs repertoire, used for many applications in pastry as well as cooking. Products commonly made from pâte à choux include cream puffs, éclairs, profiteroles, and the classic Paris-Brest.

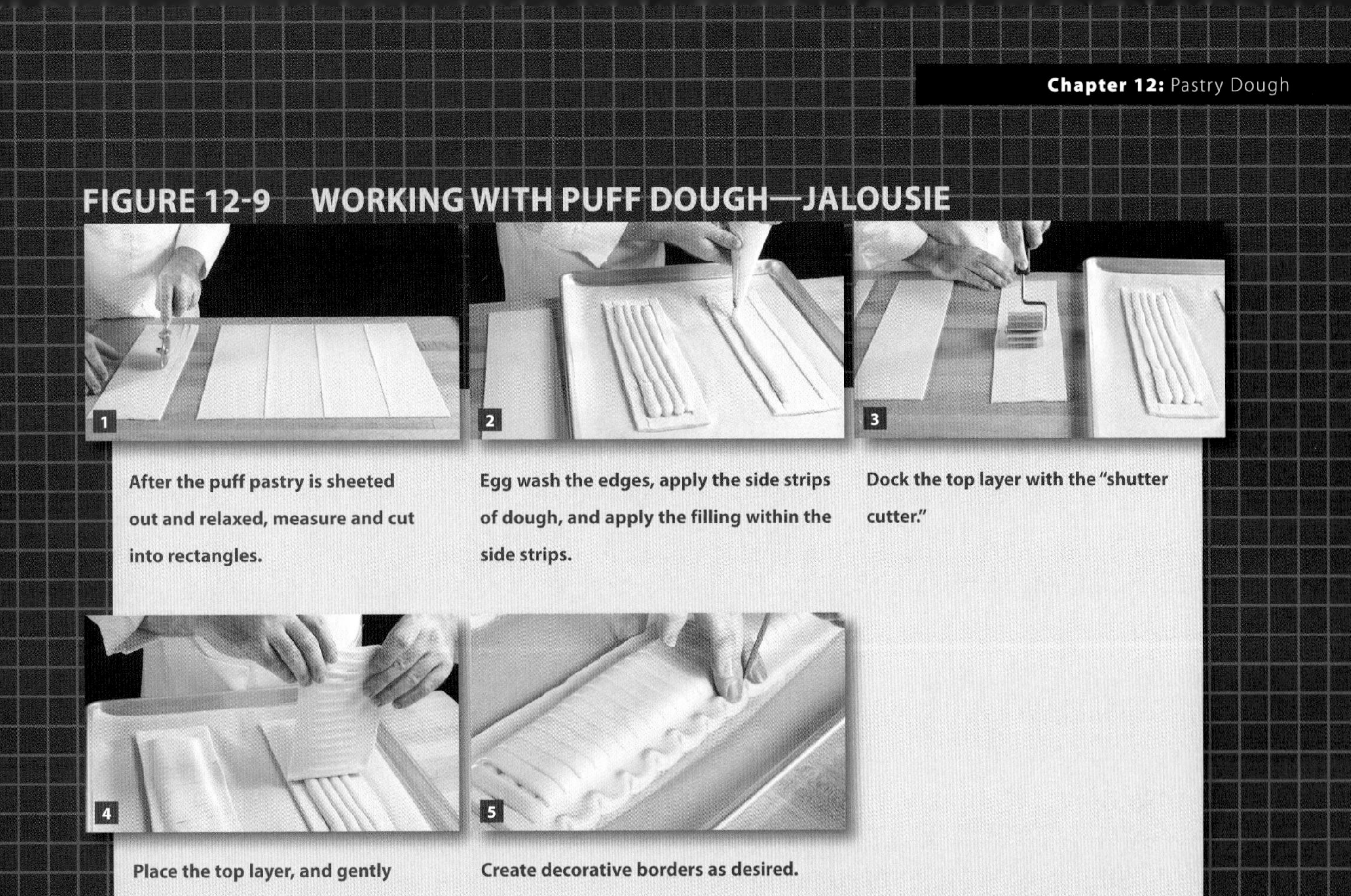

FIGURE 12-9 WORKING WITH PUFF DOUGH—JALOUSIE

1. After the puff pastry is sheeted out and relaxed, measure and cut into rectangles.
2. Egg wash the edges, apply the side strips of dough, and apply the filling within the side strips.
3. Dock the top layer with the "shutter cutter."
4. Place the top layer, and gently press onto the side strips to seal the edge.
5. Create decorative borders as desired.

Pâte à choux is a combination of milk and/or water, butter, margarine or shortening, sugar, salt, pastry flour, and whole egg. The use of milk gives the choux more color during baking and creates a more tender pastry, whereas water allows for baking at a higher temperature. Generally, a combination of both water and milk is used. Unsalted butter is typically used for the fat; however, margarine and shortening may be used as well. Pastry flour is used for its milder protein content, which prevents the dough from distorting too much during the baking process. If bread flour is used, the paste will require more hydration, and the paste may be tough and not expand well in the oven. A small quantity of sugar is typically added, and it lends a slightly sweet flavor as well as aid in coloration. Salt rounds off the flavors, helps to bind the water to the paste, and makes smoother dough. Eggs should always be fresh to ensure optimal flavor, and they should be at room temperature to ensure easy incorporation into the paste.

Cooking and Baking

To begin pâte à choux, the liquid, fat, salt, and sugar are combined in a stainless steel pot and are brought to a boil. It is important to heat this mixture slowly at first to ensure the fat melts evenly as the liquid warms. If there is too much water evaporation via steam, the emulsion could

FIGURE 12-10 PÂTE À CHOUX

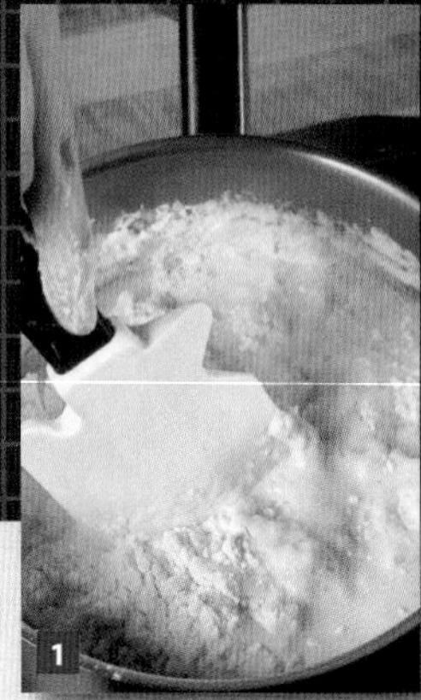
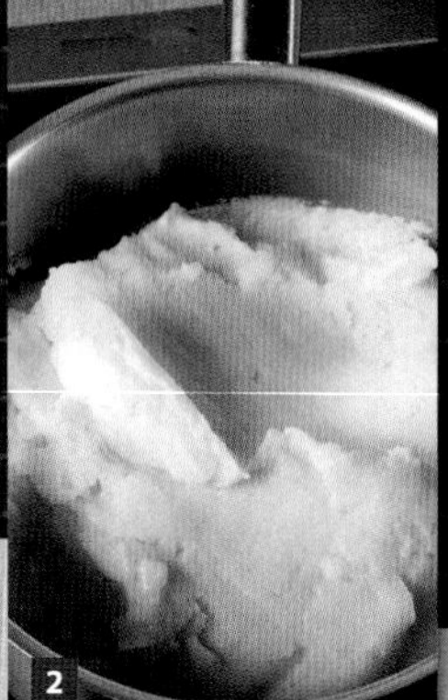
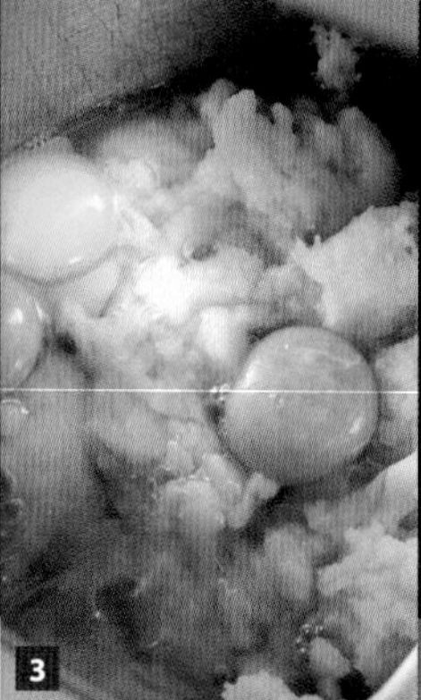
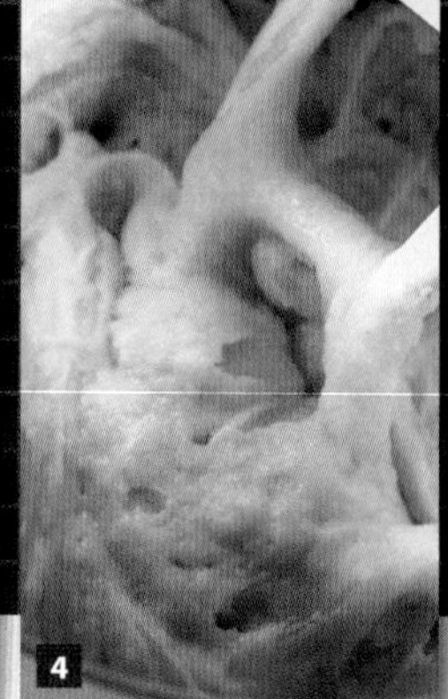
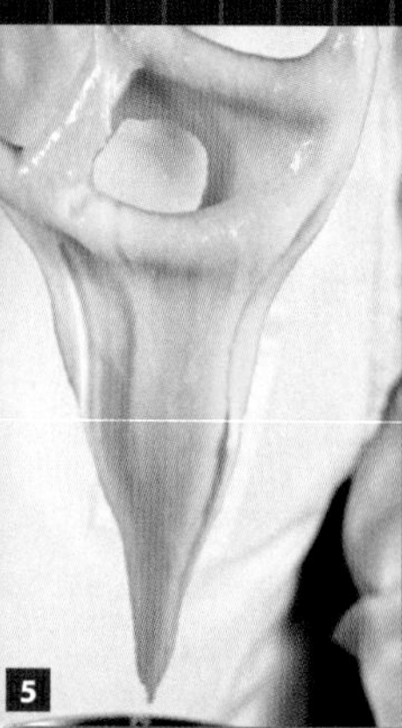

1 **After the liquid is brought to a boil, remove the pot from the heat and add the sifted flour.**

2 **Cook the paste, stirring constantly, until it clears from the side of the pot.**

3 **Transfer the paste into a mixing bowl, begin mixing, and then add 75 percent of the eggs.**

4 **Mix until smooth; adjust the consistency with the remaining eggs and hot milk if necessary.**

5 **The paste is finished with the desired consistency.**

break after the flour is added. Once this mixture has boiled, it is then removed from the heat, the flour is added all at once, and the mixture is stirred until a thick paste forms (see Pâte à Choux Figure 12-10, Step 1). The mixture is then returned to low heat and stirred just until the flour pulls away from the sides of the pot (see Pâte à Choux Figure 12-10, Step 2). During this phase, the starch in the flour is hydrated and binds with the liquid phase (butter, milk, and water), which helps to stabilize the emulsion. It is important to not overcook this paste; otherwise, the proteins will be denatured and the flour will lose its ability to hold this liquid and to then fully absorb the egg.

Next, the paste is transferred to a mixer fitted with a paddle attachment and is beaten for a few moments. Then, three-fourths of the egg is added at once (see Pâte à Choux Figure 12-10, Step 3), and after incorporation the rest is added to achieve the proper texture of batter (see Pâte à Choux Figure 12-10, Step 4). If all the egg has been added and the batter is still stiff, add warm milk to adjust the paste to the proper consistency (see Pâte à Choux Figure 12-10, Step 5). Whether or not milk is added, as well as how much milk is added, depends on the age, quality, and moisture content of the flour. It is important to not overmix pâte à choux, which can easily happen when using a machine for mixing. Pâte à choux is easily mixed by hand with almost no worry of overmixing.

The egg in pâte à choux is required to maintain the emulsion and increase the percentage of liquid in the paste. The expansion of pâte à choux is due to the creation of steam from within the pastry during the baking process. If the paste is too dry, there will not be sufficient steam generation to leaven the paste, and if it is too wet, the paste will not be able to hold the shape that the steam creates. Properly made pâte à choux should have a shiny, smooth appearance. It should not be too soft, and it should relax in shape just slightly once piped or deposited.

After pâte à choux is piped (see Piping Figure 12-11), it can be egg washed, scored, and baked. The purpose of scoring the pâte à choux is to help encourage an even expansion of the paste in the oven. An easy way to score the paste is to slightly indent it with a fork in a criss-cross pattern.

FIGURE 12-11 PIPING

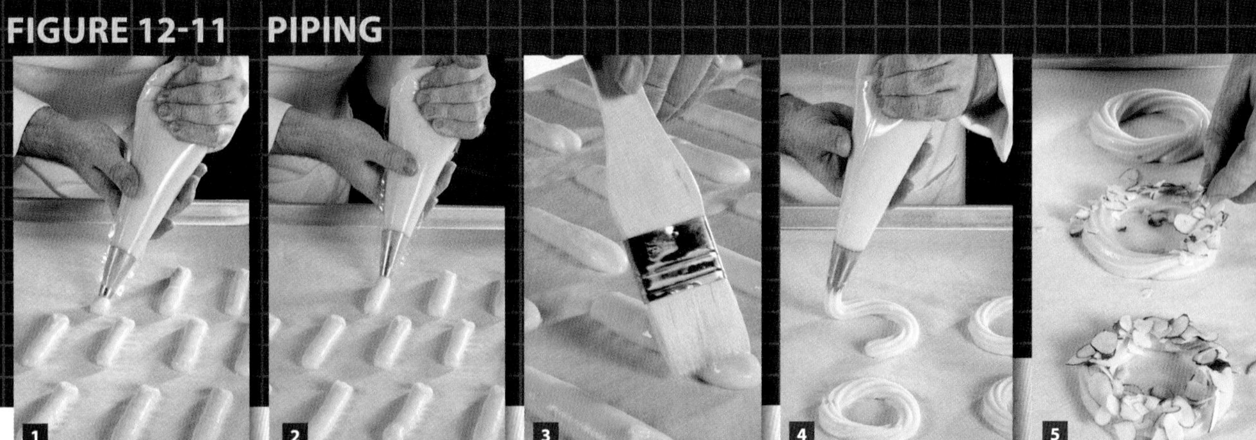

1 Pipe the éclairs to the desired length.

2 At the end of the éclair, flip the tip towards the top of the éclair to avoid a tail.

3 Egg wash the surface, smoothing out any tails.

4 Pipe Paris-Brest to the desired diameter.

5 After egg washing, top with sliced almonds.

It is best to bake the pastry in a staged oven, starting at a medium-high temperature [350°F (177°C) convection] and lowering the temperature as the bake progresses [to 325°F (163°C) after 5 to 7 minutes]. The initial temperature heats the pastry quickly, creating the steam required for leavening. If the pastry becomes too hot, too much steam can be created and a misshaped or cracked pastry will result. The proteins from the egg and flour are stretched when they are warmed and held until they are set by oven heat. Once the full volume is achieved and the crust begins to form, the temperature should be decreased and the vent should be opened. Pâte à choux should be baked until it is golden brown and "dry" in the center. This can be tested by breaking open a piece out of the oven and feeling the moisture level on the inside of the pastry. Ironically, it should feel slightly moist. If pâte à choux is prematurely removed from the oven, the pastry is at risk of collapse because the excessive moisture from within the pastry evaporates through the crust and makes it weak.

Unbaked as well as baked pâte à choux can be stored in the freezer with good results. To store pâte à choux unbaked, it is best to use a blast freezer and to freeze it for a maximum of 2 weeks. Upon thorough defrosting, the pastry can be baked as normal. To freeze baked pâte à choux, the pieces should be frozen on sheet pans and then consolidated for space-conscious storage. Once required, it can be finished as needed. All pâte à choux products have a fairly short shelf life of 24 hours because the pastry tends to soften excessively.

FORMULA

PIE DOUGH

The pursuit of the perfect pie dough has been an American obsession for generations. Each family has its own secret recipe, and each professional his or her techniques. Here we offer an expert-tested version that belongs in every baker's tool kit.

Ingredients	Baker's %	Kilogram	US decimal	Lb & Oz		Test
Pastry flour	100.00	2.191	4.831	4	13 ¼	15 ½ oz
Sugar	5.00	0.110	0.242		3 ⅞	¾ oz
Salt	2.00	0.044	0.097		1 ½	1 ½ tsp
Butter	70.00	1.534	3.382	3	6 ⅛	10 ⅞ oz
Cold water	30.00	0.657	1.449	1	7 ¼	4 ⅝ oz
Total	207.00	4.536	10.000	10	0	2 lb

Process

1. Mix the flour, sugar, salt, and butter until the pieces of butter are the appropriate size for either flaky or mealy dough, as desired.
2. Add the water to the flour mixture and mix until just incorporated. See note below.
3. Portion the dough as desired and allow it to rest in the refrigerator for at least 4 hours or store in the freezer for longer periods of time.

Note

The amount of water needed can vary according to the moisture content of the flour, as well as the degree to which the fat is being cut into the flour. The more the fat is blended, the less water will be required.

Blind Baking

1. Line the prepared pie shells with paper and weights. Bake in a convection oven at 385°F (196°C).
2. After 10 minutes, remove the paper and weights and bake for an additional 10 minutes or until golden brown.
3. Alternately, sandwich the dough between two aluminum pie tins and bake upside-down until golden brown, approximately 15 to 20 minutes.

FORMULA

PÂTE À FONCER

This French version of basic pie dough has an exceptionally fine texture that makes it perfect for use in lining tart molds. Pâte à foncer can be used for both sweet and savory applications.

Ingredients	Baker's %	Kilogram	US decimal	Lb & Oz		Test
Butter	75.00	1.680	3.704	3	11 ¼	11 ⅞ oz
Salt	2.00	0.045	0.099		1 ⅝	1 ½ tsp
Sugar	1.50	0.034	0.074		1 ⅛	1 tsp
Egg yolks	4.00	0.090	0.198		3 ⅛	⅝ oz
Milk	20.00	0.448	0.988		15 ¾	3 ⅛ oz
Pastry flour	100.00	2.240	4.938	4	15	15 ¾ oz
Total	202.50	4.536	10.000	10	0	2 lb

Process

1. Soften the butter and mix with the paddle attachment.
2. Add the salt, sugar, yolks, and milk, and then add the flour. Mix until just incorporated; be careful not to overmix.
3. Transfer to a sheet pan and reserve in the refrigerator at least 4 hours.
4. Bake at 385°F (196°C) in a convection oven or 425°F (219°C) in a deck oven until golden.

FORMULA

PÂTE BRISÉE

Pâte brisée is the French version of classic pie or tart pastry. Flavorful, quick to make, and easy to roll out, it also has a high ratio of fat to flour, which lends a tender texture and buttery flavor to this French staple. It is used in both sweet and savory applications.

Ingredients	Baker's %	Kilogram	US decimal	Lb & Oz		Test
Pastry flour	100.00	2.492	5.495	5	7⅞	1 lb 1⅜ oz
Salt	2.00	0.050	0.110		1¾	2 tsp
Butter	60.00	1.495	3.297	3	4¾	10⅜ oz
Water, cold	20.00	0.498	1.099	1	1⅝	3½ oz
Total	182.00	4.536	10.000	10	0	2 lb

Process

1. Blend the butter into the flour and salt in the bowl of a mixer fitted with the paddle attachment until mealy.
2. Gradually mix in the water until the dough comes together.
3. Cover with plastic wrap and refrigerate for at least 4 hours.
4. Bake at 385°F (196°C) in a convection oven.

FORMULA

PÂTE SUCRÉE

Sometimes referred to as a sweet tart dough, pâte sucrée is similar to pâte brisée, but it is further enriched with egg yolks and more sugar. It is similar to the American "short dough."

Ingredients	Baker's %	Kilogram	US decimal	Lb & Oz		Test
Bread flour	100.00	1.963	4.328	4	5¼	13⅞ oz
Powdered sugar	40.23	0.790	1.741	1	11⅞	5⅝ oz
Baking powder	0.57	0.011	0.025		⅜	½ tsp
Butter	50.00	0.982	2.164	2	2⅝	6⅞ oz
Eggs	25.29	0.497	1.095	1	1½	3½ oz
Almond meal	14.94	0.293	0.647		10⅜	2⅛ oz
Vanilla bean	Each	4	4		4	1 each
Total	231.03	4.536	10.000	10	0	2 lb

Process

1. Sift the flour, powered sugar, and baking powder, and add to a mixing bowl fitted with the paddle attachment.
2. Add the butter and mix on medium speed until mealy.
3. Add the eggs and once the dough begins to come together, add the almond meal and mix until the dough comes together.
4. Cover the dough in plastic film, and reserve in the refrigerator for a minimum of 4 hours.
5. Sheet to the desired thickness, dock if required, and reserve in the refrigerator for at least 30 minutes and up to 2 days. Line the tart pans as desired.
6. Blind bake at 325°F (163°C) in a convection oven for 10 to 12 minutes, or until light golden brown.

Variation

Chocolate pâte sucrée can be obtained by replacing 20 percent of the flour with cocoa powder.

FORMULA

PÂTE SABLÉE

Most often used for dessert tarts, this crust is cookie-like and crumbly, giving it the name, *sablé*, which means "sand" in French.

Ingredients	Baker's %	Kilogram	US decimal	Lb & Oz		Test
Egg yolks, cooked	17.14	0.285	0.627		10	2 oz
Butter, soft	81.43	1.352	2.981	2	15¾	9½ oz
Salt	0.29	0.005	0.011		⅛	⅛ tsp
Powdered sugar	42.86	0.712	1.569	1	9⅛	5 oz
Egg yolks	17.14	0.285	0.627		10	2 oz
Almond meal	14.29	0.237	0.523		8⅜	1⅝ oz
Pastry flour	100.00	1.661	3.661	3	10⅝	11¾ oz
Total	273.15	4.536	10.000	10	0	2 lb

Process

1. Cook the egg yolks and reserve, covered.
2. Cream the butter, salt, and sugar until well combined.
3. Press the egg yolks through a fine sieve and blend in to the butter–sugar mixture with the fresh egg yolks.
4. Add the almond meal to this mixture.

5. Add the sifted flour and mix to incorporation.
6. Cover in plastic, and store in the refrigerator until ready to use.
7. Roll out the dough and cut out circles for cookies or tarts.
8. For tarts: Line tart rings with dough; allow to rest 30 minutes.
9. For cookies: Place the circles on a parchment-lined sheet pan and brush with egg wash.
10. Bake the pâte sablée at 325°F (163°C) in a convection oven with the vent open until golden brown.

FORMULA

PÂTE BRETON

This traditional short dough from Brittany is enriched with egg yolk and a generous amount of butter. It is a slightly salty sweet dough that makes an ideal base for tarts and cakes, and can also be used for cookies.

Ingredients	Baker's %	Kilogram	US decimal	Lb & Oz		Test
Egg yolks	30.00	0.478	1.054	1	⅞	3⅜ oz
Granulated sugar	70.00	1.116	2.460	2	7⅜	7⅞ oz
Butter	75.00	1.196	2.636	2	10⅛	8⅜ oz
Salt	1.00	0.016	0.035		½	⅔ tsp
Pastry flour	100.00	1.594	3.515	3	8¼	11¼ oz
Baking powder	8.50	0.136	0.299		4¾	1 oz
Total	284.50	4.536	10.000	10	0	2 lb

Process

1. Sift together the flour and baking powder; set aside.
2. Cream the yolks and sugar until light.
3. Add the soft butter and salt and mix to incorporate.
4. Next, add the sifted ingredients. Mix until the dough comes together.
5. Use immediately or store, covered in the refrigerator, until needed.
6. Pipe or sheet to the desired shape and size.
7. Bake the pâte breton at 325°F (163°C) in a convection oven with the vent open until golden brown.

FORMULA

BLITZ PUFF PASTRY

This appropriately named quick puff pastry takes about half the time to make as standard puff pastry. It is important to not work the butter into the dough too much. It should be quite large before lamination begins to ensure an ideal final flaky texture. Blitz puff paste can be used for many of the applications that other puff pastes are used for.

Ingredients	Baker's %	Kilogram	US decimal	Lb & Oz		Test
Flour	100.00	1.981	4.367	4	5⅞	14 oz
Butter, cold	75.00	1.486	3.275	3	4⅜	10½ oz
Salt	2.00	0.040	0.087		1⅜	2 tsp
Malt	1.00	0.020	0.044		¾	1½ tsp
Lemon juice	1.00	0.020	0.044		¾	1 tsp
Water	50.00	0.990	2.183	2	2⅞	7 oz
Total	229.00	4.536	10.000	10	0	2 lb

Process

1. Combine the flour, butter, salt, and malt in a mixing bowl fitted with the paddle attachment.
2. Mix on low speed until the butter is distributed evenly and is still in large chunks.
3. Add the lemon juice and cold water to the bowl, and mix just until a dough is formed. Do not overmix.
4. Transfer the dough to a flour-dusted sheet plan and flatten it.
5. Cover the dough with plastic and place it in the refrigerator for 20 minutes.

Lamination

1. Give the dough a total of five single folds.
2. Two folds can be given back to back with a 30 minute rest between folds.
3. After the last fold (fifth single), allow the dough to rest for 30 minutes.
4. At this point, the dough can be used as desired.

FORMULA

CLASSIC PUFF PASTRY

Puff pastry is also called *pâte feuilletée* in French. The dough rises because of the stream created from the large amount of butter contained in between the many layers of dough. Puff pastry is the foundation of countless pastries, desserts, savories, and other delicacies.

Ingredients	Baker's %	Kilogram	US decimal	Lb & Oz		Test
Bread flour	100.00	2.800	6.173	6	¾	1 lb 3¾ oz
Water	48.00	1.344	2.963	2	15⅜	9½ oz
Butter	10.00	0.280	0.617		9⅞	2 oz
Salt	2.00	0.056	0.123		2	2 tsp
Lemon juice	1.00	0.028	0.062		1	1 tsp
Malt	1.00	0.028	0.062		1	1½ tsp
Total	162.00	4.536	10.000	10	0	2 lb
Butter for lamination	50.00	2.268	5.000	5	0	1 lb

Note
Butter for lamination is a percent of the total dough weight.

Process

Mixing	Mix all the ingredients (except for the butter for lamination) to incorporation (3 to 4 minutes on first speed). Transfer to a lightly floured sheet pan, form into a flat square, and cover with plastic.
Resting	Allow the dough the rest in the refrigerator for 1 hour.
Lamination	5 to 6 single folds 2 folds at a time; allow 30 minutes rest between each set of folds.
Sheeting	After a resting time of at least 30 minutes, sheet the puff pastry to ⅛ inch (2 mm). Use as desired.
Baking	350°F (176°C) in a convection oven. Time will vary according to product composition.

Shaping Option

Apple Turnover (Chausson Pomme)

Sheet out the dough to ⅛ inch (2 mm) thick. Cut into 3½ inch (90 mm) circles. Roll out into ovals, and pipe apple butter on the center. Water wash the border and fold in half to seal. Crimp the edge and egg wash. Rest in the refrigerator for at least 30 minutes. Create a vent in the top of the pastry and egg wash again before baking. Bake at 350°F (176°C) for 20 to 25 minutes, or until the edges are golden brown.

FORMULA

INVERTED PUFF PASTRY

Inverted puff pastry is formed when the butter, mixed with some flour, is placed on the outside of the dough. Though this may be intimidating to work with, the dough is actually easier to work with than classic puff pastry because it doesn't become as sticky. Additionally, it tends to retain its shape more consistently with less shrinkage during baking.

Ingredients	Baker's %	Kilogram	US decimal	Lb & Oz		Test
Bread flour	100.00	2.724	6.006	6	⅛	1 lb 3¼ oz
Water	39.00	1.062	2.342	2	5½	7½ oz
Butter	22.50	0.613	1.351	1	5⅝	4⅜ oz
Salt	3.00	0.082	0.180		2⅞	⅝ oz
Malt	1.00	0.027	0.060		1	1 tsp
Lemon juice	1.00	0.027	0.060		1	1 tsp
Total	166.50	4.536	10.000	10	0	2 lb
Butter for lamination	75.00	3.402	7.500	7	8	1 lb 8 oz
Bread flour for lamination	18.01	0.817	1.801	1	12¾	5¾ oz

Note
Butter and flour for the roll-in is a percentage of total flour weight.

Process, Détrempe

1. Mix all the ingredients (except for the butter and flour for lamination) to incorporation only, approximately 4 minutes in first speed.
2. Form the dough into a square and place on a sheet pan.
3. Reserve the dough wrapped in plastic in the refrigerator for at least 30 minutes.

Process, Beurrage

1. In a mixer with the paddle attachment, blend the butter and flour for lamination.
2. Spread the butter–flour mixture on a heavy plastic sheet or parchment paper in the form of a rectangle that is the same dimensions as the dough. Reserve in the refrigerator.

Process, Lamination

1. Ensure that the beurrage is twice the size of the dough piece.
2. Place the dough in the center of the butter and close the fat around the dough.
3. Give the dough 2 single folds and relax the dough for 1 hour under refrigeration.
4. Give the dough another 2 single folds and rest another hour in the refrigerator.
5. Finish the dough with 1 single fold and refrigerate for 1 hour.
6. Sheet the dough to ⅛ inch (2 mm) and use as desired.

FORMULA

PÀTE À CHOUX

The French named this singular pastry pâte à choux, or "cabbage," after its shape. Known since at least the 16th century, the recipe was perfected by Antoine Carême in the 19th century, and his recipe is still in use today. Exceptionally delicate before baking, pâte à choux must be either spooned or piped into shape. Once baked, the paste crusts on the outside, trapping steam inside, creating a puffed shape with a hollow interior. The crisp shells are filled with a variety of creams and finished with a glaze. Dramatic desserts such as croquembouche, profiteroles, Gâteau St. Honoré, Paris-Brest, and éclairs are all made with pâte à choux.

Ingredients	Baker's %	Kilogram	US decimal	Lb & Oz		Test
Whole milk	89.00	0.796	1.755	1	12⅛	5⅝ oz
Water	89.00	0.796	1.755	1	12⅛	5⅝ oz
Salt	3.00	0.027	0.059		1	1 tsp
Sugar	4.00	0.036	0.079		1¼	1½ tsp
Butter	79.00	0.707	1.558	1	8⅞	5 oz
Pastry flour	100.00	0.895	1.972	1	15½	6¼ oz
Eggs	143.00	1.279	2.821	2	13⅛	9 oz
Total	507.00	4.536	10.000	10	0	2 lb

Process

1. Sift the pastry flour and reserve.
2. Bring the milk, water, salt, sugar, and butter to a boil.
3. Remove from the heat, add the flour to the pot, and stir to combine.
4. Return to the heat and, stirring constantly, cook the paste for 1 minute or until it clears the side of the pot.
5. Transfer to a mixer with the paddle attachment, mix on low speed, and add three-fourths of the eggs.
6. Add the remainder of the eggs.
7. Adjust to the proper consistency using hot milk.
8. Pipe into the desired shapes, and brush lightly with the egg wash.
9. Bake at 350°F (176°C) in a convection oven for 10 minutes with the vent closed and then at 325°F (163°C) for 15 to 20 minutes with the vent open.
10. Bake until the pastry has a well browned exterior and is "dry" in the center.

CHAPTER SUMMARY

The selection of sweetened and unsweetened dough, as well as puff pastry and pâte à choux, form the bases for many traditional pastries and cakes. Undestanding their formulation and characteristics is an important step in understanding the construction and composition of cakes, tarts, quiche, and pies, just to name a few. The variations on these doughs create additional options for one to explore in order to bring the most out in what is being made.

KEY TERMS

- Blitz puff pastry
- Flaky
- Inverted puff pastry
- Italian puff pastry
- Mealy
- Mille feuille
- Pasta sfogliata
- Pâte
- Pâte à choux
- Pâte à foncer
- Pâte à sablé breton
- Pâte breton
- Pâte brisée
- Pâte sablée
- Pâte sucrée
- Pie dough
- Puff pastry
- Tart dough
- Tourrier
- Traditional puff pastry

REVIEW QUESTIONS

1. **What are the main ingredients in sweet pastry dough? What are the functions of those ingredients?**
2. **What is the process for making mealy pie dough? Flaky pie dough?**
3. **Why is it important to have a stiff dough for puff pastry?**
4. **What are the advantages of working with inverted puff pastry?**
5. **What is the leavening mechanism in pâte à choux?**

chapter
13

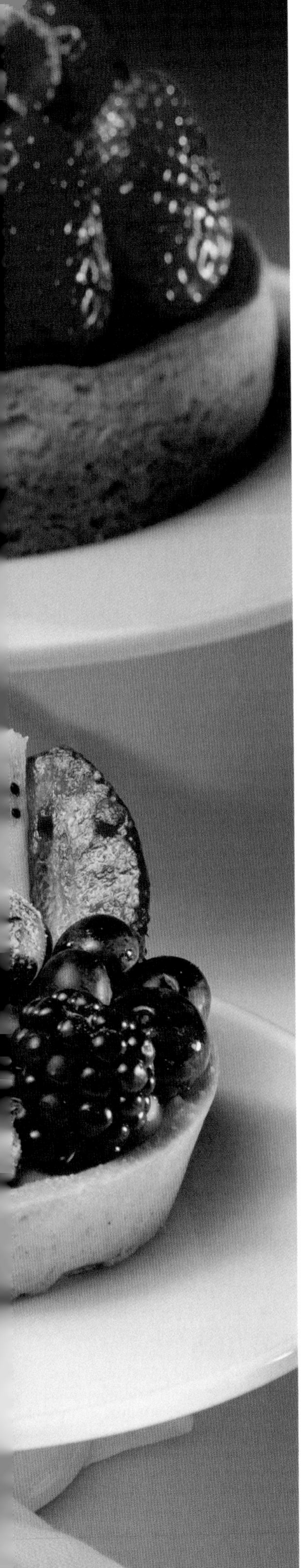

PIES AND TARTS

OBJECTIVES

After reading this chapter, you should be able to

- discuss the different types of pies and tarts and highlight what characterizes them.
- implement the various methods for producing fillings and assembling pies.
- demonstrate the ability to properly handle pie dough and properly bake pie.
- assemble various tarts using an assortment of base doughs and fillings.
- demonstrate the ability to properly handle tart dough and properly bake tart dough as well as tarts.

PIE: HISTORY AND DEFINITION

Most of what we know about pie today hasn't changed in hundreds of years. Although many consider this pastry to be as American as the flag and the Fourth of July, pie has its roots in Europe. The British, in particular, are well known for pie and are largely credited with its introduction to the New World. During the settling of America, pies of one kind or another were a staple at every meal.

Pie tends to be more popular around the winter holidays, and some bakeries offer it only during that time of year. Available in all shapes and sizes, pies are not limited to the standard image. They may be sweet or savory, highly sophisticated or extremely rustic. The variety reflects the many different tastes and memories associated with such a well-loved pastry.

The two major categories of pie, **baked pie** and **unbaked pie**, are somewhat misnomers. A baked pie begins with an unbaked pie shell that is filled with fruit or custard, and then baked. The crust may be on the bottom and/or the top. Examples of baked pies include apple, blueberry, and pumpkin.

In unbaked pies, the crust is **blind baked**, or baked alone, without filling. Then, the baked shell is filled with a prepared filling such as a flavored pastry cream. Examples of unbaked pies include chocolate cream, strawberry chiffon, and lemon meringue. There are several blind baking techniques, all of which are covered later in this chapter.

Crust and filling are the two major components to pie. To perfect the craft of both, one needs to understand a range of ingredient functions, mixing processes, filling preparations, and decoration. He or she needs to balance flavor, texture, and baking temperatures to create a delicate pastry that can meet pie lovers' near-mythic standards for perfection.

Note: An understanding of the formulation of pie dough, presented in Chapter 12, is essential background for this chapter.

WORKING WITH PIE DOUGH

Pie production can be approached in several ways, depending primarily on the quantity of pie being produced and the equipment available. When working with pie dough, several factors should be taken into consideration.

- *Portion control:* Depending on how the pie is made up, different portion control techniques may be implemented. It is important to control portions, as trimmings and excess dough should only be reused once, ideally for the bottom crust only.
- *Proper rolling and makeup techniques:* A crust should be even in thickness and diameter to maintain consistency and reduce waste.
- *Baking:* Many factors such as resting time, egg wash, oven temperature, and time in the oven contribute to the successful baking of pie dough.
- *Volume:* Techniques for production should change as volume increases. Specific equipment is available to make production more efficient.

PORTION CONTROL

A common approach to portion control is to divide the dough into a known desired weight after it is mixed. For example, if a baker gets an order for ten 9 inch (23 cm) deep-dish, double-crust apple pies, they know that they will need ten pieces of dough at 9 oz (0.250 kg) for the top crust, and ten pieces at 9 oz (0.250 kg) for the bottom crust. After the dough is portioned, it is rounded off, wrapped in plastic wrap, labeled properly, and stored under refrigeration until needed. Pie dough can be stored under refrigeration without a change in its quality for up to 3 days. For longer storage, it should be stored in the freezer.

This technique reduces waste because each portion of dough is just enough for the application. (See Figure 13-1.) Any waste that is created can be worked into the next batch of dough. Trimmings should not exceed 10 percent of the new dough weight to ensure the dough remains tender and flaky. Some may also cool the scrap pieces of dough and roll them out incorporated into existing dough.

	8 inch (20 cm) regular	9 inch (23 cm) deep dish or 10 inch (25 cm) regular	10 inch (25 cm) deep dish
Pie dough for bottom lining (double-crust)	5 oz (140 g)	9 oz (250 g)	11 oz (310 g)
Pie dough for top crust (double-crust)	5 oz (140 g)	9 oz (250 g)	9 oz (250 g)
Pie dough for lining pan (single-crust, fluted)	6 oz (170 g)	11 oz (310 g)	12 oz (340 g)

Figure 13-1

Pie Dough Weights and Sizes

ROLLING OUT PIE DOUGH

To properly roll out pie dough by hand takes practice. The goal is to end up with a circle of pie dough that is slightly larger than the inverted pan it will bake in. For large pies, the dough should be about $1/8$ inch (3 mm) thick. For individual-sized pies, the dough should be about $1/16$ inch ($1\frac{1}{2}$ mm) thick.

To maintain a circular shape, it is important to start with a round shape. The dough should also be at the proper temperature. If it is too cold, the dough may resist rolling out and may crack. If it is too warm, the butter may absorb into the flour and come out of the dough. Depending on the temperature of the dough, it may be beneficial to work the dough by hand for a few moments to make it malleable.

After the dough is ready to roll, it is important to use a slightly floured surface. The top of the pie dough should be dusted with flour as well. (See Rolling Out Pie Dough Figure 13-2, Step 1.) Using a rolling pin, start in the center of the piece of dough. The key to rolling out the dough evenly is to roll it away from you with pressure, return to the middle without pressure, and roll it toward yourself with pressure. (See Rolling Out Pie Dough Figure 13-2, Step 2.) It is equally important to roll to the ends of the dough. If this doesn't happen, the pastry will become misshapen when the dough is rotated to roll again.

After each complete roll, rotate the dough one-eighth of a turn clockwise to ensure that it rolls out evenly and into a circle. (See Rolling Out Pie Dough Figure 13-2, Step 3.) When first learning, do not roll the dough out too quickly. Try to maintain the shape of the circle. (See Rolling Out Pie Dough, Figure 13-2, Step 4.) Continue to dust the dough with flour as needed, but be careful to not use too much. If this happens, the pie will take on a dull, matte finish during baking, and the excess flour may taste bitter.

Lining Pie Pans (by Hand)

After the dough is rolled out, the pie pan can be lined. This is easier to do with cool dough. If the dough warmed up during the rolling out process, cool it for 5 minutes for easier handling.

The goal is to get an even layer of pastry over the pan with enough dough remaining for a border. (See Lining Pie Pans Figure 13-3, Step 1.) First, the pastry must be secured on the bottom of the pan, next to the edges and then on the sides from the bottom up. (See Lining Pie Pans Figure 13-3, Step 2.) The most common mistake is not resting or relaxing the dough against the side of the pan. While lining the pie pan, it is important to gently press the dough into place without stretching it. (See Lining Pie Pans Figure 13-3, Step 3.)

FIGURE 13-2 ROLLING OUT PIE DOUGH

After mixing, the pie dough should be portioned and shaped into flat discs. For rolling, place the dough on a floured surface.

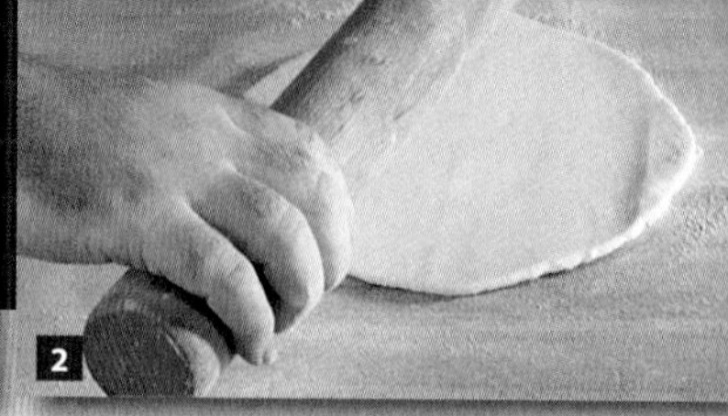

Start rolling from the center, roll it away from you with pressure, return to the middle without pressure, and roll it toward yourself with pressure.

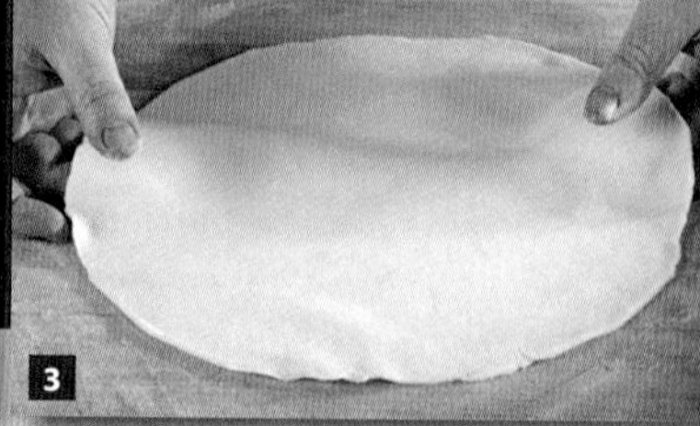

Rotate the dough 45 degrees after each complete roll.

Keep the shape evenly round with an even thickness.

FIGURE 13-3 LINING PIE PANS

Once rolled out, line the pie pan with the dough.

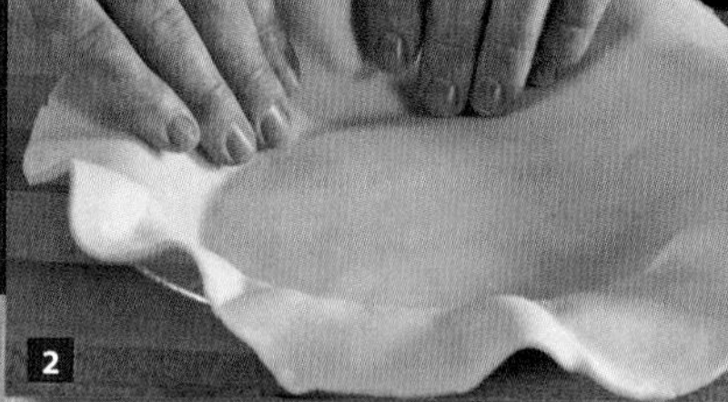

Secure the dough to the bottom of the pan first, next to the edges, and then on the sides from the bottom up.

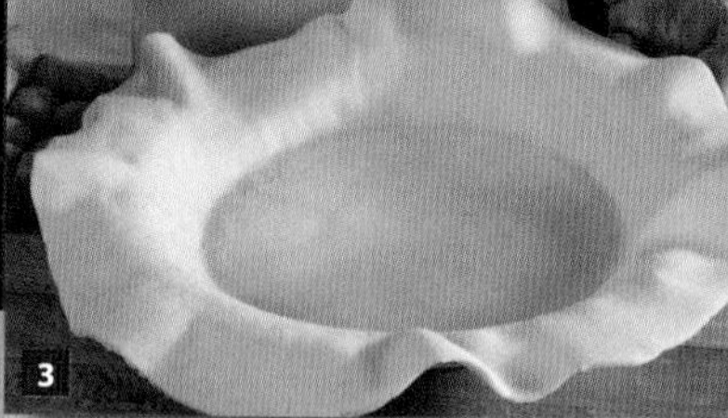

Gently press the dough into place without stretching it. Dough should extend about 1 inch (3 cm) from the edge of the pan.

To make a raised border, roll the dough under itself to create a ridge.

The dough is now ready to be crimped or pressed to create a decorative border.

Once the pie pan is lined, the border can be formed for a single-crust pie. Borders are not only decorative, but they also help the dough to remain high in the pan and they function as guards to prevent spilling wet fillings like quiche or pumpkin pie. To make a raised border, the dough must be rolled under itself to create a ridge that can be crimped, cut, or pressed to create a variety of designs. (See Lining Pie Pans Figure 13-3, Steps 4–5.) See Single-Crust Border Figure 13-4 for a step-by-step guide to making decorative borders on single-crust pies.

Double-Crust Pies

For a double-crust pie, the bottom dough should extend only 1/2 inch (1 cm) from the top of the pan after the pan is lined. The top crust should already be rolled out. When depositing the filling, it is important to make sure that it is cool and that none lands on the border of the dough. Warm filling will warm the dough and may cause the fat to soften or melt. Filling on the border will prevent a quality seal and may cause a weak spot where filling can leak. After the filling is in place, the lip of the bottom crust should be lightly brushed with water.

A vent must be placed on the top of the pie to allow moisture to escape during baking. If a pie is not vented, the steam will escape from the weakest part of the pastry, typically on the side of the pie where the top crust is formed with the bottom crust. If a pie is overvented, it can lead to excessive moisture loss in the filling. Vents can be as simple as cutting several slits in the dough, or as elaborate as making cutouts with a paring knife or specialty cutter. (See Double-Crust Pie Figure 13-5, Step 1.)

Next, the top crust is laid over the filling and secured to the bottom lip by gently pressing. (See Double-Crust Pie Figure 13-5, Step 2.) The next steps are to further seal the two pieces of dough and create a decorative border. As with the single-crust pie, the dough hanging over the edge of the pan is rolled under itself. (See Double-Crust Pie Figure 13-5, Step 3.) Once this has been completed, a crimp, rope, or other decorative style may be applied. (See Double-Crust Pie Figure 13-5, Step 4.)

Lattice Crusts

A **lattice crust** is a great decorative element that also lets large quantities of steam escape and prevents fillings from boiling out the sides of the pie. This is especially useful for fruit fillings like blueberry and cherry. To create a lattice-top pie, follow the steps for a double-crusted pie through depositing the filling into the prepared pie shell. Then, from the reserved top dough, cut strips into the desired width, making sure they are of uniform width. Follow the step-by-step guide to making the lattice top in Lattice Crust Figure 13-6, Steps 1–2.

After the lattice has been assembled, roll the dough that extends off the edges of the tin under the bottom pie dough to create the border. (See Lattice Crust Figure 13-6, Step 3.) This is important for lattice pies, since they are generally quite liquid and the filling can boil over the edge.

BAKING PIE DOUGH AND PIE

A couple of approaches to baking pie are important to know: blind baking and baking the whole pie. For blind baking, just the crust is baked, either partially or fully, depending on the needs of the baker. The baking of the pie is just as important as mixing the dough, preparing the filling, and assembling the pie because the baking determines the final quality.

FIGURE 13-4 SINGLE-CRUST BORDER

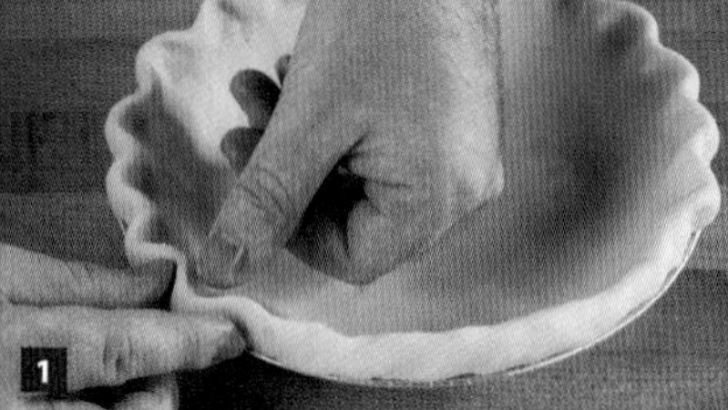

The ridge is crimped with the fingers. It is important to space evenly to achieve a clean finish.

A crimped border on a finished single-crust pie shell is both functional and attractive.

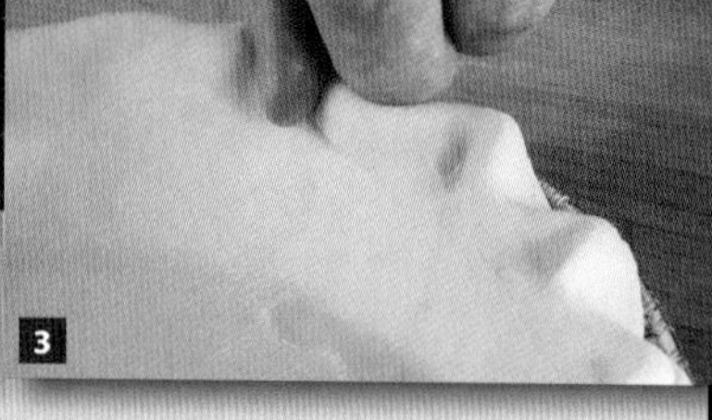

The ridge can be pinched to create a different pattern.

FIGURE 13-5 DOUBLE-CRUST PIE

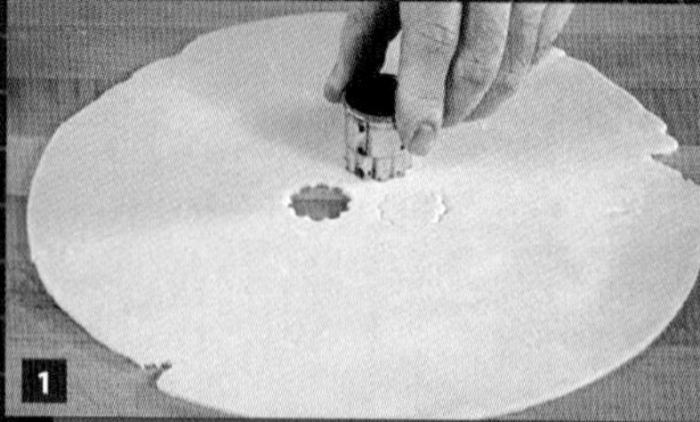

Cut out vents on the top dough to allow moisture to escape during baking.

Lay the top pie dough over the filling and secure to the bottom lip by gently pressing.

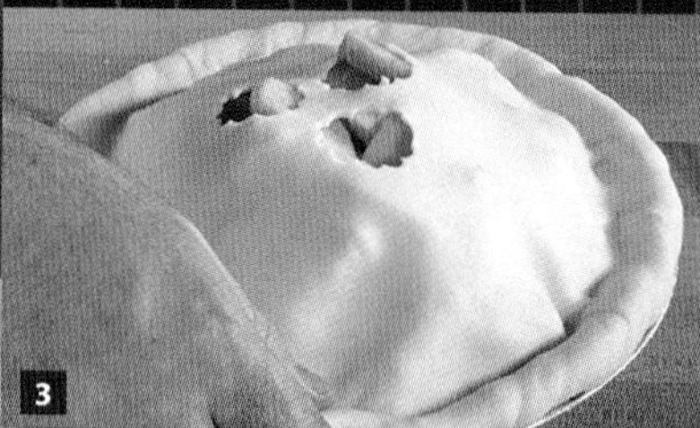

Seal the two pieces of dough to create a decorative border. As with the single-crust pie, the dough hanging over the edge of the pan is rolled under itself.

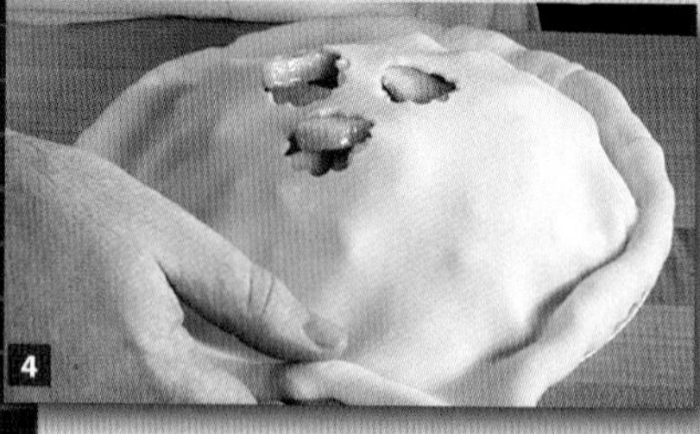

The ridge is finished. Decorative styles such as crimps and rope can be applied on the border.

FIGURE 13-6 LATTICE CRUST

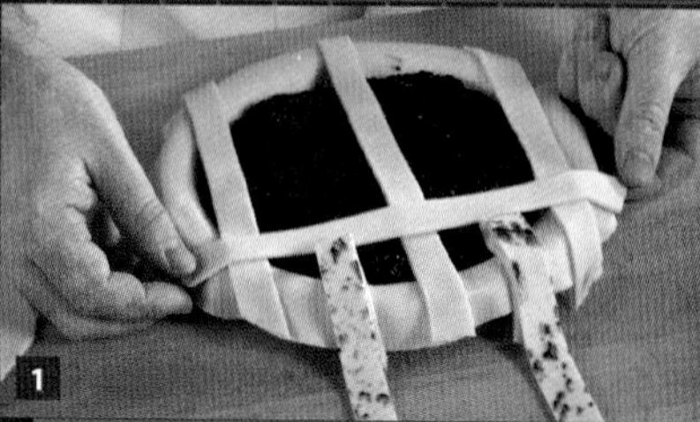

After the filling is deposited in the bottom crust, place five strips of dough running vertically on top. Lift the second and fourth strips, and position one strip running horizontally.

Return the second and fourth strips to their original position, and then lift the first, third, and fifth vertical strips in order to place the second horizontal strip.

After the lattice is finished, the dough hanging over the edge of the pan is rolled under itself to create a border.

Preparing the pie for the oven with egg or cream wash, managing the temperature of the oven, and ensuring doneness are all required to guarantee success.

Egg and Cream Washes

Before putting the made-up pie into the oven, the exposed pie dough should be given a light coating of egg wash or cream wash to promote browning and improve general quality. Egg wash will give the piecrust a shinier, darker color, while cream wash will give a duller, matte finish. Whichever wash is used, it is important to apply only a light coat. At this point, granulated, sanding, or pearl sugar may also be added for enhanced visual appearance, texture, and taste.

Pie Dough Temperature

When baking a pie shell, bakers must take into account the temperature of both the dough and the oven. Specifically, it is essential that the oven be hot and the pie dough cool. If the oven is too cool, the butter can melt out of the pastry, and it can become excessively dry. If the temperature is too hot, the pastry can bake at an uneven rate and the outside will appear baked, but the inside will be doughy.

Blind Baking Pie Dough

Blind baking is the process of baking a pie shell that has no filling in it. Pie dough may be blind baked 100 percent to a crisp shell, or it may be blind baked part way. Pie dough is blind baked for two reasons: First, the pie will be used for an unbaked pie (full blind bake), such as chiffon or lemon meringue; and second, to jump-start the baking process (partial blind bake). The latter is done to achieve a crisp crust when using wet fillings such as pumpkin or quiche.

The two methods for blind baking pie shells are using pie weights and parchment or using a second tin. The process of blind baking is fairly simple, but taking some precautions will ensure a successful end result. Pie dough should always be cold when it enters the oven, and it is recommended that the dough rest for a minimum of 30 minutes after being worked with before baking to avoid shrinkage and toughening.

Blind Baking Using Pie Weights and Parchment For the first method, weight is used to prevent the dough from moving and becoming misshapen during the baking process. Parchment paper is cut to fit the pie pan, including the sides. It is placed into the pan, above the dough, and then filled with dried beans or pie weights that help keep the dough flat and in position during the baking process. If the crust is to be partially baked and then filled and finished later, it should be baked halfway using sufficient bottom heat to make sure that the base and edges are par-baked. Depending on the baking conditions, it may be advisable to remove the beans or pie weights and continue baking for several more minutes to ensure a crisp crust.

Blind Baking Using a Second Tin A common way to blind bake pie dough is to sandwich the dough between two tins and to bake them upside-down. This method eliminates the need to use paper and weights.

FIGURE 13-7 BLIND BAKING USING SECOND TIN

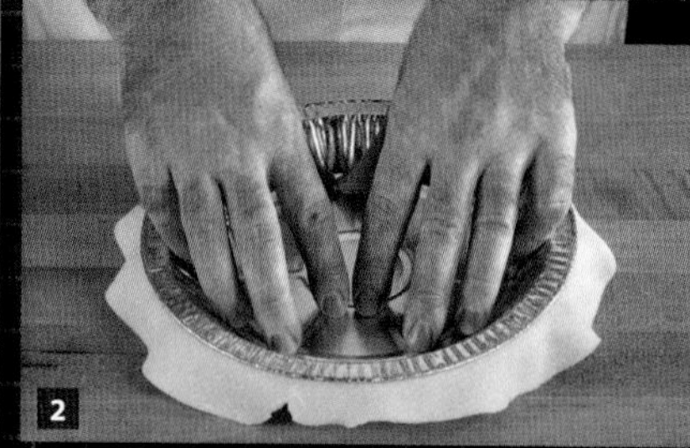

1 When using a second pan for blind baking, the second pan is placed on top of the dough after it has been placed on the first pan.

2 Press the second pan lightly to make sure there is no air gap.

3 Flip the pans upside-down, and cut the excess dough with a paring knife.

The process is to line the tin with dough as normal and then lay a second pie tin over the dough. (See Blind Baking Using Second Tin Figure 13-7.) Next, the tin sandwich is inverted, allowed to rest for at least 30 minutes, and then baked upside-down with a sheet pan over the tin to prevent it from rising. When properly executed, the result is a perfectly baked pie shell, golden brown from an even bake and no shrinkage. Additionally, after panning, the dough may be frozen in the tin and pulled for baking as needed.

STORING PIE SHELLS

Pie production may be scheduled to ease the workload of the baker. Prepared, unbaked pie shells may be stored in the refrigerator for up to 2 days, or in the freezer for up to several months if well wrapped. Frozen shells can be thawed in the refrigerator and should be baked as needed. To avoid staling, baked pie shells should not be stored in the refrigerator. If baked pie shells must be stored, they may be kept well wrapped in the freezer for up to a month.

PRODUCTION OF PIE

In small bakeries and restaurants, where pies represent a small portion of sales, an investment in a dough sheeter (or even a specialty pie press) is not merited. For bakeries that produce pies in large quantities, a pie press or a dough sheeter is a more time- and cost-efficient method of production. Dough sheeters and pie presses are useful for reducing waste and keeping production moving.

With dough sheeters, a common technique is to press the pie dough onto a sheet pan 2 inches (5 cm) thick and to cover it with plastic wrap. After the dough has chilled, a portion of dough is cut from the mass and sheeted out on the dough sheeter. Circles are cut out of the appropriate size, minimizing waste. The circles should be lightly dusted with flour to prevent sticking and then placed on a sheet pan, shingled, and reserved in the refrigerator or freezer until needed. The scrap dough can be added to the next sheeting of fresh dough but should be reused only once, as it will make the pie dough tougher and more prone to shrinkage.

Pie presses are also useful for the production of pies. The process is very simple, and a pie press can greatly reduce the amount of wasted dough if the portioning is carefully calculated. After the dough has been portioned, and rested, it is placed in the tin and the press descends, evenly spreading the dough over the tin. A heated top element prevents the dough from sticking to the unit. Some units are capable of trimming waste and for larger production there are automated pie lines that are capable of producing up to 140 large pies per minute.

PIE DOUGH PROPERTIES AND CAUSES

Many factors contribute to the success or failure of pie. Figure 13-8 contains a quick, handy reference to problems and their causes.

PIE FILLINGS

The filling of a pie is just as important as a successful crust because crust is often left on the plate, but the filling rarely remains. Numerous considerations should be made for the wide spectrum of pie fillings, with product formulation, processes, and ingredient selection playing key roles in achieving the desired results. In the fillings section, we will

Figure 13-8

Pie Dough Properties and Causes

Fault	Causes
Dough is too elastic to roll out.	◗ Flour was too strong. ◗ Dough was overmixed. ◗ Dough was not rested long enough. ◗ Not enough fat was used.
Crust is too tough.	◗ Flour was too strong. ◗ Not enough fat was used. ◗ Dough was overworked. ◗ Too much scrap was used.
Crust is too crumbly.	◗ Flour was too weak. ◗ Too much fat was used. ◗ Not enough water was added. ◗ Dough was not mixed properly.
Crust is not flaky.	◗ Not enough fat was used. ◗ Fat was blended into the dough too much. ◗ Dough was overworked. ◗ Dough was not chilled before baking.
Bottom of crust is soggy.	◗ Oven temperature was too low. ◗ Baking time was not long enough. ◗ Filling was too warm when poured into the shell. ◗ Wrong dough was used—mealy dough prevents crust sogginess.
Crust shrunk from the side of pan.	◗ Flour was too strong. ◗ Dough was overworked. ◗ Not enough fat was used. ◗ Dough did not rest enough before lining the pan. ◗ Dough was stretched out to line the pan.

review the ingredients, formulas, and processes used for fruit, custard, cream, and chiffon pies.

FRUIT PIE: INGREDIENT SELECTION

The selection of fruit to use for **fruit pie** can be divided into four main categories: fresh, frozen, canned, and dried, with each presenting its own distinct advantages and disadvantages. When choosing ingredients, the pastry chef must weigh a number of considerations, including clientele, product characteristics, flavor, food cost, labor cost, and product availability.

Fresh Fruit

Seasonal fresh fruit may be the most flavorful, yet expensive ingredient the pastry chef can use. Even so, the overall quality of the product will be high, and the chef will be able to charge more for it. The key is to choose fresh fruits that highlight local flavors. Fresh fruit may be cooked before being baked in the pie, or during the baking process.

When selecting fresh fruit to be used in baking and pastry, one needs to consider its color, taste, and texture, with an expectation of superior characteristics for fruit at its peak. For example, apple pie made in October with fresh apples will vary considerably in sweetness, tartness, and texture from apple pie made in May. Global commerce may be changing what it means for fruit to be in season, but it is important to note that some desirable characteristics may be sacrificed during the boat journey from Chile, New Zealand, or elsewhere.

When fruit is fresh, its natural textures and sugar levels can vary considerably. The chef needs to understand this and adjust formulas accordingly. In addition, in-house peeling, coring, pitting, slicing, and more add considerable time to the preparation process, which is typically reflected in a higher cost for the end product. For larger production, some fruit may be purchased fresh but already prepared into peeled and cored slices or wedges.

Canned Fruit

Canned fruit is less versatile than fresh fruit, but it has the attributes of consistent quality, year-round availability, convenience, and lower labor costs. Another benefit is that canned fruit can be stored on the shelf much longer than fresh. The selection is somewhat limited, however, with popular varieties including pears, peaches, pineapples, apricots, and cherries.

Generally, the canning process softens the fruit and standardizes its sugar content. Canned fruit is packed in syrups of various densities ranging from **light pack** to **heavy pack**, which should be taken into consideration when ordering and formulating pie fillings. Light or heavy pack refers to the syrup density that the fruit is packed in, and it affects the sweetness of the fruit.

Frozen Fruit

Frozen fruit is a very convenient, versatile ingredient in the bakery, especially for pie. The large selection includes apples, various berries, rhubarb, and pit fruits such as peaches, cherries, and plums. Some fruits, such as apples and peaches, may be processed as sliced, diced, pureed, or chopped. Whatever the variety, frozen fruit must be handled properly to ensure its integrity in the final preparation.

Many types of frozen fruit have added sugar, primarily to prevent the formation of ice crystals that can have a negative affect on the fruit's structure, color, and flavor. The quantity of added sugar averages between 10 and 15 percent by weight of the fruit.

The quality of frozen fruit varies by brand, but in general, all frozen fruit should be **individually quick frozen (IQF)**. The IQF process ensures that the fruit retains as much flavor and color as possible and that it remains separate from the other fruit. It is difficult to portion berries that are frozen into a block. When receiving, it should be checked for quality and should remain frozen at all times. As long as enough freezer space is available, storage is easy, and shelf life is good.

Dried Fruit

Dried fruit is usually treated as an inclusion for other pies, such as apple or mincemeat. It adds a unique sweetness, flavor, and difference in texture from the main ingredient in the filling.

Starch Selection

A large selection of starch is available for use as a thickening agent in fruit pie fillings. Examples include cornstarch, arrowroot, tapioca, waxy maize, and wheat flour. The gelatinization that results from the heating and swelling of the starch granules gives the filling body, mouth feel, and texture, and the extent of these results will vary depending on the thickener used and the other ingredients used in the formula.

FRUIT PIE: METHODS OF PRODUCTION

Fruit pies are an excellent way to highlight local and seasonal flavors of the field and orchard. When selecting fruit, look for high quality with natural sweetness and proper texture. Both are critical factors for success.

Whether fresh, frozen, or canned, the fruit's natural or added sugar content needs to be balanced with the additional sugar in the formula. The texture of the fruit will determine the final quality of the pie, as well as the correct method of preparation. There are three main methods for fruit pie: **uncooked fruit method**, **cooked fruit method**, and **cooked fruit juice method**.

Uncooked Fruit Method

Considered to be the classic for making fruit pie, the uncooked fruit method is also the most common for home bakers. Fresh and some frozen fruit may be used. The most common ingredient is fresh apple; however, pears, frozen apples, and frozen berries may also be used.

The process involves combining the prepared fruit with sugar, a starch such as cornstarch, flavorings, and butter and then depositing the mixture into a pie tin. It is important to pile the uncooked fruit into a dome in the center of the tin, as it will significantly shrink in volume during baking. During the baking process, the fruit will relax and settle, filling in any empty space. When the pastry is golden brown, the filling is boiling, and the fruit is tender, the pie is done.

The primary precaution for the uncooked fruit method is to not prepare the fruit mixture too far in advance. As soon as the sugar comes

FIGURE 13-9 UNCOOKED FRUIT METHOD

1 Combine the fruit, sugar, starch, and spices.

2 Deposit the fruit filling into a pie shell.

3 Dot with small chunks of butter, if applicable, and lay the top dough over it.

into contact with the fruit, it begins to draw moisture out of the fruit, and portioning becomes more difficult. Consequently, when the sugar–starch–spice mixture is added to the fruit, it should be deposited in the tin immediately to ensure that the juice that does get pulled out of the fruit remains with the fruit in proper proportion.

Uncooked Fruit Method Process

- Prepare the pie shells and reserve in the refrigerator.
- Scale all the ingredients, and prepare the fruit.
- Combine the starch, sugar, and spice.
- Combine the starch–sugar mixture with the fruit. (See Uncooked Fruit Method Figure 13-9, Step 1.)
- Deposit filling into the pie shells and finish the makeup process. (See Uncooked Fruit Method Figure 13-9, Steps 2–3.)
- Bake as soon as possible.

Cooked Fruit Method

The cooked fruit method is typically used for firmer fruits that can withstand being cooked before they are deposited into the pie. Fresh apples and crisp pears are the most common fruits used for this method.

The thickening action for cooked fruit pies happens before the pie goes into the oven. To begin, the starch is combined with the sugar and spices. The butter is melted in a pot and the apples or other fresh fruit are added to sauté. After the fruit cooks slightly, the sugar–starch mixture is added, and the mixture is cooked until the starch thickens. It is important to control the degree to which the filling cooks because the fruit will soften further as it bakes in the pie. Transfer the cooked filling to a shallow pan and allow it to cool. After it has cooled, it can be deposited and baked as normal.

Because the filling has already been cooked, it does not need to be domed as in the uncooked fruit method. It also will not shrink much during the baking process.

Cooked Fruit Method Process

- Prepare the pie shells and reserve in the refrigerator or prepare while the filling is cooling.
- Scale all the ingredients, and prepare the fruit.

- Combine the starch, sugar, and spice.
- In a large pot, melt the butter; add the prepared fruit, and sauté. (See Cooked Fruit Method Figure 13-10, Step 1.)
- Combine the starch–sugar mixture with the fruit, and stir to incorporate. (See Cooked Fruit Method Figure 13-10, Step 2.)
- Cook until the starch has swelled. Do not overwork or overcook the fruit during the cooking process. (See Cooked Fruit Method Figure 13-10, Step 3.)
- Transfer to a shallow pan, cover with plastic wrap, and allow to cool. (See Cooked Fruit Method Figure 13-10, Step 4.)
- Deposit into the pie shells, and finish the makeup process.
- Bake or freeze as soon as possible.

Cooked Fruit Juice Method

The cooked fruit juice method is used with certain, more delicate fruits, where thickening is not as consistent as it is with sturdier fruits like apples and pears. This method preserves the integrity and appearance of more fragile fruits, such as canned fruits and berries because only the juice is thickened before the pie is baked. The ingredients for this preparation include fruit juice, fruit, starch, and flavorings.

The method of preparation is to cook some of the juices from the fruit (or from another fruit) with the sugar–starch mixture and spices. The thickened juice–sugar–starch mixture is poured over the fruit, and the two are mixed just to combine. The filling should be refrigerated until cool and then deposited into the pie tin. Unlike the uncooked and cooked fruit methods, cooked fruit juice fillings are typically rather fluid and must not exceed in height the rim of the pan. Lattice crusts are generally used as the second crust for these pies because they allow a large portion of steam to escape.

Cooked Fruit Juice Method Process

- Prepare the pie shells and reserve in the refrigerator, or prepare while the filling is cooling.
- Scale all the ingredients.
- In a pot, bring the fruit juice to a boil.
- Combine the starch with the small quantity of fruit juice or water in the formula. (See Cooked Fruit Juice Method Figure 13-11, Step 1.) Add it to the boiling fruit juice, and stir to incorporate. (See Cooked Fruit Juice Method Figure 13-11, Step 2.)
- Add any sugar or spices.
- Boil for 1 minute until the starch has swelled.
- Pour over the reserved fruit and gently combine. *Note:* Be careful to not break down the fruit when folding it into the cooked fruit juice. For easiest production, defrost fruit for the pie overnight in a colander under refrigeration. (See Cooked Fruit Juice Method Figure 13-11, Step 3.)
- Transfer to a shallow pan, cover with plastic wrap, and allow to cool.
- Deposit into the pie shells and finish the makeup process. (See Cooked Fruit Juice Method Figure 13-11, Step 4.)
- Bake or freeze as soon as possible.

FIGURE 13-10 COOKED FRUIT METHOD

1 **Sauté the prepared fruit with melted butter.**

2 **Add the mixture of sugar, starch, and spices into the fruit, and mix to incorporate.**

3 **Cook until the starch is swelled and the mixture starts to thicken.**

4 **After cooked, transfer the mixture into a shallow container, and allow to cool.**

FIGURE 13-11 COOKED FRUIT JUICE METHOD

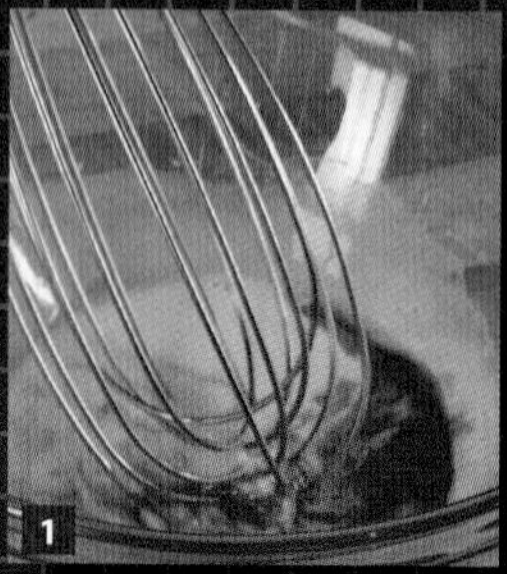

1

While bringing the fruit juice to a boil, combine the starch with a small quantity of fruit juice or water.

2

Add the starch mixture, sugar, and spices into the boiling liquid, and cook until thickened.

3

Combine the cooked juice and fruits gently. Transfer into a shallow container, cover with plastic on contact, and allow to cool.

4

Deposit the filling into a prepared pie shell.

Overview of Fruit Filling Methods

The baker or pastry chef has many options when making a fruit pie. Depending on the fruit, the uncooked method can work very well for more rustic-style, free form fruit pies known as **galettes**. This method is also favorable for holiday pie production because it is fast and requires no refrigeration of the filling. It is also much more efficient than the cooked fruit method, when cooking and cooling enough apples for 1,000 pies requires significantly more time and equipment.

The benefits of the cooked fruit method are that the thickening process is more controlled, and more fruit can be deposited into the pie tin. Only fruit that can withstand the cooking process should be used, and caution must be taken to prevent overcooking. For example, crisp pears will work, but very ripe pears will not. Canned and frozen fruits should never be used for this type of filling.

The cooked fruit juice method is ideal for canned fruits and fresh or frozen berries. Because only the juice of the fruit is thickened, fragile fruit remains whole. The drawback of the cooked fruit method is that the finished product requires refrigeration, which, for most bakeries, is at a premium.

CUSTARD PIE

Custard pie is characterized by the ingredient function of the egg acting as the main setting and thickening agent. Custard pies include varieties such as buttermilk, pumpkin, quiche, and pecan. To create a great custard pie, it is necessary to understand the baking properties of both the crust and the filling and to take appropriate measures to ensure that the crust is crisp and the filling is supple.

Custard Pie Method

The process for making custard pies is simple and straightforward. In general, all the ingredients are mixed to combine, with care taken to ensure that minimal air is mixed into the custard. After the custard filling is mixed, it may be used or reserved until needed. Some fillings can last for a couple of days under refrigeration, which is beneficial for operations that want to offer fresh pie every day but lack the time to prepare fillings on a daily basis.

Pie Dough Selection for Custard Pie When using pie dough for custard pie, it should always be mealy. Mealy pie dough will help prevent the crust from becoming soggy before and after the baking process. There are two approaches to preparing the crust for custard pies: Bake the filling in an unbaked shell or bake the filling in a blind-baked shell. Depending on the size of the pie, the type of oven, and/or the type of sheet pans being used (perforated or not), one method may be preferred over the other.

Baking Guidelines for Custard Pie For custard pies that begin the baking process with unbaked crusts, the baking process should begin at a high temperature and finish at a lower temperature. During the early stages of baking, the higher heat is essential for the pastry to bake within such a wet environment. After the crust has browned, the baking temperature should be lowered to finish baking the filling. For all custard pies, cooking the filling to the correct stage is a critical control point. If the filling is overcooked, it can curdle and lose its smoothness.

Getting a high heat to the crust of an unbaked, filled custard pie can be accomplished in a number of different ways. If a deck oven is available, baking the pie on a hearth is the easiest method of transferring heat to the dough. However, in this situation, dropping the heat rapidly enough to cook the custard evenly may be a challenge. An ideal option for the commercial baker is to bake pies in the convection oven on perforated sheet pans. This method will ensure sufficient heat transfer to bake the dough quickly. Convection ovens are also more efficient than deck ovens when temperatures must be staged in the baking process.

The other option for baking custard pies is to fill a partially blind-baked crust with the filling and bake at a low-to-medium temperature of 300°F (149°C) to 325°F (163°C) in a convection oven. At this low temperature, the crust will not readily brown, yet the heat will be sufficient to cook the filling. This method works well for smaller operations or for those without ideal baking conditions because it guarantees a baked crust.

Custard Pie Process

- Prepare the pie shells, and reserve in the refrigerator or blind bake as needed.
- Scale all the ingredients for the filling.
- Combine all the ingredients and mix well. *Note:* Be careful not to incorporate air during the mixing process.
- Deposit the filling into the pie shells.
- Bake as soon as possible.

CREAM PIE

Cream pie is always unbaked. It consists of a blind-baked crust and a cooked–stirred custard topped with whipped cream and an applicable garnish. Additional ingredients can be added to the custard to make variations such as chocolate cream, coconut cream, and peanut butter cream. To better understand cream pies, please review cooked–stirred custards and whipped cream in Chapter 15.

Crust Selection for Cream Pie

The crust for a cream pie may be mealy, flaky, or a composite, depending on the baker's requirements. If using a mealy crust, no precautions need to be taken. If using a flaky or composite crust, a moisture barrier must be created between the filling and the crust to prevent the crust from becoming soggy. Some brush a very thin layer of white or dark chocolate over the crust, while others prefer cocoa butter because it provides a more neutral taste.

Fillings for Cream Pie

In cream pies, a pastry cream or variation of a pastry cream is the main component of the custard portion. The exact formulation is based on balancing the sugars, thickeners, and fats with those of the add-in ingredients, which can include chocolate, coconut, peanut butter, and more. One needs to taste and evaluate the product for texture and flavor accordingly.

For example, a chocolate cream pie formula that calls for a 72 percent dark chocolate will have a different taste and texture if the same

FIGURE 13-12 CREAM PIE

1 Combine the warmed custard base and melted chocolate in a mixing bowl.

2 Mix to combine.

3 Deposit into a prebaked pie shell.

4 Smooth the surface and refrigerate.

weight of a 50 percent chocolate is used instead. The pie using the chocolate with a lower cocoa content will have less chocolate flavor, a sweeter taste, and a reduced setting property. To obtain a better result, the quantity of the chocolate with the lower cocoa percent should be increased, which will boost the cocoa content, flavor, and setting properties. At the same time, the amount of sugar in the custard base should be decreased because the additional chocolate will add sugar.

Depositing the Filling Depositing the filling into the crust is an important step in making cream pies, especially if it is chocolate-based. All pie shells should be baked and at room temperature before they are filled. When the filling is slightly warm, at about 90°F (32°C) to 95°F (35°C), it can be deposited into the shell. The best method for depositing depends on the formula quantity and the size of the pie. Larger pies can be poured, and smaller pies can be piped. At the desired amount, which is generally about three-fourths of the way up the crust, the filling should be smoothed out if necessary and cooled under refrigeration. After the filling has cooled, it can be topped with whipped cream and garnished as desired. It is critical to deposit the filling before it sets so that the pie will cut more easily and the slices will look cleaner.

Cream Pie Process

- Prepare the pie shells and blind bake.
- Scale all the ingredients for the filling.
- Cook the custard, and then transfer it to the bowl of a mixer fitted with the whip attachment.
- Whip on low speed and add any flavoring ingredients such as chocolate, nut pastes, and coconut. Whip until slightly warm, about 90°F (32°C) to 95°F (35°C). (See Cream Pie Figure 13-12, Steps 1–2.)
- Deposit into the pie shells, and smooth the surface. (See Cream Pie Figure 13-12, Steps 3–4.)
- Refrigerate until cool, ice with crème Chantilly, and garnish as desired.

General Considerations for Cream Pie

Precautions for cream pie composition and makeup include careful preparation of crust, filling and crème Chantilly, all of which will affect the visual and textural properties of the pie. Other precautions include sanitation and shelf life. The maximum amount of time a cream pie should be in the refrigerator or display case is two days, because the fresh cream and high ratio of liquid ingredients in the custard filling are susceptible to spoilage and microbial contamination. All equipment should be cleaned before preparations are begun and hands should never come into contact with ready-to-eat foods.

CHIFFON PIE

Chiffon pie is a classic American dessert, popular in restaurants and bakeries alike. This "light-as-air" pie relies on a base, egg foam, and sometimes whipped cream to attain its texture. Similar to a mousse in composition and preparation, chiffon requires several steps, with special attention to temperature and the degree to which the egg whites and cream are whipped.

Chiffon pies are composed of a blind-baked pie crust, the chiffon filling, whipped cream, and a garnish.

Chiffon Filling: The Base

The base gives chiffon filling its flavor and, in the case of chocolate, can potentially affect the texture as well. The base can consist of a ganache, a fruit puree, or even a flavored crème Anglaise. A portion of the sugar in the filling can be added to the base, which is typically ready to be elaborated once it cools to 95°F (35°C) to 104°F (40°C).

Chiffon Filling: Egg Foam

The egg foam for a chiffon pie is a common meringue comprised of egg whites and sugar, and it should be whipped to a medium peak before being added to the base. If the foam is underwhipped, a loss of volume will occur; if it is overwhipped, the foam will be difficult to incorporate, and the texture may be rough. For chiffon preparations to be safe to consume, it is critical to use pasteurized egg whites. Please review Chapter 15 for important information about whipping egg whites, along with the various stages of development.

Chiffon Filling: Whipped Cream

Whipped cream is an optional ingredient in chiffon preparations. To ensure optimal whipping properties and strength, it should have a fat content of 35 to 40 percent. The cream can be whipped to very soft peaks and reserved in the refrigerator until needed, or it may be whipped just before it is needed. Whipped cream is always the last ingredient added to a chiffon filling; this prevents overdeveloping the cream during incorporation. Please review Chapter 15 for a complete review of whipping cream.

Chiffon Filling: Setting Agents

Setting agents are required to stabilize the delicate matrix of the base, egg foam, and whipped cream (if used). The most common setting agent is gelatin, which must first be bloomed, melted, added to the base, and then well incorporated. The temperature of the base must be warm enough to ensure that the gelatin does not set on contact with it.

Chiffon Method

Upon acquiring an understanding of chiffon's components and its special requirements, one can learn and master a general process for the elaboration of this filling.

The first step is to scale all ingredients and whip the cream to soft peaks, if applicable. Next, the base can be prepared and the gelatin can be bloomed, melted, and well-incorporated with the base. When the base is at about 95°F (35°C) to 104°F (40°C), the meringue can be prepared to medium peaks. Next, if cream is used, it can be finished to the desired soft-peak stage.

To begin the elaboration of the base, add one-third of the meringue and incorporate it with a whisk. Next, gently add the remaining meringue in two batches, gently folding in with a rubber spatula. Take care to mix only to incorporation. Lastly, add the whipped cream in two stages, folding just to incorporation with the rubber spatula.

After the filling has been prepared, deposit it into a fully blind-baked pie shell. The filling should be mounded slightly into the tin, rising only one-half to three-fourths of the way up the side of the pan. It may be higher toward the center. The pie should then be refrigerated to allow the filling to set up slightly. When it is firmer, it can be iced with some crème Chantilly and garnished as desired.

FIGURE 13-13 LINING TART PANS

1 After sheeting the tart dough, dock it if necessary and cut into the desired shapes and sizes. Place the dough in the refrigerator until cool.

2 Lay the dough onto a tart mold, and start securing from the bottom first.

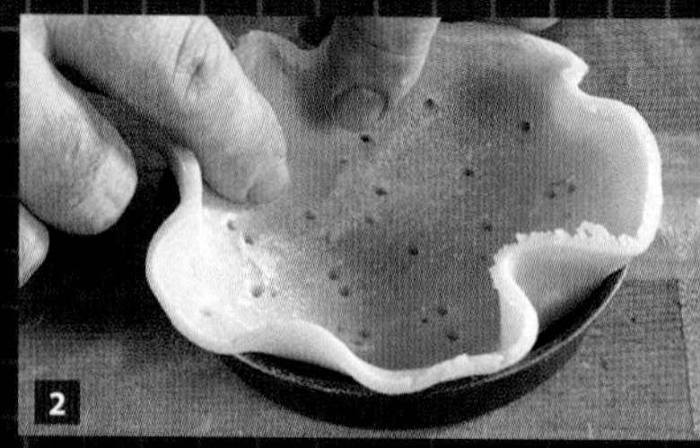

Chiffon Process

- Prepare the pie shells and blind bake.
- Scale all the ingredients for the filling.
- Whip the cream to soft peaks and reserve in the refrigerator, or whip just before it is needed.
- Prepare the base, and bloom and melt the gelatin.
- Combine the base and gelatin and prepare the meringue to medium peaks.
- Whisk one-third of the meringue into the base. Fold the remaining two-thirds in with a rubber spatula in two stages.
- Finish whipping the cream to the desired stage and add to the filling in two stages, using the rubber spatula.
- Deposit into the prepared pie shells.
- Refrigerate until set, finish with crème Chantilly, and garnish as desired.

Precautions for Chiffon

The precautions that must be observed for chiffon pies are similar to those of cream pies. The filling contains a large amount of liquid, egg white, and cream, making it essential that the egg white be pasteurized and all of the ingredients be fresh. Precautions must also be taken during the preparation of this delicate filling. Observing temperature guidelines and incorporating ingredients at the proper rate and order are critical steps in attaining the light, ethereal texture known as chiffon.

PIE CONCLUSION

In order to make a good pie, the baker must have a good understanding of several key elements: mixing the dough, making the filling, working with the dough, depositing filling, finishing and assembly, baking times and temperatures, and, potentially, decorating techniques. Whether the finished product is as simple as apple pie, or as complex as chiffon, success depends on a thorough knowledge of both the processes and techniques involved.

TARTS

Tarts are the pastry chef's answer to the baker's pie. Though tarts are based on concepts very similar to those of pie, composition dictates whether the similarities and differences are slight or drastic.

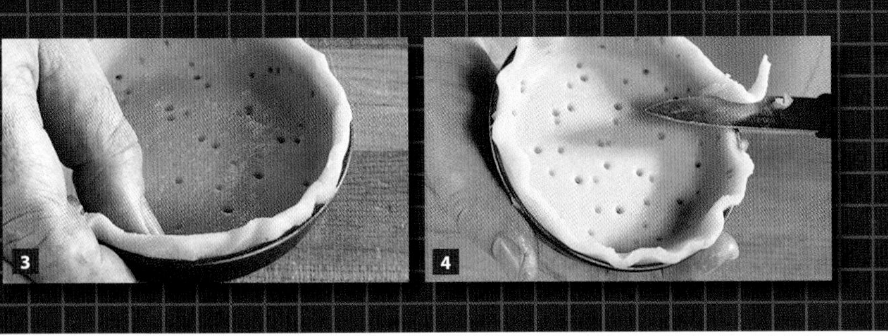

3 Make sure that every part of the dough is in contact with the mold.

4 Cut off the excess dough on the edge using a paring knife.

Tarts are generally no more than 1 inch (3 cm) thick. They always have a bottom crust and occasionally will have a top crust. Like pies, tarts may be baked or unbaked. **Baked tarts** usually contain an almond cream-based filling, such as frangipane, and fruit and the tart dough is baked with the filling. Other baked tart fillings may be based on rice, ricotta, or even jam. **Unbaked tarts** are composed of a blind-baked tart shell and may be filled with pastry cream and topped with fruit or a more complex composition such as raspberry gelée with dark chocolate mousse. In addition, some baked tarts may be combined with components often used on unbaked tarts.

There are some standard differences between tarts and pie. Tarts are usually baked in a short-sided specialty mold that may or may not have a bottom. Unlike the more fragile pie, tarts are served outside of their tin. They have straighter sides, and are made with dough that is richer and crisper than pie dough. Tarts also come in many different shapes and sizes: Contemporary tarts can be the size of petits fours or entremets and can be circular, oval, square, or a specialty shape. Finally, tarts are usually finished with apricot glaze, powdered sugar, fruit, or chocolate garnish.

WORKING WITH TART DOUGH

The working points of tart dough are very similar to those of pie dough; however, tart dough is more challenging to work with. Like pie dough, tart dough must be reserved under refrigeration for at least 4 hours before working with it to ensure that the dough is well chilled and that the gluten has relaxed.

Rolling Out Tart Dough

Tart dough may be rolled out by hand or on a dough sheeter. Either way, it is essential that tart dough be worked with quickly and efficiently because as it is rolled thinner and thinner, it warms at a faster rate. As tart dough warms, it is more prone to damage from mishandling.

Lining Tart Pans

When producing tarts, it is common practice to sheet or roll out the dough, dock it if necessary, cut out circles, transfer them to sheet pans and reserve them in the refrigerator until cool. Working with cooler dough makes it easier to line tart pans and create an end product that looks nicer in a shorter amount of working time. (See Lining Tart Pans Figure 13-13.) When lining tart pans, it is important that the tart dough

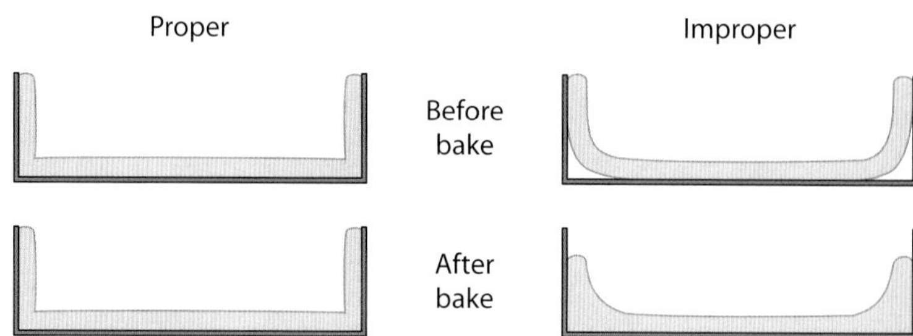

Figure 13-14
Drawing of Improper and Proper Lining Tart Pans

be relaxed into the mold, ensuring that the dough is not stretched and is in contact with all parts of the mold, especially the walls. (See Figure 13-14.)

BAKING TART DOUGH

Baking tart dough is similar to baking pie dough. Depending on the application, the dough may be blind baked or baked with a filling. Like pie dough, it is ideal for tart dough to rest at least a half hour before baking to limit the risk of shrinkage and the tart's sides falling.

Because tart dough needs to be baked until crisp, proper oven temperature is critical. If tart dough is blind baked, 350°F (175°C) in a convection oven is a good starting point, although some pastry chefs prefer to bake at a slightly lower temperature, such as 315°F (155°C) to 325°F (165°C) for a longer amount of time. This ensures that a higher level of moisture will be baked out of the dough, resulting in a dryer, crisper crust. For baked tarts, such as an almond pear tart, it is helpful to bake on a perforated sheet pan to allow maximum heat transfer to the crust.

Depending on the local climate, tart shells will have different shelf life. In climates with lower humidity, baked tart shells stored in airtight containers keep well at room temperature for about a week. For longer storage, they should be stored in an airtight container in the freezer.

Storage of Unbaked Tart Dough

Unbaked tart dough can be stored in bulk, or it can be sheeted and portioned in the refrigerator for up to several days. It is best to store tart dough on a parchment-lined sheet pan, covered with plastic wrap. Well-wrapped, unbaked tart dough can also be stored in the freezer for up to several months.

Troubleshooting Tart Dough

More things tend to go wrong with tart dough than pie dough. Insufficient mixing, improper ingredient selection and baking conditions, and mishandling of the dough can lead to problems in the final product. For troubleshooting tart dough faults and potential causes, refer to Figure 13-15.

BAKED TARTS

Whether fruit is seasonal, fresh, or frozen, baked tarts offer a sleek and sophisticated presentation. Baked tarts always start with unbaked dough, and almost always contain an additional filling, such as creamy, sweetened ricotta, a rich and flavorful frangipane, jam, or a simple pastry

Figure 13-15 Tart Dough Faults and Causes

Fault	Causes
Dough is too tough.	◗ Too little fat was used. ◗ Flour was too strong. ◗ Dough was overmixed.
Dough shrinks when rolled out.	◗ Dough was not rested enough before rolling out. ◗ Dough was overmixed. ◗ Flour was too strong.
Crust is soggy on the bottom.	◗ Filling was too fluid. ◗ Blind bake was not enough. ◗ Oven temperature was too low. ◗ Tart was underbaked.
Crust is too tough.	◗ Too strong flour was used. ◗ Dough was overmixed. ◗ Tart was overbaked.
Crust shrunk from the side of the pan.	◗ Flour was too strong. ◗ Dough was overmixed. ◗ Dough did not rest enough when cut out. ◗ Dough was stretched too much when lining the pan.

cream. For a full explanation of the preparation of assorted creams, please see Chapter 15.

Basic Assembly of Baked Tarts

When the entire mise en place is ready, tart assembly can begin, with specific steps taken to ensure successful production and baking. For example, when assembling large quantities of baked tarts using almond cream or frangipane filling, the filling must be at room temperature for ease of piping. After all of the tart pans have been lined with the dough, depositing the proper amount of almond cream is critical. If too little cream is deposited, the tart will lack in volume. If there is too much, it will take a long time to bake, and the filling may bake out of the pan. Next, the fruit or other topping may be placed atop the almond cream or frangipane filling in a decorative way. At this point, the tart may be baked, or it may be reserved under refrigeration to be baked within a day.

Fruit Selection: Baked Tarts

The type of fruit will determine the amount of filling to put in the tart. For baked tarts, canned and fresh fruits are popular. Commonly used canned fruits include pears and apricots. Fresh fruits, while endless in variety, may include apples, figs, and the pit fruits. Fruit can be prepared in a variety of ways: cut in slices or wedges, or left whole. If fresh fruit is used, it can be sprinkled with a little sugar before baking.

Baking Guidelines for Baked Tarts

When baking tarts, several components need to be considered. Fruit tarts need to be baked in a high enough heat for the dough to form a crisp crust. The filling needs to bake until it sets up, and the fruit must be tender by the time the baking is complete. For an 8 inch (20 cm) tart, 350°F (175°C) in a convection oven is a high enough temperature to ensure a crisp crust, baked filling, and tender fruit. For larger tarts, or tarts that are thicker than average, the temperature may need to be lowered to ensure even baking.

Finishing Guidelines for Baked Tarts

Baked tarts are usually finished to heighten the presentation and add protection. For baked tarts, the finishing process usually involves a simple brushing of apricot glaze. The hot glaze is brushed over the surface of the tart and acts as a protective barrier, helping to prevent baked fruit from drying out and the tart from absorbing ambient moisture. In addition to apricot glaze, fresh fruit, chocolate, powdered or pearl sugar, or nuts may be used to add additional flair to the product.

General Process for Baked Tarts

- Prepare the tart shells.
- Pipe the filling into the tart shell to the proper height. (See Baked Tarts Figure 13-16, Step 1.)
- If applicable, prepare the fruit as needed, and arrange on top of the cream. (See Baked Tarts Figure 13-16, Step 2.)
- If applicable, top the tart with the top crust (vented), and seal it securely.
- Bake until done, remove from the pan, and finish as desired.

UNBAKED TARTS

The scope of ingredients in an unbaked tart is limited only by one's imagination; however, it will always combine a blind-baked tart shell with some sort of unbaked filling. A simple unbaked tart, for example, can consist of a tart shell filled with pastry cream and topped with fresh fruit. For the more ambitious, an endless array of creams and fillings can be applied to create many different varieties, some of which can be found in the formula section of this book. No matter what the preparation, there are several key factors in creating a successful unbaked tart.

Baking Guidelines for Unbaked Tarts

To create a good unbaked tart, the tart shell must be properly blind baked to a golden brown color. Also, because the filling for unbaked tarts is usually moist, it is necessary to apply with a very light coating of chocolate or cocoa butter to prevent the crust from getting soggy.

Assembly and Composition Guidelines for Unbaked Tarts

The assembly of unbaked tarts is typically straightforward. After the optional protective coating of chocolate has been applied to the crust, the filling may be deposited. Tarts should be filled to just below the rim, taking care to not get any filling on the outside or the ridge of the crust. The ridge of the tart should remain visible and clean. The surface of the filled tart should be level. In certain instances, a filling such as a mousse or other specialty cream may rise above the ridge of the crust. In these cases, the ridge of the crust may or may not be visible, depending on the design of the dessert.

FIGURE 13-16 BAKED TARTS

1 Pipe the filling into the tart shells to the proper height.

2 Arrange the fruit on top of the filling.

Finishing Guidelines for Unbaked Tarts

Unbaked tarts allow the pastry chef to use many different components of pastry and to develop creative presentations and flavor combinations. Finishing varies by the preparation, with simple fruit tarts typically brushed with hot apricot glaze to preserve the integrity of the fruit and add to its appearance. Any tarts containing a ganache or crémeux should be glazed to protect the filling from drying and oxidation. Unbaked tarts containing mousse or more advanced components may include sprayed chocolate, sugar or chocolate décor, fresh fruit, or candied nuts.

General Process for Unbaked Tarts

- Prepare the tart shells, and blind bake.
- Remove the shells from the molds, and deposit the filling into the tart shell to the proper height.
- If applicable, prepare the fruit as needed, and arrange on top of the filling.
- If applicable, apply additional components such as previously prepared mousse or glaze.

TARTS CONCLUSION

Tarts are based on pastry dough that is typically richer and sweeter than piecrust. The creation of tarts is a more delicate process than pie making, and the scope is vast, providing many options based on available ingredients and desired product composition. Seasonal tarts, such as a fresh fruit tart in the summer, are an excellent way to highlight local, fresh produce. At the same time, a delicious almond pear tart may be made year-round. For special occasions or high-end pastry shops, the tart composition may incorporate mousse or other advanced creams as a way to elevate overall product quality.

FORMULA

OLD FASHIONED APPLE PIE

Apple pies were quite popular in Europe, especially in England, well before they became an American symbol. The popularity of the apple pie in the United States coincided with the country's growth into the world's largest apple-producing nation. This old fashioned apple pie is reminiscent of classic versions baked over several generations in American kitchens.

Components

Mealy and Flaky Pie Dough
Apple Filling

Apple Filling Formula

Ingredients	Baker's %	Kilogram	US decimal	Lb & Oz		Test
Apples, peeled, sliced	100.00	3.578	7.888	7	14¼	1 lb 9¼ oz
Lemon juice	1.46	0.052	0.115		1⅞	⅜ oz
Sugar	20.00	0.716	1.578	1	9¼	5 oz
Cornstarch	2.40	0.086	0.189		3	⅝ oz
Salt	0.15	0.005	0.012		¼	⅛ tsp
Cinnamon	0.15	0.005	0.012		¼	⅛ tsp
Nutmeg	0.05	0.002	0.004		⅛	⅛ tsp
Raisins, soaked	6.10	0.218	0.481		7¾	1½ oz
Butter	2.44	0.087	0.192		3⅛	⅝ oz
Total	132.75	4.750	10.471	10	7½	2 lb 1½ oz

Yield: 5 [9 inch (23 cm)] double-crust pies
Test: 1 [9 inch (23 cm)] double-crust pie

Mise en Place

1. Roll out the pie dough and line the pie pans with the bottom crust.
2. Reserve in the refrigerator until the filling is prepared.

Process, Apple Filling

1. Peel, core, and slice the apples.
2. Combine the apple slices and lemon juice in a large mixing bowl.
3. Mix together the sugar, cornstarch, salt, and spices.
4. Add to the apples and toss until mixed.
5. Fold in the drained, soaked raisins.

Assembly and Baking

1. Fill the pie shells. Dot the top of the filling with butter. Create vents in the top dough and secure to the bottom dough with a decorative border.

2. Brush with an egg wash or cream wash and sprinkle with granulated sugar.
3. Bake at 385°F (196°C) in a convection oven for about 40 to 45 minutes.

FORMULA

PUMPKIN PIE

When Pilgrims first arrived in the New World, they learned a variety of useful cooking methods from the Native Americans, including their use of pumpkins. The earliest version of the pumpkin pie was not really a pie at all; it was more like a pumpkin pudding. Settlers would scoop out a pumpkin, fill it with milk and pumpkin flesh, and then cook it for hours in hot ashes, often adding spices and syrup. A few decades later in France, François Pierre Varenne, the famous French chef and author, wrote *Le Vrai Cuisinier François* (*The True French Cook*), which featured a recipe for a pumpkin pie that included pastry. By the late 1600s, recipes for variations of *pumpion pie* were appearing in English cookbooks and eventually made their way to America, where serving pumpkin pie became a tradition for Thanksgiving celebrations that continues to this day.

Components

Mealy Pie Dough

Pumpkin Pie Filling

Pumpkin Pie Filling Formula

Ingredients	Baker's %	Kilogram	US decimal	Lb & Oz		Test
Eggs	23.70	0.288	0.635		10⅛	2 oz
Pumpkin puree	100.00	1.215	2.678	2	10⅞	8½ oz
Brown sugar	75.10	0.912	2.011	2	⅛	6⅜ oz
Cinnamon	0.41	0.005	0.011		⅛	⅛ tsp
Nutmeg	0.21	0.003	0.006		⅛	⅛ tsp
Ginger	0.21	0.003	0.006		⅛	⅛ tsp
Cloves	0.21	0.003	0.006		⅛	⅛ tsp
Allspice	0.21	0.003	0.006		⅛	⅛ tsp
Salt	0.62	0.008	0.017		¼	½ tsp
Evaporated milk	99.79	1.212	2.672	2	10¾	8½ oz
Butter, melted	8.23	0.100	0.220		3½	¾ oz
Total	308.69	3.750	8.267	8	4¼	1 lb 10⅜ oz

Yield: 5 [9 inch (23 cm)] single-crust pies
Test: 1 [9 inch (23 cm)] single-crust pie

Mise en Place

1. Roll out the pie dough and line the pie pans with the bottom crust.
2. Reserve in the refrigerator until the filling is prepared.

Process, Pumpkin Pie Filling

1. Break up the eggs with a whisk. Add the pumpkin, brown sugar, spices, and salt; mix well.
2. Mix in the evaporated milk and melted butter.
3. Blend with an immersion blender until smooth.

Assembly and Baking

1. Deposit the filling evenly among the pies, just below the surface of the rim of the pie.
2. Bake for 15 minutes at 385°F (196°C) in a convection oven.
3. Turn the oven down to 300°F (149°C) and bake for an additional 30 to 40 minutes or until just barely set in the center.
4. Remove from the oven and allow to cool.

FORMULA

PECAN PIE

Some say that French settlers in New Orleans invented pecan pie after learning about pecans from the Native Americans of the region. Others believe that pecan pie is a 20th century invention inspired by traditional sugar pies and sweet nut confections. Even though its origins may be in doubt, pecan pie is undeniably connected most strongly with the American South, where many other pecan-based foods are also an important element of the local cuisine. This version, based on a buttery and flaky crust, is less sweet than some others, allowing the true flavor of the pecans and rich custard to shine.

Components

Mealy Pie Dough
Custard Filling

Custard Filling Formula

Ingredients	Baker's %	Kilogram	US decimal	Lb & Oz		Test
Eggs	71.43	0.498	1.098	1	1 5/8	3 1/2 oz
Brown sugar	71.43	0.498	1.098	1	1 5/8	3 1/2 oz
Light corn syrup	100.00	0.697	1.537	1	8 5/8	4 7/8 oz
Butter, melted	21.43	0.149	0.329		5 1/4	1 oz
Vanilla extract	3.57	0.025	0.055		7/8	1 tsp
Salt	1.43	0.010	0.022		3/8	1/2 tsp
Pecans	89.29	0.622	1.372	1	6	4 3/8 oz
Total	358.58	2.500	5.511	5	8 1/8	1 lb 1 5/8 oz

Yield: 5 [9 inch (23 cm)] single-crust pies
Test: 1 [9 inch (23 cm)] single-crust pie

Mise en Place

1. Roll out the pie dough and line the pie tins with the bottom crust.
2. Reserve in the refrigerator until the filling is prepared.

Process, Custard Filling

1. Warm the eggs to 90°F (32°C), and reserve.
2. Whisk together the brown sugar and corn syrup; add the melted butter.
3. Whisk in the vanilla and salt.
4. Add the warmed, slightly beaten whole eggs to the sugar mixture slowly.
5. Avoid incorporating air into this mixture.

Assembly and Baking

1. Arrange the pecans in the unbaked pie shell and portion the custard over the nuts.
2. Bake at 365°F (185°C) for 10 minutes in a convection oven and then at 300°F (165°C) for 30 to 35 minutes or until the filling is set.

FORMULA

CHOCOLATE CREAM PIE

Many Americans fondly recall classic chocolate cream pie beckoning from the display case of their favorite roadside diner. This nostalgic dessert has been updated for a new century, with luxurious ingredients and elegant finishing, but it retains the basic elements that have made it such a lasting favorite: rich, creamy dark chocolate custard and mounds of tempting whipped cream atop a flaky all-butter piecrust.

Components

Blind-Baked Flaky Pie Dough
Chocolate Custard
Crème Chantilly
Chocolate Shavings and Powdered Sugar

Chocolate Custard Formula

Ingredients	Baker's %	Kilogram	US decimal	Lb & Oz	Test
Whole milk	60.00	0.758	1.671	1 10¾	5⅜ oz
Heavy cream	40.00	0.505	1.114	1 1⅞	3⅝ oz
Sugar #1	10.00	0.126	0.278	4½	⅞ oz
Cornstarch	5.00	0.063	0.139	2¼	½ oz
Sugar #2	20.00	0.253	0.557	8⅞	1¾ oz
Egg yolks	15.00	0.189	0.418	6⅝	1⅜ oz
Butter	13.00	0.164	0.362	5¾	1⅛ oz
72% chocolate	25.00	0.316	0.696	11⅛	2¼ oz
Total	188.00	2.375	5.235	5 3¾	1 lb ¾ oz

Yield: 5 [9 inch (23 cm)] single-crust pies
Test: 1 [9 inch (23 cm)] single-crust pie

Process, Chocolate Custard

1. In a stainless steel pot, boil the milk, cream, and first sugar.
2. Combine the second sugar with the cornstarch.
3. Combine the egg yolks and sugar–cornstarch mixture.
4. Once the milk mixture boils, temper one-third of it into the egg mixture.
5. Return the tempered sugar–yolk mixture to the milk and bring the mixture back to a boil, stirring constantly.
6. Once cooked, transfer the custard to a bowl fitted with the whip attachment.
7. Add the chocolate and mix on low speed. Add the butter and mix until smooth.
8. Once just warm to the touch, fill the blind-baked pie shells three-fourths of the way up the side of the pie shell and cool to set the filling.
9. Top with crème Chantilly. Garnish with chocolate shavings and powdered sugar.

Assorted Pies

FORMULA

QUICHE

Although most closely associated today with the French, quiche actually originated in Germany, in the medieval kingdom of Lothringen, under German rule, which the French later renamed *Lorraine*. The word *quiche* is from the German *Küchen*, meaning "cake." Originally the quiche began with a bread dough, but today pie dough or pâte brisée is the base of choice. Quiche became popular in England and in the United States during the 1940s and 1950s. Originally available in mainly vegetarian variations, the quiche evolved to include ham, seafood, and other varieties as endless as the imagination of the cook.

Custard Filling Formula

Ingredients	Baker's %	Kilogram	US decimal	Lb & Oz		Test
Heavy cream	100.00	0.848	1.869	1	13⅞	6 oz
Milk	100.00	0.848	1.869	1	13⅞	6 oz
Eggs	68.00	0.577	1.271	1	4⅜	4⅛ oz
Egg yolks	25.00	0.212	0.467		7½	1½ oz
Salt	1.80	0.015	0.034		½	½ tsp
Pepper	To taste					
Nutmeg	To taste					
Total	294.80	2.500	5.511	5	8⅛	1 lb 1⅝ oz

Yield: 5 [9 inch (23 cm)] quiches (*Note:* Yield will vary depending on quantity and type of fillings used.)
Test: 1 [9 inch (23 cm)] quiche

Process, Custard Filling

Combine all the ingredients and blend well with an immersion blender.

Assembly and Baking

1. Line quiche molds or pie tins with the pastry dough and allow to rest in the refrigerator for at least 30 minutes. Blind bake the shells before filling.
2. Prepare and cool the fillings and then deposit into the pastry shells.
3. Fill with custard to just below the surface of the pastry.
4. Bake at 300°F (149°C) in a convection oven just until the custard is set.

Note

Smaller quiches such as petits fours or single serving size do not need to have their shells blind baked. For these, start at 350°F (177°C) and then drop the temperature to 300°F (149°C). Baking on a perforated sheet pan will also improve crust color and crispness.

Assorted Quiches

Lorraine Filling Formula

Ingredients	Quantity	US decimal	Lb & Oz
Ham, diced	0.090 kg	0.198	3
Bacon, cooked	0.100 kg	0.220	3 ½
Grated emmental	0.090 kg	0.198	3

Yield: 1 [9 inch (23 cm)] quiche

Chicken and Artichoke With Roasted Red Pepper Filling Formula

Ingredients	Quantity	US decimal	Lb & Oz
Chicken	0.100 kg	0.220	3 ½
Artichoke	0.080 kg	0.176	2 ¾
Roasted pepper	0.050 kg	0.110	1

Yield: 1 [9 inch (23 cm)] quiche

Spinach, Feta, and Roma Tomato Filling Formula

Ingredients	Quantity	US decimal	Lb & Oz
Spinach	0.080 kg	0.176	2 ¾
Feta	0.120 kg	0.264	4 ¼
Tomato	0.100 kg	0.220	3 ½

Yield: 1 [9 inch (23 cm)] quiche

Mushroom and Swiss Filling Formula

Ingredients	Quantity	US decimal	Lb & Oz
Mushroom	0.150 kg	0.330	5 ¼
Thyme	0.002 kg	0.004	1 tsp
Swiss cheese	0.100 kg	0.220	3 ½

Yield: 1 [9 inch (23 cm)] quiche

Broccoli Cheddar Filling Formula

Ingredients	Quantity	US decimal	Lb & Oz
Broccoli	0.125 kg	0.275	4 ¼
Cheddar	0.125 kg	0.275	4 ¼

Yield: 1 [9 inch (23 cm)] quiche

FORMULA

PEAR ALMOND TART

This centerpiece dessert is a classic French tart often served during autumn when its key ingredient is at its finest. Pear tarts are surprisingly simple to make and are a sensational special occasion dessert because of their simple, luxurious appearance and fragrant ingredients. The combination of pears and frangipane in a buttery tart dough crust never fails to dazzle.

Components	Quantity	US decimal	Lb & Oz
Pâte sucrée	250 g	0.550	8 ½
Raspberry jam	SQ	SQ	SQ
Frangipane	500 g	1.102	1 1 ½
Pear halves, poached or canned	6	6	6
Apricot glaze	SQ	SQ	SQ

Yield: 1 [9 inch (23 cm)] tart

Process

1. Roll the dough large enough to fit a 9 inch (23 cm) tart ring.
2. Line the tart ring and trim the edges.
3. Pipe a spiral of raspberry jam on the base of the tart.
4. Pipe frangipane on the bottom of the tart to cover.
5. Slice the pear halves.
6. Arrange six pear halves on the frangipane with the small end facing toward the center.
7. Bake at 350°F (177°C) in a convection oven for about 35 minutes or until golden brown.
8. Brush with the glaze, and sprinkle sliced almonds or pearl sugar decoratively around the edge.

Pear Almond Tart

FORMULA

FRESH FRUIT TART

Fresh fruit tarts are ubiquitous in pastry shops in the United States and in Europe. The style can range from an organized presentation of fruit to an abstract arrangement. Whatever the style, it is essential to use quality ingredients and fresh components to ensure the flavors and textures of the dessert are the best that they can be. Creating a moisture barrier between the crust and the custard filling is an optional step; however, it will greatly prolong the crisp texture of the tart shell. Use seasonal fruit when it is at its best and balance the shapes and colors of the fruit for a striking appearance.

Components

Pâte Sucrée
Pastry Cream
Fresh Fruit
Apricot Glaze
Powdered Sugar

Assembly

1. Preheat the oven to 350°F (175°C).
2. Line the tart rings with the pâte sucrée, refrigerate, and then blind bake.
3. Pipe a layer of pastry cream evenly on top of the pastry shell. Place the fruit on top of the pastry cream and garnish with apricot glaze and powdered sugar.

FORMULA

PASSION FRUIT TART

The intense flavor and intoxicating fragrance of the tropical passion fruit distinguish it from other fruits commonly used in the creation of seasonal tarts. Passion fruit is the edible fruit of the passion flower, discovered by Spanish explorers who named their find in honor of the passion of Christ. This is a simple tart consisting of a pâte sucrée shell and passion crémeux, an exceptionally creamy filling composed of passion fruit puree, sugar, egg yolks, butter, and gelatin.

Components

Blind-Baked Pâte Sucrée Tart Shells
Passion Fruit Crémeux
Italian Meringue
Neutral Glaze
Chocolate Décor

Passion Fruit Crémeux Formula

Ingredients	Baker's %	Kilogram	US decimal	Lb & Oz		Test
Passion fruit puree	100.00	0.975	2.149	2	2⅜	6⅞ oz
Sugar	50.00	0.487	1.074	1	1¼	3⅜ oz
Egg yolks	30.00	0.292	0.645		10⅜	2 oz
Eggs	37.50	0.365	0.806		12⅞	2⅝ oz
Gelatin	1.50	0.015	0.032		½	2 sheets
Butter	37.50	0.365	0.806		12⅞	2⅝ oz
Total	256.50	2.500	5.512	5	8⅛	1 lb 1⅝ oz

Yield: 5 [9 inch (23 cm)] tart or 16 [4 inch (10 cm)] tartlets
Test: 1 [9 inch (23 cm)] tart

Process, Passion Fruit Crémeux

1. Bring the puree to just below a boil with half of the sugar.
2. Combine the egg yolks, whole eggs, and the remainder of the sugar.
3. Pour one-third of the puree over the egg mixture and stir with a spatula. Do not use a whisk as it will incorporate air.
4. Return the egg mixture to the pot and continue to stir constantly, agitating the bottom of the pot.
5. Cook until the mixture is 180°F (82°C) and thickened. Do not overcook.
6. Strain through a fine chinois into a clean, dry container. Add gelatin, and stir to incorporate.
7. When the mixture is at 95°F (35°C), add soft butter using an immersion blender.
8. Deposit into blind-baked tart shells ⅛ inch from the top of the tart and store covered in the freezer until ready for use.

Italian Meringue Formula

Ingredients	Baker's %	Kilogram	US decimal	Lb & Oz	
Sugar	200.00	0.600	1.322	1	5⅛
Water	60.00	0.180	0.397		6⅜
Egg whites	100.00	0.300	0.661		10⅝
Total	360.00	1.080	2.380	2	6⅛

Yield: 5 [9 inch (23 cm)] tarts

Process, Italian Meringue

1. Heat the sugar and water on the stove until it reaches the boiling point.
2. In a mixer with the whisk attachment, mix the egg whites on second speed.
3. When the sugar reaches soft ball stage [240°F (118°C)], slowly pour it into the whipped egg whites. Continue to mix for 10 minutes.

Assembly

Remove from the freezer and glaze with a very thin layer of neutral glaze, decorate the border with Italian meringue, and garnish with chocolate décor.

Assorted Unbaked Tarts

FORMULA

TARTE TATIN

This famous French dessert, basically an upside-down apple tart with caramelized apples, is supposedly the result of a happy accident. Sisters Carolina and Stéphanie Tatin ran l'Hotel Tatin in a small rural town in the Loire Valley in the late 1800s. One day, Stéphanie was preparing her special apple tart when she inadvertently placed it in the oven the wrong way round. Stéphanie served the strange tart warm, even after discovering that the pastry and apples were upside-down. Her guests raved about the unusual creation, and a star dessert was born. The French call this dessert *Tarte des Demoiselles Tatin*—"the tart of two unmarried women named Tatin." Restaurateur Louis Vaudable is usually given credit for the lasting renown of the tarte Tatin. After tasting the tart one day, he made tarte Tatin a permanent fixture on the menu at his restaurant, Maxim's of Paris.

Components

Puff Pastry
Apples
Caramel Sauce

Caramel Sauce Formula

Ingredients	Baker's %	Kilogram	US decimal	Lb & Oz		Test
Glucose	16.67	0.048	0.107		1¾	⅜ oz
Sugar	100.00	0.290	0.640		10¼	2 oz
Butter	33.33	0.097	0.213		3⅜	⅝ oz
Cream	22.22	0.065	0.142		2¼	½ oz
Total	172.22	0.500	1.102	1	1⅝	3½ oz

Yield: 5 [6 inch (15 cm)] tarts
Test: 1 [6 inch (15 cm)] tart

Process, Caramel Sauce

1. Heat the glucose and add the sugar; cook to a deep golden brown.
2. Add the butter and stir to incorporate.
3. Add the cream while stirring constantly.
4. Deposit into the molds.

Assembly

1. Sheet out the puff pastry, dock, cut out 6 inch (15 cm) rounds, and reserve.
2. Arrange the apples over the caramel decoratively.
3. Top with the pastry, and create a vent in the center of the pastry.

4. Bake at 350°F (177°C) in a convection oven until the pastry is golden brown.
5. Before removing the pastry from the pan, let it stand for 2 hours.
6. To remove the pastry, warm the pan and turn it over onto a gold board or serving tray.

FORMULA

LEMON CURD TART

This refreshing tart pleases the eye with its sunny appearance and stimulates the palate with its superb pairing of sweet and tart flavors. Lemon curd, sometimes referred to as lemon cheese, is a specialty of England, where it is has been used since the 19th century as a filling for cakes, small pastries, and tarts or as a spread for muffins or bread. The pastry used for the crust is pâte à foncer, balancing the sweet and tart in the filling and the buttery tenderness in the crust.

Components

Pâte à Foncer
Lemon Curd
Neutral Glaze
Tempered Chocolate

Lemon Curd Formula

Ingredients	Baker's %	Kilogram	US decimal	Lb & Oz		Test
Sugar	100.00	1.030	2.271	2	4	7 oz
Egg yolks	48.89	0.504	1.110	1	2	3.5 oz
Lemon juice	50.00	0.515	1.135	1	2	3.5 oz
Lemon zest	3.33	0.034	0.076		1	1 tsp
Butter	40.00	0.412	0.908		15	3 oz
Total	242.22	2.495	5.500	5	8	17 oz

Yield: 5 [9 inch (23 cm)] tarts or 16 [4 inch (10 cm)] tartlets
Test: 1 [9 inch (23 cm)] tart

Process, Lemon Curd

1. Combine the sugar, egg yolks, lemon juice, and lemon zest in a stainless steel bowl and place over a double boiler.
2. Stir occasionally. Once done, the mixture must be thick like ketchup.
3. Remove from the heat, strain into a clean container, and add butter at 90°F (32°C) to 95°F (35°C) with an immersion blender.
4. Cover to the surface, and reserve in the refrigerator.

Assembly

1. Line the tart molds with the pâte à foncer, and reserve in the refrigerator for at least a half hour.
2. Blind bake and cool.
3. Fill the tarts with the curd.
4. Place in a low oven [200°F (94°C) convection] for about 10 minutes to set the curd.
5. Cool and cover with glaze. Decorative piping with chocolate couverture is optional.

Lemon Meringue Tart Variation

1. After the curd has been deposited and set, make an Italian meringue (see pages 635–636) and apply to the surface of the tart.
2. Brown with the torch.

FORMULA

BRETON STRAWBERRY TART

Few desserts are more strikingly colorful than a strawberry tart in season. With its ruby red fruit, displayed to perfection atop a Breton tart shell, this dessert evokes summer's pleasures like nothing else. A layer of pistachio cream, along with a garnish of candied pistachios, further invigorates this tart's stimulating flavor and visual appeal.

Components

Breton Short Dough
Pistachio Cream
Fresh Strawberries
Fresh Raspberries
Apricot Glaze
Candied Pistachio Pieces
Icing Sugar

Breton Short Dough Formula

Ingredients	Baker's %	Kilogram	US decimal	Lb & Oz	Test
Egg yolks	30.00	0.132	0.291	5	1 oz
Sugar	70.00	0.307	0.678	11	2 oz
Butter	75.00	0.329	0.726	12	2 oz
Salt	1.00	0.004	0.010	0	¼ tsp
Pastry flour	100.00	0.439	0.968	15	3 oz
Baking powder	8.50	0.037	0.082	1	1 ½ tsp
Total	284.50	1.250	2.755	2 12	9 oz

Yield: 5 [6 inch (15 cm)] tarts
Test: 1 [6 inch (15 cm)] tart

Process, Breton Short Dough

1. Cream the egg yolks and sugar with the paddle until light and foamy.
2. Add the soft butter and salt and mix to incorporate.
3. Add the flour and baking powder that have been sifted together.
4. Refrigerate the dough for at least 4 hours.
5. Roll out each portion [9 oz (250 g)] to a 6 inch diameter circle and deposit into a sprayed 6 inch cake pan.
6. Bake at 350°F (177°C) for about 14 minutes.

Pistachio Cream Formula

Ingredients	Baker's %	Kilogram	US decimal	Lb & Oz	Test
Pastry cream	100.00	0.329	0.725	12	2⅜ oz
Pistachio paste	9.00	0.030	0.065	1	¼ oz
Kirsch	5.00	0.016	0.036	1	⅛ oz
Total	114.00	0.375	0.826	13	2⅝ oz

Process, Pistachio Cream

1. Whip the pastry cream until smooth.
2. Add the pistachio paste to incorporate.
3. Add the Kirsch.

Assembly

1. When cooled, remove the blind-baked breton dough shells from the cake pans.
2. Line each shell with 2.7 oz (75 g) of the pistachio cream.
3. Decorate with a selection of strawberries; glaze the strawberries to prevent from drying out.
4. Add some raspberries and dust with icing sugar.
5. Garnish with pistachio pieces.

CHAPTER SUMMARY

Pies and tarts are versatile products that allow the baker or pastry chef to highlight countless flavors and textures. From the apple pie made with fresh apples to the Breton strawberry tart, this category of pastry can be both classic and contemporary. The range of fillings that can be made for pie, the endless options for filling a variety of tart bases, and the wide selection of makeup techniques provide the baker or pastry chef with many options for product development.

KEY TERMS

- ❖ Baked pie
- ❖ Baked tarts
- ❖ Blind baked
- ❖ Chiffon pie
- ❖ Cooked fruit juice method
- ❖ Cooked fruit method
- ❖ Cream pie
- ❖ Custard pie
- ❖ Fruit pie
- ❖ Galette
- ❖ Heavy pack
- ❖ Individually quick frozen (IQF)
- ❖ Lattice crust
- ❖ Light pack
- ❖ Unbaked pie
- ❖ Unbaked tarts
- ❖ Uncooked fruit method

REVIEW QUESTIONS

1. **What are the goals when rolling out pie dough and lining pie pans?**
2. **What is the purpose for blind baking? What types of pie require it?**
3. **What are the three main methods used to prepare fruit fillings for pies? How are they prepared?**
4. **What can be done to prevent tart dough from shrinking when it is blind baked?**
5. **What preventative measures can be taken to preserve the quality of a tart crust used for a fresh fruit tart? What can be done to preserve the quality of the fruit?**

chapter
14

CAKE MIXING AND BAKING

OBJECTIVES

After reading this chapter, you should be able to

- demonstrate knowledge of the ingredient requirements and functions of cake mixing.
- mix a variety of cake bases using the processes outlined in this chapter.
- determine doneness for all types of cake presented in this chapter and implement proper storing techniques.
- troubleshoot cake mixing through an examination of the process, including conducting tests to measure temperature, pH, and specific gravity of cake batters.

INTRODUCTION TO CAKE MIXING AND BAKING

A solid understanding of cake mixing and baking is important for pastry chefs because it finds its way into many of the sweets they create. They must also have a thorough knowledge of cake characteristics and how to pair cake with other dessert components.

This chapter explores three important considerations in cake mixing for different types of cakes: ingredients, formulas, and processes. In addition, baking processes and quality monitoring by tracking specific gravity, batter pH, and batter temperature are examined.

CAKE CHARACTERISTICS

The two major categories of cake are fat-based and egg foam–based. Within these categories, several mixing types may be applicable to only one cake, or to one style of cake. For example, the angel food method is solely used for angel food cake, while the creaming method is used for many types of cake.

FAT-BASED CAKES

Fat-based cakes are typically firmer and denser than foam cakes. The high presence of fat and sugar in these cakes also makes them moister, with a finer crumb structure. Although fat-based cakes are often leavened by chemical agents, some varieties also get leavening power from air that is incorporated into the batter during creaming. Fat-based cakes tend to be more of an American-style cake because they are denser, richer, and moister than foam-based cakes and are well paired with buttercream and other rich icings.

The scope of fats used for this style of cake ranges from butter to shortening to liquid shortening. Depending on the type of fat used, the technique can differ from one method to another. For example, not all methods for high-fat cakes are based on creamed fat and sugar; they are instead based more on the thorough mixing of all ingredients in a specific order. The batter can be quite thick or rather liquid.

The most commonly used methods for fat-based cakes are creaming, modified creaming, high-ratio, and liquid shortening sponge.

FOAM-BASED CAKES

Foam-based cakes are always based on the foam of whipped whole eggs, yolks, whites, or a combination. Depending on the type of cake, the egg-based ingredient may need to be heated before being whipped in order to help increase volume. After the foam is achieved, the sifted dry ingredients are folded in gently, and the cake is baked immediately. Foam cakes are typically lighter and more fragile than fat-based cakes, with a drier and more open crumb. Examples of foam-based cakes include génoise, biscuit jaconde, chiffon, and angel food cake.

The methods used to prepare foam cakes are often particular to the products they are named after. They include sponge, separated egg sponge, chiffon, and angel food.

INGREDIENT SELECTION AND FUNCTIONALITY

Cake ingredients play essential roles in the mixing and baking process. The specific characteristics and functions described in this chapter apply to cakes only. More information on cake ingredients is available in the online companion, To download information on cake ingredients, go to http://www.delmarlearning.com/companions/.

FLOUR

Cake flour is usually milled from soft white wheat or soft red winter wheat. The relatively low extraction rate of 45 to 65 percent yields flour with low bran and protein content; on average, the protein content for cake flours is 7 to 9 percent. Even though a certain amount of protein is required to help maintain structure, too much can lead to a tough, dry crumb. Cake flour is milled to a small particle size that is beneficial for absorption, crumb uniformity, and cake symmetry (Pyler, 1988, p. 912).

After the flour is milled, it is bleached with chlorine gas to improve its baking qualities. This process lowers the pH, better enables liquid absorption, and improves volume and overall texture (Pyler, 1988, p. 914). The absorption of the flour is improved because the starch of the flour is transformed from the chlorine treatment. The texture is enhanced because the gluten is weakened by the chlorine treatment.

Other flours such as pastry flour and all-purpose flour for cakes such as chiffon and genoise may also be used for cake mixing. However, for high-ratio cake formulations, cake flour is the only flour that can absorb all of the liquid used in those formulas. In addition, chlorinated flour reacts with sodium bicarbonate (baking soda) and produces carbon dioxide.

STARCH

In addition to flour, starch can be added to cake formulations. It is preferable to use a modified starch or pregelatinized starch. These starches swell in the presence of cold water and hydrate quickly, retaining moisture and allowing a more viscous batter than is available using only flour. The increased viscosity helps retain the air cells within the emulsion created during the mixing. Regular starch is not used because the baking temperature of the cake is not high enough to set the starch, and resulting cakes will have a coarser grain. The use of modified starch can replace shortening or emulsifier in some applications like fat-free cakes or muffins.

FAT

Fat has three primary roles in cake mixing. It helps trap air from the mixing action into batter to aid in leavening, it creates a soft, light, tender texture by coating all the starch and protein of the flour and helps maintain the smooth emulsions required for smooth-textured cakes. It should also be realized that fat supplies flavor if butter is used.

The selection of fats for cake mixing includes liquid vegetable oil, butter, emulsified solid shortening, and liquid shortening. The choice of fat will require a change in the formulation, procedure, mixing time, and tools for the mixer. For example, liquid oil easily disperses, hard fat does not, and liquid shortening, which also disperses easily, has added emulsifiers and stabilizers. Less mixing is needed to create an emulsion with cakes using emulsified shortenings. The mixing time and mixing speed should be monitored closely, especially when emulsified shortening is used.

SUGAR

Sugar can be classified as a tenderizing agent. The presence of sugar in cake batters has an effect on taste, texture, physical properties, and keeping qualities because it helps to retain moisture. Superfine sugar is preferable when a granulated sugar is needed, but powdered sugar can sometimes be used, especially in some sponge cakes. Inverted sugar is also used in a few formulas. It helps to keep the crumb soft and tender, especially in chocolate and coffee-flavored cake.

EGGS

In cake mixing and baking, the combination of water content, protein, fat, and lecithin in eggs provides unique functions. Eggs are used to hydrate, tenderize, leaven, emulsify, color, and flavor cake batter. Eggs should always be of high quality.

The egg is the one ingredient that contributes the most to the emulsion by using the whole egg, the yolk, or the white. The emulsion is the most important part to establish the final texture of the crumb of the cake. The air bubbles created by the emulsion yield to the expansion of the cake batter. The air bubbles act as leavening agents and increase in size from the evaporation of the water in the batter as well as the carbon dioxide gas created by the baking powder (leavening acid + baking soda).

The formation of so many air bubbles in an emulsified state is unique to cake mixing. The stability of the egg foam emulsion is based on the introduction of air into the water–protein matrix of the egg. The mixing process and speed of mixing are important for the creation of a stable emulsion, with evenly sized air bubbles. To see how this works, let's look at a straw in water. Blowing air with a straw in water is similar to the action of whipping in slow speed. If you blow too fast with a lot of force, a few large bubbles will come very quickly to the surface. If you blow gently, the many small bubbles will slowly rise to the surface because they are small and the weight of the water slows them down.

The same phenomena can be seen inside a batter even more clearly because the sugar and fat are thicker and more viscous than water. In the mixing of egg whites or whole eggs, they should be whipped on a slower speed to start to achieve a uniform foam that is made up of small air bubbles. When this texture is achieved, mixing can take place on a higher speed to introduce air faster. The structure of the small air bubbles will help trap the air coming in on the higher speed. When the proper volume is achieved, the speed should be reduced to medium to reinforce the emulsion. This breaks any large air bubbles and makes the overall emulsion more uniform. Overwhipping the egg foam will break the emulsion, especially if lower quantities of sugar have been added to it. If the egg foam becomes "dry," it will be difficult to incorporate into the base batter, causing the emulsion to break. It is very important to monitor the development of the egg foam. For some cakes, such as angel food and genoise, the emulsion is produced only by the eggs. The stability and quality of that emulsion are critical because this is the only leavening system for the cake.

LIQUIDS

Liquids are essential components to cake mixing because they moisten the crumb and make the cake palatable. Liquids that contribute to a soft cake texture include water, sour cream, and egg and milk products. When using liquids, the appropriate hydrating properties of each ingredient must be considered.

LEAVENING AGENTS

Leavening agents create light textures in cakes. The primary leavening systems used in cake are mechanical and chemical. While whipping and creaming are very efficient ways to introduce air bubbles into batter systems, further leavening is often required (except for true sponge cakes). The most common chemical leavening agents used in smaller bakeries are baking soda and baking powder. Double-acting baking powder is available and is designed for multiple uses. Special blends with specific rates of reaction are used for large volume production for specific cake batters or dough to give the best result.

Baking powder is a mixture of a leavening acid, baking soda, and a nonreactive buffer such as cornstarch. The combination of these ingredients is balanced by what is called the **neutralizing value (NV)**. Neutralizing value is the measurement of available acidity coming from leavening acids. The NV is utilized to determine the amount of leavening acid or acids needed to provide a neutral pH when combined with baking soda. The NV represents the number of parts of baking soda that can be neutralized by 100 parts of the leavening acid. The leavening acid and soda are balanced to make sure little to none remains after baking. The balance for some products such as chocolate devil's food cake is toward a higher pH, which gives the product its signature color and flavor characteristics. The purpose of having both baking powder and baking soda for this type of cake is to create these characteristics. Most cakes have a neutral pH; however, some such as angel food cake do have a low pH. To achieve this, extra leavening acid (cream of tartar) is added to make the cake whiter and to give it a tighter crumb.

Large-scale manufacturers of cake and cookies use special blends of baking soda and leavening acids, rather than baking powder, to thoroughly control the leavening of the products being produced. To assist in this task, manufacturers who produce leavening acids have predetermined the level of acid required to reach the neutral value of sodium bicarbonate. Sophisticated processes at the manufacturing level obtain this neutral value for the food manufactures. These neutral values are representative of the acidity level determined by the process known as the titration method.

Figure 14-1 shows the most common leavening acids used in the baking industry with their abbreviations, their neutralizing values, and their reaction traits. The neutralizing value is used to calculate the quantity of sodium bicarbonate (baking soda) needed to neutralize the leavening acid.

Figure 14-1
Most Common Leavening Acids Used in the Baking Industry

Leavening Acid	Formula	Abbreviation	Neutralizing Value	Reaction
Monocalcium phosphate monohydrate	$CA(H_2PO_4)_2 \cdot H_20$	MCP	80	Intermediate
Anhydrous monocalcium phosphate	$Ca(H_2PO_4)_2$	AMCP	83	Slow intermediate
Dicalcium phosphate hydrate	$CaHPO_4 \cdot 2H_20$	DCP	33	Very slow
Sodium acid pyrophosphate	$Na_2H_2P_2O_7$	SAPP	74	Slow
Sodium aluminium phosphate anhydrous	$Na_3Al_2H_{15}(PO_4)_8$	SALP	100	Very slow
Sodium aluminum phosphate hydrous	$NaAl_3H_{14}(PO_4)_8 \cdot 4H_20$	SALP	100	Very slow
Sodium aluminum sulfate	$NaAl(SO_4)_2$	SAS	104	Very slow
Adipic acid	$HOOC(CH_2)_4COOH$	Adipic	115	Quick
Citric acid	$HOOCCH_2C(OH)(COOH)CH_2COOH$	Citric	87	Quick
Fumaric acid	HOOCHC:CHCOOH	Fumaric	145	Quick
Glucono delta lactone	$C_6H_{10}O_6$	GDL	45	Slow
Potassium acid tartrate	$COOC(HCOH)_2COOH$	Cream of Tartar	45	Very rapid
Tartaric acid	$HOOC(HCOH)_2COOH$	Tartaric	112	Very rapid

To calculate the leavening acid quantity,

- Determine the flour weight for the formula
- Calculate the soda weight: the average percentage of soda is 1.2 to 2 percent based on the weight of the flour (cake flour).
- Divide the soda weight by the neutralizing value of the acid selected; for example,

$$\frac{\text{Soda} \times 100}{\text{NV}}$$

If two leavening acids are selected, the leavening acid quantity is calculated separately for each one. To neutralize the product, the leavening acid is selected according to the final product and usage. Depending on whether the product will be baked right away or stored in cold storage, in a freezer, or as a dry mix, different leavening acids may be used. Figure 14-2 presents a few recommendations.

Here is a common mix for double-acting baking powder in a cake:

- MCP + SAPP + SALP
- SAS + MCP
- SAPP + MCP

Corn starch is often added as a carrier to minimize the damage of the acid from the moisture.

MISE EN PLACE FOR CAKE MIXING AND BAKING

Specific cake-mixing processes dictate the use of particular equipment for everything from scaling to panning and baking. Depending on the size of the operation, different configurations can be used. For example, a small bakery may mix its cake batter in a planetary mixer, whereas a larger bakery may mix the same style of batter in a continuous mixer. In the small bakery, the cake will most likely be baked in a rack oven, revolving oven, convection oven, or small deck oven, but a tunnel or traveling oven will most likely be used at a larger commercial bakery.

SMALL WARES

Efficient cake mixing relies on various small wares, including spatulas, whisks, bowl scrapers, parchment paper, palette knives, sheet pans, cake pans, and bains-marie.

Figure 14-2
Some Neutralizing Options

Leavening Acid	Abbreviation	Usage	Reaction
Monocalcium phosphate monohydrate	MCP	Double acting first reaction Angel food cake	Increases aeration during mixing Releases gas during mixing
Anhydrous monocalcium phosphate	AMCP	Cake in general	Releases during the entire process
Sodium aluminum phosphate	SALP	Cake	Helps retain moisture
Sodium acid pyrophosphate	SAPP	Cake in general and other	Releases in the oven
Dicalcium phosphate	DCP	Cake	Releases in the oven

SPECIALTY MIXERS

Two styles of mixers are typically used for cake mixing. Planetary mixers are commonly used with good results for small and mid-size bakeries. When volume increases, a continuous mixing system is beneficial for creating more consistent and productive results.

Large planetary mixers can be equipped with a vacuum or a pressurized bowl to control the emulsion as well as the temperature. The continuous mixer processes the emulsion as the ingredients are fed into the machine. It can be done in one or two stages.

For the one-stage mixer, all the ingredients are mixed together and held in a tank to be pumped to the emulsion head. The quantity is monitored. As the slurry mixture is pumped inside the emulsion head, air is introduced at the same time, and the slurry gets mixed. The quantity of slurry and air, as well as the speed of the emulsion mixer head, is controlled to achieve the proper emulsion.

For the two-stage method, the ingredients are divided according to the formula. The most common cake produced using this method is the chiffon cake. A slurry is made from the egg yolks, sugar, oil, flour, leavening agent, and water if needed, as well as any flavoring such as cocoa powder or vanilla. This slurry is held in one tank. In a separate tank, the egg whites, sugar, and some cream of tartar are mixed just to dissolve the sugar. No emulsion occurs. Then, the egg white slurry is pumped into the emulsion head to create the egg foam. The rotation is controlled to monitor the mixing and air is introduced to assist in the formation of the emulsion. After the egg whites are mixed, they are folded into the slurry batter inside the static mixer. The static mixer is a pipe with a spiral blade inside (imagine a DNA strand) that spins, folding together the two mediums as they are pumped. As the cake batter comes out of the static mixer, it can be deposited in a cake pan, a depositor, a hopper, or a tunnel oven, directly on the specially designed baking surface (especially for jelly rolls).

OVENS

A wide range of ovens can be used for cake baking, including revolving ovens, convection ovens, rack ovens, deck ovens, and tunnel ovens. Special considerations must be given for each oven type. Baking times and temperatures will vary for each.

GENERAL GUIDELINES FOR CAKE MIXING AND BAKING

There are guidelines for cake mixing and baking that, if followed, can help ensure a successful finished product. Both cake mixing and cake baking require a great deal of attention to detail, as well as a controlled approach to preparing ingredients and equipment.

SCALING

All ingredients should be scaled before any mixing or whipping begins. Any necessary preparation of ingredients, including sifting and warming, should also be complete. This preparation will allow the mixing process to be closely monitored.

PAN PREPARATION, MIXING, AND MAKEUP

Before mixing begins, all sheet pans and cake pans should be ready to be filled and placed on the appropriate baking rack. High-fat cake pans should be sprayed with nonstick spray and the bottoms should be lined with parchment paper. Foam cake pans must not be sprayed, but a parchment circle should be placed at the bottom of the pan.

Even though mixing guidelines will vary considerably according to formulas, there are some important considerations for both fat-based cakes and foam cakes. For fat-based cakes, it is especially important to scrape down the bowl as the mix progresses to ensure even incorporation of ingredients. For foam cakes, it is essential to whip the egg product to the proper stage and to fold in dry ingredients gently, efficiently, and thoroughly.

Portioning by weight is best for maintaining consistency when filling pans. A semiautomated filling system is helpful for portioning batter, especially in shops that process a lot of cake. In this case, the portioning is done by volume. Once batter is scaled, it should be spread out so that it is evenly dispersed. To get the cake into the oven as quickly and efficiently as possible, this should occur after all batter has been portioned.

BAKING

One of the first steps in making a cake is preheating the oven. It is also essential to bake at the correct temperature for the type and size of cake. As a rule, smaller cakes require higher baking temperatures and shorter baking times. The larger the cake is, the lower the baking temperature will be and the longer the product will spend in the oven.

The temperature and the bake time will affect the rate of reaction of the leavening acids. Double-acting baking powder works in two stages. The first stage releases a fast-acting leavening acid, usually the monocalcium phosphate (MCP), and carbon dioxide during mixing. The second stage releases a slow-acting leavening acid like sodium acid pyrophosphate (SAPP) or sodium aluminium phosphate (SALP). These need a temperature of at least 105°F (41°C) to 110°F (43°C) to react. If the batter does not reach this temperature fast enough, the cake will form a crust and prevent the proper expansion of the cake. The same effect can occur if the oven is too hot, creating a crust with a dark color at the bottom and top of the cake. The rate of reaction is the time it takes for a leavening acid to release 60 percent of its gas in relation to the temperature.

Sufficient space is required in the oven between cake pans to promote an even circulation of air and even baking. Steam, which can be used for high-ratio and creamed cakes to allow for better expansion by keeping the surface soft, is never used for foam cake.

Once a cake is baking, it is critical that doneness not be checked too soon. Opening the oven door or moving the pan prematurely can cause it to fall if the protein and starches have not yet gelatinized. It is impossible to provide a specific timeframe for doneness, as cakes like biscuit jaconde bake in 7 minutes, whereas others, like genoise, can take 25 minutes.

It is important to test for doneness before cakes are removed from the oven. Moving them too much before they have finished baking can result in a lack of volume and damage to the crumb. When testing, it is important to check for the following:

- A slight contraction from the sides of the pan for high-fat cakes.
- A somewhat springy texture when pressed lightly with the finger, due to the stabilized, open crumb.

- Proper coloration of the surface.
- A clean cake tester after insertion into the middle of the cake.

HIGH-ALTITUDE BAKING

High altitude creates problems for baking because the atmospheric pressure is lower than at sea level. This makes it harder for product to rise during baking. As such, fermented yeast products can be easily controlled by reducing the yeast. Cakes need a little bit more attention. The structure of cake is more fragile than the structure of yeasted dough. For yeasted products with eggs, an increase in the quantity of the egg can help to maintain the structure with additional protein. For sponge cake and genoise, which contain a lot of eggs, high-altitude baking does not create a challenge as it does in the creaming, high-ratio, and blending methods.

At elevations greater than 2,000 feet, all baking powder, baking soda, and cream of tartar should be reduced by 15 percent and by an additional 5 to 8 percent every 1,000 feet in elevation thereafter.

Any cakes with liquid shortening or cake shortening containing emulsifiers should have the mixing time reduced by 40 percent. The eggs should be reduced 4 to 10 percent of their existing weight. Water is also reduced in comparison. The baking temperature should be increased to help establish color and set up the proteins faster.

COOLING AND STORAGE

Proper cooling and storage techniques are critical for cake quality. If the cake is allowed to cool in the pan, it can sweat, and the cake can absorb the excess water. Also, a hot sheet pan can significantly dry out thinner cakes like biscuit jaconde after baking. After cakes have totally cooled, they can be wrapped in plastic wrap. If they are wrapped when warm, the moisture trapped in the cake and a warm environment will make them susceptible to mold and bacterial growth. The crust will be sticky and hard to ice.

Creamed cakes and high-ratio cakes should be turned out of their pan 10 to 15 minutes after coming out of the oven and should be left to cool to room temperature before being wrapped. Large sheet cakes should be transferred to racks to cool quickly and evenly.

Thin sheets of jaconde or genoise should be transferred to room temperature sheet pans to prevent excessive drying. Angel food cake and chiffon cake should cool in the pan, upside-down with sufficient airflow. Whenever a cake is turned out of a pan, it should be inverted onto a clean, flat, cool surface or a wire rack.

Cakes should always be wrapped airtight for storage. Undecorated cakes, which can be stored for up to 1 month in the freezer if properly wrapped, should be labeled and dated. To assure the best product, inventory should be rotated regularly.

HIGH-FAT CAKES

High-fat cakes are characterized by high levels of shortening agents, like butter, or emulsified shortenings in hard or liquid form. The typical process of mixing for butter cakes is the creaming method, which incorporates air into the batter. For liquid shortening cakes, a whipping process incorporates air into a more fluid batter. When mixing high-fat cakes, the most important step is scraping down the bowl three to four times to ensure thorough incorporation of ingredients and a well-emulsified batter.

FIGURE 14-3 CREAMING METHOD

1 After the butter and sugar are creamed to a light and fluffy stage, gradually add the beaten eggs in stages. Scrape the bowl after each incorporation.

2 Add the sifted ingredients in four stages.

3 Add the wet ingredients in three stages, alternately with the dry ingredients; scrape down the bowl and paddle occasionally.

4 Deposit the finished batter into prepared pans.

CAKE MIXING: CREAMING METHOD

Cakes made by the **creaming method** are based on the primary action of creaming butter and sugar together, a process similar to the creaming method for cookies. This method can also be the most challenging, especially if it is an all-butter cake. Alternative hard fats, such as emulsified (high-ratio) shortening, are commonly added to these cakes. Emulsifiers are also used to add stability to the emulsion of ingredients. If an all-butter cake is the goal, it requires attention to detail, including the temperature of ingredients and the speed and rate of incorporation.

Creaming Method Process

- Scale all the ingredients and have them at room temperature.
- Mix the fat until smooth and softened, and then add the sugar. Mix until light and fluffy. Scrape down the bowl.
- If melted chocolate is required, add it during the creaming stage.
- Add the eggs gradually. (See Creaming Method 14-3, Step 1.) Whip to light and fluffy. Scrape down the bowl.
- Add the sifted dry ingredients and additional liquids in the proper stages.
- Add the dry ingredients in four parts. (See Creaming Method Figure 14-3, Step 2.)
- Add the wet ingredients in three parts.
- Always start by adding the dry ingredients first, followed by the wet ingredients. (See Creaming Method Figure 14-3, Step 3.)
- Always end the mixing with the last portion of the dry ingredients. Scrape down the bowl and paddle and deposit as needed. (See Creaming Method Figure 14-3, Step 4.)

Pan Preparation and Makeup for Creaming Method

Cake pans for cakes prepared using the creaming method should be sprayed with nonstick spray or prepared with a butter–flour mixture. Next, a parchment circle should be placed on the bottom of pan to ensure easy release after baking. For cake production, some bakeries use pan liners, similar to those used for cupcakes. They cover the bottom and sides of the cake pan. By doing this, they avoid greasing and cleaning the pans. Additionally, the cakes are covered on the bottom and sides so that they can be frozen without further wrapping. Cake batter should be deposited by weight for this method. After depositing, the surface should be leveled. The batter for these cakes is typically at least halfway up the side of the pan for a 2 inch (5 cm) cake.

CAKE MIXING: MODIFIED CREAMING METHOD

The **modified creaming method** relies on the basic creaming method processes, followed by folding in a meringue that has been whipped to medium soft peaks. The addition of meringue adds extra leavening capabilities and creates a lighter final product. Once the meringue has been folded in, the batter must be deposited into prepared pans and baked without delay.

CAKE MIXING: HIGH-RATIO METHOD

High-ratio cakes are characterized by their high ratio of sugar and liquid ingredients to flour. These cakes use specialty shortenings that have added emulsifiers to help emulsify the larger quantity of liquid ingredients and fat. The process for high-ratio cake mixing begins by coating all the dry ingredients with the fat and then slowly mixing in the hydrating components. Checking mixing time and scraping down the bowl are critical concerns for mixing high-ratio cakes. Mixing occurs at different speeds and must be monitored by time for quality control and consistency.

High-Ratio Method Process

- Scale all the ingredients, and have them at room temperature.
- Add the sifted dry ingredients (excluding the sugar) to the mixing bowl and then add the emulsified shortening. (See High-Ratio Method Figure 14-4, Step 1.)
- Mix for 2 minutes on low speed, scrape down the bowl, and continue to mix for 2 more minutes on low speed. Scrape down the bowl.
- Add the sugar and part of the milk or water. Mix for 4 minutes on low speed. Scrape down the bowl several times. (See High-Ratio Method Figure 14-4, Step 2.)
- Combine the remaining liquids with the eggs, and add to the batter in three stages. (See High-Ratio Method Figure 14-4, Step 3.)
- Scrape down the bowl between each addition.
- The final mixing stage should last approximately 5 minutes.
- Deposit by weight into greased, papered pans halfway up the side of the pan, and bake without delay. (See High-Ratio Method Figure 14-4, Step 4.)

CAKE MIXING: LIQUID SHORTENING METHOD

The development of **liquid shortening** (partially hydrogenated shortening) with added emulsifiers has benefited cake makers who rely on shortenings for their fat bases. These shortenings disperse quickly and easily throughout the batter, but they require special attention to mixing time and rate. As the batter whips, air is incorporated and acts as additional leavening.

Liquid Shortening Method Process

- Place all the liquid ingredients in a mixing bowl fitted with the paddle attachment.
- Add the sifted dry ingredients on top of the wet ingredients.
- Blend on low speed for $1^1/_2$ minutes, or until all the ingredients are incorporated.
- Whip on high speed for 4 minutes.
- Scrape down the bowl well.
- Whip on medium speed for 3 minutes.
- Fill greased and papered pans halfway up the side of the pan and bake without delay.

Note: It is recommended that you get technical documentation with the shortening you select regarding the mixing time. The mixing time is related to the emulsifiers included in the shortening.

FOAM-BASED CAKES

Foam-based cakes rely on whipped egg products to act as leaveners that create a light cake. Whole eggs, yolks, and whites may be used separately

FIGURE 14-4 HIGH-RATIO METHOD

1 Sift the dry ingredients, excluding the sugar. Place in a mixing bowl with the emulsified shortening.

2 Mix as instructed; scrape the bowl and paddle occasionally. Place the sugar and milk in the bowl; continue mixing.

3 Combine the remaining liquid and eggs, and add into the bowl in three stages as it is mixing. Scrape down after each addition.

4 Deposit the finished batter into prepared molds.

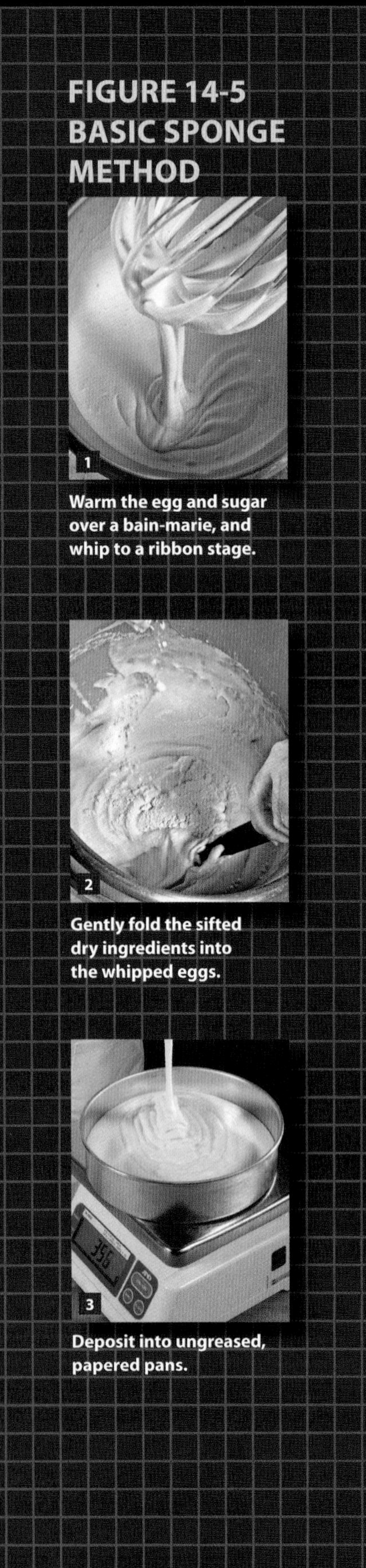

FIGURE 14-5 BASIC SPONGE METHOD

1 Warm the egg and sugar over a bain-marie, and whip to a ribbon stage.

2 Gently fold the sifted dry ingredients into the whipped eggs.

3 Deposit into ungreased, papered pans.

or in combination. For specific information about handling eggs and successfully whipping foams, please refer to the discussion of egg foams in Chapter 15. When making foam-based cakes, the mise en place must be ready because there can be no interruptions to the process. Planning ahead will ensure that egg foams are processed swiftly, and that cake quality will not suffer from time lapses during the various stages of mixing, makeup, and baking.

EGG FOAM CAKES: BASIC SPONGE METHOD

The basic sponge method is used to make **sponge cake**, which is commonly referred to as génoise. Variations include butter sponge or milk and butter sponge. Egg foam cakes made with sponges are characteristically dryer than high-fat cakes, and some consumers consider them "eggy" tasting. They are often used for more European-style cakes, and the dry texture is typically addressed by soaking the cake with a light cake syrup during assembly.

Basic Sponge Method Process

- Scale all the ingredients, and sift the dry ingredients.
- Combine the whole eggs with the sugar, and warm over a bain-marie while mixing.
- Whip on medium-high speed to a ribbon stage. Add any flavoring at the end of this stage. (See Basic Sponge Method Figure 14-5, Step 1.)
- Gently fold in the sifted dry ingredients. (See Basic Sponge Method Figure 14-5, Step 2.)
- Deposit into an ungreased, papered pan three-fourths of the way up a 2 inch (5 cm) pan. Bake without delay. (See Basic Sponge Method Figure 14-5, Step 3.)
- Cool upside-down if the cake has a tendency to deflate. This will vary, depending on the quality of the flour used.
- Remove from the pan, and use or store in the freezer for later use.

EGG FOAM CAKES: SPONGE VARIATIONS

The two main sponge cake variations add additional liquid and moisture, softening the crumb and enriching the flavor. Care must be taken to incorporate these ingredients carefully and to avoid overmixing the batter.

Butter Sponge Method

Follow the same procedure for the basic sponge method, through the addition of the dry ingredients. Then, fold in melted butter thoroughly, taking care not to overmix the batter. Process the batter as quickly as possible and in the same way as for basic sponge.

Hot Milk and Butter Sponge Method

Melt together the milk and butter. Fold the milk–butter mixture into the basic sponge base in three stages after incorporation of flour. Do not overmix.

EGG FOAM CAKES: SEPARATED EGG SPONGE METHOD

The **separated egg sponge method** combines the extreme lightening power of the egg white with the richness and lesser volume created by the whole egg and yolk. Whole eggs and yolks are used in the base foam

FIGURE 14-6 SEPARATED EGG SPONGE METHOD

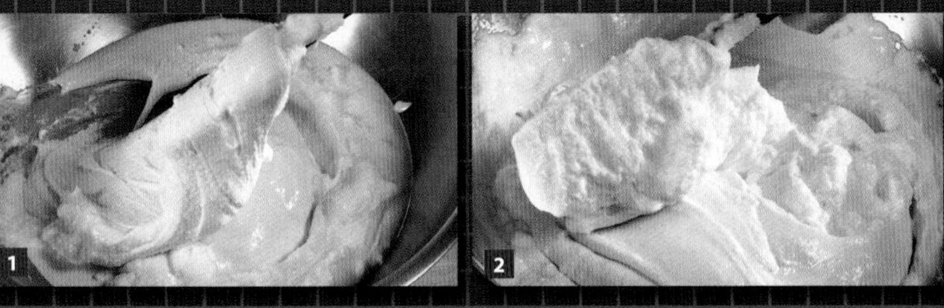

1 Whip the whole eggs and sugar to a ribbon stage, and prepare a meringue with medium-stiff peaks. Add the meringue to the whole egg mixture in stages.

2 Gently combine the two.

3 Gently fold in the sifted dry ingredients, taking caution not to overmix.

and provide a high level of fats, which gives a rich flavor to this type of cake. It is important to not over- or underwhip the whites because this will greatly affect volume. The high sugar and fat content of these cakes ensures a soft texture that makes them useful for roulade, or cakes that need to be rolled.

When panning separated egg sponge cakes for roulade, it is critical to not work the batter too much or it will lose volume. The batter should be worked the length of the sheet pan first, and then the width.

Separated Egg Sponge Method Process

- Scale all the ingredients, and have them at room temperature. Sift the dry ingredients.
- Whip the whole eggs, yolks, and sugar to ribbon stage.
- Whip the whites and sugar to medium-stiff peaks.
- Temper the whites into the whole egg mixture. (See Separated Egg Sponge Method Figure 14-6, Steps 1–2.)
- Gently fold in the sifted dry ingredients. Do not overmix. (See Separated Egg Sponge Method Figure 14-6, Step 3.)
- Deposit onto silicone mat–lined pans and bake without delay.
- After they are baked, transfer to a cool surface to prevent excessive drying of the cake.
- Use as needed, or store in the freezer, covered, for later use.

EGG FOAM CAKES: BISCUIT JACONDE METHOD

The **biscuit jaconde method** is a variation on the separated egg sponge method. It is characterized by the addition of nut flour into the cake batter, as well as by a design that is applied through a thicker batter. Biscuit jaconde is typically baked in thin sheets on sheet pans. The nut flour can be from any nut, but almond is favored for its taste and texture.

The almond flour is typically called for in **tant pour tant (TPT)**, which is one part almond flour to one part powdered sugar or granulated sugar (though in this book, all the preparations of TPT require powdered sugar). The design portion of the cake is created with a template, using a dense cake-like batter (pâte à décor) on a silicone baking mat. Parchment paper may be used but it tends to distort the cake and create wrinkles as the cake contacts during baking and pulls the paper with it into the cake. Next, the imprint of batter is frozen to firm it up and then the cake batter is portioned over it and spread with an offset spatula. The highlights adhere to the cake during baking and form one surface with a pattern.

FIGURE 14-7 BISCUIT JACONDE DESIGN OPTIONS

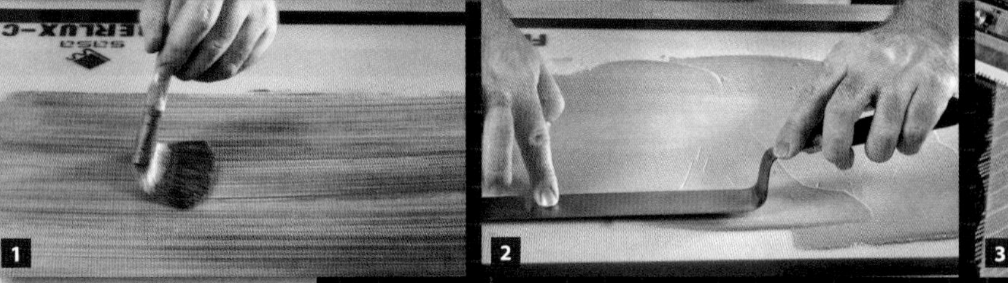

1 Option 1: Brush a small portion of softened pâte à décor onto a silicone mat.

2 Option 2: Thinly spread a portion of pâte à décor onto a silicone mat.

3 Using a comb, create a decorative pattern.

The TPT is then whipped with the whole eggs, and the egg whites are whipped separately with additional sugar to soft to medium peaks. After both foams have reached full volume, the whites are folded into the whole egg–almond base, and then the flour is folded in. Softened butter is sometimes added to the whole egg base.

Biscuit Jaconde Method Process

- Scale all the ingredients, and have them at room temperature.
- Prepare the base mixture to texture silicone baking mats with decoration. (See Biscuit Jaconde Design Options Figure 14-7.)
- Combine the TPT, whole eggs, and yolks.
- Whip the egg mixture on high speed until triple in volume.
- Make a medium-stiff meringue with the egg whites and granulated sugar.
- Fold the egg whites into the whole egg mixture and fold the flour into this mixture.
- Portion evenly between sheet pans with the design and bake. (See Biscuit Jaconde Method Figure 14-8.)

EGG FOAM CAKES: CHIFFON METHOD

Cakes made using the **chiffon method** are leavened with air from whipped egg whites, as well as from baking powder. Chiffon always contains neutrally flavored oil, which leads to a soft-textured cake. The two-step mixing process is used first to create a slurry of the wet and dry ingredients; then the egg whites are whipped and folded into the slurry base. The liquid oil in this formula makes a very tender crumb.

Because the crumb of the chiffon is so tender, it cannot be removed from the pan too soon after baking. It is important that the pans are not greased so the cake can stick to it to avoid collapse during the cooling time. For that same reason, it is cooled upside-down in the pan. To remove from the pan, slide a spatula around the perimeter of the pan, invert the pan, and tap it a little to help release the cake.

Chiffon Method Process

- Scale all the ingredients, have them at room temperature, and sift the dry ingredients together.
- Place the dry ingredients in a mixing bowl and mix on medium speed with paddle attachment. Add the oil and egg yolks; then add the water and flavoring agents. Scrape down the bowl several times to ensure a smooth batter. Do not overmix. (See Chiffon Method Figure 14-9, Steps 1–2.)
- Whip the egg whites and remaining sugar to medium-stiff peaks.

FIGURE 14-8 BISCUIT JACONDE METHOD

1 After the biscuit jaconde batter is made, deposit it onto the prepared silicone mats.

2 Spread the batter into an even thickness.

3 Once baked, the biscuit should be turned onto a parchment paper immediately after cooling slightly.

- Fold the meringue into the cake base (see Chiffon Method, Figure 14-9, Steps 3–4) and deposit into ungreased, papered pans. Bake without delay. (See Chiffon Method Figure 14-9, Step 5.)
- Cool upside-down. Remove from the pan and use or freeze, well wrapped, until needed.

EGG FOAM CAKES: ANGEL FOOD METHOD

Made using the **angel food method**, angel food cakes are named for their pure white crumb and light texture. The three basic ingredients are sugar, egg white, and flour; other ingredients like salt, flavoring, and tartaric acid are also commonlyused. The flavoring can vary from chocolate to citrus to spice. An acidic ingredient like tartaric acid is required to add strength to the egg foam, to prevent the foam from shrinking during and after baking, and to whiten and soften the crumb (Pyler, 1988, pp. 1003–1004). Egg whites must be free from contaminants, especially those that contain fat, and all equipment should be clean. Because angel food cake contains such a large ratio of sugar to flour, the egg foam is made with half of the quantity of sugar, and the remaining sugar is folded into the egg foam with the sifted flour. Time is of the essence when making angel food cake, and it is critical to get the cake into the oven as soon as possible.

Angel Food Method Process

- Scale all the ingredients, have them at room temperature, and sift the flour with half of the sugar.
- Whip the egg whites until they are frothy. Add the cream of tartar and salt. At soft peak, slowly add the remaining sugar until soft-medium peaks develop. Do not overwhip.
- Gently fold in the sifted sugar and flour mixture. (See Angel Food Method Figure 14-10, Step 1.)
- Deposit into ungreased tube pans and bake without delay. (See Angel Food Method Figure 14-10, Steps 2–3.)
- Once baked, invert the pans and allow them to cool upside-down.
- Remove from the pan when cool.

ADVANCED CAKE MIXING

Many bakers and pastry chefs mix and bake cake every day without a problem. However, if the location and ingredients change, the end results will possibly change as well. Variables that can affect cake quality include the type of oven used, the quality of ingredients, and the temperature of

FIGURE 14-9 CHIFFON METHOD

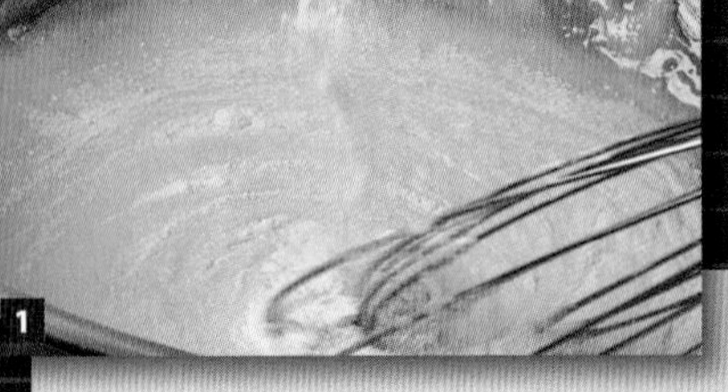

1 Add the sifted ingredients to the combined wet ingredients.

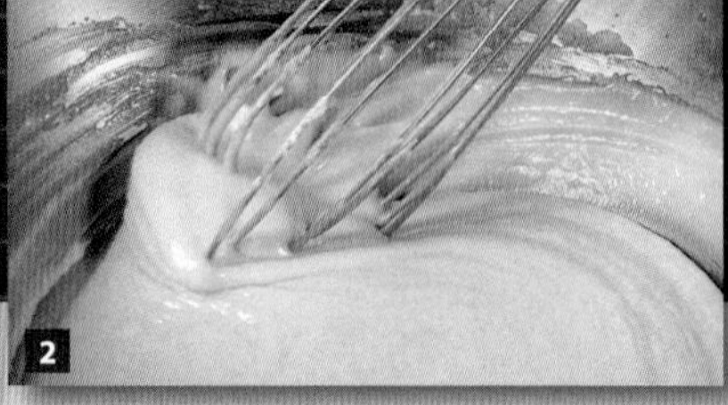

2 Mix until smooth batter is formed. Be careful to not overmix.

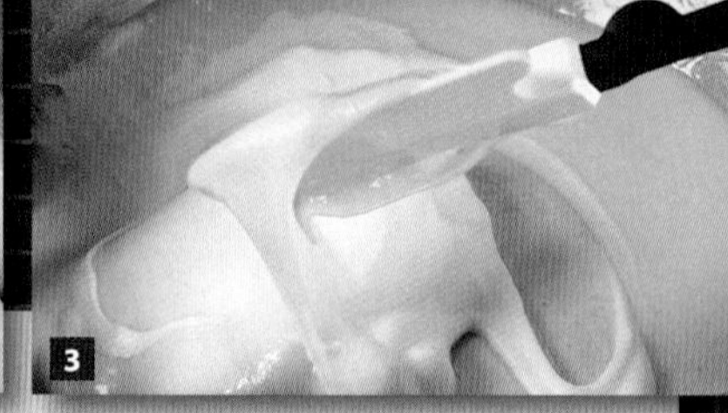

3 Prepare a medium-stiff meringue, and fold it into the egg mixture in stages.

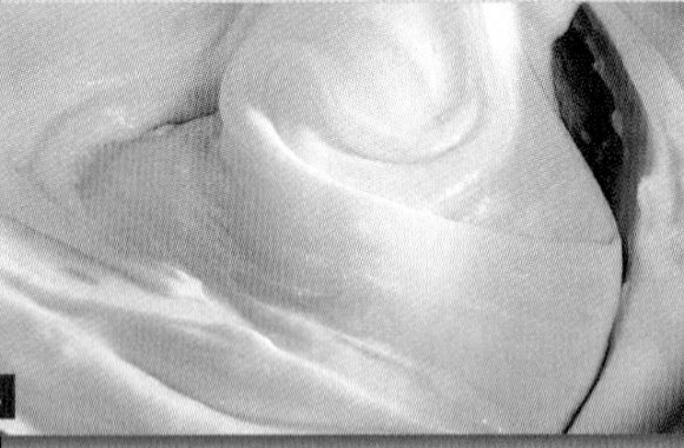

4 Gently fold the meringue in by hand.

5 Deposit into ungreased, papered pans. Bake immediately.

FIGURE 14-10 ANGEL FOOD METHOD

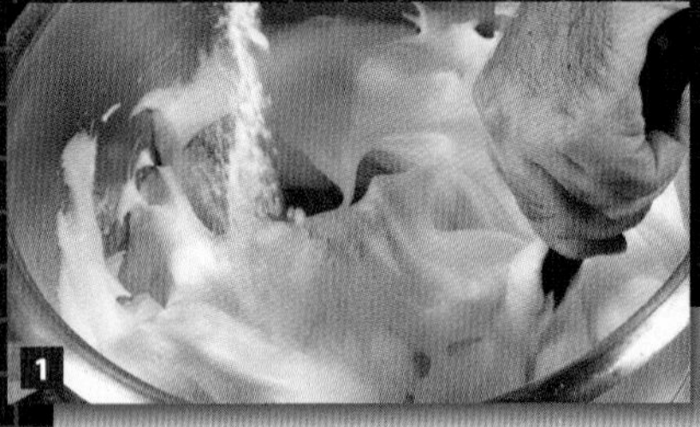

1 Gently fold in the sifted ingredients into a soft-medium peak meringue.

2 Deposit into an ungreased tube pan.

3 Smooth out the top and bake immediately.

the workroom. The established guidelines for monitoring cake mixing include measuring the temperature, pH, and specific gravity of the batter. Recording this data can help improve cake quality, because the baker or pastry chef can track results in comparison to the data recorded during mixing.

TROUBLESHOOTING CAKE FORMULATION

Use Figure 14-11 as a troubleshooting aid.

BATTER TEMPERATURE

Batter temperature affects viscosity, which, in turn, affects both aeration and stability. To achieve the best volume, batter must be the proper temperature. For example, the temperature of the fat in fat-based cakes affects

Figure 14-11
Cake Properties and Causes

Fault	Causes
Volume and Shape	
Cake does not rise properly.	◗ Too little leavening was added or chemical leavening was too old. ◗ Too much liquid or not enough flour was used. ◗ Oven was not hot enough. ◗ Oven was too hot and set the cake before the cake rose. ◗ Fat and sugar were not creamed long enough.
Cake has an uneven shape.	◗ Batter was not spread out evenly. ◗ Heat of the oven was not even. ◗ Oven racks were not leveled. ◗ Cake pan was warped.
Cake has large holes.	◗ Chemical leavening was not evenly distributed in batter, creating pockets of gas. ◗ Batter was overmixed.
Egg foam cake collapsed.	◗ Too much or too little air was incorporated into the egg foam.
Crust Color	
Crust is too dark.	◗ Oven temperature was too hot. ◗ Baking time was too long. ◗ Too much sugar was added to the batter.
Crust is too light.	◗ Oven temperature was too low. ◗ Baking time was not enough. ◗ Too little sugar was added to the batter.
Crust is soggy.	◗ Baking time was not enough. ◗ Cake was cooled in the pan with not enough ventilation. ◗ Cake was wrapped before cooled.
Crust is burst or cracked.	◗ Too much flour or too little liquid was used. ◗ Flour was too strong. ◗ Batter was improperly mixed. ◗ Oven temperature was too hot.
Texture	
Cake is heavy and dense.	◗ Not enough leavening was used. ◗ Too much liquid or too little flour was used. ◗ Too much sugar or fat was used. ◗ Oven temperature was not hot enough.
Cake falls apart and is crumbly.	◗ Flour was too weak. ◗ Too much sugar or fat was used. ◗ Batter was improperly mixed. ◗ Cake was removed from the pan while still warm.
Cake is tough.	◗ Flour was too strong. ◗ Too much flour was used. ◗ Batter was overmixed. ◗ Too little fat and sugar were used.
Flavor	
Cake has a poor flavor.	◗ Ingredients had a poor quality. ◗ Formula was unbalanced.

how much air can be incorporated into the batter. Lower temperatures inhibit incorporation of air and produce a stiffer batter. Conversely, higher temperatures melt the fat and make the batter too fluid, inhibiting its ability to hold an emulsion of the liquid ingredients, air, and fat. The temperature will also affect the baking powder and the gas released during the first stage of mixing, especially if double-acting baking powder is used.

Controlling Batter Temperature

To control batter temperature, the pastry chef should know the temperatures of all major ingredients in the batter and the friction factor from mixing, and should adjust the temperature of the liquid ingredients to compensate. Unless cake mixing is carried out in a climate-controlled facility, the temperature of the major liquid ingredient and temperature of preparation may need to vary throughout the year. Ingredient temperatures in the batter system can vary over time.

The equation in the next section can serve as a rough guide to determine final batter temperature because all formulas have varying quantities of ingredients and mixing times. Another approach is to record all the data on a cake-mixing sheet in order to understand the relationship between mixing time, ingredient temperatures, and final qualities.

Batter Temperature Factors and Calculation

Major factors affecting the calculation of batter temperature include

- FT (flour temperature)
- RT (room temperature)
- WT (water temperature)
- ST (shortening temperature)
- ET (egg temperature)
- SuT (sugar temperature)
- DesT (desired batter temperature)
- ActT (actual batter temperature)
- FF (friction factor)

To determine the temperature of the liquid ingredients to be added, we need to know the friction factor in order to understand how much heat will be generated during mixing.

$$FF = (6 \times ActT) - (RT + FT + WT + ST + ET + SuT)$$

Next, the desired water temperature needs to be calculated:

$$WT = (6 \times DesT) - (RT + FT + FF + ST + ET + SuT)$$

The adjusted temperature of the water or other major liquid ingredient will bring the batter temperature to the desired level. If the water level is too low, combine it with the egg temperature (ET) and then multiply by only five factors.

PH OF CAKE BATTER

For proper physical development and flavor, cakes need a well-balanced pH. This measure of acid and base compounds is measured on a scale of 0 to 14, with 0 indicating extreme acidity and 14 indicating extreme alkalinity. Pure water is a neutral 7.

The pH of a cake batter may be the hardest to monitor without specific tools designed for the process. However, if problems persist in producing cakes, it is important to monitor pH because too much or too little can affect the crumb structure, crumb color, flavor, and volume. Low pH in cake leads to acidic flavors and a finer texture and reduction of crumb size and cake volume. If the pH is too high, the cake will have a soapy or chemical taste, the crumb will be larger and coarser, the volume will be larger, and the cell walls will be thicker (Pyler, 1988, pp. 998–999).

Major ingredients and chemical leavening agents determine the pH of a batter.

Ingredients that have a neutral affect include white sugar, shortenings, and balanced chemical leavening agents like baking powder. Ingredients that have a lowering (more acidic) effect include and fruit juices, sour cream, milk, and buttermilk. Ingredients that have a raising effect (more alkaline) effect include baking soda, cocoa powders (natural and Dutched), and egg products (Pyler, 1988, p. 999).

Controlling pH

pH is controlled in cake batter by adjusting the chemical leavening agents. If the pH is too acidic, it is necessary to lower the level of leavening acids; if the pH is too alkaline, the quantity of sodium bicarbonate (baking soda) must be lowered. Maintaining a balance of chemical leavening agents within the cake is critical; otherwise, they may not all react during the baking process and off flavors will result.

The desired pH of the crumb should be at neutral or slightly acidic. Exceptions include angel food cake, which is more acidic from leavening acid (1.75 percent based on egg whites) and devil's food cake, which is more alkaline (8.8 to 9.2 pH) to enhance flavor and sometimes color (Pyler, 1988, p. 999). To measure the pH, equal parts of cake and distilled water (say, 0.4 oz (10 g) cake and 0.4 oz (10 g) distilled water) are mixed together to form a paste. The pH is then measured with a pH meter three times in order to obtain an average of the results (the results can vary because of changes in the temperature of the paste).

SPECIFIC GRAVITY

Specific gravity (SG) is the measure of multiple items and the comparison of their densities in relation to weight by volume. In cake mixing, specific gravity is a measurement of the incorporation of air into the batter system, which is compared by volume and weight to the same volume and weight of water divided by the water's weight. In Europe, specific gravity is realized by a different method known as "batter density." It is measured from the number of grams per milliliter of batter.

The quantity of air incorporated into a batter has a significant effect on cake characteristics such as tenderness, grain, texture, and volume. For example, overmixed cake layers are fragile, break easily, or have fissures and can excessively dome (Pyler, 1988, p. 998). Measuring specific gravity per cake formula can help determine optimum mixing time. The specific gravity is frequently taken during the mixing process for the creaming method, just before adding the remaining liquids such as eggs or water. In doing so, you can increase the mixing time before adding the liquid or reduce the mixing time after adding the liquids. The more air incorporated into the batter, the lower the specific gravity number will be.

Specific gravity is measured by dividing the weight of a given volume of batter by the weight of the same volume of water.

Specific gravity will affect the crumb texture and moisture level of the final product if it is not respected properly. When using formulas containing emulsified cake shortening, paying attention to the specific gravity is even more important.

Specific Gravity Measuring Process

- Weigh a cup and tare the scale.
- Weigh the cup filled with water to the top (but dry on the outside).
- Using the same measuring cup, weigh the cup filled with batter to the top (without dripping on the edge).
- Divide the batter weight (BW) by the water weight (WW) to find the SG:

$$BW/WW = SG$$

Example: The recommended specific gravity for selected cake types follows:

Yellow cake*:	0.725 to 0.750
Chocolate cake*:	0.750 to 0.780
Sponge cake:	0.420 to 0.480
Chiffon cake:	0.600 to 0.680

*Based on the usage of liquid shortening.

See the guidelines in Figure 14-12.

Figure 14-12
Guidelines for Temperature, Specific Gravity, and pH for Common Cakes Types

Batter Type	°F	°C	Specific Gravity	pH
Sponge	92–94	33–34	0.46–0.48	7.3–7.6
Yellow layer	70–72	21–22	0.94–0.97	7.2–7.8
White layer	70–72	21–22	0.95–0.97	7.2–7.8
Devil's food	72–74	22–23	0.95–0.97	8.8–9.2
Pound	58–60	15–16	0.83–0.85	6.6–7.1

FORMULA

MARBLE BUTTER CAKE

Seductive swirls of chocolate and yellow cake batters create the pattern that gives marble cake its name. To create the perfect marble appearance, it is important not to overmix when blending the batters together; otherwise, each element will lose its definition. Marble cakes are sometimes finished with a simple dusting of powdered sugar or drizzles of chocolate icing, but they are also quite lovely served plain.

Ingredients	Baker's %	Kilogram	US decimal	Lb & Oz		Test
Butter	60.00	0.358	0.788		12 ⅝	2 ½ oz
Sugar	83.00	0.495	1.091	1	1 ½	3 ½ oz
Trimoline	17.00	0.101	0.223		3 ⅝	¾ oz
Eggs	72.00	0.429	0.946		15 ⅛	3 oz
Vanilla extract	2.00	0.012	0.026		⅜	⅛ oz
Pastry flour	70.00	0.417	0.920		14 ¾	3 oz
Potato starch	30.00	0.179	0.394		6 ¼	1 ¼ oz
Baking powder	3.00	0.018	0.039		⅝	⅛ oz
Baking soda	1.20	0.007	0.016		¼	⅛ tsp
Salt	1.20	0.007	0.016		¼	⅛ tsp
Milk	30.00	0.179	0.394		6 ¼	1 ¼ oz
Sour cream	31.00	0.185	0.407		6 ½	1 ¼ oz
Dark cocoa powder	9.00	0.054	1.118		1 ⅞	⅜ oz
Sour cream	10.00	0.060	0.131		2 ⅛	⅜ oz
Total	419.40	2.500	5.512	5	8 ⅛	1 lb 1 ⅝ oz

Yield: 5 [8 inch (20 cm) × 4 inch (10 cm)] loaf cakes
Test: 1 [8 inch (20 cm) × 4 inch (10 cm)] loaf cake

Process

1. Sift together the pastry flour, potato starch, and baking powder; set aside.
2. Cream the butter and sugar until lightened. Add the Trimoline and then the eggs and vanilla.
3. Add the sifted dry ingredients alternately with the milk blended with the first sour cream.
4. Divide the batter in two and fold into one portion the cocoa powder and the second sour cream.

5. Deposit evenly into buttered 8 inch (20 cm) × 4 inch (10 cm) pans at 17.5 oz (500 g) per pan.
6. Swirl the batter with a knife or spatula to create a marbled effect.
7. Bake at 335°F (168°C) for about 40 to 45 minutes or until a cake tester inserted in the center comes out clean.

FORMULA

SOUR CREAM POUND CAKE

The pound cake, generally agreed to have originated in northern Europe, was named after its ingredients, as the first recipes for pound cake called for a pound each of flour, sugar, butter, and eggs. The resulting cake was very dense, with a rich and buttery flavor, but it was also difficult to mix in the days when beating by hand was the only option. Pound cakes have been a staple of American kitchens for several generations, slowly changing into lighter versions of the original, but they still retain their rewarding richness of flavor and characteristic density.

Ingredients	Baker's %	Kilogram	US decimal	Lb & Oz		Test
Unsalted butter	94.25	0.463	1.020	1	⅜	3 ¼ oz
Sugar	106.19	0.521	1.149	1	2 ⅜	3 ⅝ oz
Eggs	50.88	0.250	0.551		8 ¾	1 ¾ oz
Vanilla extract	3.10	0.015	0.034		½	1 tsp
Cake flour	100.00	0.491	1.082	1	1 ¼	3 ½ oz
Baking powder	2.65	0.013	0.029		½	½ tsp
Sour cream	100.00	0.491	1.082	1	1 ¼	3 ½ oz
Salt	1.33	0.007	0.014		¼	⅛ tsp
Total	458.37	2.250	4.960	4	15 ⅜	15 ⅞ oz

Yield: 5 [8 inch (20 cm) × 4 inch (10 cm)] loaf cakes
Test: 1 [8 inch (20 cm) × 4 inch (10 cm)] loaf cake

Process

1. Sift together the cake flour and baking powder; set aside.
2. Cream the butter and sugar until light and fluffy.
3. Slowly add the eggs and vanilla extract.
4. Add the dry ingredients alternately with the sour cream on low speed, starting and ending with the dry ingredients.

5. Deposit into buttered pans at 1 lb (450 g).
6. Bake at 325°F (163°C) in a convection oven for about 35 minutes or until a cake tester inserted in the center comes out clean.

Chocolate Pound Cake Variation

Adjustments	Baker's %	Kilogram	US decimal	Lb & Oz	Test
Reduce flour to	75	0.368	0.812	13	2 ⅝ oz
Add cocoa powder	25	0.123	0.271	4 ⅜	⅞ oz
Add baking soda	2	0.010	0.022	⅜	½ tsp

Note
New flour and cocoa powder weight is now equal to 100 percent to maintain the above percentages.

Vanilla Pound Cake Variation

Adjustments	Baker's %	Kilogram	US decimal	Lb & Oz	Test
Add vanilla bean	Each	2	2	2	0.5 each

Lemon Pound Cake Variation

Adjustments	Baker's %	Kilogram	US decimal	Lb & Oz	Test
Omit vanilla extract	—	—	—	—	—
Add lemon zest	2	0.010	0.022	⅜	½ tsp
Add lemon juice	6	0.029	0.065	1	1 ½ tsp
Add baking soda	2	0.010	0.022	⅜	½ tsp

Coffee Pound Cake Variation

Adjustments	Baker's %	Kilogram	US decimal	Lb & Oz	Test
Add coffee paste	13*	0.063	0.141	2 ¼	1 tbsp

* Coffee paste is 3 percent of total batter weight.

Pistachio Pound Cake Variation

Adjustments	Baker's %	Kilogram	US decimal	Lb & Oz	Test
Reduce sugar to	88	0.432	0.952	15 ¼	3 oz
Add pistachio paste*	14	0.069	0.151	2 ⅜	1 tbsp

* The quality of and type of pistachio paste will affect the quantity needed.

Green Tea Pound Cake Variation

Adjustments	Baker's %	Kilogram	US decimal	Lb & Oz	Test
Add green tea powder	3	0.015	0.032	½	1 tsp

FORMULA

CHOCOLATE BREAKFAST CAKE

The almond paste in this intensely flavored chocolate cake creates exceptional depth and smoothness of texture. The addition of candied fruit and almonds to this already luscious breakfast dessert further adds to the overall tone of indulgence.

Ingredients	Baker's %	Kilogram	US decimal	Lb & Oz		Test
Almond paste	50.00	0.169	0.372		6	1 ¼ oz
Eggs	125.00	0.422	0.931		14 ⅞	3 oz
Butter	100.00	0.338	0.745		11 ⅞	2 ⅜ oz
Sugar	125.00	0.422	0.931		14 ⅞	3 oz
Milk	100.00	0.338	0.745		11 ⅞	2 ⅜ oz
Bread flour	100.00	0.338	0.745		11 ⅞	2 ⅜ oz
Baking powder	2.50	0.008	0.019		¼	½ tsp
Cocoa powder	25.00	0.084	0.186		3	⅝ oz
Almond meal	25.00	0.084	0.186		3	⅝ oz
Candied orange peel	25.00	0.084	0.186		3	⅝ oz
Hazelnuts, toasted	25.00	0.084	0.186		3	⅝ oz
Chocolate chips	37.50	0.127	0.279		4 ½	⅞ oz
Total	740.00	2.500	5.512	5	8 ¼	1 lb 1 ⅝ oz

Yield: 5 [8 inch (20 cm) × 4 inch (10 cm)] loaf cakes
Test: 1 [8 inch (20 cm) × 4 inch (10 cm)] loaf cake

Process

1. Sift the flour, baking powder, and cocoa powder; set aside.
2. Warm the almond paste and then cream it using the paddle.
3. Gradually add a small amount of egg to soften the paste.
4. Add the butter and sugar slowly, mixing after each addition.
5. Add the remainder of the eggs slowly and mix until smooth.
6. Mix in the milk, then the sifted ingredients and almond meal to 50 percent incorporation.
7. Add the orange peel, hazelnuts, and chocolate chips, and mix until incorporated.
8. Deposit 17.5 oz (500 g) batter per buttered 8 inch (20 cm) × 4 inch (10 cm) loaf pan.
9. Bake at 350°F (177°C) in a convection oven for 35 to 40 minutes or until a cake tester inserted in the center comes out clean.

Creaming Method Cakes
Sour Cream Pound Cake
Chocolate Breakfast Cake
Marble Butter Cake

FORMULA

CAKE AUX FRUITS

The foundation of this complex, richly textured dessert is a butter-based cake, created using the modified creaming method. Dried apricots, currants, candied citrus peels, and almonds, along with a generous application of rum, bring robust flavor to each slice.

Ingredients	Baker's %	Kilogram	US decimal	Lb & Oz		Test
Butter	72.30	0.385	0.849		13 ⅝	2 ¾ oz
Sugar #1	38.20	0.203	0.448		7 ⅛	1 ⅜ oz
Trimoline	12.70	0.068	0.149		2 ⅜	1 tbsp
Egg yolks	25.50	0.136	0.299		4 ¾	1 oz
Pastry flour	100.00	0.533	1.174	1	2 ¾	3 ¾ oz
Baking powder	2.50	0.013	0.029		½	½ tsp
Egg whites	63.80	0.340	0.749		12	2 ⅜ oz
Sugar #2	19.10	0.102	0.224		3 ⅝	¾ oz
Candied orange peel	14.80	0.079	0.174		2 ¾	¾ oz
Currants	21.00	0.112	0.247		4	¾ oz
Golden raisins	36.00	0.192	0.423		6 ¾	1 ½ oz
Dried apricots, diced	27.60	0.147	0.324		5 ⅛	1 ½ oz
Almonds, roasted, chopped	19.00	0.101	0.223		3 ⅝	¾ oz
Dark rum	17.00	0.091	0.200		3 ¼	¾ oz
Total	469.50	2.500	5.512	5	8 ¼	1 lb 1 ⅝ oz

Yield: 5 [8 inch (20 cm) × 4 inch (10 cm)] loaf cakes
Test: 1 [8 inch (20 cm) × 4 inch (10 cm)] loaf cake

Process

1. Macerate the fruit and roasted almonds in rum for 24 hours.
2. Sift together the pastry flour and baking powder and reserve.
3. Cream the butter and first sugar until lightened. Add the Trimoline and then the egg yolks.
4. Add the sifted dry ingredients and mix until incorporated.
5. Make a medium-stiff meringue with the egg whites and second sugar and fold it into the base batter in three stages.

Cake aux Fruits

6. Fold in the macerated fruit and deposit into buttered 8 inch (20 cm) × 4 inch (10 cm) pans at 17.5 oz (500 g) per pan.
7. Bake at 335°F (168°C) for about 35 to 40 minutes, or until a cake tester inserted in the center comes out clean.

FORMULA

HIGH-RATIO CHOCOLATE CAKE

After tasting this tender cake, it may be hard to believe that it is actually the "from-scratch" version of boxed cake mix. To achieve the ideal results with this recipe, it is essential to follow the measurement and time guidelines closely because they will affect how much air is allowed into the batter and how well the cake will rise. The final outcome is what many consider the classic American layer cake, the centerpiece of countless birthday parties and special occasions.

Ingredients	Baker's %	Kilogram	US decimal	Lb & Oz		Test
Cake flour	100.00	0.551	1.214	1	3 ⅜	3 ⅞ oz
Cocoa powder	15.79	0.087	0.192		3 ⅛	⅝ oz
Salt	2.11	0.012	0.026		⅜	½ tsp
Baking powder	3.16	0.017	0.038		⅝	1 tsp
Baking soda	2.11	0.012	0.026		⅜	½ tsp
Emulsified shortening	57.89	0.319	0.703		11 ¼	2 ¼ oz
Sugar	131.58	0.724	1.597	1	9 ½	5 ⅛ oz
Milk #1	65.79	0.362	0.798		12 ¾	2 ½ oz
Vanilla extract	5.26	0.029	0.064		1	1 ½ tsp
Milk #2	50.00	0.275	0.607		9 ¾	2 oz
Eggs	65.79	0.362	0.798		12 ¾	2 ½ oz
Total	499.48	2.750	6.062	6	1	1 lb 3 ⅜ oz

Yield: 5 [8 inch (20 cm)] cakes
Test: 1 [8 inch (20 cm)] cake

Process

1. Sift together the cake flour, cocoa powder, salt, baking powder, and baking soda and add to the mixing bowl.
2. Add the emulsified shortening to the dry ingredients and cream with the paddle for 2 minutes on low speed.

3. Scrape down the bowl and the paddle.
4. Mix for another 2 minutes on low speed.
5. Gradually add the first quantity of milk alternately with the sugar and mix on low speed for 3 minutes.
6. Scrape down the bowl.
7. Combine the second quantity of milk and the eggs and add in three stages, mixing for a total of 5 minutes on low speed.
8. Deposit 1 lb 3 oz (550 g) of batter per 8 inch (20 cm) cake pan, which has been sprayed and papered.
9. Bake at 335°F (168°C) in a convection oven for about 30 to 35 minutes.

FORMULA

CHOCOLATE LIQUID SHORTENING SPONGE CAKE

This style of cake gained popularity and largely replaced the high-ratio cake mixing method because of its simplicity in mixing, ingredient handling, and "quality." This cake has a characteristic moist crumb, a good light volume, and good keeping qualities.

Ingredients	Baker's %	Kilogram	US decimal	Lb & Oz	Test
Eggs	203.84	1.037	2.286	2 4 ⅝	7 ⅜ oz
Liquid shortening	76.92	0.391	0.863	13 ¾	2 ¾ oz
Milk	76.92	0.391	0.863	13 ¾	2 ¾ oz
Vanilla extract	3.85	0.020	0.043	¾	1 tsp
Sugar	169.23	0.861	1.898	1 14 ⅜	6 ⅛ oz
Cake flour	100.00	0.509	1.122	1 2	3 ⅝ oz
Baking powder	7.69	0.039	0.086	1 ⅜	2 tsp
Salt	3.85	0.020	0.043	¾	⅔ tsp
Baking soda	3.30	0.017	0.037	⅝	1 tsp
Cocoa powder	23.08	0.117	0.259	4 ⅛	⅞ oz
Total	668.68	3.402	7.500	7 8	1 lb 8 oz

Yield: 5 [8 inch (20 cm)] cakes
Test: 1 [8 inch (20 cm)] cake

Process

1. Combine the liquid ingredients in the bowl of a mixer fitted with the whip attachment.
2. Sift all of the dry ingredients together (including cocoa powder) and add them to the bowl.
3. Blend on low speed for 1½ minutes, or until incorporated.
4. Mix on medium/high speed for 3 minutes.
5. Scrape down the bowl well.
6. Whip on medium speed for 3 minutes.
7. Deposit 1 lb 8 oz (680 g) of batter per 8 inch (20 cm) cake pan, which has been sprayed and papered.
8. Bake at 335°F (168°C) in a convection oven or 350°F (177°C) in a deck oven for 30 to 35 minutes, or just until the center is firm to the touch.

FORMULA

EMMANUEL SPONGE

This buttery cake is similar to the traditional madeleine in its preparation. The rich batter is spread thinly over a sheet pan, and then garnished with frozen raspberries and candied pistachios, or other berry and nut combinations. The inverted sugar used in the Emmanuel sponge helps this cake stay moist, while the use of melted butter produces a very tender crumb.

Ingredients	Baker's %	Kilogram	US decimal	Lb & Oz		Test
Eggs	100.00	1.191	2.625	2	10	8 ⅜ oz
Trimoline	52.70	0.628	1.383	1	6 ⅛	4 ⅜ oz
Cake flour	100.00	1.191	2.625	2	10	8 ⅜ oz
Powdered sugar	48.65	0.579	1.277	1	4 ⅜	4 ⅛ oz
Salt	1.08	0.013	0.028		½	½ tsp
Baking powder	4.05	0.048	0.106		1 ¾	1 ½ tsp
Milk	31.08	0.370	0.816		13	2 ⅝ oz
Butter, melted	81.08	0.965	2.128	2	2	6 ¾ oz
Raspberry pieces	21.62	0.257	0.568		9 ⅛	1 ⅞ oz
Candied pistachios	21.62	0.257	0.568		9 ⅛	1 ⅞ oz
Total	461.88	5.500	12.125	12	2	2 lb 6 ¾ oz

Yield: 5 full sheets
Test: 1 full sheet

Process

1. Sift together the cake flour, powdered sugar, salt, and baking powder.
2. Mix the eggs and Trimoline with the paddle.
3. Add the sifted dry ingredients to the eggs and Trimoline and mix until incorporated.
4. Add the milk and then the melted butter, and mix until incorporated.
5. Refrigerate the mix for 18 to 24 hours.
6. Deposit onto silicone mats and garnish with frozen raspberry pieces and pistachios and bake at 400°F (205°C) in a convection oven for about 8 to 10 minutes.
7. Once baked, transfer to a cool surface to prevent excessive drying.

FORMULA

ANGEL FOOD CAKE

Angel food cake is an American creation, possibly from the Pennsylvania Dutch, where the production of the cake mold, essential to a proper angel food, was a booming industry during the 1800s. Named for a texture and appearance light and airy enough to "appeal to the angels," this cake is distinguished by its use of beaten egg whites, which give it a light volume in the absence of egg yolks, fat, or baking powder.

Ingredients	Baker's %	Kilogram	US decimal	Lb & Oz		Test
Egg whites	281.25	1.393	3.072	3	1 ⅛	9 ⅞ oz
Granulated sugar #1	69.79	0.346	0.762		12 ¼	2 ½ oz
Cream of tartar	4.17	0.021	0.046		¾	⅓ tsp
Vanilla extract	2.08	0.010	0.023		⅜	½ tsp
Salt	0.42	0.002	0.005		⅛	⅛ tsp
Granulated sugar #2	208.33	1.032	2.276	2	4 ⅜	7 ¼ oz
Cake flour	100.00	0.495	1.092	1	1 ½	3 ½ oz
Total	666.04	3.300	7.275	7	4 ⅜	1 lb 7 ¼ oz

Yield: 4 [10 inch (26 cm)] tube cakes
Test: 1 [10 inch (26 cm)] tube cake

Process

1. Sift the salt, second sugar, and flour together.
2. In a mixer, whip the egg whites until volume is achieved. Combine the first sugar and cream of tartar; add the sugar mixture slowly and whip to medium peaks.
3. Fold the flour mixture into the egg white foam.

4. Scale at 1 lb 12 oz (800 g) for a 10 inch (26 cm) tube pan.
5. Bake at 310°F (155°C) in a convection oven for 30 to 35 minutes, or until golden brown. Remove from the oven and invert the pans to cool upside-down.
6. Remove the cakes from the pan when completely cooled.

Chocolate Angel Food Cake Formula

Ingredients	Baker's %	Kilogram	US decimal	Lb & Oz		Test
Egg whites	281.25	1.393	3.072	3	1 ⅛	9 ⅞ oz
Granulated sugar #1	69.79	0.346	0.762		12 ¼	2 ½ oz
Cream of tartar	4.17	0.021	0.046		¾	1 tsp
Vanilla extract	2.08	0.010	0.023		⅜	½ tsp
Salt	0.42	0.002	0.005		⅛	⅛ tsp
Granulated sugar #2	208.33	1.032	2.276	2	4 ⅜	7 ¼ oz
Cake flour	75.00	0.372	0.819		13 ⅛	2 ⅝ oz
Cocoa powder	25.00	0.124	0.273		4 ⅜	⅞ oz
Total	666.04	3.300	7.275	7	4 ⅜	1 lb 7 ¼ oz

Note

Combined flour and cocoa powder weights equal 100 percent.

Yield: 4 [10 inch (26 cm)] tube cakes

Test: 1 [10 inch (26 cm)] tube cake

Process, Chocolate Angel Food Cake

1. Sift the salt, second sugar, flour, and cocoa powder together.
2. In a mixer, whip the egg whites until volume is achieved. Combine the first sugar and cream of tartar.
3. Add the sugar mixture slowly and whip to medium peak.
4. Fold the flour mixture into the egg white foam.
5. Scale at 1 lb 12 oz (800 g) for a 10 inch (26 cm) tube pan.
6. Bake at 310°F (155°C) in a convection oven for 30 to 35 minutes, or until golden brown. Remove from the oven and invert the pans to cool upside-down.
7. Remove the cakes from the pan when completely cooled.

Angel Food Cake

Chocolate Angel Food Cake

FORMULA

BASIC GÉNOISE

Génoise, named after its place of origin, Genoa, Italy, is a member of the sponge cake family. Light and airy, this versatile cake is used as the base of many desserts. Génoise differs from other sponge cakes in that the whole eggs and sugar are beaten, flour is folded in, and a small amount of melted butter is added at the end of mixing, creating a tender and flavorful cake that has a nice buttery, slightly sweet flavor.

Ingredients	Baker's %	Kilogram	US decimal	Lb & Oz		Test
Eggs	162.00	1.388	3.060	3	1	7 ⅛ oz
Granulated sugar	90.50	0.775	1.709	1	11 ⅜	4 oz
Trimoline	11.00	0.094	0.208		3 ⅜	½ oz
Pastry flour	81.00	0.694	1.530	1	8 ½	3 ½ oz
Potato starch	19.00	0.163	0.359		5 ¾	⅞ oz
Melted butter	10.00	0.086	0.189		3	⅜ oz
Total	373.50	3.200	7.055	7	⅞	15 ⅞ oz

Yield: 7 [8 inch (20 cm)] cakes
Test: 1 [8 inch (20 cm)] cake

Process

1. Sift together the potato starch and pastry flour, and reserve.
2. Whip the eggs, sugar, and Trimoline to the ribbon stage.
3. Fold in the sifted pastry flour and potato starch.
4. Fold in the melted butter.
5. Deposit into ungreased, papered pans at 14 oz (400 g) to 16 oz (450 g) per 8 inch (20 cm) pan.
6. Bake at 335°F (168°C) in a convection oven for 25 minutes.
7. Once baked, invert onto a wire rack. Remove from the pans when completely cooled.

FORMULA

GOLDEN CHIFFON AND CHOCOLATE CHIFFON CAKE

Los Angeles insurance agent Harry Baker invented the chiffon cake in 1927 and then closely guarded his secret recipe for over two decades, making his cakes only for Hollywood stars and the famous Brown Derby Restaurant. In 1947, Baker finally sold the recipe to General Mills, which released the "secret recipe" in the May 1948 *Better Homes and Gardens* magazine, creating a nationwide sensation. The secret ingredient, vegetable oil, was revealed and *Better Homes and Gardens* advertised the cake as "the first really new cake in 100 years." Chiffon cake is moist and tender, light and airy, with the richness of a butter cake, but the springy texture of a sponge cake, relying on egg whites and baking powder for leavening. Using vegetable oil, instead of having to cream fat and sugar, makes this a quick and easy batter to create. Because of their high oil content, chiffon cakes are very moist and tend to resist dryness, even with refrigeration.

Golden Chiffon Cake Formula

Ingredients	Baker's %	Kilogram	US decimal	Lb & Oz		Test
Cake flour	100.00	0.561	1.236	1	3 ¾	4 oz
Baking powder	3.03	0.017	0.037		⅝	⅛ oz
Sugar #1	86.36	0.484	1.068	1	1 ⅛	3 ⅜ oz
Lemon zest	Each	1.5	1.5		1.5	⅓ each
Vegetable oil	50.25	0.282	0.621		10	2 oz
Egg yolks	50.00	0.280	0.618		9 ⅞	2 oz
Water	57.32	0.321	0.709		11 ⅜	2 ¼ oz
Vanilla extract	2.53	0.014	0.031		½	⅛ oz
Egg whites	100.51	0.564	1.243	1	3 ⅞	4 oz
Sugar #2	42.93	0.241	0.531		8 ½	1 ¾ oz
Cream of tartar	0.51	0.003	0.006		⅛	⅛ tsp
Total	493.44	2.767	6.100	6	1 ⅝	1 lb 3 ½ oz

Yield: 5 [8 inch (20 cm)] cakes
Test: 1 [8 inch (20 cm)] cake

Process, Golden Chiffon Cake

1. Sift together the flour, baking powder, and first sugar; add the lemon zest.
2. In a separate bowl, whisk the liquid ingredients; add the dry ingredients slowly to make a smooth batter.
3. Whip the egg whites, second sugar, and cream of tartar to medium peaks.
4. Fold the meringue into the batter in three stages until there are no streaks.
5. Deposit at 19.5 oz (550 g) into ungreased, papered pans.
6. Bake at 335°F (168°C) in a convection oven for about 30 minutes or until done.
7. Invert the cakes when cooling and remove from the pans when completely cooled.

Chocolate Chiffon Cake Formula

Ingredients	Baker's %	Kilogram	US decimal	Lb & Oz		Test
Water	60.00	0.259	0.571		9 ⅛	1 ⅞ oz
Semi-sweet chocolate	74.67	0.322	0.710		11 ⅜	2 ½ oz
Egg yolks	60.00	0.259	0.571		9 ⅛	1 ⅞ oz
Canola oil	53.33	0.230	0.507		8 ⅛	1 ⅝ oz
Vanilla extract	1.33	0.006	0.013		¼	½ tsp
Cake flour, sifted	100.00	0.431	0.951		15 ¼	3 oz
Baking powder	4.67	0.020	0.044		¾	⅛ oz
Baking soda	1.33	0.006	0.013		¼	⅛ tsp
Granulated sugar #1	120.00	0.518	1.141	1	2 ¼	3 ⅝ oz
Egg whites	105.33	0.454	1.002	1	0	3 ¼ oz
Granulated sugar #2	56.00	0.242	0.533		8 ½	1 ¾ oz
Cream of tartar	0.93	0.004	0.009		⅛	⅓ tsp
Total	637.59	2.750	6.063	6	1	1 lb 3 ⅜ oz

Yield: 5 [8 inch (20 cm)] cakes
Test: 1 [8 inch (20 cm)] cake

Process, Chocolate Chiffon Cake

1. Pour boiling water over the chopped chocolate and allow to stand for 1 minute; form an emulsion using a whisk.
2. Combine and sift together the flour, baking powder, baking soda, and first sugar.
3. In a separate bowl, whisk the liquid ingredients into the chocolate emulsion; add the dry ingredients slowly to make a smooth batter.
4. Whip the egg whites, second sugar, and cream of tartar to medium peaks.
5. Fold the meringue into the batter in three stages until there are no streaks.
6. Deposit into ungreased, papered pans at 19.5 oz (550 g) and bake at 335°F (168°C) in a convection oven for 30 to 35 minutes.
7. Invert when cooling and remove the cakes when cool.

FORMULA

ROULADE

Roulade, which is also called jelly roll by Americans and Swiss roll by the English, is a light and delicate sponge cake used for rolled desserts such as the traditional Bûche de Noël.

Ingredients	Baker's %	Kilogram	US decimal	Lb & Oz		Test
Egg yolks	80.00	0.414	0.914		14 ⅝	2 ⅞ oz
Eggs	222.22	1.151	2.538	2	8 ⅝	8 ⅛ oz
Sugar #1	86.67	0.449	0.990		15 ⅞	3 ⅛ oz
Egg whites	133.33	0.691	1.523	1	8 ⅜	4 ⅞ oz
Sugar #2	150.00	0.777	1.713	1	11 ⅜	5 ½ oz
Pastry flour	100.00	0.518	1.142	1	2 ¼	3 ⅝ oz
Total	772.22	4.000	8.819	8	13 ⅛	1 lb 12 ¼ oz

Yield: 5 full sheets
Test: 1 full sheet

Process

1. Sift the flour; set aside.
2. Warm the egg yolks, whole eggs, and first sugar to 110°F (43°C) over a bain-marie.
3. Whip the egg yolks, whole eggs, and first sugar with the whip attachment until the ribbon stage.
4. Whip the egg whites with the second sugar until medium peaks are formed.
5. Fold the egg whites into the whole egg mixture in three stages.
6. Fold the flour into the egg foam.
7. Deposit onto silicone mat–lined sheet pans at 27 oz (800 g) and bake at 400°F (205°C) for about 8 to 10 minutes.
8. Once out of the oven, transfer to another sheet pan to prevent carryover baking.

FORMULA

CHOCOLATE BISCUIT

This versatile separated egg sponge cake has a deep and rich chocolate flavor. It is used as a base cake layer in some of the mousse cake preparations; however, it may also be used for roulade style cakes.

Ingredients	Baker's %	Kilogram	US decimal	Lb & Oz		Test
Egg yolks	91.60	0.359	0.792		12 ⅝	2 ½ oz
Eggs	208.00	0.815	1.798	1	12 ¾	5 ¾ oz
Sugar #1	166.00	0.651	1.435	1	7	4 ⅝ oz
Egg whites	133.00	0.521	1.150	1	2 ⅜	3 ⅝ oz
Sugar #2	66.60	0.261	0.576		9 ¼	1 ⅞ oz
Pastry flour	50.00	0.196	0.432		6 ⅞	1 ⅜ oz
Cocoa powder	50.00	0.196	0.432		6 ⅞	1 ⅜ oz
Total	765.20	3.000	6.614	6	9 ⅞	1 lb 5 oz

Yield: 5 sheets
Test: 1 sheet

Process

1. Sift together the pastry flour and cocoa powder and reserve.
2. Whip the egg yolks, whole eggs, and first sugar to the ribbon stage.
3. Whip the egg whites and second sugar to medium-soft peaks.
4. Add the meringue to the whole egg and yolk foam in three stages and then fold in the sifted dry ingredients.
5. Deposit 21.5 oz (600 g) of batter per silicone mat–lined baking tray and spread evenly.
6. Bake at 400°F (205°C) for about 7 to 9 minutes.
7. Once out of the oven, transfer to another sheet pan to prevent carryover baking.

FORMULA

PÂTE À DÉCOR AND PÂTE À DÉCOR NOIR

Pâte à décor is most commonly used for making the colored cake walls applied for decoration. The batter is spread decoratively in a thin layer and then frozen. Next, the cake batter is applied over the frozen pâte à décor, and the cake is baked. Once baked, the two batters form one cake, which then contains the decorative element.

Pâte à Décor Formula

Ingredients	Baker's %	Kilogram	US decimal	Lb & Oz	
Butter, melted	100.00	0.227	0.500		8
Powdered sugar	100.00	0.227	0.500		8
Flour	100.00	0.227	0.500		8
Egg whites	100.00	0.227	0.500		8
Colorant	SQ	SQ	SQ		
Total	400.00	0.907	2.000	2	0

Process, Pâte à Décor

1. Combine the melted butter and powdered sugar, and then add the sifted flour.
2. Mix well and slowly add the egg whites until the batter is homogenous.
3. Color as desired.
4. Reserve in a cooler for up to 1 week or in the freezer for up to 1 month.

Pâte à Décor Noir Formula

Ingredients	Baker's %	Kilogram	US decimal	Lb & Oz	
Butter, melted	142.86	0.227	0.500		8
Powdered sugar	142.86	0.227	0.500		8
Pastry flour	100.00	0.159	0.350		5 ⅝
Cocoa powder	42.86	0.068	0.150		2 ⅜
Egg whites	142.86	0.227	0.500		8
Total	571.44	0.907	2.000	2	0

Process, Pâte à Décor Noir

1. Combine the melted butter and powdered sugar, and then add the sifted flour and cocoa powder.
2. Mix well and slowly add the egg whites until the batter is homogenous.
3. Reserve in a cooler for up to 1 week or in the freezer for up to 1 month.

FORMULA

BISCUIT VIENNOIS

Used as a base layer in many entremets, and as the layers in the classic opera cake, biscuit viennois is enhanced with almond meal, which gives the cake a very desirable texture.

Ingredients	Baker's %	Kilogram	US decimal	Lb & Oz	Test
TPT almond	250	0.887	1.955	1 15 ¼	7 ⅞ oz
Egg yolks	59	0.209	0.461	7 ⅜	1 ⅞ oz
Eggs	105	0.373	0.821	13 ⅛	3 ¼ oz
Egg whites	225	0.798	1.760	1 12 ⅛	7 oz
Granulated sugar	22	0.078	0.172	2 ¾	¾ oz
Cake flour	50	0.177	0.391	6 ¼	1 ⅝ oz
Pastry flour	50	0.177	0.391	6 ¼	1 ⅝ oz
Total	761.00	2.700	5.952	5 15 ¼	1 lb 7 ¾ oz

Yield: 4 sheets
Test: 1 sheet

Process

1. Sift together the cake flour and pastry flour; reserve.
2. Sift the TPT.
2. Combine the TPT, egg yolks, and whole eggs; whip on high speed until tripled in volume.
3. Make a medium-stiff meringue with the egg whites and granulated sugar.
4. Fold the meringue into the whole egg mixture and fold the flour into this mixture.
5. Deposit at 23 oz (650 g) on silicone baking mat–lined sheet pans and spread out evenly.
6. Bake at 400°F (205°C) in a convection oven for about 7 minutes.
7. Once baked, transfer to another sheet pan to prevent carryover baking.

Biscuit Viennois Jaconde (Decorated Cake Walls)

Components

Pâte à Décor and/or Pâte à Décor Noir
Biscuit Viennois

Process

1. Prepare silicone mats with a pâte à décor as desired. Freeze until set.
2. Make the biscuit viennois and portion over prepared silicone sheets while the pâte à décor is frozen.
3. Bake as normal for biscuit viennois.

FORMULA

APPLE BREAKFAST CAKE

This country-style cake is tasty, moist, and dense with apples. A pleasure to wake up to, apple breakfast cake is also a tempting treat throughout the day.

Apple Breakfast Cake

Ingredients	Baker's %	Kilogram	US decimal	Lb & Oz		Test
Eggs	65.38	0.404	0.891		14 ¼	2 ⅞ oz
Sugar	57.69	0.357	0.786		12 ⅝	2 ½ oz
Raisins	57.69	0.357	0.786		12 ⅝	2 ½ oz
Walnut pieces	38.46	0.238	0.524		8 ⅜	1 ⅝ oz
Butter, melted	57.69	0.357	0.786		12 ⅝	2 ½ oz
Apples, peeled, diced	384.62	2.378	5.243	5	3 ⅞	1 lb ¾ oz
Vanilla extract	1.54	0.010	0.021		⅜	½ tsp
Bread flour	100.00	0.618	1.363	1	5 ⅞	4 ⅜ oz
Baking powder	3.46	0.021	0.047		¾	1 tsp
Salt	1.54	0.010	0.021		⅜	¼ tsp
Total	768.07	4.750	10.471	10	7 ½	2 lb 1 ½ oz

Yield: 5 [8 inch (20 cm)] cakes
Test: 1 [8 inch (20 cm)] cake

Process

1. Spray the pans with nonstick spray and reserve.
2. Sift the flour, baking powder, and salt and reserve.
3. Whip the eggs and sugar to the ribbon stage.
4. Add the raisins, walnuts, and melted butter; mix to incorporate.
5. Fold in the diced apples and vanilla extract.
6. Fold the sifted ingredients into the mixture until well incorporated.
7. Portion the batter at 2 lb 2 oz (950 g) per 8 inch (20 cm) pan.
8. Bake at 335°F (168°C) for about 45 minutes.
9. Allow to cool in the pan for 15 minutes before removing the cake.
10. Turn the cake out onto a cardboard circle.
11. Glaze with a flat icing made with powdered sugar, orange juice, and orange zest.

FORMULA

HAZELNUT JAPONAISE

This meringue features hazelnut meal, baked into a light, crispy disc that can be used as a base for cakes and many other desserts. The quality of the Japonaise relies upon whipping the meringue into very stiff peaks. If this is not done, the end result may be crumbly and brittle.

Ingredients	Baker's %	Kilogram	US decimal	Lb & Oz		Test
Hazelnut meal	100.00	0.900	1.984	1	15 ¾	8 oz
Powdered sugar	100.00	0.900	1.984	1	15 ¾	8 oz
Egg whites	100.00	0.900	1.984	1	15 ¾	8 oz
Granulated sugar	100.00	0.900	1.984	1	15 ¾	8 oz
Total	400.00	3.600	7.936	7	15	2 lb

Process

1. Sift together the hazelnut meal and powdered sugar.
2. Whip the egg whites and granulated sugar to stiff peaks.
3. Fold in the sifted ingredients, taking care to not deflate the meringue.
4. Pipe into discs of the desired diameter.
5. Bake at 212°F (100°C) in a convection oven with the vent open for about 2 hours or until dry.

CHAPTER SUMMARY

Mixing and baking a successful cake is the result of high-quality ingredients, sound processes, and proper baking techniques. There are many types of cakes, each of which has a specific mixing method that is important to follow. Tracking quality by minding batter temperature, pH, and specific gravity is certainly not required; however, those tools allow the baker or pastry chef to know if key roles in the process have been observed.

KEY TERMS

- ❖ Angel food method
- ❖ Biscuit jaconde method
- ❖ Chiffon method
- ❖ Creaming method
- ❖ Fat-based cakes
- ❖ Foam-based cakes
- ❖ High-ratio cakes
- ❖ Liquid shortening
- ❖ Modified creaming method
- ❖ Neutralizing value (NV)
- ❖ Separated egg sponge method
- ❖ Specific gravity (SG)
- ❖ Sponge cake
- ❖ Tant pour tant (TPT)

REVIEW QUESTIONS

1. **What are the two main categories of cake? What distinguishes them?**
2. **What function do the following major ingredients have in a cake: flour, sugar, butter, and eggs?**
3. **How is the creaming method carried out?**
4. **How does batter temperature influence batter viscosity?**
5. **What is specific gravity? How is it found? What does it determine?**

chapter
15

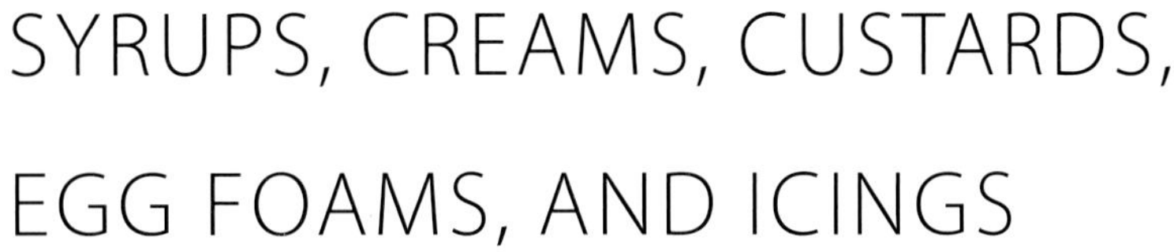

SYRUPS, CREAMS, CUSTARDS, EGG FOAMS, AND ICINGS

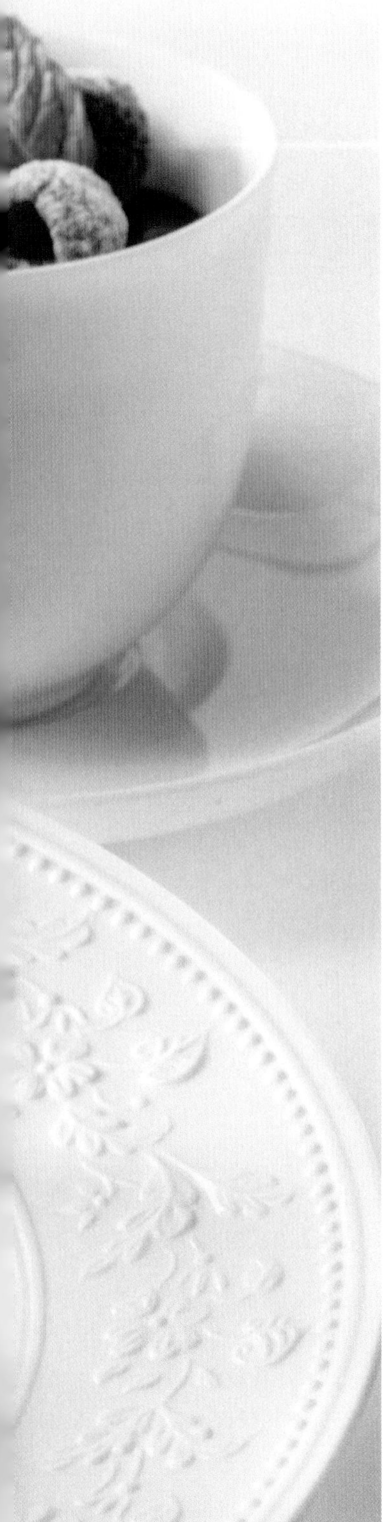

OBJECTIVES

After reading this chapter, you should be able to

- describe the functions of ingredients and the processes for assorted syrups, creams, custards, egg foams, and icings.
- practice proper sanitation, hygiene, and storage in relation to syrups, custards, creams, egg foams, and icings.
- make the various syrups, creams, custards, egg foams, and icings presented in the chapter.
- troubleshoot problems involving syrups, creams, custards, egg foams, and icings.

INTRODUCTION

This chapter presents several categories of preparations, all of which serve as foundations for elaborating and finishing pastries and cakes. These include sugar syrups, creams, egg foams, and icings; they are presented together because of their dependency on each other. For example, in order to make an Italian buttercream one first must know how to properly prepare a sugar syrup, and one must understand the whipping properties of egg whites in order to make an Italian meringue.

SUGAR SOLUTIONS

Sugar syrups are used for a wide range of pastry applications, including soaking cakes, making butter creams and meringues, and preparing for decorative sugar work. A **sugar syrup** is a combination of sugar and water that is brought to a boil and cooked to a certain temperature. In pastry, sugar syrups are defined by the ratio of sugar to water, as well as final cooking temperature.

Baumé, which is the measurement used to quantify the sugar density of any given liquid, is an important factor in determining taste and stability. Baumé is measured using a hydrometer, which is also referred to as a saccharometer. See Figure 15-1 for the relation between baumé readings and sugar density.

One of the most common sugar syrups is **simple syrup**, which is made from equal weights of sugar and water and measures 28 degrees baumé. Simple syrup can be used for soaking cakes or as a stock to pull from for other sugar syrup applications such as some decorative sugar work, glazes, and icings. **30 baumé syrup**—made with 137 parts of sugar to 100 parts of water—is also sometimes used as a simple syrup. **Cake syrup** has less sugar than water. A common ratio of water to sugar is somewhere between 2:1 and 4:3. Used to moisten cakes, it adds a minimal amount of sweetness.

Figure 15-1
Sugar Density/Baumé Readings

Degree Brix	Degree Baumé	Sugar in 1 qt Syrup	Sugar in 1 qt Water	Sugar in 1 kg Syrup	Sugar in 1 kg Water
20	11.10	6.40 oz	8.00 oz	200 g	250 g
21	11.70	6.72 oz	8.51 oz	210 g	266 g
22	12.20	7.04 oz	9.02 oz	220 g	282 g
23	12.80	7.36 oz	9.57 oz	230 g	299 g
24	13.30	7.68 oz	10.11 oz	240 g	316 g
25	13.90	8.00 oz	10.66 oz	250 g	333 g
26	14.40	8.32 oz	11.23 oz	260 g	351 g
27	15.00	8.64 oz	11.84 oz	270 g	370 g
28	15.60	8.96 oz	12.45 oz	280 g	389 g
29	16.20	9.28 oz	13.06 oz	290 g	408 g
30	16.70	9.60 oz	13.73 oz	300 g	429 g
31	17.20	9.92 oz	14.37 oz	310 g	449 g
32	17.80	10.24 oz	15.07 oz	320 g	471 g
33	18.30	10.56 oz	15.78 oz	330 g	493 g
34	18.90	10.88 oz	1 lb 0.48 oz	340 g	515 g
35	19.40	11.20 oz	1 lb 1.22 oz	350 g	538 g
36	20.00	11.52 oz	1 lb 2.02 oz	360 g	563 g
37	20.60	11.84 oz	1 lb 2.78 oz	370 g	587 g
38	21.10	12.16 oz	1 lb 3.61 oz	380 g	613 g
39	21.70	12.48 oz	1 lb 4.45 oz	390 g	639 g
40	22.20	12.80 oz	1 lb 5.34 oz	400 g	667 g
41	22.80	13.12 oz	1 lb 6.24 oz	410 g	695 g

(continues)

Figure 15-1
Sugar Density/Baumé Readings
(continued)

Degree Brix	Degree Baumé	Sugar in 1 qt Syrup	Sugar in 1 qt Water	Sugar in 1 kg Syrup	Sugar in 1 kg Water
42	23.30	13.44 oz	1 lb 7.17 oz	420 g	724 g
43	23.90	13.76 oz	1 lb 8.13 oz	430 g	754 g
44	24.40	14.08 oz	1 lb 9.15 oz	440 g	786 g
45	25.00	14.40 oz	1 lb 10.18 oz	450 g	818 g
46	25.60	14.72 oz	1 lb 11.26 oz	460 g	852 g
47	26.10	15.04 oz	1 lb 12.38 oz	470 g	887 g
48	26.70	15.36 oz	1 lb 13.54 oz	480 g	923 g
49	27.20	15.68 oz	1 lb 14.75 oz	490 g	961 g
50	27.80	1 lb 0.00 oz	2 lb 0.00 oz	500 g	1,000 g
51	28.30	1 lb 0.32 oz	2 lb 1.31 oz	510 g	1,041 g
52	28.90	1 lb 0.64 oz	2 lb 3.66 oz	520 g	1,083 g
53	29.40	1 lb 0.96 oz	2 lb 4.10 oz	530 g	1,128 g
54	30.00	1 lb 1.28 oz	2 lb 5.57 oz	540 g	1,174 g
55	30.60	1 lb 1.60 oz	2 lb 7.10 oz	550 g	1,222 g
56	31.10	1 lb 1.92 oz	2 lb 8.70 oz	560 g	1,272 g
57	31.70	1 lb 2.24 oz	2 lb 10.43 oz	570 g	1,326 g
58	32.20	1 lb 2.56 oz	2 lb 12.19 oz	580 g	1,381 g
59	32.80	1 lb 2.88 oz	2 lb 14.05 oz	590 g	1,439 g
60	33.30	1 lb 3.20 oz	3 lb 0.00 oz	600 g	1,500 g
61	34.40	1 lb 3.52 oz	3 lb 2.05 oz	610 g	1,564 g
62	33.90	1 lb 3.84 oz	3 lb 4.22 oz	620 g	1,632 g
63	35.00	1 lb 4.16 oz	3 lb 6.50 oz	630 g	1,703 g
64	35.60	1 lb 4.48 oz	3 lb 8.90 oz	640 g	1,778 g
65	36.10	1 lb 4.80 oz	3 lb 11.42 oz	650 g	1,857 g
66	36.70	1 lb 5.12 oz	3 lb 14.11 oz	660 g	1,941 g
67	37.20	1 lb 5.44 oz	4 lb 0.96 oz	670 g	2,030 g
68	37.80	1 lb 5.76 oz	4 lb 4.00 oz	680 g	2,125 g
69	38.30	1 lb 6.08 oz	4 lb 7.23 oz	690 g	2,226 g
70	38.90	1 lb 6.40 oz	4 lb 10.66 oz	700 g	2,333 g
71	39.40	1 lb 6.72 oz	4 lb 14.34 oz	710 g	2,448 g
72	40.00	1 lb 7.04 oz	5 lb 2.27 oz	720 g	2,571 g
73	40.60	1 lb 7.36 oz	5 lb 6.50 oz	730 g	2,703 g
74	41.10	1 lb 7.68 oz	5 lb 11.07 oz	740 g	2,846 g
75	41.70	1 lb 8.00 oz	6 lb 0.00 oz	750 g	3,000 g

INGREDIENTS AND PROCESS FOR SUGAR SYRUPS

A sugar syrup will always contain sugar and water. For many applications, cane sugar is preferable to beet sugar due to its purity in color and flavor. It is also more resistant to **crystallization**, which creates a rough texture in the final product. After sugar is dissolved into water and heated, it transforms into a liquid state. However, dissolved sugar naturally wants to return to crystalline form and will do so if there are any undissolved sugar crystals or foreign particles in the solution or on the walls of the pot or if there is excessive agitation. The cleanliness of the sugar is an important consideration because foreign particles will act as a catalyst for crystallization. Sugar used for syrups should be free from any foreign materials such as flour or nut meals. Finally, the water used should be of good quality. Any impurities in color and/or flavor can have a negative impact on the finished goods.

If other ingredients like zest, vanilla, and alcohol are used, they should be incorporated into the syrup during or after the cooking process. For ingredients that won't dissolve, like zest, a thinner syrup will prevent crystals from forming.

When preparing a sugar syrup of any density, following several guidelines will prevent crystallization. First, the water weight should be at least 30 percent of the sugar weight. Second, the sugar should be dissolved before the cooking process begins.

The cooking process begins when the water is placed in the pot, followed by the sugar. Next, the two are combined, but only to incorporation, and the heat is then set at medium high. If the heat is too high, it could crystallize the sugar. Also, if there is too much agitation from stirring, crystallization will occur. Finally, the sides of the pot should be washed down with cold water using a clean pastry brush to dissolve any sugar grains that are there. At a minimum, the sides of the pot should be washed down at the beginning of the cooking process and after the sugar and water have come to a boil. For sugar solutions that are boiled to higher temperatures, it may be necessary to brush down the sides more than twice.

If the sugar syrup is being used as a dessert syrup or as an element for a sorbet or if it is being reserved for other uses, the mixture should be covered and allowed to cool. Covering the syrup prevents excessive moisture loss and will help to maintain the desired sugar syrup density.

COOKING SUGAR

Cooked sugar solutions refer to sugar syrups that have been heated above the boiling point. They are often used for making sugar candies, doing decorative sugar work, or preparing items such as Italian meringue. As the temperature of the sugar syrup rises, water evaporates and the sugar syrup's density increases.

Although cooked sugar solutions may be fluid when hot, they firm up at cooler temperatures. This degree of setting during cooling is classified by terminology. For example, a sugar syrup cooked to between 300°F (149°C) and 310°F (154°C) sets up to be a firm hard mass (hard crack stage), whereas a sugar syrup cooked to 240°F (116°C) is malleable (soft ball) when cooled. Refer to Figure 15-2 to review the link between temperature, sugar concentration, and hardness.

HARDNESS	TEMPERATURE
"Thread" Stage	215°F (102°C) to 235°F (113°C)
"Soft Ball" Stage	235°F (113°C) to 240°F (116°C)
"Firm Ball" Stage	245°F (118°C) to 250°F (121°C)
"Hard Ball" Stage	250°F (121°C) to 265°F (129°C)
"Soft Crack" Stage	270°F (132°C) to 290°F (143°C)
"Hard Crack" Stage	300°F (149°C) to 310°F (154°C)
"Caramel" Stage	320°F (160°C) to 350°F (177°C)

Figure 15-2
Sugar and Hardness Temperature

BASIC CREAMS

Whether they garnish a dessert, fill a pastry, or serve as a component of an advanced preparation, creams are an essential ingredient in pastry applications. The four creams that serve as the foundations of pastry making are whipped cream, crème Chantilly, crème Anglaise, and pastry cream. These basic creams differ in composition but share one common characteristic: They are all dairy-based. Whipped cream and crème Chantilly are based on whipped heavy cream, whereas crème Anglaise and pastry cream are based on milk or a combination of milk and cream and are cooked over heat with other ingredients. The latter two creams are cooked-stirred custards and are thickened from eggs and/or starch.

This section will also cover almond cream, a classic preparation that is very different from the others, but is also considered a basic cream. Almond cream is similar to a cake batter in mixing as well as formulation. It can be used as a filling in tarts and viennoiserie, as a cake layer, and as a base for a lightened almond cream: frangipane.

WHIPPED CREAM

Whipped cream is heavy cream that has been whipped to increase its volume and lighten its texture. It is typically used as a component to create other creams, such as diplomat cream, as it is not sweetened. Cream with a fat content between 35 and 40 percent contains optimal whipping properties. Too little fat will inhibit the cream from whipping and the structure will be unstable, and too much fat will create a heavy, coarse texture.

Because fats develop and are more stable at colder temperatures, it is best to use cold cream for whipping. The bowl and whip attachment may also require cooling, depending on the room temperature. When whipping cream mechanically, use medium speed to ensure that it does not whip too quickly. This will create an imbalance in the fat and air bubble matrix, and the texture may become grainy. To fix slightly overwhipped cream, it is sometimes, though not always, possible to add some fresh cream and stir gently to incorporate.

CRÈME CHANTILLY

Crème Chantilly is sweetened, vanilla-flavored whipped cream that is usually used as a garnish for dessert or, sometimes, to ice a cake.

The degree of sweetness depends on the application; however, 15 percent sugar based on the weight of the cream is a standard starting point. Care should be taken not to overwhip the cream because the smooth texture will further develop during piping or application with an icing spatula, and it may turn grainy.

When making crème Chantilly, either powdered sugar or granulated sugar may be used and should be added during the beginning of the whipping process. Vanilla extract is usually used as a flavoring agent over fresh vanilla bean; however, some applications may use vanilla bean for flavor as well as to boost presentation.

CRÈME ANGLAISE

Crème Anglaise is a **cooked-stirred custard** (a custard cooked on the stove stop with constant agitation) that may well be considered a sauce, even though it is classified as a cream. Essentially a thickened, flavor-enhanced cream, crème Anglaise is an extremely versatile preparation with a number of uses, from dessert sauces to bases for ice cream, butter cream, or mousse.

When preparing and working with crème Anglaise, special attention must be paid to temperature and sanitation. The cream must be cooked to at least 165°F (74°C) to ensure destruction of alpha-amylase, a harmful enzyme naturally present in eggs that will break down the cream prematurely. The cream should be cooked to 180°F (82°C) and not above to ensure that the egg content does not coagulate, and proper sanitation measures must be practiced to ensure the product is not contaminated.

Crème Anglaise Ingredients and Variations

The selection and quantity of ingredients dictate the richness and flavor of the crème Anglaise. Basic ingredients include milk, sugar, and egg yolk. Additional ingredients commonly used include cream and vanilla bean or vanilla extract.

Often, the liquid for a crème Anglaise preparation will include both milk and cream as a way of adding richness. When crème Anglaise is to be used as an ice cream base, or as the primary liquid for a ganache, a lower fat content may be needed to balance the total percent of fats in the final product, and milk may be used at 100 percent of the liquid. This will ensure a smoother mouthfeel and less grainy texture.

The amount of sugar used in a crème Anglaise preparation is determined by the final product. For dessert sauces, the standard is 20 percent sugar based on the weight of the liquid. If using a crème Anglaise with other components for a composed dessert, a larger or smaller quantity of sugar may be required.

The egg content of crème Anglaise is from egg yolk, which adds richness in fats and color and also acts as the cream's primary thickening agent. An average amount is 20 percent based on the weight of the liquid, but the range can be as low as 15 percent and as high as 35 percent.

Crème Anglaise is often flavored beyond the standard vanilla, with herbs, alcohols, nut pastes, and chocolate among the more popular choices. Fruit purees are not ideal flavoring agents because the acidity and fruit flavor interfere with the richness and creaminess of the sauce. The selection of flavoring agent will determine when it is added during the mixing process. The percentage of flavoring agents is determined by their composition and the formulation of the base Anglaise sauce. For example, using the same quantity of a 72 percent chocolate, rather than a 50 percent chocolate, will create a more intense chocolate flavor that may require more sugar in the final formula.

To create custom flavors, one can use hot or cold infusions. To create a hot infusion with an herb, spice, tea, or coffee, the milk and cream are heated with the chosen flavoring agent and are allowed to infuse, covered, for a given amount of time. The duration of the hot infusion depends on the intensity of the items being infused, the quantity of the liquid, and the desired flavors. A longer infusion will supply a more intense flavor; however, care should be taken during the flavor-building process to avoid introducing tannins and other off flavors.

Cold infusions differ in that the milk and cream are not heated before the infusion begins. The item to be infused is incorporated into the dairy, covered, and left to infuse under refrigeration. Before finishing the elaboration of the crème Anglaise, the infused item is strained. For some items that absorb a lot of liquid, and depending on the preparation, additional milk may need to be added to compensate for any loss of liquid volume. It is important to not add additional cream because there is a higher percentage of fat remaining in the liquid: It is not absorbed into the product being infused. The items used for the infusion absorb water and leave a higher level of fat in the infused liquid. Adding milk helps to balance the level of fats in the final product.

Flavorings such as alcohol, nut pastes, and chocolate are incorporated simply by stirring in the flavoring after the crème Anglaise has cooked. Nut pastes and chocolate should be incorporated soon after cooking is complete so that the heat of the cream will melt the chocolate and warm the fats in the nut paste and make them easier to fully mix in. Alcohol should not be added until after the crème Anglaise is off of the stove and cool, in order to preserve its flavors.

Preparing Crème Anglaise

The basic process for making crème Anglaise is straightforward in approach. However, care must be taken to ensure that it does not overcook or become contaminated during the cooking and cooling processes.

After all ingredients are scaled, the liquid (in this example, a combination of cream and milk) is brought to a boil with half of the sugar from the formula. The remaining sugar is added to the egg yolks, and the mixture is stirred to combine. (See Preparing Crème Anglaise Figure 15-3, Step 1.) When the liquid boils, a portion of it is tempered into the yolk mixture by pouring about one-third of the liquid into the yolks and stirring to incorporate the two mediums. (See Preparing Crème Anglaise Figure 15-3, Step 2.) If these two mediums are not stirred right away, some of the egg protein could coagulate. The yolk–cream mixture is then returned to the pot, and the mixture is cooked, while stirring, to 180°F (82°C). (See Preparing Crème Anglaise Figure 15-3, Step 3.)

If the crème Anglaise does not reach the target temperature, the egg protein will not achieve its maximum thickening power. Conversely, if the cream is overheated, the egg protein can coagulate, and there will be small egg particles as well as a pronounced egg flavor. If a crème Anglaise is overcooked, some professionals chose to use an immersion blender to break down all the small egg particles, while

FIGURE 15-3 PREPARING CRÈME ANGLAISE

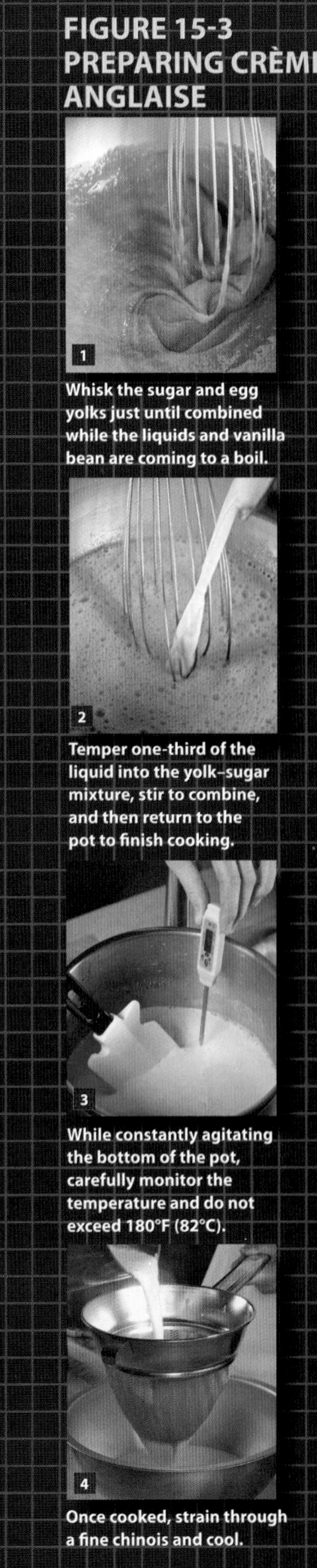

1 Whisk the sugar and egg yolks just until combined while the liquids and vanilla bean are coming to a boil.

2 Temper one-third of the liquid into the yolk–sugar mixture, stir to combine, and then return to the pot to finish cooking.

3 While constantly agitating the bottom of the pot, carefully monitor the temperature and do not exceed 180°F (82°C).

4 Once cooked, strain through a fine chinois and cool.

others prefer to start fresh. It is best to use caution and pay close attention to the temperature of the crème Anglaise to prevent any wasted product or time.

Doneness can be verified by temperature or by the viscosity of the cream on the spatula. Once the cream is cooked, it should be strained through a chinois into a clean container, covered to the surface and cooled down as quickly as possible. (See Preparing Crème Anglaise Figure 15-3, Step 4.) If the cream is not properly cooled, carryover cooking may occur and the egg protein could coagulate. When preparing larger batches, it is recommended to cool the crème Anglaise quickly over an ice bath. Proper hygiene, cooking, cooling, and storage must be practiced at all times.

With the preparation of any cream, especially cooked creams, it is always advisable to use clean, sanitized equipment made of stainless steel and silicone. This will prevent discoloration and contamination of the cream. Aluminum, non-heat-resistant plastic, or wood should never be used for cooked creams. Aluminum will react with the eggs and turn the sauce a greenish-gray color. Non-heat-resistant plastic will melt during the cooking process, and wooden utensils often harbor bacteria and off flavors and aromas.

Crème Anglaise Process

- Bring the milk, half of the sugar, and the vanilla bean (if using) to a boil.
- Combine the egg yolks and the remaining sugar and mix to incorporate, being careful not to incorporate air.
- Pour one-third of the boiled liquid over the egg yolk mixture, and stir to incorporate.
- Return the pot of liquid back to the heat and, while stirring, add the egg yolk–liquid mixture back to the pot.
- Cook over a low heat to 180°F (82°C), stirring constantly.
- Immediately strain the sauce into a clean, dry container, and cool it over an ice bath.
- Use immediately or store in the refrigerator for later use.

PASTRY CREAM

Like crème Anglaise, **pastry cream** is a cooked-stirred custard. This creamy custard is used as a filling or base cream in many classic and contemporary pastry items such as croissant and Danish, fresh fruit tarts, cream pies, butter creams, éclairs, and Napoleon cakes. It can be used fresh, for items such as a fresh fruit tart, or it can be baked as a filling for items like Danish pastry.

Pastry Cream Ingredients and Composition

Pastry cream differs from crème Anglaise in two distinct ways: composition and texture. The basic ingredients for pastry cream include milk, sugar, whole egg and/or egg yolk, cornstarch, and butter. Additional ingredients such as vanilla, zest, alcohols, chocolates, and nut pastes may be used for flavor development. Just as for crème Anglaise, cream or half-and-half can be substituted for all or a portion of the milk.

Most of the ingredients used for pastry cream are similar to crème Anglaise, with the exception of butter and cornstarch. The addition of

FIGURE 15-4 PREPARING PASTRY CREAM

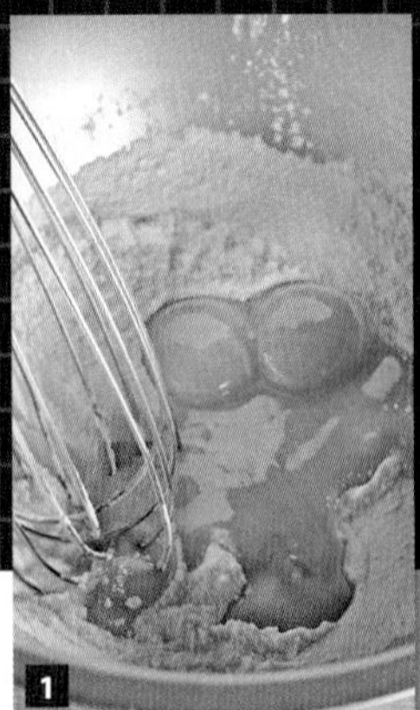

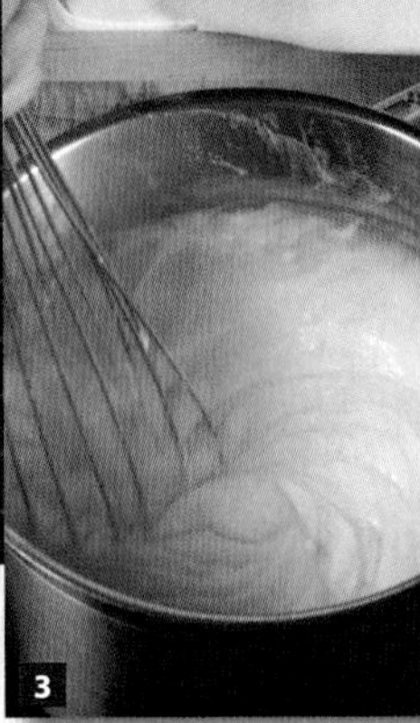

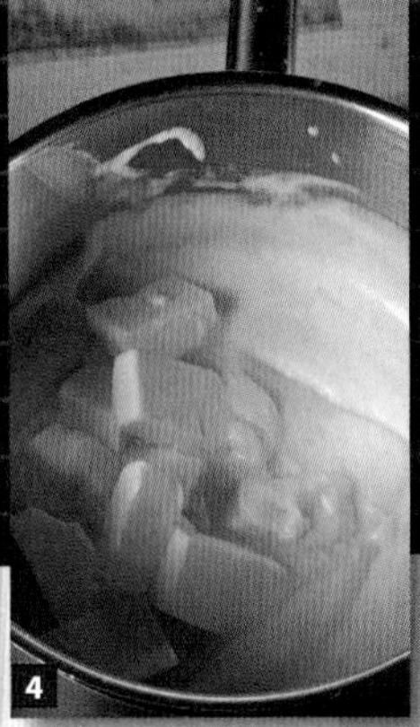

1 **After combining the sugar and starch, whisk in the egg yolks just to combine.**

2 **Once the milk and vanilla has come to a boil, temper one-third of it into the sugar–starch–yolk mixture, and then return it to the pot to finish cooking.**

3 **While whisking constantly, bring the mixture to a boil for 2 minutes.**

4 **Add the butter and whisk in to incorporate.**

5 **Pour into a clean pan and cover the surface of the cream with plastic wrap.**

butter to pastry cream softens the texture by weakening the gel phase of milk. Butter is also added to increase the richness in flavor. The starch, which bonds with the protein in the eggs and protects them from potentially curdling under higher heat, creates a thicker, more stable cream. The presence of starch requires a different temperature and final cooking process to ensure a smooth and supple product.

Instead of cornstarch, some people may use modified starches designed for use in pastry cream, or they may even use flour. Flour is the least effective of thickening agents, partly because it contains protein, which interferes with the overall starch content.

Preparing Pastry Cream

The process of making pastry cream is the same as the process for making crème Anglaise; however, pastry cream must be brought to a boil in order to thicken the cream and fully swell the starch. The same hygiene, equipment, and sanitation requirements must be in place to prevent contamination.

After all the ingredients have been scaled, the liquid can be brought to a boil with half of the sugar and the vanilla bean, if used. The remaining sugar should be combined with the starch (for even dispersal), and the eggs should be combined with the starch–sugar mixture. (See Preparing Pastry Cream Figure 15-4, Step 1.) Once the liquid comes to a boil, about one-third of it is poured over the egg–sugar–starch mixture and the two mediums are stirred to combine. (See Preparing Pastry Cream Figure 15-4, Step 2.) Next, this mixture is returned to the pot, and the cream is stirred energetically with a whisk. It is critical to stir the bottom, especially the sides, to prevent scorching. (See Preparing Pastry Cream Figure 15-4, Step 3.)

The cream should thicken quickly and boil for 2 minutes after the first sign of boiling occurs. Next, the butter can be added off heat and stirred in to incorporate. (See Preparing Pastry Cream Figure 15-4, Step 4.) Finally, the cream should be poured into a clean, shallow container and covered to the surface with plastic wrap. (See Preparing Pastry Cream Figure 15-4, Step 5.) If it is not covered, the casein protein in the milk will react with the air, and a skin will form. The pastry cream should be refrigerated as soon as possible for rapid cooling to prevent bacterial growth.

Pastry Cream Process

- Scale the whole milk and some sugar into a stainless steel pot and bring it to a boil.
- Scale the remaining sugar and cornstarch into a bowl and mix to combine.
- Scale the egg yolks into the sugar–starch mixture and whisk until smooth and pale in appearance.
- After the milk comes to a boil, pour one-third of it onto the egg yolk mixture and stir to incorporate evenly.
- Return this mixture to the pot, stirring constantly.
- Continue to cook the custard while stirring until it has boiled for 2 minutes.
- Off heat, add the butter and stir until mixed in completely.
- Pour the pastry cream onto a clean, parchment-lined sheet pan and cover the surface of the custard with plastic wrap.
- Refrigerate immediately and store until needed.

Pastry Cream Considerations

Like crème Anglaise, pastry cream should always be cooked in a pot made of stainless steel. Aluminum can discolor the pastry cream and wooden utensils should never be used. Fingers should never be put into the pastry cream. In addition, the strictest sanitation measures should be taken to avoid bacterial contamination.

The cream should be boiled for 2 full minutes, while stirring constantly, to evenly and fully swell the starch. If this happens at too slow of a rate, the pastry cream may be excessively fluid and if it is not cooked long enough, it may taste starchy and have a granular texture. Additionally, if the only egg product in the pastry cream is egg yolk, and for some reason the yolk has not coagulated by the time the pastry cream is done being made, a starch-digesting enzyme, alpha-amylase, will begin to break down the starch, and the cream will not gel once cool.

The completed cream should be poured into a clean, shallow vessel, and the top of the cream should be covered with plastic wrap and refrigerated immediately. Before using, it will be necessary to slightly whisk the cream to make it smooth. At this point, the cream may be flavored. If overworked, the starch may break down, and the result can be a runny pastry cream with not enough strength.

As pastry cream ages, the starch breaks down and water begins to "weep" from the cream. This is referred to as **syneresis**. For this reason, pastry cream should be made in batch sizes that yield enough for 2 to 3 days' use.

ALMOND CREAM

Almond cream is used as a filling for a variety of baked goods, including the classic Pithivier, various Viennoiserie, fruit tarts, and cake layers. Its ingredients typically include butter, sugar, eggs, almond meal, flour, and rum. The quantity of almond meal used is much larger than the quantity of flour, with flour used only as a binding agent. Alternative nuts other than almonds may be used to create a unique filling.

The abundance of butter, sugar, and eggs in almond cream makes it rich and decadent, and the almond meal adds a strong nut flavor and lightly textured consistency. To create a light, cake-like texture, the creaming method is typically used. Other methods of preparation include the sponge method.

Almond paste is a common alternative to almond meal. Although it creates a smoother texture in the final product, it is important to pay attention to sugar content and to balance it in the final formula. For example, a "60-percent fruit" almond paste (one of several formulations available) contains 60 percent almond and 40 percent sugar by weight.

Because of the high fat and sugar content in almond cream, it stores well under refrigeration for at least 1 week and can keep much longer in the freezer.

FRANGIPANE

Frangipane is similar to almond cream but is much lighter in texture and flavor. It has the same versatility as almond cream in that it can be used in the preparation of cakes, tarts, and Viennoiserie, yet it lends a subtler, lighter flavor and texture.

In its simplest form, frangipane combines two parts of almond cream to one part of pastry cream, but it can be easily adjusted to create a lighter or heavier texture. Preparation is simple: the cool pastry cream is added to the almond cream and is incorporated using the paddle attachment on a stand mixer. Frangipane made with pastry cream should be used within 2 to 3 days to ensure the cream is fresh and free from contamination.

BAKED CUSTARDS

A **baked custard** is created by preparing a **custard base** that can contain whole eggs, egg yolks, or both; cream, milk, or both; and additional ingredients like sugar and flavorings. The ratio of egg to liquid and the type of liquid used will dictate the texture of the final custard. Baked custards that are turned out of their mold, such as crème caramel, require a higher ratio of egg to liquid, as they need to be able to stand alone. Baked custard, such as crème brûlée and pot de crème, can be set with less egg per specified quantity of liquid because it is almost always contained within a ramekin or similar serving dish. Other baked custards include quiche and **bread pudding**.

The amount of sugar in a custard base will have an effect on its sensitivity to heat. Those that contain a small amount of sugar require gentle heating and constant attention, whereas those with a higher level of sugar are more heat-tolerant and less apt to curdle. This is due to the fact that the relatively large sugar molecules present in the liquid phase block the proteins' access to one another and slow down their bonding.

The basic process for preparing a custard base is straightforward. It mirrors the process for cooked-stirred custards up to the point of returning the mix to cook on the heat. For baked custard, all of the ingredients are tempered together and then deposited and baked.

The liquid, usually cream, should be heated with a portion of the sugar. The egg and/or egg yolk can be combined with the remaining sugar. When the liquid is close to a boil, it is slowly poured over the egg–sugar mixture and mixed to incorporate. Next, it is strained to remove any cooked egg particles, and then deposited into a ramekin or other specialty dish and baked as desired in a bain-marie.

It is important to understand a couple of key elements in this process. First, the coagulating properties of the protein within the egg set the liquid when the temperature is raised enough in the ambient heat of the oven. Often, baked custards are baked in a water bath in a low oven [300°F (149°C) deck oven] to ensure an even heat that will evenly set the custard. Second, custards should be baked just until they are barely set. The carryover cooking will finish setting the custard as it cools. If the custard is overbaked, the protein will not be able to hold the water, and the custard will curdle.

Custards and creams rely on heat to unfold the egg proteins. After this is accomplished, they reconnect in a delicate web that thickens the liquid. Heat also induces the proteins to coagulate and secure the new structure. However, as with whipping egg whites, there is danger in going too far. Loosely bound proteins hold and thicken the liquid, but excessive heat creates tight protein bonds that collapse the structure and curdle the cream or custard. The resulting graininess is formed by bits of cooked egg that separate from the mixture.

CRÈME BRÛLÉE

Crème brûlée is possibly one of the most popular desserts in the Western world. This simple dessert consists of a rich and creamy baked custard with a thin layer of crisp and caramelized sugar coating the creamy filling. When served, the sugar should still be crisp and slightly warm, and the cream should have a slight chill. The spoon should resist cracking the sugar but should make a distinct sound once it breaks through.

Crème brûlée is baked in a ramekin or a low, wide specialty dish that creates a large surface area for the most savored part of the dessert. Once baked, the crème brûlée should be reserved in the refrigerator for at least 8 hours to thoroughly cool and set before it is served in the dish it was baked in.

Before serving, the dessert should be finished with the sugar. White sugar is the most common choice; however, dried granulated brown sugar does add additional flavors. Once a thin coat has been applied to the surface of the cream, a torch is used to evenly caramelize it without burning. Alternately, the sugar may be caramelized under a Salamander or under the broiler.

CRÈME CARAMEL

Crème caramel is a classic dessert prepared from a custard base similar to that of crème brûlée. Crème caramel is formulated to be slightly firmer than crème brûlée because it is turned out of its mold before serving. The trademark characteristic of this dessert is the caramel sauce that covers the dessert after it is turned out of the mold.

Before the custard base is prepared, the ramekins are coated with sugar prior to baking. This is done by cooking sugar to the caramel stage and pouring it into the molds to coat the base and walls, where it sets up quickly. While the sugar is cooling, the custard is prepared and then deposited and baked.

The baking guidelines are the same as for crème brûlée, with care taken not to overbake. Once baked, crème caramel needs to be cooled in order to set before serving. After it has set, the crème caramel container is warmed in a bain-marie to release the caramel, and then it is inverted onto a dessert plate and garnished as desired.

POT DE CRÈME

Pot de crème is a baked custard that originated in the 18th century. Enjoyed by the elite of society, it was originally baked and served in specialty cups with ornate, hand-painted designs and gold trim. Pot de crème translates literally as "pot of cream" because the custard barely sets and is very silky in texture. Although pot de crème can have many flavors, chocolate is one of the most common. Today, it is typically served in ramekins or other specialty cups.

To prepare this dessert, the same process is followed as for crème brûlée. It is important not to incorporate any air into the cream or overwhip the egg or egg yolks. If air is incorporated, it will cause the cream to rise slightly in the oven, and cracks may appear on the surface of the custard.

Baking guidelines for pot de crème are also similar to those crème brûlée. The pot de crème should be baked at a low temperature in a water bath, and is sometimes covered during baking to prevent the formation of a crust. Once almost set, the custard is removed from the oven and allowed to thoroughly cool. Like crème brûlée, pot de crème is served in the dish in which it was baked.

CHEESECAKE

With its marked difference in texture, cheesecake is the unsuspected baked custard. The ingredient functions help it fit the profile. A creamy mixture of cream cheese, sour cream, butter, sugar, eggs, and flavoring, cheesecake is solely set by the coagulation of egg protein within the batter. Cheesecakes are often baked on top of rich, crumbly crusts made of sugar, graham cracker crumbs, and butter.

The success of cheesecake lies in the incorporation of ingredients and the baking of the batter. The ingredients, in their separate, singular states, vary in firmness and texture. Most importantly, the cream cheese is very firm, the sour cream very soft, and the eggs very fluid. To obtain a smooth batter, special attention must be paid to the mixing process and the temperature of the ingredients. All ingredients should be at room temperature to ensure even mixing and ingredient incorporation, and the bowl and paddle should be scraped down frequently to ensure even mixing.

To begin the process, the cream cheese is mixed until smooth and creamy using the paddle attachment of a stand mixer. Next, the soft butter is added and mixed until well incorporated. Next the sugar is added and mixed in well. After this, the eggs should be incorporated slowly to ensure a smooth batter. Once the eggs are well incorporated, the sour cream and any flavoring are added.

Although springform pans are commonly used for cheesecakes, they are best baked in traditional cake pans. A light coat of pan spray will ensure that the cheesecake and crust do not stick. Cheesecakes should be baked in a low oven and in a water bath to ensure an even bake. Like other baked custards, it is important that they not overbake. Once the cheesecake surface appears to "jiggle as a whole" it is a good sign that it is done.

After baking, the cake can be transferred to the refrigerator or freezer to cool and set. Once ready for removal from the pan, simply heat it in a bain-marie or with a torch and invert the pan onto a cake board. Next, invert the cake again onto another cake board so that it is right side up. The cheesecake can now be finished with fresh fruits, glazes, or lightly sweetened sour cream.

ADVANCED CREAMS

Classic and contemporary French-style pastry involves the use of a diverse range of cream preparations that are based on basic creams like whipped cream, pastry cream, and crème Anglaise. By combining basic creams with each other or additional components such as gelatin, egg foams, nut pastes, or chocolate, the pastry chef can create an impressive assortment of tastes and textures. Bordering on the qualifications of a true mousse, yet possessing equally desirable characteristics, these creams are easily prepared when key components such as pastry cream and crème Anglaise are on hand.

CRÈME ST. HONORÉ

Crème St. Honoré is a classic French cream that is not commonly used, but its preparation and special considerations are useful to know. It is also referred to as **crème Chiboust**, in honor of the pastry chef who created the cream for his famous Gateau St. Honoré in the mid-19th century. While its base components of pastry cream and French or Italian meringue make it very light, it is not as stable as other creams with similar light textures. Gelatin is added to increase stability.

The ratio of pastry cream to meringue in this classic cream is about 4:1. The temperature of the pastry cream and the Italian meringue are critical. If either is too cool, the cream could collapse or lose its emulsion. The recommended shelf life for crème St. Honoré is very short. If the cream is made with a French meringue, it is so susceptible to collapse and contamination that 12 hours is the maximum life. Preparations made with Italian meringue are more stable and should last up to 24 hours.

Crème St. Honoré Process

- Bloom the gelatin and reserve.
- Make the pastry cream, add the gelatin off heat, and cool on low speed on a stand mixer with the whip attachment to 104°F (40°C).
- While the pastry cream is cooling, prepare an Italian meringue.
- While the meringue is still warm, fold one-third of the meringue into the smooth pastry cream to lighten it.
- Fold in the remaining meringue in thirds, taking caution to not overwork the cream.
- Use immediately, respecting the time frame for serving safely.

CRÈME PARIS-BREST

Crème Paris-Brest is the classic filling for the Paris-Brest pastry. A basic preparation uses 100 percent pastry cream, 50 percent butter, and about 25 percent praline paste. The ratio of butter can be increased for a heavier cream; however, note that setting properties for this cream come from the butter, and not enough butter will create a cream that is too soft.

When making this cream, the base butter and praline paste should be at room temperature and free of lumps. The pastry cream should be cold to help set the butter and hold its shape. This cream must be used as soon as it is made. If allowed to set, it is difficult to work with and the emulsion may break. This cream is often applied using a star tip to present a larger volume without having to eat a large portion of such a rich cream.

Crème Paris-Brest Preparation

- Smooth the cold pastry cream and reserve.
- Smooth the room-temperature butter in a mixer fitted with the paddle attachment.
- Add the praline paste to the butter, and mix until just combined.
- Add the smoothed pastry cream to the butter praline mixture, and mix just until incorporated.
- Pipe immediately into pastry and refrigerate.

DIPLOMAT CREAM

Diplomat cream has its roots in a popular 19th-century French pudding: pudding Chateaubriand, which was introduced to Parisians by a famous diplomat's pastry chef. By definition, **diplomat cream** is a smooth and light cream prepared from pastry cream, whipped cream, and gelatin. It may be used as a filling in cakes, tarts, and pastries. This cream may also be referred to as crème legere.

Diplomat cream is convenient to make on short notice, or if a simple light cream is needed for desserts. Using a standard pastry cream as a base, all that is needed is whipped cream to lighten it and gelatin to stabilize and set it. For a lighter diplomat cream, a higher ratio of cream to pastry cream is used.

To begin the preparation, the whipping cream is brought to soft peaks. Next, the pasty cream is whipped until smooth. The gelatin is bloomed, melted, and tempered into the pastry cream base, and then the soft-peak whipped cream is added and folded in just to incorporation. Excessive folding may cause the cream to be overworked.

Diplomat cream must be deposited into cake molds or pastries as soon as possible because of the gelatin. Once deposited, products made with this cream can be stored under refrigeration for up to 48 hours, or they may be frozen. It is important to not freeze diplomat cream unless it is part of a finished dessert item. As with all cream preparations, sanitation guidelines must be followed to prevent contamination.

Diplomat Cream Preparation

- Follow the basic preparation method for pastry cream.
- Whip the cream to soft peaks and refrigerate.
- Bloom the gelatin in cold water.
- Add the bloomed gelatin to the hot pastry cream, and stir until dissolved.
- Mix the cream on low speed of a mixer until room temperature.
- Gently fold in the whipped cream and use immediately.

MOUSSELINE CREAM

In French, "mousseline" refers to items that are light and delicate. The traditional mousseline cream combines pastry cream and soft butter that has been whipped until light and fluffy. It creates a cross between a pastry cream and a light butter cream that is very versatile and may be used as a filling in cakes, tarts, and pastries. Some may actually use a formula that combines pastry cream and buttercream to make mousseline cream.

This cream is often served with fruit, such as the classic Le Frasier cake that combines an abundance of fresh strawberries and mousseline cream. In this and other preparations, the richness of the cream is balanced by the high quantity of fresh fruit. Mousseline cream is useful when making mille fuille or Napoleon cake as it can hold up well to the slicing of the pastry.

When preparing mousseline cream, it is important to cook the base pastry cream at a lower temperature than normal. This is because the pastry cream base has a high percentage of sugar, which is needed to sweeten the high quantity of butter that will be added, and it may scorch easily. After the pastry cream has been cooked, half of the butter is added to it. This mixture is allowed to cool, covered, in the refrigerator. After the cream is cool, but not too cold, it is placed in a mixing bowl fitted with the whip attachment and whipped until smooth. Next, the additional room-temperature butter is added and the cream is left to whip until full volume. At this point, it is ready for use.

Unused cream or finished products can be stored under refrigeration for up to 48 hours. Products made with mousseline cream freeze well and can last for several weeks in the freezer.

Mousseline Cream Process

- Prepare the pastry cream base.
- When finished, add half of the additional butter off heat with a whisk.
- Transfer the cream to a shallow container, and cool, covered with plastic, in the refrigerator.
- When it is cool, transfer it to a mixing bowl, add the remaining softened butter, and mix on medium speed to incorporate.
- Mix on high speed until the mixture doubles in volume.
- Flavor to taste and use.

CRÉMEUX

Crémeux in French means "creamy." As a pastry item, it refers to a crème Anglaise–style custard that has been thickened with butter and sometimes gelatin. The flavoring options for crémeux are plentiful and include chocolate, fruit puree, nut pastes, and caramel. Crémeux fillings can be used as the filling for a tart or as an insert for a mousse cake.

The process of creating a crémeux begins with the crème Anglaise. After it has been made, bloomed gelatin sheets may be added to the hot crème Anglaise and stirred to incorporate the gelatin. If any ingredients such as chocolate or praline paste are to be added to the crème Anglaise base, they should be added while the base cream is hot. To fully emulsify the chocolate or praline paste, it is useful to use an immersion blender.

Once the cream is 86°F (30°C) to 95°F (35°C), the softened butter is added to the base. It is critical that the temperature is within this range and that the butter is at room temperature to ensure proper creaminess. If the cream base is too warm, it will melt the butter, and the crémeux will lose texture and body. To efficiently incorporate the butter, an immersion blender is recommended. It is essential not to incorporate any air, as this will create bubbles in the thickened mixture. After the crémeux has been finished, it can be deposited into blind-baked tart shells or into FlexiMolds for entremets or other uses.

To preserve the integrity of the crémeux in tarts, a thin layer of clear mirror glaze must be applied over the creamy filling, or, if applicable, chocolate glaze. This will help prevent the moisture-rich crémeux from drying out and aging excessively, and will also help prevent oxidation and contamination. Crémeux has several special storage requirements. Finished products can be kept under refrigeration for up to 72 hours, and frozen for up to 1 week, if well wrapped.

Crémeux Process

- Prepare the basic crème Anglaise.
- Bloom the gelatin in water.
- Have the butter at room temperature.
- After the custard is cooked, add the gelatin and stir to incorporate. Strain into a clean, dry container, and cool over an ice bath.
- If using chocolate, add while the custard base is still hot, and form an emulsion. (See Crémeux Figure 15-5, Step 1.)
- When the mixture reaches 86°F (30°C) to 95°F (35°C), add the soft butter (if applicable) and incorporate it into the custard with an immersion blender. (See Crémeux Figure 15-5, Steps 2–3.) Deposit immediately into tart shells or molds for freezing. (See Crémeux Figure 15-5, Step 4.)

EGG FOAMS

Egg foams are a critical component of classic and contemporary pastry making and are used in the creation of numerous creams, cakes, and desserts. They are possible because of a family of proteins know as albumins that are naturally found in egg whites, or albumen. Egg foams are formed from whipping whole eggs, egg yolks, or egg whites with sugar to create a lightened foam, or collection of air bubbles held together by denatured protein molecules. **Meringues**, or egg foams made from egg whites and sugar, vary in composition and results depending on the production method used, as well as the ratio of egg white to sugar.

Egg foams have been used for centuries. Meringue is said to have been created in a small town in Switzerland called Mieringen by a Swiss pastry chef named Gasparini around the year 1720. The meringue was introduced to France by Stanislaus; Marie Antoinette is said to have made them regularly at Versailles.

Egg foams fall into two categories: cooked and uncooked. Both can be baked, but this is not necessary. Cooked egg foams, such as the Italian meringue and the pâte à bombe, are most likely to be used in mousse cakes or other ready-to-eat foods where an egg foam brings desired lightness.

An Italian meringue is classified as a cooked egg foam because it is made from egg whites and a sugar syrup that has been cooked to the firm ball stage. During the elaboration of the meringue, the egg whites are cooked from the heat of the sugar yet are still able to form a stable foam. Uncooked egg foams, such as the common meringue, are typically baked but are sometimes included in "raw" mousse preparations.

FIGURE 15-5 CRÉMEUX

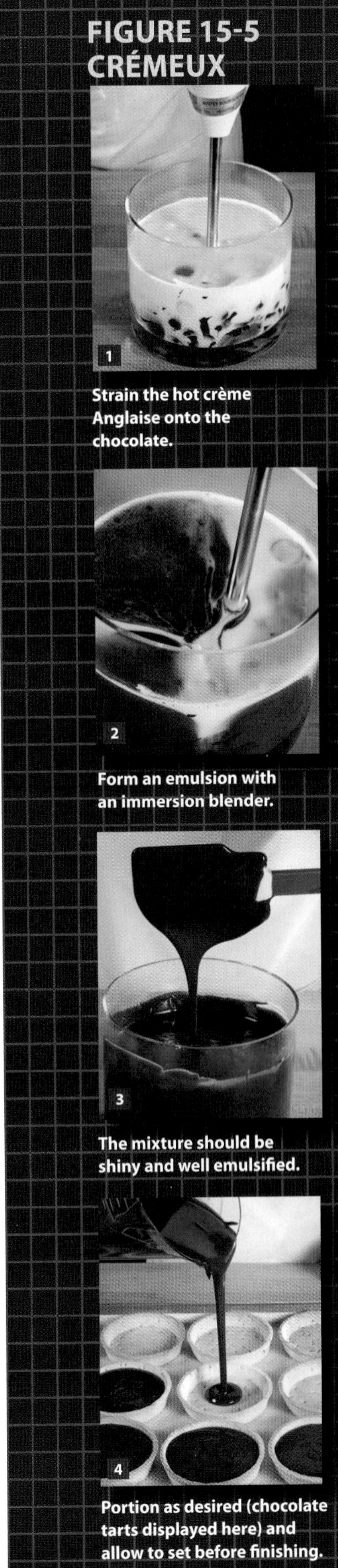

1 Strain the hot crème Anglaise onto the chocolate.

2 Form an emulsion with an immersion blender.

3 The mixture should be shiny and well emulsified.

4 Portion as desired (chocolate tarts displayed here) and allow to set before finishing.

MERINGUE

An understanding of the effects of fat on egg white foams is important to the discussion of meringue. First and foremost, it is essential that any egg white mixture be free of fat in order to obtain full volume from egg whites. Any yolk, natural skin oils, or greasy equipment will prevent egg white foams from forming, and poor meringue volume will result. Meringue is a type of egg foam that is created by beating air into the egg white and stabilizing the mixture with sugar. The albumin proteins in the egg white (primarily conalbumin and ovomucin) become denatured when agitated and unravel, securing pockets of air and water that allow the creation of a stable egg foam.

The denaturing of protein in the albumin is the unfolding of protein chains. As they unravel and are whipped, these chains of protein do not break down; rather they form new bonds, interlinking chains of molecules and eventually trapping air and water in a delicate matrix of air bubbles. The bonds continue to form and reform if broken, and as the egg foam develops, the structure becomes more stable as the molecular connections become greater and greater.

During and after the foam creation process, ovalbumin (another important protein in egg whites) provides sustained structure as it goes through multiple stages of coagulation. This happens as it comes in contact with air and during increasing temperatures in the oven or the mixer.

The addition of sugar has multiple effects on meringue. Sugar can delay the development of the meringue just as it can delay the development of gluten in bread. When higher quantities of sugar are used in a meringue, the proteins need longer to go through their process of unraveling and forming the bonds that secure the pockets of air and water. Sugar also helps reinforce the bond of water and air to the protein matrix. Without this additional bond, meringue may be more susceptible to falling or leaking water during the makeup or baking process.

Depending on the function and desired characteristics of the meringue, different formulas call for varying degrees of sugar. Higher quantities of sugar—some up to double the weight of sugar to egg white—will result in a denser foam with less volume that is more flexible and harder to overbeat. Baking at a low temperature will create a crisp meringue shell. Conversely, smaller quantities of sugar, such as equal weights sugar and egg white or less, yield softer, lighter foams with more volume. These are easier to overbeat, yet easily yield a stable meringue for piping or adding to formulas like cakes and lemon meringue pie.

Incorporating quantities of sugar that approach the 1:1 egg white–sugar ratio requires special action. To successfully produce a meringue, when whipping begins, the initial quantity of sugar with the egg white should not exceed one-third sugar to one part egg white. After the desired volume has been established, the remaining quantity of sugar can be quickly added as the machine is being turned off. If a larger ratio of sugar is needed, such as 1.5:1, any remaining sugar should be folded in with a spatula by hand.

Additional Ingredients for Meringue

A mildly acidic state adds strength to egg foams. The most commonly used ingredient for this is cream of tartar at a dosage of 0.05 percent, based on the weight of the egg whites. The slight acidification will not improve or damage the volume of the egg foam, but it will make it less likely to overcoagulate.

FIGURE 15-6 MERINGUE DEVELOPMENT

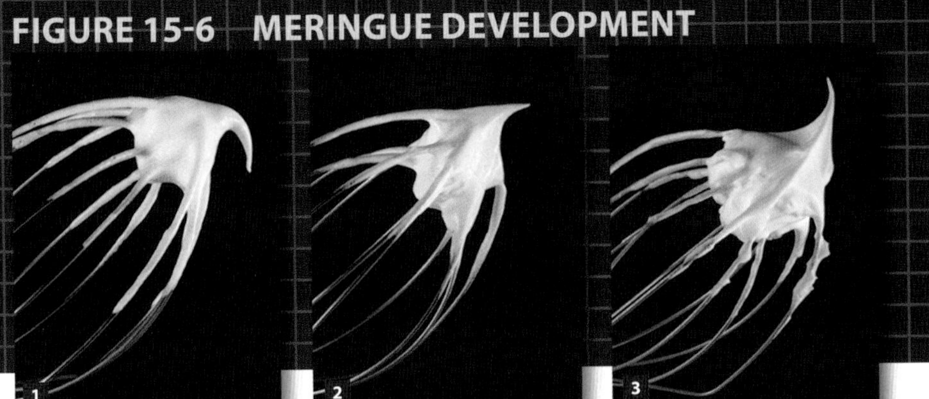

1 **Soft Peaks: The egg whites have just enough strength to form a stable foam.**

2 **Medium Peaks: The egg whites are more developed and have more strength to hold a firmer peak.**

3 **Stiff Peaks: The egg whites are fully developed and can hold stiff peaks. If whipped longer, the foam may begin to degrade.**

Contrary to the notion that a very small quantity of salt is beneficial to meringue, it has quite the opposite effect. Small additions of salt increase whipping time, penalize volume, and create less stability.

Precautions for Meringue

When creating a meringue from egg whites, it is extremely important to work with clean utensils and egg whites with no residual yolk. Any oil or fat that comes into contact with the whites inhibits the creation of a stable foam. The temperature of the egg whites is also critical for success because cold egg whites inhibit the development of egg foam. To obtain maximum volume, they should be 59°F (15°C) to 68°F (20°C).

Controlling the development of the foam is also necessary for stability. Underwhipped foam will support too few connections of the albumen, and bubbles will be large and irregular. If it is overwhipped, the albumen will overcoagulate, and the foam will become "dry," break down, and weep water.

Categories of Meringue Development

The ability of meringue to hold its own shape is a sign of how much air has been beaten into it as well as the strength of the foam. For this reason, the terms "soft peak," "medium peak," and "stiff peak" and combinations such as "medium stiff peaks" describe meringue development. (See Meringue Development Figure 15-6.)

For applications such as piping decorative meringue shells, a stiff meringue is desired. This will ensure sharp visual lines and a smooth texture. For sponge cakes, where a less-developed foam is desirable, a medium and sometimes soft peak is all that is required. Controlling the amount of leavening for the baker is a direct result of the extent of meringue development. See Chapter 14 for a close look at specific gravity of cake batters and its affect on cake characteristics.

FRENCH MERINGUE

French meringue, also known as the **common meringue**, is created with a minimum ratio of one part egg whites to one part sugar. The quantity of sugar involved in the preparation will determine the final application. A 1:1 ratio of egg whites to sugar will yield a softer meringue, ideal for the topping of pies and inclusion into mousse or soufflé items. Firmer meringues, made with a 1:2 ratio of egg whites to sugar, are used for classic, crisp results.

To begin making a French meringue (with a 1:1 egg white–sugar ratio), the whites are whipped at medium speed with a third of the sugar. The remainder of the sugar should be held back to encourage the development of the foam. During whipping, the bubbles will become smaller as the volume of the whites increases. The sugar should be added at the stage of desired meringue development, and whipping should continue only until the sugar is incorporated.

If a hard meringue is being made (2:1 egg white–sugar ratio), the second addition of sugar could take place while the machine is running on slow speed. Alternately, the second addition of sugar may be folded in by hand using a rubber spatula. If piping a number of items, it is best to keep the meringue mixing on a low speed to prevent the protein from coagulating. Additional meringue can be loaded into the pastry bag as needed.

French Meringue Process (1 : 1 Egg White–Sugar)

- In the bowl of a stainless steel mixer and using the whip attachment, begin whipping the egg whites with one-third of the sugar.
- Whip at a medium speed until the air bubbles become smaller and of uniform size.
- Increase the speed of the mixer and mix to stiff peaks.
- Add the remainder of the sugar and mix until incorporated.
- Use accordingly.
- If piping, reserve the unused meringue on a slow whipping speed to prevent coagulation.

SWISS MERINGUE

Swiss meringue is denser and more stable than French meringue. It can be used for making crisp meringue cookies, as a base for buttercream, and also as a topping for cakes and pies. Swiss meringue is characterized by heating the egg whites and sugar before final whipping, a process that involves constant agitation to prevent the egg whites from scrambling. During this process, temperatures should range from 120°F (49°C) to 160°F (71°C). If the egg whites are constantly whisked, the sugar in the mixture will prevent them from cooking.

The final temperature will have an effect on the texture and food safety of the final product. Swiss meringue heated to 120°F (49°C) will be less dense; however, the use of nonpasteurized egg whites will require heating to 160°F (71°C) as a precautionary measure to destroy any bacteria that may be present. This is especially important for items that will not be baked. Higher temperatures also have an effect on the texture of baked meringue cookies because the density of the foam will be slightly altered by the heat variation.

Swiss Meringue Process

- In the bowl of a stainless steel mixer, combine the egg whites and sugar.
- Place the bowl over boiling water and heat the mixture to a temperature between 120°F (49°C) and 160°F (71°C), whisking constantly to avoid coagulation.

- Once the desired temperature is procured, place the bowl on a mixer fitted with the whip attachment and whip on a medium-high speed until stiff peaks form.
- If piping, reserve the unused meringue, whipping slowly to prevent coagulation.

ITALIAN MERINGUE

Italian meringue is a cooked meringue that is made using egg whites and a hot, cooked sugar syrup. The sugar syrup is carefully poured over the whipping whites, and the mixture is left to whip until cool. Italian meringue is very versatile and is commonly used in mousse cakes, as an addition to sorbets, as an icing, as the base for Italian buttercream, and as a topping for Baked Alaska and meringue-topped pies.

Of all the meringues, the preparation of the Italian meringue is the most involved. It is imperative to use room-temperature [68° (20°C) to 70°F (21°C)], fat-free whites and equipment, as well as a room-temperature mixing bowl. This will help ensure that the egg whites reach at least 160°F (71°C), at which point they are considered cooked. Using cold whites and/or a cold bowl will not only hamper this goal, but it will compromise the volume of the final product.

To begin an Italian meringue, the sugar and water need to be cooked to 246°F (119°C) to 250°F (121°C), also known as the firm ball stage. While the sugar is cooking, the egg whites should be set up in a mixing bowl with the whip attachment. When the sugar reaches 240°F (116°C), the egg whites should begin whipping and should achieve half volume before the sugar is ready.

As the sugar syrup cooks, the sides of the pot should be washed down with water using a clean pastry brush to prevent crystallization. Just before the sugar reaches the firm ball stage, the pot should be taken off heat and the egg whites should be whipped at medium-high speed until a medium volume builds. As the sugar sits off heat, the temperature will continue to rise.

When the whites are at the appropriate volume and the sugar is at the correct temperature, the hot sugar syrup is slowly and carefully poured into the mixing bowl between the whipping whisk and the side of the bowl. Care should be taken to prevent the sugar from hitting the whisk and splattering around the edge of the bowl.

The rate at which sugar is added should be similar to the rate at which the sugar is incorporated into the whites. After all the sugar is added, the meringue is left to whip at medium-high speed until full volume is reached and the meringue has cooled to about 90°F (32°C).

Italian Meringue Process

- Combine the sugar and water in a pot and cook to the firm ball stage. (See Italian Meringue Figure 15-7, Step 1.)
- While it is cooking, place the egg whites in the bowl of a stainless steel mixer fitted with the whip attachment.
- When the sugar syrup is almost to the firm ball stage, at approximately 240°F (121°C), begin whipping the whites and take the sugar off the heat.
- Slowly add the sugar syrup when it reaches 246°F (119°C) to 250°F (121°C). (See Italian Meringue Figure 15-7, Step 2.)

FIGURE 15-7 ITALIAN MERINGUE

1 The sugar, water, and glucose (if any) are brought to between 246°F (119°C) and 250°F (121°C).

2 After it is cooked to the desired temperature, carefully pour the syrup onto the whipping egg whites.

3 The meringue should be whipped until full volume and proper temperature for its intended use.

- Whip at a medium-high speed for several minutes, and then mix on a lower speed until lukewarm to the touch. (See Italian Meringue Figure 15-7, Step 3.)
- Fold into mousse or use accordingly.
- If piping, slowly whip the reserved, unused meringue to prevent coagulation.

PÂTE À BOMBE

A **pâte à bombe** is an egg foam made from egg yolks and cooked sugar. Pâte à bombe bases are used for mousse cakes, as a base for French buttercream, and as a base for frozen desserts such as parfait. The pâte à bombe mixture adds both a light texture and an added richness in flavor and color.

Pâte à bombe can replace traditional meringues for producing mousse cakes and ice cream, but it lacks the structure and strength required of a meringue to stand alone and hold a peaked shape. The pâte à bombe is ready for use once it has cooled, has at least tripled in volume, and can form a ribbon when dropped from the whip.

The process used to make this egg foam is exactly the same as for the Italian meringue. The difference is only that egg yolks are substituted in place of the egg whites. The lecithin in the yolks helps to maintain a smooth emulsion in mousse. To summarize the process, the hot sugar syrup is poured over the whipping yolks and the mixture is whipped until cool. As it whips, it lightens in color, increases in volume, and takes on an airy texture.

Pâte à Bombe Process

- Combine the sugar and water in a pot, and cook to the firm ball stage.
- While it is cooking, place the egg yolks in the bowl of a stainless steel mixer fitted with the whip attachment and begin whipping.
- Slowly add the sugar syrup once it reaches 250°F (121°C).
- Whip at a medium-high speed until cool to the touch.
- Fold into mousse preparation or use accordingly.

ICING

Icing, which is sometimes referred to by the more limited term "frosting," covers a broad range of formulas that are used to fill, cover, or decorate cakes, pastries, or cookies. The main groups of icings include buttercreams, glazes, fondant, ganache, flat icing, and royal icing. Their composition, which ranges from thin to thick, depends on their specific applications.

Not only do icings improve the visual qualities of cake, but they also protect the cake from drying out. Icing can be used within the cake, or to decorate the outside. Icing can also be used to create ornamentation for the exterior of the cake, including an endless variety of borders, flowers, and other piped designs.

Specific icings are chosen for their function and appearance and because they complement the taste and texture of the composed cake or pastry. This balance of flavors, colors, textures, and taste is an integral part of success in the finished product.

BUTTERCREAM

Buttercream is the most common icing used for special occasion cakes, is widely enjoyed by many, and is a versatile choice for the baker. In its basic form, buttercream is sugar-sweetened whipped butter, though it is often further lightened with an egg foam or egg whites. Buttercream may be used to fill, ice, and decorate cakes and is sometimes used as a filling for cookies and other assorted pastries. The taste and texture of buttercream largely depend on its ingredients and the method in which it is produced.

The main types of buttercream include basic, decorator's, Italian, French, Swiss, and crème Anglaise buttercream. The method for producing each varies greatly.

Of all the ingredient choices for buttercream, the fat is the one that will explicitly determine the quality of the final product. Although butter is the favorite for flavor and mouthfeel, it is not always the first choice for two reasons. First, the high cost of butter can provide a challenge to the budget, and, second, its low melting point can be difficult to work with in warmer baking environments. Even so, it is important to keep consumer satisfaction in mind when making the choice.

Hydrogenated fats, on the other hand, lower the cost of buttercream and contain emulsifiers that can create a smoother, more stable product. The higher melting point of shortening makes buttercream easier to use. It can also be held at room temperature for longer periods of time during warmer weather. This is an important consideration for wedding cakes in hot climates, which can be displayed for long periods of time out of refrigeration.

Basic Buttercream

The essential ingredients for **basic buttercream** are powdered sugar and butter and/or icing shortening. Powdered sugar provides a better texture than granulated sugar, which does not dissolve very easily in such a low-moisture environment. The choice of fat will determine the mouthfeel, melting point, and color, with the pure white of icing-shortening producing a whiter, lighter icing, and butter imparting its natural yellow hues. If additional lightness is desired, pasteurized egg whites, water, or milk can be whipped in.

Basic Buttercream Process

- Sift the powdered sugar and add to a mixing bowl fitted with the paddle.
- Add the fat to the bowl and mix to combine.
- Whip at a medium-high speed and add pasteurized liquid egg whites, if using.

Swiss Buttercream

A **Swiss buttercream** is made with the stable base of a Swiss meringue. Once the meringue has been made, the softened butter is added slowly, and the buttercream is whipped to full volume. Swiss buttercream is not as light as one made from an Italian meringue, but the process is quicker and simpler.

Swiss Buttercream Process

- Prepare the Swiss meringue.
- When it is at full volume and cool, slowly add the softened butter.
- Whip until fully incorporated and light and fluffy.

FIGURE 15-8 ITALIAN BUTTERCREAM

1

Add the soft butter to the Italian meringue after it has dropped to about 80°F (27°C).

2

After all the butter is added, continue whipping.

3

Whip until the buttercream thickens, has good body, and is well emulsified.

Italian Buttercream

Italian buttercream, with its characteristic lightness and stability, is a common choice among pastry chefs. As the name implies, it is based on an Italian meringue that is whipped to full volume and then brought to near room temperature before slowly adding softened butter. Then, the buttercream is whipped until light and fluffy. (See Italian Buttercream Figure 15-8, Steps 1–3.)

It is important to note that if too much of a temperature differential exists between the meringue and the butter, the emulsion may break or the butter may melt. To fix a broken or curdled buttercream it is best to continue whipping on high speed. The motion of the whip and natural fluctuation of temperature will eventually emulsify the buttercream. A common mistake is to use a torch to warm the bowl and thus the buttercream. This will warm the butter, and the additional motion will emulsify the buttercream; however, the buttercream will be dense and brittle because of the melted fats.

If the butter melts because the meringue is too warm, volume will be lost. The batch can be saved if the contents of the bowl are cooled and whipped to emulsify. If the resulting buttercream is unsatisfactory but usable, one option is to temper it into a good batch to avoid any waste.

Italian Buttercream Process

- Cook the sugar syrup and make the Italian meringue.
- Once cooled to room temperature, add the softened butter. (See Italian Buttercream Figure 15-8, Step 1.)
- Whip until light and fluffy. (See Italian Buttercream Figure 15-8, Steps 2–3.)

French Buttercream

French buttercream is the richest of all the egg foam–based buttercreams. Unlike the Italian and Swiss buttercreams, which are based on meringues, the French buttercream is based on a pâte à bombe. This egg yolk–based egg foam adds an extraordinary amount of richness and color to the buttercream. Because it is significantly richer than other buttercreams, it is typically used in lower quantities to ensure that it doesn't overpower the other components of the cake or pastry.

Egg yolks reduce the shelf life of this icing. It should remain under refrigeration when not in use and can last up to 1 week in the refrigerator if well covered with plastic. Well-wrapped French buttercream can be stored for up to several months in the freezer.

French Buttercream Process

- Prepare and make the pâte à bombe.
- Add the softened butter to the pâte à bombe after it has cooled.
- Whip until light and fluffy, and store in the refrigerator until needed.

Crème Anglaise–Style Buttercream

The most flavorful of the buttercreams is **crème Anglaise–style buttercream**, also known as English buttercream. It is made using a crème Anglaise sauce, butter, and an Italian meringue. The tradeoff for crème Anglaise–style buttercream is that its high liquid content makes it the least stable and the most prone to spoilage. It must be used and served fresh. In addition, crème Anglaise–style buttercream does not freeze well because the high water content of the custard cream creates large quantities of ice crystals that damage the emulsion.

The crème Anglaise should be strained through a fine chinois and cooled as rapidly as possible in a mixer fitted with the whip attachment. At the same time, the Italian meringue can be started, and the butter can be softened. Once the custard base is at about 70°F (21°C) to 75°F (24°C), the softened butter can be added; it should then be mixed in to good incorporation. When the Italian meringue is cool, it can be mixed into the custard–butter base until well incorporated.

Crème Anglaise–Style Buttercream Process

- Prepare the crème Anglaise, strain, and whip on a stand mixer fitted with the whip.
- Prepare the Italian meringue, and whip it until it reaches room temperature.
- Soften the butter, and add it to the whipping crème Anglaise.
- Add the Italian meringue, and mix until incorporated.

Working With Buttercream

The ingredients used to formulate buttercream will determine its taste, texture, and working properties. Butter, with the lowest melting point of the hard fats, may be harder to use than a buttercream made with all or part shortening. High temperatures will cause the fats to melt and the buttercream to thin out so that the final product may not hold its form on the cake or produce clean lines. Conversely, a buttercream that is too cold will not spread easily and will be difficult to make smooth.

For these reasons, it is essential to work with the buttercream at the proper temperature. If it has been stored under refrigeration, it is best to remove it to soften approximately 1 hour before it is needed. If possible, buttercream stored in the freezer should be transferred to the refrigerator between 8 and 24 hours before it is needed, depending on the volume of the storage container. When it is at room temperature, it may be prepared for use.

It is important to ensure that buttercream for icing cakes is smooth and free of air pockets that could appear on the finished cake. The easiest way to work any air pockets out and make a smooth buttercream is to fill the bowl of a mixer to the surface (for smaller applications, a 5-quart mixer works well) and to whip the cream until smooth. It is crucial that the buttercream is over the whisk to ensure that no air is incorporated. Each pass of the whisk knocks air out of the cream. When the buttercream is smooth, it is ready to use.

The flavoring options for buttercream are endless. Fruit, chocolate, spice, nut, coffee, and liquor flavor variations are commonly created with various chocolates, nut pastes, extracts, and compounds. Because it is important not to add too much additional liquid, items like alcohol should be used as a percentage of the butter. Please refer to individual formulas for common percentages of add-in ingredients.

Of all buttercream flavorings, chocolate merits special mention. To avoid creating buttercream with chocolate chips, the chocolate must be tempered in. This tempering process has no relation to the tempering of chocolate; however, it does relate to the gradual incorporation of chocolate into the cream as a whole. To begin the process, the chocolate should be melted to 120°F (49°C). Next, an equal weight of buttercream should be warmed slightly and then mixed into the chocolate using a whisk. This will diffuse the chocolate through the buttercream and prevent it from setting up (or creating chips). Finally, this mixture can be added to the reserved buttercream.

As with any pastry or food item, buttercream waste must be kept to a minimum. For example, it is not uncommon for amateur decorators to get crumbs into the buttercream during the filling and icing process. This crumbed buttercream should be kept separate from clean buttercream and should be used only on masking applications or added to chocolate buttercream used for filling layer cakes. Keeping crumbs out of buttercream may take a lot of work, but cake quality will be higher and waste lower.

FONDANT

Fondant is a cooked sugar syrup that has been cooled and agitated in order to crystallize the sugar and produce a smooth, white, creamy icing. It is often used on napoleons, éclairs, and Danish pastries. After it is applied to the product, fondant should set up and appear shiny and white. If it has been heated improperly, it may not set up, will appear dull and cloudy, and can be very hard. The temperature guidelines depend on the fondant manufacturer. In general, ready-to-use fondants, bought from pastry supply vendors, can be heated to 120°F (49°C). Fondant made from a dry mix (often referred to as drivert sugar) can only be heated to about 100°F (38°C).

Fondant is heated to turn it into a fluid that can be poured. If the fondant is the proper temperature and is still too thick, small amounts of simple syrup can be added and mixed in to achieve appropriate viscosity. Overheated fondant will become thicker sooner and, once set, will appear dull and cloudy. To achieve a firm glaze, some people overheat fondant on purpose; however, because this process results in a loss of visual appeal, another glaze with appropriate setting properties should be considered.

Working With Fondant

It is important to heat fondant over a bain-marie, stirring to heat evenly without incorporating air. A rubber spatula is the best tool. The fondant should be heated to between 100°F (38°C) and 120°F (49°C), depending on the type being used. Other heating techniques include using a microwave or a pot over direct heat.

If the fondant reaches the proper temperature but is still too thick, it can be thinned with a little simple syrup. If it is too thin, unheated fondant can be added and stirred in just to incorporation.

Both color and flavor can be added to the fondant. If multiple colors are to be added, staged coloring is ideal to limit waste. Using primary colors with the aid of a color wheel, the pastry chef should be able to achieve any color. For example, add yellow to white to create yellow; orange to yellow to create peach; red to peach to create red; blue to red to create purple. As a rule, it's best to go easy when adding color. Pastel tones are more appealing than bold ones.

For chocolate fondant, add 18 to 20 percent melted chocolate liquor, based on total weight of fondant. Other flavorings, such as coffee paste or extract, may also be added.

CHOCOLATE GLAZE

Chocolate glaze, which is essentially a thinned ganache, is a versatile finishing medium. It may be made with white chocolate, milk chocolate, or dark chocolate, as well as a number of other ingredients that include gelatin, cocoa powder, sugar syrups, and cream. The specific formulation will determine the viscosity of the glaze. For example, hard fats like cocoa butter and cocoa solids will have a major impact on thickness.

If cocoa butter or cocoa solids are not present in high enough quantities, gelatin can be used to balance the glaze thickness and setting properties. This is especially true for white chocolate and milk chocolate glazes, which have a lower percentage of cocoa than dark chocolate. A stable emulsion is essential for smoothness and to ensure a thin glossy glaze over the finished item.

Working With Chocolate Glaze

Temperature is a critical element for working with chocolate glazes, with the proper working temperature determined by the formula used. Items to be glazed should be cold at a minimum, but some, like mousse cakes, may need to be frozen.

Typically, items to be glazed should be placed on a pouring screen over a sheet pan covered with a clean sheet of parchment paper. Excess glaze will drip off of the cake onto the parchment and can be reused. Larger, difficult-to-transfer items like full-sheet opera cake can be glazed on the pan on which they were built. Whatever the size, glazing should be quick and even to ensure all areas of the cake are covered.

CHOCOLATE GANACHE FOR GLAZING

Less popular than chocolate glaze for icing cakes is ganache. **Ganache** is a creamy mixture made when a liquid, usually cream, is poured over chocolate, and an emulsion is formed. To create a dark chocolate ganache for glazing, it is ideal to use a 1:1 ratio of cream to chocolate and to add 7 to 10 percent glucose to the cream, based on weight. Adding glucose will slow down the molecular movement of the emulsion bonds and help retain moisture and prevent cracking. Ganache may be preferred for flavor over a chocolate glaze because it will likely be less sweet. Refer to Chapter 22 for more detailed information on ganache.

Working With Chocolate Ganache

Though stable in its emulsified state, ganache is susceptible to breaking if it is agitated too much. It is ideally used when it is freshly made. If ganache sets in the bowl or container in which it was prepared, it must be melted, a process that can pose some problems for the pastry chef. Ideally, the microwave should be used to gently heat the ganache until it is the proper temperature. (See Chapter 22 for more on heating and reusing ganache.)

As with chocolate glazes, ganache temperature is critical. The ganache needs to be used at the right moment to ensure a smooth, even, and shiny coating. The temperature guidelines for ganache are similar to those for chocolate glazes. One must consider the temperature of the item being glazed, as well as its size and the viscosity of the glaze.

Chocolate ganache has less sugar than chocolate glaze and a higher concentration of hard fats. For these reasons, it sets up faster than glaze and there is greater chance for error. Pouring the cake must be a swift and concise operation. Once the cake has been glazed it should be returned to the freezer to "set up"; then it can be removed from the pouring screen and transferred as needed.

FRUIT GLAZE

Easy to make and simple to use, **fruit glaze** gives the pastry chef the opportunity to finish cakes or pastries with vibrant, fresh colors and unique flavors. The composition of fruit glazes can vary considerably. They are often made completely in-house, using ingredients such as fruit puree, glucose, water, and gelatin. Hybrid versions can be made by adding ingredients like fruit puree, glucose, and gelatin to ready-to-use products like cold process clear glaze. Fruit glaze stability is good, and it lasts several days if stored well covered in the refrigerator. Once deposited onto a cake or pastry, shelf life is usually limited to 2 days before the glaze begins to oxidize and dehydrate.

Working With Fruit Glaze

Avoiding the incorporation of air when working with fruit glazes is essential. Air bubbles will show through and remain in the glaze once poured. As with chocolate glaze, the proper temperature of the glaze is critical. The viscosity of the glaze needs to be thin enough to pour yet thick enough to leave a thin layer over the cake. The temperature-sensitive gelatin (and pectin in commercially available ready-to-use products) needs to be warmed enough so that flow properties are positive, yet the glaze must cool and gel when contact is made with the cold entremets.

ROYAL ICING

Royal icing is the classic icing. It is an icing that is easily piped, sets very firm, and can last, in decorative form, for many years. The basic ingredients include powdered sugar, water, and egg whites. It is also common to use egg white powder or meringue powder in place of fresh egg whites to ensure that it is free from bacteria. The ratio of sugar to liquid will determine the thickness of the icing. Thinner icing is used for "flood work"—a technique used to fill in piped shapes and create images. Royal icing can also be used as a medium for creating ornate decorative borders on cakes.

Royal icing is naturally white but can be colored as desired. It is best to used at room temperature. If it is made using fresh egg whites, it should be stored in the refrigerator. If it is made using meringue powder or dried egg whites, it may be stored at room temperature. Either way, it should be covered to the surface with a wet paper towel and then wrapped well with plastic wrap.

FLAT ICING

Flat icing, also known as water icing, is a quick preparation made from powdered sugar and a liquid such as milk, lemon juice, or water. If using milk, the addition of about 20 percent cream based on the weight of the milk will help the icing look whiter and creamier. Flat icing can be flavored with extracts, oils, fruit juices (especially lemon), and zest. It is frequently used as a glaze to decorate items like Danish pastries, brioche coffee cake, and hot cross buns.

Because it is important to not incorporate air bubbles, it is better to stir this product rather than whisk it. Proper consistency is important to ensure the glaze does not run out once it is piped. Flat icing may be stored in the refrigerator for up to 3 days, and items it is applied to should be sold on the same day.

OTHER ICINGS: WHIPPED TOPPING, CRÈME CHANTILLY, AND ITALIAN MERINGUE

As the American palate has shifted toward lighter textures in recent years, crème Chantilly and other whipped toppings have become increasingly popular. When using crème Chantilly, it is important to not overwhip during the whipping process, as the cream will continue to develop during icing and could turn grainy. Gelatin can be added to crème Chantilly at a percentage of 1.5 to help stabilization. **Whipped topping** is a nondairy-based whipped cream replacement and has a very smooth texture and bright appearance. The stabilizers and emulsifiers in it enable the cream to be very light and easy to work with. Many people have come to expect the light characteristics of this topping; however, it is not prized for its ingredient label and limited use (it cannot easily be used in mousse).

Italian meringue is a unique choice for icing. It is light, melts in your mouth, and can be visually textured using a torch for a dramatic visual effect. Because it is important to use Italian meringue before it sets, it should be applied while still slightly warm and the reserve should be kept in motion. Once the meringue is browned with the torch, it has a shelf life of up to 48 hours in a refrigerated case.

FORMULA

SIMPLE SYRUP

This essential ingredient is a staple in every pastry shop, where a large container of simple syrup can usually be found in the refrigerator, waiting to serve its duty in multiple preparations. The general proportions of simple syrup are a 1:1 ratio of water and sugar.

Ingredients	Baker's %	Kilogram	US decimal	Lb & Oz		Test
Water	100.00	1.000	2.205	2	3 ¼	1 lb
Sugar	100.00	1.000	2.205	2	3 ¼	1 lb
Total	200.00	2.000	4.410	4	6 ½	2 lb

Process

1. Combine the water and sugar and wash down the sides of the pot.
2. Bring to a boil, remove from the heat, cover, and reserve.

FORMULA

30 BAUMÉ SYRUP

Like simple syrup, 30 baumé syrup is an essential ingredient for the pastry chef. The difference between simple syrup and 30 baumé syrup is in the ratio between sugar and water. 30 baumé syrup calls for 137 percent sugar to 100 percent water.

Ingredients	Baker's %	Kilogram	US decimal	Lb & Oz		Test
Water	100.00	0.844	1.861	1	13 ¾	13 ⅝ oz
Sugar	137.00	1.156	2.549	2	8 ¾	1 lb 2 ⅜ oz
Total	237.00	2.000	4.410	4	6 ½	2 lb

Process

1. Combine the water and sugar and wash down the sides of the pot.
2. Bring to a boil, remove from the heat, cover, and reserve.

FORMULA

CRÈME CHANTILLY

This delicate and airy concoction first appears in history during the Age of Enlightenment. Crème Chantilly was served in the village of Hameau, with its famous dairy and dairy farm adjoining the Prince of Condé's Chantilly domain. The famous cream was served during the banquets that took place in the grand Hameau reception hall, where the most privileged of Chantilly's many guests were invited. Vanilla is optional and can be added to taste.

Ingredients	Baker's %	Kilogram	US decimal	Lb & Oz		Test
Heavy cream	100.00	2.666	5.878	5	14	1 lb 12 ½ oz
Powdered sugar	12.50	0.333	0.735		11 ¾	3 ½ oz
Total	112.50	3.000	6.613	6	9 ¾	2 lb

Process

Using a mixer with a whip attachment, whip the cream and sugar until desired stage.

FORMULA

CRÈME ANGLAISE

Crème Anglaise (English cream) is the French phrase for custard sauce. This is a rich and smooth textured sauce that can be served, warm or cold, with cakes, pies, puddings, or fruit and is ideal for plated desserts. Additionally, it is the base for numerous creams in the pastry kitchen.

Ingredients	Baker's %	Kilogram	US decimal	Lb & Oz		Test
Whole milk	50.00	1.071	2.362	2	5 ¾	11 ⅜ oz
Heavy cream	50.00	1.071	2.362	2	5 ¾	11 ⅜ oz
Vanilla bean	Each	2	2		2	½ each
Sugar	20.00	0.429	0.945		15 ⅛	4 ⅝ oz
Egg yolks	20.00	0.429	0.945		15 ⅛	4 ⅝ oz
Total	140.00	3.000	6.613	6	9 ¾	2 lb

Process

1. Scale the milk, cream, and scraped vanilla beans into a stainless steel pot and bring to a boil.
2. Meanwhile, scale the sugar and egg yolks into a bowl and mix just to combine.
3. When the liquid comes to a boil, pour one-third of it onto the egg yolk mixture, and stir to incorporate evenly.
4. Return this mixture back to the pot, constantly stirring with a heat-resistant rubber spatula.
5. Continue to cook the custard while stirring until it has reached 180°F (82°C).
6. Strain the crème Anglaise through a fine mesh chinois into a clean container.
7. Cool immediately in an ice bath to prevent any carryover cooking.
8. Cover to the surface with plastic film, and refrigerate until needed.

FORMULA

PASTRY CREAM

Pastry cream is a staple in pastry kitchens, used to fill cakes, cream puffs, éclairs, napoleons, tarts, and other pastries. It is cooked on the stove into a rich, thick custard made from a mixture of milk, eggs, sugar, and cornstarch. Vanilla beans, liqueurs, chocolate, and coffee are sometimes added to pastry creams as additional flavor.

Ingredients	Baker's %	Kilogram	US decimal	Lb & Oz		Test
Whole milk	100.00	1.829	4.032	4	½	1 lb 3 ½ oz
Sugar #1	5.00	0.091	0.202		3 ¼	1 oz
Cornstarch	7.00	0.128	0.282		4 ½	1 ⅜ oz
Sugar #2	20.00	0.366	0.806		12 ⅞	3 ⅞ oz
Egg yolks	20.00	0.366	0.806		12 ⅞	3 ⅞ oz
Butter	12.00	0.219	0.484		7 ¾	2 ⅜ oz
Total	164.00	3.000	6.613	6	9 ¾	2 lb

Process

1. Scale the whole milk and first sugar into a stainless steel pot, and bring to a boil.
2. Meanwhile, scale the cornstarch and second sugar into a bowl, and mix to combine.
3. Scale the egg yolks into the sugar–cornstarch mixture, and whisk until just combined. Do not incorporate air.
4. When the milk comes to a boil, pour one-third of it onto the egg yolk mixture, and stir to incorporate evenly.
5. Return this mixture back to the pot, constantly stirring.
6. Continue to cook the custard while stirring until it has boiled for 2 minutes.
7. Turn off the heat, add the butter and stir until mixed in completely.
8. Pour the pastry cream into a clean, shallow pan, and cover the surface with plastic wrap.
9. Refrigerate immediately until needed.

Flavor Variations

Add any of the following ingredients to pastry cream for different flavor variations. Pastry cream should be at the temperature specified below for best results. Percentages are based on the total weight of the pastry cream.

Chocolate liquor	12%	Hot
Coffee extract	3%	Hot or cold
Alcohol	5%	Warm or cold
Bittersweet chocolate	20%	Hot
Praline paste	15%–20%	Hot or cold
Vanilla beans	1 bean per 1 kg of milk, split and scraped; add to milk at the beginning of the cooking process	

FORMULA

ALMOND CREAM

One of the essential ingredients in any pastry chef's kitchen, almond cream is exceptionally versatile, used in morning pastries, cakes, and many other desserts.

Ingredients	Baker's %	Kilogram	US decimal	Lb & Oz		Test
Butter	324.62	1.319	2.907	2	14 ½	8 ½ oz
Sugar	324.62	1.319	2.907	2	14 ½	8 ½ oz
Eggs	147.69	0.600	1.323	1	5 ⅛	3 ⅞ oz
Almond meal	324.62	1.319	2.907	2	14 ½	8 ½ oz
Bread flour	100.00	0.406	0.896		14 ⅜	2 ⅝ oz
Rum	9.23	0.037	0.083		1 ⅜	¼ oz
Total	1230.78	5.000	11.023	11	⅜	2 lb

Process

1. In a mixer with the paddle attachment, cream the butter and sugar until light.
2. Add the eggs gradually.
3. Add the almond meal and bread flour, and mix until incorporated and then add rum.
4. Store covered in the refrigerator.

FORMULA

FRANGIPANE

Frangipane is the subject of one of the culinary world's more bizarre stories. It all began, legend has it, when a 16th-century Italian nobleman, Marquis Muzio Frangipani, invented almond perfume–scented gloves and created a Parisian fashion trend. Pastry chefs looking to capitalize on the latest craze experimented with different ways to capture the popular scent in desserts, and frangipane was born. Flavored with ground almonds, this rich cream, now based on two parts almond cream to one part pastry cream, is used for cakes, morning pastries, and other confections.

Ingredients	Baker's %	Kilogram	US decimal	Lb & Oz		Test
Almond cream	100.00	3.333	7.349	7	5 ⅝	1 lb 5 ⅜ oz
Pastry cream	50.00	1.667	3.674	3	10 ¾	10 ⅝ oz
Total	150.00	5.000	11.023	11	⅜	2 lb

Process

1. In a mixing bowl, combine the almond cream and the pastry cream.
2. Blend using the paddle attachment until well combined.

FORMULA

CRÈME BRÛLÉE

The origin of crème brûlée ("burnt cream" in French) is hotly debated, with the English, Spanish, and French all staking claim to this classic dish of smooth custard with a caramelized sugar topping. Crème brûlée is a staple on the menu of many of today's restaurants and is available in a wealth of diverse flavorings.

Ingredients	Baker's %	Kilogram	US decimal	Lb & Oz		Test
Heavy cream	100.00	1.709	3.767	3	12 ¼	1 lb 6 oz
Vanilla bean	each	2	2		2	½ each
Egg yolks	16.53	0.282	0.623		10	3.5 oz
Eggs	3.85	0.066	0.145		2 ⅜	1 oz
Sugar	25.77	0.440	0.971		15 ½	5.5 oz
Salt	0.20	0.003	0.008		⅛	pinch
Total	146.35	2.500	5.513	5	8 ¼	2 lb

Process

1. Scald the cream and scraped vanilla bean.
2. Combine and gently whisk the egg yolks, eggs, sugar, and salt.
3. Temper the cream into the egg–sugar mixture.
4. Next, strain it through a fine chinois.
5. Portion into crème brûlée dishes and then bake in a water bath at 300°F (149°C) in a convection oven.
6. Bake until just barely set in the middle.
7. Remove from the oven and transfer to the refrigerator, uncovered.

Finishing

To serve, apply a thin layer of sugar over the custard and brûlée with a torch or under a broiler.

FORMULA

CRÈME CARAMEL

Also referred to as flan, crème caramel is a rich custard dessert with a layer of soft caramel on top. Though the name is French, the dish has spread across Europe and the world.

Caramel Formula

Ingredients	Baker's %	Kilogram	US decimal	Lb & Oz		Test
Sugar	100.00	0.690	1.521	1	8 ⅜	11 oz
Water	30.00	0.207	0.456		7 ¼	3 ¼ oz
Glucose	15.00	0.103	0.228		3 ⅝	1 ⅝ oz
Total	145.00	1.000	2.205	2	3 ¼	1 lb

Process, Caramel

1. Combine the sugar, water, and glucose in a saucepan.
2. Stir and bring to a boil.
3. Wash down the sides and continue cooking until the sugar turns to an amber color.
4. Remove from the heat and pour the caramel sugar into the cups; let set.

Custard Formula

Ingredients	Baker's %	Kilogram	US decimal	Lb & Oz		Test
Whole milk	100.00	1.552	3.422	3	6 ¾	1 lb 3 ⅞ oz
Sugar	18.92	0.294	0.647		10 ⅜	3 ¾ oz
Vanilla bean	Each	2	2		2	⅔ each
Salt	0.50	0.008	0.017		¼	⅔ tsp
Eggs	41.67	0.647	1.426	1	6 ⅞	8 ¼ oz
Total	161.09	2.500	5.512	5	8 ¼	2 lb

Process, Custard

1. Bring the milk to a boil with the sugar, vanilla bean, and salt.
2. In another bowl whisk the eggs gently.
3. When the milk comes to a boil, remove from the heat and slowly pour the hot milk into the eggs. Strain through a mesh sieve.
4. Fill the cups with the mixture and bake in a water bath at 300°F (149°C) in a convection oven for about 1 hour, or until set.
5. Refrigerate overnight.

Serving

Once set, turn out of the cups onto the serving plate.

FORMULA

POT DE CRÈME

Pot de crème, also called petit pot de crème, is a rich, creamy custard that is named for the container it is normally served in. Pot de crème is an impressive-looking dessert that is convenient to serve for special occasions because it can be made a day ahead.

Chocolate Pot de Crème Formula

Ingredients	Baker's %	Kilogram	US decimal	Lb & Oz		Test
Heavy cream	100.00	1.471	3.243	3	3 ⅞	9 ⅜ oz
Eggs	20.00	0.294	0.649		10 ⅜	1 ⅞ oz
Granulated sugar	20.00	0.294	0.649		10 ⅜	1 ⅞ oz
Cocoa liquor	6.00	0.088	0.195		3 ⅛	⅝ oz
60% chocolate	24.00	0.353	0.778		12 ½	2 ¼ oz
Total	170.00	2.500	5.513	5	8 ¼	1 lb

Process

1. Bring the heavy cream to a boil.
2. Whisk together the eggs and granulated sugar.
3. Temper the egg mixture with the warm cream.
4. Add the hot mixture to the cocoa liquor and chocolate and emulsify with an immersion blender.
5. Pour into molds.
6. Bake at 300°F (149°C) in a bain-marie for about 30 minutes.
7. Cool at room temperature, and refrigerate until needed.
8. Serve with crème Chantilly and fresh fruit or a crisp cookie.

Crème Brûlée

Chocolate Pot de Crème

Crème Caramel

FORMULA

LEMON CURD

Lemon curd, also known as lemon cheese, is a traditional British dessert topping. In late 19th- and early 20th-century England, homemade lemon curd was served with bread or scones at afternoon tea, and was used as a filling for cakes, small pastries, and tarts. Lemon curd is distinct from lemon filling or custard, in that it contains a higher proportion of lemon juice and zest, which gives it a much more intense lemon flavor.

Ingredients	Baker's %	Kilogram	US decimal	Lb & Oz	Test
Sugar	100.00	1.238	2.730	2 11 ⅝	13 ¼ oz
Egg yolks	48.89	0.605	1.335	1 5 ⅜	6 ½ oz
Lemon juice	50.00	0.619	1.365	1 5 ⅞	6 ⅝ oz
Lemon zest	3.33	0.041	0.091	1 ½	½ oz
Butter	40.00	0.495	1.092	1 1 ½	5 ¼ oz
Total	242.22	3.000	6.613	6 9 ¾	2 lb

Process

1. Combine the sugar, yolks, lemon juice, and lemon zest in a stainless steel bowl and place over a double boiler. Stir occasionally.
2. Once done, the mixture will be thick like ketchup.
3. Remove from the heat, strain into a clean container, and add the butter at 90°F (25°C) to 95°F (32°C) with an immersion blender.
4. Cover to the surface and reserve in the refrigerator.

FORMULA

CHEESECAKE

Cheesecake is believed to have originated in ancient Greece, where it was served to athletes during the first Olympic Games held in 776 BCE. The Romans spread cheesecake from Greece across Europe, whose immigrants eventually brought it to the United States. Cream cheese, the most popular cheese used for making cheesecake today, was invented by American dairymen, who were trying to recreate the French cheese, Neufchâtel. When James L. Kraft invented pasteurized cheese in 1912, with pasteurized Philadelphia cream cheese following close on its heels, the making of cheesecakes in America accelerated significantly. Cheesecakes are esteemed for their incredible richness and endless variations.

Graham Cracker Crust Formula

Ingredients	Baker's %	Kilogram	US decimal	Lb & Oz		Test
Graham cracker crumbs	100.00	0.827	1.822	1	13 ⅛	6 oz
Granulated sugar	33.00	0.273	0.601		9 ⅝	2 oz
Butter	48.40	0.400	0.882		14 ⅛	3 oz
Total	181.40	1.500	3.306	3	4 ⅞	12 oz

Yield: 5 crusts at 10.75 oz (0.300 kg) each
Test: 1 crust at 10.75 oz (0.300 kg) each

Process, Graham Cracker Crust

1. Mix the cracker crumbs and sugar together.
2. Stir in the melted butter and mix until the crumbs are well coated.
3. Press the mixture into the bottom of the cake pans.

Cheesecake Batter Formula

Ingredients	Baker's %	Kilogram	US decimal	Lb & Oz		Test
Cream cheese	100.00	2.580	5.688	5	11	1 lb 2 ¼ oz
Sugar	30.00	0.774	1.706	1	11 ¼	5 ½ oz
Butter, softened	4.80	0.124	0.273		4 ⅜	⅞ oz
Lemon juice	1.90	0.049	0.108		1 ¾	⅜ oz
Vanilla extract	0.90	0.023	0.051		⅞	⅛ oz
Eggs	26.20	0.676	1.490	1	7 ⅞	4 ¾ oz
Heavy cream	8.70	0.224	0.495		7 ⅞	1 ⅝ oz
Sour cream	8.70	0.224	0.495		7 ⅞	1 ⅝ oz
Total	181.20	4.675	10.306	10	4 ⅞	2 lb 1 oz

Yield: 5 [8 inch (20 cm)] cakes
Test: 1 [8 inch (20 cm)] cake at 2 lb (0.935 kg)

Process, Cheesecake Batter

1. Prepare 8 inch (20 cm) pans with pan spray and the graham cracker crust and reserve. The crust should be ¼ inch (0.6 cm) thick on bottom of pan.
2. Using the paddle, cream the cream cheese until smooth. Then add the butter and sugar on medium speed, and mix until smooth. Scrape down the bowl.
3. Add the lemon juice and vanilla and mix on low speed until smooth.
4. Add the eggs in three stages, scraping the bowl between each addition.
5. When the batter is smooth, blend in the heavy cream and sour cream.
6. Place the batter in the pans, 2 lb (0.935 kg) per cake.
7. Place the pans on a sheet pan filled with water.
8. Bake at 325°F (163°C) in a deck oven for 1 hour 15 minutes or until just barely set in the middle. Or, bake at 285°F (140°C) in a convection oven for about 50 minutes.
9. Allow to cool thoroughly before removing from the pan.

Finishing

1. To remove the cake from the pan, place in a bain-marie or warm with a torch.
2. Place the cake on a 9 inch (23 cm) gold board.
3. Apply a thin layer of sour cream to the top (optional) and decorate with fresh fruit.

Cheesecake

FORMULA

BREAD PUDDING

Once known as a poor man's pudding, bread pudding originated in 13th-century England, where it was a popular dessert of its day. It was originally designed as an imaginative use for stale bread, to which sugar, spices, and other ingredients were added. Today's bread puddings are made with either fresh or stale bread soaked in a rich mixture of milk or cream, eggs, sugar, vanilla, and spices, along with a wide array of optional ingredients, including some liquors. Sweet or savory, bread puddings can be steamed or baked and are eaten both hot and cold.

Savory Bread Pudding

Savory Bread Pudding Formula

Ingredients	Baker's %	Kilogram	US decimal	Lb & Oz		Test
Olive oil	2.00	0.016	0.034		½	⅛ oz
Onion, ¼ inch (0.6 cm) dice	15.00	0.117	0.259		4 ⅛	1 ⅛ oz
Garlic, minced	3.00	0.023	0.052		⅞	¼ oz
Salt	0.50	0.004	0.009		⅛	Pinch
Black pepper	0.10	0.001	0.002		< ⅛	Pinch
Eggs	100.00	0.782	1.724	1	11 ⅝	7 ⅜ oz
Cream	70.00	0.547	1.207	1	3 ¼	5 ⅛ oz
Milk	75.00	0.586	1.293	1	4 ⅝	5 ½ oz
Bread, 1 inch (3 cm) cubes	77.00	0.602	1.327	1	5 ¼	5 ⅝ oz
Mozzarella cheese, shredded	32.00	0.250	0.552		8 ⅞	2 ⅜ oz
Parmesan, shredded	9.00	0.070	0.155		2 ½	⅝ oz
Total	383.60	3.000	6.613	6	9 ¾	1 lb 12 ¼ oz

Yield: approximately 15 at 7 oz (200 g) each
Test: approximately 4 at 7 oz (200 g) each

Note
Yields are calculated on the base mixture. The yield will increase if variations are followed.

Process, Savory Bread Pudding

1. Sauté the onions in the oil for 2 minutes, and then add the garlic, salt, and pepper. Set aside to cool.
2. Whisk together the eggs, cream, and milk.
3. Mix in the bread, cheeses, and then the onions.

4. Cover and let stand for at least 1 hour.
5. Deposit into molds and bake at 350°F (177°C) in a convection oven for 30 minutes or until golden brown.

Variations

Prepare and then fold in the following ingredients to make variations on the base. Weights are given based on a full formula or a test batch.

Red Pepper and Artichoke Variation

Ingredients	Baker's %	Kilogram	US decimal	Lb & Oz		Test
Roasted red pepper, diced	100.00	0.375	0.827		13 ¼	3 ½ oz
Artichokes, chopped	100.00	0.375	0.827		13 ¼	3 ½ oz
Total	200.00	0.750	1.653	1	10 ¼	7 oz

Mushroom and Swiss Variation

Ingredients	Baker's %	Kilogram	US decimal	Lb & Oz		Test
Roasted mushrooms	100.00	0.294	0.648		10 ⅜	2 ⅞ oz
Black olives	75.00	0.221	0.486		7 ¾	2 ⅛ oz
Swiss cheese	80.00	0.235	0.519		8 ¼	2 ¼ oz
Total	255.00	0.750	1.653	1	10 ½	7 ⅛ oz

Bacon Cheddar Variation

Ingredients	Baker's %	Kilogram	US decimal	Lb & Oz		Test
Bacon	100.00	0.225	0.496		7 ⅞	3 ½ oz
Cheddar cheese	100.00	0.225	0.496		7 ⅞	3 ½ oz
Total	200.00	0.450	0.992		15 ⅞	7 oz

FORMULA

FRENCH MERINGUE

French meringue, also referred to as a common meringue, is a versatile preparatiom. Made with more sugar than egg whites, French meringue is usually baked for meringue cookies or toppings.

Ingredients	Baker's %	Kilogram	US decimal	Lb & Oz	Test
Egg whites	100.00	0.900	1.984	1 15 ¾	12 ¾ oz
Sugar	100.00	0.900	1.984	1 15 ¾	12 ¾ oz
Powdered sugar	50.00	0.450	0.992	15 ⅞	6 ⅜ oz
Total	250.00	2.250	4.960	4 15 ⅜	2 lb

Process

1. Sift the powdered sugar and reserve.
2. Warm the egg whites to 60°F (16°C) to 65°F (18°C).
3. Add about one-third of the sugar to the egg whites and whip until stiff peaks.
4. Add the remaining sugar quickly and turn off the machine.
5. Gently fold in the sifted powdered sugar and pipe as needed.
6. To reserve a meringue that is not being actively used, hold by continuously whipping on low speed.
7. Bake the meringue at 200°F (93°C) for about 2 hours or until dry.

FORMULA

ITALIAN MERINGUE

Based on a cooked sugar syrup and egg whites, Italian meringue can be used for a multitude of applications from decoration to components of mousse cakes.

Ingredients	Baker's %	Kilogram	US decimal	Lb & Oz	Test
Sugar	200.00	1.803	3.972	3 15 ½	1 lb 1 ¾ oz
Water	60.00	0.540	1.192	1 3 ⅛	5 ⅜ oz
Egg whites	100.00	0.900	1.986	1 15 ¾	8 ⅞ oz
Total	360.00	3.243	7.150	7 2 ⅜	2 lb

Process

1. Heat the sugar and water on the stove until it reaches the boiling point.
2. Wash down the sides of the pan with plain water.
3. When the sugar reaches 240°F (116°C), whip the egg whites on second speed.
4. When the sugar reaches 246°F (119°C) to 250°F (121°C), slowly pour it down the side of the mixing bowl, into the whipping egg whites.
5. Whip until room temperature, or desired temperature.
6. To reserve a meringue that is not being actively used, hold by continuously whipping on low speed.

FORMULA

SWISS MERINGUE

Swiss meringue has a firmer texture than French meringue and is often used for making decorations or as the base for desserts.

Ingredients	Baker's %	Kilogram	US decimal	Lb & Oz	Test
Sugar	200.00	1.800	3.967	3 15 ½	1 lb 5 ⅜ oz
Egg whites	100.00	0.900	1.983	1 15 ¾	10 ⅝ oz
Total	300.00	2.700	5.950	5 15 ¼	2 lb

Process

1. Combine the egg whites and sugar in a mixing bowl.
2. Place the bowl over a bain-marie until it reaches at least 120°F (49°C), whipping constantly to avoid cooking the egg whites.
3. Transfer to a mixer and whip on medium-high speed until the meringue has reached full volume and cooled to room temperature.
4. Pipe as desired and bake in a low oven [200°F (93°C)] until dry and crisp (2 hours minimum).

Piping Meringue

FORMULA

CLASSIC CHOCOLATE BUTTERCREAM

Classic buttercream is the icing most Americans expect to find on a cake. Simple in preparation, classic buttercream has a dense, slightly grainy texture. This version is flavored with dark chocolate.

Ingredients	Baker's %	Kilogram	US decimal	Lb & Oz		Test
Butter	100.00	2.223	4.901	4	14 ⅜	14 ¼ oz
Powdered sugar	75.00	1.667	3.676	3	10 ⅞	10 ⅝ oz
Egg whites, pasteurized	11.60	0.258	0.569		9 ⅛	1 ⅝ oz
Vanilla extract	0.80	0.018	0.039		⅝	⅛ oz
Semi-sweet chocolate	37.50	0.834	1.838	1	13 ⅜	5 ⅜ oz
Total	224.90	5.000	11.023	11	⅜	2 lb

Process

1. Add the egg whites and vanilla and incorporate well.
2. Mix at high speed until light.
3. Melt the chocolate in the microwave or over a bain-marie to 120°F (49°C).
4. Temper one-fourth of the icing into the chocolate and whisk to combine.
5. Mix the chocolate icing mixture back into the remaining icing and mix until smooth.

Note

Plain buttercream can be made by eliminating the chocolate.

FORMULA

FRENCH BUTTERCREAM

The French version of buttercream is based on the pâte à bombe and achieves exceptional richness with the use of egg yolks. It has a shorter shelf life than the classic buttercream and is customarily used as a filling for cakes.

Ingredients	Baker's %	Kilogram	US decimal	Lb & Oz	Test
Sugar	45.00	1.220	2.689	2 11	7 ¾ oz
Water	12.50	0.339	0.747	12	2 ⅛ oz
Egg yolks	27.00	0.732	1.613	1 9 ¾	4 ⅝ oz
Butter	100.00	2.710	5.975	5 15 ⅝	1 lb 1 ⅜ oz
Total	184.50	5.000	11.023	11 ⅜	2 lb

Process

1. In a saucepan, heat the sugar and water as for pâte à bombe.
2. In a mixing bowl with the whip attachment, mix the egg yolks to lighten the texture.
3. When the sugar reaches the soft ball stage [244°F (118°C)], slowly pour the sugar into the whipping egg yolks, and whip until cool.
4. Add the softened butter, and mix enough to ensure good emulsion of the buttercream.

FORMULA

ITALIAN BUTTERCREAM

This buttercream is very light, based on an Italian meringue. It has a smooth, light, and airy texture and is more stable than the French buttercream.

Ingredients	Baker's %	Kilogram	US decimal	Lb & Oz	Test
Egg whites	50.00	0.926	2.041	2 ⅝	5 ⅞ oz
Sugar	90.00	1.667	3.674	3 10 ¾	10 ⅝ oz
Water	30.00	0.556	1.225	1 3 ⅝	3 ½ oz
Butter	100.00	1.852	4.083	4 1 ⅜	11 ⅞ oz
Total	270.00	5.000	11.023	11 ⅜	2 lb

Process

1. Prepare to make an Italian meringue with the egg whites, sugar, and water.
2. Combine the sugar and water and cook to 250°F (121°C) (firm ball stage).
3. Wash down the sides of the pot with water to prevent crystallization.
4. When the sugar reaches 240°F (116°C), begin whipping the egg whites on medium-high speed.
5. Once the sugar is at the proper temperature, pour slowly onto the whipping egg whites.
6. Let the mixture mix until it is room temperature, and then add the soft butter.
7. Mix until butter is fully incorporated and mixture is light and fluffy.
8. Store in the refrigerator until ready to use.

Flavor Variation Guidelines

The following flavor variations are based on the total percentage of the buttercream.

Flavor Variations	**%**
64% chocolate	20
Praline paste	10–15
Chocolate liquor	12
Coffee extract	3–4

FORMULA

CRÈME ANGLAISE–STYLE BUTTERCREAM

Some believe this is the best buttercream of them all when it comes to flavor. The balance of the thickness of butter and the lightness of meringue gives this buttercream its outstanding texture.

Custard Base Formula

Ingredients	Baker's %	Kilogram	US decimal	Lb & Oz	Test
Whole milk	100.00	0.562	1.239	1 3 ⅞	3 ⅝ oz
Egg yolks	77.00	0.433	0.954	15 ¼	2 ¾ oz
Sugar	100.00	0.562	1.239	1 3 ⅞	3 ⅝ oz
Total	277.00	1.557	3.432	3 6 ⅞	10 oz

Process, Custard Base

1. In a saucepan, heat the milk.
2. In a mixing bowl, combine the egg yolks and sugar.
3. When the milk boils, temper it into the egg yolk–sugar mixture.
4. Return this to the stove and cook until 180°F (82°C), as for a crème Anglaise.

5. Strain through a chinois into a mixer fitted with the whip. Whip on medium speed until cool.
6. See Final Buttercream Formula for the finishing of the cream.

Italian Meringue Formula

Ingredients	Baker's %	Kilogram	US decimal	Lb & Oz		Test
Water	60.00	0.077	0.171		2 ¾	1 ⅛ oz
Sugar #1	200.00	0.258	0.569		9 ⅛	3 ¾ oz
Egg whites	100.00	0.129	0.284		4 ½	1 ⅞ oz
Sugar #2	12.00	0.015	0.034		½	¼ oz
Total	372.00	0.480	1.058	1	⅞	7 oz

Process, Italian Meringue

1. In a saucepan, prepare the first sugar and the water as for Italian meringue.
2. In a mixing bowl with the whip attachment, begin to whip the egg whites with the second sugar when the sugar is cooked to the thread stage 241°F (116°C).
3. When the sugar reaches firm ball stage 250°F (121°C), slowly pour the sugar down the side of the mixing bowl.
4. Whip until cool. See Final Buttercream Formula for the finishing of the cream.

Final Buttercream Formula

Ingredients	Baker's %	Kilogram	US decimal	Lb & Oz		Test
Custard base	66.00	1.557	3.432	3	6 ⅞	10 oz
Butter	100.00	2.358	5.200	5	3 ¼	15 ⅛ oz
Italian meringue	46.00	1.085	2.392	2	6 ¼	7 oz
Total	212.00	5.000	11.023	11	⅜	2 lb

Process, Final Buttercream

1. Add the soft butter a small amount at a time to the cool, whipping custard base.
2. Continue to whip until the mixture is smooth and well emulsified.
3. Add the Italian meringue and mix to incorporate.

FORMULA

CHOCOLATE GLAZE

This glaze can be used in a variety of applications in the kitchen, even as the chocolate for mocha espresso drinks. To achieve the desired results for this glaze, it is vitally important to choose the proper chocolate, using the specified cocoa content.

Ingredients	Baker's %	Kilogram	US decimal	Lb & Oz		Test
Simple syrup	50.00	1.174	2.588	2	9 ⅜	7 ½ oz
35% cream	50.50	1.185	2.613	2	9 ⅞	7 ⅝ oz
Glucose	12.50	0.293	0.647		10 ⅜	1 ⅞ oz
Coating chocolate	37.50	0.880	1.941	1	15	5 ⅝ oz
64% chocolate	62.50	1.467	3.234	3	3 ¾	9 ⅜ oz
Total	213.00	5.000	11.023	11	⅜	2 lb

Note
The combined weight for the two chocolates equals 100 percent.

Process

1. Prepare the simple syrup and reserve.
2. Bring the cream and the glucose to a boil.
3. Chop (if in block form) the chocolates and place in a bowl.
4. Pour the boiling liquids (cream–glucose and simple syrup) over the chocolates, and let stand for 2 minutes.
5. With an immersion blender or rubber spatula, form an emulsion. Do not use a whisk, as it will incorporate air bubbles.
6. Cover to the surface with plastic wrap and store in the refrigerator.
7. When needed, reheat in microwave or over a bain-marie to pouring consistency.

Simple Syrup Formula

Ingredients	Baker's %	Kilogram	US decimal	Lb & Oz		Test
Sugar	100.00	0.587	1.294	1	4 ¾	3 ¾ oz
Water	100.00	0.587	1.294	1	4 ¾	3 ¾ oz
Total	200.00	1.174	2.588	2	9 ⅜	7 ½ oz

Process

1. Combine the water and sugar, and wash down the sides of the pot.
2. Bring to a boil, cover, and reserve.

FORMULA

BLACK GLAZE

Similar to chocolate glaze, but made with a small portion of black cocoa powder, black glaze achieves a compellingly dark color.

Ingredients	Baker's %	Kilogram	US decimal	Lb & Oz	Test
35% cream	54.00	1.204	2.654	2 10 ½	7 ¾ oz
Glucose	12.75	0.284	0.627	10	1 ⅞ oz
Black cocoa powder	5.00	0.111	0.246	3 ⅞	¾ oz
Simple syrup	52.50	1.171	2.581	2 9 ¼	7 ½ oz
64% chocolate	67.00	1.494	3.293	3 4 ¾	9 ½ oz
Coating chocolate	33.00	0.736	1.622	1 10	4 ¾ oz
Total	224.25	5.000	11.023	11 ⅜	2 lb

Note
The combined weight for the two chocolates equals 100 percent.

Process

1. Prepare the simple syrup for black glaze. Add the black cocoa powder and emulsify well; reserve.
2. Bring the cream and the glucose to a boil.
3. Chop the chocolates and place in a bowl.
4. Pour the boiling liquids (cream–glucose and simple syrup) over the chocolates, and let stand for 2 minutes.
5. With an immersion blender or rubber spatula, form an emulsion. Do not use a whisk, as it will incorporate air bubbles.
6. Cover to the surface with plastic wrap and store in the refrigerator.
7. When needed, reheat in microwave or over a bain-marie to pouring consistency.

Simple Syrup for Black Glaze Formula

Ingredients	Baker's %	Kilogram	US decimal	Lb & Oz	Test
Water	100.00	0.478	1.053	1 ⅞	3 oz
Sugar	115.00	0.549	1.211	1 3 ⅜	3 ½ oz
Glucose	30.00	0.143	0.316	5	⅞ oz
Total	245.00	1.171	2.581	2 9 ¼	7 ½ oz

Process, Simple Syrup for Black Glaze

1. Combine the water, sugar, and glucose, and wash down the sides of the pot.
2. Bring to a boil, cover, and reserve.

FORMULA

NAPPAGE

This glaze creates the nice shine necessary for fruit tarts and similar desserts. This glaze is made with pectin NH, which is critical to its success, as the pectin is thermoreversible. This glaze also freezes well.

Ingredients	Baker's %	Kilogram	US decimal	Lb & Oz		Test
Water	100.00	3.378	7.448	7	7 ⅛	1 lb 5 ⅝ oz
Used vanilla pods	Each	10	10		10	2 each
Sugar	40.00	1.351	2.979	2	15 ⅝	8 ⅝ oz
Pectin NH	4.00	0.135	0.298		4 ¾	⅞ oz
Lemon juice	4.00	0.135	0.298		4 ¾	⅞ oz
Total	148.00	5.000	11.023	11	⅜	2 lb

Process

1. Combine the water with the used vanilla pods in a stainless steel pot and bring to a boil.
2. Combine one-fourth of the sugar with the pectin NH and add to the water once it is 150°F (65°C), while stirring constantly with a whisk.
3. Add the remaining sugar over several minutes while whisking the mixture.
4. Once the mixture has boiled, remove from the heat, add the lemon juice, and cover with plastic film for 30 minutes.
5. Reboil the nappage, strain through a fine mesh chinois, and reserve in the refrigerator until needed.
6. To use, warm on the stove top or in a microwave until fluid.

FORMULA

ROYAL ICING

Royal icing is a hard white icing that is generally used for decoration only. Its taste is not comparable to other icings, but it serves its purpose well in decoration, where it hardens to a smooth and beautiful shine. Royal icing has been classically employed in decorating wedding cakes.

Ingredients	Baker's %	Kilogram	US decimal	Lb & Oz		Test
Powdered sugar	100.00	2.542	5.604	5	9 ⅝	1 lb 11 ⅛ oz
Egg whites	17.00	0.432	0.953		15 ¼	4 ⅝ oz
Lemon juice	1.00	0.025	0.056		⅞	¼ oz
Total	118.00	3.000	6.613	6	9 ¾	2 lb

Process

1. Sift the powdered sugar and place it in a mixing bowl fitted with the paddle.
2. While mixing, slowly add the egg whites and then the lemon juice. For a stiffer consistency, add less egg white; for a thinner consistency, add more.
3. For storage, cover to the surface with a moist paper towel, and cover the container with plastic wrap.

FORMULA

FLAT ICING

Flat icing is one of the simplest icings in concept and preparation. The basic ingredients of flat icing are powdered sugar and water. Flat icing can be used as the glaze on rolls, Danish, and other pastries in place of fondant. Flavorings such as citrus juices or zest can make interesting variations.

Ingredients	Baker's %	Kilogram	US decimal	Lb & Oz		Test
Powdered sugar	100.00	2.564	5.652	5	10 ⅜	1 lb 11 ⅜ oz
Lemon juice	3.00	0.077	0.170		2 ¾	⅞ oz
Water, hot	14.00	0.359	0.791		12 ⅝	3 ⅞ oz
Total	117.00	3.000	6.613	6	9 ¾	2 lb

Process

1. Sift the powdered sugar and add the water and lemon juice to it.
2. Blend carefully with a rubber spatula (by hand) or paddle attachment (by machine) so as not to incorporate air. Reserve until needed.
3. The icing can be thicker or thinner by adjusting the quantity of water.
4. Milk or juice, such as lemon or orange, may be substituted for the water.

CHAPTER SUMMARY

The preparations presented in this chapter cover a broad range of products, all bound together in that they are building blocks on one another, as well as for other work with pastry. Understanding the processes for making these sugar syrups, creams, egg foams, and icings is critical in order to work with pastry on more advanced levels. Because many of these preparations are ready to eat, it is essential that proper sanitation, hygiene, and storage procedures are practiced at all times. When one knows how to easily make and troubleshoot these base creams, icings, and egg foams, one has the tools to make an unlimited number of preparations.

KEY TERMS

- ❖ Almond cream
- ❖ Baked custard
- ❖ Basic buttercream
- ❖ Baumé
- ❖ Bread pudding
- ❖ Cake syrup
- ❖ Chocolate glaze
- ❖ Common meringue
- ❖ Cooked-stirred custard
- ❖ Crème Anglaise
- ❖ Crème Anglaise–style buttercream
- ❖ Crème brûlèe
- ❖ Crème caramel
- ❖ Crème Chantilly
- ❖ Crème Chiboust
- ❖ Crème St. Honoré
- ❖ Crystallization
- ❖ Custard base
- ❖ Diplomat cream
- ❖ Egg foam
- ❖ Flat icing
- ❖ Fondant
- ❖ Frangipane
- ❖ French buttercream
- ❖ French meringue
- ❖ Fruit glaze
- ❖ Ganache
- ❖ Icing
- ❖ Italian buttercream
- ❖ Italian meringue
- ❖ Meringue
- ❖ Pastry cream
- ❖ Pâte à bombe
- ❖ Pot de crème
- ❖ Royal icing
- ❖ Simple syrup
- ❖ Sugar syrup
- ❖ Swiss buttercream
- ❖ Swiss meringue
- ❖ Syneresis
- ❖ 30 baumé syrup
- ❖ Whipped cream
- ❖ Whipped topping

REVIEW QUESTIONS

1. **What is baumé? How is it controlled?**
2. **How is pastry cream prepared? What precautions must be taken?**
3. **What is the process for making crème Anglaise? What special precautions should be taken?**
4. **What are the baking guidelines for baked custards?**
5. **What effect does sugar have on egg whites in a French meringue at a 1 : 1 ratio and at a 2 : 1 ratio (egg white to sugar)?**
6. **What is the process for making an Italian buttercream?**

chapter
16

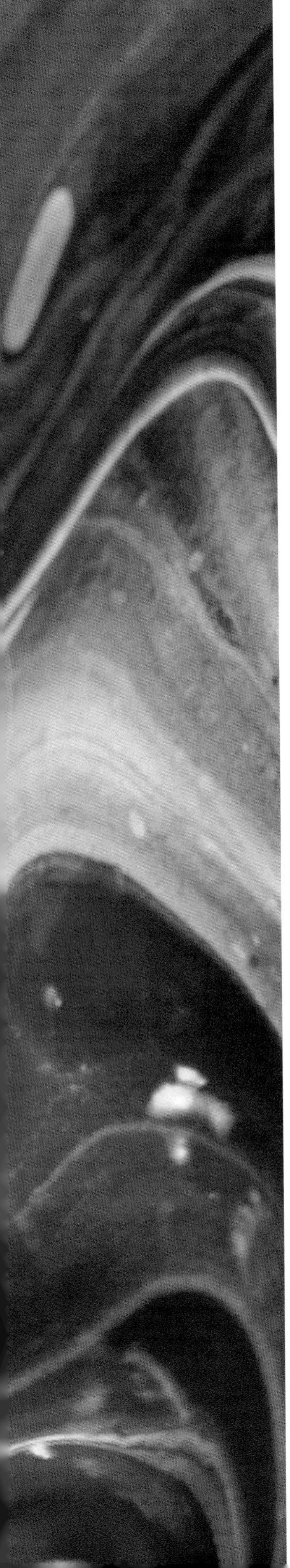

MOUSSE

OBJECTIVES

After reading this chapter, you should be able to

- explain the theory and principles regarding the components of mousse and the three major categories of mousse preparation.
- practice proper hygiene and sanitation guidelines required for working with ready-to-eat foods.
- successfully create a variety of mousse for cakes and desserts including Bavarian cream, fruit mousse, and chocolate mousse.
- troubleshoot mousse formulas and preparations for balance of ingredients and components.

HISTORY AND DEFINITION OF MOUSSE

Mousse preparations have been around since at least the mid-1800s. Fannie Farmer's 1896 cookbook includes formulas for strawberry and coffee mousse preparations and in 1918 presents the first formula for chocolate mousse.

Mousse preparations may be sweet or savory, hot or cold, but the texture should always be light. Sweet mousses are generally built on a base preparation of chocolate or fruit puree, with the addition of egg foam and/or whipped cream to lighten the mousse to its characteristic texture. Sweet mousse can be presented in many different ways: It may be a cake filling, or even the cake in its entirety. In fact, mousse cakes are becoming an increasingly popular alternative to the classic buttercream cake.

Sweet mousse preparations can be divided into three main categories: fruit mousse, chocolate mousse, and Bavarian cream. These categories of mousse are largely defined by their ingredients and base preparations. For example, fruit mousse and chocolate mousse are typically based on fruit puree or chocolate, respectively, as well as an egg foam, whipped cream, and gelatin. A Bavarian is based on a crème Anglaise, whipped cream, and gelatin. In this chapter, we will explore the components of each category of mousse preparation, as well as the processes required to make them.

MOUSSE: HYGIENE AND SANITATION

Before exploring the components and processes for mousse, we must first consider hygiene and sanitation. As with any ready-to-eat food, but especially with mousse-like preparations, the most stringent measures of sanitation must be followed. All equipment must be well cleaned and cross contamination from dirty hands or equipment must be avoided as bacteria flourish in the wet, sweet environment of mousse preparations. Gloves should be worn, clean utensils should always be used, and ingredients must be very fresh to ensure safety.

INTRODUCTION TO THE COMPONENTS OF MOUSSE

When making a mousse, one must balance flavors, textures, and setting properties through careful preparation of appropriate components. Although each type of mousse requires a different combination, the primary list includes the base, the egg foam, a setting agent, and whipped cream. Factors such as the cocoa content of the chocolate and the degree of sweetness of the base and egg foam each have a role in the overall composition.

THE BASE

As mentioned earlier, a mousse always contains a **base** preparation that is further developed to create the final product. Additional components of the mousse act as a lightening agents, which may also add sweetness. The type of base and its composition will influence the type of egg foam used and how much, if any, gelatin is required. A base can include preparations of fruit puree, cooked-stirred custards such as crème Anglaise and pastry cream, or a ganache.

Fruit Puree

Fresh or frozen fruit puree is typically the primary base for a fruit mousse. Some variations may be based on a crème Anglaise made with fruit puree, or a mixture of fruit puree and cream. However, this version of a fruit mousse requires cooking, which diminishes some of the delicate fruit flavor and colors.

As a base ingredient, the primary function of the fruit puree is to add flavor. A small quantity of lemon juice (about 5 percent, based on the weight of the puree) may be added to the fruit puree base to increase acidity and bring out the flavors of the fruit. Fresh fruit or a high-quality frozen puree may be used, both of which can make a very good mousse if handled properly. If using fresh fruit, the fruit should be as ripe as possible to obtain the best flavor and color. Whether fresh or frozen, fruit should be made into mousse immediately after it is pureed. Sitting too long can cause oxidization that will negatively affect the flavor, color, and quality.

Cooked-Stirred Custards

Crème Anglaise and pastry cream bases add specific texture and creaminess to the mousse preparation. Pastry cream, the heavier and thicker of the two, will require more lightening agents to create a more supple texture. Conversely, a mousse preparation with crème Anglaise will require more setting agent to create a mousse that can be contained within its own walls. As they are often on hand, both make very convenient bases for last-minute preparations.

The composition of a crème Anglaise or pastry cream for use in mousse cakes can vary greatly, depending on the additional components. The quantity of ingredients such as egg yolk, sugar, and butter will depend on their presence in the mousse's other components. For example, a custard-based, white chocolate mousse will require a different quantity of sugar than a custard-based, 64 percent chocolate mousse.

Ganache

When making a chocolate mousse, if the chocolate is added to the mousse improperly or at the wrong time, it will negatively affect the texture and volume of the final product. To ensure success, chocolate first needs to be transformed into a creamy texture that will ensure the smooth incorporation of other components. **Ganache**, the result of a liquid and chocolate **emulsion**, is the typical base. An emulsion is the result of two or more liquids combining to create a smooth mixture. The most common example of an emulsion is mayonnaise. There are two types of emulsions possible: a water in oil emulsion and an oil in water emulsion. Emulsions can be very stable and they can be very unstable. A ganache is an example of a water in oil emulsion, which can be considered semistable. Ganache is an extremely versatile product that can also be used for the fillings of chocolate candies, cakes, and cookies. Refer to Chapter 22 for a more detailed look at chocolate ganache.

Several factors, including temperature, viscosity, and emulsion, are important when using a ganache for a mousse. The quality of the emulsion determines the texture of the ganache, which is typically controlled by the ratio of cream to chocolate, in addition to the cocoa percent. For example, when using a 1:1 ratio of cream to chocolate, if using a chocolate with a higher cocoa percentage, it will lead to a firmer ganache.

Because some chocolates contain unknown fat quantities, a higher or lower ratio of cream to chocolate may need to be used to create a stable emulsion and an appropriate texture for the ganache base. One needs to determine the proper balance of fats and cocoa solids within the cream and the chocolate in order to create a stable emulsion and a ganache that has enough body to elaborate the mouse.

The viscosity of the ganache will dictate additional ingredients and their functions in the mousse. If a ganache is made using a higher ratio of cream to chocolate, a higher quantity of additional setting agents (other than the cocoa butter in the chocolate) will be required. The resulting mousse will be lighter in texture and chocolate flavor.

EGG FOAMS

Egg foams add lightness and volume to mousse cakes. Italian meringue and pâte à bombe are the most popular. French or common meringues are sometimes used, but they are less stable than cooked egg foams and may contain microorganisms such as *Salmonella.* See Chapter 15 for more information on egg foams.

The type of mousse and its main ingredients will determine the type of egg foam used. For fruit mousse, the typical egg foam is the Italian meringue. Its light texture adds a delicate sweetness to a fruit mousse, and it is not as vulnerable to a loss of volume as a common meringue. In addition, the pure white color of an Italian meringue lends itself well to the final color of the preparation. Another, less-used option for fruit mousse cakes is a pâte à bombe, which has a more complex flavor. The egg yolk–based pâte à bombe is high in fats, which lead to a much richer flavor and color. To mask the more intense flavor, pâte à bombe is often used in fruit mousse preparations with more intensely flavored purees such as lemon, passion fruit, grapefruit, or black currant.

For chocolate mousse cakes, the sweetness in the mousse needs to be balanced between the sugar content in the egg foam and the sugar content in the chocolate. Historically, common meringue was the most popular egg foam, but it is not commonly used today due to concerns about harmful bacteria. Instead, pâte à bombe and Italian meringue are primarily used.

Not only does pâte à bombe act as a lightening agent in chocolate mousse, but natural lecithin in the yolk helps to maintain the emulsion by suspending water in the fat content. The soft fats in the yolk also add richness and texture by retarding the rigid setting properties in cocoa butter and providing supple textures to the mousse.

Italian meringue works particularly well in chocolate mousse preparations when a crème Anglaise–based ganache has been made. The sweetness of the crème Anglaise can be adjusted to balance the sweetness of the chocolate as well as the Italian meringue. An Italian meringue will add a greater degree of lightness than a pâte à bombe because the volume achieved by whipping egg whites alone is greater than that of egg yolk.

WHIPPED CREAM

The rich taste and smooth texture of whipped cream, along with its ability to trap air, make it the perfect addition to a mousse. Because whipped fat globules add stability and mouthfeel, the right selection of cream is essential to produce a smooth texture that is strong enough to support itself and the other components of the mousse. As long as the cream is whipped to the proper degree, it will add a smooth and refreshing characteristic.

Selection of Cream

A cream with a minimum fat content of 35 percent should be used to ensure sufficient whipability and strength. A cream with too little fat will not have enough structure to hold its volume or the volume of the mousse. A cream with too high a fat content will tend to whip quickly, and the higher quantity of fat crystals will create a grainy texture that will be carried through to the mousse and create an undesired sensation on the palate. These high-fat creams typically are only available commercially and should not be used for the production of mousse.

Function and Ratio of Cream in Mousse Cakes

While the preparation of whipped cream for mousse cakes is rather straightforward when compared to its other components, the choice of base and egg foam will create a number of variables to consider. The most important of these is the quantity of whipped cream in relation to the base and egg foam.

Higher quantities of whipped cream may thin out the flavors of the base and make the texture of the mousse much lighter, which can be appropriate for purees with a more intense flavor such as passion fruit, black currant, lemon, and lime. For these more concentrated flavors, and for chocolate mousse preparations, the ratio of whipped cream to puree is about 1:1. For milder purees such as raspberry, strawberry, and white peach, the percentage of cream to puree is generally 50 to 70 percent.

Whipped cream is typically added to the base mixture after the egg foam has been folded in to prevent overmixing. As it is folded in, the cream lightens the base preparations, leading to the final texture of the mousse. Care must be taken to initially underwhip the cream and to not overdevelop the cream during the folding-in process in order to prevent the texture from turning grainy.

Whipped cream should always be used cold. When added to fruit mousse, chocolate mousse, and Bavarian creams, it acts as a catalyst to drop the temperature of the preparation and begin the setting properties of the gelatin or cocoa butter.

SETTING AGENTS

All free-standing mousse cakes need some sort of setting agent to ensure they retain their texture and shape. The primary setting agents include gelatin and the cocoa butter contained in chocolate, with the ratio of setting agents to mousse varying with the composition. For example, the percentage of cocoa content and quantity of chocolate in the mousse will determine if additional setting agents are needed. This is particularly important when dealing with chocolate mousse because the cocoa content of chocolate varies considerably by type of chocolate and brand.

When gelatin is necessary, it must always be bloomed and melted before it is added to the mousse. The blooming process moistens the gelatin for even melting. It is advisable to bloom the leaf gelatin in a larger quantities of water in order to avoid transferring any "off" flavors or smells to the mousse. The sheets of gelatin should be separated before being placed in very cold water, which will allow maximum possibility for hydration and prevent dissolving. If powdered gelatin is being used, it should be dissolved in five times its weight in cold water. After the gelatin is softened, it should be strained (gelatin sheets) and then melted and tempered into the mousse. If the gelatin is to be added to a crème Anglaise base, the bloomed, drained gelatin can be added to the hot base and stirred to dissolve.

COMPONENT REQUIREMENTS AND FUNCTIONS

In summary, each of the components of mousse has specific ingredient requirements and functions. A flavorful base is essential for taste that will carry through the mousse preparation. The base will be lightened and volume added with egg foam, typically an Italian meringue, a pâte à bombe, or potentially a common meringue. For whipped cream, a 35 to 40 percent fat content is required. The exact quantity of whipped cream will depend on the other components, along with desired results for flavor and texture, and its development will be tightly controlled to maintain the mousse's smooth texture. If any setting agent is needed, gelatin leaf will be used in just enough quantities to set the mousse.

THE GENERAL PROCESS FOR MOUSSE

Now that we have explored the major components of mousse and their functions, we can look at making mousse in general and then look at the specific processes of producing Bavarian creams, fruit mousse, and chocolate mousse. The most basic elaboration of a mousse always begins with the preparation of the base. The egg foam, if applicable, is added next, and then the whipped cream is folded in. Other ingredients or components may be included at various stages; however, this is the basic preparation.

For the production of any mousse, it is essential to combine or add components at specific times and temperatures. For example, if the gelatin is added when the preparation is too cold, or at the wrong time, it will not disperse evenly throughout the mousse. If the whipped cream is added when the base mixture is too warm, it will melt the fat globules in the cream and there will be a diminished volume and texture. Following the directions in the formulas is critical, as is paying close attention to the temperatures of the components and the physical working of the mousse.

Whenever working on the preparation of mousse cakes, or any pastry for that matter, it is imperative to work cleanly and to start the production of the formula once all ingredients and equipment have been gathered. Because mousse is particularly sensitive to temperature and timing, all components and molds must be ready before elaboration.

BAVARIAN CREAM

DEFINITION, HISTORY, AND USES

Bavarian cream, or Bavarois, is a crème Anglaise that has whipped cream added and is set by gelatin. Although its origin is somewhat mysterious, some believe that the preparation originated in Bavaria, where many French chefs worked for royalty. Carême has formulas for *fromage Bavarois* (Bavarian cheese); however, these preparations are clearly different from the Bavarian we know today (Montagne, 2001, p. 86).

Like many items, Bavarian cream was introduced to France by a member of European royalty—in this case, a Bavarian prince who was a client at Café Procope, one the most famous cafés of the time (Bilheux & Escoffier, 2000, p. 60). A meeting place for intellectuals, writers, revolutionaries, actors, and other notable personalities, the café was the first established coffee house in France and was decorated to appeal to the aristocracy (Montagne, 2001, pp. 937–38).

The original Bavarian creams were very frothy beverages that were often based on an infusion with ferns and later included eggs, yolks, kirsch, and milk (Bilheux & Escoffier, 2000, p. 60). Over the years, Bavarian cream has evolved to be the mousse-like dessert we know today. Bavarian creams are very versatile and are often used in charlottes and Bavarian cakes.

BAVARIAN CREAM: INGREDIENTS AND COMPOSITION

The main ingredients of a Bavarian cream are milk, cream, egg yolks, sugar, and gelatin. Its main components include a crème Anglaise base, gelatin, and whipped cream. The choice for flavoring additives is virtually unlimited and may include chocolate, coffee, caramel, teas, fruit puree, spices, and vanilla.

Composition of the Crème Anglaise

Depending on the flavor of the Bavarois, the crème Anglaise may be differently formulated than a crème Anglaise used for a dessert sauce. The main variables will be the quantity of sugar, as determined by other ingredients such as chocolate, nut paste, and fruit purees, and the quantity of egg yolk as a ratio to the weight of the liquid in the formula. The quantity of egg yolk may fluctuate slightly, but an average range is 20 to 35 percent of the liquid in the formula. Although the thickening and enriching role of the egg yolk is important, using too much may lead to problems like coagulation and an egg taste. If a fruit-based Bavarois is desired, 100 percent fruit puree should be used in place of the liquid in the crème Anglaise preparation in order to obtain full fruit flavor.

Whipped Cream for Bavarians

Unlike other cakes in the mousse category, Bavarian creams always have whipped cream as a main component because it adds lightness to the base. The whipped cream should always be underwhipped to soft peaks, just as for fruit and chocolate mousse. It may be folded into the crème Anglaise base in two stages after the base has reached a temperature of 75°F (24°C) to 85°F (29°C).

Setting Agents for Bavarians

Gelatin is the setting agent used in Bavarian creams. The quantity of gelatin to use as a percentage of the total formula is about 1 percent, or about 3 percent based on the weight of the liquid in the crème Anglaise.

Balancing Sugar in Bavarians

An important step in the success of a Bavarian is balancing the quantities of ingredients in the crème Anglaise, including the sugar and any additional ingredients such as chocolate or praline paste. The fresh flavors of the whipped cream or added flavoring agents should shine and not be overpowered by sweetness. A total sugar content for the finished cream should be in the range of 15 to 25 percent, depending on the flavor preferences of the audience.

BAVARIAN CREAM: PROCESS

The process for Bavarian cream is fairly straightforward. Like all mousse preparations, the gelatin should be bloomed in advance (see Bavarian Cream Figure 16-1, Step 1) and the cream may be whipped to soft peaks and reserved under refrigeration. (See Bavarian Cream Figure 16-1, Step 2.) Next, the crème Anglaise base is made, and the bloomed gelatin is added and stirred to dissolve. After the custard has cooled to 75°F (24°C) to 85°F (29°C), the soft-peak whipped cream is folded in, and the Bavarian cream is deposited into molds. (See Bavarian Cream Figure 16-1, Steps 3–4.)

FIGURE 16-1 BAVARIAN CREAM

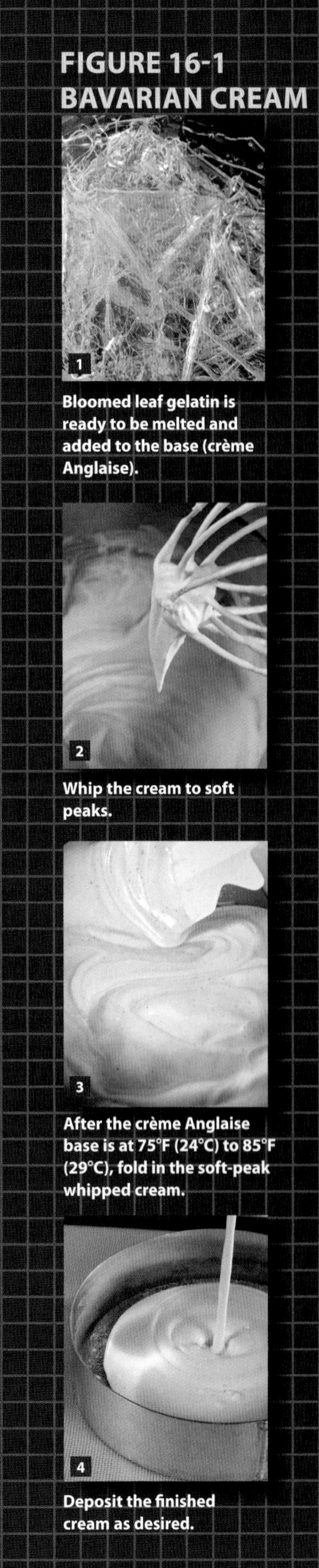

1 Bloomed leaf gelatin is ready to be melted and added to the base (crème Anglaise).

2 Whip the cream to soft peaks.

3 After the crème Anglaise base is at 75°F (24°C) to 85°F (29°C), fold in the soft-peak whipped cream.

4 Deposit the finished cream as desired.

Most variations on this process will happen during the preparation of the crème Anglaise. For a coffee Bavarois, freshly ground coffee can be infused into the liquid ingredients for the custard sauce, or a coffee extract may be used. For a chocolate Bavarois, the chocolate is added to the hot Anglaise and an emulsion is formed before adding the whipped cream. Additional ingredients, such as alcohol, gelée or chocolate pearls, and liquors, may be added after the whipped cream has been folded in.

Process for Bavarian Cream

- Prepare all the molds and scale all the ingredients.
- Bloom the gelatin in cold water.
- Whip the cream to soft peaks and reserve in the refrigerator (or whip just before it is needed).
- Cook the crème Anglaise.
- Add the bloomed, drained gelatin to the crème Anglaise while hot and stir well to incorporate.
- When the base is 75°F (24°C) to 85°F (29°C), finish the whipped cream to soft peaks.
- Fold in the whipped cream in two stages.
- If needed, fold in any additional ingredients.
- Deposit into the molds and place in freezer.

BAVARIAN CREAM: SHELF LIFE

The shelf life of a Bavarian cream is similar to that of a mousse or other fresh cream preparation. The maximum amount of time under refrigeration should be 48 hours, and a well-wrapped cake may be frozen for up to 2 weeks with good results.

FRUIT MOUSSE

Fruit mousse cakes offer an opportunity to create seasonal cakes or desserts using fresh local fruits as the base of their creations. The end result is a light, fruit-flavored cream that dissolves in the mouth and leaves a fresh taste of the season. Rather than relying on fresh fruit to use as the base, a consistent and popular option is to use high-quality, commercially made frozen fruit purees.

Fruit mousse is usually composed of a base, an egg foam, whipped cream, and a setting agent, the selection of which will have an effect on the final texture and flavor. This section will explore the formulation and process of making fruit mousse.

ASSEMBLING THE COMPONENTS FOR A FRUIT MOUSSE

The type of fruit used will dictate how to prepare it for the base. For berries and fruit with small seeds, puree and then strain the fruit through a chinois. For pit fruits such as nectarines or apricots, peel the fruit, remove the pit, and puree it. There is no need to strain pit fruits. Process the fruit just before starting the preparation and then store it covered and in the refrigerator until needed. If using a frozen fruit puree, defrost it in the refrigerator overnight.

One of the first steps in mousse preparation is to prewhip the cream to soft peaks and to return it to the refrigerator. Some may prefer to whip the cream to soft peak just before incorporation into the final mousse; however, the number of mixing bowls that are available is sometimes a consideration in when the cream is whipped. Whipping should stop once it has gained volume and the trail of the whisk can barely be seen on the surface of the cream. It is always better to underwhip the cream for finishing later.

The next step is to prepare the Italian meringue and bloom the gelatin in very cold water until it is soft. Once softened, it can be held off to the side until it is needed in the formula.

When the meringue is in its last minutes of whipping, the gelatin can be melted and added into the fruit puree base. (See Fruit Mousse Figure 16-2, Step 1.) To ensure even distribution, this is best done by a process of tempering.

A small portion of the puree (about five times the quantity of gelatin) should be heated to about 115°F (46°C). Separately, the gelatin should be melted to about the same temperature. This can be done in a microwave or bain-marie. At this point, the melted gelatin can easily be incorporated into the warmed puree, and then added to the remaining fruit puree base and fully incorporated.

When the Italian meringue is lukewarm, it can be folded into the base. (See Fruit Mousse Figure 16-2, Step 2.) To ensure that maximum volume will be retained in the mousse, light components such as Italian meringue or whipped cream should be folded in using a two-stage process. Some like to incorporate the first addition of Italian meringue with a whisk until fully mixed and then fold in the rest with a rubber spatula in two stages.

The temperature of the fruit mousse preparation should still be about 80°F (27°C) to 85°F (29°C), at which point the cream can be whipped to its final consistency of soft peaks. (See Fruit Mousse Figure 16-2, Step 3.) The cream will further develop as it is folded into the mousse in a couple of stages, and it should be mixed in just until there are no more streaks of white. At this point the mousse is ready to be molded. (See Fruit Mousse Figure 16-2, Steps 4–5.)

Fruit Mousse Process

- Prepare the cake rings or molds.
- Prepare the fruit puree as required.
- Whip the cream to soft peaks.
- Bloom the gelatin.
- Make the Italian meringue.
- Add the gelatin to the base.
- Fold the Italian meringue into the base in two or three stages.
- Fold in the whipped cream in two stages.
- Deposit the mousse into the cake rings or molds and freeze.

CHOCOLATE MOUSSE

Chocolate mousse can be a rich, intoxicating rush of chocolate with smooth flavors and a creamy mouthfeel. There are numerous preparations and formulas for chocolate mousse, from a simple combination of crème Chantilly and ganache to a formulation of several elements such

FIGURE 16-2 FRUIT MOUSSE

1 Add the bloomed, melted gelatin to the base.

2 Using a whisk, gently whip in the Italian meringue.

3 Add the whipped cream in two stages.

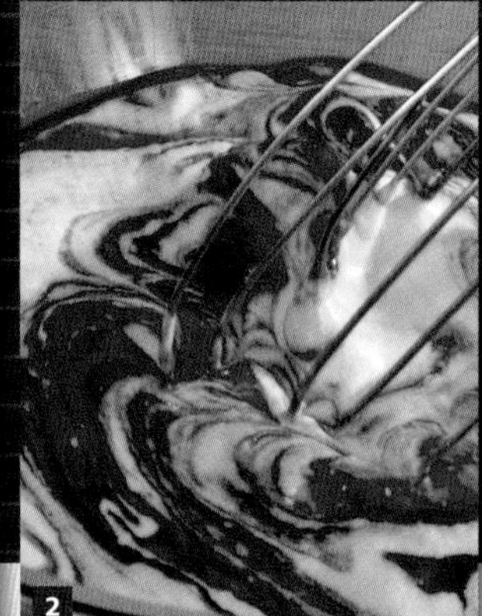

as ganache, various egg foams (pâte à bombe, Italian meringue, Swiss meringue, and common meringue), and whipped cream. Numerous options for composition and flavor development can be created from the three major categories of chocolate—white, milk, and dark.

Because there are several key variables concerning cocoa content alone, one must understand the working properties of chocolate in order to have consistent results. For a detailed look at chocolate, refer to Chapter 22. Whatever preparation is chosen, the formulas and processes are all bound by common practices and techniques.

ESSENTIAL GUIDELINES FOR CHOCOLATE MOUSSE

To make a successful chocolate mousse, specific guidelines should be followed in the following areas:

- Ingredients and formulation
- Temperature
- Emulsion
- Handling and sanitation

Ingredients and Formulation

The quality of ingredients used in a chocolate mousse will be evident in its final structure and flavor. In particular, the percentages of cocoa butter and cocoa content in chocolate provide essential functions in the mousse, including setting properties, workability, and mouthfeel. If a couverture-grade chocolate is not used, for example, the chocolate may not be supple enough, and other hard fats in the preparation may interfere with the makeup process and have a negative effect on mouthfeel and flavor. In addition to the texture of the final product, the percentage of cocoa will affect the quantity of chocolate and additional sweet elements such as pâte à bombe and Italian meringue.

As previously discussed, successful chocolate mousse is always based on a ganache because decrystallizing the cocoa butter (which contains hard crystalline fats) before elaboration enables easy incorporation of the remaining components. The ganache may be made with milk, pastry cream, cream, or crème Anglaise. Each liquid contains a different amount

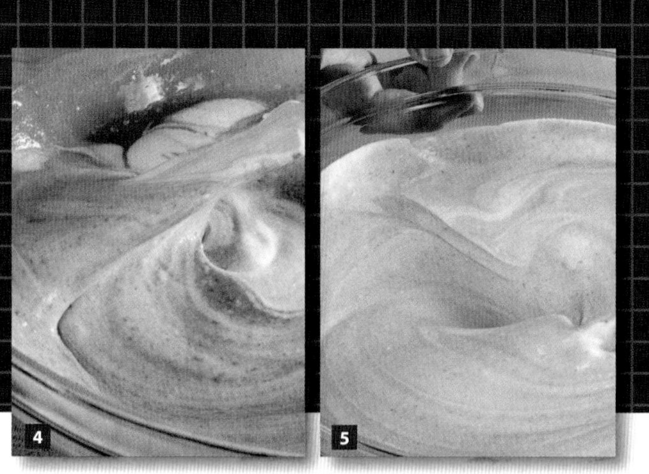

4 Fold the whipped cream in gently with a spatula.

5 When no streaks of cream can be seen, the mousse is ready for depositing.

and variety of fats that will affect the texture of the ganache and ultimately the final mousse texture.

As for the egg foam component, pâte à bombe adds a rich flavor, and the egg yolks help maintain a smooth emulsion. For these reasons, it is commonly used in chocolate mousse. Italian meringue may also be used; however, due to its lighter nature, it will provide somewhat more lightening capacity than the pâte à bombe. Some mousse may be made without an egg foam.

Almost all chocolate mousse calls for whipped cream with a 35 to 40 percent fat content. The quantity of whipped cream added will thin the network of cocoa butter–setting properties, yet the developed cream should have enough strength from the developed fats to hold its own weight. As with fruit mousse, the temperature will drop and the final process of depositing the mousse should begin after the soft-peak whipped cream is incorporated.

Depending on the type and quantity of chocolate used for a mousse, additional setting agents may be required. A dark chocolate mousse should be able to set on its own, whereas white and milk chocolate mousse cakes generally require the addition of gelatin to ensure proper setting and texture. The quantity of gelatin will vary by process and the quantity of cocoa butter in the formula, but, in general, the lower the cocoa content, the higher the amount of alternative setting agents that will be needed for the final product.

Cocoa Percent and Sugar in Chocolate Mousse Formulas

The brand, percentage of cocoa, and type of chocolate are important considerations when determining the quantity of chocolate required for a mousse. The higher the percentage of cocoa is, the less chocolate will be required to substantiate a full chocolate flavor and set a specific amount of the mousse. Particular attention must be paid to the amount of chocolate used because the cocoa butter in it is the major setting agent for chocolate mousse cake. As a rule, cocoa butter makes up at least 50 percent of the cocoa content.

Balancing the cocoa and sugar content of the chocolate with the other fats and sugars in the mousse is essential to maintaining a smooth emulsion, proper mouthfeel, and taste. Cocoa content acts as a stabilizer and

FIGURE 16-3 CHOCOLATE MOUSSE

1 The base of this chocolate mousse is ganache.

2 The pâte à bombe is ready to be folded into the mousse.

3 Fold the pâte à bombe into the mousse.

setting agent, and if the formula does not contain enough pâte à bombe or whipped cream in relation to the chocolate, the mousse will be very firm. Conversely, too little cocoa content may not provide enough flavor or setting properties.

Temperature

Temperature control is as essential to a great mousse as the selection of high-quality ingredients. Because of the unique crystallization properties of the cocoa butter and its behavior over different temperature ranges, it is necessary to have a solid understanding of temperature guidelines before mousse preparation begins. The discussion of the properties of chocolate in Chapter 22 will serve as a good review for this section.

Chocolate needs to reach 110°F (43°C) to 120°F (49°C) for the fat crystals to melt completely. When ganache is used as the base for a mousse, the temperature should be between 110°F (43°C) and 120°F (49°C) to ensure that all cocoa butter is melted and that production is not rushed. After the ganache has cooled to 95°F (35°C) to 105°F (41°C), the egg foam may be folded in and the whipped cream added.

Mousse should always be deposited before it cools to the point of cocoa butter crystallization, which occurs between 80°F (27°C) and 84°F (29°C). If the cocoa butter crystallizes before the mousse is deposited in the mold, it becomes difficult to portion, and quality is compromised. The mousse should set up in the mold after it has been deposited and not before.

Emulsion

A key step in producing a palatable mousse is to create a stable emulsion, or blend of water and oil. Considering the high fat and water content in a mousse, proper formulation, temperature control, and rate of incorporation must be observed. If not, the end product will have a sticky and greasy mouthfeel, will have a dense consistency, and will not cut cleanly.

Handling

For the mousse to maintain proper volume, overworking the mousse at all stages of production as well as makeup must be avoided. Mousse should be ladled into larger molds and piped into smaller ones. It should

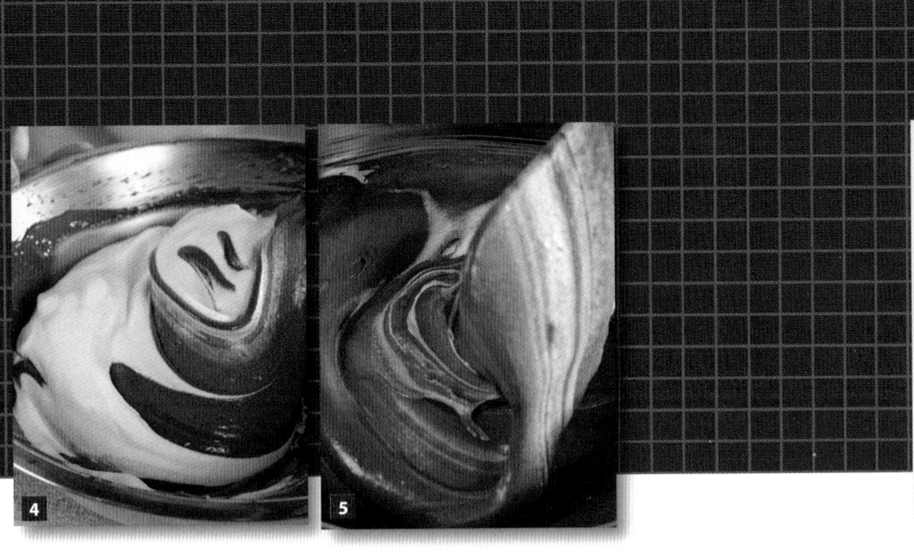

4 Fold the whipped cream into the mousse in two stages.

5 Fold in the cream just until there are no more streaks and then deposit as needed.

be noted that applying mousse with a spatula or piping bag may decrease the volume by 15 to 20 percent, which in turn may lead to increased costs for labor and ingredients, because more weight is needed to create the same volume.

CHOCOLATE MOUSSE: PROCESS

The general process for chocolate mousse is to begin by whipping the cream to soft peaks and reserving it in the refrigerator. Note, however, that some people prefer to whip the cream just before it is needed. The next step is to make the base ganache. (See Chocolate Mousse Figure 16-3, Step 1.) Depending on the formulation, this may be based on cream, crème Anglaise, or pastry cream and chocolate. If gelatin is used in the formula, it may be added to the warm ganache after blooming and melting. Next, the egg foam should be started. (See Chocolate Mousse Figure 16-3, Step 2.) After the egg foam has cooled to 95°F (35°C) to 105°F (41°C) and the ganache–base is the same temperature, the egg foam may be added to the ganache. (See Chocolate Mousse Figure 16-3, Step 3.) It should be mixed in only to incorporation to avoid breaking the emulsion. Next, the soft-peak whipped cream may be added. (See Chocolate Mousse Figure 16-3, Steps 4–5.) Once all the cream is incorporated, the mousse should be deposited and frozen or kept in the refrigerator if it is not being unmolded.

Variations on chocolate mousse may include the addition of nut pastes, chocolate nibs, cubed gelée, or alcohol. Denser items such as nut pastes should be added to the ganache, whereas lighter ingredients and inclusions may be added after the whipped cream has been folded in. Caution must be taken to avoid overmixing the mousse during the addition of alcohol or other inclusions. The more the mousse is stirred, the more the fat develops, and the grainier the texture becomes.

General Process for Chocolate Mousse

- Scale all the ingredients and prepare all the molds.
- Whip the cream to soft peaks and reserve in the refrigerator (this may also be done right before it is needed for incorporation).
- Prepare the base ganache.
- Prepare the egg foam.

- After the base is 95°F (35°C) to 105°F (41°C), fold in the egg foam (if applicable).
- Finish whipping the cream to soft peaks and fold into the base.
- Gently fold in any inclusions (if applicable).
- Deposit into the molds and freeze or refrigerate.

CHOCOLATE MOUSSE: MUCH TO CONSIDER

The possibilities for flavor and presentation of chocolate mousse are quite vast. Careful selection of chocolate can produce a tremendous array of results, and using different egg foams, add-in ingredients, and different quantities of whipped cream will allow any chocolate to be transformed into virtually any mousse.

FORMULA

BASIC BAVARIAN CREAM WITH VARIATIONS

This classic Bavarian cream formula can easily be adjusted with a flavoring such as praline paste or chocolate.

Ingredients	Baker's %	Kilogram	US decimal	Lb & Oz		Test
Cream #1	50.00	0.242	0.532		8 ½	6 ⅛ oz
Milk	50.00	0.242	0.532		8 ½	6 ⅛ oz
Sugar	25.20	0.122	0.268		4 ¼	3 ⅛ oz
Egg yolks	31.40	0.152	0.334		5 ⅜	3 ⅞ oz
Gelatin leaf	2.22	0.011	0.024		⅜	¼ oz
Cream #2	100.00	0.483	1.065	1	1	12 ⅜ oz
Total	258.82	1.250	2.756	2	12 ⅛	2 lb

Note
Combined weight of the milk and the first cream is 100 percent.

Process

1. Bloom the gelatin in very cold water and reserve.
2. Whip the second cream to soft peaks and reserve.
3. Boil the first cream and the milk and proceed with the base preparation as for a crème Anglaise and cook to 180°F (82°C).
4. Strain through a fine chinois into a clean bowl and add the bloomed, melted gelatin and mix to incorporate.
5. When the base mixture has cooled to 75°F (24°C) to 85°F (29°C), fold in the whipped cream.

Note
A large batch of basic Bavarian cream can be made, and after straining but before folding in the whipped cream, it can be flavored accordingly.

Flavor Variations

Dark Chocolate Bavarian Cream
Scale out 6 ½ oz (0.188 kg) of 64 percent couverture (15 percent total weight of Bavarian cream). Melt the chocolate in a microwave to 110°F (44°C), and fold it into the crème Anglaise while it is hot.

Praline Bavarian Cream
Scale out 3 ½ oz (0.100 kg) of praline paste (8 percent total weight of Bavarian cream). Mix it in the hot crème Anglaise base after straining.

FORMULA

WILLIAMS PEAR MOUSSE WITH AND WITHOUT ITALIAN MERINGUE

The Williams pear mousse formula creates a delicately flavored mousse. For the classic version, there is no Italian meringue; however, a version that uses one is presented here. The puree for this mousse formula can also be switched out using apricot, blackberry, blueberry, orange, and blood orange to create a variety of other flavors, using the same ratios of ingredients.

William Pear Mousse Without Italian Meringue Formula

Ingredients	Baker's %	Kilogram	US decimal	Lb & Oz	Test
Williams pear puree	100.00	0.692	1.526	1 8 ⅜	1 lb 1 ¾ oz
Sugar	8.00	0.055	0.122	2 1 ⅜ oz	
Cream	70.00	0.485	1.068	1 1 ⅛	12 ⅜ oz
Gelatin leaf	2.60	0.018	0.040	⅝	½ oz
Total	180.60	1.250	2.756	2 12 ⅛	2 lb

Note

The Williams pear puree can be substituted with one of the following purees: apricot, blackberry, blueberry, orange, or blood orange.

Process

1. Whip the cream to soft peaks. Reserve in the refrigerator.
2. Bloom the gelatin in cold water and reserve.
3. Warm 7 ¼ oz (208 g) of the puree (30 percent of the puree weight) and sugar to 110°F (44°C). Add the bloomed, melted gelatin, and stir well to dissolve.
4. Add the puree with gelatin to the remaining puree and adjust the temperature to 75°F (24°C) to 85°F (29°C).
5. Gently fold the whipped cream into the puree mixture. Fold until there are no more white streaks.
6. Deposit into the desired molds.

Williams Pear Mousse With Italian Meringue Formula

Ingredients	Baker's %	Kilogram	US decimal	Lb & Oz		Test
Williams pear puree	100.00	0.724	1.597	1	9 ½	1 lb 2 ½ oz
Sugar	11.00	0.080	0.176		2 ¾	2 oz
Water	2.20	0.016	0.035		½	⅜ oz
Egg whites	6.80	0.049	0.109		1 ¾	1 ¼ oz
Cream	50.00	0.362	0.798		12 ¾	9 ¼ oz
Gelatin leaf	2.60	0.019	0.042		⅝	½ oz
Total	172.60	1.250	2.756	2	12 ⅛	2 lb

Note
The Williams pear puree can be substituted with one of the following purees: apricot, blackberry, blueberry, orange, or blood orange.

Process

1. Whip the cream to soft peak. Reserve in the refrigerator.
2. Bloom the gelatin in cold water and reserve.
3. Combine the sugar and water and cook to prepare an Italian meringue. Prepare the egg whites.
4. Warm the fruit puree to 80°F (27°C).
5. Take a small portion of the fruit puree, warm it to 120°F (49°C), and add the bloomed, melted gelatin to it. Stir to dissolve. Temper this gelatin–puree mixture back into the main stock of puree.
6. When the Italian meringue is room temperature, fold it into the fruit puree base.
7. Lastly, at 80°F (27°C) to 85°F (29°C), fold in the soft peak whipped cream, and deposit into the desired molds.

FORMULA

CHOCOLATE MOUSSE

This is a basic chocolate mousse formula, which can be used in many ways for desserts, entremets, tarts, and petits fours, among others. Proper ingredient selection, temperatures, and processes must be followed to achieve a light, flavorful mousse that has enough strength to stand without gelatin.

Ingredients	Baker's %	Kilogram	US decimal	Lb & Oz	Test
35% cream	100.00	0.338	0.745	11 ⅞	8 ⅝ oz
64% couverture	100.00	0.338	0.745	11 ⅞	8 ⅝ oz
Egg yolks	30.00	0.101	0.223	3 ⅝	2 ⅝ oz
Sugar	30.00	0.101	0.223	3 ⅝	2 ⅝ oz
Water	10.00	0.034	0.074	1 ¼	⅞ oz
40% cream	100.00	0.338	0.745	11 ⅞	8 ⅝ oz
Total	370.00	1.250	2.756	2 12 ⅛	2 lb

Process

1. Make a ganache with the 35 percent cream and chocolate.
2. Make a pâte à bombe with the egg yolks, sugar, and water.
3. Whip the 40 percent cream to soft peaks and reserve in the refrigerator.
4. When the pâte à bombe is between 100°F (38°C) and 105°F (40°C), add it to the ganache, which should be the same temperature.
5. Fold in the soft peak whipped cream in two stages.
6. Deposit into molds and freeze.

Note

One 8 inch (20 cm) cake with two inserts (one bottom cake and one frozen insert) requires approximately 33 ⅓ (950 g) of the chocolate mousse.

CHAPTER SUMMARY

Mousse, which has been around for over a century, has a light and creamy texture as its trademark characteristic. It can be used in making cakes, or it can stand alone as a component to a plated dessert. To ensure the taste, texture, and mouthfeel that are the trademarks of a successful mousse, proper ingredient selection and formulation are essential. Taking into consideration the main components of a mousse, the base, the egg foam, the whipped cream, and the gelatin, there are many options for flavor and texture development. Proper temperature and mixing processes must also be practiced to ensure good results.

Mousse cakes have waned in and out of popularity, possibly due to the misuse of gelatin and its effect on consumers who have grown accustomed to sweet layer cakes. Today's trends point toward a growing demand for and enjoyment of a variety of mousse cakes with the rich, delicate tastes and textures featured at quality pastry shops. (See Chapter 17 for a closer look at specialty and mousse cakes.)

KEY TERMS

- ❖ Base
- ❖ Bavarian cream
- ❖ Chocolate mousse
- ❖ Emulsion
- ❖ Fruit mousse
- ❖ Ganache
- ❖ Mousse

REVIEW QUESTIONS

1. **Describe the typical components of the three main types of mousse and their functions.**
2. **What is the basic process for making a Bavarian cream?**
3. **What are the considerations of temperature when making chocolate mousse? Why are they important?**
4. **What hygiene and sanitation precautions need to be taken when making mousse? Why?**

chapter
17

CLASSIC AND MODERN CAKE ASSEMBLY

OBJECTIVES

After reading this chapter, you should be able to

- present the concepts of composition and balance and the evolution of ideas regarding cake, including wedding cake.
- split, fill, mask, ice, and decorate a layer cake using classic assembly techniques.
- construct contemporary specialty cakes, including mousse cakes, using assorted decorative techniques and sensible production.
- recognize and understand coordinating the production of wedding cakes.
- practice proper hygiene, sanitation, and storage guidelines in regard to classic and specialty cakes.

INTRODUCTION

Ever since flour was combined with water to make bread, people have added ingredients like honey and spices to make sweetened confections. Sweetened breads have been enjoyed since ancient Egypt, where they were often a part of ritual and celebration. Today, cakes are globally enjoyed as desserts that have become synonymous with public and private celebrations. Because they can be a symbol of one's perceived worth, designer cakes have turned into high art and are often regarded as such.

This chapter serves as the culmination of several chapters, including cake mixing, cream preparation, egg foams, glazes, mousse processes, and decorative techniques, all of which must be understood to make a wide variety of cakes. A number of base formulas must be understood and mastered, and the skills involved in the various steps of assembly and finishing must be understood and practiced to be able to create everything from a simple layer cake to an extravagant **entremets**, or cake designed to serve at least several people. The common expectation for cakes is perfection, with the quality and presentation of all components seen as an extension of the quality of the pastry shop. This chapter will explore classic cakes, specialty cakes, and wedding cakes, and it will consider taste, texture, color, visual balance, and the appeal of décor.

COMPOSITION AND BALANCE: CLASSIC AND CONTEMPORARY CAKES

Cake composition and balance begin with component planning and design. The main components used in classic **layer cakes** include cake bases, filling, icing, and decoration. The filling and icing can be made from the same component such as buttercream, or layers of buttercream can alternate with layers of ganache as the filling, with buttercream for the icing and a combination of buttercream and ganache for the decoration. As classic cake assembly becomes more complex, increasing numbers of components are required to finish the cake. To be appealing, these components must be well balanced in flavor, texture, color, and presentation.

Depending on the complexity of the cake being assembled, product composition considerations can include

- Flavor of the cake, filling, and icing
- Texture of the cake, filling, and icing
- Color schemes of the cake, filling, and icing
- Assembly style
- Decoration and garnish

FLAVOR OF CAKE, FILLING, AND ICING

The flavors of the cake base, filling, and icing should all be complementary. What is obviously complementary to one person, however, may not necessarily be obvious to another. Flavor choices include chocolate, vanilla, sugary, buttery, nutty, fruity, coffee, tea, and alcohol. For each of these profiles, there are even more considerations, such as dark chocolate, vanilla bean, hazelnut praline paste, fresh raspberries, coffee syrup, and tea-infused ganache. Flavors may also be analogous as in a chocolate layer cake.

Most importantly, many different flavors can be combined from various cake bases, fillings, and icing components to create signature cake, and these flavors must harmonize. Their intensity should vary according to the goals of the person making the cake, especially when working with multiple flavors. Components within the cake may act as balancers between opposing qualities, such as cake flavors that balance lightness or sweetness of filling. This balance can only be learned by tasting, which is different from eating because the flavors are allowed to diffuse in the mouth and attention is paid to their introductory notes, high notes, and tail ends, hopefully from just one bite.

TEXTURE OF CAKE, FILLING, AND ICING

The texture of the cake, filling, and icing will have an effect on not only the mouthfeel experience of the person eating the cake but also in determining its shelf life and stability. The textures of the components are determined by their composition, including the formula used to prepare them, ingredient selection, and method of production. While texture elements are usually flavor elements, texture can also be manipulated through setting agents.

Soft, crisp, firm, crunchy, brittle, creamy, light, dense, airy, wet, and dry are just some of the words used to describe how the cake structurally appears in the case and how it is experienced when eaten. The combination of textures can create unique sensations in the mouth and should be considered in planning.

Opposing qualities that complement each other include a crisp meringue with a creamy filling, a soft mousse with crunchy praline, and a syrup-soaked cake with chocolate ganache. Basic ingredients that create texture include sugar, chocolate, flour, eggs, butter, cream, gelatin, and nuts. Elements that create texture include short crusts, meringues, mousse, ganache, buttercream, glazes, assorted creams, nougatine, praline, cake bases, and sugar syrups.

COLOR SCHEMES OF CAKE, FILLING, ICING, AND DECORATION

As a general rule, applying color to cakes should relate to the flavor and presentation/theme of the cake. Because the color schemes of cake components combine to create visual appeal, a basic understanding of color is beneficial. Questions that should be asked include: Is there a color that applies to the theme of the cake? Where do the colors come from? What is the subtlety/intensity of the color?

As a guideline, pastel tones are better for lighter icings such as buttercreams. The exceptions to this are naturally colored fresh fruit, fruit glazes, and chocolate. These bolder colors are well tolerated because consumers expect the vibrant colors of strawberry or raspberry and the rich color of dark chocolate.

ASSEMBLY STYLE

Assembly style refers to the way in which the cake is prepared as well as the complexity of the composition. Cakes can be round or square or formed in a number of specialty shapes. Some classic cakes consist of only a cake round that has been iced and decorated, whereas others are split, filled, iced, and decorated. The difference is more cake with less filling, or more filling with less cake. It would be impossible to choose one style over the other because each application has a different purpose and clientele. Classic cakes made for mass-market distribution are typically iced rather than split and filled. Cakes in an upscale pastry shop can contain several layers of cake alternating with filling.

DECORATION AND GARNISH

Decoration and garnish are extremely important because they are often the consumer's first impression of the cake. They not only provide a way for pastry chefs to display their decorative abilities but also communicate something about what is in the cake. Icing, fruit, nuts, chocolate work, sugar work, rolled fondant, marzipan, and more can be used to create a wide variety of display work. Applications can range from piping script onto the cake to an intricate application of rolled fondant garnished with gum paste flowers to a display of fresh fruit with chocolate or sugar decoration.

CLASSIC CAKE ASSEMBLY

Most classic cake assembly is based on the construction of cake layers that are alternately layered with a filling such as buttercream, ganache, or whipped cream and then encased in an icing and decorated with more icing. The selection of cake, filling, and decoration can vary greatly, and many different types of finished cakes can be made from several base formulas. The degree of decoration can range from the minimalist's rosettes to gaudy flowers of every color to intricate, rococo-style piping characterized by thinly piped, intricate, stacked layers of royal icing.

CLASSIC CAKE MISE EN PLACE

Before cake assembly begins, the pastry chef should have proper mise en place, with all ingredients, components, and related tools and equipment ready for use. For cake assembly, the following are generally required:

- Cake bases
- Fillings and icing
- Decoration and garnish
- Hand tools, equipment, and cake boards

Cake Bases

All cakes should be baked and cooled before starting the assembly process. Bakeries that sell a lot of cake typically have a "team" dedicated to cake mixing and baking. Once they have appropriately cooled, cakes can be used the same day or wrapped and frozen for later use, with storage time in the freezer dependent on the type of cake. Refer to Chapter 14 for additional information on freezing cake bases.

Fillings and Icings

Not all cakes require filling. For those that do, fillings should be ready to use when assembly begins. As with cake base preparation, larger bakeries often have people dedicated to the proper mixing and preparation of fillings and icings to maintain consistency and improve efficiency.

Before beginning cake assembly, fillings and icings should possess proper flavor, consistency, and quantity. It is essential to maintain efficient assembly so that enough filling and icing are prepared to fill and ice all the cakes required.

Decoration and Garnish

Decoration and garnish mediums can include fresh fruit, chocolate décor, roasted sliced almonds, gum paste flowers, and much more. Some of these items can be bought ready to use (for example, fresh raspberries), others may need to be prepared (such as roasted sliced almonds), and still others can be made completely in-house (such as gum paste flowers). Regardless of the scope and origin of the decoration and garnish, they should complement the style and flavors of the cake.

Hand Tools, Equipment, and Cake Boards

Depending on the method of assembly, different hand tools, equipment, and cake boards will be required to make, finish, and easily move the cake.

A sample list of hand tools includes a serrated knife, a palette knife, an offset palette knife, a paring knife, piping bags, paper cones, piping tips, scissors, and assorted icing combs. Equipment used to prepare components can include mixers for preparing whipped cream, sheeters for preparing rolled fondant, and the turntable on which the

1 Cut the cake on a level surface and from one direction, turning the cake as you cut.

2 When ready to cut subsequent layers, leave the cake stacked for ease of handling.

cake will be assembled. (Turntables enable the decorator to turn the cake without turning the body too much, which can become tiresome and uncomfortable.)

A variety of cake boards are needed to easily move the cake. These can include round, square, or rectangular shapes. Cake boards can also be classified as white or gold (they can also be silver or other colors). White boards are typically used during the initial assembly of the cake, after which the cake is transferred to a gold board. If the cake is large and needs extra support, white boards can remain under it. In these cases, they are trimmed flush to the edge of the finished cake.

SPLITTING, FILLING, AND MASKING CAKES

Splitting, **filling**, and **masking** are the terms used to describe the initial process of assembling a cake. Splitting refers to cutting the cake base into layers, filling refers to the application of filling in between the cake layers, and masking refers to covering the assembled cake with an initial coat of icing.

Splitting

Depending on the size of the cake base, the desired size of the finished cake, and the required thickness of the layers, cakes can be cut into two to four layers for assembly. (See Splitting Figure 17-1.)

When splitting cakes, it is necessary to use a good-quality serrated knife so that the knife does not do more damage than good. Some knives tend to tear the cake, creating lots of crumbs. Although not necessary, a specialty knife designed for cake has a long blade with fine serration and a slight convex shape and helps cut cake layers without pulling out or damaging the crumb.

Cakes should always be cut after they have totally cooled because cutting when warm will result in a damaged crumb structure. The key to splitting cakes evenly and achieving consistent, uniform results is for the knife to cut at a constant rate without changing the angle of the blade. If the angle of the blade shifts, an uneven layer will result. Cakes that have been split and are ready for filling should be put aside and the crumbs should be cleared.

Filling

After the cakes have been split, they are ready to be filled. This process begins by determining which layer should be in which position within

FIGURE 17-2 FILLING

1 On a cake turntable, apply a thin, even and level layer of icing, being sure to bring it all the way out to the edges.

2 Apply the next layer of cake and then the next layer of icing.

3 Apply the top layer of cake, ensuring it is well centered and level.

the assembled cake. The most damaged layers should be used within the cake, so that they can be hidden with the assistance of the icing. The flattest layer, which is usually the bottom layer flipped upside-down, should be reserved for the top.

The base layer should be placed on a cake board that is slightly larger than the cake round. Some pastry chefs prefer to brush the bottom of the bottom cake layer with coating chocolate so that it is easy to move later. Depending on the type and size of cake used, this can be a good idea.

Next, the filling can be placed in the center of the cake round and drawn out toward the edge of the cake using a palette knife. (See Filling Figure 17-2, Step 1.) This can be done with or without a turntable. However, it is definitely beneficial to use a turntable when learning how to assemble cakes. After spreading the filling evenly to the edges, the next layer of cake is placed on top of it and the filling and stacking process continues. (See Filling Figure 17-2, Steps 2–3.)

Additional steps may be required during the filling process. Cakes are sometimes moistened with cake syrup or have a thin layer of jam applied before the filling is added. If this is the case, the syrup or jam is applied just before the primary filling is applied to the cake and spread.

Masking

After the cake has been filled, it can be masked, which refers to the process of putting a thin coat of icing over the sides and top of the cake. (See Masking Figure 17-3.) Some call this the **crumb coat**. The purpose for masking is to secure all of the crumbs to the cake to ensure that none make their way onto the icing. Masking also acts as an intermediate stage to establish the final form of the cake between icing and filling. For example, if the cake is not level after filling, it can be leveled during masking to lessen the amount of work once it is time to ice.

After cakes, especially buttercream cakes, are masked, they should remain in the refrigerator for at least 10 minutes, but can remain for up to one day, depending on the icing. For cakes masked with whipped cream, less time is required because the whipped cream will never really set up. Some cake decorators skip the masking stage because they are able to quickly and easily ice the cake without crumbs showing in the final icing. This is fine as long as the results are good.

ICING AND GLAZING CAKES

Icing and glazing is the final step in cake assembly of the cake. All that remains is the decoration and garnishing. Special attention must be paid

FIGURE 17-3 MASKING

1 Apply a thin coat of icing on the top of the cake and push the excess over the edge to mask the sides.

2 Apply additional icing on the sides of the cake as needed to achieve the masked cake.

3 Work the upsurge of icing over the top of the cake. Once the sides and top are evenly covered, the cake should cool for at least 10 minutes before applying the final icing.

to this process because the quality of the work will be apparent throughout cake consumption.

Once iced or glazed, the cake can be frozen for later use or shipping, or it can be decorated and sold. Some icings and glazes hold up differently in the freezer. For this reason, pastry chefs who rely on freezing techniques should conduct tests to understand icing or glaze durability.

Icing

Cakes are iced with thicker mediums like buttercream, whipped cream, or whipped ganache. The concept is the same as for masking, although the coat of icing is thicker.

Icing should be placed in the middle of the surface of the cake and should then be worked toward the outer edges using a palette knife and turntable. Once an even layer has been created on the surface of the cake, icing should hang over the edge. (See Icing Figure 17-4, Step 1.) This icing is then used to coat the sides of the cake. If more icing is required, it can be applied directly to the sides of the cake. (See Icing Figure 17-4, Steps 2–3.)

When a coat of icing has been applied to the walls of the cake, excess icing should extend above the surface. (See Icing Figure 17-4, Step 4.) This should be smoothed onto the surface of the cake and removed as needed using an offset palette knife or a large palette knife, depending on the decorator's preference. Swift motions are used to clear the icing from the edge, drawing it in toward the center and removing any excess. This process is completed toward the decorator to ensure control over how much icing is removed from the cake. After the surface and walls of the cake are smooth and the edges are crisp, the cake can be decorated or frozen for later use. (See Icing Figure 17-4, Steps 5–6.)

Glazing

Glazing creates a smooth, seamless finish to cakes without nearly as much work as icing. Several precautions must be taken, though, to ensure a successful glaze and to minimize waste. Masking and the temperature of the cake and glaze play important roles in success.

Because glaze is poured over the cake, it reveals any imperfections in the construction and masking; it does not fill in gaps or holes and can't hide raised surface areas. For these reasons, a good final masking is required to ensure that there is an even surface for the glaze to flow over.

Almost all glazes need to be warmed before use, and care must be taken to ensure the glaze is not too warm to melt the icing that was used for masking. A chocolate glaze warmed to 80°F (27°C) is sufficient to glaze a buttercream-masked cake removed from the refrigerator. A hot glaze, however, will most likely melt the butterfat in the buttercream and the glaze will slide off the cake.

When ready to glaze, it is important that cakes are placed on a pouring screen over a clean sheet pan lined with a clean sheet of parchment paper. When the glaze is the appropriate consistency and temperature, it can be applied to the cake. The glaze should be poured around the perimeter of the surface of the cake first, ensuring that it reaches the bottom of the side walls (see Glazing Figure 17-5, Step 1), and then the center should be poured with enough glaze to fill in the unglazed center (see Glazing Figure 17-5, Step 2). This process should happen relatively quickly, especially with a quick-setting glaze. Any runoff glaze should be strained to remove crumbs before being reused. A torch may be used to pop any air bubbles. (See Glazing Figure 17-5, Step 3.) Use caution to not heat the glaze too much, or it may burn.

After the cake has been glazed, it should be returned to the refrigerator or freezer to set the glaze. Once set, the cake should be transferred to a gold board, where it can be decorated as required.

DECORATION OF CLASSIC LAYER CAKES

The decoration and garnishes for classically assembled cakes typically consist of icing, fruits, nuts, chocolate, and other similar items. The choice of decoration should be related to the theme of the cake, the fillings used, and the flavors present. Fruit is a great way to highlight seasonal flavors, which can be important for cakes designed to sell during certain times of the year.

Basic Piping Techniques

Proper use of a piping bag and the ability to pipe a variety of shapes and styles is essential. Figure 17-6 shows examples of piping rosettes, shells, and reversed shells.

Figure 17-6
Piping Rosettes, Shells, and Reversed Shells

SPECIALTY CAKE ASSEMBLY

Specialty cakes differ from classic layer cakes in composition and presentation. Many of their components have classical roots and have been around for decades, but what sets them apart is the approach to assembly and presentation. Specialty cakes are often made from multiple components that draw on different techniques of preparation and have varying textures. Often, these cakes achieve their unique shapes from specialty molds made out of metal, plastic, or silicone. Although many modern cakes feature mousse components, specialty cake bases and other cream preparations are common as well.

Specialty cakes are notable for their range of shapes and sizes. The vast array of commercially available and custom-designed specialty molds makes very unique presentations possible. In addition, the same dessert can often be seen in multiple sizes, including petits fours, individual, and entremets.

SPECIALTY CAKE MISE EN PLACE

Just as for classic cakes, specialty cakes have their own set of mise en place. Cake components, hand tools, acetate strips and sheets, textured

FIGURE 17-4 ICING

Apply icing to the top of the cake and work it toward and over the edge, creating a level surface on top of the cake.

Work the icing around the side of the cake, ensuring that enough icing is built up that the cake cannot be seen.

Smooth the icing on the sides of the cake to establish the vertical sides.

A metal scraper may be useful to establish vertical sides.

Carefully work the upsurge of icing over the surface of the cake, removing any excess.

The finished iced cake is ready for decoration.

FIGURE 17-5 GLAZING

With the cake on a pouring screen, pour the glaze around the edges of the cake.

Fill in the center.

Using a torch, warm the surface of the cake to pop any air bubbles.

plastic sheets, cake molds, and silicone molds may all be used. The complexity of the cake is typically reflected by the number of components used as well as the formula processes used.

Cake Components

All specialty cake components should be prepared before assembly begins. In some bakeries, a supply of basic components is reserved in the freezer or prepared daily. They are set up in this way so the person or division of the business responsible for making specialty cakes only has to make the main component of the dessert, such as the mousse. In addition, depending on the size of the pastry shop, the pastry chef may make up specialty cakes once a week and freeze them, thawing and finishing as needed. This allows for easier production scheduling and less waste.

Completing all prep work and organizing the workstation minimizes distraction and streamlines cake production. If cake rounds require cutting before depositing in a dessert, it should happen before the assembly begins. If the mousse should be at a particular temperature while depositing, everything should be prepared and readied before the mousse is elaborated.

Hand Tools

The same basic hand tools that are used for classic cakes are used for specialty cakes. They include a chef's knife, serrated knife, an assortment of palette knives, and bowl scrapers, among others. Pastry cutters can be used to cut out cake rounds from biscuit jaconde sheets, and ladles may be used frequently for portioning mousse.

Acetate Strips and Sheets

Plastics have become an indispensable product in the pastry kitchen. They are usually used to line ring molds for cake assembly, to line mousse cakes with no cake walls, and to do decorative chocolate work. They can be acquired in many widths, which make adjusting cake heights simple and economical. Acetate strips and sheets can be reused if washed and dried well before storing. *Note:* Reuse is not a good idea for chocolate work because it will be a challenge to get a perfect shine.

Cake Molds

Cake molds are metal or plastic molds in which mousse cakes are built. They are excellent for this use because they ensure efficiency and consistent results with softer fillings. Cake molds typically have no base, which makes it easy to produce intricate cakes and easily remove them from the mold. They come in many shapes and sizes and can be lined or extended with acetate strips. Preparing cake molds can be labor-intensive, but they allow for quick assembly of items that typically sell for more than classic cakes.

Silicone Molds

Silicone molds are very popular for individual-sized desserts and are a very easy way to add visual texture to cake or shape to mousse. They can be used to create inserts, individual-sized desserts, entremets, cake bases, and much more. Desserts are easily removed from silicone molds once frozen, which makes them ideal for dessert production, even for very soft mousse. Silicone molds can be used for baking as well. This improves efficiency by eliminating steps, such as a roulade or roll cake that can be rolled with the assistance of the silicone baking mat on which the cake is baked.

Cake Frames

Cake frames are metal frames that are available in the size of a sheet pan or a half sheet pan and are designed for building specialty cakes. When using cake frames, one sheet of the cake is produced and then cut and sold as slices and cakes of desired size.

These are essentially large rectangular cake molds. Some stackable varieties are used to ensure even layers of dessert components. For example, a different mousse can be prepared and deposited into three different frames of the same height. Once frozen, they can be stacked to create a perfect, flat, even layer of mousse or other component for each of the selections.

ASSEMBLING MOUSSE CAKES

The production options for specialty and mousse cakes include cake molds, cake pans, cake frames, silicone molds, and acetate strips. Some of the easiest methods use cake molds or silicone molds, sometimes in conjunction with acetate strips. It is easier to approach production methods in terms of how the cake is assembled than what it is assembled in because equipment can easily change.

There are at least two techniques for portioning mousse for the assembly of cakes: the upside-down technique and the bottom-up technique. These two techniques can be used depending on what type of mold is being used, and both will be described in detail. Before considering the techniques of assembling specialty cakes made in molds, it will be useful to consider the preparation of the cake base as well as the special handling considerations of mousse.

Preparing Cake Bases for Molded Cakes

To prepare the cake for use with a ring mold or Flexipan, cut out circles of cake that are slightly smaller than the base diameter of the mold. If using a ring mold, place it on a silpat or sheet of acetate and place the cake layer in the center, and optionally moisten the cake with a light cake syrup. To prepare a Flexipan, place it on a flat sheet pan, and keep the cake circles ready for later use.

Special Considerations for Portioning Mousse

No matter what type of specialty cake is being made, the portioning of mousse into molds should be done as quickly and efficiently as possible. As soon as the whipped cream is added, the temperature will drop, and the gelatin and/or chocolate will begin to set. If the mousse is mishandled during this stage, texture and volume will suffer.

It is best to portion larger mousse cakes with a ladle, which is unobtrusive and will not alter integrity. For petit four or individual-sized cakes, it may be best to use a pitcher or piping bag with a large plain tip. A piping bag can be used for a thicker mousse; forcing the medium out of the tip will reduce air and volume. After the mousse is portioned, it should be smoothed out and made flush with the top of the mold.

After the molds are filled, the cakes should be frozen for at least 6 hours. A shorter freezing time is possible with a blast freezer, but a longer period will ensure the product is frozen through. At this point, the cakes may be finished or stored in the freezer for later use. Some cakes with mousse components may not require freezing, especially if the cake does not rely on the shape of the mold for its structure. Cakes that are stored frozen can have their molds removed for reuse and should be well wrapped and used within 2 weeks for best results.

FIGURE 17-7 BOTTOM-UP ASSEMBLY

1 Insert the cake wall into the mold, which has been lined with an acetate strip. Next, insert the cake base.

2 Pipe the mousse one-third of the way up the mold.

3 Press the frozen insert into the mousse.

Bottom-Up Assembly

Bottom-up assembly refers to the method of assembling cake from the bottom up. These cakes can be assembled in ring molds, cake frames, or other molds with no bottom. This may be required due the presence of a **cake wall**, or strip of thin cake that surrounds the dessert and can extend all the way up the side of the dessert.

For bottom-up construction, molds should be prepared with an acetate liner and a cake base. The acetate liner will assist in the release of the dessert from the mold, and if a cake wall is to be used, it should be cut to perfectly fit the inner circumference of the mold. If the wall is cut short, a piece of cake should be cut to fit in the gap. The cake should not be squeezed into the mold because it can spring away from the dessert and expose the center after the ring is removed. For cakes with a cake wall, it is important that the cake base fits inside the base of the cake wall. For preparations that do not require a cake wall, the cake base should be trimmed to a diameter that is less than the diameter of the cake so no cake shows.

After the acetate strip and then the base have been deposited, the mousse can be deposited. If additional components are to be included within the cake, such as frozen inserts or biscuit, the cake is partially filled and then topped off after the insertion takes place. **Frozen inserts** are components of a cake that are too soft to add to the preparation when just refrigerated or at room temperature. Their texture is usually soft, such as a crémeux, a gelée, or gelatin-based crème brûlée filling, but it may be crunchy such as for a crispy praline layer. Alternating layers of mousse or specialty creams with the frozen insert may take place several times, depending on the number of inserts. (See Bottom-Up Assembly Figure 17-7.) After the cake has been filled with the appropriate components, it should be frozen for at least 6 hours before unmolding.

Upside-Down Assembly

Upside-down assembly is best used with silicone molds and some specialty molds such as Bûche de Noël and half dome or pyramid molds.

For upside-down assembly, the mousse is deposited in the mold, any inserts are added, and the cake base is placed on top of the mousse and made flush with the top of the mold. After the dessert is frozen, it is inverted so the cake base is on the bottom. At this point, it can be stored in the freezer for later use or finished for immediate use.

The pastry chef should always work on a flat surface and ensure that the molds are appropriately filled. After the insert is added, any additional mousse is added, taking care to leave approximately 1/8 to 1/4 inch

4 Pipe on additional mousse.

5 Level the mousse so it is flush with the surface of the mold.

(0.5 cm) at the top, depending on cake size. Then, the base of the cake is placed into the mold and pressed so that the bottom is flush with the top of the mold. Any air gaps or mounds are repaired by working the top with an offset spatula. (See Upside-Down Assembly Figure 17-8.)

Use of Silicone Mold for Upside-Down Assembly Once frozen, the cakes can be popped out of their molds but they should remain frozen until ready for finishing. Only enough molds should be taken out of the freezer as can be released to prevent the cakes from softening. The frozen cakes are returned to the freezer and finished as needed, and the mold is ready for reuse.

FINISHING AND PRESENTATION FOR MOUSSE CAKES

Finishing techniques vary for mousse and specialty cakes, and, in general, the techniques are faster than icing a cake. The finishing process for mousse cakes is not merely aesthetic. The glaze or gelée also preserves the mousse from oxidation and rancidity by creating a barrier between the cake, the cream and the air. This limits the flow of contaminants and oxygen and slows the process of degradation.

Depending on the finishing technique, the still-frozen mousse cake is released from the Flexipan, silpat, or acetate sheet and placed on a cake board or pouring screen. When removing cakes from Flexipans, the cake should be very frozen. If the whole cake is to be glazed, the cake should be placed directly on a pouring screen and the cake ring removed. However, if the glaze is to cover just the surface of the cake, it may be applied while the cake ring or acetate is still surrounding the cake, to guarantee that the glaze covers only the surface and not the sides of the cake.

To remove the cake ring, heat it lightly with a hot towel or a torch, taking great care to warm only the ring mold and not the mousse. The ring should then be lifted off the cake.

Decoration and Presentation Techniques

Specialty cake decoration should be of higher caliber than that for the classic cakes. This does not necessarily mean more expensive components or more decoration. Specialty cakes can be highly refined and aesthetically pleasing using easy, yet interesting, techniques. Cakes can also be presented seasonally by highlighting local flavors. The pastry chef's goal should be to use the best of what is available.

Clientele often dictate the type of décor used, and bakeries, pastry shops, high-end food service suppliers and wholesale accounts can all

FIGURE 17-8 UPSIDE-DOWN ASSEMBLY

1
Pipe the mousse into the mold just below the surface of the mold.

2
Place the cake base on top of the mousse, and press it down to be flush with the surface of the mold.

3
Clean the edges of the pastry, and fill in any gaps.

have different presentations for the same dessert. Wholesale suppliers typically use the smallest amount of decoration because they need to keep costs low and ensure stable movement of the product.

Other considerations for specialty cakes are temperature guidelines and serving instructions for customers, which are the responsibility of the sales staff. Many bakeries do this with a pamphlet that describes serving suggestions for each product.

The choice of finishing should be considered in relation to the flavor and style of the dessert and the appearance of other desserts within the line. Differences in appearance and dessert "autonomy" can help the line look more diversified, even if only several techniques are used to yield a dozen presentations.

Fruit and chocolate glazes are commonly used on specialty cakes. They are simple to make, relatively simple to use, and have an elegant simplicity. Other options include clear or cold process glazes. One very fast technique is to use spray chocolate for a velvety chocolate finish. Fruit mousse cakes should always be presented with complementary fresh fruit. If the cake is not glazed, the fruit should cover the majority of its surface in orderly or more abstract arrangements. If the cake is glazed, fruit can be arranged decoratively around the border or as a minicenterpiece. Glaze and powdered sugar should be applied to the fruit to preserve it and to add another visual element.

A small arrangement of fruit and chocolate or sugar work can also add a very nice visual element to entremets. Focus should be placed on balancing the contrast of colors, use of various mediums (chocolate, fresh fruit, sugar work), flow, and height. For a more detailed look at decoration, please refer to Chapter 21.

PRODUCTION AND SHELF LIFE OF MOUSSE CAKES

For a bakery or other business, cakes can be produced in larger quantities and pulled from the freezer as needed for finishing and sale. This cuts labor costs and reduces waste. During the finishing process, cakes should remain frozen until they are ready to be displayed for sale. If a cake is for a special order and is not needed right away, it may be sold frozen to eliminate any damage that could happen during transit.

If mousse cakes are for wholesale delivery, they should remain packed in their shipping boxes in the freezer until just before the delivery person leaves. Quality control methods must be in place to ensure that the desserts arrive to their destinations safely and are stored properly once they arrive.

Once unfrozen, mousse cakes on display can be stored under refrigeration for about 48 hours before quality starts to deteriorate. The high percentage of fresh cream and fresh fruit in mousse cakes creates a medium that is highly susceptible to breaking down. Mousse made with chocolate and higher quantities of sugar and acidity may last longer, but much depends on the elements and quality of the ingredients. Finished cakes should always be stored away from off odors as cream readily absorbs the smells of its environs. This is mostly a concern in restaurants and grocery stores, where a walk-in refrigerator is used for both sweet and savory preparations.

COMPOSITION, DESIGN, AND EVOLUTION

When composing cakes, pastry chefs need a solid understanding of ingredient functions, formula processes, and assembly techniques.

In addition, imagination and creativity in flavor, presentation, texture, and surprise all play major roles. Other factors in cake composition include current trends, flavor profiles of the customer base, ingredient availability, and personal goals.

WEDDING CAKES

A wedding cake is the visual showpiece of any marriage celebration. Some consider it one of the most elaborate practices of the pastry arts, and there is no denying that the wedding cake business is a large and growing part of the pastry industry.

Wedding cakes represent the accumulation of the pastry chef's skill, talent, and creativity. An intricate cake may require days, or even weeks, to complete using a variety of techniques, flavors, colors, designs, and mediums.

When creating a wedding cake, it is very important to communicate with the customer—to make the bride's wishes a reality, to make the wedding day memorable, and, most importantly, to be at the site on time with the cake completed as planned. For these reasons, advance planning and organization are absolute requirements for wedding cake production.

This section will explore how wedding cakes have evolved, including historical and contemporary wedding cakes, as well as characteristics of cakes from different cultures. It will then describe the practical process of planning, producing, and delivering a wedding cake, including advice on how to work with clients through every step.

EVOLUTION OF WEDDING CAKES

Although wedding cakes have greatly evolved in style over the centuries, their symbolic purpose has not changed. They represent the uniting of a new family, as well as best wishes for the future. Today, the custom of celebrating a wedding with a cake is practiced worldwide.

History of Wedding Cakes

Wedding cakes date as far back as the Roman Empire, around 400 BCE. Bread was initially used, but wedding cakes have elaborated into sweeter pastry over time. As early as 100 BCE, a piece of dense fruitcake or sweet bread was eaten by the groom, and the remainder of the cake was crumbled over the bride's head so that she would be blessed by the gods with fertility. This symbolic ceremony has changed to today's common custom, in which the bride and groom cut the cake together and then feed each other.

Sugar icing was invented during the 17th century, but for a long time it remained a luxury available only to the wealthy. Early wedding cakes, like wedding dresses, were white, symbolizing the bride's virginity.

Wedding cakes similar to today's style evolved in Great Britain, a major sugar importer with many refined varieties that led to the creation of royal icing, pastillage, and rolled fondant. Piping tips and other decorating tools were also invented during this time, and the technique of cake decoration rapidly grew.

In the 19th century, Queen Victoria's own wedding cake created the fundamentals seen today. Decorated with royal icing, it measured 14 inches (36 cm) deep, 3 yards (2.8 m) across, and over 7 feet (2.2 m) high. Although it consisted of multiple tiers, only the bottom tier was a real cake. The top tiers consisted of pastillage and royal icing.

By the end of the 19th century, wedding cake decoration became more artistic. The quality of cake improved, due to the invention of chemical leavenings and more advanced tools and equipment. By the early 20th century, tiered cakes were becoming very common. Colors other than white began to be used, as were different shapes and flavors of cakes and fillings. Today, the wedding cake business has grown to $32 billion annually and keeps growing.

Wedding Cakes From Different Cultures

As the centerpiece of marriage celebrations throughout the world, wedding cakes vary in shape and function, but many are firmly rooted in the British tradition.

Great Britain Today's British wedding cakes are similar to the cakes of the 19th century. The traditional cake is a dense fruitcake soaked in liqueur and covered in white marzipan or rolled fondant. Stacked or tiered, it is decorated with layers of intricate piping of royal icing and pastillage. The flavor of this style of cake matures as time passes: It does not require refrigeration and has a very long shelf life.

France The French tradition of wedding cakes is very different. The most traditional style of pastry for weddings is croque en bouche or small profiteroles filled with pastry cream or crème Chiboust, which are then dipped in hot caramel and stacked to make a cone shape. This is usually placed on a nougatine base and decorated with sugar flowers, pulled sugar ribbons, and marzipan fruits. Assembly must be done just before the wedding because croque en bouche is very sensitive to humidity.

When served, the decorations are removed and individual profiteroles are broken off and served to guests, with the number of profiteroles per guest dictating the size of the croque en bouche. Today, a growing number of French couples are breaking with this tradition and opting for layer cakes, with some choosing a combination of a layer cake base with a croque en bouche set on top.

Australia and New Zealand The strong British influence on Australia and New Zealand includes the style of wedding cakes. In Australia, rolled fondant is commonly used to cover fruitcake to give it a softer edge. White is the traditional color, but soft pastel colors can be used as well. Cakes are then decorated with extensive royal icing décor, including ornaments, embroidery, laces, and string work. Intricate sugar and gum paste works, such as ribbons and flowers, are often used. Wedding cakes in New Zealand are very similar to Australia's; however, rolled fondant is more popular in New Zealand, and much less royal icing décor is used. Instead, flowers made with gum paste are the major decoration.

South Africa South African wedding cakes closely resemble those of Great Britain and Australia. They usually have multiple tiers and are covered with rolled fondant. The distinct characteristics of South African wedding cakes are royal icing "wings," which are piped on waxed paper, released when dry, and attached to rolled fondant. This is a time-consuming and labor-intensive process, but it adds a very elaborated and delicate dimension to the cake.

United States American wedding cakes are also influenced by British style; however, pound cake, sponge, or butter cake takes the place of fruitcake. American wedding cakes normally consist of multiple stacked or tiered cakes, and different colors and shapes are often used. Classic wedding cakes are iced with buttercream and decorated with buttercream roses and piping, plastic decorations, pearls, and cake toppers that are often figures of the bride and groom.

Contemporary American wedding cakes are not restricted by traditional wedding cake styles. Unusually shaped cakes are often created to reflect the couple's tastes, hobbies, and personalities; however, tiered cakes are still the most common because of the structural support they provide. Styles are constantly evolving, and many artistically designed cakes regularly appear in wedding magazines and professional publications that specialize in cake decoration.

When it comes to ingredients, any type of cake and icing can be used, including more fragile components like whipped cream, chocolate or fruit mousse, and fresh fruit. Fresh and seasonal ingredients are preferred, and a clean, light appearance is favored. For décor, pastillage cutouts and chocolate decorations are popular, as are gum paste flowers, marzipan figures, and fresh flowers and fruit.

Groom's cake is a popular custom in the southern United States. It is commonly made with chocolate cake and is smaller than the wedding cake, but more uniquely decorated. There is no single groom's cake style or shape. Some choose a classic glazed chocolate cake, while others prefer something playful that reflects their personality, such as a guitar shape, or a cake decorated like a football stadium. Groom's cake can be served at the rehearsal dinner, or next to the wedding cake at the reception.

COORDINATING WEDDING CAKE PRODUCTION

A well-planned schedule for cake production ensures a successful wedding cake business. This is largely a seasonal business, and simultaneous work on multiple wedding cakes is often required. It is important to plan accordingly by establishing a good relationship with clients and by making it clear that you need to be informed immediately if there are any changes to the initial plan—and that you will do the same.

Designing

There are numerous possibilities when designing a wedding cake. Many techniques and materials can be incorporated, making it a great showcase for the pastry chef's skill. This section is divided into two parts: the first explains types of structural supports used in wedding cakes, while the second includes a list of materials used to decorate wedding cakes and examples of how they are used.

Structure There are two basic types of structures for building multitiered wedding cakes: a cake stand and columns. When choosing the style, the structural stability of the cake itself must be considered.

A variety of cake stands are available in different designs, and many of them can be rented. Usually made from plastic or metal, cake stands feature multiple horizontal platforms for each cake, with the largest typically on the bottom and smaller ones toward the top. During assembly, decorated cakes are simply placed on their corresponding platforms. The advantages of using a cake stand are ease of assembly and suitability for fragile cakes like tiramisu and charlotte. The major disadvantage is the initial purchase or rental cost.

When cakes are stacked, there is typically no visible support. Cakes are placed directly onto one another, straight or offset. Support comes from columns or dowels inserted into the cake. These columns are the same height as the cake and provide support for additional cakes above.

The tiered style has a more elegant and elaborate appearance, with visible support columns between each cake. These columns, which are usually made with durable plastic, are extended into the cake below and touch the bottom cardboard. The tiered style is suitable for any type of cake, but the tiers must be built with perfect balance. When using columns, be sure to choose those that are made with food-safe materials or are specially made for wedding cakes.

Materials This section explores different materials that are commonly used in the composition of wedding cakes. The consideration is to use elements that meet the bride and groom's preference, as well as something that is structurally sound in the given environment at the wedding. The characteristics of each material are important to understand when determining the composition of a wedding cake.

Buttercream Buttercream is the most basic material to ice and fill wedding cakes. It usually has a natural yellow tint from butter, but it can be colored as desired. On the surface of a cake, buttercream can be spread flat or piped into a pattern, such as basket weaves. It can also be used to pipe rosettes, shell borders, decorative patterns, roses, and other flowers.

Due to its stiff consistency and durability, basic buttercream is suitable for decorating wedding cakes that will be set up in a place without air-conditioning. Italian buttercream has the best mouthfeel but not the best stability, and it cannot be out of refrigeration for an extended period of time in warmer climates. For a thorough discussion of buttercream, please see Chapter 15.

Rolled Fondant Rolled fondant is used to cover cakes that are usually already iced with a very thin layer of buttercream. It forms a seamless coat, providing a clean, elegant appearance. Unlike buttercream, rolled fondant has many versatile applications. It can tightly cover a cake, or it can be draped to create a soft look. Color can be kneaded into rolled fondant before the cake is covered, or airbrushed on afterward, with designs ranging from simple gradation of colors to intricate drawings. Rolled fondant can also be textured and embossed. For more detailed information about rolled fondant, please refer to Chapter 21.

Pastillage Pastillage is suitable for making small decorative pieces or decorations to place on top of a cake. Because it dries out very fast and becomes very hard when completely dry, it is also used to make support pieces for pulled and blown sugar. Pastillage is pure white, which makes it a great canvas for paint or airbrushing. It is made with edible ingredients but is not meant to be consumed, so every piece of pastillage must be removed when the cake is served. More information about pastillage appears in Chapter 21.

Gum Paste Gum paste is typically used to make various flowers and leaves. It is a time-consuming and labor-intensive process, but the end result is breathtaking: flowers made by very experienced artisans look exactly like the real thing. Once dried out, gum paste flowers are not sensitive to humidity and can last indefinitely when properly stored. Detailed information about gum paste appears in Chapter 21.

Marzipan Marzipan can be used to cover cakes or to create small figures such as flowers, fruits, and animals. Color can be kneaded into marzipan, or figures can be painted and/or airbrushed. It is an easy material to work with because it does not dry out quickly and remains soft for a long time. Flowers as intricate as gum paste flowers cannot be made with marzipan because of its much coarser grain.

Pulled Sugar Skill and experience are required to create pulled sugar pieces, which can include elaborate, colorful ribbons and shiny sugar flowers. Pulled sugar pieces are very sensitive to humidity, so they must be stored in airtight boxes with humectants and placed on the cake at the last minute. For more information about pulled sugar, please refer to Chapter 21.

Blown Sugar Elegant swans and figures of the bride and groom are examples of pieces that can be created with blown sugar. Although blowing sugar requires a high level of skill and specialized equipment, these pieces create very elegant and beautiful artwork. Like pulled sugar, blown sugar pieces must be kept away from humidity. More information about blown sugar can be found in Chapter 21.

Royal Icing Even though royal icing was used to cover cakes hundreds of years ago, it is no longer used for this purpose. Instead, royal icing is commonly used to create intricate piped decorations, as seen in examples of Australian and South African wedding cakes. More information about royal icing can be found in Chapter 15.

Modeling Chocolate **Modeling chocolate** is a combination of couverture chocolate and inverted sugar, such as corn syrup, glucose, or simple syrup. Inverted sugar provides a pliable and workable consistency that sets up as the paste cools down. Modeling chocolate can be made with dark, milk, or white chocolate, with the ratio of chocolate to inverted sugar varying, depending on the ratio of cocoa butter and a specific cocoa mass in each chocolate.

Modeling chocolate can be textured (including a fabric-like texture), or shaped into ribbons and bows, or flowers and leaves. Coating chocolate cannot be substituted for couverture chocolate because cocoa butter and cocoa mass content are required for pliability and stability (once set).

Modeling Chocolate Formula

18.8 percent simple syrup (1:1 ratio)

31.3 percent glucose

100 percent dark couverture chocolate

Modeling Chocolate Process

Bring the simple syrup to a boil. Add the glucose to the simple syrup.

Cool the mixture to 90°F (32°C).

Add the cooled mixture to the tempered chocolate, and mix until well blended using a rubber spatula.

Spread the mixture 1 to 1 ½ inches (2 to 4 cm) thick on parchment paper.

Cover lightly with plastic wrap, and make sure no moisture collects on the surface of the chocolate.

Let the modeling chocolate rest in the refrigerator overnight before using.

Planning

When meeting with prospective clients, be sure to describe your philosophy and how it differs from the competitors. Whether the focus is on a well-balanced combination of flavors or intricate sugar decoration, it should be mentioned at this stage so that your work can be distinguished from others. Ask prospective clients to fill out a brief form that will enable you to collect as much information about the wedding as possible, including vendors, florists, and caterers. This will help to determine the overall quality of the wedding. One should also be prepared to provide an approximate price for the wedding cake, or the price per slice.

Date, Time, and Venue The first information to be determined from the client is the date, time, and location of the wedding. Make sure that refrigerator space is available on-site, in case some components need refrigeration. It is also important to establish the location of the cake; for example, if it will be outside in summer, a shaded space should be reserved. If the reception will occur late at night, the cake will need to hold for long hours. Also, be sure to ask if the reception hall will be air-conditioned. All of these factors will affect the design and components of a well-structured cake.

Next, ask who will serve the cake. Some clients prefer to have the caterer do it, whereas others prefer that the pastry chef serve. Finally, after you learn the location, consider the mode of transportation. The date and time of day can have a significant influence on travel time; for example, if the wedding is held during a holiday season, traffic can have an effect on the timely delivery of the cake.

Size So that you can give the client a realistic cost estimate, you should determine the size of the cake. Ask the client how many guests are expected to attend, and explain that it is better to have enough cake to serve everyone at the wedding, including photographers, musicians, and wedding coordinators. And, although some guests can be expected to leave before the cake is served, some guests will eat more than one slice.

Next, ask if the bride and groom want to save the top tier of the cake; many couples follow the tradition of saving this tier for their first anniversary. If this is the case, the top tier cannot be part of the estimated size for serving at the reception. Ask if there is a chance that the number of guests will change drastically before the wedding, and explain that it will be very helpful to let you know as soon as they know. If the client does not anticipate that the number of guests will grow by more than 10 percent, ask for a confirmation of the final number 2 weeks before the wedding.

Figure 17-9 shows the number of servings that can be yielded per tier. These are general numbers because serving sizes change depending

Figure 17-9 Serving Yield per Tier

Tier Size, Diameter	Estimated Number of Servings
5 inch (13 cm)	6
6 inch (15 cm)	8
7 inch (18 cm)	10 to 12
8 inch (20 cm)	12 to 14
9 inch (23 cm)	16 to 20
10 inch (25 cm)	24 to 28
12 inch (31 cm)	36 to 42
14 inch (36 cm)	48 to 64
16 inch (41 cm)	72 to 84
18 inch (46 cm)	92 to 108

of the type of cake chosen. Richer cakes yield more than lighter cakes because the serving size is typically smaller.

Portfolio When designing a wedding cake, it is very helpful for the bride and groom to see actual photos of cakes. For this reason, presenting a portfolio that displays work you have done in the past is highly recommended. It can also include photographs from books and magazines, as long as it is noted that they are taken from outside sources, along with photographs of the same work recreated, if applicable.

When clients can visualize a wide variety of cakes, they have a better idea of what they prefer in terms of shape (round, square, or heart-shaped), stacked or separate tiers, type of finish (buttercream icing, rolled fondant, glaze, etc.), gum paste or fresh flowers, and more. Whenever creating a new cake, bring a camera to the wedding and take as many photographs as possible. Some wedding photographers will be happy to provide photographs of the cake for your portfolio.

Selecting Style When deciding flavor, ask the bride and groom if they have a preference. Be prepared to present some examples of past work because people like to know what has been successfully done. Prepare a list of cakes and fillings, as well as a list of current best sellers. If the client isn't sure, be prepared make some recommendations. Incorporate seasonal ingredients, if available.

It is possible to have two types of cakes with different flavors in one wedding cake, as long as the flavors complement each other. Avoid similar flavors, or flavors that do not go well together: Ideally, a lighter flavor should contrast with a heavier one. Also note that incorporating a combination of flavors is a way to up-sell the cake because it increases the price.

Structure of the cake is another concern. Wedding cakes usually stand in the reception hall for hours, and they must have enough structure to hold up under any condition. If softer cake bases and fillings are used, use separate pillars for multiple tiers. If the cake will be standing where there is no air-conditioning, avoid using temperature- and humidity-sensitive components, such as sugar garnishes and mousse fillings.

If time allows, and the bride and groom prefer, arrange a cake tasting before the final decision is made. This will help provide clarity, especially if they are deciding between several types of cakes. It also presents an excellent opportunity to sell upgraded versions of cakes and fillings by introducing several new flavors.

For large weddings, the composition of the cake should be focused on. Even though the cake is made exclusively for the bride and groom, it showcases work that has been done over months of planning and days or even weeks of production. Keep in mind that a wedding with over 200 guests is likely to include at least one potential client.

Finally, the cake's appearance should match the theme of the wedding, including colors and flowers of choice. Utilize the portfolio to provide visual examples and explain the materials used, including their characteristics and technical differences. For example, buttercream has limited applications in cake finishes, while rolled fondant can be colored, airbrushed, textured, shaped, and draped. In addition, marzipan and gum paste flowers last much longer than fresh flowers, which look good only for a couple of hours. This discussion also provides an opportunity to introduce components that can up-sell the cake: the more advanced the techniques used, the higher the price will be.

Contract and Deposit It is very important to have a contract that contains detailed information. The form should be filled out while you are talking to the client, to ensure that all necessary details are included and mutually agreed upon. After the contract is signed, the initial deposit is paid. The amount of the deposit should be based on the estimated number of guests and estimated price of the cake and should cover the cost of food and equipment, as well as a cancellation penalty. The final balance can be calculated after the number of guests is confirmed. Be sure to receive final payment on the day of wedding, before the reception starts.

Assembly and Transportation One day before the wedding, confirm the time when the cake is arriving and the time it needs to be finished. Also, be clear about where to unload the cake and where it can be assembled.

The first suggestion for wedding cake delivery is to transport the cake unassembled. Cakes can be filled and iced, and stable decorations such as buttercream piping can be done on each tier. However, fragile decorations like sugar flowers should be placed on the cake at the reception site. This is the safest way to prevent cake deformation and damage to the decorations. Depending on distance of travel, the type of vehicle available, the weather, and the size of the cake, some stacked wedding cakes may be able to be delivered already assembled.

Before transport, each cake should be placed in a different box and secured by placing nonslip mats underneath the cake. In addition, take care to ensure that the cake boxes do not move around in the vehicle by placing nonslip mats between the boxes and the floor. Upon arrival at the wedding site, you can assemble and apply the final decorations to the finished cake.

As a rule, always bring extra icing, piping bags and tips, and tools to assemble or fix the cake in case any damage occurs during transport or assembly. If you are cutting and serving the cake, bring your own tools because they may not be available on-site. If you are expected to make an appearance to wedding guests, bring an extra, clean jacket.

Pricing

As discussed, a wedding cake should be priced based on the number of servings. Factors that determine the base price per serving are the cost of labor, food, and equipment.

- Labor costs include the actual time that you and/or your staff work on the cake, plus the day of the wedding, from transporting the cake until leaving the site. Hourly labor costs may vary depending on the location and level of difficulty of the project.
- Food costs include the prices of all ingredients, as well as decorative elements on the cake.
- Equipment costs include other tools and equipment, such as cardboard, plastic cake toppers, pillars, and pearls.

When calculating a base price, start with a basic sponge cake and buttercream icing and calculate price per serving. The base price can also vary depending on the location and reputation.

The next step is to calculate the cost of the cake once the flavor and design of the cake are determined. It is important to remember that customers often have a budget when shopping for a wedding cake. It can be your goal to help the couple get the best cake possible within their budget. Add on flat fees for special fillings, liqueur and fresh fruits, specialty garnishes, and flowers as needed. When the number of the guests is confirmed, calculate the final price of the cake to create an official invoice.

WEDDING CAKES CONCLUSION

Wedding cakes have a long and interesting history, and it is now a common custom to have one at a wedding in many different countries. By knowing what materials are suitable to a given situation and what are not, it is possible to create a cake that is structurally practical and meets the bride and groom's desires. Close communication with the clients and advanced production planning ensures a well-organized production of the cake, which leads to a successful presentation of the cake. Wedding cakes can be the most memorable pastry for anyone who has been married. The success of this relies on the pastry chef's skill and creativity to compose one unique wedding cake for every marrying couple.

Lemon Curd Cake

FORMULA

LEMON CURD CAKE

This delightful cake is a striking medley of tart and sweet flavors, with bright visual appeal. Lemon curd cake is made with light génoise moistened with lemon cake syrup. The filling is a light crème Chantilly, with accents of lemon curd and fresh raspberries. Other seasonal fruit can be used as desired. It is a perfectly light and refreshing dessert for a warm summer evening.

Mise en Place

Components	Kilogram	US decimal	Lb & Oz
Génoise	1 each	1 each	1 each
Cake syrup	0.100	0.220	4
Lemon curd	0.200	0.441	7
Crème Chantilly	0.500	1.100	1 2
Fresh raspberries or blueberries	SQ	SQ	SQ
Snow icing	SQ	SQ	SQ

Yield: 1 [8 inch (20 cm)] cake

Process

1. Split the génoise into three layers.
2. Place the bottom layer on a 9 inch (23 cm) cake board.
3. Apply a light layer of cake syrup to the cake with a pastry brush.
4. Next, apply a thin layer of lemon curd with a palette knife.
5. Spread a layer of Chantilly over the curd layer ¼ inch (0.5 cm) thick and press raspberries into the cream.
6. Repeat the process twice more until the last layer has been placed.
7. Mask the cake with a thin layer of Chantilly, and reserve the cake in the refrigerator until ready to finish.
8. To finish, transfer the cake to a 9 inch (23 cm) gold board, ice the cake with a ¼ inch (0.5 cm) layer of Chantilly, and place in the freezer for 1 hour.
9. Apply a layer of curd on the top of the cake, leaving about a border ½ inch (1 cm) from the edge.
10. Dust about 8 to 12 fresh raspberries with snow icing and place them around the border of the curd. Place three dusted raspberries in the center of the cake.
11. Store under refrigeration.

FORMULA

CHOCOLATE HAZELNUT CAKE

This cake takes the classic flavor combination of chocolate and hazelnuts and gives it a twist with unexpected texture. The hazelnut japonaise is a surprising crunch in the mouth and a refreshing palate cleanser balanced with the rich praline buttercream. The chocolate cake is moist, and even though it calls for a high-ratio chocolate cake, any chocolate cake can reasonably be substituted.

Mise en Place

Components	Kilograms	US decimal	Lb & Oz
High-ratio chocolate cake	1 each	1 each	1 each
Hazelnut japonaise disc	1 each	1 each	1 each
Apricot jam	0.150	0.331	5
Praline buttercream	0.550	1.213	1 3
Plain buttercream	0.075	0.165	3
Chocolate shavings	0.100	0.220	4
Roasted hazelnuts	8 each	8 each	8 each
Cocoa powder	0.050	0.110	2

Yield: 1 [8 inch (20 cm)] cake

Process

1. Trim the japonaise disc to match the diameter of the cake. Reserve.
2. Split the cake into three layers (only two will be used) and place the bottom layer on a 9 inch (23 cm) cake board.
3. Apply a very thin layer of apricot jam to the cake, pressing it into the crumb.
4. Spread praline buttercream over the jam at ¼ inch (0.5 cm) thick.
5. Place the Japonaise layer over the buttercream.
6. Spread more praline buttercream over the Japonaise layer at ¼ inch (0.5 cm) thick.
7. Place another cake layer over the buttercream and apply another thin layer of jam.
8. Mask the cake with a thin layer of praline buttercream and reserve the cake in the refrigerator until ready to finish.
9. To finish, transfer the cake to a 9 inch (23 cm) gold board. Ice the cake with a ¼ inch (0.5 cm) layer of praline buttercream.
10. Pipe three rings of shells of marbled buttercream [¾ inch (2 cm) in height].
11. Pipe chocolate glaze between the rings of shells.
12. Place candied hazelnuts in the center of the shells.
13. Store in a refrigerated case or refrigerator.

Chocolate Hazelnut Cake

FORMULA

BLACK FOREST CAKE

This light cake, layered with Kirsch cake syrup, cherry cream, chocolate whipped cream, sour cherries, and chocolate curls, probably originated in the late 16th century in the Black Forest region (Der Schwarzwald) of Germany. This region is known for its sour cherries and Kirschwasser. Our version honors the combination of chocolate chiffon, brandy-soaked cherries, and two flavors of whipped cream, which has made this traditional German delicacy a lasting classic.

Mise en Place

Components	Kilogram	US decimal	Lb & Oz
Chocolate chiffon cake	1 each	1 each	1 each
Cake syrup with Kirsch	0.100	0.220	4
Cherry cream	0.400	0.892	14 ¼
Chocolate crème Chantilly	0.200	0.446	7 ⅛
Morello cherries	16 each	16 each	16 each
Crème Chantilly (décor)	0.075	0.165	3
Brandied cherries, drained	8 each	8 each	8 each
Chocolate shavings	SQ	SQ	SQ

Yield: 1 [8 inch (20 cm)] cake

Cherry Cream Formula

Ingredients	Baker's %	Kilogram	US decimal	Lb & Oz		Test
Whipping cream	100.00	1.465	3.229	3	3 ⅝	10 ⅜ oz
Powdered sugar	21.00	0.308	0.678		10 ⅞	2 ¼ oz
Cherry puree	24.00	0.352	0.775		12 ⅜	2 ½ oz
Gelatin leaf	2.20	0.032	0.071		1 ⅛	¼ oz
Kirsch	6.40	0.094	0.207		3 ¼	⅝ oz
Total	153.60	2.250	4.960	4	15 ⅜	1 lb

Yield: 5 [8 inch (20 cm)] cakes
Test: 1 [8 inch (20 cm)] cake

Process, Cherry Cream

1. Whip the cream and powdered sugar to soft peaks and reserve.
2. Bloom the gelatin and warm the puree. Temper the two together.
3. Continue to whip the cream and slowly add the cherry mixture, whipping to medium peaks.
4. Add the alcohol last and continue whipping just until proper consistency for icing.
5. Use immediately.

Chocolate Créme Chantilly Formula

Ingredients	Baker's %	Kilogram	US decimal	Lb & Oz
Whipping cream	100.00	0.189	0.417	6 ⅝
Powdered sugar	15.00	0.028	0.063	1
Atomized couverture	17.00	0.032	0.071	1 ⅛
Total	132.00	0.250	0.551	8 ⅞

Process, Chocolate Crème Chantilly

Whip the cream, powdered sugar, and atomized couverture to medium peaks.

Assembly

1. Split the cake into three layers and brush the bottom layer with melted coating chocolate.
2. Once set, place the bottom layer on a 9 inch (23 cm) cake board. Brush lightly with cake syrup.
3. Spread cherry cream on the cake ¼ inch (0.5 cm) thick. Dot with Morello cherries.
4. Place the next cake layer over the cream, and repeat the process of adding syrup, cream, and cherries until the third layer has been placed on the cake.
5. Mask the cake with a thin layer of cherry cream; reserve in the refrigerator until ready to finish.

6. To finish, transfer the cake to a 9 inch (23 cm) gold board, and ice the cake with a ¼ inch (0.5 cm) layer of chocolate crème Chantilly.
7. Pipe rosettes of Chantilly blended with cherry cream [1 inch (2.5 cm) in height] at eight portion markings. Top each rosette with a dry, brandied cherry.
8. Place chocolate shavings in the center of the rosettes and dust with powdered sugar or sucraneige.
9. Store in a refrigerated case or refrigerator.

FORMULA

MOCHA CAKE

Lush coffee buttercream is paired with light chocolate chiffon cake in this addictive layer cake with classic appeal. A hint of apricot jam pressed into the crumb of the cake adds a refreshing note of acidity to balance the richness of the buttercream and chocolate glaze in this delectable mocha cake.

Mise en Place

Components	Kilogram	US decimal	Lb & Oz	
Chocolate chiffon cake	1 each	1 each	1 each	
Cake syrup	0.100	0.220		4
Apricot jam (optional)	0.150	0.331		5
Coffee buttercream	0.500	1.102	1	2
Chocolate glaze	0.250	0.551		9

Yield: 1 [9 inch (23 cm)] cake

Assembly

1. Split the cake into four layers.
2. Place the bottom layer on a 9 inch (23 cm) cake board.
3. Apply a light layer of cake syrup to the cake with a pastry brush.
4. Next, apply a thin layer of jam with a palette knife (if using).
5. Spread a layer of buttercream ⅛ inch thick (0.5 cm).
6. Repeat this process three more times until the last layer has been placed.
7. Mask the cake with a thin layer of buttercream, and reserve in the refrigerator until ready to finish.
8. Ice the cake with a ¼ inch (0.5 cm) layer of coffee buttercream. Create a level top and next level the sides. Leave the upsurge of buttercream to create a border to hold the glaze.
9. Pour the glaze onto the cake, refrigerate, and then transfer to a gold board.
10. Store in a refrigerated case or refrigerator.

Mocha Cake

Black Forest Cake

FORMULA

SACHER CAKE

Sacher cake consists of two layers of dense chocolate cake with a thin layer of apricot jam in the middle and dark chocolate icing on the top and sides. It is traditionally eaten with whipped cream and coffee, as most Viennese consider the Sachertorte too dry to be eaten without.

Ingredients	Baker's %	Kilogram	US decimal	Lb & Oz		Test
50% almond paste	333.00	0.768	1.694	1	11 ⅛	5 ⅜ oz
Sugar #1	125.00	0.288	0.636		10 ⅛	2 oz
Eggs	114.00	0.263	0.580		9 ¼	1 ⅞ oz
Egg yolks	208.00	0.480	1.058	1	⅞	3 ⅜ oz
Melted butter	100.00	0.231	0.509		8 ⅛	1 ⅝ oz
Pastry flour	100.00	0.231	0.509		8 ⅛	2 ⅝ oz
Cocoa powder	100.00	0.231	0.509		8 ⅛	2 ⅝ oz
Egg whites	312.00	0.720	1.587	1	9 ⅜	5 ⅛ oz
Sugar #2	125.00	0.288	0.636		10 ⅛	2 oz
Total	1517.00	3.500	7.715	7	11 ½	1 lb 8 ¾ oz

Yield: 5 [8 inch (20 cm)] cakes
Test: 1 [8 inch (20 cm)] cake

Process

1. Line the cake pans.
2. Warm the almond paste in a microwave.
3. In a mixing bowl with the paddle attachment, mix the almond paste with the first sugar.
4. Add the egg yolks slowly, mix well, and then add the eggs slowly. Mix for approximately 10 minutes.
5. Add the cooled melted butter, flour, and cocoa powder.
6. In a mixer with a whip attachment, whip the egg whites with the second sugar to soft peaks.
7. Fold the whipped egg whites into the cake batter.
8. Deposit 1 lb 8 oz (700 g) into each cake pan.
9. Bake at 335°F (168°C) in a convection oven for approximately 30 to 35 minutes.

Assembly

1. Divide the cake into two equal layers.
2. Spread apricot jam between the two layers.
3. Cover the cake with chocolate glaze and pipe *Sacher* on the top decoratively with cooled and thickened chocolate glaze.

Sacher Cake

FORMULA

CARROT CAKE

According to food historians, our modern carrot cake most likely descended from cakes made during the Middle Ages in Europe, when sugar was scarce and carrots were used as sweeteners. Although they were baked in the United States early in the 18th century, carrot cakes do not appear in American cookbooks until well into the 1900s. They enjoyed a revival in the United States in the last quarter of the 20th century, when they were perceived to be "health food." In 2005, Food Network listed carrot cake, with its cream cheese icing, as number five of the top five fad foods of the 1970s. The worthy carrot cake is now ready for yet another revival, as evidenced by this deliciously updated, wholesome, and delectable treatment.

Ingredients	Baker's %	Kilogram	US decimal	Lb & Oz	Test
Canola oil	50.60	0.477	1.051	1 ⅞	3 ⅜ oz
Buttermilk	57.00	0.537	1.184	1 3	3 ¾ oz
Sugar	145.60	1.372	3.025	3 ⅜	9 ⅝ oz
Vanilla	5.10	0.048	0.106	1 ¾	⅜ oz
Eggs	50.60	0.477	1.051	1 ⅞	3 ⅜ oz
Bread flour	75.90	0.715	1.577	1 9 ¼	5 oz
Pastry flour	24.10	0.227	0.501	8	1 ⅝ oz
Baking soda	3.80	0.036	0.079	1 ¼	¼ oz
Cinnamon	1.50	0.014	0.031	½	⅛ oz
Salt	1.00	0.009	0.021	⅜	⅛ oz
Pineapple, crushed	75.90	0.715	1.577	1 9 ¼	5 oz
Carrots, grated	83.50	0.787	1.735	1 11 ¾	5 ½ oz
Coconut, shredded	24.10	0.227	0.501	8	1 ⅝ oz
Walnuts, toasted	38.00	0.358	0.789	12 ⅝	2 ½ oz
Total	636.70	6.000	13.228	13 3 ⅝	2 lb 10 ⅜ oz

Yield: 5 [8 inch (20 cm)] cakes
Test: 1 [8 inch (20 cm)] cake

Process

1. Sift together the dry ingredients and reserve.
2. Combine the oil, buttermilk, vanilla extract, sugar, and eggs.
3. Slowly add the sifted dry ingredients to this mixture.
4. Fold in the pineapple, carrots, coconut, and nuts. Deposit into papered and greased cake pans at 1 lb 5 oz (600 g) each.
5. Bake at 325°F (163°C) in a convection oven for about 25 to 30 minutes.

Cream Cheese Icing Formula

Ingredients	Baker's %	Kilogram	US decimal	Lb & Oz		Test
Unsalted butter	11.00	0.145	0.321		5 ⅛	1 oz
White chocolate	16.00	0.212	0.467		7 ½	1 ½ oz
Cream cheese	100.00	1.323	2.916	2	14 ⅝	9 ⅜ oz
Powdered sugar	51.00	0.675	1.487	1	7 ¾	4 ¾ oz
Sour cream	11.00	0.145	0.321		5 ⅛	1 oz
Total	189.00	2.500	5.511	5	8 ⅛	1 lb 1 ⅝ oz

Yield: 5 [8 inch (20 cm)] cakes
Test: 1 [8 (20 cm)] cake

Process, Cream Cheese Icing

1. Melt the butter and chocolate together, taking caution to not overheat. Reserve.
2. In a bowl fitted with the paddle attachment, blend the cream cheese until smooth.
3. Add the sifted powdered sugar and mix well.
4. Add the butter and chocolate mixture; mix just until blended.
5. Mix in the sour cream just to incorporation.

Assembly

1. Place a carrot cake on a cake board.
2. Spread 9 oz (250 g) of cream cheese icing on top of one layer of the cake, using caution not to get any on the side of the cake.
3. Add a second cake layer and apply another 9 oz (250 g) of icing on top, just to the edges of the cake.
4. If desired, garnish with traditional piped carrot décor.

FORMULA

NAPOLEON

This noble French dessert is constructed from several lush layers of baked puff pastry and pastry cream. Traditional napoleons are poured with white fondant and then chocolate fondant is piped laterally and feathered throughout the white fondant. The more contemporary approach here uses powdered sugar, which is "branded" with a hot metal rod. Another modern method is to lightly dust the puff pastry with sugar and then brûlée it as one would a crème brûlée, producing a pleasantly shiny crisp crunch.

Mise en Place

Puff dough sheet, baked, 1 each

Pastry cream for napoleon, 3 lb 4 ⅞ oz (1.5 kg)

Powdered sugar, SQ

Yield: ⅓ sheet

Pastry Cream for Napoleon Formula

Ingredients	Baker's %	Kilogram	US decimal	Lb & Oz	
Whole milk	100.00	0.920	2.028	2	½
Vanilla bean	Each	1	1		1
Cornstarch	8.00	0.074	0.162		2 ⅝
Sugar	20.00	0.184	0.406		6 ½
Egg yolks	20.00	0.184	0.406		6 ½
Butter	15.00	0.138	0.304		4 ⅞
Total	163.00	1.500	3.306	3	4 ⅞

Process

1. Scale the whole milk and vanilla beans into a stainless steel pot and bring to a boil.
2. Meanwhile, scale the sugar and cornstarch into a bowl, and mix to combine.
3. Scale the egg yolks into the sugar–starch mixture, and whisk until just combined. Do not incorporate air.
4. After the milk comes to a boil, pour one-third of it onto the egg yolk mixture, and stir to incorporate evenly.

5. Return this mixture to the pot, constantly stirring.
6. Continue to cook the custard while stirring until it has boiled for 2 minutes.
7. Turn off the heat, add the butter and stir until mixed in completely.
8. Pour the pastry cream into a clean, shallow container and cover to the surface with plastic wrap.
9. Refrigerate immediately until needed.

Assembly

1. Trim the edges of the puff dough sheet and reserve.
2. Cut the sheet into three strips lengthwise, about 4 inch (10 cm) wide each.
3. Whip the pastry cream until smooth.
4. Apply half the pastry cream to the base strip and spread evenly.
5. Gently press the second strip of puff pastry onto the pastry cream.
6. Apply the second layer of pastry cream and top with the last strip of puff pastry.

Finishing

1. Dust the top of the cake with powdered sugar.
2. Cut slices to the desired size [approximately 4 inches (10 cm) × 1 ½ inches (4 cm)].
3. "Brand" the powdered sugar with a hot metal rod and garnish as desired.

FORMULA

PITHIVIER

Traditionally served as a Twelfth Night cake, when it is baked with a fava bean, this large round puff pastry tart with scalloped edges usually contains almond cream, but has been open to many interpretations since its origin in the city of Pithivier, in the Orleans region of France. Some versions call for a filling of crystallized fruits and a frosting of white fondant.

Mise en Place

Puff pastry with six single folds

Process

1. Sheet the puff pastry down to ¹⁄₁₆ inch (2 mm) and relax the dough.
2. For one finished Pithivier, cut two 8 inch (20 cm) diameter circles and a strip ½ inch (1 cm) wide, long enough to circumnavigate the circle.
3. Chill the pastry if it warms while handling.
4. Place one circle of dough on a parchment-lined sheet pan. Lightly brush the edges with water and place the ½ inch (1 cm) strips around the perimeter.
5. Pipe frangipane in the center of circle, spiraling out toward the edge. Do not cover the strips. Optional: Place fruit over the frangipane.
6. Brush the top of the strips lightly with water.
7. Top with the second piece of puff pastry; press lightly to secure it to the moist sides.
8. To crimp the edges: Press down firmly with two fingers (index and middle finger recommended). Using a nonsharp, straight edge object such as the stem of a thermometer, draw the outside edge of the dough between the two fingers. Move the fingers over one finger's width (that is, one finger will be placed in the formed indent). Proceed in this manner around the edge of the circle to form a decorative, scalloped pattern.
9. Lightly egg wash the puff pastry top, and reserve at least ½ hour in the refrigerator.
10. Before baking, apply a second egg wash and lightly score the traditional Pithivier pattern (curved radial lines that originate at the center and reach almost to the crimped edge).
11. Vent the pastry with a center hole.
12. Bake at 350°F (177°C) in a convection oven for about 30 to 40 minutes or until golden brown on the sides.
13. Brush with apricot glaze (optional).

Pithivier

Napoleons

FORMULA

JALOUSIE

The jalousie consists of two long rectangular pieces of puff pastry dough filled with almond cream or frangipane. The top crust is lined with slices to create the appearance of a window shutter when baked. The inclusion of fruits such as apples, pears, peaches, or berries adds seasonal color, placed just atop the filling. After baking, the pastry is often glazed and garnished with a shimmer of pearl sugar. Jalousie is typically sold by the slice.

Mise en Place

Puff pastry with six single folds

Process

1. Sheet the puff pastry to 1⁄16 inch (2 mm) and relax the dough.
2. Cut two wide strips of puff pastry, one with a width of 4 inches (10 cm) will be used for the bottom and the other 4 ½ inches (11.5 cm) wide will be used for the top.
3. In addition, cut enough ½ inch (1 cm) wide strips to run the length of each of the sides of the wider strips of dough.
4. If the pastry warms while handling, place it in the refrigerator to chill.
5. Place a 4 inch (10 cm) wide bottom strip of dough on a parchment-lined sheet pan.
6. Lightly brush the sides with water.
7. Place a ½ inch (1 cm) strip along each side of the rectangle, as if creating a frame.
8. Pipe frangipane down the center, between the two side strips, using caution not to cover the strips. Optional: Place fruit over the frangipane.
9. Brush the tops of the strips lightly with water.
10. Using the "shutter" cutter, cut the 4 ½ inch (11.5 cm) wide piece of puff pastry down the center.
11. Transfer to the assembled pastry and secure the top dough to the moist sides.
12. Crimp the edges and seal with the stem of a thermometer.
13. Lightly egg wash, and reserve at least ½ hour in the refrigerator.
14. Egg wash again, and bake at 350°F (177°C) in a convection oven for about 30 minutes or until golden brown on the sides.
15. Brush with apricot glaze and garnish with pearl sugar.

FORMULA

ST. HONORÉ CAKE

St. Honoré cake is named for the French patron saint of bakers and pastry chefs, Saint Honoré, Bishop of Amiens. This sophisticated confection is built from a gâteau consisting of a layer of puff pastry, which is then crowned with choux paste, and decorated with delicate caramel-glazed choux balls. The extravagant presentation of this traditional French cake is stunning to behold, perfect for special occasions.

Components

Traditional puff pastry

Pâte à choux

Caramel

Crème Chiboust

Crème Chantilly

Yield: 5 [8 inch (20 cm)] cakes
Test: 1 [8 inch (20 cm)] cake

Process

1. Cut one 8 inch (20 cm) round circle of puff pastry dough for each cake; dock with a dough docker.
2. Using a pastry bag with a round tip, pipe a circle of pâte à choux around the outside edge of the puff piece. Also, pipe a loose, open spiral that starts at the outside and finishes in the center, decreasing in height as it moves to the center.
3. Egg wash the puff pastry and pâte à choux.
4. Bake at 350°F (177°C) in a convection oven until golden brown.
5. On a parchment-lined sheet pan, pipe small pâte à choux puffs. Each cake will need 12 to 15 puffs.
6. Bake at 350°F (177°C) in a convection oven until golden brown.

Crème Chiboust Formula

Ingredients	Baker's %	Kilogram	US decimal	Lb & Oz		Test
Milk	100.00	1.069	2.358	2	5 ¾	13 ¾ oz
Vanilla bean	Each	1	1		1	½ each
Sugar #1	5.00	0.053	0.118		1 ⅞	5/7 oz
Cornstarch	10.00	0.107	0.236		3 ¾	1 ⅜ oz
Egg yolks	24.00	0.257	0.566		9	3 ¼ oz
Gelatin	1.75	0.019	0.041		¾	3 sheets
Butter	10.00	0.107	0.236		3 ¾	1 ⅜ oz
Rum	10.00	0.107	0.236		3 ¾	1 ⅜ oz
Water	10.00	0.107	0.236		3 ¾	1 ⅜ oz
Sugar #2	33.00	0.353	0.778		12 ½	4 ½ oz
Glucose	6.00	0.064	0.141		2 ¼	⅞ oz
Egg whites	24.00	0.257	0.566		9	3 ¼ oz
Total	233.75	2.500	5.511	5	8 ⅛	2 lb

Process, Crème Chiboust

Make Pastry Cream

1. Bloom the gelatin in cold water, and reserve.
2. Scale the whole milk, vanilla beans, and half of the first sugar into a stainless steel pot and bring to a boil.
3. Meanwhile, scale the other half of the first sugar and cornstarch into a bowl, and mix to combine.
4. Scale the egg yolks into the sugar–starch mixture, and whisk until just combined. Do not incorporate air.
5. Once the milk comes to a boil, temper one-third of it into the egg yolk mixture; stir to incorporate evenly.
6. Return this mixture back to the pot, stirring constantly.
7. Continue to cook the custard while stirring until it has boiled for 2 minutes.
8. Off heat, add the butter and bloomed gelatin; stir until mixed in completely. Next, add the rum.
9. Pour the pastry cream into a bowl and cover with plastic wrap to prevent a skin from developing. Reserve and make the Italian meringue.

Make Italian Meringue

1. Heat the water, glucose, and second sugar until it reaches the boiling point.
2. Wash down the sides of the pan with water.
3. When the sugar reaches 241°F (116°C), start whipping the egg whites on medium speed.

5. When the sugar reaches soft ball stage [246°F (119°C) to 250°F (121°C)], slowly pour it into the whipping egg whites.
6. Whip until 104°F (40°C).

Finish Crème Chiboust

Once the desired temperatures are achieved, fold the warm meringue into the pastry cream and use immediately.

Caramel Formula

Ingredients	Baker's %	Kilogram	US decimal	Lb & Oz		Test
Sugar	100.00	0.524	1.156	1	2 ½	9 ¼ oz
Glucose	40.00	0.210	0.462		7 ⅜	3 ¾ oz
Water	33.00	0.173	0.382		6 ⅛	3 oz
Total	173.00	0.907	2.000	2	0	1 lb

Process, Caramel

1. In a saucepan, combine the sugar, glucose, and water.
2. Cook over medium heat until the sugar mixture reaches the caramel stage and has a golden brown color.
3. Remove the caramel from the heat, and shock the pan in cold water to stop the cooking.

Assembly and Finishing

1. Fill the pâte à choux puffs with crème Chiboust and reserve.
2. When the puff pastry is cooled, pipe the crème Chiboust over the base using a plain tip leaving the puffed edges of pâte à choux uncovered.
3. Using the caramel, seal the custard-filled cream puff all around the pâte à choux edges.
4. Using a pastry bag with a St. Honoré tip, pipe crème Chantilly over the crème Chiboust in a decorative pattern.

FORMULA

PARIS-BREST

Paris-Brest was created in 1891 when an industrious Parisian pastry cook recognized an opportunity in owning a *pâtisserie* situated along the route of a bicycle race (precursor to the Tour de France) from Paris to Brest. Filled with crème Paris-Brest and garnished with sliced almonds and powdered sugar, Paris-Brest are baked in the shape of bicycle wheels in honor of the race's cyclists. Today this winning confection continues to tempt customers in pastry shops throughout France.

Components

Pâte à choux (Paris-Brest) 4 inch (10 cm) diameter
Sliced almonds
Granulated sugar
Crème Paris-Brest
Powdered sugar

Process, Pâte à Choux (Paris-Brest)

1. Prepare the pâte à choux, and load into a piping bag fitted with a star tip.
2. Pipe 4 inch (10 cm) diameter circles of choux.
3. Lightly egg wash, garnish with sliced almonds, and sprinkle with granulated sugar.
4. Bake as for pâte à choux.
5. Reserve until needed.

Crème Paris-Brest Formula

Ingredients	Baker's %	Kilogram	US decimal	Lb & Oz		Test
Pastry cream	100.00	2.057	4.535	4	8 ½	8 ⅛ oz
Praline paste	25.00	0.514	1.134	1	2 ⅛	6 oz
Butter	50.00	1.028	2.267	2	4 ¼	12 ⅛ oz
Total	175.00	3.600	7.936	7	15	10 ⅜ oz

Yield: 30 [4 inch (10 cm)] diameter Paris-Brest
Test: 10 [4 inch (10 cm)] diameter Paris-Brest

Process, Crème Paris-Brest

1. For best results, pastry cream, praline paste, and butter should be at room temperature [65°F (18°C) to 70°F (21°C)].
2. In a mixer with the paddle attachment, smooth the praline paste and add the soft butter, and mix until incorporated.
3. Mix the pastry cream until smooth and then fold the butter/praline mixture into it.

Assembly

1. Split the choux pastry in half and pipe the cream filling onto the base with a star tip.
2. Place the top over the piped cream and dust with powered sugar.
3. Store under refrigeration.

Paris-Brest

St. Honoré Cake

FORMULA

BABA SAVARIN

The Baba Savarin is a yeast dough baked in a ring mold and soaked in rum syrup. The center hole can contain pastry cream, crème Chantilly, or fresh fruit. It may have been invented in the 1600s by Polish King Leszczynski, who soaked his stale Kugelhopf in rum and named the resulting dessert after Ali Baba, the hero of the king's favorite book, *A Thousand and One Nights.* Many years later, a Parisian pastry maker decided to experiment with the original baba recipe, changing the shape of the ring mold and adjusting other details, such as leaving out the raisins. The culmination of his efforts was the rich and tasty Baba Savarin. Baba Bouchon is a similar pastry, but in the shape of a cork.

Ingredients	Baker's %	Kilogram	US decimal	Lb & Oz		Test
Bread flour	100.00	1.916	4.223	4	3 ⅝	13 ½ oz
Water	44.00	0.843	1.858	1	13 ¾	6 oz
Eggs	30.00	0.575	1.267	1	4 ¼	4 oz
Yeast (instant)	2.40	0.046	0.101		1 ⅝	⅜ oz
Salt	2.40	0.046	0.101		1 ⅝	⅜ oz
Sugar	8.00	0.153	0.338		5 ⅜	1 ⅛ oz
Melted butter	30.00	0.575	1.267	1	4 ¼	4 oz
Macerated raisins	20.00	0.383	0.845		13 ½	2 ¾ oz
Total	236.80	4.536	10.000	10	0	2 lb

0.040 kg (1.5 ounce) per piece for 1 individual portion, 0.300 kg (10.7 ounce) per piece for 1 entremets
Yield: about 110 individual babas
Test: about 22 individual babas

Process, Baba Savarin

1. Combine the flour, water, eggs, yeast, salt, and sugar and mix with the dough hook.
2. Mix for 5 to 7 minutes after incorporation to cleanup stage, using medium-high speed.
3. Once the dough is developed, add the melted butter on slow speed.
4. Next add the raisins.
5. After mixing, divide and shape the dough into loose balls.
6. Deposit the dough into appropriate molds halfway up the mold, and let ferment 25 to 30 minutes.
7. The dough is ready to bake once it reaches the top of the mold.
8. Bake at 400°F (205°C) in a convection oven until golden brown.

Baba Syrup Formula

Ingredients	Baker's %	Kilogram	US decimal	Lb & Oz		Test
Water	100.00	3.024	6.667	6	10 ⅝	2 lb 3 ¼ oz
Sugar	50.00	1.512	3.333	3	5 ⅜	1 lb 1 ⅝ oz
Vanilla bean	Each	6	6		6	2 each
Lemons, zested	Each	3	3		3	1 each
Dark rum	To taste					To taste
Total	75.00	4.536	10.000	10	0	3 lb 4 ⅞ oz

Process, Baba Syrup

1. Boil the water, sugar, vanilla, and zest.
2. Add the rum when slightly warm.

Assembly

1. Soak the babas until no longer dry.
2. Garnish with crème Chantilly and fruits.

Baba Savarin

FORMULA

CONCORD CAKE

Layers of chocolate meringue and dark chocolate whipped cream are the harmonious elements of this unusual cake, notable for its decoration of miniature chocolate meringue "logs."

Components

Chocolate meringue

Concord cream

Powdered sugar

Chocolate Meringue Formula

Ingredients	Baker's %	Kilogram	US decimal	Lb & Oz		Test
Egg whites	100.00	0.933	2.058	2	⅞	6 ⅝ oz
Sugar	100.00	0.933	2.058	2	⅞	6 ⅝ oz
Powdered sugar	100.00	0.933	2.058	2	⅞	6 ⅝ oz
Dark cocoa powder	12.00	0.112	0.247		4	¾ oz
Cocoa powder	8.80	0.082	0.181		2 ⅞	⅝ oz
Total	320.80	2.995	6.602	6	9 ⅝	1 lb 5 ⅛ oz

Yield: 5 [8 inch (20 cm)] cakes
Test: 1 [8 inch (20 cm)] cake

Process, Chocolate Meringue

1. Preheat the oven to 250°F (122°C).
2. Sift together the powdered sugar and cocoa powders. Set aside.
3. In a mixing bowl with the whip attachment, whip the egg whites and the granulated sugar to stiff peaks.
4. Fold in the sifted powdered sugar and cocoa powders.
5. Using a pastry bag with a large round pastry tip, pipe the meringue into 7 inch (18 cm) round disks, and pipe logs for the top and side of the cake.
6. Bake until the meringue is dry to the touch.

Concord Cream Formula

Ingredients	Baker's %	Kilogram	US decimal	Lb & Oz		Test
Cream	100.00	2.952	6.508	6	8 ⅛	1 lb 4 ⅞ oz
64% chocolate	35.00	1.033	2.278	2	4 ½	7 ¼ oz
Gelatin leaf	0.50	0.015	0.033		½	⅛ oz
Total	135.50	4.000	8.818	8	13 ⅛	1 lb 12 ¼ oz

Yield: 5 [8 inch (20 cm)] cakes
Test: 1 [8 inch (20 cm)] cake

Process, Concord Cream

1. Bloom the gelatin in cold water and reserve.
2. Bring the cream to a boil, and then cool to 180°F (83°C). Add the gelatin.
3. Next, pour the cream over the chocolate and form an emulsion.
4. Cool the mixture completely and allow to rest in the refrigerator for at least 12 hours.

Assembly

1. Before assembly, whip the concord cream to medium peaks.
2. In an 8 inch (20 cm) cake ring, place a disk of chocolate meringue.
3. Using a pastry bag with a round pastry tip, fill the ring or pan with a thin layer of concord cream.
4. Place the next layer of chocolate meringue on top of the cream. Add enough concord cream to fill the ring or pan.
5. Smooth and level the cream with a pastry spatula.
6. Refrigerate the cake for at least 2 hours.
7. To unmold, warm the cake ring with a torch and lift it off.
8. To finish, break the meringue logs into pieces that are slightly longer than the height of the cake. Arrange vertically around the side of the cake, lightly pressing the flat side of the meringue into the chocolate cream.
9. Cover the top of the cake with broken meringue pieces, mounding in the center.
10. Dust the top with powdered sugar.

Concord Cake

FORMULA

TIRAMISU

Desserts similar to tiramisu are noted as far back as the Renaissance, and folklore relates fanciful tales about tiramisu as a favorite dessert of Venetian courtesans, who relied on the espresso-laden treat as a "pick me up" (the literal translation of *tirami-su*) to fortify themselves between amorous encounters. But the version of tiramisu we are familiar with today originated quite recently in a restaurant called Le Beccherie, in Treviso, northwest of Venice. In the 1970s, Le Beccherie introduced the dessert as ladyfingers soaked in strong espresso coffee, mascarpone-zabaglione cream, and bitter cocoa powder. The dessert became immediately popular and was copied by many restaurants throughout Italy. In America, the tiramisu trend started in San Francisco and soon spread to restaurants throughout the United States.

Components

Ladyfinger sponge

Rum and coffee cake syrup

Tiramisu cream

Chocolate powder

Powdered sugar

Chocolate décor

Ladyfinger Sponge Cake Formula

Ingredients	Baker's %	Kilogram	US decimal	Lb & Oz		Test
Egg whites	142.00	0.511	1.127	1	2	3 ⅝ oz
Egg white powder	0.70	0.003	0.006		⅛	⅛ tsp
Sugar	89.00	0.320	0.706		11 ¼	2 ¼ oz
Trimoline	7.00	0.025	0.056		⅞	⅛ oz
Egg yolks	78.00	0.281	0.619		9 ⅞	2 oz
Pastry flour	50.00	0.180	0.397		6 ⅜	1 ¼ oz
Potato starch	50.00	0.180	0.397		6 ⅜	1 ¼ oz
Total	416.70	1.500	3.307	3	4 ⅞	10 ⅝ oz

Note

Combined pastry flour and potato starch weights equal 100 percent.

Yield: 5 [8 inch (20 cm)] cakes
Test: 1 [8 inch (20 cm)] cake
Each cake requires 3 [7.5 inch (19 cm)] discs of ladyfinger sponge.

Process, Ladyfinger Sponge Cake

1. Preheat the oven to 350°F (83°C).
2. Sift together the pastry flour and potato starch.
3. Whip the egg whites and egg white powder in the bowl of a mixer fitted with the whip attachment to stiff peaks with the sugar.
4. Combine the Trimoline and the egg yolks and add them to the stiff peak meringue, while mixing on low speed.
5. Fold in the sifted flour–starch mixture and pipe 7 ½ inch (19 cm) diameter circles.
6. Dust with powered sugar and bake until the cake is golden brown, about 10 minutes.

Rum and Coffee Syrup Formula

Ingredients	Baker's %	Kilogram	US decimal	Lb & Oz		Test
Coffee, strong and hot	100.00	0.909	2.004	2	0	6 ⅜ oz
Sugar	50.00	0.454	1.002	1	0	3 ¼ oz
Dark rum	15.00	0.136	0.301		4 ¾	1 oz
Total	165.00	1.500	3.306	3	4 ⅞	11 ⅝ oz

Process, Rum and Coffee Syrup

1. Add the sugar to the hot coffee and stir to dissolve the sugar.
2. Next, add the alcohol.

Tiramisu Cream Formula

Ingredients	Baker's %	Kilogram	US decimal	Lb & Oz		Test
Mascarpone cheese	71.00	1.402	3.092	3	1 ½	9 ⅞ oz
Coffee extract	7.00	0.138	0.305		4 ⅞	1 oz
Powdered sugar, sifted	19.00	0.375	0.827		13 ¼	2 ⅝ oz
Dark rum	4.40	0.087	0.192		3 ⅛	⅝ oz
Heavy cream	100.00	1.975	4.355	4	5 ⅝	13 ⅞ oz
Gelatin, leaves	1.10	0.022	0.048		¾	⅛ oz
Total	202.50	4.000	8.818	8	13 ⅛	1 lb 12 ¼ oz

Process, Tiramisu Cream

1. Bloom the gelatin in cold water.
2. Temper the gelatin into the heavy cream.
3. Whip the cream, sugar, and mascarpone cheese on medium speed until soft peaks.
4. Add the coffee extract and then rum and mix just until incorporated. Do not overmix.

Assembly

1. Place a 7 ½ inch (19 cm) diameter ladyfinger disc in an 8 inch (20 cm) cake ring lined with an acetate strip.
2. Brush the cake base with the cake syrup.
3. Deposit some of the tiramisu cream and top with a layer of ladyfinger sponge. Soak the cake with syrup.
4. Next, deposit some more tiramisu cream.
5. Add another disc of ladyfinger brushed with coffee syrup.
6. Fill the ring to the top with the cream and smooth the top of the cake with a pastry spatula.
7. Reserve in the freezer for at least 2 hours.
8. Once well chilled, garnish the cake with chocolate powder and powdered sugar.
9. Next, transfer to a gold board, remove the cake ring, and garnish with a chocolate band.

Tiramisu

Opera Cake

FORMULA

OPERA CAKE

The elegant opera cake premiered as the Clichy, introduced by Louis Clichy, with his name written across the top, at the 1903 Exposition Culinaire in Paris. Years later, the renowned Parisian pâtisserie Dalloyau reintroduced and popularized it as L'Opéra. This classic gâteau is composed of exquisitely thin layers of biscuit viennois soaked in coffee syrup and then layered with coffee-flavored buttercream and bittersweet chocolate ganache. The top of the cake is iced with a very thin chocolate glaze, creating a pleasantly firm texture. This cake is traditionally square or rectangular with the sides of the cake exposed to reveal its tempting layers.

Components

Biscuit viennois (per full sheet of opera cake, three sheets of biscuit viennois are required)

Coffee buttercream

Coffee soaker

Chocolate ganache

Glacage opera

Coating chocolate

Yield: 1 full sheet opera cake

Coffee Buttercream Formula

Ingredients	Baker's %	Kilogram	US decimal	Lb & Oz
Italian buttercream	100.00	1.443	3.181	3 2 ⅞
Coffee extract (Trablit)	3.93	0.057	0.125	2
Total	103.93	1.500	3.306	3 4 ⅞

Process

Add the Trablit to the Italian buttercream and whip until smooth and light.

Coffee Soaker Formula

Ingredients	Baker's %	Kilogram	US decimal	Lb & Oz
Strong coffee	100.00	1.000	2.204	2 3 ¼
Sugar	35.00	0.350	0.772	12 ⅜
Coffee extract (Trablit)	3.00	0.030	0.066	1
Total	138.00	1.380	3.042	3 ⅝

Process, Coffee Soaker

Dissolve the sugar in the hot coffee and then add the coffee extract.

Chocolate Ganache Formula

Ingredients	Baker's %	Kilogram	US decimal	Lb & Oz
Cream	100.00	0.500	1.102	1 1 ⅝
64% couverture	100.00	0.500	1.102	1 1 ⅝
Total	200.00	1.000	2.204	2 3 ¼

Process, Chocolate Ganache

1. Bring the cream to a boil and pour over the chocolate.
2. Form an emulsion, and cover to the surface until ready to use.
3. For use, ganache must be soft enough to spread, yet not too soft.

Glacage Opera

Ingredients	Baker's %	Kilogram	US decimal	Lb & Oz
Dark coating chocolate	100.00	1.298	2.861	2 13 ¾
64% couverture	40.00	0.519	1.144	1 2 ¼
Salad oil	14.00	0.182	0.400	6 ⅜
Total	154.00	1.998	4.405	4 6 ½

Process, Glacage Opera

1. Melt the two chocolates together to 120°F (49°C), and add the oil.
2. Reserve until needed, and use at 90°F (37°C).

Assembly (for a full sheet)

1. Spread a thin layer of coating chocolate over a sheet of biscuit viennois.
2. Once set, flip this over onto a sheet of parchment paper onto the back of a sheet pan.
3. Soak the cake through with the coffee soaker.
4. Apply 2 lb (900 g) of buttercream over the cake, making sure to build up the sides of the cake.
5. Set the next cake layer over the buttercream, and soak with the coffee soaker.
6. Apply 2 lb 3 oz (1000 g) of ganache evenly over the second layer of cake.
7. Place the last cake layer over the ganache and soak with the coffee soaker.
8. Apply 1 lb 3 oz (550 g) of buttercream to the top of the cake, being careful to make the top smooth and even.
9. Freeze the cake until needed.
10. Pour the cake with the glacage opera, trim the sides if required, and cut to the desired sizes using a hot, dry knife.
11. Optionally, pipe the word *Opera* on top of the cake or cake slices.

FORMULA

LE FRAISIER

Le Fraisier is a classic composition of crème mousseline, sponge cake, and fresh strawberries. The strawberries crown a layer of sponge cake, with cream piped in between them and another layer of cake on top. The version shown here is topped with marzipan, cut with a design of three concentrically smaller holes. The top of the cake is sprayed with green-colored white chocolate to create a velvety finish, and the holes in the marzipan are filled with a strawberry gelée for a delightful medley of flavors and colors.

Components

Génoise layer 6 inch (15 cm) diameter, ¼ inch (0.6 cm) thick, two each per cake

Grand Marnier cake syrup

Mousseline cream

Fresh strawberries

Marzipan

Green-colored chocolate spray

Strawberry coulis

Yield: 5 [6 inch (15 cm) × 2½ inch (6.5 cm)] cakes
Test: 1 [6 inch (15 cm) × 2½ inch (6.5 cm)] cake

Grand Marnier Cake Syrup Formula

Ingredients	Baker's %	Kilogram	US decimal	Lb & Oz		Test
Water	100.00	0.310	0.683		10 ⅞	2 ⅛ oz
Sugar	84.08	0.260	0.574		9 ⅛	1 ⅞ oz
Grand Marnier	9.55	0.030	0.065		1	¼ oz
Total	193.63	0.600	1.322	1	5 ⅛	4 ¼ oz

Process, Grand Marnier Cake Syrup

1. In a sauce pan, bring the water and sugar to boil. Remove from the heat and cool to room temperature.
2. Stir in the Grand Marnier.

Mousseline Cream Formula

Ingredients	Baker's %	Kilogram	US decimal	Lb & Oz		Test
Milk	100.00	0.784	1.727	1	11 ⅝	5 ¼ oz
Vanilla bean	Each	1	1		1	¼ each
Sugar	34.00	0.266	0.587		9 ⅜	1 ¾ oz
Cornstarch	8.00	0.063	0.138		2 ¼	⅜ oz
Egg yolks	28.00	0.219	0.484		7 ¾	1 ½ oz
Butter	85.00	0.666	1.468	1	7 ½	4 ⅜ oz
Total	255.00	1.998	4.405	4	6 ½	13 ¼ oz

Process, Mousseline Cream

1. In a saucepan over medium heat, warm the milk and vanilla bean. When the milk reaches 90°F (32°C), stir in half of the sugar. Allow the milk to come to a boil.
2. In a mixing bowl, combine the remaining sugar with the cornstarch and add the egg yolks to this mixture to combine all ingredients.
3. Whisk about one-third of the boiling milk into the egg yolk–sugar mixture and then pour the tempered egg yolk–milk mixture into the boiled milk and return the pot to the stove. Boil for an additional 2 minutes, stirring with a whisk.
4. Once cooked, add half of the softened butter to the cream, mix thoroughly, and then refrigerate the cream for 30 minutes.
5. In a mixer with the whip attachment, mix the chilled cream, and add the other half of the softened butter.
6. Mix the cream for 5 minutes, or until it becomes light and fluffy.

Strawberry Coulis Formula

Ingredients	Baker's %	Kilogram	US decimal	Lb & Oz	Test
Strawberry puree	100.00	0.397	0.876	14	2 ¾ oz
Sugar	20.00	0.079	0.175	2 ¾	½ oz
Gelatin	5.85	0.023	0.051	⅞	⅛ oz
Total	125.85	0.500	1.102	1 1 ⅝	3 ½ oz

Process, Strawberry Coulis

1. Bloom the gelatin in cold water.
2. Combine the strawberry puree and sugar, and heat it to 120°F (49°C).
3. Melt the bloomed gelatin in the puree; stir thoroughly.
4. Use immediately, or keep under refrigeration.

Green Chocolate Spray Formula

Ingredients	Baker's %	Kilogram	US decimal	Lb & Oz
White couverture	100.00	0.833	1.837	1 13 ⅜
Cocoa butter	20.00	0.167	0.367	5 ⅞
Liposoluble green colorant	SQ			
Total	120.00	1.000	2.204	2 3 ¼

Process, Green Chocolate Spray

1. Melt the white chocolate, cocoa butter, and colorant. Emulsify well.
2. Spray at 120°F (49°C).

Assembly

1. Slice the génoise cake into three layers. Reserve one of the layers for another use.
2. Line a 6 inch (16 cm) × 2 inch (5 cm) cake ring with a 2 ½ inch (6.5 cm) high acetate strip and place it on a cake board.
3. Place the cake layer in the ring mold, and using a pastry brush, soak the cake with Grand Marnier syrup.
4. Using a piping bag, pipe a thin layer of mousseline cream evenly on the cake, leaving a ½ inch (1 cm) border unpiped around the edge.
5. Place strawberry halves around the perimeter of the cake facing out.
6. Next, cover the entire surface of the cake with whole hulled strawberries.
7. Using a piping bag, cover the strawberries with mousseline cream. Fill in the area above them by spreading the cream evenly on the surface of the cake.
8. Place another layer of the cake on top of the mousseline cream, and press to make flush.
9. Using a cake spatula, apply a very thin layer of mousseline cream over the cake layer.
10. Refrigerate the cake for at least 1 hour.
11. For the final decoration, roll out marzipan and cover just the top of the cake. Make three round indentations on the surface of the marzipan. Reserve in the freezer for at least 30 minutes to prepare for chocolate spray.
12. Spray the marzipan with the green-colored chocolate spray. Deposit the strawberry coulis in the three cavities.

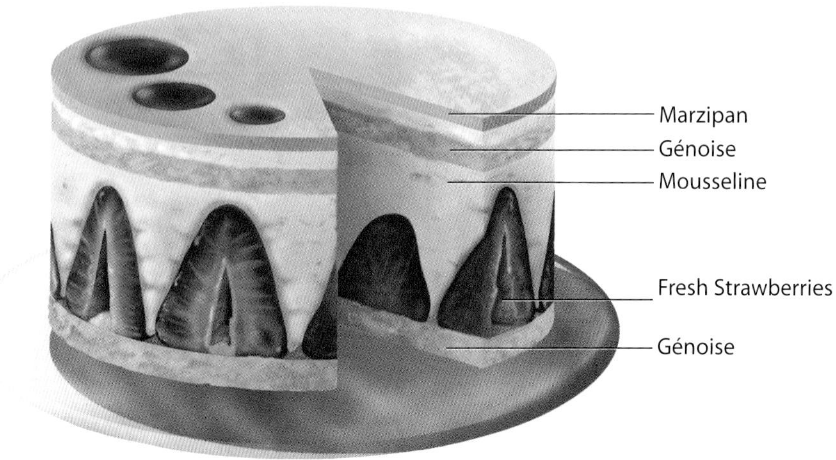

Le Fraisier

FORMULA

FRESH FRUIT CHARLOTTE

Charlotte is a timeless French cake composed of a light cream, such as Bavarian cream or diplomat cream, which is placed in a mold lined with ladyfinger sponge cake. This version is filled with diplomat cream, layered with red berry compote and lemon crémeux. Fresh seasonal berries and a touch of snow sugar are all the decoration needed for the rustically appealing Charlotte.

Components

Ladyfinger sponge
Kirschwasser simple syrup
Berry compote
Lemon crémeux
Vanilla diplomat cream
Fresh fruit
Powdered sugar

Yield: 5 [8 inch (20 cm)] cakes
Test: 1 [8 inch (20 cm)] cake

Ladyfinger Sponge Formula

Ingredients	Baker's %	Kilogram	US decimal	Lb & Oz		Test
Egg whites	142.00	0.375	0.826		13 ¼	2 ⅝ oz
Egg white powder	0.70	0.002	0.004		⅛	⅛ tsp
Sugar	89.00	0.235	0.518		8 ¼	1 ⅝ oz
Egg yolks	78.00	0.206	0.454		7 ¼	1 ½ oz
Trimoline	7.00	0.018	0.041		⅝	⅛ oz
Pastry flour	50.00	0.132	0.291		4 ⅝	⅞ oz
Potato starch	50.00	0.132	0.291		4 ⅝	⅞ oz
Total	416.70	1.100	2.425	2	6 ¾	7 ¾ oz

Each cake will require approximately 160 g for 2 [7 inch (18 cm)] ladyfinger bases and 100 g for 1 [24 inch (61 cm) × 2 ½ inch (6 cm)] band of ladyfingers.

Process, Ladyfinger Sponge

1. Preheat the oven to 350°F (175°C).
2. Sift together the pastry flour and potato starch.
3. Whip the egg whites and egg white powder in the bowl of a mixer fitted with the whip attachment to stiff peaks with the sugar.
4. Combine the Trimoline and the egg yolks, and add them to the stiff peak meringue.
5. Fold in the sifted flour–starch mixture and pipe the desired sizes.
6. Dust with powdered sugar and bake until the cake is golden brown, approximately 7 to 10 minutes.

Kirschwasser Syrup Formula

Ingredients	Baker's %	Kilogram	US decimal	Lb & Oz	Test
Water	100.00	0.258	0.569	9 ⅛	1 oz
Sugar	84.08	0.217	0.479	7 ⅝	⅞ oz
Kirschwasser	9.55	0.025	0.054	⅞	⅛ oz
Total	193.63	0.500	1.102	1 1 ⅝	2 oz

Process, Kirschwasser Syrup

Bring the water and sugar to boil and cool. Then add the alcohol.

Berry Compote Formula

Ingredients	Baker's %	Kilogram	US decimal	Lb & Oz	Test
Raspberry	40.00	0.226	0.498	8	1 ⅝ oz
Blackberry	20.00	0.113	0.249	4	¾ oz
Blueberry	40.00	0.226	0.498	8	1 ⅝ oz
Raspberry puree	40.00	0.226	0.498	8	1 ⅝ oz
Blackberry puree	40.00	0.226	0.498	8	1 ⅝ oz
Vanilla bean	Each	1	1	1	⅕ each
Sugar	38.00	0.214	0.473	7 ⅝	1 ½ oz
Gelatin	3.00	0.017	0.037	⅝	⅛ oz
Total	221.00	1.247	2.750	2 12	8 ¾ oz

Process, Berry Compote

1. Bloom the gelatin in cold water.
2. Combine and heat the berries and puree; add the vanilla bean and the sugar.
3. Simmer the berry mixture for 1 minute. Discard the vanilla bean.
4. Cool slightly and add the bloomed, melted gelatin.
5. Stir well, deposit into a 6 inch (15 cm) diameter FlexiMold, and freeze.

Lemon Crémeux Formula

Ingredients	Baker's %	Kilogram	US decimal	Lb & Oz	Test
Lemon juice	100.00	0.367	0.809	13	2 ⅝ oz
Sugar	60.00	0.220	0.485	7 ¾	1 ½ oz
Egg yolks	56.00	0.205	0.453	7 ¼	1 ½ oz
Eggs	64.00	0.235	0.518	8 ¼	1 ⅝ oz
Butter	60.00	0.220	0.485	7 ¾	1 ½ oz
Total	340.00	1.247	2.750	2 12	8 ¾ oz

Process, Lemon Crémeux

1. Bring the lemon juice to just below the boil with half of the sugar.
2. Combine the egg yolks, whole eggs, and the remainder of the sugar.
3. Pour one-third of the lemon juice over the egg mixture and stir with a spatula. Do not use a whisk as it will incorporate air.
4. Return the egg mixture to the pot and continue to stir constantly, agitating the bottom of the pot.
5. Cook until the mixture is 180°F (82°C) and thickened. Do not overcook.
6. Strain through a fine chinois into a clean, dry container.
7. When the mixture is at 95°F (35°C), add the soft butter using an immersion blender.
8. Deposit into a 6 inch (15 cm) diameter FlexiMold and freeze.

Pastry Cream for Diplomat Cream Formula

Ingredients	Baker's %	Kilogram	US decimal	Lb & Oz	Test
Whole milk	100.00	0.856	1.888	1 14 ¼	6 oz
Sugar #1	12.50	0.107	0.236	3 ¾	¾ oz
Vanilla bean	Each	1	1	1	¼ each
Cornstarch	7.50	0.064	0.142	2 ¼	½ oz
Sugar #2	25.00	0.214	0.472	7 ½	1 ½ oz
Egg yolks	16.25	0.139	0.307	4 ⅞	1 oz
Butter	12.50	0.107	0.236	3 ¾	¾ oz
Lemon zest	Each	1 ¼	1 ¼	1 ¼	¼ each
Total	173.75	1.488	3.281	3 4 ½	10 ½ oz

Process, Pastry Cream for Diplomat Cream

1. Scale the whole milk, the first sugar, and the vanilla bean into a stainless steel pot and bring to a boil.
2. Meanwhile, scale the second sugar and cornstarch into a bowl, and mix to combine.
3. Scale the egg yolks into the sugar–starch mixture, and whisk until combined.
4. When the milk comes to a boil, pour one-third of it onto the egg yolk mixture, and stir to incorporate evenly.
5. Return this mixture back to the pot, constantly stirring.
6. Continue to cook the custard while stirring until it has boiled for 2 minutes.
7. Turn off the heat, and add the butter and lemon zest. Stir until mixed in completely.
8. Pour the pastry cream onto a clean, parchment-lined sheet pan, and cover the surface of the custard with plastic wrap.
9. Refrigerate immediately until needed.

Diplomat Cream Formula

Ingredients	Baker's %	Kilogram	US decimal	Lb & Oz		Test
Pastry cream	100.00	1.488	3.281	3	4 ½	10 ½ oz
Whipped cream	100.00	1.488	3.281	3	4 ½	10 ½ oz
Gelatin	1.60	0.024	0.052		⅞	⅛ oz
Total	201.60	3.000	6.614	6	9 ⅞	1 lb 5 ⅛ oz

Process

1. Whip the cream to soft peaks and reserve in the refrigerator.
2. Meanwhile, bloom the gelatin in cold water.
3. Take the pastry cream (five times the weight of the gelatin), and warm to 120°F (49°C) in a microwave.
4. Melt the bloomed gelatin in a microwave, and add to the warmed pastry cream.
5. Whip the reserved pastry cream until smooth, and then temper in the gelatin and pastry cream mix.
6. Fold in the soft peak whipped cream.

Assembly

1. Place a 7 inch (18 cm) diameter ladyfinger in an 8 inch (20 cm) cake ring with an acetate strip, and line the perimeter of the cake with the ladyfinger band.
2. Brush the cake base with the cake syrup.
3. Pour over 8 oz (230 g) of the diplomat cream.
4. Place a disc of frozen berry compote insert.
5. Pour over 8 oz (230 g) of the diplomat cream.
6. Place a disc of frozen lemon crémeux insert.
7. Fill the cake ¼ inch (0.6 cm) below to the top of the ladyfingers with the diplomat cream and smooth the top of the cake with a pastry spatula.
8. Reserve in the refrigerator for at least 6 hours.

Finishing

1. Transfer to a gold board and remove the ring mold.
2. To finish, garnish the cake abundantly with fresh fruit, and apply apricot glaze and powdered sugar as applicable.

Fresh Fruit Charlotte

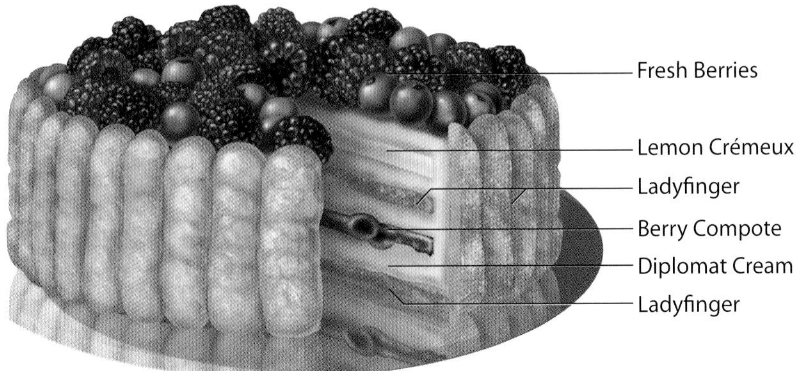

FORMULA

VANILLA BEAN BAVAROIS

Bavarois, the French name for Bavarian cream, is based on crème Anglaise. It can be enjoyed as a dessert by itself or used as filling in cakes, tarts, and pastries. This rich version is fragrant with the addition of vanilla bean, but Bavarois can be combined with a wide variety of flavorings, such as chocolate, coffee, or liqueurs. This cake stores well in the freezer, unfinished, for up to 1 week. After it is thawed, it should just be held for 48 hours.

Components

Golden chiffon, 7 inch (18 cm) diameter
Vanilla-rum syrup
Muscovado sablé breton
Bavarian cream
Vanilla glaze
Fresh raspberries
Chocolate décor

Yield: 5 [8 inch (20 cm)] cakes
Test: 1 [8 inch (20 cm)] cake

Mise en Place

Prepare the golden chiffon by splitting it in fourths. One fourth will be used per Bavarian cake formula.

Vanilla-Rum Syrup Formula

Ingredients	Baker's %	Kilogram	US decimal	Lb & Oz
Water	125.00	0.094	0.208	3 ⅜
Sugar	100.00	0.075	0.166	2 ⅝
Rum	40.00	0.030	0.067	1 ⅛
Vanilla bean	Each	1	1	1
Total	265.00	0.200	0.441	7

Process, Vanilla-Rum Syrup

1. Bring the water, sugar, and vanilla bean to a boil.
2. Turn off the heat, and cool down. Stir in the rum when completely cooled.

Muscovado Sablé Breton Formula

Ingredients	Baker's %	Kilogram	US decimal	Lb & Oz		Test
Butter	92.00	0.404	0.890		14 ¼	2 ⅞ oz
Muscovado	31.00	0.136	0.300		4 ¾	1 oz
Fleur de sel	2.00	0.009	0.019		¼	⅛ tsp
Cooked egg yolks	3.00	0.013	0.029		½	⅛ oz
Pastry flour	83.00	0.364	0.803		2 ⅞	2 ⅝ oz
Potato starch	17.00	0.075	0.164		2 ⅝	½ oz
Total	228.00	1.000	2.205	2	3 ¼	7 oz

Process, Muscovado Sablé Breton

1. Sift the flour and potato starch together and reserve.
2. Place the soft butter, muscovado, and fleur de sel in a mixing bowl. The butter must be very soft.
3. Mix on low speed for 30 seconds, just to incorporate the ingredients.
4. Press the egg yolks through a fine sieve. Add to the mixer and mix until combined.
5. Add the sifted dry ingredients, and mix until combined.
6. Wrap with plastic wrap, and chill in the refrigerator for at least 4 hours.
7. Roll the dough out to ⅜ inch (1 cm) thickness × 7 inch (18 cm) diameter and bake in a 7 inch (18 cm) flan ring on a silicone baking mat and bake at 365°F (180°C) for 12 minutes or until the edge of the dough starts to brown.
8. Cool, and keep wrapped until needed.

Vanilla Bavarian Cream Formula

Ingredients	Baker's %	Kilogram	US decimal	Lb & Oz		Test
Cream	50.00	1.134	2.501	2	8	8 oz
Milk	50.00	1.134	2.501	2	8	8 oz
Vanilla bean	Each	3	3		3	½ each
Sugar	20.70	0.470	1.035	1	⅝	3 ⅜ oz
Egg yolks	24.30	0.551	1.215	1	3 ½	3 ⅞ oz
Gelatin, leaf	2.40	0.054	0.120		1 ⅞	⅜ oz
Heavy cream	73.00	1.656	3.651	3	10 ⅜	11 ⅝ oz
Total	220.40	5.000	11.023	11	⅜	2 lb 3 ¼ oz

Note
Combined weight of milk and cream is 100 percent.

Process, Vanilla Bavarian Cream

1. Bloom the gelatin in very cold water and reserve.
2. Whip the heavy cream to soft peaks and reserve.
3. Boil the milk, cream, and vanilla and allow to infuse, covered, for 15 minutes minimum.

4. Return the liquid to a boil, and proceed with the base preparation as for a crème Anglaise using the sugar and egg yolks and cook to 180°F (82°C).
5. Strain into a clean bowl and add the bloomed, melted gelatin. Mix to incorporate.
6. When the base mixture has cooled to 75°F (24°C) to 85°F (30°C), fold in the whipped cream.
7. See the assembly instructions for makeup procedures.

Vanilla Glaze Formula

Ingredients	Baker's %	Kilogram	US decimal	Lb & Oz		Test
Neutral glaze	100.00	0.500	1.102	1	1 ⅝	3 ½ oz
Vanilla bean	Each	1	1		1	⅕ each
Total	100.00	0.500	1.102	1	1 ⅝	3 ½ oz

Process, Vanilla Glaze

1. Blend together the neutral glaze and the vanilla bean.
2. Reserve until needed.

Assembly

1. On a cake board, place a disc of sablé breton. Place an 8 inch (20 cm) × 2 inch (5 cm) cake ring around it. Line it with a strip of acetate.
2. Pour the Bavarian cream halfway up and place a circle of the prepared golden chiffon. Place in the freezer for 10 minutes to secure the cake.
3. Moisten the cake with the vanilla-rum syrup. Pour the Bavarian cream up to the top of the ring. Flatten the top, and keep in the freezer.
4. Once frozen, apply a thin layer of vanilla glaze over the top of the cake and return to the freezer.

Finishing

Unmold the cake, and transfer it to a gold board. Decorate with fresh raspberries around the perimeter and place a textured chocolate ring over the berries, and place lattice chocolate décor around the sides of the cake.

Vanilla Bean Bavarois

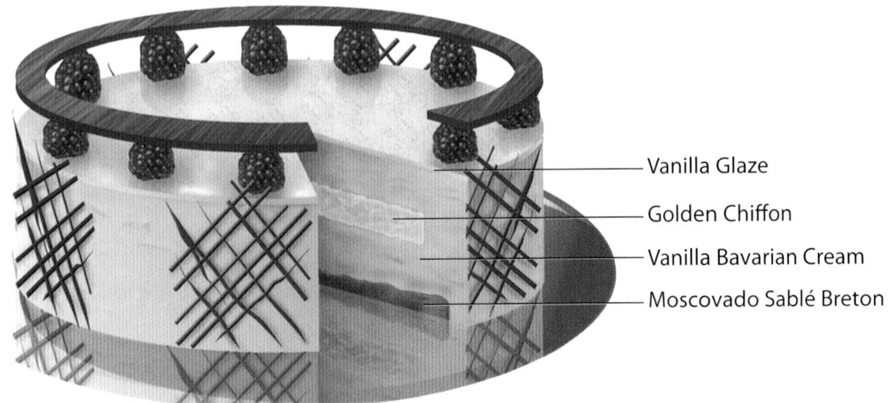

FORMULA

RASPBERRY CRÈME BRÛLÉE MACARON

This is the larger version of a Parisian macaron, filled with a crème brûlée and garnished with fresh raspberries and mint. Allow the entremets to "mature" for several hours in order to soften the macaron discs to an ideal texture and allow the flavors to properly infuse.

Components

Vanilla crème brûlée

Special macaron

Fresh raspberries and mint

Fruit, chocolate, and dried vanilla bean decoration

Powdered sugar

Yield: 5 [7 inch (18 cm)] cakes
Test: 1 [7 inch (18 cm)] cake

Vanilla Crème Brûlée Formula

Ingredients	Baker's %	Kilogram	US decimal	Lb & Oz	Test
35% cream	85.00	0.736	1.623	1 10	5 ¼ oz
Whole milk	15.00	0.130	0.286	4 ⅝	⅞ oz
Vanilla bean	Each	1 ¼	1 ¼	1 ¼	¼ each
Sugar	22.00	0.191	0.420	6 ¾	1 ⅜ oz
Egg yolks	20.00	0.173	0.382	6 ⅛	1 ¼ oz
Gelatin (leaves)	2.30	0.020	0.044	¾	⅛ oz
Total	144.30	1.250	2.756	2 12 ⅛	8 ⅞ oz

Process, Vanilla Crème Brûlée

1. Bring the cream, milk, and vanilla bean to a boil.
2. Mix the sugar with the egg yolks.
3. Temper part of the cream mixture into the egg yolk mixture and stir.
4. Return the tempered mixture to the cream mixture, and warm to 180°F (82°C) using a spatula to continuously stir the bottom.
5. Strain though a chinois into a clean container, and add the bloomed gelatin.
6. Cool until 85°F (29°C), and then deposit 8 ½ oz (0.250 g) into 6 inch (16 cm) diameter molds and freeze.

Special Macaron Formula

Ingredients	Baker's %	Kilogram	US decimal	Lb & Oz		Test
Egg whites	100.00	0.505	1.113	1	1 ⅞	3 ⅝ oz
Sugar	100.00	0.505	1.113	1	1 ⅞	3 ⅝ oz
Powdered sugar	100.00	0.505	1.113	1	1 ⅞	3 ⅝ oz
Pastry flour	22.67	0.114	0.252		4	¾ oz
Almond flour	73.33	0.370	0.816		13 ⅛	2 ⅝ oz
Color as desired						
Total	396.00	2.000	4.409	4	6 ½	14 ⅛ oz

Process, Special Macaron

1. Sift the powdered sugar, flour, and almond flour together. Reserve.
2. Whip the egg whites with a third of the sugar until stiff peak. Add colorant to achieve a pastel pink color. Mix until there are no streaks of white. Add the remaining sugar and mix just to incorporation.
3. Gently fold in the sifted dry ingredients.
4. Immediately pipe the batter into 7 inch (18 cm) discs on a silicone mat–lined perforated sheet pan.
5. Bake at 325°F (163°C) for 5 minutes and then at 300°F (149°C) for 30 to 35 minutes, or until baked through. The product should retain the pink color.
6. Reserve covered in the freezer until needed.

Assembly

1. Place one disc of macaron on a gold board.
2. Unmold the crème brûlée from the molds and place one on top of the macaron base and allow to defrost slightly.
3. Line the border of the crème brûlée insert with fresh raspberries.
4. Apply a small amount of fresh, chopped mint to the surface of the crème brûlée, and press split raspberries into the crème brûlée surface.
5. Place the second macaron disc on top of the base preparation.

Finishing

With a template, dust a 1 inch (2.5 cm) wide line of powdered sugar down one side of the top macaron. Use this as a guide for placing the décor. As the décor approaches the front of the entremets, curve it in toward the center of the cake.

Raspberry Crème Brûlée Macaron

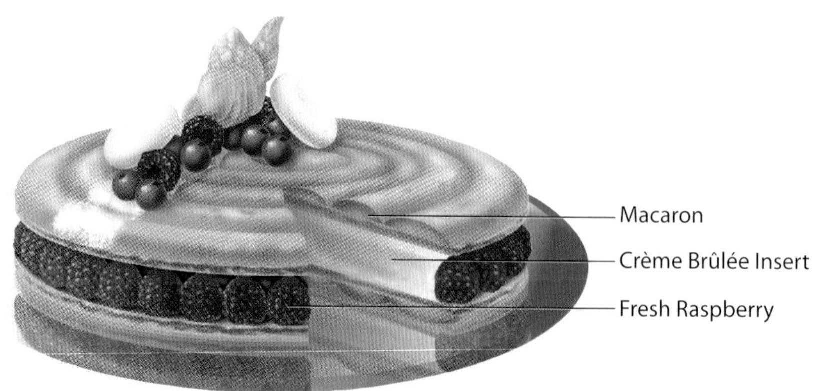

FORMULA

RASPBERRY MOUSSE CAKE

This beautiful mousse cake inspires daydreams of summer with its irresistible layers of moist chocolate cake, creamy chocolate spread, fresh raspberries, light raspberry mousse, and raspberry gelée.

Components

Chocolate chiffon, half sheet, split into thirds (one-third cake per one raspberry mousse cake)

Chocolate spread

Fresh raspberries

Raspberry mousse

Raspberry gelée

Yield: 5 [11 inch (28 cm) × 16 inch (41 cm)] cakes
Test: 1 [11 inch (28 cm) × 16 inch (41 cm)] cake

Mise en Place

Prepare the chocolate chiffon by trimming to 11 inch (28 cm) ×16 inch (41 cm) and splitting into thirds.

Chocolate Spread Formula

Ingredients	Baker's %	Kilogram	US decimal	Lb & Oz	Test
Heavy cream	100.00	1.644	3.625	3 10	11 ⅝ oz
Glucose	2.39	0.039	0.087	1 ⅜	¼ oz
Milk couverture chocolate	67.16	1.104	2.435	2 7	7 ¾ oz
58% couverture	17.91	0.295	0.649	10 ⅜	2 ⅛ oz
Unsweetened chocolate	25.37	0.417	0.920	14 ¾	3 oz
Total	212.83	3.500	7.716	7 11 ½	1 lb 8 ¾ oz

Process, Chocolate Spread

1. Bring the cream and glucose to a boil.
2. Pour over the combined chocolates, and allow to stand for 1 minute.
3. Form an emulsion and cover to the surface with plastic wrap, and reserve for at least 12 hours or until set. The texture will be soft, but pliable.

Raspberry Mousse Formula

Ingredients	Baker's %	Kilogram	US decimal	Lb & Oz		Test
Raspberry puree	100.00	4.368	9.629	9	10	1 lb 14 ¾ oz
Gelatin	2.39	0.104	0.230		3 ⅝	¾ oz
Whipping cream	67.16	2.933	6.467	6	7 ½	1 lb 4 ¾ oz
Egg whites	17.91	0.782	1.724	1	11 ⅝	5 ½ oz
Sugar	25.37	1.108	2.443	2	7 ⅛	7 ⅞ oz
Water	7.46	0.326	0.718		11 ½	2 ¼ oz
Total	220.29	9.621	21.211	21	3 ⅜	4 lb 3 ⅞ oz

Process, Raspberry Mousse

1. Whip the cream to soft peaks and refrigerate.
2. Bloom the gelatin in cold water and reserve.
3. Combine the sugar and water and cook to prepare an Italian meringue. Prepare the egg whites.
4. Warm the fruit puree to 100°F (38°C).
5. Take a small portion of the fruit puree, and warm it to 120°F (49°C). Add the bloomed, melted gelatin to it, and stir to dissolve. Temper this gelatin–puree mixture back into the main stock of puree.
6. When the Italian meringue is room temperature, fold it into the fruit puree base.
7. Lastly, at 80°F (27°C) to 85°F (29°C), fold in the soft peak whipped cream, and deposit into molds as required.

Raspberry Gelée Formula

Ingredients	Baker's %	Kilogram	US decimal	Lb & Oz		Test
Simple syrup	100.00	0.968	2.135	2	2 ⅛	6 ⅞ oz
Gelatin	6.50	0.063	0.139		2 ¼	½ oz
Raspberry puree	100.00	0.968	2.135	2	2 ⅛	6 ⅞ oz
Total	206.50	2.000	4.409	4	6 ½	14 ⅛ oz

Process, Raspberry Gelée

1. Bloom the gelatin and reserve.
2. Warm the simple syrup, melt the gelatin, and add it to the warm syrup. Mix well.
3. Temper the simple syrup into the puree, and emulsify with the immersion blender.
4. Use at 90°F (33°C).

Assembly

1. Prepare an 11 inch (28 cm) × 16 inch (41 cm) sheet cake mold with acetate on the sides on a cake board. Place a ½ inch (1.5 cm) thick 11 inch (28 cm) × 16 inch (41 cm) chocolate chiffon cake in the mold on the cake board. Spread 1 lb 8 ½ oz (700 g) of chocolate spread over the cake.

2. Line fresh raspberries on top of the chocolate spread.
3. Deposit the raspberry mousse in the mold and level off the top.
4. Place the cake in the freezer.

Finishing

1. Prepare the gelée and glaze the cake. Return to the freezer to set the gelée.
2. Unmold the mousse, cut to the desired sizes, and transfer to gold boards.
3. Decorate with fresh raspberries.

Note

When making an 8 inch (20 cm) cake, the required components and weights per one cake are:

8 inch (20 cm) chocolate chiffon cake, split into fourths
Chocolate spread, 10 ¼ oz (291 g)
Raspberry gelée, 5 ⅞ oz (166 g)
Fresh raspberries
Raspberry mousse, 1 lb 12 ⅛ oz (800 g)

Raspberry Mousse Cake

FORMULA

LEMON MOUSSE CAKE WITH BLACKBERRY

Lemon and blackberry perform perfectly together in this sublime mousse cake. The lemon mousse is based on a pâte à bombe made with fresh lemon juice for the intense, rich, and pure flavor that sets this dessert apart. Best results are achieved with fresh lemon juice or high-quality frozen puree, rather than juice from concentrate. When making the mousse, it is important that the butter is very soft when it is added to the cooled pâte à bombe, and that the whole is then mixed minimally to retain the light texture necessary for a truly sensational mousse cake.

Components

Biscuit jaconde with purple stripes
Blackberry insert
Dacquoise
Lemon mousse
Blackberry glaze
Fresh fruit décor
White chocolate décor

Yield: 5 [8 inch (20 cm)] cakes
Test: 1 [8 inch (20 cm)] cake

Process, Biscuit Jaconde With Purple Stripes

1. Prepare the jaconde with purple stripes.
2. Run diagonal lines of décor on a silicone baking mat and freeze.
3. Prepare the biscuit viennois and deposit over the frozen pâte décor.
4. Bake, and store as normal.

Cake Setup Mise en Place

1. Cut strips of biscuit jaconde that are three-fourths the height of the mold and that can circumnavigate the mold.
2. Line the cake mold with an acetate strip.

Note

This can be done after the blackberry insert and dacquoise have been made.

Blackberry Insert Formula

Ingredients	Baker's %	Kilogram	US decimal	Lb & Oz	Test
Blackberry puree	100.00	0.940	2.071	2 1 ⅛	6 ⅝ oz
Sugar	30.00	0.282	0.621	10	2 oz
Gelatin	3.00	0.028	0.062	1	¼ oz
Total	133.00	1.250	2.755	2 12 ⅛	8 ⅞ oz

Process, Blackberry Insert

1. Bloom the gelatin in cold water and reserve.
2. Warm the puree to 180°F (82°C) with the sugar.
3. Melt the bloomed gelatin, add to the warmed puree, and emulsify well.
4. Deposit into 6 inch (15 cm) diameter Flexipans and freeze until ready for use.

Dacquoise Formula

Ingredients	Baker's %	Kilogram	US decimal	Lb & Oz	Test
Almond meal	80.00	0.370	0.815	13	2 ⅝ oz
Powdered sugar	80.00	0.370	0.815	13	2 ⅝ oz
Egg whites	100.00	0.462	1.019	1 ¼	3 ¼ oz
Sugar	32.00	0.148	0.326	5 ¼	1 oz
Total	292.00	1.350	2.976	2 15 ⅝	9 ½ oz

Process, Dacquoise

1. Sift the almond meal and powdered sugar together.
2. Whip the egg whites and sugar to a stiff peak.
3. Gently fold in the sifted dry ingredients.
4. Pipe into 7 inch (18 cm) rounds; bake at 300°F (149°C) with the vent open for 30 to 35 minutes.

Lemon Mousse Formula

Ingredients	Baker's %	Kilogram	US decimal	Lb & Oz	Test
Lemon juice	27.00	0.349	0.770	12 ⅜	1 ⅞ oz
Sugar, split	46.00	0.595	1.311	1 5	3 ⅛ oz
Egg yolks	33.00	0.427	0.941	15	2 ¼ oz
Butter	26.00	0.336	0.741	11 ⅞	1 ¾ oz
Lemon zest	Each	7	7	7	1 each
Whipped cream	100.00	1.293	2.851	2 13 ⅝	6 ⅞ oz
Total	232.00	3.000	6.614	6 9 ⅞	23 oz

Process, Lemon Mousse

1. Whip the cream to soft peaks and reserve.
2. Boil the lemon juice and half of the sugar. Combine the remaining sugar and the egg yolks, and then temper them into the boiling juice.
3. Whisk constantly and bring the mixture to a boil. Quickly transfer to a mixer fitted with the whip, and whip on medium-high speed until cool.
4. Add the soft butter and zest, and stop mixing when incorporated (15 seconds maximum).
5. Fold in the soft peak whipped cream.

Blackberry Glaze Formula

Ingredients	Baker's %	Kilogram	US decimal	Lb & Oz	Test
Blackberry puree	100.00	0.286	0.630	10 ⅛	2 ⅛ oz
Simple syrup	100.00	0.286	0.630	10 ⅛	2 ⅛ oz
Gelatin	10.00	0.029	0.063	1	¼ oz
Total	210.00	0.600	1.323	1 5 ⅛	4 ⅜ oz

Process, Blackberry Glaze

1. Bloom the gelatin in cold water and reserve.
2. Warm the puree to 180°F (82°C) with the sugar.
3. Melt the bloomed gelatin, add to the warmed puree, and emulsify well. Reserve in the refrigerator.
4. Use at 85°F (29°C) to 90°F (32°C).

Assembly

1. Place the strip of biscuit jaconde with lines on the inside perimeter of the mold.
2. Place a disc of dacquoise on the bottom of the mold.
3. Once the mousse has been made, pipe or ladle the mixture into the prepared molds, filling halfway.
4. Place the blackberry insert into the mousse and then fill the molds to the top with lemon mousse. Level the top of the mousse cake so it is smooth, and then freeze until set.

Finishing

1. To finish, remove from the mold, being careful to not take off the plastic. Apply the blackberry glaze and then take off the plastic and place onto a gold board.
2. Garnish with fresh fruit and chocolate decorations.

Lemon Mousse Cake
With Blackberry

FORMULA

CHOCOLATE MOUSSE WITH SWEET RISOTTO

Creamy, slightly sweetened vanilla risotto and a layer of milk chocolate with crispy praline are the seductive elements of this rich chocolate mousse cake. The unexpected addition of risotto balances wonderfully with the familiar flavor combination of chocolate and hazelnut.

Components

Chocolate cake with 7 inch (18 cm) diameter
Sweet risotto
Crispy praline layer
Chocolate mousse
Chocolate glaze
Orange chips
Candied hazelnuts
Dried vanilla bean
Chocolate décor

Yield: 5 [8 inch (20 cm)] cakes
Test: 1 [8 inch (20 cm)] cake

Mise en Place

Set up 8 inch (20 cm) × 2 inch (5 cm) ring molds and insert the chocolate cake for the base. Reserve.

Sweet Risotto Formula

Ingredients	Baker's %	Kilogram	US decimal	Lb & Oz		Test
Olive oil	7.00	0.029	0.063		1	¼ oz
Arborio rice	100.00	0.408	0.900		14 ⅜	2 ⅞ oz
Milk	439.00	1.793	3.952	3	15 ¼	12 ½ oz
Vanilla bean	Each	2	2		2	½ each
Sugar	15.00	0.061	0.135		2 ⅛	⅜ oz
Lemon zest	Each	1	1		1	¼ each
Orange zest	Each	1	1		1	¼ each
Total	561.00	2.291	5.050	5	¾	1 lb

Process, Sweet Risotto

1. Heat the olive oil in a sauté pan.
2. Add the rice in the pan; toast until the rice becomes fragrant.
3. Meanwhile, bring the milk, vanilla bean, and sugar to a simmer.
4. Add a small amount of hot milk into the rice. Stir continuously. Once the rice absorbs all the liquid, add more milk. Continue this process until the rice is tender. *Note:* Some varieties of rice may require more or less liquid.

5. Once cooked, remove the pan from the heat. Cool slightly, and then add the zest.
6. Deposit into a 6 inch (15 cm) diameter FlexiMold at 1 lb (450 g) each, and then place in the freezer.

Crispy Praline Layer Formula

Ingredients	Baker's %	Kilogram	US decimal	Lb & Oz		Test
Milk chocolate	20.63	0.197	0.435		7	1 ⅜ oz
Hazelnut praline paste	100.00	0.957	2.110	2	1 ¾	6 ¾ oz
Pailleté feuilletine	47.62	0.456	1.005	1	⅛	3 ¼ oz
Total	168.25	1.610	3.550	3	8 ¾	11 ⅜ oz

Process, Crispy Praline Layer

1. Melt the milk chocolate over a bain-marie or in a microwave.
2. Add the praline paste and stir to incorporate.
3. Fold in the pailleté feuilletine.
4. Deposit the mixture into a 7 inch (18 cm) diameter mold at 10 ½ oz (300 g) each, and freeze.

Chocolate Mousse Formula

Ingredients	Baker's %	Kilogram	US decimal	Lb & Oz		Test
35% cream	100.00	1.013	2.234	2	3 ¾	7 ⅛ oz
64% couverture	100.00	1.013	2.234	2	3 ¾	7 ⅛ oz
Egg yolks	30.00	0.304	0.670		10 ¾	2 ⅛ oz
Sugar	30.00	0.304	0.670		10 ¾	2 ⅛ oz
Water	10.00	0.101	0.223		3 ⅝	¾ oz
40% cream	100.00	1.013	2.234	2	3 ¾	7 ⅛ oz
Total	370.00	3.750	8.267	8	4 ¼	1 lb 10 ⅜ oz

Process, Chocolate Mousse

1. Make a ganache with the 35% cream and chocolate.
2. Make a pâte à bombe with the egg yolks, sugar, and water.
3. Whip the 40 percent cream to soft peaks and reserve in the chiller.
4. Once the pâte à bombe is 100°F (38°C) to 105°F (40°C), add it to the ganache, which should be the same temperature.
5. Lastly, fold in the soft peak whipped cream in two stages.
6. Deposit into molds and freeze.

Assembly

1. On a 9 inch (23 cm) cake board, place a round disk of chocolate cake with a 7 inch (18 cm) diameter. Place an 8 inch (20 cm) cake ring around it. Line a 2 inch (5 cm) high sheet of acetate inside of the mold.
2. Deposit chocolate mousse on top of the cake, pressing the mousse between the cake and the mold, about ½ inch (1.5 cm) thick.
3. Place a disk of crispy praline layer over the mousse.

Chocolate Mousse With Sweet Risotto

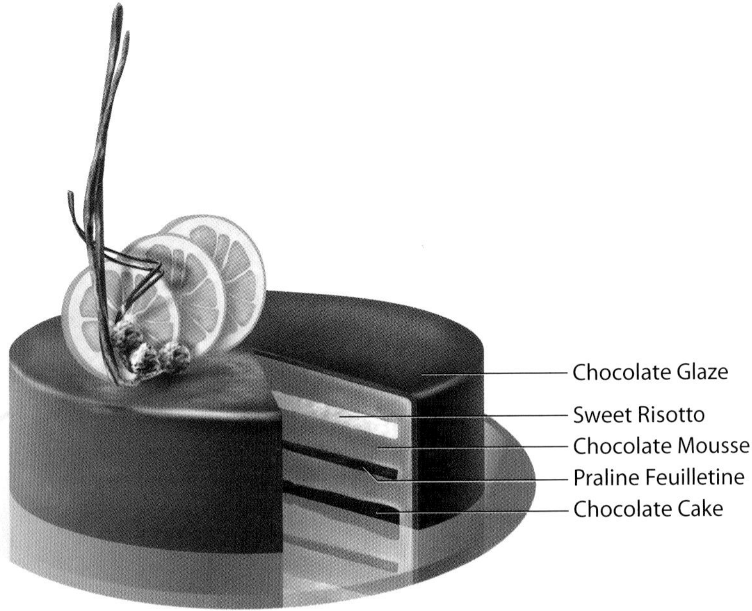

4. Deposit chocolate mousse on top of the crispy praline.
5. Next, insert the sweet risotto.
6. Deposit chocolate mousse up to the top of the mold and level with a palette knife. Place the cake in the freezer.

Finishing

1. When completely frozen, remove the cake ring and acetate.
2. Transfer the cake to a pouring screen, and prepare the chocolate glaze.
3. Glaze the cake, and return it to the freezer.
4. Transfer to a gold board and garnish with orange chips, candied hazelnuts, dried vanilla bean, and chocolate décor.

FORMULA

CHOCOLATE MINT MOUSSE CAKE

Chocolate and mint are an enduringly popular combination of flavors that finds flawless expression in this chocolate mint mousse cake with a blend of milk and dark chocolate mousse and a mint crème brûlée insert. Infusing fresh mint into the crème brûlée results in a sensation of amazingly clean flavors.

Components

Chocolate biscuit
Mint cake syrup
Mint crème brûlée insert
Chocolate mousse
Dark chocolate spray

Yield: 5 [8 inch (20 cm)] cakes
Test: 1 [8 inch (20 cm)] cake

Mise en Place

Cut out a 7 inch (18 cm) diameter circle from a sheet of chocolate biscuit, one per finished cake. Place in the middle of an 8 inch (20 cm) × 2 inch (5 cm) ring mold on a silpat-lined sheet pan.

Mint Cake Syrup Formula

Ingredients	Baker's %	Kilogram	US decimal	Lb & Oz		Test
Fresh mint leaves	13.00	0.032	0.071		1 ⅛	¼ oz
Sugar	70.00	0.174	0.383		6 ⅛	1 ¼ oz
Water	100.00	0.248	0.546		8 ¾	1 ¾ oz
Total	183.00	0.454	1.000	1	0	3 ¼ oz

Process, Mint Cake Syrup

1. Remove the stems from the mint; weight is for the leaf only. Wash thoroughly, and then dry in a salad spinner. Roughly chop the leaves and reserve.
2. Make a simple syrup, and then add the chopped mint. Infuse for 15 minutes, and then strain off the mint leaves.

Mint Crème Brûlée Insert Formula

Ingredients	Baker's %	Kilogram	US decimal	Lb & Oz		Test
Fresh mint	29.00	0.225	0.496		7 ⅞	1 ⅝
Whole milk	12.00	0.093	0.205		3 ¼	⅝ oz
35% cream	88.00	0.683	1.505	1	8 ⅛	4 ⅞ oz
Sugar	32.00	0.248	0.547		8 ¾	1 ¾ oz
Egg yolks	23.00	0.178	0.393		6 ¼	1 ¼ oz
Gelatin leaves	2.30	0.018	0.039		⅝	⅛ oz
Total	186.30	1.445	3.186	3	3	10 ¼ oz

Note
The final weight of the crème brûlée mix will be 1.250 kg due to the discarded mint.

Process, Mint Crème Brûlée Insert

1. Remove the stems from the mint; weight is for the leaf only. Wash thoroughly, and then dry in a salad spinner. Roughly chop the leaves and reserve.
2. Bring the milk and cream to a boil and then add the mint.
3. Cover the pot, and let the mint infuse for 30 minutes.
4. Strain the mixture through a chinois, and rescale the liquid to the original quantity by adding additional cream.
5. Add half of the sugar to this mixture and return to a boil.
6. Mix the remaining sugar with the egg yolks.
7. Temper part of the cream mixture into the egg yolk mixture and stir.
8. Return tempered mixture to cream mixture and warm the liquid to 180°F (82°C), cooking as for crème Anglaise.

9. Once cooked, strain through a chinois.
10. Add the bloomed gelatin off heat and stir to incorporate thoroughly.
11. Deposit into Flexipan molds at 8 ¾ oz (250 g) each and freeze.

Milk and Dark Chocolate Mousse Formula

Ingredients	Baker's %	Kilogram	US decimal	Lb & Oz		Test
35% cream	94.00	1.014	2.236	2	3 ¾	2 ¾ oz
64% couverture	47.00	0.507	1.118	1	1 ⅞	1 ⅜ oz
38% milk chocolate	53.00	0.572	1.261	1	4 ⅛	1 ⅝ oz
Sugar	28.00	0.302	0.666		10 ⅝	⅞ oz
Water	14.00	0.151	0.333		5 ⅜	⅜ oz
Egg yolks	28.00	0.302	0.666		10 ⅝	⅞ oz
Gelatin leaves	0.95	0.010	0.023		⅜	½ sheet
40% cream, soft peak	94.00	1.014	2.236	2	3 ¾	2 ¾ oz
Total	358.95	3.874	8.540	8	8 ⅝	10 ⅝ oz

Note
The total weight of chocolate is at 100 percent.

Process, Milk and Dark Chocolate Mousse

1. Make a ganache with the 35 percent cream and the chocolates.
2. Make a pâte à bombe with the sugar, water, and egg yolks.
3. Whip the 40 percent cream to soft peaks, and reserve in the refrigerator.
4. Once the pâte à bombe is at 80°F (27°C), add it to the ganache at 80°F (27°C).
5. Lastly, fold in the soft peak whipped cream in two stages.
6. See assembly for makeup notes.

Assembly

1. Place a 7 inch (18 cm) diameter round of chocolate biscuit on a silpat-lined sheet pan and place an 8 inch (20 cm) × 2 inch (5 cm) ring mold around it. Brush with the mint syrup.
2. Deposit the mousse halfway up the mold, over the chocolate biscuit cake base.
3. Remove the mint crème brûlée insert from the freezer, and press into the mousse.
4. Deposit the mousse into the mold to the top, level it off with a palette knife, and place it in the freezer.

Finishing

1. Warm the chocolate spray, assemble the spray gun, and reserve.
2. Unmold the cakes and place on a parchment-lined sheet pan for spraying.
3. While the cakes are still frozen, spray with the chocolate spray, and return to the freezer.

4. Warm the chocolate glaze to a pipable consistency, 85°F (29°C) to 90°F (35°C), and reserve.
5. Place a white board template over the cake that has a cutout that is 1 ¼ inch (3 cm) wide that is off center. The cutout must not extend to the edge of the cake board. (Refer to the templates section of the online companion at http://www.delmarlearning.com/companions/ for an example of the template required.)

6. With a gloved hand, splash some glaze quickly over the cake. Remove the template, transfer to a cake board, and garnish with a mint leaf.

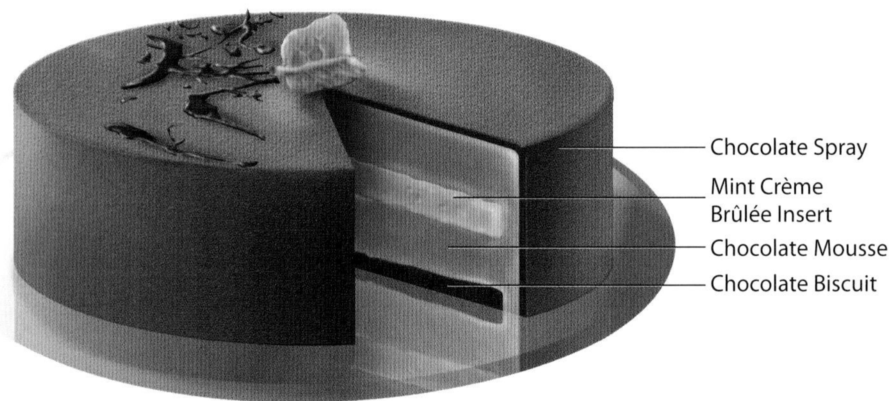

Chocolate Mint Mousse Cake

FORMULA

WHITE CHOCOLATE MOUSSE CAKE WITH RASPBERRY

The white chocolate mousse cake with raspberry does not contain an egg foam as one of its components, which leads to a very creamy mousse, enhanced by an intensely flavored white chocolate ganache base elaborated with vanilla bean–infused cream. A raspberry insert adds the striking visual dimension of red berries contrasted with white mousse. The Emmanuel sponge base cake is moist and tender, studded with raspberries and candied pistachios. All of these memorable elements combine for a dramatic and delicious dessert.

Components

Biscuit jaconde with vertical red lines (cake wall)

Emmanual sponge with raspberry and pistachios (cake bottom)

Raspberry insert

White chocolate mousse

Raspberry gelée

White chocolate décor

Fresh raspberries

Yield: 5 [8 inch (20 cm)] cakes
Test: 1 [8 inch (20 cm)] cake

Mise en Place

Before making the mousse, prepare the 8 inch (20 cm) × 2 inch (5 cm) cake molds with the acetate sheet; place the cake wall with biscuit jaconde and then the Emmanuel sponge cake bottoms at 7 inch (18 cm) diameter circle. The height of the cake wall should be approximately three-fourths the height of the mold.

Raspberry Insert Formula

Ingredients	Baker's %	Kilogram	US decimal	Lb & Oz	Test
Raspberry puree	100.00	0.940	2.071	2 1 ⅛	6 ⅝ oz
Sugar	30.00	0.282	0.621	10	2 oz
Gelatin leaf	3.00	0.028	0.062	1	¼ oz
Total	133.00	1.250	2.755	2 12 ⅛	8 ⅞ oz

Process, Raspberry Insert

1. Bloom the gelatin and warm the puree and the sugar to 120°F (49°C).
2. Melt the gelatin and temper it into the puree then emulsify, deposit into 6 inch (15 cm) diameter Flexipans, and freeze.

White Chocolate Mousse Formula

Ingredients	Baker's %	Kilogram	US decimal	Lb & Oz		Test
Milk	52.40	0.610	1.345	1	5 ½	4 ¼ oz
Vanilla bean	Each	2	2		2	¾ each
Sugar	3.20	0.037	0.082		1 ⅜	¼ oz
Egg yolks	12.00	0.140	0.308		4 ⅞	1 oz
Gelatin	1.40	0.016	0.036		⅝	⅛ oz
White chocolate	100.00	1.164	2.567	2	9 ⅛	8 ¼ oz
Heavy cream	153.00	1.782	3.928	3	14 ⅞	12 ⅝ oz
Total	322.00	3.749	8.266	8	4 ¼	1lb 10 ½ oz

Process, White Chocolate Mousse

1. Bloom the gelatin in very cold water and reserve.
2. Melt the white chocolate and reserve.
3. Whip the heavy cream to soft peaks and reserve.
4. Make a crème Anglaise with the milk, vanilla, sugar, and egg yolks.
5. Strain the crème Anglaise through a fine chinois into a clean dry bowl, and add the bloomed melted gelatin to it. Stir to emulsify.
6. Add the melted white chocolate to the crème Anglaise, and form an emulsion.
7. When this mixture reaches 80°F (27°C), fold in the soft peak whipped cream.

Raspberry Gelée

Ingredients	Baker's %	Kilogram	US decimal	Lb & Oz		Test
Raspberry puree	100.00	0.422	0.930		14 ⅞	6 ⅞ oz
Simple syrup	100.00	0.422	0.930		14 ⅞	6 ⅞ oz
Gelatin	6.50	0.027	0.060		1	½ oz
Total	206.50	0.871	1.921	1	14 ¾	14 ⅛ oz

Process, Raspberry Gelée

1. Bloom the gelatin and reserve.
2. Warm the simple syrup; melt the gelatin, add it to the warm syrup, and mix well.
3. Temper the simple syrup into the puree and emulsify with the immersion blender.
4. Use at 90°F (33°C).

Assembly

1. After the mousse has been made, pipe or ladle the mixture into the prepared molds halfway.
2. Place the raspberry insert into the mousse and then fill the molds to the top with the mousse. Level the top of the mousse cake with a palette knife and then freeze until set.

Finishing

1. To finish, remove from the mold, being careful to not take off the plastic.
2. Apply the raspberry gelée, take the plastic off, and place cake onto a gold board.
3. Garnish with fresh raspberries and white chocolate lattice decorations.

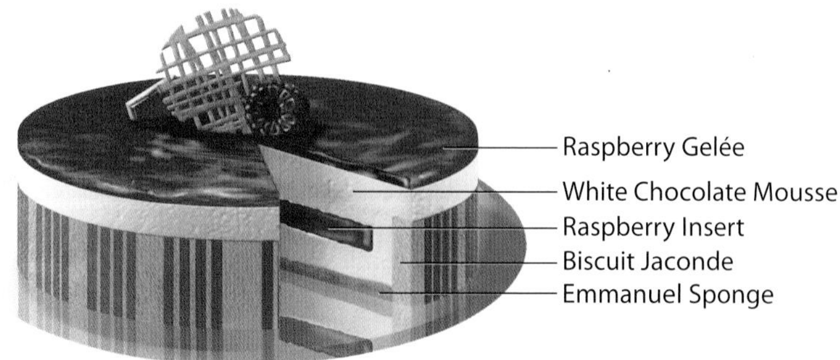

White Chocolate Mousse Cake With Raspberry

FORMULA

WHISKEY HAZELNUT MOUSSE

Deeply flavorful, yet very light in texture, this chocolate mousse, made with both milk and dark chocolates, is a decadent treat flavored with praline paste and Scotch whiskey. The mousse is layered with thin dark chocolate discs, studded with fleur de sel de Guérande, a very flavorful sea salt from the northwest of France. The cake is then poured with an alluring black glaze and garnished with chocolate plaques and a cluster of caramelized hazelnuts for an intoxicating presentation.

Components

Chocolate biscuit

Crispy praline layer

Dark chocolate discs for décor

Dark chocolate sheets for décor

Whiskey hazelnut mousse

Black glaze

Caramelized hazelnut clusters

Yield: 5 [7 inch (18 cm) x 3 ½ inch (9 cm)] domes
Test: 1 [7 inch (18 cm) x 3 ½ inch (9 cm)] dome

Crispy Praline Layer Formula

Ingredients	Baker's %	Kilogram	US decimal	Lb & Oz	Test
Milk chocolate	20.63	0.074	0.162	2 ⅝	½ oz
Praline paste	100.00	0.357	0.786	12 ⅝	2 ½ oz
Pailleté feuilletine	47.62	0.170	0.374	6	1 ¼ oz
Total	168.25	0.600	1.323	1 5 ⅛	4 ¼ oz

Yield: 1 full sheet

Process, Crispy Praline Layer

1. Melt the milk chocolate over a bain-marie or in a microwave.
2. Add the praline paste, and stir to incorporate.
3. Fold in the pailleté feuilletine.
4. Spread a thin layer over the prepared chocolate biscuit.
5. Once the praline layer is set, cut out circles that measure 6 ½ inches (16.6 cm) in diameter, and reserve in the freezer until ready for finishing.

Process, Dark Chocolate Discs for Décor

Spread tempered dark chocolate over a sheet of acetate. Before the chocolate sets, sprinkle with fleur de sel de Guérande and cut out discs with diameters of 5 ½ inches (14 cm), 4 ½ inches (11.5 cm), 3 ½ inches (9 cm), and 2 inches (5 cm). One of each will be required for each cake. Once cut, place a sheet of parchment paper over the chocolate décor and weigh down to prevent warping.

Process, Dark Chocolate Sheets for Décor

Spread tempered dark chocolate in a thin layer over a sheet of acetate that is the size of a sheet pan. Before it sets, cover with another sheet of acetate. Weigh down during crystallization and reserve until needed.

Whiskey Hazelnut Mousse Formula

Ingredients	Baker's %	Kilogram	US decimal	Lb & Oz		Test
Milk	45.00	0.441	0.972		15 ½	3 ⅛ oz
35% cream	45.00	0.441	0.972		15 ½	3 ⅛ oz
Vanilla bean	Each	1 ½	1 ½		1 ½	½ each
Sugar	5.00	0.049	0.108		1 ¾	⅜ oz
Egg yolks	21.00	0.206	0.454		7 ¼	1 ½ oz
38% milk chocolate	86.00	0.843	1.858	1	13 ¾	6 oz
64% dark chocolate	14.00	0.137	0.303		4 ⅞	1 oz
Gelatin leaf	2.90	0.028	0.063		1	¼ oz
Praline paste 60%	32.00	0.314	0.691		11 ⅛	2 ⅛ oz
Scotch whiskey	25.00	0.245	0.540		8 ⅝	1 ¾ oz
40% cream	173.00	1.696	3.738	3	11 ¾	12 oz
Total	448.90	4.400	9.700	9	11 ¼	1 lb 15 oz

Process, Whiskey Hazelnut Mousse

1. Bloom the gelatin in very cold water.
2. Whip the 40 percent cream to medium peaks and reserve.
3. Bring the milk, 35 percent cream, vanilla bean, and half of the sugar to a boil in a stainless steel pot.
4. Combine the egg yolks with the other half of the sugar.
5. Once the milk boils, temper one-third of it into the egg mixture.
6. Return the tempered mixture back to the stove and cook it 180°F (82°C), as for a crème Anglaise.
7. Strain the crème Anglaise over the partially melted chocolates, and form an emulsion.
8. Melt the gelatin and mix it into the ganache before the ganache cools down to 115°F (46°C).
9. Add the praline paste and then the whiskey.
10. When this mixture reaches 80°F (27°C), fold in the medium peak whipped cream.

Assembly

1. Ladle into the dome molds, which have been secured on a tart pan so they do not shift. When depositing the mousse, insert the chocolate discs in between the mousse layers to create four layers of chocolate and five layers of mousse.
2. Place a piece of chocolate biscuit with crispy praline layer as the base, being careful to place it flush with the mold.
3. Place the cake in the freezer until it is needed for finishing.

Process, Candied Hazelnut Clusters

Prepare the formula for dragées; however, substitute whole blanched, skinned hazelnuts for the almonds. Cook until the sugar caramelizes and then add butter at 10 percent of the weight of the nuts to retard the sticking. Pour the caramelized nuts into a silpat or a lightly oiled granite surface and separate into flat clusters. Allow to cool, and then reserve until needed.

Finishing

1. When the cake is frozen, unmold and place on a pouring screen.
2. Warm the black glaze to pouring consistency and pour over the cake.
3. Tap off the excess glaze and return the cake to the freezer.
4. When the glaze is set, remove the cake from the screen, and place it on a gold board.
5. Decorate with pieces of the chocolate sheet that are broken into geometric shapes.
6. Leave one spot blank, and garnish with a caramelized hazelnut cluster.

Whiskey Hazelnut Mousse

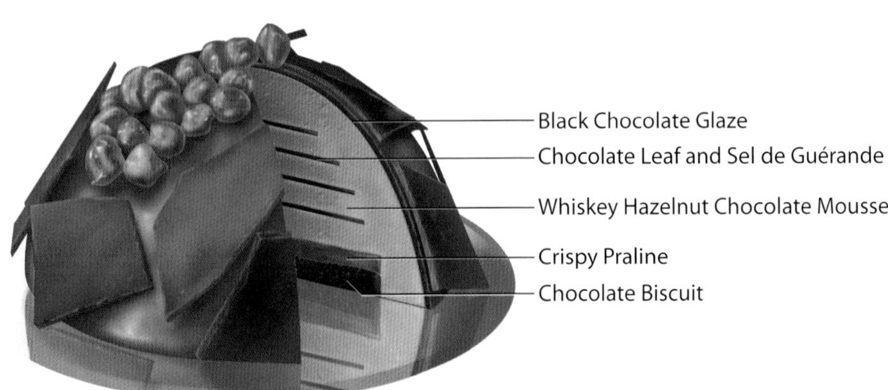

BÛCHE DE NOËL

The origins of this famous French celebration cake can be traced to pagan times when Celtic tradition called for burning a log at winter solstice, as a symbol of the rebirth of the sun. During the Middle Ages, the ceremony of the burning log became more elaborate, and the logs were decorated with ribbons and greenery before being set ablaze in the hearth. The tradition of actually burning the log began to disappear with the arrival of small stoves and the subsequent disappearance of large hearths. The log was replaced by a smaller branch, set in the middle of the table and surrounded by tiny *friandises* (sweets or delicacies) offered as treats to guests. This branch eventually transformed into the cake we know today as the Bûche de Noël or yule log. Bûches are often served with a portion of one end of the cake cut off and set on top of the cake to resemble a chopped off branch, while a bark-like texture is achieved with textured buttercream. To create the further illusion of realism, bûches are sometimes decorated with powdered sugar to resemble snow, along with representations of tree branches, fresh berries, and mushrooms made of meringue.

FORMULA

LEMON AND RED FRUIT BÛCHE DE NOËL

The lemon and red fruit Bûche de Noël is prepared in the traditional manner, using a roulade sponge cake and buttercream as the filling and icing. The unusual addition of citrus acts as a refreshing note at a time of year when people tend to overeat before dessert arrives. The red fruit compote spread over half of the cake before it is rolled is a tribute to the old custom of preserving fruits from the summer. Of course, with the availability of high-quality fruits year round, preserved fruits are no longer necessary. Because of its use of lemons and seasonal red fruit, this bûche, while traditionally prepared for Christmas, could be a nice treat at any time of the year.

Components

Roulade, one full sheet

Lemon soaking syrup

Red fruit compote

Lemon buttercream

Fruit and meringue decoration

Yield: 3 [7 inch (18 cm)] cakes
Test: 1 [7 inch (18 cm)] cake

Lemon Soaking Syrup Formula

Ingredients	Baker's %	Kilogram	US decimal	Lb & Oz
Simple syrup	100.00	0.129	0.284	4 ½
Lemon juice	16.67	0.021	0.047	¾
Lemon zest	Each	1 ¼	1 ¼	1 ¼
Total	116.67	0.150	0.331	5 ¼

Process, Lemon Soaking Syrup

Add the lemon juice and zest to the simple syrup. Reserve until needed.

Red Fruit Compote Formula

Ingredients	Baker's %	Kilogram	US decimal	Lb & Oz
Cherries, frozen	33.33	0.062	0.138	2 ¼
Raspberry, frozen	33.33	0.062	0.138	2 ¼
Blackberry, frozen	33.33	0.062	0.138	2 ¼
Lemon juice	8.33	0.016	0.034	½
Sugar #1	16.67	0.031	0.069	1 ⅛
Vanilla pod, used	Each	1	1	1
Sugar #2	6.67	0.013	0.028	½
Pectin NH	1.67	0.003	0.007	⅛
Total	133.33	0.250	0.551	8 ⅞

Process, Red Fruit Compote

1. Combine and heat the frozen fruit, lemon juice, first sugar, and vanilla bean.
2. When the mixture reaches 150°F (65°C), add the second sugar blended well with the pectin NH.
3. Cook the mixture until it boils for 1 minute, then transfer to a clean container and store covered to the surface in the refrigerator.

Lemon Buttercream

Custard Base for Buttercream Formula

Ingredients	Baker's %	Kilogram	US decimal	Lb & Oz
Lemon juice	100.00	0.118	0.260	4 ⅛
Egg yolks	77.00	0.091	0.200	3 ¼
Sugar	100.00	0.118	0.260	4 ⅛
Total	277.00	0.327	0.720	11 ½

Process, Custard Base for Buttercream

1. In a saucepan, heat the lemon juice.
2. In a mixing bowl, combine the egg yolks and sugar.
3. When the lemon juice boils, temper it into the egg yolk–sugar mixture.
4. Return this to the stove and cook until 180° F (82°C) as for a crème Anglaise.
5. Strain through a chinois into a mixer fitted with the whip and mix on medium speed until the mixture is 80°F (27°C).
6. See the final buttercream process for finishing instructions.

Italian Meringue Formula

Ingredients	Baker's %	Kilogram	US decimal	Lb & Oz
Water	30.00	0.037	0.081	1 ¼
Sugar #1	100.00	0.122	0.269	4 ¼
Egg whites	50.00	0.061	0.134	2 ⅛
Sugar #2	6.00	0.007	0.016	¼
Total	186.00	0.227	0.500	8

Process, Italian Meringue

1. In a saucepan, prepare the first sugar and the water as for an Italian meringue.
2. In a mixing bowl with the whip attachment, begin to whip the egg whites with the second sugar when the first sugar is cooked to the thread stage 241°F (116°C).
3. When the sugar reaches firm ball stage 250°F (121°C), slowly pour the sugar down the side of the mixing bowl.
4. Whip until cool.
5. See the final buttercream process for finishing instructions.

Final Buttercream Formula

Ingredients	Baker's %	Kilogram	US decimal	Lb & Oz
Custard base	66.00	0.326	0.719	11 ½
Butter, soft	100.00	0.494	1.090	1 1 ⅜
Lemon zest	2.60	0.013	0.028	½
Italian meringue	46.00	0.227	0.501	8
Total	212.00	1.048	2.310	2 5

Process, Final Buttercream

1. Add the soft butter a small amount at a time to the cool, whipping custard base.
2. Continue to whip until the mixture is smooth and well emulsified, and then add the zest.
3. Add the Italian meringue and mix to incorporate.

Final Assembly

1. Release the roulade from the silpat and brush with the 5 ¼ oz (150 g) lemon syrup.
2. On the half of the roulade closest, apply a layer of the red fruit compote [7 oz (200 g)].
3. On the other half of the roulade, apply a layer of the lemon buttercream [10 ½ oz (300 g)].
4. Roll the cake and tighten with parchment paper.
5. Ice the cake with 13 ⅛ oz (375 g) lemon buttercream and decorate as for Bûche de Noël.

Finishing

Transfer to a gold board and decorate with French meringue décor, chocolate décor, and candied fruits.

FORMULA

CHOCOLATE PRALINE BÛCHE DE NOËL

Celebrating the time-honored flavor combination of chocolate and hazelnut, this Bûche de Noël is formed in a contemporary Bûche de Noël mold. Rich chocolate mousse accounts for the majority of the cake, with layers of crispy praline and praline crème brûlée, and a base of chocolate biscuit. A black glaze lends a dramatic finish, garnished with a whimsical adornment of candied nuts, chocolate décor, and raspberries.

Components

Chocolate biscuit

Praline crème brûlée insert

Crispy praline layer

Chocolate mousse

Black chocolate glaze

Chocolate décor

Candied nuts

Yield: 2 bûches at 19 inch (49 cm) long × 3¼ inch (8 cm) wide × 3¼ inch (8 cm) high
Test: 1 bûche at 19 inch (49 cm) long × 3¼ inch (8 cm) wide × 3¼ inch (8 cm) high

Mise en Place

Cut the chocolate biscuit to 2 ¾ inches (7 cm) wide × 19 inches (49 cm) long.

Praline Crème Brûlée Insert Formula

Ingredients	Baker's %	Kilogram	US decimal	Lb & Oz	Test
Whole milk	11.70	0.060	0.133	2 ⅛	1 ⅛ oz
35% cream	88.30	0.455	1.004	1 0	8 oz
Vanilla bean	Each	1	1	1	½ each
Sugar	32.30	0.167	0.367	5 ⅞	3 oz
Egg yolks	20.00	0.103	0.227	3 ⅝	1 ⅞ oz
Gelatin leaf	2.30	0.012	0.026	⅜	¼ oz
Praline paste	20.00	0.103	0.227	3 ⅝	1 ⅞ oz
Total	174.60	0.900	1.985	1 15 ¾	15 ⅞ oz

Process, Praline Crème Brûlée Insert

1. Bloom the gelatin and reserve.
2. Bring the milk, cream, and vanilla bean to a boil.
3. Mix the sugar with the egg yolks.
4. Temper part of the cream mixture into the egg yolk mixture and stir.
5. Return the tempered mixture to the cream mixture and warm to 180° F (82°C) using a spatula to continuously stir the bottom.
6. Strain through a fine mesh chinois into a clean container and add the bloomed, melted gelatin.
7. Add the praline paste and mix to incorporate and deposit into a one-fourth sheet pan lined with plastic wrap and freeze.

Crispy Praline Layer Formula

Ingredients	Baker's %	Kilogram	US decimal	Lb & Oz	Test
Milk chocolate	20.63	0.065	0.143	2 ¼	1 ⅛ oz
Praline paste	100.00	0.315	0.694	11 ⅛	5 ½ oz
Pailleté feuilletine	47.62	0.150	0.331	5 ¼	2 ⅝ oz
Total	168.25	0.530	1.168	1 2 ¾	9 ⅜ oz

Process, Crispy Praline Layer

1. Melt the milk chocolate over a bain-marie or in a microwave.
2. Add the praline paste and stir to incorporate.
3. Fold in the pailleté feuilletine.
4. Spread over a silpat or parchment paper to the size of one-half sheet pan, and store in the freezer until ready to use.

Chocolate Mousse Formula

Ingredients	Baker's %	Kilogram	US decimal	Lb & Oz	Test
35% cream	100.00	0.811	1.788	1 12 ⅝	14 ¼ oz
64% couverture	100.00	0.811	1.788	1 12 ⅝	14 ¼ oz
Egg yolks	30.00	0.243	0.536	8 ⅝	4 ¼ oz
Sugar	30.00	0.243	0.536	8 ⅝	4 ¼ oz
Water	10.00	0.081	0.179	2 ⅞	1 ⅜ oz
40% cream	100.00	0.811	1.788	1 12 ⅝	14 ¼ oz
Total	370.00	3.000	6.614	6 9 ⅞	3 lb 4 ⅞ oz

Process, Chocolate Mousse

1. Make a ganache with the 35 percent cream and chocolate.
2. Make a pâte à bombe with the egg yolks, sugar, and water.
3. Whip the 40 percent cream to soft peaks, and reserve in the refrigerator.
4. Once the pâte à bombe is 100°F (38°C) to 105°F (40°C), add to the ganache, which should be the same temperature.
5. Lastly, fold in the soft peak whipped cream in two stages.

Assembly

1. Deposit the mousse into the bûche mold one-third of the way up, and spread some mousse over the sides of the mold.
2. Cut a strip of the frozen praline crème brûlée to 1½ inches (4 cm) wide × 19 inches (49 cm) long, and lightly press it into the mousse.
3. Deposit a layer of mousse over the praline crème brûlée, and then deposit a 2¾ inch (7 cm) wide × 19 inch (49 cm) long strip of the crispy praline layer. *Note:* To achieve 19 inches (49 cm) long, there will need to be two sections.
4. Deposit mousse to just below the surface of the mold and apply the chocolate biscuit base.
5. Reserve in the freezer until needed for finishing.

Finishing

Remove the cake from the mold and place on a pouring screen. Warm the black glaze to pouring consistency, and pour over the cake. Return the cake to the freezer to set the glaze. Garnish with chocolate decoration, candied nuts, meringue decoration, and fresh raspberries.

Chocolate Praline
Bûche de Noël

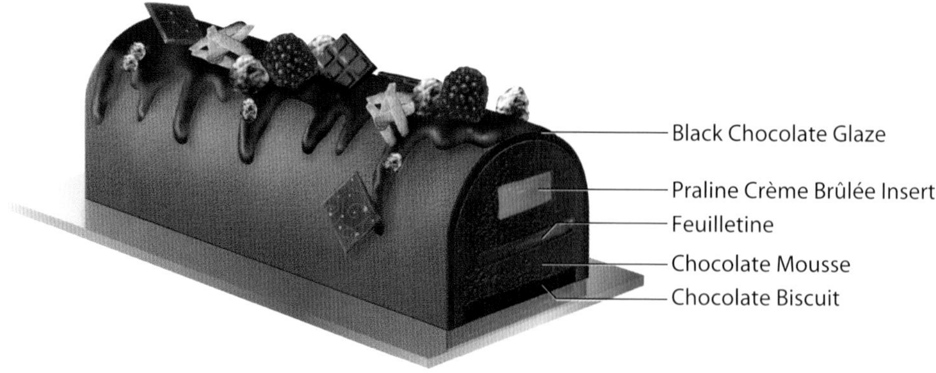

CHAPTER SUMMARY

Being prepared with proper mise en place and having a solid understanding of all cake components and equipment functions are required for success in cake assembly, whether it is a layer cake, a mousse cake, or a wedding cake. That being said, all the knowledge in the world about splitting, filling, and masking a cake, and the assembly techniques associated with the use of ring molds or silicone molds is totally subjective until the pastry chef does it over and over. Only then can one learn what can go wrong. Following the guidelines presented in this chapter can help to steer one in the right direction; however, it must be realized that it takes practice and determination to properly ice a cake. Experience and learning from others are extremely valuable in learning the subtle techniques that can make the difference between a good cake and a great one.

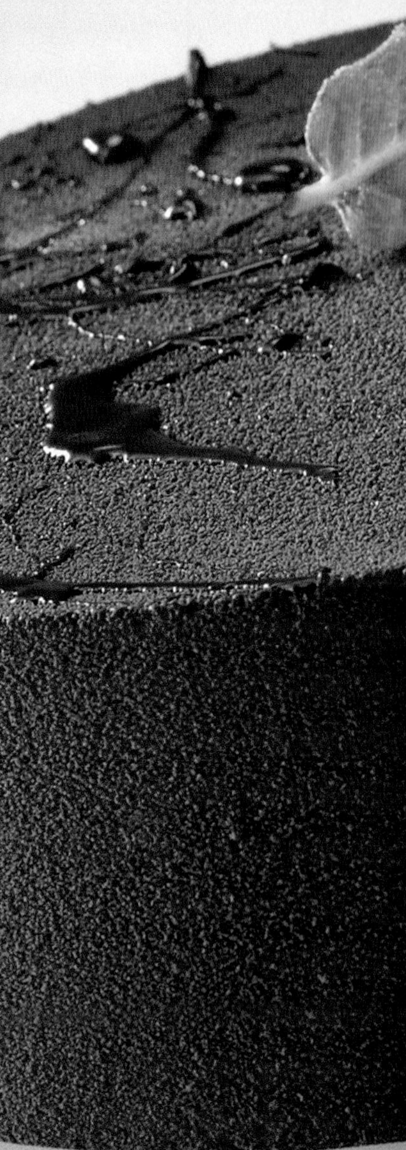

KEY TERMS

- ❖ Bottom-up assembly
- ❖ Cake frames
- ❖ Cake wall
- ❖ Crumb coat
- ❖ Entremets
- ❖ Filling
- ❖ Frozen inserts
- ❖ Ice
- ❖ Layer cakes
- ❖ Masking
- ❖ Modeling chocolate
- ❖ Specialty cakes
- ❖ Splitting
- ❖ Upside-down assembly

REVIEW QUESTIONS

1. **What is the distinction between a classic layer cake and a specialty cake?**
2. **Why is it essential to have all mise en place prepared before beginning a cake project?**
3. **Why are timing and preparedness essential for making specialty mousse cakes?**
4. **What is a cake wall? How is it used?**
5. **Why are the date, time, and venue the first information to be determined when producing a wedding cake?**

chapter
18

PETITS FOURS AND CONFECTIONS

OBJECTIVES

After reading this chapter, you should be able to

- define the classical categories of petits fours and the characteristics of the items.
- describe the contemporary categories of petits fours and to be able to make a selection of them.
- define the properties of saturated and supersaturated sugar solutions and to be able to make them successfully.
- make a selection of sugar confections including crystalline, noncrystalline, aerated, and jelly.

HISTORY AND EVOLUTION OF PETITS FOURS

The term **petits fours** is traditionally used to describe the miniature cookies, tartlets, and cakes that may accompany an afternoon coffee or tea or that are served after a meal. Petits fours have numerous characteristics, including light, delicate, crisp, and refreshing. The common defining characteristic of petits fours is that they can be eaten in one or two bites. The name of these small treats, which literally means "small ovens," refers to the tradition of baking small pastries in a slow oven after large pastries have been removed and oven temperature is reduced.

Petits fours are often based on larger versions of traditional pastries and are made up from all the different types of bases—dough, batters, creams, fillings, and icings—that are found in the pastry shop. Petits fours are largely a concept of size and delicacy and can be adapted from many traditional larger items. Some adjustments may need to occur in the handling of the dough, the baking process, and the assembly. Examples of petits fours adapted from larger products include opera cake, tarte Tatin, crémeux fruit tarts, madeleines, and Baba Savarin.

There are two styles of sweet petits fours, traditional and contemporary, both of which are explored in this chapter. Traditional petits fours include petits fours sec, petits fours glacés, petits fours frais, and petits fours déguisés. Contemporary petits fours include petits fours prestige, as well as the list of the traditional petits fours.

The presentation and overall quality of petits fours plays an important role in the perception of these sweets. Because these creations are small and designed for a discriminating palate, care should be taken in their preparation to ensure they are as perfect as can be. Petits fours are sometimes described as **mignardise**, essentially small, delicate bites, and **friandise**, which refers to a treat often enjoyed with coffee or tea or after a dessert course. Usually found in fine dining settings such as restaurants and hotels, they are the pastry kitchen's version of the savory **amuses bouche**, or taste teasers.

CATEGORIES OF PETITS FOURS

PETITS FOURS SEC

Petits fours sec are usually unfilled cookies. These have a signature dry, crisp texture from being baked at a lower temperature for longer periods of time. The simple nature of this category makes attention to detail a crucial consideration to ensure the quality and presentation. These cookies often include various shapes and assembly procedures, which may include the following cookie processes: icebox, molded, piped, and sheeted. Common dough used for petits fours sec include shortbread, sablé breton, and puff pastry to make items like duchesses, sablé beurre, Spritz, speculos, palmiers, allumettes glacées, tuiles, and langue du chats.

A popular petit four sec is the **Parisian macaron**, a delicate cookie made with sugar, egg whites, and ground almonds. The Parisian variety of macaron is becoming increasingly popular and is defined by two cookies, sandwiched together with a flavored filling. Macarons should be shiny and smooth on the outside with color representative of the filling inside. The inside of the cookie should be soft and moist, never crunchy or tough. It is common for these cookies to go through a "curing" stage in the refrigerator to soften the cookie and infuse the flavor of the filling throughout the treat. At 70 percent relative humidity, macarons can remain in the refrigerator uncovered for up to 3 days. If the humidity is too high, the cookie can soften too much and take on a very soft texture. Macarons are most commonly flavored with buttercream or ganache, which may be flavored as vanilla, pistachio, chocolate, praline, lemon, and raspberry, among others.

PETITS FOURS GLACÉS

Petits fours glacés are small, bite-sized cakes with a thin coating of glaze, typically fondant, which is applied at the end of the production process. Assembled in large sheets and then cut after setting up, petits fours glacés contain thin layers of cake alternating with jam and/or buttercream. The top of the cake is adorned with a thin layer of **marzipan** to add flavor, as well as a smooth surface for the glaze to settle on. Marzipan is made from almond paste, with the addition of sugar, a cooked sugar syrup, and sometimes glucose and/or egg white. After the cake is cut, it can be enrobed in fondant, or sometimes chocolate. Petits fours glacés are typically finished with intricate, stylized piping. This type of petit four is not as common as it once was as petits fours frais and petits fours prestige have become more popular.

PETITS FOURS FRAIS

Petits fours frais are characterized by items that are served the day they are made because their composition leads to deterioration of quality the longer they sit. This group includes cream-filled items, such as éclairs, tartlets (fruit, crémeux, ganache), and some petits fours déguisés. Parisian macarons may be classified as petits fours frais when they are filled with fresh fruit and a mousse or similar light-textured cream. Petits fours frais may also include "spongy" petits fours such as almond cakes, madeleines, and financiers.

PETITS FOURS DÉGUISÉS

Petits fours déguisés are made from fresh, dried, or candied fruits that are coated in cooked sugar, fondant, chocolate, or any combination of the three. Fruits commonly dipped in sugar include gooseberries, kumquats, cherries, grapes, and candied fruits such as pineapple or mango. The fruit is simply dipped into the cooked sugar solution and then transferred to a silicone mat or lightly oiled granite. Some fruit, such as kumquat, may benefit from drying out slightly before dipping. Any fruit dipped in sugar should be used in a timely fashion or should be stored with humectants, to avoid the softening of the sugar.

A standard syrup for dipping includes

100 percent sugar
35 percent water
35 percent glucose
5 drops of tartaric acid solution per 1 kg sugar

This syrup should be prepared as other supersaturated syrups by bringing the water and sugar to a boil, brushing down the sides of the pot with cold water and then adding the glucose. The syrup needs to be cooked to 320°F (160°C). The sugar should then be removed from the heat, and the cooking should be stopped in cold water. After the bubbles have subsided, the fruit can be dipped in the sugar. The sugar syrup may be colored to enhance the presentation of the petits fours.

Traditional fruit petits fours déguisés are usually first coated in marzipan and then dipped in sugar. Decorator's marzipan (20 percent fruit content) is commonly used as a filling to replace the pit in pitted fruits, and as a thin outside layer used to cover some dried fruit before dipping in sugar. Whenever marzipan is used to cover fruit to be dipped, it should be allowed to dry for a couple of days before dipping in sugar. After the marzipan is dry, it may be dipped in the sugar syrup. If fruit is coated with fondant, the fondant should be dry and slightly hard before it is dipped into an additional ingredient like chocolate.

Products that are dipped in fondant should be candied or of relatively low moisture to ensure the fondant sets. To partially enrobe petits fours déguisés which have been dipped in fondant with chocolate, the fondant must set first. Common fruits using this technique include strawberries, candied orange slices, and candied citrus peels.

Considerations for Dipping Fruits in Sugar

Two factors should be considered when whole or sliced fruits are dipped in cooked sugar. First, fruit should be properly cleaned and thoroughly dried before dipping to avoid sugar crystallization, as well as problems where the water dissolves the fondant, seizes the chocolate, or deteriorates the fruit pieces. Second, fruits with a higher moister level on the surface should be coated with marzipan to keep the sugar from crystallizing due to the presence of natural liquids or moisture. In addition, syrup for dipped fruit can range from hard crack to caramel, depending on the flavor and desired color. Please refer to the sugar cooking guidelines in Chapter 21 to create the best quality coating.

PETITS FOURS PRESTIGE

Petits fours prestige, which are composed of more advanced preparations, mirror current trends in pastry. Petits fours prestige may be smaller versions of contemporary entremets or other desserts. Components used for petits fours prestige may include cake bases such as biscuit or Dacquoise, creams such as crème mousseline or crémeux, egg foams like Italian meringue, and fresh fruit. Additionally, many of the finishing techniques used for advanced cake production may be used for petits fours prestige such as glazing and chocolate spraying. Often these small pastries will even include small decorative chocolate or sugar elements. The production of these items is labor intensive; however, with the use of specialty molds and working out of the freezer, petits fours prestige can look consistent and sharp and can be produced efficiently.

STORAGE AND SERVICE OF PETITS FOURS

Storage plays an important role in the production and serving of petits fours. Consideration needs to be given both to the environment and the individual characteristics of each item. If the item is susceptible to humidity, it should be held airtight, vacuum-sealed when possible, and with antihumectants.

Many petits fours are produced as close to serving time as possible, due to the element of freshness that is a defining characteristic. Petits fours sec may have a shelf life of roughly 1 to 2 weeks. Petits fours frais, déguisés, and prestige are fresh for shorter periods of time, which varies by product. Freezing is a good option for many of the bases and doughs that can be made up ahead of time and held until ready to bake or assemble.

Figure 18-1
Assorted Confections: Pâtes de Fruits, Marshmallows, and Chartreuse Marshmallow Lollipops

AN INTRODUCTION TO SUGAR CONFECTIONS

Confections can be broken into three distinct categories: chocolate, flour, and sugar. **Chocolate confections** are described in detail in Chapter 22. **Flour confections** represent a vast array of products, including cookies, cakes, and pastries. The focus of this portion of the chapter, **sugar confections**, includes products like caramels, cordials, fondants, marzipan candies, pâtes de fruits, nougat, and marshmallows, all of which are sugar based. (See Figure 18-1.) Sugar confections can be eaten as snacks or served after a meal as petits fours.

SUGAR CONFECTIONS IN HISTORY

India was the first country to establish a method for extracting sugar from sugar cane. Persians soon adopted these techniques, and eventually the Arabs introduced sugar to Spain and countries in North Africa. Sugar was first introduced to inland Europe in the 12th century, where it was traded along with exotic spices. At the time, sugar was largely treated as a flavoring used in medicine, electuaries, and other solid pills made by apothecaries, where the sweetener acted as a binding agent and masked unpleasant flavors from medicinal ingredients. By the 15th century, a distinct separation of medical and nonmedical confections had been established.

SUGAR SOLUTIONS

The common component of sugar confections is a **sugar solution** made from sugar and water. At sea level, and under normal atmospheric conditions, water boils at 212°F (100°C). As a sugar solution is boiled and water turns to steam, the sugar remains in a liquefied state. The dissolved sugar in the solution allows it to rise above the boiling point of pure water; as the concentration of sugar becomes higher, so does the boiling point. The final ratio of sugar to water determines the density of the syrup (which affects the boiling point), as well as the degree of setting that occurs after cooling.

Confectioners were making candies long before thermometers were widely available to gauge solution temperature. Instead, the degree of cooking was determined by dropping a small amount of the boiling sugar solution in cold water and feeling its texture as it quickly cooled. This technique is still widely practiced today. Figure 18-2 displays the relationship between the temperature of the cooking solution, its setting property, and the confections for which it is commonly used.

Saturation of Sugar

When sugar is dissolved into water, the ratio of water to sugar and the temperature of the solution will determine the point of saturation. At any given temperature, water can only dissolve a certain amount of sugar. For example, water at room temperature dissolves approximately 66 percent of its weight in sugar. In order to dissolve more sugar, the temperature of the solution must be increased. A **saturated solution** is achieved when the maximum quantity of sugar is dissolved into water.

Supersaturated solutions contain dissolved sugar at a higher ratio than is normally possible at a given temperature. This is achieved when a saturated sugar solution is boiled to evaporate part of the water, and then cooled. It is important to cool supersaturated solutions in a controlled environment in order to prevent the formation of crystals. Agitation or the introduction of dust, granular sugar, or any other foreign material into the solution can create a **seed**. Agitation or a seed can start a chain reaction of crystallization.

Figure 18-2
Common Sugar Solution Temperatures for Confections

Cooked Texture	Temperature	Uses
"Thread"	215°F (102°C) to 235°F (113°C)	Fruit syrups
"Soft Ball" Stage	235°F (113°C) to 240°F (116°C)	Fondant, fudge
"Firm Ball" Stage	245°F (118°C) to 250°F (121°C)	Soft caramels
"Hard Ball" Stage	250°F (121°C) to 265°F (129°C)	Marzipan, marshmallow
"Soft Crack" Stage	270°F (132°C) to 290°F (143°C)	Taffy
"Hard Crack" Stage	300°F (149°C) to 310°F (154°C)	Hard candy, toffee, brittle
"Caramel" Stage	320°F (160°C) to 350°F (177°C)	Caramel, decorative sugar work

Crystallization

Understanding and controlling the crystallization of sugar is essential in the production of sugar confections. Whether or not the sugar has been crystallized defines the subcategory to which the confection belongs. For example, sugar is purposefully crystallized during the cooking process for **crystalline confections** like fondants and fudge because controlled crystallization forms thousands of microscopic sugar crystals that create smooth and creamy characteristics.

Conversely, crystallization must be avoided during the production of **noncrystalline confections** such as caramels, hard candies, and toffees. The characteristics of noncrystalline confections range from hard and brittle to soft and chewy, depending on the degree to which the sugar solution was cooked and the quantity of glucose or inverted sugars in the formula.

When cooking saturated sugar solutions, adhere to the following important guidelines to prevent crystallization.

- *Avoid Impurities:* Always use clean tools, equipment, and ingredients. Caution should be taken if using a sugar that may be contaminated with flour so it is a good idea to work from a sugar source that is known to be pure.
- *Temperature:* Begin cooking at a medium-high temperature because too high of an initial heat can promote crystallization. After the sugar solution has boiled, it is possible to increase the temperature. If cooking with gas, be sure the flames do not go up the sides of the pot, as this can produce uneven heat and may result in premature browning.
- *Sugar Grains:* Before the sugar and water mixture comes to a boil, make sure that the sugar is completely dissolved. Wash down the sides of the pot with a clean pastry brush and water to ensure that there are no undissolved sugar particles. This should be done as soon as the cooking process begins, when the solution comes to a boil, and periodically as needed. Note that excessive washing down will introduce more water into the solution and will lengthen the time required to achieve the desired temperature.
- *Agitation:* Unless specified in the process of the formula, sugar solutions should not be stirred after the solution comes to a boil because stirring promotes crystallization.

Additional ingredients, referred to as **doctors** by confectioners, can be added to sugar solutions to help prevent crystallization. Common doctors include glucose (the most favored), inverted sugar, and acids such as tartaric acid. Doctors should be added to the solution after it has come to a boil because it is easier for sugar to dissolve without the presence of glucose or inverted sugar. The molecular structures of glucose and inverted sugar, which are longer than sugar (sucrose), can inhibit the bonding of sucrose molecules. A solution of tartaric acid can help prevent the sugar syrup from crystallizing by partially inverting of the solution through hydrolysis.

Caramelization and the Maillard Reaction

Caramelization occurs when sugar is heated above 320°F (160°C). The sugar changes color from clear to light yellow and progresses to darker tones of brown. Caramelization evolves the initial sweet flavors into richer, nutty, and slightly bitter flavors. The darker the sugar becomes, the more intense the bitterness will be.

The Maillard reaction occurs when amino acids from protein and monosaccharides (glucose and fructose) are combined in the presence of heat. The reaction is complicated; however, it is an important one for the confectioner, pastry chef, and baker to understand. This reaction takes place during the processing of many foods and results in familiar flavors in caramels, bread, coffee beans, chocolate, dark beers, and grilled meats, to name just a few.

In the production of confections, this reaction can be observed when making toffee and caramels. In theory, when there are more amino acid proteins in the dairy being cooked, more browning and flavor development will occur. In addition, if the cooking process happens at a slower rate, the degree of browning and flavor development will be increased.

CATEGORIES OF SUGAR CONFECTIONS

Sugar confections can be divided into four main categories: crystalline, noncrystalline, aerated, and jelly. The textures of sugar confections (hard, soft, chewy, jelly, and supple) are largely determined by the concentration of the sugar solution, the ingredients, the formula, and the manufacturing process.

CRYSTALLINE CONFECTIONS

This group of confections is defined by the formation of sugar crystals during cooking. Examples include fondant, fudge, pralines, dragées, and liqueur pralines. Most crystalline confections are based on a supersaturated sugar solution that is agitated to create fine sugar crystals. The pastry chef can control all these factors (temperature, saturation, and agitation) to create specific outcomes.

For example, crystal size is determined by the rate at which the temperature of the sugar solution is lowered; the number of crystals depends on the level of agitation during the cooling process. Hot syrup that is stirred occasionally while cooling will have fewer larger crystals, and syrup that is not stirred until it has cooled to 110°F (43°C) will have more crystals with a finer texture. Saturation, or the amount of water left in a solution after cooking, will also effect overall crystallization. If a syrup is not cooked enough, the solution will crystallize but remain runny. If it is overcooked, it will be dry and brittle.

Fondant

Fondant has applications for both pastry and confections. As presented in Chapter 15, fondant is an icing that is often used on items like napoleon cake, éclairs, and Danish pastries. This sweet, thick, opaque, finely crystallized sugar paste should not be confused with the rolled fondant used in cake decoration. There are two main types of fondant: **pastry fondant** and **confectionary fondant**.

Pastry fondant is used as a glaze because it is cooked to a lower temperature, has more free water in it, and is less viscous. In confectionary fondant, because the sugar syrup is cooked to a higher temperature, the crystalline structure is finer and the viscosity is greater. The higher temperature creates a firmer texture and enables the pastry chef to thin the fondant to add flavorings in the form of alcohols and oils. Herbs or spices can also be added.

Figure 18-3
Temperature Guidelines for Cooking Syrup for Fondant

Temperature	Texture	Uses
235°F (113°C)	Soft	Pastry, glaze
242°F (117°C)	Medium	Multipurpose
257°F (125°C)	Firm	Confectionary, fillings

Figure 18-3 presents temperature guidelines for cooking syrup for fondant, along with the corresponding texture.

Confectionary fondant can be formed by hand or heated and poured into **starch molds** to set until firm. Starch molds are made from a thick, contained layer of dry starch that has been carefully imprinted with cavities in which fillings can be deposited and left to set. Some preparations for fondants include invertase, an enzyme that breaks down the sugars contained in the fondant to produce a more liquid filling. Invertase enables the confectioner to produce very soft fondants at a stage when they are easy to handle. Its use must be closely monitored because the quantity (0.5 to 1.5 percent based on the total weight of the fondant) will affect the amount of time (days to weeks) that it takes for sugar conversion. It is very common, though not necessary, to finish fondants by enrobing them in chocolate.

Process for Fondant

- Combine the sugars, inverted sugars, and liquids. Cook to the required temperature, depending on the final use.
- If the formula contains salt, stir it in at the end of the cooking process.
- Pour the hot mixture onto a granite slab that has some ice water on it and allow it to cool to approximately 122°F (50°C).
- If seeding the fondant, add about 10 percent based on the total weight, and place it on the syrup.
- Agitate the mixture using a scraper until it reaches to the desired level of crystallization.
- Keep in an airtight container and allow to mature overnight.

Starch Molds for Fondant Fillings Starch molds can be used to form a fine crust on soft fondant, which is then dipped in chocolate to finish. To make fondant interiors, the fondant is warmed to approximately 150°F (66°C), and liqueur or flavoring is added. Using a warmed fondant funnel, the fondant is deposited into the starch molds and allowed to set for 3 to 5 hours to form a crust. Then, it is removed from the starch, excess starch is dusted off with a dry, clean pastry brush, and the fondant is enrobed in tempered chocolate.

Fudge

Fudge is based on the formulation of fondant (fine sugar crystals surrounded by a supersaturated sugar solution) with additional ingredients, such as dairy products, fat, nuts, and chocolate. Because each additional ingredient affects the stability of the mass by altering the texture, appearance, and shelf life, the formulation of fudge requires a fine balance of all ingredients. Fudge does not have an extreme hygroscopic property, but it can dry out if it is exposed to air for too long. Therefore, fudge should be enrobed or wrapped immediately after cutting.

Process for Fudge

- Combine the sugars, inverted sugars, and liquids. Cook to the specified temperature.
- If the formula contains salt, stir it in at the end of cooking process.
- Pour the hot mixture onto a lightly oiled granite slab and allow it to cool without agitation to the desired temperature.
- Place flavorings and additional ingredients such as chocolate or nuts on top of the mixture.
- Agitate the mixture using a scraper, first to incorporate the added ingredients and then until it reaches the desired level of crystallization.
- Deposit into a frame to crystallize.
- After the fudge has set for approximately 1 hour, it is ready to be portioned and wrapped for storage.

Liqueur Cordials

Liqueur cordials are crystalline confections that are filled with a liqueur-flavored, supersaturated sugar solution. When this syrup is deposited into a starch mold, a fine crystalline shell is formed through a very controlled crystallization. The use of a starch mold is the classic choice for liqueur cordials; however, these confections can also be molded in chocolate shells. If a starch mold is used, the starch must be very dry so that the process of crystallization can begin. If it is too moist, or if there is a lot of humidity in the air, the liqueur could absorb into the starch and result in a misshapen confection. A thin sugar skin that holds in the liqueur-flavored syrup characterizes these bite-sized candies. When the seal is broken, the liqueur is released all at once.

The desired cooking temperature for cordial syrup varies by formula because the type of alcohol used has an effect on the rate of crystallization. For a solution using an alcohol with 45 percent alcohol, the solution should be cooked to 240°F (116°C). It is important to not use a doctor, which will prevent the most critical part of the process, the formation of fine sugar crystals. Proper techniques for cooking sugar solutions should be carefully carried out, including brushing down the side of the pot with a clean pastry brush and water in order to prevent crystallization, and the temperature must be closely monitored. A cordial syrup that has not been cooked to a high-enough temperature will not be saturated enough to begin the process of crystallization. Conversely, syrup that has been overcooked will crystallize too much, possibly to the point of total crystallization.

After the sugar has cooled slightly, warmed liqueur is added, and the syrup is cooled to below 120°F (49°C) with minimal agitation. The type of liqueur should not be too acidic because this can prohibit crystals from forming properly. The syrup is then deposited into the starch or other specialized molds. Once deposited, warm starch should be sifted over the syrup, and the cordials should be allowed to crystallize for at least 4 hours. Next, a lid is placed over the box, to the surface of the starch, and the box is inverted for at least 10 hours. At this point, the candies can be removed from the starch, dusted off, and enrobed in chocolate or packaged in plastic. If the syrup is to be deposited into chocolate shells, it should first be cooled to 78°F (26°C). The technique for these candies is very detailed and should be followed very closely to ensure final product quality.

To determine the ratios of sugar, water, and alcohol in a liqueur cordial, the percent of alcohol in the liqueur must be known. Per liter of alcohol, based on the degree of alcohol, 50 g sugar is required per percentage point of alcohol. For example, for 1 liter of Calvados (45 percent), we can use the following formula to determine how much sugar is required: 45 × 50 = 2,250. The quantity of alcohol in the solution should always be 50 percent of the sugar weight. This can be expressed as 2,250 × 50% = 1,125. Next, we need to figure out the weight of the water, which should be 45 percent of the sugar weight. (The percentage of the water is not connected with the percentage of the alcohol; they are coincidentally the same in this example). To achieve the water weight, multiply the water percentage by the sugar weight: 2,250 × 45% = 1,012.5. The results of our calculation follow:

Sugar, 2.250 kg

Water, 1.012 kg

Calvados (45 percent), 1.125 kg

Process for Liqueur Cordials

- Loosely deposit the sifted and dried starch into a metal frame.
- Make depressions in the starch.
- Place the starch box in a warm, dry place or a very low oven to "dry" before depositing the syrup solution.
- Using a fondant funnel, deposit the syrup into the indentations, and then sift more warm starch over the exposed sugar solution to ensure even crystallization.
- After 4 to 6 hours, a fine layer of crystallization should have developed. At this point, the candies should be inverted to allow for an even thickening of the "crust." This is an optional step but improves the quality of the cordial.
- Place the lid over the starch box, directly to the surface of the starch, and flip it over.
- After 10 to 12 hours, the crust of the candy should be completely stable and ready for handling. Remove and dust with a clean, dry pastry brush. Leaving the candies longer will create a thicker, less desirable crust.
- If desired, dip the candies into tempered chocolate to provide a protective coating and prevent breaking the fine crust.

Dragées

Dragées represent a category of crystalline confections made from slow-roasted nuts that have gone through two distinct processes: candying and coating. The first step involves coating the nuts in sugar syrup and going through a process of cooking and agitation. Next, the nuts are coated in a smooth sugar or chocolate coating. This latter process is referred to as panning.

The sugar syrup for dragée is cooked to the thread stage [240°F (116°C)], typically in a round-bottomed copper pot. The copper pot is useful because it is an efficient heat conductor, and the curved sides of the pot make it easy to tumble the nuts to promote crystallization. If a round bottom is not available, dragée should be made in smaller-sized batches using stainless steel, if possible. Once the syrup is ready, the roasted nuts are added and stirred to evenly coat them with the sugar syrup. Continued stirring triggers the crystallization of the sugar, which will appear opaque and wet as it begins to crystallize. As agitation continues, it will become whiter and drier until it appears sandy.

The cooking process can stop when the sugar has crystallized to a white, sandy state, or it can continue if caramelization is desired. If the latter method is used, the nuts should be constantly stirred to evenly remelt and caramelize the sugar. It may be necessary to turn down the heat to prevent burning.

Once the sugar coating of the nuts has caramelized, a small portion of butter or cocoa butter should be added to the nuts and stirred in to evenly coat the candy. This will help prevent the nuts from sticking to each other. However, if too much fat is added, the final product will be oily and greasy. It is common practice to add a pinch of salt to blend the flavors of the caramel and butter. The nuts can then be turned out onto a nonstick baking mat or a lightly oiled granite surface. They can be separated by hand to ensure they don't stick, or they can be left in clusters. If the sugar is not caramelized, the added butter is not required. Dragées can be used plain, in candied or caramel form, or they can be coated with a layer of chocolate before serving.

Process for Dragées

- Roast the nuts in a low oven to brown them to the core. Reserve until needed.
- In a round-bottomed copper pot, combine the sugar, water, and vanilla bean, and cook to the thread stage.
- Add the nuts and stir constantly to crystallize the sugar to the point of at least being white, dry, and sandy. If stopping here, turn out of the pot onto a clean surface and allow to cool to room temperature before storing.
- If cooking the dragées to the caramel stage, continue stirring the nuts. The heat may need to be reduced to avoid uneven cooking.
- After the nuts have taken on a caramel color, remove the pot from the heat and add the butter or cocoa butter and stir to incorporate. Turn the nuts out onto a silpat or lightly oiled granite surface and separate as desired to cool.
- Store cooled dragées in an airtight container until ready for panning or other use.

Panning

The process for coating nutmeats or other confectionary centers is referred to as **panning**. There are three types of panning: soft sugar panning, hard sugar panning, and **chocolate panning**. Because the process for soft sugar panning and hard sugar panning is highly technical and requires specialized equipment, only chocolate panning will be presented here in detail.

Classically, *dragée* can refer to the process of dredging nutmeats through something to coat them. Sugar is the classic coating, but chocolate became a favorite once it was discovered and mass-produced. There are two possible approaches to coating centers with chocolate: panning using mechanized systems and stirring chocolate and nuts together by hand. The mechanized process merits special attention because specific temperature and motion controls are required to obtain the desired results.

To evenly coat nuts or dried fruit with chocolate, it is important to start off with uniform pieces. For larger commercial production, nuts are commonly tumbled in a mixture of a gum solution and starch or cocoa powder (depending on the finishing techniques employed). This creates a fine preliminary layer around the center, which makes the piece more symmetrical, helps the chocolate adhere to the center, and helps to limit fat migration from the center through the chocolate.

The temperature of both workroom and chocolate are important considerations for panning. The ideal temperature for the chocolate is between 90°F (32°C) and 95°F (35°C), just above and several degrees above the point at which chocolate can be tempered. For a detailed description of tempering and the properties of cocoa butter crystallization in chocolate, refer to Chapter 22. The temperature of the workroom should be between 55°F (13°C) and 60°F (16°C). This cooler temperature helps initiate the process of crystallizing the cocoa butter from within the chocolate, which results in building layers of chocolate.

The process is quite simple. For a small shop or a test kitchen, a panning drum that fits onto KitchenAid mixers is available; however, for larger production, highly specialized equipment is available. To begin, the drum is set to spin at approximately 25 rpm, and nuts are added to it. The quantity of nuts should not reach more than halfway up the bottom of the mold. Enough space is needed to ensure a complete coating process, which requires that the nuts have enough room to tumble. As the nuts tumble, the warm chocolate is ladled into the pan.

Where the chocolate falls is a critical point because it determines how the chocolate will coat the centers. To promote the most even coating, the chocolate should be released from the ladle in a slow, steady stream toward the front of where the nuts are tumbling. As the nuts tumble they may congregate and cluster. It is essential to break these up as early as possible, because their size will grow considerably as more chocolate is added.

Once the initial chocolate coating has set, additional chocolate can be ladled in using the same method. This process of settling and ladling continues until the confectioner reaches the desired point of thickness; a typical quantity of chocolate is two to three times the weight of the nuts. Panned confections are usually finished with powdered sugar or cocoa powder, but can also be smooth and shiny. Although the technique of coating nuts and dried fruits through chocolate panning requires some skill and practice, it is easy to achieve very consistent and desirable results once the confectioner establishes a workable technique.

NONCRYSTALLINE CONFECTIONS

Noncrystalline confections are characterized by a lack of crystal formation during the cooking process. Whether hard and crunchy or smooth and soft, the texture is established by controlling how much water is evaporated during the cooking process and the ingredients used in the formula. Two of the most commonly added ingredients are cream and butter, which cause browning to occur through the Maillard reaction and provide characteristic caramel and toffee flavors. In order to prevent crystal formation, it is very important to closely follow several guidelines while making these candies:

- Combine all applicable ingredients in a pot, and dissolve the sugar.
- In order to prevent "seeding," wash down the sides of the cooking pan with a clean, wet brush while heating to a boil to ensure that no sugar crystals are present.
- For preparations without dairy products, do not stir after a boil is reached because the agitation will induce crystallization. For prepara-

tions containing dairy, such as caramels and toffee, stirring is required to prevent scorching.

- Skim the residual sugar impurities from the top of the mixture during boiling.
- Add an invert sugar such as glucose, corn syrup, or honey. An acid like lemon juice, tartaric acid, or cream of tartar will also help block crystal formation.

Hard Candies

One of the oldest forms of confections, **hard candies** were once largely associated with pharmacists. Today, due to mass-market appeal, they are most commonly produced on an industrial scale using highly specialized equipment. For small-scale production, such as for a restaurant or hotel, several styles of hard candies are more common than others. Hard candies achieve their texture due to minimal water content in the final product. Most hard candies do not reach the point of any Maillard reaction, because the sugar syrup does not go over 320°F (160°C).

Ingredients for hard candies always include sugar, as well as glucose and flavoring. For small batch production, a common ratio of sugar to glucose is 7:3. The glucose syrup is required to stabilize the sugar to prevent crystallization and to help make the medium easier to mold and form. To a point, the glucose assists in retarding the degradation of the hard candy because the glucose prevents the sugar from easily absorbing water from the environment. However, if too much inverted sugar is present in the formulation—either through inversion during the cooking process, use of inverted sugar, or excessive use of glucose syrup—the candies will attract more humidity.

If any acids are added while the sugar is cooking, hydrolysis can occur and cause the sugar to be too soft, which will encourage moisture attraction. Acidic ingredients such as citric acid and tartaric acid are sometimes added to the cooked sugar after it has begun to cool to complement added flavorings with notes of acidity.

At the artisan level, processing is mostly done by hand using specialty low-tech tools that form or mold the candies. If there is more to be done than simply depositing the syrup in a mold, a review of working with pulled sugar (found in Chapter 21) will be helpful. As with pulled sugar, hard candies present issues related to working with very hot mediums. When multiple colors and flavors are required, a large batch of cooked sugar syrup can be divided for cooling, then flavored and colored as desired. Stretching, folding, forming, and shaping hard candies takes practice before the skill of the confectioner can show through.

Process for Hard Candies

- Dissolve the sugar with the water, and bring to a boil.
- Add the glucose, and dissolve and cook to the desired temperature.
- Add colorant as needed.
- Cool the mass on a silicone mat, and add any flavors, acids, or colors as needed.
- Satinize the mass as needed.
- Shape the product as desired.
- Wrap in plastic to preserve against humidity.

Brittles

Brittles are crunchy sugar confections based on cooked sugar syrup that have added nuts or seeds. This confection can be considered an offshoot of hard candies because it is based on sugar syrup cooked to a high temperature with added ingredients. The base formula of sugar, water, and glucose, which is similar to that of hard candies, is cooked to a high temperature to evaporate the maximum amount of liquid. When nuts or seeds are added to the confection, it takes on a caramelized flavor and color, due to the Maillard reaction. Once nuts are added to the sugar syrup, it should be stirred to ensure that the nuts don't fall to the bottom of the pot and scorch.

Additional ingredients can be added, like salt, baking soda and butter, as well as flavorings like vanilla. Baking soda is added after the cooking process to lighten the texture and to allow the layers of brittle to be thicker, while still remaining edible. If used, baking soda should be added at the end of the cooking process, just before pouring, to ensure that the carbon dioxide is trapped in the mass. There is also a technique that stretches and folds the brittle to create thin layers.

Process for Brittles

- Combine the sugar and water and bring to a boil.
- After a boil is achieved, add the glucose, and stir to dissolve.
- Cook the sugar syrup to 230°F (110°C), and then add the nuts or seeds.
- Continue to cook, stirring the mixture until it reaches 311°F (155°C).
- Remove the pot from the heat, and add any additional ingredients (salt, flavorings, baking soda, and butter).
- Pour onto a lightly oiled granite surface or a silicone baking mat to cool, and spread into a thin layer.
- If desired, pull the brittle into thin sheets when it is cool enough.
- Store in a covered environment with humectants to avoid moisture absorption.

Caramel and Toffee

The difference between **caramel** and **toffee** can be measured by the difference in moisture content at the end of the cooking process. Temperatures that promote the caramelization of sugar are never reached for these items; instead, the characteristic flavors and colors that mimic caramel are produced when dairy proteins go through the Maillard reaction. Both are very flavorful, with buttery caramel notes, but the texture is very different: caramel ranges from soft and creamy to firm and chewy, while toffee is characterized by hard and crunchy textures. Caramel and toffee both rely on the controlled cooking of sugar, a doctor, and dairy. Several types of dairy can be used, including cream, milk, evaporated milk, or sweetened condensed milk.

Process for Caramel and Toffee

- Combine the sugar and liquid ingredients, and bring to a boil while stirring.
- Add the glucose, inverted sugar, or honey, and continue to cook while stirring over medium heat.
- Monitor the temperature to ensure proper moisture content in the final product.

- When it is done cooking, add salt or other flavorings as applicable.
- Pour the mixture into metal frames, or deposit as needed.
- For caramel, cut when cool and wrap in applicable packaging or enrobe in chocolate.
- For toffee, cut while still malleable and wrap to avoid attracting moisture.

AERATED CONFECTIONS

Aerated confections, which consist of a stable foam, are created by both the formulation and the process of whipping. The two most common examples of aerated confections are the light, spongy marshmallow and firmer, chewy nougat. The two most common approaches to making aerated confections are adding a gelling agent to meringue while it is whipping and adding a gelling agent to cooked sugar syrup and whipping it to the desired stage.

When a stable foam is created by whipping egg whites or a gelling agent (most frequently gelatin), the incorporated air provides a lighter texture. Once the stable foam is created, it must be further stabilized for the end product to retain its characteristics. The ingredients used to elaborate the foam are often the same ingredients responsible for its stability. For example, the coagulation of egg white protein stabilizes the foam as it cools and is not thermoreversible, while gelatin whipped with sugar creates a foam that jellifies and becomes stable when set.

Marshmallows

Marshmallows date back to ancient Eqypt where they were made from the sap of the marsh mallow plant (*Althaea officinalis*) and honey. Reserved for the upper classes, they were highly regarded for their medicinal properties of acting as a cough suppressant. Today, marshmallows are made using at least two methods: one with egg whites and one without. Both methods include sugar, glucose, gelatin, and optional flavoring.

Gelatin or a combination of egg white and gelatin can be used to create the foam for marshmallows. Gelatin-based marshmallows are more common; however, the added flavor and lighter texture of marshmallows based on both egg white and gelatin is more appropriate for artisan confections.

Commercially produced marshmallows are extruded in a cylinder form and cut into segments. Artisan marshmallows are usually deposited into a frame, cut into squares or other shapes, and then dredged in a 50/50 blend of potato starch and powdered sugar. (When cutting marshmallows, it is best to use a lightly oiled knife that will keep the sugar from sticking.) Additionally, marshmallow can be molded in silicone molds like Flexipans to create unique shapes.

Process for Marshmallows With Egg Whites and Gelatin

- Bloom the gelatin in cold water five times its weight.
- Warm the egg whites to 65°F (18°C) to 70°F (21°C), and put them in the bowl of a mixer fitted with the whip attachment.
- Begin cooking the sugar syrup to 284°F (140°C).
- Begin whipping the egg whites when the sugar syrup reaches 248°F (120°C).

- When the sugar syrup reaches 284°F (140°C), remove from the heat, add the bloomed, melted gelatin, and thoroughly incorporate.
- Turn the mixer onto high speed.
- Pour the sugar–gelatin mixture down the side of the mixing bowl into the whipping egg whites and mix at a high speed until full volume and just warm to the touch [113°F (45°C)].
- Deposit into molds or frames while still warm, allow to set, and then portion and finish as desired.

Process for Marshmallows With Gelatin

- Bloom the gelatin in cold water five times its weight.
- Cook the sugar syrup to the temperature specified in the formula.
- Allow to cool to 212°F (100°C) without agitation.
- Add the bloomed, melted gelatin to this mixture, and thoroughly incorporate.
- In a mixer fitted with the whip attachment, mix on a high speed until full volume and just warm to the touch [113°F (45°C)].
- Deposit into molds or frames while still warm, allow to set, and then portion and finish as desired.

Nougat

Nougat is a dense, aerated confection with textures that range from soft and chewy to firm, depending on the degree to which the sugar syrup is cooked, as well as the ingredients used in the formula. Even though the texture is significantly denser than marshmallow, nougat relies on the formation of an egg white foam to achieve its characteristics. European nougat is white and firm, while most American-style nougat used in candy bars is much softer and lighter.

Nougat comes in many styles, with a number of possible inclusions and flavor combinations. Common additives include hazelnuts, pistachios, and whole, blanched almonds. With the exception of pistachios, it is best to roast the nuts and hold them in a warm place until they are needed, so that the nougat does not cool too quickly and is easier to mold and roll out. Nougat can also be flavored with coffee, chocolate, or other flavorings like pistachio paste. When mixing is complete, the nougat is deposited on a silicone baking mat in a frame or between metal confectionary bars. Some confectioners deposit the nougat onto rice paper, which helps limit flow.

One of the most popular types of nougat, nougat de Montélimar, is named after a French town in the Rhone Valley. The formula consists of a meringue made with cooked honey and a sugar syrup. The common technique, which can vary slightly from formula to formula, is to cook the honey to the specified temperature and then add it to a meringue whipped to soft peaks. When the meringue–honey elaboration has achieved full volume, sugar syrup that has been cooked to a specified temperature is added. Because there is a low water content in the meringue, it is best to switch to the paddle before the sugar syrup is added. It is very important that the syrup not be allowed to brown, or it will give the nougat an undesirable, uncharacteristic color.

Whipping continues until the mixture has cooled, but is still warm. When the meringue is approximately 130°F (55°C), additional ingredients can be added. The most common added ingredients include powdered sugar, cocoa butter, and roasted nuts. Powdered sugar is added to induce crystallization to alter the texture of the confection, whereas cocoa butter is often added to make the texture shorter and softer.

If adding cocoa butter and/or nuts, the temperature of the added ingredients must be similar to the nougat. Otherwise, it will cause separation, and portions of the nougat will prematurely set in the bowl. If this happens, the bowl can be warmed with a torch or heat gun to soften the nougat and warm the mix.

After nougat has set, it can be cut to desired sizes using a serrated knife (this will ensure that the shape is maintained) After it is cut, nougat should be wrapped or dipped partially or entirely in chocolate. If it is partially coated, brushing the exposed surface with cocoa butter will prevent it from absorbing moisture.

Process for Nougat

- Before beginning the nougat, roast the nuts. Next, combine with pistachios (if using) and hold in a warm oven [150°F (66°C)] until needed.
- Boil the honey to the specified temperature.
- Bring the sugar and water to a boil. As soon as it boils, add the glucose, and cook the syrup to the specified temperature.
- Begin to whip the egg whites, sugar, and salt when the honey is at 212°F (100°C).
- Pour the honey onto the egg whites, and whip with the whisk attachment. When the cooked sugar has reached the desired temperature, switch to the paddle attachment before adding.
- Continue to whip with the paddle on medium speed.
- At 125°F (50°C), add the powdered sugar, and mix to incorporation.
- Next, add the melted cocoa butter, and mix to incorporation.
- Last, add the warm nuts and dried fruit (if any), and mix just to incorporation.
- Pour onto a silicone mat, and roll out between metal bars. If desired, deposit the nougat in an even layer onto rice paper, and top with another sheet of rice paper.
- Allow to set, and then cut to the desired size.
- Dip the sides or the whole confection in tempered dark couverture.
- If not coating with tempered couverture, wrap the nougat in plastic after it is cut.

JELLY CONFECTIONS

Jellies, or **jelly confections**, are popular sugar confections, and many of the commercially available varieties can be quite whimsical, including Gummy Worms, Sour Patch Kids, Swedish Fish, and jelly beans. An artisan confectioner's approach to jellies can include items like Turkish Delight and pâtes de fruits.

In general, jelly products always contain a supersaturated sugar solution, flavorings, and binding agents. The four categories of jellies—gelatin, pectin, agar, and starch—are classified by the type of gelling agent used. This section will explore gelatin, pectin, and agar because they are the most applicable to the artisan confectioner.

Gelification Ingredient Technology

All formulations for jellies are based on a supersaturated sugar solution, which provides texture, sweetness, and shelf life. The presence of water in sugar solutions affects the degree of softness or toughness in the solution's setting properties. Water activity and solids count also have an effect on the microbiological stability of the confection. In order to be stable, the solids count of the base syrup must be at least 75 percent.

Flavorings Flavorings for jellies range from natural fruit juices or purees, to acidic powders such as tartaric acid or citric acid, to commercially produced artificial and natural flavors. Flavorings provide the pleasure in eating jellies. There are very classic flavors, such as licorice or assorted fruit flavors (banana, cherry, green apple, watermelon), as well as contemporary flavors that can be quite wild, including vomit, sardines, and rotten egg. The artisan confectioner is pretty much guaranteed to steer away from these latter flavors and focus on fruit, herbs, spices, and acidic powders. Acidic ingredients not only highlight fruit flavors but are also required to initiate jellification in pectin-based jellies.

Binding Agents **Binding agents** such as gelatin, agar powder, modified starch, and pectin help to stabilize and set the formula, which allows the product to take on the shape of the mold and to be handled for cutting and packaging. Using gelling agents from starch and protein sources enables the confectioner to gel supersaturated solutions into stable states. The choice of gel will have an effect on the formula, the process, and, of course, the texture of the final jelly.

Gelatin Gelatin is the most common gelling agent in the confection industry. Gelatin is able to form an elastic, thermoreversible gel that enables products to melt in the mouth, yet still retain a chewy texture when gelatin is present at levels of about 4.5 to 7.5 percent of the total weight of the candy. Leaf or powdered gelatin can be used.

Protein in gelatin denatures when it is held for longer periods of time at temperatures above 176°F (80°C). The use of gelatin in hot liquids is quite common in confection work (marshmallows, for example), and the rate at which degradation occurs increases along with the temperature. Additionally, acidic environments and certain natural enzymes in some fruits can denature gelatin. When acidic ingredients are required to provide flavors, they should be added at the last possible moment before depositing the jelly in the mold. When using papaya, kiwi, mango, or pineapple, the puree must first be boiled to kill the denaturing enzymes.

Agar Powder When it is not possible to use animal products, agar powder can sometimes be substituted for gelatin. Extracted from various seaweeds and red algae, agar is a powerful thermoreversible binding agent that requires only 0.5 to 1.5 percent of the finished confection weight to form a stable gel.

Because agar is harvested from many parts of the world, it comes in different forms, and there are no standards of identity as there are for pectin, gelatin, and starches. As a result, the quality and strength of gelling using agar can vary considerably. Once a reliable source has been established and formulas balanced, the confectioner should try to remain with that source to maintain consistency.

The properties of a confection made with agar are significantly different than one made with gelatin or pectin. The texture tends to be short and slightly rubbery, and products made with agar lack the tender qualities that are possible with gelatin. One reason for this has to do with the melting point of gels formed with agar.

Agar does not melt until 185°F (85°C) to 194°F (90°C), and agar solutions set at approximately 90°F (32°C) to 105°F (40°C). This wide range between when agar is activated and when it sets, also referred to as **hysteresis**, is beneficial to the confectioner because it provides a wide working window for depositing. Some gels, like those made with pectin, are much less tolerant in their working properties and begin gelification when cooking ceases.

Pectin **Pectin**, a polysaccharide**,** is obtained from plant sources, most notably apples and citrus fruits. It produces a tender but short-textured jelly that allows very clean flavors in the mouth. Three types of pectin are commonly used in pastry: **yellow pectin** (also called **apple pectin**), **pectin NH**, and **medium rapid set pectin**. They are used for different applications, depending on the desired results, and are not interchangeable. (See Figure 18-4.)

Regardless of what type of pectin is used, heat and acidity are required to trigger the gelification properties. Additionally, the solids count must be high (above 60 for apple pectin) to create a stable candy. The solids count for pâtes de fruits is always over 75 because low water content is required for shelf stability.

The acidity of the mixture for apple pectin should be in the range of 3.0 to 3.6 to ensure there is ample catalyst for setting. If there is too much acidity and the cooking process happens at a slow rate, the pectin can break down and lose gelification properties. For this reason, items with pectin should always be cooked as quickly as possible, and procedures in the formula followed carefully and accurately.

Pâtes de Fruits

Pâtes de fruits are a specialty confection in France. They are made from fruit juice or puree, sugar, glucose, yellow pectin, and an acid. Some formulas call for gelatin; however, these make a less stable confection with a considerably softer, more tender texture. Pâtes de fruits should be slightly firm in texture yet still have tender qualities.

Pâtes de fruits are small candies that contain the flavors of the orchard, the field, or the garden. Depending on the fruit, they can range from opaque to translucent. They should always have a slight shine and should never appear dull or cloudy; these are signs of overcooking. On the outside of the candy, there should be an ever-so-slight crust that is covered in granulated sugar. Some variations exist for pâtes de fruits, including multiple-layered flavors or layering on ganache or praline. If layered on ganache, enrobing in chocolate is essential.

Formulas for pâtes de fruits are typically available through purveyors of quality frozen fruit puree. Most often, these purees have 10 percent added sugar, which must be taken into account if substitutions are made

Type of Pectin	Uses	Thermoreversibility
Yellow pectin	Pâtes de fruits	Irreversible
Pectin NH	Nappage, glazes	Reversible
Medium rapid set pectin	Confiture, jams	Mixture of reversible and irreversible

Figure 18-4
Types and Uses of Pectin

to the pâtes de fruits formulas in this book. In the formula section, there is a chart of formulas for pâtes de fruits using commercially available frozen fruit purees.

The process for pâtes de fruits is very simple. However, if the steps are not followed carefully and attention is not paid to temperature, the concentration of the sugar solution may be off. This will cause the final product to be too tough or to not set enough. After the pectin has been added, the preparation should be constantly whisked to encourage liquid content evaporation. When making pâtes de fruits, the goal is to cook quicker rather than slower.

To begin pâte de fruits, the puree should be warmed and brought to a boil. Next, the pectin should be combined with one-fourth of the weight of the sugar in the formula. This is a critical step: Not doing so will cause the pectin to form irreversible clumps when it comes into contact with the heat and moisture. Once the puree has reached 122°F (50°C), the pectin–sugar blend should be added to the puree in a slow, steady stream while constantly whisking. The puree mixture should then be brought to a boil.

After the puree has come to a boil, the remaining sugar should be added in three stages. It is critical that the additions happen in slow, steady streams while whisking, and that the temperature increases before the next addition of sugar. After all the sugar has been added, the glucose should be added, and the mixture should continue to be whisked and cooked to the required temperature. At this point, the acid should be added and stirred in thoroughly, and then the mixture must be deposited right away.

Depositing should be done quickly and efficiently because the acid and drop in temperature will initiate the gelling process. For the easiest depositing, a silicone mold with shallow sides is ideal; however, a silicone mat and metal bars or a frame are also acceptable. Pouring pâtes de fruits should be done on a flat, solid surface, ideally made of granite. The heat from the cooked mixture can warp metal tables, resulting in an uneven layer of product.

Pâtes de fruits should be firm, yet still warm, 20 minutes after depositing. Covering the top with plastic is advised for two reasons: first, to ensure that it doesn't dry out and, second, to provide the sugar with a surface to stick to. If making a layered pâte de fruit, it is critical to cover the first layer, which should be slightly sticky and still warm when the second layer is poured on top of it.

It is very important to cook pâtes de fruits to the temperature specified in the formula, which guarantees a specific concentration of solids and liquids. If the confection is overcooked, it will be dry and tough and will lack brilliance. If it is undercooked, there will be too much free water, and the confection may not set up, or it may sweat water.

Because the temperature relates to the degree of water evaporation, the density of sugar solids can also be determined. Most pâtes de fruits formulas have a column with a number relating to the Brix scale, which corresponds to sugar density. If this is to be measured, a tool called a refractometer must be used, and the pâte de fruits solution must be cooled enough to appropriately measure sugar concentration.

After a pâte de fruit has cooled and set, it can be stored in the freezer, used as part of mise en place, or cut and finished. The finishing process has a determining effect on the quality of the finished product and should not be rushed. Pâtes de fruits are traditionally cut in squares.

The most efficient way to do this is by using a **guitar**. A guitar is a tool used to evenly cut a variety of confectionary items including pâtes de fruits, ganache, pralines, and cake. To ensure easy handling and clean cuts, the product should be coated in sugar on both sides, and the wires of the guitar must be wiped clean between each cut.

Cut pâtes de fruits are covered entirely in granulated sugar and left covered for at least one day. Next, they are removed from the sugar, the excess is shaken off, and the candies are placed on a sheet pan with parchment paper that has been dusted very lightly with sugar (to ensure the pâte de fruit is slightly above the paper's surface). The candies should be allowed to "dry" for at least 24 hours in a well-ventilated area. After 24 hours, they should be flipped to dry on the other side. It is important not to rush this process because the formation of a small "crust" is important for preserving the confection. At this point, the candies can be packaged, or wrapped in plastic and stored for later use.

Process for Pâtes de Fruits

- Scale all the ingredients, warm the puree, and blend one-fourth of the sugar with the pectin.
- At 122°F (50°C), begin to add the sugar–pectin blend, whisking constantly.
- When the mixture boils, begin to add the remaining sugar in three stages, ensuring that the temperature does not drop too much.
- After all the sugar has been added and the mixture returns to a boil, add the glucose, and continue whisking until the desired temperature is reached.
- Add the acid, stir well to incorporate, and deposit the mixture in applicable frames.
- After the product is set, dredge it in sugar and cut as desired.
- Submerge the cut pieces in sugar for at least 24 hours.
- Remove the candies from the sugar, and shake off the excess sugar.
- Place on a sheet pan lined with parchment paper and dusted with granulated sugar to "dry" for 24 hours.
- Flip over the candies to dry the other side for 24 hours.
- Package as desired, or cover in plastic and store for later use.

SUGAR CONFECTIONS CONCLUSION

Sugar confections encompass a wide range of specialty products, including classics like hard candies, toffee, caramels, nougats, pâtes de fruits, and marshmallows. The common thread is that they are all based on supersaturated sugar solutions. These solutions can be crystalline or noncrystalline, aerated or gelled. Additionally, many ingredients can be added as inclusions or to create unique chemical reactions. One clear example of this is the presence of protein in cooked sugar syrups, which initiates the Maillard reaction to create the color and flavor of caramel.

To practice and become proficient in sugar confections, the confectioner must understand the properties of cooking sugar solutions, understand the process of crystallization, and have the technical skills required for working with hot sugar solutions, including manipulating them quickly into desired shapes.

FORMULA

PETIT FOUR FRUIT TARTS

These smaller versions of the classic fruit tart consist of a crisp pâte sucrée shell that is filled with pastry cream and topped with seasonal fruit and glaze.

Mise en Place

Pâte sucrée, 1 lb 1 ½ oz (500 g)

White chocolate or cocoa butter

Pastry cream, 10 ¾ oz (300 g)

Fresh fruit

Nappage

Yield: 50 petit four tartlets

Assembly

1. Sheet the dough to 1⁄16 inch (2 mm) on a dough sheeter.
2. Dock the dough, and cut out circles to just fit in the molds.
3. Line the molds with the pâte sucrée, and blind bake until lightly golden brown.
4. Brush with white chocolate or cocoa butter to create a moisture barrier between the pastry cream and the pastry shell (optional).

Finishing

1. Gently whisk the pastry cream to smooth it and pipe into tart shells to just below the surface.
2. Garnish with fresh fruit and glaze with nappage.
3. Store in a refrigerated case for service.

FORMULA

ALMOND SABLÉ WITH CHOCOLATE MOUSSE AND RASPBERRIES

Raspberry gelée enclosed in chocolate mousse sits atop a tender almond cookie in this flavorful petit four, finished with chocolate spray, fruit, and simple décor.

Mise en Place

Raspberry gelée, 9 oz (250 kg)

(Flexipan half-spheres: 23 mm x 11 mm, Ref 1242)

Chocolate mousse, 1 lb 10½ oz (0.750 kg)

(Flexipan petit four: 40 mm diameter x 20 mm deep, Ref 1129)

Almond sablé, 4 lb 6½ oz (2 kg)

Chocolate spray

Chocolate décor

Fresh raspberries

Yield: 50

Assembly

1. Prepare the raspberry gelée and deposit it into small half-sphere molds and freeze.
2. Prepare the chocolate mousse and pipe into the petit four Flexipan, depositing the raspberry insert halfway, and depositing the rest of the way with mousse to be level with the surface of the mold and freeze.
3. Sheet out the almond sablé between two silicone baking mats to ⅛ inch (3 mm). Bake at 325°F (163°C) between two baking mats until barely set and cut out circles with a 2 inch (50 mm) diameter fluted cutter.
4. Return the almond sablé to the oven to finish baking until golden brown.
5. Reserve until needed.

Finishing

1. Remove the chocolate mousse from the freezer and place on a sheet pan. Spray with the dark chocolate spray and then transfer to an almond sablé base.
2. Garnish with the chocolate décor and a fresh raspberry.

FORMULA

WHITE CHOCOLATE MOUSSE CAKES WITH FRUITS

Tender cake, white chocolate mousse, and fresh, seasonal fruit come together for this tasty little petit four prestige.

Components

Biscuit viennois, plain, 1 ¼ sheet

White chocolate mousse, 1.1 kg

White chocolate décor for lattice

Fresh fruit, assorted

Nappage

Yield: 50
Petit four cake mold round: 1 inch (2.5 cm) high and 1 ⅔ inch (4.1 cm) wide

Assembly

1. Cut the biscuit viennois to form a cake wall that is as high as the mold.
2. Place the strip of biscuit on the inside perimeter of the mold, which has been lined with acetate.
3. Place a disc of biscuit on the bottom of the mold.
4. After the mousse has been made, pipe the mixture into the prepared molds just below the surface of the cake.

Finishing

1. To finish, remove from the mold, take off the acetate strip, and place on a gold board.
2. Decorate the top of the cake with a selection of fresh fruit.
3. Glaze the fruit as applicable and garnish the petit four with white chocolate décor.

FORMULA

ASSORTED PETITS FOURS CHOUX: ÉCLAIR, PARIS-BREST

Versatile pâte à choux is a perfect option for petits fours as it adapts well to small shapes. Éclair, Paris-Brest, and choquette can all be created in appealing one- to two-bite versions.

Mise en Place, Éclair

Pastry cream: vanilla, chocolate, pistachio, praline, among others

Éclair shells, 1 ½ inches (38 mm) to 2 inches (50 mm) long

Fondant, couverture

Assembly, Éclair

1. Bake the choux paste, and reserve until cool.
2. In a piping bag fitted with a small plain tip, pipe the pastry cream into the choux shells.
3. Dip the tops in fondant or couverture.

Mise en Place, Paris-Brest

Paris-Brest shells 1 ½ inch (38 mm) diameter

Crème Paris-Brest

Powdered sugar

Assembly, Paris-Brest

1. To pipe Paris-Brest shells, pipe 1 ½ inch (38 mm) diameter circles on parchment-lined sheet pans, using a medium star tip.
2. Egg wash lightly, garnish with sliced almonds, and sprinkle with sugar.
3. Bake the choux paste and reserve until cool.
4. Cut the baked Paris-Brest in half.
5. Prepare the crème Paris Brest, and load into a piping bag fitted with a medium star tip.
6. Pipe the filling into the base of the pastry and then place the top on.
7. Dust with powdered sugar.

FORMULA

CHOCOLATE MOUSSE AND RASPBERRY MACARON

The decadent flavors of chocolate mousse and fresh raspberry make for a happy marriage in this French delicacy, a macaron distinguished by its exceptional flavor, texture, and color.

Mise en Place

Chocolate macaron base piped at 1 ½ inch (38 mm) diameter, approximately 2 ⅝ lb (1.2 kg) of batter

Chocolate mousse: approximately 2 ¾ lb (1.3 kg)

Raspberries: 6 to 7 per petit four

Yield: 50

Assembly and Finishing

1. Pipe the chocolate mousse onto the center of the macaron base.
2. Place raspberries around the perimeter of the macaron base, secured into the mousse. The center of the mousse should be slightly taller than the raspberry to ensure the top macaron can be set in place.
3. Top with a second macaron to finish.

Assorted Petits Fours

(opposite, left to right) Passion Fruit Crémeux Tart, White Chocolate Mousse Cake With Fruits, Almond Sable With Chocolate Mousse and Raspberry, Fresh Fruit Tart, Chocolate Crémeux Tart

FORMULA

GRAPEFRUIT AND VANILLA CREAM MACARON

The distinctive flavors of slightly acidic fresh grapefruit and rich vanilla mousseline cream align perfectly in this refreshing and creamy macaron. A touch of spice is introduced with delicate slices of ginger confit. Because of the moist fruit and the mousseline cream used in this macaron, the shelf life should be limited to 24 hours.

Mise en Place

Plain macaron base with vanilla bean variation, 2 ¼ lb (1 kg) macaron base piped at 1 ½ inch (3.8 cm) diameter

Vanilla mousseline cream, 1 lb 10 oz (0.75 kg)

Fresh grapefruit

Ginger confit

Yield: 50

Process, Fresh Grapefruit

1. Cut off the skin, and segment the grapefruit.
2. Slice the segments in half to achieve thin slices.
3. Cut the slices in thirds to obtain small segments of the pulp.
4. Place the pulp segments between paper towels for several hours to draw out excess moisture.

Assembly and Finishing

1. Pipe the vanilla mousseline cream onto the base of the vanilla macaron, and top it with a thin slice of ginger confit.
2. Place two grapefruit pulp segments over the mousseline.
3. Pipe a small dot of mousseline over the grapefruit to secure the top macaron.
4. Place the top cookie over the mousseline. Garnish with a thin slice of ginger confit.

FORMULA

PRALINE CREAM WITH SALTED CARAMEL MACARON

Hazelnut and salted caramel merge effortlessly in this cream based on crème Paris-Brest. The salted caramel is coated in cocoa butter, helping it to remain crunchy for a longer period of time. Because of the cream used in this macaron, the shelf life should be limited to 24 hours.

Mise en Place

Parisian macaron base

Praline cream with salted caramel

Yield: 50 pieces
Test: 25 pieces

Salted Caramel Formula

Ingredients	Baker's %	Kilogram	US decimal	Lb & Oz
Trimoline	100.00	0.080	0.176	2 ¾
Sugar	100.00	0.080	0.176	2 ¾
Salted butter	35.00	0.028	0.061	1
Unsalted butter	60.00	0.048	0.105	1 ⅝
Cocoa butter	15.00	0.012	0.026	⅜
Total	313.88	0.250	0.551	8 ⅞

Process, Salted Caramel

1. Heat the Trimoline, and add the sugar to it to make a caramel.
2. After the sugar has turned to caramel stage, add the salted butter and the unsalted butter to deglaze.
3. Cook this mixture, stirring constantly.
4. Drop a small quantity in cold water. When it is ready, it will set up to the hard crack stage.
5. Pour the mixture on a silpat, place another silpat on top of it, and roll it out thin. Allow to cool.
6. When it is cool, break up the caramel to make small pieces.
7. Melt the cocoa butter, and toss it with the caramel to coat it.
8. Place this mixture in the freezer for 20 minutes to set the cocoa butter. Reserve until needed.

Praline Cream With Salted Caramel Formula

Ingredients	Baker's %	Kilogram	US decimal	Lb & Oz		Test
Praline paste	38.00	0.232	0.511		8 ⅛	3 ¼ oz
Butter	52.00	0.317	0.699		11 ⅛	4 ½ oz
Pastry cream	100.00	0.610	1.344	1	5 ½	8 ⅝ oz
Salted caramel	15.00	0.091	0.202		3 ¼	1 ¼ oz
Total	205.00	1.250	2.756	2	12 ⅛	1 lb 1 ⅝ oz

Process, Praline Cream With Salted Caramel

1. In a mixer with the paddle attachment, smooth the praline paste, add the soft butter, and mix until incorporated.
2. Mix the pastry cream until smooth, and then fold the butter–praline mixture into it.
3. Fold in the salted caramel.

Assembly

Pipe the praline cream with caramel onto the base of the macaron. Place the top on and reserve until needed.

Assorted Macarons

(top to bottom) Chocolate Mousse and Raspberry Macaron, Grapefruit and Vanilla Cream Macaron, Praline Cream With Salted Caramel Macaron

FORMULA

PETIT FOUR CRÉMEUX TART

A small version of the standard tart, this petit four tart is based on pâte sucrée and passion fruit crémeux. The tart shell is baked until golden and crisp, and then brushed with a thin layer of white chocolate or cocoa butter and garnished with a circle of white chocolate lattice. Store in the freezer for up to 1 week with the crémeux already deposited.

Mise en Place

Pâte sucrée tartlet shells, 5 lb 8 oz (2.5 kg) for full batch, 2 lb 3 oz (1 kg) for test

Assorted crémeux: raspberry, lemon, passion fruit, 64 percent chocolate

Chocolate glaze

Neutral glaze

Yield: 200–250 [1 inch (2.6 cm)] tartlets per formula
Test: 70–90 [1 inch (2.6 cm)] tartlets
Flexipan for tartlets (42 mm x 10 mm, Ref 1413)

Raspberry Crémeux Formula

Ingredients	Baker's %	Kilogram	US decimal	Lb & Oz		Test
Raspberry fruit pulp	100.00	0.528	1.165	1	2 ⅝	6 ¾ oz
Gelatin leaves	1.50	0.008	0.017		¼	⅛ oz
Egg yolks	30.00	0.159	0.349		5 ⅝	2 oz
Eggs	37.50	0.198	0.437		7	2 ½ oz
Sugar	30.00	0.159	0.349		5 ⅝	2 oz
Butter	37.50	0.198	0.437		7	2 ½ oz
Total	236.50	1.250	2.755	2	12 ⅛	1 lb

Lemon Crémeux Formula

Ingredients	Baker's %	Kilogram	US decimal	Lb & Oz		Test
Lemon juice	100.00	0.368	0.810		13	4 ¾ oz
Egg yolks	56.00	0.206	0.454		7 ¼	2 ⅝ oz
Eggs	64.00	0.235	0.519		8 ¼	3 oz
Sugar	60.00	0.221	0.486		7 ¾	2 ⅞ oz
Butter	60.00	0.221	0.486		7 ¾	2 ⅞ oz
Total	340.00	1.250	2.755	2	12 ⅛	1 lb

Process, Raspberry and Lemon Crémeux

1. Bring the lemon juice or raspberry puree to just below the boiling point with half of the sugar.
2. Combine the egg yolks, whole eggs, and the remainder of the sugar.

3. Pour one-third of the puree over the egg mixture and stir with a spatula. Do not use a whisk as it will incorporate air.
4. Return the egg mixture to the pot and continue to stir constantly, agitating the bottom of the pot.
5. Cook until the mixture is 180°F (82°C) and thickened. Do not overcook.
6. Strain through a fine chinois into a clean, dry container.
7. When the mixture reaches 95°F (35°C), add tepid butter using an immersion blender.
8. Deposit into the blind-baked tart shells, and store covered in the refrigerator until ready for use.

Chocolate Crémeux Formula

Ingredients	Baker's %	Kilogram	US decimal	Lb & Oz	Test
Cream	100.00	0.741	1.634	1 10 ⅛	9 ½ oz
Gelatin leaves	0.60	0.004	0.010	⅛	1/16 oz
Egg yolks	24.00	0.178	0.392	6 ¼	2 ¼ oz
64% chocolate	44.00	0.326	0.719	11 ½	4 ⅛ oz
Total	168.60	1.250	2.755	2 12 ⅛	1 lb

Process, Chocolate Crémeux

1. Bring the cream to a boil.
2. Temper the egg yolk–sugar mixture (like crème Anglaise).
3. Cook (like crème Anglaise) with a spatula to 180°F (82°C) using caution to not overcook.
4. Strain through a fine chinois, and add the bloomed melted gelatin.
5. Add the chocolate and form an emulsion with a rubber spatula. Improve the emulsion with an immersion blender, using caution to not get any air bubbles into the mix. Let cool to 95°F (35°C) and then deposit.

Assembly

1. Coat the pate sucrée shells with a thin layer of cocoa butter or chocolate. For fruit crémeux, use white chocolate; for chocolate crémeux use the corresponding chocolate as is in the crémeux.
2. Deposit the crémeux into the blind-baked tart shells, just below the surface. Be sure that the crémeux is warm enough that it relaxes in the shell. If it is too cold, it will not create a smooth surface. Allow to set in the refrigerator or freezer.

Finishing

Apply a thin layer of neutral glaze over the fruit crémeux tarts and a thin layer of black chocolate glaze over the chocolate crémeux. Garnish with the applicable fresh fruit as desired or chocolate décor.

FORMULA

MARZIPAN

Unlike the other edible decorative mediums, marzipan actually has a pleasing taste and texture. Composed primarily of almonds and sugar, it can be rolled into thin sheets for wrapping cakes, used as a layer in pastries or a filling for chocolates, or molded into various shapes such as fruits, animals, or other figures.

Ingredients	Baker's %	Kilogram	US decimal	Lb & Oz		Test
Almond paste	100.00	1.249	2.753	2	12	8 oz
Powdered sugar	100.00	1.249	2.753	2	12	8 oz
Kirsch	0.25	0.003	0.007		⅛	¼ tsp
Total	200.25	2.500	5.512	5	8 ¼	1 lb

Process

1. Blend the almond paste with the powdered sugar in the bowl of a mixer fitted with the paddle attachment on low speed.
2. Mix until the dough just comes together, adding the kirsch as needed.
3. Transfer to a clean work surface and knead to a uniform mass.
4. Wrap well in plastic and allow to rest for 12 hours before using.

Notes

Adding powdered sugar is not a remedy for wet marzipan.
Use less liquid if you will be adding color (only use gel colors).
If mixed too long, oil from almonds will come out and the marzipan will be greasy.

FORMULA

PÂTE DE FRUIT

Pâte de fruit, loosely translated as "fruit paste," is a classic French confection. Pâte de fruit can be made with any fruit puree but is most commonly made from high-quality frozen purees. The process must be followed very carefully (refer to the text for more detailed information). Temperatures are very important to consider because they determine the quantity of water in the fruit paste, which affects the gelling capacity of the pectin. The formulas presented here are from Ravi Fruit and most manufacturers of high-quality fruit purees will supply their customers with a similar sheet.

Proportion Chart for Pâte de Fruit

Fruit	Pectin (g)	Sugar (g)	Powdered Glucose (g)	Citric Acid Diluted at 50% (g)	Total Weight	Cooking Temperature (°C)	Cooking Temperature (°F)	Brix Degree
Apricot	24	1,140	350	14	2,528	105	221	72
Banana	24	900	120	16	2,060	105	221	73
Blackberry	24	1,260	170	16	2,470	106	222	73
Black currant	25	1,170	200	14	2,409	107	224	75
Blueberry	22	1,050	70	14	2,156	107	224	74
Boysenberry	20	1,150	150	16	2,036	106	222	74
Fig	25	850	150	16	2,041	105	221	73
Fruit of the forest	22	1,100	150	14	2,286	105	221	73
Green apple	18	950	80	14	2,062	106	222	74
Guanabana (soursop)	26	1,100	120	16	2,262	105	221	73
Guava	24	1,350	200	16	2,590	105	221	73
Kiwi	24	1,050	60	16	2,150	105	221	73
Lemon	28	1,350	200	8	2,586	108	226	73
Lime	26	1,450	150	8	2,634	107	224	73
Lychee	30	1,050	200	16	2,296	106	222	74
Mandarin	26	1,150	70	14	2,260	106	222	73
Mango	25	1,150	200	16	2,391	105	221	73
Melon	25	1,050	100	16	2,191	106	222	75
Mirabelle plum	25	800	200	16	2,041	106	222	74
Morello (sour) cherry	24	950	20	16	2,010	106	222	73

(continues)

Proportion Chart for Pâte de Fruit *(continued)*

Fruit	Pectin (g)	Sugar (g)	Powdered Glucose (g)	Citric Acid Diluted at 50% (g)	Total Weight	Cooking Temperature (°C)	Cooking Temperature (°F)	Brix Degree
Orange	24	1,100	200	12	2,336	106	222	75
Pabana cocktail	25	800	120	14	1,959	105	221	74
Papaya	26	800	20	16	1,862	106	222	74
Passion fruit	21	1,150	250	10	2,431	107	224	74
Ruby peach	24	900	160	16	2,100	105	221	73
White peach	25	900	200	12	2,137	105	221	72
Pineapple	30	1,100	100	14	2,244	106	222	75
Red currant	20	1,000	150	14	2,184	107	224	73
Raspberry	20	1,140	200	16	2,376	105	221	73
Strawberry	24	1,100	100	16	2,240	105	221	74
Strawberry mara des bois	24	1,100	140	16	2,280	105	221	74
Wild strawberry	22	1,150	150	14	2,336	105	221	74

For 1 kg of fruit puree.

Process, Pâte de fruit

1. Scale all the ingredients, warm the puree, and blend one-fourth of the sugar with the pectin.
2. At 122°F (50°C), begin to add the sugar–pectin blend, whisking constantly.
3. When the mixture boils, begin to add the remaining sugar in three stages, ensuring that the temperature does not drop too much.
4. After all the sugar has been added and the mixture returns to a boil, add the powdered glucose, and continue whisking until the desired temperature is reached.
5. Add the acid, stir well to incorporate, and deposit the mixture in the applicable frames.
6. After the product is set, dredge it in sugar and cut as desired.
7. Submerge the cut pieces in sugar for at least 24 hours.
8. Remove the candies from the sugar, and shake off the excess sugar.
9. Place on a sheet pan lined with parchment paper and dusted with granulated sugar to "dry" for 24 hours.
10. Flip over the candies to dry the other side for 24 hours.
11. Package as desired, or cover in plastic and store for later use.

FORMULA

MARSHMALLOW SQUARES

Marshmallows date back to ancient times, derived from plants called marsh mallows, which were indigenous to Europe and Asia. The fluffy white confection we are familiar with today originated in France during the 19th century, but manufacturing was expensive and slow because it involved the casting and molding of each individual marshmallow. When mass production was introduced in America in 1948, marshmallows became much easier to make, and their popularity exploded. These marshmallow squares showcase the best properties of marshmallow, with appealing texture and sweetness.

Ingredients	Baker's %	Kilogram	US decimal	Lb & Oz		Test
Gelatin	13.30	0.178	0.392		6 ¼	1 ⅝ oz
Sugar	250.00	3.339	7.360	7	5 ¾	1 lb 13 ½ oz
Water	83.40	1.114	2.455	2	7 ¼	9 ⅞ oz
Glucose	62.50	0.835	1.840	1	13 ½	7 ⅜ oz
Egg whites	100.00	1.335	2.944	2	15 ⅛	11 ¾ oz
Total	509.20	6.800	14.991	14	15 ⅞	3 lb 12 oz

Yield: 2 full sheets
Test: 1 half sheet

Process

1. Bloom the gelatin in cold water.
2. Heat the sugar, water, and glucose to 285°F (140°C).
3. Start whipping the egg whites on medium speed, when the sugar mixture reaches 248°F (120°C).
4. When the sugar mixture reaches 266°F (130°C) begin to mix on high speed.
5. At 284°F (140°C), pour the bloomed, drained gelatin on the sugar and pour into the whipping egg whites.
6. Once the foam is full volume and is stabilized, portion into a sheet pan lined with a silicone baking mat.
7. Cool at room temperature.
8. Once at room temperature, cover with a 1:1 mixture of potato starch and powdered sugar.
9. Cut into the desired sizes. Roll in the starch–sugar mixture to cover the sides after cutting.

FORMULA

CHARTREUSE MARSHMALLOW LOLLIPOP

Chartreuse, a color resting somewhere between yellow and green, was named for its resemblance to the French liqueur, green Chartreuse, itself named after the Grande Chartreuse monastery where it is produced. This whimsical little marshmallow lollipop is certain to bring smiles wherever it is found.

Ingredients	Baker's %	Kilogram	US decimal	Lb & Oz		Test
Gelatin	5.00	0.009	0.020		⅜	⅛ oz
Chartreuse	41.70	0.076	0.167		2 ⅝	1 oz
Sugar	416.70	0.756	1.668	1	10 ⅝	9 ⅝ oz
Water	125.00	0.227	0.500		8	2 ⅞ oz
Egg whites	100.00	0.182	0.400		6 ⅜	2 ⅜ oz
Pastel green colorant	SQ	SQ	SQ		SQ	SQ
Total	688.40	1.250	2.755	2	12 ⅛	1 lb

Yield: variable depending on mold

Process

1. Bloom the gelatin in the Chartreuse.
2. Cook the sugar and water to 261°F (127°C), and pour over the egg whites once whipped to 50 percent volume. Add the green colorant.
3. Whip until full volume and slightly warm.
4. Deposit into a small half-dome Flexipan.
5. Once set, remove the marshmallow, toss in potato starch, and stick to a lollipop stick with some melted chocolate.
6. Dip in tempered dark couverture.

FORMULA

MARSHMALLOW WITHOUT EGG WHITES

The absence of egg whites in the formula is no mistake. This formula and its process represent the majority of contemporary marshmallow production.

Ingredients	Baker's %	Kilogram	US decimal	Lb & Oz		Test
Gelatin leaf	8.34	0.195	0.430		6 ⅞	1 ¾ oz
Sugar	100.00	2.341	5.162	5	2 ⅝	4 ⅝ oz
Water	41.66	0.975	2.150	2	2 ⅜	8 ⅝ oz
Honey	37.50	0.878	1.936	1	15	7 ¾ oz
Glucose	62.50	1.463	3.226	3	3 ⅝	12 ⅞ oz
Water	37.50	0.878	1.936	1	15	7 ¾ oz
Vanilla extract	2.92	0.068	0.151		2	1 oz
Total	290.42	6.800	14.991	14	15 ⅞	3 lb 12 oz

Process

1. Bloom the gelatin in cold water. Reserve.
2. Combine the sugar, water, honey, and glucose and cook to 245°F (118°C).
3. Cool the mixture to 215°F (102°C), and then mix with the gelatin.
4. Whip on high speed until soft peaks form, and add the vanilla.
5. Deposit into a frame on a silicone mat–lined sheet pan, and allow to set.
6. When it reaches room temperature, cover with a 1:1 mixture of potato starch and powdered sugar.
7. Cut into the desired sizes. Roll in the starch–sugar mixture to cover the sides after cutting.

Assorted Confections

FORMULA

NOUGAT DE MONTÉLIMAR

The Provencal region of Montélimar, with its proliferation of almond trees, has specialized in nougat making for hundreds of years. This beloved confection is a based on a meringue made with sugar syrup and honey and the addition of almonds or pistachios. Some insist that, in order for nougat to be classified as nougat de Montélimar, it must contain lavender honey.

Ingredients	Baker's %	Kilogram	US decimal	Lb & Oz		Test
Orange blossom honey	500.37	0.978	2.157	2	2 ½	9 ⅛ oz
Sugar #1	620.77	1.214	2.676	2	10 ⅞	11 ¾ oz
Water	250.47	0.490	1.080	1	1 ¼	4 ⅝ oz
Glucose	100.00	0.196	0.431		6 ⅞	1 ⅞ oz
Egg whites	100.00	0.196	0.431		6 ⅞	1 ⅞ oz
Sugar #2	24.02	0.047	0.104		1 ⅝	½ oz
Salt	0.62	0.001	0.003		< ⅛	⅛ tsp
Powdered sugar	214.60	0.420	0.925		14 ¾	3 ⅞ oz
Cocoa butter	214.60	0.420	0.925		14 ¾	3 ⅞ oz
Almonds	623.83	1.220	2.689	2	11	11 ⅜ oz
Pistachio	623.83	1.220	2.689	2	11	11 ⅜ oz
Total	3273.11	6.400	14.109	14	1 ¾	3 lb 12 oz

Yield: 4 [8 inch (20 cm) × 11 inch (28 cm)] sheets
Test: 1 [8 inch (20 cm) × 11 inch (28 cm)] sheet

Process

1. Roast the almonds. Then, combine with the pistachios and hold in a warm oven, 212°F (100°C), until needed.
2. Boil the honey to 250°F (120°C).
3. Bring the first sugar, water, and glucose to 300°F (150°C).
4. Begin to whip the egg whites, second sugar, and salt when the honey is at 212°F (100°C).
5. Pour the boiling honey on the egg whites and whip with the whisk attachment.
6. Switch to the paddle attachment before adding the cooked sugar.
7. Continue to whip with the paddle on medium speed.
8. At 125°F (50°C) add the powdered sugar, cocoa butter, almonds, and pistachios.
9. Pour onto a silicone mat and roll out between metal bars. Optional: Cover the surface of the nougat with rice paper.
10. Cut to ¾ inch (21 mm) x 1 ⅛ inch (28 mm) or the desired size.
11. Dip the sides in 70% dark couverture.
12. Wrap in plastic when cooled.

FORMULA

CHOCOLATE NOUGAT

French historians think that the nougat traces back to a Greek walnut confection known as *nux gatum* or *mougo* that was originally made using walnuts. In the 17th century, Olivier of Serres planted almond trees close to Montélimar. It is thought that the almonds replaced the walnuts in the Greek recipe and evolved into nougat. Today, nougat is central to the history of the city of Montélimar and the traditions of Provence. This nougat emphasizes rich chocolate along with its characteristic nuts.

Ingredients	Baker's %	Kilogram	US decimal	Lb & Oz		Test
Sugar #1	830.00	1.880	4.146	4	2 ⅜	1 lb ½ oz
Glucose	180.00	0.408	0.899		14 ⅜	3 ⅝ oz
Water	250.00	0.566	1.249	1	4	5 oz
Honey	500.00	1.133	2.497	2	8	9 ⅞ oz
Egg whites	100.00	0.227	0.499		8	2 oz
Sugar #2	40.00	0.091	0.200		3 ¼	¾ oz
Chocolate liquor	170.00	0.385	0.849		13 ⅝	3 ⅜ oz
Hazelnuts	275.00	0.623	1.374	1	6	5 ½ oz
Whole almonds	350.00	0.793	1.748	1	12	7 oz
Pistachios	130.00	0.295	0.649		10 ⅜	2 ⅝ oz
Total	2825.00	6.400	14.110	14	1 ¾	3 lb 8 oz

Yield: 4 [8 inch (20 cm) × 11 inch (28 cm)] sheets
Test: 1 [8 inch (20 cm) × 11 inch (28 cm)] sheet

Process

1. Toast the hazelnuts and almonds until golden to the core. Add the pistachios and keep the nut mixture warm.
2. Cook the first sugar, glucose, and water to 302°F (150°C).
3. When the sugar mixture reaches 248°F (120°C), start cooking the honey.
4. Cook the honey to 266°F (130°C). The goal is to have both mixtures finish cooking close to the same time.
5. Using the whisk attachment, whip the egg whites with the second sugar.
6. Make a meringue by slowly pouring the hot honey onto the whipping whites.
7. Switch to the paddle attachment, and add the hot sugar mixture.
8. When full volume is reached, add the melted chocolate liquor, and mix until blended.
9. Next, add the warm nuts, and mix to incorporation.
10. Deposit into a metal frame lined with rice paper. Press the rice paper into the top of the nougat.
11. Allow to set. When the nougat is cool, cut into the desired sizes.

FORMULA

CARAMELS

According to *The New Larousse Gastronomique* the name *caramel* comes from the Latin *Cannamella* ("sugar cane"), and it is also the French word for "burnt sugar." Food historians place the first mentions of caramelization in 17th-century France. Known for their incredibly chewy texture, and requiring a good set of teeth, perfect caramels should melt in the mouth for a while, giving the taste buds time to savor each sweet moment.

Creamy Caramel Formula

Ingredients	Baker's %	Kilogram	US decimal	Lb & Oz		Test
Heavy cream	29.70	0.215	0.475		7 ⅝	1 ¾ oz
Half and half	29.70	0.215	0.475		7 ⅝	1 ¾ oz
Sugar	100.00	0.725	1.598	1	9 ⅝	5 ¾ oz
Salt	3.70	0.027	0.059		1	¼ oz
Glucose	112.80	0.818	1.803	1	12 ⅞	½ oz
Vanilla bean	Each	2	2		2	½ each
Total	275.90	2.000	4.410	4	6 ½	1 lb

Process, Creamy Caramel

1. Bring all of the ingredients to a boil in a stainless steel or copper pot.
2. Stir constantly and cook to the desired temperature. (See the list of temperatures.)
3. After the bubbles have subsided, pour the caramel into arranged metal bars on top of a silicone mat to a depth of ½ inch (1 cm).
4. When it is set, cut to the desired size, and wrap or enrobe with chocolate.

Final Temperature	Texture
250°F (121°C)	Soft
255°F (124°C)	Chewy
266°F (130°C)	Hard

Note

The resulting texture of the caramels will be determined by the maximum temperature reached in cooking. Humidity will also have an effect. When working in a humid environment, it is advisable to add a few degrees to the chosen temperature.

Vanilla Caramel Formula

Ingredients	Baker's %	Kilogram	US decimal	Lb & Oz		Test
Heavy cream	47.60	0.544	1.200	1	3 ¼	4 ⅜ oz
Honey	21.80	0.249	0.550		8 ¾	2 oz
Sugar	100.00	1.144	2.521	2	8 ⅜	9 ⅛ oz
Vanilla bean	Each	4	4		4	1 each
Butter	5.50	0.063	0.139		2 ¼	½ oz
Total	174.90	2.000	4.410	4	6 ½	1 lb

Process, Vanilla Caramel

1. Bring all the ingredients, except the butter, to a boil in a stainless steel or copper pot.
2. Stir constantly and cook to the desired temperature. (See the list of temperatures.)
3. After reaching the chosen temperature, stir in the butter.
4. After the bubbles have subsided, pour the caramel into arranged metal bars on top of a silicone mat to a depth of ½ inch (1 cm).
5. When it is set, cut to the desired size, and wrap or enrobe with chocolate.

Final Temperature	Texture
250°F (121°C)	Soft
255°F (124°C)	Chewy
266°F (130°C)	Hard

Note

The resulting texture of the caramels will be determined by the maximum temperature reached in cooking. Humidity will also have an effect. When working in a humid environment, add a few degrees to the chosen temperature.

Coffee Caramel Formula

Ingredients	Baker's %	Kilogram	US decimal	Lb & Oz		Test
Heavy cream	47.60	0.473	1.043	1	¾	3 ¾ oz
Honey	45.60	0.453	0.999	1	0	3 ⅝ oz
Sugar	100.00	0.994	2.192	2	3 ⅛	8 oz
Coffee extract	2.50	0.025	0.055		⅞	¼ oz
Butter	5.50	0.055	0.121		1 ⅞	½ oz
Total	201.20	2.000	4.410	4	6 ½	1 lb

Process, Coffee Caramel

1. Bring all of the ingredients, except the butter, to a boil in a stainless steel or copper pot.
2. Stir constantly and cook to the desired temperature. (See the list of temperatures.)
3. After reaching the chosen temperature, stir in the butter.

4. After the bubbles have subsided, pour the caramel into arranged metal bars on top of a silicone mat to a depth of ½ inch (1 cm).
5. When it is set, cut to the desired size, and wrap or enrobe with chocolate.

Final Temperature	Texture
250°F (121°C)	Soft
255°F (124°C)	Chewy
266°F (130°C)	Hard

Note

The resulting texture of the caramels will be determined by the maximum temperature reached in cooking. Humidity will also have an effect. When working in a humid environment, add a few degrees to the chosen temperature.

Chocolate Nougat

Vanilla Caramel

FORMULA

SWISS ROCHER

These delicate, candied almonds are great on their own, or they may be coated in chocolate, either milk or dark.

Ingredients	Baker's %	Kilogram	US decimal	Lb & Oz		Test
Sugar	36.67	0.367	0.808		12 ⅞	3 ¼ oz
Water	11.67	0.117	0.257		4 ⅛	1 oz
Vanilla bean	Each	1	1		1	¼ each
Toasted almonds	100.00	1.000	2.204	2	3 ¼	8 ¾ oz
Total	148.34	1.483	3.270	3	4 ⅜	13 oz

Process

1. Bring the sugar, water, and vanilla to 241°F (116°C).
2. Add the toasted almonds and stir, creating constant agitation.
3. When the nuts become white and sandy, transfer them to a sheet pan lined with parchment paper.
4. After they are cool, store in a covered, airtight container.

FORMULA

DRAGÉE

A dragée, from the Greek *tragêmata* or "sweets," is used primarily as a decorative element. The town of Verdun, France, had acquired a reputation for these ancient confections by the 13th century. Historic dragées, called confetti in Italian and Jordan almonds in English, are whole almonds coated with a pastel colored sugar shell. Traditionally associated with weddings and special celebrations, throwing dragées or confetti has been symbolic for centuries to ensure prosperity, fertility, happiness, and good luck. Dragées have evolved to include chocolate versions and varieties with nonedible metallic coating.

Mise en Place

Candied nuts, SQ
Chocolate couverture at 92°F (34°C) to 95°F (35°C), SQ
Cocoa powder, SQ
Powdered sugar, SQ
Cool work room [65°F (58°C)]

Note

If a cool work room is not available, use tempered chocolate.

Process

1. In a tumbler, turn the nuts and add the melted chocolate in a slow, steady stream at the crashing point of the nuts. Use caution to not coat the tumbling unit.
2. Once the nuts have been coated once, break up any pieces using a spatula. Allow the nuts to tumble for a few minutes to crystallize the chocolate. Continue this process until the nuts have been sufficiently coated (three or four times).
3. After the last addition of chocolate, and before the chocolate has crystallized, add either cocoa powder or powdered sugar to coat the nuts.
4. Scoop out of the tumbler and repeat the process as needed.

Assorted Confections

FORMULA

HARD CANDY

Hard candies are one of the oldest confections. The key to a successful hard candy is in cooking the sugar syrup. It is essential to prevent crystallization for these candies. Flavorings and colors can vary according to preference. Essential oils provide the best flavors and should be added to taste.

Ingredients	Baker's %	Kilogram	US decimal	Lb & Oz	Test
Sugar	100.00	0.804	1.772	1 12 ⅜	10 ¼ oz
Glucose	33.33	0.268	0.591	9 ½	3 ⅜ oz
Water	22.26	0.179	0.394	6 ¼	2 ¼ oz
Flavoring	SQ				
Coloring	SQ				
Total	155.59	1.250	2.756	2 12 ⅛	1 lb

Note
Some examples of flavoring are orange oil and cinnamon oil.

Process

1. Cook the sugar and glucose with the water to 284°F (140°C).
2. Add the coloring.
3. Continue cooking the syrup to 311°F (155°C), and then add the flavoring.
4. Pour the cooked syrup onto a silicone mat to cool.
5. Satinize the mass as needed.
6. Cut into the desired shapes or pillows. Package as soon as the candies are at room temperature.
7. Alternately, after cooking the syrup, deposit into molds for nonpillow hard candies.

FORMULA

ENGLISH TOFFEE

Traditional English toffee is slightly salty and very rich in butter; its full caramel flavor is a result of the Maillard reaction. For an American version, enrobe in dark chocolate and roll in chopped, roasted almonds.

Ingredients	Baker's %	Kilogram	US decimal	Lb & Oz		Test
Butter, salted	80.00	0.446	0.983		15 ¾	5 ¾ oz
Water	22.00	0.123	0.270		4 ⅜	1 ⅝ oz
Sugar	100.00	0.558	1.229	1	3 ⅝	7 ⅛ oz
Salt	0.50	0.003	0.006		⅛	⅛ tsp
Lecithin powder	0.20	0.001	0.002		0	⅛ tsp
Almond, raw, chopped	21.50	0.120	0.264		4	2 oz
Total	224.20	1.250	2.756	2	12 ⅛	1 lb

Process

1. Place the butter in a large and heavy pot, and melt the butter over medium heat.
2. Add the water, sugar, salt, and lecithin and continue cooking over medium heat while continuously stirring.
3. When the mixture reaches 260°F (127°C), add the almonds.
4. Continue cooking until the mixture turns a golden brown color. The temperature should be between 305°F (152°C) and 310°F (154°C).
5. Pour the cooked syrup onto a buttered granite slab or a silicone baking mat. Spread out quickly and as thinly as possible. Be careful not to overly agitate the toffee.
6. While the toffee is still plastic, score to a desired size with a knife or a pastry wheel.
7. Cut or break the toffee into pieces.
8. Place the toffee in an airtight container until ready to dip it in chocolate.
9. To finish, dip the cut toffee in tempered couverture chocolate.

FORMULA

TOFFEE SQUARES

This toffee is made without nuts and is flavored with vanilla.

Ingredients	Baker's %	Kilogram	US decimal	Lb & Oz		Test
Sugar	100.00	0.619	1.364	1	5 ⅞	7 ⅞ oz
Glucose	13.73	0.085	0.187		3	1 ⅛ oz
Water	29.73	0.184	0.405		6 ½	2 ⅜ oz
Butter	57.19	0.354	0.780		12 ½	4 ½ oz
Salt	0.81	0.005	0.011		⅛	⅛ oz
Vanilla	0.65	0.004	0.009		0	¼ tsp
Total	202.11	1.250	2.756	2	12 ⅛	1 lb

Process

1. Combine the sugar, glucose, and water, and cook to 275°F (135°C).
2. Stir in the butter, and continue to cook to 315°F (157°C); stir in the salt.
3. Cook the mixture until it reaches 320°F (160°C), and stir in the vanilla.
4. Prepare the confectionery bars by setting to a desired size on a silicone baking mat, and adjust the bars to contain the toffee in an even layer. Pour the candy between the bars.
5. The toffee must be scored while it is still warm with an oiled knife; this will allow the toffee to be broken easily.
6. Break along the score marks and dip in tempered chocolate to coat.

FORMULA

CHOCOLATE NUT FUDGE

This chocolate fudge is rich in chocolate flavor and crunchy with nuts. Follow the formula carefully; the specified temperatures and proper agitation are necessary to the desired crystallization of the sugars.

Ingredients	Baker's %	Kilogram	US decimal	Lb & Oz		Test
Inverted sugar	10.00	0.032	0.070		1 ⅛	⅜ oz
Evaporated milk	65.00	0.206	0.455		7 ¼	2 ⅝ oz
Sugar	100.00	0.317	0.700		11 ¼	4 oz
Glucose	35.40	0.112	0.248		4	1 ½ oz
Butter #1, salted	25.00	0.079	0.175		2 ¾	1 oz
Lecithin powder	0.20	0.001	0.001		0	1⁄16 tsp
Cream	40.00	0.127	0.280		4 ¾	1 ⅝ oz
Butter #2, salted	10.08	0.032	0.071		1 ⅛	⅜ oz
Chocolate liquor	36.13	0.115	0.253		4	1 ½ oz
Walnuts	39.50	0.125	0.276		4 ⅜	1 ⅝ oz
Fondant	30.25	0.096	0.212		3 ⅜	1 ½ oz
Vanilla extract	2.40	0.008	0.017		¼	⅛ oz
Total	393.96	1.250	2.756	2	12 ⅛	1 lb

Process

1. Toast the walnuts lightly. Cool completely and reserve.
2. Combine the inverted sugar, evaporated milk, sugar, glucose, first butter, and lecithin in a heavy pot. Stir with a spatula for 5 minutes to dissolve the sugars.
3. Place the pot over low to medium heat, and cook the mixture to 250°F (121°C).
4. Add the cream, and bring the temperature back to 241°F (116°C).
5. Remove the pot from the heat and mix in the second butter.
6. Once the butter is incorporated, stir in the chocolate, then the walnuts.
7. Let the mixture cool to 180°F (82°C) and then add the fondant and vanilla, and stir to incorporate.
8. Deposit the mixture into a frame on a silicone mat and allow to crystallize.
9. Cut into the desired shapes, and enrobe in chocolate or wrap in plastic for storage.

FORMULA

PEANUT BRITTLE

Peanut brittle is an old-fashioned confection popular in the South. The flavors and crunchy texture of caramel candy loaded with rich nuts make for a timeless treat.

Ingredients	Baker's %	Kilogram	US decimal	Lb & Oz		Test
Sugar	100.00	0.410	0.904		14 ½	5 ¼ oz
Glucose	50.00	0.205	0.452		7 ¼	2 ⅝ oz
Water	25.12	0.103	0.227		3 ⅝	1 ⅜ oz
Peanuts, raw	125.12	0.513	1.131	1	2 ⅛	6 ⅝ oz
Baking soda	2.20	0.009	0.020		⅜	⅛ oz
Vanilla	0.98	0.004	0.009		⅛	½ tsp
Butter	0.98	0.004	0.009		⅛	½ tsp
Salt	0.49	0.002	0.004		⅛	¼ tsp
Total	304.89	1.250	2.756	2	12 ⅛	1 lb

Process

1. Cook the sugar, glucose, and water to 280°F (138°C).
2. Add the peanuts, and cook to a golden brown.
3. Remove from the heat and stir in the soda, vanilla, butter, and salt.
4. Stir well and pour out onto a lightly greased granite slab or silicone mat.
5. Spread and pull into thin sheets.

FORMULA

FONDANT

Fondant is a versatile confection that can be used as icing or a filling for chocolates.

Ingredients	Baker's %	Kilogram	US decimal	Lb & Oz		Test
Sugar	100.00	0.453	0.999	1	0	5 ¾ oz
Glucose	20.00	0.091	0.200		3 ¼	1 ⅛ oz
Water	20.00	0.091	0.200		3 ¼	1 ⅛ oz
Total	140.00	1.250	2.756	2	12 ⅛	1 lb

Process

1. Combine the sugar, glucose, and water in a heavy pot. Cook to 244°F (118°C), while washing down the sides to prevent crystallization.
2. Pour the hot syrup onto a marble table, and cool to 110°F (43°C).
3. Agitate the mixture by folding and pressing it, using a wide metal spatula. Continue until the mass completely crystallizes.
4. Reserve in an airtight container for at least 24 hours to "cure," and then use as needed.

Fondant for Enrobing

For use in starch molds or free form.

Process

1. Heat the fondant to 160°F (71°C).
2. Add flavorings and colorant as desired.
3. Pour into a confectionary funnel that has been warmed.
4. Deposit into a starch mold or onto a silicone baking mat to the desired size.
5. Allow to crystallize.
6. If using a starch mold, dust off the starch.
7. Enrobe in chocolate.

FORMULA

LIQUEUR CORDIAL

These confections are a surprise in the mouth when the delicate sugar crust breaks and slightly sweetened alcohol fills the mouth. Try this with any alcohol, but when substituting for alcohols with a different percentage of alcohol, be sure to recalculate the sugar solution using the guidelines in this chapter.

Ingredients	Baker's %	Kilogram	US decimal	Lb & Oz		Test
Sugar	100.00	0.641	1.413	1	6 ⅝	8 ¼ oz
Water	45.00	0.288	0.636		10 ⅛	3 ¾ oz
Calvados 45%	50.00	0.321	0.707		11 ¼	4 ⅛ oz
Total	195.00	1.250	2.756	2	12 ⅛	1 lb

Note
Some examples of other liqueurs to use are Pear Brandy or Armagnac.

Process

1. Prepare the starch molds or truffle shells of desired shapes.
2. Cook the sugar and water to 246°F (119°C).
3. Remove the syrup from the heat. Gently mix in the liqueur, which has been warmed to 105°F (41°C). Be careful not to overly agitate the syrup, but make sure that the liqueur is completely mixed in.
4. Carefully deposit the warm syrup into the prepared molds. The temperature of the syrup should be below 120°F (49°C) for starch molds, and below 78°F (28°C) for chocolate shells.
5. If using starch molds, sift a thin layer of warm starch to bury the molds.
6. Allow to set for 4 to 5 hours.
7. Place a lid over the starch mold and flip it over to allow for even crystallization. Let set for at least another 10 hours.

Finishing

1. When using starch molds, carefully brush off the starch and dip in tempered couverture chocolate.
2. When using truffle shells, seal the shells with a drop of tempered couverture chocolate. Enrobe carefully, and decorate as desired.

CHAPTER SUMMARY

It is possible for a pastry shop to have a variety of sugar confections and petits fours available. The petits fours may include miniature versions of the items already offered. The range of products (which can be made as petits fours sec, glacés, frais, déguisés, and prestige) can add an exciting product line to a pastry shop, hotel, or catering company. Common sugar confections in a pastry shop may include marshmallow, caramels, nougats, and fudge. Even though petits fours take more labor than entremets to produce by number of units, the food cost is significantly less by weight. For confections, skilled employees are required to carry out the work, which utilizes cooked sugar syrups and techniques like pulling sugar and whipping hot egg foams. Customers get excited about small treats and may take interest in having one for an afternoon snack or in bringing several dozen to a party. In hotels, their use ranges from amenities to welcome guests, to high tea service, to complements from the chef after dinner. Wherever petits fours and confections are served, it is important to maintain a balance of products for presentation and display.

KEY TERMS

- Aerated confections
- Amuses bouche
- Binding agents
- Brittles
- Caramel
- Caramelization
- Chocolate confections
- Chocolate panning
- Confectionary fondant
- Confections
- Crystalline confections
- Doctors
- Dragées
- Flour confections
- Friandise
- Fudge
- Guitar
- Hard candies
- Hysteresis
- Jelly confections
- Liqueur cordials
- Marshmallows
- Nougat
- Marzipan
- Medium rapid set pectin
- Mignardise
- Noncrystalline confections
- Panning
- Parisian macaron
- Pastry fondant
- Pâtes de fruits
- Pectin
- Pectin NH
- Petits fours
- Petits fours déguisés
- Petits fours frais
- Petits fours glacés
- Petits fours prestige
- Petits fours sec
- Saturated solution
- Seed
- Starch molds
- Sugar confections
- Sugar solution
- Supersaturated solution
- Toffee
- Yellow pectin (apple pectin)

REVIEW QUESTIONS

1. **What are petits fours?**
2. **What are the main categories of petits fours? What distinguishes them from one another?**
3. **How does a saturated sugar solution differ from a supersaturated sugar solution?**
4. **What will be the differences between a marshmallow made with egg whites and gelatin and one made with gelatin (no egg whites)?**
5. **When making pâtes de fruits, why is it important to cook the solution as quickly as possible and to add the sugar in stages?**

chapter
19

FROZEN DESSERTS

OBJECTIVES

After reading this chapter, you should be able to

- discuss the ingredients used in frozen desserts and the role each plays in creating texture, and if applicable, flavor.
- describe the distinction between churned and still-frozen desserts.
- calculate and balance a churned frozen dessert formula for ice cream and sorbet.
- discuss the physical structure of ice cream and the challenges faced in maintaining its quality during storage and transport.
- make a selection of churned and still-frozen desserts.
- practice proper hygiene, sanitation, and storage for frozen desserts.

FROZEN DESSERTS

The category of frozen desserts represents a wide range of sweet preparations that are served in a frozen state. The most popular of these is ice cream, along with similar products such as sorbet, gelato, and frozen yogurt. Others include granita, frozen mousse, parfait, and a long list of variations. The light, smooth, creamy textures of these frozen concoctions have universal appeal. Air bubbles contribute the lightness, and sugar lowers the **freezing point**, thus preventing the mixture from becoming rock-solid at typical freezer temperatures.

Based on the process used to make them, frozen desserts can be divided into two general categories: **churned desserts** and **still-frozen desserts**. Churned desserts are constantly agitated during freezing to break up the ice crystals as they form. Smaller crystals result in a smoother texture. Air is also incorporated during the churning. This process is usually done with an ice cream machine but can also be performed by hand, as is the case with granita. In contrast, still-frozen desserts are prepared, assembled, and left undisturbed in the freezer until they reach a somewhat solid state. They are composed of a liquid base plus a foam, such as whipped egg whites or cream. The foam provides air bubbles and gives the dessert a light texture.

PHYSICAL STRUCTURE

Frozen desserts, and ice cream in particular, are physically complex, unstable mixtures. Stability is maintained primarily through low storage temperature, but support also comes from special physical properties of the core ingredients.

Ice cream is a unique mixture of all three states of matter: gas, liquid, and solid. It consists of fat globules, air bubbles, and ice crystals that are evenly dispersed in an aqueous solution. The solution is able to remain liquid at freezer temperatures due to its high concentration of sugar, a substance that can lower the freezing point of water. Low storage temperatures maintain the existing ice crystals and prevent the trapped air bubbles from escaping. Frozen desserts that contain dairy products benefit from fat's ability to trap air bubbles, but it also introduces the instability of a water–fat emulsion. Again, freezer temperatures help to slow the separation that occurs naturally between these two substances. The lecithin in the egg yolk and milk proteins in the milk and cream work as **emulsifiers**. Their molecules are surface active, meaning that one end is attracted to water and the other is attracted to fat. This relationship works to help maintain an even dispersion of fat globules within the water-based liquid.

BASIC INGREDIENTS

When preparing any edible product, the best results are achieved by using high-quality, flavorful ingredients. Likewise, this should be a guide in selecting ingredients for frozen desserts. It is equally important, however, to consider the role each ingredient plays in determining the texture of the final product. Frozen dessert formulations are a delicate balance between flavor and texture. Ingredients contribute to the flavor but can also affect melting point, mouthfeel, and smoothness. The ingredients detailed in this section pertain specifically to those commonly used in frozen desserts. The guidelines set forth by the US Department of Agriculture (USDA) for ice cream production specify the minimum and maximum amounts of specific ingredients that must be included to classify the product as ice cream. General information about these ingredients may also be found in the online companion. To download information about the ingredients in this section, go to http://www.delmarlearning.com/companions/.

MILK/CREAM

Dairy products form the basis of most frozen desserts. Not only do they provide the desired richness and characteristic dairy flavor expected in high-quality ice cream, gelato, frozen mousse, and more, but the fat and proteins in milk and cream are also responsible for the smooth, creamy texture found in these desserts. As in whipped cream, milk fat's unique ability to trap air bubbles lends a pleasant lightness to the texture. The milk proteins, casein and whey, assist by stabilizing the foam.

Dairy products that are used in frozen desserts are available in many different forms. They are selected based on the quality and type of ice cream to be produced. The following products include the most commonly used products:

Whole, concentrated, and skimmed liquid milk
Skimmed milk powder and whey powder
Buttermilk and buttermilk powder
Cream
Butter

Skimmed or nonfat milk powder has had its water and fat components removed. It consists of a mixture of proteins, lactose, and minerals that are also referred to as **milk solids nonfat (MSNF)**. Adding powdered milk to an ice cream mix reinforces its framework, resulting in an improved texture and overrun percentage. MSNF helps stabilize the water that is present from milk and other ingredients, but too much will cause lactose crystals to form. These triangular lactose crystals are noticeable to the tongue and will be perceived as a sandy texture. Whey, a by-product of cheese manufacturing, is sometimes used for low-cost ice cream. Buttermilk may be used to replace skim milk. In general, the selection of raw material is based on availabilities, cost, and final product quality.

Milk fat is one of the most expensive ingredients used in ice cream. For this reason, lower-quality products contain less of it than premium ice creams. The average fat content in ice cream is between 7 and 20 percent, most commonly falling between 7 and 12 percent. The combination of milk solids nonfat and milk fat ranges from 16 to 22 percent. USDA regulations specify the minimum amounts of fat required for each classification of ice cream. They range from standard, with 10 percent milk fat by weight, to super premium, with as much as 20 percent. (See Figure 19-1 for more details.)

Figure 19-1
Dairy Product Specifications

Product	Percentage Water	Percentage Solids	Percentage Fat	Percentage NFMS	Weight Per Quart (kg)	Percentage Lactose
Whole milk	88	12	3.60	8.40	1.036	
Nonfat milk	91	9.30	0.06	9.24	1.035	
Condensed milk	66	34	10	24.00		
Condensed nonfat milk	68.50	31.50	0.50	31		
Sweet condensed	26	74	9	23		
26% fat milk powder	4	94	26	71		37
Nonfat milk powder	3	97	0	97		50
18% fat cream	74.46	25.54	18.00	7.54	1.015	
20% fat cream	72.46	27.36	20	7.36	1.000	
25% fat cream	68.10	31.90	25	6.90	1.005	
30% fat cream	63.56	36.44	30	6.44	1.000	
35% fat cream	59.02	40.98	35	5.98	0.998	
40% fat cream	54.48	45.52	40	5.52	0.993	
Butter*	16	84	82	2.00		
Concentrated butter	0.10	99.90	99.90	0.00		

*Water in dairy butter varies. This butter listed is considered a high fat butter.

It is possible to recombine milk solids and fat to achieve whole milk. Through the combination of water, milk solids, and butter, ice cream manufacturers can create whole milk at a fraction of the cost for fresh whole milk. Figure 19-2 shows the formulas to make a liter of whole milk when using 26 percent milk powder and with nonfat milk powder.

In ice cream formulations, whole milk, cream, and butter are the most common sources of fat. Other frozen products are sometimes made with vegetable oils or a combination of milk fat and vegetable oil. Whichever fat is used, it is important that the melting point fall within a particular temperature range: high enough to allow for the creation of a stable foam and low enough to melt at body temperature. Fats that have a melting point higher than human body temperature coat the mouth and leave an unpleasant, greasy, waxy residue when consumed. Palm oil and coconut oil are two alternative fats with melting profiles similar enough to those of dairy fat to produce a reasonable product.

EGGS

Many ice cream formulas include egg yolks or occasionally, whole eggs. This type is referred to as **custard-style** or **French custard ice cream** since the ice cream base preparation is similar to that of custard (that is, the eggs are cooked with milk, cream, sugar, and flavoring). The eggs add richness and the lecithin in the egg yolk acts as an emulsifier, stabilizing the even dispersion of water and fat in the mixture. Egg yolk contains approximately 30 percent fat and 10 percent lecithin. Further information on egg yolk composition is detailed in Figure 19-3.

Figure 19-2
Formulas to Make Whole Milk

Recombine	Using 26% Fat Milk Powder	Using Nonfat Milk Powder
Water*	914 g	908 g
26% fat milk powder	114 g	N/A
Nonfat milk powder	N/A	84 g
Butter	8 g	44 g

* The water is reduced to compensate for water contained in the butter.

Figure 19-3
Egg Yolk Composition and Egg Conversion and Lecithin Equivalencies

Egg Yolk Composition

	Water	Lecithin	Protein	Other Fats	Minerals
Egg yolk	50%	9%	16%	23%	2%

Egg Conversion and Lecithin Equivalencies

1 kg whole egg	20 whole eggs
1 kg egg white	30 egg whites
1 kg egg yolk	56 egg yolks
1 egg yolk	18 g
1 egg yolk	2 g lecithin
10 g lecithin	90 g egg yolk

Note

Frozen egg yolk contains an average of 10 percent sugar to minimize freezing damage. This quantity of sugar should be considered in the sugar calculation of the final formula.

SUGAR

Sugar plays an essential role in the taste and texture of frozen desserts. It raises sweetness to the desired level and balances bitter or acidic flavorings such as fruit, coffee, or chocolate. In addition, sugar is the primary ingredient responsible for giving ice cream and like products its "scoopable" texture. This means that it is soft enough to scoop, yet solid enough to maintain its shape once served. As the amount of sugar in a solution increases, the freezing point is lowered. This prevents ice cream from being rock-solid at freezer temperatures. At the typical serving temperature of 5°F (−15°C) to 10°F (−12°C), about 28 percent of the water present in ice cream remains in a liquid state.

Sucrose is the primary sweetener for frozen desserts, although various other sugars are commonly used in combination with it. Invert sugars such as glucose, dextrose, and corn syrup are often included due to their ability to prevent crystallization and extend the shelf life of a product. These sugars are available in liquid or dry form and in varying levels of sweetness. Sweetness levels are measured relative to sucrose, which has been assigned a value of 100. This system provides an easy way to identify the sweetening power of a particular sugar and the corresponding effect it will have on the freezing point of a mixture. The combined sweetening level in a mix has a very important influence on the final texture. For more information about different sugars and their sweetening power, refer to Figure 19-4.

Another system for measuring sweetness applies exclusively to products that are obtained through **hydrolysis**, a process that converts starch to glucose (dextrose) by the application of heat and an acid or enzymes. Hydrolysis can be full or partial. The extent of conversion is expressed as its **dextrose equivalent (DE)**. A higher DE indicates a higher level of sweetness. Starch has a DE of 0, as it has undergone no

Product	Percentage Water	Percentage Solids	Sweetening Power
Sugar	1 to 5	95	100
Inverted sugar	22	78	125
Honey*	20	80	130
Glucose DE 38	30	70	45
Glucose DE 60	30	70	60
Glucose powder DE 38	1 to 5	95	45
Dextrose	1 to 5	95	70
Fructose	1 to 5	95	130
Sorbitol	1 to 5	95	55
Lactose	1 to 5	95	15 to 20
Lactose powder	1 to 5	95	65 to 85
Maltose	1 to 5	95	33
Isomalt	1 to 5	95	40

Note

This chart is presented with sugar at the top because the sweetening power of all other products is based on it. The presentation of ingredients is based on an approximation of how frequently they are used in the industry.

*In a natural product such as honey, water and solids can vary.

Figure 19-4
Sugar Composition and Sweetening Power

conversion. Dextrose, obtained through full conversion, has a DE of 100. Commercial corn syrups have DE in the range of 35 to 65.

There is some confusion regarding terminology with these products. Technically, dextrose is a specific form of glucose. In the food industry, the two terms are often used interchangeably, but commercial products labeled glucose and dextrose can be quite different. In general, glucose syrup or powder refers to a starch-based sweetener obtained through partial hydrolysis. At least 20 percent of the starch has been converted to dextrose. In contrast, products sold as dextrose imply that they have undergone a fuller conversion and have a considerably higher DE. It is important to note that two dry sweeteners commonly used in ice cream production, glucose powder and dextrose powder, can have different composition and sweetening levels.

Selection of various sugars provides a means of modifying the sweetness, texture, and **overrun** of the product. Overrun is the air that is incorporated during the churning phase of ice cream production. When using powdered glucose, 6 percent is recommended, and 10 percent is the maximum suggested amount. Glucose DE 50 is known to provide the best overrun. Dextrose DE 75 will reduce the freezing point by 0.9°F (0.5°C) for each percentage point added and is also known to reduce overrun. The maximum amount of dextrose used should not exceed 2 percent. An excess of either glucose or dextrose will produce an ice cream with a rubbery texture. The invert sugar, Trimoline, is sometimes used in ice cream formulas that have high fat content. It contains an emulsifier and has a high DE of 127 which will soften the texture. Powdered sugar is never used for ice cream since it contains starch, a potential source of spoilage if not fully cooked.

The sweetness of an ice cream mix can be measured with a **refractometer**, an optical instrument that is capable of determining the sugar concentration in most substances. It is a very precise tool, but to obtain an accurate reading, the user must follow proper procedures. To start, the glass must be cleaned with distilled water, then a drop of ice cream mix is set on it and the cover is closed. With the refractometer held level and pointed toward a light source, the user looks through the eyepiece. A reading will correspond to the percentage of sugar in the solution. This percentage is also referred to as **Brix**.

An alternative method of determining the percentage of sugar is to reference the table of all ingredients and calculate the total sugar compared to the total weight of the mix. Everything must be considered, including the lactose in the milk, which has a sweetening power of 16.

EMULSIFIERS AND STABILIZERS

In order to protect against the temperature fluctuations that are likely to occur during transport and storage, many manufacturers enlist the aid of emulsifiers and/or **stabilizers**. When ice crystals in a product melt, they tend to migrate and join other water droplets. Once refrozen, the crystals formed are larger and the ice cream takes on a coarse, icy texture. This explains the condition commonly found in an old container of ice cream that has been sitting in the freezer or one that is left out to melt and is later refrozen.

A fine-textured, smooth ice cream is composed of evenly dispersed tiny ice crystals, small enough to be undetectable by the tongue. When ice cream is inevitably subjected to varying temperatures, it undergoes a sequence of melting and refreezing called **heat shock**. This is the process that takes place when the tiny ice crystals melt and water droplets join together as they migrate within the solution. When the mixture is refrozen, the larger water drops become larger ice crystals and create a coarse ice cream texture, with crystals often visible on the surface. Heat shock, which damages both the texture and the flavor of the product, is one of manufacturers' biggest concerns.

Emulsifiers maintain a homogenous water–fat mixture and work to keep the two disparate substances from separating. Egg yolks traditionally provide this function in ice cream and still do in many natural products; however, some ice cream manufacturers choose to include other commercially produced emulsifiers such as polysorbates and mono- and diglycerides due to their increased strength and relative low cost.

Stabilizers are also used to prevent water migration by increasing the viscosity of the solution. After ice crystals melt, they are held in isolation, and then, once refrozen, the crystal size and numbers are maintained and little damage is done. An additional benefit of the viscous texture is that it helps to mask detection of larger crystals when they do form. However, too much stabilizer in a mix will produce an unpleasant rubbery consistency. Common stabilizers include sodium alginate, carrageenan, locust bean gum/carob gum, guar gum, xanthan gum, pectin, and gelatin.

Best results are obtained by using a combination of stabilizers to take advantage of the particular characteristics of each. Some differences to consider are how well a particular substance reacts to acid, heat, or milk proteins and how easily it dissolves. Special formulations designed specifically for sorbet or ice cream can be purchased. Emulsifier–stabilizer compound products also provide an easy alternative for small producers.

Selection of an appropriate mix of stabilizers is important to achieve the best results. Comments on some of the popular ones follow, and see Figure 19-5 for their recommended usages.

- *Alginate* is extracted from seaweeds. It dissolves easily in water. The gelling properties of alginate diminish in highly acidic mixtures (3.4 pH). In a well-balanced mixture, it provides very good viscosity.
- *Agar* is a gelatinous substance that is extracted from certain species of seaweed and red algae native to the Pacific and Indian Oceans. It is not often used in ice cream production. To dissolve fully, it requires boiling liquid, higher temperatures than are used for ice cream.
- *Carrageenan* is also a seaweed. It reacts very well with milk proteins and protects the casein in a highly acidic mix.

Product	Suggested Percentage Usage
Sodium alginate	0.20 to 0.30
Agar	0.30 to 0.35
Carrageenan	0.15 to 0.25
Carob flour	0.15 to 0.30
Guar flour	0.15 to 0.30
Pectin	0.30 to 0.50
Gelatin	0.25 to 0.50

Figure 19-5
Stabilizers and Suggested Percentage Usage

- *Guar flour*, like guar gum, is produced from guar seeds. The flour dissolves more easily than guar gum. It is cold water soluble and reacts very nicely in a neutral pH mixture.
- *Carob flour* comes from the carob fruit. It has similar properties as the guar flour but produces an ice cream texture that is less elastic.
- *Pectin* is extracted from citrus skin, apples, and beets. There are two types of pectin: low methoxy (LM) pectin and high methoxy (HM) pectin. HM pectin gives a better result in solutions that are acidic and have a high sugar concentration. Pectin has very good gelling properties and is often used for vegetarian or Kosher production.
- *Gelatin* is an animal protein product that is produced from the bones, cartilage, skin, and connective tissue of animals, primarily pigs and cows. It is frequently used as a stabilizer because it has no taste, odor, or color. Gelatin gives a nice viscosity and smooth texture and retards thawing.
- *Egg whites* are not generally used because heat diminishes their stabilizing properties. Powdered egg whites are sometimes used in cold sorbet mixes.

Emulsifiers increase the ability of an ice cream mix to hold air bubbles and maintain its volume. Mono- and diglycerides are chemical emulsifiers that are made from partially hydrolyzed vegetable fat, such as soybean or palm oil. See Figure 19-6 for suggested usage of emulsifiers.

FLAVORINGS

Possibilities for flavoring an ice cream mix are limited only by one's imagination and a few factors that may affect texture and taste. For example, when including ingredients that are high in fat, sugar, or alcohol, it is important to consider their impact on the final texture. Like sugar, alcohol lowers the freezing point and will produce a softer product.

Flavor ingredients are generally added to the base mixture. Others may be added at the end of the process, depending on the desired result. Base flavorings in liquid, powder, or paste form can easily be blended into the mix. Strong flavors such as herbs or spices are more suited to flavoring by infusion. In this case, the base is cooked as usual with the flavorings added. Heat encourages extraction of the flavors but harsh and bitter notes are avoided by straining the substances from the mix prior to freezing. In order to maintain their size and texture, solid pieces, referred to as **inclusions**, are folded in at a later stage, after churning. Examples of popular inclusions are fruit chunks, nuts, candies, and baked goods. It is important to consider that solid inclusions will take on moisture from the ice cream mix. To help prevent soggy textures, nuts can be toasted, baked pieces can be fully dried, and items can be coated in a protective layer of chocolate or cocoa butter. Rippled sauces and swirls are also added at the stage between churning and freezing. Sauces should contain an appropriate level of sugar or alcohol to ensure a soft texture that is consistent with the base when frozen.

Figure 19-6
Emulsifiers and Suggested Percentage Usage

Product	Suggested Percentage Usage
Mono- and diglyceride	0.10 to 0.30
Polysorbate	0.10 to 0.20

FRUITS

Fruit is a very popular flavoring for frozen desserts. It can be added as a puree to flavor the base, mixed in as bite-size pieces, or inserted in the form of fruit swirls. Figure 19-7 shows suggested percentages of fruit to be used in sorbet. When using fresh fruit, it is important to choose ripe, full-flavored produce. Following the seasons is the best way to find the highest quality fruit at the lowest price. Clean the fruit well, select only the best portions, and remove coarse pieces such as seeds or skins. Mix fruits that have a tendency to oxidize with lemon juice or citric acid to prevent them from discoloring.

Most fruits contain a high percentage of water which, when incorporated into a frozen dessert, can have detrimental effects on taste and texture. Extra water can bleed from the fruit, form large ice crystals, and result in an icy texture. Equally unpleasant are fruit inclusions that become hard as ice cubes when frozen. Both of these conditions can easily be avoided.

To remove excess water from pureed or chunk fruit, mix it with an amount of sugar equal to 25 percent of its weight and then refrigerate it for 12 to 24 hours to draw out the natural juices. The pulp will fall to the bottom of the container and the water can be easily drained. Alternatively, fruit can be cooked or roasted to remove moisture and intensify flavor. The textural changes that occur, especially in fruits high in pectin, have the added benefit of producing a creamier base for sorbet or granita. Cooked fruit has a very different flavor than fresh, which may or may not be desired.

Ingredients such as sugar and alcohol lower the freezing point of water. This behavior is exploited to give frozen desserts a soft texture, but it can also be applied to fruit inclusions to give them softness at typical

Fruit	Percentage	Fruit	Percentage
Apricot	50 to 60	Mandarin	45 to 55
Pineapple	45 to 60	Mango	50 to 60
Banana	35 to 40	Melon	60 to 80
Black currant	30 to 35	Mirabelle prune	50 to 60
Lime	15 to 20	Blackberry	45 to 5
Lemon	20 to 30	Muroise	40 to 50
Coconut	50	Blueberry	45 to 55
Strawberry	47 to 70	Orange	55 to 70
Raspberry	45 to 55	Peach	50 to 70
Passion Fruit	30 to 35	Pear	50 to 70
Morello cherry	40 to 50	Grapefruit	35 to 50
Gooseberry	35 to 45	Prune	50 to 60
Kiwi	50 to 60	Lychee	50

Note

Fruit puree added sugar content, 10 percent; recommended solid content in sorbet, 31 to 33 percent; recommended solid content with alcohol, 22 to 28 percent; recommended sugar with alcohol, 14 to 16 percent; recommended sugar, 20 to 33 percent; recommended glucose, 10 percent max; recommended fat, 2 percent max; recommended MSNF, 3 percent max; recommended fresh fruits, 1.25.

Figure 19-7
Recommended Percentage of Fruit in Sorbet

freezer temperatures. Macerate fruit pieces in sugar syrup or alcohol, drain, and add to the dessert mixture prior to the hardening phase. Dried fruits also benefit from being rehydrated in this manner. Candied or glazed fruits such as cherries, pineapple, and candied citrus peels do not require this extra step because they have ample sugar content.

Using prepack fruit puree has some advantages. The producer often has a purchase agreement with the farmers allowing the fruits to be closely monitored and harvested at the peak of ripeness. This arrangement allows them to obtain the best flavor and sweetness. Immediately after harvest, the fruit is processed to remove the seeds or pit, sifted to eliminate excess skin and foreign particles, and then frozen to a low temperature. Fruits may also be analyzed for acidity and sweetness levels to maintain a consistent product and to monitor for potential contamination. Sucrose, generally added at an average of 10 percent, heightens flavors and helps shorten the defrosting time.

NUTS

Nuts, valued both for their flavor contribution and textural contrast, are a delicious addition to ice cream and frozen desserts. Whole nuts or pieces can be folded in as crunchy inclusions or they can be ground and used as a base ingredient. Toasting the nuts beforehand enhances their flavors and increases crispness. Candying or coating them in chocolate or cocoa butter before adding to a creamy dessert will further prevent them from softening.

CHOCOLATE

Chocolate is one of the most popular flavoring ingredients used in ice cream. It can be incorporated in a multitude of ways: as a flavoring for the base, as solid bits, as coating for inclusions, or as a rippled sauce. When adding chocolate to the base mixture, it is important to consider the composition of the specific chocolate being used, namely, its sugar, solids, and fat content. These components have an important impact on the texture as well as flavor of the ice cream. The amounts of each vary considerably between types of chocolate as well as between different brands. Figure 19-8 details the composition of Valrhona chocolates. It is important to determine this information for the particular brand and type of chocolate being used.

CHURNED FROZEN DESSERTS

Churned frozen desserts are generally produced using an ice cream machine. Exceptions to this rule are granita and similar frozen ices. In both cases, the mixture is stirred or churned during freezing in order to break up the size of the ice crystals that form. Ice cream machines are very efficient at this task and produce smooth desserts with tiny ice crystals. The ice crystals in granita are periodically broken up manually as the mixture freezes. This creates a refreshing crunchy, icy texture.

PRODUCTION

Though the scale of the operation and the equipment are very different in commercial ice cream production, the procedure is quite similar to home production. An ice cream base is made by mixing and

Figure 19-8 Valrhona Chocolate Composition

Product	Percentage Cocoa	Percentage Sugar	Percentage Fat	Percentage Cocoa Solid	Percentage Milk Powder
Dark					
Caraibe	66.5	33	40.6	26.5	
Caraque	56	43.5	37	19	
Equatoriale noire	55.5	44	37.4	18	
Extra amer	67	32	38	30	
Extra bitter	61	38	38	23	
Guanaja	70.5	29	42.5	28	
Manjari	64.5	35	40	24.5	
Noir extra	53	46.5	30	23.5	
Milk					
Equatoriale lait	35	44.5	36.8		20
Guanaja lait	41				
Jivara	40	36	40.4		23.5
Super alpina	39				
White					
Ivoire	30	43.5	37		20

Cocoa Powder—Paste

	Solids	Water	pH	Fat
Cocoa paste	99%	1%		54%
Cocoa powder 22%	98%	2%	8	22%
Low-fat cocoa powder	98%	2%	8	10%

heating milk and/or cream, sweetener, flavoring, and, optionally, eggs. After reaching a temperature suitable for pasteurization, the mixture is refrigerated and aged for a number of hours. It then goes into the ice cream maker, where it is subjected to freezing temperatures and constant churning. Eventually, the liquid becomes a semifrozen solid and is placed in a freezer for further hardening.

Preparing the Base

Blending the base ingredients and heating the mix are the first steps in ice cream production. Heat helps to dissolve dry ingredients like milk powder and stabilizers and encourages flavor extraction when flavoring by infusion. Even more important though is the need to pasteurize the mix. **Pasteurization** is an essential step to ensuring a safe product. Heating to a specified temperature for a determined length of time prevents the development of dangerous microbes that are present in eggs and dairy products.

There are two pasteurization options for frozen products. **High-temperature short-time (HTST)** pasteurization is the most commonly used method for ice cream. It requires the mixture be heated to 185°F (85°C) for 2 to 3 minutes. An alternate method, **low-temperature long-time (LTLT)** pasteurization requires that the mixture be heated to a minimum temperature of 149°F (65°C) for 30 minutes. This method may be preferable for mixtures that contain ingredients whose flavors or composition would be adversely affected by high heat.

Making the Ice Cream Mix Using HTST Pasteurization

- Scale all the ingredients and keep in separate sanitized containers.
- Mix the stabilizer with 10 times its weight of sugar to dilute it.
- In a stainless steel pan, heat the milk or water, if powdered milk is being used.
- When the temperature reaches 39°F (4°C), add the powdered milk, and mix with a wire whip.
- At 77°F (25°C), add all the sugar and spices, coffee flavor, and tea if part of the formula.
- At 95°F (35°C), add the cream (35 percent milk fat) or melted butter or oil.
- At 104°F (40°C), add the egg yolks that have been mixed with a little milk. Make sure to whip continuously while the egg yolks are being added.
- At 111°F (45°C), add the stabilizer–sugar mixture. Stir constantly to prevent burning. Bring the mixture to 185°F (85°C) for 2 minutes.
- Remove from the heat, and add the melted chocolate, peanut butter, or any nut paste, if part of the ice cream base.
- Cool the ice cream very rapidly to 39°F (4°C), and refrigerate in a closed container. The refrigerator should be 36°F (2°C) to 42°F (6°C).

If you have some concern about the quality of the nut's source or about contamination of any flavor, the addition of the paste should be part of the pasteurization stage: 185°F (85°C) for 2 minutes for HTST or 149°F (65°C) for 30 minutes for LTLT.

Aging

After pasteurization, the mixture is quickly cooled to 40°F (4°C). This temperature should be reached within 1 hour to minimize the time spent in the critical temperature zone of 50°F (10°C) to 140°F (60°C), a range that is most conducive to dangerous bacteria growth. During the aging or ripening stage, the mixture is held in a refrigerated compartment in a sanitized covered container. Specific times and temperatures are as follows: 24 hours maximum at 42°F (6°C) or 48 hours maximum at 35°F (2°C); maturation can be achieved in as few as 4 hours at 35°F (2°C) with the assistance of slow agitation. Extended resting time is highly recommended, however, because it allows the fat inside the globules to begin to crystallize, the emulsifiers to adhere to water droplets, and the stabilizers to hydrate fully. The mixture will become thicker and creamier. All these conditions build a better, more stable environment for the air bubbles that will be incorporated in the next step. Heat-sensitive ingredients like flavorings, colorings, or fruit purees can also be added this time. Also, large productions may test the mix for viscosity and microbiological safety before going to the freezing.

Freezing

The three structural components of ice cream are fat globules, ice crystals, and air bubbles. By the end of the aging phase, the partially crystallized fat globules have created a network that provides a structure to hold the ice crystals and air bubbles, which will be formed during the freezing stage. The chilled mix is placed into the freezing tank of an ice cream maker where a central vertical paddle, called a **dasher**, spins. The action simultaneously aerates the mix and continuously scrapes frozen crystals off the sides of the canister, preventing them from growing too large.

Air that is incorporated, also referred to as overrun, gives ice cream its characteristic lightness. The amount can be significant, with overrun accounting for up to half the volume of some lower quality ice creams. Heavy use of emulsifiers allows for such high overrun amounts. When the mix has reached a consistency similar to that of soft-serve ice cream, it is removed from the freezing tank. At this point, inclusions such as fruits, nuts, and baked items may be gently folded in, and sauces can be inserted. If left in the freezing tank too long, the ice cream will harden and air will be forced out.

Overrun

Overrun is the measure of additional volume the ice cream acquires during churning, as a result of air bubbles becoming trapped by the fat. Emulsifiers encourage higher overrun. Typical overrun for ice cream is between 50 and 100 percent and for sorbet from 30 to 40 percent. Premium products have levels at the lower range, whereas economy brands contain significantly more. Overrun provides lightness and good mouthfeel, yet too much dilutes the flavor and produces an undesirable, overly airy texture.

How to Calculate Overrun Using the same container, weigh the ice cream mix before and after freezing. Be careful to fill to the top to ensure that there are no air pockets.

Example

1 quart ice cream mix before freezing = 1,200 g

1 quart ice cream after freezing = 750 g

$$\frac{1200 - 750}{750} \times 100\% = 60\% \text{ overrun}$$

Hardening

After removal from the ice cream maker, about half of the liquid has been frozen into ice crystals, and the ice cream is in a very unstable state. It is essential to lower the temperature as quickly as possible to prevent water migration and a coarse texture. Once inclusions have been added, the ice cream is packaged and its temperature quickly lowered. Because colder temperatures produce a smoother product, the ideal range is −22°F (−30°C) to −40°F (−40°C). Once the product is hardened, ice cream can be stored indefinitely at −13°F (−25°C) or colder. Ice crystal growth is prevented at these extreme low temperatures.

ICE CREAM

Ice cream at its simplest is made with dairy products, sugar, various flavorings, and sometimes eggs. There are two main styles: **Philadelphia-style ice cream** and custard-style ice cream. Philadelphia-style ice cream is made from an uncooked mixture of cream, sugar, and flavorings. It can have a slightly grainy texture because it lacks the emulsifying capabilities of egg yolk, and larger ice crystals may form. However, the addition of bulky flavoring ingredients such as chocolate or fruit puree can help emulsify the mixture and produce a smooth-textured ice cream. A custard-style ice cream base is a cooked mixture of milk, cream, whole eggs or egg yolks, and sugar that is similar to crème Anglaise. It produces a rich, smooth ice cream. To define ice cream as French or custard-style, the USDA requires that it contain a minimum of 1.4 percent egg solids. Processing methods for both styles are the same.

GELATO

Gelato is an Italian frozen dessert that is similar to ice cream. Although the process for making gelato and ice cream is almost identical, the two differ slightly in taste and texture. While ice cream is loved for its lightness and creamy, rich taste, a good gelato is valued for its dense consistency and intense flavor. In gelato, the proportion of flavoring to fat is substantially higher than that of ice cream. The dense texture is a result of minimal air incorporation.

SORBET

Sorbet is composed primarily of fruit or vegetable juice or puree, sugar syrup, and an acid. They are characteristically light and refreshing. Some formulations include alcohol or infusions of tea, coffee, herbs, and spices. Sorbet is often served as a palate cleanser between courses or as a light dessert.

Sorbet, like ice cream, has a smooth and creamy texture that is the result of careful control of ice crystal size. The process for making it is basically the same as for ice cream; however, sorbet contains no fat or dairy. This results in lower overrun levels because fat is responsible for trapping most of the air in ice cream. Maximum overrun levels for sorbet can reach 30 to 60 percent compared to 100 percent or more for ice cream. The high percentage of fruit puree in some sorbet formulas provides bulk that can help trap air and produces a light texture. Emulsifiers are unnecessary due to an absence of fat, but stabilizers may be added to prevent the texture from coarsening, which can occur over time from water recrystallization.

The balance of solids and sugar is important to maintain overrun and hold the scoop shape. The content of solids should fall between 31 to 33 percent, and the sugar should be between 20 and 33 percent. Up to 10 percent powdered glucose may be added to create a firmer texture. This is due to it having a lower sweetening power than sucrose and consequently less impact on the freezing point. Some sorbets may add low levels of fat or nonfat milk solids to help trap air. The amounts should not exceed 2 and 3 percent, respectively. Sorbets that include alcohol may require a reduction in sugar content because alcohol also depresses the freezing point.

GRANITA

Granita, or **granité**, is a crisp, refreshing ice that can be made from a wide assortment of flavorings, including fruit purees, fruit or vegetable juices, wine, alcohol, coffee, or tea. It can also be infused with unlimited variations of zests, herbs, and spices. Ingredients are mixed with simple syrup or water, depending on the flavoring ingredients used and desired level of sweetness. Granita is frequently served as an intermezzo or light dessert, although a growing trend is to offer savory versions that provide texture and temperature contrast to other courses.

The basic ratio for granita is three parts juice to one part simple syrup. The ideal sugar content for ice crystal formation is between 8° and 12° baumé. When making a savory granita, sugar can be substituted with salt and alcohol to achieve the desired texture. These ingredients also lower the freezing point and prevent the mixture from becoming a solid block of ice. A small amount of salt is recommended, even for sweet granitas, because it helps balance and enhance flavors.

STILL-FROZEN DESSERTS

Still-frozen desserts offer a delicious alternative to traditional ice cream. They do not require an ice cream machine for their preparation and therefore are a good option for kitchens with limited equipment.

Desserts that fall into this category are largely composed of the ingredients that go into a classic mousse. Whipped foam made of egg whites or yolks and heavy cream may be folded into a flavored base. Any of the inclusions that are used for ice cream can be incorporated into the mixture. And, there are endless possibilities for creating sophisticated desserts by layering multiple flavors and contrasting textural elements such as cake, crisp cookies, or meringue.

Some examples of still-frozen desserts follow:

- **Frozen mousse**, the simplest of these preparations, is a combination of a Swiss or Italian meringue, whipped cream, and a flavoring base.
- **Frozen parfait** is a mixture of pâte à bombe or Italian or Swiss meringue, with flavoring and whipped cream folded in. In the United States, parfait also refers to a dessert of ice cream layered with fruit and whipped cream.
- **Frozen soufflé** is similar to a frozen mousse. The distinction is attributed to its presentation, made to mimic the appearance of a hot soufflé. Frozen and served in ramekins that have been fitted with a collar, the additional height that is exposed when the collar is removed mimics the puff of a classic hot soufflé.
- **Semifreddo**, which means "half frozen" in Italian, is a frozen dessert composed of a custard base lightened with whipped cream or meringue. Chocolate, nuts, fruits, or other inclusions can be incorporated. Semifreddo is served frozen, but the incorporated air softens it and makes it seem less cold.
- **Bombe** is a molded frozen dessert named for its classic dome shape. It is traditionally comprised of multiple layers of parfait-type mixtures.

ICE CREAM FORMULA CREATION AND BALANCE CALCULATION

Creation of an ice cream or sorbet formula requires careful balance of the substances that affect both flavor and texture, especially fat, MSNF, sugars, solids, and water. These components are found in a number of the ingredients in the mix so it is necessary to evaluate all to determine an accurate total. For example, sugar concentration is calculated from the lactose in milk or milk powder, sugar included in fruit puree or other ingredients, and any type of sugar that is added directly to the base.

The formula calculation spreadsheet (Figure 19-9) included later in this chapter contains recommended percentage levels for each component, allowing for easy formula creation or modification of an existing formula. Breaking a formula down into component percentages can help identify problems with texture or sweetness when compared against the recommended ranges. For large-scale production there are computer programs available that do similar analysis.

To balance a formula, the fat, MSNF, water, and total solids in the dairy products and other ingredients must be calculated. For each component, add the weights contributed from the various ingredient sources and divide by the total weight of the batch to obtain a percentage. These numbers can then be compared to the recommended percentages noted on the spreadsheet. These guidelines help to create the ice cream/sorbet texture and flavor desired. For large commercial production it is necessary to observe the USDA guidelines in order to label the ice cream/sorbet according to the classification. Smaller production such as that in restaurant or pastry shops does not require as strict adherence.

In the ice cream example below, metric measurements are used to facilitate calculation; however, US decimal point can also be used.

Ice Cream Calculation Example

Formula Guidelines

9% fat
14% MSNF
17% sucrose
0.2% stabilizer
0.2% emulsifier
Total weight of batch: 10,000 g

Ingredient Composition Selected

Butter 82% butterfat
Skim milk powder 97% solids
Sucrose
Stabilizer
Emulsifier

Quantity of butter needed to make 9% fat in the final formula using butter with 82% butterfat

Formula	*Batch*	*Butterfat*
9% fat	10,000	82%

$$\frac{9 \times 10{,}000}{82} = 1{,}097 \text{ g butter}$$

Quantity of powdered skim milk needed for 14% solids or 1,400 g

First, determine the weight of solids in the amount of butter calculated previously. This particular butter has 2 percent MSNF.

$$\text{Weight of butter} \times \text{MSNF in butter} = 1{,}097 \text{ g} \times 2\%$$

$$\frac{1{,}097 \text{ g} \times 2}{100} = 21.94 \text{ g MSNF in the butter}$$
$$= 22 \text{ g when rounded up}$$

Deduct this amount (22 g) from the total number of solids needed for the batch (1,400 g). Then, determine the amount of milk powder needed to provide the rest. The skim milk powder chosen has 97 percent MSNF.

Desired	*MSNF in butter*
14% of 10,000	22 g

$$1{,}400 \text{ g} - 22 \text{ g} = 1{,}378 \text{ g}$$

$$\frac{1{,}378 \text{ g} \times 100}{97} = 1{,}420 \text{ g}$$

Amount of sucrose needed for 17% of 10,000 g batch

$$\frac{10{,}000 \times 17}{100} = 1{,}700 \text{ g}$$

or

$$10{,}000 \times 0.17 = 1{,}700 \text{ g}$$

Amount of stabilizer needed for 0.2% of 10,000 g batch

$$\text{Total batch} = \frac{10{,}000 \text{ g} \times 0.2\%}{100} = 20 \text{ g}$$

or

$$10{,}000 \times 0.002 = 20 \text{ g}$$

Amount of emulsifier needed for 0.2% of 10,000 g batch

$$\text{Total batch} = \frac{10{,}000 \text{ g} \times 0.2\%}{100} = 20 \text{ g}$$

or

$$10{,}000 \text{ g} \times 0.002 = 20 \text{ g}$$

Now that we have the total of all ingredients, we can determine the amount of water needed.

Quantity of water needed

$$\text{Batch} = 10{,}000 \text{ g} - (1{,}097 \text{ g butter} + 1{,}420 \text{ g milk powder} + 1{,}700 \text{ g sugar} + 20 \text{ g emulsifier} + 20 \text{ g stabilizer}) = 5{,}743 \text{ g}$$

So, 5,743 g of water is 57.43 percent of the total 10,000 g batch.

Replacing Water With Fresh Whole Milk

If fresh whole milk is used instead of water, we need to calculate the composition of the whole milk considering that whole milk contains 3.6 percent fat, 8.4 percent MSNF, and 88 percent water, the sum of which equals 100 percent.

First, we calculate the amount of fresh milk needed to replace the water. Then, we evaluate the fat and MSNF in this quantity and adjust the butter and powdered skim milk to reflect the change.

Quantity of milk to replace the water

Water weight	*Water in milk*
5,473	88%

$$\frac{5{,}743\ \text{g} \times 100}{88} = 6{,}526\ \text{g milk}$$

This is the total weight of whole milk needed to replace the water. Next, calculate the fat and MSNF and deduct the result from your earlier calculation.

Fat weight in the milk (3.6%)

$$\frac{6{,}526\ \text{g} \times 3.6}{100} = 235\ \text{g}$$

or

$$6{,}526\ \text{g} \times 0.036 = 235\ \text{g}$$

MSNF weight in the whole milk (8.4%)

$$\frac{6{,}526\ \text{g} \times 8.4}{100} = 548\ \text{g}$$

or

$$6{,}526\ \text{g} \times 0.084 = 548\ \text{g}$$

These two components can be deducted from the other ingredients.

Final Formula Comparison

	Using Water	Change Required	Using Whole Milk
Water	5,743 g		0 g
Whole milk	0 g		6,526 g
Powdered skim milk	1,420 g	−548 g	872 g
Sugar	1,700 g		1,700 g
Butter	1,097 g	−235 g	862 g
Emulsifier	20 g		20 g
Stabilizer	20 g		20 g
Total	10,000 kg		10,000 kg

If cream is an ingredient of the ice cream mix, it is necessary to determine its fat content, which can vary from 18 to 40 percent. The water and MSNF contribution from the cream should also be reflected.

The composition of each ingredient is the most important part to consider. What is added with one must be balanced with the others. To balance the solids, first calculate the other ingredients, then the MSNF, and finally the water. Information on dairy products, sugars, and egg yolks are detailed in their associated composition tables found in the ingredients section of this chapter. Enter values into the formula calculation spreadsheet (Figure 19-9) later in this chapter to organize the calculation of an ice cream or sorbet formula.

One equation can be used to calculate the MSNF. Add the other solid percentages and subtract from 100. The result is then divided by 6.9 for short conservation and 6.4 for longer conservation. Short conservation applies to a product that will be stored up to 1 week. Long conservation refers to storage of a month or longer. A larger quantity of solids helps stabilize the ice cream structure for extended storage.

Example of MSNF Calculation

		Percentage Solid of the Mix
Butter	1097 g	2%
Sugar	1700 g	17%
Emulsifier	20 g	0.2%
Stabilizer	20 g	0.2%
		19.4%

100% − 19.4% = 80.6%

Short Conservation

80.6 / 6.9 = 11.68% MSNF

Total solid = 11.68% + 19.4% = 30.91% solids

Long Conservation

80.6 / 6.4 = 12.6% MSNF

Total solid = 12.6% + 19.4% = 32% solids

These calculated MSNF and total solids percentages fall within the recommended ranges.

SORBET FORMULA CALCULATION

Sorbet is slightly easier to calculate because fewer ingredients are involved. First, add the percentage of the solids in the ingredients used. Keep in mind that frozen puree generally includes 10 percent sugar for better flavor, easier usage, and increased shelf life. For best results, follow this guide, which applies the average rule.

Guidelines for Sorbet Formulas

			Percentage Solid*
Sugar	20% to 33%		100%
MSNF	0.5% to 3%	If used	Varies by product
Fat	0.5% to 2%	If used	Varies by product
Fruit pulp			Varies
Stabilizer	0.2% to 0.3%		100%
Emulsifier	None		

*Total solids from 31 to 33 percent.

Sorbet Calculation Example

Batch Mix Formula

31% of solid (7,000 g strawberry puree with 10% sucrose included)

0.2% stabilizer

Total weight of the batch: 10,000 g

Actual quantity of strawberry puree: 7,000 g with 10% sucrose

$$\frac{7{,}000 \text{ g} \times (10\% \text{ sugar})}{100} = 700 \text{ g sucrose}$$

or

$$7{,}000 \text{ g} \times 0.10 = 700 \text{ g}$$
$$7{,}000 \text{ g} - 700 \text{ g} = 6{,}300 \text{ g puree}$$

Actual quantity of solids considering the puree has 11% solid

Actual strawberry puree × Solid = 6,300 g − 11%

$$\frac{6{,}300 \times 11}{100} = 693 \text{ g}$$

or

$$6{,}300 \times 0.11 = 693 \text{ g}$$

Actual quantity of stabilizer: 0.2%

$$\frac{10{,}000 \text{ g} \times 0.2}{100} = 20 \text{ g}$$

or

$10{,}000 \times 0.002 = 20$ g

Total solids known = 693 + 20 = 713 g solids

Solids selected: 31%

Batch size × Solid selected = 10,000 × 31%

$$\frac{10{,}000 \times 31}{100} = 3{,}100 \text{ g}$$

or

$$10{,}000 \times 0.31 = 3{,}100 \text{ g}$$

Sugar to add to balance the solids 3,100 g with 31%

Selected solids − (Existing solid + Sucrose in puree)

= 3,100 g − (713 + 700) = 1,687 g sucrose

Water to be added

Batch − (Sucrose + Stabilizer + Puree)

$$= 10{,}000 - (1{,}687 + 20 + 7{,}000) = 1{,}292 \text{ g water}$$

Mineral water can be used for ice cream/sorbet to avoid off flavors and potential contamination.

Calculate sugar percentage to compare to guideline

Sucrose + Sucrose in puree = 1,687 g + 700 g = 2,387 g total sugar

$$\frac{2{,}387 \times 100}{10{,}000} = 3.87\%$$

or

$$2{,}387 \times 0.010 = 23.87\%$$

Final Formula Balance

Solid

713 + 2,387 = 3,100 g or 31% (31 to 33%) recommended

Sugar

700 + 1,687 = 2,387 g or 23.87% (20 to 30%) recommended

Water

$$\frac{1{,}293 \times 100}{10{,}000 \text{ g}} = 12.93\%$$

or

$$1{,}293 \times 0.010 = 12.93\%$$

If fat, MSNF, or powdered glucose are selected for this formula, add the solids of those ingredients and make adjustments to stay within the 31 percent range. Make the same calculation when adding chocolate to make chocolate sorbet. Refer to Figure 19-9 for an example of a formula calculation spreadsheet.

Figure 19-9 Formula Calculation Spreadsheet

Products	Weight	% Fat	Fat Weight	% MSNF	MSNE Dry Extract	% Solids	Solids	% Water
Whole milk		3.6%		8%				88.0%
Nonfat milk powder				97%				3%
Butter		82.0%		2%				16%
Cream								
Sucrose		0.0%		0%		95%		5%
Inverted sugar		0.0%		0%				22%
Other sweetener								
Other sweetener								
Egg yolk		33.5%		0%				50%
Stabilizer		0.0%		0%				
Emulsifier		0.0%		0%				
Vanilla powder		0.0%		0%				
Cocoa								
Fruit puree								
Water								
Total weights								
Actual %								
Suggested %								
Ice cream %		**7%–12%**		**8%–11%**		**35%–45%**		
Sorbet %		**2%**		**3%**		**31%–32%**		

***Process to Calculate Sweetness Concentration (SC)**

To calculate the SC from the casein take the MSNF and divide it by 2 (50%). This gives the casein content since the casein is 16 DE. Multiply the result by 0.16 and then place the result in the column SC.

All the other sweeteners are multiplied by the DE given number. Sucrose is 100 percent.

When you have all the sweetness concentration numbers, add them up and divide the result by 100 to give the actual percentage.

Water	Lactose	SC*	% Sugar	Sugar	Egg Yolk	Stabilizer	Emulsifier	Flavoring	Alcohol
		16%–23%	**18%–22%****			**0.2%–0.3%**	**0.25%**		
			20%–33%						

****Suggested Percentages of Select Ingredients for Sorbet and Ice Cream**

Sugar percentage for ice cream with alcohol 14 to 15 percent

Sorbet with alcohol 22 to 28 percent

Alcohol maximum in sorbet 7 percent

Glucose powder in sorbet 10 percent

MSNF plus fat in sorbet 16 to 22 percent

NOTES ON READING AN ICE CREAM FORMULA

- For simplicity and consistency, formulas are presented in kilograms only, as is the example on how to balance an ice cream formula.
- The low storage temperatures specified in this section provide the ideal environment for sorbet and ice cream. As explained in this chapter, such low temperatures prevent water migration and the formation of large crystals, which destroy the desirable smooth texture. If a blast freezer is unavailable, frozen desserts may be stored for shorter periods at typical freezer temperatures. Note that degradation will occur over time.
- Mineral water is specified in a number of formulas due to its neutral taste and lack of bacteria. If you are lucky enough to have good tap water, it can be substituted.
- Monostearate, an ingredient listed in most of the ice cream formulas, is a fat emulsifier. It is used in combination with an ice cream stabilizer for improved texture. Commercially available stabilizer–emulsifier blends can be substituted. Follow the manufacturer's guidelines for usage. Lecithin powder or egg yolks can also be used as emulsifiers. Keep in mind that these ingredients will affect the flavor of the product. Additional egg yolks will also increase the fat level and mouthfeel of the ice cream.
- Commercially available inverted sugar is a liquid sweetener composed of equal parts fructose and glucose. The sweetening power is higher than sucrose by weight. Glucose and corn syrup are not appropriate replacements.

FORMULA

VANILLA ICE CREAM

A classic favorite, our version of vanilla ice cream features a generous amount of vanilla bean, which lends a clean, refreshing vanilla flavor. This ice cream makes a great base for additions of fresh fruit, liqueur, cookies, and more.

Ingredients	Kilogram
Whole milk	1.129
Nonfat powdered milk	0.080
Sugar	0.220
Glucose powder	0.060
Vanilla bean (1 per kg mix)	2
Inverted sugar	0.040
35% cream	0.400
Egg yolks	0.060
Stabilizer	0.006
Monostearate	0.005
Total	2.000

Process

1. Scale all the ingredients, and hold them in separate sanitized containers.
2. Mix the stabilizer and monostearate with 10 times their combined weight of sugar (from the sugar already in the formula) to dilute it for better incorporation.
3. In a stainless steel pan, heat up the milk.
4. When the temperature reaches 39°F (4°C), add the powdered milk, and mix with a whisk.
5. At 77°F (25°C), add all the sugar, glucose powder, and vanilla bean.
6. At 95°F (35°C), add the cream.
7. At 104°F (40°C), add the egg yolks, which have been mixed with a little milk. Make sure to whip continuously while the egg yolks are added.
8. At 111°F (45°C), add the monostearate and stabilizer mixed with the sugar and the inverted sugar.
9. Stir constantly to prevent scorching. Bring the mixture to 185°F (85°C) for 2 minutes.

10. Cool the ice cream very rapidly to 39°F (4°C), cover to the surface with plastic wrap, and refrigerate at 42°F (6°C) to 35°F (2°C).
11. Let the ice cream mature/age for at least 4 hours or overnight under refrigeration.
12. Blend the ice cream mix with an immersion blender to ensure a smooth mix and distribution of ingredients, especially the monostearate.
13. Sanitize the ice cream machine mixing tank and all applicable components.
14. Pour the mix into the ice cream machine tank.
15. Churn until the ice cream reaches the desired consistency.
16. Remove from the ice cream machine, and transfer to a clean, frozen container.
17. Freeze right away at −31°F (−35°C).
18. Storage temperature before serving should be 0°F (−18°C) to −4°F (−20°C).
19. Serve at 5°F (−15°C) to 10°F (−12°C).

FORMULA

CHOCOLATE ICE CREAM

The rival to vanilla ice cream is almost certainly chocolate ice cream. Rich with cream and flavored with bittersweet couverture, this chocolate ice cream will please the most discerning of palates.

Ingredients	Kilogram
Whole milk	1.165
Nonfat powdered milk	0.050
Sugar	0.150
35% cream	0.280
Stabilizer	0.005
Monostearate	0.005
Inverted sugar	0.080
67% chocolate couverture	0.265
Total	2.000

Process

1. Scale all the ingredients, and hold them in separate sanitized containers.
2. Melt the couverture in a microwave to 120°F (49°C) and reserve.
3. Mix the stabilizer and monostearate with 10 times their combined weight of sugar (from the sugar already in the formula) to dilute it for better incorporation.
4. In a stainless steel pan, heat the milk.
5. When the temperature of the milk reaches 39°F (4°C), add the powdered milk, and mix with a wire whip.
6. At 77°F (25°C), add the sugar.
7. At 95°F (35°C), add the cream.
8. At 111°F (45°C), add the stabilizer and monostearate mixed with the sugar and then the inverted sugar.
9. Next, add the melted chocolate.
10. Stir constantly to prevent scorching. Bring the mixture to 185°F (85°C) for 2 minutes.
11. Cool the ice cream very rapidly to 39°F (4°C), cover to the surface with plastic wrap, and refrigerate at 42°F (6°C) to 35°F (2°C).
12. Let the ice cream mature/age for at least 4 hours or overnight under refrigeration.
13. Blend the ice cream mix with an immersion blender to ensure a smooth mix and distribution of ingredients, especially the monostearate and stabilizers.
14. Sanitize the ice cream machine mixing tank and all applicable components.
15. Pour the mix into the ice cream machine tank.
16. Churn until the ice cream reaches the desired consistency.
17. Remove from the ice cream machine, and transfer to a clean, frozen container.
18. Freeze right away at −31°F (−35°C).
19. Storage temperature before serving should be 0°F (−18°C) to −4°F (−20°C).
20. Serve at 5°F (−15°C) to 10°F (−12°C).

FORMULA

COFFEE ICE CREAM

A perfect treat after a meal, this coffee ice cream is made with fresh ground coffee and espresso powder for an extra kick.

Ingredients	Kilogram
Whole milk	1.060
Nonfat powdered milk	0.080
Sugar	0.230
Instant coffee	0.020
Ground coffee	0.040
35% cream	0.400
Egg yolks	0.060
Stabilizer	0.006
Monostearate	0.005
Glucose	0.060
Inverted sugar	0.040
Total	2.001

Process

1. Scale all the ingredients, and hold them in separate sanitized containers.
2. Mix the stabilizer and monostearate with 10 times their combined weight of sugar (from the sugar already in the formula) to dilute it for better incorporation.
3. In a stainless steel pan, heat the milk.
4. When the temperature reaches 39°F (4°C), add the powdered milk, and mix with a wire whip.
5. At 77°F (25°C), add all the sugar, the instant coffee, and the crushed coffee.
6. At 95°F (35°C), add the cream.
7. At 104°F (40°C), add the egg yolks, whipping continuously.
8. At 111°F (45°C), add the stabilizer and monostearate mixed with the sugar; then add the glucose and inverted sugar.
9. Stir constantly to prevent scorching. Bring the mixture to 185°F (85°C) for 2 minutes.
10. Strain through a fine mesh chinois to extract the ground coffee.

11. Cool the ice cream very rapidly to 39°F (4°C), cover to the surface with plastic wrap, and refrigerate at 42°F (6°C) to 35°F (2°C).
12. Let the ice cream mature/age for at least 4 hours or overnight under refrigeration.
13. Blend the ice cream mix with an immersion blender to ensure a smooth mix and distribution of ingredients, especially the monostearate.
14. Sanitize the ice cream machine mixing tank and all applicable components.
15. Pour the mix into the ice cream machine tank.
16. Churn until the ice cream reaches the desired consistency.
17. Remove from the ice cream machine, and transfer to a clean, frozen container.
18. Freeze right away at −31°F (−35°C).
19. Storage temperature before serving should be 0°F (−18°C) to −4°F (−20°C).
20. Serve at 5°F (−15°C) to 10°F (−12°C).

Coffee Ice Cream
Chocolate Ice Cream
Vanilla Ice Cream

FORMULA

GREEN TEA ICE CREAM

In Japan, this product is referred to as matcha ice cream. Matcha is a fine powdered green tea. It is popular in the United States, especially at small ice cream shops and Japanese restaurants.

Ingredients	Kilogram
Whole milk	1.130
Heavy cream	0.355
Green tea powder	0.045
Sugar	0.240
Nonfat powdered milk	0.110
Glucose powder	0.110
Stabilizer	0.010
Total	2.000

Process

1. Boil the milk, cream, and green tea powder. Add the sugar, powdered milk, glucose powder, and stabilizer mix.
2. Cook to 185°F (85°C).
3. Mix and cool to 39°F (4°C).
4. Let the ice cream mature/age for at least 4 hours or overnight in a covered container at 35°F (2°C).
5. Stir the ice cream mix.
6. Pour the mix into the ice cream machine tank.
7. Churn until the ice cream gets the desired consistency.
8. Remove from the ice cream machine, and transfer to a clean container.
9. Freeze right away at −31°F (−35°C).
10. Storage temperature before serving should be 0°F (−18°C) to −4°F (−20°C).
11. Serve at 5°F (−15°C) to 10°F (−12°C).

FORMULA

HAZELNUT PRALINE ICE CREAM

The rich flavors of hazelnut praline shine through in this ice cream, making it a perfect finish to any meal or a delightful afternoon treat.

Ingredients	Kilogram
Whole milk	1.185
Nonfat powdered milk	0.045
35% cream	0.280
Sugar	0.070
Stabilizer	0.005
Monostearate	0.005
Inverted sugar	0.080
Hazelnut praline 50% fruit	0.330
Total	2.000

Process

1. Scale all the ingredients, and hold them in separate sanitized containers.
2. Mix the stabilizer and monostearate with all of the sugar to dilute it for better incorporation.
3. In a stainless steel pan, heat the milk.
4. When the temperature reaches 39°F (4°C), add the powdered milk, and mix with a wire whip.
5. At 95°F (35°C), add the cream.
6. At 111°F (45°C), add the stabilizer mixed with sugar, the inverted sugar, and the hazelnut praline.
7. Stir constantly to prevent burning. Bring the mixture to 185°F (85°C) for 2 minutes.
8. Cool the ice cream very rapidly to 39°F (4°C), cover to the surface with plastic wrap, and refrigerate at 42°F (6°C) to 35°F (2°C).
9. Let the ice cream mature/age for at least 4 hours or overnight under refrigeration.
10. Blend the ice cream mix with an immersion blender to ensure a smooth mix and distribution of ingredients, especially the monostearate.

11. Sanitize the ice cream machine mixing tank and all applicable components.
12. Pour the mix into the ice cream machine tank.
13. Churn until the ice cream reaches the desired consistency.
14. Remove from the ice cream machine, and transfer to a clean, frozen container.
15. Freeze right away at −31°F (−35°C).
16. Storage temperature before serving should be 0°F (−18°C) to −4°F (−20°C).
17. Serve at 5°F (−15°C) to 10°F (−12°C).

FORMULA

RASPBERRY SORBET

The color and flavor of this sorbet is bright and fresh. It can be enjoyed at the end of a meal or as a treat on a hot summer afternoon.

Ingredients	Kilogram
Water	0.490
Sugar	0.270
Glucose powder	0.120
Stabilizer	0.010
Raspberry puree, 10% sugar	1.090
Lemon juice	0.020
Total	2.000

Process

1. Combine the sugar, glucose powder, and stabilizer.
2. Bring the water toward the boiling point.
3. When the water is at 113°F (45°C), add the sugar mixture.
4. Bring the liquid to a boil: 212°F (100°C).
5. Add the raspberry puree and lemon juice and mix.
6. Quickly cool to 39°F (4°C), and cover to the surface with plastic wrap.

7. Let the sorbet mature/age for at least 4 hours or overnight in a covered container at 35°F (2°C).
8. Blend the sorbet mix with an immersion blender.
9. Sanitize the ice cream machine mixing tank and all applicable components.
10. Pour the mix in the ice cream machine tank.
11. Churn until the sorbet gets the desired consistency.
12. Remove from the machine, and transfer to a clean, frozen container.
13. Freeze right away at −31°F (−35°C).
14. Storage temperature before serving should be 0°F (−18°C) to −4°F (−20°C).
15. Serve at 5°F (−15°C) to 10°F (−12°C).

FRUIT ICE CREAM CHART

Use this chart to make a variety of fruit ice creams.

Ice Creams Using Fruit Puree

Ingredients	Apricot	Banana	Strawberry	Raspberry	Lychee	Chestnut	Pabana	Passion	Coconut
Fruit puree	800 g	750 g	1,200 g	800 g	700 g	650 g	850 g	700 g	600 g
Whole milk	1,036 g	1,036 g	1,036 g	1,036 g	1,036 g	1,036 g	1,036 g	1,036 g	1,036 g
Nonfat powdered milk	140 g	130 g	240 g	150 g	110 g	120 g	140 g	150 g	120 g
Heavy cream 35% fat	360 g	600 g	700 g	360 g	330 g	550 g	350 g	450 g	140 g
Butter	90 g		100 g	110 g	70 g		110 g	80 g	
Sugar	300 g	270 g	400 g	320 g	290 g	250 g	240 g	310 g	160 g
Glucose powder	90 g	120 g	150 g	95 g	110 g		90 g	100 g	40 g
Inverted sugar						90 g			90 g
Cognac or Armagnac						20 g			
Stabilizer–emulsifier	10 g	8 g	20 g	10 g	10 g	8 g	10 g	10 g	7 g
Total weight	2,826 g	2,914 g	3,846 g	2,356 g	2,658 g	2,724 g	2,826 g	2,836 g	2,193 g

Process

1. Put the milk in a stainless steel pot, and bring toward a boil.
2. At 77°F (25°C), add the nonfat powdered milk, and whisk constantly.
3. At 86°F (30°C), add three-fourths of the sugar, which has been blended with the powdered glucose. Next add the inverted sugar.
4. Blend the remainder of the sugar with the stabilizer–emulsifier.
5. At 95°F (35°C), add the cream and the butter (if needed).
6. At 113°F (45°C), add the sugar, which has been mixed with the stabilizer–emulsifier.
7. Pasteurize at 185°F (85°C) in a machine or at 188°F (87°C) in a saucepan.
8. Let mature/age for 1 to 4 hours.
9. Combine the puree and the base, and put in the ice cream machine.
10. For recipes using alcohol, place the alcohol in the cold mix.

FRUIT SORBET CHART

Use this chart to make a variety of fruit sorbets. *Note:* All formulas are based on 1 kg of puree.

Sorbets Using Fruit Puree

Flavor	Fruit Puree Percentage	Sugar	Glucose Powder	Dextrose	Stabilizer	Water
Apricot	75%	130 g	50 g	25 g	4 g	110 g
Pineapple	75%	115 g	65 g	25 g	4 g	125 g
Banana	70%	100 g	70 g		4 g	255 g
Boysenberry	70%	160 g	70 g		4 g	200 g
Black currant	55%	230 g	70 g		5 g	430 g
Lemon	40%	510 g	150 g		8 g	830 g
Lime	40%	510 g	150 g		8 g	830 g
Coconut	60%	210 g	50 g	35 g	5 g	370 g
Fig	75%	85 g	55 g	25 g	4 g	170 g
Strawberry	75%	155 g	80 g		4 g	95 g
Wild strawberry	55%	215 g	110 g	35 g	5 g	455 g
Mara des bois strawberry	70%	210 g	85 g		4 g	130 g
Raspberry	70%	130 g	85 g	30 g	5 g	180 g
Fruits of the forest	70%	145 g	85 g	30 g	5 g	165 g
Guava	70%	200 g	55 g	25 g	4 g	145 g
Morello cherry	70%	115 g	85 g		5 g	225 g
Red currant	65%	200 g	90 g		5 g	240 g
Kiwi	70%	185 g	55 g	30 g	4 g	155 g
Lychee	70%	130 g	85 g		4 g	210 g
Mandarin	75%	135 g	55 g	25 g	4 g	115 g
Mango	70%	120 g	70 g	30 g	5 g	205 g
Melon	75%	145 g	55 g	25 g	4 g	105 g
Mirabelle	75%	70 g	50 g	25 g	4 g	180 g
Blackberry	70%	140 g	85 g		3 g	200 g
Blueberry	70%	170 g	70 g		5 g	180 g
Orange	70%	145 g	85 g		4 g	190 g
Blood orange	70%	170 g	85 g		5 g	165 g
Pabana	70%	90 g	85 g		4 g	250 g
Pink grapefruit	65%	190 g	90 g		4 g	250 g
Papaya	70%	165 g	70 g		3 g	190 g
Passion	45%	335 g	135 g		7 g	745 g
White peach	75%	150 g	50 g	25 g	4 g	105 g

(continues)

Sorbets Using Fruit Puree *(continued)*

Flavor	Fruit Puree Percentage	Sugar	Glucose Powder	Dextrose	Stabilizer	Water
Yellow peach	75%	140 g	50 g	25 g	4 g	110 g
Vine peach	70%	145 g	55 g	25 g	3 g	195 g
Comice pear	75%	100 g	55 g	25 g	4 g	150 g
Williams pear	75%	110 g	55 g	25 g	4 g	140 g
Green apple	70%	145 g	55 g	30 g	4 g	190 g
Pruneau	70%	10 g	55 g	25 g	4 g	330 g
Chestnut	70%	70 g	55 g		4 g	240 g

Process for Fruit Sorbets Using High Percentages of Fruit Purees

1. Weigh all the ingredients.
2. Mix the stabilizer with one-fourth of the total weight of sugar.
3. Mix the rest of the sugar with atomized glucose and dextrose.
4. Warm the water to 77°F (25°C).
5. At 86°F (30°C), add the mix sugar–atomized glucose and dextrose and mix.
6. At 113°F (45°C), add the sugar–stabilizer and mix.
7. Boil the mix.
8. Remove from the heat, and cover the surface with a plastic film. Cool the mix as quickly as possible (with ice).
9. Let mature for 4 hours minimum.
10. Mix the syrup with the purée thawed at 46°F (8°C).
11. Put in the ice cream machine.

FORMULA

RED WINE GRANITÉ

This style of slow stirred frozen dessert is perfect for anyone who wants to serve frozen desserts but lacks the required equipment. The more the granité is stirred, the smaller the ice crystals will be. For an even quicker preparation, freeze the mix proportioned by weight (2 or 2½ oz, etc.) and when needed, turn the frozen granité onto a cutting board and chop it up quickly.

Ingredients	Kilogram
Sugar	0.295
Orange zest	2 each
Orange juice	0.135
Lemon juice	0.051
Cinnamon stick	2 each
Cloves	4 each
Water	0.253
Red wine	1.266
Total	2.000

Process

1. Combine the sugar, orange zest, orange juice, lemon juice, cinnamon stick, and cloves in a pot.
2. Add the water and red wine, and heat over low heat to dissolve the sugar.
3. After the sugar is completely dissolved, bring it to a simmer and keep simmering for 3 minutes.
4. Strain the liquid, pour in a shallow metal container, and place in the freezer.
5. Allow to harden for at least 6 hours.
6. To serve, scrape the surface of the ice and place in glassware that has been kept in the freezer.

Red Wine Granité

FORMULA

MEYER LEMON BOMBE GLACÉE

The distinctive flavor of meyer lemon adds a floral note to this bombe.

Ingredients	Kilogram
Cream	1.067
Egg yolks	0.267
Sugar	0.267
Water	0.133
Meyer lemon juice	0.267
Lemon zest	1 each
Total	2.000

Process

1. Whip the cream to medium peaks. Reserve in the refrigerator.
2. Combine the egg yolks with a third of the sugar, and whip on medium speed of a stand mixer until triple in volume.
3. Combine the remaining sugar and water, and cook to 248°F (120°C).
4. Turn the mixer on high speed, and slowly pour the cooked sugar into the egg yolk mixture. Be careful to pour between the whip and the side of bowl. Continue whipping until cool.
5. Lighten the lemon juice with a small amount of the egg yolk mixture, and then add it to the remaining egg yolk mixture. Mix in the lemon zest.
6. Add the whipped cream into the egg yolk mixture in three stages.
7. Deposit in the desired molds, and freeze until ready to serve.

FORMULA

NOUGAT GLACÉE

The pleasing flavors of this traditional candy are delicious in a frozen dessert.

Ingredients	Kilogram
Sliced almond	0.235
Sugar	0.235
Egg whites	0.294
Sugar	0.118
Honey	0.176
Cream	0.588
Dried fruits and nuts*	0.353
Total	2.000

* Some examples are candied orange peel, candied lemon peel, currants, roasted whole almonds, and pistachios.

Process

1. Whip the cream to soft peaks. Reserve in the refrigerator.
2. Cook the first quantity of sugar until it begins to caramelize and add the sliced almonds, stirring until completely coated. Spread onto a silicone mat and let cool; then crush coarsely.
3. Combine the sugar and honey in a saucepan. Place the egg whites in a mixer to whip. When the honey mixture reaches 230°F (110°C), start whipping the whites on medium speed.
4. Cook the sugar to 255°F (124°C), remove from the heat, and slowly pour into the whipping egg whites; continue whipping the egg whites until cool.
5. Fold the nuts and fruits into the meringue and then fold in the cream.
6. Deposit in the desired molds and freeze until ready to serve.

FORMULA

MANDARIN ORANGE SOUFFLÉ GLACÉE

The intense flavor of mandarin orange in this soufflé glacée comes from a reduction of mandarin orange juice. Paired with the super-light texture due to the use of an Italian meringue as well as whipped cream, this is a very refreshing frozen dessert.

Ingredients	Kilogram
Mandarin orange juice	0.507
Sugar	0.320
Egg whites	0.159
Cream	1.014
Total	2.000

Process

1. Reduce the mandarin orange juice by half and cool completely.
2. Cook the sugar with a third of its weight in water.
3. When the sugar reaches 240°F (116°C), whip the egg whites on second speed.
4. When the sugar reaches 246° F (119°C) to 250°F (121°C), slowly pour it down the side of the mixing bowl into the whipping egg whites.
5. Whip until room temperature.
6. Lighten the mandarin reduction with a small amount of meringue to make a similar texture to the lightness of the meringue.
7. Combine into the remaining meringue, and then fold in the cream.
8. Deposit in the desired molds, and freeze until ready to serve.

CHAPTER SUMMARY

Ice cream, sorbet, and other frozen desserts are extremely popular and quite easy to produce. The variety of texture combinations and endless flavor possibilities can offer the pastry chef much creative inspiration. Whether still-frozen or churned, produced with an ice cream machine or manually, there is a process that works for every kitchen. However, the simplicity in creating a satisfying frozen dessert belies its physically complex structure and delicate balance of ingredients. Technical knowledge about structure and the role each ingredient plays in texture and flavor is essential for modifying and creating frozen dessert formulas as well as product storage.

KEY TERMS

- ❖ Bombe
- ❖ Brix
- ❖ Churned desserts
- ❖ Custard-style (French custard) ice cream
- ❖ Dasher
- ❖ Dextrose equivalent (DE)
- ❖ Emulsifier
- ❖ Freezing point
- ❖ Frozen mousse
- ❖ Frozen parfait
- ❖ Frozen soufflé
- ❖ Granita (granité)
- ❖ Heat shock
- ❖ High-temperature short-time (HTST)
- ❖ Hydrolysis
- ❖ Inclusions
- ❖ Low-temperature long-time (LTLT)
- ❖ Milk solids nonfat (MSNF)
- ❖ Overrun
- ❖ Pasteurization
- ❖ Philadelphia-style ice cream
- ❖ Refractometer
- ❖ Semifreddo
- ❖ Stabilizer
- ❖ Still-frozen desserts

REVIEW QUESTIONS

1. **What is the function of fat in ice cream?**
2. **What is the function of milk protein in ice cream derived from MSNF?**
3. **What is DE? Why is it important to consider in ice cream formulation?**
4. **Why is it necessary to use emulsifiers and stabilizers for ice cream?**
5. **What is hardening? Why is it important?**
6. **What is overrun? How does it differ for sorbet and ice cream?**

chapter
20

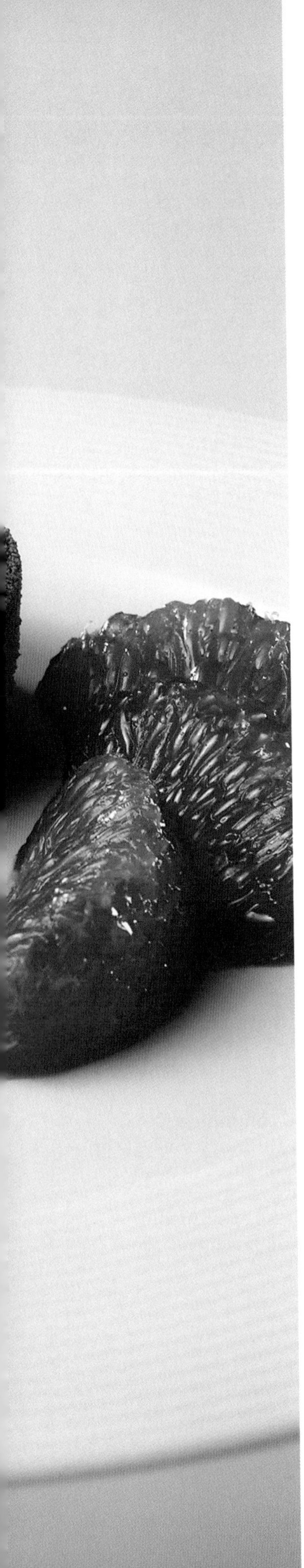

PLATED DESSERTS

OBJECTIVES

After reading this chapter, you should be able to

- discuss the factors that should be considered when creating a menu of plated desserts.
- describe the importance of representing seasons in a dessert menu.
- plan the production of a selection of plated desserts, using multiple components.
- prepare a selection of plated desserts that include multiple components, as described and presented in this chapter.

INTRODUCTION TO PLATED DESSERTS

Plated desserts, typically served in restaurants and hotels, contain several elements that contribute to the flavor and presentation of the dessert. Plated desserts are different from **à la carte** desserts, those of which are composed of a single item, such as a slice of apple pie. The level of craft involved with plated desserts has risen substantially in the past 15 to 20 years. The elements of a plated dessert, such as sauce, tuile, fruit, and chocolate or sugar decoration add to the flavor as well as visual composition. A well-balanced plated dessert will contain several different textures as well as multiple temperatures. Dessert is likely to be the last experience of the customers at a restaurant and will possibly leave the final impression of the dining experience on their mind, thus the importance of dessert cannot be overstated.

CATEGORIES OF PLATED DESSERTS

To compose plated desserts as well as assemble them, the pastry chef must understand a range of base ingredients as well as processes for making everything from cake bases to meringue to mousse to ice cream. The most common categories for plated desserts fall into the following categories: frozen, warm and hot, custard- and cream-based, fruit-based, chocolate-based, and cheese-based.

FROZEN DESSERTS

Frozen desserts, which are covered in detail in Chapter 19, can be served or manipulated into many plated desserts. Combining frozen desserts with different textures allows for endless variations and flavor combinations. For example, ice creams or sorbets can be rolled in crepes or layered with puff pastry or short dough for mille feuille. Shapes like balls, quenelles, and even squares can be scooped, molded, or cut from most frozen desserts. Examples of common frozen desserts include:

- *Coupe:* Ice cream layered with a fruit sauce and whipped cream served in a bowl
- *Bombe Glacée:* Molded and cut ice cream bases and other bases, such as dacquoise assembled using specialty molds in much the same way as mousse cakes
- *Vacherin:* Airy and crunchy baked meringue with ice cream
- *Profiteroles:* Pâte à choux puffs which have been split and filled with ice cream
- *Baked Alaska:* Layers of ice cream or ice cream and sorbet that have been sealed with thin layers of sponge cake, masked and decorated with Italian meringue, and baked in a high oven until the meringue is golden

WARM AND HOT DESSERTS

Desserts that are served warm or hot allow for a great deal of personal interpretation. Because their flavors have no rules, this category is made up of basic techniques. Classic hot desserts include the classic soufflé and table-side flambé like crepes Suzette and bananas Foster. Baked desserts include crumbles, cobblers, turnovers, and phyllo parcels, whereas fried desserts can include any kind of fritter.

CUSTARD- AND CREAM-BASED DESSERTS

Most custards served as desserts are variations of the basic crème Anglaise. They can be baked, cooked on the stovetop, poured into molds and set with gelatin, or whipped and served soft. Custard-based desserts can be served baked in specialized ramekins, molded, served in a tart shell, or served in a glass or bowl. Custard preparation and considerations are covered in Chapter 15.

Crème brûlée is one of the most traditional and commonly found custards. It is a combination of cream, egg yolks, and sugar that is baked in a shallow dish until lightly set and then given a thin dusting of sugar that is cooked until the sugar is caramelized. Crème caramel is an inverted version of crème brûlée that is made by placing caramel in the bottom of a baking dish before adding the custard. It is then baked in the oven.

FRUIT-BASED DESSERTS

Fruit generally finds its way onto a plated dessert as a secondary component or garnish, though it can also be a major part of the main component. However, when choosing fruit as a main component, many methods of preparation can be used. Ways to utilize fruit in a dessert include fresh, grilled, baked, dried, and poached.

- *Fresh fruit:* Fresh, ripe fruit can be cut, sliced, fanned, macerated, or molded in a gelée. It is commonly found layered with pastry bases to make up fresh napoleons and shortcakes. When cutting fruit, it is important to keep in mind that the shape and size of the final product will lend to the overall texture.
- *Grilled fruit:* Grilling fruit creates a smoky flavor and an original presentation. The fruit is most commonly sliced and skewered before grilling.
- *Baked fruit:* Fruit can be baked whole or used as a filling for pies, tarts, crumbles, and cobblers. It can also be baked in a custard or parchment parcel or with a batter, as is the case with upside-down cakes. Another example, tarte Tatin, is a caramelized fruit baked with puff pastry or pâte brisée.
- *Dried fruit:* Dried fruit can add flavor and texture in many different ways. It can be made into stuffing, candied for compote, baked into a batter, and folded into a cream or mousse.
- *Poached fruit:* Poaching is a moist heat cooking method that uses transfer heat from a liquid to cook the food submerged in it. This method is best used on fruit that is a little firm. It can be poached whole or in pieces, depending on the final presentation of the fruit. This method also includes compotes.

CHOCOLATE-BASED DESSERTS

Chocolate dessert is almost always the best seller on the menu and is also the most expensive to produce. It is used as a main dessert component in a number of ways, including:

- Mousse, which is commonly found in dessert cups, molded and formed into numerous shapes, or layered with cakes or biscuits
- Classic gateau and layered cakes
- Batter baked with a molten chocolate center
- Tarts filled with truffle-like filling and served warm and gooey or soft and dense
- Numerous chocolate-based custards, creams, and parfaits

CHEESE-BASED DESSERTS

Many dessert menus include a cheese plate or a dessert with some kind of cheese ingredient. For the latter, cream cheese, ricotta cheese, cottage cheese, curd cheese, fromage frais, mascarpone cheese, and goat cheese are all good choices. The most popular and well-known cheese dessert is cheesecake; however, others include filled crepes, phyllo dough parcels, puff pastry turnovers, soufflés, and ricotta or goat cheese fritters.

THE MENU

Before plated desserts can be created, a dessert menu must be developed. The dessert menu should complement the main course menu in style, theme, and presentation to ensure the experience of the customer is guided along a smooth course. Many factors should be considered to create a balanced dessert menu, including venue, season, style of presentation, current trends, ease of production, and execution of service.

Only after these factors have been realized can the main component of the dessert and supporting flavors be chosen and the presentation of the plate begin.

When developing a menu, the pastry chef should establish a range of items whose textures and temperatures are diverse, to ensure there is a choice for everyone. The addition of low or nonfat desserts is well appreciated from health-conscious diners. Dairy-free or wheat-free specialty desserts may also be appreciated and can create a positive professional challenge for the pastry chef. Moderate portions are equally important: Dessert should complement the main course, not be the main course. No more than seven or eight dessert items should be available to make selection easier. A well-planned menu can include frozen desserts (ice cream or sorbet selections), warm or hot desserts, chocolate desserts, fruit desserts, custard desserts, cheese plates, or cheese-based sweet desserts. Fine dining restaurants or hotels also often include composed plates of petits fours (Chapter 18). The pastry chef should view plated desserts as an outlet for limitless creativity, with the goal of supplying a source of enjoyment and excitement to the guests.

THE VENUE AND MARKET

The venue of the restaurant or hotel and the market it caters to has a direct effect on the types of desserts offered. Customers at fine dining restaurants have different expectations from customers at neighborhood diners. Guests at fine dining restaurants often expect more advanced and refined dessert service, and the skill involved with its preparation is notably more intricate and labor-intensive than plating simple desserts à la carte. To compose a dessert plate with several elements takes skill as well as time, both of which can only be carried out if the market has a desire for it and is willing to pay for it.

When taking into consideration the venue, volume and resources must be realized. A dessert menu for a restaurant that serves 100 tables a night will differ from dessert service for 1,000 at a hotel function. Both may require spectacular plated desserts; however, the approach should mirror the resources available to the pastry chef.

THE SEASON

The season plays an important role in determining the ingredients and types of desserts to highlight on the menu. Each season has signature holidays, traditions, flavor characteristics, and fruits that can merit special preparations. Seasonal dessert preparation allows the pastry chef to have a selection of menu items that rotate out and help to keep staff and guests engaged.

Seasonal nonfruit items include chocolate, nuts, and alcohols. Also, warmer months merit cooler desserts and cooler flavors (mint, lemon); cooler months require warmer dishes using warmer components and heartier components.

Seasonal fruit (and, if possible, identity-preserved fruit) is one of the pastry chef's most important ingredients. Fruit enables the pastry chef to highlight the best of local flavors when they are at their peak. Farmer's markets are ideal venues in which to buy fruit. Fruit from these markets is typically picked when ripe and is usually organic.

What follows is a list of the seasons and the fruit and other specialties commonly available during those months.

- *Winter:* Even though winter is one of the busiest seasons for pastry chefs, it offers the smallest variety of fruits. The selection includes many varieties of apples and pears, along with pomegranates, citrus fruits, and imported tropical fruits like pineapples, lychees, mangoes, papayas, and passion fruit. During winter, dried fruits and preserved fruits are commonly used, with nuts, spices, wine, and liquor typically added to provide variety and depth of flavor.
- *Spring:* The true fruits of spring (where applicable), include local strawberries, rhubarb, and, later in the season, cherries. Also fresh herbs like mint begin to bloom as do flowers, which may be used for infusions or garnishes. The general characteristics of spring fruits are refreshing flavors that are more tart than sweet.
- *Summer:* Summer is by far the most exciting season for pastry chefs. Available produce includes berries like strawberries, blackberries, boysenberries, blueberries, and raspberries; stone fruits like peaches, plums, nectarines, and apricots; and melons like honeydew, cantaloupe, and watermelon. Along with their blossoms, fresh herbs like mint, lemon verbena, thyme, and lavender are also available during these months. They can be added to desserts by infusion or used fresh.
- *Fall:* Cooler weather brings slightly heavier desserts that utilize apples, pears, persimmons, quince, squash, figs, kumquats, and grapes. Spices, wines, and liquors are common ingredients at this time of year, as are dried fruits and nuts, marking a return to winter.

DESSERT SERVICE

How each dessert will be served, who will prepare (plate) it, and who will serve it are additional considerations when writing a menu. The dessert menu can only be as good as the staff involved in the production and service of the dessert. If the restaurant lacks staff, the proper equipment, or time for the pastry chefs desired execution and plating, then the dessert menu should feature items that are easier to produce. For example, if a pastry chef wants to prepare chocolate or sugar decorations to garnish the plates, the kitchen cannot be too humid or too hot. Additionally, if the venue lacks the equipment, it could be difficult or impossible to create certain products. For example, to serve frozen desserts, there must be an ice cream machine as well as the proper amount of freezer space for storage of ice creams, sorbets, and granités.

As the menu is being written, the pastry chef should know how each dessert will be made, who will be responsible for making it (if they are not on site), how it will be "picked up" during service, and how these variables will affect the rest of the menu, staff, and consistency of the desserts.

CONSIDERATIONS FOR PLATED DESSERTS

After the market, style, and season are determined, the plate and its presentation can be created. The number of components per plated dessert ranges from two to five items, depending on the style. The main component is generally chosen first, and the rest of the plate is designed around it, including sauces and garnishes that add flavor, texture, shape, color, and style. Whichever elements are chosen, they should be complementary and balanced.

Flavor is largely considered more important than presentation. Achieving the best flavors in the plated dessert should be the ultimate goal of the pastry chef, and these flavors need to match the menu description of the dessert. When creating new plates, the components should be tasted alone and together to ensure overall quality and to determine the final balance of flavor. The sweeter dessert components can be enhanced by adding a little salt or an acidic ingredient. Tart or acidic elements can be enhanced by adding varying degrees of sweetness. Many flavors automatically complement each other and can be found regularly paired together; however, going beyond what we think goes well together to find new unexpected flavor combinations is exciting.

The texture of the components, individually and as a whole, is one of the most important considerations of a dessert plate. Mouthfeel can range from monotonous to surprising. Opposing qualities of texture complement each other in the mouth: creamy and crunchy, smooth and textured, moist and crisp, and firm and soft. A surprise element may be a crunchy component, such as crisp caramel bits here and there in a mousse. To add to the surprise, the caramel could be lightly salted. The ability of the pastry chef to combine texture and flavor is one of the most important achievements in the creation of desserts.

The shape of the plate, the material of the plate, the dessert components, and the garnishes all create an overall perception that adds to the quality of the dessert. Shape and size of the dessert components also create eye appeal. To achieve visual balance, round and circular items are often paired with linear or angular garnishes. Along with height and width, these different elements are used to create a pleasing effect.

In more intricate compositions, various temperatures are combined to entertain the palate. Warm or hot desserts are often served with a cold or frozen element, and cold desserts are complemented when served with warm ones. A scoop of ice cream or sorbet next to a warm tart will enhance the warmth of the main component. For desserts that are served hot, textures can be manipulated. For example, a sweet vanilla risotto with a (baked to order) ganache studded phyllo purse adds a surprise to guests as they puncture the purse and warm ganache flows out to add another dimension to the risotto.

The combination of colors provides one of the first impressions of the dessert plate. However, this does not mean that there should be one or more accent colors on the plate. Relying on the colors of the ingredients and components is the pastry chef's best way to keep the dessert in the realm of the natural while providing fresh colors. Introducing fruit, sauces, tuile, ice cream, chocolate, and sugar decorations all add pleasing colors.

THE MAIN COMPONENT

The main component of a dessert is the star of the plate and is usually why the guest will order the dessert. The flavor of the main component should have a theme based on highlighting the predominant ingredient or ingredients. These theme-based creations, based on flavor, can be elaborated from all of the preparations the pastry chef knows. The final product is only limited by imagination (and ingredients and equipment). Once the main component is chosen, it is elaborated with more components (sauce, compote, ice cream, tuile, décor, and more) to complement the creation. Sometimes there may be no true main component, just a dessert base that is elaborated with several small main components.

Plated desserts can be created from existing lines of product and used as dessert bases. Dessert bases are considered items that can be paired with other preparations and turned into plated desserts. These items may be served or prepared à la carte or combined with other components to compose a plated dessert. Even though the dessert base may commonly be prepared to serve multiple people, finer dessert preparations can be assembled individually. The following are common dessert bases that may be served alone or assembled using components from here and there.

- *Pies:* single crust, double crust, baked, unbaked
- *Tarts:* assorted creams, custards, fruit, chocolate, nuts
- *Cakes:* roulades, gateaux, classic layered, pain de genes, upside-down
- *Custards:* pot de crème, crème brûlée, bread pudding
- *Pâte à choux:* profiteroles, Paris-Brest, éclair, St. Honoré, fried for a fritter
- *Puff pastry:* mille feuille, turnovers, cookies (palmier)
- *Frozen desserts:* ice creams, sorbets, granité, frozen parfait
- *Yeasted dough:* baba, donut
- *Assorted dough:* phyllo (used for layering, rolling, making dessert containers and for crispy parcels and turnovers) and strudel dough

ADDITIONAL COMPONENTS FOR PLATED DESSERTS

The components for plated desserts can range from simple to complicated. No matter what style is used, the goal is to add flavor, texture, spatial dimension, and color to highlight the main component. Common components for garnishes and decorations include various sauces, foams, tuile, fruit, flowers and herbs, and decorative chocolate and sugar work.

Sauces

Sauces add texture, flavor, color, and design to desserts. The many varieties include cream-based (which may include chocolate and caramel), fruit-based, gelée, and syrup or oil. Textures can be smooth and creamy, heavy and rich, or light and delicate with colors that vary from vibrant to neutral. See Figure 20-1 for samples of each style of sauce.

Figure 20-1
Plate With Samples of Different Styles of Sauce: (top to bottom) Caramel, Fruit Coulis, Fruit Sauce, Oil

Cream-Based Sauces Cream-based sauces can be thickened with eggs, caramel, starch, and/or chocolate. Many dessert sauces are based on crème Anglaise, the "master sauce" of pastry that can be infused with herbs, spices, coffee, nut pastes, tea, or alcohol to add flavor, and is thick enough to be variegated with other sauces to create decorative designs on the plate. Other sauces that use cream as a main ingredient include chocolate and caramel sauces.

- *Chocolate sauce* can have different variations in color and consistency. Dark, milk, and white chocolate or cocoa powder can all be used to flavor cream-based sauces, including crème Anglaise.
- *Caramel sauce* is made by caramelizing sugar and then deglazing with cream, butter, or water. Cream and butter produce an opaque sauce, while water produces a transparent sauce. The more liquid added, the thinner the sauce will be.

Fruit Sauces and Fruit Coulis Fruit sauces and coulis are used to incorporate flavor and color into a plated dessert. The method of preparation in conjunction with the type of fruit used will largely determine the quality of the sauce. **Fruit sauces** are sauces made from fruit that still contains some of the pulp from the fruit. **Coulis** are sauces that are clearer and contain no pulp. Whenever fresh fruit is being used for sauce or coulis, it must be washed and hulled as needed.

These sauces can be approached using several forms of fruit: fresh fruit, frozen fruit, or commercially available frozen fruit puree. Furthermore, the fruit or puree may be cooked to thicken or reduce it, it may be thickened with neutral glaze (add 10 percent neutral glaze to fruit puree by weight), or it may be used solely in its puree form. The level of sweetness in fruit sauce needs to be balanced with the flavors of the fruit, and caution must be used to ensure the fruit flavor, and not the sugar, is the focal point of the flavor. Use caution when cooking fruit puree because overcooking may damage the flavors and colors. The technique of cooking fruit for a sauce should be reserved for fruit that should be cooked to create a sauce (such as frozen fruit) or to thicken fruit purees with starch or pectin to achieve a thicker consistency.

Fruits most commonly used for sauces and coulis include the following:

- *Berries:* Used either fresh, frozen, or pureed, berries can add exciting flavor and color to desserts. The sweetness must be controlled, and the flavor of the berry should be well balanced with the sweetening power. Puree may be combined with neutral glaze or cooked with sugar and thickened with starch or pectin to control the thickness of the sauce.
- *Tree fruits:* Characteristic of summer and fall, the tree fruits include stone fruits. Tree fruits benefit from cooking with sugar and spices. The puree can be very thick due to higher pulp levels. When stone fruits are cooked with the skins, the puree can develop a deep, rich color.
- *Tropical fruits:* Either fresh or pureed, tropical fruits make a flavorful, colorful sauce. If precooking is required, roasting before pureeing creates a very appealing quality to most tropical fruits, especially pineapple.

Gelée In its simplest form, a **gelée** is a sauce made from liquid, sugar, and gelatin. When made with the proper proportions, gelée-based sauces have a very pleasant texture, mouthfeel, and appearance. Any sweetened puree, juice, wine, or alcohol can be used, and the sauce should "set" overnight before using. When making a gelée using certain fresh fruit puree, the pastry chef should know whether or not it contains **proteolytic enzymes**. These enzymes break down gelatin molecules into shorter chains, thus preventing gels from forming. Examples of fruits with proteolytic enzymes are pineapples (**bromelain**), mangoes, papayas (**papain**), figs (**ficin**), and kiwi (**asctinidin**). To kill the proteolytic enzymes, the puree must be heated to denature the proteins. The texture of gelée should be like a thicker fruit coulis instead of the gelée that is used for glazing a Bavarian cake.

Syrups and Oils Syrups and oils add flavor and color to a plate through the process of **infusion**. Thickened sugar syrup creates a canvas for vanilla beans, citrus zests, spices, and blanched blended herbs, which are used to subtly enhance the flavor of a dessert. The inclusion of "specks" of specific flavors that are used and the natural shine of the syrup gives it a pleasant appearance. Sugar syrup is a little thinner than other sauces, but should puddle naturally.

Oils are often used on the savory side of the kitchen, but if used properly, they can also enhance the appearance and flavor of a plated dessert. Like sugar syrups, oils may be infused with herbs, fruit zest, or spices. A range of oils (hazelnut oil, walnut oil, almond oil, and olive oil are just a few) already have an inherent flavor that may be beneficial to a plated dessert.

Sauce as a Decorative Element When using sauce for a decorative element, one of the most important rules is to make sure that the sauces to be used have similar consistencies. This makes sauces easier to arrange and combine into the many patterns and styles that lend to the overall look of the plate. The ways to use sauce on a plate include drizzling, pooling, decorative blending, outlining, and using bottle designs.

- Drizzling uses a spoon to apply the sauce to a plate. It is common to overlap a couple of different sauces.
- Pooling or flooding refers to pooling sauce or allowing it to flood the plate before placing the dessert on top.
- Decorative blending is done by combining two or more sauces in various amounts and styles, and using the tip of a knife or a toothpick to create beautiful visual effects.
- Outlines are made using a paper cone filled with chocolate and creating a design that is later filled with a sauce. These designs can range from simple to complex.
- Squeeze bottles allow for more control than a spoon and are best used when a controlled line or design on a plate is desired. They are best used for dots and straight lines but can produce any number of creative effects on the plate.

Foams

Foams are commonly used in pastry work, especially with egg products and whipping cream. There is a trend to include extremely light and delicate foam as part of plated desserts. These foams are usually prepared from dairy; however, they may be flavored with fruit puree, nut paste, or alcohol. By definition, **foam** is a dispersion of gas throughout a continuous solid phase (which may be liquid). The gas (air) is produced when agitation of the continuous phase solution occurs and is stretched into thin sheets. The gas becomes interspersed between them.

Common examples of foam used outside of pastry include milk foams used for coffee drinks. Foams for plated desserts require a similar process, though the agitation is not through steam injection. The prepared liquid should remain refrigerated at all times to ensure easy foaming properties. To foam, a small hand blender is used, which should be done to order. The foam will rise to the surface of the liquid and can be skimmed off to garnish the plate. See the Strawberry Foam formula in the Strawberries and Cream plated dessert later in this chapter.

Tuile

Tuile, a decorative cookie made from a batter that can have a varied formulation, may include a thin batter based on egg whites, flour, and sugar, with corn syrup and nut or seed variations. The common theme to tuile batter is the creation of malleable, crisp, thin cookies. Tuile is easily colored, and piping can be applied with a paper cone to create an intricate design. Tuile batter can be prepared and stored in bulk in the refrigerator for several days. It is then easily spread into a template or portioned free form on parchment or a silpat and baked until golden, when it is formed into decorative shapes. Tuile, which absorb moisture easily, should be prepared in small batches. Their quality also needs to be checked regularly. Tuile can be stored in small containers to protect them from humidity. Larger production may merit storing tuile on a covered rack with humectants such as limestone or silica.

Fruit

Fruit can be used in many ways to add freshness and flavor to a dessert plate and to heighten the presentation. Because fruit, in one form or another, is available year round, it is easy to incorporate into desserts all year. A brief description of the main types of fruit used in plated desserts follows:

- *Fresh fruit:* Common types of fresh fruit include berries and tropical fruits. They can be "marinated" to create a softer, more tender fruit.
- *Dried fruit:* Commonly used in the fall or winter, dried fruits may be used to make compotes. Additionally, they may be rehydrated in water, tea, or alcohol to soften the texture and create a surprise flavor.
- *Cooked fruit:* The cooking process, which may include poaching, roasting, or grilling, can bring out unique flavors and textures from fresh and some dried fruit.
- *Candied fruit and zest:* Boiled in salted water and then a sugar syrup, candied fruit and zest can be used to highlight flavors on the plate and make attractive garnishes.
- *Frozen fruit:* Frozen fruit can be broken into small bits in a food processor, spread thin over a silpat, and dried in a low oven to make a fruit powder. The fruit powder can then be ground in a spice grinder for powdered fruit flavor to garnish plates with (or add to formulas such as meringue).

Flowers and Herbs

Flowers, especially the many edible varieties available today, add a simple, elegant element to desserts. The flavor of certain herbs, such as thyme or basil, may be well suited to complement the rest of the dessert. Both flowers and herbs may be used fresh, dried, or as an infusion. Flowers and herbs can be used whole, or the leaves may be cut into a chiffonade and sprinkled around the plate. It is extremely important to know that the herbs or flowers are in fact safe and to obtain them from a reputable source. See Figure 20-2 for a reference of edible fresh flowers and herbs and their uses.

Figure 20-2 Edible and Safe Fresh Flowers and Herbs

Species	Taste	Suggested Use
Anise hyssop	Licorice, sweet	Herb best used fresh or infused
Basil	Spicy and sweet; flower mild	Leaves fresh, infused; flower mild, décor
Bergamot	Tea-like, fragrant, aromatic	Flower more aromatic than leaves; infusion
Chervil	Citrus, tarragon, parsley-like	Herb infusions, flower garnish
Coriander	Spicy, floral, fragrant	Herb fresh, infused, decor; flower décor
Dandelion	Bitter	Cooked or infused
Dill	Spicy, fragrant, earthy	Fresh, cooked, infused; flower garnish
Elderberry	Mild floral	Garnish, accent
Fennel	Licorice, sweet; flower mild	Candied, cooked, infused, garnish
Lavender	Perfumy, floral	Infusion, fresh, garnish
Lemon balm	Sweet lemony	Herb, infusion
Lilac	Perfumy, floral, bitter	Garnish, candies well
Marjoram	Spicy, sweet	Herb, infusion, garnish
Oregano	Spicy, pungent	Herb, infusion, fresh, chopped
Mint	Spicy, sweet; varies by varietal	Herb, fresh; flowers garnish
Nasturtium	Piquant, spicy	Flower, garnish
Orange blossom	Perfumed, citrusy	Candies well, garnish
Plum blossom	Sweet, floral	Candies well, garnish
Rose	Perfumed, sweet—bitter	Garnish, candies well
Rosemary	Spicy, floral, delicate	Infusion, flower—don't cook as garnish only
Sage	Slightly musky, flowery	Infusion, candies well, flower garnish
Pineapple sage	Slight musk, pineapple hint	Infusion, flowers garnish
Summer savory	Sweet, mild, peppery	Herb infusions, flower garnish
Winter savory	Sweet, mild, spicy	Herb infusions, flower garnish
Geranium	Slightly sour, bitter	Garnish
Thyme	Sweet, floral, delicate	Herb infusion, flower garnish
Violet	Sweet, mild, leafy green	Garnish, candies well
Pansy	Sweet, mild, earthy	Garnish, candies well
Kaffir lime	Aromatic	Infusion
Lemon grass	Citrus, pungent	Infusion

Chocolate and Sugar Decorations

Chocolate and sugar decorations allow the pastry chef to show talent at two of the most difficult mediums to master within the pastry arts. Not only is skill required, but specific workroom conditions are essential as well. Restaurant pastry chefs often share small work areas with other kitchen staff and are often in close proximity to high levels of heat (ovens) and humidity (stocks, etc.), which both have detrimental effects on chocolate and sugar. Chocolate decorations are presented in Chapter 22, and sugar decorations are presented in Chapter 21.

MISE EN PLACE AND SERVICE

Mise en place is a French term used to describe the preparation of all necessary ingredients and equipment for cooking. With plated desserts, mise en place is a critical part of preparing for service. It requires a well-planned menu, constant readiness of prepared ingredients, and the ability to plate desserts as needed. The scope of mise en place will determine production and storage requirements for each of the plated dessert elements. For example, fresh tuile may need to be baked every day; however, the batter is good for several days under refrigeration. Other desserts can be made in bulk, stored in the freezer, and pulled as needed before service. Balancing the production of dessert components so that not everything has to be prepared every day is a requirement for the pastry chef. Even so, the quality of all components must be closely monitored for intended flavor, texture, color, and more.

The preparation and service of desserts, as previously described in this chapter, is a critical planning point where timing, attention to detail, and mise en place are essential. The preparation of foods to order, also know as **á la minute**, is the ideal approach to dessert service. The planning, preparation, and execution of dessert are all carried out for the customer to have the ultimate flavor and presentation. Advanced preparation of foods sacrifices the freshness and quality of any food, and the pastry chef should strive to have control over how dessert is served. This last-minute preparation, drawing on the entire mise en place, enables the textures to be appropriate, the flavors true, the colors preserved, and the temperatures as desired.

FORMULA

STRAWBERRIES AND CREAM

This almond cake, rich with toasted almonds, is served with ripe strawberries and a cloud of strawberry foam. A stroke of Marsala reduction enhances the character of the fruit with a tart kick, while clean ice milk unites all the flavors. A hint of pistachio on the plate accentuates the bright color palette of this springtime dessert.

Components

Toasted almond cake

Marsala reduction

Fresh strawberries

Ice milk

Strawberry foam

Blanched pistachio

Note

The following formulas will yield 15 servings of Strawberries and Cream plated dessert.

Toasted Almond Cake Formula

Ingredients	Baker's %	Kilogram	US decimal	Lb & Oz
Almonds, sliced	250.00	0.125	0.276	4 ⅜
Almond paste	625.00	0.313	0.691	11
Granulated sugar	75.00	0.038	0.083	1 ⅜
Salt	10.00	0.005	0.011	⅛
Eggs	575.00	0.288	0.635	10 ⅛
Pastry flour	50.00	0.025	0.055	⅞
Potato starch	50.00	0.025	0.055	⅞
Butter, melted	175.00	0.088	0.193	3 ⅛
Total	1810.00	0.907	2.000	2 0

Process, Toasted Almond Cake

1. Butter a 4½ inch (11 cm) × 9 inch (23 cm) metal loaf pan. Set aside.
2. Spread the sliced almonds into an even layer on a sheet pan and toast in an oven until lightly golden, stirring occasionally. Remove and cool.
3. Meanwhile, sift the pastry flour and potato starch together. Reserve.
4. In a stand mixer with the paddle attachment, mix the almond paste, sugar, salt, and about one-fourth of the eggs on low speed until an even consistency.

5. Increase the speed to medium, and add the rest of the eggs gradually, scraping down the bowl occasionally, allowing each addition to be incorporated fully into the almond paste base.
6. On low speed, incorporate the sifted flours, butter, and toasted almonds; mix until just combined.
7. Pour the batter into the prepared pan, and level with a spatula.
8. Bake at 325°F (163°C) until evenly browned and a cake tester inserted in the center comes out clean, approximately 30 minutes. Unmold immediately, and cool on a rack.

Marsala Reduction Ingredients

7 oz (200 g) Marsala wine

Process, Marsala Reduction

Reduce the wine to a syrupy consistency.

Ice Milk Formula

Ingredients	Baker's %	Kilogram	US decimal	Lb & Oz	
Whole milk	71.11	0.503	1.110	1	1 ¾
Heavy cream	28.89	0.204	0.451		7 ¼
Dry nonfat milk	6.67	0.047	0.104		1 ⅝
Sugar	12.44	0.088	0.194		3 ⅛
Dextrose	3.11	0.022	0.049		¾
Trimoline	5.33	0.038	0.083		1 ⅜
Ice cream stabilizer	0.62	0.004	0.010		⅛
Total	128.17	0.907	2.000	2	0

Process, Ice Milk

1. Mix the stabilizer with approximately one-fourth of the sugar and set aside.
2. Heat the milk, cream, dry milk, dextrose, Trimoline, and remaining sugar in a heavy saucepan over medium heat, stirring periodically to ensure that the bottom does not scorch.
3. When the mixture reaches 110°F (44°C), whisk in the reserved sugar–stabilizer mixture. Bring the mixture to 185°F (85°C), stirring constantly with a spatula.
4. Pour into a deep container, and mix with an immersion blender for 1 minute.
5. Cool in an ice bath, and then cover to the surface. Refrigerate, covered, for at least 12 hours (up to 24 hours).
6. Process in an ice cream machine according to the manufacturer's instructions. Reserve at 0°F (−18°C) for best conservation; for service hold at 5°F (−15°C) to 10°F (−12°C).

Strawberry Foam Formula

Ingredients	Baker's %	Kilogram	US decimal	Lb & Oz
Water	100.00	0.204	0.450	7 ¼
Sugar	20.00	0.041	0.090	1 ½
Lecithin powder	2.00	0.004	0.009	⅛
Strawberry puree	100.00	0.204	0.450	7 ¼
Total	222.00	0.454	1.000	1 0

Process, Strawberry Foam

1. Boil the water and sugar, and whisk in the lecithin.
2. Remove from the heat and cool to room temperature. Add the puree. Reserve refrigerated.

Assembly

1. Brush the Marsala reduction on the center of a plate.
2. Place three triangles of almond cake next to the brush stroke.
3. Slice the fresh strawberries into 1/16 inch (2 mm) thickness using a meat slicer.
4. Make a loose pile of the sliced strawberries behind the almond cake.
5. Line the chopped pistachios along with the brush stroke.
6. Cube the strawberries into ¼ inch (6 mm) cubes; place on the right side of the plate.
7. Mix the strawberry emulsion with an immersion blender, holding the container at an angle; blend until frothy. Spoon the foam in front of the almond cake, forming a nice dome. Make a quenelle of the ice milk and place on the cubed strawberries.

Strawberries and Cream

FORMULA

DONUTS

A sophisticated take on an American favorite, this dessert features two warm donuts dusted in sugar with a touch of spice, creating a stimulating contrast of soft and warm, sweet and spicy. The donuts nestle alongside a frozen parfait loaded with vanilla beans and a tiny shot of hot chocolate. The miniature drink contains a trio of luscious layers: rich ganache on the bottom, hot chocolate in the middle, and a feather-light milk foam topping. The three layers can be swirled together, adding an interactive element to this modern interpretation of comfort food at its most tempting.

Components

Spicy raised donuts

Chocolate donuts

Spiced sugar

Layered hot chocolate

Vanilla bean parfait

Dark chocolate plaques

Note

The following formulas will yield 15 servings of Donuts plated dessert.

Sponge for Spicy Raised Donuts Formula

Ingredients	Baker's %	Kilogram	US decimal	Lb & Oz
Bread flour	100.00	0.124	0.274	4 ⅜
Water	68.75	0.086	0.189	3
Yeast (instant)	3.75	0.005	0.010	⅛
Total	172.50	0.215	0.473	7 ⅝

Process, Sponge for Spicy Raised Donuts

1. Mix all the ingredients until well incorporated with a DDT of 70°F (21°C).
2. Allow to ferment 1 ½ hours at room temperature [65°F (18°C) to 70° F (21°C)], or until triple in size.

Final Dough for Spicy Raised Donuts Formula

Ingredients	Baker's %	Kilogram	US decimal	Lb & Oz
Bread flour	53.33	0.124	0.274	4 3/8
Pastry flour	46.67	0.109	0.240	3 7/8
Eggs	66.70	0.156	0.343	5 ½
Salt	2.70	0.006	0.014	¼
Sponge	92.00	0.215	0.473	7 5/8
Sugar	26.70	0.062	0.137	2 ¼
Butter	33.30	0.078	0.171	2 ¾
Total	321.40	0.750	1.653	1 10 ½

Process, Final Dough for Spicy Raised Donuts

Mix	Intensive mix
DDT	73°F (23°C) to 76°F (25°C)
First fermentation	20 minutes at 65°F (18°C) to 70°F (21°C), then 1 hour at 40°F (4°C)
Shaping	Roll to ¼ inch (6 mm) thickness. Cut out 2 inch (5 cm) rounds, ¾ inch (2 cm) holes.
Final proof	Proof on oiled plastic wrap for 15 minutes at 78°F (26°C) at 65% rh. Place in the refrigerator.

1. Mix the flours, eggs, salt, and sponge on first speed for 5 minutes.
2. Turn the mixer up to second speed, and begin to develop the gluten.
3. Gradually add the sugar after the dough pulls from the side of the bowl.
4. When the gluten is well developed, add the softened butter all at once.
5. Mix to incorporate.
6. Line the dough on a dusted sheet pan; cover with plastic wrap.
7. Proof for 20 minutes at room temperature [65°F (18°C) to 70°F (21°C)], then for 1 hour at 40°F (4°C) .
8. Roll out the dough to 3/8 inch (1 cm), cut out to 2 ½ inch (6 cm) diameter donuts.
9. Place on an oiled, plastic-lined sheet pan, and cover with a large plastic bag inflated with air to prevent skin from forming. Proof for 15 minutes, and then place in the refrigerator until needed.
10. For service, heat peanut oil to 365°F (185°C).
11. Fry the cold donuts in the oil for 1 minute on each side.
12. See the assembly instructions for plating direction.

Sponge for Chocolate Donuts Formula

Ingredients	Baker's %	Kilogram	US decimal	Lb & Oz
Bread flour	100.00	0.118	0.261	4 ⅛
Water	68.75	0.081	0.179	2 ⅞
Yeast (instant)	3.75	0.004	0.010	⅛
Total	172.50	0.204	0.450	7 ¼

Process, Sponge for Chocolate Donuts

1. Mix all the ingredients until well incorporated with a DDT of 70°F (21°C).
2. Allow to ferment 1 ½ hours at room temperature [65°F (18°C) to 70°F (21°C)], or until triple in size.

Final Dough for Chocolate Donuts Formula

Ingredients	Baker's %	Kilogram	US decimal	Lb & Oz
Sugar	26.70	0.059	0.131	2 ⅛
Atomized couverture	16.00	0.036	0.078	1 ¼
Bread flour	90.00	0.200	0.441	7
Pastry flour	10.00	0.022	0.049	¾
Eggs	66.70	0.148	0.326	5 ¼
Salt	2.70	0.006	0.013	¼
Yeast (instant)	0.30	0.001	0.001	0
Sponge	92.00	0.204	0.450	7 ¼
Butter	33.30	0.074	0.163	2 ⅝
Total	337.70	0.750	1.653	1 10 ½

Process, Final Dough for Chocolate Donuts

Mix	Intensive mix
DDT	73°F (23°C) to 76°F (25°C)
First fermentation	20 minutes at 65°F (18°C) to 70°F (21°C), then 1 hour at 40°F (4°C)
Shaping	Roll to ¼ inch (6 mm) thickness. Cut out 2 inch (5 cm) rounds, ¾ inch (2 cm) holes.
Final proof	Proof on oiled plastic wrap for 15 minutes at 78°F (26°C) at 65% rh. Place in the refrigerator.

1. Combine the sugar and atomized couverture.
2. Mix the flours, eggs, salt, yeast, and sponge on first speed for 5 minutes.
3. Turn the mixer up to second speed, and begin to develop the gluten.
4. Alternately add the sugar and the atomized couverture after the dough is pulled from the side of the bowl.
5. Once the gluten is well developed, add the softened butter all at once.
6. Mix to incorporate.
7. Line the dough on a dusted sheet pan, and cover with plastic wrap.

8. Proof for 20 minutes at room temperature [65°F (18°C) to 70°F (21°C)], and then for 1 hour at 40°F (4°C).
9. Roll out the dough to ⅜ inch (1 cm), cut out to 2 ½ inch (6 cm) diameter donuts.
10. Place on an oiled, plastic-lined sheet pan, and cover with a large plastic bag inflated with air to prevent skin from forming. Proof for 15 minutes, and then place in the refrigerator until needed.
11. For service, heat peanut oil to 365°F (185°C).
12. Fry the cold donuts in the oil for 1 minute on each side.
13. See the assembly instructions for plating direction.

Spiced Sugar Formula

Ingredients	Baker's %	Kilogram	US decimal	Lb & Oz
Coriander seeds	1.00	0.009	0.019	¼
Szechwan peppercorns	2.00	0.017	0.038	⅝
Star anise	1.50	0.013	0.029	½
Sugar	100.00	0.872	1.923	1 14 ¾
Cayenne	1.00	0.009	0.019	¼
Total	104.00	0.907	2.000	2 0

Process, Spiced Sugar

1. Toast the coriander, Szechwan peppercorns, and star anise on a sheet pan until very fragrant, about 15 minutes. Cool thoroughly.
2. Process as finely as possible in a spice or coffee grinder; sift through a fine tamis.
3. Combine the spices with the sugar and cayenne, mixing all together thoroughly. Reserve in a covered container at room temperature.

Layer 1 for Layered Hot Chocolate Formula

Ingredients	Baker's %	Kilogram	US decimal	Lb & Oz
Cream	150.00	0.218	0.480	7 ⅝
58% chocolate	75.00	0.109	0.240	3 ⅞
Unsweetened chocolate	25.00	0.036	0.080	1 ¼
Total	250.00	0.363	0.800	12 ¾

Process, Layer 1 for Layered Hot Chocolate

1. Bring the cream to a boil.
2. Pour over the chocolates, and let sit for 1 minute.
3. Stir the mixture with a whisk until forming a smooth emulsion.
4. Cover with plastic to the surface. Let cool. Keep at room temperature for service.

Layer 2 for Layered Hot Chocolate Formula

Ingredients	Baker's %	Kilogram	US decimal	Lb & Oz
Milk	100.00	0.544	1.200	1 3 ¼
Layer 1	25.00	0.136	0.300	4 ¾
Total	125.00	0.680	1.500	1 8

Process, Layer 2 for Layered Hot Chocolate

1. Bring the milk to a boil.
2. Add layer 1, and whisk to dissolve. Reserve.
3. See the assembly instructions for plating direction.

Vanilla Bean Parfait Formula

Ingredients	Baker's %	Kilogram	US decimal	Lb & Oz
Milk	100.00	0.239	0.526	8 ⅜
Vanilla bean	Each	1	1	1
Egg yolks	40.00	0.095	0.211	3 ⅜
Sugar	40.00	0.095	0.211	3 ⅜
Cream	200.00	0.477	1.053	1 ⅞
Total	380.00	0.907	2.000	2 0

Process, Vanilla Bean Parfait

1. Bring the milk and scraped vanilla beans to a boil, remove from the heat, cover with plastic film, and let infuse at room temperature for 10 minutes. Strain through chinois.
2. Combine the egg yolks and the sugar. Gradually mix in the warm milk while mixing.
3. Place the mixture back into the pot and cook until the mixture is thickened. Stir continuously with a heat-resistant rubber spatula to prevent curdling. Strain through chinois and cool in the refrigerator.
4. Whip the cream to soft-medium peaks. Fold it into the cooled mixture, and pour it into a 4 ½ inch (11 cm) × 9 inch (23 cm) cake pan lined with plastic wrap.
5. Freeze at least 6 hours until set. After it is set, remove from the pan by lifting the plastic. Cut quickly with a hot knife into 1 ¼ inch (3 cm) cubes, and return to the freezer in a tightly covered container.

Process, Dark Chocolate Plaques

1. Temper the dark couverture chocolate.
2. Spread the chocolate 1⁄32 inch (1 mm) thick on a sheet of acetate.
3. When the chocolate begins to set, use two oval cutters to make oval rings.
4. After the rings are cut, place a sheet of parchment paper over the chocolate décor, and weight down the chocolate décor to prevent warping.

Assembly

1. Deep fry two cold donuts (one plain, one chocolate) in 365°F (185°C) peanut oil, for about 1 minute on each side. Drain well.
2. Cut a slit on one donut, and link the two donuts together.
3. Dust in the spiced sugar, and then place on the center of a plate.
4. Rewarm layer 2 for the hot chocolate.
5. Carefully pour layer 1 into a glass to about one-fifth the way up from the bottom.
6. Gently pour warmed layer 2 on top, leaving about a ¼ inch (6 mm) gap from the top of the glass.
7. Steam some milk to create foam, as for cappuccino. Spoon the foam in the glass, forming a nice dome on top.
8. Place the glass on the right side of the donuts. Place an oval chocolate plaque on the left of the donuts. Place a cubed parfait on top of the chocolate, and cover with another oval chocolate plaque.

Donuts

FORMULA

ROASTED PEAR WITH CHAMOMILE

Chamomile and pear create a delightful harmony of flavors in this cool-weather dessert. The pears are roasted with chamomile until tender and served warm atop a buttery hazelnut financier. A pear chip and caramel décor add a light crunch and refined appearance, while lemony chamomile brings cohesiveness to the whole dessert. Pear sorbet at the finish serves as a refreshing counterpoint to the warmth and richness of the other elements.

Components

Chamomile jus
Pear sorbet
Pear chip
Sugar garnish
Chamomile sugar
Roasted pear with chamomile

Note

The following formulas will yield 10 servings of Roasted Pear With Chamomile plated dessert.

Chamomile Jus Formula

Ingredients	Baker's %	Kilogram	US decimal	Lb & Oz
Water	100.00	0.166	0.366	5 ⅞
Chamomile flowers, dried	3.00	0.005	0.011	⅛
Sugar	62.50	0.104	0.229	3 ⅝
Lemon juice	15.00	0.025	0.055	⅞
Total	180.50	0.299	0.660	10 ½

Process, Chamomile Jus

1. Bring the water to a boil, and pour over the chamomile in a heatsafe container. Cover and allow to steep for 5 minutes. Strain though a coffee filter, and discard the solids.
2. Place the infused liquid into a small saucepan; keep covered.
3. In a medium heavy-bottomed saucepan, caramelize the sugar over medium heat to a light brown, stirring constantly with a long-handled heat-resistant spatula.
4. Meanwhile, bring the infusion back to a boil.
5. Remove the caramelized sugar from the heat, and very carefully add a small amount of the hot chamomile infusion, stirring constantly. Place back over low heat and gradually add the rest of the liquid, stirring.
6. Remove from the heat, and stir in the lemon juice. Keep covered, and store at room temperature.

Pear Sorbet Formula

Ingredients	Baker's %	Kilogram	US decimal	Lb & Oz	
Sorbet stabilizer	0.40	0.003	0.006		⅛
Sugar	11.00	0.075	0.165		2 ⅝
Dextrose	2.50	0.017	0.037		⅝
Powdered glucose	5.50	0.037	0.082		1 ⅜
Water	14.00	0.095	0.210		3 ⅜
Pear puree	100.00	0.680	1.499	1	8
Total	133.40	0.907	2.000	2	0

Process, Pear Sorbet

1. Mix the stabilizer with approximately one-fourth of the sugar and set aside. Mix the rest of the sugar with the dextrose and powdered glucose.
2. Warm the water in a saucepan to 77°F (25°C).
3. At 86°F (30°C), add the sugar, dextrose, and atomized glucose mixture. Stir well.
4. At 113°F (45°C), add the sugar and stabilizer mixture. Stir well.
5. Bring the mixture to a boil.
6. Remove the pan from the stove, cover with plastic wrap, and cool as soon as possible on an ice bath.
7. Let the mixture mature at least 4 hours.
8. Combine the mixture and the puree thawed at 46°F (8°C).
9. Process in an ice cream machine according to the manufacturer's instructions. Reserve at 0°F (−18°C) for best conservation; for service hold at 5°F (−15°C) to 10°F (−12°C).

Hazelnut Financier Formula

Ingredients	Baker's %	Kilogram	US decimal	Lb & Oz	
Hazelnut flour	125.00	0.093	0.205		3 ¼
Butter	234.38	0.174	0.384		6 ⅛
Sugar	203.13	0.151	0.333		5 ⅜
Egg whites	250.00	0.186	0.410		6 ½
Pastry flour	100.00	0.074	0.164		2 ⅝
Baking powder	1.56	0.001	0.003		¼ tsp
Baking soda	1.56	0.001	0.003		¼ tsp
Total	915.63	0.680	1.500	1	8

Note
Use Demarle Fleximold, Savarin Shape, Ref. 2476.

Process, Hazelnut Financier

1. Toast the hazelnut flour in an oven until golden brown. Cool completely.
2. Brown the butter in a sauce pot. Cool completely.
3. Mix half of the sugar and egg whites; whisk to a very soft peak.

4. Fold the sifted dry ingredients, the other half of the sugar, and the hazelnut flour into the egg whites.
5. Incorporate the browned butter.
6. Pipe into the mold; bake at 350°F (176°C) in a convection oven for 15 to 20 minutes.

Pear Chips Ingredients

Pear, sliced to 1/16 inch (2 mm) thick
Simple syrup, 30° baumé

Process, Pear Chips

1. Dip the sliced pears in the syrup.
2. Place between two silpats, bake in a 225°F (107°C) oven until the pears are crisp.

Process, Sugar Garnish

1. Cook the granulated sugar to a caramelized stage.
2. Using a fork, spin sugar over a silpat to create a fine mesh of sugar.
3. Place the silpat in the oven at 250°F (122°C), and warm until the surface of the sugar is tacky.
4. While the sugar is still soft, cut out with a 4 inch (105 mm) round cutter.
5. Place the rounds on a silpat, and place it in the oven to soften again.
6. Form the rounds into a cone shape, and let cool to set.

Chamomile Sugar Formula

Ingredients	Baker's %	Kilogram	US decimal	Lb & Oz
Sugar	100.00	0.072	0.159	2 ½
Chamomile flowers, dried	11.00	0.008	0.017	¼
Total	111.00	0.080	0.176	2 ⅞

Process, Chamomile Sugar

1. In a food processor, blend the sugar and chamomile together thoroughly. Pass through a fine-mesh sieve, discarding any chamomile that will not pass through.
2. Reserve the sugar in a tightly sealed container at room temperature in a cool, dry place.

Roasted Pear With Chamomile Ingredients

5 firm pears, peeled, halved, cored
3 oz (80 g) chamomile sugar
1 ¼ oz (35 g) butter

Process, Roasted Pear With Chamomile

1. Toss the halved pears with the chamomile sugar.
2. Heat the butter in a sauté pan; sear the cut-side of the pears until golden brown.

3. Transfer the pears onto a parchment-lined sheet pan, and continue baking at 350°F (177°C) for 20 to 25 minutes or until the pears are softened.

Additional Components

Fresh chamomile blossoms (if available)

Assembly

1. Place a financier off-center on a plate.
2. Place half a roasted pear on top.
3. Carefully place a sugar garnish on the pear to support a pear chip at an angle.
4. Draw one streak of chamomile jus around the financier toward the front of the plate.
5. Slice and fan out a piece of pear; place a quenelle of pear sorbet on top.
6. Place one or two fresh chamomile blossoms on the sorbet.

Roasted Pear With Chamomile

FORMULA

CHOCOLATE GRAPEFRUIT TART

Grapefruit-infused dark chocolate ganache lines a buttery and tender sablé breton with cocoa nibs. The tart is paired with juicy, refreshing grapefruit segments marinated in a slightly bitter Campari caramel sauce. A touch of grapefruit curd adds to the creaminess of the ganache and the crisp flavor of the tender and crunchy cocoa nib sablé breton. Grapefruit tuiles contribute height and a lovely pink shimmer to this unusual and arresting dessert.

Components

Grapefruit-infused ganache
Cocoa nib sablé breton
Grapefruit curd
Fresh grapefruit
Campari caramel
Grapefruit tuiles
Dark chocolate spray

Note

The following formulas will yield 10 servings of Chocolate Grapefruit Tart plated dessert.

Grapefruit-Infused Ganache Formula

Ingredients	Baker's %	Kilogram	US decimal	Lb & Oz	
64% couverture	100.00	0.319	0.703		11 ¼
Cream	100.00	0.319	0.703		11 ¼
Glucose	25.00	0.080	0.176		2 ¾
Salt	1.00	0.003	0.007		⅛
Butter	25.00	0.080	0.176		2 ¾
Grapefruit zest	1.00	0.003	0.007		0
Total	252.00	0.804	1.764	1	12 ¼

Process, Grapefruit-Infused Ganache

1. Pulse the chocolate several times in a food processor until the pieces are no larger than a pea.
2. Bring the cream, glucose, salt, and grapefruit zest to a boil, stirring so the glucose does not stick to the bottom of the pan. Remove from the heat, cover with plastic wrap, and allow to infuse for approximately 15 minutes.
3. Strain the infused cream through a chinois, discarding the zest. Reheat the cream just to a simmer, and pour over the chocolate in the bowl of the food processor.

4. Process the chocolate and cream mixture until very smooth, stopping to scrape the bowl a few times. Add the butter at 95°F (35°C), and blend until incorporated.
5. On a very flat sheet pan lined with acetate or alternatively plastic wrap, pour the ganache into 3 inch (75 mm) × ⅜ inch (10 mm) ring molds that are lined with acetate on the sides.
6. Cover thoroughly with plastic, without touching the ganache, and refrigerate for at least 2 hours.
7. Remove from the refrigerator, and with a hot small spoon, scoop out a small impression from the top of each ganache round.
8. Cover and refrigerate until hard, remove from the rings, and peel off the acetate. Place in the freezer for at least 2 hours.
9. Spray the ganache with the dark chocolate spray. Wrap tightly with plastic wrap without touching the ganache, then refrigerate. Allow to come to room temperature before serving.

Cocoa Nib Sablé Breton Formula

Ingredients	Baker's %	Kilogram	US decimal	Lb & Oz
Butter	88.00	0.121	0.266	4 ¼
Sugar	70.00	0.096	0.212	3 ⅜
Salt	0.80	0.001	0.002	0
Egg yolks	34.00	0.047	0.103	1 ⅝
Pastry flour	100.00	0.137	0.303	4 ⅞
Baking powder	4.80	0.007	0.015	¼
Cocoa nibs	30.00	0.041	0.091	1 ½
Total	327.60	0.450	0.992	15 ⅞

Process, Cocoa Nib Sablé Breton

1. In the bowl of a food processor, process the butter, sugar, and salt until creamy. Scrape down the sides of the bowl.
2. Add the egg yolks and approximately one-third of the flour. Process just until smooth, several seconds. Scrape the bowl, and add the rest of the flour, baking powder, and cocoa nibs. Process just until the mixture is homogenous, several seconds.
3. Pat the dough into a rectangle approximately ½ inch (12 mm) thick on plastic wrap; wrap and refrigerate at least 4 hours (preferably overnight).
4. Roll the dough to approximately ⅛ inch (4 mm) between two silpats. Bake at 325°F (203°C) with the silpats on contact, for 10 minutes or until the edge of the dough starts to brown.
5. Cut out with 3 inch (75 mm) round cutters. Finish baking in an oven until the cookies are golden brown.
6. Allow to cool, and reserve in a tightly covered container in a dry place at room temperature.

Grapefruit Curd Formula

Ingredients	Baker's %	Kilogram	US decimal	Lb & Oz
Sugar	119.44	0.108	0.239	3 ⅞
Eggs	55.55	0.050	0.111	1 ¾
Egg yolks	33.33	0.030	0.067	1 ⅛
White grapefruit juice	83.33	0.076	0.167	2 ⅝
Lemon juice	16.67	0.015	0.033	½
Grapefruit zest	3.00	0.003	0.006	⅛
Butter	44.44	0.040	0.089	1 ⅜
Total	352.76	0.320	0.706	11 ¼

Process, Grapefruit Curd

1. Combine the sugar, eggs, egg yolks, grapefruit juice, lemon juice, and grapefruit zest in a stainless steel bowl and place over a double boiler. Stir occasionally.
2. When the mixture is done, it will be thick like ketchup.
3. Remove the mixture from the heat, strain into a clean container, and add the butter at 90°F (32°C) to 95°F (35°C) with an immersion blender.
4. Cover to the surface, and reserve in the refrigerator.

Campari Caramel and Marinated Grapefruit Formula

Ingredients	Baker's %	Kilogram	US decimal	Lb & Oz
Water	40.00	0.227	0.500	8
Sugar	100.00	0.567	1.250	1 4
Vanilla bean	Each	½	½	½
Campari	20.00	0.113	0.250	4
White grapefruit	Each	2	2	2
Total	160.00	0.907	2.000	2 0

Process, Campari Caramel and Marinated Grapefruit

1. Prepare the grapefruit by cutting off the peel and then cutting out the segments. Reserve.
2. Place the water into a small covered saucepan over low heat.
3. In a large heavy-bottomed saucepan, caramelize the sugar over medium heat, stirring constantly with a heat-resistant spatula until light golden.
4. Remove from the heat, and very carefully pour in a small amount of the hot water, stirring quickly.
5. Add the vanilla, place back over medium-low heat, and gradually stir in the rest of the water. Bring just to a simmer, remove from the heat, and add the Campari.
6. Pour over the grapefruit segments in a heatsafe container, cover, and refrigerate for 24 hours. Remove the grapefruit, and reserve under refrigeration.
7. Reduce the liquid over medium heat until syrupy; remove and discard the vanilla pod. Reserve covered at room temperature.

Grapefruit Tuiles Ingredients

White grapefruit

Simple syrup, 30° baumé

Process, Grapefruit Tuiles

1. With a meat slicer, slice the grapefruit as thin as possible, approximately 1⁄16 inch (2 mm).
2. Dip in the simple syrup, shake off the excess, and lay on sheet pans lined with silpats. Dry at 225°F (107°C) until dry but still pliable.
3. While warm, remove gently from the silpats, and manipulate into abstract crumpled shapes.
4. Reserve in a tightly sealed container in a dry place at room temperature until use.

Assembly

1. Pipe a small amount of grapefruit curd into the cavity on the surface of the ganache.
2. Place the ganache on a disc of sablé breton.
3. Place the tart off-center on the plate.
4. To the side, arrange several marinated grapefruit segments into a fan shape.
5. Arrange two grapefruit tuiles beside.
6. Spoon sauce on the plate around the marinated grapefruit.

Chocolate Grapefruit Tart

FORMULA

PANNA COTTA

This delicate dessert owes its unique flavor to chèvre, which brings a slightly tangy twist to the Italian classic. Veiling the panna cotta are translucent slices of vanilla-infused Granny Smith apples, which are then crowned with a tangle of crisp nutmeg tuiles. This panna cotta's intricate flavors are complemented by the sweetness and distinctive texture of an agar-based port sauce, along with a surprising herbal accent from a bright green thyme gelée.

Components

Chèvre panna cotta

Tawny port sauce

Vanilla Granny Smith apples

Nutmeg tuiles

Thyme gelée

Note

The following formulas will yield 10 servings of Panna Cotta plated dessert.

Chevre Panna Cotta Formula

Ingredients	Baker's %	Kilogram	US decimal	Lb & Oz
Milk	100.00	0.463	1.020	1 ⅜
Chèvre (fresh)	66.67	0.309	0.680	10 ⅞
Sugar	15.00	0.069	0.153	2 ½
Gelatin	2.00	0.009	0.020	⅜
Total	183.67	0.850	1.874	1 14

Process, Chevre Panna Cotta

1. Warm approximately one-third of the milk with the chèvre and sugar over low heat, using a spatula to break up the cheese. Stir until melted, and remove from the heat.
2. Soften the gelatin in cold water until completely bloomed.
3. Whisk the gelatin into the hot chèvre mixture in a metal bowl; whisk in the remaining milk.
4. Immerse the bottom of the bowl in an ice bath and stir constantly until cool to the touch and slightly thickened.
5. Pour 3 oz (85 g) of the panna cotta mixture into the timbale molds. Allow to set in the refrigerator, covered, for at least 4 hours.

Tawny Port Sauce Formula

Ingredients	Baker's %	Kilogram	US decimal	Lb & Oz
Tawny port	100.00	0.299	0.659	10 ½
Powdered agar	1.00	0.003	0.007	⅛
Total	101.00	0.302	0.666	10 ⅝

Process, Tawny Port Sauce

1. Reduce the port by half over low heat.
2. When it is reduced, bring to a boil and gradually whisk in the powdered agar.
3. Pour into a shallow heatsafe container and leave at room temperature until firmly set, about 1 to 2 hours.
4. Process in a food processor until smooth, scraping down the sides with a spatula as needed. Reserve under refrigeration in a covered container.

Vanilla Granny Smith Apples Formula

Ingredients	Baker's %	Kilogram	US decimal	Lb & Oz
Simple syrup	100.00	0.907	2.000	2 0
Vanilla bean	Each	1	1	1
Granny Smith apples	Each	2	2	2
Total	100.00	0.907	2.000	2 0

Process, Vanilla Granny Smith Apples

1. Bring the simple syrup and vanilla bean to a simmer. Lower the heat, and keep the syrup hot.
2. Peel the apples, and slice them as thinly as possible. Immerse the apple slices immediately in the hot syrup.
3. Poach the apples over low heat until the apples are cooked through and semitranslucent, about 5 minutes. Store in the syrup under refrigeration.
4. After the apples have cooled, remove any visible apple cores from the slices with a small round cutter.

Nutmeg Tuiles Formula

Ingredients	Baker's %	Kilogram	US decimal	Lb & Oz
Butter	133.33	0.239	0.526	8 ⅜
Powdered sugar	133.33	0.239	0.526	8 ⅜
Egg whites	140.00	0.251	0.553	8 ⅞
Pastry flour	100.00	0.179	0.395	6 ⅜
Nutmeg, grated	2.00	0.004	0.008	⅛
Coffee extract	3.00	0.005	0.012	¼
Total	506.66	0.907	2.000	2 0

Process, Nutmeg Tuiles

1. Sift the sugar, and then cream with softened butter until light in color.
2. Gradually add the egg whites; mix to incorporation.
3. Sift the flour and nutmeg together. Add to the butter mixture along with the coffee extract; mix to achieve a smooth paste. Cover and let rest in the refrigerator for at least 1 hour.
4. Pipe onto silpats in thin, straight lines approximately 10 inches (25 cm) long.
5. Bake at 325°F (163°C) until just golden brown on the edge, several minutes. Working quickly, use an offset spatula to loosen the tuiles and, with gloved hands, twist and fold to form abstract "nests."
6. When fully cooled, reserve in a sealed container at room temperature until use.

Thyme Gelée Formula

Ingredients	Baker's %	Kilogram	US decimal	Lb & Oz
Parsley or spinach	1.67	0.005	0.012	¼
Water #1	16.67	0.055	0.121	1 ⅞
Fresh thyme	6.67	0.022	0.048	¾
Water #2	100.00	0.329	0.725	11 ⅝
Sugar	10.00	0.033	0.072	1 ⅛
Gelatin	3.00	0.010	0.022	⅜
Total	138.00	0.454	1.000	1 0

Process, Thyme Gelée

1. Blanch the parsley or spinach in the first boiling water until bright green, for approximately 5 seconds.
2. Drain and plunge immediately in ice water. Drain again, and process in a blender with the first water until smooth. Strain through a coffee filter, discarding solids. Reserve the liquid.
3. Bring the thyme, second water, and sugar to a boil. Remove from the heat, cover the pan with plastic wrap, and let infuse for 20 minutes. Strain, discarding solids. Allow to cool to room temperature.
4. Bloom the gelatin in cold water. Melt in the microwave with a small amount of the thyme infusion. Stir the mixture back into the remaining infusion. Stir in the reserved parsley or spinach infusion.
5. Pour it into a flat shallow pan, cover, and refrigerate until fully set, at least 4 hours.

Assembly

1. On a plate, draw two curved streaks of port sauce using a spoon.
2. Gently ease away the panna cotta from the mold and dip the mold into hot water for a couple of seconds. If it will not release, hold it upside-down until the natural vacuum breaks and the panna cotta releases. Place it on the plate.
3. Loosely wrap the panna cotta with 3 or 4 slices of vanilla apple.
4. Cut out a ¾ inch (2 cm) circle of thyme gelée, and place it next to the panna cotta.
5. Place a pile of tuiles on top of the panna cotta.

Panna Cotta

FORMULA

RED VELVET OPERA CAKE

An ode to France's famous opera cake, this classic specialty of the American South gets a stylish makeover here. Nutty pecan dacquoise, subtly tangy molasses ganache, and rich milk chocolate buttercream are layered with the strikingly colored flourless chocolate biscuit from which the finished cake takes its name. Further reinforcing the flavor profile, an airy bourbon sabayon incorporates the gentle sourness of crème fraîche—a nod to the buttermilk that would normally be present in a traditional Southern version of this cake. Pecan croquant adds a subtly crunchy visual dimension to the elegant appearance of the unforgettable Red Velvet Opera.

Components

Flourless chocolate cake

Pecan dacquoise

Molasses ganache

Milk chocolate buttercream

Bourbon sabayon

Pecan croquant

Candied pecan

Dark chocolate décor

Note

These formulas will make a half sheet of Red Velvet Opera, which yields about 30 servings. For establishments that do not require a large production of this dessert, the cake will keep well after it is assembled and then frozen.

Flourless Chocolate Cake Formula

Ingredients	Baker's %	Kilogram	US decimal	Lb & Oz
70% couverture	100.00	0.375	0.826	13 ¼
Butter, melted	24.00	0.090	0.198	3 ⅛
Egg yolks	20.00	0.075	0.165	2 ⅝
Egg whites	200.00	0.750	1.653	1 10 ½
Sugar	34.00	0.127	0.281	4 ½
Red food coloring	SQ			
Total	378.00	1.417	3.124	3 2

Yield: 1 full-sheet cake and 1 half-sheet cake

Process, Flourless Chocolate Cake

1. Melt the chocolate in a microwave. Combine with the butter and egg yolks.
2. Whip the egg whites and the sugar to a stiff meringue.
3. Add the coloring to the whipping egg whites to make a very bright red.
4. Fold the chocolate mixture into the meringue. Deposit the batter on a parchment-lined sheet pan: 2 lb 1 ¼ oz (945 g) for a full sheet pan, and 1 lb ⅔ oz (473 g) for a half-sheet pan. Spread evenly.
5. Bake at 340°F (171°C) in a convection oven for 10 minutes. Once cooled, cover and store in the freezer until needed.

Pecan Dacquoise Formula

Ingredients	Baker's %	Kilogram	US decimal	Lb & Oz	
Pecans, toasted	80.00	0.199	0.438		7
Powdered sugar	80.00	0.199	0.438		7
Egg whites	100.00	0.249	0.548		8 ¾
Sugar	32.00	0.080	0.175		2 ¾
Cream of tartar	1.60	0.004	0.009		⅛
Total	293.60	0.730	1.609	1	9 ¾

Yield: 1 half-sheet

Process, Pecan Dacquoise

1. Process the toasted pecans and powdered sugar in a food processor. Sift the mixture.
2. Whip the sugar and egg whites with the cream of tartar to a stiff peak.
3. Fold the egg foam and pecan–sugar mixture together, and spread the batter on a parchment-lined half-sheet pan.
4. Bake at 350°F (177°C) in a convection oven with the vent closed for 5 minutes. Open the vent, and continue baking for another 25 minutes.

Molasses Ganache Formula

Ingredients	Baker's %	Kilogram	US decimal	Lb & Oz	
64% couverture	100.00	0.137	0.302		4 ⅞
Milk	100.00	0.137	0.302		4 ⅞
Molasses	125.00	0.171	0.378		6
Butter	40.00	0.055	0.121		1 ⅞
Total	365.00	0.500	1.102	1	1 ⅝

Process, Molasses Ganache

1. Bring the milk to a boil. Pour it over the chocolate, and form an emulsion.
2. Add the molasses, stirring to incorporate. Next, add the soft butter when the mixture reaches 95°F (35°C).
3. Cover to the surface with plastic wrap and reserve until needed.

Italian Meringue for Milk Chocolate Buttercream Formula

Ingredients	Baker's %	Kilogram	US decimal	Lb & Oz
Sugar	200.00	0.067	0.148	2 ⅜
Water	60.00	0.020	0.044	¾
Egg whites	100.00	0.033	0.074	1 ⅛
Total	360.00	0.120	0.266	4 ¼

Process, Italian Meringue for Milk Chocolate Buttercream

1. Heat the water and sugar until it reaches the boiling point.
2. Wash down the sides of the pan with water.
3. When the sugar reaches 241°F (116°C), start whipping the egg whites on medium speed.
4. When the sugar reaches soft ball stage 246°F (119°C) to 250°F (121°C), slowly pour it into the whipping egg whites.
5. Whip until 104°F (40°C). See the final buttercream formula for finishing instructions.

Final Formula

Ingredients	Baker's %	Kilogram	US decimal	Lb & Oz
Milk	40.00	0.161	0.354	5 ⅝
Egg yolks	24.00	0.096	0.213	3 ⅜
Sugar	5.00	0.020	0.044	¾
Butter	100.00	0.402	0.886	14 ⅛
Milk chocolate	50.00	0.201	0.443	7 ⅛
Italian meringue	30.00	0.121	0.266	4 ¼
Total	249.00	1.001	2.205	2 3 ¼

Process, Final

1. Bring the milk to a boil. Meanwhile, whisk the egg yolks and sugar together.
2. Temper the hot milk into the egg yolk mixture. Place the mixture back in the pot; cook until the mixture reaches 180°F (82°C).
3. Place the cooked mixture into a mixing bowl. Whip on medium speed until cooled.
4. Add the soft butter, and mix until fully incorporated. Then add the melted milk chocolate, and mix until fully incorporated.
5. Fold in the Italian meringue.

Assembly, Red Velvet Opera

1. Place the dacquoise on a parchment-lined sheet pan.
2. Spread 12 ¼ oz (350 g) of buttercream evenly over the dacquoise.
3. Place a half-sheet of flourless chocolate cake over the buttercream.
4. Spread 17 ½ oz (500 g) of molasses ganache over the cake, and then place a half-sheet of cake over the ganache.

5. Spread 12 ½ oz (350 g) of buttercream, and then place the last sheet of cake over the buttercream.
6. Next, spread 10 ½ oz (300 g) of buttercream over the top cake layer and smooth evenly. Then decorate the top layer with an icing comb, creating grooved lines that run the length of the cake.
7. Place the cake in the freezer for at least 3 hours.

Bourbon Sabayon Formula

Ingredients	Baker's %	Kilogram	US decimal	Lb & Oz	
Egg yolks	35.56	0.198	0.436		7
Sugar	26.67	0.148	0.327		5 ¼
Bourbon	17.78	0.099	0.218		3 ½
Crème fraîche	100.00	0.556	1.225	1	3 ⅝
Total	180.01	1.001	2.205	2	3 ¼

Process, Bourbon Sabayon

1. Prepare a double boiler.
2. Combine the egg yolks, sugar, and bourbon, and cook over the double boiler while whisking until the mixture has a pale yellow color and is fully thickened.
3. Fold in the crème fraîche. Reserve in the refrigerator until needed.

Pecan Croquant Formula

Ingredients	Baker's %	Kilogram	US decimal	Lb & Oz
Pecan flour	8.00	0.018	0.039	⅝
Pastry fondant	60.00	0.133	0.294	4 ¾
Glucose	40.00	0.089	0.196	3 ⅛
Total	108.00	0.240	0.529	8 ½

Process, Pecan Croquant

1. Toast the pecan flour. Cool completely and reserve.
2. Cook the fondant and glucose to a desired level of caramel. Add the pecan flour; stir thoroughly.
3. Pour over a silicone mat, and make it leveled.
4. Once cooled, break the caramel into ¼ oz (8 g) pieces. Place the pieces between two silicone mats on a flat sheet pan, with a 4 inch (10 cm) gap between each piece.
5. Warm it up in the oven at 350°F (177°C) until softened. Using a rolling pin, roll out the caramel very thin.
6. Place the sheet pan back in the oven for a few minutes to soften the caramel again. Roll out again, and then peel off the top silicone mat. Wait until slightly cooled. Using gloved hands, form the caramels into abstract shapes.
7. Once cooled, keep the croquant in an airtight container at room temperature.

Process, Caramelized Pecans

Melt a small amount of sugar in a saucepan, stirring constantly. Once all the sugar is melted, add 30 pieces of pecan halves. Keep stirring until the sugar around the nuts caramelizes. Reserve until needed.

Process, Chocolate Décor

1. Spread tempered dark chocolate onto a sheet of acetate 12 inches (31 cm) long.
2. Using a comb, create a straight stripe pattern lengthwise.
3. Before the chocolate is set, curve the sheet using a 6 inch (15 cm) cake ring. Wait until set, and reserve until needed.

Assembly

1. Slice the red velvet opera lengthwise, ⅜ inch (8 mm) wide. Cut two short sides to form a parallelogram. Place it on a rectangular plate at an angle, the cut-side down.
2. Place loops of the chocolate décor on one side of the cake, placing the ends of the chocolate strips underneath the cake.
3. Make a small indentation on the cake with a small knife, to allow the pecan croquant to stand up by the chocolate décor.
4. Place a piece of caramelized pecan on the other end of cake, and pipe a small round of the Bourbon sabayon sauce on a corner of the plate.

Red Velvet Opera Cake

CHAPTER SUMMARY

When dining out, dessert is the final course and is intended to offer the diner a sweet, pleasurable moment. This course is often shared with a companion and enjoyed with coffee, a sweet wine, or liquor; it can be seen as a time of slight indulgence. The pastry chef can and should tailor the plated dessert to the diners' needs and provide them with something memorable that complements the previous courses, as well as the experience of being in the restaurant. Dessert is not just about eating something sweet and sharing it with another; it is also important that the power of the course allows feelings of satisfaction and the inclination to reflect on the past and to remember similar flavors, textures, and company.

To produce plated desserts and plan a menu for a restaurant or hotel, the pastry chef must have significant knowledge of the pastry arts as well as a developed ability to plan and artistically present creations. Plated desserts always include multiple components, and the organization of the workplace, production schedule, and service is part of ensuring that the dessert makes it to the table as the guest envisions it as well as how the pastry chef and chef envision it.

KEY TERMS

- ❖ Actinidin
- ❖ À la carte
- ❖ À la minute
- ❖ Bromelain
- ❖ Coulis
- ❖ Ficin
- ❖ Foam
- ❖ Fruit sauces
- ❖ Gelée
- ❖ Infusion
- ❖ Mise en place
- ❖ Papain
- ❖ Plated desserts
- ❖ Proteolytic enzymes
- ❖ Tuile

REVIEW QUESTIONS

1. **What are the main concerns of the pastry chef when planning a dessert menu?**
2. **What impact do the market and venue have on the presentation of plated desserts?**
3. **What are the different ways in which fruit can be used as a plated dessert?**
4. **What is the range of components involved for plated desserts?**
5. **What is the purpose of having all appropriate mise en place completed before service?**

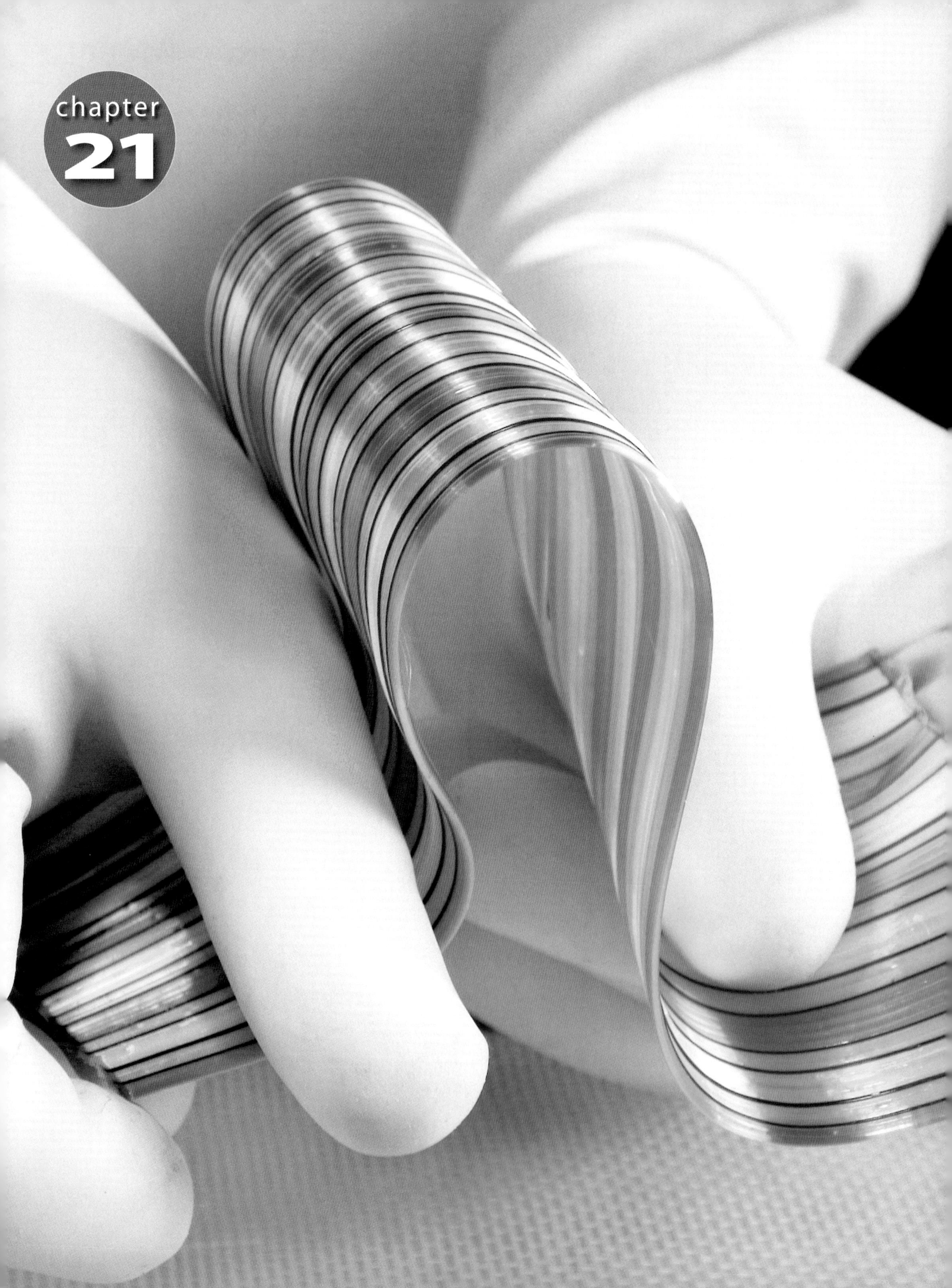
chapter
21

ADVANCED DECORATION

OBJECTIVES

After reading this chapter, you should be able to

- implement advanced piping techniques that use paper cones.
- make and use elements used for decoration including pastillage and gum paste.
- prepare sugar syrups for decorative work.
- make simple decorations such as bubble sugar, rock sugar, and spun sugar.
- approach more advanced decorative work such as cast sugar, pulled sugar, and blown sugar.

DECORATIVE ELEMENTS IN HISTORY

The use of sugar as a decorative element can be traced back to the 16th century. Pastillage and marzipan were commonly used. Its use for decoration rose in popularity at a time when the presentation of food on the table was becoming important. By the 19th century, this "designing" of the table began to incorporate influences from landscape art and architecture, which was made possible by the use of sugar pastes, biscuit dough, and colored sanding sugars.

The scope of decorative elements has evolved over time to the elaborate showpieces that are commonly found in high-end hotels and at pastry competitions. Pastry chefs use many different applications of sugar art to provide a finishing touch to items that range from plated desserts to specialty cakes. Designs can range from classical, resembling finely detailed pieces of art, or whimsical and creative, incorporating different elements such as cast, blown, and pulled sugars or pastillage. Modern uses highlight fragility, lightness, and gravity-defying displays of craftsmanship.

ELEMENTS OF ADVANCED DECORATION

There are many elements and techniques used for advanced decoration in the pastry shop. Those covered in this chapter include

- Paper cones, which are used for decorative piping with mediums such as royal icing or chocolate. They are also used to hold melted sugar or chocolate for assembling decorative display pieces made from sugar, pastillage, or chocolate.
- Pastillage, which is used to create centerpieces. It may be molded or rolled out thin and cut into shapes and assembled.
- Gum paste, which is similar to pastillage and is commonly used to make delicate flowers and leaves.
- Sugar, which is used for many decorative elements including rock sugar, spun sugar, blown sugar, and pulled sugar, just to name a few.

PAPER CONES

Piping plays a large role in advanced pastry decoration, which is reflected by the many types of piping bags, tips, icings, and techniques. Piping bags are made of plastic, acetate, nylon, and paper. **Paper cones** are generally considered to be the most convenient, inexpensive, sanitary, and versatile for fine decorative work. Paper cones are made from a triangular sheet of parchment paper, which is rolled into a cone shape. In general, the finer the work that needs to be done, the smaller the cone should be to allow for maximum control. When piping with a paper cone, it is important to fill the bag to only half full to keep the icing from seeping out during piping. The bag should be held with two hands. One hand should be at the top of the bag and the other uses the tip of an index or pointer finger to guide the bag.

PROCESS FOR MAKING A PAPER CONE

- Cut a triangle out of a sheet of parchment paper. The smaller the triangle, the finer the details should be.
- Holding the triangle with the longest side up and away from you, fold the right point down and over to meet the bottom point. Curl the remaining paper around until the left-hand point can be folded over the cone.
- Bring all three points together and fold the tips over twice to secure the cone.
- If a tip is being used, cut ¼ to ½ inch (1 cm) off the tip to fit.
- Fill the bag with the piping medium half full.
- Fold the top down, securing the paper cone as well as the piping medium in the bag.
- If no tip is being used, cut a small hole.

PIPING MEDIUMS

Numerous mediums can be used for piping such as royal icing, buttercream, fondant, chocolate, chocolate glaze, and sugar. To effectively pipe anything, the medium must be a uniform consistency so that there is no blockage in the tip. Before piping, icing can be colored using paste colors. The contents of the coloring should be taken into consideration to ensure there are no ingredients that can interfere with drying. Royal icing can be painted or airbrushed after it dries.

Using Chocolate in a Paper Cone

When piped from a small paper cone, chocolate makes a great medium for filigree work and lettering. **Filigree** is fine piping used for decoration. It is piped from a bag without a tip because the work is very fine. Two types of chocolate mixtures are primarily used for paper cone techniques. The first is a chocolate liquor paste made by mixing chocolate liquor with a simple syrup to a pipable consistency. The second is "seized" chocolate that is created by adding a couple of drops of water to give the chocolate a firmer, pipable consistency. Only the amount of chocolate being used at any given moment should be seized. Leftover seized chocolate can be saved and used in glaze formulas that call for couverture. Whichever type of chocolate is used, it must be smooth and free from lumps, and care should be taken to not overfill the cone. Filling it half full prevents overflow and ensures that the bag, as well as the piper, will stay clean.

Using Royal Icing in a Paper Cone

Royal icing is one of the most versatile mediums a pastry chef can work with. This mixture of powdered sugar, egg whites, and lemon juice is discussed in more detail in Chapter 15. Depending on its particular use, royal icing can range from a firm peak to a very liquid icing for glazing cakes or doing decorative flood work. If royal icing is to be used for run-outs and flood work, care should be taken to not incorporate air, which leaves small, unstable air pockets that will lead to the breakdown of the decoration after drying.

Because royal icing can dry very hard, the pastry chef can be very creative with the filigree or any of the fine piping as these may be applied to items after the icing dries. It can be painted on, used for three-dimensional creations, stenciled, and dried in a low oven to garnish plated desserts.

DECORATION TECHNIQUES

There are three basic techniques for decorating with a paper cone. These traditional French techniques are known as the sliding method, the thread method, and the applied method (Buys & Decluzeau, 1996, p. 14). By learning and mastering these three techniques, the pastry chef can present an unlimited array of decorative piping techniques. When choosing which technique to use, the pastry chef needs to consider several things about the mediums being worked with, including the texture of the surface to be piped on, the piping medium, the angle needed to apply the piping medium, the length of time the work must last, and the environment in which it will be stored.

- **Sliding method**: In the sliding method, the tip of the cone barely touches the surface of the product, which allows the pastry chef more control. This method can be used on a variety of surfaces, ranging from hard to delicate, and can be used to make borders, letters, and lines.
- **Thread method**: When using the thread method, the pastry chef applies the piping medium from above the surface of the cake. This can be done from a distance of ½ inch (1 cm) to 2 inches (5 cm), depending on the application. This technique allows for more control for decorative piping.

FIGURE 21-1 CUTTING PASTILLAGE

1 **Roll the pastillage to 1⁄16 inch (2 mm).**

2 **Cut out the desired shapes using a very sharp, fine-pointed knife.**

3 **Remove the trim carefully.**

Applications for this method include ornate letters and borders, as well as thread work like decorative borders made with royal icing. As with the sliding method, the surface of the product can be hard or soft.

- **Applied method**: The applied method uses the cone to apply embellishments that highlight existing decoration or design. The surface can be any texture because the tip of the cone is usually held just above the surface. This style provides more "stop-and-go" control and can be used in conjunction with the other methods like the sliding method.

With all three methods, paper cones should be freshly made and maintained in a clean, sanitary way, and each cone should be used only for its designated application. Sliding can dirty the tip. If the tip becomes dirty, it should be carefully cleaned to prevent any contamination and any damage to the physical integrity of the paper. Maintaining a clear and clean opening is a good way to ensure easy piping.

PASTILLAGE

Pastillage is one of the oldest of the decorative elements used for display pieces. It is made with totally edible ingredients, but it is not meant to be consumed; pastillage is tasteless and very hard once it dries. Pastillage is usually used for making display pieces for dessert buffet tables and pastry competitions, as well as for small baskets or boxes to hold candies and petit gateaux. Pastillage is left white most of the time, although there are two possible ways to color the pieces; colorant can be mixed into the dough or food coloring can be airbrushed onto a dried surface.

Pastillage is made of powdered sugar, cornstarch, water, cream of tartar, and gelatin. Powdered sugar, the main ingredient in pastillage, gives the dough its body and white color. Cornstarch helps to dry out the pastillage piece faster, and it is not used when slow-drying is required. Cream of tartar helps to maintain the whiteness of the dough, and gelatin assists in stabilizing the paste and keeping it pliable. Proportions of these ingredients change according to the desired consistency of pastillage paste after mixing.

The mixing of the pastillage can have a large impact on the final qualities of the dough. When a strong piece is desired, keep mixing to a minimum so that the piece will dry slowly. If there is a time constraint when making pastillage pieces, the paste can be mixed for a longer time

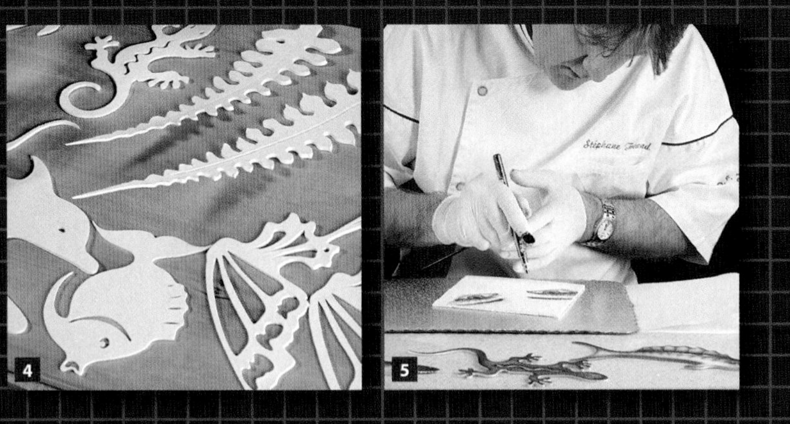

4 **Assorted pastillage cut-outs are shown drying on a wooden board.**

5 **Pastillage cut-outs can be airbrushed.**

to incorporate more air, which leads to faster drying. However, when too much air is incorporated, the piece can become fragile after drying.

Pastillage can be rolled out and cut or molded into different shapes fairly easily (see Cutting Pastillage Figure 21-1, Step 1). It is very important to work on a clean surface and use dry and clean tools. A granite table is desirable for working with pastillage, but a stainless steel table is fine as well. The work surface should be dusted with cornstarch or a mixture of powdered sugar and cornstarch to prevent the dough from sticking. When it is not being worked with, pastillage should be kept in an airtight container or plastic bag because it forms a crust very easily when exposed to air.

To cut pastillage, it is best to use an Exacto knife or sharp paring knife to ensure clean cuts (see Cutting Pastillage Figure 21-1, Steps 2–3). If the pastillage dries too quickly and cutting becomes difficult, roll out a second sheet of pastillage and place it over the one to be cut. This will preserve the one being cut and prevent it from drying. If the pastry chef is working at a bakery with a walk-in proofing room, the pastillage can be cut there as long as the humidity is not above 80 percent.

After they are cut or molded into desired shapes, pastillage pieces are dried out. When drying flat pieces, they should be on a flat sheet that has been lined with foam to allow drying on both sides. Wooden boards can also be used for drying because they help to allow moisture to escape from the bottom side of the cut-outs. Pastillage should dry on each side for at least one day. After the first day, the pastillage pieces should be turned over and dried for another day to ensure even drying. The time it takes to dry out a pastillage piece depends on the size of the piece and length of mixing time. (See Cutting Pastillage Figure 21-1, Step 4.)

When the pieces are completely dried, they can be sanded with extra-fine sandpaper to achieve very smooth edges and surfaces. After being sanded, the pieces can be glued with royal icing or **pastillage glue**, which is a mixture of melted gelatin and powdered sugar (a simple mixture of powdered sugar at five times the weight of bloomed gelatin). Pieces need to be supported until set; royal icing and pastillage glue do not dry out as fast as melted chocolate or sugar. Pieces are pure white when finished but may be hand-painted or airbrushed either before or after building the piece (see Cutting Pastillage Figure 21-1, Step 5).

Figure 21-2
Pastillage Centerpieces

The completed pastillage piece must be kept at room temperature and in a dry environment (See Figure 21-2.). A well-built pastillage piece should last indefinitely if properly stored.

PASTILLAGE PROCESS

- Bloom the gelatin leaves in water.
- Place three-fourths of the powdered sugar into a mixing bowl fitted with the paddle attachment.
- Melt the gelatin and vinegar together in the microwave, and stir to combine evenly.
- Pour the gelatin mixture into the mixing bowl and mix to incorporate to a smooth paste.
- Add the remaining powdered sugar until a smooth dough forms.
- If the dough becomes too dry, add more vinegar.
- Place the finished dough in an airtight container until ready for use.
- When ready to work with the dough, quickly roll the pastillage on a granite or nonstick surface dusted with cornstarch, using rulers as guides to ensure even thickness.
- Cut into the desired shapes, and form or mold.
- Allow to dry on each side for at least one day.

SUGAR WORK

The scope of sugar work is vast including preparations that the novice can make and others that the most advanced pastry chefs practice devotedly to master. The art of sugar is part science, knowing the working properties of the sugar (including crystallization and heat transfer), and part art, recognizing color, shape, design, implementation, and technical considerations such as balance and assembly. This section on sugar work presents ingredients, tools, and the processes for a number of sugar preparations beginning with the easier ones such as bubble, rock, spun, and piped sugar and progressing to the more challenging ones including cast, pulled, and blown sugar.

INGREDIENTS

Selecting the ingredients used for sugar work is basic; however, careful consideration must be taken to ensure consistent results. The basic ingredients used for sugar work include sugar, water, and glucose. A recent alternative to sugar is isomalt, and its use merits special considerations. Acidic ingredients are needed for cast, pulled, and blown sugar to create a degree of inversion and tartaric acid should be used for this. If an opaque quality is desired, calcium carbonate can be added. Colorants can also be added during the cooking process or immediately after the sugar base has been poured onto the slab.

Sugar

Working with sugar involves numerous precautions, most of which are driven by the need to work with a "clean" sugar. The purity of the sugar, as well as the type of sugar being used, must be considered because it can determine the working properties of the sugar for casting, pulling, or blowing. The three main types of available refined sugar are superfine sugar, granulated sugar, and sugar cubes. Sugar quality is most important for pulled sugar. To achieve a good working quality, it is most advisable to use cane sugar, which has fewer impurities than beet sugar.

Glucose

Glucose is used in sugar work to modify the texture of the sugar and to help prevent crystallization. The use of glucose in sugar work allows the final piece to be of a higher quality, making it set harder, shinier, and drier. Additionally, the addition of glucose adds protection against humidity, leading to a longer shelf life. However, if too much glucose is used, the sugar retains more heat and is more difficult to work with because it may have a softer texture. Good-quality glucose is transparent and thick. During the cooking process, glucose is added after the syrup reaches a boil to ensure that it completely dissolves.

Water

The use of spring water is preferred over tap water. Mineral water also gives better and more consistent results than tap water, which contains lime that may generate crystals. Water contributes the function of dissolving the sugar granules through moisture and the conduction of heat. It is important for the sugar to melt slowly and dissolve completely in water before it starts to cook in order to minimize formation of crystals.

Isomalt

Isomalt has become very popular as an alternative to sugar for decorative work in recent years. Isomalt is most often used for cast sugar. Its glass-like aspect makes it the ingredient of choice to build artistic pieces. It can be purchased as small granules or as a powder depending on the brand. Isomalt has been successful because it is easy to use. It can be used as is and does not require any water or glucose. It can be melted slowly in a pan until it becomes a transparent liquid. Isomalt can reach higher temperatures than regular sugar and still retain a clear aspect. It is cooked and used at temperature between 338°F (170°C) and 356°F (180°C) with no change in color. The techniques used to get a satin finish and for coloring are the same as with traditional sugars. Although the final satin finish will be less desirable than that attained with sugar, isomalt does have a higher resistance to humidity.

Water can be added to isomalt. The addition of 10 percent water allows isomalt to melt easily and without as much stirring. It will take longer to cook but the cooking should stop at 329°F (165°C). Under this condition, isomalt will be less fragile and less breakable than if it were cooked without adding water. In a very dry environment, it is also advisable to add 10 percent water during cooking to minimize breakage during assembling. As for regular sugars, always wait until isomalt cools down to 284°F (140°C) and bubbles disappear before starting working with it.

Another advantage of isomalt is that it can be remelted after cooling down without forming crystals. Broken pieces can easily be remelted to be worked with again.

Acid

Tartaric acid helps to prevent crystallization of the sugar and helps the sugar to be more elastic when it's being pulled or blown. Additionally, the sugar can be worked with for longer periods of time under the heat lamp without losing any gloss or shine. A lack of tartaric acid would make the sugar hard to pull, whereas too much would make it too soft and would not allow the sugar to keep its shape. Signs of too much acid include soft, sticky sugar that does not easily set. Tartaric acid can be found in the form of small crystal white powder. Tartaric acid must be reconstituted with boiling water before it can be used. The ratio is 1:1 tartaric acid to water. This solution should be kept in a small bottle with an eyedropper for easy measuring.

EQUIPMENT, TOOLS, AND WORKSPACE

The necessary equipment for cooking sugar is the same for all sugar techniques. The specific pieces of equipment used may differ according to the technique and how the sugar is to be used. Here is the most common equipment list for cast, pulled, and blown sugar:

- Granite slab
- Copper or stainless steel pan
- Ice bath
- Candy thermometer
- Clean brush and cold water
- Silicone mat
- Sugar lamp
- Blow torch
- Scissors
- Fan
- Sugar pump
- Gloves
- Cutting molds and silicone molds
- Airbrush
- Airtight boxes with humidity repellant such as calcium chloride, limestone, or silica
- Hygrometer
- Pan liner or parchment paper
- Foil and plastic wrap

Work Environment

Cooked sugar is very sensitive to humidity, which implies a few precautions mostly regarding pulled sugar. Avoid cooking sugar too close to a **sugar lamp** and working in areas with lots of steam. Under normal working conditions, try to avoid pulling sugar in a drafty area and with high temperature gradients. The most recommended place to work with sugar is in a small room equipped with a sugar lamp and a dehumidifier. The room temperature should be between 68°F (20°C) and 75°F (24°C) with a humidity level lower than 50 percent.

SUGAR SYRUPS

When cooking sugar, pay close attention to the temperature of the syrup because the difference of a few degrees can render the sugar unusable for different applications. For this reason, follow all the steps in the sugar-cooking process carefully. To ensure that the sugar dissolves easily, the water should be added to the pan first. Next, the sugar is added, and the mixture is stirred over medium heat just until the sugar is dissolved. If stirring continues after this point, crystallization can occur. To prevent crystallization, the mixture should be cooked over medium heat, and heat should be increased only after the syrup has come to a boil. Sugar that is cooked too slowly is also at risk of crystallization. The flame must be kept beneath the pot and not allowed to crawl up the sides, which could result in uneven cooking and off colors.

During cooking, the sides of the pan should be washed down with a clean, wet pastry brush that has been dipped in cold water. This action will wash any sugar crystals off the side of the pan and back into the solution. If any of these crystals fall into the solution after it has become saturated, it can cause the syrup to crystallize. The washing down process continues until the sugar reaches 235°F (113°C), at which point there should be no more crystals.

If a thin layer of residue from impurities appears when the syrup comes to a boil, it should be removed and discarded. The glucose should be added after the syrup has come to a boil to ensure better incorporation and to prevent the sugar from decrystallizing before the mixture becomes hot enough. Then, the mixture should be brought back to a boil. At this point, the top of the syrup should be cleaned one more time if necessary. The degree to which the sugar is cooked is determined by its application.

If calcium carbonate is required, it should be added when the mixture reaches 260°F (127°C). **Calcium carbonate** is a powder used to make the sugar syrup opaque. Tartaric acid is added in solution at 280°F (138°C). If it is added too soon, the sugar can invert, causing premature and extreme softening of the sugar art. Any colorants should also be added at this time.

Sugar is ready for its different uses between 315°F (157°C) and 330°F (166°C). If heated beyond 330°F (166°C), it can take on color. At this point, it should be removed from the stove. It can be shocked in an ice bath to stop heat conduction and discontinue cooking and then allowed to cool naturally in the pot for a couple of minutes before it is used. Some sugar for decorative work can be prepared up to the point of satinizing and then either be used or stored in airtight containers. This is a common practice in kitchens that do a lot of sugar work and want to shorten the time involved with decorative sugar work.

Safety precautions should always be taken when working with a product at this temperature. If care is not taken, severe burns are possible.

For this reason, some people work with a bowl of ice water so that they can submerge their hands into it if hot sugar gets on them.

BUBBLE SUGAR

Bubble sugar is a simple way to add an interesting decoration to a dessert or a showpiece. It is the result of the loose, free bubbles that occur in sugar when hot sugar hits a layer of alcohol on parchment paper or silicone sheets. Special care should be taken with this method, as the hot sugar can very easily get on the skin. A much more practical approach to making bubble sugar is to spread or pipe glucose onto a silpat and bake it in a low oven until set. The glucose can be colored before baking to any desired color.

Formula for Bubble Sugar Using Alcohol

Sugar	1.000 kg
Water	0.350 kg
Glucose	0.200 kg

Process for Making Bubble Sugar Using Alcohol

- Prepare parchment paper or silicone sheets by rubbing them with a thin layer of clear alcohol.
- Bring the sugar and water to a boil, add the glucose, and cook to 312°F (156°C). Remove from heat.
- As quickly as possible, pour sugar into a thin layer over the sheet of alcohol-rubbed parchment or silicone mat or disperse it in small uniform puddles for individual garnishes.
- Carefully lift the sheet from its edges, and gently shake it. As the sugar hits the alcohol, it will bubble up.
- When the sheet has reached the desired thinness, carefully set it down and allow it to cool completely. It can then be broken into desired sizes and stored with humectants.

Process for Making Bubble Sugar With Glucose

- Warm the glucose and add colors as desired.
- Pipe or spread onto a silicone mat on a sheet pan.
- Bake in a low oven until crisp, bubbly, and set.
- When the glucose is cool, remove from the silpat and reserve with humectants until needed.

ROCK SUGAR

Rock sugar is a decorative element largely used in the construction of showpieces. It combines a cooked sugar syrup, royal icing, and agitation. This combination creates a foam that aerates the sugar syrup, creating millions of bubbles that set once "cool." Rock sugar is less susceptible to humidity, so it keeps well and is relatively easy to make. Rock sugar creates a very interesting effect in showpieces and is an excellent base on which to attach other types of sugar elements. It is also given great effect by airbrushing or filing down to a smoother texture.

Formula for Rock Sugar

Sugar	1.000 kg
Water	0.300 kg
Royal icing	0.050 kg

Process for Making Rock Sugar

- Line a bowl or dish with foil, and lightly oil it.
- Cook the sugar and water to 290°F (143°C). Add any color to the sugar between 248°F (120°C) and 260°F (127°C).
- At 290°F (143°C), quickly stir in the royal icing. The mixture will rise and then collapse.
- Reheat the mixture, and allow it to rise a second time before pouring it into molds.
- The mixture will rise again in the mold. When it has cooled, remove it, and work with it as desired.

SPUN SUGAR

Spun sugar is commonly used for decorating plated desserts. Spun sugar is a very fine element that is used on plated desserts, especially frozen ones. The syrup for spun sugar should be cooked to between 305°F (152°C) and 310°F (154°C). The pan should then be cooled in cold water to stop the cooking and reserved on a granite slab for a couple of minutes until a consistency similar to molasses is obtained. Two lightly sprayed metal bars are needed to catch the strands as they are thrown back and forth. To create "spin," dip the tines of a fork or a whisk with the curved ends into the cooled sugar, and then quickly toss the syrup over the bars. This action allows fine threads to form. The finished threads are gathered into a light, loose ball or nest and transferred to garnish the dessert or pastry. Because the threads are so thin, spun sugar is more susceptible to humidity than other types of sugar decoration, and its shelf life is very short. For this reason, it is best to make spun sugar as needed or to make enough for a few hours and store it in an airtight container with humectants.

Formula for Spun Sugar

Sugar	1.000 kg
Water	0.350 kg
Glucose	0.200 kg

Process for Making Spun Sugar

- Bring the sugar and water to a boil.
- Add the glucose once the sugar syrup boils and cook the syrup to 320°F (160°C).
- The sugar may be boiled higher, but it will take on color.
- Shock the sugar pot in ice water to stop the cooking.
- Dip a sugar wand (whisk with curved ends cut off) into the sugar.
- Shake the sugar over two metal bars hanging over the edge of the table. Once enough sugar is on the bars, pick it up and form a nest or ball, as desired.

PIPED SUGAR

The spun sugar solution can also be used for **piped sugar**. For piping, sugar is poured into a double- or even triple-thick paper cone and then piped into various designs on a nonstick sheet or a lightly oiled piece of parchment. Piping with a fine-tipped paper cone allows both the flow and thickness of the line to be controlled. Piped sugar can be used for filigree work and for shapes that are detailed; for example, spirals that are lifted in the center while cooling to form a modern form of a dessert cage. Piping sugar can be dangerous, and special care should be taken to avoid the serious burns that can occur if the piping bag breaks or overflows from being overfilled. When not actively piping, the tip should be kept warm to ensure the sugar doesn't begin to harden.

CAST SUGAR

Cast sugar is most often used for making showpiece bases or structures for art or commercial (sturdier) pieces and is defined by pouring sugar into greased metal forms, metal bars, food grade silicone molds or forms made from plasticine, a modeling paste that is used to make templates. Casting sugar is quick and simple so that different colors, shapes, and interesting textures can easily be made. Even though the components may be easy to create, care must be taken in their assembly. The same precautions exist for any sugar work and must be avoided: fingerprints, dust, and messy assembly. A clean and neat assembly is required for the quality and beauty of a nice poured sugar piece to show.

Formula for Cast Sugar

Sugar	1,000 g
Water	400 g
Glucose	350 g

Process for Making Cast Sugar

The process for this formula is straightforward. The sugar is combined with the water in a clean copper or stainless steel pan until boiling. The sugar is cleaned by skimming the surface of foreign particles and then the inside of the pan is cleaned with a wet brush. After the syrup comes to a boil, the glucose can be added. It may be necessary to clean the surface of the sugar again. The temperature should always be controlled with the thermometer. Cook the sugar to 320°F (160°C). Next, stop the cooking by placing the bottom of the pan in cold water. Reserve the pan on the work surface and wait the necessary time for the air bubbles to disappear. Finally, fill the forms carefully with the sugar. Sugar Casting Using a Silicone Noodle Figure 21-3, Alternate Sugar Casting Techniques Figure 21-4, and Casting in Sugar Figure 21-5 detail the application of cast sugar.

Coloring Cast Sugar

Cast sugar can be colored in different ways. To get a vibrantly colored sugar, the coloring should be added at the end of cooking, at about 284°F (140°C). By adding the color at this time, the liquid coloring is absorbed by the cooking and does not cool down the sugar. On the contrary, when a less colored, still transparent sugar is needed, a few drops of coloring can be added after cooking. It is important to slowly mix the coloring to avoid making bubbles by incorporating air. To get marbled effects, add some coloring drops in a pan or on the sugar surface, without mixing, then pull something through the colorant, spreading the marbled color through the sugar before pouring into the molds.

Casting

The art of working with cast sugar primarily involves working with shape and color. For flat shapes, always work on a flat and smooth granite surface. Sugar can be poured on silicone mats, in metallic rulers or cake rings lightly oiled to make geometric forms, or into silicone molds as silicone is the ideal material for poured sugar. Sugar can also be poured on different materials (such as pan liners, foil paper, silicone mats, or vinyl) that have been placed on the granite. To obtain the best

FIGURE 21-3 SUGAR CASTING USING A SILICONE NOODLE

A design is airbrushed on the pastillage puzzle to be cast in the sugar.

A Silicone Noodle is used to create a poured sugar piece.

Air bubbles are removed with the torch.

After the sugar sets, the Silicone Noodle can be easily removed.

FIGURE 21-4 ALTERNATE SUGAR CASTING TECHNIQUES

Modeling paste has been rolled out and cut as a template for poured sugar showpiece components.

A Silicone Noodle is used to create bases for a sugar showpiece.

A silicone Showpeel is used to create the wing of a butterfly.

FIGURE 21-5 CASTING IN SUGAR

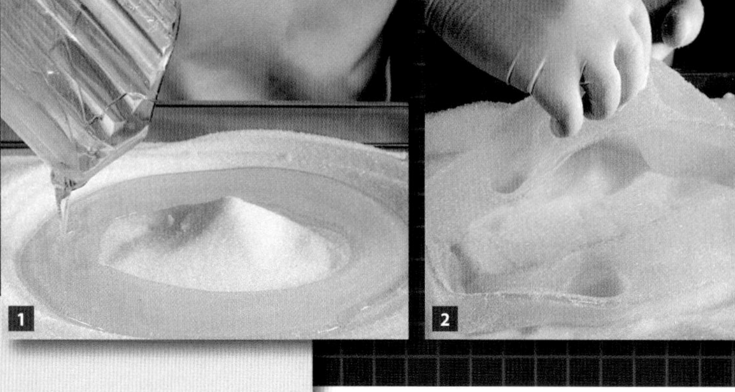

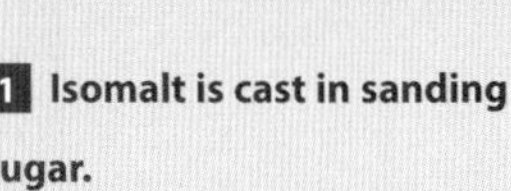

1 Isomalt is cast in sanding sugar.

2 As the sugar cools, it can be manipulated into different shapes.

3 The cooled sugar cast element is removed from the sanding sugar.

looking finish and regular, consistent shapes, let the sugar cool and thicken slightly in the pan before pouring it in the center of the molds. Also, if pouring a large or detailed piece, it may be better to work on a wooden surface to ensure that the sugar doesn't set up as quickly as it would on granite.

Materials such as silicone mats or vinyl (transparent thick plastic) have a vacuum effect when placed flat on a marble top. Air trapped under the material warms and expands once the hot sugar is poured on top of it. Always place a pan liner under these items to let the silicone molds cool by sliding them on the marble top.

Process for Casting With Modeling Paste

- On a silicone mat or flat surface, roll the modeling paste or plasticine between metal candy bars to the desired thickness.
- Place a template on the paste, cut around the outline, and remove the centers.
- Oil the base (if applicable) and sides of the mold.
- Pour in the sugar, and fill to the top of the mold.
- Once set, cut the side away from the paste to remove the cast piece.
- If any paste is sticking to the edges, gently scrape it away with a knife.

See Figure 21–6 for an example of a showpiece that uses cast sugar.

PULLED SUGAR

Pulled sugar is an advanced sugar technique that is used to create delicate decorations like ribbons, flowers, leaves, and corkscrews. Before pulling can occur, the sugar must be cooked and then cooled and stretched and folded over itself repeatedly to achieve a satin-like consistency. This is called **satinizing** the sugar and it helps add strength. Next, it can be pulled into very thin, fine, shiny creations that hold have a glass-like final quality and hold their shape as they cool.

Of all the sugar work, pulled sugar is certainly the technique that requires the most practice and training to reach an acceptable level. Pulled sugar is the most technical and the most interesting medium to work with. Without doubt, the pastry chef will develop his art and, little by little, express a personal style through pulled sugar. The balance of colors in a composed piece, the pulling and shaping of the sugar, and the composition must all be mastered for the artist to succeed at this craft.

Many recipes for pulled sugar give good results. It is important is to keep one after performing some tests and never change it. This will allow progress and the ability to concentrate on the technique and the art.

Figure 21-6
A Sugar Showpiece Using Pastillage and Cast Sugar

Formula for Pulled Sugar

Sugar cubes (preferably cane sugar)	1,000 g
Water	400 g
Glucose	200 g
Tartaric acid solution	10 drops
Cook to 329°F (165°C).	

Process for Pulled Sugar

In a very clean pan, let the sugar melt slowly with the water, mixing it from the beginning with a whisk. Clean the sides of the pan with a wet brush and clean, cold water and bring to a boil. Next, add the glucose. Cook at a high temperature and monitor the cooking using a thermometer. Keep cleaning the pan sides during cooking and skim impurities from sugar if necessary. The thermometer can be used to slowly mix the sugar and to control a constant and homogeneous cooking throughout the pan. Take care, however, because too much agitation could introduce air bubbles or promote crystallization. About 10 drops of tartaric acid per 1,000 grams of sugar is added at the end of cooking, around 320°F (160°C), using a dropper.

When the sugar reaches 329°F (165°C), turn off the heat, and stop the cooking by immersing the pan in cold water or letting it rest on a granite work surface. Let all the bubbles dissolve, and pour on a silicone sheet before it gets a satin appearance.

Sugar Syrup Considerations for Pulled Sugar

It is possible to use an induction hot plate to cook the sugar; however, the use of a special pan is required. Because induction hot plates are more powerful than gas heat, it is advisable not to use full power. When cooked too fast, sugar crystallizes; it becomes white, dry, and very hard to work with. If cooked too slowly, it may become yellowish, soft, and unable to keep its shape during assembly. The higher the temperature is when cooking sugar, the grainier the sugar may become from crystallization. Grains are a real problem when pulling ribbons.

Because a small quantity of sugar will cook too fast, and a large quantity will take a long time to cook, it is best to cook at least 1,000 grams of sugar, and no more than 1,500 grams, at a time.

To avoid or, at least, limit grains, the syrup should be prepared one day in advance: Bring the water, sugar, and glucose to a boil; remove it from the heat; and cover it directly with a food plastic film to avoid surface crystallization. On the next day, filter the syrup directly in the pan and start cooking. Using this method will greatly reduce the amount of grains in the ribbon mainly because the sugar crystals will dissolve completely in the water overnight.

Coloring Pulled Sugar

Alcohol-based colorings are recommended for pulled sugar. The heat from the sugar evaporates the alcohol, which would bring additional moisture to the syrup. Pulled sugar can be colored in several different ways. When only one color is needed, coloring can be added during cooking at 284°F (140°C). To obtain several colors during one cooking, cook the sugar syrup as normal at 329°F (165°C), and then add a few drops of the lighter colorant. Mix and pour the desired amount onto a silicone sheet. To create other colors, add some drops of another darker coloring directly in the pan. Stir to incorporate, and pour out on the pan again. You will then have several colors of sugar coming from the same stock of syrup. This method is only good if you want to use a little coloring to obtain pastel colors.

Another coloring technique involves coloring the sugar after pouring it onto the silicone sheet. This allows several masses of sugar from the same cooking to be colored. The advantage of this method is to get colors that have not been diluted by other coloring in the pan. Additionally, color pigments are less affected by the heat when poured on sugar that is already on the silicone sheet. After coloring the sugar on the silicone sheet, bring the sides toward the center in order to form a block, which allows the colors to mix and the sugar to cool down the sugar before satinizing.

To satinize the sugar, turn the sugar over to get a more homogenous cooling. Always bring the sides toward the center and then turn over until the sugar forms a firm ball and keeps its shape.

Gloves should be worn when satinizing to protect the hands from heat and to protect the sugar from sweaty hands. At this time, the sugar is still too hot to be handled with bare hands, although it has cooled down from boiling. It is very important not to satin a sugar too early. The sugar must be "cool" so that it does not quickly lose its shape.

Start by pulling the sugar and folding it over several times. Repeat this process in order to cool the sugar down and satin it. Pulled sugar is the most shiny when it is satined at cooler temperatures (however the sugar is still very hot at this point). Sugar is well satined when it "snaps" and when shaped as a ball becomes very firm. At this point, it should be placed under the heat lamp to maintain its temperature, after which it is ready to be shaped.

Considerations for Satinizing Sugar for Pulling

Care must be taken to not oversatin the sugar by pulling sugar that is too hot or by pulling it for too long. This creates an end result that is dull and opaque. The coloring needs to be strong enough to retain its coloration after satinizing.

Pulled Sugar Shaping

After the sugar has been satined, it is ready to be pulled and shaped into leaves, flowers, ribbons, and more. The sugar has to be at the right consistency, and most of all it must not be too hot to be pulled. The sugar has to be "cold" to be properly satined and to achieve the maximum brightness. It is important to always maintain a good consistency of the sugar under the lamp by folding it to maintain the temperature and consistency of the mass. A good sugar consistency means that it is soft enough to allow pulling but not so soft that it can't hold a shape and stay bright once set.

The way to pull sugar depends on the various shapes you want to make. Generally, the pastry chef will start by pinching the sides of the cooked sugar using both hands with spread thumbs, in order to spread out the center part. Then, holding it between the thumb and the forefinger, a petal, a flower, or a leaf can be pulled and then shaped.

Knowing the difference between pulling sugar and shaping sugar is very important. When the sugar is pulled and cooled at the same time, it becomes beautiful and bright. It is decisive timing that enhances pulled sugar. On the other side, pulled sugar depends on technical hand moves to make the difference. Shaping has to be done very quickly in order for the piece to look alive, natural, and "spontaneous." As a matter of fact, a sugar that has been well cooked and well satined cools down and hardens as it is pulled.

Pulled sugar requires more practice and patience than any other technique. To start with granules of sugar and to end up with flowers or ribbons is not an easy task. The whole purpose is to make progress and have fun at the same time.

Process for Making Pulled Sugar

- Pour cooked sugar onto a silicone mat, and let it cool until it can be picked up. It will still be very hot. (See Coloring and Satinizing Sugar Figure 21-7, Steps 1–2.)
- If using preformed, cooled sugar, heat it in a microwave on low until it is soft but not liquid, or place it under heat lamps, gently moving it around until it is melted and pliable.
- Hold the ends and pull the sugar away from the center, folding the sugar back on itself into the middle and completely attaching the ends to each other before pressing flat again. Continue with this process until it has cooled to a more manageable temperature and consistency.
- Pull and twist the sugar to incorporate very small air molecules and to strengthen it. When finished, it will be slightly opaque and shiny due to the incorporation of air.
- Stretch the sugar into a coil. While twisting, fold it back in on itself, and squeeze out any excess air. Continue this process until it has reached a cooler temperature. (See Coloring and Satinizing Sugar Figure 21-7, Steps 3–5.)
- Return the sugar to the heat lamp. When a high-gloss shine develops on the surface, fold the sugar in on itself to form a ball until the total product has heated and become pliable again. (See Coloring and Satinizing Sugar Figure 21-7, Step 6.)

Flowers and Leaves

To create the petals of a flower, it is important to first create a thin edge by grasping the sugar with the fingers held close together and pulling them away from each other. The edge can then be cut and formed into petals of various sizes and manipulated into desired fineness and thickness. A flower is built by overlapping and attaching these petals. After it is complete, the edge can be brushed with coloring for effect, and a stamen can be added by making fine strands from yellow or gold sugar. This same method is used for different types of leaves. For special effect, the pulled sugar can be pressed into silicone textured leaf forms that apply detailed indentations and enhance the satin. Figures 21-8 and 21-9 detail the making of leaves and roses from pulled sugar.

FIGURE 21-7 COLORING AND SATINIZING SUGAR

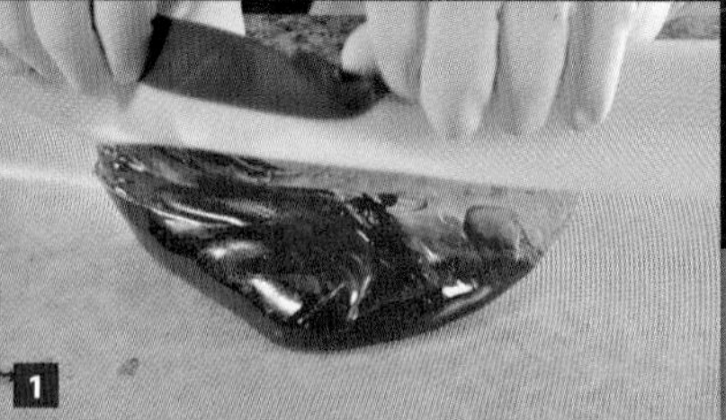
1 Cool the sugar for satinizing and incorporating the color.

2 When the sugar forms a mass and can be picked up, it is ready for satinizing.

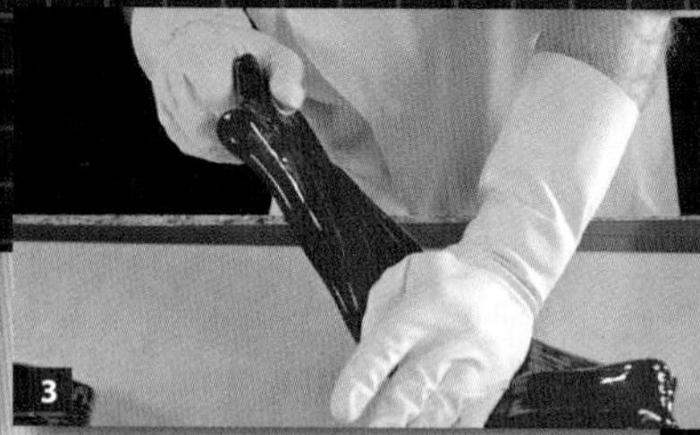
3 Stretch the sugar.

4 Fold the sugar in half, and stretch the sugar again.

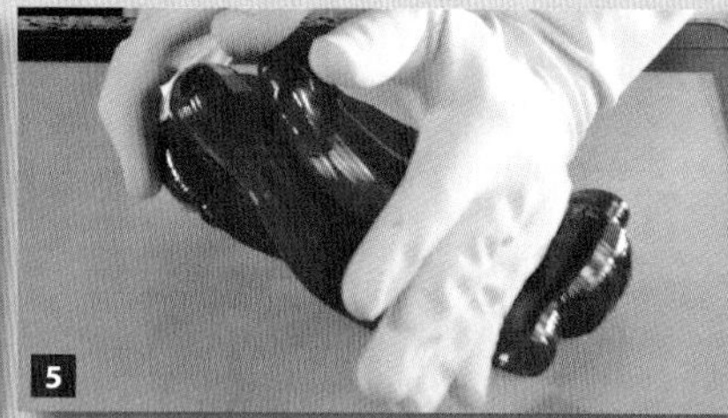
5 Form the sugar into a more compact mass.

6 The satinized sugar is ready to be used for pulling and blowing.

FIGURE 21-8 LEAVES

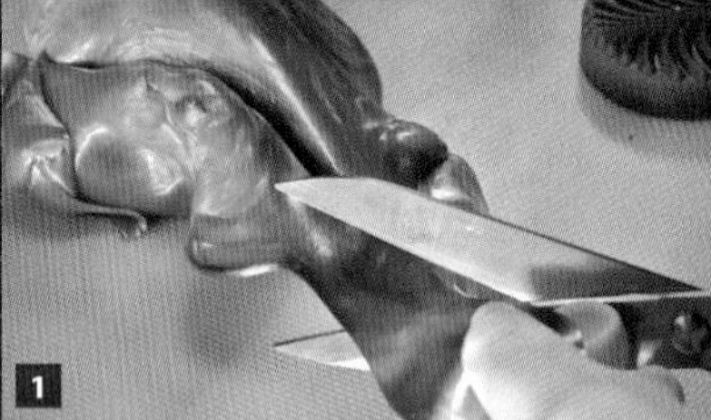
1 Stretch a thin sheet of sugar from the satinized mass, and cut it off on an angle.

2 Quickly lay it on the silicone press.

3 Quickly press it using the top.

4 Remove the leaf and shape as desired.

5 Assorted leaves are ready to be added to the sugar creation.

FIGURE 21-9 ROSES

Cut off a rounded edge of satinized sugar to create the center of the rose.

Stretch the satinized sugar out from one edge using two hands to form a thin sheet of sugar.

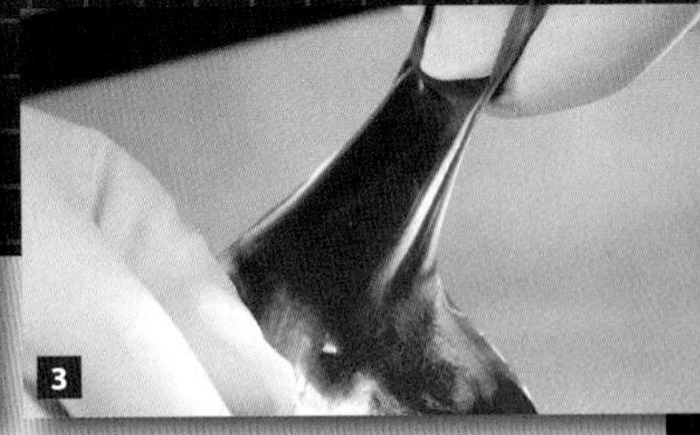

Secure the sheet between the thumb and index finger to continue forming the petal.

Or, form the petal using the thumb.

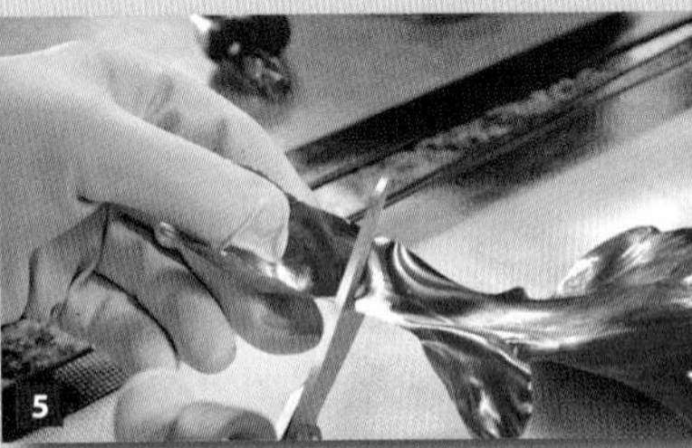

Cut the petal off of the satinized mass and tuck the thin sugar back to the mass to retain the heat.

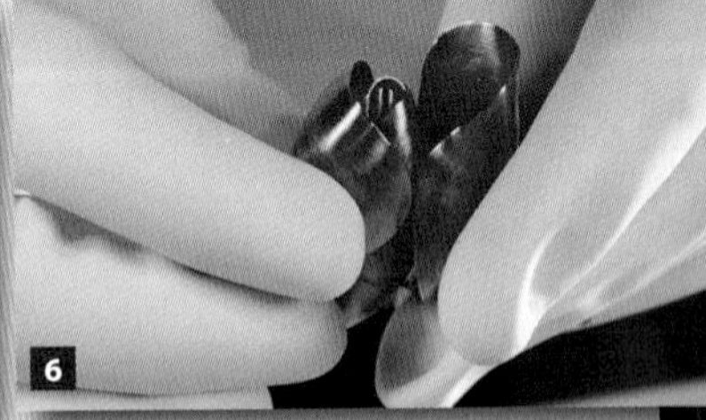

Secure the first petal to the bud and then subsequent petals to the other petals.

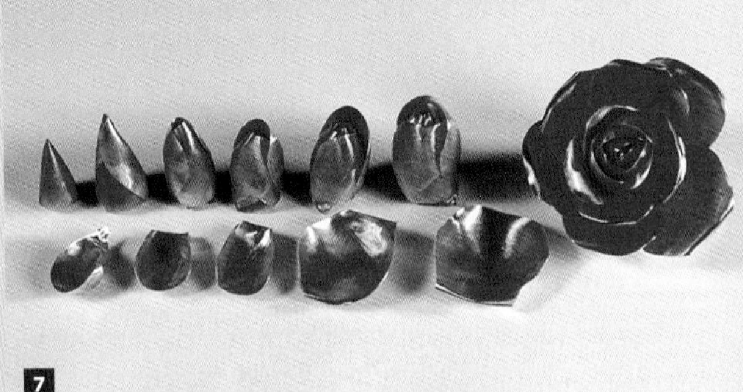

As the rose becomes larger, the petal sizes increase.

FIGURE 21-10 RIBBON MAKING

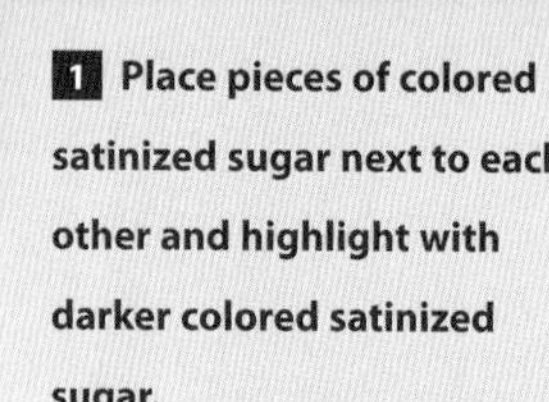

1 Place pieces of colored satinized sugar next to each other and highlight with darker colored satinized sugar.

2 Gently and evenly pull the ribbon.

3 Once some length has been established, bring the two ends together, side by side, cut the bottom loop, and continue to stretch the ribbon, now with more lines.

4 Continue to elongate the ribbon.

Ribbons

To make a basic ribbon, four pieces of satinized sugar, of at least two colors, are rolled into the shape of a cigar. They are placed next to each other and joined together. Starting from one end, the sugar is held with the hand in the air and the other hand gently pulls straight down and out to elongate the strip. The piece is then folded in half, the two halves are laid out parallel to each other, and the bottom is cut (it will be curved). It is then inverted and this process is repeated three times. The side of the table or one's leg can be used to smooth the ribbon and make it thinner. Once it is the desired length, it is cut and shaped into the desired length and form. If the ribbon hardens before shaping is complete, it can be heated under a lamp just until it becomes pliable again. To cut the ribbon into portions, it can be cut with a hot knife See Ribbon Making Figure 21-10 for step-by-step photographs of the process.

BLOWN SUGAR

Blown sugar is sugar art that mirrors glass blowing. Pumps or metal pipes are used to inflate sugar pieces, and with careful manipulation with hands and gravity, many shapes can be created. Accomplished blown sugar artists are capable of creating amazing pieces of sugar art. However, because not everything is easily represented with blown sugar, it is often augmented with other types of sugar work. For this reason, a solid knowledge of decorative sugar work should be obtained, and the base processes of pulled sugar and sugar-casting techniques should be mastered before learning sugar blowing.

Sugar Syrup for Blown Sugar

Syrup for blown sugar is based on the same formula as that for pulled sugar. Blown sugar should be cooked to 315°F (157°C) to 320°F (160°C). The tartaric acid can be added at 300°F (149°C). Although colorants can be added to the sugar base, they usually are not. Instead, the finished piece is typically airbrushed.

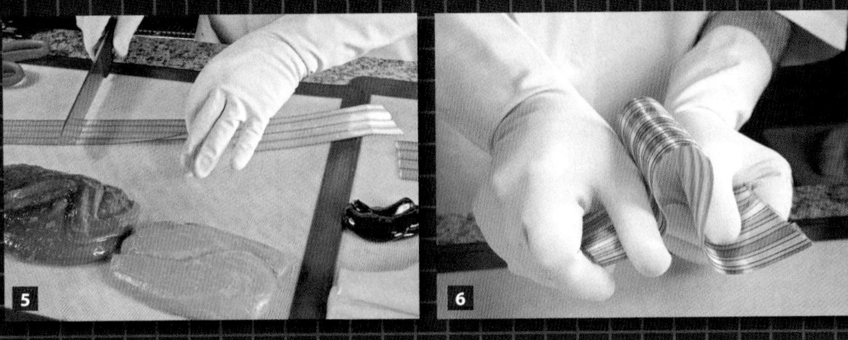

5 With a hot knife, cut the ribbon to the desired length.

6 Briefly warm the ribbon segment under the heat lamp, and then manipulate it into the desired forms.

7 Assorted ribbon components are ready to be added to the sugar creation.

Process for Blown Sugar

- After the syrup is cooked, pour it onto a silpat, and satinize it in the same way as sugar for pulling. Reserve and keep warm under a heat lamp. (See Blowing Sugar Figure 21-11, Steps 1–2.)
- To prepare for blowing, pull off the required size, form it into a ball, and mold it around the top portion of your thumb.
- Warm the tip of the sugar pump with a torch, and attach a small piece of sugar to it to act as a liaison to the sugar to be blown.
- Insert the warmed end of the sugar pump halfway into the indentation, and attach the sugar to the sides with the sugar acting as a liaison and ensuring the seal is secure. The natural air left by the indentation that is not attached to the sugar pump will allow the beginning expansion of air when blowing starts.
- Hold the sugar pump slightly perpendicular to the ground.
- Pump slowly and softly, using the hands to guide the expanding sugar and to allow for even air distribution. Gravity will help form the finished piece as will holding it at different levels while pumping more air to play a part in its overall form. (See Blowing Sugar Figure 21-11, Steps 3–4.)
- Using your hands to insulate the piece, cover areas that need to remain warmer.
- During pumping, stop frequently to check the item for consistency in form. (See Blowing Sugar Figure 21-11, Steps 5–6.)
- When the piece is ready, pinch between the margin of the sugar pump and the blown sugar piece.
- Cut with scissors at the pinch and cool completely in front of a fan and finish as desired. (See Blowing Sugar Figure 21-11, Steps 7–9).

Elements Made by Blowing

Figures, forms, fruit, dessert cups, vases, and animals are just a few of the items that can be made from blown sugar. It is best to start simply to get a feel for the technique and then to move on to more detailed items.

FIGURE 21-11 BLOWING SUGAR

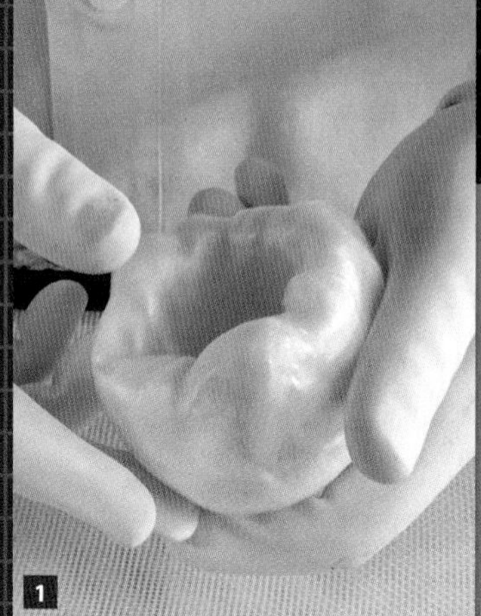

Form a ball from satinized sugar, and create a cavity in it.

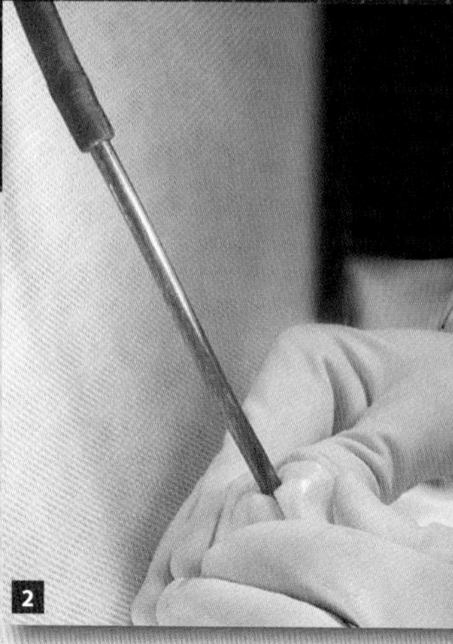

Secure the pump or pipe to the sugar piece.

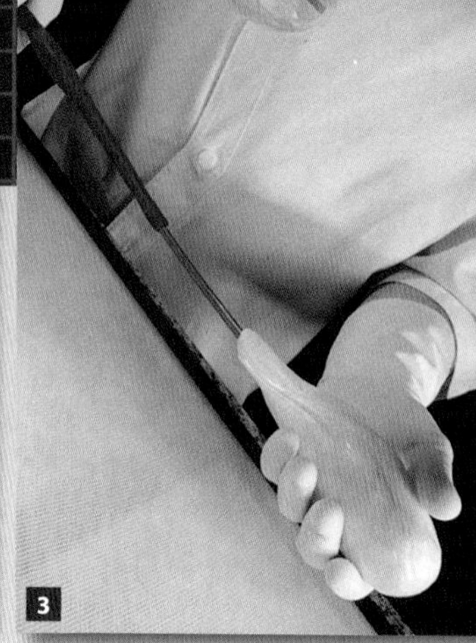

Begin to inflate the sugar piece, molding it as it becomes larger.

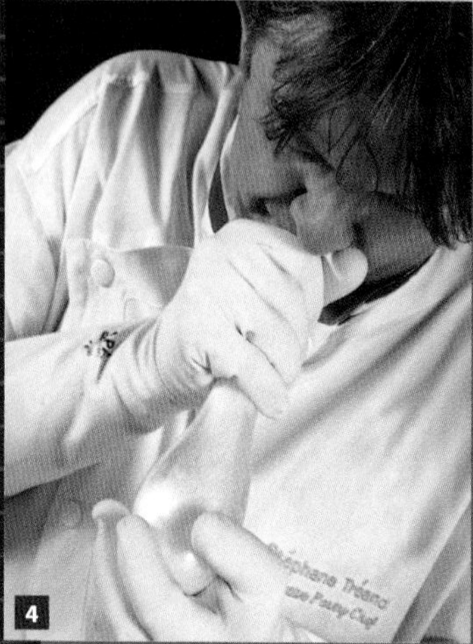

Here is an alternate method of blown sugar where just a pipe is attached to the sugar piece.

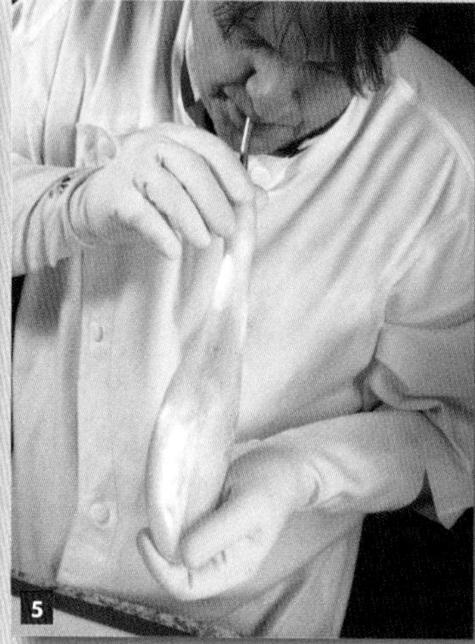

Use gravity to help form the shape of the sugar piece, at the same time shaping it with your hands.

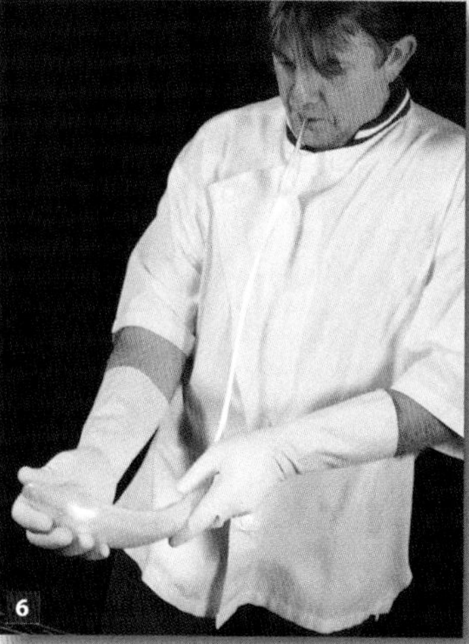

Form the blown sugar into its final shape.

Cut off the remaining sugar not needed for the piece.

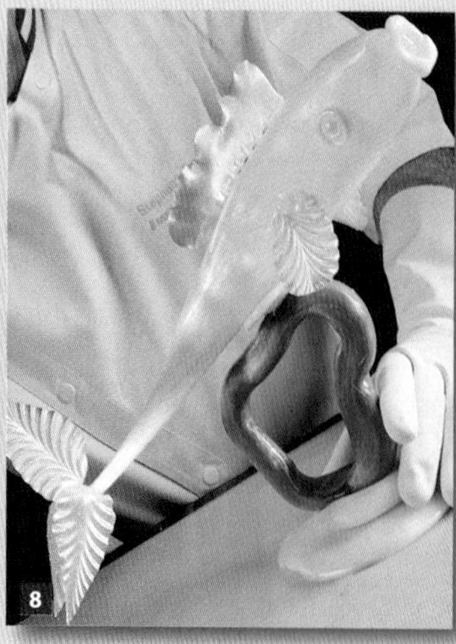

The blown fish has added sugar components for gills and fins.

Airbrush the finished piece.

SUGAR SHOWPIECES

Making quality sugar showpieces takes practice and mastery of all the components, which can include rock, cast, bubble, pulled, and blown sugar. All showpieces require a strong base and support system to make sure they remain standing. The base and support system should be incorporated into the design of the piece and have good color and flow.

With any event, competition, or display window project, having a detailed plan of execution is best. This should take into account required base syrups, color schemes, templates for casting, and other details that will add efficiency to the process. Before beginning the piece, it is beneficial to do a mock-up out of cardboard. The pastry chef should carefully plan the base, the support system, and all components. After the components have been made, assembly can begin. When it has been made, the finished piece must be stored properly, usually in special cases with crushed limestone under the pedestal to maintain the shape, height, and integrity of the color and shine.

Showpiece Bases

To ensure the stability of a showpiece, the thickness of the base should be directly related to the size and use of the showpiece. It is important to pour the sugar slightly away from the edge to prevent it from riding up the side of the mold and making a lip. The sugar can be marbled after it is poured by using coloring or luster dust that is added in the center and swirled into the base. This will give the poured piece the look of marble.

Sugar that has added tartaric acid for blowing and pulling should only be used to make bases up to 6 inches (15 cm) in diameter and 1/4 inch (6 mm) thick. Due to the softening effects of the acid, larger bases will have inadequate stability.

Showpiece Support Systems

Essential to producing stability, support pieces should be in harmony with the design of a showpiece. Consideration should be given to which shapes will provide the most support, as well as to how many will be needed for a particular design. For specialty designs, some people make custom molds with modeling paste or custom silicone molds and then cast them.

Attaching Sugar Pieces

Showpiece elements are attached to a base by heating the small area of the base targeted for attachment. Larger items must be heated before they are attached, but they can be reinforced by piping cooked sugar into their seams. Showpiece elements are attached to one another by touching them together, slightly pulling them away and putting them together again. This process of welding produces a very strong bond.

A piece of sugar heated for attachment goes through three stages. In the first stage, the surface appears to liquefy. In the second stage, tiny air bubbles appear on the surface as they escape from the sugar. This is the stage that forms the strongest bond. In the third stage, the bubbles brown and caramelize. If sugar is overheated during this process, the result can be a weak bond.

HANDLING AND STORING FINISHED SUGAR PIECES

Wearing surgical gloves makes manipulating hot sugar easier and prevents fingerprints on finished pieces. Because sugar pieces are fragile and decorations made with cooked sugar can absorb moisture from the air, care must be taken when storing. Spraying with a fine coating of sugar lacquer helps preserve the original quality, especially during display. In addition, anti-humectants can also aid in preservation during storage.

Finished sugar pieces or components should be stored in an airtight box with calcium chloride or other humectants to deter humidity from affecting the sugar. Depending on the work done, always use clear airtight boxes of different sizes for small pieces such as flowers, leaves, or ribbons made with pulled sugar. A good way to store large pieces made of poured sugar is to use an old, out-of-service reach-in freezer or refrigerator, which even if in nonworking condition will still be airtight. Always remember to place calcium chloride in boxes and reach-ins in order to avoid humidity before storing sugar pieces inside.

Sugar pieces must be stored right after they are made because humidity creates a less shiny and less satin finish forever, even if it is stored in a dry box afterwards. Boxes containing sugar pieces should be opened as little as possible in order to retain the good-looking quality of the sugar. Sugar pieces can be left outside only in a very dry climate such as that found in Las Vegas or Phoenix.

FORMULA

SUGAR SYRUPS (POURED, PULLED, BLOWN)

These sugar syrups are used for decorative sugar work. The use of "clean" cane sugar is required to create a sugar syrup with minimal impurities, and techniques for cooking sugar syrups should be followed carefully.

Poured Sugar Formula

Ingredients	Baker's %	Kilogram	US decimal	Lb & Oz
Sugar	100.00	1.000	2.205	2 3¼
Water	40.00	0.400	0.882	14⅛
Glucose	35.00	0.350	0.772	12⅜
Total	175.00	1.750	3.858	3 13¾

Process, Poured Sugar

1. Combine the sugar and water in a clean copper or stainless steel pan until boiling.
2. Wash down the sides of the pot with a wet brush.
3. Add the glucose, and clean the sides of the pot again if necessary.
4. Monitor the temperature with a thermometer.
5. Cook the sugar to 320°F (160°C).
6. Stop the cooking by placing the bottom of the pan in cold water.
7. Wait the necessary time for the air bubbles to disappear, then fill the forms with the sugar.

Pulled Sugar and Blown Sugar Formula

Ingredients	Baker's %	Kilogram	US decimal	Lb & Oz
Sugar	100.00	1.000	2.205	2 3¼
Water	40.00	0.400	0.882	14⅛
Glucose	20.00	0.200	0.441	7
Tartaric acid*	Drops	10	10	10
Total	160.00	1.600	3.527	3 8½

*10 drops of tartaric acid per 1 kg of sugar

Process, Pulled Sugar and Blown Sugar

1. In a very clean pan, let the sugar melt slowly with the water, mixing from the start constantly with a whip.
2. Clean the pan sides with a wet brush and bring to a boil.
3. Add the glucose. Cook at high temperature, and control the cooking using a thermometer.
4. Keep cleaning the pan sides during cooking and skim impurities from the sugar if necessary.
5. Use the thermometer to slowly mix the sugar and to control a constant and homogeneous cooking throughout the pan.
6. When the temperature reaches 329°F (165°C), turn off the heat, and stop the cooking by immersing the pan in cold water or letting it rest on a cold marble top.
7. Let all the bubbles dissolve, and pour on a silpat sheet before it gets a satin aspect.

FORMULA

PASTILLAGE

Pastillage, or sugar paste, is a sugar-based dough that can be used for modeling intricate showpieces. It can be left in its strikingly white state, or it can be airbrushed. For a dramatic effect, try putting some pastillage in the microwave to create a modern, yet very white rock sugar. It is an easier technique that yields an open structure.

Ingredients	Baker's %	Kilogram	US decimal	Lb & Oz		Test
Powdered sugar	100.00	2.329	5.135	5	2 ⅛	1 lb 13 ¾ oz
Gelatin leaf	0.67	0.016	0.034		½	¼ oz
White vinegar	6.67	0.155	0.343		5 ½	2 oz
Total	107.34	2.500	5.512	5	8 ¼	2 lb

Process

1. Bloom the gelatin leaves in cold water.
2. Warm up the white vinegar in a microwave to 120°F (49°C), and stir in the bloomed gelatin to melt.
3. Sift the powdered sugar, and place in a mixing bowl fitted with the paddle attachment. Mix on low speed, and pour in the vinegar mixture while mixing. Hold on to add a small amount of liquid.
4. Mix on medium-low speed until smooth. Adjust the consistency by adding the remaining liquid if the paste looks too dry.
5. Place the pastillage in a sealable plastic bag, and seal airtight. Reserve at room temperature until use.

Sugar Showpiece Using Pulled and Cast Sugar

Sugar Showpiece Using Poured Sugar, Pastillage, and Pulled Sugar

FORMULA

GUM PASTE

Also called flower paste, this is another medium used for delicate decorations. Gum paste can be rolled quite thin and, as a result, is well-suited for producing realistic flowers and leaves. It is not as strong as pastillage, but it is easier to form delicate floral representations.

Ingredients	Baker's %	Kilogram	US decimal	Lb & Oz		Test
Egg whites	12.50	0.243	0.536		8 ⅝	3 ⅛ oz
Tylose powder	3.50	0.068	0.150		2 ⅜	⅞ oz
Powdered sugar	100.00	1.946	4.289	4	4 ⅝	8 ⅞ oz
Shortening	12.50	0.243	0.536		8 ⅝	3 ⅛ oz
Total	128.50	2.500	5.512	5	8 ¼	2 lb

Process

1. Lightly beat the egg whites.
2. Add the sugar gradually, beating at medium speed for 2 to 3 minutes.
3. Add the tylose powder, and mix for a few seconds. The mixture will thicken quickly.
4. Scrape the mixture out of the mixer.
5. Mix the shortening into the mixture, and knead well until smooth.
6. Wrap the gum paste in plastic wrap, close tightly, and keep in the refrigerator.
7. Allow the paste to warm to room temperature before using.

FORMULA

ROLLED FONDANT

Rolled fondant is a sugar dough that is not based on a cooked sugar syrup as is confectionary or pastry fondant. Rolled fondant is used primarily in the cake decorating business and is one of the most popular choices for finishing wedding cakes. It can be colored using gel colors, and it can also be airbrushed.

Ingredients	Baker's %	Kilogram	US decimal	Lb & Oz	Test
Gelatin	0.78	0.015	0.033	½	¼ oz
Cold water	7.03	0.136	0.299	4 ¾	1 ¾ oz
Powdered sugar	100.00	1.928	4.250	4 4	1 lb 8 ⅝ oz
Glucose	17.18	0.331	0.730	11 ⅝	4 ¼ oz
Glycerin	1.56	0.030	0.066	1	⅜ oz
Shortening	3.13	0.060	0.133	2 ⅛	¾ oz
Total	129.68	2.500	5.512	5 8 ¼	2 lb

Process

1. Bloom the gelatin in cold water.
2. Sift the powdered sugar and place in a mixing bowl, and make a well in the center.
3. Heat the gelatin to melt completely.
4. Add the glucose and glycerin to the melted gelatin.
5. Stir the shortening into this mixture, and heat to 110°F (43°C), stirring constantly.
6. Pour the mixture immediately into the well in the powdered sugar, without pouring onto the sides. Avoid allowing the gelatin to set, which will cause specks in the final product.
7. Mix on low speed with the paddle attachment, and scrape as needed until a soft white dough is formed.
8. Remove from the mixer and knead, dusting with equal parts cornstarch and powdered sugar until a smooth dough is formed.
9. Wrap airtight or use immediately.

FORMULA

CANDIED NUTS

This formula and process coat nuts with a thin layer of sugar syrup, which crystallizes, through agitation, giving a sandy, white coating to the nuts. After this stage, the nuts could be cooked until the sandy sugar turns into a caramel. Almonds are specified, but any nut can be used.

Ingredients	Baker's %	Kilogram	US decimal	Lb & Oz	Test
Almonds, toasted	100.00	1.692	3.730	3 11 ⅝	1 lb 6 oz
Sugar	36.67	0.620	1.368	1 5 ⅞	8 oz
Water	11.11	0.188	0.414	6 ⅝	2 oz
Vanilla bean	Each	2	2	2	1 each
Total	147.78	2.500	5.512	5 8 ¼	2 lb

Process

1. Roast the nuts in a low oven until the cores of the nuts are golden brown.
2. Combine the sugar, water, and vanilla bean seeds, and cook until 240°F (116°C).
3. Add the nuts, and stir constantly until the sugar crystallizes and the nuts are dry, white, and sandy.
4. Transfer to a sheet pan to cool, and then store in a covered container for up to 1 month.

FORMULA

CITRUS CONFIT

Slowly cooking fruit in sugar syrup preserves it and changes its flavor and appearance. Candied fruit is often eaten as a confection, used for decoration, or chopped and included as an ingredient in cakes or cookies. Fruits with a sturdy texture such as citrus, pineapples, cherries, and apricots are well suited to this preparation.

Mise en Place

Water for blanching

Sugar syrup (formula follows)

Citrus fruits

Sugar Syrup Formula

Ingredients	Baker's %	Kilogram	US decimal	Lb & Oz	Test
Sugar	100.00	0.546	1.204	1 3 ¼	7 oz
Glucose	42.73	0.233	0.514	8 ¼	3 oz
Water	86.18	0.471	1.038	1 ⅝	6 oz
Total	228.91	1.250	2.756	2 12 ⅛	1 lb

Process, Sugar Syrup

1. Place the sugar, glucose, and water in a pot. Heat until the sugar is completely dissolved.
2. Cool and reserve in the refrigerator until needed.

Process, Citrus Confit

1. Cut the fruits in quarters, and remove the skins. Blanch the skin in boiling water three times, changing the water each time.
2. Bring the syrup to a boil in a pot. Place the blanched skins in the syrup; keep simmering for 1 to 1 ½ hours. Make sure that the syrup does not boil and that the skins are immersed in the syrup.
3. Remove the pot from the heat, and allow the skins to cool in the syrup.
4. Cover well and reserve in the refrigerator until needed.

CHAPTER SUMMARY

There are many ways to apply creativity and design to the products that come out of the pastry kitchen. The pastry chef's decorative repertoire can span from intricate piping for a birthday cake, to pastillage centerpieces, to vibrant sugar showpieces. When deciding on the appropriate elements for a finished item, the pastry chef should always ask what it is for, where it will be served, and how it will be presented. With this information, the project is sure to be a success and the customer, satisfied.

KEY TERMS

- Applied method
- Blown sugar
- Bubble sugar
- Calcium carbonate
- Cast sugar
- Filigree
- Isomalt
- Paper cone
- Pastillage
- Pastillage glue
- Piped sugar
- Pulled sugar
- Rock sugar
- Satinizing
- Sliding method
- Spun sugar
- Sugar lamp
- Tartaric acid
- Thread method

REVIEW QUESTIONS

1. **What is pastillage used for? How is it made? Are there any special considerations?**
2. **Why is tartaric acid used in sugar art? What is the result if the tartaric acid is added to the sugar syrup too soon?**
3. **Why is it important to add glucose to the sugar syrup after it has reached a boil?**
4. **What can be done to ensure the integrity of finished sugar pieces?**
5. **What is satinizing? How is it done?**

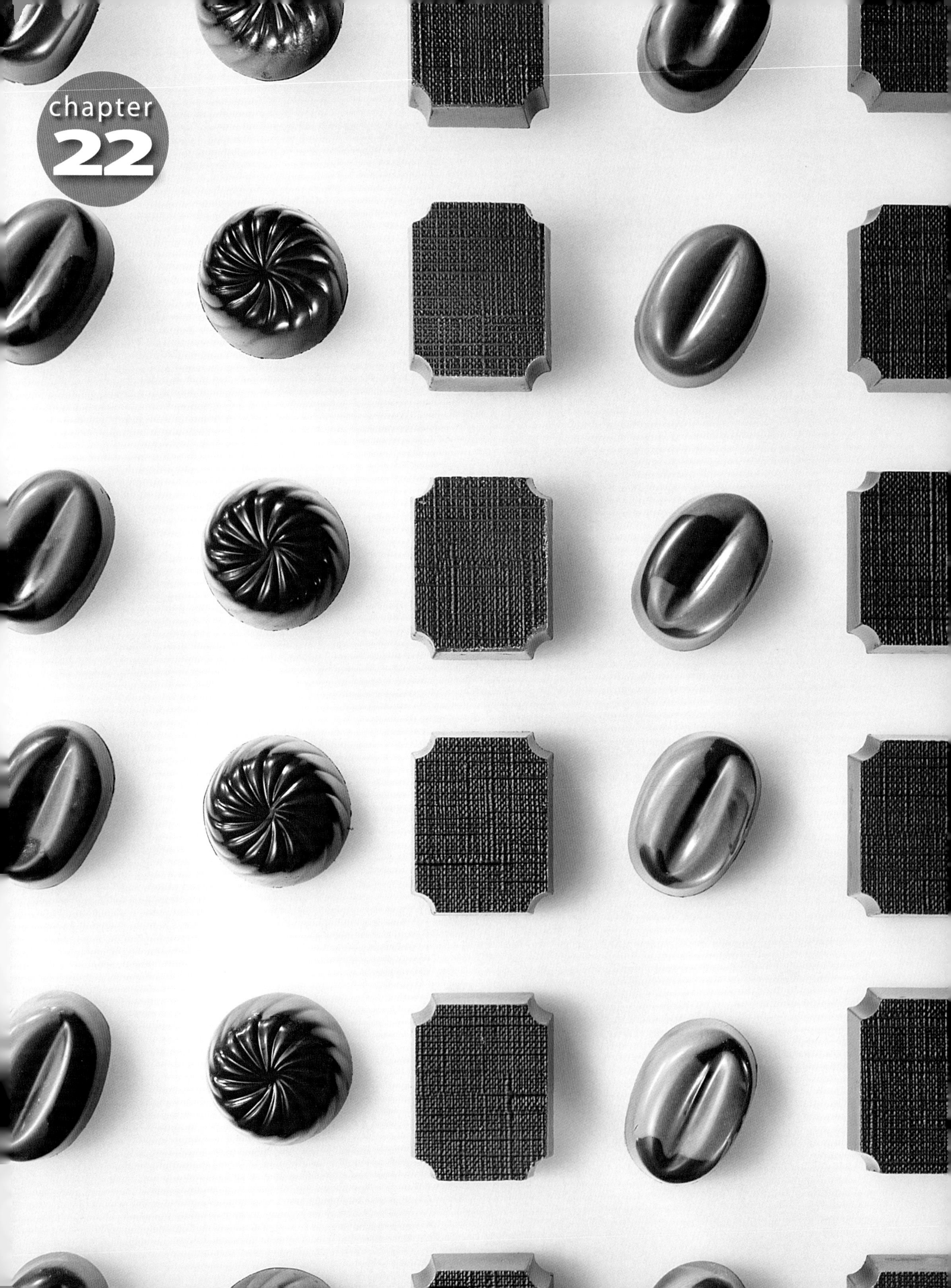
chapter
22

CHOCOLATE AND CHOCOLATE WORK

OBJECTIVES

After reading this chapter, you should be able to

- describe the processes involved in making chocolate and the impact the process has on the flavor and working properties of chocolate.
- temper white, milk, and dark chocolate.
- make a chocolate ganache.
- make an assortment of chocolates and chocolate decorations.

A BRIEF HISTORY OF CHOCOLATE

Chocolate is made from the **cacao bean**, which comes from the pod of the ***Theobroma cacao*** (*Theobroma* translates as "food of the gods"). The global history of chocolate dates to 200 BCE. By 600 CE, the Maya had established cacao plantations in the Yucatan. In their culture, cacao beans were used among the elite as currency, for beverages, and as digestive aids.

In 1502, Christopher Columbus was introduced to cacao but dismissed its importance. Instead, Cortez is typically credited with bringing the popular cocoa beverage process to Spain in 1520. Coe and Coe dispute this attribution because there is no mention of cacao or a cocoa-related product in the plunder lists of Cortez's conquered goods. It was not until 1585 that the first official commerce between Veracruz and Spain brought cocoa to Europe (Coe and Coe, 1996, p. 133).

After cocoa was introduced to Europe, only the wealthy and ruling classes enjoyed cocoa beverages for more than 100 years. These beverages were rich and frothy but became grainy if their temperature was too cool due to the high concentration of fat in the bean. To solve this problem, a press was invented to de-fat the cocoa, turning the drink into a smoother, less fatty beverage. A byproduct of this press was **cocoa butter**, a hard fat in the cocoa bean. Confectioners were asked if there was a use for cocoa butter in candy production. As a result of this effort to prevent waste, the first eating chocolate was produced in 1847. By the late 19th century, cacao plantations were established and producing large quantities of cocoa for export.

THE IMPORTANCE OF THE BEAN

Theobroma cacao is native to northern areas of South America and Central America, but cacao trees are now grown in many regions of the world between 20° north and 20° south. Areas that are well suited to cacao production have high average temperatures, high rainfall, low wind, and rich, deep soil. The trees, which grow up to 30 feet (9 m) high, are native to rainforests where they thrive under the shade-bearing canopy and larger trees. Plantations have adapted to these natural environments by "inter-cropping" coconut, banana, and mango trees to provide shade.

Depending on the variety, cacao trees begin to produce pods after 2 or 3 years of initial growth, but they can take up to 6 years to produce a full yield. The pods, which can contain 30 to 45 beans (technically cotyledons), take about 6 months to develop and vary considerably in color, shape, and size. The cacao bean, also known as the **cotyledon**, is approximately 54 percent cocoa butter and 46 percent cocoa solids.

CACAO VARIETIES

To produce higher yields, resistance to disease and particular flavor profiles, three types of cacao have been developed by interbreeding. They are Criollo, Forastero, and Trinitario.

Criollo is prized for its mild, yet deep chocolate flavor. However, these trees do not have high yields. Criollos grow commonly in Mexico, Nicaragua, Venezuela, Colombia, Madagascar, and the Comoros. The yield from Criollos represents about 10 percent of the worldwide cacao harvest.

The **Forastero** has a well-rounded chocolate flavor, and the trees produce high yields of beans. Forastero is commonly grown in the West African countries of the Ivory Coast, Ghana, and Nigeria, and in the Americas in Brazil, Venezuela, Colombia, Ecuador, Costa Rica, and the Dominican Republic. At 70 percent of the total harvest, the Forastero variety supplies the largest quantity of beans worldwide.

The **Trinitario** is a hybrid of the Criollo and Forastero and can be seen as a compromise between the two. It has higher and more consistent yields than the Criollo and more flavor than Forastero. Trinitario commonly grows in the Criollo's native regions, such as Central and South America. Trinitario makes up the final 20 percent of worldwide cacao yield.

The development of cacao evolved as cultivation spread, higher yields were in demand, and the disease and infestation became more of a problem to growers. Flavor and working properties of cocoa depend on the type of bean as well as the local soil and climate. **Terroir** is the term used to describe the chocolate properties that are developed through the region in which the cacao was grown and can include rainfall, soil conditions, and more. Beans grown closer to the equator will have a harder fat, which is more desirable.

The major cacao-producing areas of the world include West Africa, Southeast Asia, and South America (see Figure 22-1). Production levels are largely influenced by the economy, the political stability of the region, and local infestations and diseases. The chocolate industry is one of the last industries in the modern world to rely heavily on slave labor. In the Ivory Coast, where approximately 70 percent of the world's chocolate is produced, child slave labor continues to be a major problem. In response to this concern, boutique chocolate companies that promote fair trade and organic chocolate often deal directly with the farmer or farmer-owned co-ops to ensure that a larger portion of the money will reach the farm.

CACAO PREPARATION

From the soil the cacao grows in to the type of pile the beans ferment in (heap or bin), cacao preparation is as integral a step in the chocolate-making process as bean processing. Knowing when to harvest and how long to ferment and dry the beans takes experience and knowledge. For cacao beans to be transformed into chocolate, they must be harvested, fermented, dried, and packaged, steps that sound simple yet involve exact measures and critical quality control points.

Harvest

The harvest season lasts for several months. Pods are harvested by machete as they ripen, and only mature pods are removed from the tree.

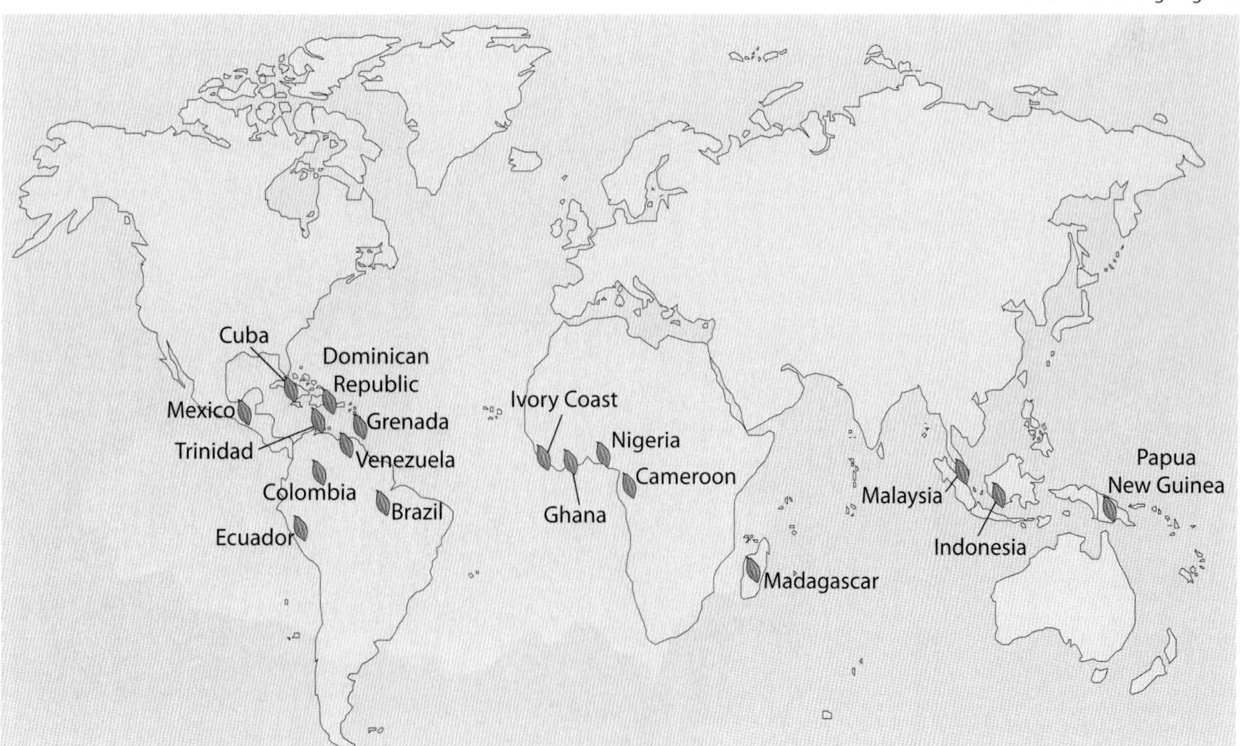

Figure 22-1
Cocoa-Producing Regions

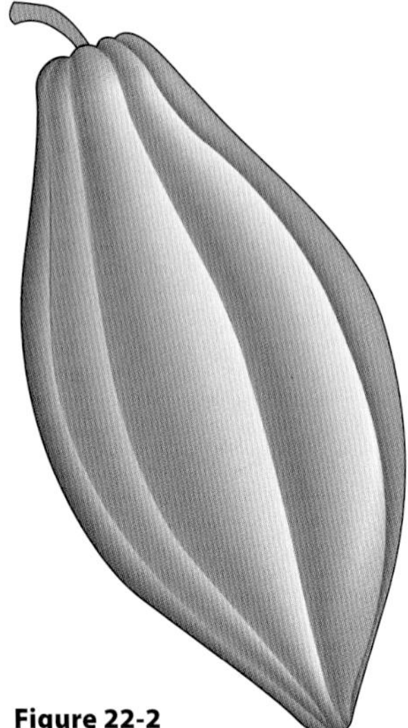

Figure 22-2
Mature Cacao Pod

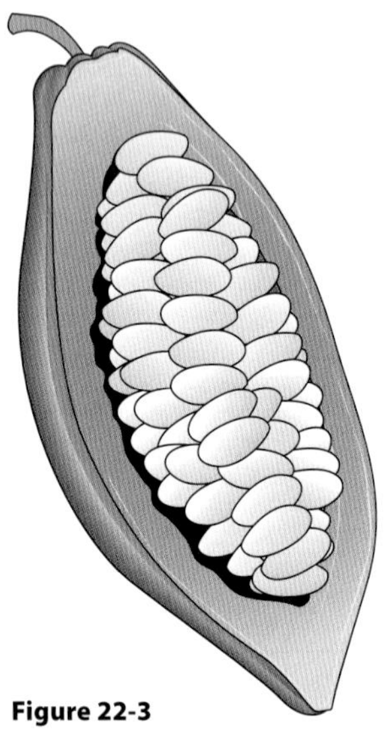

Figure 22-3
Split Cacao Pod

Growers and field workers determine the optimum harvest time. After the pods are harvested, they are opened, and the beans are removed from most of the white, fibrous pulp. At this point in the process, the beans contain approximately 65 percent moisture content. (See Figures 22-2 and 22-3.)

Fermentation

Cacao becomes cocoa when the fermentation process is initiated. Proper fermentation is essential for proper flavor development of the bean, which is alive up until this point. Fermentation, which is typically carried out by the cacao farmer, kills beans within 2 to 3 days.

The two main fermentation techniques are heap and box. Heap fermentation, in which beans are mounded into 55 lb (25 kg) to 5,500 lb (2,500 kg) piles and covered with banana leaves, is typically more popular in Africa (Figure 22-4). Heap fermentation lasts for 5 to 6 days, with the beans typically agitated once or twice. Box fermentation is more popular in Asia and is known to produce more acidity because of increased airflow and production of ethanoic acids (Figure 22-5). Bins designed to generate airflow hold up to 2 tons of beans; however, lower bins with less volume are known to produce better flavors. The beans are transferred to a new bin every day, a process that encourages even fermentation because of easy access to oxygen.

Compared to bread, where yeast breaks down sugars to create alcohol and carbon dioxide, cotyledon fermentation is not a true fermentation. Instead, all fermentation happens on the outside of the bean from microorganisms native to the cacao. Enzymes break down the bean's energy reserve and create sugars and acids. On the outside of the bean, pulp sugars that are fermented by yeast form acids and ethanol. Bacteria activated by the ethanol break it down into acetic acid and lactic acid, which can penetrate the shell and affect the flavor of the bean. The bacteria are "refreshed" from oxygen exposure, increasing the rate of fermentation and flavor profiles. After the beans are fermented, they are washed to remove any remaining pulp and then dried.

Drying

After fermentation is over, the beans are dried to lower the moisture content to 7 to 8 percent, which is required for shipping and further

Figure 22-4
Heap Fermentation

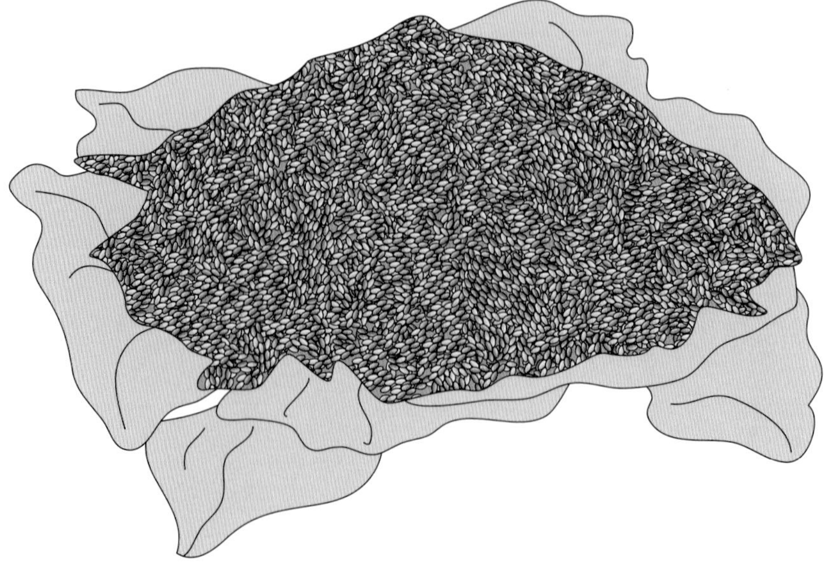

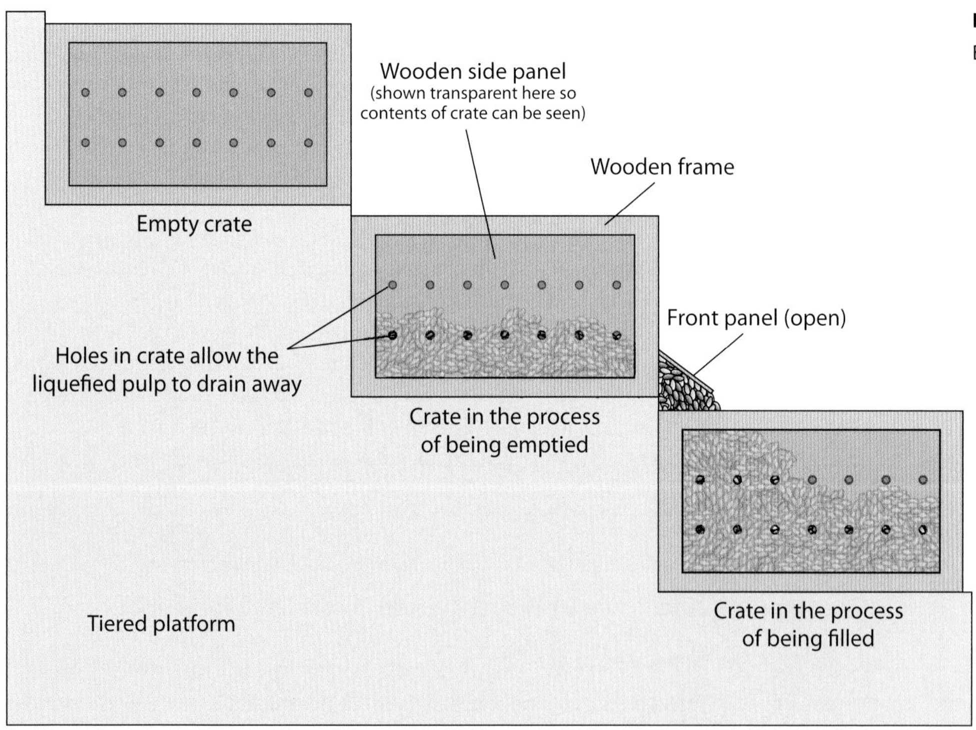

Figure 22-5
Box Fermentation

processing. If the beans are too moist, they can easily mold, and the cocoa flavor would be sacrificed. If the beans are too dry, with less than 6 percent moisture content, the beans can break easily. Beans grown in remote areas with little access to electricity or advanced drying systems frequently become too dry.

The drying process varies largely by region. For example, in some regions, beans are dried in thin layers spread out on large trays. In others, cocoa beans are dried on mats on the ground, which can create a problem if bacteria like *Salmonella* or viruses attach to the bean. Mechanized drying is common in wet climates like Asia, or in areas with a larger volume in a concentrated area. The mechanized drying process is designed to mimic the effects of sun drying with a low, gentle heat that minimizes acidity in the bean.

Storage and Shipping

The dried beans are stored in breathable jute sacks in 132 lb (60 kg) quantities. After they are packed, the beans must be stored away from off odors and condensable surfaces because they can absorb odor and humidity that can lower the quality of the cocoa. During transportation, the hulls of cargo ships can condensate, making proper ventilation and placement away from the walls essential. While excess humidity can cause mold to grow on the beans, a lack of humidity can cause them to dry out.

PROCESSING THE BEAN INTO CHOCOLATE LIQUOR, COCOA BUTTER, AND COCOA POWDER

The goal of the initial processing of the bean is to make chocolate liquor or cocoa butter and cocoa powder. The process involves five steps that transform the bean from a solid to a liquid, including cleaning, roasting, winnowing, grinding, and pressing. To produce quality chocolate, each of these processes needs to be carried out to exact specifications.

There are two options for the manufacturing of cocoa bases. They can either be produced in the country of origin or in the country of processing. Because of the fragility of the bean, processing in the country of origin is best. Chocolate manufacturers do not always consider this approach beneficial because they do not have control over the process.

CLEANING

The first priority of cleaning is to remove foreign materials. Because beans may be dried close to the ground, they may contain foreign contaminates ranging from pebbles to pieces of metal. Removing these contaminates is essential to maintaining integrity over the chocolate and ensuring that there is no damage to machinery. Various techniques are used for this purpose, including agitators that cause denser materials to sink and beans to rise, blowing air that causes lighter pieces of debris to be blown away from the beans, and magnetic devices that attract metals.

ROASTING

Roasting is a critical step in the flavor and color development of cocoa products. It is carried out by applying varying degrees of heat [from 284°F (140°C) to 302°F (150°C)] and constant motion to the cotyledons, a process that alters the flavor precursors and chemicals associated with chocolate flavor. The process of roasting removes astringent and bitter elements from the cocoa and lowers its acidic properties, which is essential in obtaining a cleaner chocolate flavor. During the roasting process, the water content of the bean is reduced to about 3 percent.

There is not one prescribed way to roast cocoa. Depending on origin and size of the cotyledons, different temperatures and temperature combinations can be used to achieve multiple characteristics in a single cacao variety. Different roasting durations also develop different flavor profiles. In addition, beans can be roasted whole, in pieces (nibs), or in liquor form after the shells are removed. Whichever form is chosen, all the cocoa being roasted must be of uniform size. If mixed sizes are roasted in the same batch, the smaller pieces will burn and the larger ones will be underroasted.

High heat also kills bacteria such as *Salmonella* and any enzymes that have survived the fermentation process. Roasting is such a critical control point that beans are considered to be wholesome only after it is complete. Roasting is typically carried out in a controlled environment that is closed off from the rest of chocolate production to ensure no cross contamination.

WINNOWING

Winnowing is the process of separating the shell and germ from the bean before grinding to ensure chocolate purity. Several techniques are used for the winnowing process, in which nibs or bean pieces are separated out early in the process to prevent further breakage and the remaining whole beans are projected at high speeds against plates that cause them to crack. The shells are then separated through vibration that causes the nibs to sink and the shells to rise to the surface. Whole cotyledon pieces are easier to separate and generate less waste. If pieces of the nib are attached to shells, they are usually thrown away. After the nib has been extracted from the shell and the germ has been removed, the next step is to grind the cocoa.

GRINDING

Grinding is the phase of production when the cocoa is transformed from a solid state to one that has liquid-like flow properties when warm and solid properties at room temperature (chocolate liquor). A two-step process is used to make the cocoa particles small enough for further processing into chocolate, and to extract the fat from the cells of the bean so it can coat all of the solid, nonfat particles. The friction created during this two-stage process generates enough heat to melt the cocoa butter within the chocolate liquor. It reduces the nibs by 100 times from an initial size of about one half of a centimeter to about 25 to 30 microns.

Two stages of processing are needed for the production of chocolate liquor. First, an impact mill is used to break up the nibs into smaller pieces by hitting them with hammers against screens. The force of the blow heats the cocoa butter, and it falls through the sieve along with any solids. This is repeated until all of the nibs have passed through the screen. The next step is to further reduce the size of the cocoa paste using a disc mill or ball mill that further refine the paste and reduce the particle size by grinding the cocoa down to a very small size. Once this stage is complete, the end result is chocolate liquor.

It is possible to overgrind chocolate liquor. If all of the fat is pressed out of the cells, the cells begin to break down and are then coated with fat. This has an undesirable thickening effect on the chocolate. After the chocolate liquor has been made it can be sold as is, processed into cocoa butter and cocoa powder, or processed to make chocolate.

PRESSING CHOCOLATE LIQUOR

Hydraulic presses are used to press cocoa butter from chocolate liquor. Because no more than half of the cocoa butter is pressed out of the liquor, the remaining solids form a compressed cocoa cake that is later milled into cocoa powder. Cakes can contain 8 to 24 percent fat, depending on pressure.

Cocoa Butter

Cocoa butter, the natural hard fat found in the cacao, exists within the cotyledon at about 55 percent of the total weight. Although it occurs naturally in the shell, it is of a lesser quality and is infrequently used. Cocoa butter has a unique melting property in that it can be solid at room temperature and yet melt at body temperature.

Due to these unique melting properties, cocoa butter has many applications in various industries, including pharmaceuticals and cosmetics. In chocolate making, cocoa butter is added to chocolate liquor to improve viscosity and mouthfeel. It is also used in other confectionary and pastry making because of its setting properties.

Cocoa Powder

Cocoa powder is milled from the cocoa cake left over after the cocoa butter has been pressed out of the chocolate liquor. The classic fat ranges of cocoa powder include 20 to 22 percent, 10 to 12 percent, and 8 percent. Cocoa powder is used in a wide range of baking, pastry, and beverage applications.

Dutched Cocoa Powder **Dutched cocoa powder** is made from processing chocolate liquor or cocoa beans that have been treated with an alkali, usually potassium carbonate. This process was invented in the Netherlands in the 19th century by Conrad van Houten as a way to make cocoa powder less likely to clump or sink to the bottom when combined with liquids. The addition of an alkali to the cocoa powder intensifies the color and makes the flavor mellower, yet stronger.

CHOCOLATE COUVERTURE PRODUCTION

After the base chocolate liquor has been made, it can be further processed into chocolate **couverture**. In French, *couverture* means "coating," and couverture grade chocolate refers to chocolate that contains *only* cocoa butter as fat. To make the couverture, the chocolate liquor, sugar, extra cocoa butter, and any other additional ingredients such as milk powder, vanilla bean, and lecithin are combined and milled to a particle size of at least 30 microns.

REFINER MILL

The initial process of combining and milling ingredients is carried out in succession in two machines called the two roll and five roll refiner mills. These mills utilize increasing pressure of cylindrical rollers to decrease the particle size of the chocolate. The purpose of these processes is to coat all the solid particles with fat and to reach a particle size between 15 and 25 microns to ensure smooth taste. A particle size larger than 30 microns is noticeable to the palate and a particle size smaller than 15 microns makes a pasty chocolate that sticks to the mouth.

CONCHE

The conche was invented to further refine chocolate in late 19th-century Switzerland by Rudi Lindt. Although modern processes using roller refiners are efficient enough to reach the desired 15 to 25 micron particle size, the refinement process was not so exact 100 years ago. The conche was and still is a required step in the chocolate-making process to achieve the finer textures of quality chocolate. Today conching is done to improve flavor and viscosity and flow properties.

During the **conching** process, milk chocolate is heated to between 140°F (60°C) and 185°F (85°C) and dark chocolate is heated to 140°F (60°C). This rise in temperature, in conjunction with constant agitation, reduces the water content of the chocolate from approximately 4 percent to about 0.5 percent (Lenôtre, 2000, p. 21). It is thought that through the evaporation of water content, any remaining volatile acids produced during fermentation are released through vents on the top of the conche (Beckett, 2000, p. 57). The action of the chocolate pressed against the side of tank repeatedly further coats the solid particles and creates chocolate with more fluid properties. As the mixing continues, additional cocoa butter and lecithin are added to adjust viscosity. The conching of the chocolate, depending on the equipment, can take anywhere from 8 hours to 2 days. It is a common misconception that longer conching creates better flavor, but the opposite is actually the case.

TEMPERING AND MOLDING

After chocolate has been conched, it must be tempered before molding. Tempering allows the chocolate to set quickly and creates a firm, crisp texture and shiny finish. Untempered chocolate takes a long time to set and has a dull finish with white streaks. In general, the better the tempering, the easier it is to mold chocolate. Although molding is often thought of in terms of commercial chocolate manufacturing, it is equally important for the confectioner or pastry chef.

Tempering refers to the process of precrystallizing a portion of the cocoa butter within the chocolate so that it can later crystallize the remainder of the fats and set the chocolate. Careful control over crystallization is accomplished by moving the chocolate, changing the temperature, and introducing precrystallized fat crystals into the chocolate. Commercial tempering involves a heating and cooling process that is designed to precrystallize a portion of the cocoa butter so that it can properly set in the mold. After the chocolate is tempered, it can be used immediately for molding. After the molds are filled, they are cooled, and the chocolate is later extracted, wrapped, and shipped. Figure 22-6 is a flowchart of chocolate production from cacao bean to bars. The tempering process will be covered in depth later in this chapter.

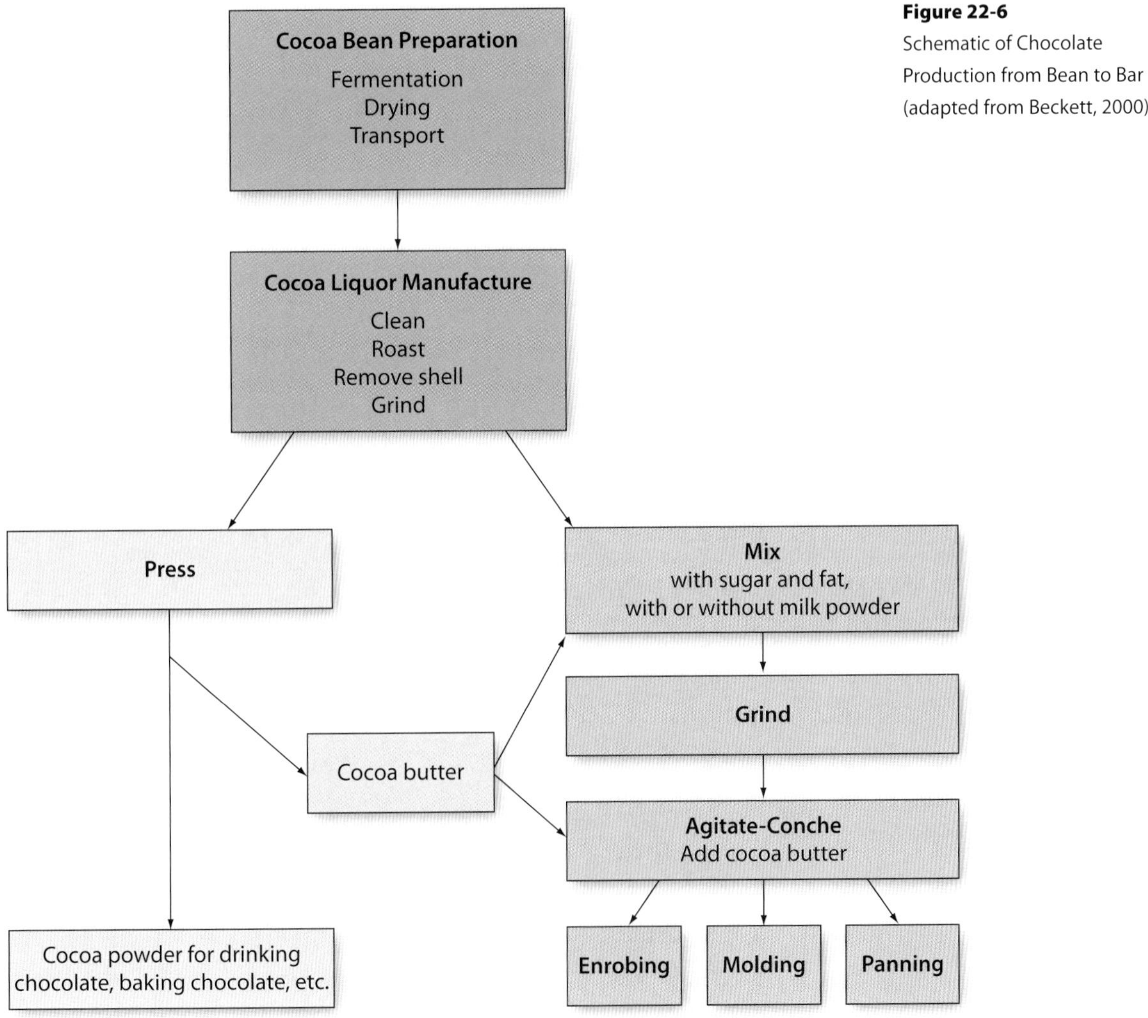

Figure 22-6
Schematic of Chocolate Production from Bean to Bar (adapted from Beckett, 2000)

COCOA PRODUCTS

STANDARDS OF IDENTITY: CHOCOLATE

A vast number of products are made from cocoa. To prevent adulteration and maintain certain standards, many countries have Standards of Identity for Chocolate. These standards dictate ingredients and the levels at which they must be present to be used in chocolate-related products. (See Figure 22-7.)

UNDERSTANDING CHOCOLATE PERCENTAGES

Chocolates are often referred to with percentages that tell the consumer the amount of cocoa ingredients in the chocolate in relation to other ingredients. Cocoa ingredients include chocolate liquor, which is roughly 54 percent cocoa butter and 46 percent cocoa solids.

For example, a dark chocolate bar is made from 100 parts that include cocoa, sugar, vanilla, and lecithin. A 70 percent chocolate contains 70 parts of cocoa product and about 29 parts of sugar. The remaining part is combined and contains flavoring such as vanilla and lecithin.

Figure 22-7

Chart of Standards of Identity for US and Canadian Chocolate Products

US Food and Drug Administration (FDA) Regulation—April 1, 2003

	Chocolate Liquor	Semi-Sweet Chocolate	Sweet Chocolate	Milk Chocolate	White Chocolate
Cocoa butter	Min. 50% Max. 60%	—	—	—	Min. 20%
Chocolate liquor	100%	Min. 35%	Min. 15%	Min. 10%	—
Milk solids	—	< 12%	< 12%	Min. 12%	Min. 14%
Milk fat	—	—	—	Min. 3.39%	Min. 3.5%
Sugar	—	—	—	—	Max. 55%
Emulsifiers	—	Max. 1%	Max. 1%	Max. 1%	Max. 1.5%
Antioxidants	No	No	No	No	Yes
Whey Products	No	No	No	No	Max. 5%

Health & Welfare Canada: Food and Drug Regulations—June 11, 1997

	Chocolate Liquor	Semi-Sweet Chocolate	Sweet Chocolate	Milk Chocolate	White Chocolate
Cocoa butter	Min. 50%	Min. 18%	Min. 18%	Min. 15%	Min. 20%
Total cocoa solids	100%	Min. 35%	Min. 30%	Min. 25%	—
Fat-free cocoa solids	—	Min. 14%	Min. 12%	Min. 2.5%	—
Milk solids	—	< 5%	< 12%	Min. 12%	Min. 14%
Milk fat	—	—	—	Min. 3.39%	Min. 3.5%
Sugar	—	—	—	—	—
Emulsifiers		Max. 1.5%	Max. 1.5%	Max. 1.5%	Max. 1.5%
Antioxidants	Yes (through fats)	Yes (through fats)	Yes (through fats)	Yes (through fats)	Yes (through fats)
Whey products	No	No	No	No	No

The 70 parts of cocoa product are a combination of chocolate liquor and added cocoa butter. All chocolate manufacturers add additional cocoa butter during the conching stage to improve chocolate flow properties and eating qualities. Not all manufacturers make the cocoa solids content known to consumers, however. This can be determined for dark chocolate couverture only by the consumer. If a 0.100 kg bar of 70 percent chocolate has a total of 0.040 kg of fat, the total known quantity of fat can be subtracted from the total cocoa percentage to determine that the cocoa solid content is 0.030 kg. This formula will not work for milk and white chocolate, which have additional fat content from the milk solids.

The higher the percentage of cocoa, the more bitter the chocolate will taste. Even though the percentage of cocoa in chocolate has an effect on quality, it does not mean that more cocoa content makes better quality chocolate.

Chocolate Liquor

Chocolate liquor, which is produced from the whole cocoa bean after it has gone through the initial production process, often has cocoa butter added to improve flow properties. Chocolate liquor is a base product that can be turned into cocoa powder and cocoa butter, can be sold as unsweetened chocolate, or can be further processed into dark or milk chocolate products. Other names for chocolate liquor are **cocoa mass** and **cocoa paste**.

Cocoa Powder

Cocoa powder is made from chocolate liquor by pressing out a portion of the fat with hydraulic presses. Depending on the quantity of fat extracted, the cocoa will have a variable fat content ranging from 8 to 24 percent. Most cocoa powder is alkalized during processing to make the chocolate flavor and colors more pronounced.

Dark Chocolate

Dark chocolate is made using chocolate liquor, additional cocoa butter, and sugar. Additional ingredients like vanilla and lecithin can be added. The range of cocoa in the chocolate will determine the cocoa percentage, with most quality dark chocolates containing between 55 and 80 percent cocoa. The terms sweet, semi-sweet, and bittersweet are used to differentiate categories of sweetness as the percentage changes.

Sweet Chocolate **Sweet chocolate** is made from a combination of chocolate liquor, cocoa butter, and sugar, and must contain at least 15 percent chocolate liquor. This chocolate, which has ranges from 15 to 50 percent, is uncommon in quality confectionary work.

Semi-Sweet Chocolate **Semi-sweet chocolate** is more flavorful than sweet dark chocolate because it has higher percentage of cocoa solids. This type of chocolate can be used for confectionary work (coatings, fillings), as well as pastry and entremets. The average percentages are 50 to 64 percent.

Bittersweet Chocolate **Bittersweet chocolate**, with cocoa content ranges from 64 to 85 percent, is becoming increasingly popular as the consumption of quality chocolate grows. Bittersweet chocolate can be used in chocolate confections, baked goods, and entremets.

Milk Chocolate

Milk chocolate is made from chocolate liquor, sugar, milk solids, vanilla, and lecithin. It can range in cocoa content from 10 to 45 percent. European-style milk chocolate is darker than what most American palates are accustomed to and may taste of caramel due to a high temperature during the conching process. By law, milk chocolate in the United States must contain at least 10 percent cocoa mass and 12 percent milk solids.

White Chocolate

White chocolate is not a true chocolate because it contains no cocoa solids. Instead, it is made from cocoa butter, milk solids, sugar, and flavoring ingredients. In 2002, the FDA revised the standards of identity for white chocolate by determining that it must contain at least 20 percent cocoa butter and 14 percent milk solids.

Specialty Chocolates

This category includes products like **gianduja** (chocolate, usually milk chocolate, combined with a nut paste, usually hazelnut) and flavored chocolates like cappuccino, coffee, or orange. This lesser category of specialty chocolates is emerging as consumers become more aware of quality cocoa and more adventurous in taste. Some confectioners have begun producing chocolate bars with the addition of spices, dried fruits, and nuts. These items are not regulated because the manufacturer typically adds flavorings to chocolate that is already made.

Origin Chocolates

Origin chocolates are made using beans from one growing region. The result is a uniquely flavored chocolate with flavor that highlights local cocoa varieties and production nuances. Like estate wines, origin chocolates are prized for their unique and unadulterated flavor.

Coating and Compound Chocolate

Coating chocolate, also called compound chocolate, is made with **cocoa butter equivalents (CBEs)** and is designed for use without tempering. Palm kernel oil, a common CBE, is fractionated to mirror cocoa butter's crystallization properties. CBEs eliminate the need to temper the coating or compound chocolate after it has melted.

The taste of coating chocolate is not as good as couverture because the unique melting properties of cocoa butter create superior quality in mouth release and flavor. CBEs, which have a higher melting point, take away from chocolate flavor.

Coating chocolate has less sheen, as well as less-appealing taste and mouthfeel. It is, however, a convenient product for applications when there is no knowledge of couverture working properties and is often called for in conjunction with couverture for chocolate glazes. The working temperature of coating chocolate is 95°F (35°C).

PROPERTIES OF COCOA BUTTER IN CHOCOLATE

To successfully understand chocolate and how to work with it, it is important to understand cocoa butter. This is because the ability to control cocoa butter is necessary for successful chocolate and confectionary work. Cocoa butter is responsible for melting properties, setting properties, brilliant sheen, and the crisp snap of well-tempered chocolate. If it is not properly precrystallized in the tempering process, a phenomenon known as **fat bloom**, or migration of the cocoa butter to the surface of the chocolate, occurs. Fat bloom appears as a harmless, cloudy white dust over chocolate. Chocolate with fat bloom can still be used in confectionary work after it has been properly tempered.

Like all fats, cocoa butter is a **triglyceride** composed of three fatty acids connected to a glycerol molecule. The triglyceride in cocoa butter is composed of oleic acid (35 percent), stearic acid (34 percent), and palmitic acid (26 percent). The simple composition of cocoa butter adds to the unique melting range of chocolate. It has a fusion point of 97°F (36°C) and can go from solid to liquid with no real intermediate state, unlike butter, which softens before it liquefies.

Cocoa butter is a **polymorphic** substance that can crystallize into six different forms, all which have different melting properties and stability. The chocolate-manufacturing industry has named these six forms using Roman numerals, and the oil and fat industry using letters from the Greek alphabet (Beckett, 2000, p. 89). This text uses Roman numerals in reference to crystal structure.

Cocoa butter crystals set depending on the way in which they are formed. Form I, which is very unstable, creates very loose crystal structure and is mostly used as an ice cream topping. However, it eventually reaches a firmer form IV crystalline structure (Beckett, 2000, p. 90). The most desirable of these forms is **form V crystallization**, which confectioners and chocolate manufacturers require to ensure a shelf stable product that is resistant to fat bloom. Form V is characterized by the "dense compacting" of the fat crystals into an organized structure. The six forms of crystallization are shown in Figure 22-8.

The existence of form VI crystallization has been debated in the scientific community. Form VI crystallization occurs when solid cocoa butter migrates through the chocolate to bloom on the surface after extended storage under normal conditions. Granular cocoa butter (form VI) can be used as seeds in tempering chocolate and even in setting mousse applications.

WORKING WITH CHOCOLATE

In the pastry shop, working with chocolate has long been considered a special privilege. There is much to consider when working with this ingredient because every part of the process, from harvesting to decoration, is carried out by people who understand the nuances of cocoa products and how to not waste any of it.

		Melting Point (°F)
Unstable	I	60.8–64.4 Loose Compacting
	II	71.6–75.2
	III	75.2–78.8
	IV	78.8–82.4
	V	89.6–93.2
Stable	VI	93.2–96.8 Dense Compacting

Figure 22-8
Melting Points of Cocoa Butter (adapted from Beckett, 2000, p. 90)

STORAGE OF CHOCOLATE

Although a seasoned **chocolatier** (one who works professionally with chocolate) will know how to store chocolate, it is a major factor in quality control that the novice must understand. Chocolate should always be well wrapped and stored in a cool dry place. It should never be stored in the refrigerator or freezer because it will form damage-causing condensation and sweat which will result in **sugar bloom**. Sugar bloom happens when chocolate is stored in high humidity areas and forms condensation on its surface. The sugar attracts the humidity to the surface of the chocolate; this makes the surface moist and draws out some of the sugar from the chocolate. Once the water content evaporates, the sugar remains on the surface of the chocolate in a crystallized form. Chocolate should also be stored away from direct sunlight and should not be stored on the floor.

MELTING CHOCOLATE

Chocolate must be melted before it can be tempered for use in decorative or confectionary work. The following are guidelines for melting chocolate; however, the manufacturer's directions, which should be printed on the packaging, should be consulted and followed.

- Dark chocolate should be melted to 120°F (49°C).
- Milk and white chocolate should be melted to 110°F (43°C).

Due to the higher milk and sugar content of white and milk chocolates, they should not be heated as much as dark chocolate. If overheated, white, milk, and dark chocolate can thicken at an increased rate.

Before adding chocolate to any vessel for melting, it should first be inspected for cleanliness and water contamination. Even small quantities of water in chocolate can cause a phenomenon called **seizing**, which thickens the chocolate into a paste.

Some pastry chefs heat chocolate over a bain-marie. This technique will work, but the steam generated from the water is a potential threat. In addition, steam is a very effective heat generator that can cause the chocolate to become overheated. If using this technique, moderate heat should be used, and the chocolate should be stirred often to ensure even heating.

If used properly, the microwave can be used for melting chocolate. If the microwave is large enough to melt the quantity desired, this is an economical choice. To prevent overheating and burning, the chocolate should be stirred every 30 seconds until it is fluid. When the chocolate is in a fluid state, it can withstand more time in the microwave without burning.

The best way to melt chocolate is slowly in an ambient heat of about 135°F (57°C) for dark and 125°F (52°C) for milk and white. Although these temperatures may seem high, the chocolate should melt to the proper temperature within 12 to 18 hours. The slower the chocolate melts, the more fluid it will be. Caution must be taken to ensure that chocolate is not left for a long time without being stirred; this can cause the cocoa butter to rise to the surface and the solids to sink to the bottom. In addition, if the storage temperature is above 113°F (45°C) for milk and white chocolate, the flavor can be affected, and the proteins from the milk solids can combine and thicken (Beckett, 2000, p. 105).

Overheated chocolate is difficult to use for fine confectionary work. This is not to suggest that it should be discarded, however. Overheated chocolate works extremely well for showpieces because thicker chocolate is sometimes beneficial in molding larger items. It is also possible to add some fresh chocolate (50 percent) to overheated chocolate to help it cool faster and to add a material with lower viscosity to the batch.

TEMPERING CHOCOLATE

Tempering chocolate involves the process of melting and precrystallizing the cocoa butter to have it set in an organized way. This creates a nice gloss, resistance to fat bloom, and a good snap. Poorly crystallized, improperly stored, and old chocolate can form fat bloom or become untempered. Even though this chocolate is perfectly edible, it is not attractive.

Because cocoa butter is so sensitive to temperature variation, there are ideal requirements for tempering that should serve as guidelines. The ideal ambient temperature for tempering chocolate is 70°F (21°C). It is possible to temper chocolate in an environment that is outside of this figure, but it will create some challenges. For example, if the pastry maker is working in a room that is colder than 70°F (21°C), the chocolate will set up at an accelerated rate, and the pastry chef will have to work faster to keep up with the chocolate's behavior. In a room that is too warm, the chocolate may never be able to be tempered because appropriate precrystallization cannot take place due to the high ambient temperatures.

For chocolate to be tempered, it must be heated, cooled, and then warmed to specific temperatures. Although individual brands of chocolate provide temperature goals for tempering, it is helpful to know the guidelines. After dark chocolate is melted to 120°F (49°C) and milk and white chocolate is be melted to 110°F (43°C), it must be cooled to 82°F (28°C) and then reheated to 88°F (31°C) to 91°F (33°C) for dark chocolate and 84°F (49°C) to 86°F (49°C) for white and milk chocolate, respectively (see Figure 22-9).

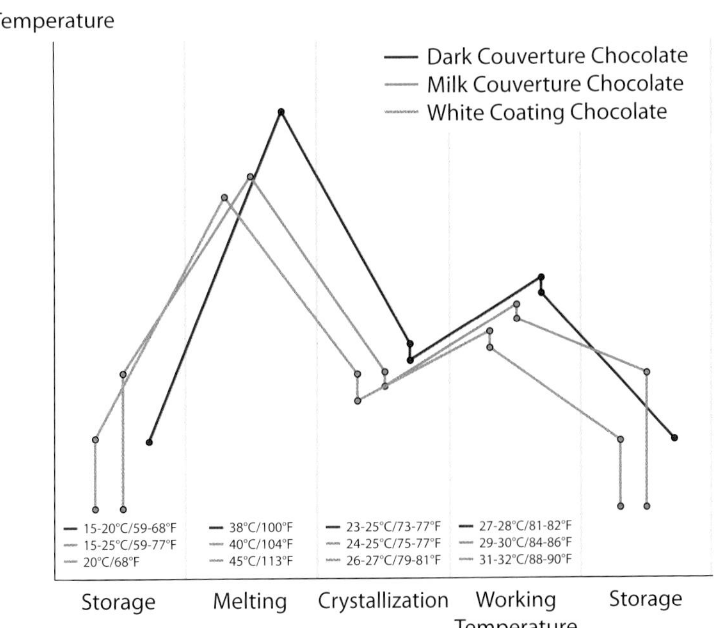

Figure 22-9
Guidelines for Tempering Chocolate

FIGURE 22-10 TEMPERING CHOCOLATE

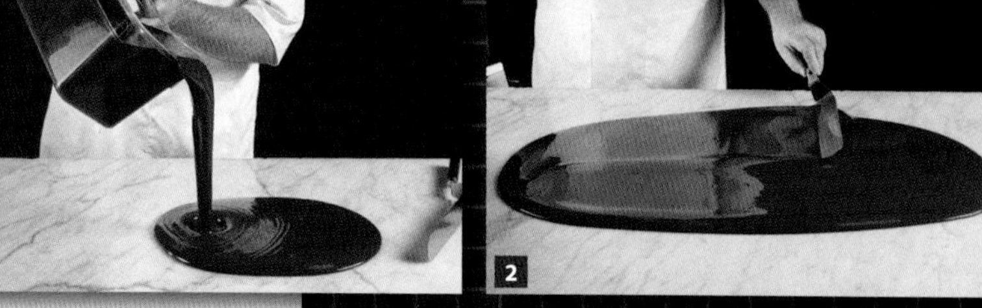

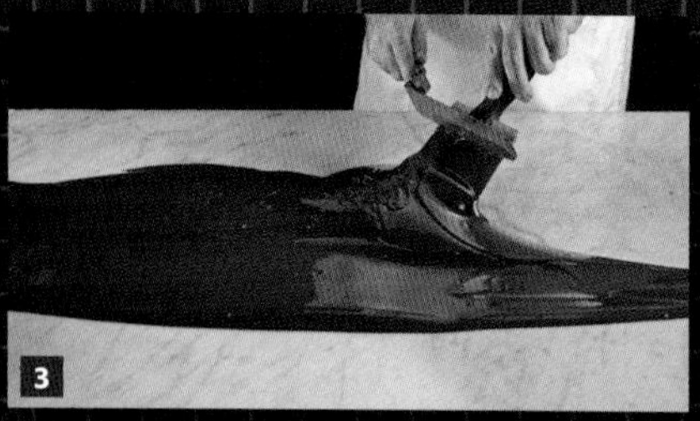

1 Once the chocolate is melted to 120°F, pour three-fourths of it onto the granite slab.

2 Spread the chocolate out to cool it down.

3 Bring the chocolate in toward the center and then spread it out again.

The three primary methods for successful chocolate tempering are seed, table, and mechanical. Using one of these three techniques, anyone can temper chocolate, provided the work is done in proper ambient conditions. After this section on the major tempering techniques, what to do with the chocolate as well as how to maintain its temper will be explored.

Seed Method

The seed method is the most approachable method for the serious home pastry cook, as it does not require a machine or a granite slab. In theory, melted, decrystallized chocolate is "seeded" with crystallized cocoa butter by adding well-tempered chocolate.

Once the chocolate is melted, one-fourth of the weight of the batch is added in seed. For example, for 4.4 lb (2 kg) of melted chocolate, 1.1 lb (0.5 kg) is required to seed. After the seed chocolate is added to the melted chocolate, it should be stirred briefly to incorporate and then left to sit. As the seed chocolate melts, it cools the decrystallized chocolate and provides a stable form of cocoa butter for the unstable cocoa butter to begin crystallizing around.

After a couple of minutes, the batch should be stirred using a clean, dry rubber spatula, taking care to not incorporate air. Stirring should continue until all the added chocolate has been melted. The motion of stirring will help the seeds melt and will also help the precrystallized cocoa butter become organized into the required form V crystallization configuration.

The next step is to check the temperature of the chocolate and to do a **test strip** to see if it is in temper. A test strip is made by applying a thin strip of chocolate over a small piece of parchment paper and observing the setting properties of the chocolate to determine whether the chocolate is in temper, and if it is, what the quality of the temper is. The desired temperature is between 82°F (28°C) and 86°F (30°C) for white and milk chocolate, and between 88°F (31°C) and 91°F (33°C) for dark chocolate. Stirring should continue while waiting for the results of the test strip.

Table Method

The table method can be a quick and easy way to temper chocolate. It is also the most theatrical because it involves spreading the chocolate over a cool granite surface and successfully getting it back into the reserved warm chocolate container. Anywhere from 2 lb (1 kg) to 22 lb (10 kg) can easily be tempered on a granite slab. The only limitation is the size of the table. See Tempering Chocolate Figure 22-10 for an entire tempering process using the table method.

For this method, once the chocolate is melted to its appropriate temperature, three-fourths of the chocolate is poured onto the clean, dry

4 After the chocolate has cooled to the proper temperature, return it to the container with the reserved warm chocolate, stir the two together, and take the temperature.

5 Make a test strip to determine whether or not the chocolate is in temper.

6 These test strips show properly tempered chocolate on left, which set within 2 minutes, and undertempered chocolate on right, which was still unset after 30 minutes.

granite slab and the remaining chocolate is reserved. The chocolate on the granite is spread out and moved back and forth periodically using a palette knife and a scraper. When the temperature has dropped to between 79°F (26°C) and 81°F (27°C) for milk chocolate and between 82°F (28°C) and 84°F (29°C) for dark chocolate, sufficient precrystallization will have taken place and the cooling must be stopped to prevent the cocoa butter from overcrystallizing. This is accomplished by quickly returning the chocolate to the reserved, warm chocolate and stirring for at least 1 minute to incorporate the two temperatures and spread the precrystallized cocoa butter throughout the mass.

After the chocolate has been stirred for at least a minute, the temperature should be checked and a test strip should be made. The desired temperature is between 82°F (28°C) and 86°F (30°C) for white and milk chocolate and between 88°F (31°C) and 91°F (33°C) for dark chocolate. While the test strip is setting, the chocolate should continue to be stirred.

Mechanical Methods

Because chocolate can be a challenging medium to work with, and is so dependent on the appropriate application of heat, motion, and duration of motion, machines have been developed to assist everyone from the home pastry cook to the largest commercial producer. The tempering capacity varies greatly and can range from 2 lb (1 kg) to several tons an hour. Even though it is being accomplished by machine, the main principles of tempering remain the same.

The two main styles of machines are automatic and manual. Automatic machines are able to measure temperature and make changes accordingly based on the type of chocolate. The operator must double-check the temper of the chocolate for quality control. Automatic tempering machines are frequently used for only large manufacturers. Manual machines are run by the operator and can have a range of controls and capabilities. While basic manual tempering units often melt the chocolate without motion, other manual models melt the chocolate in motion, with temperature changes controlled by the operator.

Either type of tempering unit can be a continuous tempering or batch tempering unit. Continuous tempering units supply a continuous feed of tempered chocolate, while batch tempering units temper only a given quantity of chocolate. Whatever machine is used, the operator needs to have a full understanding of it and the tempering process.

Reacting to the Initial Temper Once the initial tempering of the chocolate has occurred, the technician needs to verify the degree of temper and take appropriate action. At this point, the chocolate may be perfectly tempered, **undertempered**, or **overtempered**. The way to determine this is by examining the test strip and looking for the degree to which the chocolate is set, the presence of fat bloom, and the sheen.

If the chocolate is perfectly tempered, continue on to work with chocolate, being sure to maintain the temper.

An undertempered chocolate will appear dull and will have visible cocoa butter migration to the surface of the chocolate. It will not set up within 2 minutes and will never have a shine, or characteristics of well-tempered chocolate. For undertempered chocolate, more precrystallized cocoa butter should be introduced into the chocolate, and stirring should continue to encourage the organization of the fat crystals into the proper form V. If adding more chocolate, ground chocolate that melts easily is recommended. If pistoles (small, flat "buttons" of chocolate) are added, they may take too long to melt and could begin to overcrystallize the chocolate.

Chocolate is easily ground in a food processor, where it is pulsed until it is mealy. It is important to not mix it too much because the increased temperature rise from friction can cause it to melt. The chocolate should be stirred and checked periodically until the appropriate temper is achieved.

A sign that chocolate is overtempered is a quick setting time of the chocolate. If the test strip sets in 30 seconds, or if the chocolate bows a lot during the setting process, it is overtempered. Overtempered chocolate should be warmed in order to prevent rapid crystallization of the cocoa butter. Care must be taken, however, to not create undertempered chocolate in the process. A couple of techniques work well in this situation. Chocolate that has been melted to full decrystallization can be added to the overtempered chocolate to raise the temperature and increase the number of decrystallized fat crystals. Another option is to apply direct heat to the too cool chocolate by microwave or heat gun.

After undertempered and overtempered chocolate is remedied, it should be tested for the quality of the temper. Well-tempered chocolate should set within 2 minutes [in a room with a temperature of 70°F (21°C)]. Additionally, the surface of the chocolate should not have any visible fat migration, and there should be minimal bowing of the chocolate. When the temper is good, confectionary or decorative work can begin.

Maintaining Form V To work efficiently, a good temper must be maintained. This will provide fluid chocolate that does not thicken quickly and sets within 2 minutes under an ambient 70°F (21°C) temperature.

Because the working temperature range for chocolate is so narrow, the temperature must be closely monitored. As it fluctuates, the chocolate can become too cold or too warm to work with. An experienced chocolatier can do this visually, taking cues from the well of chocolate, as well as from how it falls off of enrobed candies or out of molds. For novices, temperatures are best measured with a digital thermometer.

Temperature can be maintained with a heat gun, with a bain-marie, or by adding 120°F (49°C) chocolate. The two benefits to this last technique are an increase of temperature and volume of the couverture. Using this method, the chocolatier should be able to work from one batch of tempered chocolate for many hours. Optimum crystallization must occur, though, and care must be taken to avoid overcrystallization.

In addition to monitoring the temperature, the chocolatier must continue to stir the chocolate while working with it. Just as a lack of stirring can result in chocolate that becomes prematurely overcrystallized, so an excessive amount of motion can also result in overcrystallized chocolate. If working out of a container that is not temperature-controlled, care must be taken to not stir the sides, as there will most likely be a buildup of chocolate. This chocolate has crystallized due to the contact with a cold surface and if it is stirred into the fluid chocolate, it will introduce an abundance of crystals that can overcrystallize the rest of the batch.

APPLICATIONS USING CHOCOLATE COUVERTURE

Chocolate couverture is not limited to confectionary or decorative work. Couverture-grade chocolate may be used in a number of applications, including cookies, quick breads, pie, assorted creams, and mousse cakes. The quality of the chocolate used in those applications does not always need to be as high as it should be for confectionary work. For example, a brownie can be successfully made using a midgrade couverture; however, a mousse cake for a high-end restaurant or pastry shop will benefit from a high-grade couverture. Below are the general processes for applications using chocolate couverture that do not appear in other chapters. The processes for chocolate confections and decorative work are also explored.

GANACHE

In its simplest form, a ganache is a smooth emulsion made from chocolate and a liquid like cream, milk, or fruit puree. The ratio of chocolate to liquid varies depending on the type of chocolate used, the percentage of cocoa in the chocolate, and the desired results. A ganache can be formulated for many uses, including as a component in cakes, as an icing or as the center of a chocolate.

Ingredients of Ganache

Ganaches made for filling candies rely on a basic set of ingredients that guarantee good flavor and optimal shelf life without the use of added preservatives. Many chocolate companies achieve a longer shelf life for ganache-filled candies because they rely heavily on inverted syrups rather than fresh cream or fruit purees when preparing their base ganache. However, the proper selection of ingredients is a crucial step in making quality candy fillings, and the freshest ingredients should always be chosen.

Cream The cream for ganache should be fresh cream with a fat content of 35 percent. Too high of a fat content can create problems forming a good emulsion, and too little fat can create a lack of creaminess.

Chocolate The chocolatier or pastry chef has a broad selection of chocolate to use as a base for ganache, as well as an unlimited number of chocolate combinations. In any case, couverture-grade chocolate should always be chosen. Chocolate for ganache is selected based on flavor and cocoa content and how the flavor interacts with additional flavoring ingredients such as coffee, mint, or vanilla. To achieve the best combination, the chocolatier should understand flavor balancing and how to taste chocolate.

Inverted Sugar Inverted sugar retains moisture and maintains a creamy texture in ganache. The inverted sugar should be flavorless. In the process of making ganache, inverted sugar should be added to cream at 7 to 10 percent, based on the total weight of the filling.

Butter When incorporated properly into the emulsion, butter adds texture and body to ganache. It should be added to the ganache when it is at 95°F (35°C) and should be soft and pliable to ensure easy incorporation. If it is added too early, butter will create a greasy and undesirable mouthfeel. So as not to distract flavor from the filling, a neutral tasting butter is preferred, because a cultured butter will compete with the flavors of the chocolate.

Nut Pastes Any type of nut paste can be added to ganache in varying degrees, depending on the flavor desired. The nut paste can be made in-house for added control over flavor and texture, or it can be from a commercially available source, which is typically much smoother. Nut pastes should utilize fresh nuts and should be added to the ganache after the emulsion has formed.

Alcohol Alcohol acts as a preservative and flavor enhancer in ganache. Any type desired by the pastry chef can be used. Alcohol is generally added at about 5 to 10 percent of the total weight; however, this can be increased or decreased as desired. Alcohol is one of the last ingredients to be added to a ganache after the emulsion.

Process for Basic Ganache

When making ganache, it is important to work with very clean utensils and to keep the hands out of the mixture. A good sanitation program will help add shelf life.

The general process for making a shiny, elastic ganache is straightforward. It can be achieved only through the proper use of ingredients and the use of balanced formulas. Although there are variations, the basic guidelines are presented here. Students are encouraged to review the processes in the formula section for instructions regarding special considerations.

It is important to scale all ingredients into appropriately sized containers. For example, the chocolate should be scaled into the bowl in which the ganache is made. If possible, the cream should be scaled into the pot in which it will be boiled.

After all ingredients have been scaled, the cream and inverted sugar can be brought to a boil. Because it is important that the ganache not become too hot, it can be helpful to slightly cool the cream before it is poured over the chocolate. (This will depend on the room temperature. If the room is very cold, use the boiled cream right away.) A rubber spatula is used to form an emulsion in the center of the bowl after the cream has been poured over the chopped chocolate or chocolate pieces. When the elastic core forms, the movement of the spatula should draw out to emulsify the cream and chocolate.

As soon as the emulsion is achieved, the temperature should be measured and the butter should be added at 95°F (35°C) and mixed in just to incorporation. If any nut pastes are to be included, they are added next. Lastly, alcohol is added in a slow and steady stream and should be incorporated as it is added. When the ganache is finished,

FIGURE 22-11 GANACHE

1 Pour the boiled liquid over the chocolate.

2 Begin forming the emulsion in the center of the bowl.

3 When the emulsion begins to form, slowly work toward the outer edges of the bowl.

4 The finished ganache should be slightly elastic, shiny, and very smooth

it should be covered with plastic wrap until it is ready to use. See Ganache Figure 22-11 for step-by-step details on how to make ganache.

Basic Ganache Process

- Boil the liquid and inverted sugar (include vanilla bean if applicable) and cool to 190°F (88°C).
- Pour over the chopped chocolate, and let rest for 1 minute.
- Begin to form an emulsion in the center of the bowl with a rubber spatula and work outward.
- At 95°F (35°C), add the soft butter.
- Add any nut paste if used.
- Add the alcohol if used.
- Cover the surface with plastic wrap, and reserve until needed.

TRUFFLES

Chocolate **truffles** are made from ganache that is firm enough to hold its shape when piped or otherwise portioned. Although a softer ganache can be used, specialty premade shells are required to hold the soft filling. These rustic-style confections are traditionally meant to mimic the wild truffle but have evolved into many different shapes and presentations.

Truffles are coated in a layer of chocolate and cocoa powder, powdered sugar, or any number of other ingredients such as cocoa nibs, roasted coconut, and chopped candied nuts. Sometimes truffles are only coated in chocolate, but are recognizable because of their round shape.

Hand-Rolled Truffles Figure 22-12 and Lining Chocolate Molds Figure 22-13 illustrate the steps necessary for producing various truffles and show some of the finishing techniques.

Hand-Rolled Truffle Process

- Pipe ganache into mounds on a parchment-lined sheet pan using a large plain tip.
- Allow to set.
- Roll the ganache into balls using gloved hands lightly dusted with powdered sugar. (See Hand-Rolled Truffles Figure 22-12, Step 1.)
- Roll and coat in untempered couverture by hand. (See Hand-Rolled Truffles Figure 22-12, Steps 2–3.)

FIGURE 22-12 HAND-ROLLED TRUFFLES

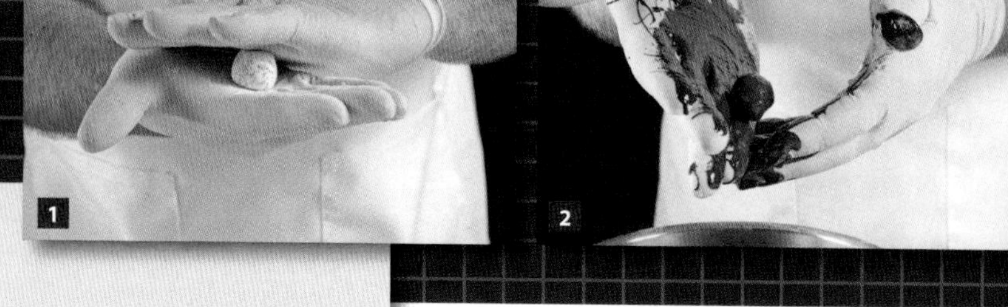

1 Once the centers are piped and partially crystallized, roll them lightly in powdered sugar.

2 Roll the truffle centers in untempered couverture [90°F (32°C)].

3 The truffles rolled in couverture are ready to be dipped.

- Dip in tempered couverture, deposit into cocoa powder, and dredge. (See Hand-Rolled Truffles Figure 22-12, Steps 3–5.)

Piped Truffle Process

- Pipe ganache in short lines approximately 1 inch (2.5 cm) long, or as desired, onto a parchment-lined sheet pan using a large plain tip.
- Allow to set.
- Dip in tempered couverture and then deposit into cocoa powder and dredge.

Deposited Truffle Process

- Pipe ganache into truffle shells and allow to crystallize.
- Pipe chocolate over the opening to seal the ganache.
- Dip in tempered couverture and then deposit into cocoa powder and dredge.
- Alternately, dip in tempered couverture for finishing.

Specialty Ingredient–Coated Truffle Process

- Have rolled, piped, or deposited truffles on hand.
- Dip in tempered couverture and roll in the selected ingredient to coat.

Enrobed Truffle Process (Hand-Dipped)

- Have rolled, piped, or deposited truffles on hand.
- Dip in tempered couverture, and transfer to parchment paper to set.
- Decorate accordingly.

MOLDED CHOCOLATES

Molded chocolates require both skill and stamina to produce by hand. There are automated and semiautomated lines to aid in the process, but it is entirely possible to create elegant molded candied without them. The process for molded candies is more involved than that for truffles and enrobed candies.

Chocolate molds made from polycarbonate plastic are required for efficient molding. Flimsy plastic molds should not be considered as they will bend and will not provide attractive candy. Molds must be clean and free from fingerprints and chocolate from previous batches.

Preparing the Mold

The first step in making molded chocolates is to prepare the molds, although some chocolatiers prefer to prepare the fillings first. The molds

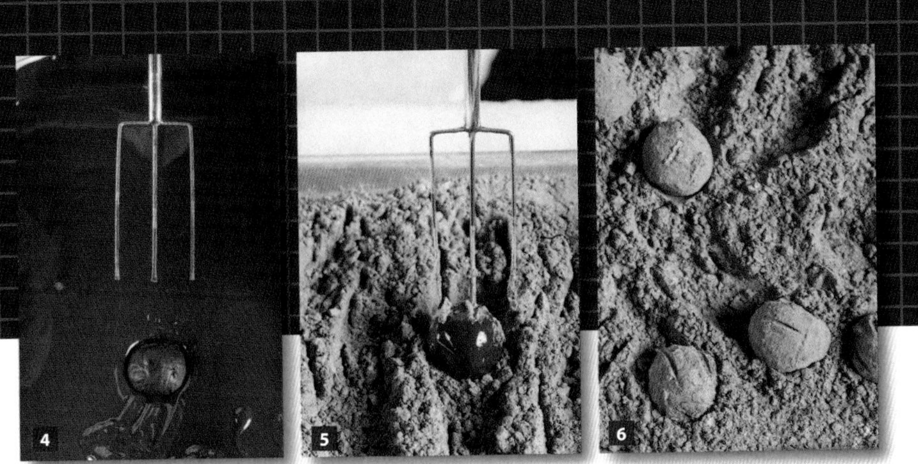

4 Dip the truffle in tempered couverture, and tap off any excess chocolate.

5 Deposit onto a tray of a sifted cocoa powder/powdered sugar blend and roll the truffle with the dipping fork before the chocolate sets.

6 Let the truffles remain in the cocoa powder until the chocolate is set.

can be lined with chocolate without any issues if the workroom is not too cold. If it is, the filling should be made before the molds are lined. This is because the chocolate will contract more in a cold workroom and can pop out of the mold more easily during chocolate making. Molds should be warmed slightly to prevent a large differential in temperature between the mold and the chocolate. A heat gun is a good choice for warming the mold. If the mold is too cold, the chocolate will set at a faster rate, and a thin shell will be harder to obtain.

Lining the Mold

The lining of the mold with chocolate should be quick and clean. A palette knife, two chocolate scrapers, and a 4 to 6 ounce ladle are required. Some pastry chefs pipe the chocolate into the cavities, but this is a time-consuming process that results in low-quality molded candies with thick shells. To make the task go quickly and to minimize waste, it is important to keep chocolate off the hands and tools as much as possible. The longer the lining process takes, the thicker the candy shells will be.

When molding, it is important not to touch any of the cavities, which can warm them and throw the chocolate out of temper. The mold is held in one hand, and the chocolate is ladled evenly over the cavities of the mold until just filled (see Lining Chocolate Molds Figure 22-13, Step 1). Next, the excess chocolate is removed from the top of the mold and the sides are cleaned (see Lining Chocolate Molds Figure 22-13, Step 2). The mold is tapped on the edge of the table to remove air bubbles and is inverted over the supply of reserved chocolate and tapped with the chocolate scraper to remove excess chocolate (see Lining Chocolate Molds Figure 22-13, Steps 3–5). With the mold still inverted, dangling chocolate is scraped off, and the mold is placed upside-down on a sheet of parchment paper (see Lining Chocolate Molds Figure 22-13, Step 6).

After 1 minute, the mold is picked up without being turned over, and the chocolate on the surface is scraped off to create an even coat of chocolate that covers only the cavities. The molds are reserved until ready for filling.

Depositing Fillings

Depending on the approach used for filling the molds, the ganache should be made or prepared for depositing. It must be pipable and soft enough to fall into the crevices of the mold and leave a flat surface. If it is too thick and leaves an uneven surface, it will be difficult to close properly.

FIGURE 22-13 LINING CHOCOLATE MOLDS

Using a ladle, line the cavities of the mold with tempered chocolate.

Scrape off any excess chocolate back into the reserve chocolate.

Tap the mold on the table to remove any air bubbles.

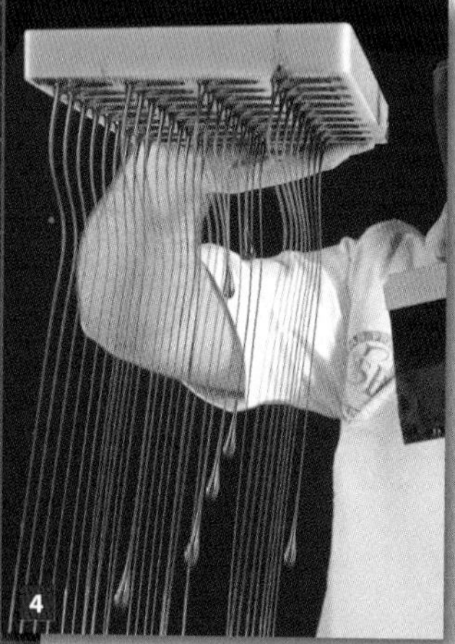

Invert the mold over the reserve chocolate and tap out the chocolate.

While the mold is inverted, scrape off any remaining chocolate that is not lining the cavities of the mold.

Place the mold on a sheet of parchment paper until the chocolate is partially crystallized; then remove the mold from the parchment paper, and scrape off any chocolate that is in the surface of the mold.

If this happens, air gaps between the filling and the base may host bacterial and mold growth. If the temperature of the ganache rises above 80°F (27°C) to 82°F (28°C), the lining can decrystallize.

When the ganache is ready to be deposited, it should be piped into the cavities using a clean (preferably disposable) piping bag (Figure 22-14). The ganache should be deposited within 1/16 inch (2 mm) of the surface of the mold. If too much space is between the top of the filling and the top of the mold, the base will be excessively thick. If there is not enough room between the filling and the mold, the base will not be sufficiently thick and the chocolate may not be able to be close. After the fillings are deposited, the mold should be gently tapped on the table to ensure that the filling is settled into the mold. Any filling on the mold's surface should be removed.

The fillings should crystallize in the mold for 24 to 48 hours before they are closed. If this does not happen, excess moisture will be created, and bacterial contamination can occur. If the filling is left to crystallize for too long, it can dry and pull away from the side of the chocolate, creating a perfect breeding ground for mold and bacteria. Filling based on white and milk chocolate requires longer times (up to 48 hours) for crystallization because of the increased quantities of sugar and lower quantities of cocoa content. The molds should be stored in a covered transit rack in a workroom that is about 60°F (16°C) to 65°F (18°C).

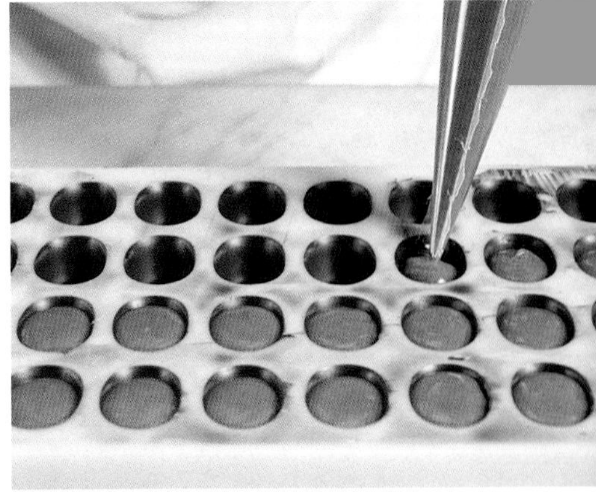

Figure 22-14
Fill the cavities with the fillings that have cooled to below 78°F (26°C). Leave a few millimeters space between the top of the filling and the top of the mold.

Closing the Molds

When the ganache is properly crystallized in the molds, they can be closed. This process requires the same care and precautions as lining. It is important to work cleanly and efficiently and at the proper temperature. Molded candies benefit from a slight warming before the base is applied to encourage better bonding. This can be accomplished with a quick pass of the heat gun.

The mold is held in one hand, while the other hand ladles a sufficient quantity of chocolate over the cavities of the mold. Next, it is tapped into the depressions on the surface of the filling. Excess chocolate is removed, and the mold is tapped on the table to remove air bubbles. If any air bubbles show, they must be covered to cut off the chocolate center from the air. Once the bases are clean, the sides of the molds are be cleaned and set aside for the chocolate to crystallize. (See Closing the Mold Figure 22-15.)

Extracting Molded Candies

Twenty minutes before extracting the candies from the mold, they should be placed in the refrigerator to cool. This makes the candies easier to remove and helps to prevent fingerprints.

The molds should be turned over in one swift motion onto a silicone baking mat, which acts as a cushion for the candies during extraction. If candies remain in the mold, it should be tapped on an angle until the candies fall out. It is essential to not crush any candies during this process. After they are turned out of the molds, the candies are transferred to appropriate storage containers or packed as needed.

ENROBED CHOCOLATES

Enrobed chocolates are candies with ganache or praline centers that have been coated with a thin layer of chocolate. This can be achieved by hand dipping the chocolates with a dipping fork or by using an enrobing

FIGURE 22-15 CLOSING THE MOLD

1 Ladle chocolate over the filled cavities.

2 Tap the mold to settle the chocolate onto the surface of the filling.

3 Scrape off the excess chocolate.

4 Tap the mold to pop any air bubbles while the chocolate is still fluid. If there are any holes, cover with couverture and level the surface as needed.

machine for higher volumes. An experienced chocolatier can hand dip at least 300 pieces per hour, while an enrobing machine can easily process 3,000 an hour, depending on the model and configuration.

Enrobed candies must to be handled in a different way than truffles and molded chocolates. Special attention must be paid to the handling of the ganache before it is enrobed. Failure to follow basic guidelines can result in a loss of shelf life.

Typically, the ganache is slightly firmer so that it is movable. It should not be too firm, however, as soft-textured, supple ganache is preferred. The ganache for enrobed candies is typically prepared in a sheet and must be cut before it can be further processed. Special cutters called guitars cut upwards of 200 pieces in two presses of the cutting strings.

The basic equipment required for enrobed candies includes parchment paper, a clean and dry pastry brush, a palette knife, a straight edge, a candy frame, and a flat sheet pan or plaque.

Preparing the Ganache

Four equally important steps are involved in the preparation of the ganache for enrobed candies. The steps are preparing the base and portioning, cutting, and spacing the ganache.

Preparing the Base The ganache base ensures that the candies will be easy to handle during cutting and spacing and that they will hold their intended shape, especially the corners. To prepare the base, a mixture of 90°F (32°C) chocolate that has had 10 percent cocoa butter added to it is brushed onto a sheet of parchment paper over the footprint of the candy frame. The frame is secured to the paper using the chocolate solution and then brushed in the center area with a thin layer of the chocolate solution. This is allowed to set for 10 minutes or until dry before the ganache is added. If it remains unfilled for too long, the base may crack and buckle, rendering it useless. Timing of this preparation is critical.

Even though the chocolate is not tempered, the motion of brushing will promote crystallization of the cocoa butter, and the chocolate will set up. It is essential that this base is just thick enough to prevent the ganache from sticking to the parchment paper and the guitar.

Portioning the Ganache The ganache should be portioned into the frame by weight for ease of production. The weight is determined when the mold is filled to the surface and cleared of any excess. After the weight has been determined and the filling has been deposited, the filling should be spread out using a palette knife. Next, the straight edge should be used to ensure that the filling is flush with the top of the frame.

After the ganache has been portioned, it is beneficial to place it in the refrigerator for 15 to 20 minutes to help promote crystallization. The ganache should then be stored at workroom temperature [65°F (18°C) to 70°F (21°C)] until enough time has passed to ensure sufficient crystallization.

Cutting and Spacing the Ganache Before the centers can be enrobed, the ganache must first be removed from the frame, cut, and separated to slightly dry the surface. This is because chocolate coating applied while the candies are moist will create a gap between the filling and the chocolate shell when the filling dries. This gap is a perfect breeding ground for bacteria and mold.

The most efficient tool to cut ganache centers is a guitar, but a ruler and knife will work equally well. Once centers of the desired size are cut, they must be separated and allowed to rest for at least 3 hours before enrobing to dry the surfaces of the ganache.

Enrobing the Ganache

Enrobing can begin as soon as the centers have been sufficiently air-dried. Whether this is done by hand or with a machine, the chocolate must be well tempered because overtempering will create thick coatings and will make removing excess chocolate more difficult. The quality of the temper should be closely monitored to ensure a thin, even coating of chocolate.

When enrobing by hand, several practices help move the task along. Candies are placed on a piece of clean parchment paper on a sheet pan or plaque. Candies should be within close reach and the station should be set up for workflow to occur in one direction. After being dipped, the candy should be placed in the far corner of the tray, and as dipping progresses, the lines toward the dipper should be filled from the back to the front of the tray. This is to guarantee that no chocolate drips on finished candies. (See Hand-Dipping Process Figure 22-16.)

Removing the candy from the dipping fork must be done swiftly and in a way that will not allow feet and or marks on the bottom of the candy. Although this requires practice, it is easy to achieve.

When enrobing candies by machine, all centers should be ready to be enrobed because tempered chocolate should be utilized as soon as it is ready. Once the temper is assured, enrobing begins. The size of the machine and finishing techniques used on the candy will determine how many workers are required. For example, a small operation that utilizes a cooling tunnel will use two people: one to load the candies, and one to catch them. Additional people can be added for decoration and catching, depending on the volume, while smaller units without cooling tunnels can be operated by only one technician.

Throughout the enrobing process, the quality of the temper and the quality of the enrobing must be monitored. If the chocolate becomes too thick, adjustments can be made to the machine, such as increasing the working temperature, adding fresh chocolate at 120°F (49°C), or decrystallizing and retempering the chocolate.

Decorating Candies

Candy decoration showcases the chocolatier's style and provides differentiation from colleagues. Decorations can be complex or very simple, depending on the volume being produced and the caliber of the

FIGURE 22-16 HAND-DIPPING PROCESS

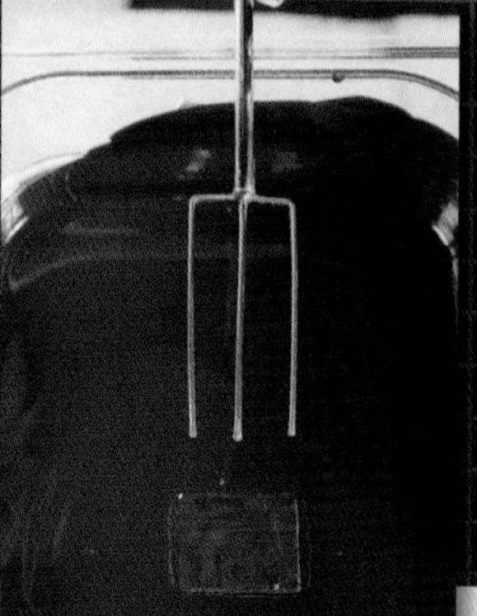

1 Drop the center in the tempered couverture with the base facing up.

2 With the fork, press the base to invert the chocolate.

3 Lift the enrobed center out of the chocolate.

4 Tap off any excess chocolate and then deposit the candy on a parchment-lined sheet pan.

chocolates. They include textured, cocoa butter, or house-made transfer sheets; base ingredients like gru de cacao, candied ginger, and crushed nuts; chocolate piping; fork design; and even the application of forced air. Whatever decoration is chosen should be applied efficiently during production.

SPECIALTY PROCESSES FOR DECORATIVE WORK

Specialty processes are used for applications like garnished desserts, retail cakes and pastries, and chocolate candies and decorative pieces.

CHOCOLATE TRANSFER SHEETS

Chocolate transfer sheets are plastic sheets that have been printed on one side with colored cocoa butter. They come in a variety of designs, and can be custom made with any logo or words printed on them.

To use chocolate transfer sheets, tempered chocolate is spread in a thin and even layer over the side of the sheet that has been printed on (see Chocolate Transfer Sheets Figure 22-17, Steps 1–2). Just before it sets, it is cut into desired shapes using the back of knife (see Chocolate Transfer Sheets Figure 22-17, Step 3). Alternatively, the chocolate can be "cut" using pastry cutters to achieve the desired shapes. Once cut (see Chocolate Transfer Sheets Figure 22-17, Step 4), transfer sheets should be placed under a flat weight to prevent warping until the cocoa butter is fully crystallized. The plastic should not be removed from the chocolate until it ready to use and should remain on the chocolate for at least 4 hours.

TEXTURED SHEETS

Textured plastic sheets are useful tools for creating visual texture on candies or showpieces. They come in a variety of textures and are easily cut into strips or other shapes for custom work.

HOUSE-MADE TRANSFER SHEETS

Custom transfer sheets can be easily made using white, milk, or dark chocolate thinned with cocoa butter. Designs are applied to plastic sheets, and an additional layer of chocolate of contrasting color is applied to act as the "back" after they have set. From this point, the application process is the same.

Examples of house-made transfers include marbled dark and white chocolate designs or delicate milk chocolate brush strokes with a white

FIGURE 22-17 CHOCOLATE TRANSFER SHEETS

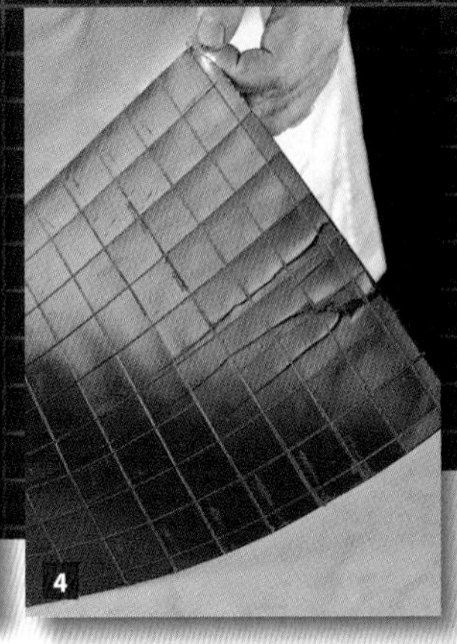

1 **Pour tempered chocolate on the acetate sheet.**

2 **Spread the tempered chocolate into a very thin layer.**

3 **Using a ruler, cut strips to make squares or rectangles.**

4 **Next, transfer the prepared transfer sheets to a flat surface and cover with a flat object and allow the cocoa butter to crystallize for at least several hours.**

back. Fat-soluble colorants can also be used, as can things like poppy seeds or vanilla seeds.

CHOCOLATE CURLS AND BOWS

Chocolate curls and bows are frequently used to decorate entremets and chocolate showpieces. They are quick and easy to make and store well for long periods of time. The specialty equipment needed to make curls and bows includes acetate plastic sheets, an icing comb, a squeegee, and a slightly damp cloth. The process for making curls is highlighted in Chocolate Curls Figure 22-18, while the technique for making bows is outlined in Chocolate Bows Figure 22-19.

CHOCOLATE CIGARETTES

Several techniques can be used to make chocolate cigarettes, which can be single- or duo-toned. A thicker, slightly overtempered chocolate works well because it remains more pliable for a longer period of time. The basic tools required for cigarette making includes a chef knife, a palette knife, a chocolate scraper. and an icing comb (see Chocolate Cigarettes Figure 22-20).

CASTING CHOCOLATE

Casting chocolate is a simple technique that can be applied to showpiece components. Tempered chocolate is simply deposited into molds or templates and is allowed to set. Because chocolate contracts as it cools, it is important to cast only the inside of molds or templates to prevent cracking. For thicker casts, the chocolate piece should be refrigerated for up to 20 minutes to ensure a thorough and quick crystallization of the cocoa butter.

MOLDING LARGE PIECES

Showpiece production often uses large molds that are brushed with chocolate until the surface is thick enough to bear the weight it must support. For example, an egg mold 2 feet (61 cm) tall should be molded to approximately 3/4 inch (2 cm) thick to ensure appropriate strength.

When brushing the mold with chocolate, it is best to take an organized approach that will ensure an even coat. First, chocolate is applied to the entire mold and then worked around it systematically to ensure an even coat on the upper edges as well as in the depths. Simple molds work best because unmolding less-detailed areas is much easier than

FIGURE 22-18 CHOCOLATE CURLS

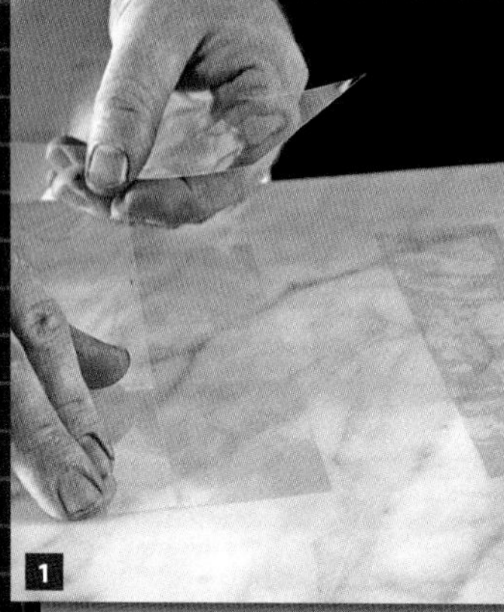

Line up the acetate strips on a granite surface.

Ladle some chocolate on the top of the strips.

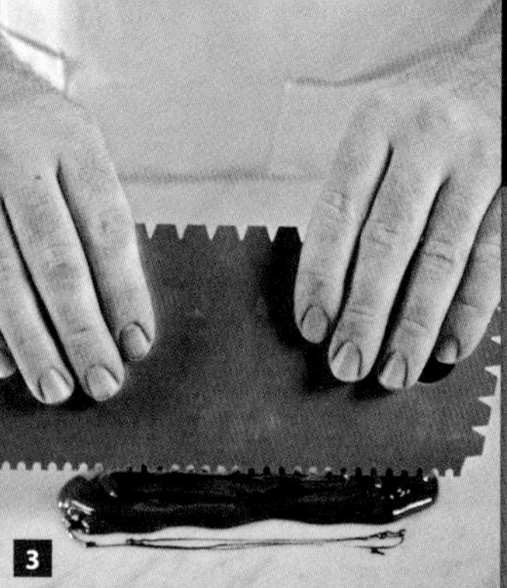

Drag the icing comb down the length of the chocolate to form the thin lines of chocolate.

Release the strips from the table.

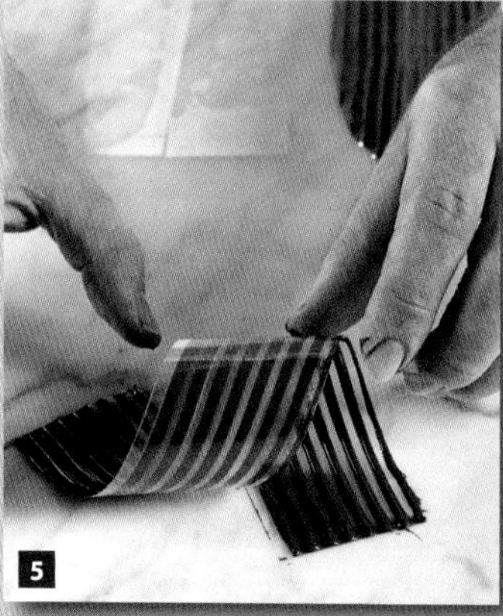

Before the chocolate sets, form the curl.

FIGURE 22-19 CHOCOLATE BOWS

Release the strips from the table.

Bring the two ends of the acetate strip to meet.

Line up the chocolate lines, and join them to form the bows.

FIGURE 22-20 CHOCOLATE CIGARETTES

1 Spread a thin layer of tempered chocolate on a granite slab, and quickly scrape it with a scraper when it is "leathery."

2 It will form a classic cigarette.

3 For a different result, use a chef knife to push the chocolate into more open cigarette shapes as shown here.

unmolding detailed ones. Building up a flat edge of the mold is also important to create a sufficient surface for joining the pieces to be assembled.

SPRAYING CHOCOLATE AND COCOA BUTTER

The use of chocolate spray is not limited to creating a velvety texture with thinned chocolate on cakes. Spraying has many applications in the preparation of molded chocolate pieces and showpiece finishing. The following ratios of chocolate to cocoa butter should serve as guidelines for creating spray chocolate. In general, as the cocoa solid content decreases, less cocoa butter is required to thin the couverture. All ratios are chocolate to cocoa butter:

- Dark Spray: 50:50 to 70:30
- Milk Spray: 65:35
- White Spray: 80:20

For frozen desserts, spray chocolate should be 120°F (49°C). For molds and showpieces, the solution should be approximately 90°F (32°F). The actual temperature will vary according to equipment being used and the temperature of the workroom. If the work is being done in a cold room and a compressor is in use with the spray gun, the chocolate solution will need to be warmer than if it is being used with a self-contained unit such as a Wagner spray gun.

COMPOSING AND ASSEMBLING CHOCOLATE CENTERPIECES AND SHOWPIECES

The culmination of the pastry chef's and the chocolatier's experience is the creation of decorative showpieces or centerpieces that serve to display the quality of their work and artistic expression. The combination of many techniques (some of which have already been discussed), the vision of the artist, and the ability to construct all the components serve as the basis for making eye-catching showpieces and centerpieces.

Several basic concepts should be known regarding composition and building. The theme of the project, visual balance, structural integrity, and construction techniques need to be well understood and planned. The process can be broken into two categories: planning the theme and visual balance, and producing and constructing components.

Theme is important from the beginning of the project because it provides the artist with a direction for style, including shapes, colors, and sizes for the project. When the theme and components are known, the piece should be drawn and life-size cutouts of the components made,

Figure 22-21
Simple Chocolate Showpiece With an Easter Theme

if desired, to help the artist better visualize how they will fit together. This will also help to identify problems present in the design.

After the final plan is established, component production can begin. Structural integrity and strength are important aspects because pieces at the bottom will need to support their own weight, in addition to the weight above them. After the components have been made, assembly can begin. The main objective during the assembly is to attach the elements together without the appearance of the "glue" used to do so.

Before joining two items, it is best to score them and then apply tempered chocolate to the items being joined. When the couverture is three-fourths set, the join should take place. If it happens too soon, the chocolate will be too thin and will not hold. Excess chocolate that can leak out from two joined pieces can be removed carefully using a paring knife or other sharp object.

Some pieces are finished with a chocolate spray after assembly. There are two options for spraying: spraying tempered, thinned couverture for a shiny chocolate finish or spraying warm, thinned couverture onto a cold item for a dramatic velvet finish. In the latter case, leaving chocolate in the freezer for too long is not advisable because the extreme cold can compact the fat crystals, causing it to break. Pieces should be placed in the freezer for a maximum of 20 to 30 minutes.

See Figure 22-21 for an example of a simple chocolate showpiece.

HEALTH AND CHOCOLATE

This section is not supposed to replace information provided by medical professionals and additional research, and a consultation with appropriate medical personnel should be considered before changing any diet.

Recently, the benefits of dark chocolate have been extolled in the press. Dark chocolate contains flavonoids, a type of antioxidant that naturally occurs in plants as defense mechanisms. Plants and foods that are high in flavonoids include cranberries, apples, onions, cacao, peanuts, and red wine. Of the chocolates, only dark contains flavonoids, the quantity of which is related to how much the chocolate has been processed. As the chocolate goes through more processing, more of these natural flavonoids are lost.

An additional consideration is the type of chocolate that is being eaten. Eating a candy bar filled with nuts, cookies, and caramel is very different from eating a small piece of dark chocolate. The type of fat in the chocolate will have an impact on the health of the consumer as well. Cocoa butter substitutes are not as healthy as cocoa butter, which is a naturally occurring fat. Research has shown the fats from cocoa are of mixed benefit to health. The **oleic acid** component of cocoa butter, which makes up one-third of its fat content, is a monounsaturated fat that is also found in olive oil. The other two-thirds of the molecule are composed of **stearic acid** and **palmitic acid**, which are saturated fats. Saturated fats have been shown to increase the risk of heart disease and increase LDL cholesterol. The good news is that stearic acid has been shown to have a neutral affect on cholesterol, which means that only one-third of the fat in chocolate has a negative affect on cholesterol (Cleveland Clinic Heart and Vascular Institute).

FORMULA

CHOCOLATE SPRAY

A blend of cocoa butter and chocolate, these chocolate sprays are used to create a quick and easy velvet finish on cakes. For best results, ensure that the cake, or item being sprayed, is frozen and that the spray is the proper temperature.

Dark Chocolate Spray Formula

Ingredients	Baker's %	Kilogram	US decimal	Lb & Oz	Test
64% chocolate	50.00	0.227	0.500	8	8 oz
Cocoa butter	50.00	0.227	0.500	8	8 oz
Total	100.00	0.454	1.000	1 0	1 lb

Milk Chocolate Spray Formula

Ingredients	Baker's %	Kilogram	US decimal	Lb & Oz	Test
35% milk chocolate	65.00	0.295	0.650	10 ⅜	10 ⅜ oz
Cocoa butter	35.00	0.159	0.350	5 ⅝	5 ⅝ oz
Total	100.00	0.454	1.000	1 0	1 lb

White Chocolate Spray Formula

Ingredients	Baker's %	Kilogram	US decimal	Lb & Oz	Test
White couverture	80.00	0.363	0.800	12 ¾	12 ¾ oz
Cocoa butter	20.00	0.091	0.200	3 ¼	3 ¼ oz
Total	100.00	0.454	1.000	1 0	1 lb

Process

Melt the chocolate and cocoa butter to 120°F (49°C), and spray onto the frozen item using a spray gun.

FORMULA

MACARON FILLINGS

These macaron fillings are all based on ganaches. They create very flavorful fillings that have a smooth and creamy mouthfeel.

Dark Chocolate Macaron Filling Formula

Ingredients	Baker's %	Kilogram	US decimal	Lb & Oz		Test
35% cream	72.00	0.471	1.039	1	⅝	12 ⅛ oz
Inverted sugar	9.00	0.059	0.130		2	1 ⅜ oz
70% couverture	100.00	0.654	1.442	1	7 ⅛	¾ oz
Butter	10.00	0.065	0.144		2 ⅜	1 ⅝ oz
Total	191.00	1.250	2.755	2	12 ⅛	2 lb

Uses: Macaron fillings, enrobed or molded chocolates

Process, Dark Chocolate Macaron Filling

1. Bring the cream and inverted sugar to boil, and form an emulsion with the chocolate.
2. Next, add the soft butter at 90°F (32°C) and emulsify well.
3. For storage, cover to the surface with plastic wrap.

Raspberry Macaron Filling Formula

Ingredients	Baker's %	Kilogram	US decimal	Lb & Oz		Test
Raspberry puree	126.00	0.455	1.003	1	0	11 ⅝ oz
Sugar	63.00	0.228	0.502		8	5 ⅞ oz
Glucose	32.00	0.116	0.255		4 ⅛	3 oz
White chocolate	100.00	0.361	0.796		12 ¾	9 ¼ oz
Cocoa butter	9.00	0.033	0.072		1 ⅛	⅞ oz
Butter	16.00	0.058	0.127		2	1 ½ oz
Total	346.00	1.250	2.755	2	12 ⅛	2 lb

Uses: Macaron fillings, molded chocolates

Process, Raspberry Macaron Filling

1. Warm the puree and reserve.
2. Cook the sugar dry to caramel stage. Add the glucose to deglaze.
3. Next, add the warmed puree.
4. Strain through chinois over the chocolate and cocoa butter and form an emulsion.
5. Once cooled to 95°F (35°C), add the soft butter.
6. For storage, cover to the surface with plastic wrap.

Cappuccino Macaron Filling Formula

Ingredients	Baker's %	Kilogram	US decimal	Lb & Oz		Test
35% cream	40.00	0.239	0.526		8 ⅜	6 oz
Trimoline	8.00	0.048	0.105		1 ⅝	1 oz
Trablit	13.33	0.080	0.175		2 ¾	2 oz
White chocolate	100.00	0.597	1.316	1	5	15 oz
Butter, soft	48.00	0.287	0.632		10 ⅛	7 oz
Total	209.33	1.250	2.755	2	12 ⅛	2 lb

Uses: Macaron fillings, enrobed or molded

Process, Cappuccino Macaron Filling

1. Melt the white chocolate and reserve.
2. Bring the cream and the inverted sugar to a boil and form an emulsion with the chocolate.
3. Add the coffee extract.
4. Next, add the soft butter at 95°F (35°C) and emulsify well.
5. For storage, cover to the surface with plastic wrap.

Lemon Macaron Filling Formula

Ingredients	Baker's %	Kilogram	US decimal	Lb & Oz		Test
Lemon zest	2.73	0.016	0.036		⅝	⅜ oz
Lemon juice	29.09	0.172	0.378		6	4 ⅜ oz
Egg yolks	29.09	0.172	0.378		6	4 ⅜ oz
Sugar	18.18	0.107	0.236		3 ¾	2 ¾ oz
Butter #1, soft	5.45	0.032	0.071		1 ⅛	⅞ oz
White chocolate	100.00	0.590	1.301	1	4 ¾	15 ⅛ oz
Butter #2, soft	27.27	0.161	0.355		5 ⅝	4 ⅛ oz
Total	211.81	1.250	2.755	2	12 ⅛	2 lb

Uses: Macaron filling, molded chocolates

Process, Lemon Macaron Filling

1. Melt the white chocolate, and deposit into a food processor.
2. Cook the lemon zest, lemon juice, egg yolks, and sugar to 190°F (88°C), stirring constantly.
3. When the temperature is reached, take off the heat, add the first butter, and mix in to stabilize.
4. Pour over the melted white chocolate, and form an emulsion. Add the second butter at 95°F (35°C).
5. For storage, cover to the surface with plastic wrap.

Pistachio Macaron Filling Formula

Ingredients	Baker's %	Kilogram	US decimal	Lb & Oz	Test
35% cream	47.76	0.304	0.669	10 ¾	7 ¾ oz
Cinnamon	0.30	0.002	0.004	⅛	¼ tsp
Inverted sugar	5.22	0.033	0.073	1 ⅛	⅞ oz
White chocolate	100.00	0.636	1.402	1 6 ⅜	1 lb ¼ oz
Pistachio paste	20.90	0.133	0.293	4 ⅝	3 ⅜ oz
Butter	22.39	0.142	0.314	5	3 ⅝ oz
Total	196.57	1.250	2.755	2 12 ⅛	2 lb

Uses: Macaron filling, enrobed or molded chocolates

Process, Pistachio Macaron Filling

1. Melt the white chocolate and reserve.
2. Bring the cream, cinnamon, and inverted sugar to a boil, and form an emulsion with the chocolate.
3. Add the pistachio paste.
4. Next, add the soft butter at 95°F (35°C), and emulsify well.
5. For storage, cover to the surface with plastic wrap.

Passion Fruit Macaron Filling Formula

Ingredients	Baker's %	Kilogram	US decimal	Lb & Oz	Test
Passion fruit puree	45.21	0.331	0.730	11 ⅝	8 ½ oz
Trimoline	5.48	0.040	0.088	1 ⅜	1 oz
Milk chocolate	100.00	0.732	1.614	1 9 ⅞	1 lb 2 ¾ oz
Butter	20.00	0.146	0.323	5 ⅛	3 ¾ oz
Total	170.69	1.250	2.755	2 12 ⅛	2 lb

Uses: Macaron filling, molded chocolates

Process, Passion Fruit Macaron Filling

1. Melt the milk chocolate over a bain-marie or in the microwave and reserve.
2. Combine the passion fruit puree and the inverted sugar, and bring to a light boil.
3. Pour the fruit puree over the melted milk chocolate, and form an emulsion.
4. Add the butter at 95°F (35°C), and emulsify well.
5. For storage, cover to the surface with plastic wrap.

Enrobed Candies

FORMULA

RUM RAISIN GANACHE

Raisins, dark rum, and vanilla are highlighted against a backdrop of creamy white chocolate ganache. Enrobed in milk or dark chocolate, or as a molded candy, this is sure to be a favorite.

Ingredients	Baker's %	Kilogram	US decimal	Lb & Oz		Test
35% cream	43.00	0.302	0.666		10 ⅝	7 ¾ oz
Vanilla bean	Each	2	2		2	1 ½ each
Inverted sugar	8.00	0.056	0.124		2	1 ½ oz
White chocolate	100.00	0.702	1.548	1	8 ¾	1 lb 2 oz
Butter	11.00	0.077	0.170		2 ¾	2 oz
Raisins	11.00	0.077	0.170		2 ¾	2 oz
Spiced rum	5.00	0.035	0.077		1 ¼	⅞ oz
Total	178.00	1.250	2.755	2	12 ⅛	2 lb

Uses: Enrobed or molded chocolates

Process

1. Macerate the raisins with the rum for 24 hours.
2. Melt the chocolate, and set aside.
3. Bring the cream, vanilla bean, and inverted sugar to a boil.
4. Pour over the chocolate and form an emulsion.
5. Add the butter when the emulsion reaches 95°F (35°C).
6. Form a paste out of the macerated raisins, and fold into the ganache.
7. For storage, cover to the surface with plastic wrap.

Enrobed Candies

FORMULA

EARL GREY GANACHE

Earl Grey tea is a blend of black tea flavored with the aromatic oil of bergamot orange. By infusing the tea into the cream to make the ganache, a strong flavor of bergamot is achieved. When combined with milk and dark chocolate, the result is a complex and sophisticated ganache. Enrobed or molded in dark chocolate, this can be garnished with some tea leaves.

Ingredients	Baker's %	Kilogram	US decimal	Lb & Oz		Test
35% cream	50.00	0.360	0.794		12 ¾	9 ¼ oz
Earl Grey tea	8.33	0.060	0.132		2 ⅛	1 ½ oz
Inverted sugar	2.10	0.015	0.033		½	⅜ oz
Honey	2.10	0.015	0.033		½	⅜ oz
35% milk chocolate	83.00	0.598	1.318	1	5 ⅛	14 ¼ oz
58% chocolate	17.00	0.122	0.270		4 ⅜	3 ⅛ oz
Butter	11.00	0.079	0.175		2 ¾	2 oz
Total	173.53	1.250	2.755	2	12 ⅛	2 lb

Uses: Molded chocolates

Process

1. Melt the chocolates together and set aside.
2. Boil the cream, and add the tea.
3. Cover the pot with plastic wrap, and let infuse for 10 minutes.
4. Strain the tea from the cream.
5. Rescale the cream to the original amount, using whole milk.
6. Add the inverted sugar and honey to the cream and bring back to a boil.
7. Pour over the chocolate, and form an emulsion.
8. When the emulsion reaches 95°F (35°C), add the butter.
9. For storage, cover to the surface with plastic wrap.

FORMULA

MADAGASCAN VANILLA GANACHE

The finest vanilla comes from Madagascar, the world's largest producer. It is prized for its rich mellow flavor and consistent quality. This candy features a robust vanilla flavor through using a hot infusion of the vanilla into the cream.

Ingredients	Baker's %	Kilogram	US decimal	Lb & Oz		Test
35% cream	70.00	0.490	1.080	1	1 ¼	12 ½ oz
Trimoline	8.57	0.060	0.132		2 ⅛	1 ½ oz
Vanilla bean	Each	3	3		3	2.5 each
58% chocolate	100.00	0.700	1.543	1	8 ⅝	1 lb 1 ⅞ oz
Total	178.57	1.250	2.755	2	12 ⅛	2 lb

Uses: Enrobed and molded chocolates

Process

1. Partially melt the chocolate and set aside.
2. Bring the cream, inverted sugar, and vanilla bean to a boil.
3. Cover with plastic wrap, and let infuse for 20 minutes.
4. Bring the cream back to a boil.
5. Pour the cream over the chocolate, and form an emulsion.
6. For storage, cover to the surface with plastic wrap.

Molded Candies

FORMULA

70 PERCENT GANACHE

This rich, dark chocolate ganache with a hint of vanilla bean is perfect for truffles or molded or enrobed chocolates. For an interesting variation and highlight of flavor, try using an identity-preserved couverture.

Ingredients	Baker's %	Kilogram	US decimal	Lb & Oz		Test
35% cream	81.75	0.466	1.026	1	⅜	11 ⅞ oz
Inverted sugar	17.54	0.100	0.220		3 ½	2 ½ oz
Vanilla bean	Each	1 ½	1 ½		1 ½	1 each
70% couverture	100.00	0.569	1.255	1	4 ⅛	14 ⅝ oz
Butter	20.17	0.115	0.253		4	3 oz
Total	219.46	1.250	2.755	2	12 ⅛	2 lb

Uses: Molded and enrobed chocolates

Process

1. Bring the cream, inverted sugar, and vanilla bean to a boil.
2. Cover with plastic wrap, and allow to infuse for 15 minutes.
3. Bring the cream back to a boil.
4. Pour the cream over the chocolate, and form an emulsion.
5. At 95°F (35°C), add the butter.
6. For storage, cover to the surface with plastic wrap.

FORMULA

COFFEE GANACHE

This treat is an irresistible mixture of two favorite flavors: chocolate and espresso. Enrobed or molded in milk or dark chocolate, this candy has the full flavor of coffee and a smooth and creamy texture.

Ingredients	Baker's %	Kilogram	US decimal	Lb & Oz		Test
35% cream	66.15	0.407	0.897		14 ⅜	10 ⅜ oz
Espresso beans	10.76	0.066	0.146		2 ⅜	1 ¾ oz
Inverted sugar	9.23	0.057	0.125		2	1 ½ oz
58% chocolate	100.00	0.615	1.357	1	5 ¾	15 ¾ oz
Butter	16.92	0.104	0.230		3 ⅝	2 ⅝ oz
Total	203.06	1.250	2.755	2	12 ⅛	2 lb

Uses: Enrobed or molded chocolates

Process

1. Melt the chocolate and set aside.
2. Grind the coffee beans.
3. Boil the cream, and add the ground coffee beans.
4. Cover the pot with plastic wrap, and let infuse for 10 minutes.
5. Strain the grounds from the cream.
6. Add the inverted sugar to the cream, and bring back to a boil.
7. Pour over the chocolate, and form an emulsion.
8. When the emulsion reaches 95°F (35°C), add the butter.
9. For storage, cover to the surface with plastic wrap.

FORMULA

CASSIS GANACHE

This smooth milk and dark chocolate ganache is enlivened by the acidity of cassis puree.

Ingredients	Baker's %	Kilogram	US decimal	Lb & Oz	Test
Cassis puree	33.00	0.267	0.588	9 ⅜	7 oz
Glucose	8.50	0.069	0.152	2 ⅜	1 ¾ oz
Milk couverture	54.00	0.437	0.963	15 ⅜	11 ⅜ oz
58% couverture	46.00	0.372	0.820	13 ⅛	9 ¾ oz
Butter	10.00	0.081	0.178	2 ⅞	2 ⅛ oz
Crème de cassis	3.05	0.025	0.054	⅞	⅝ oz
Total	154.55	1.250	2.755	2 12 ⅛	2 lb

Uses: Enrobed or molded chocolate

Process

1. Melt the chocolates and set aside.
2. Bring the puree and glucose to a boil.
3. Pour the puree over the chocolate, and form an emulsion.
4. At 95°F (35°C), add the butter, and form an emulsion.
5. Add the crème de cassis, and stir to incorporate.
6. For storage, cover to the surface with plastic wrap.

FORMULA

WHISKEY GANACHE

The evolution of flavor when eating this chocolate candy is a pleasure for the senses. Out of a rich and creamy base, the whiskey rises out for a robust and complex experience in this adult chocolate filling.

Ingredients	Baker's %	Kilogram	US decimal	Lb & Oz	Test
35% cream	40.00	0.280	0.617	9 ⅞	7 ⅝ oz
Inverted sugar	11.42	0.080	0.176	2 ⅞	2 ⅛ oz
Milk couverture	57.15	0.400	0.882	14 ⅛	11 oz
58% couverture	42.85	0.300	0.661	10 ⅝	8 ¼ oz
Butter	15.71	0.110	0.242	3 ⅞	3 oz
Scotch whiskey	11.42	0.080	0.176	2 ⅞	2 ⅛ oz
Total	178.55	1.250	2.755	2 12 ⅛	2 lb

Uses: Molded and enrobed chocolates

Process

1. Melt the chocolates and set aside.
2. Bring the cream and inverted sugar to a boil.
3. Pour the cream over the chocolate, and form an emulsion.
4. At 95°F (35°C), add the butter, and form an emulsion.
5. Add the whiskey, and stir to incorporate.
6. For storage, cover to the surface with plastic wrap.

FORMULA

CINNAMON HAZELNUT PRALINE

Spiced with cinnamon and flavored with two types of hazelnut paste, sweetened and unsweetened, this candy is loaded with textures and flavors that are rich, yet melt delicately in the mouth.

Ingredients	Baker's %	Kilogram	US decimal	Lb & Oz		Test
Praline paste 60% fruit	38.23	0.260	0.573		9 ⅛	6 ¾ oz
Hazelnut paste	40.44	0.275	0.606		9 ¾	7 ⅛ oz
Cinnamon	1.47	0.010	0.022		⅜	¼ oz
Inverted sugar	3.67	0.025	0.055		⅞	⅝ oz
Milk couverture	29.41	0.200	0.441		7	5 ⅛ oz
Gianduja	70.58	0.480	1.058	1	⅞	12 ⅜ oz
Total	183.80	1.250	2.755	2	12 ⅛	2 lb

Uses: Enrobed or molded chocolates

Process

1. Melt the milk chocolate and gianduja and set aside.
2. Combine the praline paste, hazelnut paste, and cinnamon with the inverted sugar, and warm to 120°F (49°C).
3. Combine with the melted chocolate, and form an emulsion.
4. Cool to 72°F (22°C) on a sanitized, dry granite slab, and use as desired.

Note

Hazelnut paste is unsweetened. If hazelnut paste is not available, roast hazelnuts in a low oven until golden brown. Then, process in a food processor until a fine paste is achieved.

FORMULA

PEANUT BUTTER PRALINE

This praline is a sophisticated version of a child's favorite flavor combination: chocolate and peanut butter. Slightly salty, sweet, creamy, and crunchy, the sensation of peanut butter just slightly lingers in the mouth, leaving one wanting more.

Ingredients	Baker's %	Kilogram	US decimal	Lb & Oz		Test
Milk couverture	100.00	0.165	0.365		5 ⅞	4 ½ oz
Cocoa butter	42.42	0.070	0.155		2 ½	1 ⅞ oz
Powdered sugar	60.60	0.100	0.221		3 ½	2 ¾ oz
Peanut butter, unsalted	509.00	0.842	1.856	1	13 ¾	1 lb 6 ⅝ oz
Salt	7.27	0.012	0.027		⅜	⅜ oz
Pailleté feuilletine	36.36	0.060	0.133		2 ⅛	1 ⅝ oz
Total	755.65	1.250	2.755	2	12 ⅛	2 lb

Uses: Enrobed or molded chocolates

Process

1. Melt the chocolate and cocoa butter to 110°F (44°C), and set aside.
2. Sift the powdered sugar.
3. Combine the peanut butter with the chocolate mixture.
4. Fold in the sifted powered sugar and salt.
5. Fold in the pailleté feuilletine.
6. Cool to 72°F (22°C) on a sanitized, dry granite slab and use as desired.

FORMULA

CRISPY MILK CHOCOLATE PRALINE

This praline is a blend of milk chocolate, praline paste, butter, and pailleté feuilletine. The result is a slightly firm, yet melts-in-the-mouth sensation with a strong hazelnut flavor and crispy highlights provided by the pailleté feuilletine.

Ingredients	Baker's %	Kilogram	US decimal	Lb & Oz		Test
Milk couverture	100.00	0.660	1.455	1	7 ¼	1 lb ⅞ oz
Praline paste 60% fruit	62.87	0.415	0.915		14 ⅝	10 ⅝ oz
Soft butter	21.21	0.140	0.309		4 ⅞	3 ⅝ oz
Pailleté feuilletine	5.30	0.035	0.077		1 ¼	⅞ oz
Total	189.38	1.250	2.755	2	12 ⅛	2 lb

Uses: Enrobed or molded chocolates

Process

1. Melt the chocolate to 120°F (49°C) and set aside.
2. Heat the praline noisette to 120°F (49°C), and add to the chocolate.
3. When 95°F (35°C), add the butter and emulsify.
4. Fold in the pailleté feuilletine.
5. Cool to 72°F (22°C) on a sanitized, dry granite slab, and use as desired.

Cinnamon Hazelnut Praline

Peanut Butter Praline

Crispy Milk Chocolate Praline

Assorted Pralines

FORMULA

MENDIANTS

Also referred to as beggars, the term *mendiant* is commonly applied to preparations that include a mixture of dried fruits and nuts. The combination symbolized the original mendicant orders from the Middle Ages and the colors of their robes: raisins for the Dominicans, hazelnuts for the Augustans, dried figs for the Franciscans, and almonds for the Carmelites.

Mise en Place

Tempered couverture

Nut/fruit mixture:

- Candied nuts (almond, pistachio, hazelnut)
- Candied fruit (orange peel, lemon peel)
- Dried fruit (raisin, cherry)

Process

1. Pipe dots of chocolate onto a sheet of parchment paper.
2. Before the chocolate sets, garnish with a selection of fruits and nuts.

CHAPTER SUMMARY

Chocolate is a dynamic ingredient and is used in many types of confections, pastries, and even some breads and savory foods. Understanding its origins and processing better enables one to know its working properties and understand variations in chocolate characteristics. The process of tempering must be understood and put into practice in order to produce chocolate confections, decorations, and showpieces. Being able to work with the three main types of chocolate (white, milk, and dark) enables one to make a wide range of confections and decorations. Furthermore, it enables one to have a better understanding of how chocolate reacts in preparations such as ganache, pralines, and mousse. When learning to work with chocolate, it is mandatory to observe temperature as it relates to crystallization, which affects the working properties of chocolate and, in turn, the final product. Practice, patience, and attention to detail are required for learning how to control chocolate and achieve the desired results.

KEY TERMS

- ❖ Bittersweet chocolate
- ❖ Cacao bean
- ❖ Chocolate liquor
- ❖ Chocolatier
- ❖ Coating chocolate
- ❖ Cocoa butter
- ❖ Cocoa butter equivalent (CBE)
- ❖ Cocoa mass
- ❖ Cocoa paste
- ❖ Cocoa powder
- ❖ Conching
- ❖ Cotyledon
- ❖ Couverture
- ❖ Criollo
- ❖ Dark chocolate
- ❖ Dutched cocoa powder
- ❖ Enrobed chocolates
- ❖ Fat bloom
- ❖ Forastero
- ❖ Form V crystallization
- ❖ Gianduja
- ❖ Grinding
- ❖ Milk chocolate
- ❖ Molded chocolates
- ❖ Oleic acid
- ❖ Origin chocolate
- ❖ Overtempered
- ❖ Palmitic acid
- ❖ Polymorphic
- ❖ Seizing
- ❖ Semi-sweet chocolate
- ❖ Stearic acid
- ❖ Sugar bloom
- ❖ Sweet chocolate
- ❖ Tempering
- ❖ Terroir
- ❖ Test strip
- ❖ *Theobroma cacao*
- ❖ Triglyceride
- ❖ Trinitario
- ❖ Truffles
- ❖ Undertempered
- ❖ White chocolate
- ❖ Winnowing

REVIEW QUESTIONS

1. **Why are cacao beans fermented? What are two main fermentation techniques?**
2. **What is the relationship between the percentage of cocoa and flavor in chocolate?**
3. **Why is chocolate tempered? How is this accomplished?**
4. **What does it mean if chocolate is undertempered? Overtempered?**
5. **Why should ganache filling crystallize for 24 to 48 hours in the mold or before being cut for enrobing?**

APPENDIX A: Conversions

Basic Baking Ingredients: Weight in Grams		
	1 Teaspoon	1 Tablespoon
Ammonium Carbonate	3.5	10.5
Baking Powder	4	12
Baking Soda	4	12
Cornstarch	3	9
Cream of Tartar	2	6
Bread Flour	2.5	7.5
Butter	5	15
Cinnamon, ground	1.5	4.5
Spices, ground (other than cinnamon)	2	6
Cocoa powder, unsweetened	2	6
Brown Sugar	4	12
Granulated Sugar	5	15
Powdered Sugar	3	9
Kosher Salt	3.5	10.5
Table Salt	6	18
Gelatin, powder	3	9
Pectin, powder	3	9
Vanilla Extract	4	12

Equivalents and Substitutions		
Yeast		
	substitute...	with...
By weight or volume	Fresh compressed yeast	50% active dry yeast*
	Fresh compressed yeast	33% instant yeast
*Note: Must be rehydrated in 105°F to 110°F (41°C to 43°C) water for 5 to 10 minutes		
1 consumer packet of active dry yeast equals:		
weight	0.25 oz (7 g)	
volume	2 ¼ teaspoons (11 ml)	
Gelatin		
	substitute...	with...
By weight	Gelatin powder	Gelatin sheet
1 consumer packet of unflavored gelatin powder equals:		
weight	0.25 oz (7 g)	
volume	2 ½ teaspoons (12.5 ml)	

Volume Conversions

Multiply fluid ounces by 30 to convert to milliliters.

Volume Measure	Fluid Ounces	Milliliters
1 teaspoon	0.15	5
1 tablespoon	0.5	15
2 tablespoons	1	30
1 cup	8	240
1 pint	16	480
1 quart	32	960
1 gallon	128	3.84 liters

Weight Conversions

Multiply ounces by 28.349 to convert to grams.

Pounds	Ounces	Grams
0.016	0.25	7
0.031	0.5	14
0.063	1	28
0.25	4	113
0.5	8	227
1	16	454
1.5	24	680
2	32	907
2.5	40	1.13 kg
3	48	1.13 kg

APPENDIX B: Baker's Percentages

Why are baker's percentages important for the baker?

- Consistency in production
- Ease of calculating the absorption rate of the flour
- Simple increase or decrease in dough size using the same formula
- Ease in comparing formulas
- Ability to check if a formula is well-balanced
- Ability to correct defects in the formula

What are the important characteristics of baker's percentages?

- Baker's percentages are always based on the total weight of the all the flour in the formula.
- Flour is always represented by the value of 100 percent (i.e., all other ingredients are calculated in relationship to the flour). If more than one type of flour is in the formula, the sum of the flour is 100 percent.
- Baker's percentages can only be calculated if the amount of all the ingredients in the formula is expressed in the same unit of measure; for example, you cannot mix grams and ounces, or pounds and kilograms, in the same formula.
- Units of measure must be expressed in terms of weight, not volume (e.g., you cannot mix pounds and quarts in the same formula). Additionally, weights given in pounds and ounces cannot easily be calculated with baker's percents. The easiest system of measurement with baker's percentages is the metric system. The US decimal system may also be used.
- Baker's percentages work best with the metric system because metrics are based on units of 10, as are percentages (e.g., 100 = 10 × 10).

Percentage Basics

0.01 = 1%	0.1 = 10%
1/100 = 1%	10/100 = 10%
1 ÷ 100 = 1%	10 ÷ 100 = 10%

- If the percentage is greater than 100, the number is larger than the number that represents 100 percent.
- If the percentage is less than 100, the number is less than the number that represents 100 percent.

Math Basics

$$a/b = a \div b$$

$$(23 \times a = b) = (a = b \div 23) = (a = b/23)$$

Typical Formula Calculations Using Baker's Percentages

Example 1: From Weight to Baker's Percentages

In this example, we have a formula, and we want to express the amounts of the ingredients in baker's percentages.

Flour : 50 kg
Water : 30 kg
Salt : 1 kg
Yeast : 0.75 kg

Step 1. Determine the baker's percentage for the flour. We know that flour is always 100%. In this formula, 50 kg = 100%.

Step 2. Determine the baker's percentage for the water. We need to calculate what percentage the weight of the water is in relation to the weight of the flour. Another way to state this calculation is: How many parts of water would be needed to achieve the same hydration ratio if there were 100 parts of flour?

Two calculation methods are possible.

Calculation Method 1: Cross Multiplication

Using this method, crossed lines are drawn.

Flour : 50 kg ╲╱ 100%
Water : 30 kg ╱╲ W

(W = the percentage of water we want to find)

The necessary calculation can be expressed as an equation, following the crossed lines, beginning with the flour:

$$50 \times W = 30 \times 100$$

Applying math basics to isolate the unknown variable:

$$W = (30 \times 100) \div 50$$

$$W = 60$$

In this formula, the baker's percentage for the water is 60 percent (i.e., the weight of the water represents 60 percent of the weight of the flour).

Calculation Method 2: Fractions

Using this method, the necessary calculation can be expressed as a fraction with the weight of the water on top and the weight of the flour on the bottom:

$$W = 30/50$$

Applying math basics, we know that

$$W = 30/50 = 30 \div 50 = 0.6 = 60\%$$

Step 3. Determine the baker's percentages for the yeast and salt using one of the two calculation methods described in Step 2.

Two calculation methods are possible.

Calculation Method 1: Cross Multiplication

Flour :	50 kg	100%	Flour :	50 kg	100%
Water :	30 kg	60%	Water :	30 kg	60%
Salt :	1 kg	S	Yeast :	0.75 kg	Y

Expressed as equations:

$$50 \times S = 1 \times 100 \qquad 50 \times Y = 0.75 \times 100$$

$$S = (1 \times 100) \div 50 \qquad Y = (0.75 \times 100) \div 50$$

$$S = 2 \qquad Y = 1.5$$

Calculation Method 2: Fractions

$$S = 1/50 = 1 \div 50 = 0.02 = 2\%$$

$$Y = 0.75/50 = 0.75 \div 50 = 0.015 = 1.5\%$$

The complete formula with baker's percentages:

Flour :	50 kg	100%
Water :	30 kg	60%
Salt :	1 kg	2%
Yeast :	0.75 kg	1.5%

Example 2: From Baker's Percentages to Weight

In this example, we have the baker's percentages, we want to make a dough using 40 kg of flour, and we want to express the formula in quantities for each of the ingredients.

Flour : 100%
Water : 65%
Salt : 2%
Yeast : 1%

Remember that flour is always 100 percent and that other amounts are calculated in relationship to flour.

$$\text{Flour} = 100\% = 40 \text{ kg}$$

$$\text{Water} = 65\% = 40 \times 0.65 = 26 \text{ kg}$$

$$\text{Salt} = 2\% = 40 \times 0.02 = 0.8 \text{ kg} = 800 \text{ g}$$

$$\text{Yeast} = 1\% = 40 \times 0.01 = 0.4 \text{ kg} = 400 \text{ g}$$

The complete formula with baker's percentages:

Flour :	40 kg	100%
Water :	26 kg	65%
Salt :	800 g	2%
Yeast :	400 g	1%

Example 3: From Baker's Percentages to Weights Using Desired Production Quantity

In this example, we have a production order to fill:

50 baguettes @ 350 g of dough
40 balls @ 400 g of dough
300 rolls @ 80 g of dough

All these breads will be made from the same dough. The baker's percentages for the formula are

Flour : 100%
Water : 67%
Salt : 2%
Yeast : 1%

We want to express the formula in quantities for each of the ingredients.

Step 1. Determine the total amount of dough needed:

$$50 \times 350 \text{ g} = 17{,}500 \text{ g} = 17.5 \text{ kg}$$

$$40 \times 400 \text{ g} = 16{,}000 \text{ g} = 16 \text{ kg}$$

$$300 \times 80 \text{ g} = 24{,}000 \text{ g} = 24 \text{ kg}$$

$$\text{Total Dough} = 57{,}500 \text{ g} = 57.5 \text{ kg}$$

Step 2. Determine the amount of flour needed. The baker's percentages for all the ingredients in this formula total 170 percent. Here is another way to state this is: We know that with 100 parts of flour, we can produce 170 parts of dough. We need to calculate the amount of flour needed to make 57.5 kg of dough.

Two calculation methods are possible.

Calculation Method 1: Cross Multiplication

Flour :	100%	F
Water :	67%	
Salt :	2%	
Yeast :	1%	
Total :	170%	57.5 kg

Expressed as an equation:

$$100 \times 57.5 = 170 \times F$$

$$F = (100 \times 57.5) \div 170$$

$$F = 33.82$$

Calculation Method 2: Fractions

First, we need to calculate what proportion of the total dough in the formula is represented by the flour. The necessary calculation can be expressed as a fraction with the baker's percentage of the flour on top and the total of baker's percentages on the bottom:

$$F\% = 100/170 = 100 \div 170 = 0.5882 = 58.82\%$$

We now know that 58.82 percent of the total dough in the formula is flour. Now we need to calculate the weight of the flour for the quantity of total dough we need to make.

$$F = 57.5 \text{ kg} \times 58.82\% = 57.5 \text{ kg} \times 0.5882 = 33.82 \text{ kg}$$

Now we know that 33.82 kg of flour will be necessary to obtain 57.5 kg of dough.

To simplify the rest of the calculations and to make sure we will produce enough dough, we will round up the amount of flour to the next whole number: 33.82 kg will become 34 kg. However, we only round up the weight of the flour; we do not round up the weights of the other ingredients.

Step 3. We must apply the baker's percentages of the formula to the weight of the flour to determine the desired weights of the remaining ingredients:

Flour = 100% = 34 kg

Water = 67% = 34 × 0.67 = 22.78 kg

Salt = 2% = 34 × 0.02 = 0.68 kg = 680 g

Yeast = 1% = 34 × 0.01 = 0.34 kg = 340 g

To verify our calculations, if we total the weights of all the ingredients, we should find the amount of dough needed to accommodate this order:

Flour :	34 kg	100%
Water :	22.78 kg	67%
Salt :	680 g	2%
Yeast :	340 g	1%
Total :	57.8	kg

With 57.5 kg of dough needed, this formula will produce 57.8 kg of dough. We have a small amount of extra dough because we rounded up the amount of flour.

Using Baker's Percentages with Preferments

When using preferments, the principles of baker's percentage stay the same. However, because a preferment is a preparation made from a portion of a formula's total flour, water, yeast, and sometimes salt, and because the proportion of those ingredients in the preferment may differ from the proportion in the total formula, additional calculations are often necessary.

Example 1: From Formula for Total Dough to Formulas for Preferment and Final Dough

In this example, we have a formula, with baker's percentages. We want to make the dough using 20 percent of the flour in a preferment (sponge).

Flour :	10 kg	100%
Water :	6.7 kg	67%
Salt :	200 g	2%
Yeast :	150 g	1.5%

For this example, the baker's percentage for the water in the sponge will be 64 percent, and the baker's percentage for the yeast will be 0.1%. The sponge will contain no salt.

Step 1. Determine the weight of the flour to use in the preferment.

10 kg × 20% = 10 kg × 0.2 = 2 kg

Step 2. Determine the weight of the water and the yeast to use in the preferment.

Water = 64% = 2 kg × 0.64 = 1.28 kg

Yeast = 0.1% = 2 kg × 0.001 = 0.002 kg = 2 g

If the preferment contained salt, the weight of the salt would be determined in the same way.

The complete formula for the preferment, with baker's percents, is

Flour :	2 kg	100%
Water :	1.28 kg	64%
Yeast :	2 g	0.1%

Step 3. Determine the weight of the ingredients in the final dough. We need to subtract the quantity of each ingredient used in the preferment from the quantity in the total formula.

Flour = 10 kg − 2kg = 8 kg

Water = 6.7 kg − 1.28 kg = 5.42 kg

Salt = 200 g − 0 = 200 g

Yeast = 150 g − 2 g = 148 g

The formula for the final dough is

Flour :	8 kg
Water :	5.42 kg
Salt :	200 g
Yeast :	148 g

Step 4. Determine the baker's percentages for all the ingredients in the final dough. We know that flour is always 100 percent. Baker's percentages for all the other ingredients are calculated using the cross multiplication or fractions method.

Two calculation methods are possible.

Calculation Method 1: Cross Multiplication

Water

$$8 \times W = 5.42 \times 100$$
$$W = (5.42 \times 100) \div 8$$
$$W = 67.75$$

Salt

$$8 \times S = 0.2 \times 100$$
$$S = (0.2 \times 100) \div 8$$
$$S = 2.5$$

Yeast

$$8 \times Y = 0.148 \times 100$$
$$Y = (0.148 \times 100) \div 8$$
$$Y = 1.85$$

Sponge

$$8 \times P = 3.282 \times 100$$
$$P = (3.282 \times 100) \div 8$$
$$P = 41.02$$

Calculation Method 2: Fractions

$$W = 5.42/8 = 5.42 \div 8 = 0.6775 = 67.75\%$$
$$S = 0.2/8 = 0.2 \div 8 = 0.025 = 2.5\%$$
$$Y = 0.148/8 = 0.148 \div 8 = 0.0185 = 1.85\%$$
$$P = 3.282/8 = 3.282 \div 8 = 4102 = 41.02\%$$

The complete formula with baker's percents:

Flour :	8 kg	100%
Water :	5.42 kg	67.75%
Salt :	200 g	2.5%
Yeast :	148 g	1.85%
Preferment :	3.282 kg	41.02%

Note: For a poolish preferment, the weight of the water is determined in Step 1 (usually 1/3 or 1/2). The weight of the flour in the poolish is always equal to weight of the water. Therefore, the baker's percentage for the water in the preferment is 100 percent.

Example 2: From Baker's Percentages for Total Dough and Preferment to Formula for Final Dough Using Desired Production Quantity

In this example, we have a production order to fill for which we need 40 kg of sourdough dough. This method is important for scheduling production using sourdough so enough can be on hand for all production needs.

We know the baker's percentages for the total dough. We already have a sufficient quantity of the levain that was prepared according to a formula with known baker's percentages, and we want to incorporate this levain into the final dough in the ratio of 50 percent in relation to the weight of the flour in the final dough.

The formula for the total dough is

Flour : 100%
Water : 67%
Salt : 2%

The formula for the preparation of the levain is

Flour : 100%
Water : 50%
Culture : 150%

Note: In this example, the number of feedings of the culture is not important, but we will assume that the same formula has been used for all the feedings.

Step 1. Determine the baker's percentages for the final dough. Starting with the flour, we know that flour is always 100 percent.

To calculate the correct amount of water and salt in the final dough, we must consider that the flour in the levain will be added to the final dough. For 100 parts of flour in the final dough, there are 50 parts of levain. We must calculate how much of those 50 parts is flour.

Two calculation methods are possible.

Calculation Method 1: Cross Multiplication

Flour :	100%	F
Water :	50%	W
Total :	150%	50 parts

Expressed as an equation:

$$F \times 150 = 50 \times 100$$
$$F = (50 \times 100) \div 150$$
$$F = 33.33$$

Calculation Method 2: Fractions

First, we need to calculate what proportion of the 150 parts is represented by the flour:

$$F = 100/150 = 100 \div 150 = 0.6667 = 66.67\%$$

We now know that 66.67 percent of the 50 parts is flour. Now we need to calculate the number of parts.

$$F = 50 \text{ parts} \times 66.67\% = 50 \text{ parts} \times 0.6667 = 33.33 \text{ parts}$$

Now we know that we must take into consideration 133.33 parts of flour when we calculate the amount of water and salt in the final dough.

The total amount of water in the final dough will be

$$133.33 \text{ parts} \times 67\% = 89.33 \text{ parts}$$

We must consider that the water in the levain will be added to the final dough. Because we know that 33.33 parts of the 50 parts of levain are flour, the number of parts that are water is

$$50 \text{ parts} - 33.33 \text{ parts} = 16.67 \text{ parts}$$

The number of parts of water in the final dough is

$$89.33 \text{ parts} - 16.67 \text{ parts} = 72.66 \text{ parts}$$

The baker's percentage for the water in the final dough is 72.66 percent.

The total amount of salt in the final dough will be

$$133.33 \text{ parts} \times 2\% = 2.67 \text{ parts}$$

There is no salt in the levain, so the baker's percentage for the salt in the final dough is 2.67 percent.

The baker's percentages for the final dough are

Flour : 100%
Water : 72.66%
Salt : 2.67%
Levain : 50%

Step 2. Determine the weight of the flour in the final mix to make 40 kg of total dough.

Two calculation methods are possible.

Calculation Method 1: Cross Multiplication

Flour	: F	100%
Water	: W	72.66%
Salt	: S	2.67%
Levain	: L	50%
Total	: 40 kg	225.33%

Expressed as an equation:

$$F \times 225.33 = 400 \times 100$$

$$F = (40 \times 100) \div 225.33$$

$$F = 17.75$$

Calculation Method 2: Fractions

First, we need to calculate what proportion of the total dough is represented by the flour. The necessary calculation can be expressed as a fraction with the baker's percentage of the flour on top and the total of baker's percentages on the bottom:

$$F\% = 100/225.33 = 100 \div 225.33 = 4438 = 44.38\%$$

We now know that 44.38 percent of the total dough is flour. Now we need to calculate the weight of the flour.

$$F = 40\text{ kg} \times 44.38\% = 40\text{ kg} \times 0.4438 = 17.75$$

Now we know that 17.75 kg of flour will be necessary to obtain 40 kg of dough.

To simplify the rest of the calculations and to make sure we will produce enough dough, we will round up the amount of flour to the next whole number: 17.75 kg will become 18 kg. However, we only round up the weight of the flour; we do not round up the weights of the other ingredients.

Step 3. We must apply the baker's percentages of the formula to the weight of the flour to determine the desired weights of the remaining ingredients:

Flour	= 100%	= 18 kg		
Water	= 72.66%	= 18 × 0.7266	=	13 kg
Salt	= 2.67%	= 18 × 0.0267	=	0.48 kg
Levain	= 50%	= 18 × 0.5	=	9 kg

To verify our calculations, if we total the weights of all the ingredients, we should find the amount of dough needed to accommodate this order:

Flour :	18 kg	100%
Water :	13 kg	72.66%
Salt :	480 g	2.67%
Levain :	9 kg	50%
Total :	40.48 kg	225.33%

With 40 kg of dough needed, this formula will produce 40.48 kg of dough. We have a small amount of extra dough because we rounded up the amount of flour.

APPENDIX C: Temperature Conversions

C°	F°	C°	F°	C°	F°	C°	F°	C°	F°	C°	F°	C°	F°
1	**33.8**	41	**105.8**	81	**177.8**	121	**249.8**	161	**321.8**	201	**393.8**	241	**465.8**
2	**35.6**	42	**107.6**	82	**179.6**	122	**251.6**	162	**323.6**	202	**395.6**	242	**467.6**
3	**37.4**	43	**109.4**	83	**181.4**	123	**253.4**	163	**325.4**	203	**397.4**	243	**469.4**
4	**39.2**	44	**111.2**	84	**183.2**	124	**255.2**	164	**327.2**	204	**399.2**	244	**471.2**
5	**41**	45	**113**	85	**185**	125	**257**	165	**329**	205	**401**	245	**473**
6	**42.8**	46	**114.8**	86	**186.8**	126	**258.8**	166	**330.8**	206	**402.8**	246	**474.8**
7	**44.6**	47	**116.6**	87	**188.6**	127	**260.6**	167	**332.6**	207	**404.6**	247	**476.6**
8	**46.4**	48	**118.4**	88	**190.4**	128	**262.4**	168	**334.4**	208	**406.4**	248	**478.4**
9	**48.2**	49	**120.2**	89	**192.2**	129	**264.2**	169	**336.2**	209	**408.2**	249	**480.2**
10	**50**	50	**122**	90	**194**	130	**266**	170	**338**	210	**410**	250	**482**
11	**51.8**	51	**123.8**	91	**195.8**	131	**267.8**	171	**339.8**	211	**411.8**	251	**483.8**
12	**53.6**	52	**125.6**	92	**197.6**	132	**269.6**	172	**341.6**	212	**413.6**	252	**485.6**
13	**55.4**	53	**127.4**	93	**199.4**	133	**271.4**	173	**343.4**	213	**415.4**	253	**487.4**
14	**57.2**	54	**129.2**	94	**201.2**	134	**273.2**	174	**345.2**	214	**417.2**	254	**489.2**
15	**59**	55	**131**	95	**203**	135	**275**	175	**347**	215	**419**	255	**491**
16	**60.8**	56	**132.8**	96	**204.8**	136	**276.8**	176	**348.8**	216	**420.8**	256	**492.8**
17	**62.6**	57	**134.6**	97	**206.6**	137	**278.6**	177	**350.6**	217	**422.6**	257	**494.6**
18	**64.4**	58	**136.4**	98	**208.4**	138	**280.4**	178	**352.4**	218	**424.4**	258	**496.4**
19	**66.2**	59	**138.2**	99	**210.2**	139	**282.2**	179	**354.2**	219	**426.2**	259	**498.2**
20	**68**	60	**140**	100	**212**	140	**284**	180	**356**	220	**428**	260	**500**
21	**69.8**	61	**141.8**	101	**213.8**	141	**285.8**	181	**357.8**	221	**429.8**	261	**501.8**
22	**71.6**	62	**143.6**	102	**215.6**	142	**287.6**	182	**359.6**	222	**431.6**	262	**503.6**
23	**73.4**	63	**145.4**	103	**217.4**	143	**289.4**	183	**361.4**	223	**433.4**	263	**505.4**
24	**75.2**	64	**147.2**	104	**219.2**	144	**291.2**	184	**363.2**	224	**435.2**	264	**507.2**
25	**77**	65	**149**	105	**221**	145	**293**	185	**365**	225	**437**	265	**509**
26	**78.8**	66	**150.8**	106	**222.8**	146	**294.8**	186	**366.8**	226	**438.8**	266	**510.8**
27	**80.6**	67	**152.6**	107	**224.6**	147	**296.6**	187	**368.6**	227	**440.6**	267	**512.6**
28	**82.4**	68	**154.4**	108	**226.4**	148	**298.4**	188	**370.4**	228	**442.4**	268	**514.4**
29	**84.2**	69	**156.2**	109	**228.2**	149	**300.2**	189	**372.2**	229	**444.2**	269	**516.2**
30	**86**	70	**158**	110	**230**	150	**302**	190	**374**	230	**446**	270	**518**
31	**87.8**	71	**159.8**	111	**231.8**	151	**303.8**	191	**375.8**	231	**447.8**	271	**519.8**
32	**89.6**	72	**161.6**	112	**233.6**	152	**305.6**	192	**377.6**	232	**449.6**	272	**521.6**
33	**91.4**	73	**163.4**	113	**235.4**	153	**307.4**	193	**379.4**	233	**451.4**	273	**523.4**
34	**93.2**	74	**165.2**	114	**237.2**	154	**309.2**	194	**381.2**	234	**453.2**	274	**525.2**
35	**95**	75	**167**	115	**239**	155	**311**	195	**383**	235	**455**	275	**527**
36	**96.8**	76	**168.8**	116	**240.8**	156	**312.8**	196	**384.8**	236	**456.8**	276	**528.8**
37	**98.6**	77	**170.6**	117	**242.6**	157	**314.6**	197	**386.6**	237	**458.6**	277	**530.6**
38	**100.4**	78	**172.4**	118	**244.4**	158	**316.4**	198	**388.4**	238	**460.4**	278	**532.4**
39	**102.2**	79	**174.2**	119	**246.2**	159	**318.2**	199	**390.2**	239	**462.2**	279	**534.2**
40	**104**	80	**176**	120	**248**	160	**320**	200	**392**	240	**464**	280	**536**

GLOSSARY

A

acidification
Production of acids as a byproduct of fermentation activity in dough.

actinidin
Proteolytic enzyme in kiwi.

adulteration
Modification of a product by the inclusion of cheaper, inferior materials.

aerated confections
Whipped confections (such as marshmallow and nougat) consisting of a stable foam. The two most common approaches to making these confections are adding a gelling agent to meringue while it is whipping and adding a gelling agent to cooked sugar syrup and whipping it to the desired stage.

à la carte
Dessert item served without accompanying sauces or other components, unlike plated desserts. À la carte may also refer to an item which is not part of a prix fixe menu.

à la minute
Preparation of food to order.

almond cream
Filling for a variety of baked goods, including the classic Pithivier, various Viennoiserie, fruit tarts, and cake layers. Its ingredients typically include butter, sugar, eggs, almond meal, flour (sometimes), and rum.

alum
Sodium aluminum sulfate. Used as a chemical leavener due to its ability to react with baking soda in the presence of heat and produce carbon dioxide.

alveograph
Instrument that discerns specific physical characteristics of dough, quantifying the balance between elasticity and extensibility and strength. These values appear on the spec sheet as *P*, *L*, *P/L*, and *W*, respectively.

alveoles
Holes, or cell structure of the crumb.

amino acids
Basic components of protein.

amuses bouche
Tiny savory treats served as an introduction to the meal.

analytical data
Spec sheet details of flour characteristics such as moisture content, ash content, protein content, and enzyme activity.

angel food method
Angel food cakes are named for their pure white crumb and light texture. The three basic ingredients are sugar, egg white, and flour. Due to the large ratio of sugar to flour, the egg foam is made with half of the quantity of sugar and the remaining sugar is folded into the egg foam with well-sifted flour.

applied method
Piping technique that uses a cone to apply an embellishment that highlights existing decoration or design. The surface can be any texture because the tip of the cone is usually held just above it.

arrival time
Time required for the top of a farinograph curve to reach the 500 FU line after the mixer has been started and the water introduced. This value is a measurement of the rate at which flour takes up water during the formation of the dough.

ash content
Amount of bran present in flour after milling. Ash content affects dough characteristics and fermentation activity.

autolyse
Process that involves premixing the flour and water and allowing it to rest for a minimum of 15 to 20 minutes. This step increases hydration of the flour, which leads to a better gluten structure. Also, the increased enzyme activity that occurs enhances extensibility of the dough.

B

baked custard
Custard that is baked and set in the oven. An example of this type of custard is crème brûlée.

baked pie
Style of pie that begins with an unbaked shell that is filled with fruit or custard and then baked. It may have a single or double crust. Examples of baked pies include apple, blueberry, and pumpkin.

baked tarts
Tarts in which the tart dough is baked with the filling. Common fillings for this style of tart include frangipane, almond cream, ricotta cheese, or rice.

baking ammonia
Also known as ammonium bicarbonate. In the presence of moisture and heat, this chemical leavener reacts rapidly to produce carbon dioxide and ammonia gas that leavens the batter or dough and then dissipates once the item is baked.

baking powder
Combination of baking soda, acidic salts, and a small amount of starch for stabilization.

baking soda
Also known as sodium bicarbonate or bicarbonate of soda. When it comes into contact with moisture and acid, carbon dioxide gas is produced. Baking soda is also used to balance the neutralizing value for baking powder.

barley
Earliest known cereal to be cultivated. Historically, its flour was relied upon for making bread; the high-starch, low-gluten content produced dense, flat loaves. Today it is used mostly in beer brewing.

base
Primary flavoring component of mousse. The egg foam or whipped cream is folded into this mixture to add lightness. The base may be fruit puree, ganache, or a cooked-stirred custard such as crème Anglaise.

basic buttercream
Sugar-sweetened whipped butter, often lightened with egg foam or egg whites. The essential ingredients for basic buttercream are powdered sugar and butter and/or shortening.

baumé
Measurement used to quantify the sugar density of any given liquid.

Bavarian cream
Type of mousse based on crème Anglaise, whipped cream, and gelatin.

beurrage
Fat component in laminated dough that is enclosed in the détrempe. Also referred to as roll-in fat.

biga
Historically an Italian preferment, a biga is prepared using flour, water, and yeast, with a hydration of approximately 50 to 55 percent. It is allowed to ferment at 60°F (16°C) for 18 hours. Today, the term biga is often improperly used as a generic name for a preferment.

binding agents
Stabilizers such as gelatin, agar powder, modified starch, and pectin; such agents help to set the formula, which allows the product to take on the shape of a mold and to be handled for cutting and packaging.

biofilm
Community of microorganisms that attaches to solid surfaces exposed to water and excretes a slimy, glue-like substance.

Bioterrorism Act
Laws enacted in 2002 to protect the health and safety of Americans from an intended or actual terrorist attack on the nation's food supply.

biscuit jaconde method
Variation on the separated egg sponge method. It is characterized by the addition of nut flour into the cake batter, as well as by a design that is applied through a thicker batter. Biscuit jaconde is baked in thin sheets.

biscuit method
Mixing method that produces a flaky structure as desired in biscuits and scones. First, cold fat is cut into flour and other dry ingredients. Liquid ingredients are then added to the mixture and blended to incorporation.

bittersweet chocolate
Dark chocolate in which the cocoa content averages between 64 and 85 percent.

blast freezer
Freezer used to freeze products quickly, minimizing the dryness and crystal formation inside products.

blending method
Fastest and easiest mixing method for muffins, quick breads, and scones. The dry ingredients are simply added to the liquid ingredients. Also called the muffin method.

blind baked
Pie or tart dough baked alone, without filling.

blitz puff pastry
Pastry dough similar to a very flaky pie dough. Cold butter is mixed into the dough with large pieces remaining visible. The dough is then rolled out and folded a number of times to create flaky layers.

blown sugar
Decorative application of cooked sugar in which air is pumped or blown into satinized sugar and the piece is manipulated to represent the vision of the pastry chef.

bombe
Molded frozen dessert named for its classic dome shape. It is traditionally comprised of multiple layers of parfait-type mixtures.

book fold
Book folds can be done by folding the sheeted dough in four, with the center spine offset to ensure consistent layering. Also known as a double fold.

bottom-up assembly
Refers to the method of assembling cake from the bottom up. These cakes can be assembled in ring molds, cake frames, or other molds with no bottom. This may be required due the presence of a cake wall.

bread pudding
Popular dessert made from a baked mixture of dried bread, custard base, and flavorings.

brittles
Crunchy sugar confections based on cooked sugar syrup to which nuts or seeds have been added.

brix
The percentage of sugar in a solution.

bromelain
Proteolytic enzyme in pineapple.

bubble sugar
Result of the bubbles that occur in sugar when it hits a layer of alcohol on parchment paper or silicon sheets.

bulk fermentation
See first fermentation

butter press
Hydraulic press that efficiently and consistently forms uniform blocks of butter at the push of a button.

C

cacao bean
Seeds from the pod of the *Theobroma cacao* tree. Cacao beans are processed to make chocolate.

cake frames
Metal frames (available in the size of a sheet pan or a half sheet pan) that are designed for assembling specialty cakes.

cake syrup
Sugar syrup made with less sugar than water (commonly 2:1, water to sugar). Used to moisten cakes, it adds a minimal amount of sweetness.

cake wall
Strip of thin cake that surrounds the sides of the dessert.

calcium carbonate
Mineral added to sugar to make it opaque.

Calvel, Raymond
A French Master Baker known for his in-depth studies of the dough system. Also known as the developer of the autolyse process.

caramel
Sugar that has been cooked dry, or in solution to a light to dark brown color. Also a sugar confection with a caramel flavor and a texture which can range from soft and chewy to firm.

caramelization
Process that occurs when sugar is heated above 320°F (160°C). The sugar changes color from clear to light yellow and progresses to darker tones of brown, evolving the initial sweet flavors into richer, nutty, and slightly bitter flavors.

carbonates of soda
Ash produced from the burning of certain plants that live in or by the sea. This alkaline substance was one of the first leaveners used in baking.

carbon dioxide
Gas produced as yeast metabolizes sugars.

carotenoid pigments
Natural components of the wheat kernel that are responsible for the creamy color of flour and some aroma production.

cast sugar
Technique of pouring sugar into lightly greased metal forms, metal bars, food grade rubber mats, or silicone molds.

certificate of analysis (COA)
Fact sheet detailing information about a particular batch of flour.

chemical leavening agents
Substances that aerate and leaven batter as a result of the gases produced from their reaction with water, acid, and/or heat.

chevron cut
Series of angled, parallel cuts that run along the top and bottom edges of the loaf. The chevron cut is typically used for short, elongated shapes like batards. It encourages a round cross-section in the baked loaf.

chiffon method
Two-step mixing process: First, a slurry of wet and dry ingredients is created. Then, egg whites are whipped and folded into the base. Liquid oil in this type of cake makes a very tender crumb.

chiffon pie
Classic American dessert composed of a blind-baked crust, mousse-like filling, and sometimes a whipped cream topping.

chocolate confections
Confections made from chocolate or that are covered in chocolate.

chocolate glaze
Thin, shiny chocolate coating made from a thinned ganache.

chocolate liquor
Product of the whole cocoa bean after it has gone through the initial production process. Chocolate liquor can be turned into cocoa powder and cocoa butter, can be sold as unsweetened chocolate, or can be further processed into dark or milk chocolate products.

chocolate mousse
Mousse preparation that includes chocolate, whipped cream, usually egg foam, and sometimes gelatin. If the cocoa content of the mixture is high enough to set the mousse, gelatin is not necessary.

chocolate panning
Process in which nutmeats or other confectionary centers are coated in chocolate.

chocolatier
One who works professionally with chocolate.

churned desserts
Mixture that is stirred or churned during freezing in order to break up the size of the ice crystals as they form. Churned frozen desserts are generally produced using an ice cream machine. Ice cream and sorbet are two examples of churned desserts.

classic cut
Scoring technique used for baguettes and batards. To make a classic cut, the baker holds the blade as flat as possible, or at least with a 45 degree angle to the surface, and creates a horizontal incision.

coating chocolate
Convenience product designed for use without tempering. It is made with cocoa butter equivalents and consequently has inferior taste and texture qualities.

cocoa butter
Natural hard fat found in the cocoa bean; cocoa butter is a triglyceride composed of three fatty acids connected to a glycerol molecule. It is roughly 54 percent of the chocolate liquor.

cocoa butter equivalent (CBE)
Fats that mimic the crystallization properties of cocoa butter.

cocoa mass
See chocolate liquor.

cocoa paste
See chocolate liquor.

cocoa powder
Powder milled from the cocoa cake left over after the cocoa butter has been pressed out of the chocolate liquor.

common meringue
Meringue made with sugar and egg whites that is often characterized by having less sugar than egg whites. Commonly used as a leavening agent in cake mixing applications. A common meringue may be referred to as a French Meringue.

complete metamorphosis
Life cycle of an insect.

conching
Process to further refine chocolate to reach the desired 15 to 25 micron particle size and to improve flavor, viscosity, and flow properties.

confectionary fondant
Type of fondant in which the initial sugar syrup is cooked to a higher temperature; the resulting firm texture enables the pastry chef to thin the fondant to add flavorings.

confections
Term describing a vast array of products that can be broken into three categories: chocolate, flour, and sugar.

consistency
Level of hardness or softness of the dough system.

cooked fruit juice method
Method used to enhance thickening for fillings made with delicate fruits and berries. Fruit juice is cooked with sugar, starch, and optional spices until thick. The mixture is then mixed with the fruit. When it is cool, the filling is deposited into the pie shell and baked.

cooked fruit method
Method in which fresh fruit, along with sugar and starch, is precooked prior to baking in the pie shell. This method is best for firmer fruits such as apples or pears.

cooked-stirred custard
Custard that is cooked over heat. Constant stirring is necessary to prevent scorching. Two examples of this style of custard are pastry cream and crème Anglaise.

cookie spread
Amount of outward expansion that occurs during the baking of cookie dough.

cooling
In reference to the cooling bread, this is one of the last steps of the baking process.

cotyledon
First leaf or pair of leaves created by the embryo of a seed plant.

coulis
Clear fruit sauce that contains no pulp.

couverture
High-quality chocolate that contains only cocoa butter as fat.

creaming method
Mixing method in which fat and sugar are blended together to the desired stage. Next, eggs are added, followed by alternating additions of dry and wet ingredients (if any).

cream pie
Unbaked pie that is composed of a blind-baked crust and a cooked-stirred custard filling. Examples include chocolate cream, banana cream, and coconut cream pies.

crème Anglaise
Cooked-stirred custard that can be employed in a number of applications, including dessert sauces, bases for ice cream, buttercream, or mousse.

crème Anglaise–style buttercream
Icing that combines crème Anglaise, Italian meringue, and butter.

crème brûlée
Rich and creamy baked custard with a thin layer of crisp and caramelized sugar coating the creamy filling.

crème caramel
Custard formulated to be slightly firmer than crème brûlée because it is turned out of its mold before serving. The trademark characteristic of this dessert is the caramel that covers the dessert after it is turned out of the mold.

crème Chantilly
Sweetened, vanilla-flavored whipped cream that can be used as garnish or an icing.

crème Chiboust
Rich, light cream that is a component of the classic French dessert St. Honoré. Pastry cream is combined with French or Italian meringue at a ratio of 4:1. Gelatin is added to increase stability.

crème St. Honoré
See crème Chiboust.

criollo
Type of cacao prized for its mild, yet deep chocolate flavor and low acidity levels. It is the rarest and most expensive of the three types of cacao.

cross contamination
Transfer of bacteria from one food, typically raw, to other foods. It is one of the major causes of food poisoning.

crumb coat
See masking.

crystalline confections
Style of confections defined by the formation of sugar crystals during the cooking process. Examples include fondant, fudge, pralines, dragées and liqueur pralines.

crystallization
Process that occurs when a crystalline substance such as salt or sugar precipitates from the liquid in which it was dissolved.

culture
Collection of wild yeast and Lactobacillus bacteria living in a mixture of flour and water. These microorganisms need three things to thrive and reproduce: food, which is provided by simple sugars in the flour or from enzymatic activity; water added to the flour; and oxygen incorporated during mixing.

custard base
Mixture containing whole eggs, egg yolks, or both; cream, milk, or both; and additional ingredients like sugar and flavorings. As it cooks, proteins in the eggs thicken the liquid.

custard pie
Baked pie in which the liquid filling is set by eggs. Examples include pumpkin and pecan pies, and quiche.

custard-style (French custard) ice cream
Type of ice cream that utilizes egg yolks or whole eggs in the preparation of the ice cream base.

cut-out cookie
Cookie that is cut from rolled-out dough. Sugar cookies and gingerbread cookies are examples.

D

danger zone
Most hospitable temperature range for disease-causing microorganisms. For those capable of causing foodborne illness, this range is 41°F (5°C) to 140°F (60°C).

dark chocolate
Chocolate made from chocolate liquor with the addition of cocoa butter and sugar.

dasher
Central vertical paddle that churns, or spins, inside the freezing tank of an ice cream maker.

departure time
Time from the first addition of water until the top of a farinograph curve leaves the 500 FU line. Longer time indicates stronger flour as the mixing time can be longer without degradation of the gluten structure.

desired dough temperature (DDT)
Ideal temperature to create an environment favorable for fermentation of most dough; in most cases, this range is 74°F (23°C) to 77°F (25°C).

détrempe
The dough portion of laminated Viennoiserie.

dextrose equivalent (DE)
Value assigned to a substance that indicates its sweetening power relative to dextrose. Dextrose has a DE of 100.

diplomat cream
Smooth and light cream prepared from pastry cream, whipped cream, and gelatin.

dividing
Process in which the bulk of the dough is divided into small pieces according to the desired final weight of the bread, accounting for the weight loss that will occur during baking.

doctors
Ingredients that can be added to sugar solutions to help prevent crystallization. Common doctors include glucose, inverted sugar, and acids such as tartaric acid.

double-acting baking powder
Chemical leavener that contains both low- and high-temperature reacting leavening acids.

double fold
See book fold.

dough conditioners
Optional ingredients that can be added to dough in order to improve the processing characteristics of the dough and the final product characteristics. Dough conditioners can be natural, chemical, or microbial.

dough development
Formation of the structure of the dough.

dough development time
Time in minutes between the first addition of water to the dough and the development of dough's maximum consistency.

dough rheology
Physical properties of the dough.

dragées
Category of crystalline confections made from slow-roasted nuts that have gone through two distinct processes: candying and coating.

dropped cookie
Cookie named for the portioning and releasing action of the dough. The thick batter is generally portioned using a scoop or cookie depositor.

Dutched cocoa powder
Baking cocoa made from cacao beans that have been treated with an alkaline solution. The resulting powder is darker, milder, and less acidic than nonalkalized or natural cocoa powder.

E

egg foam
Whipped whole eggs, egg yolks, or egg whites that create a lightened foam, or collection of air bubbles held together by denatured protein molecules.

elasticity
Refers to the dough's ability to return to its initial position after stretching.

emulsifier
Chemical or natural substance that is soluble at low concentrations in both water and fat. Emulsifiers' main function in a dough system is to better link water and the lipids naturally contained in the flour; as a result, the dough has a stronger texture and is better able to withstand mechanical mixing.

emulsion
Combination of two or more liquids that are naturally repellent into a smooth mixture. One substance is dispersed in the other. Emulsions are usually water-in-oil or oil-in-water blends.

endosperm
Main component of wheat that contains starch and protein.

enrichment
Flour enrichment is used to increase the nutritional value of white flour. Since the 1930s, the natural vitamins and minerals taken out during the milling process have been replaced with vitamins such as thiamin, niacin and riboflavin, and minerals like iron. As of January 1998, folic acid has also been included.

enrobed chocolates
Chocolate confections that are produced by covering or dipping solid fillings in melted chocolate.

entremets
Composed cake of a size sufficient to serve a small group.

enzyme
Protein that catalyzes a chemical reaction of degradation.

esters
Organic compounds that are formed by the reaction between an alcohol and an acid. In baking, esters are aromatic components important to the flavor of the final product.

extensibility
Stretching property of dough.

F

falling number
Number that represents the enzyme activity of the flour.

farinograph
Device that characterizes the quality of the flour by measuring the mixing properties of its dough to determine absorption capacity, development time, and structure stability.

fat-based cakes
Moist, dense, rich, cakes that are high in fat and sugar. Techniques used to make these cakes include the creaming method, the high-ratio method, and the liquid shortening method.

fat bloom
Migration of cocoa butter to the surface of chocolate. Fat bloom appears as a cloudy white dust over chocolate. Improper tempering, warm storage conditions, or abrupt temperature changes can cause fat bloom.

Federal Food, Drug and Cosmetic Act (FDCA)
Act of Congress passed in 1938 that gave the Food and Drug Administration the authority to govern the safety and accurate labeling of drugs, cosmetics, medical devices, and the nation's food supply (meat and poultry excluded).

feeding
Periodic mixing of a portion of a culture with flour and water to keep the flora alive and active. Maintenance of a culture requires that the vital conditions (food, water, and air) are constantly refreshed.

fermentation
Breakdown of compound molecules in organic substances under the effect of yeast or bacteria (ferments).

ficin
Proteolytic enzyme in figs.

filigree
Fine decorative piping.

filling
In reference to cake assembly: elements such as buttercream, ganache, or curd spread between layers of cake.

final proof
Fermentation period that takes place between dough shaping and the beginning of the bake. Throughout this process, the gas produced by the yeast will accumulate and create internal pressure on the gluten structure.

first fermentation
Process in which dough is allowed to ferment as a large mass. This creates conditions that are optimal for the development of all of the benefits fermentation brings to the dough. Also called bulk fermentation or floor time.

first-in, first-out (FIFO)
Stock rotation methodology that ensures that foods are used in a timely manner, well before their "use by" date.

flaky
Type of pie dough characterized by a light and flaky texture.

flat icing
Also known as water icing, flat icing is a quick preparation made from powdered sugar and a liquid such as milk, lemon juice, or water.

floor time
See first fermentation.

flour confections
Category of pastry characterized by the use of flour as a primary ingredient for the creation of confections. Examples include but are not limited to cookies, cakes, quick breads, etc.

foam
Dispersion of gas throughout a continuous solid phase (which may be liquid).

foam-based cakes
Light cakes that are based on a foam of whipped whole eggs, egg yolks, egg whites, or a combination. Examples include chiffon, sponge and angel food cakes.

fondant
Smooth, white icing that is prepared from a sugar syrup that has been cooled and agitated to crystallize the sugar.

food allergen
Product or ingredient that contains proteins that can potentially cause severe, occasionally fatal, reactions in a person who is allergic to that food.

food-stored insects
Insects that live in stored food.

forastero
Type of cacao that is used to produce 80 percent of the world's chocolate.

form V crystallization
Level of crystallization confectioners and chocolate manufacturers require to ensure a shelf stable product that is resistant to fat bloom. Form V is characterized by the "dense compacting" of the fat crystals into an organized structure.

fornarii
Professional bread bakers of the 12th century. Fornarii performed the task of baking the townspeoples' dough in communal ovens.

frangipane
Cream similar to almond cream, but lighter in texture and flavor. Like almond cream, frangipane can be used in the preparation of cakes, tarts, and Viennoiserie.

freezer burn
Degradation of quality that occurs when a frozen food dries out during storage.

freezing point
Temperature at which a liquid becomes a solid.

French buttercream
Based on a pâte à bombe. This egg yolk–based egg foam adds richness and color to the buttercream.

French meringue
An egg foam created with a minimum ratio of one part egg whites to one part sugar.

friandise
Small treats that are served with coffee or tea or after a dessert course.

frozen dough process
Dough that is mixed, minimally fermented, shaped, and then frozen. When the dough is required for baking, it is defrosted and then proofed as usual. Special considerations required for this process include mixing, fermentation, the type of yeast, dough conditioner selection, the freezing process, and the defrosting process.

frozen inserts
Components of specialty cakes that are soft and fragile at room temperature. Examples are mousse, crémeux, and crème brûlée. Freezing before assembly allows these elements to be handled and inserted easily.

frozen mousse
Frozen combination of a Swiss or Italian meringue, whipped cream, and a flavoring base.

frozen parfait
Frozen mixture of pâte à bombe or Italian or Swiss meringue, with flavoring and whipped cream folded in. In the United States, parfait also refers to a dessert of ice cream layered with fruit and whipped cream.

frozen soufflé
Similar to frozen mousse; its distinction is its appearance, which is made to resemble that of a hot soufflé.

fruit glaze
Pourable yet viscous icing made with ingredients such as fruit puree, glucose, water, and gelatin.

fruit mousse
Mousse preparation that includes fruit puree, whipped cream, egg foam (optional), and gelatin.

fruit pie
Pie in which the filling is made from fresh, frozen, canned, or dried fruit.

fruit sauces
Sauces that contain some pulp of the fruit.

fudge
Confection based on the formulation of fondant (fine sugar crystals surrounded by a supersaturated sugar solution) with additional ingredients, such as dairy products, fat, nuts, and chocolate.

G

galette
Rustic, freeform pie that may be sweet or savory. Galette may also refer to any flat, round, rustic tart such as galette de rois, which is made with puff pastry. Furthermore, in Brittany, a local specialty is referred to as galette; it is a buckwheat-based crepe batter cooked and filled with savory items.

ganache
Creamy mixture made when a liquid, usually cream, is poured over chocolate and an emulsion is formed.

gelée
Substance made from fruit juice, sugar solution, and a gelling agent like gelatin, agar, or pectin.

germination
Sprouting phase of the plant life cycle.

gianduja
Blend of chocolate and hazelnut.

gliadin
One of the two proteins that combine to form gluten. Gliadin affects the extensibility of the dough.

glucides
Group of carbohydrates including sugars, starches, and cellulose that are present naturally in flour.

glucoamylases
Enzymes that break down the dextrin chains generated by amylases into glucose sugar, which is easier for yeast to process (thus improving yeast activity during fermentation). Glucoamylases are sometimes used to partially replace other sugars in the formula, creating a final product that is a bit leaner but retains a sweet flavor.

glucose oxidase
Enzyme that converts glucose into gluconic acid, which acts as an oxidizer and increases gluten strength.

gluten
Three-dimensional matrix that occurs when water and flour are combined and developed.

gluten coagulation
Coagulation of gluten begins at 165°F (74°C).

gluten development
Development of the gluten structure of the dough.

glutenin
One of two primary proteins in wheat. Glutenin has some effect on the elasticity of dough.

Good Manufacturing Practices (GMPs)
Guidelines that provide a system of processes, procedures, and documentation that ensure the bread or pastry produced has the identity, strength, composition, quality, and purity it is represented to possess.

granita (granité)
Frozen dessert that can be made from a wide assortment of flavorings; granita is frequently served as an intermezzo or light dessert.

grinding
Shelled, roasted cacao beans (nibs) are finely ground into a liquid mass called chocolate liquor.

guitar
Cutting tool made up of a series of wires; the guitar is used to evenly cut a variety of confectionary items including pâtes de fruits, ganache, pralines, and cake.

H

hard candies
Noncrystalline confections made from a saturated sugar syrup that is cooked to a specific temperature and then cooled.

Hazard Analysis Critical Control Point (HACCP)
Program in which the original purpose was to produce defect- and hazard-free food for astronauts to consume during space flights. Today, HACCP programs are seen as essential elements of food safety in bakery and food service operations throughout the world.

heat shock
Texture and flavor damage in frozen desserts caused by fluctuating temperatures. The melting and refreezing causes water in the mixture to migrate and form larger ice crystals.

heavy pack
Sugar density in the syrup of canned fruit. Heavy pack is sweeter than light pack.

heterofermentative
One of the two types of lactic bacteria, heterofermentative bacteria convert the sugars in dough into lactic acid, acetic acid, and carbon dioxide, all of which affect dough characteristics and bread flavor.

high-ratio cakes
Cakes characterized by their high ratio of sugar and liquid ingredients to flour. These cakes use specialty shortenings that have added emulsifiers to help emulsify the larger quantity of liquid ingredients and fat.

high-temperature short-time (HTST)
Pasteurization process in which a mixture must be heated to 185°F (85°C) for two to three minutes.

homofermentative
One of the two types of lactic bacteria, homofermentative bacteria convert the sugars in dough into lactic acid, which affects dough characteristics and bread flavor.

humectants
Substances that promote moisture retention.

hydrolysis
Process that converts starch to glucose (dextrose) by the application of heat and an acid or enzymes. Hydrolysis can be described as full or partial.

hygroscopic
Ability to attract and retain moisture.

hysteresis
Difference between the point at which a liquid is fluid and the point at which it is set. For example, agar does not melt until 185°F (85°C) to 194°F (90°C), and agar solutions set at approximately 90°F (32°C) to 105°F (40°C).

I

ice
Final step in layer cake assembly. A thick, even layer of an icing component is applied to the cake sides and top.

icebox cookie
Cookie in which dough is formed into cylinders or blocks that are refrigerated, sliced, and baked, or frozen until needed. Intricate geometric or marbled designs may be created from multiple flavors of dough.

icing
Refers to a broad range of formulas that are used to fill, cover, or decorate cakes, pastries, or cookies. Types of icing include buttercreams, glazes, fondant, ganache, flat icing, and royal icing.

improved mix
Compromise between the short mix and the intensive mix. Improved mix allows the baker to achieve the efficiencies of intensive mixing, while retaining most of the product quality obtained with a short mix method. With this technique, ingredients are incorporated in first speed and dough is mixed to half development in second speed.

inclusions
Ingredients that add flavor and texture components to items such as cookies or frozen desserts. They do not have a structural function, and are usually added near the end of the mixing process. Examples of inclusions are chocolate chips, rolled oats, nuts, candies, and dried fruits.

individually quick frozen (IQF)
Freezing process that ensures a high retention of flavor and color in fruit. Pieces are frozen individually rather than in one block so that they can be easily portioned.

infusion
Method of adding flavor to water or oil-based liquids. Ingredients such as zest, herbs, or spices are allowed to steep in warm liquid until the desired strength is reached but are strained out to prevent overly strong or bitter flavors.

integrated pest management
Series of pest management evaluations, monitoring, prevention, and controls.

intensive mix
Mixing technique in which ingredients are incorporated in first speed, and the dough is then fully developed in second speed.

intermediate proof
See rest.

inverted puff pastry
Type of puff pastry produced by enclosing the dough layer (détrempe) within the butter (beurrage).

isomalt
Manufactured sugar substitute derived from sucrose. Isomalt is frequently used in sugar sculpture because it is more resistant to crystallization and less hygroscopic than sugar.

Italian buttercream
Light buttercream based on Italian meringue. Softened butter is added to the meringue and whipped in to incorporation.

Italian meringue
Cooked meringue that is made using egg whites and cooked sugar syrup. The sugar syrup is carefully poured into the whipping whites and the mixture is whipped until it is just slightly warm or cool.

Italian puff pastry
Version of puff pastry characterized by a dough that contains eggs and white wine.

J

jelly confections
Popular sugar confections (including pâtes de fruits and Turkish Delight) containing a supersaturated sugar solution, flavorings, and binding agents.

L

laminated dough
Dough that has had fat enclosed in it and has undergone a series of folds to create a light and flaky final product.

lamination
Process by which layers of dough and butter are created in order to make flaky pastries such as croissants and Danish.

lattice crust
Decorative top crust for a pie or tart. The lattice appearance is formed by an open weave of dough strips.

layer cakes
Cakes composed of alternating layers of filling and cake.

leavening acids
Acidic substances added for the purpose of reacting with sodium bicarbonate and producing carbon dioxide.

letter fold
See single fold.

levain
Mature sourdough culture used to ferment the dough.

light pack
Sugar density in the syrup of canned fruit. Light pack is less sweet than heavy pack.

liqueur cordials
Crystalline confections filled with a liqueur-flavored, supersaturated sugar solution. When this syrup is deposited into a starch mold, a fine crystalline shell is formed.

liquid shortening
Liquid (partially hydrogenated) shortenings with added emulsifiers are used mostly by cake makers who rely on shortenings for their fat bases. These shortenings disperse quickly and easily throughout the batter but require special attention to mixing time and rate.

low-temperature long-time (LTLT)
Pasteurization process in which a mixture must be heated to a minimum temperature of 149°F (65°C) for 30 minutes.

M

Maillard reaction
Reaction of residual sugars, amino acids, and heat that contributes to a desirable browned appearance and roasted flavor.

maize
Also known as corn, this starchy grain is native to North America. While certain varieties are grown and consumed as a vegetable, others whose kernels are small and hard are ground into meal or flour.

marshmallows
Aerated sugar confections made with a saturated sugar syrup, gelatin and egg whites (optional).

marzipan
Confection made from almond paste with the addition of sugar, a cooked sugar syrup, and sometimes glucose and/or alcohol.

masking
Applying a thin coat of icing to the sides and top of a cake prior to icing. Its purpose is to secure any crumbs and prevent them from appearing in the icing layer.

Material Safety Data Sheets (MSDS)
Information designed to provide workers and emergency personnel with the proper procedures for handling or working with a particular substance.

maturation
Process wherein flour is allowed to age for two to three weeks after milling. The natural oxidation process improves protein quality and the baking performance of the flour.

mealy
Type of pie dough characterized by a compact yet tender texture.

medium peak
Peak that forms when a whipped medium (egg whites, whipped cream), has enough stability to form a peak, but the top of the peak bends.

medium rapid set pectin
One of the three most common types of pectin used in pastry, medium rapid set pectin is most often used in confiture and jams.

meringue
Egg foam created by beating air into egg whites. Sugar helps to stabilize the foam and it may be cooked or uncooked.

microorganisms
Organisms such as yeast or bacteria that are too small to see with the naked eye.

mignardise
Small, delicate sweets presented with after-dinner coffee service. Items may include chocolates, caramels, dipped fruits and nuts, mints, small cookies, or pastries.

milk chocolate
Chocolate made from chocolate liquor, sugar, milk solids, vanilla, and lecithin. In the United States, milk chocolate must contain a minimum of 10 percent cocoa and 12 percent milk solids.

milk solids nonfat (MSNF)
Components of skim or nonfat milk powder (which have had their water and fat components removed) including proteins, lactose, and minerals.

mille feuille
Dessert utilizing puff pastry. Literally translated as "thousand layers," a reference to the many layers created in the dough during the lamination process.

millet
Grain harvested from a group of cereal grasses grown for human and animal consumption. It is an important element of the diet in many African and Asian countries.

mise en place
French term meaning "put in place" used to describe the preparation of all necessary ingredients and equipment for cooking.

mixing
In reference to yeasted dough mixing: The step of the baking process during which the baker combines all of the ingredients together to make the dough. Mixing may also refer to the process of combining ingredients for assorted pastry doughs or batters.

mixing tolerance index (MTI)
Difference in FU between the top of a farinograph curve at the peak and the top of the curve measured five minutes after the peak is reached. The higher the MTI is, the weaker the flour will be.

modeling chocolate
Combination of couverture chocolate and inverted sugar, such as corn syrup, glucose, or simple syrup. Modeling chocolate can be used to cover a cake or to create textured decorative elements like ribbons, bows, flowers, and leaves.

modified creaming method
Basic creaming method process, followed by the folding in of a common meringue.

molded chocolates
Chocolate confections prepared in a mold.

molded cookie
Cookie dough is deposited into dye plates and then extracted for baking. The most common type of molded cookie is shortbread, produced from molds made of metal.

mousse
French term meaning "foam" or "froth." This light, elegant preparation consists of a flavored base into which egg foam and/or whipped cream has been folded, giving it its airy texture.

N

neutralizing value (NV)
Measurement of available acidity coming from leavening acids. The NV is utilized to determine the amount of leavening acid or acids needed to provide a neutral pH when combined with baking soda; this value represents the number of parts of baking soda that can be neutralized by 100 parts of the leavening acid.

noncrystalline confections
Confections in which crystallization must be avoided, such as caramels, hard candies, and toffees. The characteristics of noncrystalline confections range from hard and brittle to soft and chewy.

nonlaminated dough
Enriched dough that is not composed of alternating dough and fat layers.

nougat
Dense, aerated confection with a texture that ranges from soft and chewy to firm. Nougat relies on the formation of an egg white foam to achieve its characteristics.

Nutrition Labeling Education Act (NLEA)
1990 amendment to the FDCA that mandates nutritional labeling on all commercially produced bakery products.

O

oat
Grain that is well suited to growing in cold, wet climates. It is especially popular in Scotland, Wales, Germany, and Scandinavia.

oleic acid
Monounsaturated omega-9 fatty acid found in various animal and vegetable sources. Oleic acid comprises 35 percent of the triglycerides in cocoa butter.

one-stage method
Mixing method wherein all ingredients, once scaled and brought to room temperature (if needed), are mixed until incorporation.

origin chocolate
Chocolate made using beans from one growing region. The result is a uniquely flavored chocolate with flavor that highlights local cocoa varieties and production nuances.

osmotolerant yeast
Strain of yeast that is tolerant of high osmotic pressure conditions, a situation that arises in dough that has a high sugar or acidity content. The yeast is forced to compete with the sugar for moisture, increasing the pressure on the yeast cell wall. Osmotolerant yeast is available in fresh and dried forms.

oublies
Crisp, thin, flat or cone-shaped wafer made from batter cooked between hot, patterned iron molds. A predecessor to the modern waffle, these small cakes were popular in the Middle Ages.

oubloyers
Guild of bakers established in France in the Middle Ages who sold small cakes from stalls on the street and at festivals and fairs.

oven kick or oven spring
Quick temperature increase that occurs during the initial four to six minutes of baking time and stimulates yeast and enzyme activity in the dough. A large amount of carbon dioxide is produced and retained by the gluten structure, which develops the volume of the bread.

oven loading
Process in which loaves are placed in the oven for baking. This can be done by hand, using an oven peel or loader, or with an automatic loading system for larger production.

overrun
Amount of air that is incorporated during churning. It is expressed as a percentage and calculated as follows: Using the same volume for both the weight of the ice cream and the mix complete the following calculation: (Weight of ice cream × Weight of mix) / (Weight of mix × 100).

overtempered
Chocolate that has an excess of cocoa butter precrystalized, resulting in a chocolate that is thick and quick to set.

oxidation
Series of reactions that occur as a result of oxygen being incorporated into the dough during mixing. Gluten bonds that reinforce the structure and tolerance of the dough are formed. Overmixing and too much oxidation will result in a bleached appearance and diminished flavor.

oxidizers
Additives that strengthen the gluten structure by fixing the oxygen incorporated into the dough during mixing.

P

palmitic acid
One of the most common saturated fatty acids found in animals and plants. Palmitic acid comprises 26 percent of the triglycerides in cocoa butter.

panning
Process of coating nutmeats or other confectionary centers; the three types of panning are soft sugar panning, hard sugar panning, and chocolate panning. Panning may also refer to the action of placing pastries on pans before baking them.

papain
Proteolytic enzyme in papaya.

paper cone
Used for decorative piping with mediums such as royal icing or chocolate. Paper cones are also used to hold melted sugar or chocolate for assembling decorative display pieces made from sugar, pastillage, or chocolate.

par-baked process
Refers to the process wherein the dough is baked until the starch is gelatinized and the protein coagulates. At this point, the structure of the product is solid, and its volume is almost final. Par-baked breads are taken out of the oven when the crust is still a light beige color. The product is cooled, stored in a freezer or vacuum pack and at a future point undergoes a second bake to achieve appropriate product color.

Parisian macaron
Delicate meringue-like cookie made with sugar, egg whites, and ground almonds. Two cookie halves sandwich a sweet filling such as buttercream or ganache.

parts per million (ppm)
System used for measuring small quantities of very reactive ingredients such as dough conditioners. A specific quantity of the required ingredient is diluted in a specific quantity of a neutral carrier (such as flour) to combine a blend. From this blend, the ppm is obtained.

pasta sfogliata
See Italian puff pastry.

pasteurization
Application of heat at a specific temperature for a determined length of time prevents the development of dangerous microbes that are present in such foods as eggs and dairy products.

pastillage
White, tasteless, decorative dough similar to rolled fondant that dries very hard and is commonly used for making centerpieces or showpieces.

pastillage glue
Mixture of melted gelatin and powdered sugar used for gluing together pastillage for decorative display pieces.

pastry cream
Thick custard made from a mixture of milk, eggs, sugar, and cornstarch, often used to fill cakes, cream puffs, éclairs, napoleons, tarts, and other pastries.

pastry fondant
Type of fondant in which the initial sugar syrup is cooked to a lower temperature; the resulting liquid texture allows it to be used as a glaze.

pâte
French for "dough," "paste," or "batter."

pâte à bombe
Egg foam made from egg yolks and cooked sugar syrup.

pâte à choux
Precooked batter that is sometimes classified as dough. Choux (French for "cabbage") originally referred to the irregular shape it took on as it baked.

pâte à foncer
French for "lining pastry." The ingredients are similar to those in pie dough but also include variable quantities of sugar and egg.

pâte à sablé breton
Based on pâte breton cookies from Brittany, France, this dough is used for tarts or bases for petits fours.

pâte breton
Specialty dough that originated in Brittany, France, baked traditionally as a cookie with a characteristic open crumb, a very sandy texture and a slightly salty taste.

pâte brisée
Basic pie or pastry dough made with butter. It can be used for sweet or savory fillings.

pâtes de fruits
Specialty French confection made from fruit juice or puree, sugar, glucose, yellow pectin, and an acid. Pâtes de fruits should be slightly firm in texture yet still have tender qualities.

pâte sablée
Tender dough that can be used for lining tart molds, or as a base for cake or other pastry.

pâte sucrée
"Sweet pastry" is the literal translation. This enriched dough is often used for lining tart molds.

pathogens
Disease-causing microorganisms.

pâtissiers
French baking guild established in the 15th century. This trade group was given exclusive rights to make and sell tarts and pies filled with various meats, fish, and cheeses.

pectin
Polysaccharide obtained from plant sources (most notably apples and citrus fruits) that produces clean-flavored, tender, yet short-textured jellies.

pectin NH
One of the three most common types of pectin used in pastry, pectin NH is most often used in nappage and glazes because of its thermoreversible properties.

pentosans (hemicelluloses)
Long-chained carbohydrate molecules that are naturally present in flour. Their function in a dough system is to attract and distribute water. The two types of pentosans found in cereals are soluble and insoluble.

personal hygiene
Cleaning practices that fight infection by removing substances that allow bacteria to grow on the human body. Good personal hygiene includes bathing, shampooing, handwashing, wearing clean clothes and mouth cleanliness.

pesticides
Substances or mixtures of substances intended for preventing, destroying, or repelling any pest. Pests are living organisms that occur where they are not wanted or that cause damage to crops, humans, or other animals.

petits fours
Traditionally used to describe an assortment of miniature biscuits and fancy cakes that accompany afternoon coffee or tea, as well as the confections served at the end of a meal. Light, delicate, and fresh, the essential characteristic of petits fours is that they can be eaten in one or two bites.

petits fours déguisés
Also referred to as fruit déguisé. Fresh, dried or candied fruits that are coated in chocolate, fondant, cooked sugar, or any combination of the three.

petits fours frais
Tiny, fresh pastries that must be served the day they are made. This group includes filled items, such as éclairs; cream-filled choux pastries that are dipped in fondant, chocolate, or caramel; fruit, curd, or fancy tartlets; and filled cookies and biscuits.

petits fours glacés
Miniature confections that are comprised of thin layers of cake filled with jam or buttercream, topped with a thin layer of marzipan and coated with fondant icing or sometimes chocolate.

petits fours prestige
Tiny versions of contemporary entremets or other desserts.

petits fours sec
Dry, crisp, unfilled biscuits and cookies. This category includes shortbread and sablé dough creations like duchesses, sablé beurre, Spritz, and speculoos; puff pastry–based palmiers and allumettes glacés; and butter-based tuiles and langue du chats.

Philadelphia-style ice cream
Ice cream made from an uncooked mixture of cream, sugar, and flavorings. It can have a slightly grainy texture because it lacks the emulsifying capabilities of egg yolk.

pièces montées
Centerpieces of artistic design.

pie dough
Unsweetened pastry dough made from flour, fat, and water. Additional basic ingredients can include salt, sugar, and an acidic liquid such as lemon juice.

piped cookie
Cookie that is portioned using a piping bag, cookie press, or depositor, often in decorative shapes. Spritz cookies are an example of piped cookies.

piped sugar
Sugar that is poured into a double- or even triple-thick paper cone and then piped into various designs on a nonstick sheet or a lightly oiled piece of parchment.

pistores
At the turn of the 13th century in Paris, pistores gained the exclusive right to be the city's bread makers and bakers.

plasticity
Firm yet pliable texture. Used to describe characteristics of fat used in laminated dough.

plated desserts
Final course of a meal typically served in a restaurant or hotel. A plated dessert is a composition of elements that contribute supporting or contrasting flavors, textures, and sometimes temperatures. Presentation is often playful or thematic.

polka cut
Series of diagonal cuts that are made first in one direction and then at an opposing angle. The result is a criss-cross pattern that is frequently used for batards and specialty breads and rolls. It produces a loaf that has a flattened top.

polymorphic
Refers to the ability for something to exist in numerous states. In the context of chocolate, cocoa butter is polymorphic as it is able to set in different forms. Form V is the ideal form and is a sign of the chocolate being in temper.

poolish
Liquid preferment that consists of equal parts flour and water and is allowed to ferment at room temperature. Hydration is at 100 percent.

porridge
Dish made from cereal grains boiled in milk or water.

potash
Early chemical leavener made from the ashes of certain land plants.

pot de crème
Baked custard that is barely set and has a very fine, silky texture. Pot de crème is served in the dish in which it was baked.

preferment
Dough or batter that is created from a portion of the total formula's flour, water, yeast (natural or commercial), and sometimes salt. It is prepared prior to mixing the final dough, allowed to ferment for a controlled period of time at a controlled temperature, and added to the final dough.

prefermented dough
Also referred to as old dough. A portion of regular dough (made with white flour, water, yeast, and salt) that has fermented for three to six hours is then incorporated into a final dough mix. This method improves the quality of breads that are allowed only a short fermentation period.

preproof frozen process
Process for dough that allows the end user the ability to remove a yeasted product from the freezer and bake it without thawing and proofing. The degree of proofing can vary; however, 75 percent proofed is the most common. Special baking processes must be used, as these items require a progressive rise in baking temperature.

preshaping
In this step, cut pieces of dough are formed by hand or by machine using an automatic rounder. This process is done with the desired final shape in mind; for example, loose balls are appropriate for short shapes like batards or boules, while cylinders are used for longer shapes like baguettes.

product specification sheet (spec sheet)
Sheet provided by the miller per lot of flour which highlights assorted properties and qualities of the flour.

Professor Raymond Calvel
See Calvel, Raymond.

protease
Enzyme responsible for protein degradation. Protease enzymes break down gluten and increase extensibility of the dough.

proteolytic enzymes
Enzymes that break the long, chainlike molecules of gelatin into shorter fragments. This destroys gelatin's ability to hold and set liquids.

puff pastry
Non-yeasted laminated dough. The four main types of puff pastry are blitz, traditional, Italian, and inverted.

pulled sugar
Cooked sugar that is stretched and folded over itself repeatedly into a satin-like consistency that helps add strength to the sugar. Then, it is pulled into very thin, fine, shiny creations that hold their shape as they cool and have a glass-like final quality.

Q

quick breads
Wide range of nonyeasted products such as muffins, scones, biscuits, and coffee cakes. Quick breads are leavened by chemical leavening agents and steam.

R

reducing agents
Additives that remove oxygen, thereby creating a gluten network that is easier to stretch. Reducing agents are used to decrease mixing time and to improve dough flow and machinability.

refractometer
Instrument that measures the concentration of sugar in a liquid.

residual sugars
Sugars that have not been metabolized by yeast and are left over after fermentation.

rest
Time between pre-shaping and shaping during which the gluten in the dough is allowed to relax, thereby making the dough easier to shape. Also called intermediate proof or bench time.

ribbon stage
Refers to an egg foam made from whole eggs and sugar that displays ribbon-like texture when the whisk is lifted.

rock sugar
Combination of cooked sugar syrup and royal icing with enough agitation to cause it to aerate and bubble while setting. It is less resistant to humidity, so it keeps well.

roll-in fat
See beurrage.

roll-in shortening
Fat specifically designed for the lamination process.

royal icing
Classic icing made from powdered sugar and egg whites.

run out
Condition that occurs during cookie baking when the butter–sugar phase melts and flows out of the cookie. This condition is generally caused by uneven mixing.

rye
Cereal grain capable of growing in poor soil and a cool climate. It is especially popular in Nordic countries for bread baking. Rye flour proteins are able to form gluten but fermentation tolerance is improved when mixed with wheat flour.

S

sanding method
Also called the sablér method (sablé is the French term for "sandy"), this technique creates a sandy, tender texture in cookies.

Sanitation Standard Operating Procedures (SSOPs)
Written, step-by-step cleaning and sanitizing procedures for each scheduled task.

sanitizing
Going beyond cleaning to make a food contact surface free from bacteria or other contamination.

satinizing
Process in which sugar is cooked and then cooled, stretched and folded over itself repeatedly to achieve a satin-like consistency.

saturated solution
Type of solution achieved when the maximum quantity of sugar is dissolved into water.

sausage cut
Series of parallel cuts that run perpendicular to the length of the loaf. This pattern is often used for batards, specialty breads such as rye, and Viennese baguettes. It encourages a round cross-section in the baked loaf.

scoring
Incisions made on the surface of the dough prior to baking. Scores control expansion and add a decorative element to bread.

seed
Foreign material such as dust or granular sugar added (often inadvertently) to a sugar solution; such seeds create chain reactions of crystallization in sugar solutions, which may or may not be desirable.

seizing
Undesirable phenomenon that occurs when even a tiny bit of water interacts with melting chocolate, turning the chocolate into a thick paste.

semifreddo
Italian word meaning "half frozen"; semifreddo is a frozen dessert composed of a custard base lightened with whipped cream or meringue. It is served frozen, but the incorporated air softens it and makes it seem less cold.

semi-sweet chocolate
Chocolate made up of 50 to 64 percent cocoa content. Semi-sweet chocolate can be used for coatings, fillings, pastry, and entremets.

separated egg sponge method
Cake mixing process characterized by the separate preparation of a whole egg foam and a common meringue. These are combined and flour is then folded in. This technique is often used for thin sheets of cake.

shaping
Forming of the dough into its final shape; this can be achieved by hand or machine.

sheet cookie
Style of cookie representing a diverse range of products usually baked on a sheet pan and then portioned into individual-sized servings. Examples include lemon bars and brownies.

short mix
Gentle mixing method that utilizes first speed only. This method most closely approximates the characteristics of hand mixing. A short mix incorporates the ingredients with very little gluten development. The under-developed gluten structure requires a long fermentation time.

simple sugars
Monosaccharides, the simplest form of carbohydrate. Examples are fructose and glucose.

simple syrup
Sugar syrup made from equal weights of sugar and water.

single-acting baking powder
Substance used in baking that contains only low-temperature reacting leavening salt.

single fold
Single folds can be done by folding the sheeted dough in three sections, similar to a business letter.

sliced cookie
Cookie made from a long piece of dough that is baked and then cut into individual pieces. Biscotti is one example of this style of cookie.

sliding method
Piping technique where the tip of the cone barely touches the surface of the product, allowing the pastry chef more control for fine detailed work.

soft peak
Foam that has a smooth, developed look, yet lacks defined, rigid peaks.

specialty cakes
Cakes with multiple components; texture and preparation techniques may vary substantially. Molds are frequently used to create unique and dramatic presentations.

specific gravity (SG)
Measure found by dividing the weight of a given volume of batter by the weight of the same volume of water. In cake mixing, finding the specific gravity is a method of determining the amount of air in a batter.

spelt
Ancient variety of wheat.

splitting
Slicing a baked cake horizontally into layers.

sponge
Stiff preferment that, like poolish, consists of only flour, water and yeast, and is allowed to ferment at room temperature or at a controlled temperature.

sponge cake
Cake that contains whole eggs warmed and whipped with sugar to the ribbon stage. Sifted dry ingredients are gently folded into the batter.

sponge method
Mixing method used for light, fine-textured cookies. The first step involves development of an egg foam stabilized with sugar. Sifted dry ingredients are then folded into the foam. As the whipped eggs incorporate air, they gain volume, and the foam is transformed into a physical leavening agent.

spun sugar
Sugar decoration often used for plated desserts. To achieve a very silky, angel-hair sugar strand, a whisk whose curved ends have been cut off or the tines of a fork are dipped into hot sugar syrup, the instrument is waved back and forth, and strings of sugar are created.

stability
Characteristic of flour determined by calculating the difference in time between the point at which the top of a farinograph curve intercepts the 500 FU line (arrival time) and the point at which the top of the curve leaves the 500 FU line (departure time). The stability gives some indication of the flour's tolerance during mixing.

stabilizer
Substance used in baking to prevent water migration by increasing the viscosity of the solution.

stage
Common approach to ongoing professional development; the baker or pastry chef completes a short work period to learn techniques and processes at a workplace other than his or her own.

staling
Degradation of the crumb due mostly to the migration of water. Water that surrounds the starch particles in the dough moves to the inside during gelatinization and baking, bursting the starch particle and extending some chains of starch molecules. As the bread cools, these chains retract to their original position, making the crumb denser and causing it to lose softness.

starch gelatinization
Process wherein starch granules burst at 140°F (60°C), liberating numerous chains of starch that form a very complex, gelatin-like matrix. The process is complete at 153°F (67°C).

starch molds
Molds made from a thick, contained layer of dry starch that has been carefully imprinted with cavities in which fillings can be deposited and left to set.

starter
Portion of the levain that is retained and fed (given flour and water) to continue a sourdough culture.

stearic acid
Saturated fat making up one-third of the fat content in cocoa butter.

stencil cookie
Cookies that are made from a thin, basic batter that is mixed, allowed to rest, spread freeform or into a template, and then baked.

stiff peak
Meringue that has a glossy look and forms spikes when the whisk is lifted.

still-frozen desserts
Preparations that are largely composed of the ingredients that go into a classic mousse: whipped foam made of egg whites, egg yolks, or heavy cream is folded into a flavored base.

storage freezer
Freezer in which packaged pieces of frozen dough can be kept from two weeks to six months at temperatures ranging from 0°F (−18°C) to −4°F (−20°C).

sugar bloom
Occurs when chocolate is stored in high humidity areas and forms condensation on its surface. The sugar attracts the humidity to the surface of the chocolate, making the surface moist and drawing out some of the sugar from the chocolate. Once the water content evaporates, the sugar remains in a crystallized form.

sugar confections
Wide variety of sugar-based products including caramels, cordials, fondants, marzipan candies, pâtes de fruits, nougat, and marshmallows.

sugar lamp
Heat lamp used to maintain the high temperature of sugar.

sugar solution
Stable mixture of water and dissolved sugar.

sugar syrup
Combination of sugar and water that is brought to a boil and cooked to a certain temperature.

supersaturated solution
Type of solution achieved when sugar is dissolved in water at a higher ratio than is normally possible at a given temperature; requires a saturated sugar solution to be boiled to evaporate part of the water, and then cooled.

sweet chocolate
Chocolate that must contain at least 15 to 50 percent cocoa content. It is uncommon in quality confectionary work.

Swiss buttercream
Icing made with the stable base of Swiss meringue. Once the meringue has been made, the softened butter is added slowly, and the buttercream is whipped to full volume.

Swiss meringue
Meringue characterized by heating the egg whites and sugar before final whipping, a process that involves constant agitation to prevent the egg whites from coagulating.

syneresis
Process that occurs as pastry cream ages; the starch in the cream begins to break down and water begins to "weep" from the cream.

T

tant pour tant (TPT)
Mixture containing one part almond flour to one part powdered or granulated sugar.

tartaric acid
Also known as cream of tartar, tartaric acid is a leavening acid; also used in sugar work to prevent crystallization and to increase elasticity in sugar that is being pulled or blown.

tart dough
Dough suited for use with tarts. It will not shrink or fall down the sides of the pan. Pâte sucrée, pâte sablé, and even puff pastry are all tart doughs.

tempering
Process of melting and precrystallizing a portion of cocoa butter to establish form V crystals. Tempered chocolate has a nice gloss, resistance to bloom, and a good snap.

tenderizing ingredients
Ingredients that soften, enable spread, and prevent the product from becoming crisp and chewy. Tenderizers include granulated, liquid, and invert sugars, natural and manufactured fats, leavening agents, egg yolks, and starches derived from corn or wheat.

terroir
French word that refers to the idea that, like wine and coffee, cacao beans derive their individual characteristics from the conditions of the environment in which they are grown and processed. Terroir can be loosely defined as "a sense of place."

test strip
Method to check if chocolate is in temper; a thin strip of chocolate is applied over a piece of parchment paper, and the setting properties are observed.

Theobroma cacao
Tree that produces cacao beans. *Theobroma* is a Greek composite word meaning "food of gods," an appropriate description for chocolate.

30 baumé syrup
Sugar syrup make with 137 parts sugar to 100 parts water. Sometimes used as a simple syrup.

thread method
Piping technique in which the pastry chef applies the piping medium from above the surface of the cake. This can be done from a distance of 1/2 inch (1 cm).

toffee
Confection characterized by a hard and crunchy texture. Toffee is made from the controlled cooking of sugar, a doctor, and dairy.

toughening ingredients
Ingredients that create a viable structure for the dough, thereby reducing spread and producing a firmer shape. The major toughening ingredients include flour, water, cocoa powder, egg whites, whole eggs, and nonfat milk solids.

tourrier
Person whose job responsibilities include the mixing and proper handling of various dough preparations. *Tour* refers to the marble or granite table this person usually works on.

traditional method
Basic steps of the baking process used for thousands of years. This process begins with the elaboration and development of the preferment, continues with the final dough mixing, and ends with baking.

traditional puff pastry
Pastry in which butter (beurrage) is enclosed in a dough (détrempe) and is given a series of turns. This produces alternating layers of dough and butter, which, after baking, results in a crisp, flaky texture.

triglyceride
Fat molecule made up of three fatty acids.

trinitario
Hybrid of the criollo and forastero varieties of cacao. Trinitario combines the benefits of the higher, more consistent yields of the forastero with the more delicate flavor notes of the criollo.

truffles
Chocolate confections that are composed of a ganache coated with chocolate. Originally they were named for their resemblance to the wild truffle, but today they can be found in many different shapes and presentations.

tuile
Crisp, lacey cookie made from a thin batter based on egg whites, flour, and sugar. Variations may include corn syrup, nuts, seeds, or fruit purees.

tunneling
Holes that run diagonally along the product. They are the result of overmixing a batter, which also causes a toughening of the crumb.

U

unbaked pie
Pie shell that is blind-baked and then filled with ingredients that do not require baking. Examples of unbaked pies are lemon meringue and chocolate cream.

unbaked tarts
Blind-baked tart shells are filled with a combination of pastry cream and fresh fruit or any variety of fillings that do not require baking.

uncooked fruit method
Classic method for fruit pie preparation. Fresh or frozen fruit is mixed with sugar and a starch and baked inside an unbaked pie shell.

undertempered
Chocolate that appears dull and will have visible cocoa butter migration to the surface of the chocolate. It will not set up within two minutes and will never have a shine, or the characteristics of well-tempered chocolate

upside-down assembly
Cake assembly technique best used with silicon molds and some specialty molds such as Bûche de Nöel and half dome or pyramid molds. In upside-down assembly, the mousse is deposited in the mold, any inserts are added, and the cake base is placed on top of the mousse and made flush with the top of the mold. After the dessert is frozen, it is inverted so the cake base is on the bottom.

US Food and Drug Administration (FDA)
Scientific, regulatory, and public health agency that is responsible for ensuring the safety, efficacy, and security of drugs, medical devices, food, and cosmetics.

V

Viennoiserie
Yeast-raised products that are sweetened with sugar and enriched with butter and eggs. They may be laminated or nonlaminated.

W

wheat
Most widely cultivated grain for human consumption. The flour produced from wheat is a staple in the world's diet. It is an essential ingredient in most breads, baked goods, pastas, noodles, and pastry items.

whipped cream
Heavy cream that has been whipped to increase its volume and lighten its texture. It is typically used as a component to create other creams.

whipped topping
Nondairy-based whipped cream replacement incorporating stabilizers and emulsifiers to make it very light and easy to work with.

white chocolate
Chocolate made from cocoa butter, milk solids, sugar, and flavoring ingredients. White chocolate is not considered a true chocolate because it contains no cocoa solids.

winnowing
Process of separating the shell and germ from the cacao bean before grinding.

Y

yellow pectin (apple pectin)
One of the three most common types of pectin used in pastry, yellow pectin is most often used in pâtes de fruits.

REFERENCES

Bachmann, W. (1955). *Continental confectionery: The pastrycooks' art.* London: Maclaren & Sons.

Beckett, S. T. (2000). *The science of chocolate.* Cambridge, UK: Royal Society of Chemistry.

Bennion, E. B. & Bamford, G. S. T. (1973). *The technology of cake making.* Bucks, Great Britain: Leonard Hill Books.

Bilheux, R., & Escoffier, A. (2000). *Doughs, batters, and meringues.* New York: John Wiley and Sons.

Bilheux, R., & Escoffier, A. (2000). *Creams, confections, and finished desserts.* New York: John Wiley and Sons.

Buys, A., & Decluzeau, J.-L. (1996). *Decorating with a paper cone.* New York: John Wiley & Sons.

Calvel, R. (2001). *The taste of bread.* (R. L. Wirtz, Trans.). Gaithersburg, MD: Aspen Publishers, Inc.

Chaboissier, D., & Lebigre, D. (1993). *Compagnon et maître pâtissier: Tome I technologie de patisserie.* France: Editions Jérôme Villette.

Clarke, C. (2004). *The science of ice cream.* Cambridge, UK: The Royal Society of Chemistry.

Cleveland Clinic Heart and Vascular Institute. (n.d.). *The health benefits of chocolate unveiled.* Retrieved from http://www.clevelandclinic.org/heartcenter/pub/guide/prevention/nutrition/chocolate.htm.

Coe, S., & Coe, M. (1996). *The true history of chocolate.* New York: Thames and Hudson.

"Current good manufacturing practice in manufacturing, packing, or holding human food," 21 C.F.R. § 110. Washington DC: US Government Printing Office. GPO access via http://www.access.gpo.gov/nara/cfr/waisidx_07/21cfr110_07.html.

Darenne, E., & Duval, E. (1974). *Traité de pâtisserie moderne.* Paris: Flammarion.

Ecole Lenôtre. (1995). *Les recettes glacées.* Les Lilas, France: Jérôme Villette.

Ecole Lenôtre (2000). *Chocolats et confiserie.* Les Lilas, France: Jérôme Villette.

Ecole Lenôtre. (2006). *Ecole Lenôtre: La pâtisserie—grands classiques et créations.* Les Lilas, France: Jérôme Villette.

Edwards, W. P. (2000). *The science of sugar confectionary.* Cambridge, UK: The Royal Society of Chemistry.

Flandrin, J.-L., Montanari, M., & Sonnenfeld, A. (Eds.) (1999). *Food: A culinary history from antiquity to the present.* New York: Columbia University Press.

Gisslen, W. (2001). *Professional baking.* New York: John Wiley and Sons.

Glacier, Stephane. (2001). *Sucre d'art: l'envers du décor.* Paris, France: Les Editions de L'if.

Goff, D. (1995). *Dairy science and technology education series.* Retrieved February 2006, from University of Guelph, Canada Web site: http://www.foodsci.uoguelph.ca/dairyedu/home.html.

Greweling, Peter P. (2007). *Chocolates and confections: Formula, theory and technique for the artisan confectioner.* Hoboken, NJ: John Wiley and Sons.

Guinet, R., & Godon, B. (1994). *La panification française.* Paris, France: Lavoisier.

Jacob, H. E. (1944). *Six thousand years of bread: Its holy and unholy history.* New York: Lyons Press.

Matz, S. A. (1987). *Formulas and processes for bakers.* McAllen, Texas: Pan-Tech International.

Matz, S. A. (1992). *Cookie and cracker technology.* McAllen, Texas: Pan-Tech International.

McGee, H. (2004). *On food and cooking: The science and lore of the kitchen.* New York: Scribner.

MacLauchlan, Andrew. (1995). *New classic desserts.* New York: John Wiley and Sons.

MacLauchlan, Andrew. (1999). *The making of a pastry chef.* New York: John Wiley and Sons.

McWilliams, M. (2001). *Foods: experimental perspectives.* Upper Saddle River, NJ: Prentice Hall.

Meyer, A. L. (1998). *Baking across America.* Austin, TX: University of Texas Press.

Montagné, P. (Ed.) (2001). *Larousse gastronomique.* New York: Clarkson Potter/Publishers.

Perruchon, J. M. & Bellouet, G. J. (2002). *Apprenez l'art des petits fours sucres et sales.* Barcelona, Spain: Montagud Editions.

Pyler, E.J. (1988). *Baking science and technology.* (Vols. 1–2). Kansas City, MO: Sosland Publishing Company.

Revel, J.-F. (1982). *Culture and cuisine: A journey through the history of food.* Garden City, NY: Doubleday.

Tannahill, R. (1988). *Food in history.* New York: Three Rivers Press.

Trotter, Charlie. (1998). *Charlie Trotter's desserts.* Berkeley, CA: Ten Speed Press.

Note: As with any dynamic informational tool, Web sites will change and even disappear from time to time. Any Internet user must be aware of this fact and be prepared to investigate and discover other comparable Web sites.

FORMULA INDEX

Note: Page numbers followed by *f* refer to figures.

O

P

Q

R

SUBJECT INDEX

Note: Page numbers followed by *f* refer to figures.

D

G